The Essential
HOUSE PLAN
COLLECTION

The *Essential*
HOUSE PLAN
COLLECTION

The Essential
HOUSE PLAN COLLECTION

hanley▲wood

Published by Hanley Wood
One Thomas Circle, NW, Suite 600
Washington, DC 20005

Vice President, House Plans, Andrew Schultz
Associate Publisher, Development, Jennifer Pearce
Manager, Customer Service, Michael Morgan

Director, Marketing, Mark Wilkin
Editor, Simon Hyoun
Assistant Editor, Kimberly R. Johnson
Publications Manager, Brian Haefs
Production Manager, Theresa Emerson
Senior Plan Merchandiser, Nicole Phipps
Plan Merchandiser, Hillary Huff
Graphic Artist, Joong Min
Director, Audience Development, Erik Schulze

Most Hanley Wood titles are available at quantity discounts with bulk
purchases for educational, business, or sales promotional use. For information,
please contact Jennifer Pearce at jpearce@hanleywood.com.

VC Graphics
Creative Director, Veronica Vannoy
Graphic Designer, Jennifer Gerstein
Graphic Designer, Denise Reiffenstein
Graphic Designer, Jeanne-Erin Worster

PHOTO CREDITS
Front Cover, Main Image
HPK2101527 on page 672, Exposures Unlimited, Ron & Donna Kolb

Front Cover, Insets (Left to Right)
HPK2101472 on page 862, Alan Mascord; HPK2101354 on page 790, ©Kim
Sargent; HPK2100345 on page 204, Bob Greenspan

Back Cover (in Reading Order)
HPK2100188 on page 119, ©1994 Donald A. Gardner Architects, Inc.;
HPK2100860 on page 498, Get Decorating, courtesy Garrell Associates, Inc.;
HPK2101122 on page 650, Stephen Fuller, Inc.; HPK2100791 on page 453, Bob
Greenspan; HPK2100916 on page 527, Stephen Moore, courtesy of Stephen
Fuller, Inc.; HPK2100927 on page 532, Russell Kingman/HDS; HPK2101393 on
page 813, Peter Fownes/Backlight Photography, courtesy Garrell Associates;
HPK2101460 on page 856, William E. Poole Designs, Inc. Wilmington NC;
HPK2101337 on page 781, John Sciarrino, courtesy Giovanni Photography

Distribution Center
PBD
Hanley Wood Consumer Group
3280 Summit Ridge Parkway
Duluth, Georgia 30096

10 9 8 7 6 5 4 3 2 1

Printed in the United States of America

Library of Congress Control Number: 2006935045

ISBN-13: 978-1-931131-70-4
ISBN-10: 1-931131-70-8

CONTENTS

House plans offer a great balance between custom-built looks and production-built savings.

The book you're holding is the definitive collection of home plans created by North America's most celebrated and trusted residential designers and architects. The plans are for homes in a broad range of sizes—from the tiny and super-efficient 840 square-foot, one-bedroom vacation design that starts the book (page 8), to a grand European manor home (page 896), measuring in just over 10,000 square feet. The architectural styles included in the collection are just as varied. You'll find plenty of the familiar favorites—Neoclassical, Traditional, Craftsman—and a great selection of regional styles—Southwestern, Floridian, Farmhouse, and more. In short, *The Essential House Plan Collection* is your best bet for finding a design that fits your taste and understands your family's needs.

ALL HERE ALL READY

As always, our goal is to help you realize what your family is looking for in a new home and to help you find it. To that purpose, we've divided *Essential* into seven sections, organized by square footage. But if you don't yet know how big of a home you need, turn to the index at the back of the book to search homes by architectural style. For more complicated searches, as well as to see any photos of finished homes, take your query to www.eplans.com. There you'll see all the plans collected in this book, as well as a few thousand more.

We've also included a brief collection of garage plans (pages 182-183), in case you're considering a smaller home that doesn't include a garage—or if you simply prefer a detached garage. Remember that all house plans can be modified to your preference. Our customization consultation package (turn to the last set of fold-out pages, starting on page 896, for details) puts you in touch with a qualified plan designer who can modify the plan you have purchased or are considering for purchase. Does your home need an extra bedroom? Would you like higher ceilings in the great room? Can the plan accommodate a larger garage? The budget-friendly price of a predrawn plan combined with the customization options available through a modification designer equals an affordable and satisfying way to build a brand new home.

You may notice in *Essential* four sets of fold-out pages, called gatefolds. The first gatefold (opposite page 64) discusses the natural advantages of a smaller home, such as energy efficiency and easy maintenance. For comparison, the third gatefold (opposite page 672) helps you find the most comfortable and attractive larger home—and how to avoid inelegantly oversized designs. The second gatefold (opposite 352) will be useful to those who are new to browsing house plans and may have trouble, at first, imagining the three-dimensional space represented by a floor plan. Lastly, turn to the gatefold opposite page 896 to see what is included in a basic house plan package, as well as all the options and upgrades available for most plans. This is also where you'll find package pricing and instructions for ordering a plan. If at any point you would like to ask specific questions about a home you see—or would just like a second opinion—our knowledgeable staff is on hand to assist you.

Comfortable and elegant spaces are
ready to receive your final touches.

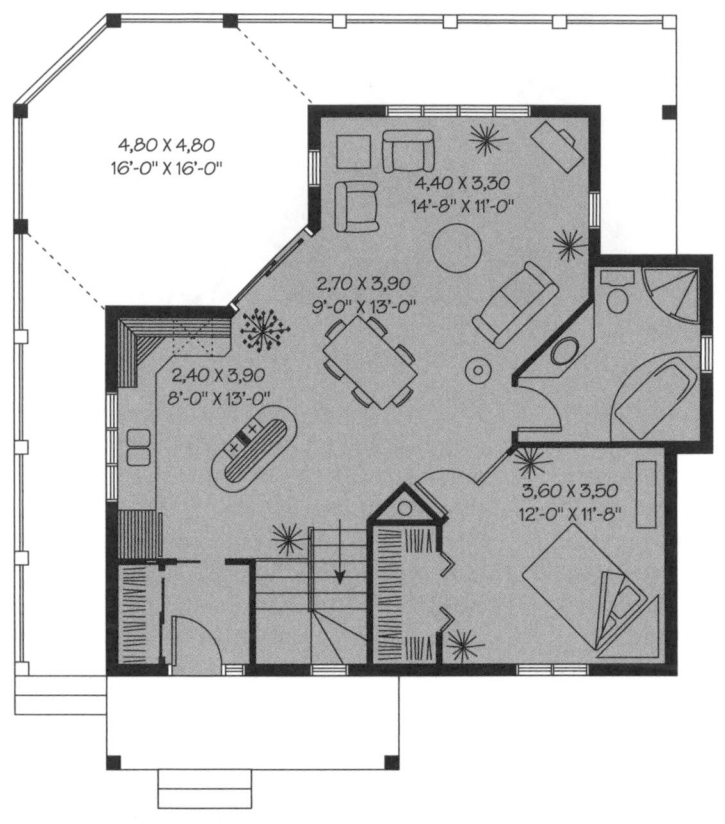

4,80 X 4,80
16'-0" X 16'-0"

4,40 X 3,30
14'-8" X 11'-0"

2,70 X 3,90
9'-0" X 13'-0"

2,40 X 3,90
8'-0" X 13'-0"

3,60 X 3,50
12'-0" X 11'-8"

HPK2100001

Style: Cottage

Square Footage: 840

Bedrooms: 1

Bathrooms: 1

Width: 33' - 0"

Depth: 31' - 0"

Foundation: Unfinished Walkout Basement

EPLANS.COM

This charming home is ideal for waterfront property with a generous wraparound porch that features a corner gazebo perfect for outdoor living. The vestibule offers an energy- and space-efficient pocket door that opens to the island kitchen and dining room, where sliding glass doors open to the gazebo. The living room views in three directions, bringing the outside in. A bedroom and lavish bath complete the floor plan.

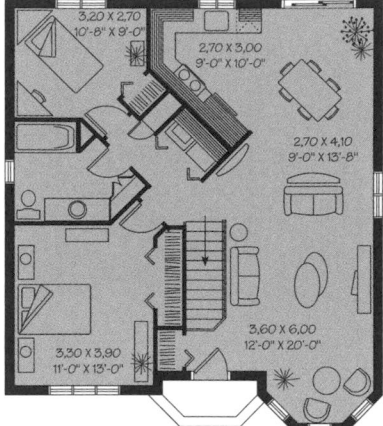

HPK2100002

Style: Cottage

Square Footage: 972

Bedrooms: 2

Bathrooms: 1

Width: 30' - 0"

Depth: 35' - 0"

Foundation: Unfinished Basement

EPLANS.COM

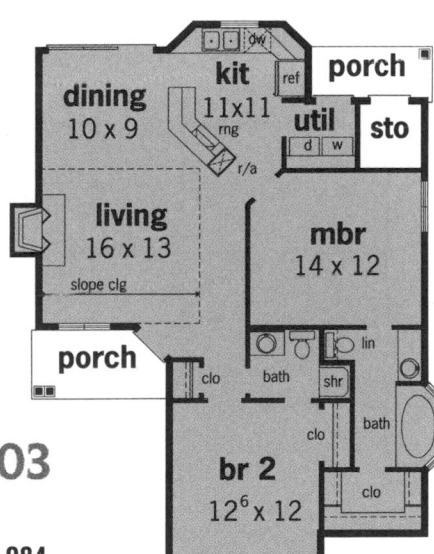

HPK2100003

Style: Bungalow

Square Footage: 984

Bedrooms: 2

Bathrooms: 2

Width: 33' - 9"

Depth: 43' - 0"

Foundation: Crawlspace, Slab, Unfinished Basement

EPLANS.COM

HPK2100004

Style: **Bungalow**

Square Footage: **996**

Bedrooms: **3**

Bathrooms: **1**

Width: **24' - 4"**

Depth: **43' - 8"**

Foundation: **Crawlspace**

EPLANS.COM

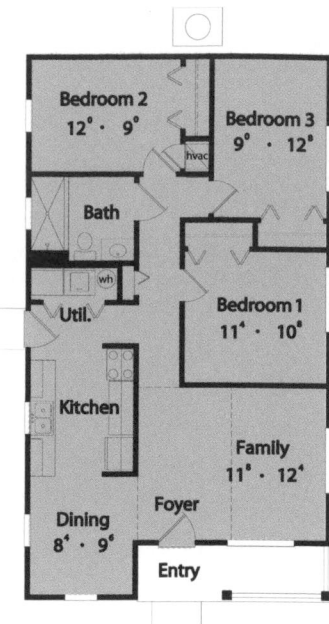

Bedroom 2
12⁰ · 9⁰

Bedroom 3
9⁰ · 12⁰

hvac

Bath

Util.

wh

Kitchen

Bedroom 1
11⁴ · 10⁰

Family
11⁸ · 12⁴

Dining
8⁴ · 9⁶

Foyer

Entry

HPK2100005

Style: **Ranch**

Square Footage: **1,070**

Bedrooms: **3**

Bathrooms: **2**

Width: **29' - 0"**

Depth: **47' - 2"**

Foundation: **Crawlspace, Slab**

EPLANS.COM

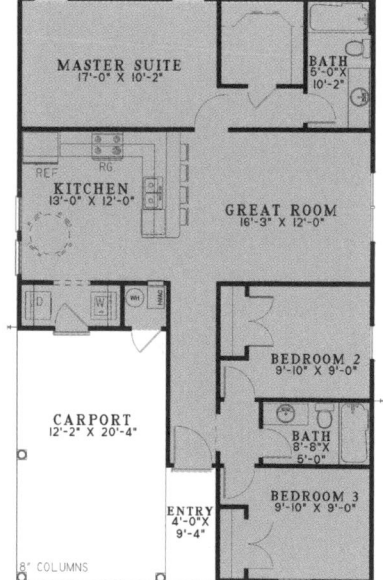

MASTER SUITE
17'-0" X 10'-2"

BATH
5'-0" X
10'-2"

KITCHEN
13'-0" X 12'-0"

REF   RG.

GREAT ROOM
16'-3" X 12'-0"

W   D   WH

CARPORT
12'-2" X 20'-4"

BEDROOM 2
9'-10" X 9'-0"

BATH
8'-8" X
5'-0"

ENTRY
4'-0" X
9'-4"

BEDROOM 3
9'-10" X 9'-0"

8" COLUMNS

ORDER BLUEPRINTS ANYTIME AT EPLANS.COM OR 1-800-521-6797

HPK2100006

Style: Country
Square Footage: 1,080
Bedrooms: 3
Bathrooms: 2
Width: 36' - 0"
Depth: 34' - 0"
Foundation: Unfinished Basement

EPLANS.COM

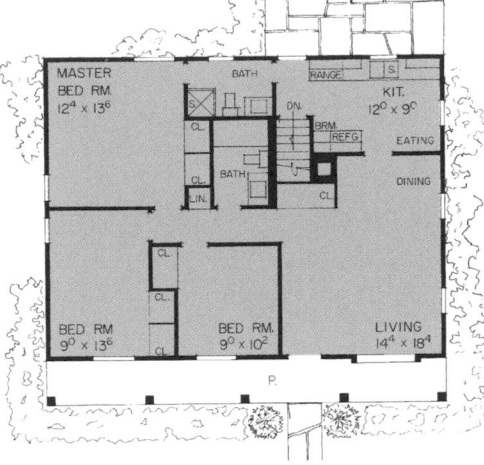

HPK2100007

Style: Cottage
Square Footage: 1,085
Bedrooms: 3
Bathrooms: 2
Width: 48' - 0"
Depth: 36' - 0"
Foundation: Crawlspace, Unfinished Walkout Basement

EPLANS.COM

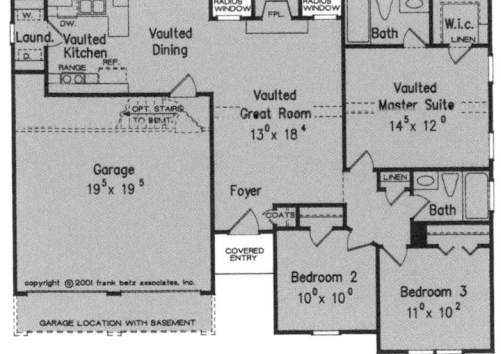

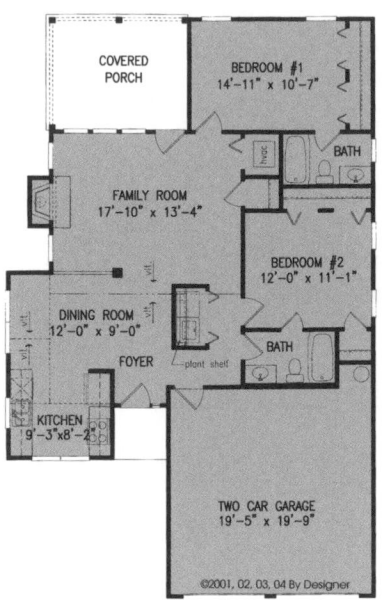

HPK2100008

Style: Country

Square Footage: 1,093

Bedrooms: 2

Bathrooms: 2

Width: 35' - 0"

Depth: 56' - 0"

Foundation: Slab

EPLANS.COM

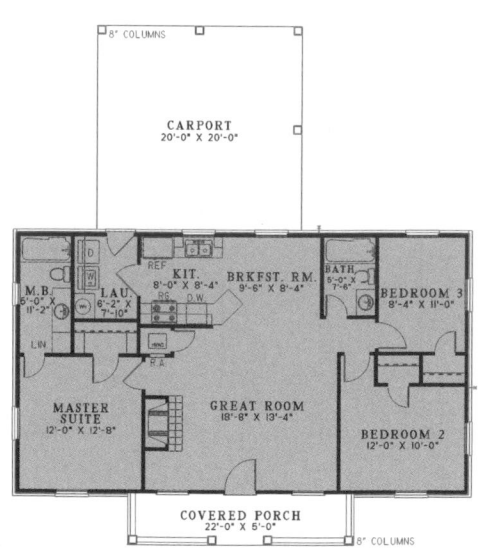

HPK2100009

Style: Bungalow

Square Footage: 1,100

Bedrooms: 3

Bathrooms: 2

Width: 44' - 0"

Depth: 50' - 0"

Foundation: Crawlspace, Slab

EPLANS.COM

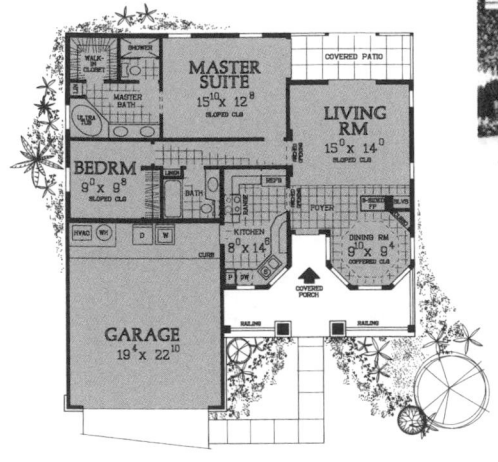

HPK2100010

Style: Country

Square Footage: 1,118

Bedrooms: 2

Bathrooms: 2

Width: 44' - 4"

Depth: 47' - 4"

Foundation: Slab

HPK2100011

Style: Cottage

Square Footage: 1,124

Bedrooms: 3

Bathrooms: 2

Width: 43' - 4"

Depth: 31' - 6"

Foundation: Unfinished Walkout Basement

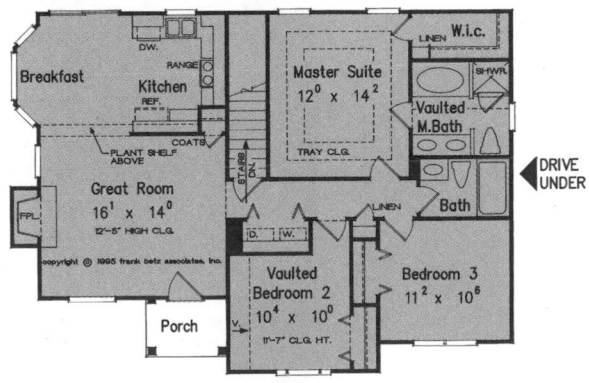

UNDER 1,500 SQUARE FEET

HPK2100012

Style: Cottage

Square Footage: 1,149

Bedrooms: 3

Bathrooms: 2

Width: 47' - 6"

Depth: 42' - 4"

Foundation: Crawlspace, Unfinished Walkout Basement

EPLANS.COM

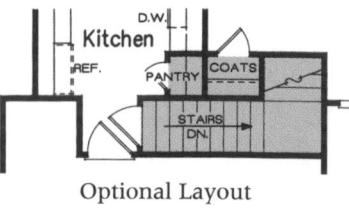

Optional Layout

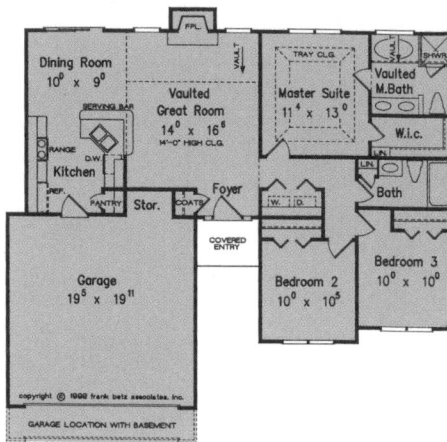

HPK2100013

Style: Cottage

Square Footage: 1,151

Bedrooms: 3

Bathrooms: 2

Width: 39' - 3"

Depth: 42' - 1"

Foundation: Slab

EPLANS.COM

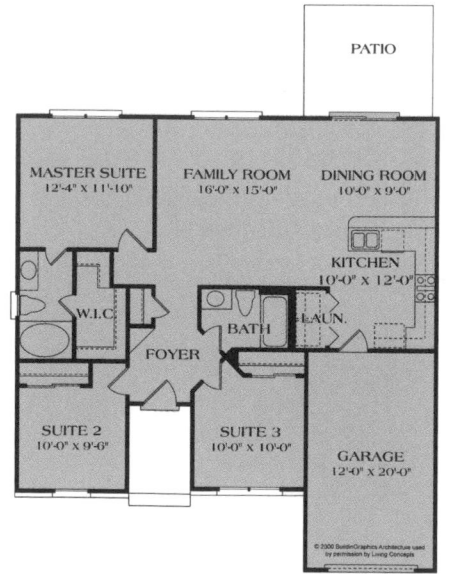

ORDER BLUEPRINTS ANYTIME AT EPLANS.COM OR 1-800-521-6797

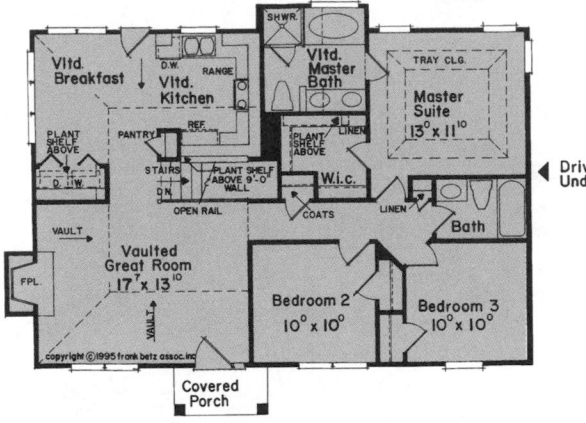

HPK2100014

Style: Cottage
Square Footage: 1,166
Bedrooms: 3
Bathrooms: 2
Width: 43' - 4"
Depth: 34' - 0"
Foundation: Unfinished Walkout Basement

HPK2100015

Style: Cottage
Square Footage: 1,195
Bedrooms: 3
Bathrooms: 2
Width: 40' - 0"
Depth: 48' - 8"

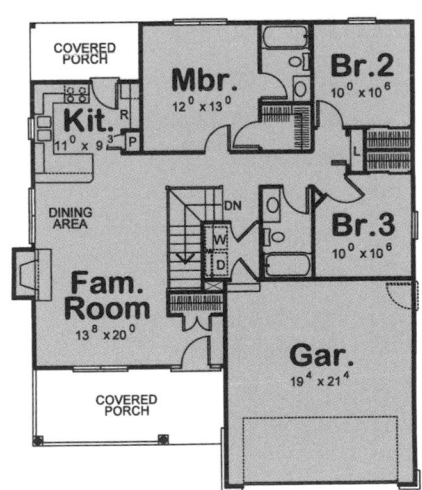

C Larry E. Belk Designs

HPK2100016

Style: Cottage

Square Footage: 1,202

Bedrooms: 3

Bathrooms: 2

Width: 51' - 10"

Depth: 43' - 10"

Foundation: Crawlspace, Slab

EPLANS.COM

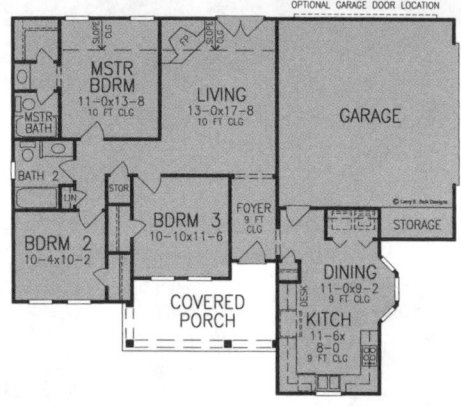

HPK2100017

Style: Cottage

Square Footage: 1,208

Bedrooms: 3

Bathrooms: 2

Width: 48' - 0"

Depth: 29' - 0"

Foundation: Unfinished Walkout Basement

EPLANS.COM

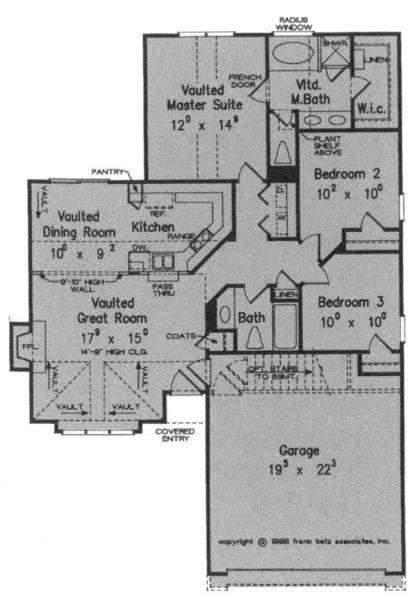

HPK2100018

Style: Cottage

Square Footage: 1,209

Bedrooms: 3

Bathrooms: 2

Width: 40' - 0"

Depth: 55' - 6"

Foundation: Crawlspace, Unfinished Walkout Basement

EPLANS.COM

HPK2100019

Style: Cottage

Square Footage: 1,218

Bedrooms: 3

Bathrooms: 2

Width: 54' - 0"

Depth: 36' - 4"

Foundation: Unfinished Walkout Basement

EPLANS.COM

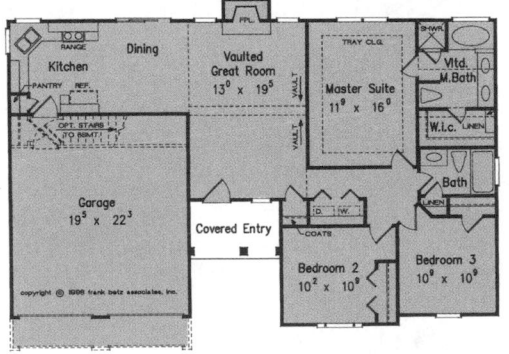

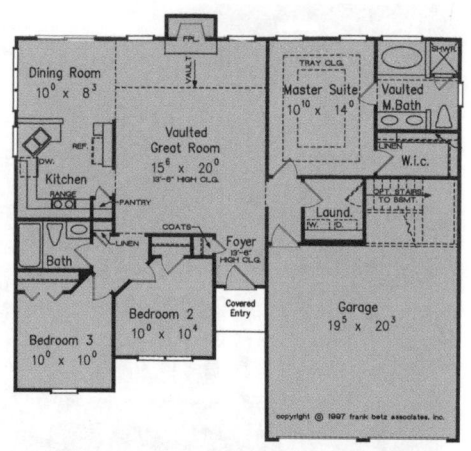

HPK2100020

Style: Cottage
Square Footage: 1,232
Bedrooms: 3
Bathrooms: 2
Width: 46' - 0"
Depth: 44' - 4"
Foundation: Crawlspace, Slab, Unfinished Walkout Basement

EPLANS.COM

HPK2100021

Style: Country
Square Footage: 1,246
Bedrooms: 3
Bathrooms: 2
Width: 60' - 0"
Depth: 60' - 0"

EPLANS.COM

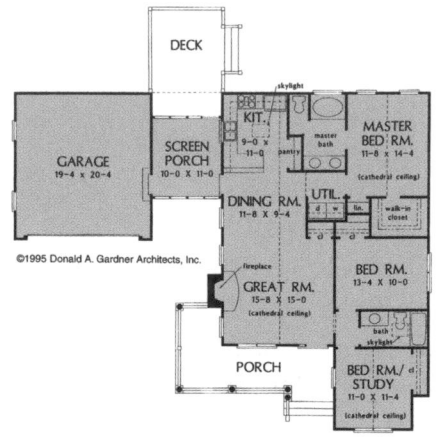

©1995 Donald A. Gardner Architects, Inc.

© 1995 Donald A. Gardner Architects, Inc.

ORDER BLUEPRINTS ANYTIME AT EPLANS.COM OR 1-800-521-6797

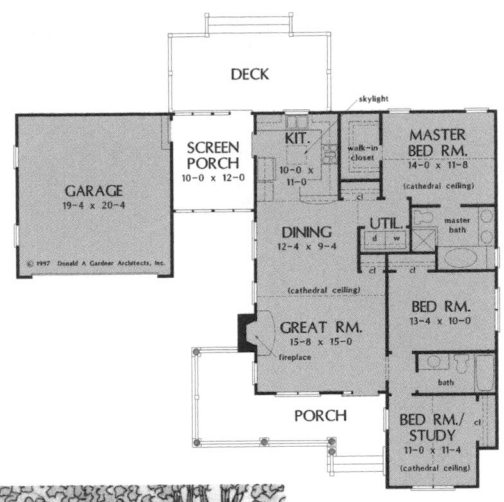

DECK

SCREEN PORCH
10-0 x 12-0

GARAGE
19-4 x 20-4

KIT.
10-0 x 11-0

walk-in closet

MASTER BED RM.
14-0 x 11-8
(cathedral ceiling)

skylight

DINING
12-4 x 9-4

UTIL.

master bath

(cathedral ceiling)

BED RM.
13-4 x 10-0

GREAT RM.
15-8 x 15-0
fireplace

bath

PORCH

BED RM./ STUDY
11-0 x 11-4
(cathedral ceiling)

© 1997 Donald A. Gardner Architects, Inc.

© 1997 Donald A. Gardner Architects, Inc.

HPK2100022

Style: Country
Square Footage: 1,246
Bedrooms: 3
Bathrooms: 2
Width: 60' - 0"
Depth: 48' - 0"

HPK2100023

Style: Cottage
Square Footage: 1,248
Bedrooms: 3
Bathrooms: 2
Width: 36' - 0"
Depth: 61' - 6"
Foundation: Crawlspace, Slab

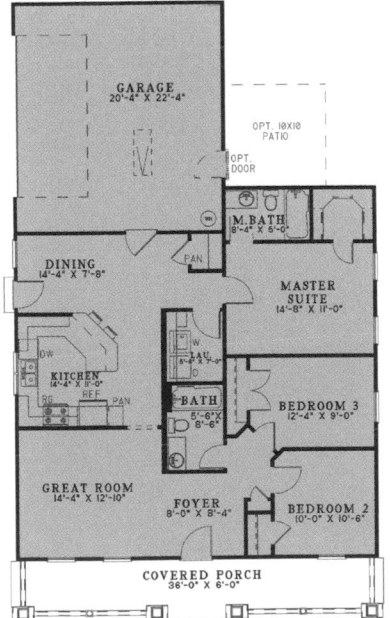

GARAGE
20'-4" X 22'-4"

OPT. 10X10 PATIO

OPT. DOOR

M. BATH
8'-4" X 6'-0"

DINING
14'-4" X 7'-8"

MASTER SUITE
14'-8" X 11'-0"

KITCHEN
14'-4" X 11'-0"

BATH
8'-6" X 8'-0"

BEDROOM 3
12'-4" X 9'-0"

GREAT ROOM
14'-4" X 12'-10"

FOYER
8'-0" X 8'-4"

BEDROOM 2
10'-0" X 10'-6"

COVERED PORCH
36'-0" X 6'-0"

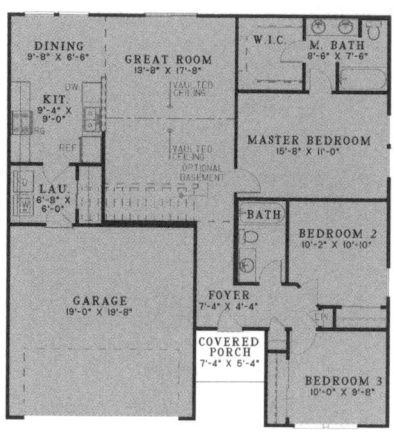

HPK2100024

Style: Colonial

Square Footage: 1,250

Bedrooms: 3

Bathrooms: 2

Width: 40' - 0"

Depth: 43' - 2"

Foundation: Crawlspace, Slab

EPLANS.COM

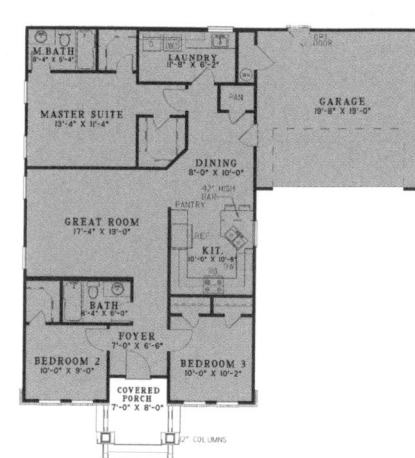

HPK2100025

Style: Country

Square Footage: 1,252

Bedrooms: 3

Bathrooms: 2

Width: 48' - 4"

Depth: 45' - 6"

Foundation: Crawlspace, Slab

EPLANS.COM

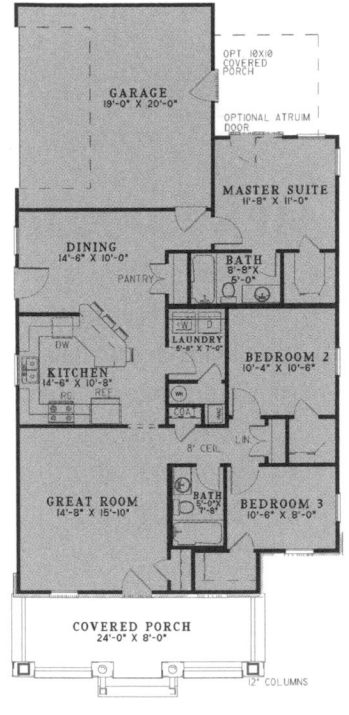

COVERED PORCH
24'-0" X 8'-0"

HPK2100026

Style: Cottage

Square Footage: 1,256

Bedrooms: 3

Bathrooms: 2

Width: 31' - 8"

Depth: 66' - 2"

Foundation: Crawlspace, Slab

EPLANS.COM

HPK2100027

Style: New American

Square Footage: 1,259

Bedrooms: 3

Bathrooms: 2

Width: 49' - 0"

Depth: 51' - 6"

Foundation: Crawlspace, Slab, Unfinished Walkout Basement

EPLANS.COM

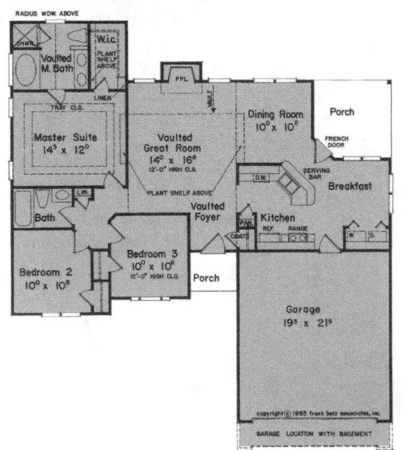

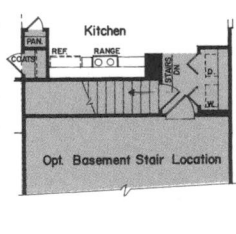

UNDER 1,500 SQUARE FEET

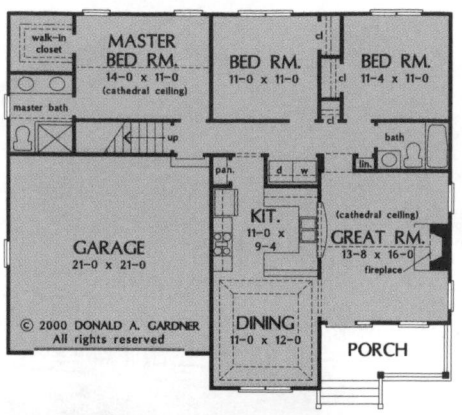

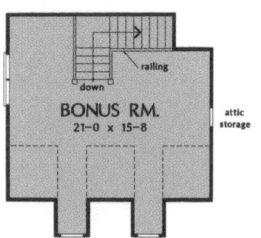

HPK2100028

Style: Cottage
Square Footage: 1,264
Bonus Space: 397 sq. ft.
Bedrooms: 3
Bathrooms: 2
Width: 47' - 0"
Depth: 40' - 4"

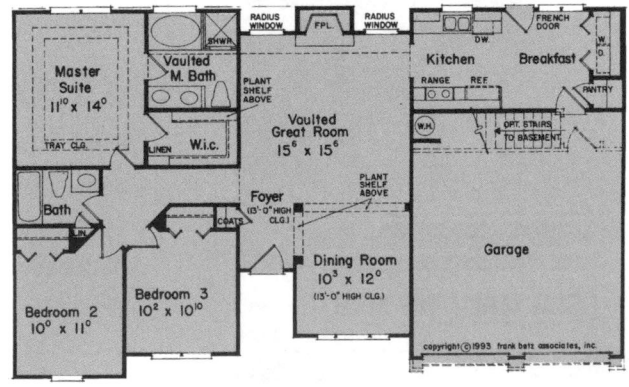

HPK2100029

Style: New American
Square Footage: 1,271
Bedrooms: 3
Bathrooms: 2
Width: 56' - 6"
Depth: 33' - 10"
Foundation: Crawlspace, Unfinished Walkout Basement

HPK2100030

Style: Bungalow

Square Footage: 1,275

Bedrooms: 3

Bathrooms: 2

Width: 40' - 0"

Depth: 58' - 0"

Foundation: Crawlspace

EPLANS.COM

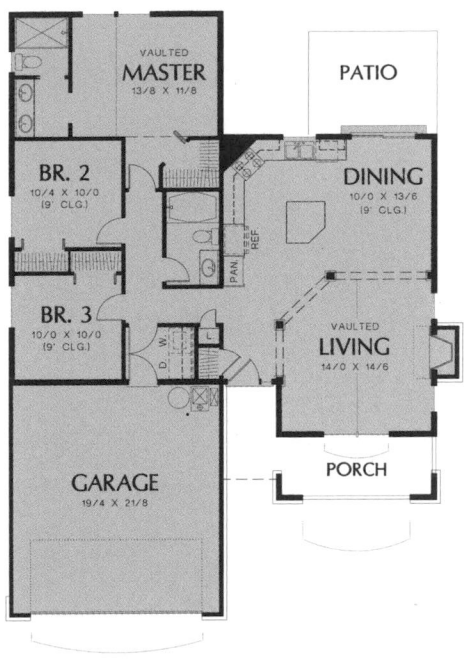

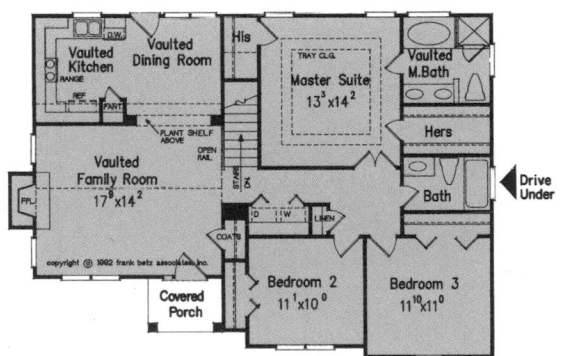

HPK2100031

Style: Cottage

Square Footage: 1,281

Bedrooms: 3

Bathrooms: 2

Width: 46' - 4"

Depth: 32' - 6"

Foundation: Unfinished Walkout Basement

EPLANS.COM

UNDER 1,500 SQUARE FEET

© 1992 Donald A. Gardner Architects, Inc.

HPK2100032

Style: Country

Square Footage: 1,287

Bedrooms: 3

Bathrooms: 2

Width: 66' - 4"

Depth: 48' - 0"

EPLANS.COM

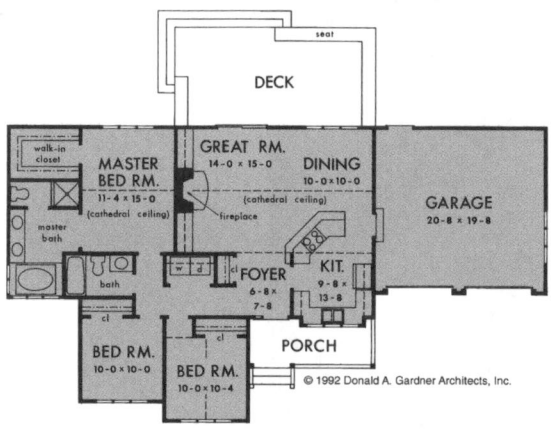

© 1992 Donald A. Gardner Architects, Inc.

© Sater Design Collection, Inc.

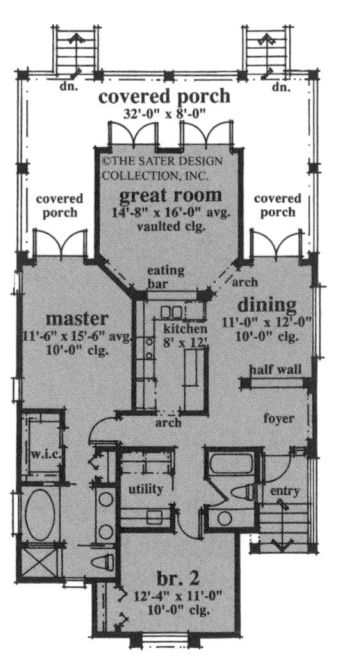

HPK2100033

Style: Tidewater

Square Footage: 1,288

Bedrooms: 2

Bathrooms: 2

Width: 32' - 4"

Depth: 60' - 0"

Foundation: Crawlspace

EPLANS.COM

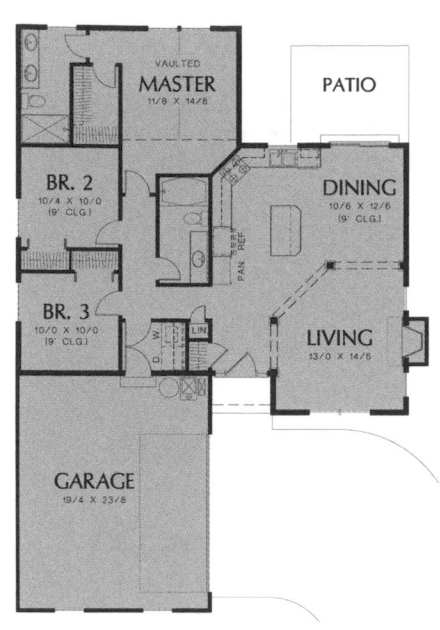

HPK2100034

Style: Ranch

Square Footage: 1,292

Bedrooms: 3

Bathrooms: 2

Width: 40' - 0"

Depth: 60' - 0"

Foundation: Crawlspace

EPLANS.COM

HPK2100035

Style: Colonial

Square Footage: 1,294

Bonus Space: 374 sq. ft.

Bedrooms: 3

Bathrooms: 2

Width: 64' - 6"

Depth: 29' - 10"

Foundation: Crawlspace, Slab

EPLANS.COM

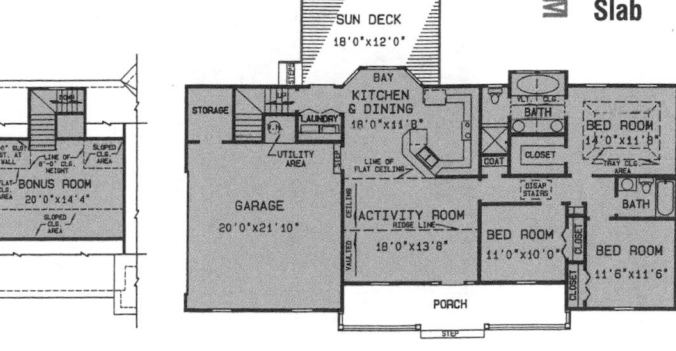

UNDER 1,500 SQUARE FEET

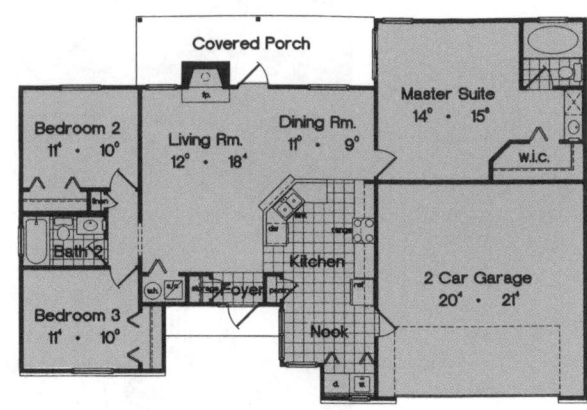

Covered Porch

Bedroom 2
11⁰ · 10⁰

Living Rm.
12⁰ · 18⁴

Dining Rm.
11⁰ · 9⁰

Master Suite
14⁰ · 15⁰

w.i.c.

Bath 2

Kitchen

2 Car Garage
20⁴ · 21⁴

Bedroom 3
11⁰ · 10⁰

Foyer

Nook

HPK2100036

Style: Ranch

Square Footage: 1,300

Bedrooms: 3

Bathrooms: 2

Width: 56' - 0"

Depth: 38' - 0"

Foundation: Slab

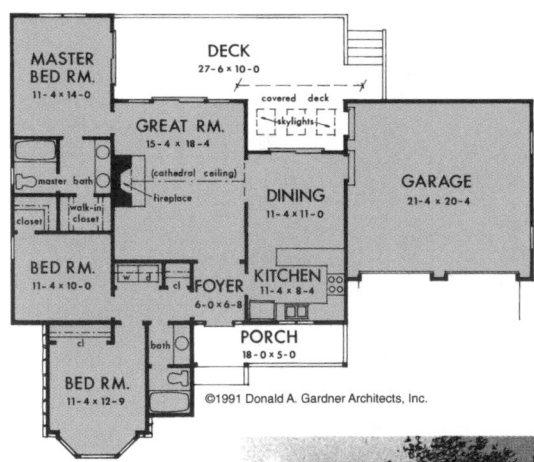

MASTER
BED RM.
11-4 x 14-0

DECK
27-6 x 10-0

covered deck
skylights

GREAT RM.
15-4 x 18-4

(cathedral ceiling)
fireplace

DINING
11-4 x 11-0

GARAGE
21-4 x 20-4

master bath

walk-in
closet

BED RM.
11-4 x 10-0

KITCHEN
11-4 x 8-4

FOYER
6-0 x 6-8

cl

bath

PORCH
18-0 x 5-0

BED RM.
11-4 x 12-9

©1991 Donald A. Gardner Architects, Inc.

HPK2100037

Style: Country

Square Footage: 1,310

Bedrooms: 3

Bathrooms: 2

Width: 61' - 0"

Depth: 51' - 5"

© 1991 Donald A. Gardner, Architects, Inc.

HPK2100038

Style: Cottage

Square Footage: 1,315

Bedrooms: 3

Bathrooms: 2

Width: 50' - 0"

Depth: 54' - 8"

Foundation: Unfinished Walkout Basement

EPLANS.COM

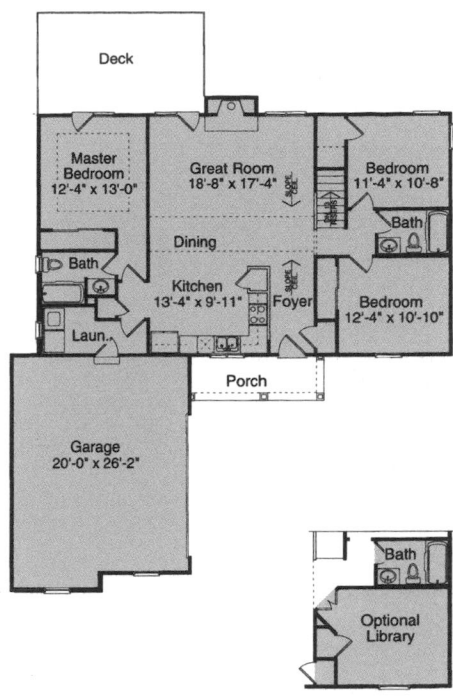

Optional Layout

HPK2100039

Style: Cottage

Square Footage: 1,317

Bedrooms: 3

Bathrooms: 2

Width: 45' - 0"

Depth: 52' - 4"

Foundation: Slab

EPLANS.COM

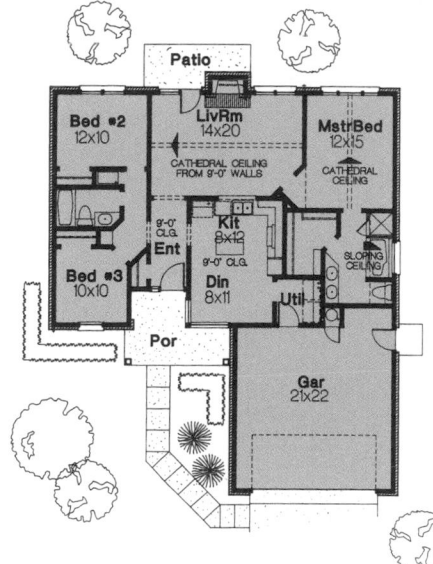

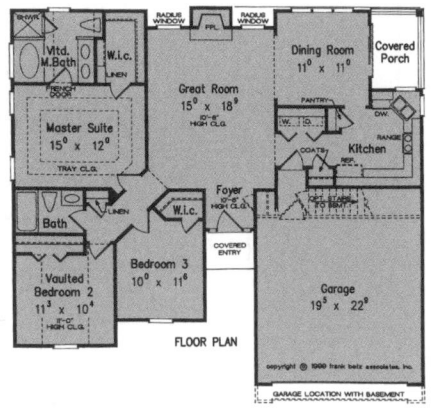

HPK2100040

Style: Cottage

Square Footage: 1,324

Bedrooms: 3

Bathrooms: 2

Width: 48' - 0"

Depth: 44' - 4"

Foundation: Crawlspace, Slab, Unfinished Walkout Basement

EPLANS.COM

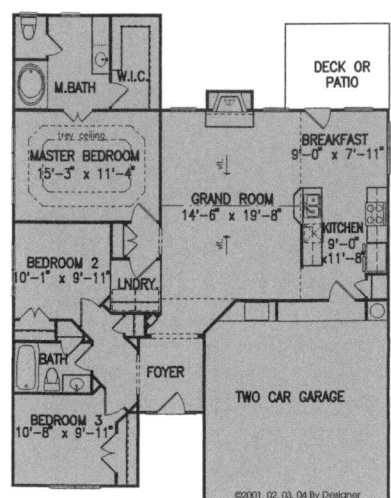

HPK2100041

Style: Cottage

Square Footage: 1,328

Bedrooms: 3

Bathrooms: 2

Width: 40' - 0"

Depth: 52' - 0"

Foundation: Slab

EPLANS.COM

HPK2100042

Style: Cottage

Square Footage: 1,333

Bedrooms: 3

Bathrooms: 2

Width: 47' - 0"

Depth: 47' - 0"

EPLANS.COM

HPK2100043

Style: Cottage

Square Footage: 1,342

Bonus Space: 350 sq. ft.

Bedrooms: 3

Bathrooms: 2

Width: 52' - 6"

Depth: 39' - 10"

Foundation: Crawlspace, Slab, Unfinished Walkout Basement

EPLANS.COM

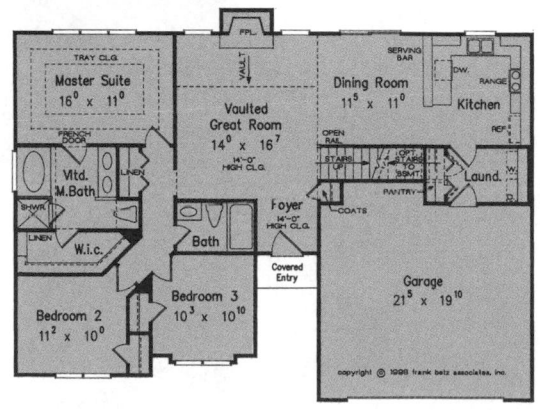

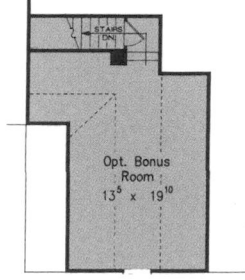

UNDER 1,500 SQUARE FEET

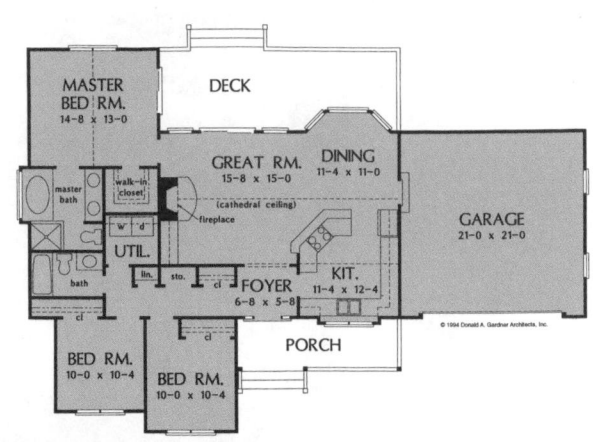

© 1994 Donald A. Gardner Architects, Inc.

HPK2100044

Style: Country

Square Footage: 1,346

Bedrooms: 3

Bathrooms: 2

Width: 65' - 0"

Depth: 44' - 2"

EPLANS.COM

HPK2100045

Style: Ranch

Square Footage: 1,356

Bedrooms: 3

Bathrooms: 2

Width: 37' - 6"

Depth: 56' - 10"

Foundation: Crawlspace, Slab

EPLANS.COM

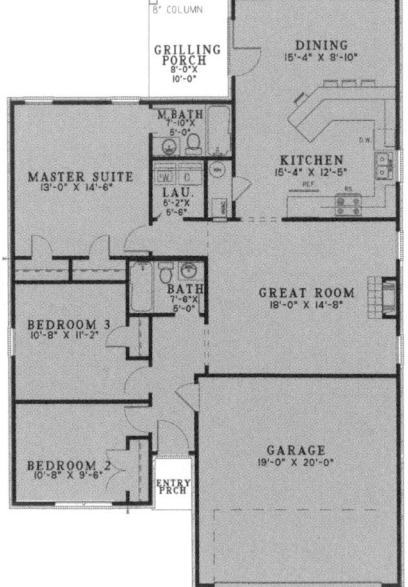

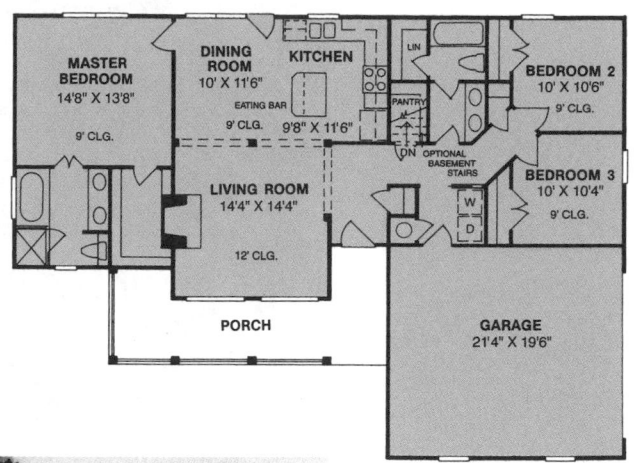

HPK2100046

Style: Ranch

Square Footage: 1,359

Bedrooms: 3

Bathrooms: 2

Width: 57' - 0"

Depth: 42' - 0"

EPLANS.COM

HPK2100047

Style: Cottage

Square Footage: 1,360

Bedrooms: 3

Bathrooms: 2

Width: 40' - 0"

Depth: 49' - 10"

Foundation: Slab

EPLANS.COM

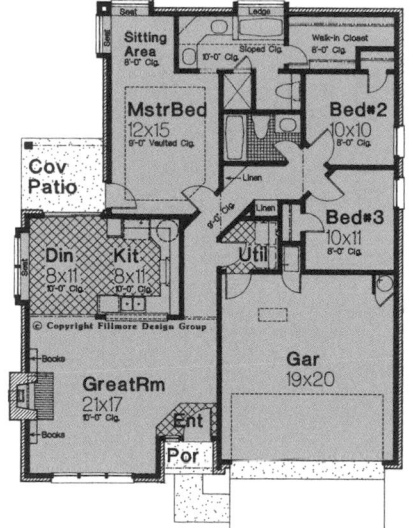

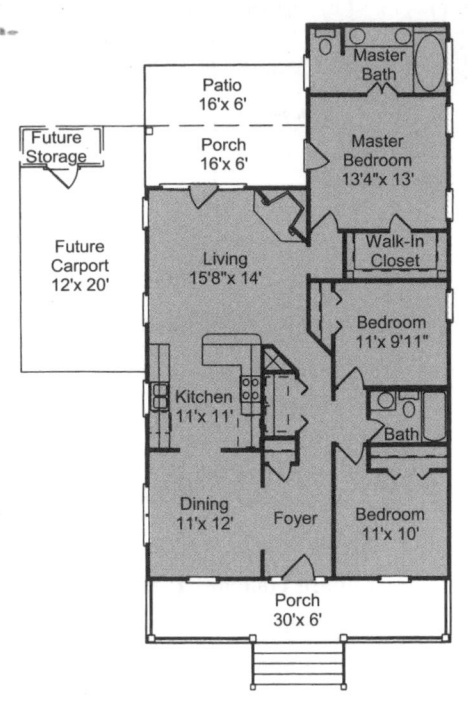

HPK2100048

Style: Cracker

Square Footage: 1,363

Bedrooms: 3

Bathrooms: 2

Width: 30' - 0"

Depth: 60' - 0"

Foundation: Slab

EPLANS.COM

HPK2100049

Style: Victorian Eclectic

Square Footage: 1,370

Bedrooms: 3

Bathrooms: 1

Width: 58' - 0"

Depth: 36' - 0"

Foundation: Unfinished Basement

EPLANS.COM

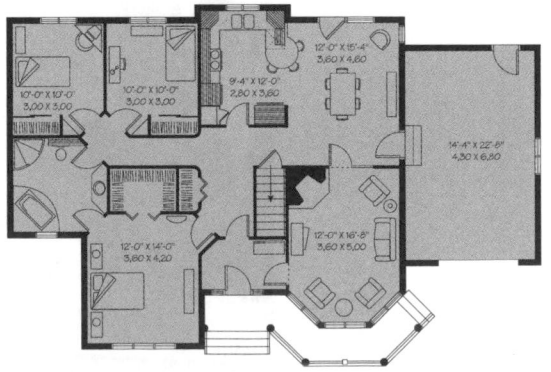

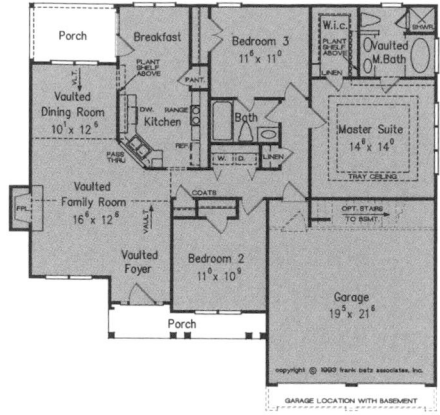

HPK2100050

Style: Country

Square Footage: 1,373

Bedrooms: 3

Bathrooms: 2

Width: 50' - 4"

Depth: 45' - 0"

Foundation: Crawlspace, Unfinished Walkout Basement

EPLANS.COM

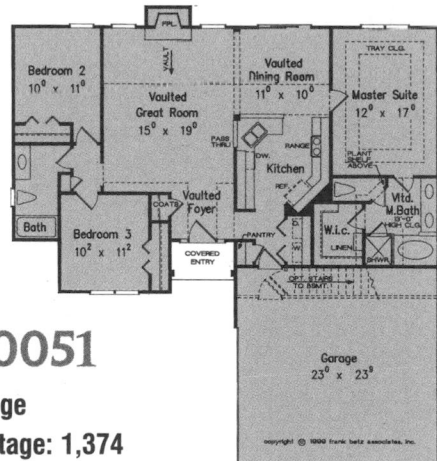

HPK2100051

Style: Cottage

Square Footage: 1,374

Bedrooms: 3

Bathrooms: 2

Width: 49' - 0"

Depth: 55' - 4"

Foundation: Crawlspace, Unfinished Walkout Basement

EPLANS.COM

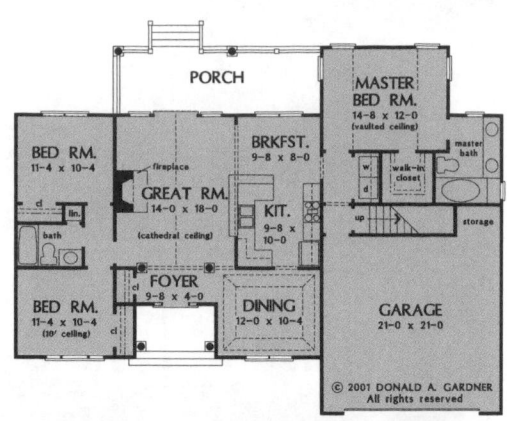

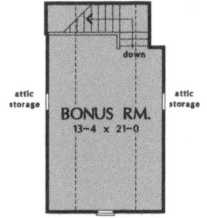

HPK2100052

Style: Cottage
Square Footage: 1,377
Bonus Space: 322 sq. ft.
Bedrooms: 3
Bathrooms: 2
Width: 57' - 8"
Depth: 44' - 0"

EPLANS.COM

HPK2100053

Style: French Country
Square Footage: 1,379
Bedrooms: 3
Bathrooms: 2
Width: 38' - 4"
Depth: 68' - 6"
Foundation: Crawlspace, Slab

EPLANS.COM

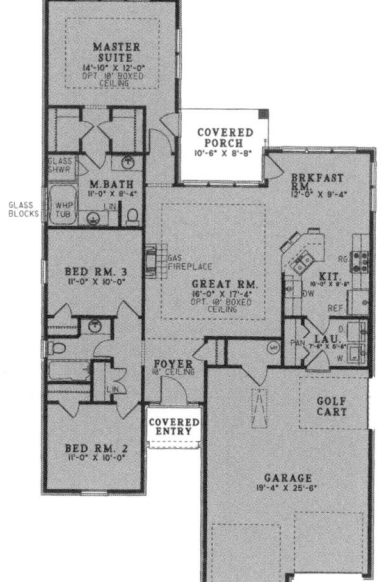

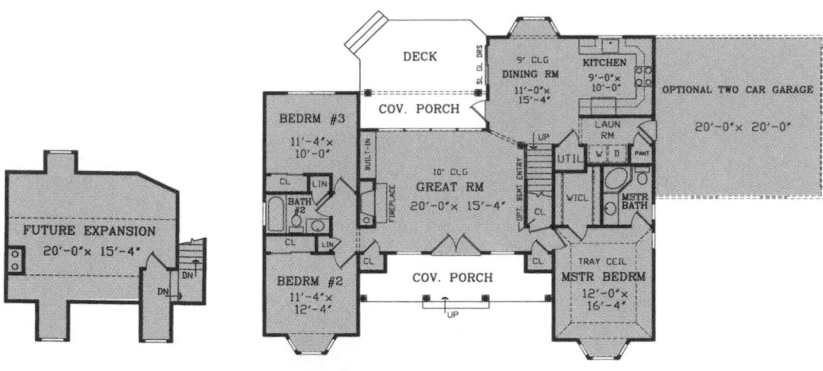

HPK2100054

Style: Cottage
Square Footage: 1,380
Bonus Space: 372 sq. ft.
Bedrooms: 3
Bathrooms: 2
Width: 48' - 0"
Depth: 43' - 4"
Foundation: Crawlspace, Slab, Unfinished Basement

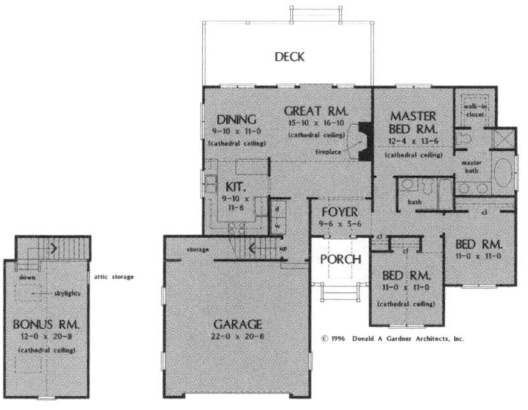

HPK2100055

Style: Cottage
Square Footage: 1,386
Bonus Space: 314 sq. ft.
Bedrooms: 3
Bathrooms: 2
Width: 54' - 10"
Depth: 48' - 0"

© 1996 Donald A. Gardner Architects, Inc.

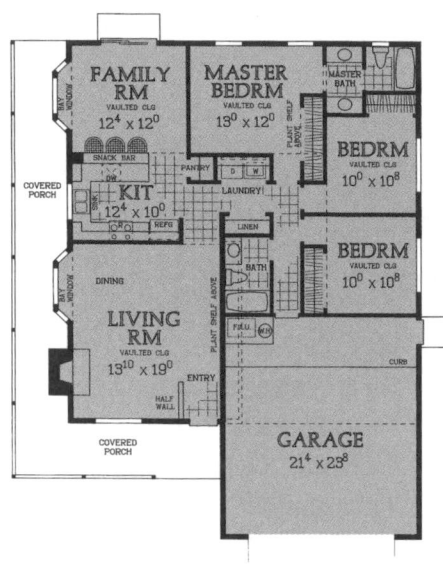

UNDER 1,500 SQUARE FEET

HPK2100056

EPLANS.COM

Style: Cottage
Square Footage: 1,389
Bedrooms: 3
Bathrooms: 2
Width: 44' - 8"
Depth: 54' - 6"
Foundation: Slab

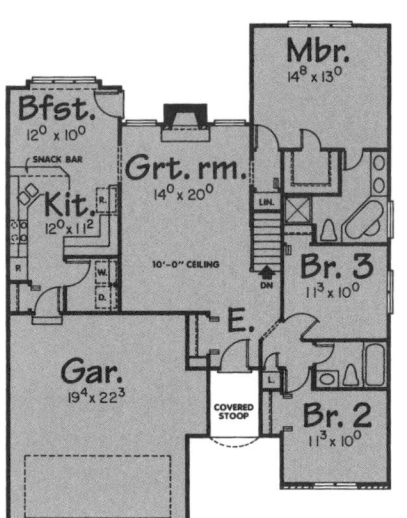

HPK2100057

EPLANS.COM

Style: Cottage
Square Footage: 1,392
Bedrooms: 3
Bathrooms: 2
Width: 42' - 0"
Depth: 54' - 0"

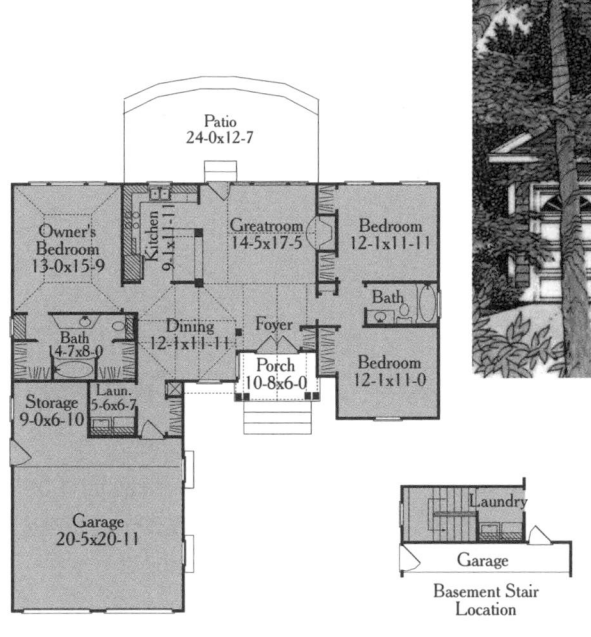

Patio
24-0x12-7

Owner's
Bedroom
13-0x15-9

Kitchen
9-1x11-1

Greatroom
14-5x17-5

Bedroom
12-1x11-11

Bath

Dining
12-1x11-11

Foyer

Bath
4-7x8-0

Porch
10-8x6-0

Bedroom
12-1x11-0

Storage
9-0x6-10

Laun.
5-6x6-7

Garage
20-5x20-11

Laundry

Garage

Basement Stair
Location

HPK2100058

Style: Cottage

Square Footage: 1,392

Bedrooms: 3

Bathrooms: 2

Width: 52' - 6"

Depth: 52' - 8"

**Foundation: Crawlspace,
Slab, Unfinished Basement**

EPLANS.COM

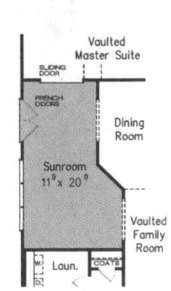

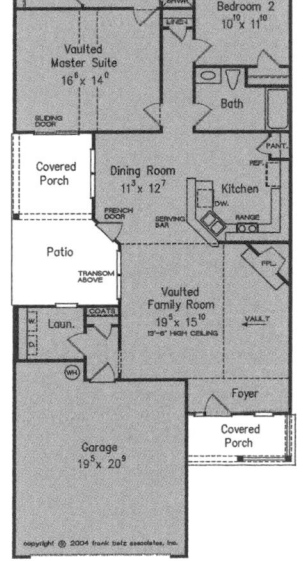

Vaulted
Master Suite

Dining
Room

Sunroom
11⁹x 20⁰

Vaulted
Family
Room

Laun.

Optional Layout

W.i.c.   M. Bath   Bedroom 2
10¹⁰ x 11¹⁰

Vaulted
Master Suite
16⁶ x 14⁶

Bath

Covered
Porch

Dining Room
11³ x 12⁷

Kitchen

Patio

Vaulted
Family Room
19⁵ x 15¹⁰

Laun.

Garage
19⁵ x 20⁸

Foyer

Covered
Porch

copyright © 2004 frank betz associates, inc.

HPK2100059

Style: Cottage

Square Footage: 1,393

Bonus Space: 206 sq. ft.

Bedrooms: 2

Bathrooms: 2

Width: 32' - 0"

Depth: 70' - 0"

**Foundation: Crawlspace,
Unfinished Walkout
Basement**

EPLANS.COM

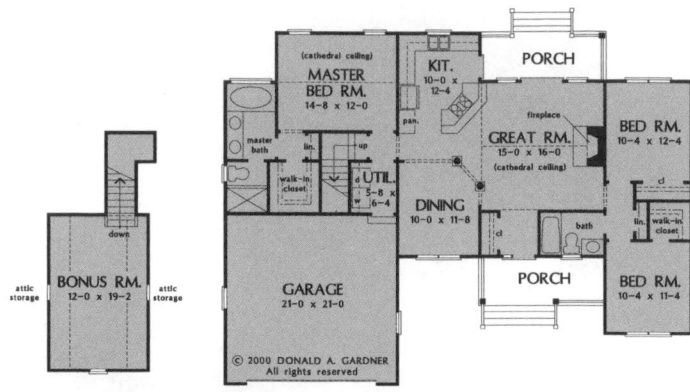

© 2000 Donald A. Gardner, Inc.

HPK2100060

Style: Country
Square Footage: 1,399
Bonus Space: 296 sq. ft.
Bedrooms: 3
Bathrooms: 2
Width: 58' - 0"
Depth: 44' - 4"

EPLANS.COM

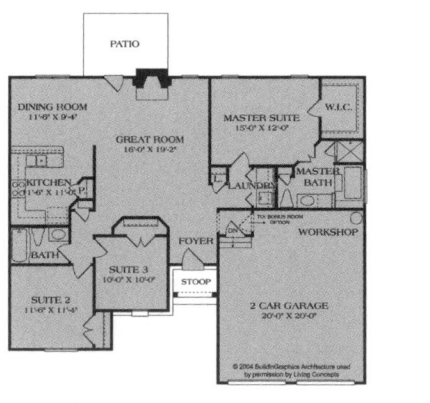

HPK2100061

Style: French Country
Square Footage: 1,400
Bonus Space: 297 sq. ft.
Bedrooms: 3
Bathrooms: 2
Width: 50' - 0"
Depth: 42' - 8"
Foundation: Crawlspace

EPLANS.COM

HPK2100062

Style: Contemporary

Square Footage: 1,401

Bedrooms: 3

Bathrooms: 2

Width: 48' - 0"

Depth: 58' - 0"

Foundation: Crawlspace, Slab

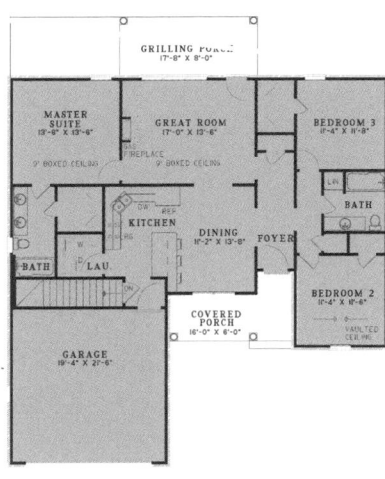

HPK2100063

Style: Cottage

Square Footage: 1,402

Bedrooms: 3

Bathrooms: 2

Width: 45' - 4"

Depth: 50' - 1"

Foundation: Slab

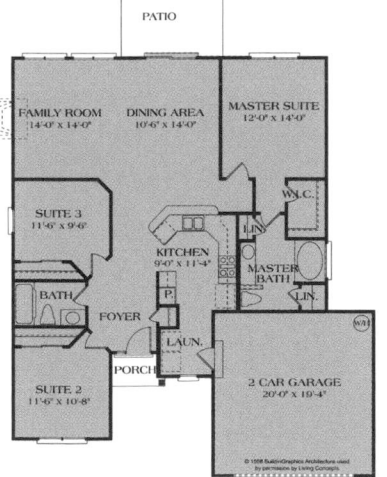

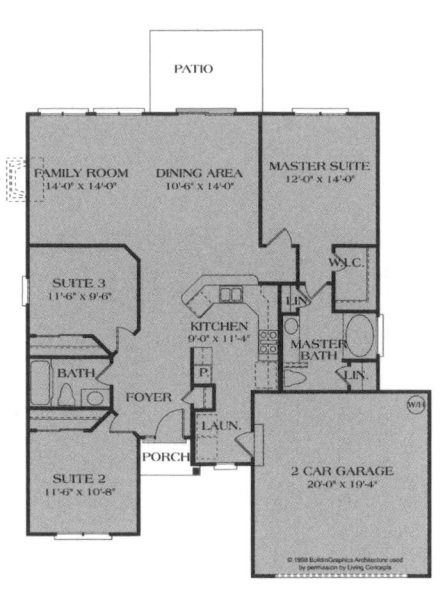

HPK2100064

Style: Cottage

Square Footage: 1,402

Bedrooms: 3

Bathrooms: 2

Width: 45' - 8"

Depth: 50' - 6"

Foundation: Slab

EPLANS.COM

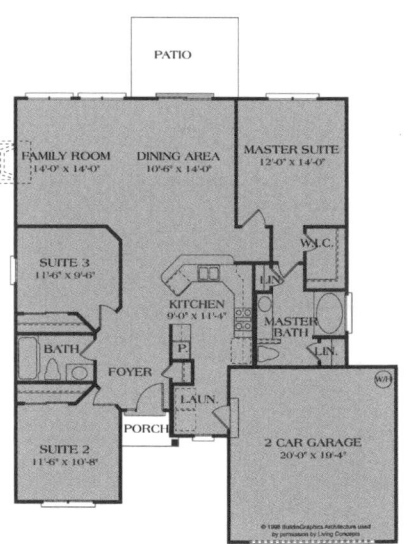

HPK2100065

Style: Cottage

Square Footage: 1,402

Bedrooms: 3

Bathrooms: 2

Width: 44' - 11"

Depth: 50' - 1"

Foundation: Slab

EPLANS.COM

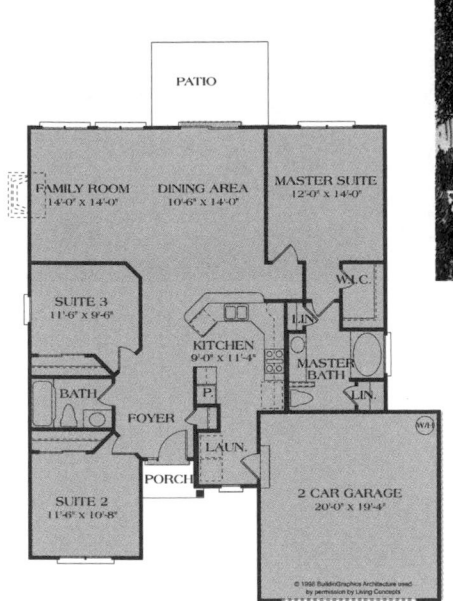

HPK2100066

Style: Cottage

Square Footage: 1,402

Bedrooms: 3

Bathrooms: 2

Width: 45' - 4"

Depth: 50' - 1"

Foundation: Slab

HPK2100067

Style: Country

Square Footage: 1,404

Bonus Space: 256 sq. ft.

Bedrooms: 2

Bathrooms: 2

Width: 54' - 7"

Depth: 46' - 6"

Foundation: Crawlspace

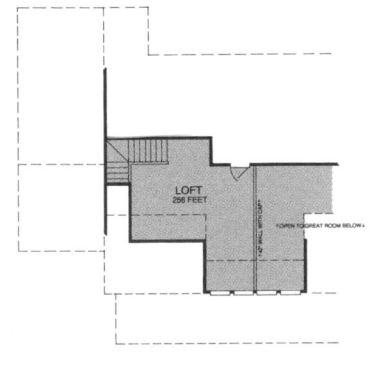

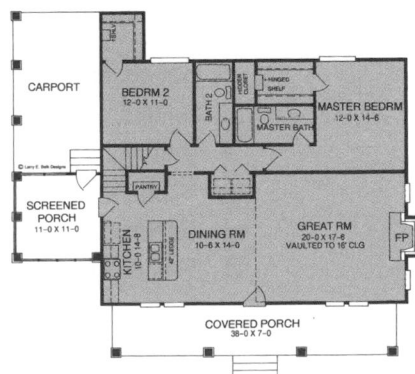

UNDER 1,500 SQUARE FEET

HPK2100068

Style: Greek Revival

Square Footage: 1,404

Bedrooms: 3

Bathrooms: 2

Width: 48' - 4"

Depth: 62' - 0"

Foundation: Crawlspace, Slab

EPLANS.COM

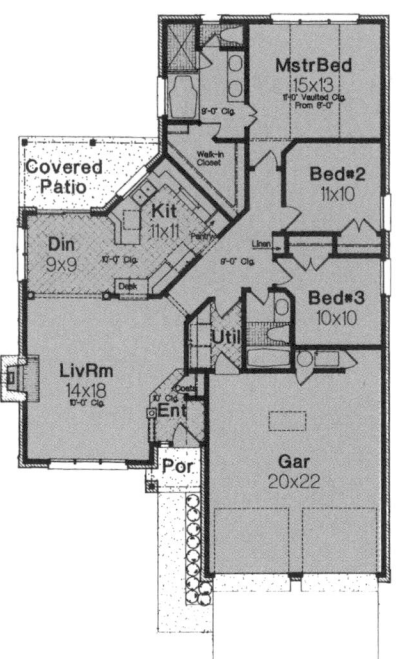

HPK2100069

Style: Cottage

Square Footage: 1,405

Bedrooms: 3

Bathrooms: 2

Width: 40' - 0"

Depth: 60' - 8"

Foundation: Slab

EPLANS.COM

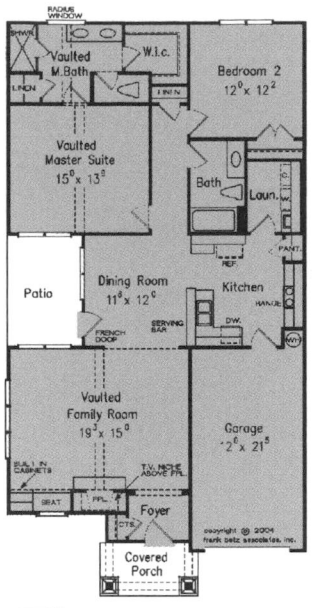

Optional Layout

HPK2100070

Style: Bungalow

Square Footage: 1,407

Bedrooms: 2

Bathrooms: 2

Width: 32' - 0"

Depth: 61' - 7"

Foundation: Slab, Unfinished Walkout Basement

HPK2100071

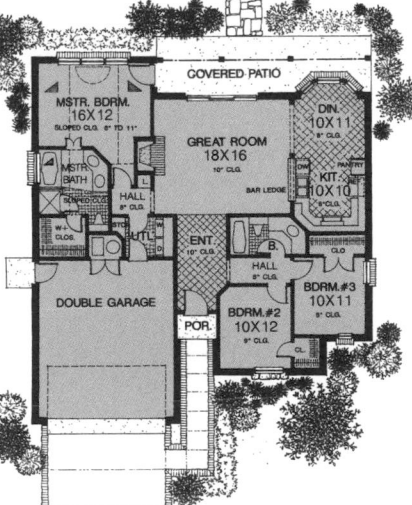

Style: French Country

Square Footage: 1,416

Bedrooms: 3

Bathrooms: 2

Width: 45' - 0"

Depth: 49' - 10"

Foundation: Slab

UNDER 1,500 SQUARE FEET

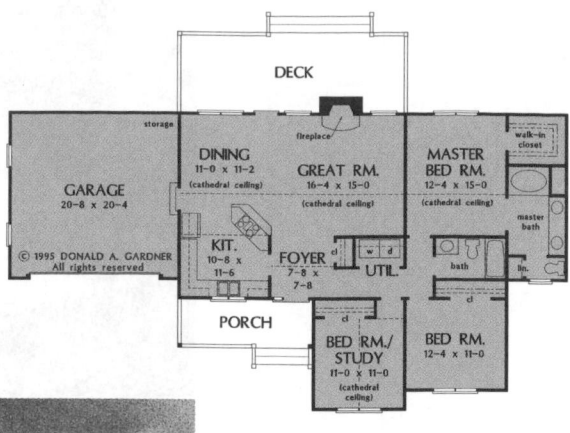

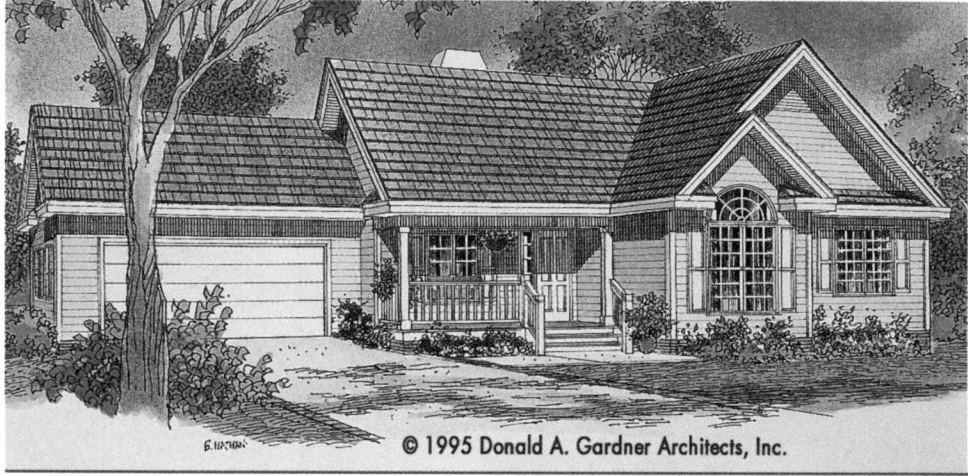

© 1995 Donald A. Gardner Architects, Inc.

HPK2100072

Style: Country
Square Footage: 1,417
Bedrooms: 3
Bathrooms: 2
Width: 69' - 0"
Depth: 39' - 0"

EPLANS.COM

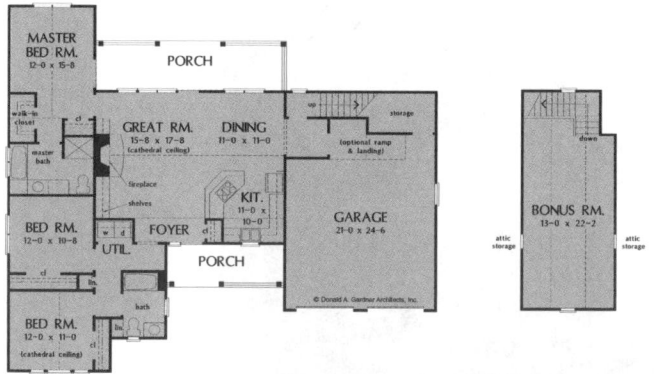

HPK2100073

Style: Cottage
Square Footage: 1,425
Bonus Space: 424 sq. ft.
Bedrooms: 3
Bathrooms: 2
Width: 61' - 0"
Depth: 51' - 8"

EPLANS.COM

©1999 Donald A. Gardner, Inc.

HPK2100074

Style: Cottage

Square Footage: 1,425

Bedrooms: 3

Bathrooms: 2

Width: 40' - 0"

Depth: 53' - 0"

Foundation: Crawlspace, Unfinished Walkout Basement

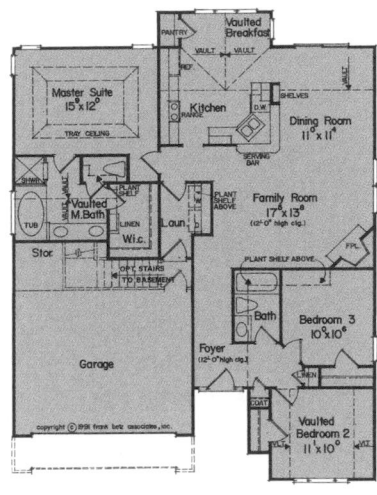

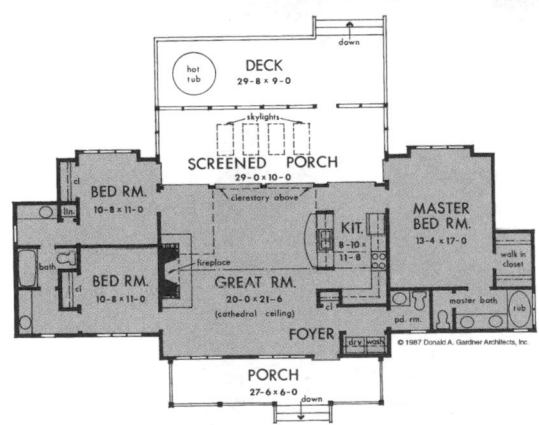

HPK2100075

Style: Country

Square Footage: 1,426

Bedrooms: 3

Bathrooms: 2 ½

Width: 67' - 6"

Depth: 36' - 8"

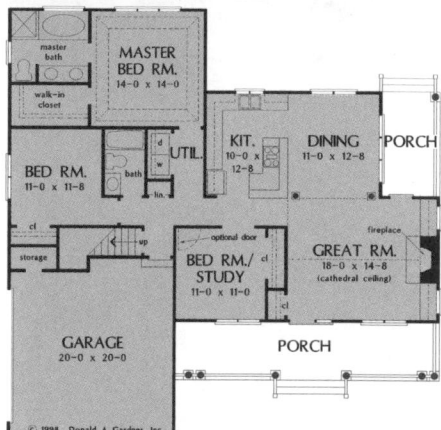

©1998 Donald A. Gardner, Inc.

HPK2100076

Style: Country
Square Footage: 1,428
Bonus Space: 313 sq. ft.
Bedrooms: 3
Bathrooms: 2
Width: 52' - 8"
Depth: 52' - 4"

EPLANS.COM

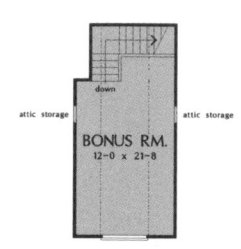

HPK2100077

Style: French Country
Square Footage: 1,429
Bedrooms: 3
Bathrooms: 2
Width: 49' - 0"
Depth: 53' - 0"
Foundation: Crawlspace, Slab,
Unfinished Walkout Basement

EPLANS.COM

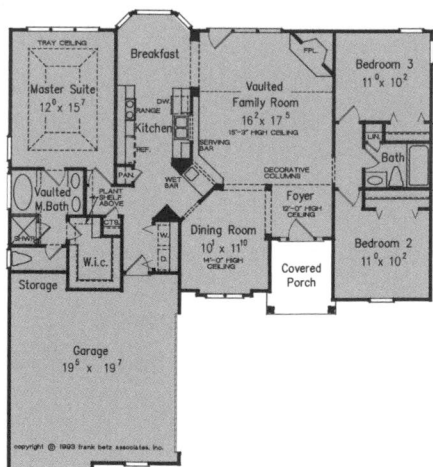

HPK2100078

Style: Cottage

Square Footage: 1,432

Bedrooms: 3

Bathrooms: 2

Width: 49' - 0"

Depth: 52' - 4"

Foundation: Crawlspace, Slab, Unfinished Walkout Basement

EPLANS.COM

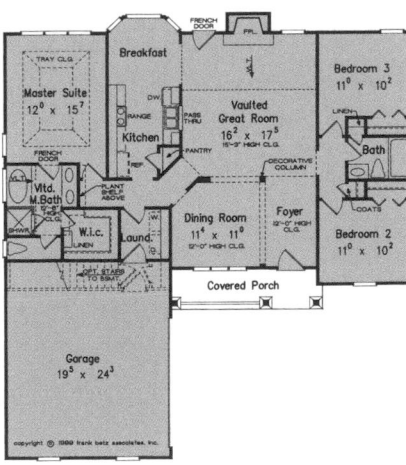

HPK2100079

Style: Country

Square Footage: 1,439

Bedrooms: 3

Bathrooms: 2

Width: 49' - 0"

Depth: 54' - 10"

Foundation: Crawlspace, Slab, Unfinished Walkout Basement

EPLANS.COM

HPK2100080

Style: Cottage
Square Footage: 1,442
Bedrooms: 3
Bathrooms: 2
Width: 54' - 0"
Depth: 50' - 0"
Foundation: Crawlspace, Slab

EPLANS.COM

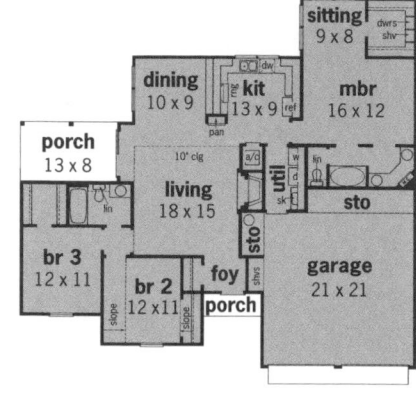

HPK2100081

EPLANS.COM

Style: Country
Square Footage: 1,442
Bedrooms: 3
Bathrooms: 2
Width: 52' - 8"
Depth: 45' - 0"
Foundation: Unfinished Walkout Basement

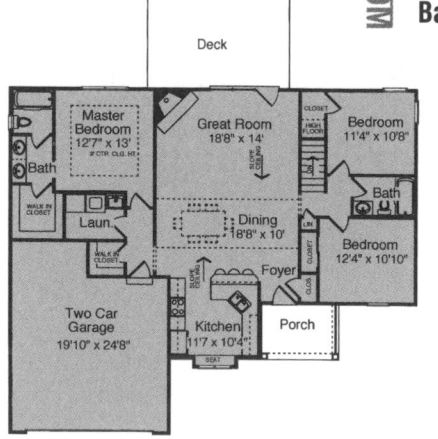

HPK2100082

Style: Cracker

Square Footage: 1,456

Bedrooms: 3

Bathrooms: 2

Width: 54' - 0"

Depth: 45' - 6"

Foundation: Crawlspace

Expansive rear and front porches extend living space outward, and the master suite enjoys private access to a deck. A cozy fireplace is tucked into the corner of the main living room. The center island in the kitchen eases meal preparation. The deluxe master suite, with a walk-in closet and a private bath, is on the left, and two more bedrooms are on the right side of the home. A laundry room is close by.

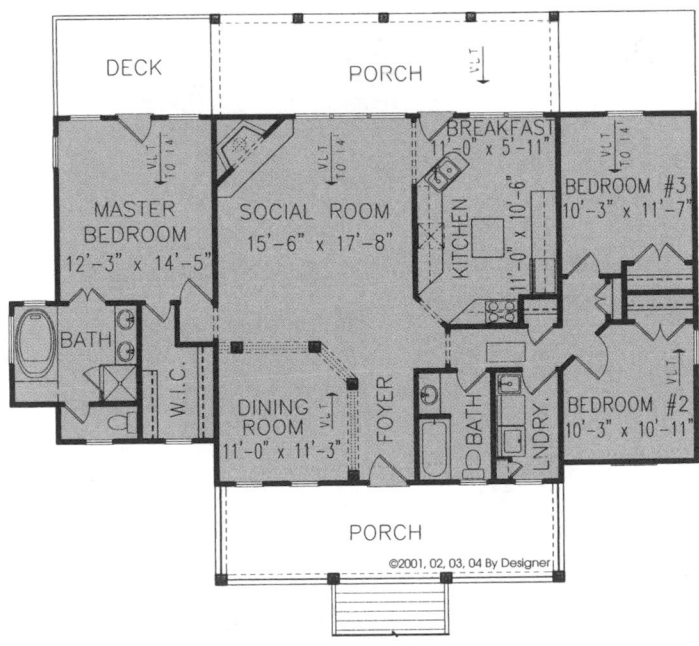

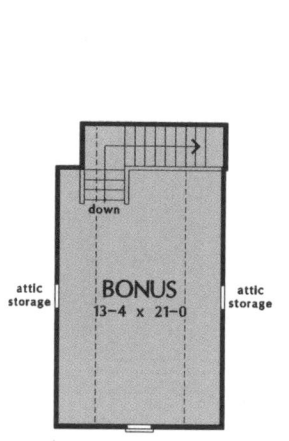

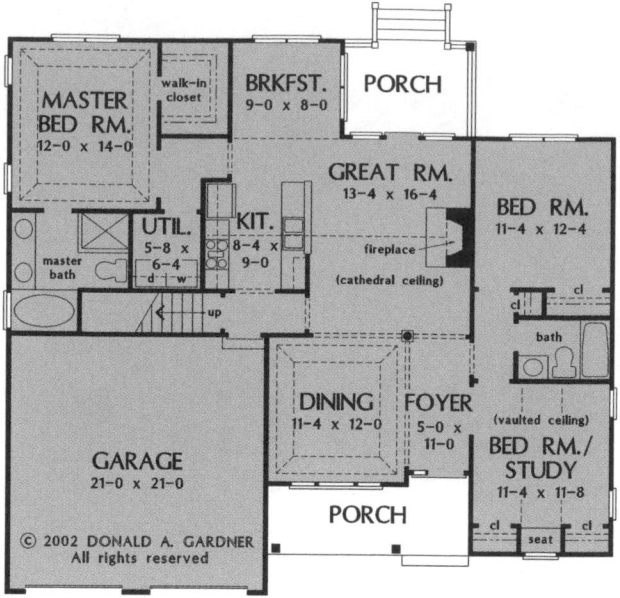

attic storage

BONUS
13-4 x 21-0

attic storage

down

MASTER BED RM.
12-0 x 14-0

walk-in closet

BRKFST.
9-0 x 8-0

PORCH

GREAT RM.
13-4 x 16-4

BED RM.
11-4 x 12-4

master bath

UTIL.
5-8 x 6-4
d — w

KIT.
8-4 x 9-0

fireplace
(cathedral ceiling)

cl
cl

bath

up

cl

DINING
11-4 x 12-0

FOYER
5-0 x 11-0

(vaulted ceiling)

GARAGE
21-0 x 21-0

BED RM./ STUDY
11-4 x 11-8

PORCH

cl
cl

seat

Sunny rooms and elegant ceiling treatments give a feeling of spaciousness in an adorable home that is less than 1,500 square feet. Enter from the covered front porch to find the dining room to the left of the foyer and a vaulted bedroom/study—with a window seat—to the right. The great room soars with a cathedral ceiling and comforts with an extended-hearth fireplace. In the quiet master bedroom, a tray ceiling and sumptuous bath will pamper morning and night.

EPLANS.COM

HPK2100083

Style: Cottage
Square Footage: 1,457
Bonus Space: 341 sq. ft.
Bedrooms: 3
Bathrooms: 2
Width: 50' - 4"
Depth: 46' - 4"

HPK2100084

Style: Cottage

Square Footage: 1,458

Bonus Space: 256 sq. ft.

Bedrooms: 3

Bathrooms: 2

Width: 47' - 7"

Depth: 46' - 5"

Foundation: Slab

This picturesque cottage was designed with a small family in mind. The spacious living room is a likely gathering area and the proximity to the kitchen snack bar invites the opportunity for informal meals. Suite 3 is useful as guest lodging or a home office. The well-appointed master suite is tucked away for privacy.

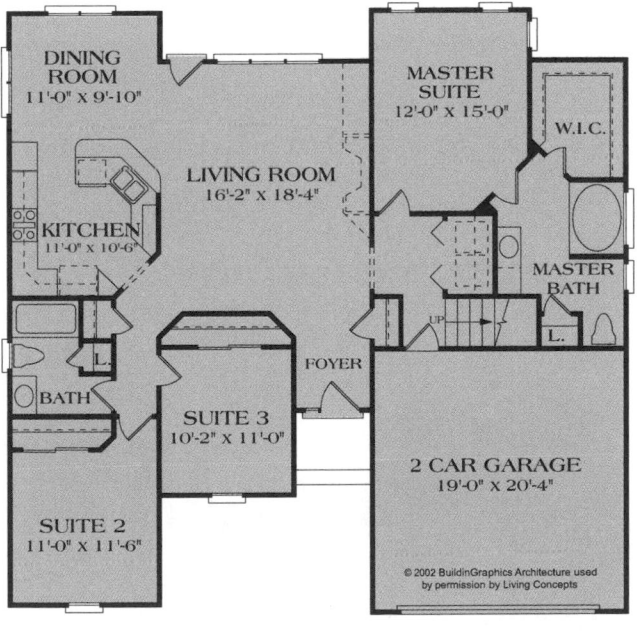

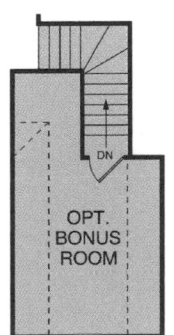

© 2002 BuildinGraphics Architecture used by permission by Living Concepts

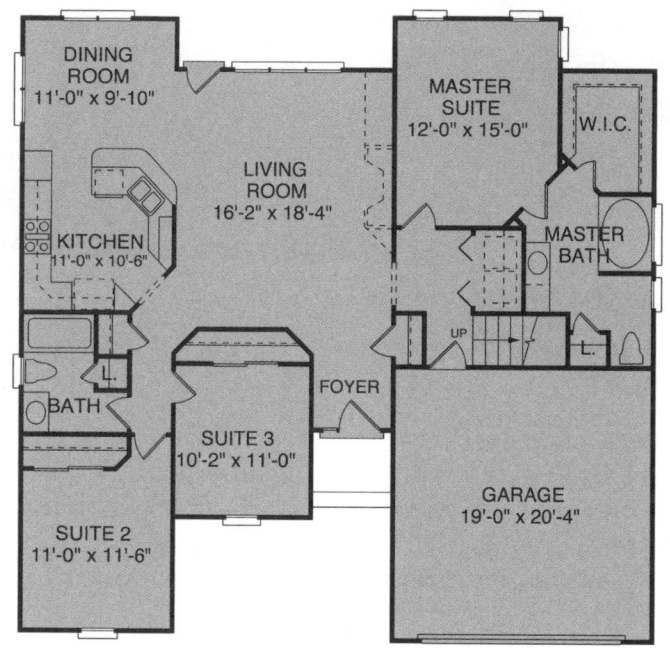

This efficient design looks good anywhere—in an established neighborhood or a new lot. The foyer opens directly onto a sunlit living room with an optional fireplace. The kitchen features a serving bar to both the dining and living rooms. Two family bedrooms share a bath. To the right of the living room sits a luxurious master suite. A set of stairs between the master suite and garage leads to an optional bonus room.

HPK2100085

Style: Cottage
Square Footage: 1,458
Bonus Space: 256 sq. ft.
Bedrooms: 3
Bathrooms: 2
Width: 47' - 7"
Depth: 47' - 5"
Foundation: Slab

EPLANS.COM

HPK2100086

Style: Ranch
Square Footage: 1,467
Bedrooms: 3
Bathrooms: 2
Width: 49' - 0"
Depth: 43' - 0"
Foundation: Crawlspace

This charming traditional design boasts a cozy, compact floor plan. Vaulted ceilings add spaciousness to the dining area, living room, and master bedroom. The kitchen is open to the dining room and includes an island cooktop and corner sink. A service entry leads to the two-car garage and holds the laundry alcove and a storage closet. The master suite is as gracious as those found in much larger homes, with a walk-in closet and a bath with a spa tub, separate shower, and double sinks.

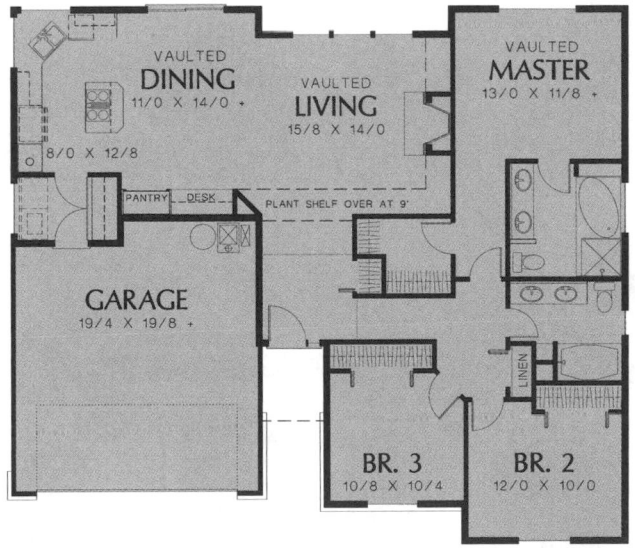

UNDER 1,500 SQUARE FEET

EPLANS.COM

HPK2100087

Style: New American

Square Footage: 1,467

Bedrooms: 3

Bathrooms: 2

Width: 51' - 6"

Depth: 54' - 10"

Foundation: Crawlspace, Unfinished Walkout Basement

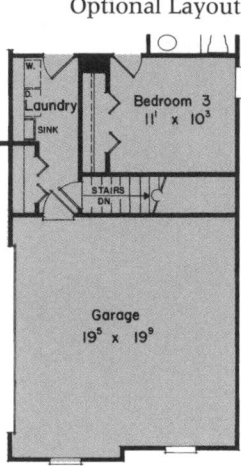

Optional Layout

This stucco one-story home offers graceful details fitting for any neighborhood. With its window detailing, hipped and gabled rooflines, and welcoming entrance, it's sure to be a winner. The efficient kitchen provides a pantry and plenty of counter and cabinet space. Split for privacy, the master suite sits on the left side of the home. The two family bedrooms on the right side of the home share a full hall bath.

© 2002 Donald A. Gardner, Inc.

HPK2100088

Style: Cottage
Square Footage: 1,472
Bedrooms: 3
Bathrooms: 2
Width: 46' - 6"
Depth: 56' - 4"

Cedar shake and siding combine with arched transoms to add architectural interest to this Craftsman cottage. A cathedral ceiling and fireplace make a grand impression upon entry. The dining room is distinguished by a tray ceiling. A pass-through between the kitchen and dining room facilitates ease of service. Both the kitchen and study/bedroom have French doors leading to the rear porch. The sleeping quarters are located away from the gathering rooms.

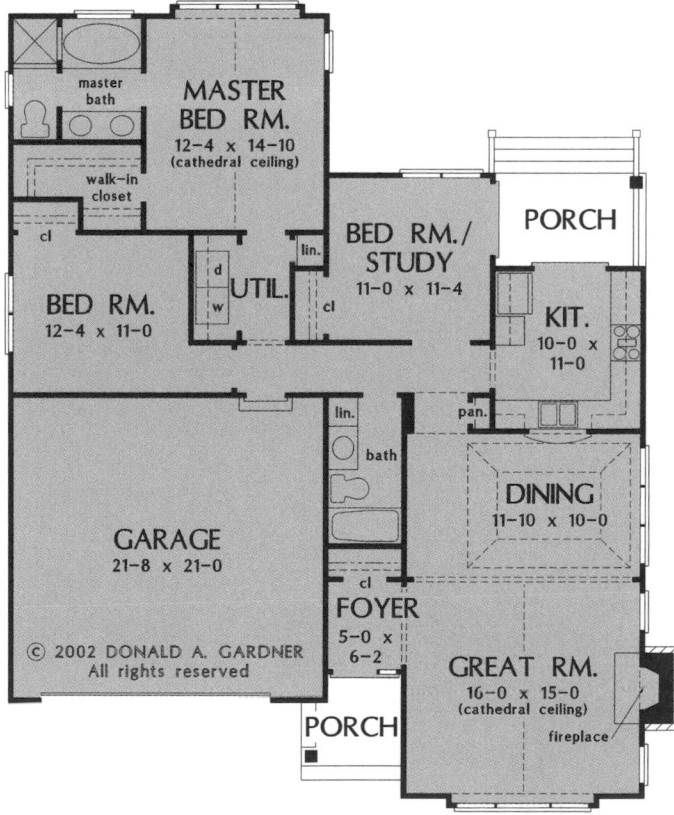

© 2002 DONALD A. GARDNER
All rights reserved

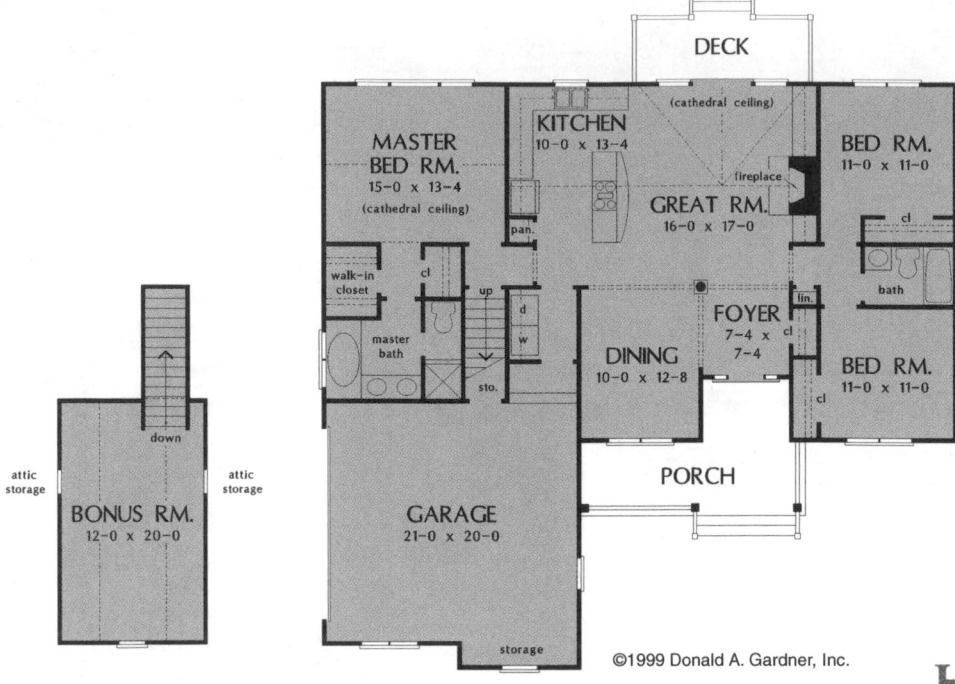

DECK

MASTER BED RM.
15-0 x 13-4
(cathedral ceiling)

KITCHEN
10-0 x 13-4

(cathedral ceiling)

fireplace

GREAT RM.
16-0 x 17-0

BED RM.
11-0 x 11-0

walk-in closet

cl

up

pan.

d
w

bath

master bath

sto.

DINING
10-0 x 12-8

FOYER
7-4 x 7-4

lin.

cl

BED RM.
11-0 x 11-0

cl

down

attic storage

attic storage

BONUS RM.
12-0 x 20-0

GARAGE
21-0 x 20-0

PORCH

storage

©1999 Donald A. Gardner, Inc.

Form and function blend wonderfully in this cottage-style home. To maximize space, the foyer, great room, dining room, and kitchen are completely open to one another. The bedrooms are split for ultimate master suite privacy, and a cathedral ceiling caps the master bedroom for an added sense of space. Two family bedrooms and a hall bath are located on the opposite side of the home.

HPK2100089

Style: Bungalow
Square Footage: 1,473
Bonus Space: 297 sq. ft.
Bedrooms: 3
Bathrooms: 2
Width: 53' - 4"
Depth: 49' - 8"

EPLANS.COM

© 1999 Donald A. Gardner, Inc.

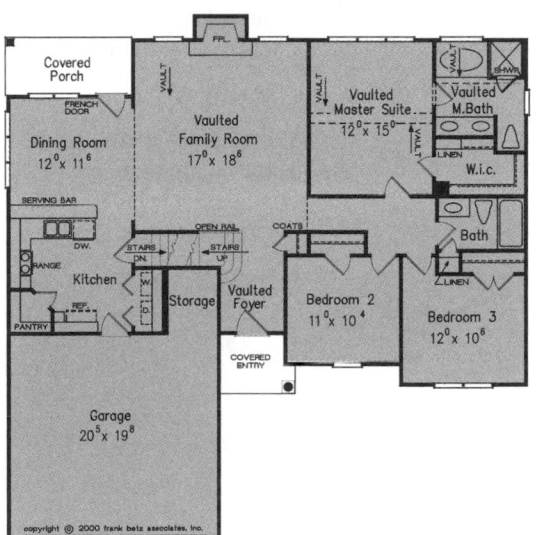

This adorable three-bedroom home will provide a pleasant atmosphere for your family. The communal living areas reside on the left side of the plan. The L-shaped kitchen includes a serving bar that opens to the dining area. The vaulted family room features a fireplace and leads to three bedrooms.

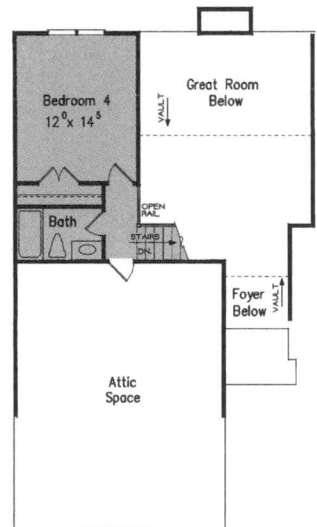

HPK2100090

Style: Cottage

Square Footage: 1,477

Bonus Space: 283 sq. ft.

Bedrooms: 3

Bathrooms: 2

Width: 51' - 0"

Depth: 51' - 4"

Foundation: Crawlspace, Unfinished Walkout Basement

EPLANS.COM

FRENCH SLID DRS

BDRM #2
10'-0"x12'-0"

BDRM #3
10'-0"x10'-0"

CL

BATH

GREAT ROOM
24'-0"x14'-4"
11'-0" HIGH
STEPPED CEILING

BUILT-IN

MASTER
BDRM
11'-6"x15'-8"
11'-0" HIGH
STEPPED CEILING

4' WIDE HALL

CL

OPTIONAL RAMP

OPT DOOR
WITHOUT RAMP

LOCATION OF OPT
BASEMENT STAIR

UTIL

LAUN

W D

CL

UP

FOY

REF

KIT
9'-0"x10'-0"

SNACK COUNTER

DINING
10'-0"x10'-0"
9' CEILING

LIN

CAB

CL

MASTER
BATH

WIC

STORAGE

TWO CAR
CAR
22'-0"x24'-0"

COVERED PORCH

Optional Layout

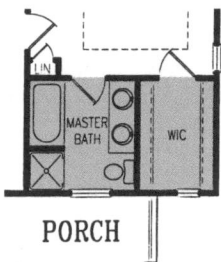

LIN

MASTER
BATH

WIC

PORCH

HPK2100091

Style: Country
Square Footage: 1,480
Bedrooms: 3
Bathrooms: 2
Width: 69' - 8"
Depth: 39' - 4"
Foundation: Crawlspace, Slab, Unfinished Basement

EPLANS.COM

This modest farmhouse ranch home is attractive and practical. The split bedroom plan with a private master suite includes a large bath and walk-in closet. The fabulous great room features an 11-foot-high step ceiling, a fireplace, and a media center. This home is designed to be fully handicap-accessible throughout.

© 1998 Donald A. Gardner, Inc.

B. NATHAN.

Soaring gables make this narrow-lot design seem larger than its modest square footage; cathedral and tray ceilings enhance interior spaciousness. A flowing floor plan positions the great room, dining room, and kitchen in convenient proximity. The great room features a fireplace with flanking built-in cabinets and bookshelves, access to the back porch, and a pass-through to the efficient kitchen.

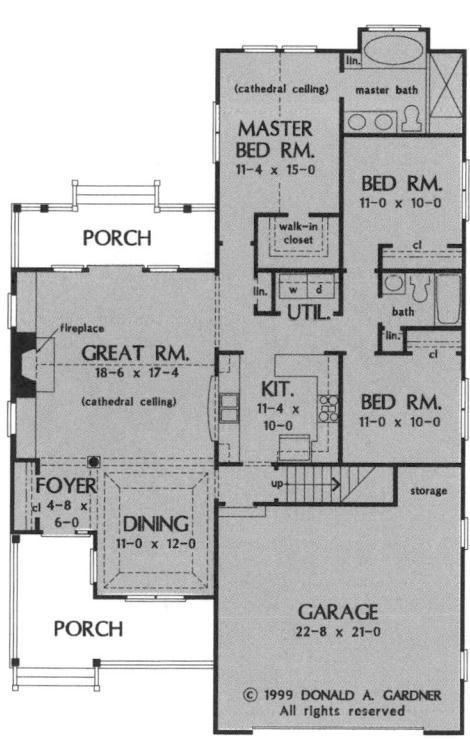

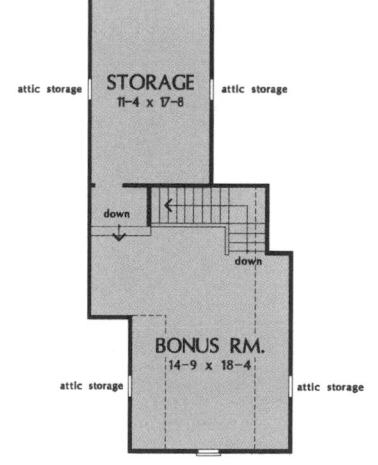

HPK2100092

Style: Cottage

Square Footage: 1,481

Bonus Space: 643 sq. ft.

Bedrooms: 3

Bathrooms: 2

Width: 42' - 4"

Depth: 65' - 10"

EPLANS.COM

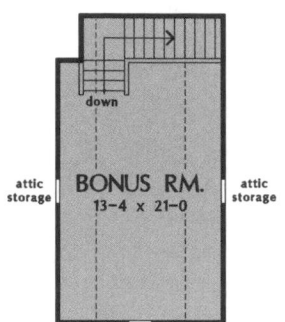

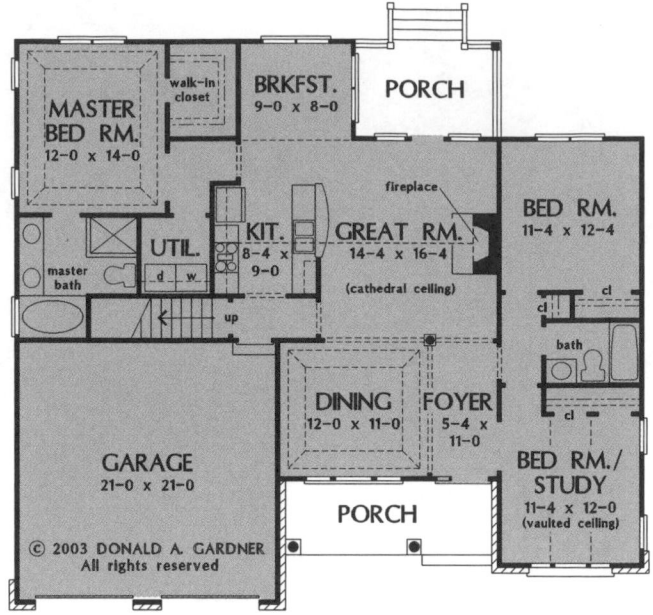

Brick and siding combine to create curb appeal in a low-maintenance facade. A sidelight and transom highlight the front door and allow natural light into the home. With tray ceilings in the dining room and master bedroom, along with a vaulted ceiling in the study/bedroom, this home showcases custom-styled elements. The family-efficient floor plan defines rooms without enclosing space. Note the savings on plumbing made possible by having the kitchen, utility room, and master bath adjacent to each other.

HPK2100093

Style: Cottage
Square Footage: 1,486
Bonus Space: 341 sq. ft.
Bedrooms: 3
Bathrooms: 2
Width: 52' - 3"
Depth: 46' - 10"

EPLANS.COM

© 2003 Donald A. Gardner, Inc.

HPK2100094

Style: New American
Square Footage: 1,486
Bedrooms: 3
Bathrooms: 2
Width: 52' - 8"
Depth: 44' - 4"
Foundation: Unfinished Basement

EPLANS.COM

This traditional home offers many of the amenities of a much grander house, including high ceilings, a great room, and large open spaces. This compact home lives large. Its master bedroom suite is close to the other bedrooms, a perfect configuration for young families. The eat-in kitchen is sure to please.

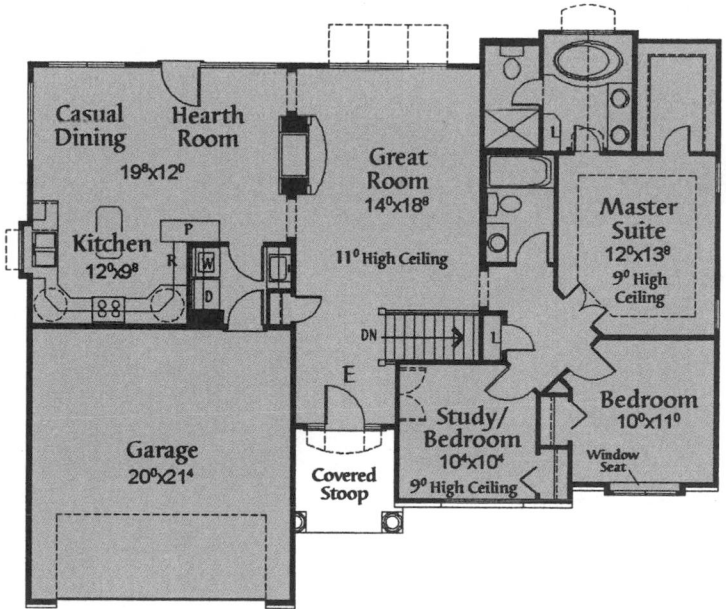

lanai
48'-0" x 10'-0"

nook
9'-4" x 10'-0"
vaulted clg.

great room
16'-0" x 14'-0"
vaulted clg.

master suite
13'-0" x 15'-0"
8' clg.

br. 1
12'-0" x 10'-0"
8' clg.

br. 2
11'-8" x 12'-4"
8' clg.

foyer

dining
11'-6" x 10'-4"
vaulted clg.

util.

entry

garage
20'-0" x 21'-4"

© THE SATER DESIGN COLLECTION, INC.

HPK2100095

Style: Mediterranean
Square Footage: 1,487
Bedrooms: 3
Bathrooms: 2
Width: 58' - 0"
Depth: 58' - 0"
Foundation: Slab

EPLANS.COM

Stucco styling, elegant arches, and a wealth of modern livability is presented in this compact one-story home. Inside, a great room with a vaulted ceiling opens to the lanai, offering wonderful options for either formal or informal entertaining. Step out onto the lanai and savor the outdoors from the delightful kitchen with its bay-windowed breakfast nook. Two secondary bedrooms (each with its own walk-in closet) share a full bath. Finally, enjoy the lanai from the calming master suite, which includes a pampering bath with a corner tub, a separate shower, and a large walk-in closet.

© The Sater Design Collection, Inc.

HPK2100096

Style: Cottage
Square Footage: 1,488
Bonus Space: 338 sq. ft.
Bedrooms: 3
Bathrooms: 2
Width: 69' - 7"
Depth: 42' - 0"

There's not a bit of wasted space in this cozy, well-designed home. The foyer opens to a spacious great room with a cathedral ceiling, a fireplace, and access to the rear porch. The formal dining room features a bay window that offers wide views of the property. Split sleeping quarters include a master suite with a walk-in closet, oversized shower, garden tub, as well as two secondary bedrooms that share a full bath.

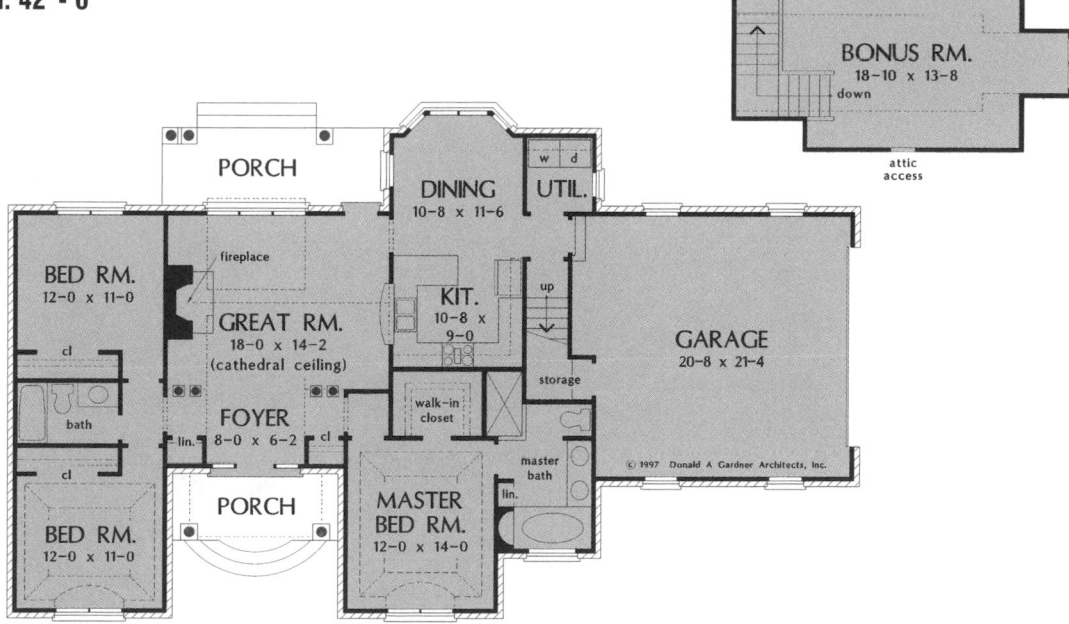

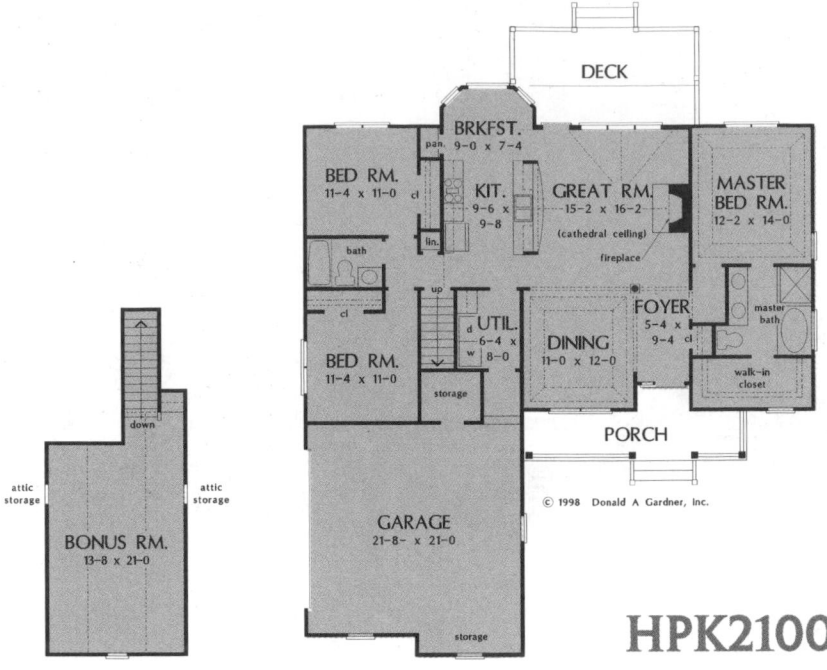

© 1998 Donald A Gardner, Inc.

HPK2100097

Style: Bungalow

Square Footage: 1,488

Bonus Space: 375 sq. ft.

Bedrooms: 3

Bathrooms: 2

Width: 51' - 10"

Depth: 58' - 0"

Rustic on the exterior, this appealing one-story home is a paragon of fine floor planning inside. Tray ceilings decorate both the dining room and the master bedroom. The great room features a cathedral ceiling and a large fireplace. To pamper the homeowner, the master retreat offers a huge walk-in closet and a bath with a shower, a spa tub, and dual sinks. The breakfast room is set in a bay-windowed area for sunny, casual meals.

1998 Donald A. Gardner, Inc.

HPK2101521

Style: Cottage

Square Footage: 1,496

Bonus Space: 301 sq. ft.

Bedrooms: 3

Bathrooms: 2

Width: 55' - 0"

Depth: 58' - 0"

Foundation: Slab

EPLANS.COM

This charming 1,496 sq.ft. country cottage features spacious open rooms and an easy flow from the welcoming stone front porch to the breezy screened porch off the family room and master suite. Perfect for entertaining, the well-appointed kitchen serves a breakfast room as well as a spacious dining room. The family room features a cozy corner fireplace. Isolated from the secondary bedrooms, the master suite is an owner's retreat with a sitting area, large walk-in closet and private bath with separate tub and shower. The secondary bedrooms share a hall bath. A laundry room is conveniently located off the breakfast room. Garage access to a bonus room and handy workshop complete this delightful design.

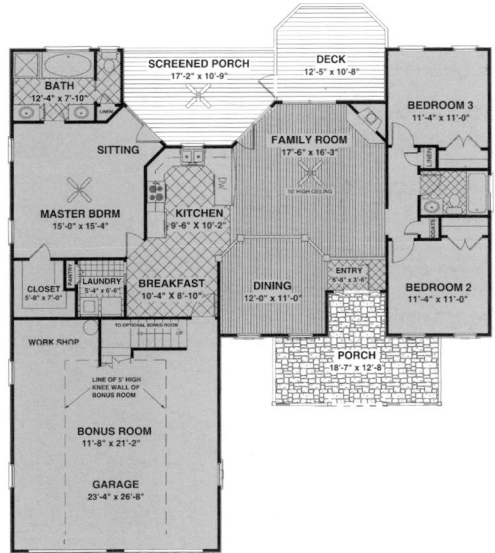

A Palladian window and covered porch contribute toward a well-balanced facade. For dimensions and order information on this home, turn to page 60.

BUILD SMALL, LIVE LARGE

A smaller home is ideal for anyone looking to build a smart, flexible, cost-efficient, and energy-saving residence that is no larger than what the family needs or what the plot allows. In general, smaller structures cost less at initial construction because they require fewer raw materials. Similarly, small designs need less power to heat and illuminate, which means cost and energy savings over time. In fact, by investing what will be saved at initial construction toward environmentally safe methods and materials, a small home can reinforce its fundamental design efficiencies to become a truly "green" home. At the same time, also reinvesting those initial savings toward custom finishes and fine amenities can turn a smaller design into an especially comfortable and beautiful home.

The fireplace facilitates this sitting area. The built-in shelves can hold a media center.

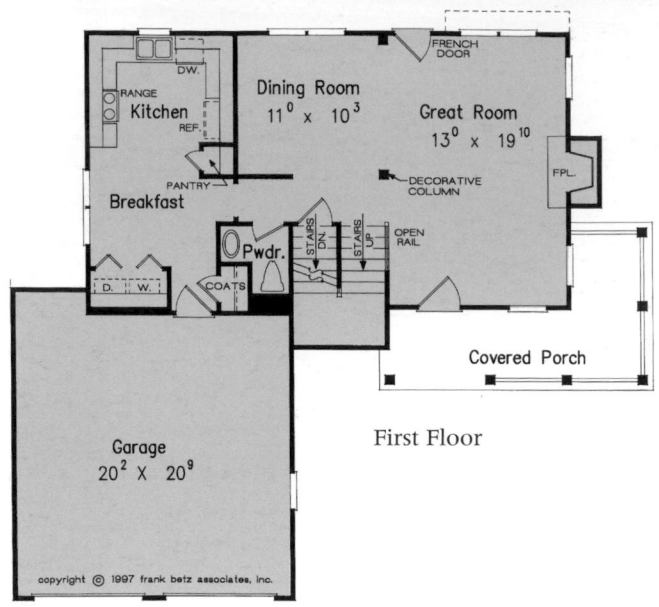

First Floor

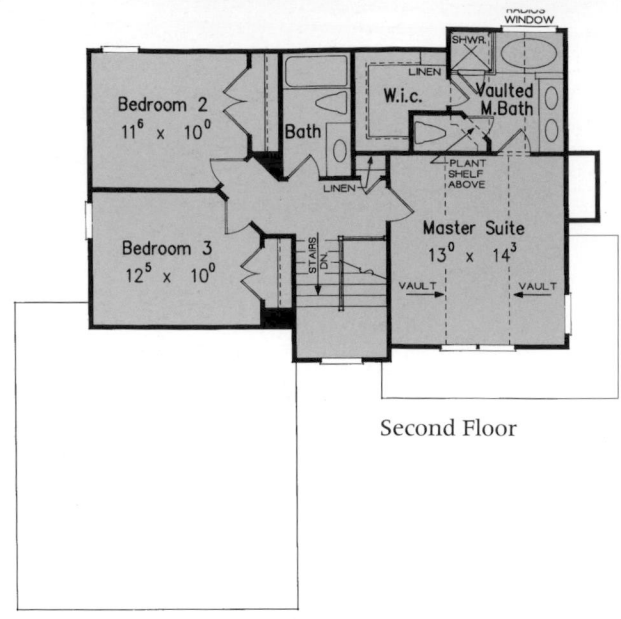

Second Floor

HPK2101522

Style: New American

First Floor: 757 sq. ft.

Second Floor: 735 sq. ft.

Total: 1,492 sq. ft.

Bedrooms: 3

Bathrooms: 2 ½

Width: 47' - 0"

Depth: 42' - 0"

Foundation: Crawlspace, Slab, Unfinished Walkout Basement

EPLANS.COM

The foyer announces the living and dining areas, defined by decorative columns. A kitchen serves both the breakfast area and the dining room. The great room opens to the rear property through a French door. The master suite provides a vaulted ceiling, garden tub with radius window, and walk-in closet. Each of two additional bedrooms offers a wide wardrobe.

© 1993 Donald A. Gardner, Architects, Inc.

HPK2100098

Style: Country
Square Footage: 1,498
Bedrooms: 3
Bathrooms: 2
Width: 59' - 8"
Depth: 46' - 8"

The great room commands attention with a cathedral ceiling and leads to the kitchen and breakfast nook through an archway defined by columns. A tray ceiling accents the master bedroom. Two secondary bedrooms and a hall bath are located at the opposite end of the house for privacy.

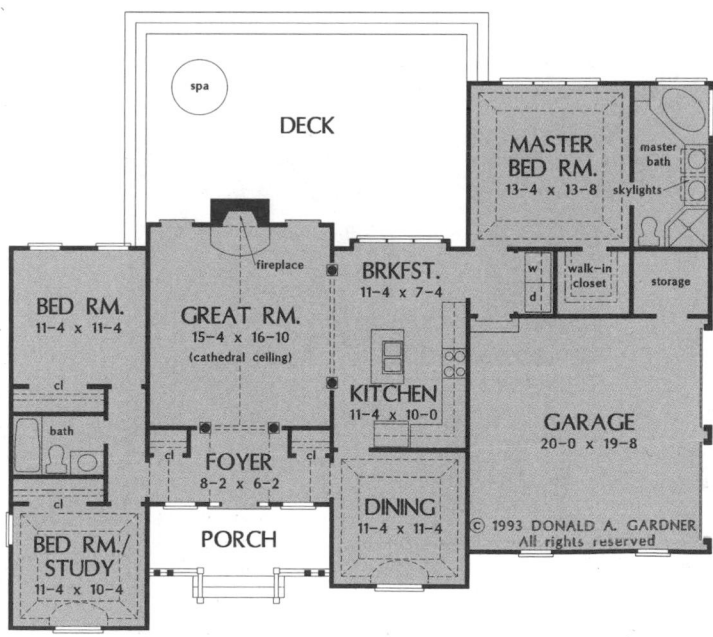

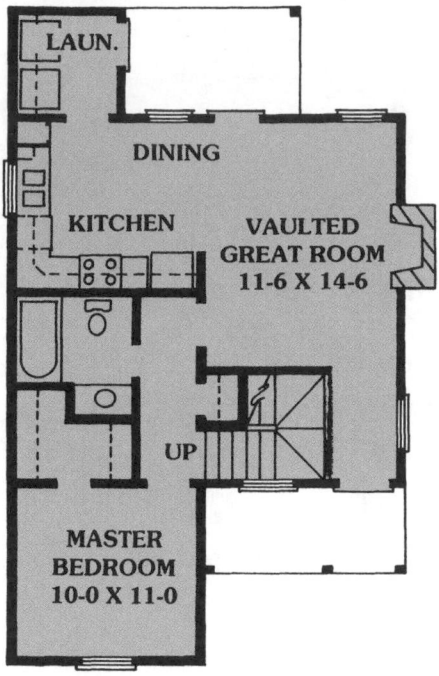

First Floor

This quaint country home, with outside pillars and a front porch, is chock full of living space. It's hard to believe that this modest-sized plan holds three bedrooms with walk-in closets, two baths, and a laundry room. This is in addition to an open area that contains a farm-sized kitchen, a sunlit dining space, and a great room with a vaulted ceiling and fireplace. A rear deck, entered from the dining room, helps extend the living space to the outdoors.

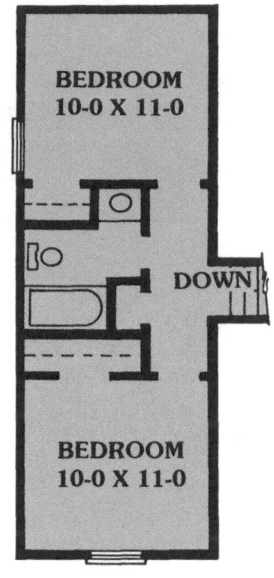

Second Floor

HPK2100099

Style: Cottage
First Floor: 702 sq. ft.
Second Floor: 396 sq. ft.
Total: 1,098 sq. ft.
Bedrooms: 3
Bathrooms: 2
Width: 26' - 0"
Depth: 40' - 0"
Foundation: Crawlspace

EPLANS.COM

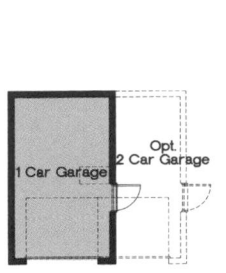

Optional Layout

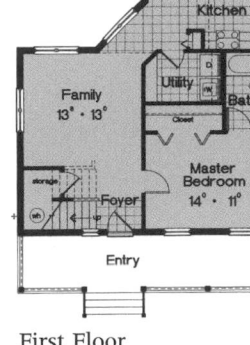

First Floor

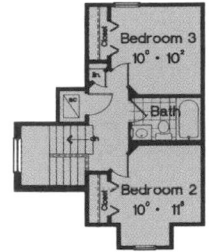

Second Floor

HPK2100100

Style: Country
First Floor: 820 sq. ft.
Second Floor: 350 sq. ft.
Total: 1,170 sq. ft.
Bedrooms: 3
Bathrooms: 2
Width: 37' - 0"
Depth: 67' - 0"
Foundation: Slab

EPLANS.COM

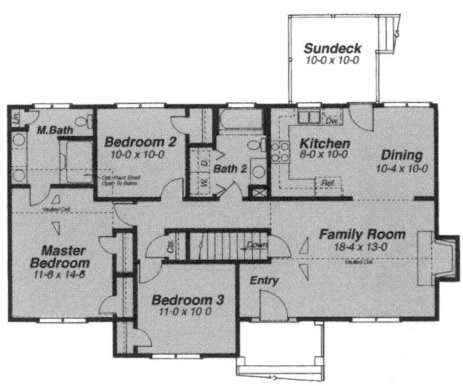

HPK2100101

Style: Contemporary
Square Footage: 1,208
Bedrooms: 3
Bathrooms: 2
Width: 50' - 4"
Depth: 29' - 0"
Foundation: Unfinished Walkout Basement

EPLANS.COM

UNDER 1,500 SQUARE FEET

HPK2100102

Style: Craftsman

First Floor: 852 sq. ft.

Second Floor: 374 sq. ft.

Total: 1,226 sq. ft.

Bedrooms: 2

Bathrooms: 2

Width: 37' - 10"

Depth: 33' - 4"

Foundation: Crawlspace

EPLANS.COM

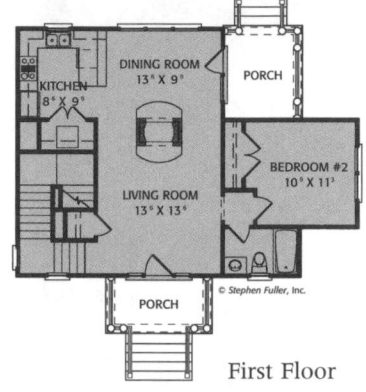

First Floor

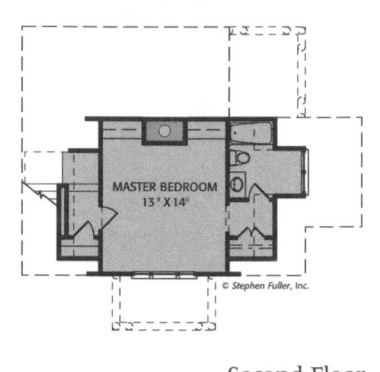

Second Floor

HPK2100103

Style: Cottage

First Floor: 628 sq. ft.

Second Floor: 660 sq. ft.

Total: 1,288 sq. ft.

Bedrooms: 3

Bathrooms: 2 ½

Width: 42' - 10"

Depth: 41' - 0"

Foundation: Crawlspace, Slab, Unfinished Walkout Basement

EPLANS.COM

First Floor

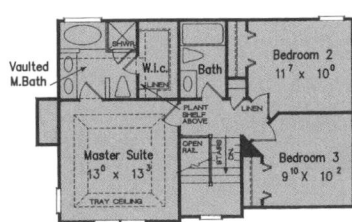

Second Floor

HPK2100104

Style: Country
First Floor: 603 sq. ft.
Second Floor: 694 sq. ft.
Total: 1,297 sq. ft.
Bedrooms: 3
Bathrooms: 2 ½
Width: 42' - 0"
Depth: 43' - 0"

EPLANS.COM

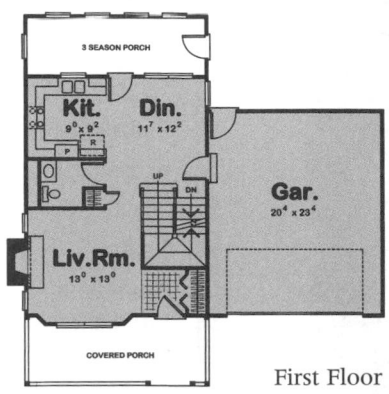

First Floor

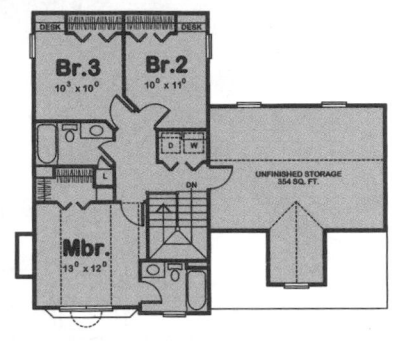

Second Floor

© 1991 Donald A. Gardner, Architects, Inc

HPK2100105

Style: Country
First Floor: 1,002 sq. ft.
Second Floor: 336 sq. ft.
Total: 1,338 sq. ft.
Bedrooms: 3
Bathrooms: 2
Width: 36' - 8"
Depth: 44' - 8"

EPLANS.COM

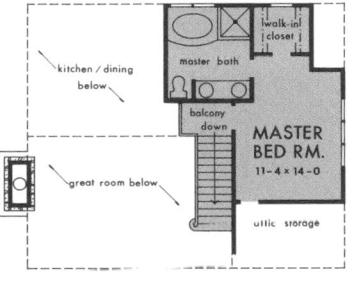

Second Floor

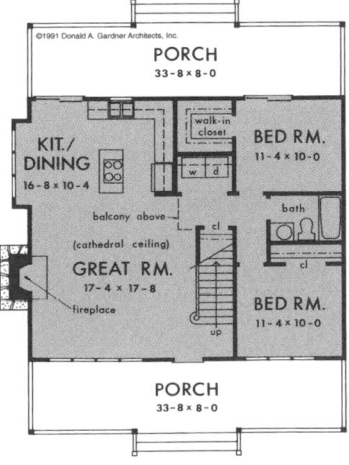

First Floor

UNDER 1,500 SQUARE FEET

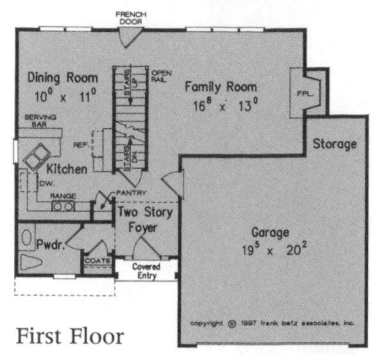

First Floor

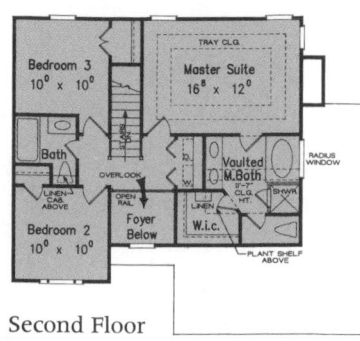

Second Floor

HPK2100106

Style: Colonial Revival

First Floor: 637 sq. ft.

Second Floor: 730 sq. ft.

Total: 1,367 sq. ft.

Bedrooms: 3

Bathrooms: 2 ½

Width: 37' - 6"

Depth: 34' - 0"

Foundation: Crawlspace, Unfinished Walkout Basement

EPLANS.COM

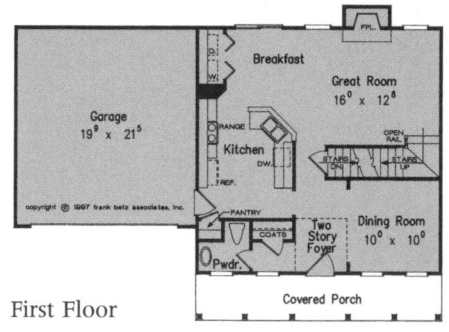

First Floor

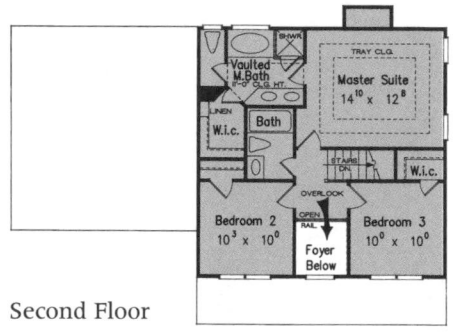

Second Floor

HPK2100107

Style: Farmhouse

First Floor: 729 sq. ft.

Second Floor: 670 sq. ft.

Total: 1,399 sq. ft.

Bedrooms: 3

Bathrooms: 2 ½

Width: 47' - 0"

Depth: 34' - 4"

Foundation: Crawlspace, Slab, Unfinished Walkout Basement

EPLANS.COM

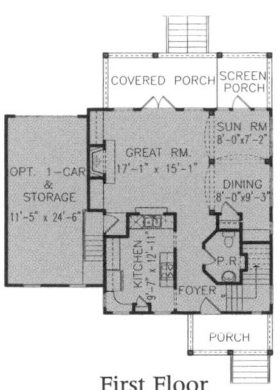
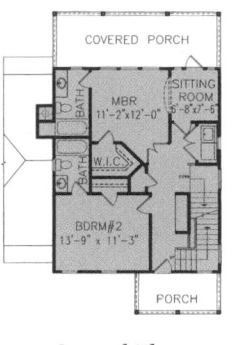

First Floor   Second Floor

HPK2100108

Style: Italianate

First Floor: 754 sq. ft.

Second Floor: 662 sq. ft.

Total: 1,416 sq. ft.

Bedrooms: 2

Bathrooms: 2 ½

Width: 38' - 0"

Depth: 44' - 0"

Foundation: Crawlspace

EPLANS.COM

HPK2100109

Style: Bungalow

First Floor: 436 sq. ft.

Second Floor: 792 sq. ft.

Third Floor: 202 sq. ft.

Total: 1,430 sq. ft.

Bedrooms: 2

Bathrooms: 2

Width: 16' - 0"

Depth: 54' - 0"

Foundation: Crawlspace

EPLANS.COM

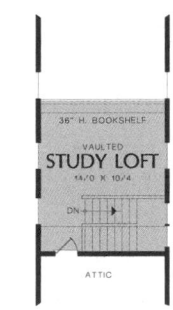

First Floor   Second Floor

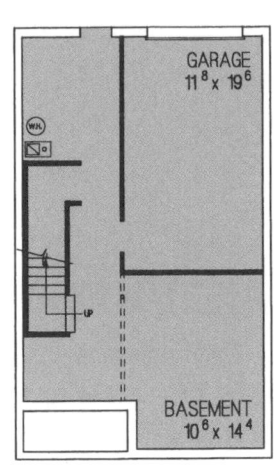

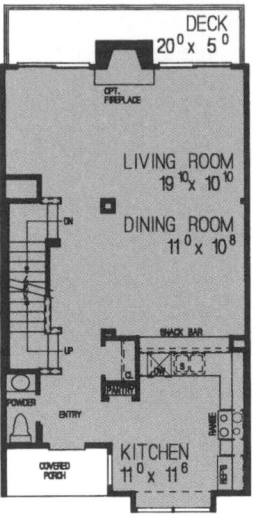

First Floor

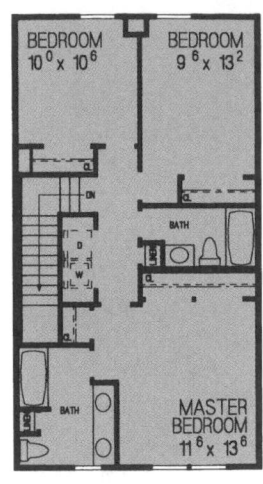

Second Floor

Here's a plan with lots of flexibility. It comes with two garage alternatives—rear-loading or front-loading—and open space to organize the living and dining areas to suit your needs. There's also an option of adding a fireplace. The kitchen is marked off from the living/dining area by a handy snack bar. Upstairs, a master suite with a dual-sink vanity enjoys a private bath; two family bedrooms share a bath. This plan is well-suited for a narrow lot.

EPLANS.COM

HPK2100110

Style: Cottage
First Floor: 685 sq. ft.
Second Floor: 760 sq. ft.
Total: 1,445 sq. ft.
Bedrooms: 3
Bathrooms: 2 ½
Width: 21' - 0"
Depth: 36' - 0"
Foundation: Unfinished Basement

HPK2100111

Style: Colonial Revival
First Floor: 771 sq. ft.
Second Floor: 681 sq. ft.
Total: 1,452 sq. ft.
Bedrooms: 3
Bathrooms: 2 ½
Width: 53' - 4"
Depth: 34' - 0"
Foundation: Unfinished Walkout Basement

EPLANS.COM

A little asymmetry puts a twist on the traditional center-gabled farmhouse design. Beyond the long entry porch, a time-tested layout exhibits sensitivity to contemporary lifestyles. A large family room replaces the formal living room. The C-shaped kitchen is open to the breakfast nook. On the second level, the master suite contains all the amenities you've come to expect: dual vanities, soaking tub, shower, and large walk-in closet. Two family bedrooms share a bath.

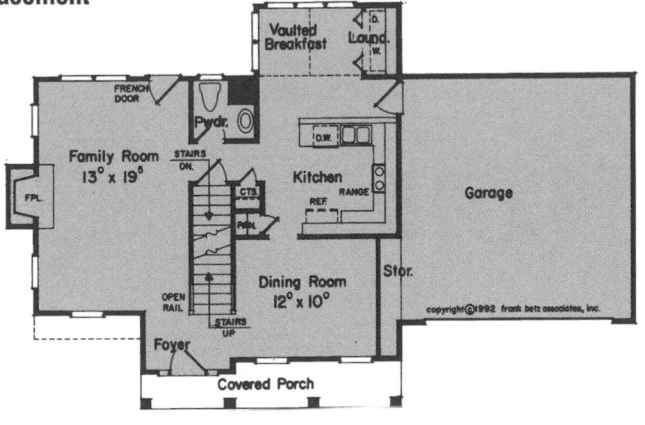

First Floor

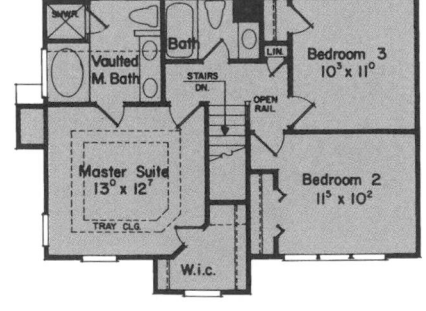

Second Floor

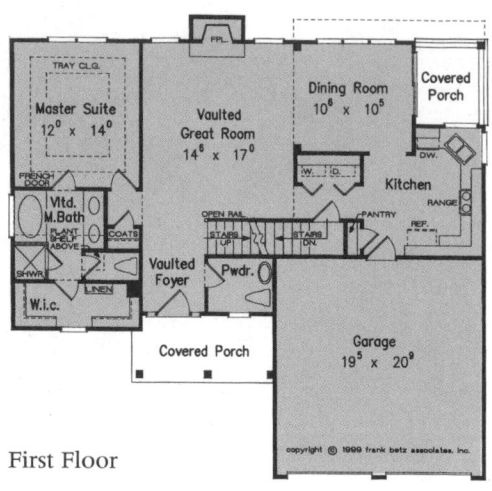

First Floor

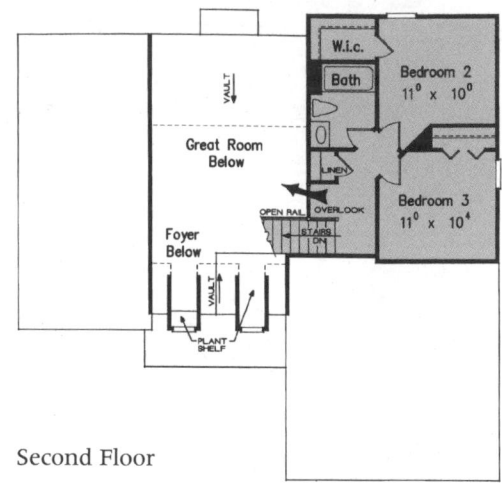

Second Floor

HPK2100112

This lovely two story cottage home is complemented by two front facing planter boxes on either side of the main entrance and a charming covered porch. The foyer leads to a vaulted great room complete with a fireplace and powder room for guests. On the left side resides the master suite accented with french doors that lead to the vaulted full bath and walk-in closet. On the upper level, two additional bedrooms share a full bath.

Style: Cottage
First Floor: 1,051 sq. ft.
Second Floor: 411 sq. ft.
Total: 1,462 sq. ft.
Bedrooms: 3
Bathrooms: 2 ½
Width: 45' - 0"
Depth: 44' - 4"
Foundation: Crawlspace, Unfinished Walkout Basement

EPLANS.COM

HPK2100113

Style: Cottage
First Floor: 655 sq. ft.
Second Floor: 809 sq. ft.
Total: 1,464 sq. ft.
Bedrooms: 3
Bathrooms: 2 ½
Width: 30' - 0"
Depth: 42' - 0"
Foundation: Crawlspace

EPLANS.COM

A towering entry is set off by twin-gabled rooflines and a long clerestory window that lights up the foyer in this two-story home. The foyer leads to a deceptively simple floor plan that owes a great view in the back to large windows in the great room and the dining room. The great room is further enhanced by a fireplace and sits near the island kitchen for convenience.

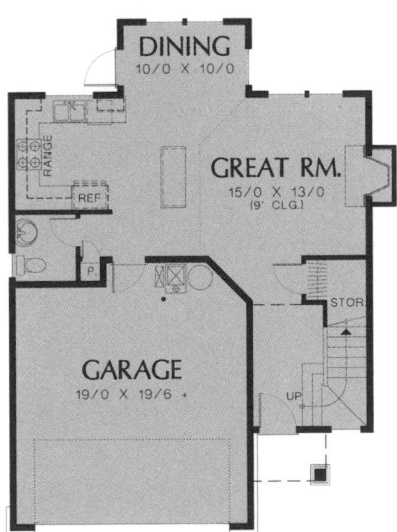

First Floor

Second Floor

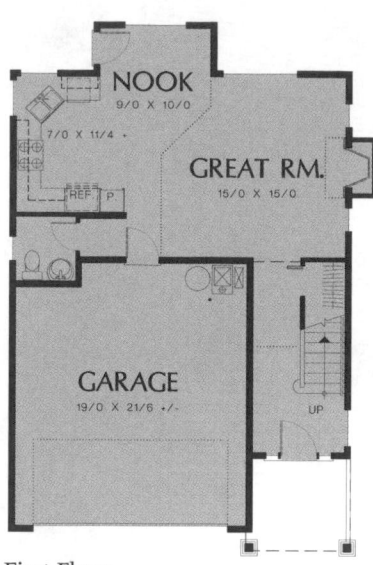

First Floor

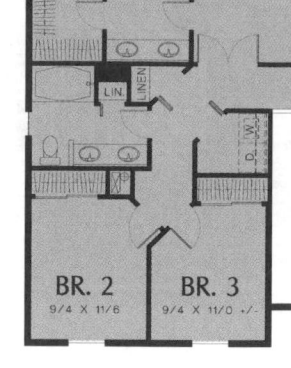

Second Floor

Traditional and Craftsman elements shape the exterior of this lovely family home. The two-story foyer leads down the hall to a great room with a warming fireplace. The U-shaped kitchen is open to the breakfast nook. A powder room is located near the garage. Upstairs, the master suite provides a private bath and a walk-in closet. The two family bedrooms share a full hall bath across from the second-floor washroom.

HPK2100114

Style: Craftsman
First Floor: 636 sq. ft.
Second Floor: 830 sq. ft.
Total: 1,466 sq. ft.
Bedrooms: 3
Bathrooms: 2 ½
Width: 28' - 0"
Depth: 43' - 6"
Foundation: Crawlspace

EPLANS.COM

©The Sater Design Collection, Inc.

HPK2100115

Style: Country

Square Footage: 1,487

Bedrooms: 3

Bathrooms: 2

Width: 52' - 6"

Depth: 66' - 0"

Foundation: Crawlspace

EPLANS.COM

Precious Victorian accents highlight this outstanding design. An open dining space and the spacious great room feature stepped ceilings. The kitchen acts as the hub of the house, convenient to all areas, and features a walk-in pantry. The master suite is split from the two family bedrooms.

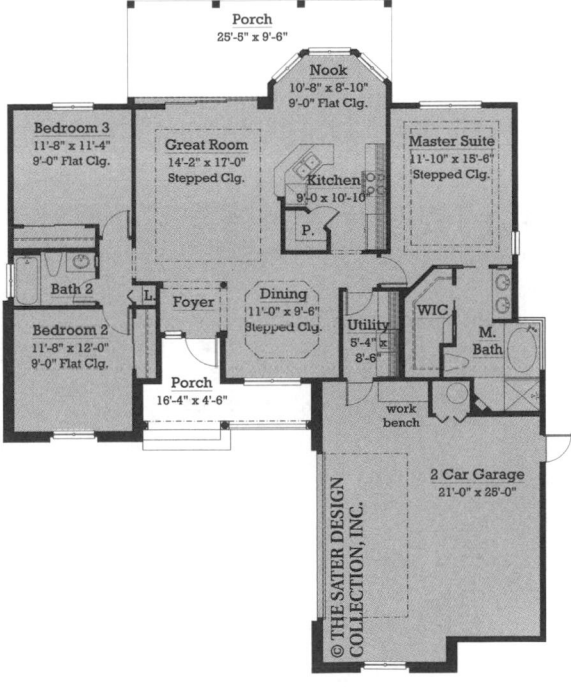

First Floor

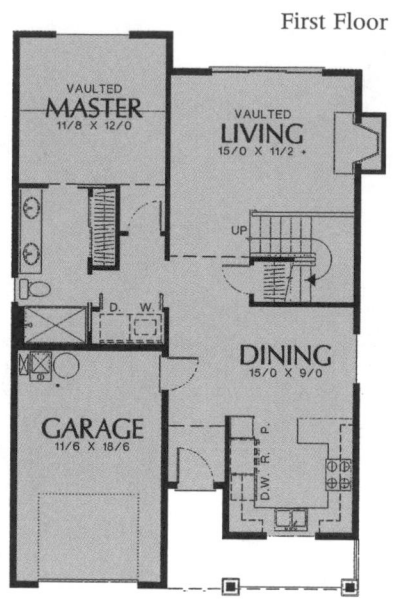

Second Floor

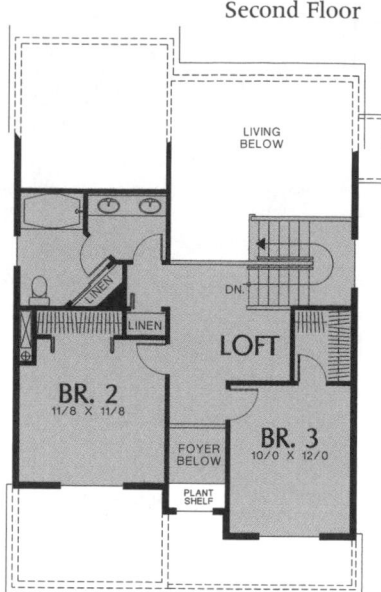

HPK2100116

Style: Craftsman
First Floor: 902 sq. ft.
Second Floor: 586 sq. ft.
Total: 1,488 sq. ft.
Bedrooms: 3
Bathrooms: 2
Width: 28' - 0"
Depth: 45' - 0"
Foundation: Crawlspace

EPLANS.COM

Quaint Craftsman living is defined in this two-story home. Aromas from the adjacent U-shaped kitchen greet friends and family from the entry foyer. The open layout of the dining room expands this space. To the left, the first-floor master suite sits in quiet seclusion from the remaining family bedrooms upstairs. The spacious living room boasts a fireplace on the side wall. Upstairs, two bedrooms—each with a walk-in closet—share a full hall bath.

HPK2100117

Style: Country
Square Footage: 1,488
Bedrooms: 3
Bathrooms: 2
Width: 54' - 0"
Depth: 48' - 0"
Foundation: Unfinished Basement

EPLANS.COM

Don't miss this charming family home. Flexibility is an attractive feature of this design. The open floor plan with a split-bedroom layout is sure to please, not to mention the secluded master suite. There are two additional bedrooms on the right side of the plan. A full basement provides additional space for all storage needs.

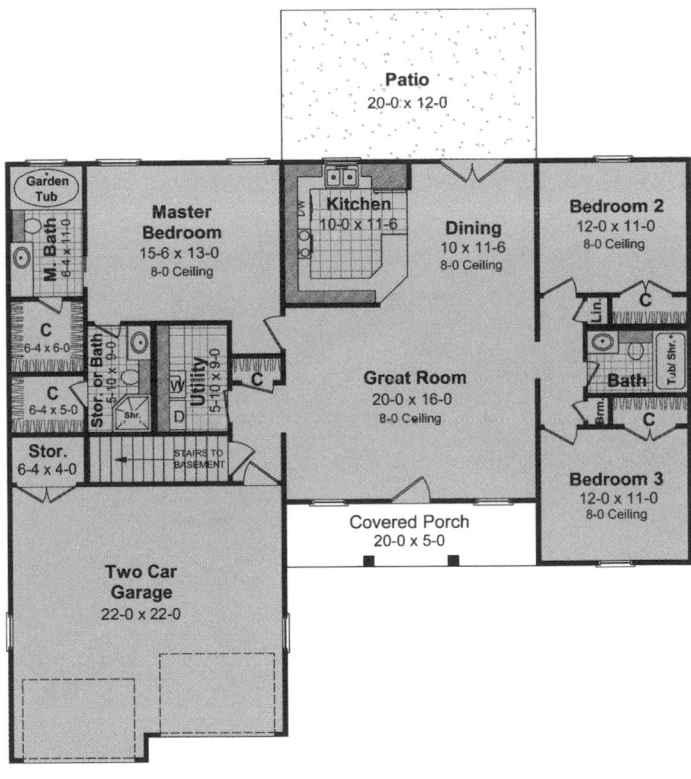

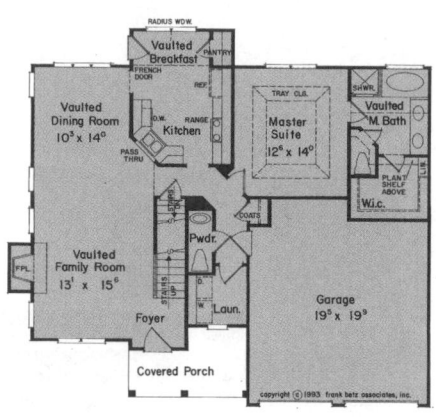

First Floor

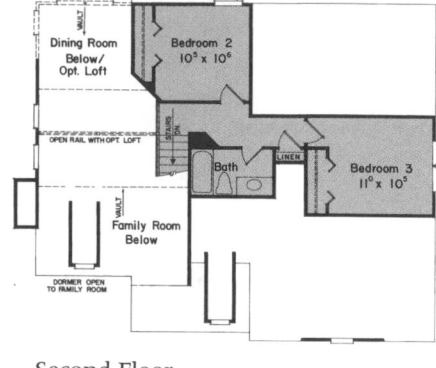

Second Floor

HPK2100118

Style: Cottage
First Floor: 1,073 sq. ft.
Second Floor: 418 sq. ft.
Total: 1,491 sq. ft.
Bonus Space: 167 sq. ft.
Bedrooms: 3
Bathrooms: 2 ½
Width: 45' - 10"
Depth: 41' - 0"
Foundation: Crawlspace, Unfinished Walkout Basement

EPLANS.COM

This cozy cottage design is filled with details that you might expect only in much larger plans. The master suite is on the first floor and boasts luxurious amenities. Two family bedrooms on the second floor share a full bath. An optional loft may also be included.

HPK2100119

Style: Country

First Floor: 1,061 sq. ft.

Second Floor: 430 sq. ft.

Total: 1,491 sq. ft.

Bedrooms: 3

Bathrooms: 2 ½

Width: 40' - 4"

Depth: 36' - 2"

Foundation: Unfinished Walkout Basement

EPLANS.COM

This sporty hideaway retreat is great for being in the wilderness. Adorned with dormers and a covered front porch, this two-story home warms family and guests with a vaulted family room, which features a cozy fireplace and radius windows on each side. The kitchen includes a serving bar and a pantry. The master bedroom boasts a tray ceiling, a walk-in closet, and a sumptuous private bath. The second floor holds two family bedrooms that share a full bath. Note the open rail overlooking the family room below.

First Floor

Second Floor

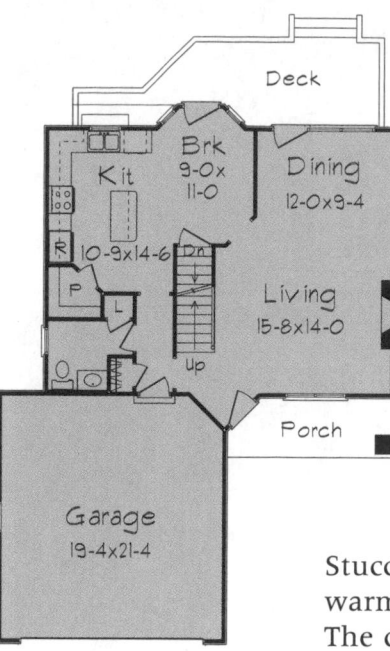

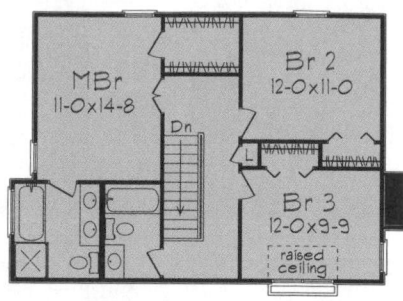

Deck

Kit
10-9x14-6

Brk
9-0x
11-0

Dining
12-0x9-4

Living
15-8x14-0

Dn

Up

Garage
19-4x21-4

Porch

First Floor

MBr
11-0x14-8

Br 2
12-0x11-0

Dn

Br 3
12-0x9-9

raised ceiling

Second Floor

Stucco and Dutch hipped roofs add warmth and charm to this home. The cleverly angled entry spills into the living and dining rooms that share the warmth of the fireplace. The L-shaped kitchen features an island and connects to the well-lit breakfast nook. Upstairs, the master suite includes a double-door entry, a huge walk-in closet, and a bath with a picture window. Also on this floor, two family bedrooms share a full bath.

HPK2100120

Style: Cottage
First Floor: 760 sq. ft.
Second Floor: 732 sq. ft.
Total: 1,492 sq. ft.
Bedrooms: 3
Bathrooms: 2 ½
Width: 35' - 0"
Depth: 47' - 8"
Foundation: Unfinished Basement

EPLANS.COM

HPK2100121

Style: Country
First Floor: 1,065 sq. ft.
Second Floor: 432 sq. ft.
Total: 1,497 sq. ft.
Bedrooms: 3
Bathrooms: 2 ½
Width: 50' - 0"
Depth: 37' - 4"
Foundation: Crawlspace,
Unfinished Walkout Basement

Although this home would work well on a narrow lot, it would fit just as comfortably on a lot surrounded by land. A vaulted great room with a fireplace and rear-yard access will be ideal for family gatherings. The master suite is located on the first floor for privacy and features a vaulted bath with a walk-in closet and a separate tub and shower. Two bedrooms and a full bath are available upstairs, as well as an optional bonus room that can be developed later as needed.

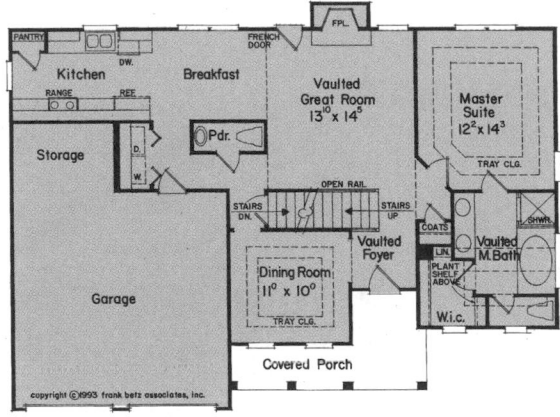

First Floor

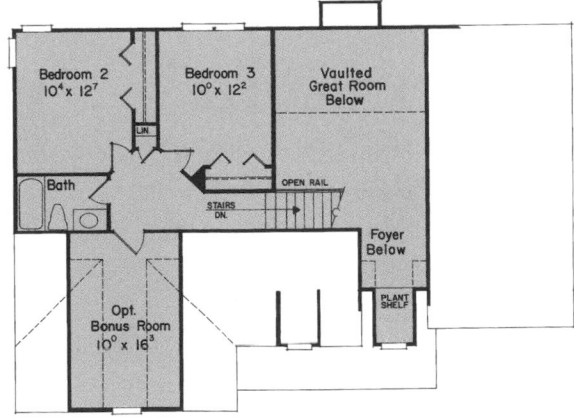

Second Floor

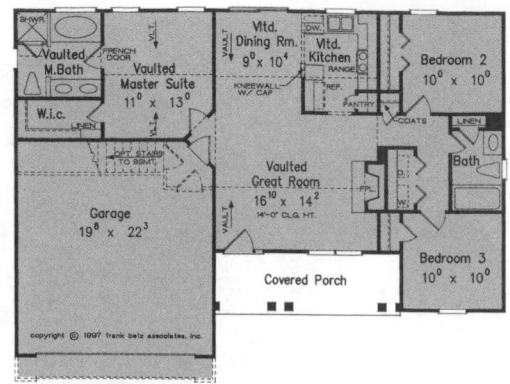

GARAGE LOCATION WITH BASEMENT

HPK2100122

Style: Country
Total: 1,080 sq. ft.
Bedrooms: 3
Bathrooms: 2
Width: 50' - 0"
Depth: 36' - 0"
Foundation: Crawlspace, Unfinished Walkout Basement

EPLANS.COM

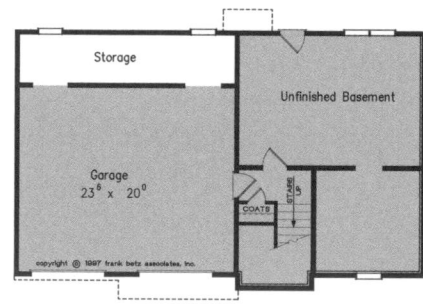

Lower Level

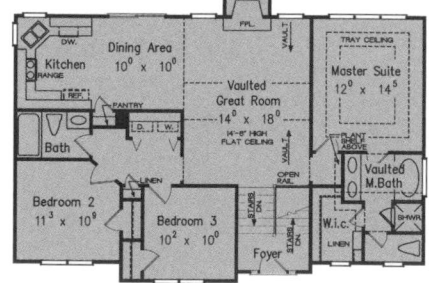

Main Level

HPK2100123

Style: Colonial Revival
Main Level: 1,249 sq. ft.
Lower Level: 46 sq. ft.
Total: 1,295 sq. ft.
Bedrooms: 3
Bathrooms: 2
Width: 45' - 0"
Depth: 31' - 4"
Foundation: Unfinished Walkout Basement

EPLANS.COM

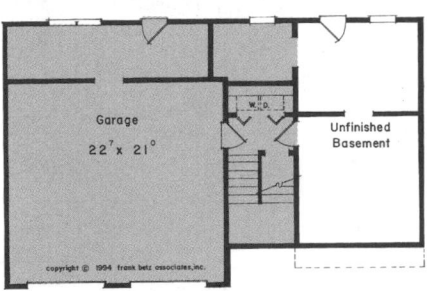

Lower Level

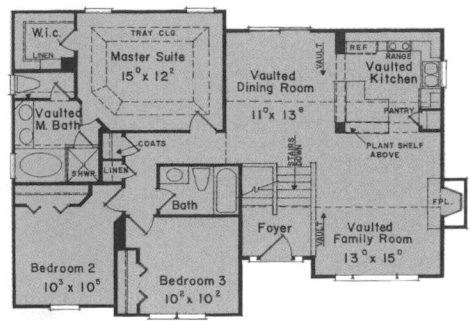

Main Level

HPK2100124

Style: Contemporary

Main Level: 1,258 sq. ft.

Lower Level: 60 sq. ft.

Total: 1,318 sq. ft.

Bedrooms: 3

Bathrooms: 2

Width: 46' - 4"

Depth: 32' - 0"

Foundation: Unfinished Walkout Basement

EPLANS.COM

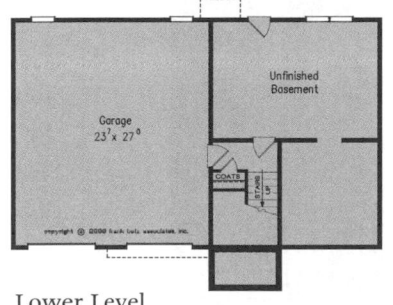

Lower Level

Main Level

HPK2100125

Style: Craftsman

Main Level: 1,273 sq. ft.

Lower Level: 47 sq. ft.

Total: 1,320 sq. ft.

Bedrooms: 3

Bathrooms: 2

Width: 48' - 0"

Depth: 35' - 4"

Foundation: Unfinished Walkout Basement

EPLANS.COM

UNDER 1,500 SQUARE FEET

HPK2100126

Style: Country
Main Level: 628 sq. ft.
Upper Level: 743 sq. ft.
Total: 1,371 sq. ft.
Bedrooms: 3
Bathrooms: 2 ½
Width: 37' - 0"
Depth: 40' - 4"
Foundation: Crawlspace, Unfinished Walkout Basement

EPLANS.COM

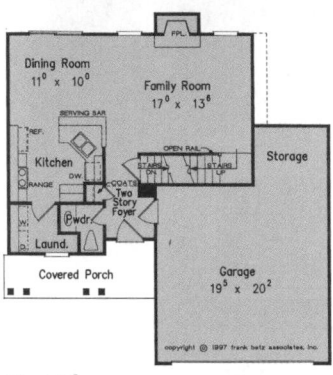

First Floor

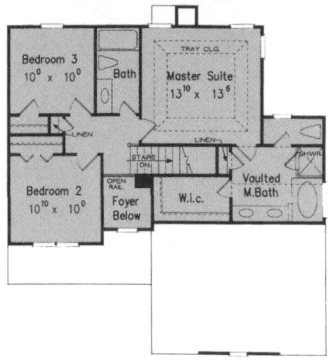

Second Floor

HPK2100127

Style: Farmhouse
First Floor: 819 sq. ft.
Second Floor: 579 sq. ft.
Total: 1,398 sq. ft.
Bedrooms: 3
Bathrooms: 2
Width: 39' - 9"
Depth: 29' - 4"
Foundation: Unfinished Basement

EPLANS.COM

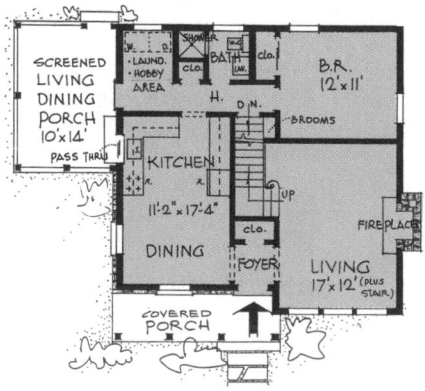

First Floor

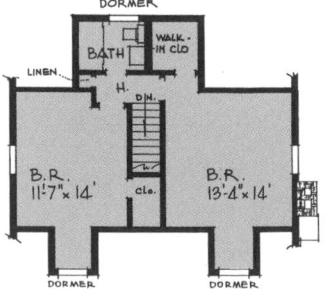

Second Floor

HPK2100128

Style: Cottage
Square Footage: 1,441
Bedrooms: 3
Bathrooms: 2
Width: 50' - 0"
Depth: 50' - 4"
Foundation: Crawlspace,
Unfinished Walkout Basement

Brick and siding are great country touches to this traditional neighborhood home. A foyer makes a grand entrance. Ahead, the great room and dining room share a continuous vaulted ceiling for an elegant feel. Here, a fireplace warms and sliding glass doors extend the living area. The vaulted master suite features a sumptuous spa bath and a walk-in closet. Two additional bedrooms, one with a vault, share a full bath.

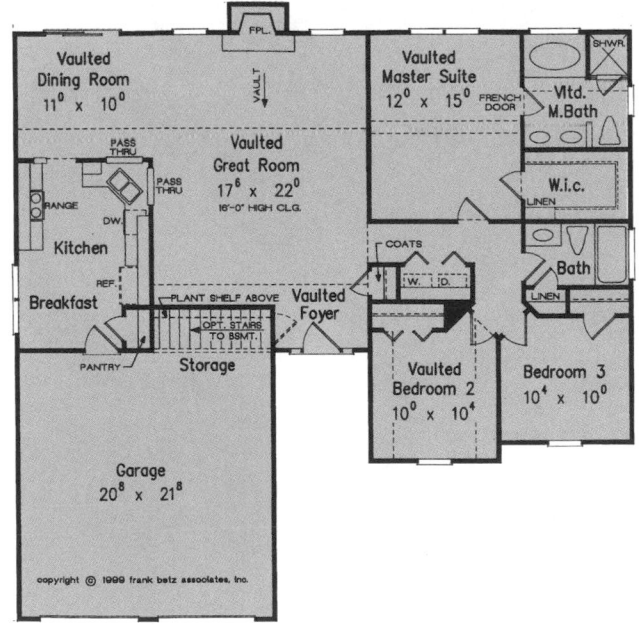

UNDER 1,500 SQUARE FEET

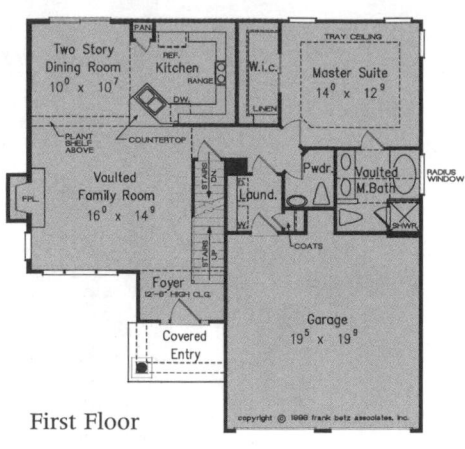

First Floor

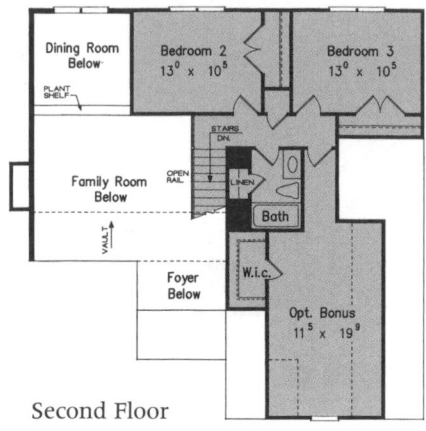

Second Floor

HPK2100129

Style: Cottage

First Floor: 1,001 sq. ft.

Second Floor: 466 sq. ft.

Total: 1,467 sq. ft.

Bonus Space: 292 sq. ft.

Bedrooms: 3

Bathrooms: 2 ½

Width: 42' - 0"

Depth: 42' - 0"

Foundation: Crawlspace, Slab, Unfinished Walkout Basement

EPLANS.COM

Arched transoms set off by keystones add the final details to a traditional exterior. The foyer opens to a vaulted family room that enjoys a warm fireplace. The U-shaped kitchen features an angled countertop and spacious pantry. Down the hall, the abundant master suite boasts a tray ceiling and can be found in its own secluded area. Upstairs, two additional bedrooms are found sharing a full bath—note that both bedrooms enjoy French doors. An optional bonus room with a walk-in closet is included in this plan.

HPK2100130

Style: Cottage

First Floor: 696 sq. ft.

Second Floor: 786 sq. ft.

Total: 1,482 sq. ft.

Bonus Space: 141 sq. ft.

Bedrooms: 3

Bathrooms: 2 ½

Width: 33' - 0"

Depth: 41' - 4"

Foundation: Crawlspace, Slab, Unfinished Walkout Basement

EPLANS.COM

Charming as a vacation home, retirement cottage, or full-time residence, this Cape Cod-style plan packs a lot of living space into less than 1,500 square feet. Outside, brick accents, a flower box, and a covered front porch add country flavor; inside, an open design is modern and full of amenities. Don't miss the ultra-convenient upstairs laundry area.

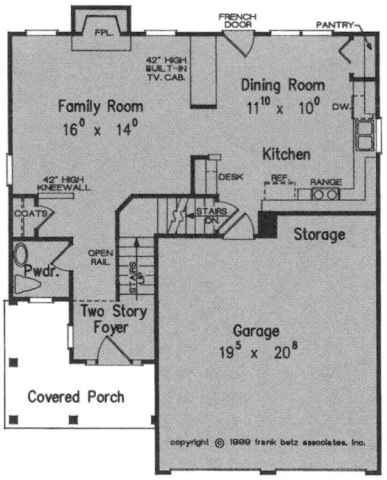

First Floor

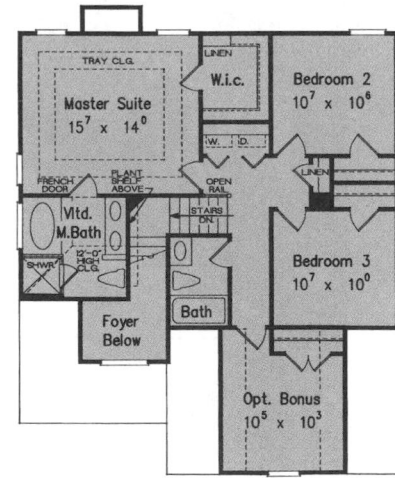

Second Floor

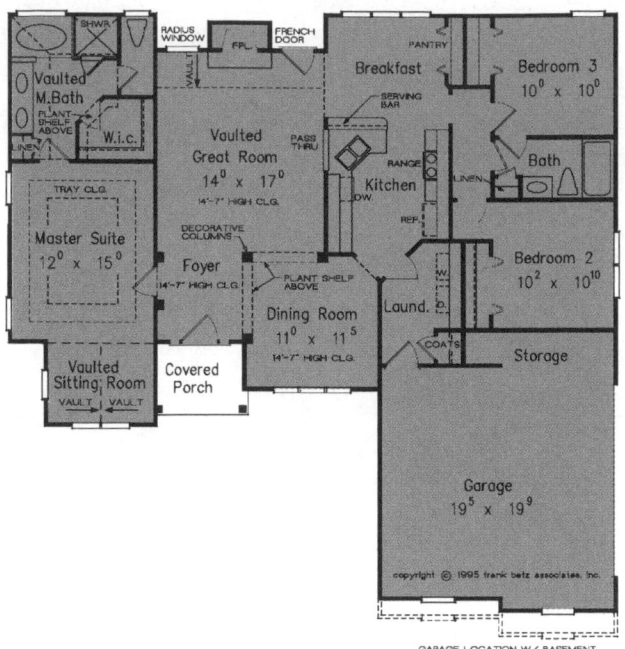

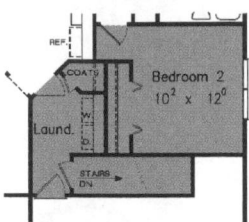

Optional Layout

This plan masterfully combines architectural style with a smaller square footage. Elegant ceiling details and window treatments prevail throughout this three-bedroom home. Livability is also a part of the design with the kitchen conveniently located next to the garage and a sitting room in the master suite.

HPK2100131

Style: New American
Square Footage: 1,502
Bedrooms: 3
Bathrooms: 2
Width: 51' - 0"
Depth: 50' - 6"
Foundation: Crawlspace, Slab, Unfinished Walkout Basement

EPLANS.COM

HPK2100132

Style: Cottage

Square Footage: 1,506

Bedrooms: 3

Bathrooms: 2

Width: 40' - 0"

Depth: 52' - 0"

Foundation: Crawlspace, Slab, Unfinished Walkout Basement

EPLANS.COM

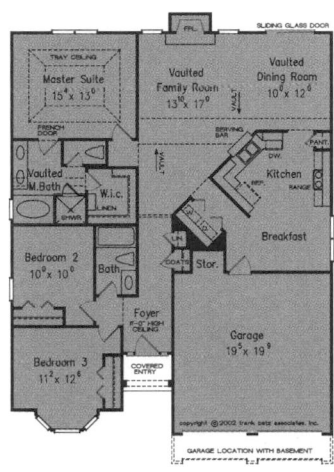

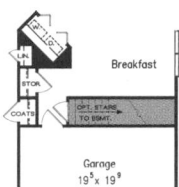

Optional Layout

HPK2100133

Style: Bungalow

Square Footage: 1,509

Bedrooms: 3

Bathrooms: 2

Width: 59' - 4"

Depth: 46' - 4"

Foundation: Crawlspace, Unfinished Basement

EPLANS.COM

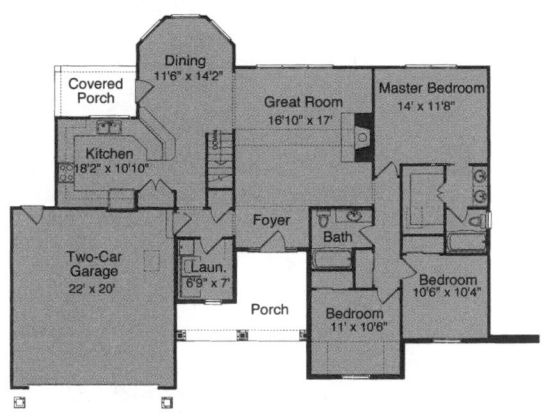

1,500 TO 1,999 SQUARE FEET

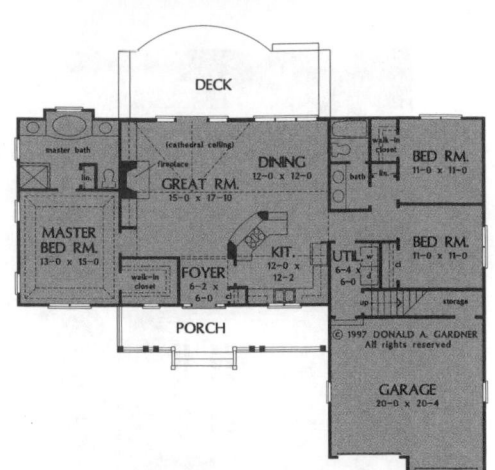

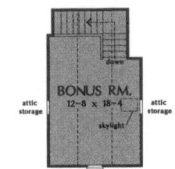

BONUS RM.

© 1997 Donald A. Gardner Architects, Inc.

HPK2100134

Style: Country

Square Footage: 1,517

Bonus Space: 287 sq. ft.

Bedrooms: 3

Bathrooms: 2

Width: 61' - 4"

Depth: 48' - 6"

© THE SATER DESIGN COLLECTION, INC.

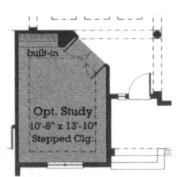

HPK2100135

Style: French Country

Square Footage: 1,526

Bonus Space: 336 sq. ft.

Bedrooms: 3

Bathrooms: 2

Width: 65' - 0"

Depth: 54' - 0"

Foundation: Crawlspace

© Sater Design Collection, Inc.

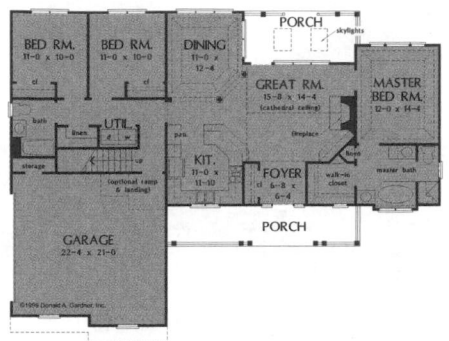
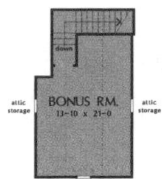

HPK2100136

Style: Country
Square Footage: 1,540
Bonus Space: 277 sq. ft.
Bedrooms: 3
Bathrooms: 2
Width: 63' - 4"
Depth: 46' - 10"

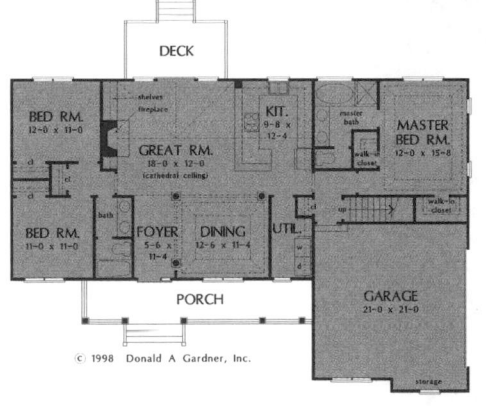

HPK2100137

Style: Craftsman
Square Footage: 1,544
Bonus Space: 320 sq. ft.
Bedrooms: 3
Bathrooms: 2
Width: 63' - 0"
Depth: 43' - 0"

1,500 TO 1,999 SQUARE FEET

HPK2100138

Style: Country
Square Footage: 1,559
Bedrooms: 3
Bathrooms: 2
Width: 54' - 4"
Depth: 52' - 0"

© 1999 Donald A. Gardner, Inc.

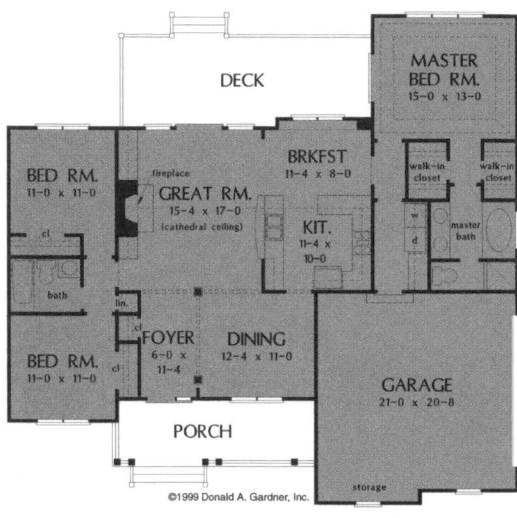

©1999 Donald A. Gardner, Inc.

© 1995 Donald A. Gardner Architects, Inc.

HPK2100139

Plan: HPK2100139
Style: Country
Square Footage: 1,561
Bedrooms: 3
Bathrooms: 2
Width: 60' - 10"
Depth: 51' - 6"

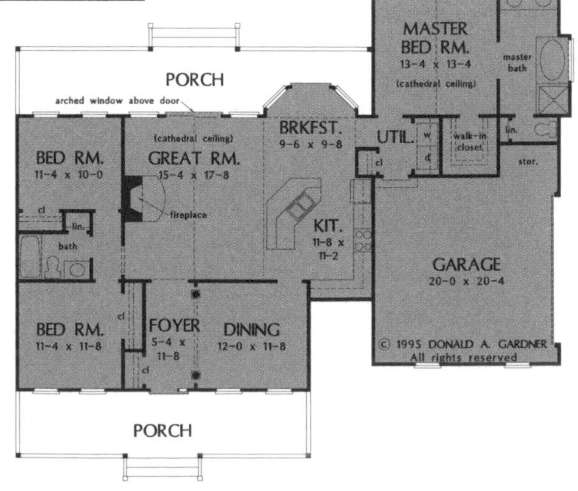

ORDER BLUEPRINTS ANYTIME AT EPLANS.COM OR 1-800-521-6797

HPK2100140

Style: New American

Square Footage: 1,575

Bedrooms: 3

Bathrooms: 2

Width: 50' - 0"

Depth: 52' - 6"

Foundation: Crawlspace, Unfinished Walkout Basement

EPLANS.COM

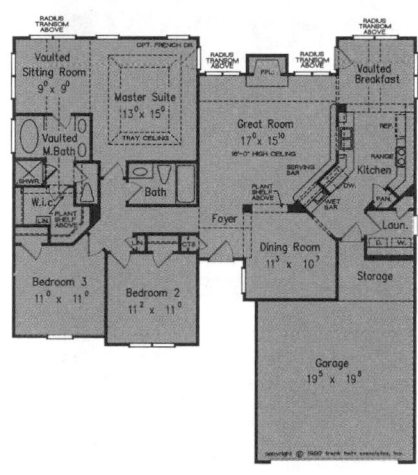

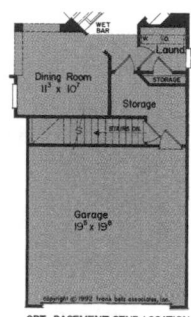

OPT. BASEMENT STAIR LOCATION

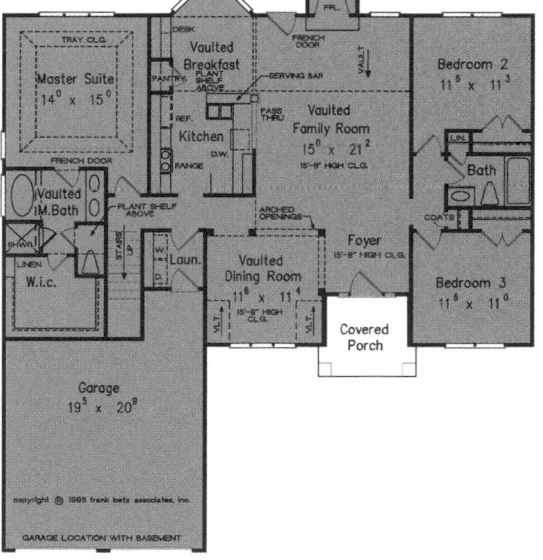

GARAGE LOCATION WITH BASEMENT

HPK2100141

Style: New American

Square Footage: 1,575

Bedrooms: 3

Bathrooms: 2

Width: 52' - 0"

Depth: 52' - 6"

Foundation: Crawlspace, Slab, Unfinished Walkout Basement

EPLANS.COM

1,500 TO 1,999 SQUARE FEET

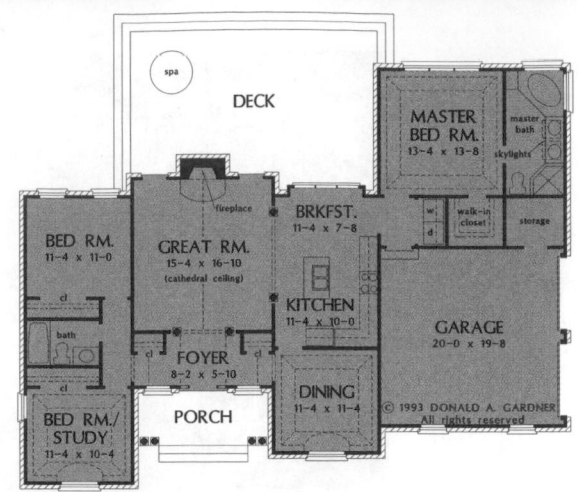

HPK2100142

EPLANS.COM

Style: New American
Square Footage: 1,576
Bedrooms: 3
Bathrooms: 2
Width: 60' - 6"
Depth: 47' - 3"

HPK2100143

EPLANS.COM

Style: Cottage
Square Footage: 1,580
Bedrooms: 3
Bathrooms: 2 ½
Width: 50' - 0"
Depth: 48' - 0"
Foundation: Crawlspace

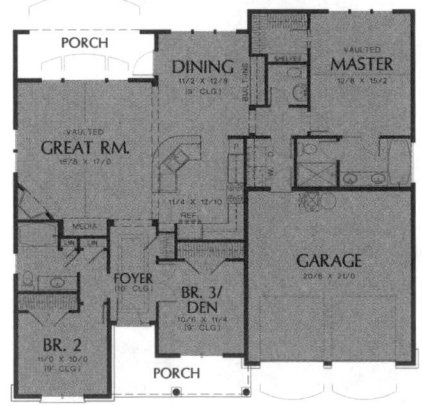

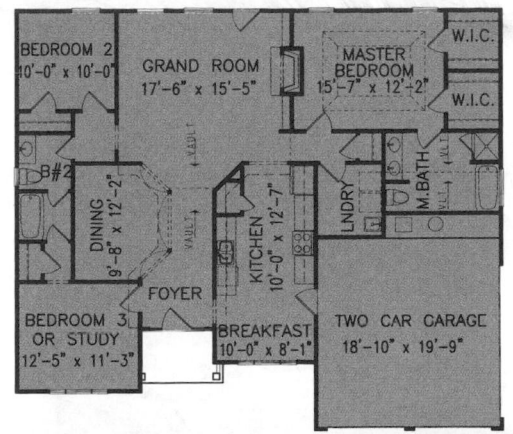

HPK2100144

Style: Ranch
Square Footage: 1,580
Bedrooms: 3
Bathrooms: 2
Width: 50' - 0"
Depth: 44' - 0"
Foundation: Slab

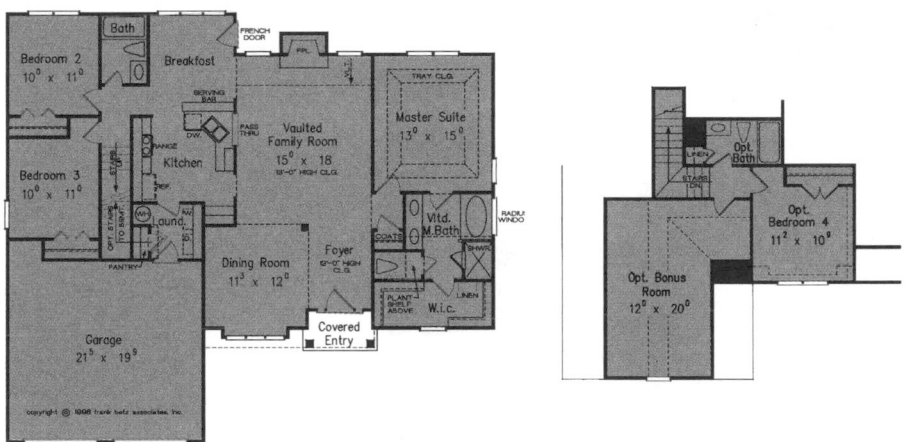

HPK2100145

Style: Cottage
Square Footage: 1,583
Bonus Space: 544 sq. ft.
Bedrooms: 3
Bathrooms: 2
Width: 54' - 0"
Depth: 47' - 0"
Foundation: Crawlspace, Slab, Unfinished Walkout Basement

© 2000 Donald A. Gardner, Inc.

HPK2100146

Style: Cottage

Square Footage: 1,593

Bonus Space: 332 sq. ft.

Bedrooms: 3

Bathrooms: 2

Width: 50' - 0"

Depth: 54' - 0"

EPLANS.COM

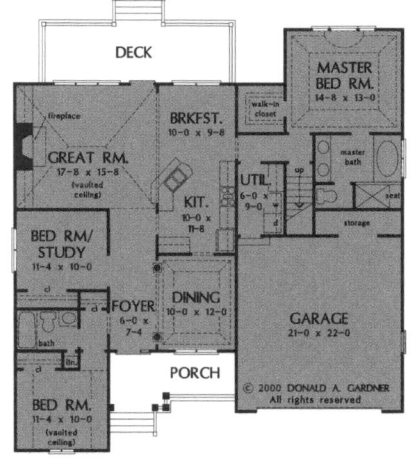

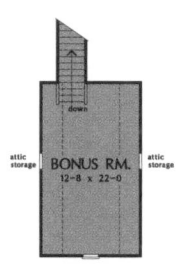

HPK2100147

Style: French Country

Square Footage: 1,593

Bedrooms: 3

Bathrooms: 2

Width: 60' - 0"

Depth: 48' - 10"

Foundation: Unfinished Basement

EPLANS.COM

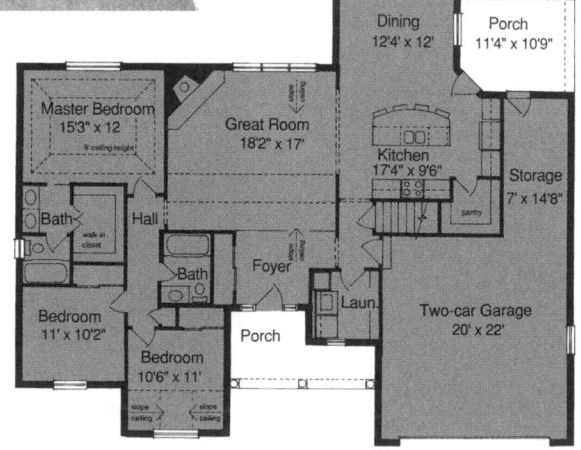

HPK2100148

Style: European

Square Footage: 1,595

Bedrooms: 3

Bathrooms: 2

Width: 52' - 8"

Depth: 42' - 8"

Foundation: Unfinished Basement

EPLANS.COM

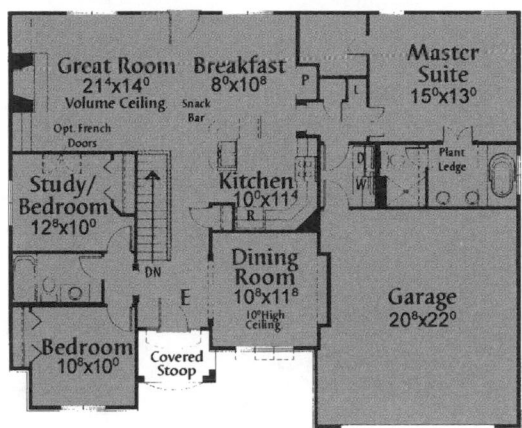

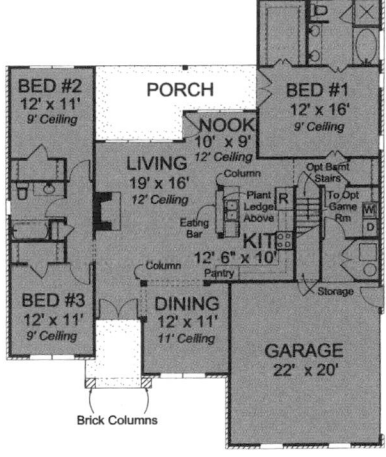

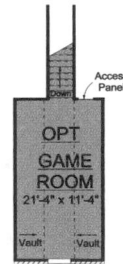

HPK2100149

Style: European

Square Footage: 1,595

Bonus Space: 312 sq. ft.

Bedrooms: 3

Bathrooms: 2

Width: 49' - 0"

Depth: 60' - 0"

EPLANS.COM

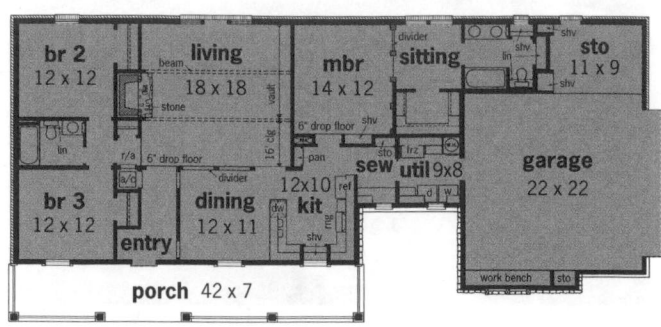

HPK2100150

Style: Farmhouse

Square Footage: 1,600

Bedrooms: 3

Bathrooms: 2

Width: 75' - 0"

Depth: 37' - 0"

Foundation: Crawlspace, Slab, Unfinished Basement

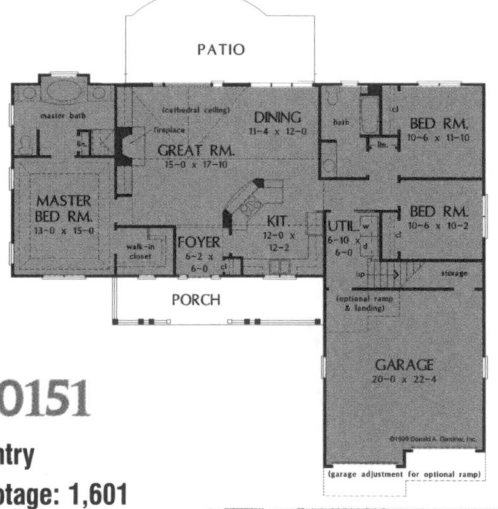

HPK2100151

Style: Country

Square Footage: 1,601

Bonus Space: 237 sq. ft.

Bedrooms: 3

Bathrooms: 2

Width: 61' - 4"

Depth: 50' - 6"

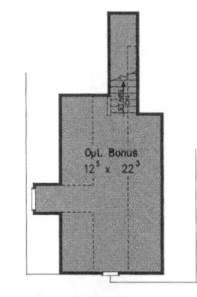

HPK2100152

Style: Country

Square Footage: 1,604

Bonus Space: 334 sq. ft.

Bedrooms: 3

Bathrooms: 2

Width: 53' - 6"

Depth: 55' - 10"

Foundation: Crawlspace, Slab, Unfinished Walkout Basement

EPLANS.COM

HPK2100153

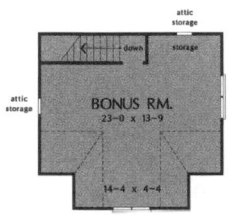

EPLANS.COM

Style: Cottage

Square Footage: 1,608

Bonus Space: 437 sq. ft.

Bedrooms: 3

Bathrooms: 2

Width: 40' - 8"

Depth: 62' - 8"

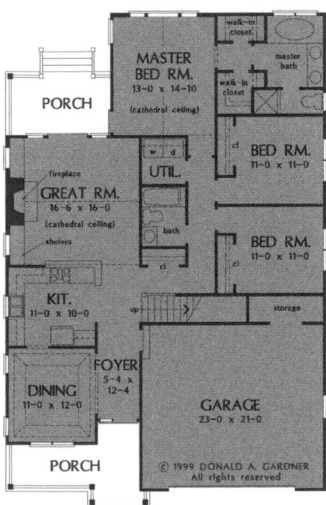

1,500 TO 1,999 SQUARE FEET

HPK2100154

Style: Cottage
Square Footage: 1,610
Bonus Space: 353 sq. ft.
Bedrooms: 3
Bathrooms: 2
Width: 49' - 11"
Depth: 55' - 1"

EPLANS.COM

© 2001 Donald A. Gardner, Inc.

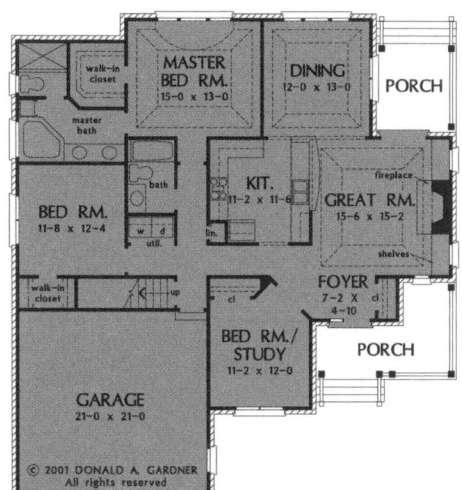

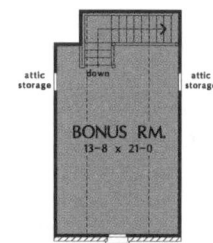

©The Sater Design Collection, Inc.

© THE SATER DESIGN COLLECTION, INC.

HPK2100155

Style: French Country
Square Footage: 1,616
Bonus Space: 362 sq. ft.
Bedrooms: 3
Bathrooms: 2
Width: 64' - 0"
Depth: 55' - 0"
Foundation: Crawlspace

EPLANS.COM

HPK2100156

Style: Farmhouse

Square Footage: 1,616

Bonus Space: 362 sq. ft.

Bedrooms: 3

Bathrooms: 2

Width: 64' - 0"

Depth: 55' - 0"

Foundation: Crawlspace

EPLANS.COM

HPK2100157

EPLANS.COM

Style: Country

Square Footage: 1,628

Bonus Space: 300 sq. ft.

Bedrooms: 3

Bathrooms: 2

Width: 56' - 0"

Depth: 50' - 4"

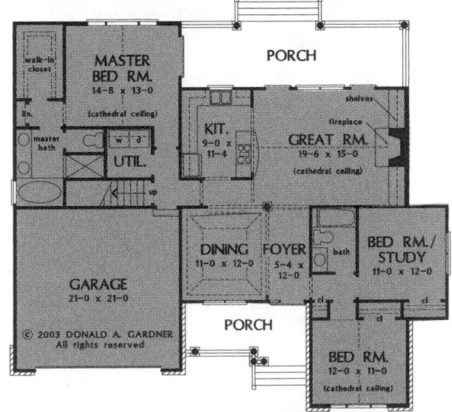

1,500 TO 1,999 SQUARE FEET

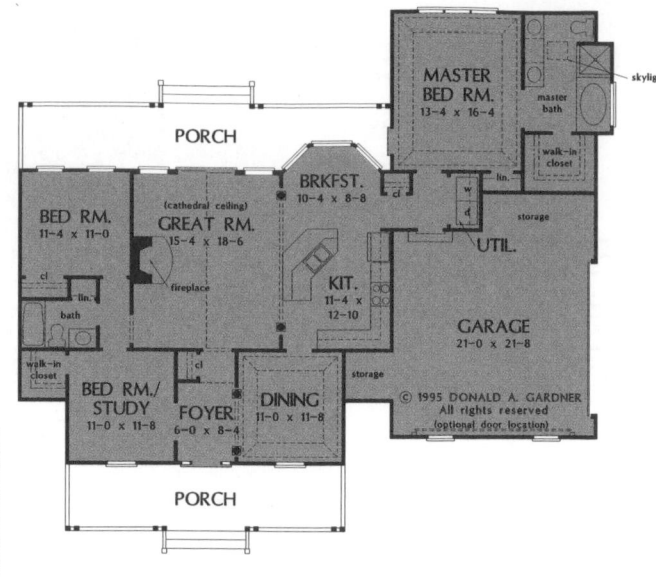

HPK2100158

Style: Country
Square Footage: 1,632
Bedrooms: 3
Bathrooms: 2
Width: 62' - 4"
Depth: 55' - 2"

EPLANS.COM

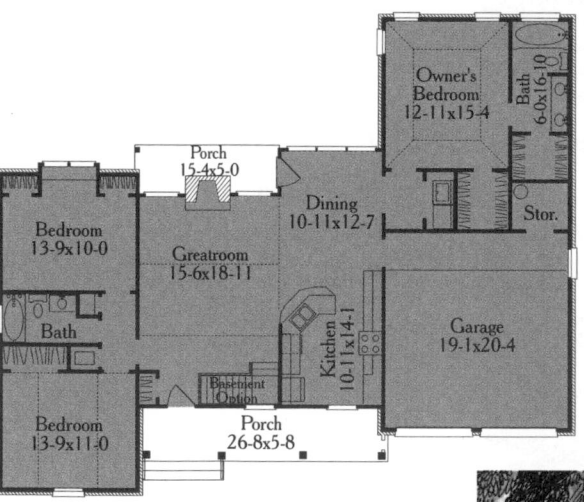

HPK2100159

Style: Country
Square Footage: 1,643
Bedrooms: 3
Bathrooms: 2
Width: 62' - 2"
Depth: 51' - 4"
Foundation: Crawlspace, Slab, Unfinished Basement

EPLANS.COM

HPK2100160

Style: Country

Square Footage: 1,644

Bonus Space: 922 sq. ft.

Bedrooms: 3

Bathrooms: 2

Width: 63' - 0"

Depth: 52' - 2"

Foundation: Crawlspace, Slab, Unfinished Basement

EPLANS.COM

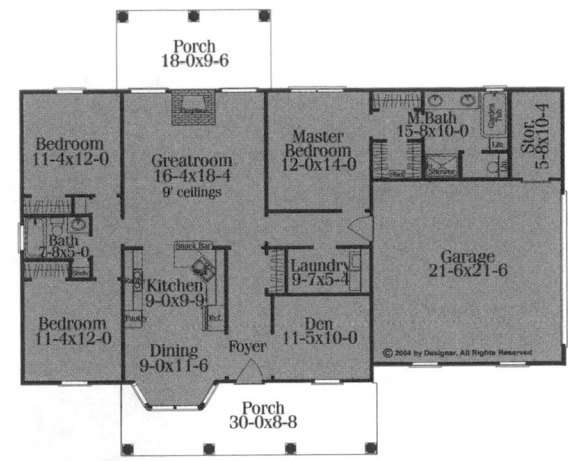

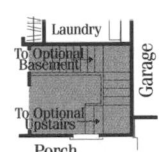

HPK2100161

Style: New American

Square Footage: 1,644

Bedrooms: 3

Bathrooms: 2

Width: 55' - 0"

Depth: 41' - 10"

Foundation: Slab

EPLANS.COM

© 1997 Donald A. Gardner Architects, Inc.

HPK2100162

EPLANS.COM

Style: Country
Square Footage: 1,652
Bonus Space: 367 sq. ft.
Bedrooms: 3
Bathrooms: 2
Width: 64' - 4"
Depth: 51' - 0"

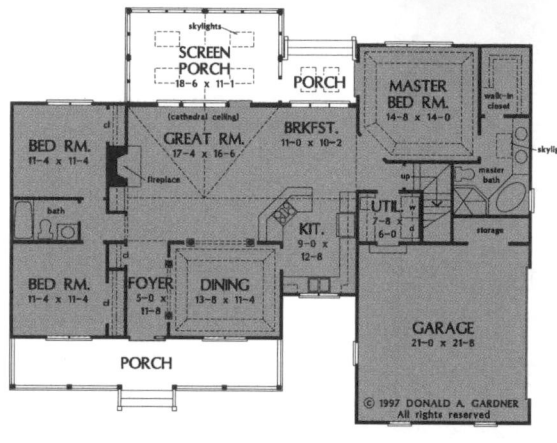

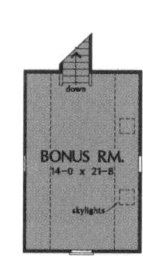

© 1993 Donald A. Gardner, Architects, Inc.

HPK2100163

EPLANS.COM

Style: Country
Square Footage: 1,655
Bedrooms: 3
Bathrooms: 2
Width: 61' - 0"
Depth: 49' - 8"

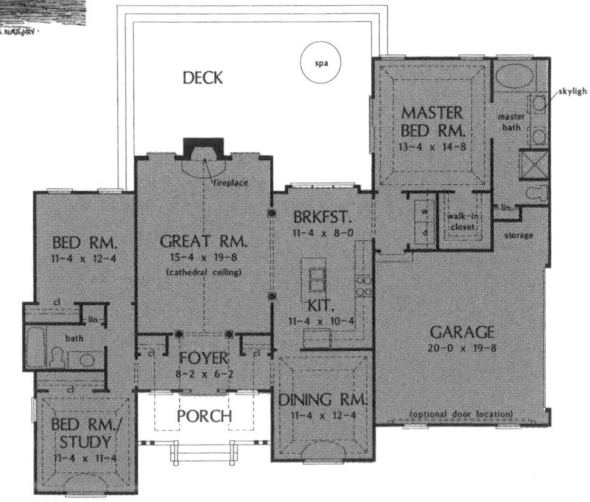

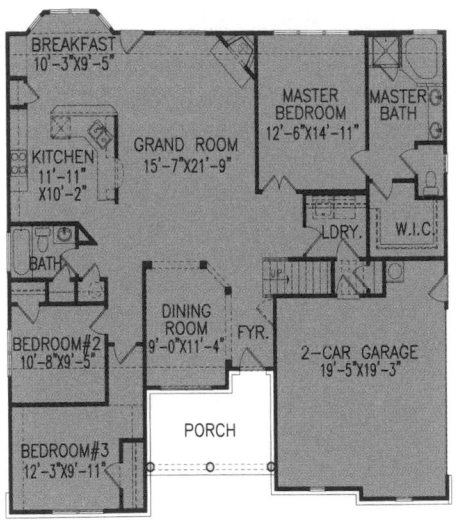

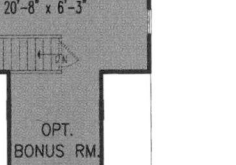

HPK2100164

Style: Country

Square Footage: 1,656

Bonus Space: 368 sq. ft.

Bedrooms: 3

Bathrooms: 2

Width: 50' - 0"

Depth: 48' - 0"

Foundation: Slab

EPLANS.COM

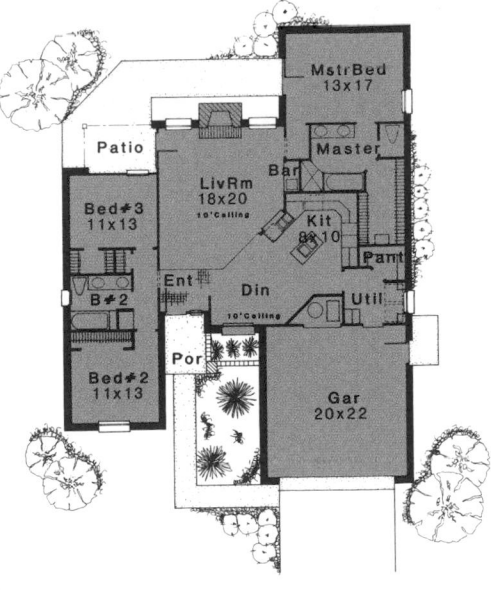

HPK2100165

Style: Cottage

Square Footage: 1,664

Bedrooms: 3

Bathrooms: 2

Width: 48' - 0"

Depth: 63' - 1"

Foundation: Crawlspace, Slab

EPLANS.COM

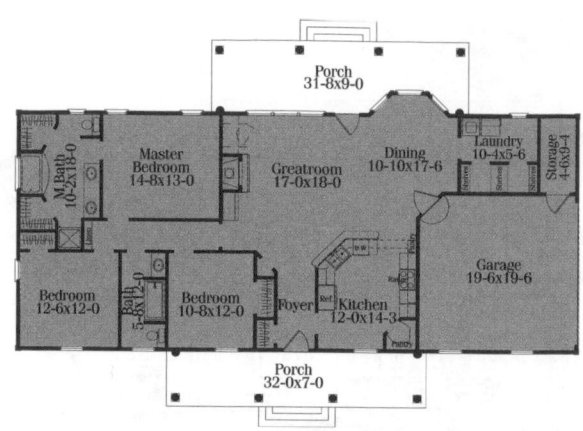

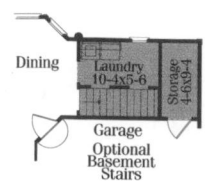

HPK2100166

Style: Colonial Revival

Square Footage: 1,670

Bedrooms: 3

Bathrooms: 2

Width: 70' - 0"

Depth: 46' - 0"

Foundation: Crawlspace, Slab, Unfinished Basement

EPLANS.COM

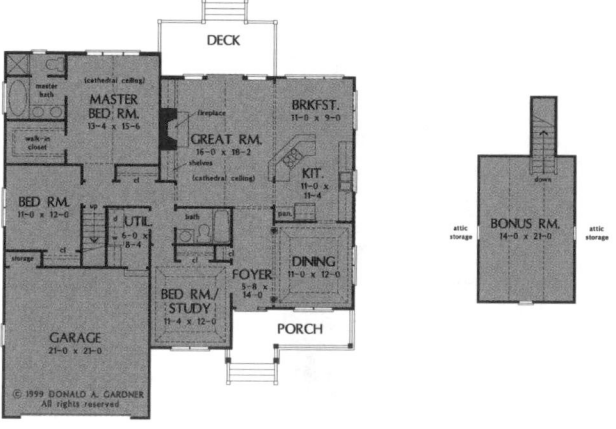

HPK2100167

Style: Country

Square Footage: 1,671

Bonus Space: 348 sq. ft.

Bedrooms: 3

Bathrooms: 2

Width: 50' - 8"

Depth: 52' - 4"

EPLANS.COM

HPK2100168

Style: Country

Square Footage: 1,671

Bedrooms: 3

Bathrooms: 2

Width: 50' - 0"

Depth: 51' - 0"

Foundation: Crawlspace, Slab, Unfinished Walkout Basement

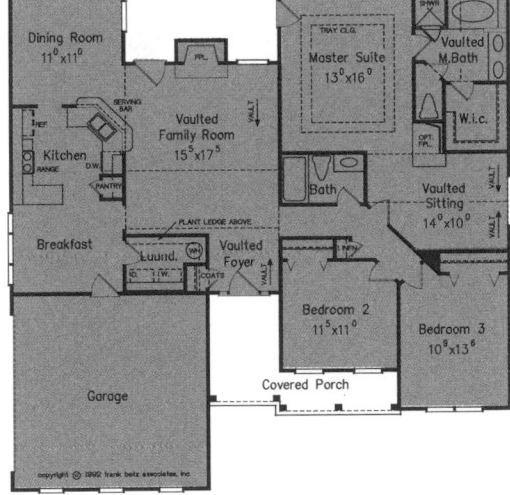

HPK2100169

Style: Country

Square Footage: 1,674

Bonus Space: 336 sq. ft.

Bedrooms: 3

Bathrooms: 2

Width: 56' - 4"

Depth: 50' - 0"

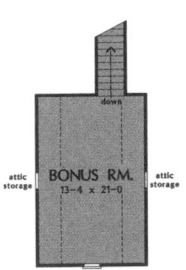

1,500 TO 1,999 SQUARE FEET

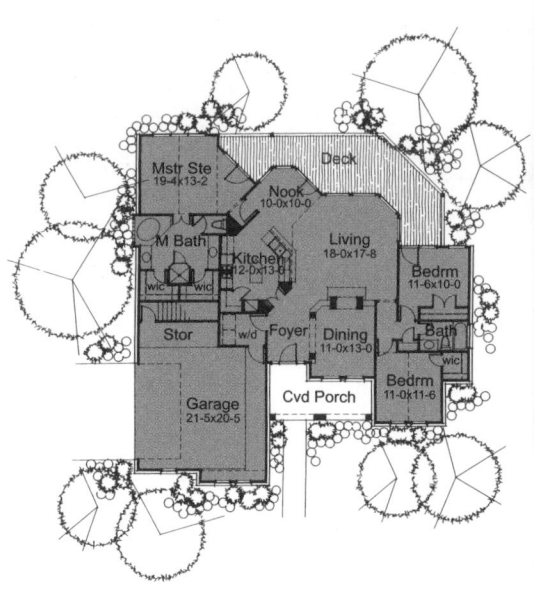

HPK2100170

Style: New American

Square Footage: 1,675

Bedrooms: 3

Bathrooms: 2

Width: 57' - 5"

Depth: 59' - 6"

Foundation: Crawlspace, Slab, Unfinished Basement

EPLANS.COM

© 1997 Donald A. Gardner Architects, Inc.

HPK2100171

Style: Country

Square Footage: 1,680

Bedrooms: 3

Bathrooms: 2

Width: 62' - 8"

Depth: 59' - 10"

EPLANS.COM

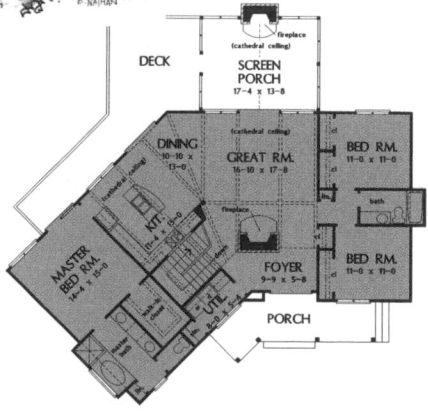

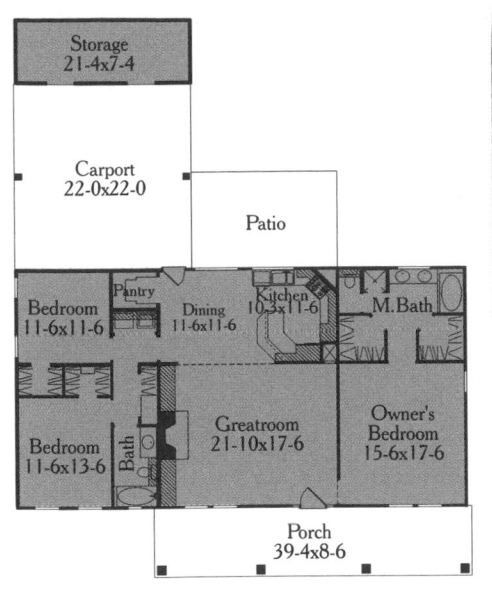

Storage
21-4x7-4

Carport
22-0x22-0

Patio

Bedroom
11-6x11-6

Pantry

Kitchen
10-3x11-6

Dining
11-6x11-6

M. Bath

Bedroom
11-6x13-6

Bath

Greatroom
21-10x17-6

Owner's
Bedroom
15-6x17-6

Porch
39-4x8-6

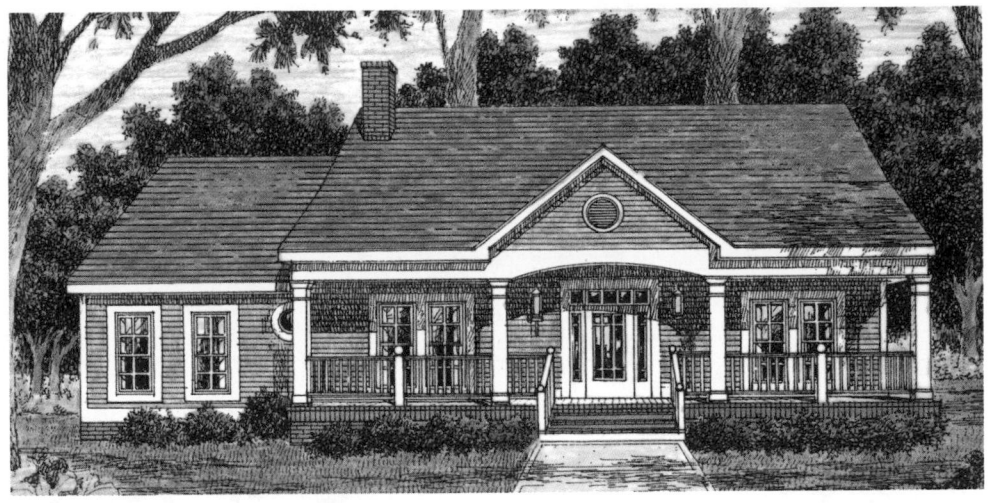

HPK2100172

Style: Country

Square Footage: 1,680

Bedrooms: 3

Bathrooms: 2

Width: 56' - 6"

Depth: 68' - 6"

Foundation: Crawlspace, Slab, Unfinished Basement

EPLANS.COM

© 1996 Donald A. Gardner Architects, Inc.

B. NATHAN

HPK2100173

Style: Country

Square Footage: 1,685

Bonus Space: 331 sq. ft.

Bedrooms: 3

Bathrooms: 2

Width: 62' - 4"

Depth: 57' - 4"

EPLANS.COM

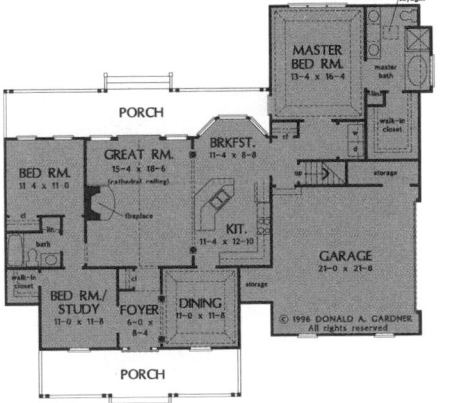

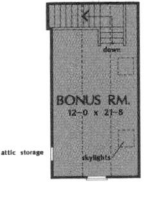

1,500 TO 1,999 SQUARE FEET

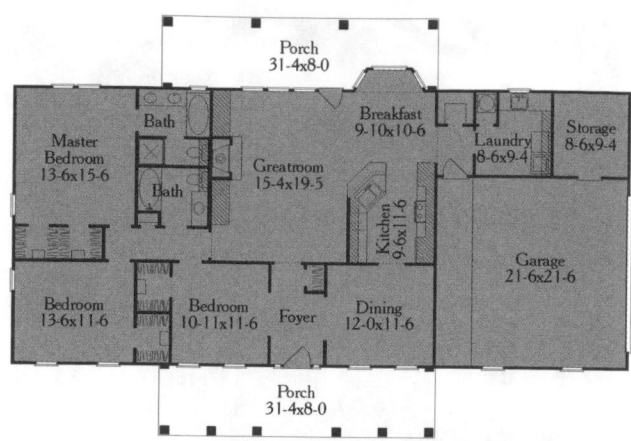

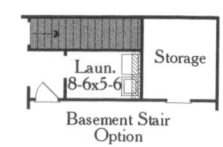

HPK2100174

Style: Colonial Revival

Square Footage: 1,688

Bedrooms: 3

Bathrooms: 2

Width: 70' - 1"

Depth: 48' - 0"

Foundation: Crawlspace, Slab, Unfinished Basement

EPLANS.COM

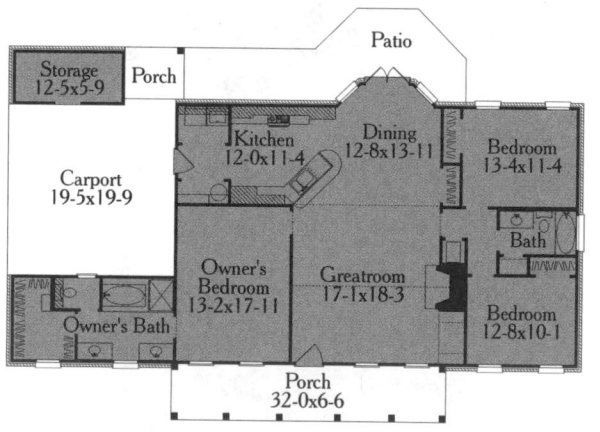

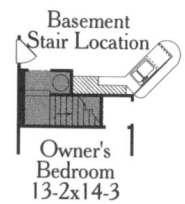

HPK2100175

Style: Colonial Revival

Square Footage: 1,689

Bedrooms: 3

Bathrooms: 2

Width: 67' - 0"

Depth: 43' - 0"

Foundation: Crawlspace, Slab, Unfinished Basement

EPLANS.COM

HPK2100176

Style: Country

Square Footage: 1,700

Bonus Space: 333 sq. ft.

Bedrooms: 3

Bathrooms: 2

Width: 49' - 0"

Depth: 65' - 4"

EPLANS.COM

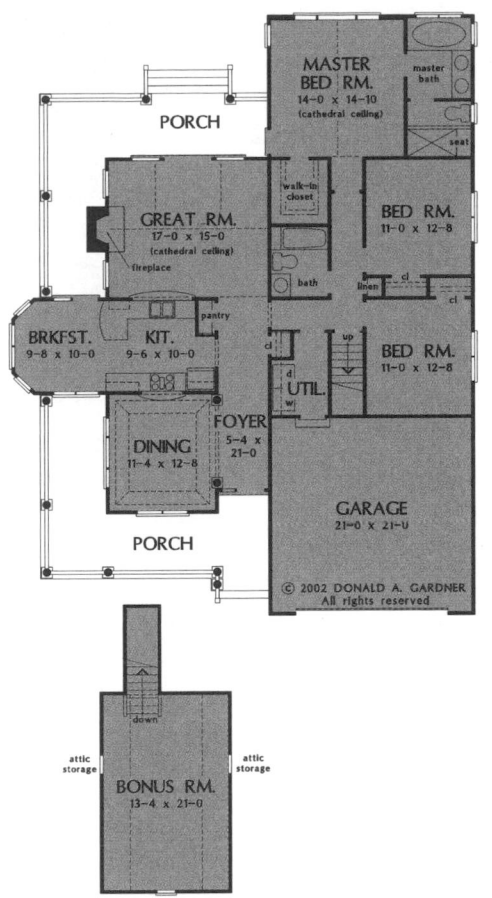

HPK2100177

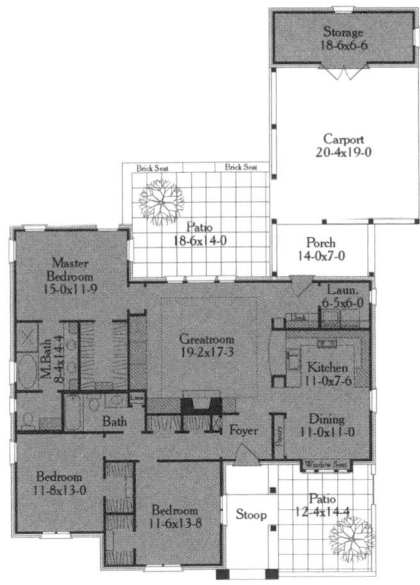

Style: Cottage

Square Footage: 1,702

Bedrooms: 3

Bathrooms: 2

Width: 55' - 0"

Depth: 76' - 4"

Foundation: Crawlspace, Slab, Unfinished Basement

EPLANS.COM

Optional Layout

HPK2100178

Style: New American

Square Footage: 1,715

Bedrooms: 3

Bathrooms: 2

Width: 55' - 0"

Depth: 49' - 0"

Foundation: Crawlspace, Slab, Unfinished Walkout Basement

EPLANS.COM

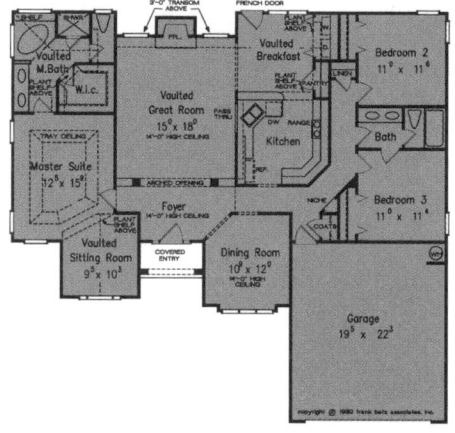

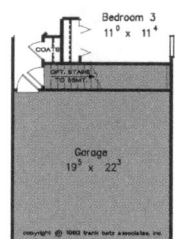

Optional Layout

HPK2100179

Style: Country

Square Footage: 1,721

Bedrooms: 3

Bathrooms: 2

Width: 83' - 0"

Depth: 42' - 0"

Foundation: Unfinished Walkout Basement

EPLANS.COM

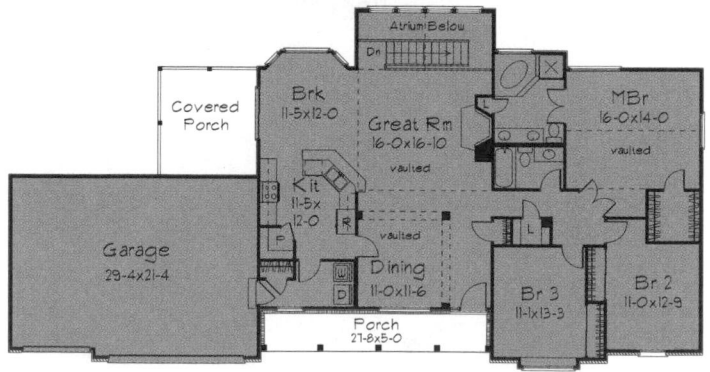

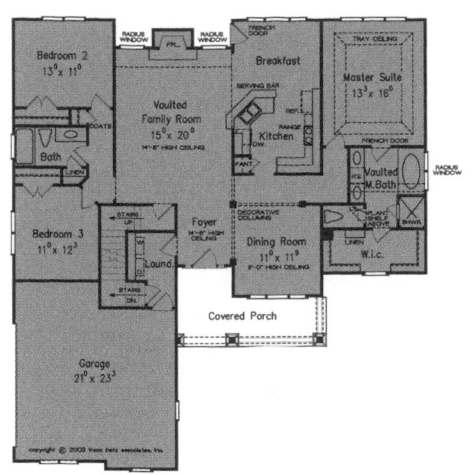

HPK2100180

Style: Craftsman

Square Footage: 1,724

Bonus Space: 375 sq. ft.

Bedrooms: 3

Bathrooms: 2

Width: 53' - 6"

Depth: 58' - 6"

Foundation: Crawlspace, Slab, Unfinished Walkout Basement

EPLANS.COM

HPK2100181

Style: Cottage

Square Footage: 1,725

Bonus Space: 256 sq. ft.

Bedrooms: 3

Bathrooms: 2

Width: 58' - 0"

Depth: 54' - 6"

Foundation: Crawlspace, Slab, Unfinished Walkout Basement

EPLANS.COM

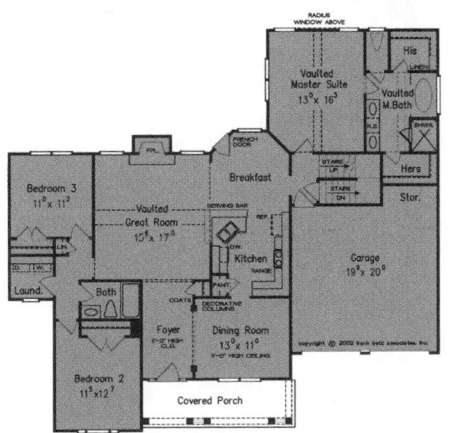

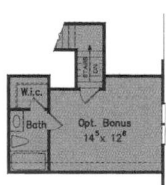

Rear Exterior

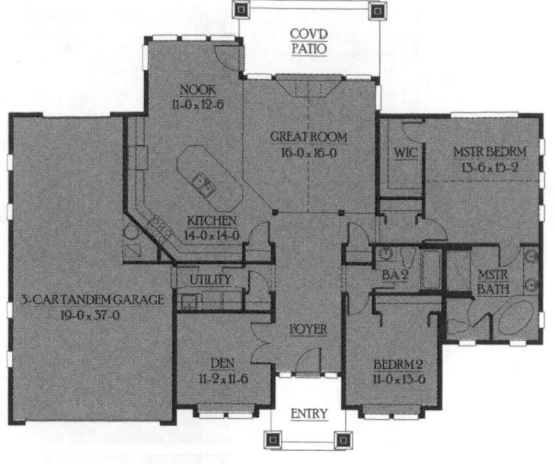

HPK2100182

Style: Craftsman

Square Footage: 1,725

Bedrooms: 2

Bathrooms: 2

Width: 64' - 0"

Depth: 53' - 6"

Foundation: Crawlspace

EPLANS.COM

HPK2100183

Style: Country

Square Footage: 1,727

Bonus Space: 346 sq. ft.

Bedrooms: 3

Bathrooms: 2

Width: 46' - 0"

Depth: 66' - 4"

EPLANS.COM

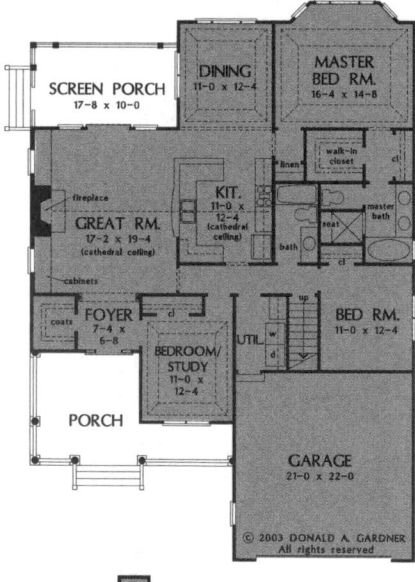

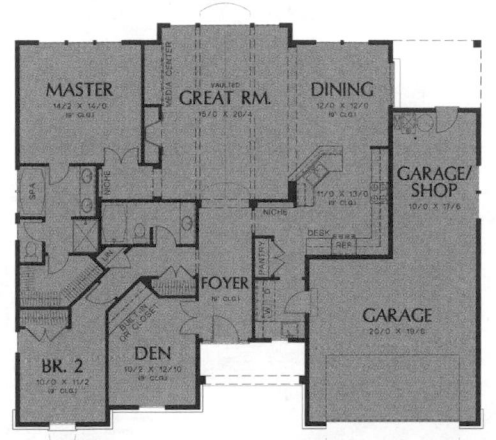

HPK2100184

Style: French Country

Square Footage: 1,728

Bedrooms: 2

Bathrooms: 2

Width: 55' - 0"

Depth: 48' - 0"

Foundation: Crawlspace

EPLANS.COM

HPK2100185

Style: Bungalow

Square Footage: 1,728

Bedrooms: 2

Bathrooms: 2

Width: 55' - 0"

Depth: 48' - 0"

Foundation: Crawlspace

EPLANS.COM

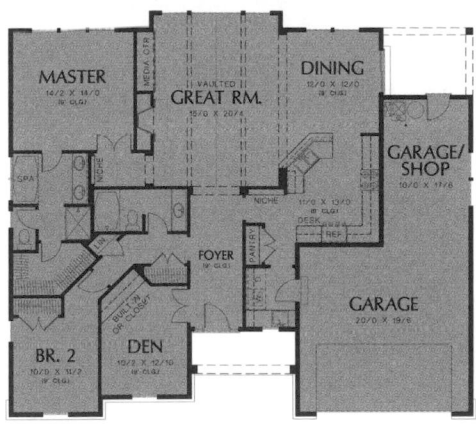

HPK2100186

Style: Colonial Revival

Square Footage: 1,730

Bonus Space: 520 sq. ft.

Bedrooms: 3

Bathrooms: 2

Width: 61' - 0"

Depth: 62' - 0"

Foundation: Crawlspace, Slab, Unfinished Basement

EPLANS.COM

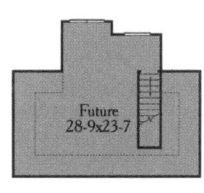

© Stephen Fuller, Inc.

HPK2100187

Style: Cottage

Square Footage: 1,733

Bedrooms: 3

Bathrooms: 2 ½

Width: 55' - 6"

Depth: 57' - 6"

Foundation: Walkout Basement

EPLANS.COM

HPK2100188

EPLANS.COM

Style: Country

Square Footage: 1,737

Bedrooms: 3

Bathrooms: 2

Width: 65' - 10"

Depth: 59' - 8"

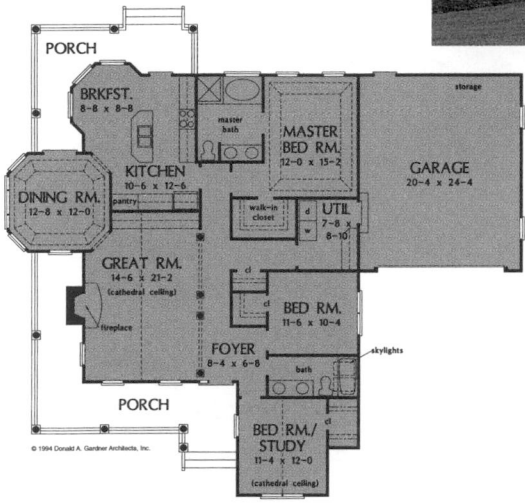

HPK2100189

EPLANS.COM

Style: Colonial

Square Footage: 1,742

Bedrooms: 3

Bathrooms: 2

Width: 78' - 10"

Depth: 40' - 10"

Foundation: Crawlspace, Slab

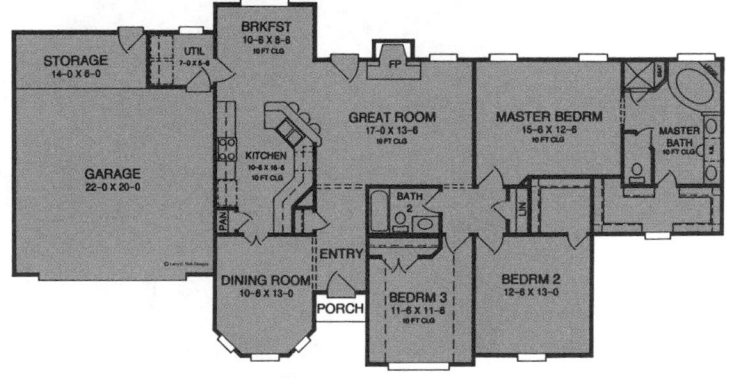

1,500 TO 1,999 SQUARE FEET

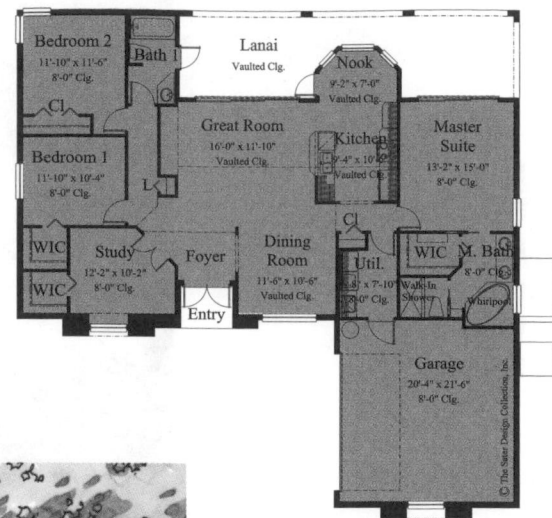

HPK2100190

Style: Spanish Revival

Square Footage: 1,746

Bedrooms: 3

Bathrooms: 2

Width: 58' - 0"

Depth: 59' - 4"

Foundation: Slab

EPLANS.COM

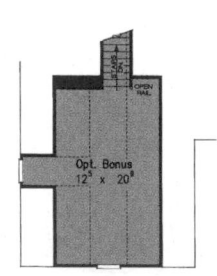

HPK2100191

Style: Country

Square Footage: 1,749

Bonus Space: 308 sq. ft.

Bedrooms: 3

Bathrooms: 2

Width: 54' - 0"

Depth: 56' - 6"

Foundation: Crawlspace, Slab, Unfinished Walkout Basement

EPLANS.COM

HPK2100192

Style: Cottage
Square Footage: 1,768
Bonus Space: 354 sq. ft.
Bedrooms: 3
Bathrooms: 2
Width: 54' - 0"
Depth: 59' - 6"
Foundation: Crawlspace, Slab, Unfinished Walkout Basement

EPLANS.COM

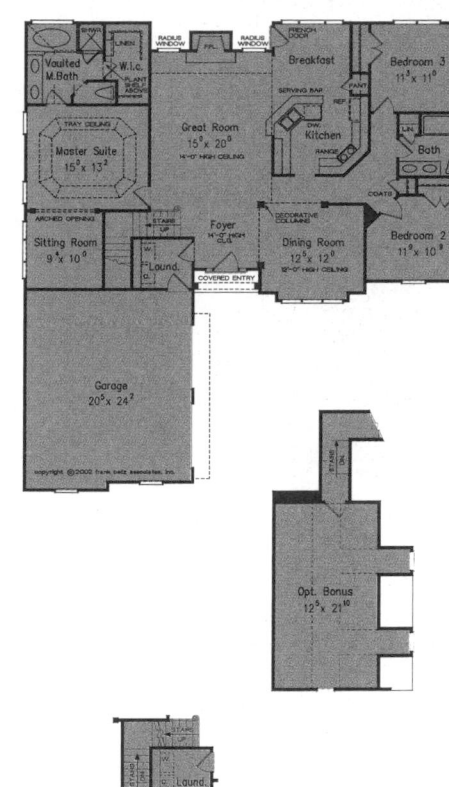

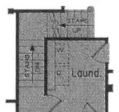

Optional Layout

HPK2100193

Style: Country
Square Footage: 1,768
Bedrooms: 3
Bathrooms: 2
Width: 36' - 0"
Depth: 61' - 5"
Foundation: Slab

EPLANS.COM

1,500 TO 1,999 SQUARE FEET

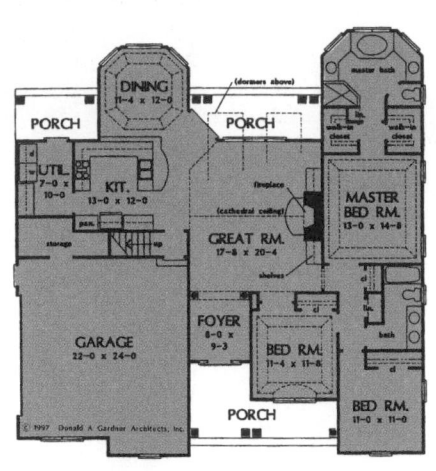

© 1997 Donald A. Gardner Architects, Inc.

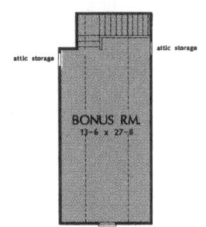

HPK2100194

Style: Country

Square Footage: 1,770

Bonus Space: 401 sq. ft.

Bedrooms: 3

Bathrooms: 2

Width: 54' - 0"

Depth: 57' - 8"

EPLANS.COM

HPK2100195

Style: Bungalow

Square Footage: 1,771

Bedrooms: 3

Bathrooms: 2

Width: 50' - 0"

Depth: 70' - 0"

Foundation: Crawlspace

EPLANS.COM

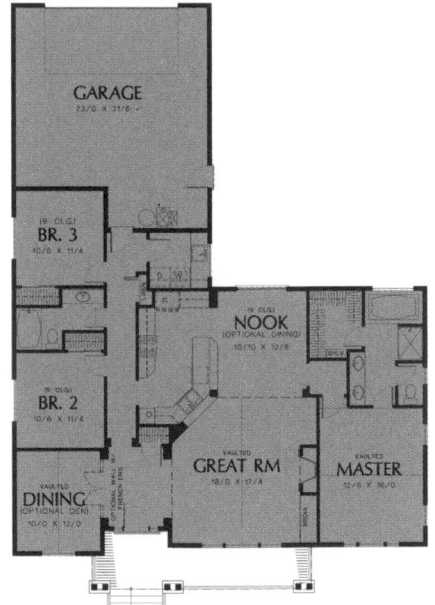

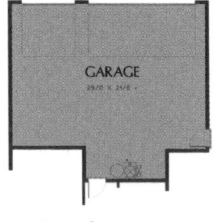

Optional Layout

ORDER BLUEPRINTS ANYTIME AT EPLANS.COM OR 1-800-521-6797

HPK2100196

Style: New American

Square Footage: 1,779

Bedrooms: 3

Bathrooms: 2

Width: 57' - 0"

Depth: 56' - 4"

Foundation: Crawlspace, Unfinished Walkout Basement

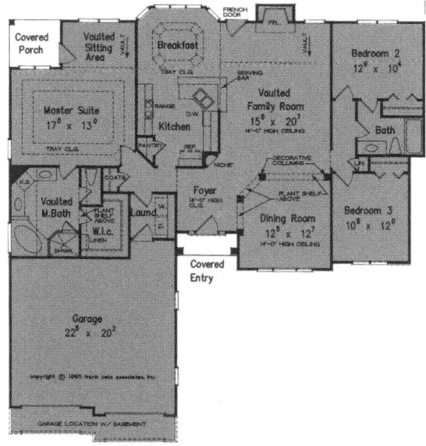

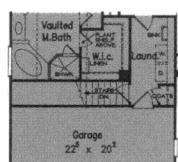

Optional Layout

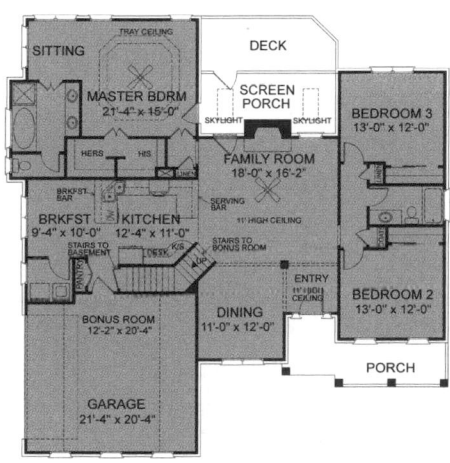

HPK2100197

Style: Country

Square Footage: 1,787

Bonus Space: 263 sq. ft.

Bedrooms: 3

Bathrooms: 2

Width: 55' - 8"

Depth: 56' - 6"

Foundation: Crawlspace, Slab, Unfinished Walkout Basement

1,500 TO 1,999 SQUARE FEET

HPK2100198

Style: Country
Square Footage: 1,787
Bonus Space: 326 sq. ft.
Bedrooms: 3
Bathrooms: 2
Width: 66' - 2"
Depth: 66' - 8"

EPLANS.COM

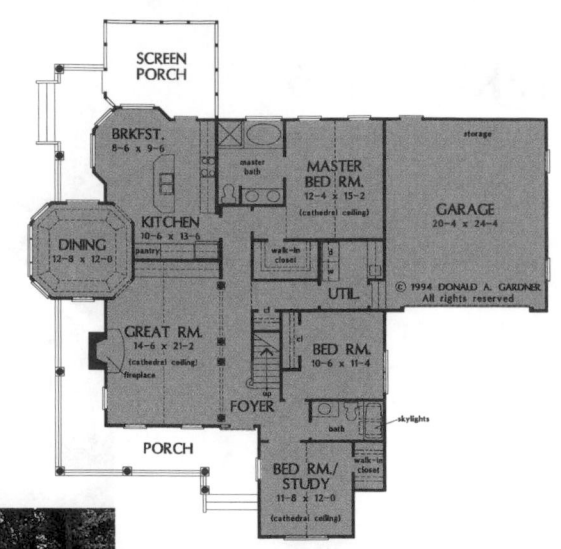

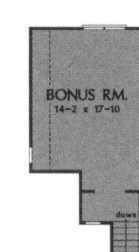

HPK2100199

Style: New American
Square Footage: 1,792
Bedrooms: 3
Bathrooms: 2
Width: 68' - 0"
Depth: 62' - 0"
Foundation: Crawlspace, Slab, Unfinished Basement

EPLANS.COM

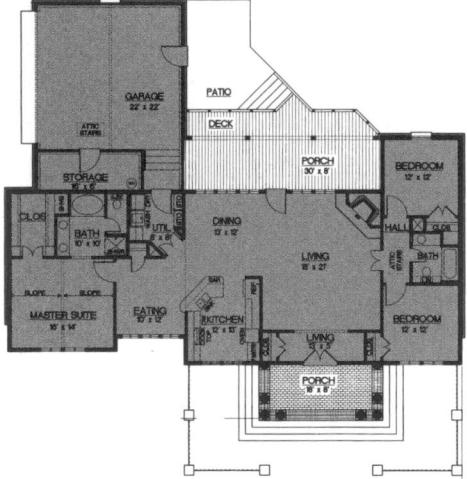

ORDER BLUEPRINTS ANYTIME AT EPLANS.COM OR 1-800-521-6797

HPK2100200

Style: Country
Square Footage: 1,792
Bonus Space: 255 sq. ft.
Bedrooms: 3
Bathrooms: 2
Width: 50' - 0"
Depth: 62' - 6"
Foundation: Crawlspace, Unfinished Walkout Basement

EPLANS.COM

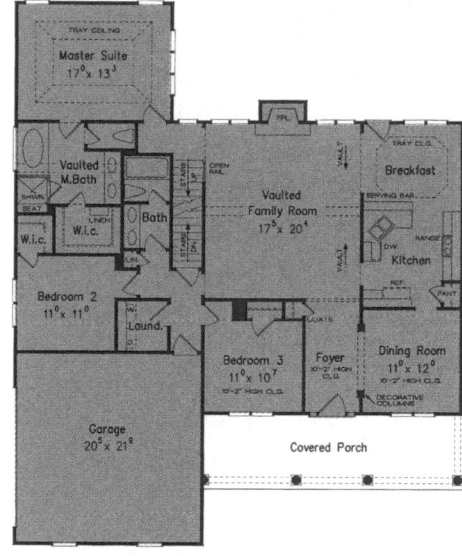

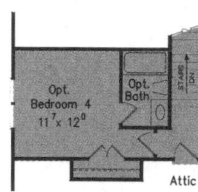

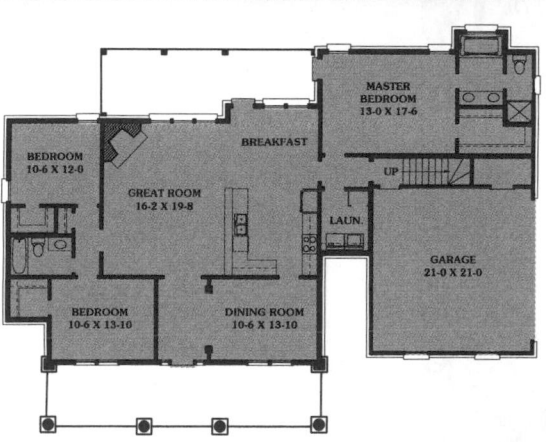

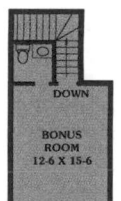

HPK2100201

Style: Farmhouse
Square Footage: 1,794
Bonus Space: 253 sq. ft.
Bedrooms: 3
Bathrooms: 2
Width: 69' - 4"
Depth: 51' - 0"
Foundation: Crawlspace

EPLANS.COM

1,500 TO 1,999 SQUARE FEET

HPK2100202

Style: Bungalow

Square Footage: 1,797

Bedrooms: 3

Bathrooms: 2

Width: 45' - 0"

Depth: 45' - 2"

Foundation: Unfinished Walkout Basement

EPLANS.COM

© 1994 Donald A. Gardner Architects, Inc.

HPK2100203

Style: Country

Square Footage: 1,807

Bonus Space: 419 sq. ft.

Bedrooms: 3

Bathrooms: 2

Width: 70' - 8"

Depth: 52' - 8"

EPLANS.COM

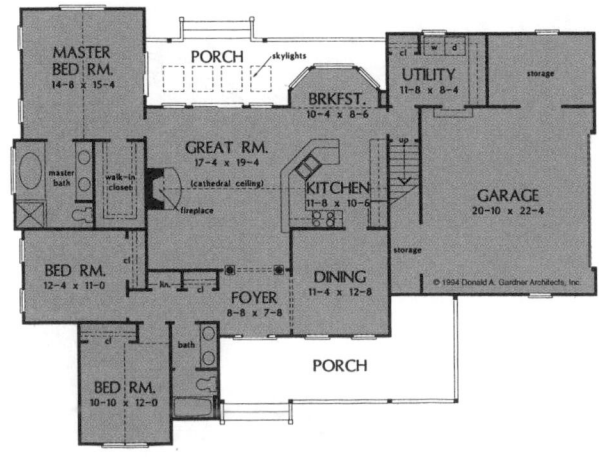

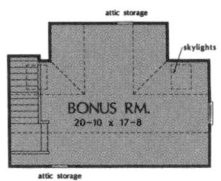

© 1994 Donald A. Gardner Architects, Inc.

ORDER BLUEPRINTS ANYTIME AT EPLANS.COM OR 1-800-521-6797

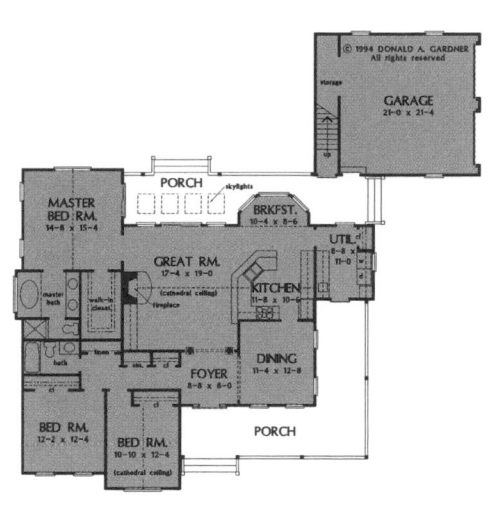

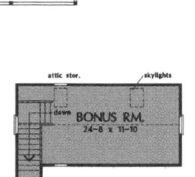

HPK2100204

Style: Farmhouse

Square Footage: 1,815

Bonus Space: 336 sq. ft.

Bedrooms: 3

Bathrooms: 2

Width: 70' - 8"

Depth: 70' - 2"

EPLANS.COM

HPK2100205

Style: New American

Square Footage: 1,815

Bedrooms: 3

Bathrooms: 2 ½

Width: 60' - 0"

Depth: 60' - 6"

Foundation: Walkout Basement

EPLANS.COM

1,500 TO 1,999 SQUARE FEET

HPK2100206

Style: Craftsman
Square Footage: 1,821
Bonus Space: 409 sq. ft.
Bedrooms: 3
Bathrooms: 2
Width: 54' - 4"
Depth: 61' - 6"

EPLANS.COM

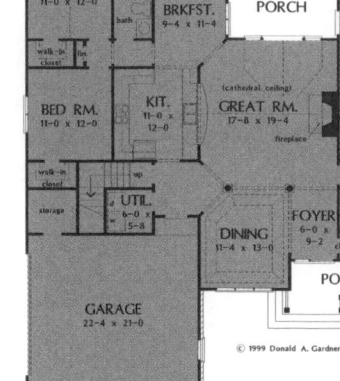

© 1999 Donald A. Gardner, Inc.

© 1999 Donald A. Gardner, Inc.

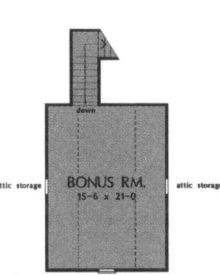

HPK2100207

Style: Country
Square Footage: 1,821
Bonus Space: 191 sq. ft.
Bedrooms: 3
Bathrooms: 2
Width: 54' - 0"
Depth: 54' - 0"
Foundation: Slab

EPLANS.COM

HPK2100208

Style: Country

Square Footage: 1,822

Bedrooms: 3

Bathrooms: 2

Width: 58' - 0"

Depth: 66' - 8"

Foundation: Unfinished Basement

EPLANS.COM

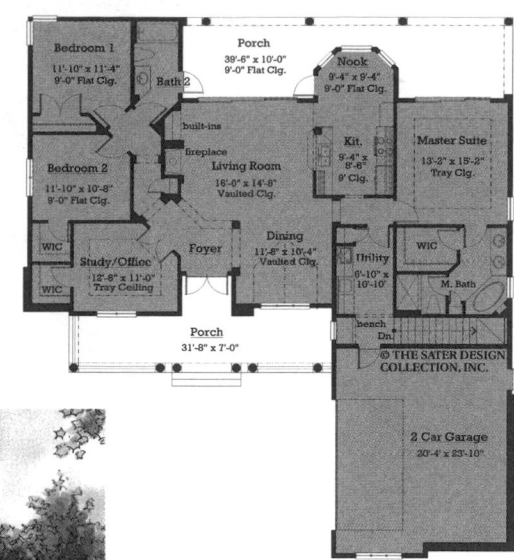

© The Sater Design Collection, Inc.

HPK2100209

Style: Country

Square Footage: 1,827

Bonus Space: 384 sq. ft.

Bedrooms: 3

Bathrooms: 2

Width: 61' - 8"

Depth: 62' - 8"

EPLANS.COM

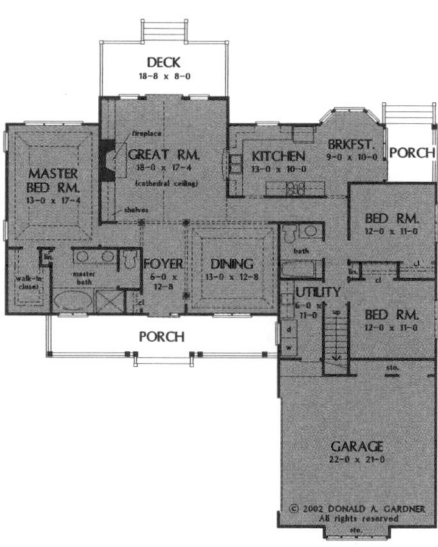

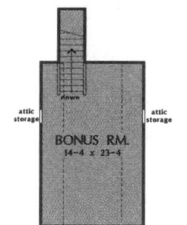

© 2002 Donald A. Gardner, Inc.

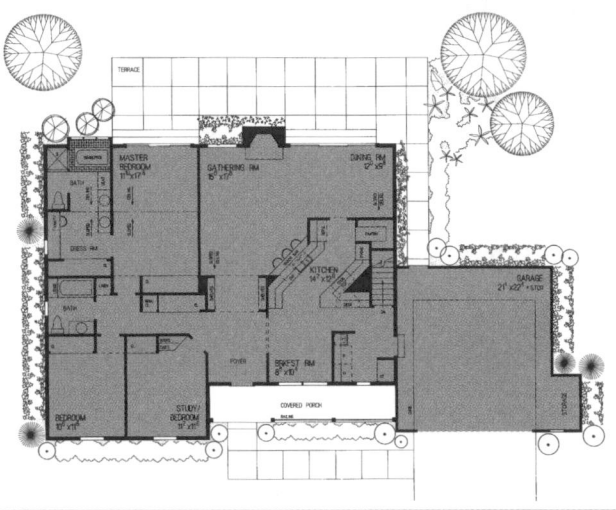

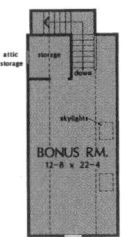

HPK2100210

Style: Country

Square Footage: 1,830

Bedrooms: 3

Bathrooms: 2

Width: 75' - 0"

Depth: 43' - 5"

Foundation: Unfinished Basement

EPLANS.COM

HPK2100211

Style: Country

Square Footage: 1,832

Bonus Space: 425 sq. ft.

Bedrooms: 3

Bathrooms: 2

Width: 65' - 4"

Depth: 62' - 0"

EPLANS.COM

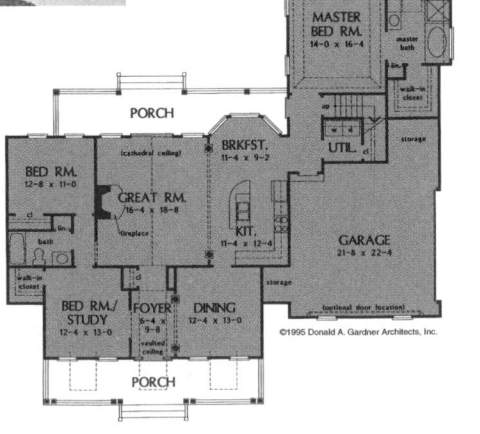

HPK2100212

Style: New American

Square Footage: 1,832

Bonus Space: 68 sq. ft.

Bedrooms: 3

Bathrooms: 2 ½

Width: 59' - 6"

Depth: 52' - 6"

Foundation: Crawlspace, Slab, Unfinished Walkout Basement

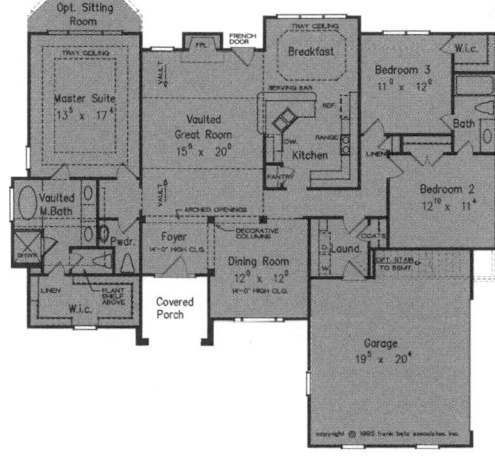

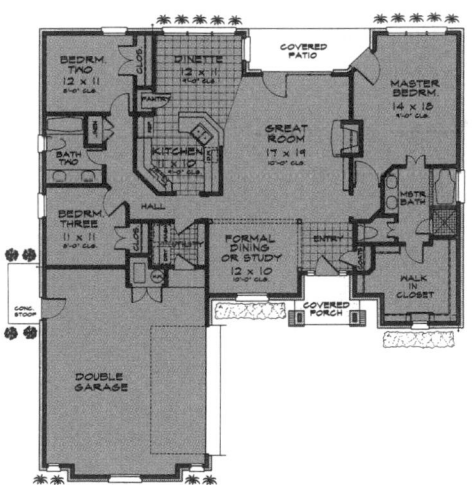

HPK2100213

Style: Cottage

Square Footage: 1,834

Bedrooms: 3

Bathrooms: 2

Width: 55' - 0"

Depth: 60' - 4"

Foundation: Slab

EPLANS.COM

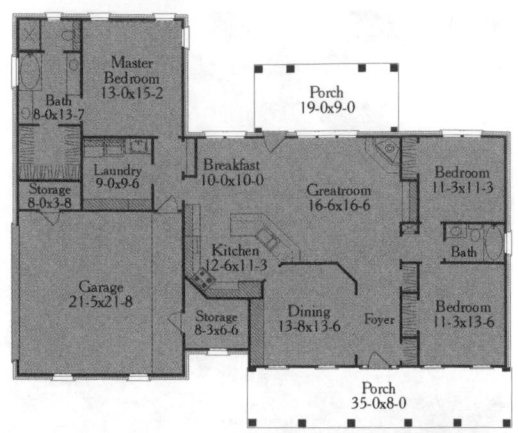

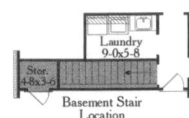

HPK2100214

Style: Colonial Revival

Square Footage: 1,836

Bedrooms: 3

Bathrooms: 2

Width: 65' - 8"

Depth: 55' - 0"

Foundation: Crawlspace, Slab, Unfinished Basement

EPLANS.COM

HPK2100215

Style: French Country

Square Footage: 1,848

Bedrooms: 3

Bathrooms: 2

Width: 58' - 0"

Depth: 60' - 0"

Foundation: Crawlspace

EPLANS.COM

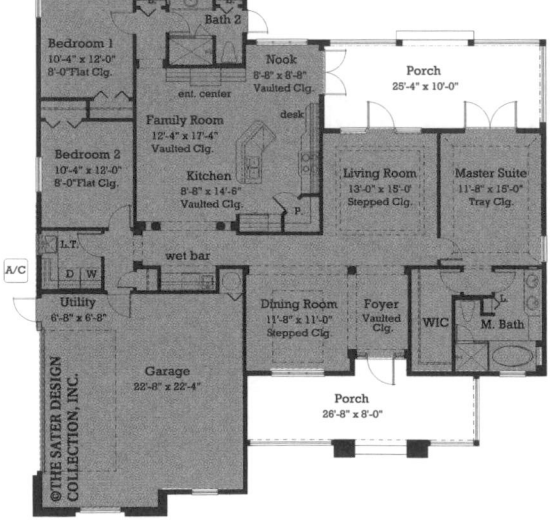

HPK2100216

Style: Bungalow
Square Footage: 1,850
Bedrooms: 3
Bathrooms: 2
Width: 44' - 0"
Depth: 68' - 0"
Foundation: Crawlspace

EPLANS.COM

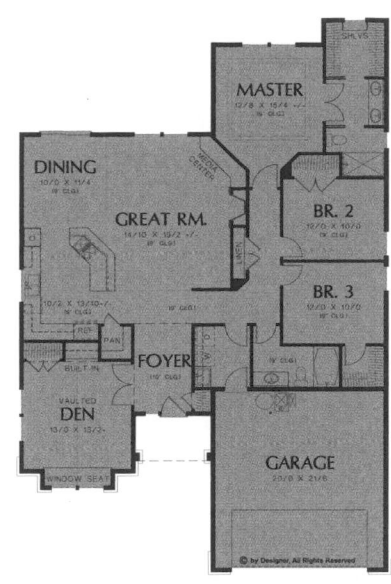

HPK2100217

Style: Country
Square Footage: 1,850
Bedrooms: 3
Bathrooms: 2
Width: 62' - 0"
Depth: 48' - 0"

EPLANS.COM

1,500 TO 1,999 SQUARE FEET

HPK2100218

Style: Ranch

Square Footage: 1,852

Bedrooms: 3

Bathrooms: 2

Width: 70' - 0"

Depth: 45' - 0"

Foundation: Crawlspace

EPLANS.COM

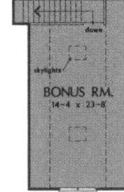

HPK2100219

Style: Country

Square Footage: 1,864

Bonus Space: 420 sq. ft.

Bedrooms: 3

Bathrooms: 2 ½

Width: 71' - 0"

Depth: 56' - 4"

EPLANS.COM

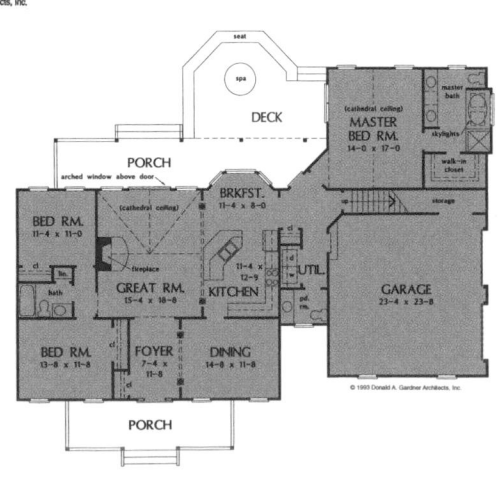

HPK2100220

Style: French Country
Square Footage: 1,869
Bonus Space: 336 sq. ft.
Bedrooms: 3
Bathrooms: 2
Width: 54' - 0"
Depth: 60' - 6"
Foundation: Crawlspace, Slab, Unfinished Walkout Basement

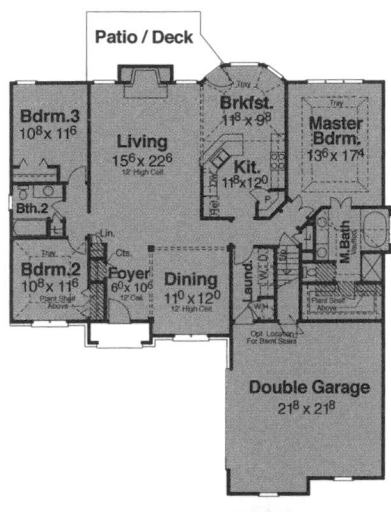

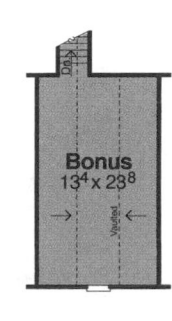

HPK2100221

Style: Ranch
Square Footage: 1,873
Bedrooms: 3
Bathrooms: 2
Width: 70' - 0"
Depth: 51' - 6"
Foundation: Crawlspace

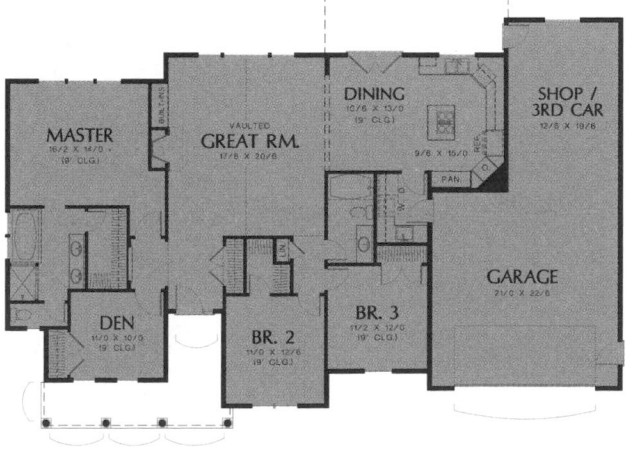

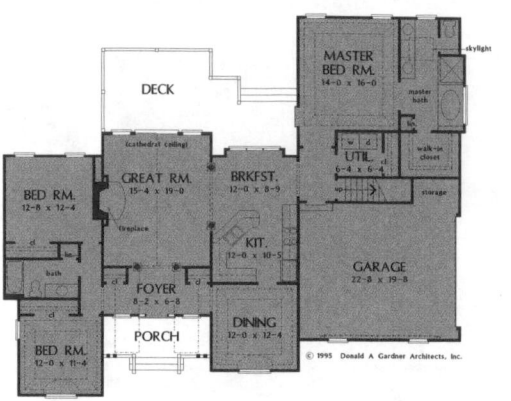

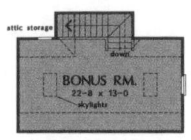

HPK2100222

Style: Country
Square Footage: 1,879
Bonus Space: 360 sq. ft.
Bedrooms: 3
Bathrooms: 2
Width: 66' - 4"
Depth: 55' - 2"

EPLANS.COM

HPK2100223

Style: Country
Square Footage: 1,882
Bonus Space: 363 sq. ft.
Bedrooms: 3
Bathrooms: 2 ½
Width: 61' - 4"
Depth: 55' - 0"

EPLANS.COM

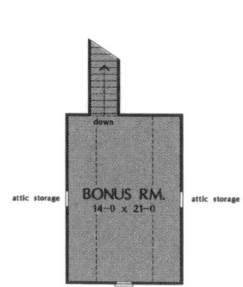

ORDER BLUEPRINTS ANYTIME AT EPLANS.COM OR 1-800-521-6797

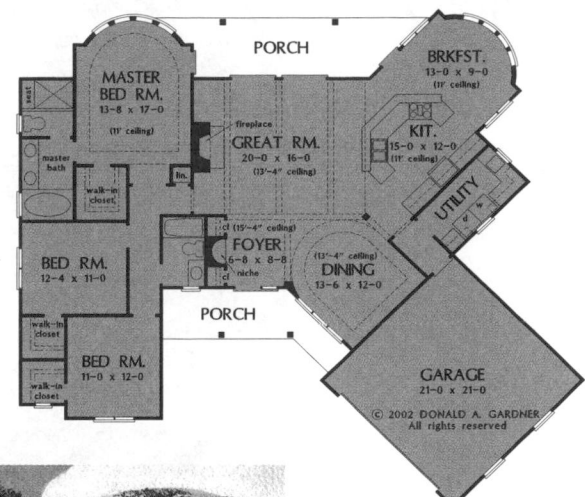

HPK2100224

Style: Pueblo

Square Footage: 1,883

Bedrooms: 3

Bathrooms: 2

Width: 66' - 2"

Depth: 59' - 8"

© 2002 Donald A. Gardner, Inc.

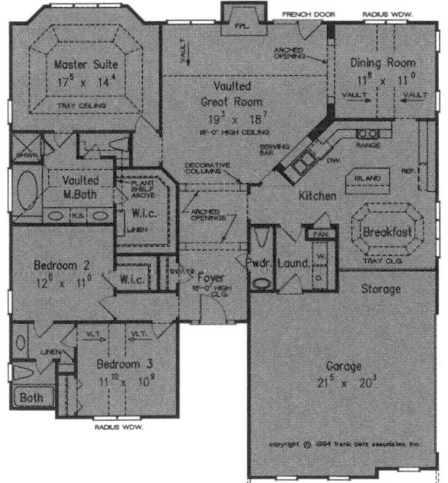

HPK2100225

Style: New American

Square Footage: 1,884

Bedrooms: 3

Bathrooms: 2 ½

Width: 50' - 0"

Depth: 55' - 4"

Foundation: Crawlspace, Slab, Unfinished Walkout Basement

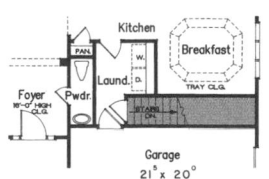

Optional Layout

HPK2100226

Style: New American
Square Footage: 1,890
Bedrooms: 3
Bathrooms: 2
Width: 65' - 10"
Depth: 53' - 5"
Foundation: Crawlspace, Slab

EPLANS.COM

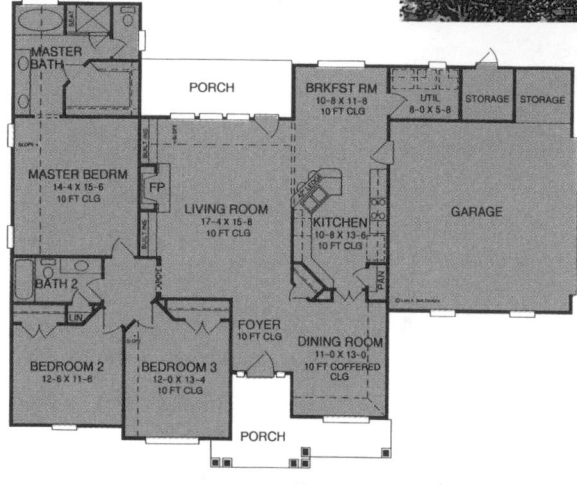

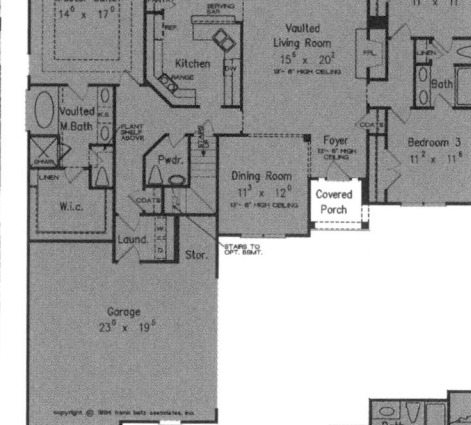

HPK2100227

Style: New American
Square Footage: 1,891
Bonus Space: 409 sq. ft.
Bedrooms: 3
Bathrooms: 2 ½
Width: 56' - 0"
Depth: 60' - 0"
Foundation: Crawlspace, Slab, Unfinished Walkout Basement

EPLANS.COM

HPK2100228

Style: Cottage
Square Footage: 1,892
Bonus Space: 285 sq. ft.
Bedrooms: 3
Bathrooms: 2 ½
Width: 65' - 4"
Depth: 45' - 10"
Foundation: Crawlspace, Slab, Unfinished Basement

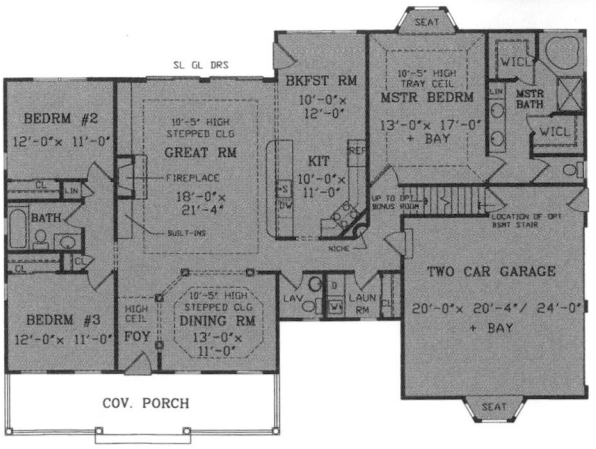

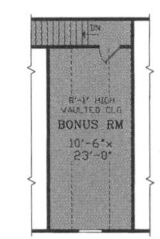

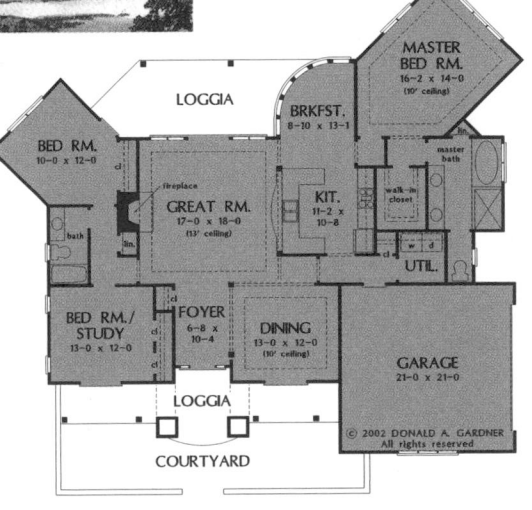

HPK2100229

Style: Pueblo
Square Footage: 1,895
Bedrooms: 3
Bathrooms: 2
Width: 65' - 10"
Depth: 59' - 9"

© 2002 Donald A. Gardner, Inc.

1,500 TO 1,999 SQUARE FEET

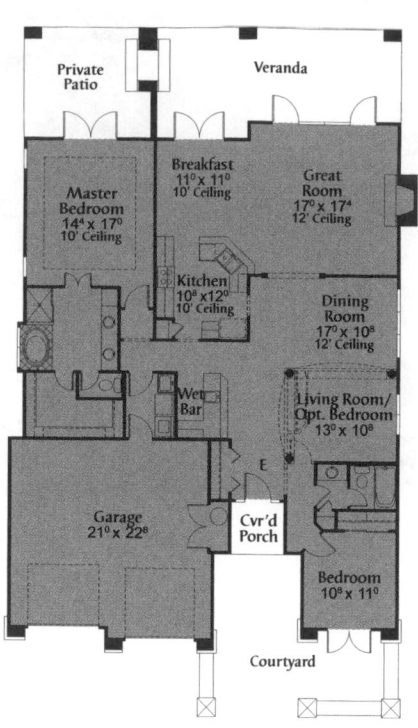

Private Patio

Veranda

Master Bedroom
14⁴ x 17⁰
10' Ceiling

Breakfast
11⁰ x 11⁰
10' Ceiling

Great Room
17⁰ x 17⁴
12' Ceiling

Kitchen
10⁸ x 12⁰
10' Ceiling

Dining Room
17⁰ x 10⁸
12' Ceiling

Wet Bar

Living Room/Opt. Bedroom
13⁰ x 10⁸

Garage
21⁰ x 22⁸

Cvr'd Porch

Bedroom
10⁸ x 11⁰

Courtyard

HPK2100230

Style: Pueblo
Square Footage: 1,899
Bedrooms: 3
Bathrooms: 2
Width: 43' - 4"
Depth: 79' - 6"
Foundation: Slab

EPLANS.COM

© 2002 Donald A. Gardner, Inc.

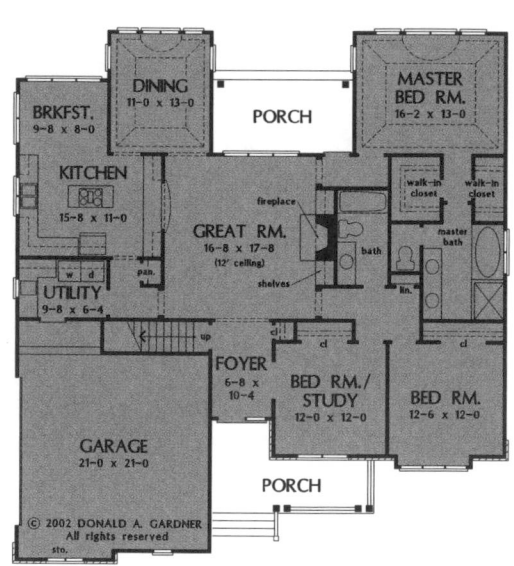

BRKFST.
9-8 x 8-0

DINING
11-0 x 13-0

PORCH

MASTER BED RM.
16-2 x 13-0

KITCHEN
15-8 x 11-0

fireplace

walk-in closet

walk-in closet

master bath

GREAT RM.
16-8 x 17-8
(12' ceiling)

bath

shelves

UTILITY
9-8 x 6-4

w d

pan.

up

FOYER
6-8 x 10-4

BED RM./STUDY
12-0 x 12-0

BED RM.
12-6 x 12-0

GARAGE
21-0 x 21-0

PORCH

© 2002 DONALD A. GARDNER
All rights reserved

sto.

HPK2100231

Style: French Country
Square Footage: 1,904
Bonus Space: 366 sq. ft.
Bedrooms: 3
Bathrooms: 2
Width: 53' - 10"
Depth: 57' - 8"

EPLANS.COM

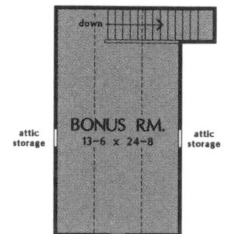

down

BONUS RM.
13-6 x 24-8

attic storage

attic storage

ORDER BLUEPRINTS ANYTIME AT EPLANS.COM OR 1-800-521-6797

HPK2100232

Style: New American

Square Footage: 1,906

Bedrooms: 3

Bathrooms: 2 ½

Width: 72' - 0"

Depth: 44' - 8"

Foundation: Unfinished Basement

EPLANS.COM

This hip-roofed ranch has an exterior that tastefully mixes brick and siding. The recessed entrance fills the formal entry with glowing light. The foyer opens to the large living room with high ceilings and a fireplace, the perfect spot for family gatherings. There is a large kitchen with ample cupboard space. The spacious master bedroom, with sweeping windows overlooking the rear yard, has a large walk-in closet. Two additional bedrooms share a full bath and each has a large closet.

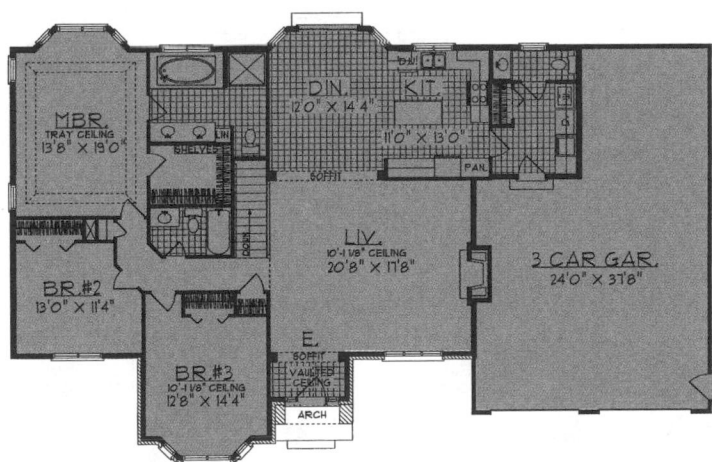

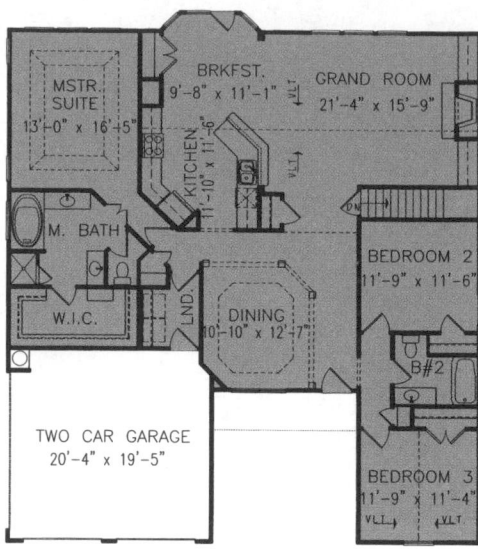

MSTR. SUITE
13'-0" x 16'-5"

BRKFST.
9'-8" x 11'-1"

GRAND ROOM
21'-4" x 15'-9"

KITCHEN
11'-10" x 11'-6"

M. BATH

BEDROOM 2
11'-9" x 11'-6"

W.I.C.

LND

DINING
10'-10" x 12'-7"

B#2

TWO CAR GARAGE
20'-4" x 19'-5"

BEDROOM 3
11'-9" x 11'-4"

HPK2100233

Style: Colonial
Square Footage: 1,923
Bedrooms: 3
Bathrooms: 2
Width: 48' - 0"
Depth: 53' - 0"
Foundation: Unfinished Walkout Basement

EPLANS.COM

Brick with a hint of siding, keystone lintels, and window shutters complement this home's exterior. To the right of the foyer, find two family bedrooms and a hall bath. To the left, the dining room features a decorative ceiling and defining columns. The grand room, with built-ins and a fireplace, shares a breakfast space and the open kitchen. A private hall leads to the master suite. Full bath amenities and a walk-in closet complete this space.

HPK2100234

Style: Country

Square Footage: 1,932

Bedrooms: 4

Bathrooms: 3

Width: 63' - 0"

Depth: 45' - 0"

Foundation: Crawlspace, Unfinished Walkout Basement

EPLANS.COM

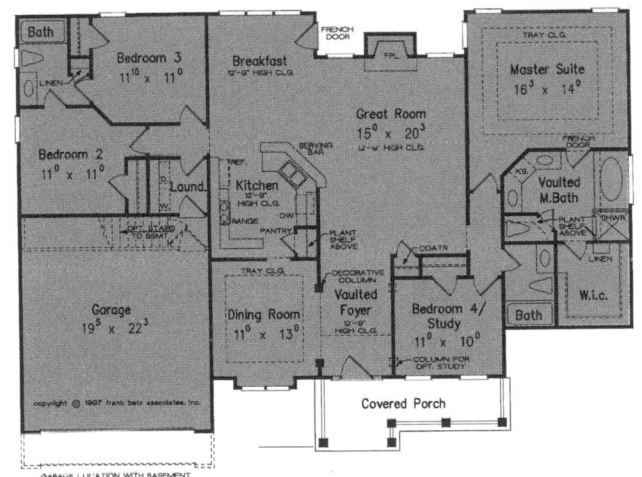

Special architectural aspects turn this quaint home into much more than just another one-story ranch design. A central great room acts as the hub of the plan and is graced by a fireplace. It is separated from the kitchen by a convenient serving bar. Two bedrooms to the left share a full bath. The master suite and one additional bedroom are to the right.

Graceful curves welcome you into the courtyard of this Santa Fe home. Inside, a gallery directs traffic to the work zone on the left or the sleeping zone on the right. A pantry offers extra storage space for kitchen items. The covered rear porch is accessible from the dining room, gathering room, and secluded master bedroom. The master bath has a whirlpool tub, a separate shower, a double vanity, and lots of closet space.

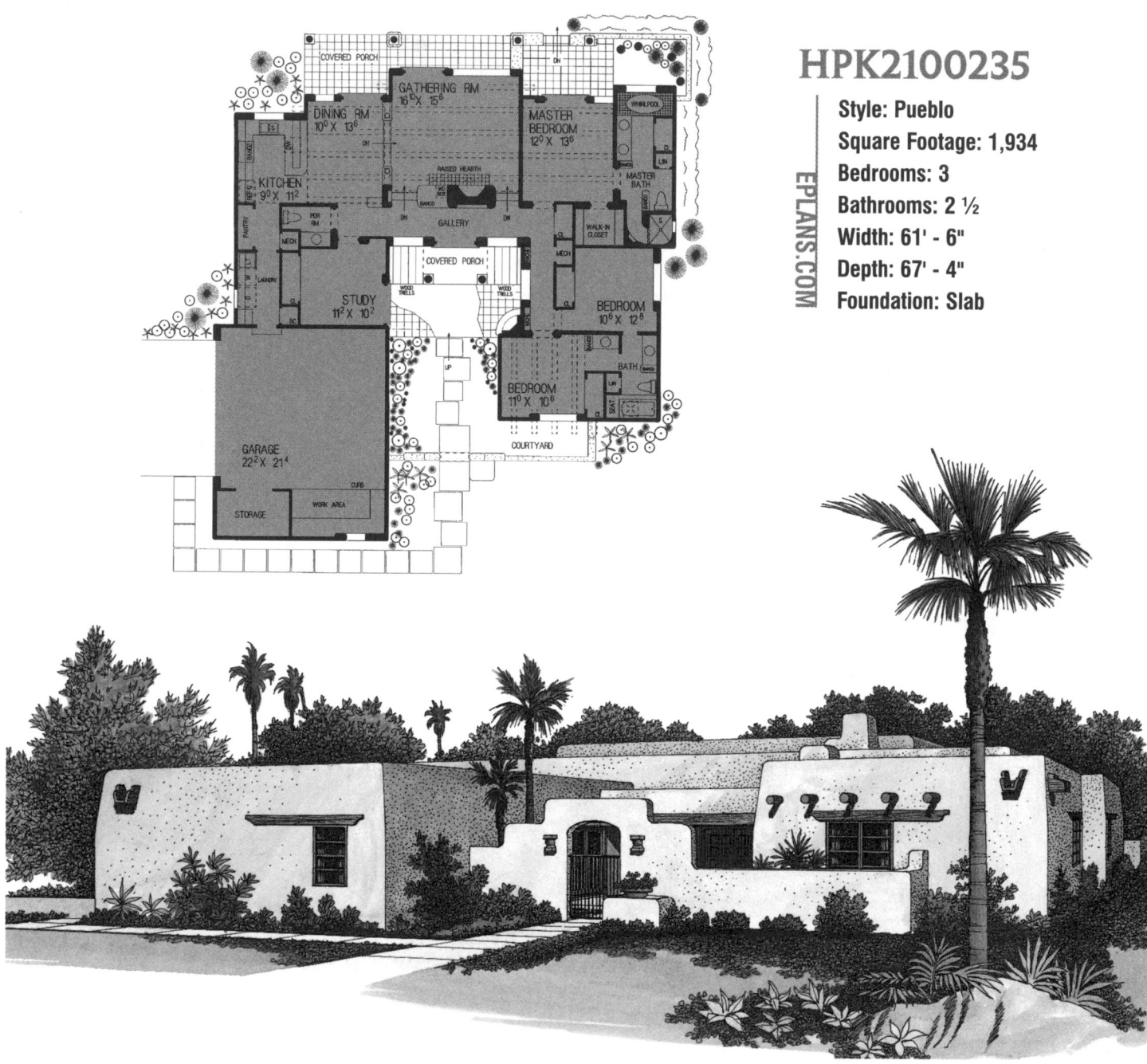

HPK2100235

Style: Pueblo

Square Footage: 1,934

Bedrooms: 3

Bathrooms: 2 ½

Width: 61' - 6"

Depth: 67' - 4"

Foundation: Slab

EPLANS.COM

HPK2100236

Style: Country

Square Footage: 1,937

Bonus Space: 414 sq. ft.

Bedrooms: 3

Bathrooms: 2

Width: 62' - 8"

Depth: 56' - 0"

Foundation: Crawlspace

Gables, dormers, and an old-fashioned covered porch create a winsome country look for this transitional exterior. Inside, an upscale, educated floor plan starts with the great room, which offers a sloped ceiling, a fireplace with an extended hearth, and built-in shelves for an entertainment center. Gourmet features in the kitchen include a cooktop island counter, easy-care ceramic tile flooring, and a divided sink. A split bedroom plan allows a separate wing for the master suite.

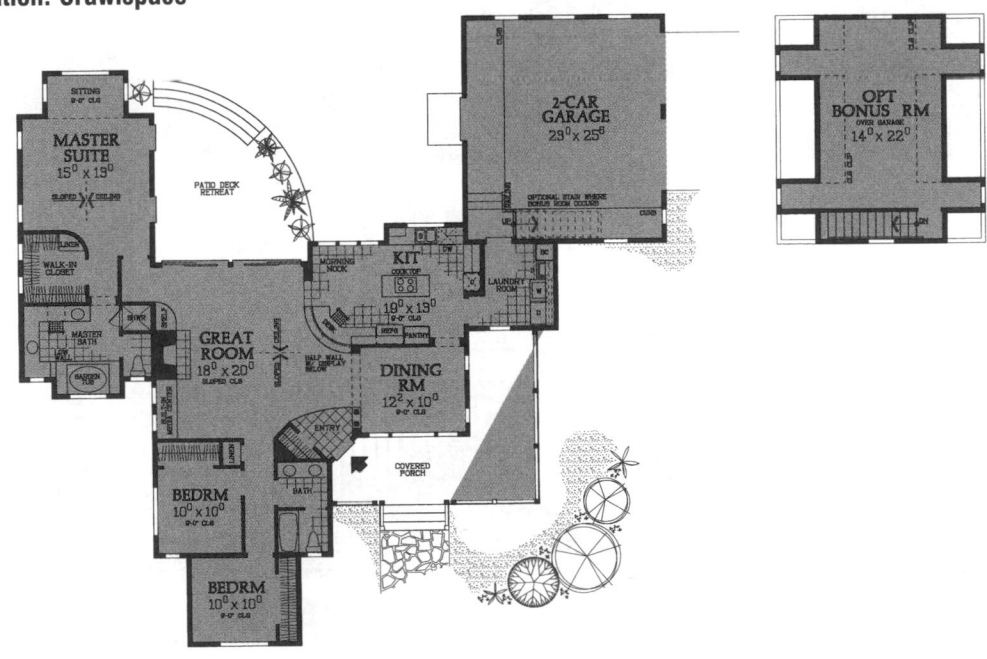

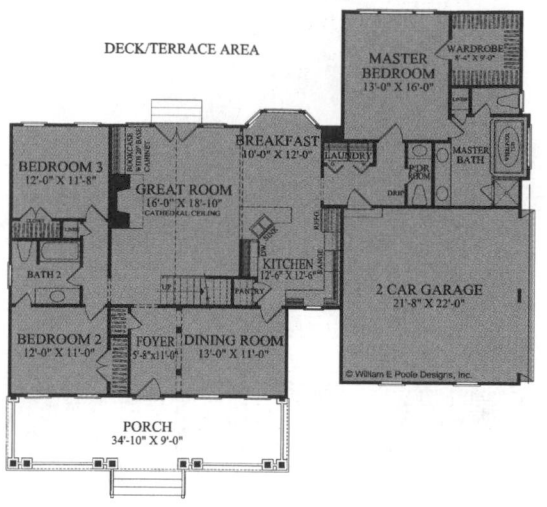

Welcome to the perfect starter home. Classical elements lend an air of formality. A wealth of bonus space on the second floor invites expansion as your family grows and matures. Elegant touches include paired columns supporting a pedimented porch roof, oculus windows in the great room and master suite, and a built-in bookcase beside the great room's fireplace. Two family bedrooms share a full bath on the first floor.

HPK2100237

Style: Farmhouse

Square Footage: 1,942

Bonus Space: 1,040 sq. ft.

Bedrooms: 3

Bathrooms: 2 ½

Width: 64' - 10"

Depth: 58' - 2"

Foundation: Crawlspace, Unfinished Basement

EPLANS.COM

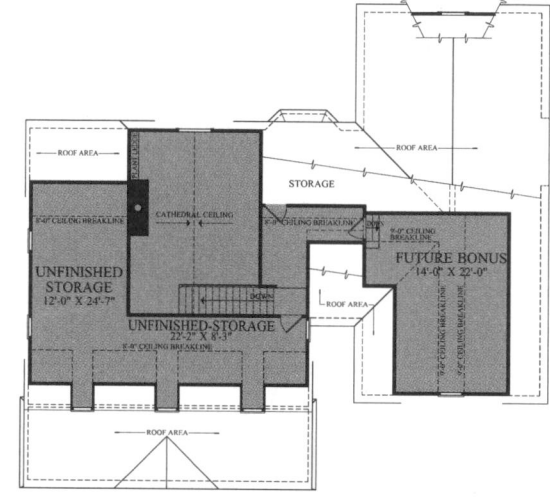

© William E Poole Designs, Inc.

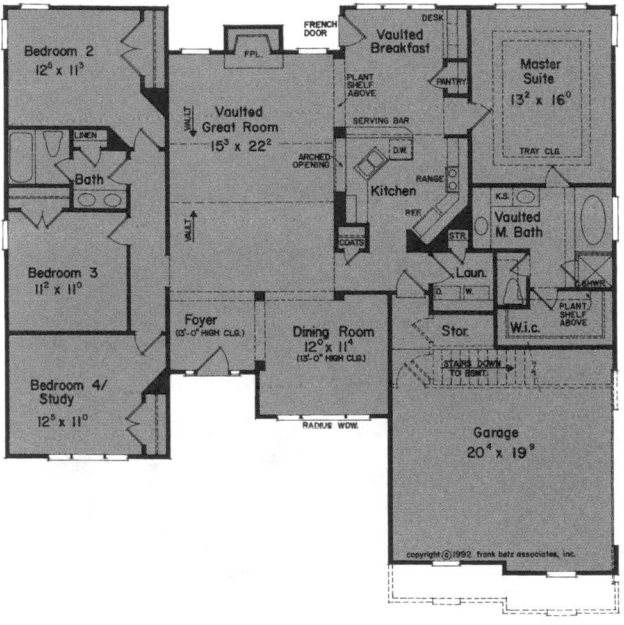

Corner quoins and keystones above graceful window treatments have long been a hallmark of elegant European-style exteriors—this home has all that and more. This becomes apparent upon entering the foyer, which is beautifully framed by columns in the dining room and the entrance to the vaulted great room. The left wing holds three secondary bedrooms—one doubles as a study—and a full bath. To the right of the combined kitchen and vaulted breakfast room, you will find the private master suite. A relaxing master bath and a large walk-in closet complete this splendid retreat.

HPK2100238

Style: New American

Square Footage: 1,945

Bedrooms: 4

Bathrooms: 2

Width: 56' - 6"

Depth: 52' - 6"

Foundation: Crawlspace, Slab, Unfinished Walkout Basement

EPLANS.COM

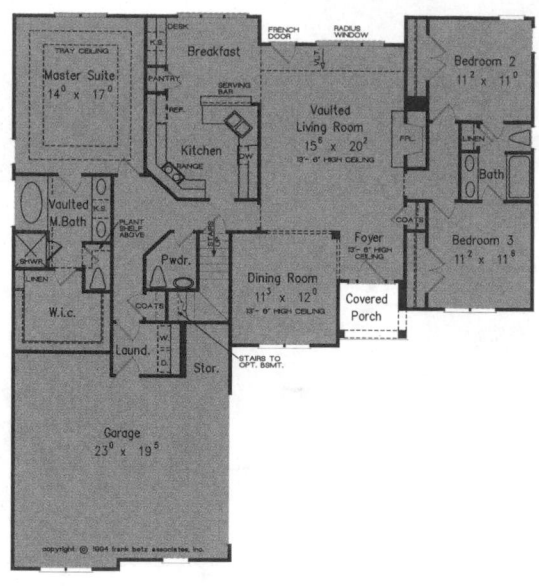

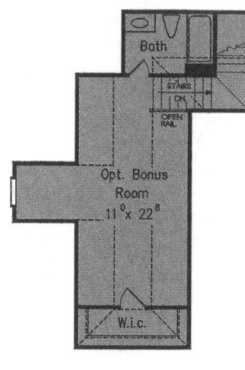

HPK2100239

Style: New American
Square Footage: 1,949
Bonus Space: 398 sq. ft.
Bedrooms: 3
Bathrooms: 2 ½
Width: 56' - 0"
Depth: 65' - 0"
Foundation: Crawlspace, Slab, Unfinished Walkout Basement

EPLANS.COM

Red brick enhances the facade of this traditional design and brings to mind a Colonial influence. Tall arched windows allow natural light into the foyer and formal dining room. On the right side of the plan, two family bedrooms share a full bath. The master suite is secluded from activity on the left side of the plan and features an opulent bath and large walk-in closet. Family and guests will enjoy gathering in the open spaces of the vaulted living room, kitchen, and breakfast nook.

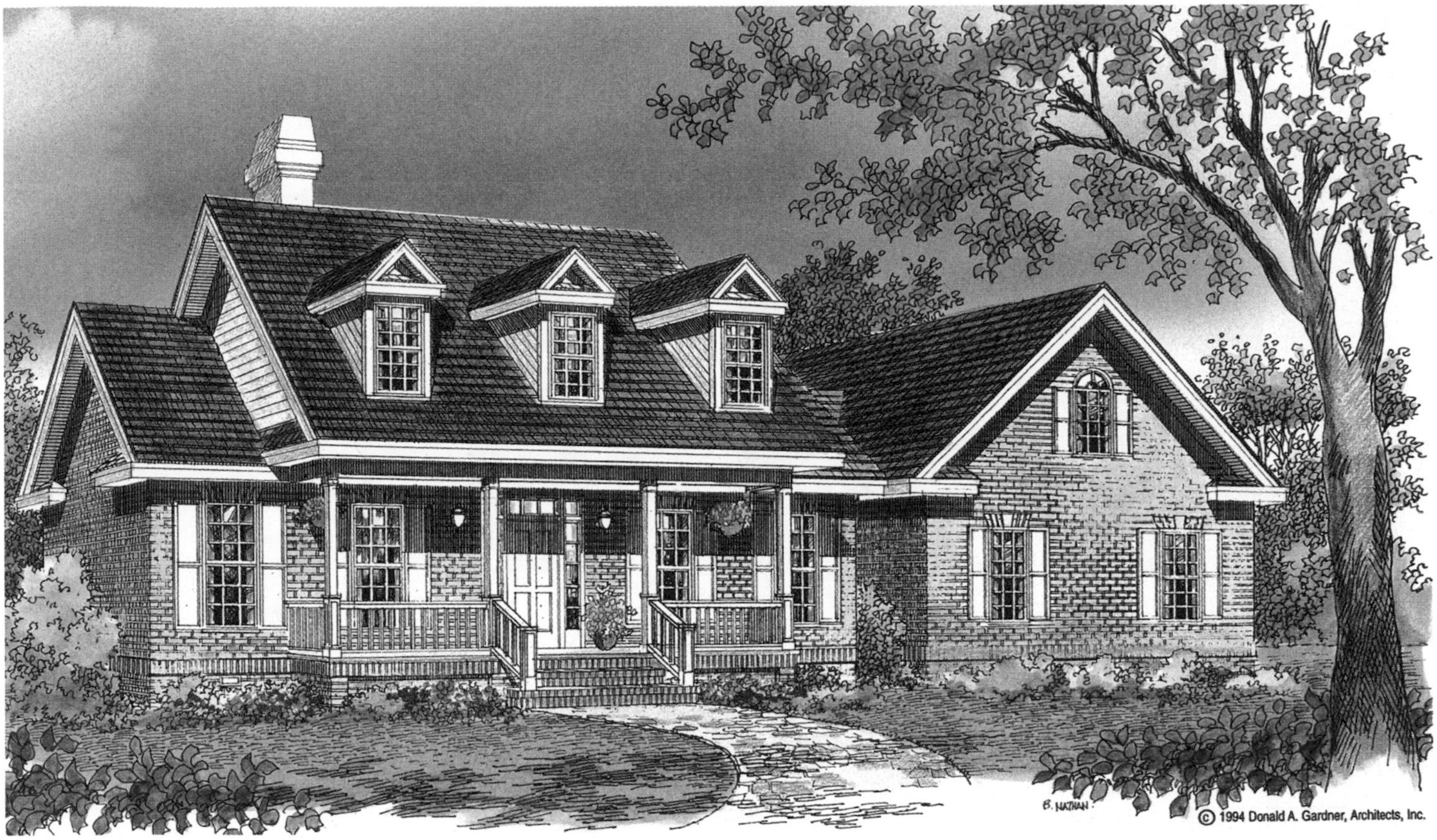

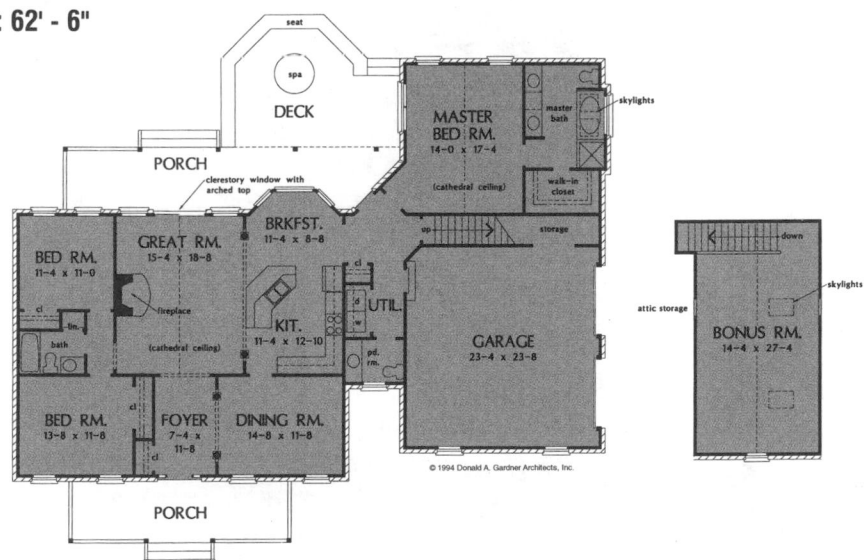

HPK2100240

Style: Country
Square Footage: 1,954
Bonus Space: 436 sq. ft.
Bedrooms: 3
Bathrooms: 2 ½
Width: 71' - 3"
Depth: 62' - 6"

EPLANS.COM

This beautiful brick country home offers style and comfort for an active family. Two covered porches and a rear deck with a spa invite enjoyment of the outdoors. A cathedral ceiling soars above the central great room, warmed by an extended-hearth fireplace and by sunlight through an arch-top clerestory window. The splendid master suite enjoys its own secluded wing and provides a skylit whirlpool bath, a cathedral ceiling, and private access to the deck.

1,500 TO 1,999 SQUARE FEET

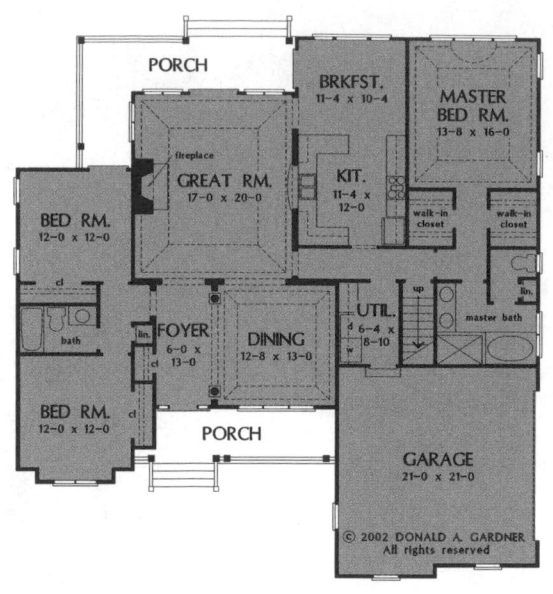

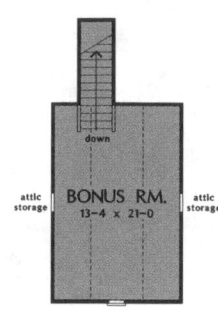

This plan's facade offers traditional, down-home appeal, yet its interior boasts elegance and convenience. Graceful ceiling detail brings the great room, dining room, and master bedroom to new heights of style. Two bedrooms share a bath to the left of the plan. The spacious master suite, tucked behind the garage on the right, offers ample closet space and a deluxe bath. Bonus space awaits expansion above the two-car garage.

HPK2100241

Style: Cottage
Square Footage: 1,955
Bonus Space: 329 sq. ft.
Bedrooms: 3
Bathrooms: 2
Width: 56' - 0"
Depth: 58' - 4"

EPLANS.COM

HPK2100242

EPLANS.COM

Style: Greek Revival

Square Footage: 1,955

Bedrooms: 3

Bathrooms: 2 ½

Width: 56' - 4"

Depth: 67' - 4"

Foundation: Crawlspace, Slab, Unfinished Basement

Double pillars, beautiful transoms, and sidelights set off the entry door and draw attention to this comfortable home. The foyer leads to a formal dining room and a great room with a pair of French doors framing a warming fireplace. Privacy is assured with a master bedroom set in its own section of the U-shaped plan. Two family bedrooms share a full bath at the front of the design.

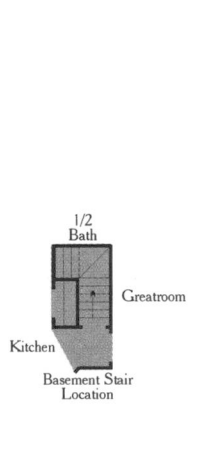

1,500 TO 1,999 SQUARE FEET

This narrow-lot plan has all the appeal and romance of a European cottage. The island kitchen easily serves the dining room, which accesses a private garden and the casual breakfast room. The spacious family room offers a warming fireplace, built-ins, and back-porch access. The plan is completed by the master suite, which features a private bath and walk-in closet.

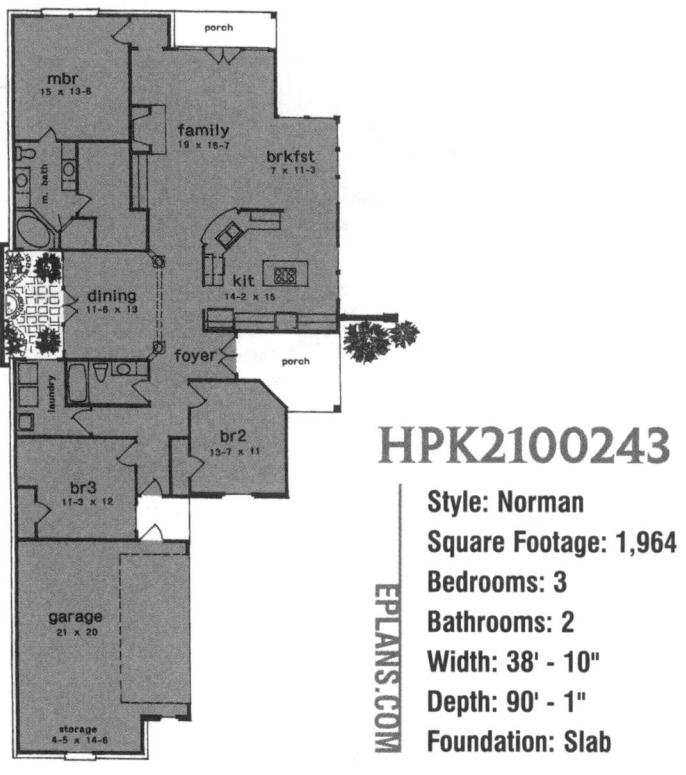

HPK2100243

Style: Norman
Square Footage: 1,964
Bedrooms: 3
Bathrooms: 2
Width: 38' - 10"
Depth: 90' - 1"
Foundation: Slab

EPLANS.COM

HPK2100244

Style: Cottage
Square Footage: 1,966
Bedrooms: 3
Bathrooms: 2
Width: 54' - 11"
Depth: 65' - 9"

Old World charm mingles and merges with traditional detailing upon the facade of this three-bedroom home. The covered entry opens to the foyer, where open planning allows views through the stately great room and out beyond the skylit rear porch. The formal dining room enjoys a tray ceiling, the master bedroom has a vaulted ceiling, and the great room boasts a stepped-ceiling treatment.

© 2000 DONALD A. GARDNER
All rights reserved

1,500 TO 1,999 SQUARE FEET

This beautiful home, with its covered porch, stone facade, and many windows, is wonderful for a family to enjoy. This design features a study reached by double doors, a great room with a cozy fireplace, and a spacious kitchen with a dinette area accessing the rear covered patio. The master bedroom has a luxurious bath and a huge walk-in closet plus access to the private patio.

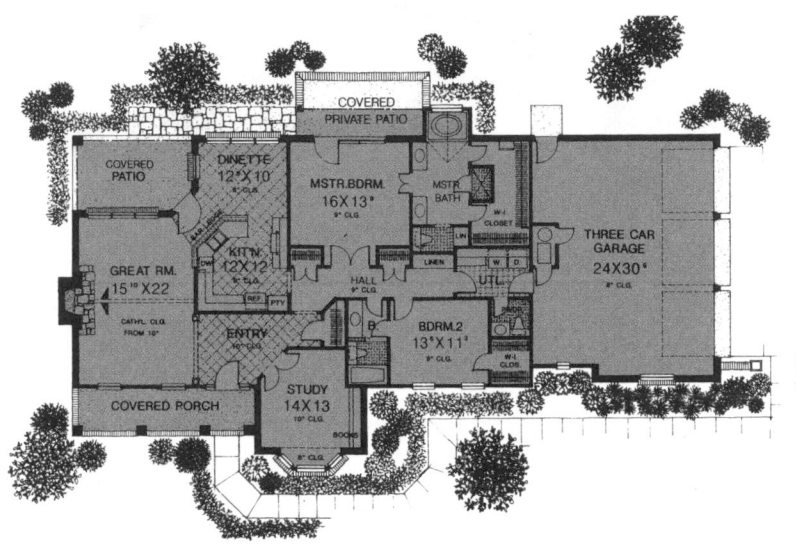

EPLANS.COM

HPK2100245

Style: French Country
Square Footage: 1,966
Bedrooms: 2
Bathrooms: 2 ½
Width: 85' - 0"
Depth: 46' - 4"
Foundation: Slab

HPK2100246

Style: Craftsman

Square Footage: 1,971

Bonus Space: 358 sq. ft.

Bedrooms: 3

Bathrooms: 3

Width: 62' - 6"

Depth: 57' - 2"

EPLANS.COM

This Craftsman cottage combines stone, siding, and cedar shake to create striking curb appeal. The interior features an open floor plan with high ceilings, columns, and bay windows to visually expand space. Built-in cabinetry, a fireplace, and a kitchen pass-through highlight and add convenience to the great room. The master suite features a tray ceiling in the bedroom and a bath with garden tub, separate shower, dual vanities, and a walk-in closet. On the opposite side of the home is another bedroom that could be used as a second master suite. Above the garage, a bonus room provides ample storage and space to grow.

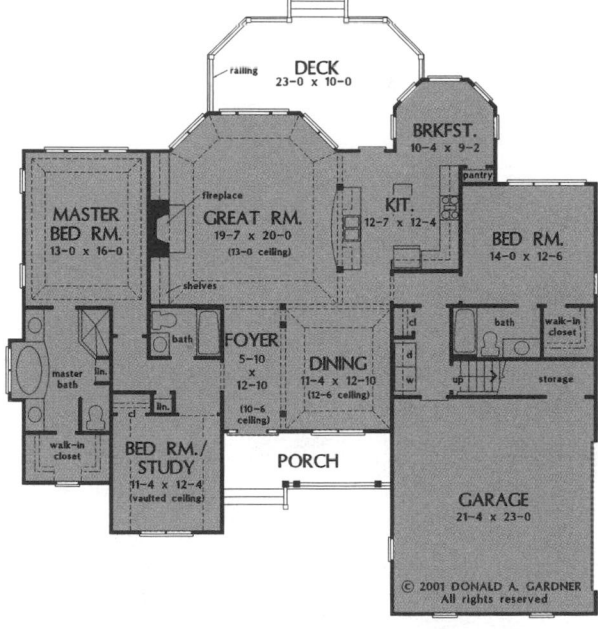

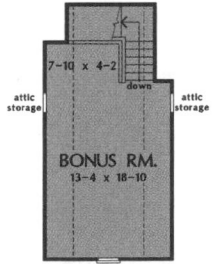

1,500 TO 1,999 SQUARE FEET

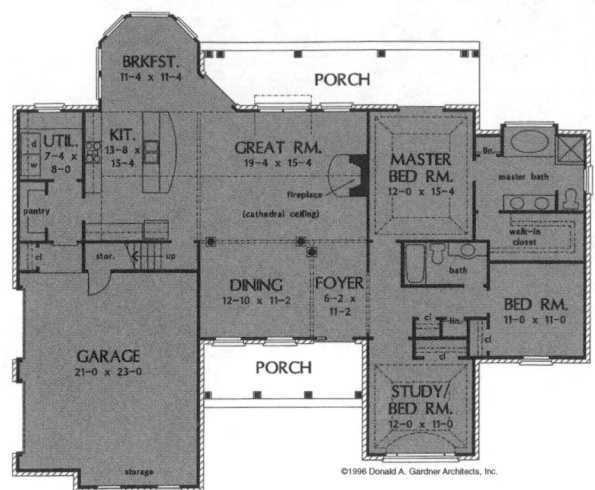

HPK2100247

Style: Country
Square Footage: 1,972
Bonus Space: 398 sq. ft.
Bedrooms: 3
Bathrooms: 2
Width: 67' - 7"
Depth: 56' - 7"

EPLANS.COM

This delightful country cottage elevation gives way to a modern floor plan. The formal dining room is set off from the expansive great room with decorative columns. Amenities in the nearby kitchen include an abundance of counter and cabinet space, a bilevel island with a snack bar, and a gazebo breakfast nook. The master bedroom is detailed with a tray ceiling and features a lush master bath with a large walk-in closet.

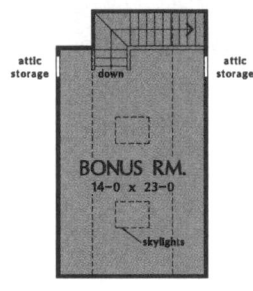

© 1996 Donald A. Gardner Architects, Inc.

B. NATHAN.

© William E. Poole Designs, Inc.

HPK2100248

Style: Country

Square Footage: 1,973

Bonus Space: 368 sq. ft.

Bedrooms: 3

Bathrooms: 2

Width: 64' - 10"

Depth: 58' - 2"

Foundation: Crawlspace, Unfinished Basement

EPLANS.COM

An inviting columned porch, flower-box window, and pinnacled cupola make this three-bedroom home a classic neighborhood charmer. Past the foyer, enter the great room, exquisite with a cathedral ceiling, built-in bookcase, and warming fireplace. The kitchen accesses the breakfast nook and dining room, both accented with bay windows. The secluded master suite features a walk-in closet and a luxurious bath with a whirlpool tub. Two bedrooms, a relaxing terrace, and a convenient utility room complete the plan.

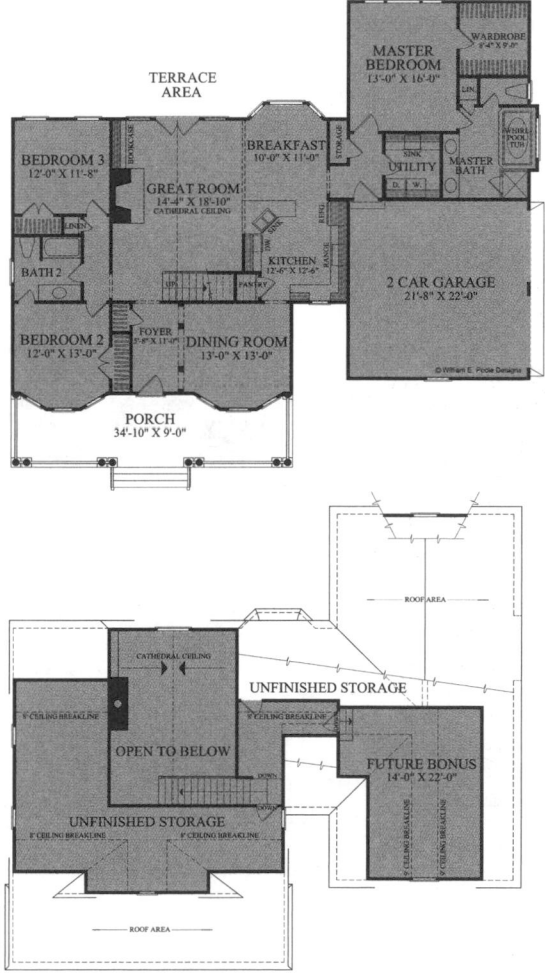

DECK

seat

spa

SCREEN PORCH
16-0 x 11-0
skylights

wet bar

BED RM.
12-4 x 11-8

GREAT RM.
16-0 x 17-4

fireplace

cabinets

cl

lin.

bath

BRKFST.
12-0 x 8-6

KITCHEN
12-0 x 12-8

up

MASTER BED RM.
13-4 x 18-8

master bath
skylights

walk-in closet

UTIL.
d w
lin.

storage

GARAGE
22-0 x 20-4

© 1994 Donald A. Gardner Architects, Inc.

FOYER
12-4 x 5-6

cl

BED RM./STUDY
12-0 x 12-0

PORCH

DINING
12-0 x 13-8

storage

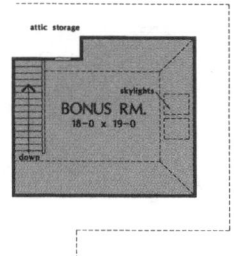

attic storage

BONUS RM.
18-0 x 19-0
skylights

down

HPK2100249

Style: New American
Square Footage: 1,977
Bonus Space: 430 sq. ft.
Bedrooms: 3
Bathrooms: 2
Width: 69' - 8"
Depth: 59' - 6"

EPLANS.COM

A two-story foyer with a Palladian window above sets the tone for this sunlit home. Columns mark the passage from the foyer to the great room, where a centered fireplace and built-in cabinets are found. Hidden quietly at the rear, the master suite includes a bath with dual vanities and sky-lights. Two family bedrooms (one an optional study) share a bath that has twin sinks.

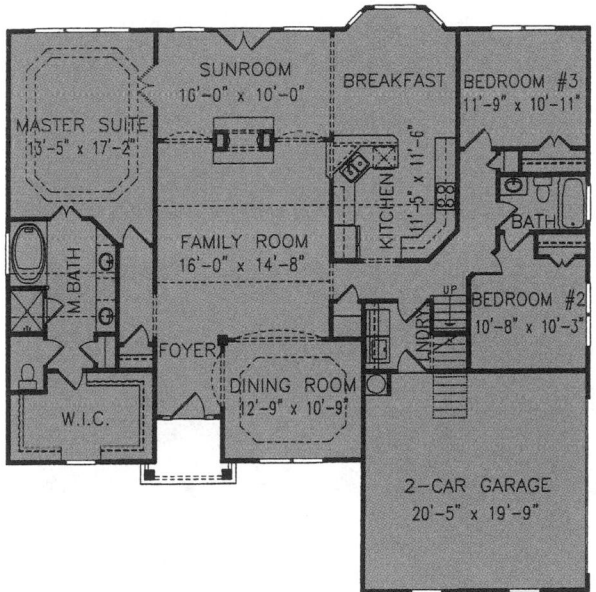

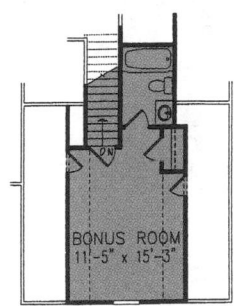

Gracious living starts with a balanced and appealing facade. A formal dining room offers just the right amount of space for get-togethers. The family room does double duty for guests and casual time. An adjoining sunroom is a perfect spot to close the evening or start the day. Breakfast will be bright with natural light from the bay just off the kitchen.

HPK2100250

Style: Country

Square Footage: 1,985

Bonus Space: 191 sq. ft.

Bedrooms: 3

Bathrooms: 2

Width: 54' - 0"

Depth: 54' - 0"

Foundation: Slab

EPLANS.COM

Vaulted and volume ceilings highlight this extraordinary one-story design. Amenities include a spacious family room with a fireplace, a formal dining room, and a breakfast area with access to the screened porch. The master suite features a sitting area and access to the rear deck. Each of two secondary bedrooms boasts a walk-in closet and separate access to a shared bath.

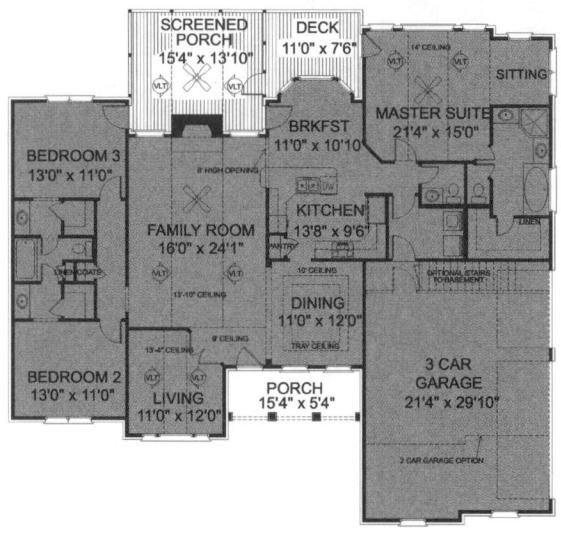

HPK2100251

Style: Ranch

Square Footage: 1,992

Bedrooms: 3

Bathrooms: 2 ½

Width: 63' - 0"

Depth: 57' - 2"

Foundation: Crawlspace, Slab, Unfinished Basement

EPLANS.COM

HPK2100252

Style: Colonial Revival

Square Footage: 1,997

Bedrooms: 4

Bathrooms: 2 ½

Width: 56' - 4"

Depth: 67' - 4"

Foundation: Crawlspace, Slab, Unfinished Basement

EPLANS.COM

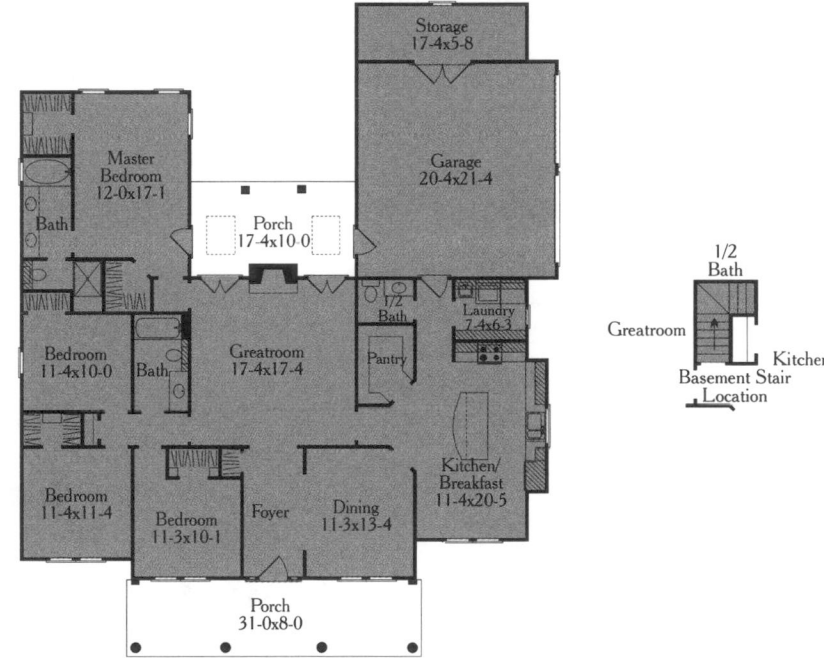

The curved front steps, columned porch, and symmetrical layout give this charming home a Georgian appeal. The central great room offers radiant French doors on both sides of the fireplace. The large kitchen with its adjoining walk-in pantry will gratify any cook. Three family bedrooms share a hall bath; the master suite features a pampering bath and two walk-in closets.

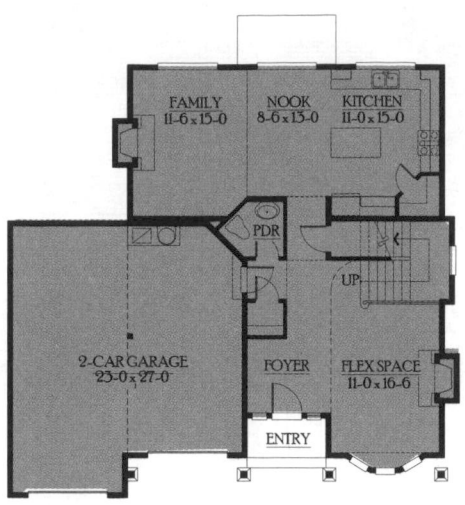

First Floor

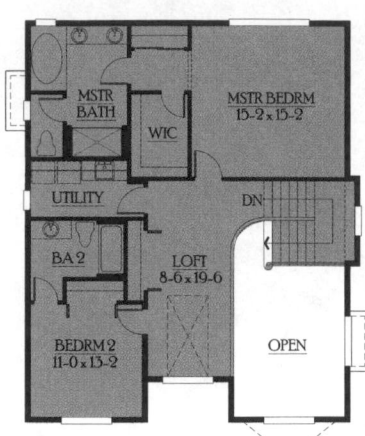

Second Floor

HPK2100253

EPLANS.COM

Style: Craftsman
First Floor: 978 sq. ft.
Second Floor: 984 sq. ft.
Total: 1,962 sq. ft.
Bedrooms: 2
Bathrooms: 2 ½
Width: 44' - 0"
Depth: 44' - 0"
Foundation: Crawlspace

The pleasing facade inspires entry into this two-story Craftsman home. A bayed window near the main entrance provides a scenic view from the private sitting area. The open layout cleverly blends common living spaces. The second floor master suite amply accomodates two. The adjacent laundry room is an added convenience.

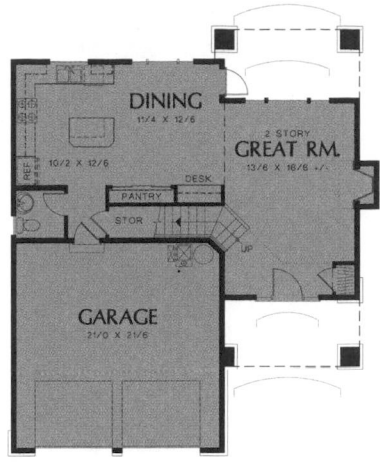

First Floor

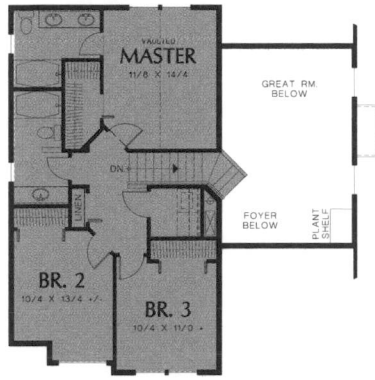

Second Floor

HPK2100254

Style: Cottage

First Floor: 716 sq. ft.

Second Floor: 784 sq. ft.

Total: 1,500 sq. ft.

Bedrooms: 3

Bathrooms: 2 ½

Width: 36' - 0"

Depth: 44' - 0"

Foundation: Crawlspace

EPLANS.COM

HPK2100255

Style: Country

First Floor: 767 sq. ft.

Second Floor: 738 sq. ft.

Total: 1,505 sq. ft.

Bedrooms: 3

Bathrooms: 2 ½

Width: 47' - 10"

Depth: 36' - 0"

Foundation: Crawlspace, Slab, Unfinished Walkout Basement

EPLANS.COM

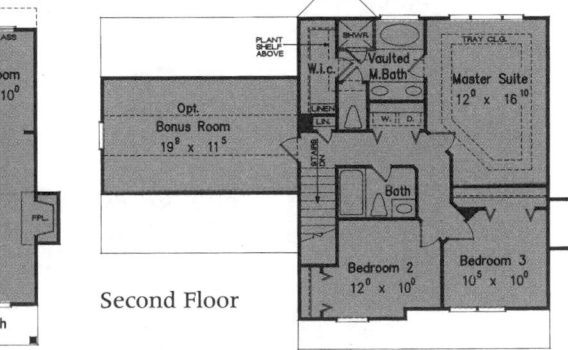

First Floor

Second Floor

1,500 TO 1,999 SQUARE FEET

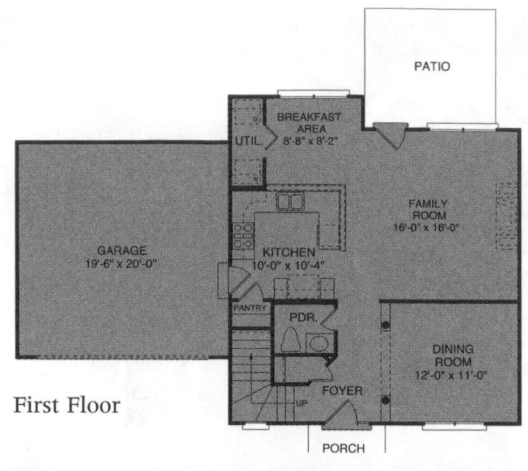

First Floor

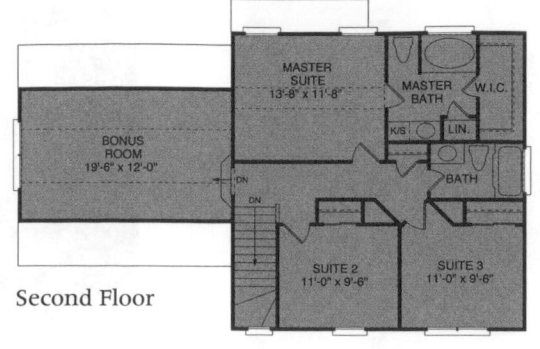

Second Floor

HPK2100256

Style: Colonial Revival

First Floor: 794 sq. ft.

Second Floor: 756 sq. ft.

Total: 1,550 sq. ft.

Bonus Space: 251 sq. ft.

Bedrooms: 3

Bathrooms: 2 ½

Width: 46' - 11"

Depth: 35' - 1"

Foundation: Slab

First Floor

HPK2100257

Style: Country

First Floor: 1,116 sq. ft.

Second Floor: 442 sq. ft.

Total: 1,558 sq. ft.

Bedrooms: 3

Bathrooms: 2 ½

Width: 49' - 0"

Depth: 52' - 0"

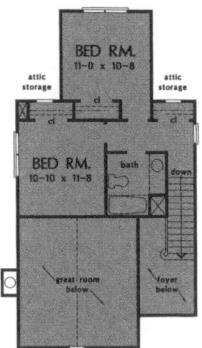

Second Floor

HPK2100258

Style: Cottage
First Floor: 1,185 sq. ft.
Second Floor: 398 sq. ft.
Total: 1,583 sq. ft.
Bedrooms: 3
Bathrooms: 2 ½
Width: 47' - 4"
Depth: 45' - 6"
Foundation: Unfinished Basement

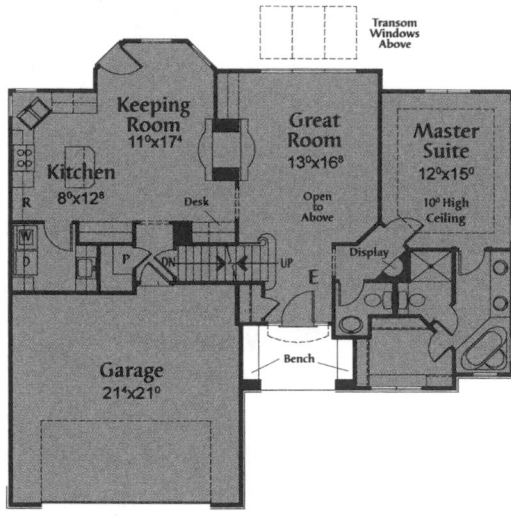

First Floor

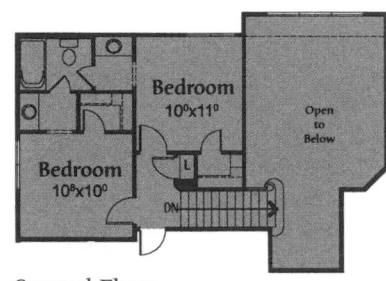

Second Floor

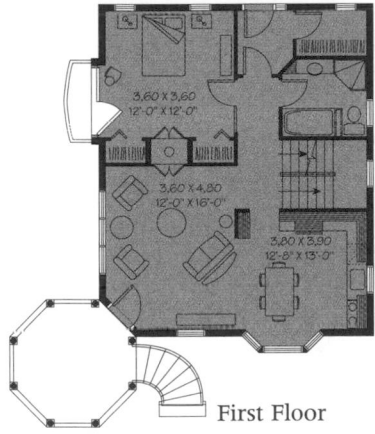

First Floor

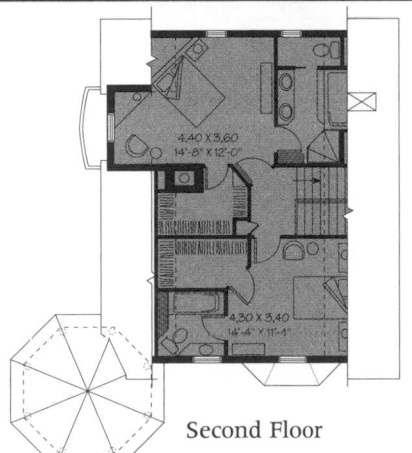

Second Floor

HPK2100259

Style: Queen Anne
First Floor: 840 sq. ft.
Second Floor: 757 sq. ft.
Total: 1,597 sq. ft.
Bedrooms: 3
Bathrooms: 3
Width: 26' - 0"
Depth: 32' - 0"
Foundation: Unfinished Basement

1,500 TO 1,999 SQUARE FEET

HPK2100260

Style: Country
First Floor: 1,205 sq. ft.
Second Floor: 392 sq. ft.
Total: 1,597 sq. ft.
Bonus Space: 190 sq. ft.
Bedrooms: 3
Bathrooms: 2 ½
Width: 50' - 6"
Depth: 42' - 0"
Foundation: Crawlspace, Slab, Unfinished Walkout Basement

EPLANS.COM

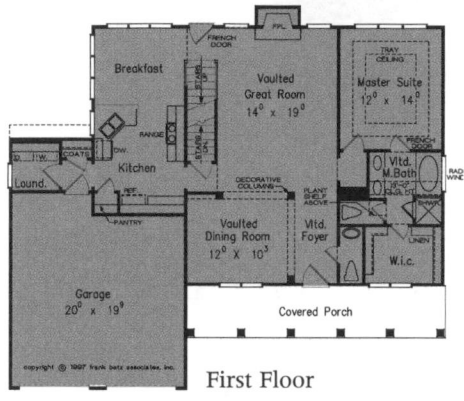

First Floor

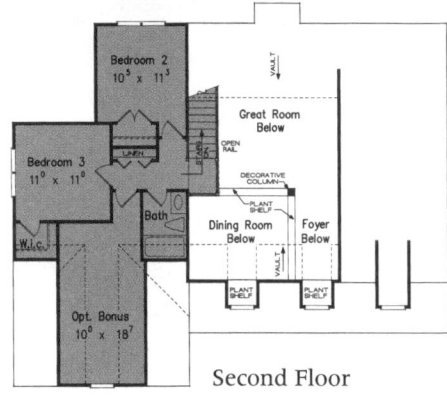

Second Floor

First Floor

HPK2100261

Style: Bungalow
First Floor: 872 sq. ft.
Second Floor: 734 sq. ft.
Total: 1,606 sq. ft.
Bedrooms: 3
Bathrooms: 3
Width: 40' - 0"
Depth: 29' - 6"
Foundation: Crawlspace

EPLANS.COM

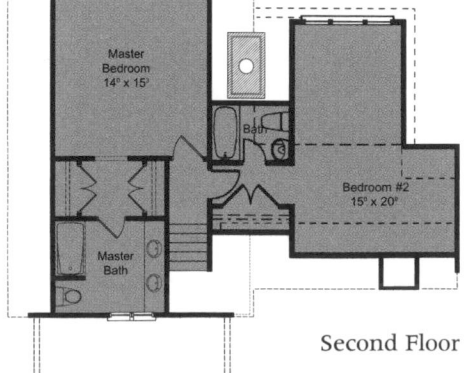

Second Floor

ORDER BLUEPRINTS ANYTIME AT EPLANS.COM OR 1-800-521-6797

HPK2100262

Style: Tidewater
First Floor: 1,027 sq. ft.
Second Floor: 580 sq. ft.
Total: 1,607 sq. ft.
Bedrooms: 3
Bathrooms: 2
Width: 37' - 4"
Depth: 44' - 8"

EPLANS.COM

© 1992 Donald A. Gardner Architects, Inc.

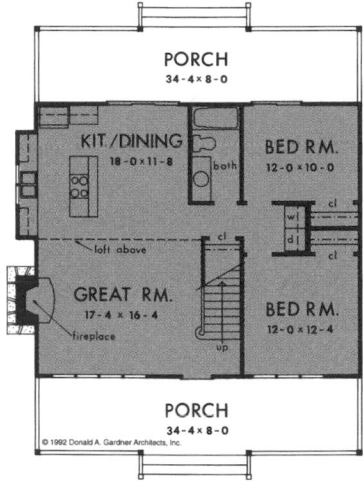

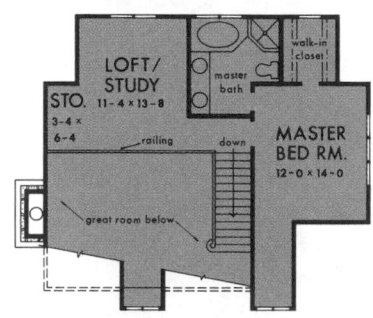

First Floor

Second Floor

HPK2100263

Style: Craftsman
First Floor: 1,108 sq. ft.
Second Floor: 517 sq. ft.
Total: 1,625 sq. ft.
Bedrooms: 3
Bathrooms: 2
Width: 36' - 0"
Depth: 36' - 0"
Foundation: Unfinished Basement

EPLANS.COM

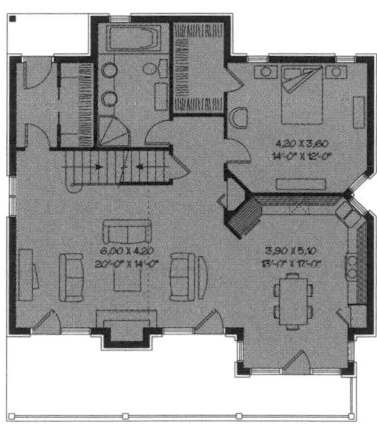

First Floor

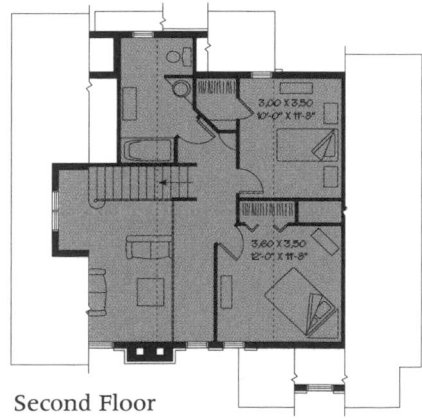

Second Floor

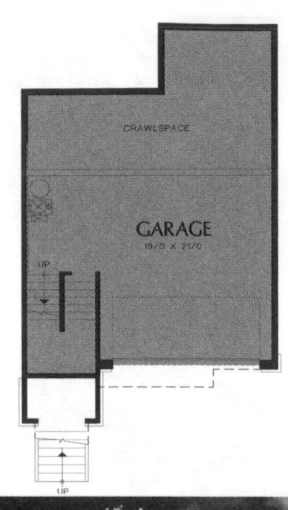

First Floor

Second Floor

HPK2100264

Style: Cottage
First Floor: 993 sq. ft.
Second Floor: 642 sq. ft.
Total: 1,635 sq. ft.
Bedrooms: 2
Bathrooms: 2 ½
Width: 28' - 0"
Depth: 44' - 0"
Foundation: Finished Walkout Basement

EPLANS.COM

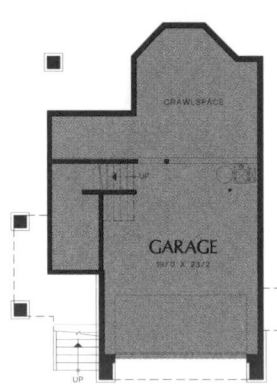

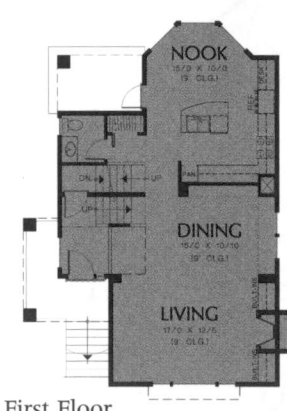

First Floor

Second Floor

HPK2100265

Style: Bungalow
First Floor: 897 sq. ft.
Second Floor: 740 sq. ft.
Total: 1,637 sq. ft.
Bedrooms: 3
Bathrooms: 2 ½
Width: 30' - 0"
Depth: 42' - 6"
Foundation: Unfinished Walkout Basement

EPLANS.COM

HPK2100266

Style: Colonial

First Floor: 740 sq. ft.

Second Floor: 898 sq. ft.

Total: 1,638 sq. ft.

Bedrooms: 3

Bathrooms: 2 ½

Width: 35' - 0"

Depth: 31' - 6"

Foundation: Slab

EPLANS.COM

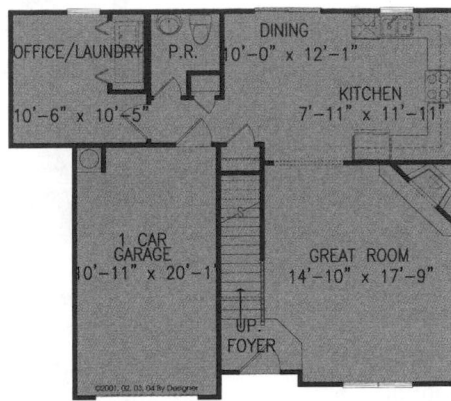

First Floor

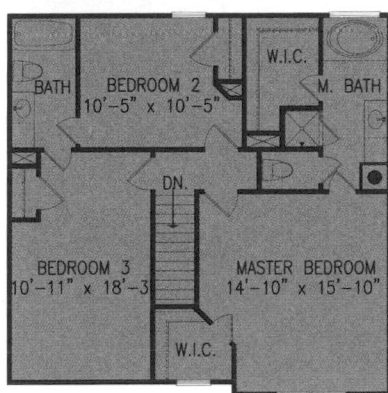

Second Floor

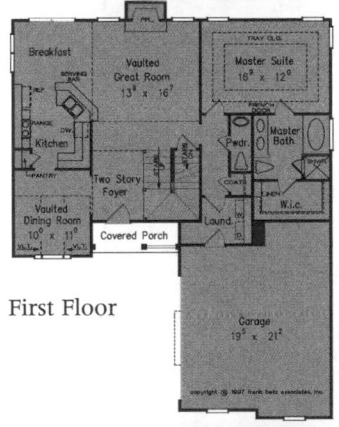

First Floor

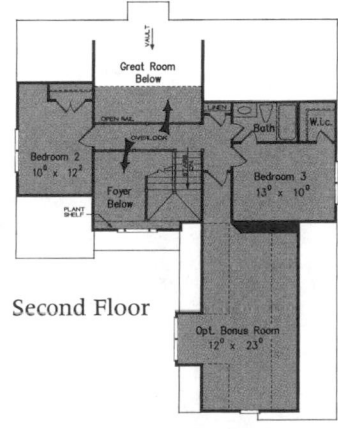

Second Floor

HPK2100267

Style: New American

First Floor: 1,179 sq. ft.

Second Floor: 479 sq. ft.

Total: 1,658 sq. ft.

Bonus Space: 338 sq. ft.

Bedrooms: 3

Bathrooms: 2 ½

Width: 41' - 6"

Depth: 54' - 4"

Foundation: Crawlspace, Slab, Unfinished Walkout Basement

EPLANS.COM

HPK2100268

Style: Farmhouse
First Floor: 1,145 sq. ft.
Second Floor: 518 sq. ft.
Total: 1,663 sq. ft.
Bonus Space: 380 sq. ft.
Bedrooms: 3
Bathrooms: 2 ½
Width: 59' - 4"
Depth: 56' - 6"

EPLANS.COM

© 1992 Donald A. Gardner Architects, Inc.

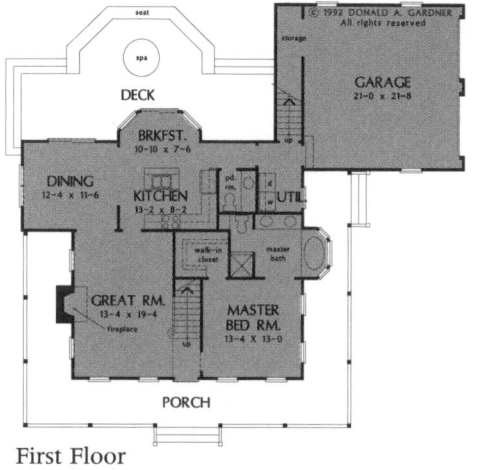

First Floor

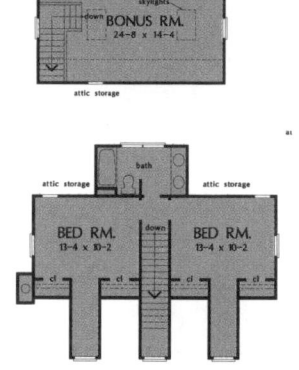

Second Floor

HPK2100269

Style: French Country
First Floor: 1,233 sq. ft.
Second Floor: 433 sq. ft.
Total: 1,666 sq. ft.
Bedrooms: 3
Bathrooms: 2 ½
Width: 49' - 0"
Depth: 47' - 4"
Foundation: Unfinished Basement

EPLANS.COM

First Floor

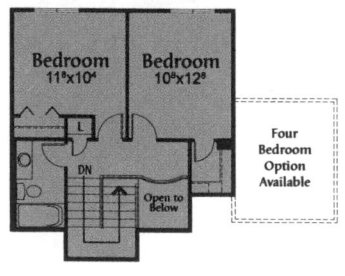

Second Floor

ORDER BLUEPRINTS ANYTIME AT EPLANS.COM OR 1-800-521-6797

HPK2100270

Style: Country
First Floor: 1,219 sq. ft.
Second Floor: 450 sq. ft.
Total: 1,669 sq. ft.
Bonus Space: 406 sq. ft.
Bedrooms: 3
Bathrooms: 2 ½
Width: 50' - 4"
Depth: 49' - 2"

EPLANS.COM

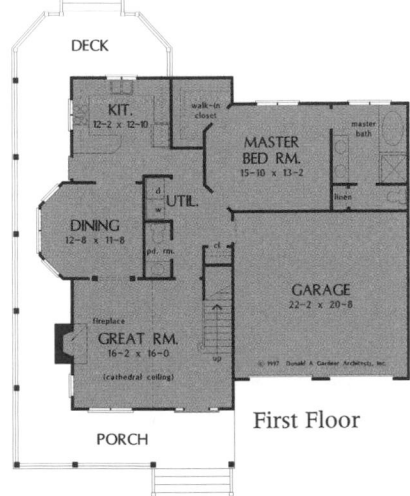

First Floor

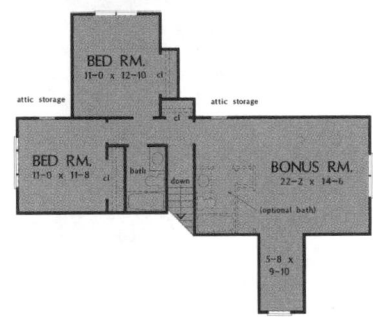

Second Floor

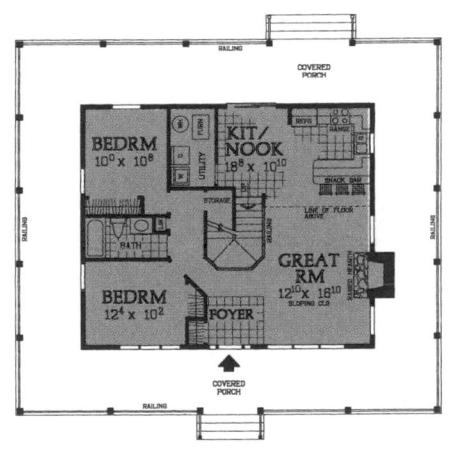

First Floor

HPK2100271

Style: Log House
First Floor: 1,093 sq. ft.
Second Floor: 576 sq. ft.
Total: 1,669 sq. ft.
Bedrooms: 3
Bathrooms: 2
Width: 52' - 0"
Depth: 46' - 0"
Foundation: Crawlspace

EPLANS.COM

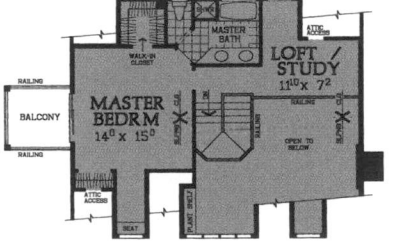

Second Floor

1,500 TO 1,999 SQUARE FEET

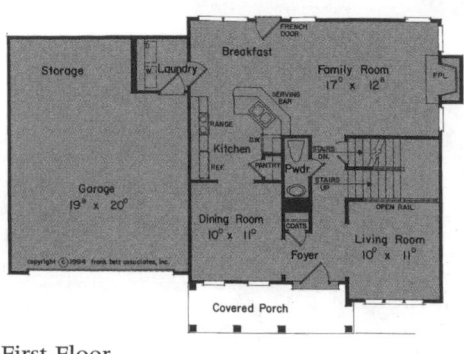

First Floor

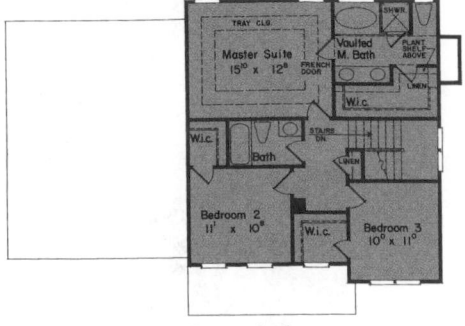

Second Floor

HPK2100272

Style: Colonial Revival

First Floor: 887 sq. ft.

Second Floor: 784 sq. ft.

Total: 1,671 sq. ft.

Bonus Space: 406 sq. ft.

Bedrooms: 3

Bathrooms: 2 ½

Width: 50' - 4"

Depth: 35' - 0"

Foundation: Crawlspace, Slab, Unfinished Walkout Basement

EPLANS.COM

HPK2100273

Style: Farmhouse

First Floor: 1,093 sq. ft.

Second Floor: 580 sq. ft.

Total: 1,673 sq. ft.

Bedrooms: 3

Bathrooms: 2

Width: 46' - 0"

Depth: 52' - 0"

Foundation: Crawlspace

EPLANS.COM

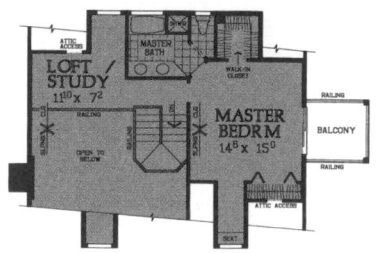

First Floor

Second Floor

ORDER BLUEPRINTS ANYTIME AT EPLANS.COM OR 1-800-521-6797

HPK2100274

Style: Farmhouse

First Floor: 979 sq. ft.

Second Floor: 694 sq. ft.

Total: 1,673 sq. ft.

Bedrooms: 3

Bathrooms: 2

Width: 52' - 0"

Depth: 63' - 4"

Foundation: Unfinished Basement

EPLANS.COM

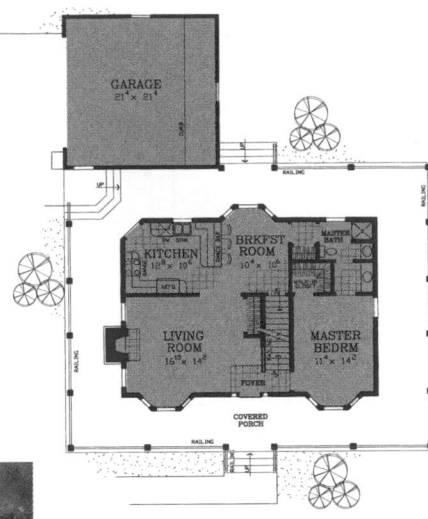

First Floor

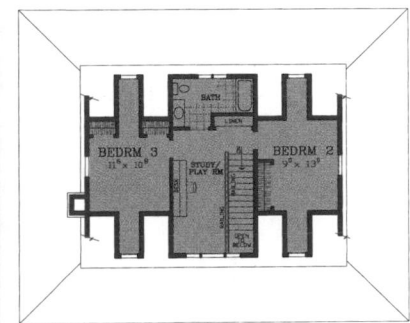

Second Floor

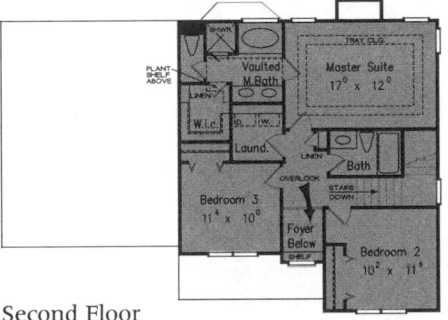

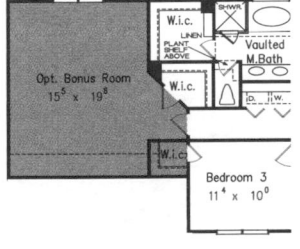

First Floor

Second Floor

Optional Layout

HPK2100275

Style: Colonial Revival

First Floor: 882 sq. ft.

Second Floor: 793 sq. ft.

Total: 1,675 sq. ft.

Bonus Space: 416 sq. ft.

Bedrooms: 3

Bathrooms: 2 ½

Width: 49' - 6"

Depth: 35' - 4"

Foundation: Crawlspace, Slab, Unfinished Walkout Basement

EPLANS.COM

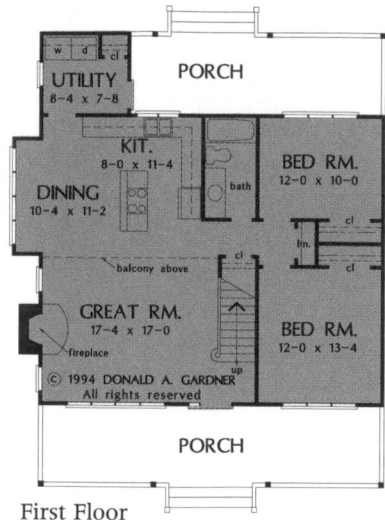

First Floor

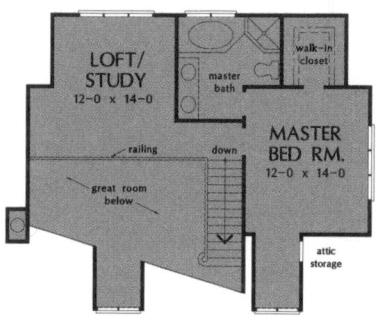

Second Floor

HPK2100276

Style: Country
First Floor: 1,100 sq. ft.
Second Floor: 584 sq. ft.
Total: 1,684 sq. ft.
Bedrooms: 3
Bathrooms: 2
Width: 36' - 8"
Depth: 45' - 0"

EPLANS.COM

HPK2100277

Style: Country
First Floor: 875 sq. ft.
Second Floor: 814 sq. ft.
Total: 1,689 sq. ft.
Bedrooms: 3
Bathrooms: 2 ½
Width: 37' - 0"
Depth: 51' - 0"

EPLANS.COM

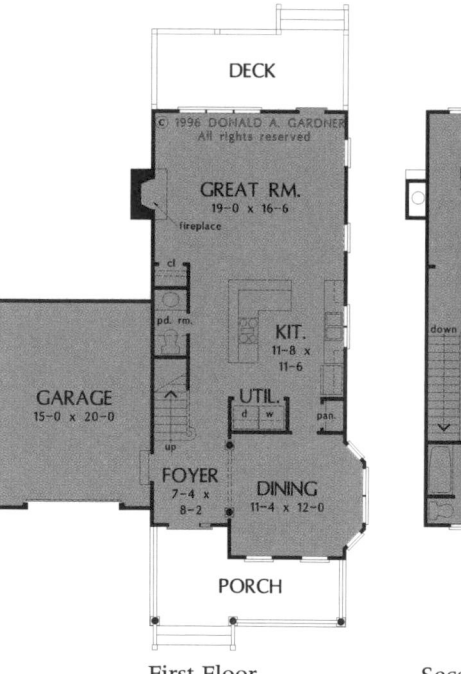

First Floor   Second Floor

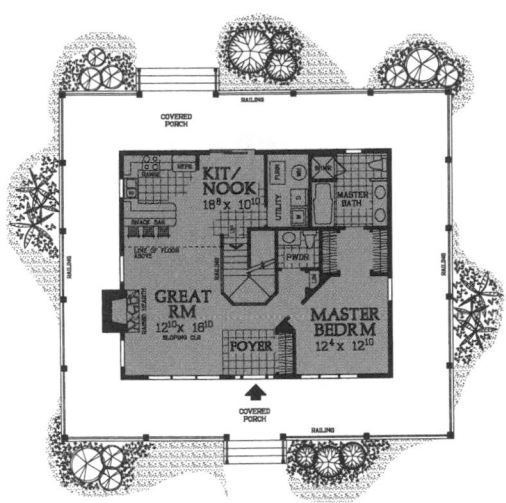

First Floor

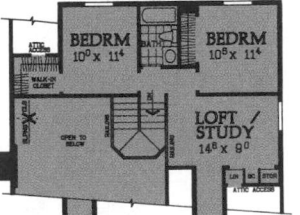

Second Floor

HPK2100278

Style: Farmhouse

First Floor: 1,093 sq. ft.

Second Floor: 603 sq. ft.

Total: 1,696 sq. ft.

Bedrooms: 3

Bathrooms: 2 ½

Width: 52' - 0"

Depth: 46' - 0"

Foundation: Crawlspace

EPLANS.COM

HPK2100279

Style: Cottage

First Floor: 1,230 sq. ft.

Second Floor: 477 sq. ft.

Total: 1,707 sq. ft.

Bonus Space: 195 sq. ft.

Bedrooms: 3

Bathrooms: 2 ½

Width: 40' - 0"

Depth: 52' - 10"

Foundation: Crawlspace

EPLANS.COM

First Floor

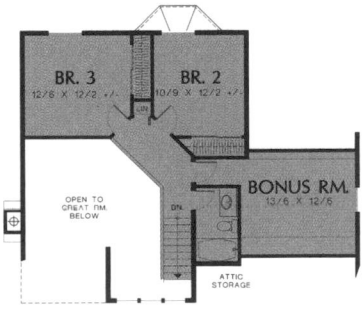

Second Floor

HPK2100280

Style: Cottage
First Floor: 1,292 sq. ft.
Second Floor: 423 sq. ft.
Total: 1,715 sq. ft.
Bedrooms: 3
Bathrooms: 2 ½
Width: 40' - 0"
Depth: 59' - 8"

EPLANS.COM

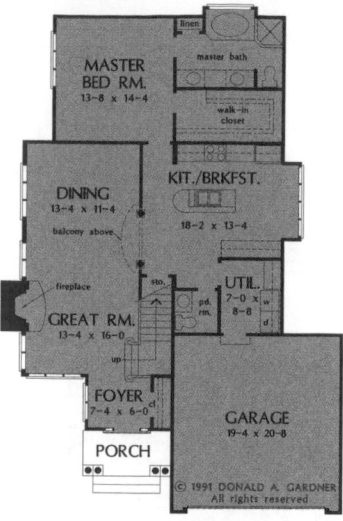

First Floor

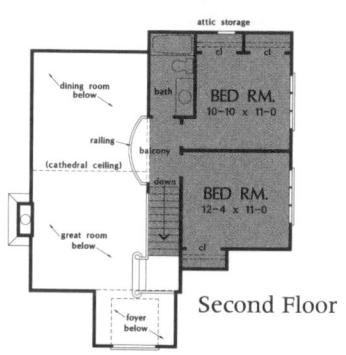

Second Floor

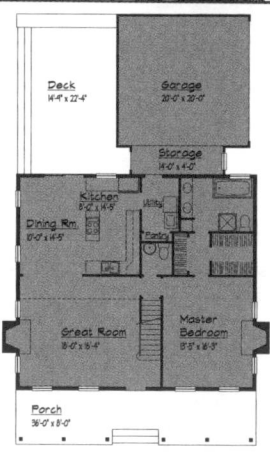

First Floor

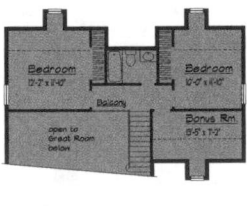

Second Floor

HPK2100281

Style: Country
First Floor: 1,152 sq. ft.
Second Floor: 567 sq. ft.
Total: 1,719 sq. ft.
Bonus Space: 115 sq. ft.
Bedrooms: 3
Bathrooms: 2 ½
Width: 36' - 0"
Depth: 64' - 0"
Foundation: Crawlspace,
Unfinished Basement

EPLANS.COM

ORDER BLUEPRINTS ANYTIME AT EPLANS.COM OR 1-800-521-6797

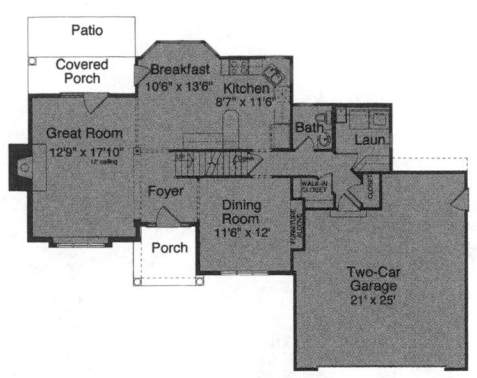

First Floor

Second Floor

HPK2100282

Style: New American

First Floor: 941 sq. ft.

Second Floor: 786 sq. ft.

Total: 1,727 sq. ft.

Bedrooms: 3

Bathrooms: 2 ½

Width: 57' - 10"

Depth: 42' - 4"

Foundation: Unfinished Basement

EPLANS.COM

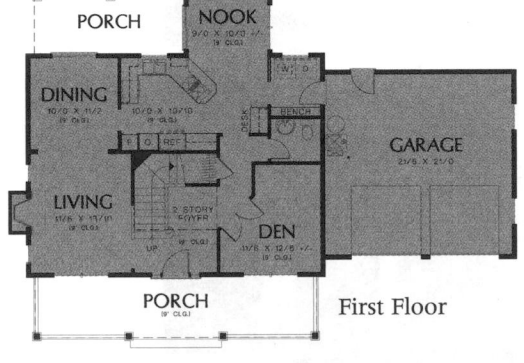

First Floor

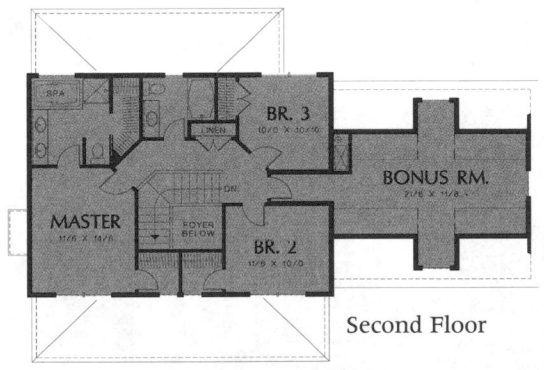

Second Floor

HPK2100283

Style: Country

First Floor: 954 sq. ft.

Second Floor: 783 sq. ft.

Total: 1,737 sq. ft.

Bonus Space: 327 sq. ft.

Bedrooms: 3

Bathrooms: 2 ½

Width: 56' - 0"

Depth: 40' - 0"

Foundation: Crawlspace

EPLANS.COM

1,500 TO 1,999 SQUARE FEET

HPK2100284

Style: Cottage
First Floor: 1,251 sq. ft.
Second Floor: 505 sq. ft.
Total: 1,756 sq. ft.
Bonus Space: 447 sq. ft.
Bedrooms: 3
Bathrooms: 2 ½
Width: 50' - 0"
Depth: 39' - 0"
Foundation: Crawlspace, Slab

EPLANS.COM

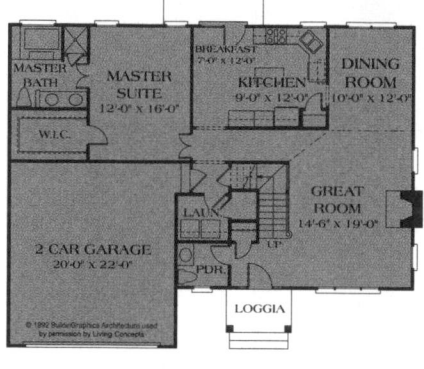

First Floor

Second Floor

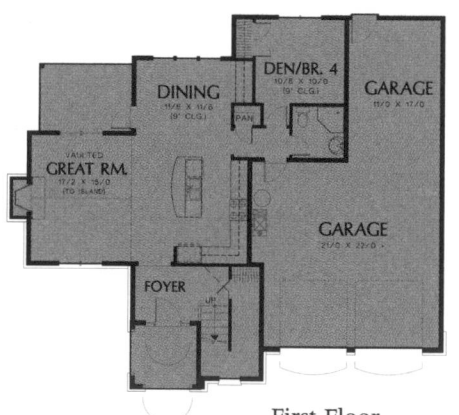

First Floor

HPK2100285

Style: French Country
First Floor: 941 sq. ft.
Second Floor: 819 sq. ft.
Total: 1,760 sq. ft.
Bedrooms: 3
Bathrooms: 3
Width: 50' - 0"
Depth: 44' - 6"
Foundation: Crawlspace

EPLANS.COM

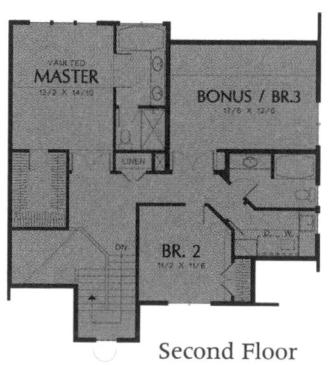

Second Floor

©1996 William E Poole Designs, Inc.

HPK2100286

Style: Cottage

First Floor: 1,211 sq. ft.

Second Floor: 551 sq. ft.

Total: 1,762 sq. ft.

Bonus Space: 378 sq. ft.

Bedrooms: 3

Bathrooms: 2 ½

Width: 64' - 4"

Depth: 39' - 4"

Foundation: Crawlspace, Unfinished Basement

EPLANS.COM

An endearing and enduring American original that is straightforward and of spare design, yet warm, cozy, and uncomplicated, this home brings the past into sharp focus. The openness of the floor plan pairs the great room with the dining area for convenience and a modern flow. Two family bedrooms share a bath upstairs. Above the garage is future space that is easily converted into livable space as needed.

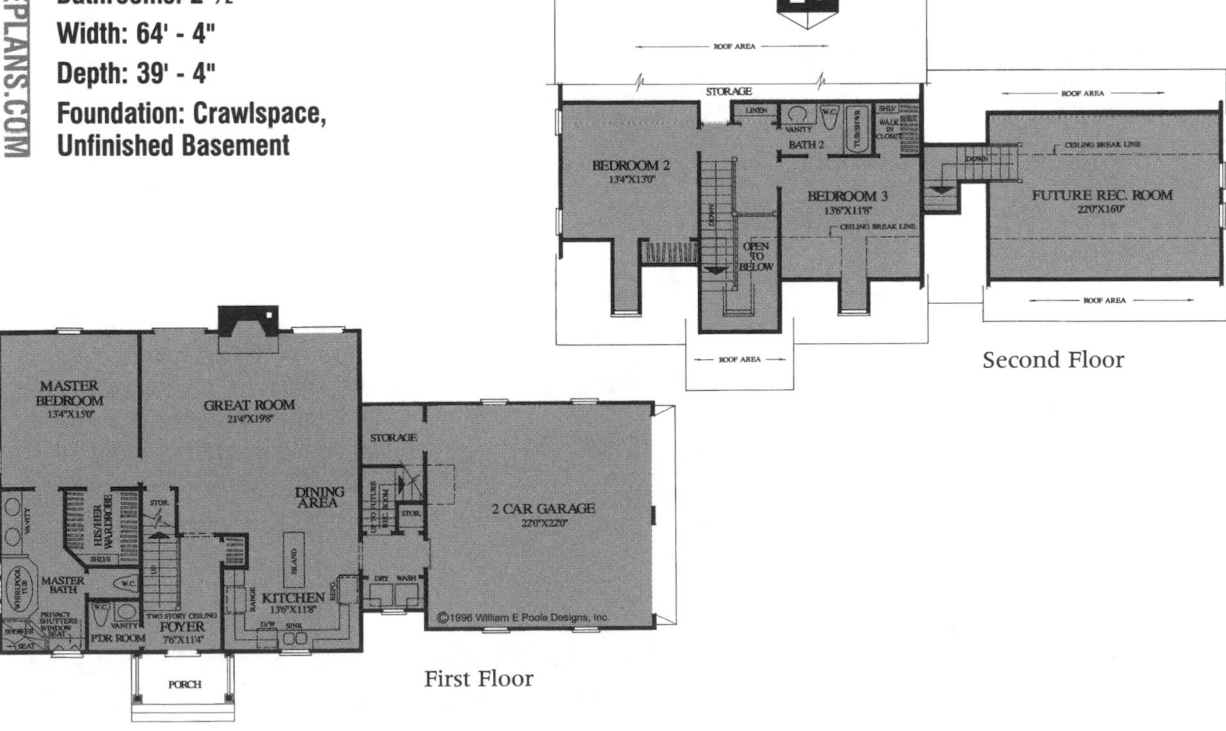

Second Floor

First Floor

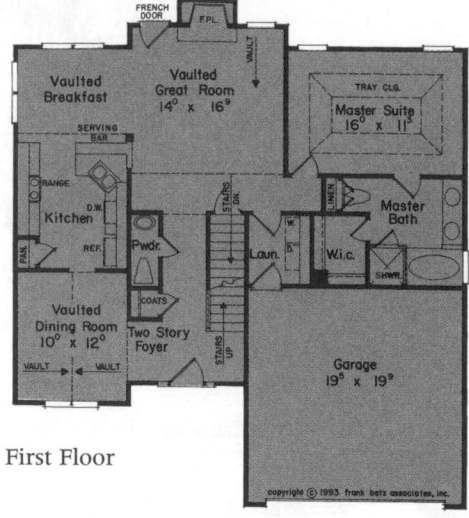

First Floor

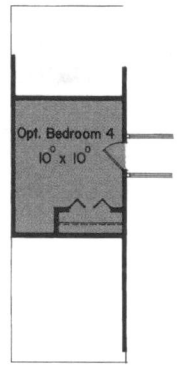

Second Floor

Optional Layout

Stucco and stone provide a pleasing contrast to the large-pane windows on the exterior of this two-story family home. Open planning joins the great room and the breakfast room under a dramatic vaulted ceiling. The modified galley kitchen features a serving bar to the breakfast room and has easy access to the formal dining room. The master suite has a tray ceiling, a compartmented bath, and a walk-in closet. Stairs lead up to a balcony overlooking the great room and two family bedrooms. An optional loft can be converted to a fourth bedroom, if desired.

HPK2100287

Style: French Country
First Floor: 1,144 sq. ft.
Second Floor: 620 sq. ft.
Total: 1,764 sq. ft.
Bedrooms: 3
Bathrooms: 2 ½
Width: 41' - 0"
Depth: 46' - 4"
Foundation: Crawlspace, Slab, Unfinished Walkout Basement

EPLANS.COM

© Stephen Fuller

HPK2100288

Style: Greek Revival

First Floor: 900 sq. ft.

Second Floor: 870 sq. ft.

Total: 1,770 sq. ft.

Bonus Space: 198 sq. ft.

Bedrooms: 3

Bathrooms: 2 ½

Width: 45' - 0"

Depth: 36' - 11"

Foundation: Unfinished Basement

EPLANS.COM

A pediment gable echoed over the entry and the garage and pilastered corners reveal the Georgian heritage of this design. Inside, columned arches mark the boundaries of the great room, kitchen, and breakfast room. The second floor offers three bedrooms, including a master suite with a deluxe bath.

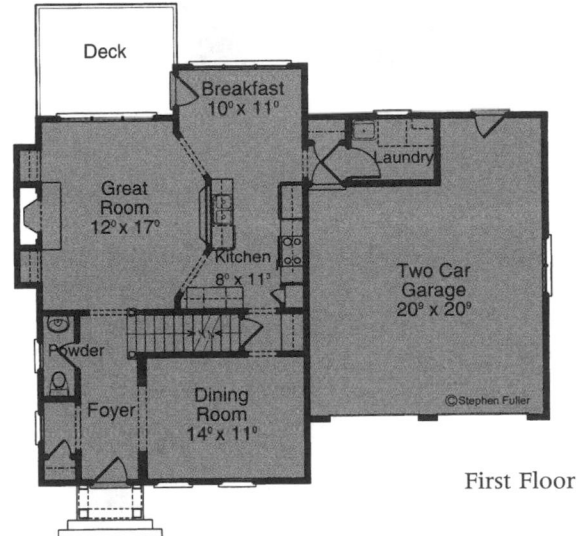

First Floor

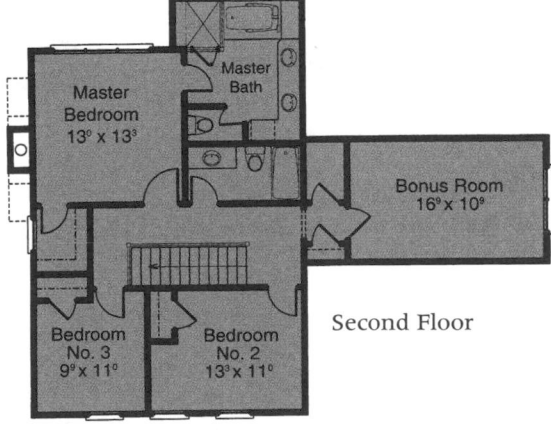

Second Floor

HPK2100336

Square Footage: 741
Width: 24' - 8"
Depth: 32' - 0"
Foundation: Slab

HPK2100337

Square Footage: 840
Width: 36' - 0"
Depth: 26' - 0"
Foundation: Slab

HPK2100338

First Floor: 576 sq. ft.
Second Floor: 334 sq. ft.
Total: 910 sq. ft.
Width: 24' - 0"
Depth: 24' - 0"
Foundation: Slab

HPK2100339

First Floor: 606 sq. ft.
Second Floor: 374 sq. ft.
Total: 980 sq. ft.
Width: 21' - 4"
Depth: 28' - 4"
Foundation: Slab

HPK2100340

First Floor: 624 sq. ft.
Second Floor: 374 sq. ft.
Total: 998 sq. ft.
Width: 24' - 0"
Depth: 26' - 0"
Foundation: Slab

HPK2100341

First Floor: 576 sq. ft.
Second Floor: 455 sq. ft.
Total: 1,031 sq. ft.
Width: 18' - 0"
Depth: 32' - 0"
Foundation: Slab

HPK2100342

First Floor: 600 sq. ft.
Second Floor: 450 sq. ft.
Total: 1,050 sq. ft.
Width: 20' - 0"
Depth: 30' - 0"
Foundation: Slab

HPK2100343

First Floor: 776 sq. ft.
Second Floor: 295 sq. ft.
Total: 1,071 sq. ft.
Width: 34' - 0"
Depth: 24' - 0"
Foundation: Slab

HPK2100344

First Floor: 192 sq. ft.
Second Floor: 888 sq. ft.
Total: 1,080 sq. ft.
Bedrooms: 2
Bathrooms: 1 ½
Width: 24' - 0"
Depth: 42' - 0"
Foundation: Slab

HPK2100290

Square Footage: 336
Width: 14' - 0"
Depth: 24' - 0"
Foundation: Slab

HPK2100291

Square Footage: 336
Width: 14' - 0"
Depth: 24' - 0"
Foundation: Slab

HPK2100292

Square Footage: 384
Width: 16' - 0"
Depth: 24' - 0"
Foundation: Slab

HPK2100293

Square Footage: 576
Width: 24' - 0"
Depth: 24' - 0"
Foundation: Slab

HPK2100294

First Floor: 345 sq. ft.
Second Floor: 261 sq. ft.
Total: 606 sq. ft.
Width: 15' - 0"
Depth: 23' - 0"
Foundation: Slab

HPK2100295

First Floor: 384 sq. ft.
Second Floor: 272 sq. ft.
Total: 656 sq. ft.
Width: 16' - 0"
Depth: 24' - 0"
Foundation: Slab

HPK2100296

Square Footage: 662
Width: 28' - 0"
Depth: 26' - 0"
Foundation: Slab

HPK2100297

First Floor: 384 sq. ft.
Second Floor: 320 sq. ft.
Total: 704 sq. ft.
Width: 16' - 0"
Depth: 24' - 0"
Foundation: Slab

HPK2100298

First Floor: 112 sq. ft.
Second Floor: 601 sq. ft.
Total: 713 sq. ft.
Bedrooms: 1
Bathrooms: 1
Width: 28' - 0"
Depth: 26' - 0"
Foundation: Slab

HPK2100299

Style: Farmhouse
First Floor: 959 sq. ft.
Second Floor: 833 sq. ft.
Total: 1,792 sq. ft.
Bonus Space: 344 sq. ft.
Bedrooms: 3
Bathrooms: 2 ½
Width: 52' - 6"
Depth: 42' - 8"

EPLANS.COM

© 1995 Donald A. Gardner Architects, Inc.

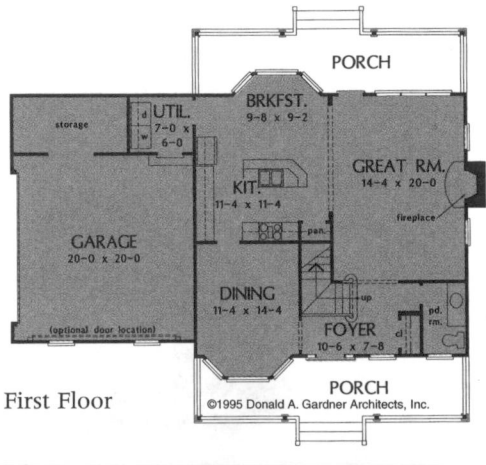

First Floor
©1995 Donald A. Gardner Architects, Inc.

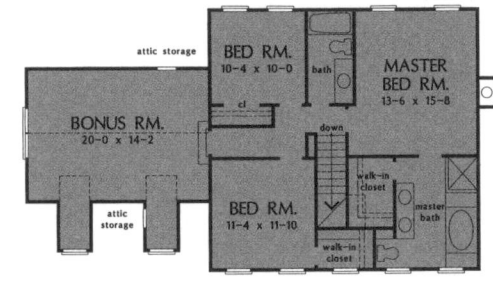

Second Floor

HPK2100300

Style: French Country
First Floor: 1,345 sq. ft.
Second Floor: 452 sq. ft.
Total: 1,797 sq. ft.
Bonus Space: 349 sq. ft.
Bedrooms: 3
Bathrooms: 2 ½
Width: 63' - 0"
Depth: 40' - 0"

EPLANS.COM

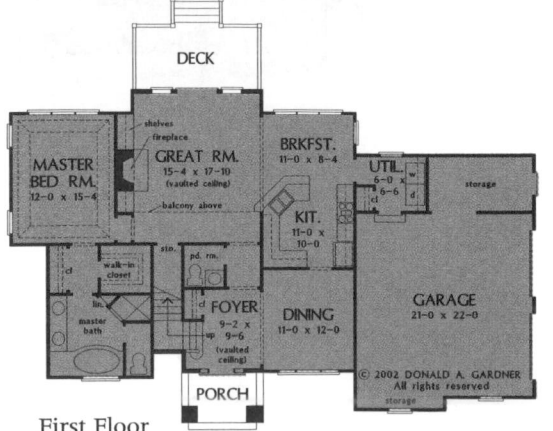

First Floor

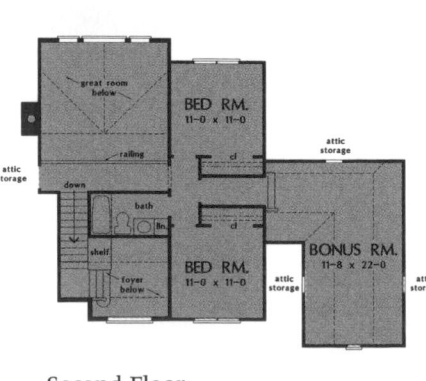

Second Floor

ORDER BLUEPRINTS ANYTIME AT EPLANS.COM OR 1-800-521-6797

HPK2100301

Style: Country
First Floor: 916 sq. ft.
Second Floor: 895 sq. ft.
Total: 1,811 sq. ft.
Bonus Space: 262 sq. ft.
Bedrooms: 3
Bathrooms: 2 ½
Width: 44' - 0"
Depth: 38' - 0"
Foundation: Crawlspace, Slab, Unfinished Walkout Basement

EPLANS.COM

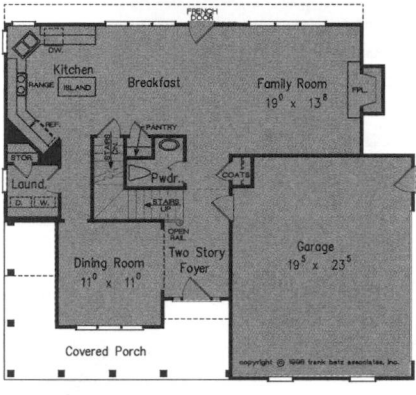

First Floor

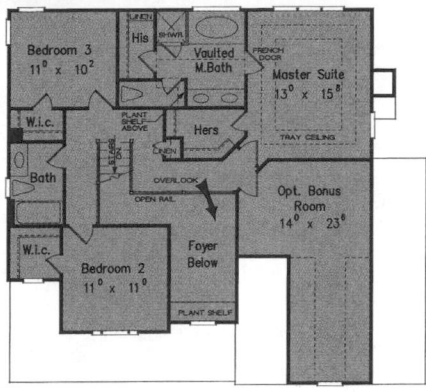

Second Floor

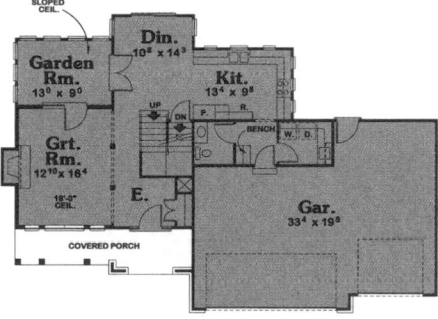

First Floor

HPK2100302

Style: New American
First Floor: 837 sq. ft.
Second Floor: 977 sq. ft.
Total: 1,814 sq. ft.
Bedrooms: 4
Bathrooms: 2 ½
Width: 58' - 4"
Depth: 41' - 4"

EPLANS.COM

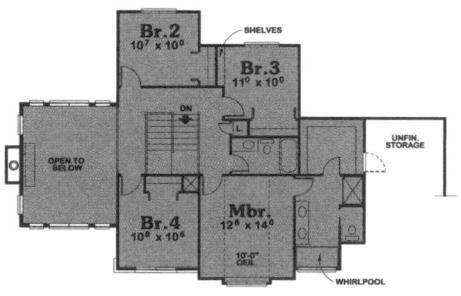

Second Floor

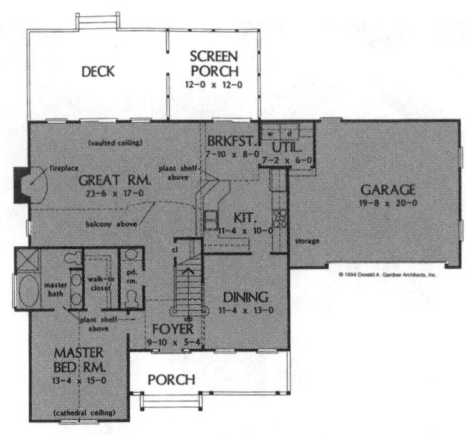

First Floor

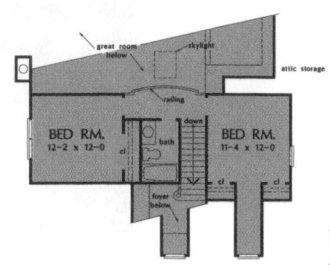

Second Floor

HPK2100303

Style: Country
First Floor: 1,335 sq. ft.
Second Floor: 488 sq. ft.
Total: 1,823 sq. ft.
Bedrooms: 3
Bathrooms: 2 ½
Width: 61' - 6"
Depth: 54' - 0"

EPLANS.COM

© 1994 Donald A. Gardner Architects, Inc.

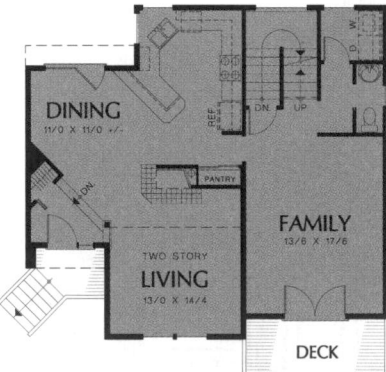

First Floor

Second Floor

HPK2100304

Style: New American
First Floor: 1,022 sq. ft.
Second Floor: 813 sq. ft.
Total: 1,835 sq. ft.
Bedrooms: 3
Bathrooms: 2 ½
Width: 36' - 0"
Depth: 33' - 0"
Foundation: Slab

EPLANS.COM

HPK2100305

Style: Country
First Floor: 919 sq. ft.
Second Floor: 927 sq. ft.
Total: 1,846 sq. ft.
Bedrooms: 4
Bathrooms: 2 ½
Width: 44' - 0"
Depth: 40' - 0"

EPLANS.COM

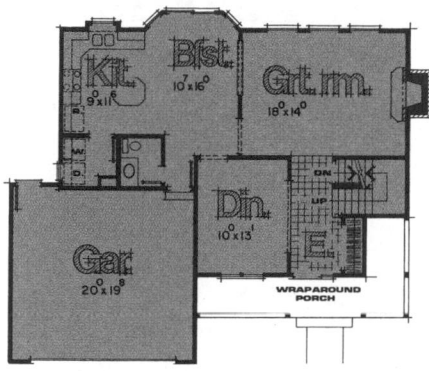

First Floor

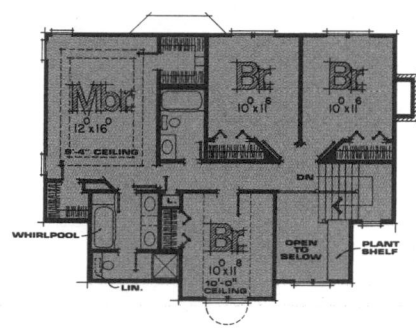

Second Floor

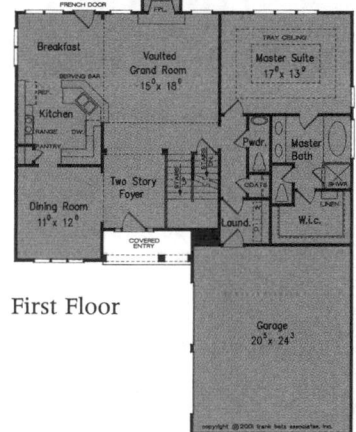

First Floor

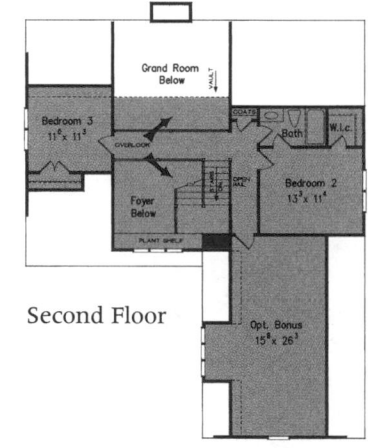

Second Floor

HPK2100306

Style: Colonial Revival
First Floor: 1,335 sq. ft.
Second Floor: 515 sq. ft.
Total: 1,850 sq. ft.
Bonus Space: 368 sq. ft.
Bedrooms: 3
Bathrooms: 2 ½
Width: 44' - 0"
Depth: 57' - 4"
Foundation: Crawlspace, Slab, Unfinished Walkout Basement

EPLANS.COM

1,500 TO 1,999 SQUARE FEET

HPK2100307

Style: Cottage

First Floor: 1,342 sq. ft.

Second Floor: 511 sq. ft.

Total: 1,853 sq. ft.

Bedrooms: 3

Bathrooms: 2

Width: 44' - 0"

Depth: 40' - 0"

Foundation: Pier (same as Piling)

EPLANS.COM

© The Sater Design Collection, Inc.

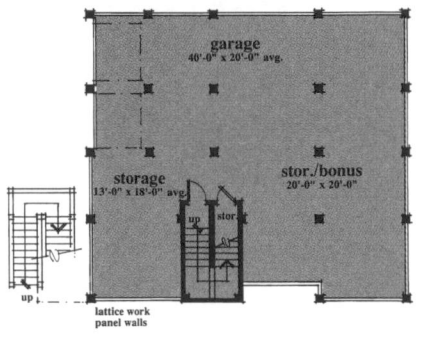

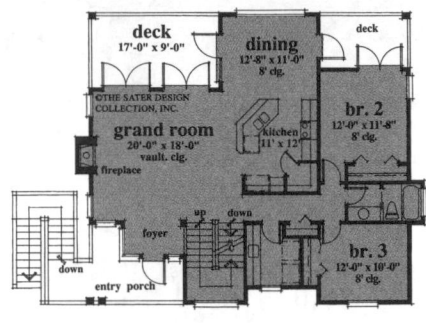

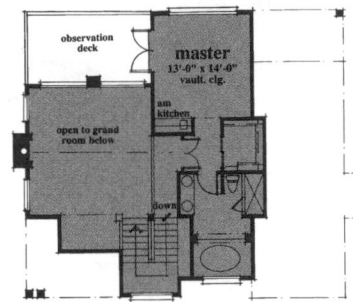

First Floor

Second Floor

© Sater Design Collection, Inc.

HPK2100308

Style: New American

First Floor: 1,342 sq. ft.

Second Floor: 511 sq. ft.

Total: 1,853 sq. ft.

Bedrooms: 3

Bathrooms: 2 ½

Width: 44' - 0"

Depth: 44' - 0"

Foundation: Island Basement

EPLANS.COM

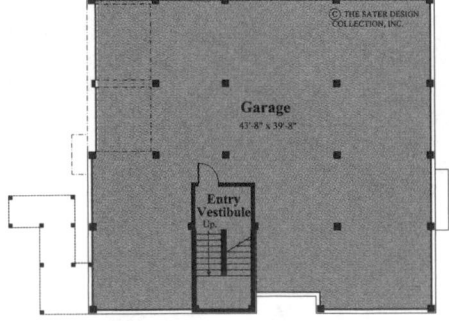

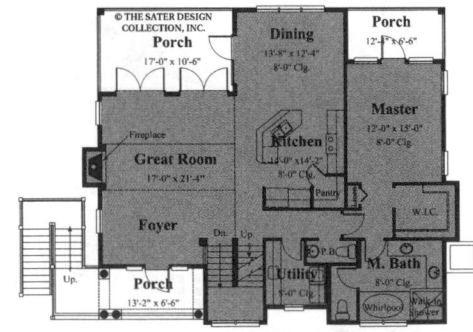

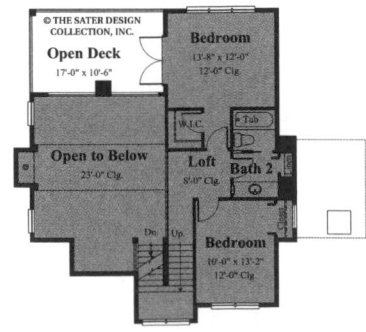

First Floor

Second Floor

ORDER BLUEPRINTS ANYTIME AT EPLANS.COM OR 1-800-521-6797

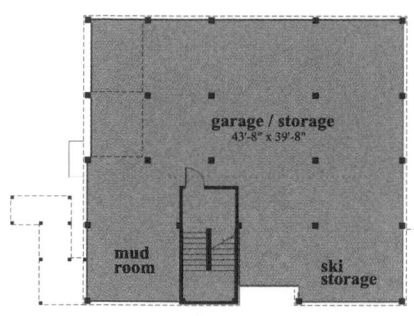

garage / storage
43'-8" x 39'-8"

mud room

ski storage

Porch
17'-0" x 10'-6"

Dining
13'-8" x 12'-4"
8'-0" Clg.

Porch
12'-5" x 6'-6"

Master
12'-6" x 15'-0"
9'-0" Clg.

Kitchen
10'-0" x 14'-2"
8'-0" Clg.

Great Room
17'-0" x 21'-4"

Fireplace

Foyer

Pantry

Do.   Up.

W.I.C.

Utility
4'-0" Clg.

M. Bath
8'-0" Clg.

Porch
13'-2" x 6'-6"

Up.

Whirlpool

Walk-in Shower

First Floor

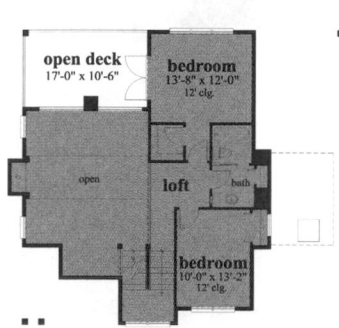

open deck
17'-0" x 10'-6"

bedroom
13'-8" x 12'-0"
12' clg.

open

loft

bath

bedroom
10'-0" x 13'-2"
12' clg.

Second Floor

HPK2100309

Style: New American

First Floor: 1,342 sq. ft.

Second Floor: 511 sq. ft.

Total: 1,853 sq. ft.

Bedrooms: 3

Bathrooms: 2

Width: 44' - 0"

Depth: 40' - 0"

Foundation: Unfinished Basement

EPLANS.COM

©1998 Donald A. Gardner, Inc.

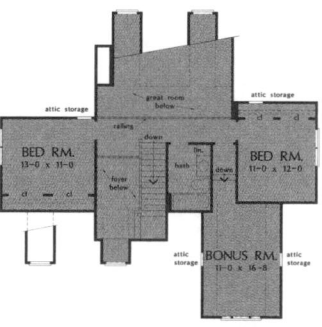

PORCH

DINING
11-0 x 10-0

MASTER
BED RM.
13-0 x 15-0

GREAT RM.
19-0 x 17-0
(cathedral ceiling)
Fireplace

KIT.
11-0 x
13-0

UTIL.
6-5 x
5-8

storage

master bath

FOYER
6-0 x
11-11

GARAGE
21-0 x 21-0

walk-in closet

PORCH

First Floor

HPK2100310

Style: Country

First Floor: 1,336 sq. ft.

Second Floor: 523 sq. ft.

Total: 1,859 sq. ft.

Bonus Space: 225 sq. ft.

Bedrooms: 3

Bathrooms: 2 ½

Width: 45' - 0"

Depth: 53' - 0"

EPLANS.COM

attic storage

great room below
ceiling

attic storage

BED RM.
13-0 x 11-0

down

bath

foyer below

BED RM.
11-0 x 12-0

attic storage

BONUS RM.
11-0 x 16-8

attic storage

Second Floor

HPK2100311

Style: New American
First Floor: 1,416 sq. ft.
Second Floor: 445 sq. ft.
Total: 1,861 sq. ft.
Bonus Space: 284 sq. ft.
Bedrooms: 3
Bathrooms: 2 ½
Width: 58' - 3"
Depth: 68' - 6"

EPLANS.COM

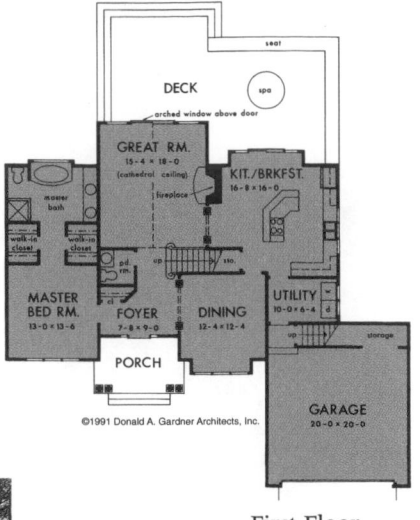

First Floor

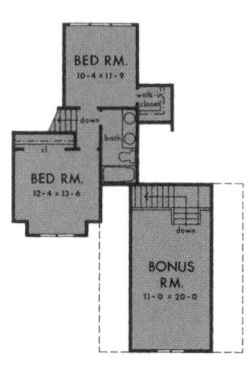

Second Floor

©1991 Donald A. Gardner Architects, Inc. Photography courtesy of Donald A. Gardner Architects, Inc. This home, as shown in photographs, may differ from the actual blueprints. For more detailed information, please check the floor plans carefully.

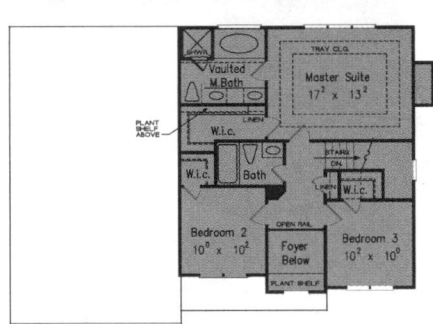

First Floor

Second Floor

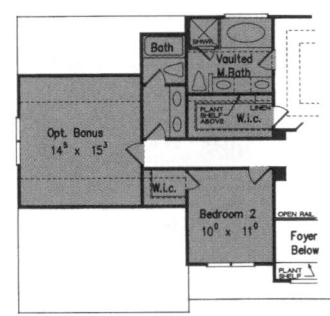

Optional Layout

HPK2100312

Style: Country
First Floor: 1,103 sq. ft.
Second Floor: 759 sq. ft.
Total: 1,862 sq. ft.
Bonus Space: 342 sq. ft.
Bedrooms: 4
Bathrooms: 3
Width: 50' - 4"
Depth: 35' - 0"
Foundation: Crawlspace, Slab, Unfinished Walkout Basement

EPLANS.COM

ORDER BLUEPRINTS ANYTIME AT EPLANS.COM OR 1-800-521-6797

HPK2100313

Style: Tidewater

First Floor: 1,056 sq. ft.

Second Floor: 807 sq. ft.

Total: 1,863 sq. ft.

Bedrooms: 4

Bathrooms: 3

Width: 33' - 0"

Depth: 54' - 0"

Foundation: Crawlspace, Pier (same as Piling)

EPLANS.COM

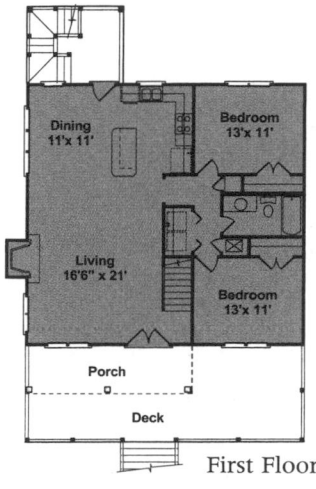

First Floor

Second Floor

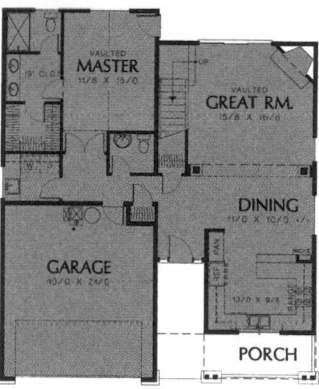

First Floor

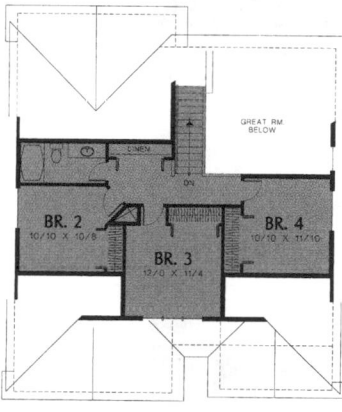

Second Floor

HPK2100314

Style: Bungalow

First Floor: 1,198 sq. ft.

Second Floor: 668 sq. ft.

Total: 1,866 sq. ft.

Bedrooms: 4

Bathrooms: 2 ½

Width: 40' - 0"

Depth: 47' - 0"

Foundation: Crawlspace

EPLANS.COM

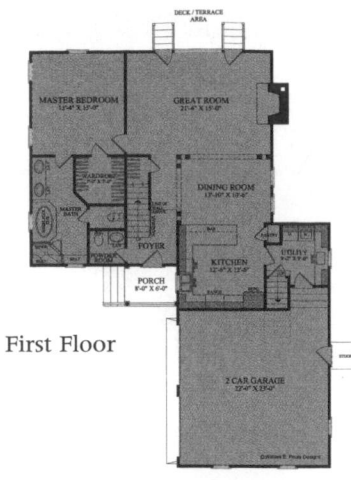

First Floor

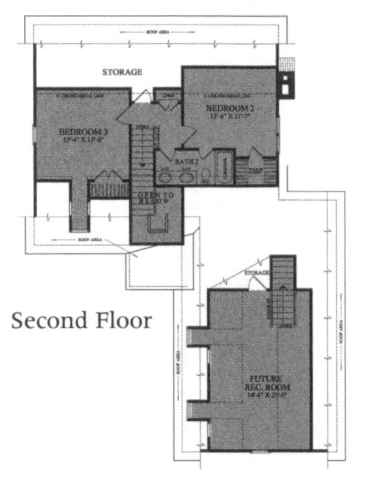

Second Floor

© William E. Poole Designs, Inc.

HPK2100315

Style: Cottage

First Floor: 1,314 sq. ft.

Second Floor: 552 sq. ft.

Total: 1,866 sq. ft.

Bonus Space: 398 sq. ft.

Bedrooms: 3

Bathrooms: 2 ½

Width: 44' - 2"

Depth: 62' - 0"

Foundation: Crawlspace

EPLANS.COM

© 1998 William E. Poole Designs, Inc.

HPK2100316

Style: Federal - Adams

First Floor: 1,028 sq. ft.

Second Floor: 843 sq. ft.

Total: 1,871 sq. ft.

Bonus Space: 304 sq. ft.

Bedrooms: 3

Bathrooms: 2 ½

Width: 40' - 0"

Depth: 61' - 0"

Foundation: Crawlspace, Unfinished Basement

EPLANS.COM

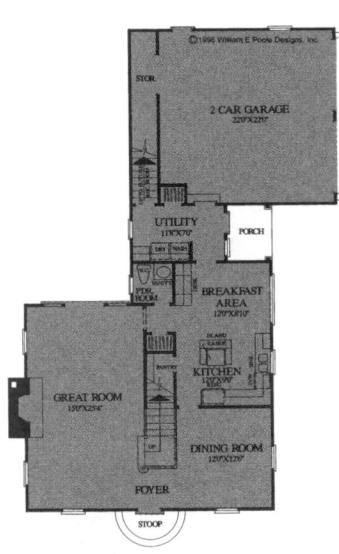

First Floor

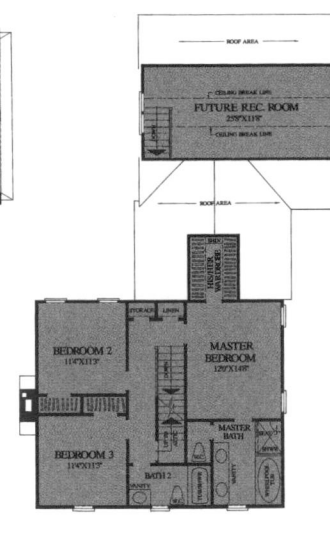

Second Floor

First Floor

Second Floor

HPK2100317

Style: Greek Revival

First Floor: 870 sq. ft.

Second Floor: 1,007 sq. ft.

Total: 1,877 sq. ft.

Bonus Space: 263 sq. ft.

Bedrooms: 4

Bathrooms: 2 ½

Width: 40' - 0"

Depth: 49' - 0"

Foundation: Crawlspace

EPLANS.COM

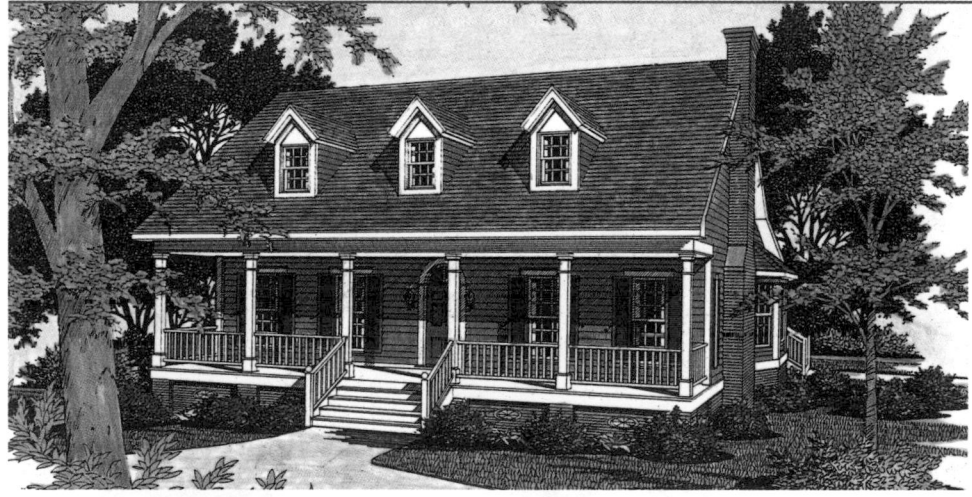

HPK2100318

Style: Country

Square Footage: 1,879

Bonus Space: 965 sq. ft.

Bedrooms: 3

Bathrooms: 2

Width: 45' - 0"

Depth: 62' - 0"

Foundation: Crawlspace, Slab, Unfinished Basement

EPLANS.COM

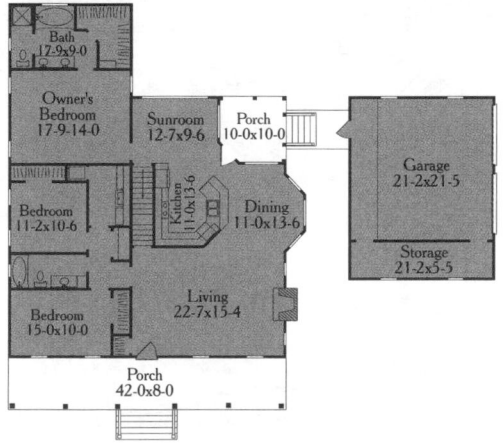

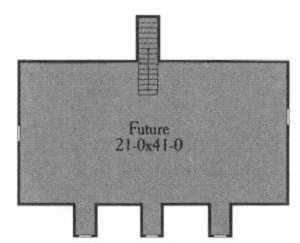

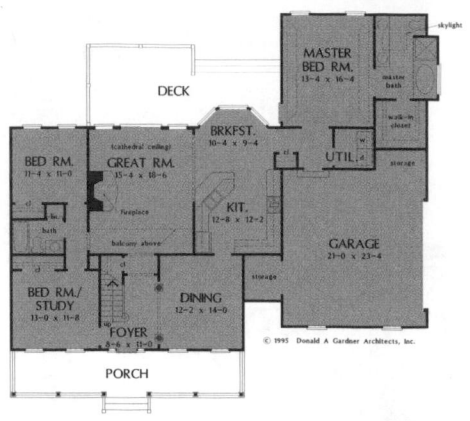

First Floor

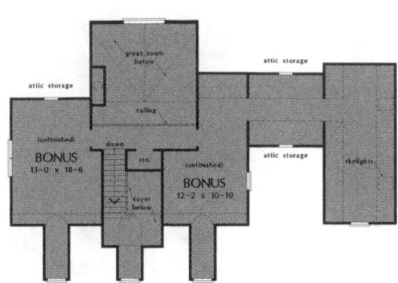

Second Floor

HPK2100319

Style: Farmhouse

First Floor: 1,803 sq. ft.

Second Floor: 80 sq. ft.

Total: 1,883 sq. ft.

Bonus Space: 918 sq. ft.

Bedrooms: 3

Bathrooms: 2

Width: 63' - 8"

Depth: 57' - 4"

EPLANS.COM

©1995 Donald A. Gardner Architects, Inc.

HPK2100320

Style: Cottage

First Floor: 1,408 sq. ft.

Second Floor: 476 sq. ft.

Total: 1,884 sq. ft.

Bedrooms: 3

Bathrooms: 2 ½

Width: 41' - 8"

Depth: 56' - 4"

EPLANS.COM

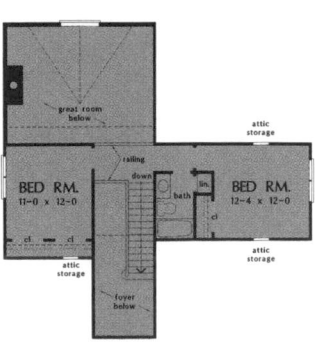

First Floor

Second Floor

© 2003 Donald A. Gardner Inc.

HPK2100321

Style: Neoclassical
First Floor: 1,347 sq. ft.
Second Floor: 537 sq. ft.
Total: 1,884 sq. ft.
Bedrooms: 3
Bathrooms: 2 ½
Width: 32' - 10"
Depth: 70' - 10"
Foundation: Crawlspace

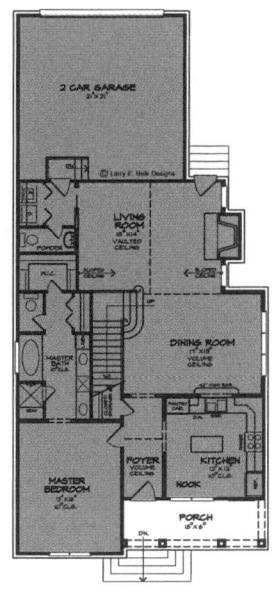

First Floor

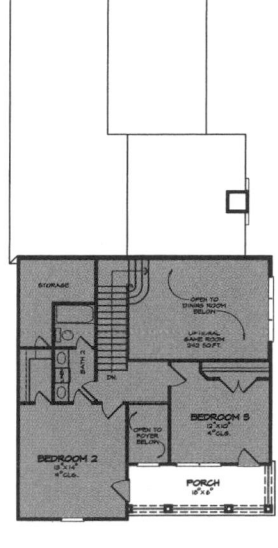

Second Floor

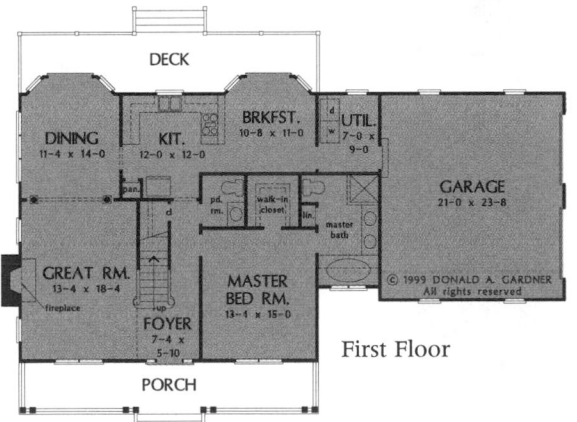

First Floor

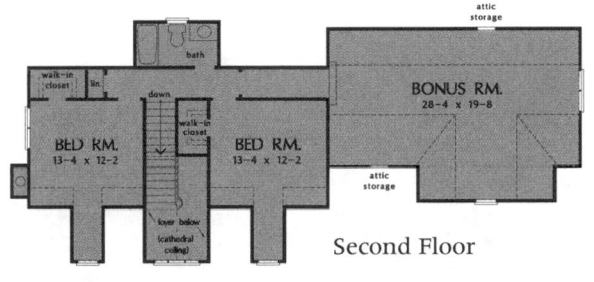

Second Floor

HPK2100322

Style: Country
First Floor: 1,309 sq. ft.
Second Floor: 582 sq. ft.
Total: 1,891 sq. ft.
Bonus Space: 572 sq. ft.
Bedrooms: 3
Bathrooms: 2 ½
Width: 65' - 8"
Depth: 39' - 4"

© 1999 Donald A. Gardner, Inc.

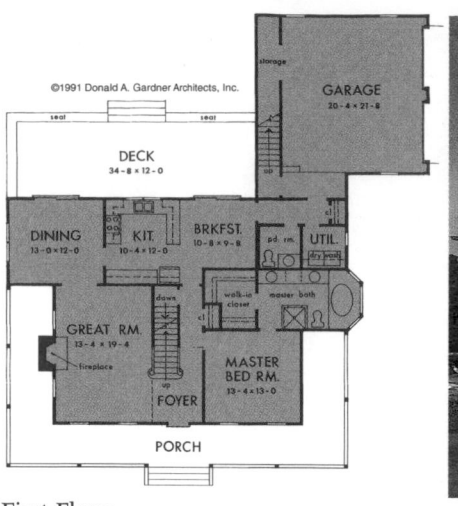

©1991 Donald A. Gardner Architects, Inc.

First Floor

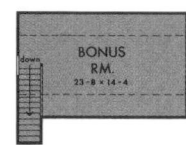

BONUS RM.
23-8 x 14-4

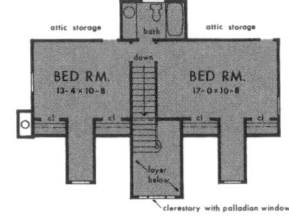

Second Floor

HPK2100323

Style: Tidewater
First Floor: 1,356 sq. ft.
Second Floor: 542 sq. ft.
Total: 1,898 sq. ft.
Bonus Space: 393 sq. ft.
Bedrooms: 3
Bathrooms: 2 ½
Width: 59' - 0"
Depth: 64' - 0"

EPLANS.COM

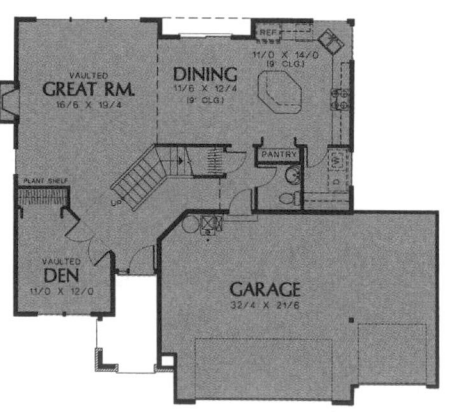

First Floor

HPK2100324

Style: Bungalow
First Floor: 1,097 sq. ft.
Second Floor: 807 sq. ft.
Total: 1,904 sq. ft.
Bedrooms: 3
Bathrooms: 2 ½
Width: 40' - 0"
Depth: 45' - 0"
Foundation: Crawlspace

EPLANS.COM

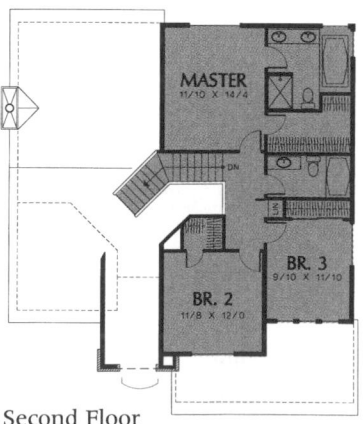

Second Floor

HPK2100325

Style: New American

First Floor: 915 sq. ft.

Second Floor: 994 sq. ft.

Total: 1,909 sq. ft.

Bedrooms: 3

Bathrooms: 2 ½

Width: 38' - 0"

Depth: 38' - 0"

Foundation: Unfinished Basement

EPLANS.COM

First Floor

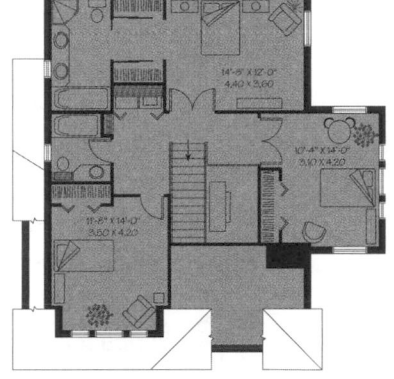

Second Floor

©1996 William E Poole Designs, Inc.

HPK2100326

Style: Cottage

First Floor: 1,201 sq. ft.

Second Floor: 708 sq. ft.

Total: 1,909 sq. ft.

Bedrooms: 3

Bathrooms: 2 ½

Width: 56' - 8"

Depth: 39' - 8"

Foundation: Crawlspace

EPLANS.COM

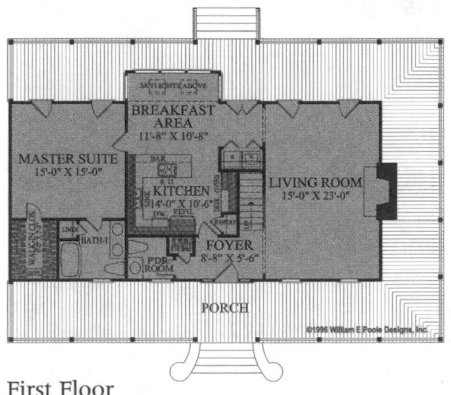

First Floor

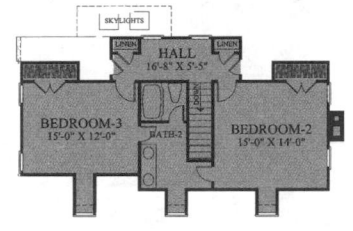

Second Floor

1,500 TO 1,999 SQUARE FEET

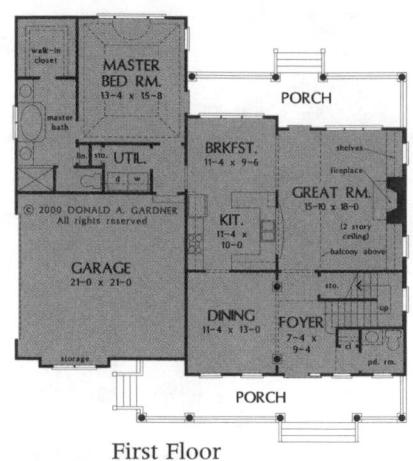

First Floor

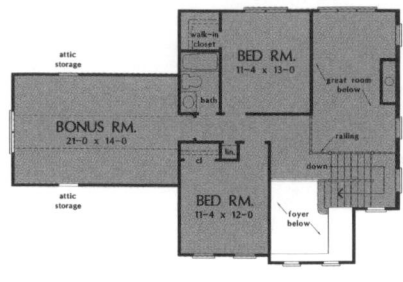

Second Floor

© 2000 Donald A. Gardner, Inc.

HPK2100327

Style: Country

First Floor: 1,412 sq. ft.

Second Floor: 506 sq. ft.

Total: 1,918 sq. ft.

Bonus Space: 320 sq. ft.

Bedrooms: 3

Bathrooms: 2 ½

Width: 49' - 8"

Depth: 52' - 0"

EPLANS.COM

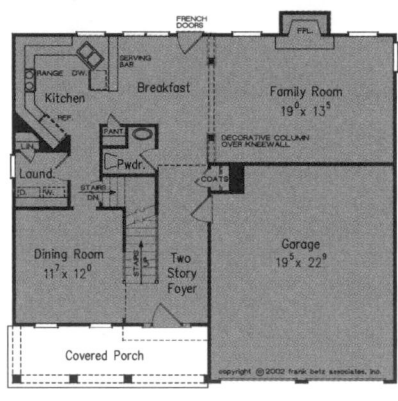

First Floor

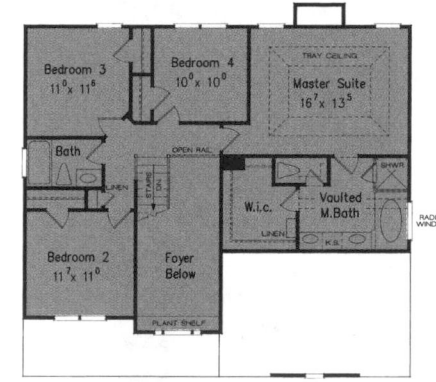

Second Floor

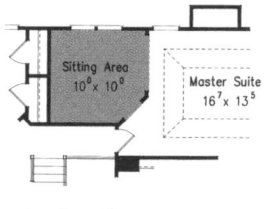

Optional Layout

HPK2100328

Style: Country

First Floor: 947 sq. ft.

Second Floor: 981 sq. ft.

Total: 1,928 sq. ft.

Bedrooms: 4

Bathrooms: 2 ½

Width: 41' - 0"

Depth: 39' - 4"

Foundation: Crawlspace, Slab, Unfinished Walkout Basement

EPLANS.COM

HPK2100329

Style: Colonial Revival

First Floor: 1,314 sq. ft.

Second Floor: 616 sq. ft.

Total: 1,930 sq. ft.

Bedrooms: 3

Bathrooms: 2 ½

Width: 40' - 0"

Depth: 54' - 6"

Foundation: Unfinished Walkout Basement

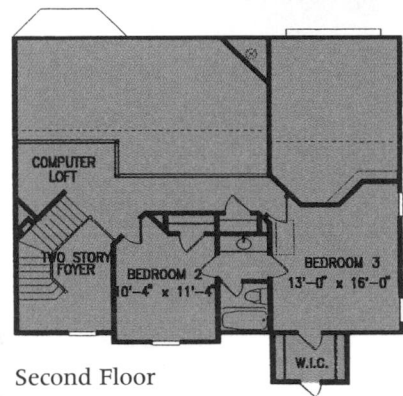

First Floor

Second Floor

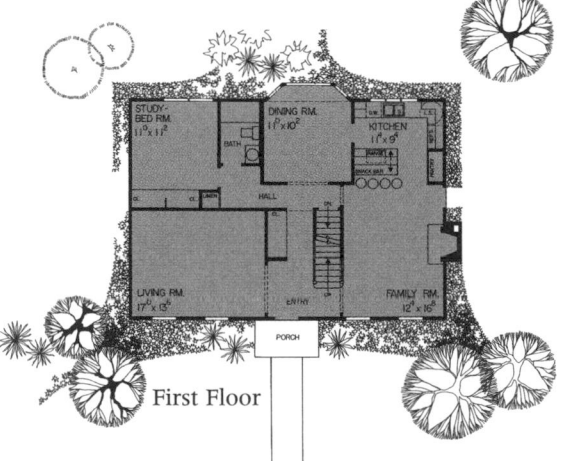

First Floor

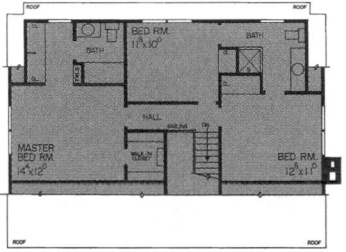

Second Floor

HPK2100330

Style: Cape Cod

First Floor: 1,137 sq. ft.

Second Floor: 796 sq. ft.

Total: 1,933 sq. ft.

Bedrooms: 4

Bathrooms: 3

Width: 40' - 0"

Depth: 28' - 0"

Foundation: Unfinished Basement

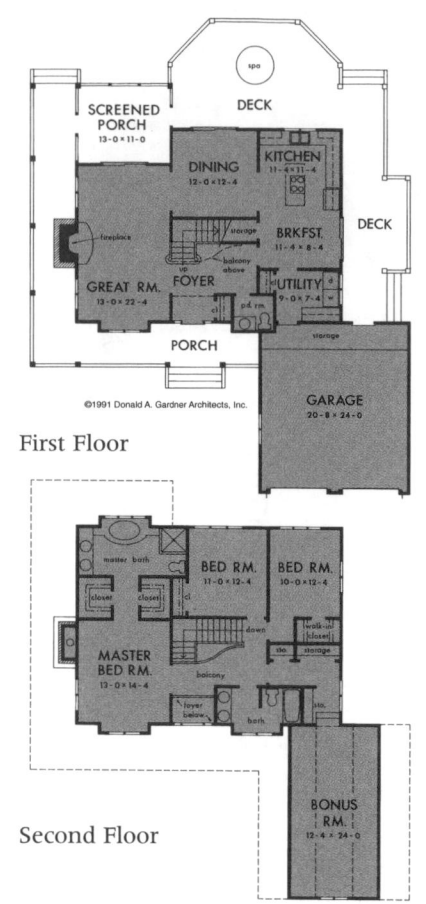

SCREENED PORCH
13-0 × 11-0

DECK

spa

DINING
12-0 × 12-4

KITCHEN
11-4 × 11-4

DECK

BRKFST.
11-4 × 8-4

GREAT RM.
13-0 × 22-4

FOYER

UTILITY
9-0 × 7-4

balcony above

storage

PORCH

GARAGE
20-8 × 24-0

©1991 Donald A. Gardner Architects, Inc.

First Floor

master bath

BED RM.
11-0 × 12-4

BED RM.
10-0 × 12-4

closet

closet

cl.

walk-in closet

MASTER BED RM.
13-0 × 14-4

down

sto.

storage

balcony

foyer below

bath

BONUS RM.
12-4 × 24-0

Second Floor

© 1991 Donald A. Gardner Architects, Inc.

HPK2100331

Style: Country

First Floor: 1,025 sq. ft.

Second Floor: 911 sq. ft.

Total: 1,936 sq. ft.

Bonus Space: 410 sq. ft.

Bedrooms: 3

Bathrooms: 2 ½

Width: 53' - 8"

Depth: 67' - 8"

EPLANS.COM

HPK2100332

Style: Cottage

First Floor: 1,021 sq. ft.

Second Floor: 915 sq. ft.

Total: 1,936 sq. ft.

Bonus Space: 378 sq. ft.

Bedrooms: 3

Bathrooms: 2 ½

Width: 66' - 8"

Depth: 38' - 8"

Foundation: Crawlspace, Unfinished Basement

EPLANS.COM

©1997 William E Poole Designs, Inc.

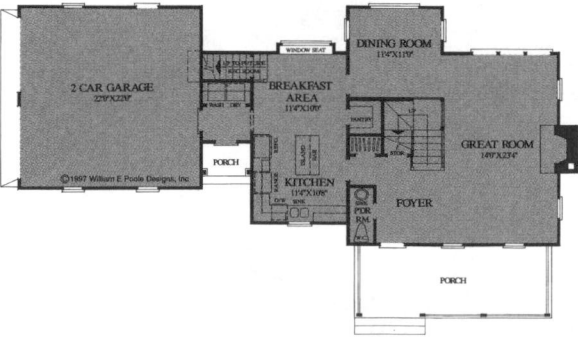

2 CAR GARAGE
22'0"×22'0"

WINDOW SEAT

DINING ROOM
11'4"×11'9"

BREAKFAST AREA
11'4"×10'9"

GREAT ROOM
14'9"×23'4"

KITCHEN
11'4"×10'8"

PORCH

FOYER

POR. RM.

PORCH

©1997 William E Poole Designs, Inc

First Floor

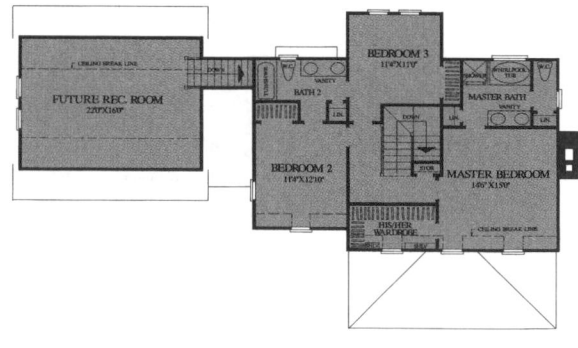

FUTURE REC. ROOM
22'0"×16'0"

BATH 2

VANITY

BEDROOM 3
11'4"×11'9"

MASTER BATH

VANITY

BEDROOM 2
11'4"×12'0"

MASTER BEDROOM
14'0"×15'0"

HIS/HER WARDROBE

Second Floor

ORDER BLUEPRINTS ANYTIME AT EPLANS.COM OR 1-800-521-6797

HPK2100333

Style: Craftsman

First Floor: 1,341 sq. ft.

Second Floor: 598 sq. ft.

Total: 1,939 sq. ft.

Bedrooms: 3

Bathrooms: 2

Width: 50' - 3"

Depth: 46' - 3"

Foundation: Crawlspace

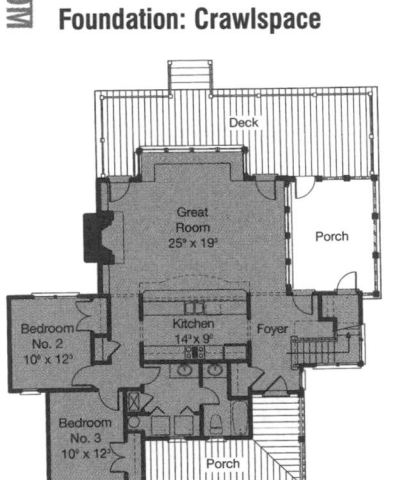

First Floor

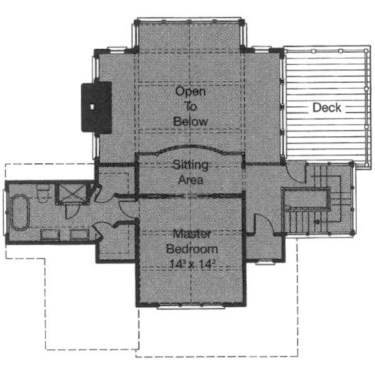

Second Floor

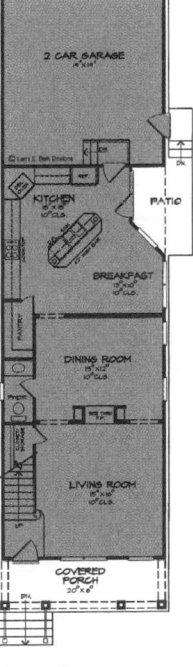

First Floor

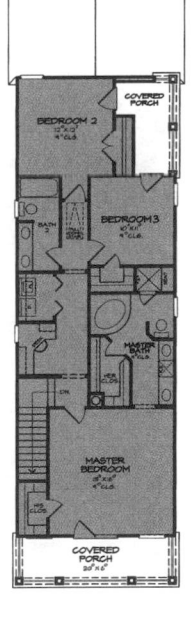

Second Floor

HPK2100334

Style: Cottage

First Floor: 911 sq. ft.

Second Floor: 1,029 sq. ft.

Total: 1,940 sq. ft.

Bedrooms: 3

Bathrooms: 2 ½

Width: 20' - 10"

Depth: 75' - 10"

Foundation: Crawlspace

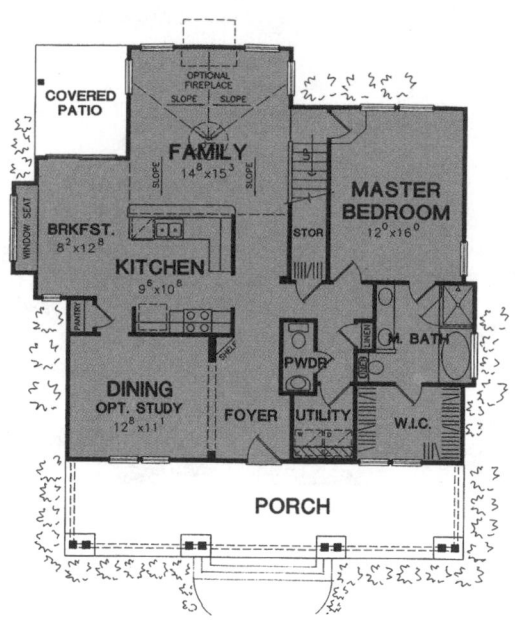

First Floor

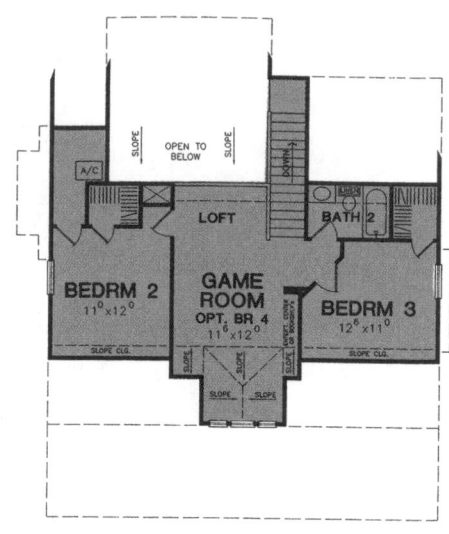

Second Floor

HPK2100335

Style: Bungalow
First Floor: 1,305 sq. ft.
Second Floor: 636 sq. ft.
Total: 1,941 sq. ft.
Bedrooms: 3
Bathrooms: 2 ½
Width: 42' - 4"
Depth: 46' - 10"
Foundation: Crawlspace, Slab, Unfinished Basement

EPLANS.COM

Craftsman-style windows decorate the facade of this beautiful bungalow design. Inside, the formal dining room to the left of the foyer can double as a study. The family room offers a sloping ceiling and a fireplace option. In the breakfast nook, a window seat and sliding glass doors that open to the covered patio allow homeowners to enjoy the outdoors. The master bedroom dominates the right side of the plan. Upstairs, two secondary bedrooms—both with walk-in closets and one with a private bath—sit to either side of a game room.

ORDER BLUEPRINTS ANYTIME AT EPLANS.COM OR 1-800-521-6797

HPK2100289

EPLANS.COM

Style: New American

Square Footage: 1,944

Bedrooms: 3

Bathrooms: 3

Width: 71' - 10"

Depth: 66' - 10"

Foundation: Slab

Upscale design takes on a new meaning with open gables, a hipped roof, arch-topped windows and a side-loading garage as enhancements. The dining room features decorative columns that offer spatial definition. The living room enjoys a tray ceiling, central fireplace and rear-porch access. To the right, the breakfast room, kitchen with utility room and the luxurious master suite with full amenities offer privacy and comfort. Two family bedrooms on the left share a full bath.

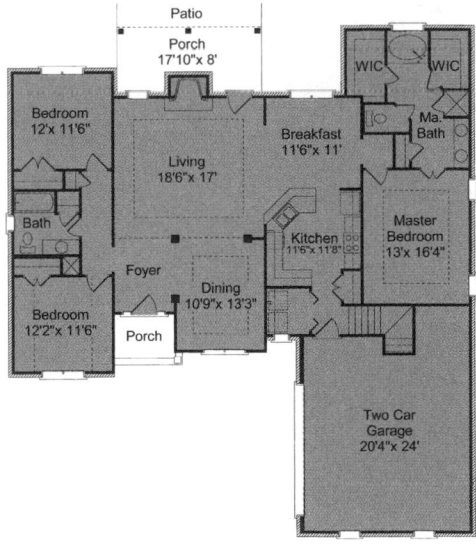

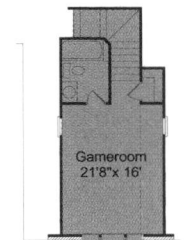

HPK2100345

Style: Craftsman
First Floor: 1,082 sq. ft.
Second Floor: 864 sq. ft.
Total: 1,946 sq. ft.
Bonus Space: 358 sq. ft.
Bedrooms: 3
Bathrooms: 2 ½
Width: 40' - 0"
Depth: 52' - 0"
Foundation: Crawlspace

EPLANS.COM

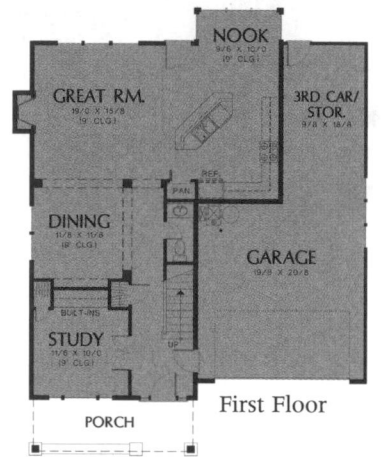

First Floor

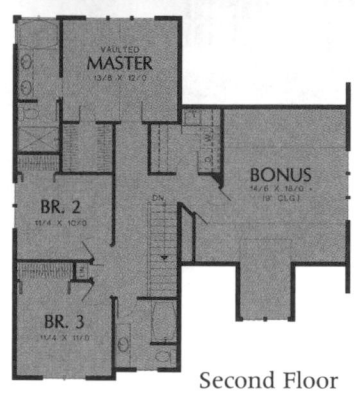

Second Floor

HPK2100346

Style: Country
First Floor: 1,113 sq. ft.
Second Floor: 835 sq. ft.
Total: 1,948 sq. ft.
Bedrooms: 3
Bathrooms: 2 ½
Width: 54' - 0"
Depth: 34' - 8"
Foundation: Unfinished Basement

EPLANS.COM

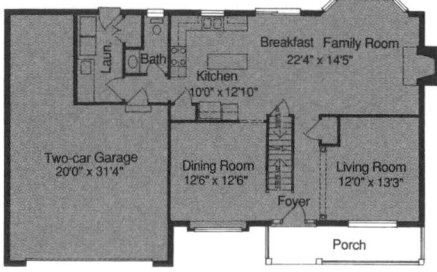

First Floor

Second Floor

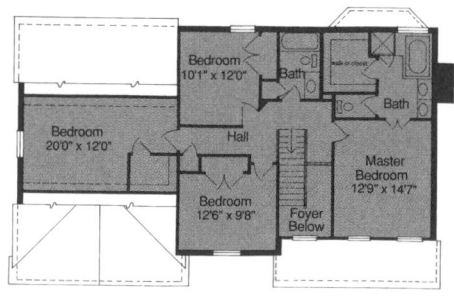

Optional Layout

HPK2100347

Style: Craftsman

First Floor: 1,301 sq. ft.

Second Floor: 652 sq. ft.

Total: 1,953 sq. ft.

Bonus Space: 342 sq. ft.

Bedrooms: 3

Bathrooms: 2 ½

Width: 58' - 0"

Depth: 55' - 0"

Foundation: Unfinished Basement

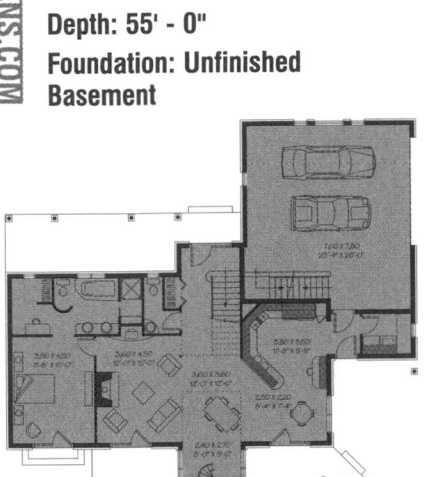

First Floor

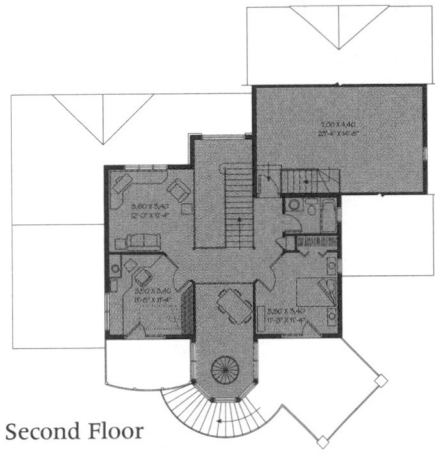

Second Floor

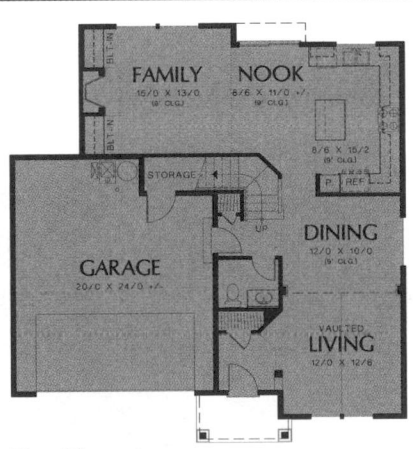

First Floor

HPK2100348

Style: Craftsman

First Floor: 970 sq. ft.

Second Floor: 988 sq. ft.

Total: 1,958 sq. ft.

Bedrooms: 3

Bathrooms: 2 ½

Width: 40' - 0"

Depth: 43' - 0"

Foundation: Crawlspace

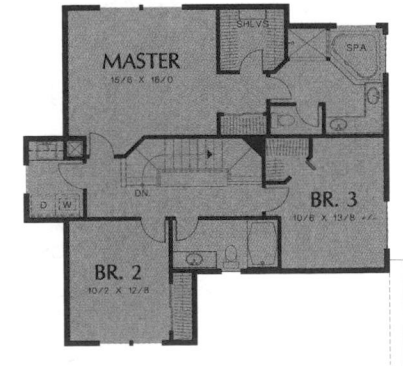

Second Floor

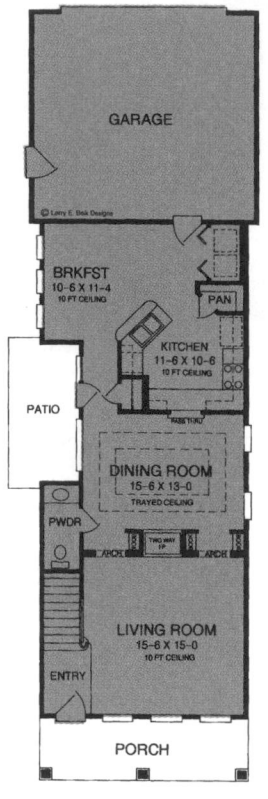

First Floor

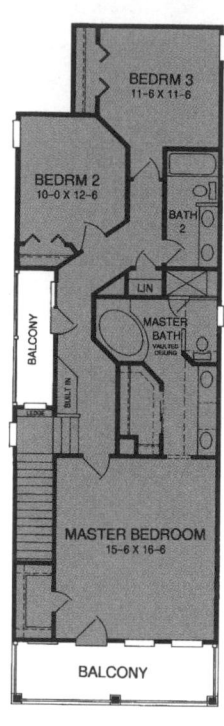

Second Floor

Reminiscent of the popular townhouses of the past, this fine clapboard home is perfect for urban or riverfront living. Two balconies grace the second floor—one at the front and one on the side. A two-way fireplace between the formal living and dining rooms provides visual impact. Built-in bookcases flank an arched opening between these rooms. A pass-through from the kitchen to the dining room simplifies serving, and a walk-in pantry provides storage.

HPK2100349

Style: Neoclassical
First Floor: 904 sq. ft.
Second Floor: 1,058 sq. ft.
Total: 1,962 sq. ft.
Bedrooms: 3
Bathrooms: 2 ½
Width: 22' - 0"
Depth: 74' - 0"
Foundation: Crawlspace, Slab

EPLANS.COM

© Larry E. Belk Designs

© 2000 Donald A. Gardner, Inc.

This sophisticated country home is economical and cozy, yet it has all the amenities of a larger plan. From the wraparound porch to the vaulted great room, this floor plan provides space for family togetherness as well as personal privacy. The secluded master suite contains two spacious walk-in closets, double lavatories, and a garden tub.

HPK2100350

Style: Farmhouse
First Floor: 1,437 sq. ft.
Second Floor: 531 sq. ft.
Total: 1,968 sq. ft.
Bedrooms: 3
Bathrooms: 2 ½
Width: 51' - 4"
Depth: 41' - 6"

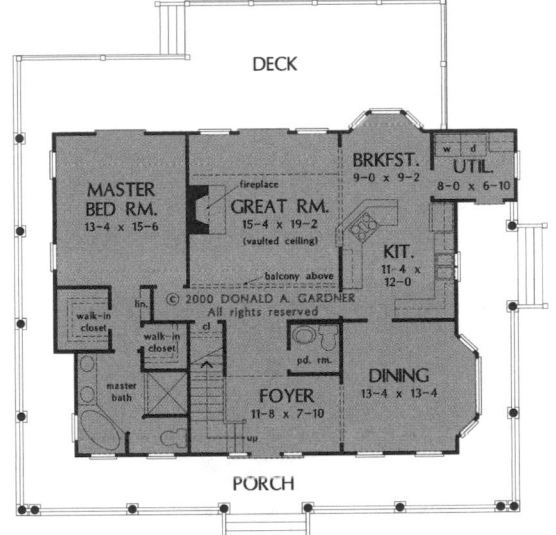

First Floor

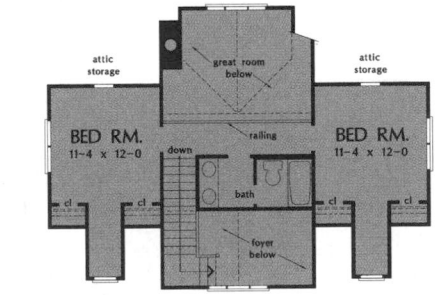

Second Floor

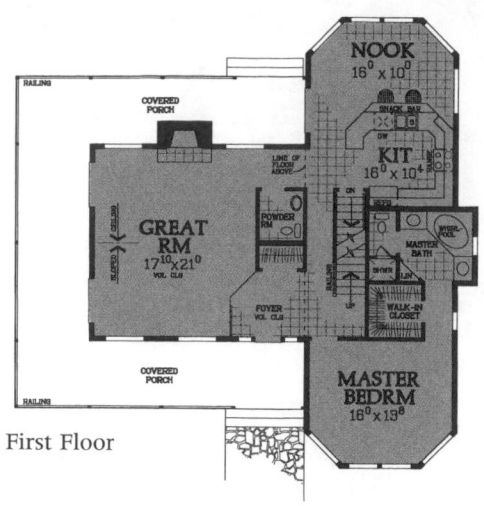

First Floor

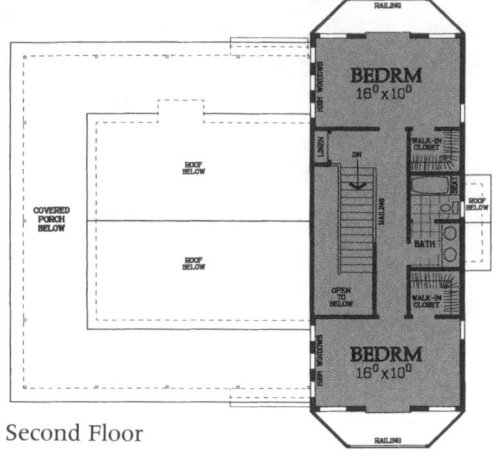

Second Floor

HPK2100351

Style: Farmhouse
First Floor: 1,374 sq. ft.
Second Floor: 600 sq. ft.
Total: 1,974 sq. ft.
Bedrooms: 3
Bathrooms: 2 ½
Width: 51' - 8"
Depth: 50' - 8"
Foundation: Unfinished Basement

EPLANS.COM

Balustrades and brackets, dual balconies, and a wraparound porch create a country-style exterior meant for soft summer evenings. An aura of hospitality pervades the well-planned interior, starting with a tiled foyer that opens to an expansive two-story great room filled with light. The sunny, bayed nook invites casual dining and shares its natural light with a snack counter and a well-appointed U-shaped kitchen. A spacious master suite offers a sumptuous bath with corner whirlpool, dual lavatories, and a walk-in closet.

HPK2100352

Style: Cottage

First Floor: 1,448 sq. ft.

Second Floor: 527 sq. ft.

Total: 1,975 sq. ft.

Bonus Space: 368 sq. ft.

Bedrooms: 3

Bathrooms: 2 ½

Width: 46' - 0"

Depth: 62' - 0"

Foundation: Crawlspace, Slab, Unfinished Walkout Basement

On the outside, the facade incorporates stone, siding, and dormers to create a traditional facade with an attractive courtyard entry. Inside, fantastic open floor plan unites all of the family living areas in one unrestricted space. Personal interaction will be at a maximum level whether entertaining a large group or just going about household chores.

EPLANS.COM

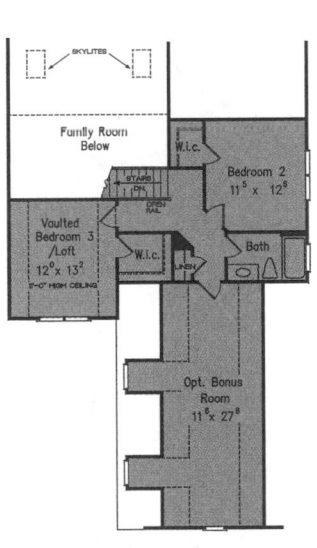

Second Floor

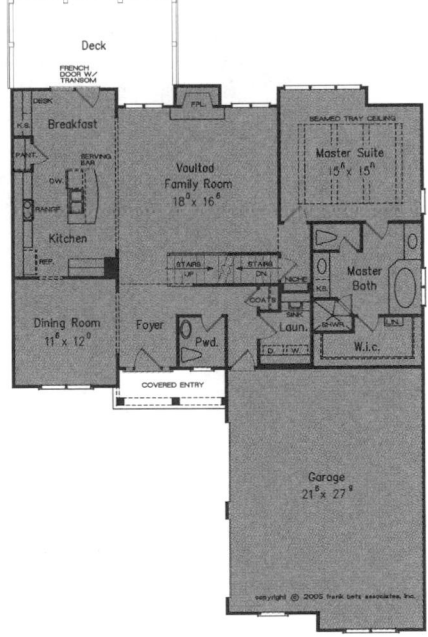

First Floor

HPK2100353

Style: Mediterranean
First Floor: 1,383 sq. ft.
Second Floor: 595 sq. ft.
Total: 1,978 sq. ft.
Bonus Space: 617 sq. ft.
Bedrooms: 3
Bathrooms: 2
Width: 48' - 0"
Depth: 42' - 0"
Foundation: Island Basement

EPLANS.COM

The mixture of grand details with a comfortable layout makes this home a perfect combination of elegance and easy living. Those who prefer a spacious master suite set apart from the rest of the home will love this arrangement. The top story is devoted to a master suite with double doors leading to a private porch and a loft that overlooks the vaulted great room below. On the first floor, each of the two family bedrooms has an adjoining porch. The built-ins and fireplace in the great room give a feeling of casual sophistication.

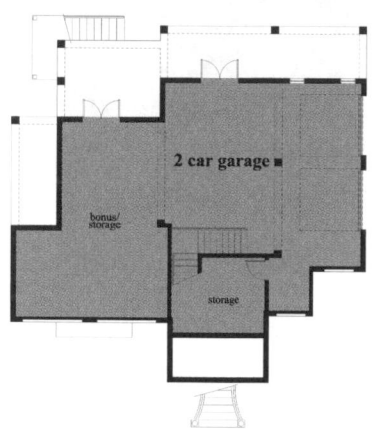

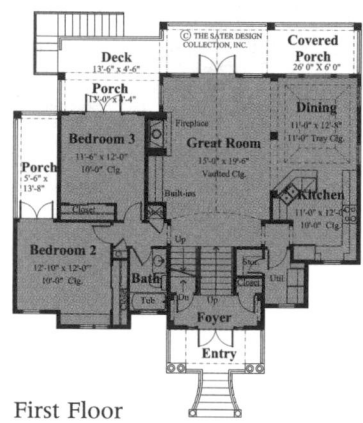

First Floor

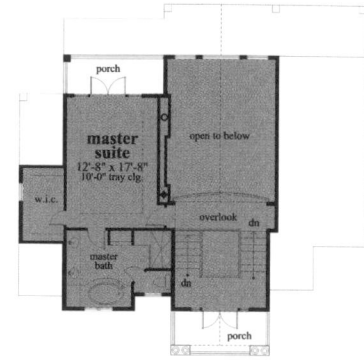

Second Floor

© The Sater Design Collection, Inc.

ORDER BLUEPRINTS ANYTIME AT EPLANS.COM OR 1-800-521-6797

© Sater Design Collection, Inc.

HPK2100354

Style: New American

First Floor: 1,383 sq. ft.

Second Floor: 595 sq. ft.

Total: 1,978 sq. ft.

Bedrooms: 3

Bathrooms: 2

Width: 48' - 0"

Depth: 48' - 8"

Foundation: Unfinished Walkout Basement

EPLANS.COM

The stone facade and woodwork detail give this home a Craftsman appeal. The great room features a fireplace flanked by built-ins and French-door access to the rear covered porch. The open dining room with a tray ceiling offers convenience to the spacious kitchen. Two family bedrooms share a bath and enjoy private porches. The second level is devoted to the master suite with a spacious walk-in closet, private porch, and a private bath.

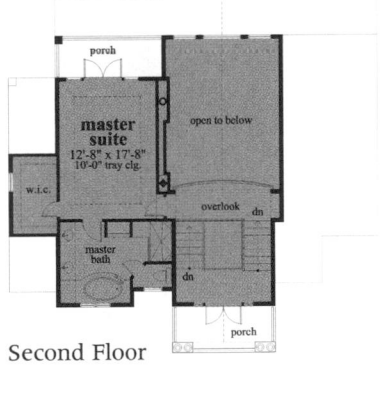
Second Floor

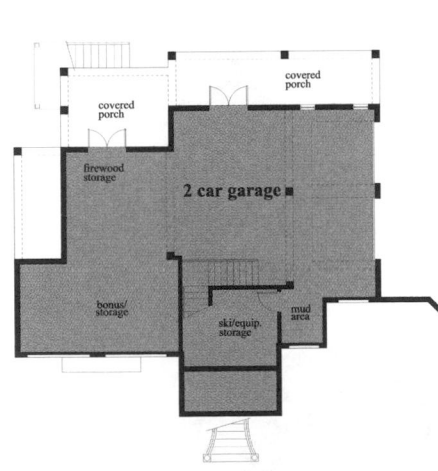

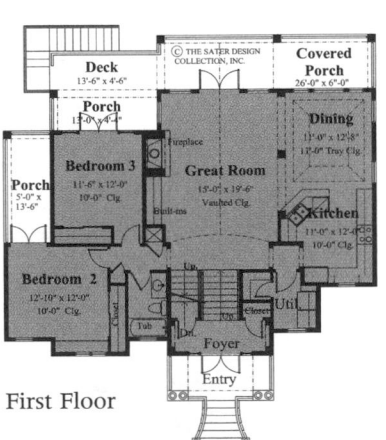
First Floor

First Floor

Second Floor

HPK2100355

Style: Cottage
First Floor: 1,383 sq. ft.
Second Floor: 595 sq. ft.
Total: 1,978 sq. ft.
Bonus Space: 617 sq. ft.
Bedrooms: 3
Bathrooms: 2
Width: 48' - 0"
Depth: 42' - 0"
Foundation: Island Basement

EPLANS.COM

This fabulous Key West cottage blends interior space with the great outdoors, boasting access from every area of the home to expansive porches and decks. A sun-dappled foyer leads via a mid-level staircase to the great room. Highlighted by a wall of glass that opens to the rear porch, this two-story living space opens to the dining room and kitchen. Upstairs, a 10-foot tray ceiling highlights a private master suite, which provides French doors to an upper-level porch.

ORDER BLUEPRINTS ANYTIME AT EPLANS.COM OR 1-800-521-6797

HPK2100356

Style: Cottage

First Floor: 803 sq. ft.

Second Floor: 1,182 sq. ft.

Total: 1,985 sq. ft.

Bedrooms: 4

Bathrooms: 2 ½

Width: 36' - 0"

Depth: 43' - 4"

Foundation: Crawlspace, Slab, Unfinished Walkout Basement

EPLANS.COM

This narrow-lot home would be perfect nestled into an in-fill lot or standing prominently in a new development. Subtle angles direct traffic into the family room, where a warming fireplace awaits. An efficient kitchen opens to both the sunny breakfast nook and formal dining room, catering to any occasion. Upstairs, four bedrooms include a vaulted master suite with a lavish bath.

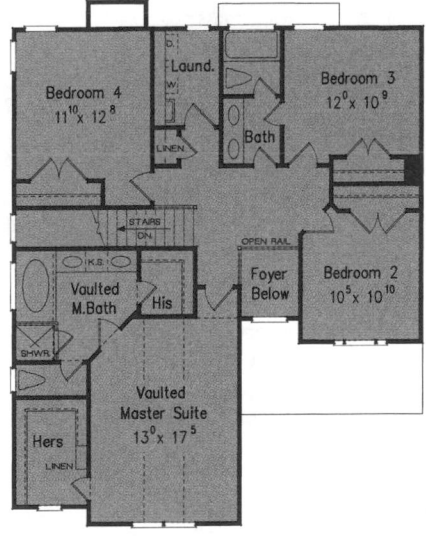

Second Floor

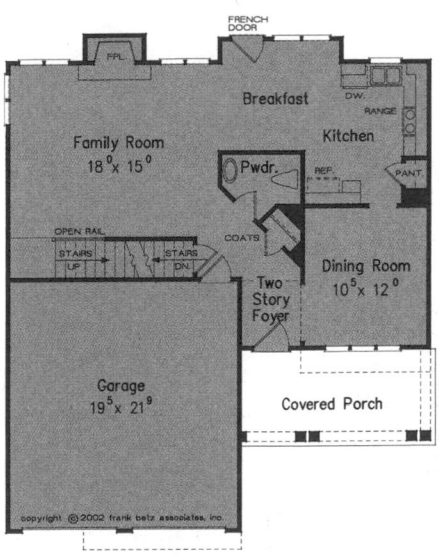

First Floor

1,500 TO 1,999 SQUARE FEET

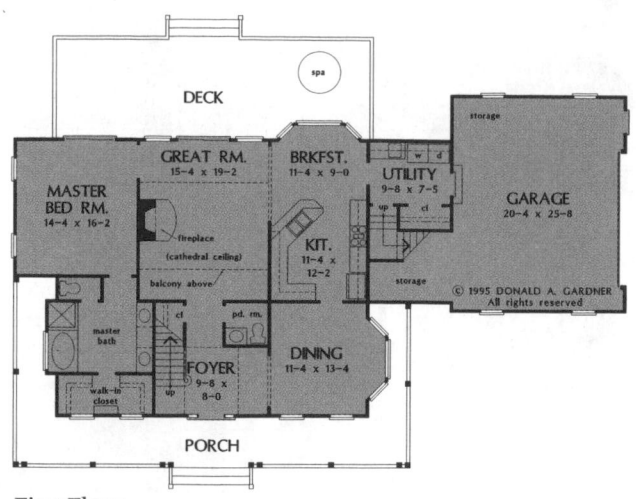

First Floor

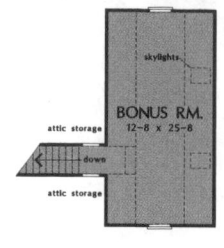

Second Floor

This farmhouse has plenty to offer, from its covered front porch to its rear deck with a spa. Inside, the amenities continue, with a bayed formal dining room, a great room, and a bayed breakfast nook. A nearby kitchen is spacious and shares a snack bar with the breakfast/great room area. A deluxe master bedroom pampers with access to the rear deck and a luxurious bath comprising a whirlpool tub, a separate shower, twin vanities, and a walk-in loset. Upstairs, two family bedrooms share a full hall bath and a balcony overlooking the great room.

HPK2100357

Style: Farmhouse
First Floor: 1,480 sq. ft.
Second Floor: 511 sq. ft.
Total: 1,991 sq. ft.
Bonus Space: 363 sq. ft.
Bedrooms: 3
Bathrooms: 2 ½
Width: 73' - 0"
Depth: 51' - 10"

EPLANS.COM

© 1995 Donald A. Gardner Architects, Inc.

© Larry E. Belk Designs

HPK2100358

Style: Country

Square Footage: 1,993

Bonus Space: 307 sq. ft.

Bedrooms: 3

Bathrooms: 2

Width: 66' - 10"

Depth: 71' - 5"

Foundation: Crawlspace, Slab

A gabled roof tops the welcoming front porch of this country charmer. Inside, a formal dining room opens through decorative columns off the foyer. The nearby living room offers a warming fireplace and access to the rear covered porch. Angled counters in the kitchen contribute to easy food preparation. The master suite opens through double doors from a private vestibule and offers a relaxing retreat for the homeowner. On the other side of the plan, two family bedrooms share a full hall bath.

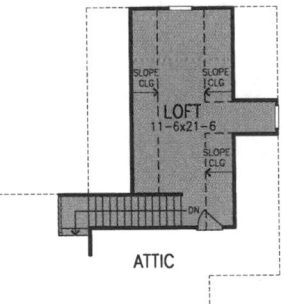

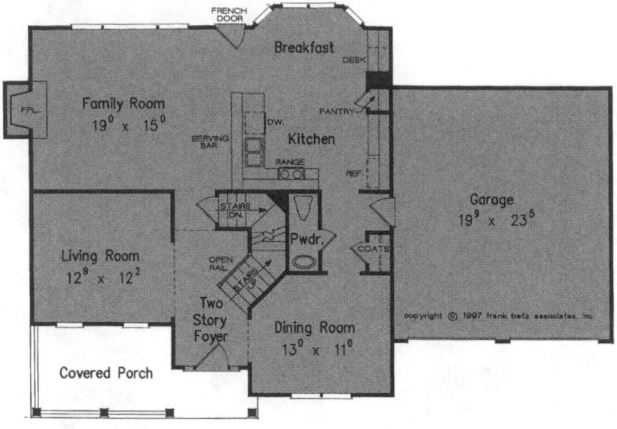

First Floor

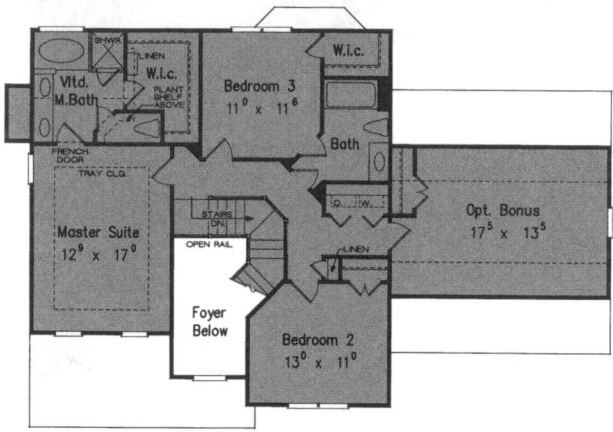

Second Floor

Move-up buyers can enjoy all the luxuries of this two-story home, highlighted by an angled staircase separating the dining room from casual living areas. A bay window and built-in desk in the breakfast area are just a few of the plan's amenities. The sleeping zone occupies the second floor—away from everyday activities—and includes a master suite and two secondary bedrooms.

HPK2100359

Style: Country

First Floor: 1,071 sq. ft.

Second Floor: 924 sq. ft.

Total: 1,995 sq. ft.

Bonus Space: 280 sq. ft.

Bedrooms: 3

Bathrooms: 2 ½

Width: 55' - 10"

Depth: 38' - 6"

Foundation: Crawlspace, Slab, Unfinished Walkout Basement

EPLANS.COM

HPK2100360

Style: Tudor

First Floor: 999 sq. ft.

Second Floor: 997 sq. ft.

Total: 1,996 sq. ft.

Bedrooms: 3

Bathrooms: 2 ½

Width: 60' - 0"

Depth: 28' - 10"

Foundation: Unfinished Basement

EPLANS.COM

The exterior of this English Tudor-style home reflects the craftsmanship that lifts this design above others. Flanking the foyer is a spacious family room and a comfortable living room with a fireplace. Two family bedrooms with a shared bath and a master suite are located on the second floor. A walk-in closet, a built-in vanity, a private bath, and an adjoining nursery/study complete the master suite.

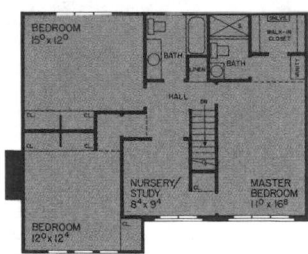

Second Floor

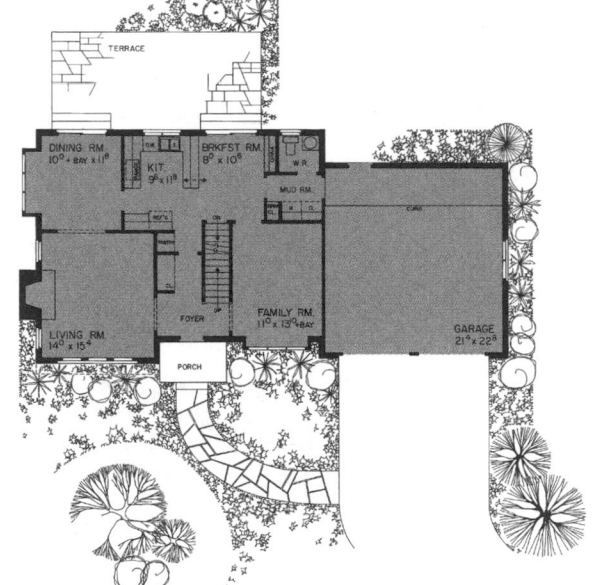

First Floor

1,500 TO 1,999 SQUARE FEET

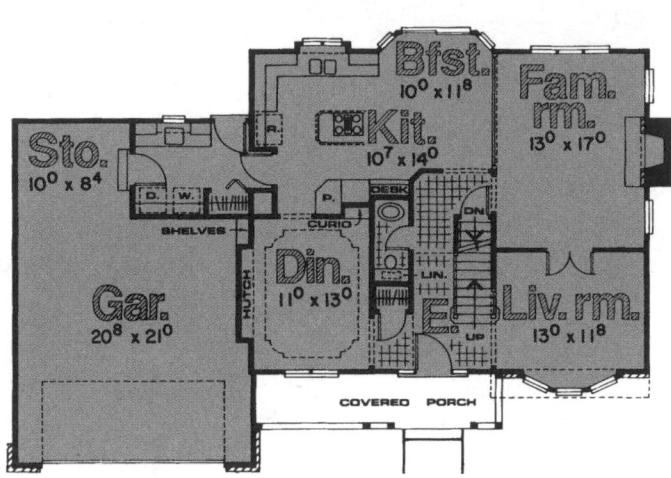

First Floor

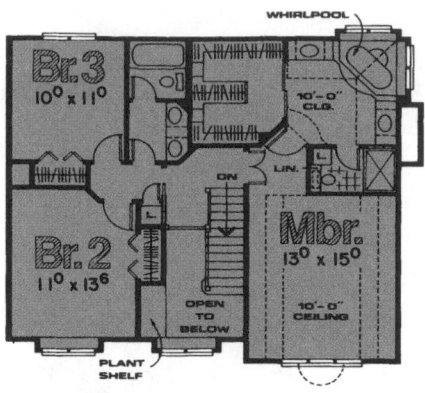

Second Floor

HPK2100361

This homes distinctive design personality is complemented by a large covered porch with a wood railing. The living room is distinguished by the warmth of a bay window and French doors leading to the family room. An island cooktop will save you steps in the well-appointed kitchen. The master suite on the second floor delights with special ceiling treatment and a spacious bath. Two family bedrooms share a full hall bath on this level.

Style: Country
First Floor: 1,093 sq. ft.
Second Floor: 905 sq. ft.
Total: 1,998 sq. ft.
Bedrooms: 3
Bathrooms: 2 ½
Width: 55' - 4"
Depth: 37' - 8"

EPLANS.COM

HPK2100362

Style: Neoclassical
First Floor: 1,078 sq. ft.
Second Floor: 921 sq. ft.
Total: 1,999 sq. ft.
Bedrooms: 3
Bathrooms: 3
Width: 24' - 11"
Depth: 73' - 10"
Foundation: Crawlspace

EPLANS.COM

This charming home is loaded with character and is perfect for a narrow lot. The kitchen includes a window view and a bayed breakfast area with access to the rear porch. Upstairs, the master suite features a vaulted ceiling and a bath with dual vanities and a whirlpool tub. A secondary bedroom and a full bath are also located on the second floor with a large rear balcony.

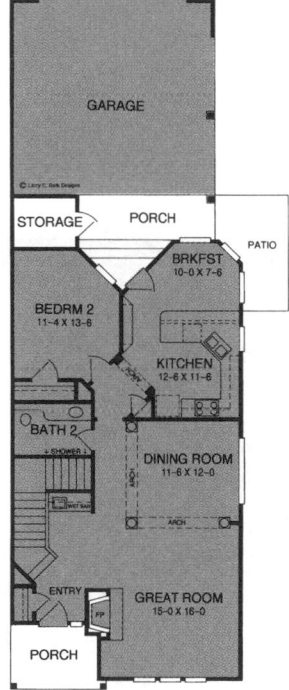

First Floor

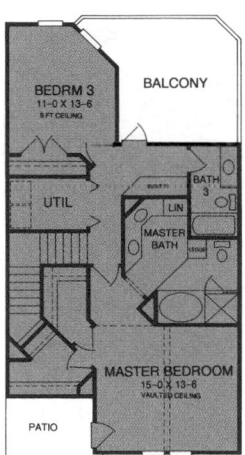

Second Floor

This lovely brick-and-siding home will be a welcome addition to any neighborhood. The illusion of two stories elevates this traditional home, with the garage and unfinished basement/storage area below and a well-planned layout above. A vaulted family room invites family and friends to delight in an extended-hearth fireplace. On the far right, the master suite is secluded for privacy, with a pampering vaulted bath and plenty of natural light.

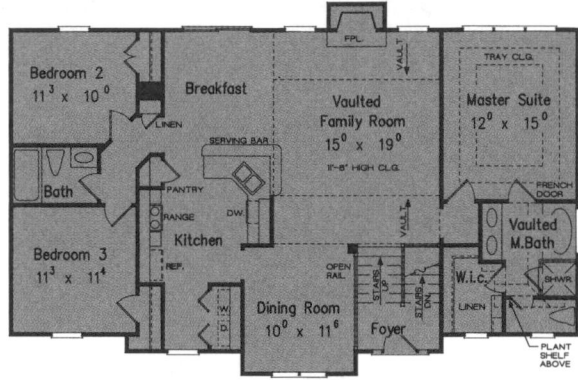

Lower Level

HPK2100363

Style: Colonial Revival

Main Level: 1,480 sq. ft.

Lower Level: 36 sq. ft.

Total: 1,516 sq. ft.

Bedrooms: 3

Bathrooms: 2

Width: 51' - 6"

Depth: 31' - 0"

Foundation: Unfinished Walkout Basement

EPLANS.COM

Main Level

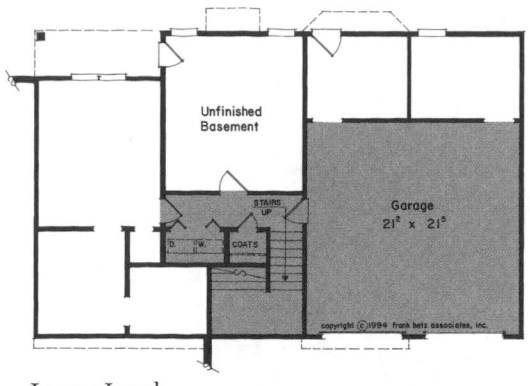

Lower Level

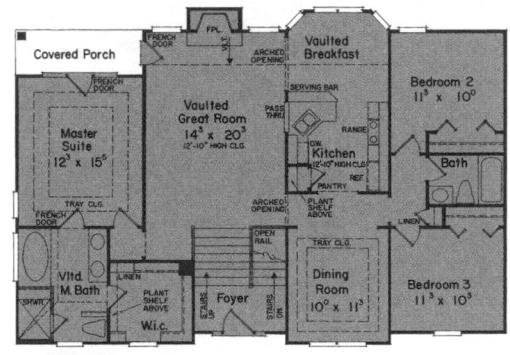

Main Level

HPK2100364

Style: New American

Main Level: 1,509 sq. ft.

Lower Level: 100 sq. ft.

Total: 1,609 sq. ft.

Bedrooms: 3

Bathrooms: 2

Width: 49' - 0"

Depth: 34' - 4"

Foundation: Unfinished Walkout Basement

EPLANS.COM

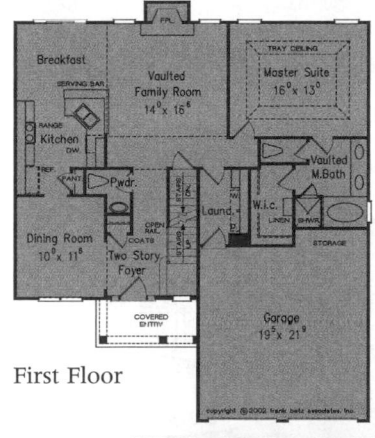

First Floor

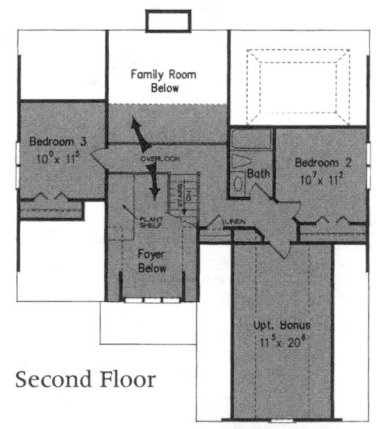

Second Floor

HPK2100365

Style: Cottage

First Floor: 1,177 sq. ft.

Second Floor: 457 sq. ft.

Total: 1,634 sq. ft.

Bonus Space: 249 sq. ft.

Bedrooms: 3

Bathrooms: 2 ½

Width: 41' - 0"

Depth: 48' - 4"

Foundation: Crawlspace, Unfinished Walkout Basement

EPLANS.COM

HPK2100366

Style: New American

Square Footage: 1,684

Bedrooms: 3

Bathrooms: 2 ½

Width: 55' - 6"

Depth: 57' - 6"

Foundation: Walkout Basement

EPLANS.COM

© Stephen Fuller, Inc.

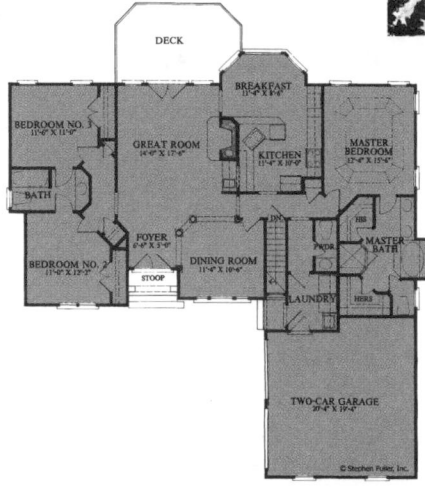

© Stephen Fuller, Inc.

HPK2100367

Style: Split Level

Main Level: 745 sq. ft.

Upper Level: 544 sq. ft.

Lower Level: 443 sq. ft.

Total: 1,732 sq. ft.

Bedrooms: 3

Bathrooms: 2 ½

Width: 43' - 0"

Depth: 40' - 0"

Foundation: Finished Basement

EPLANS.COM

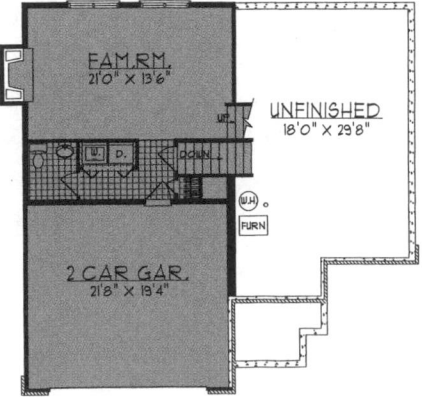

Lower Level

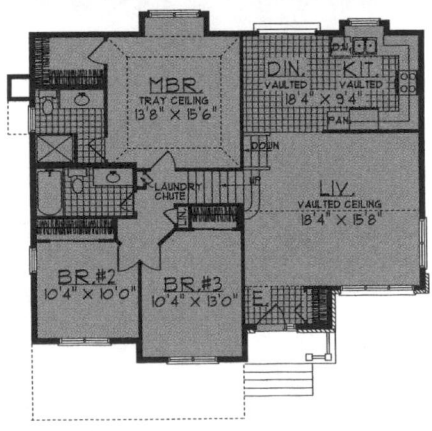

Main/Upper Level

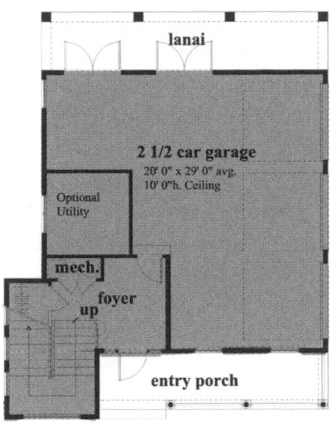

lanai

2 1/2 car garage
20' 0" x 29' 0" avg.
10' 0"h. Ceiling

Optional Utility

mech.

foyer up

entry porch

Lower Level

©Sater Design Collection, Inc.

HPK2100368

Style: Italianate

Main Level: 874 sq. ft.

Upper Level: 880 sq. ft.

Lower Level: 242 sq. ft.

Total: 1,754 sq. ft.

Bedrooms: 3

Bathrooms: 2 ½

Width: 34' - 0"

Depth: 43' - 0"

Foundation: Island Basement

EPLANS.COM

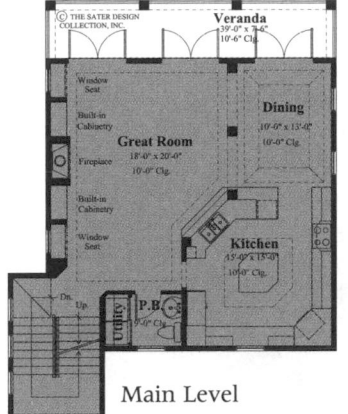

THE SATER DESIGN COLLECTION, INC.

Veranda
39'-0" x 9'-6"
10'-6" Clg.

Window Seat

Built-in Cabinetry

Great Room
18'-0" x 20'-0"
10'-6" Clg.

Fireplace

Built-in Cabinetry

Window Seat

Dining
10'-6" x 13'-0"
10'-0" Clg.

Kitchen
15'-0" x 13'-0"
10'-0" Clg.

Dn. Up

Utility

P.B.

Main Level

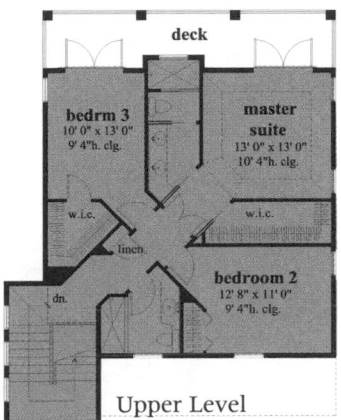

deck

bedrm 3
10' 0" x 13' 0"
9' 4"h. clg.

master suite
13' 0" x 13' 0"
10' 4"h. clg.

w.i.c.

w.i.c.

linen

bedroom 2
12' 8" x 11' 0"
9' 4"h. clg.

dn.

Upper Level

HPK2100369

Style: New American

First Floor: 1,382 sq. ft.

Second Floor: 436 sq. ft.

Total: 1,818 sq. ft.

Bonus Space: 298 sq. ft.

Bedrooms: 3

Bathrooms: 2 ½

Width: 52' - 4"

Depth: 45' - 10"

Foundation: Crawlspace, Slab, Unfinished Walkout Basement

EPLANS.COM

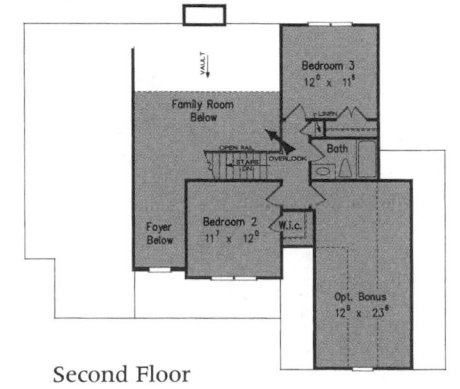

Master Suite
13⁹ x 16⁰

Vaulted Family Room
18⁴ x 15⁸

Breakfast

Kitchen

Laund.

Two Story Foyer

Dining Room
11' x 12⁶

Garage
20⁰ x 21⁶

W.I.C.

Covered Porch

RADIUS WINDOW

Mstd M.Bath

First Floor

VAULT

Bedroom 3
12⁴ x 11⁸

Family Room Below

Bath

Foyer Below

Bedroom 2
11⁷ x 12⁸

W.I.C.

Opt. Bonus
12⁸ x 23⁸

Second Floor

HPK2100370

Style: Farmhouse

Square Footage: 1,822

Bedrooms: 3

Bathrooms: 2

Width: 58' - 0"

Depth: 67' - 2"

Foundation: Unfinished Basement

EPLANS.COM

© The Sater Design Collection, Inc.

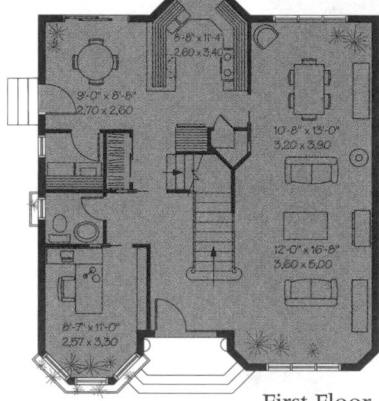

First Floor

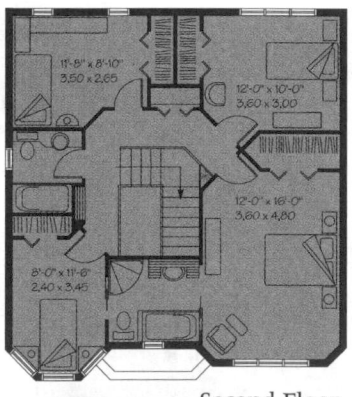

Second Floor

HPK2100371

Style: Victorian Eclectic

First Floor: 923 sq. ft.

Second Floor: 900 sq. ft.

Total: 1,823 sq. ft.

Bedrooms: 4

Bathrooms: 2 ½

Width: 30' - 0"

Depth: 34' - 2"

Foundation: Unfinished Basement

EPLANS.COM

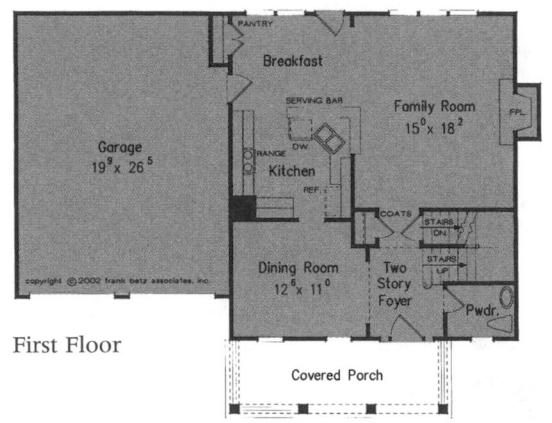

First Floor

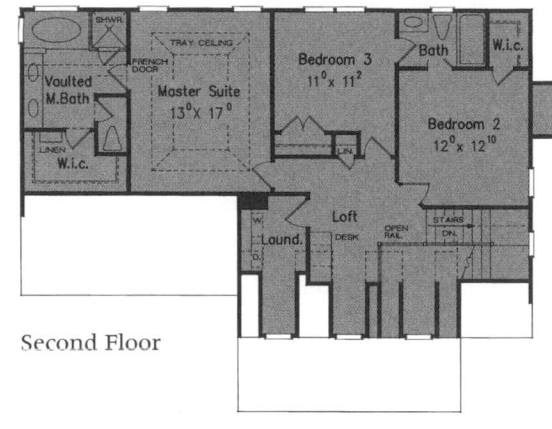

Second Floor

HPK2100372

Style: Greek Revival

First Floor: 846 sq. ft.

Second Floor: 998 sq. ft.

Total: 1,844 sq. ft.

Bedrooms: 3

Bathrooms: 2 ½

Width: 49' - 4"

Depth: 38' - 0"

Foundation: Crawlspace, Unfinished Walkout Basement

EPLANS.COM

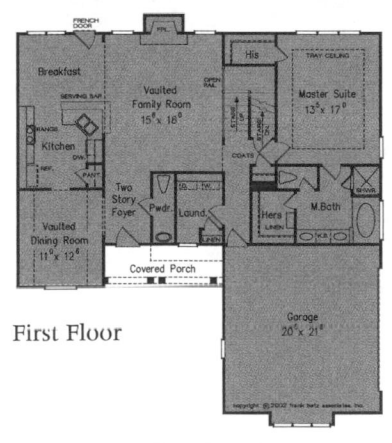

First Floor

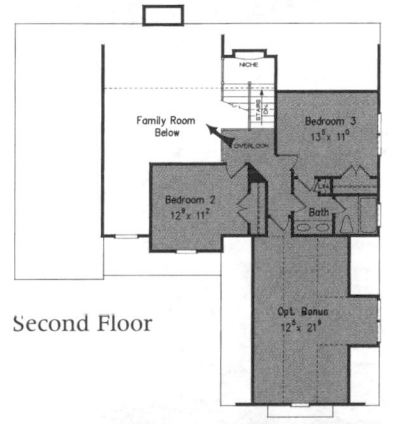

Second Floor

HPK2100373

Style: French Country

First Floor: 1,407 sq. ft.

Second Floor: 472 sq. ft.

Total: 1,879 sq. ft.

Bonus Space: 321 sq. ft.

Bedrooms: 3

Bathrooms: 2 ½

Width: 48' - 0"

Depth: 53' - 10"

Foundation: Crawlspace, Unfinished Walkout Basement

EPLANS.COM

HPK2100374

Style: Cottage
Main Level: 1,342 sq. ft.
Upper Level: 511 sq. ft.
Lower Level: 33 sq. ft.
Total: 1,886 sq. ft.
Bedrooms: 3
Bathrooms: 2 ½
Width: 44' - 0"
Depth: 40' - 0"
Foundation: Island Basement

EPLANS.COM

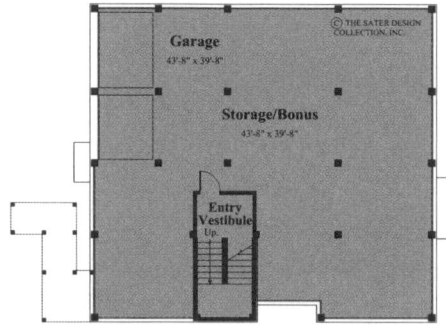

Lower Level

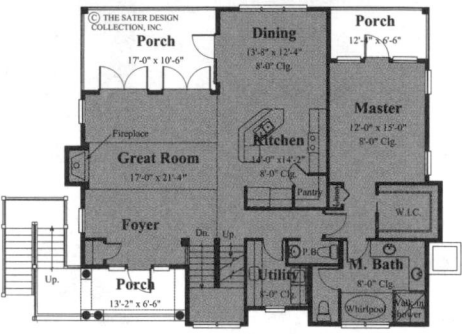

Main Level

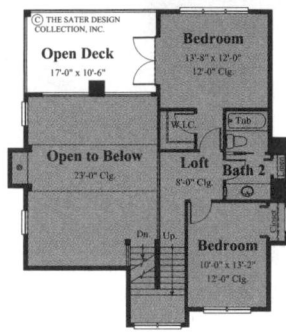

Upper Level

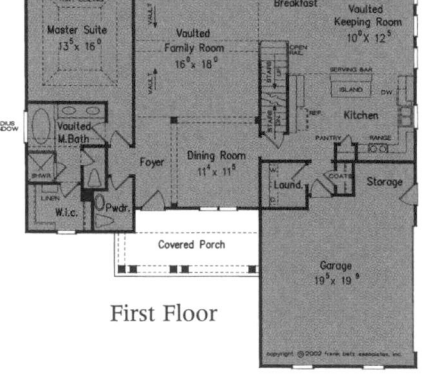

First Floor

HPK2100375

Style: Country
First Floor: 1,506 sq. ft.
Second Floor: 426 sq. ft.
Total: 1,932 sq. ft.
Bedrooms: 3
Bathrooms: 2 ½
Width: 50' - 0"
Depth: 52' - 6"
Foundation: Crawlspace, Unfinished Walkout Basement

EPLANS.COM

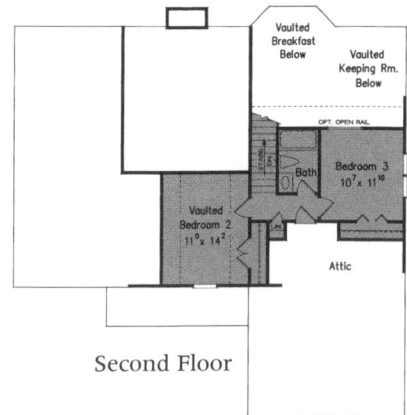

Second Floor

HPK2100376

Style: Greek Revival
Square Footage: 1,933
Bonus Space: 519 sq. ft.
Bedrooms: 3
Bathrooms: 2 ½
Width: 62' - 0"
Depth: 50' - 0"
Foundation: Crawlspace, Unfinished Walkout Basement

EPLANS.COM

Traditional in every sense of the word, you can't go wrong with this charming country cottage. A sunny bayed breakfast nook flows into the angled kitchen for easy casual meals. Down the hall, two bedrooms share a full bath, tucked behind the two-car garage to protect the bedrooms from street noise. The master suite is indulgent, pampering home-owners with a bayed sitting area, tray ceiling, vaulted spa bath, and an oversize walk-in closet. A fourth bedroom and bonus space are available to grow as your family does.

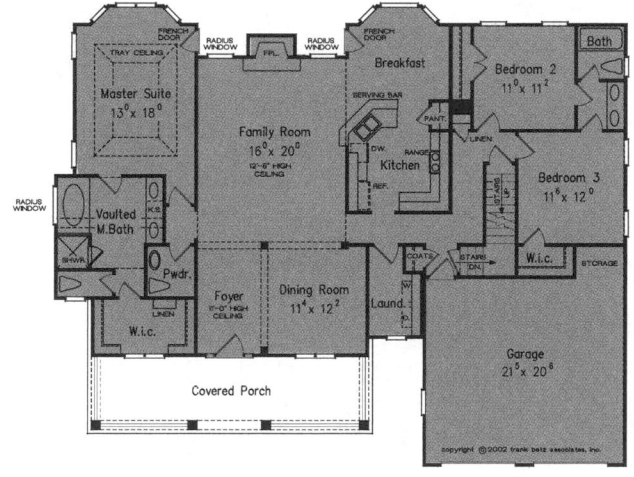

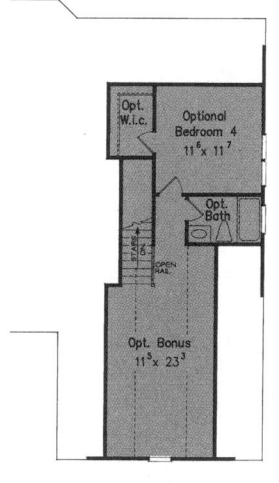

First Floor

Second Floor

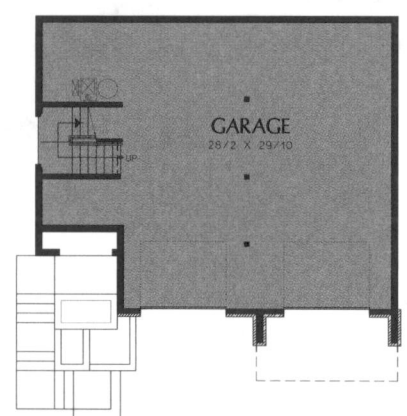

HPK2100377

Style: Craftsman

First Floor: 1,106 sq. ft.

Second Floor: 872 sq. ft.

Total: 1,978 sq. ft.

Bedrooms: 3

Bathrooms: 2 ½

Width: 38' - 0"

Depth: 35' - 0"

Foundation: Slab, Unfinished Basement

EPLANS.COM

Craftsman style is evident both on the outside and the inside of this three-bedroom home. From the foyer, the two-story living room is just a couple of steps up and features a two-way fireplace. The U-shaped kitchen has a cooktop work island, an adjacent nook, and easy access to the formal dining room. A spacious family room shares the fireplace with the living room. A two-car, basement garage has plenty of room for storage.

This petite country cottage design is enhanced with all the modern amenities. Inside, through a pair of double doors, the family den is illuminated by a large window. The vaulted master bedroom includes a private full bath and a walk-in closet. Downstairs, two additional family bedrooms share a hall bath.

HPK2100378

Style: Cottage

Main Level: 1,230 sq. ft.

Lower Level: 769 sq. ft.

Total: 1,999 sq. ft.

Bedrooms: 3

Bathrooms: 2 ½

Width: 40' - 0"

Depth: 52' - 6"

Foundation: Finished Walkout Basement

EPLANS.COM

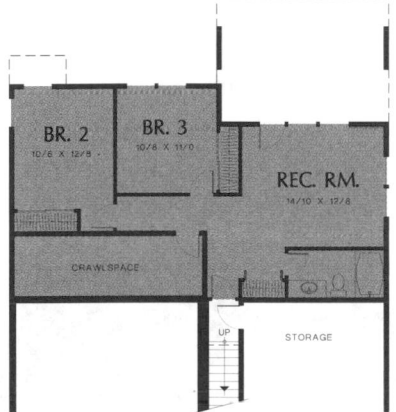

Lower Level

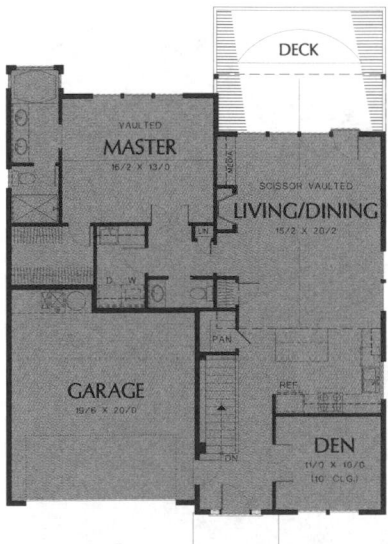

Main Level

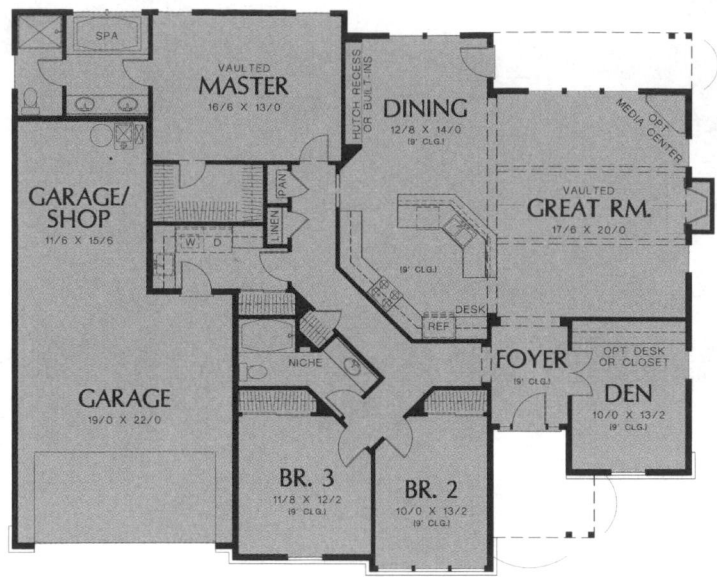

HPK2100379

This lovely design combines fresh country style with old-fashioned values. From the arched entry, the foyer leads to a sprawling great room with vaulted ceilings, a fireplace, and an optional media center. Looking out over the rear property, the master suite includes a vaulted ceiling, pampering spa bath, and abundant closet space. Two bedrooms at the front of the home share an angled bath; a nearby den may also be used as a fourth bedroom.

Style: Cottage
Square Footage: 2,001
Bedrooms: 3
Bathrooms: 2
Width: 60' - 0"
Depth: 50' - 0"
Foundation: Crawlspace

EPLANS.COM

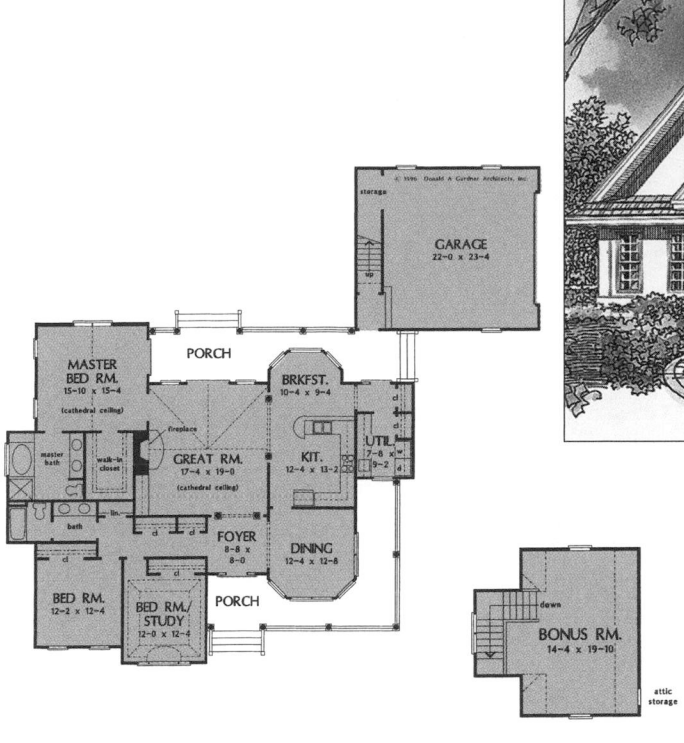

© 1996 Donald A. Gardner Architects, Inc.

HPK2100380

Style: Country
Square Footage: 2,006
Bonus Space: 329 sq. ft.
Bedrooms: 3
Bathrooms: 2
Width: 76' - 10"
Depth: 72' - 2"

EPLANS.COM

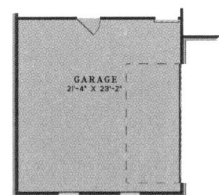

HPK2100381

Style: European
Square Footage: 2,014
Bedrooms: 3
Bathrooms: 2
Width: 59' - 0"
Depth: 62' - 10"
Foundation: Crawlspace, Slab

EPLANS.COM

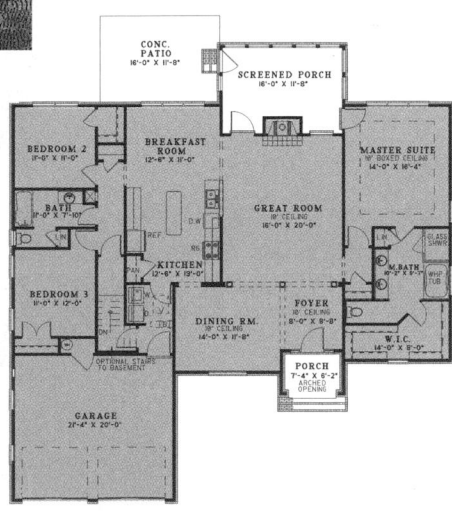

2,000 TO 2,499 SQUARE FEET

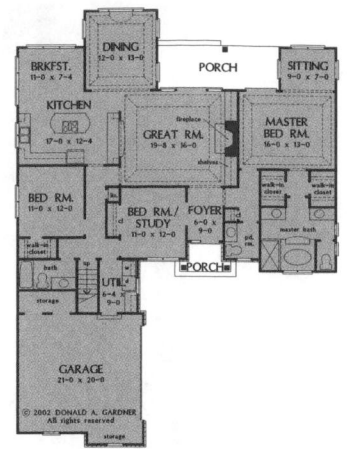

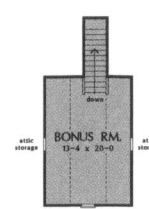

© 2002 Donald A. Gardner, Inc.

HPK2100382

Style: Cottage
Square Footage: 2,017
Bonus Space: 319 sq. ft.
Bedrooms: 3
Bathrooms: 2 ½
Width: 54' - 0"
Depth: 74' - 0"

HPK2100383

Style: Bungalow
Square Footage: 2,019
Bonus Space: 368 sq. ft.
Bedrooms: 3
Bathrooms: 2
Width: 56' - 0"
Depth: 56' - 3"
Foundation: Crawlspace

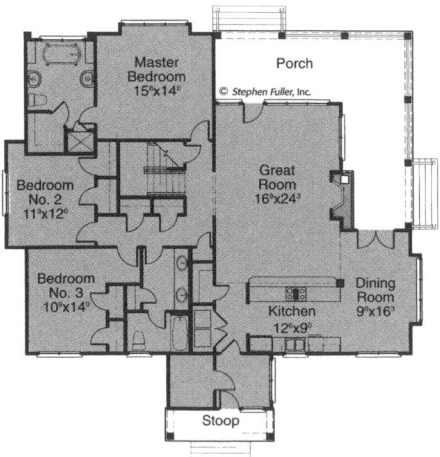

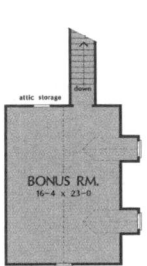

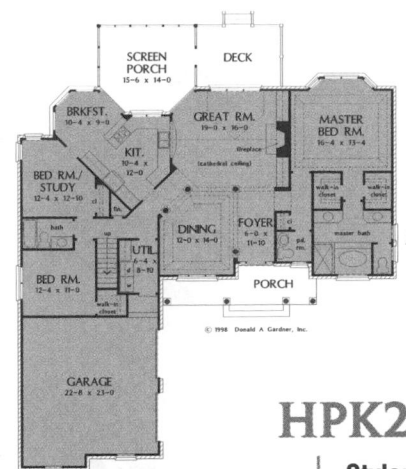

HPK2100384

Style: Country
Square Footage: 2,024
Bonus Space: 423 sq. ft.
Bedrooms: 3
Bathrooms: 2 ½
Width: 62' - 3"
Depth: 74' - 9"

EPLANS.COM

© 1998 Donald A. Gardner, Inc.

HPK2100385

Style: Country
Square Footage: 2,037
Bonus Space: 361 sq. ft.
Bedrooms: 3
Bathrooms: 2 ½
Width: 62' - 4"
Depth: 61' - 8"

EPLANS.COM

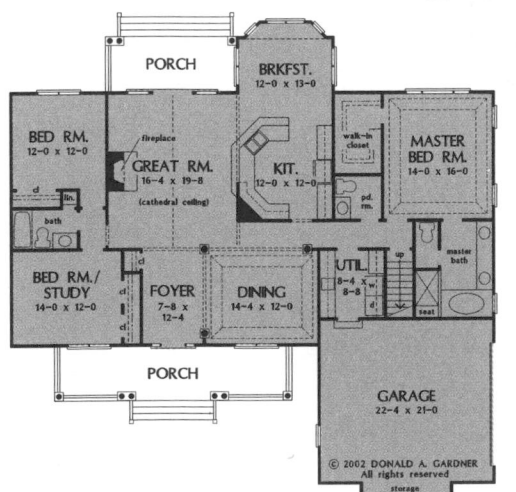

© 2002 Donald A. Gardner, Inc.

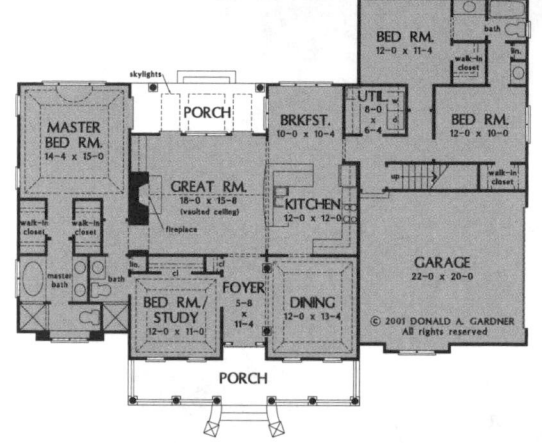

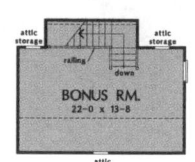

© 2001 Donald A. Gardner, Inc.

HPK2100386

Style: Country

Square Footage: 2,038

Bonus Space: 365 sq. ft.

Bedrooms: 4

Bathrooms: 3

Width: 68' - 0"

Depth: 54' - 4"

EPLANS.COM

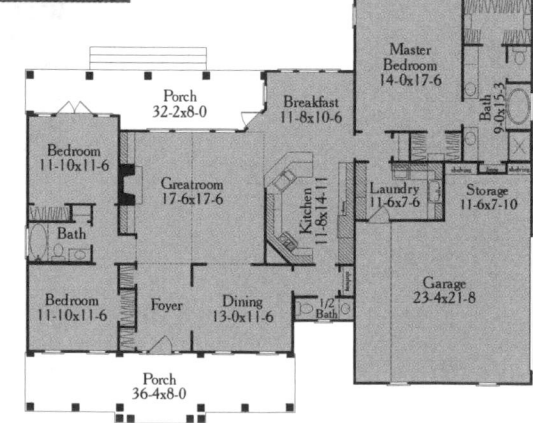

HPK2100387

Style: Federal - Adams

Square Footage: 2,046

Bedrooms: 3

Bathrooms: 2 ½

Width: 68' - 2"

Depth: 57' - 4"

Foundation: Crawlspace, Slab, Unfinished Basement

EPLANS.COM

HPK2100388

Style: Country

Square Footage: 2,050

Bonus Space: 418 sq. ft.

Bedrooms: 4

Bathrooms: 3

Width: 60' - 0"

Depth: 56' - 0"

Foundation: Crawlspace, Slab, Unfinished Walkout Basement

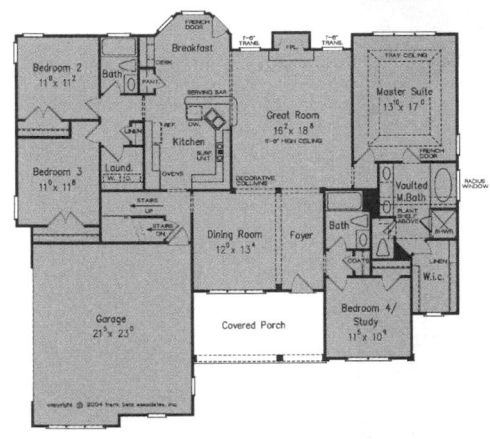

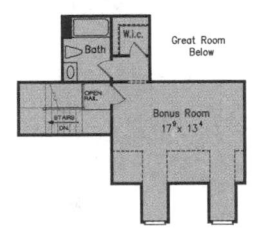

© 1997 Donald A. Gardner Architects, Inc.

HPK2100389

Style: Country

Square Footage: 2,057

Bonus Space: 444 sq. ft.

Bedrooms: 3

Bathrooms: 3

Width: 80' - 10"

Depth: 61' - 6"

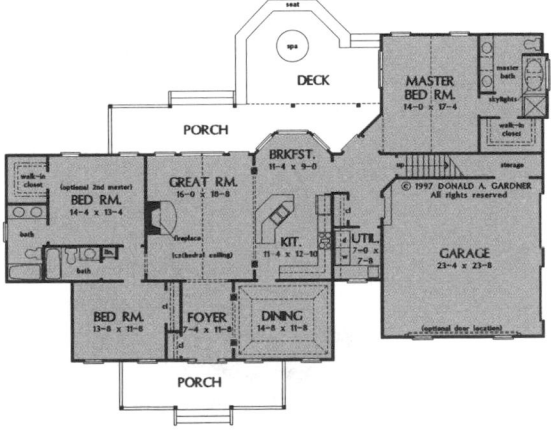

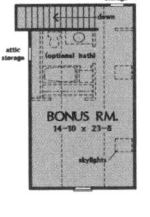

© 1997 DONALD A. GARDNER All rights reserved

2,000 TO 2,499 SQUARE FEET

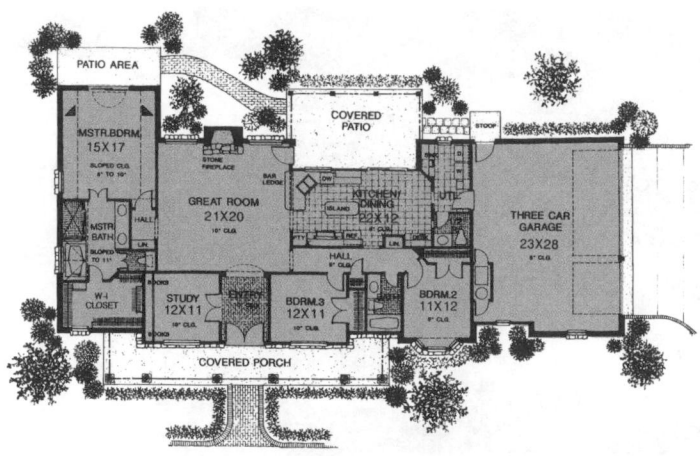

HPK2100390

Style: French Country
Square Footage: 2,061
Bedrooms: 3
Bathrooms: 2 ½
Width: 88' - 10"
Depth: 40' - 9"
Foundation: Crawlspace, Slab

EPLANS.COM

HPK2100391

Style: French Country
Square Footage: 2,065
Bedrooms: 4
Bathrooms: 2 ½
Width: 60' - 0"
Depth: 65' - 10"
Foundation: Crawlspace, Slab

EPLANS.COM

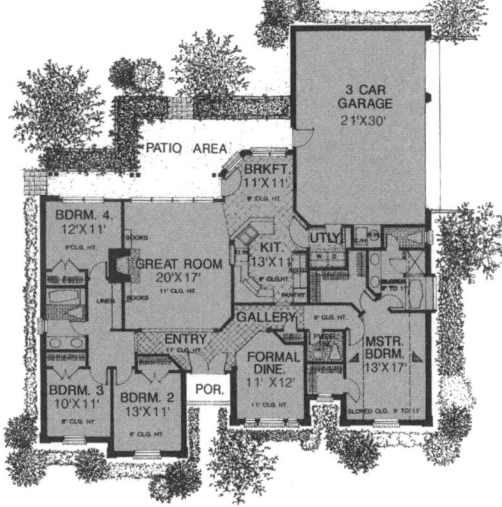

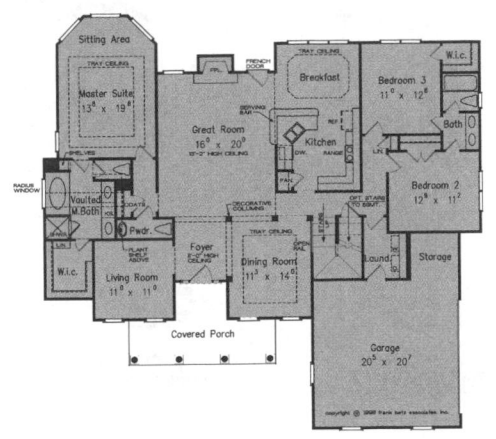

HPK2100392

Style: Greek Revival

Square Footage: 2,072

Bonus Space: 372 sq. ft.

Bedrooms: 3

Bathrooms: 2 ½

Width: 61' - 0"

Depth: 58' - 6"

Foundation: Crawlspace, Unfinished Walkout Basement

EPLANS.COM

HPK2100393

Style: Country

Square Footage: 2,076

Bedrooms: 3

Bathrooms: 2

Width: 64' - 8"

Depth: 54' - 7"

Foundation: Unfinished Basement

EPLANS.COM

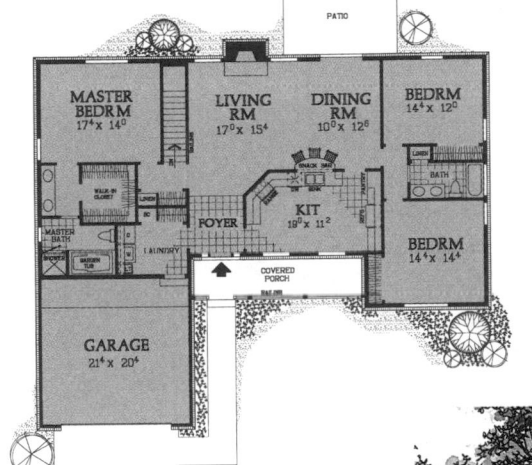

HPK2100394

EPLANS.COM

Style: Country
Square Footage: 2,078
Bonus Space: 339 sq. ft.
Bedrooms: 3
Bathrooms: 2 ½
Width: 62' - 2"
Depth: 47' - 8"

© 1999 Donald A. Gardner, Inc.

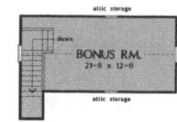

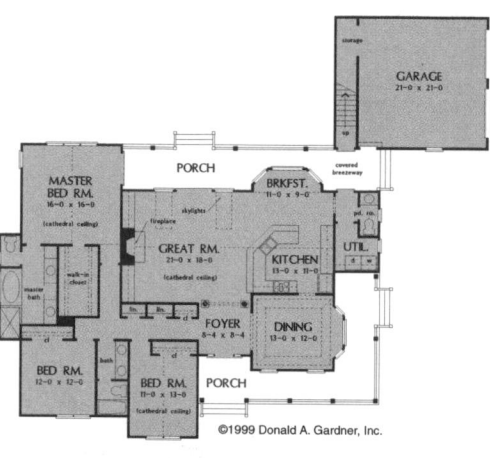

©1999 Donald A. Gardner, Inc.

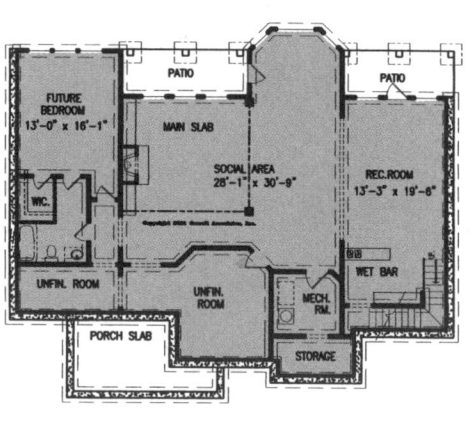

HPK2100395

EPLANS.COM

Style: Cottage
Square Footage: 2,086
Bedrooms: 3
Bathrooms: 3
Width: 57' - 6"
Depth: 46' - 6"
Foundation: Unfinished Basement

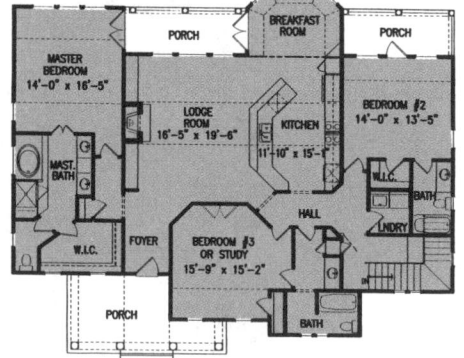

HPK2100396

Style: Mediterranean

Square Footage: 2,089

Bedrooms: 4

Bathrooms: 3

Width: 61' - 8"

Depth: 50' - 4"

Foundation: Slab

EPLANS.COM

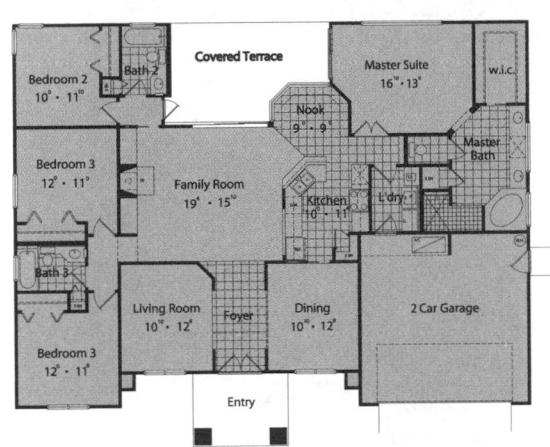

HPK2100397

Style: Farmhouse

Square Footage: 2,090

Bedrooms: 3

Bathrooms: 2 ½

Width: 84' - 6"

Depth: 64' - 0"

Foundation: Crawlspace

EPLANS.COM

2,000 TO 2,499 SQUARE FEET

HPK2100398

Style: Farmhouse
Square Footage: 2,096
Bonus Space: 374 sq. ft.
Bedrooms: 3
Bathrooms: 2
Width: 64' - 8"
Depth: 60' - 0"
Foundation: Crawlspace, Unfinished Basement

EPLANS.COM

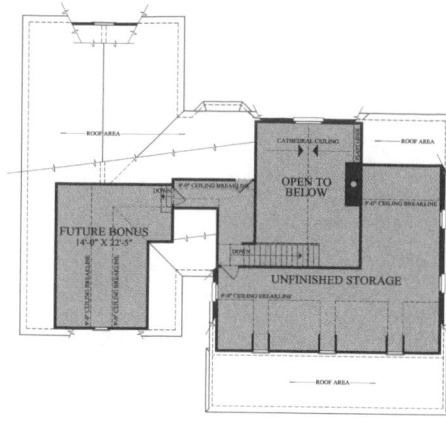

© William E. Poole Designs, Inc.

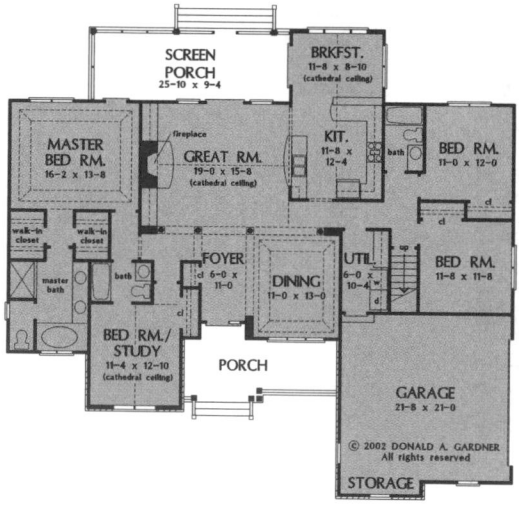

© 2002 DONALD A. GARDNER All rights reserved

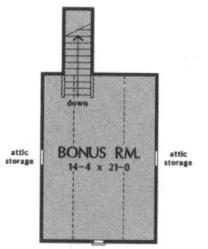

HPK2100399

Style: Cottage
Square Footage: 2,097
Bonus Space: 352 sq. ft.
Bedrooms: 4
Bathrooms: 3
Width: 64' - 10"
Depth: 59' - 6"

EPLANS.COM

© 2002 Donald A. Gardner, Inc.

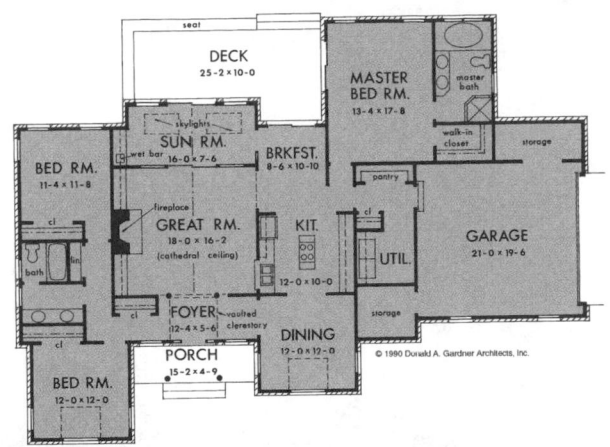

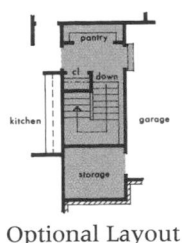

Optional Layout

HPK2100400

Style: New American

Square Footage: 2,099

Bedrooms: 3

Bathrooms: 2

Width: 72' - 6"

Depth: 53' - 10"

EPLANS.COM

HPK2100401

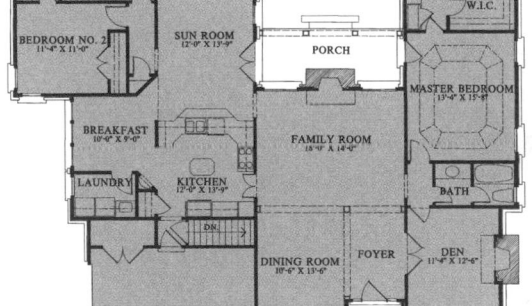

Style: New American

Square Footage: 2,120

Bedrooms: 3

Bathrooms: 3

Width: 62' - 0"

Depth: 62' - 6"

Foundation: Unfinished Walkout Basement

EPLANS.COM

2,000 TO 2,499 SQUARE FEET

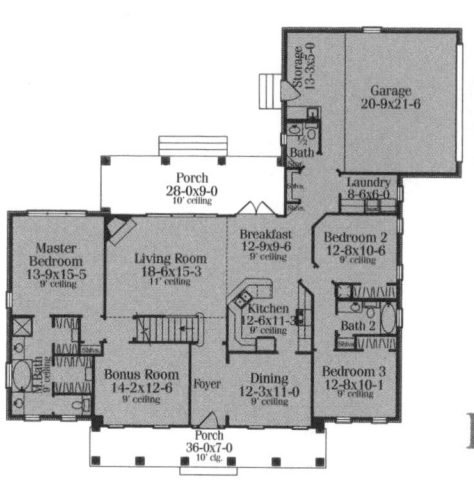

HPK2100402

Style: Greek Revival

Square Footage: 2,122

Bonus Space: 965 sq. ft.

Bedrooms: 3

Bathrooms: 2 ½

Width: 69' - 0"

Depth: 67' - 10"

Foundation: Crawlspace, Slab, Unfinished Basement

EPLANS.COM

HPK2100403

Style: Ranch

Square Footage: 2,133

Bedrooms: 3

Bathrooms: 2 ½

Width: 74' - 4"

Depth: 58' - 0"

EPLANS.COM

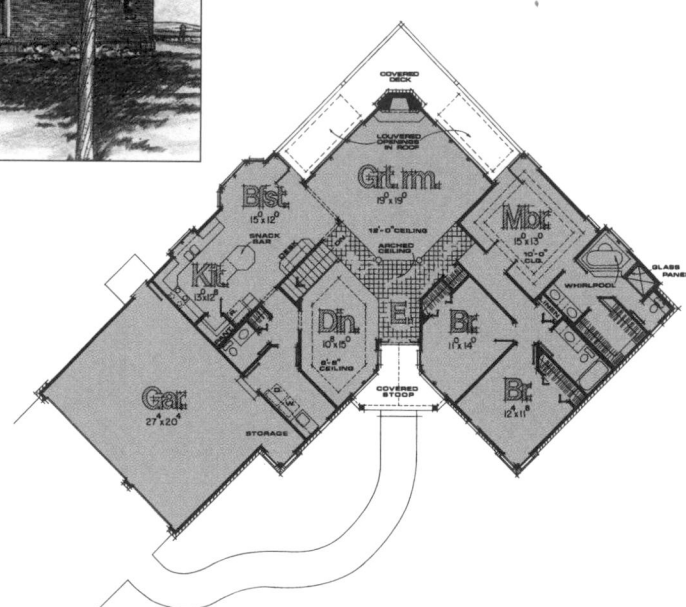

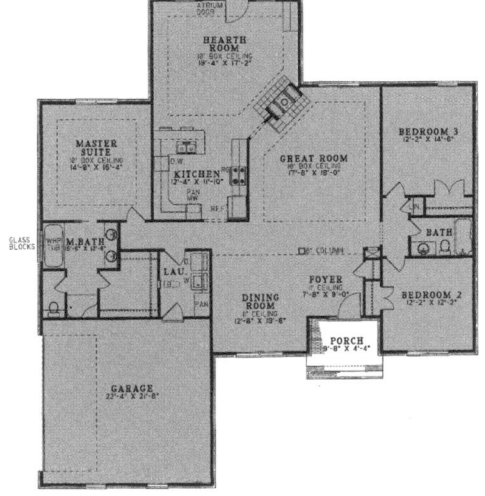

HPK2100404

Style: New American

Square Footage: 2,133

Bedrooms: 3

Bathrooms: 2

Width: 58' - 6"

Depth: 64' - 6"

Foundation: Crawlspace, Slab, Unfinished Basement

EPLANS.COM

© 1994 Donald A. Gardner Architects, Inc.

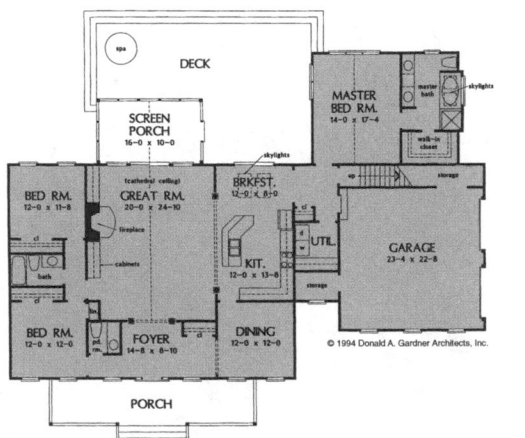

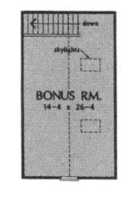

© 1994 Donald A. Gardner Architects, Inc.

HPK2100405

Style: Country

Square Footage: 2,136

Bonus Space: 405 sq. ft.

Bedrooms: 3

Bathrooms: 2 ½

Width: 76' - 4"

Depth: 64' - 4"

EPLANS.COM

© Stephen Fuller, Inc.

HPK2100406

Style: French Country

Square Footage: 2,150

Bedrooms: 3

Bathrooms: 2 ½

Width: 64' - 0"

Depth: 60' - 4"

Foundation: Finished Walkout Basement

EPLANS.COM

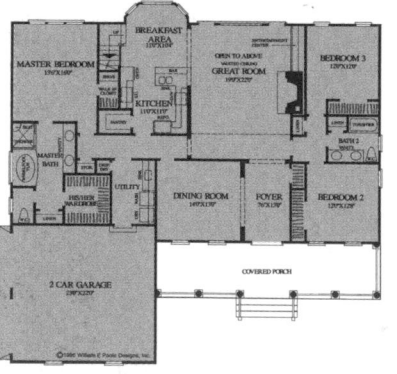

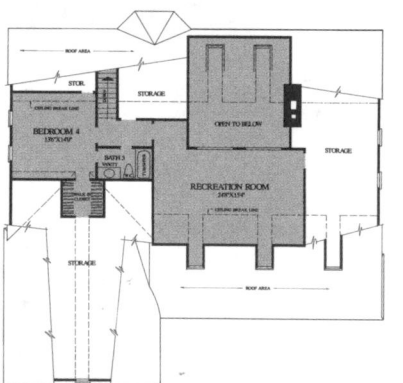

HPK2100407

Style: Cottage

Square Footage: 2,151

Bonus Space: 814 sq. ft.

Bedrooms: 3

Bathrooms: 2

Width: 61' - 0"

Depth: 55' - 8"

Foundation: Crawlspace, Unfinished Basement

EPLANS.COM

HPK2100408

Style: New American
Square Footage: 2,158
Bedrooms: 4
Bathrooms: 3
Width: 63' - 0"
Depth: 63' - 6"
Foundation: Crawlspace, Unfinished Walkout Basement

EPLANS.COM

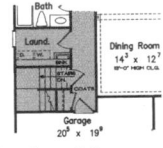

Optional Layout

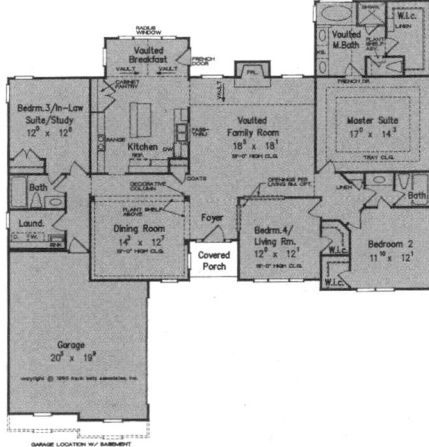

HPK2100409

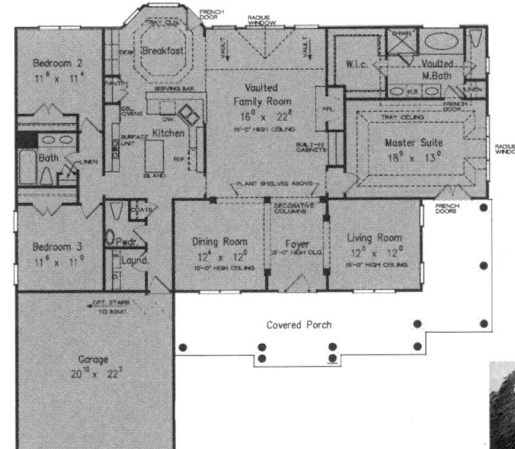

Style: Country
Square Footage: 2,170
Bedrooms: 3
Bathrooms: 2 ½
Width: 63' - 6"
Depth: 61' - 0"
Foundation: Crawlspace, Unfinished Walkout Basement

EPLANS.COM

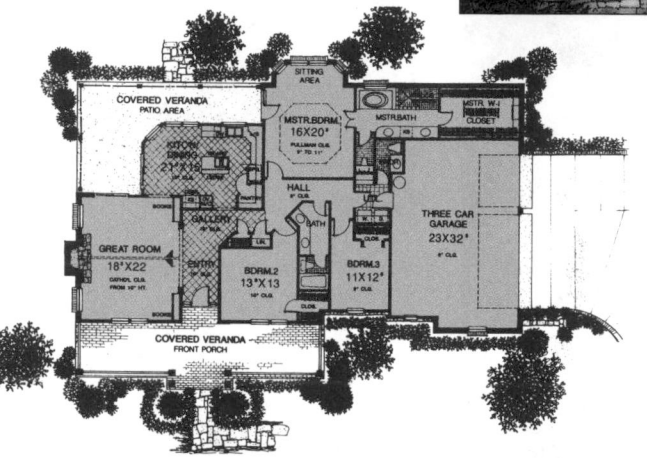

HPK2100410

Style: Country

Square Footage: 2,172

Bedrooms: 3

Bathrooms: 2

Width: 79' - 0"

Depth: 47' - 0"

Foundation: Crawlspace, Slab

EPLANS.COM

HPK2100411

Style: Mediterranean

Square Footage: 2,173

Bedrooms: 3

Bathrooms: 2 ½

Width: 74' - 4"

Depth: 56' - 0"

Foundation: Slab

EPLANS.COM

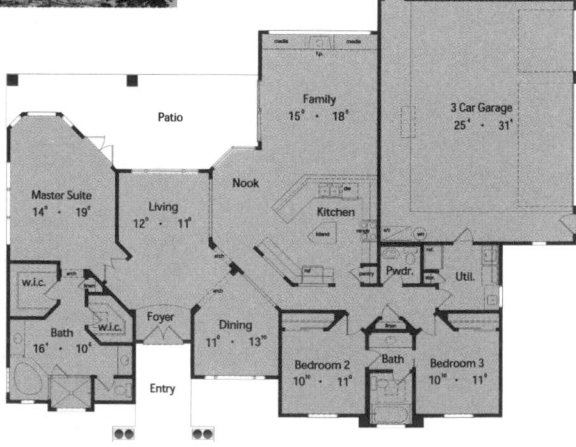

HPK2100412

Style: Bungalow

Square Footage: 2,184

Bedrooms: 3

Bathrooms: 2 ½

Width: 63' - 4"

Depth: 63' - 4"

© 2000 Donald A. Gardner, Inc.

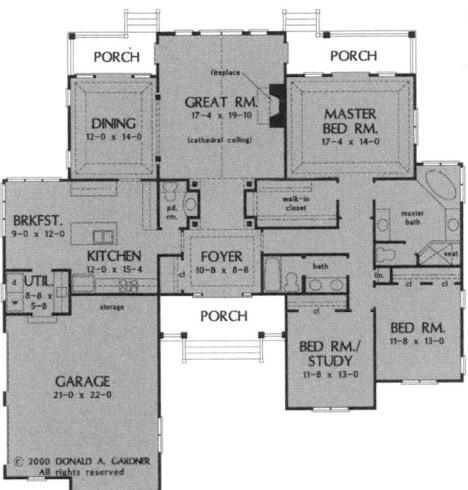

HPK2100413

Style: Cottage

Square Footage: 2,190

Bedrooms: 3

Bathrooms: 2

Width: 59' - 8"

Depth: 54' - 0"

Foundation: Slab

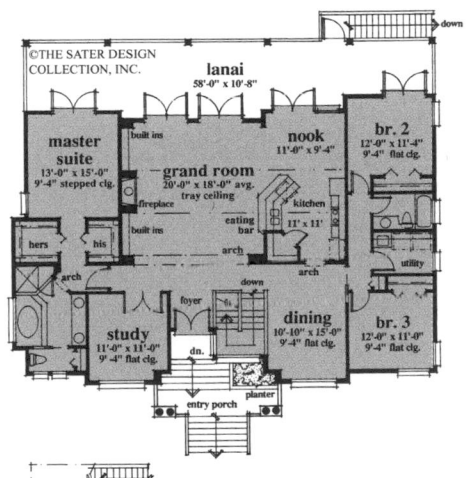

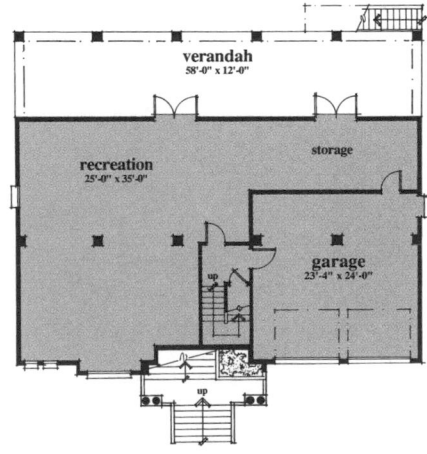

2,000 TO 2,499 SQUARE FEET

HPK2100414

Style: Mediterranean
Square Footage: 2,191
Bedrooms: 3
Bathrooms: 2 ½
Width: 62' - 10"
Depth: 73' - 6"
Foundation: Slab

EPLANS.COM

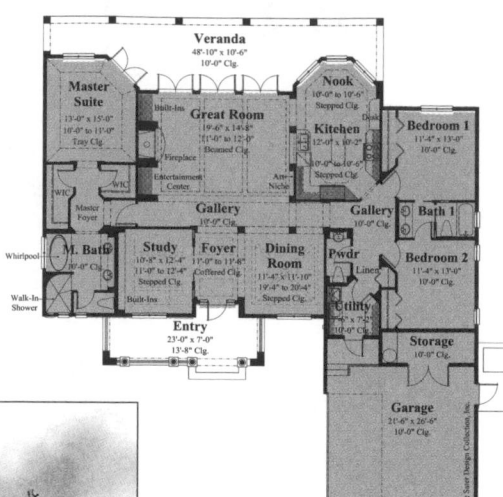

© The Sater Design Collection, Inc.

HPK2100415

Style: Colonial Revival
Square Footage: 2,191
Bedrooms: 3
Bathrooms: 2 ½
Width: 62' - 10"
Depth: 73' - 6"
Foundation: Slab

EPLANS.COM

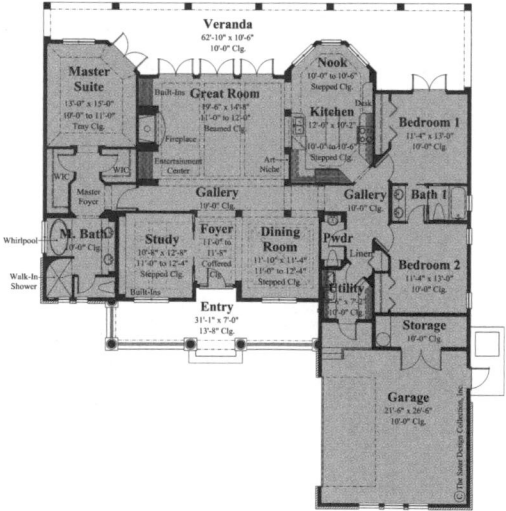

© The Sater Design Collection, Inc.

HPK2100416

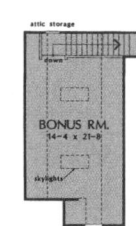

Style: Country

Square Footage: 2,192

Bonus Space: 390 sq. ft.

Bedrooms: 4

Bathrooms: 2 ½

Width: 74' - 10"

Depth: 55' - 8"

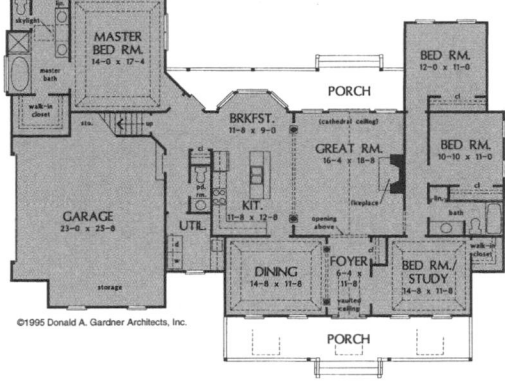

©1995 Donald A. Gardner Architects, Inc.

© 1995 Donald A. Gardner Architects, Inc.

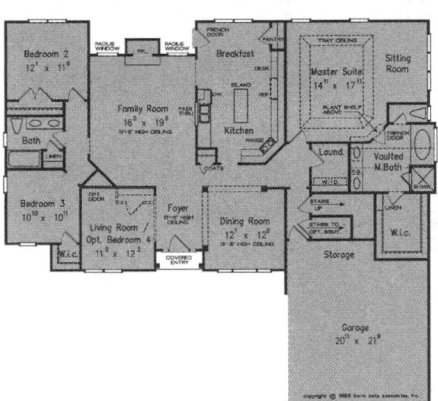

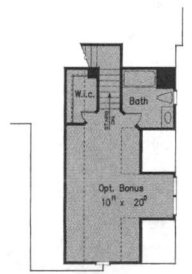

HPK2100417

Style: New American

Square Footage: 2,193

Bonus Space: 400 sq. ft.

Bedrooms: 4

Bathrooms: 2

Width: 64' - 6"

Depth: 59' - 0"

Foundation: Crawlspace, Slab, Unfinished Walkout Basement

EPLANS.COM

2,000 TO 2,499 SQUARE FEET

© 1999 Donald A. Gardner, Inc.

HPK2100418

Style: Farmhouse
Square Footage: 2,195
Bonus Space: 556 sq. ft.
Bedrooms: 4
Bathrooms: 3
Width: 71' - 8"
Depth: 54' - 4"

EPLANS.COM

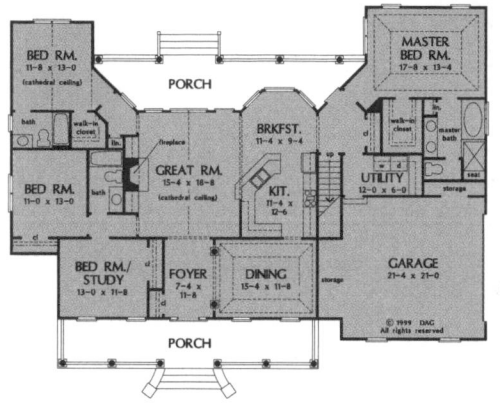

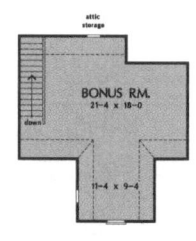

HPK2100419

Style: French Country
Square Footage: 2,199
Bedrooms: 3
Bathrooms: 2 ½
Width: 74' - 8"
Depth: 60' - 7"
Foundation: Unfinished Basement

EPLANS.COM

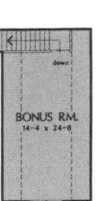

BONUS RM.
14-4 x 24-8

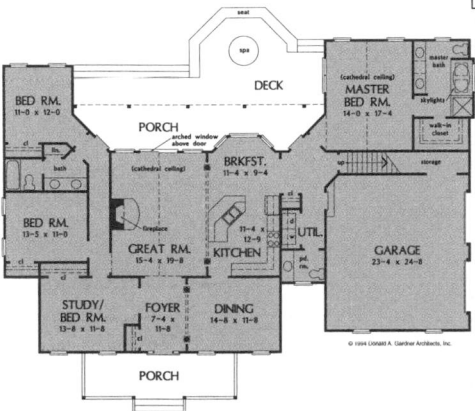

HPK2100420

Style: Country

Square Footage: 2,207

Bonus Space: 435 sq. ft.

Bedrooms: 4

Bathrooms: 2 ½

Width: 76' - 1"

Depth: 50' - 0"

EPLANS.COM

HPK2100421

Style: Country

Square Footage: 2,207

Bonus Space: 441 sq. ft.

Bedrooms: 4

Bathrooms: 2 ½

Width: 76' - 9"

Depth: 57' - 4"

EPLANS.COM

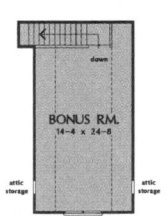

BONUS RM.
14-4 x 24-8

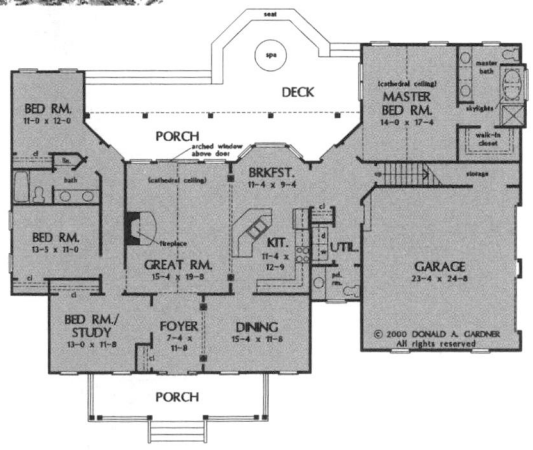

HPK2100422

Style: Cottage
Square Footage: 2,215
Bedrooms: 3
Bathrooms: 3
Width: 69' - 10"
Depth: 62' - 6"
Foundation: Crawlspace, Unfinished Basement

EPLANS.COM

© 1997 William E Poole Designs, Inc

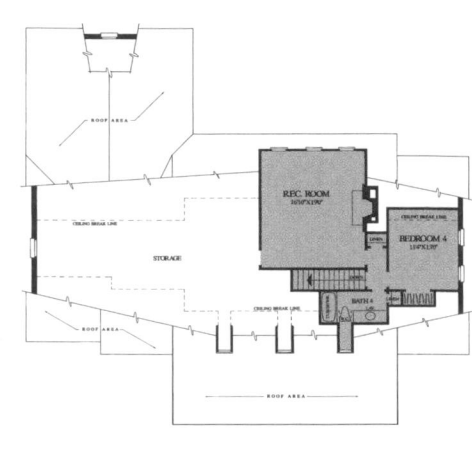

HPK2100423

Style: Mediterranean
Square Footage: 2,227
Bedrooms: 3
Bathrooms: 3 ½
Width: 65' - 0"
Depth: 77' - 0"
Foundation: Slab

EPLANS.COM

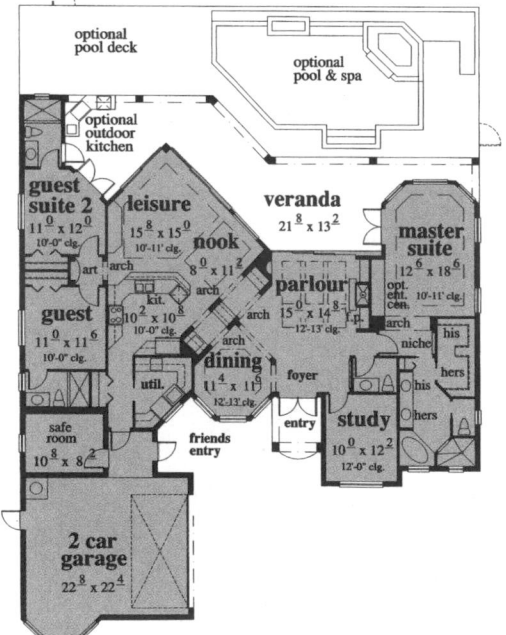

HPK2100424

Style: New American

Square Footage: 2,233

Bonus Space: 289 sq. ft.

Bedrooms: 3

Bathrooms: 2 ½

Width: 60' - 3"

Depth: 74' - 11"

EPLANS.COM

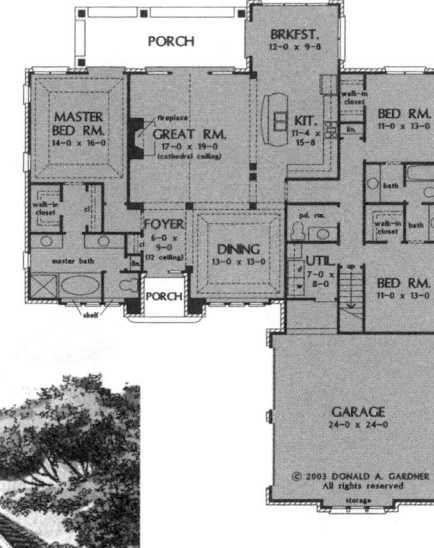

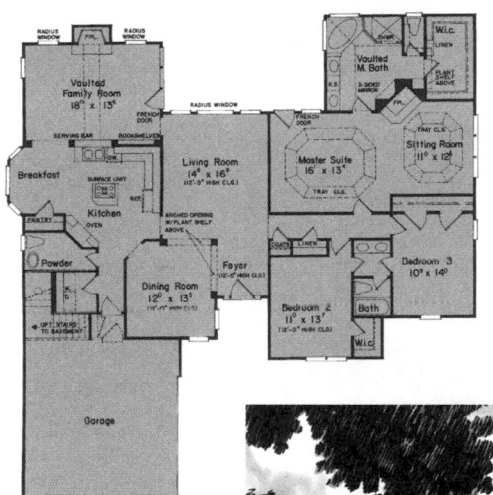

HPK2100425

Style: New American

Square Footage: 2,236

Bedrooms: 3

Bathrooms: 2 ½

Width: 63' - 0"

Depth: 67' - 0"

Foundation: Crawlspace, Unfinished Walkout Basement

EPLANS.COM

©1993 William E Poole Designs, Inc

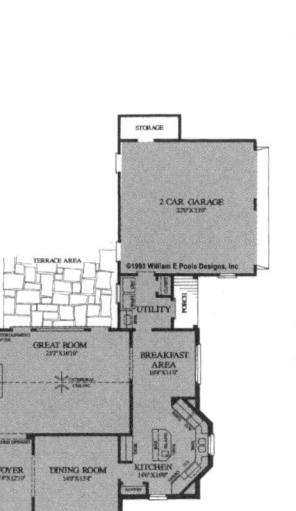

©1993 William E Poole Designs, Inc

HPK2100426

Style: Federal-Adams

Square Footage: 2,249

Bedrooms: 3

Bathrooms: 2

Width: 72' - 6"

Depth: 76' - 8"

Foundation: Crawlspace

EPLANS.COM

© 1998 Donald A. Gardner Architects, Inc.

HPK2100427

Style: French Country

Square Footage: 2,250

Bedrooms: 3

Bathrooms: 2 ½

Width: 84' - 10"

Depth: 62' - 4"

EPLANS.COM

© 1998 Donald A. Gardner Architects, Inc.

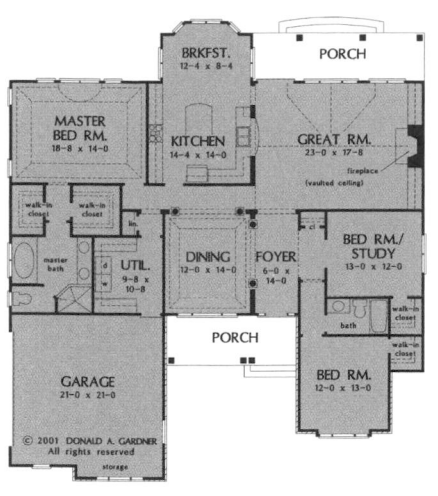

HPK2100428

Style: Cottage

Square Footage: 2,252

Bedrooms: 3

Bathrooms: 2

Width: 57' - 8"

Depth: 64' - 4"

EPLANS.COM

HPK2100429

Style: Cottage

First Floor: 1,634 sq. ft.

Second Floor: 619 sq. ft.

Total: 2,253 sq. ft.

Bonus Space: 229 sq. ft.

Bedrooms: 3

Bathrooms: 2 ½

Width: 46' - 0"

Depth: 54' - 5"

Foundation: Crawlspace, Slab

EPLANS.COM

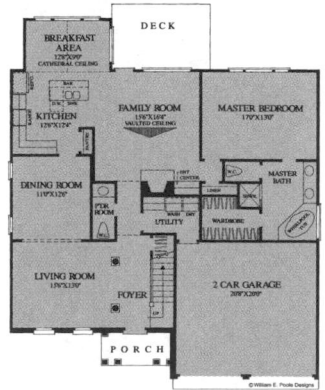

First Floor

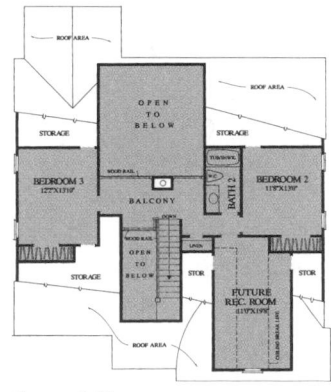

Second Floor

HPK2100430

Style: Mediterranean
Square Footage: 2,258
Bedrooms: 4
Bathrooms: 3
Width: 66' - 0"
Depth: 73' - 4"
Foundation: Slab

HPK2100431

Style: Cottage
Square Footage: 2,259
Bonus Space: 352 sq. ft.
Bedrooms: 4
Bathrooms: 3
Width: 64' - 10"
Depth: 59' - 6"

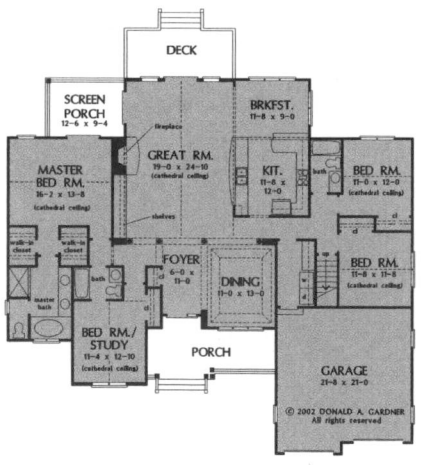

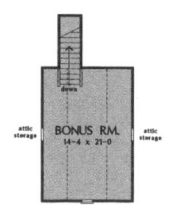

© 2002 Donald A. Gardner, Inc.

HPK2100432

Style: Italianate

Square Footage: 2,259

Bedrooms: 4

Bathrooms: 3

Width: 59' - 8"

Depth: 54' - 4"

Foundation: Slab

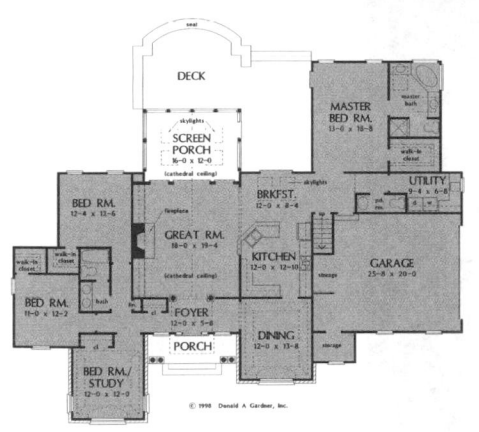

HPK2100433

Style: Country

Square Footage: 2,262

Bonus Space: 388 sq. ft.

Bedrooms: 4

Bathrooms: 2 ½

Width: 77' - 4"

Depth: 62' - 0"

© 1998 Donald A. Gardner, Inc.

2,000 TO 2,499 SQUARE FEET

HPK2100434

Style: Country
Square Footage: 2,273
Bonus Space: 342 sq. ft.
Bedrooms: 4
Bathrooms: 2 ½
Width: 74' - 8"
Depth: 75' - 10"

© 1997 Donald A. Gardner Architects, Inc.

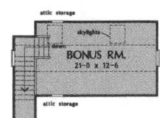

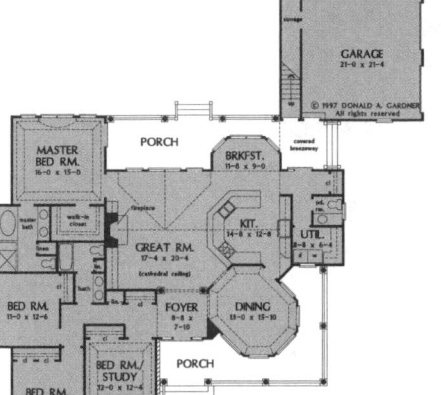

HPK2100435

Style: French Country
Square Footage: 2,275
Bonus Space: 407 sq. ft.
Bedrooms: 3
Bathrooms: 2 ½
Width: 59' - 4"
Depth: 69' - 0"
Foundation: Crawlspace, Unfinished Walkout Basement

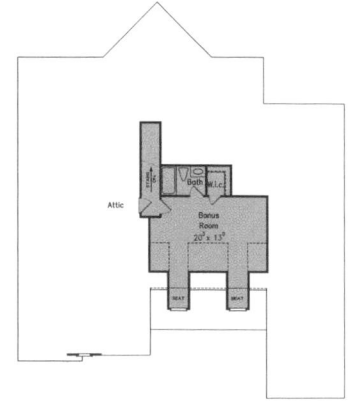

HPK2100436

Style: Ranch

Square Footage: 2,276

Bedrooms: 3

Bathrooms: 2 ½

Width: 72' - 0"

Depth: 56' - 0"

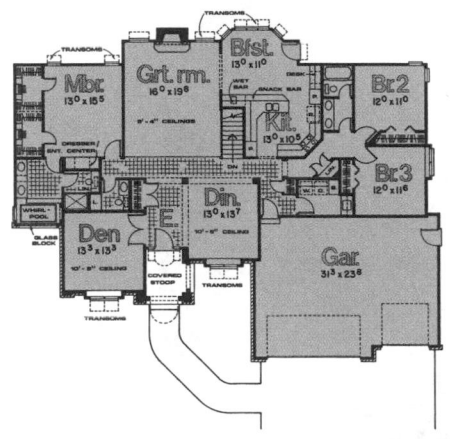

HPK2100437

Style: French Country

Square Footage: 2,282

Bonus Space: 629 sq. ft.

Bedrooms: 3

Bathrooms: 2 ½

Width: 60' - 0"

Depth: 75' - 4"

Foundation: Crawlspace, Unfinished Walkout Basement

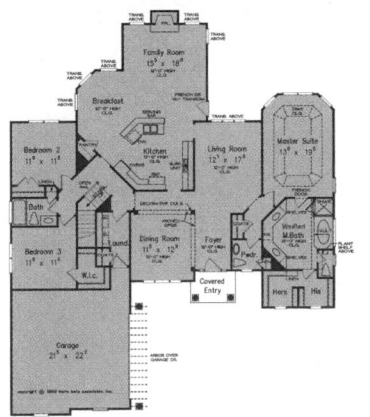

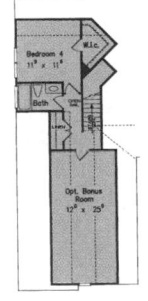

Optional Layout

HPK2100438

Style: French Country

Square Footage: 2,282

Bedrooms: 4

Bathrooms: 3

Width: 63' - 10"

Depth: 71' - 1"

Foundation: Crawlspace, Slab

EPLANS.COM

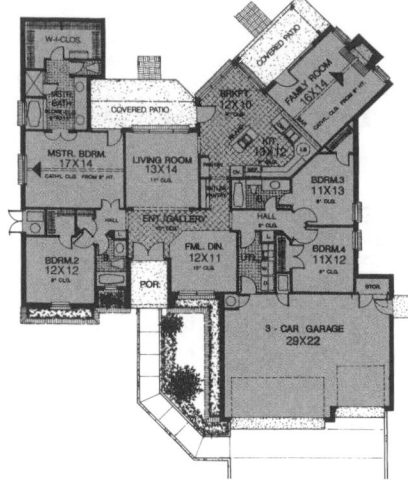

HPK2100439

Style: Country

Square Footage: 2,290

Bonus Space: 355 sq. ft.

Bedrooms: 4

Bathrooms: 3

Width: 53' - 0"

Depth: 80' - 10"

EPLANS.COM

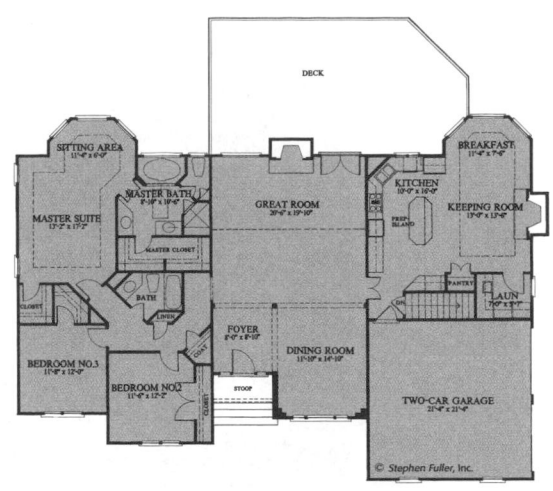

HPK2100440

Style: New American

Square Footage: 2,295

Bedrooms: 3

Bathrooms: 2

Width: 69' - 0"

Depth: 49' - 6"

Foundation: Unfinished Walkout Basement

EPLANS.COM

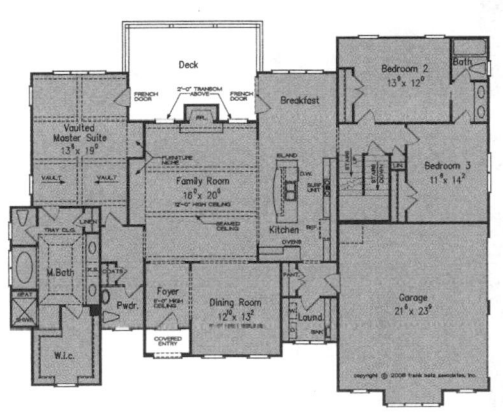

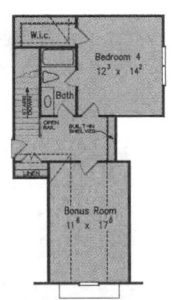

HPK2100441

Style: French Country

Square Footage: 2,302

Bonus Space: 595 sq. ft.

Bedrooms: 3

Bathrooms: 2 ½

Width: 69' - 0"

Depth: 53' - 0"

Foundation: Crawlspace, Unfinished Walkout Basement

EPLANS.COM

© 2005 Donald A. Gardner, Inc.

HPK2100442

Style: Country
Square Footage: 2,304
Bonus Space: 397 sq. ft.
Bedrooms: 3
Bathrooms: 2 ½
Width: 67' - 8"
Depth: 63' - 6"

EPLANS.COM

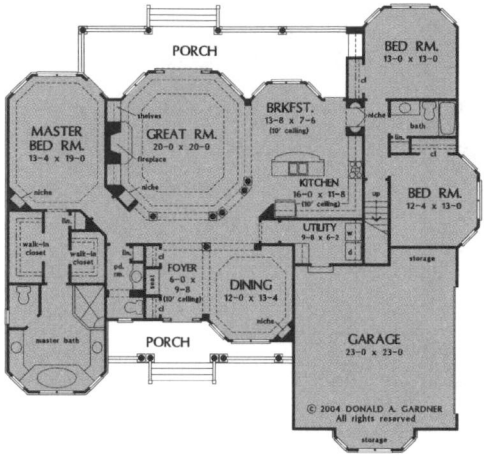

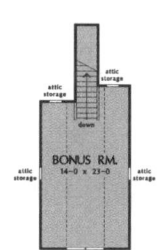

© 2004 Donald A. Gardner
All rights reserved

HPK2100443

Style: New American
Square Footage: 2,311
Bonus Space: 425 sq. ft.
Bedrooms: 4
Bathrooms: 2 ½
Width: 61' - 0"
Depth: 65' - 4"
Foundation: Crawlspace, Slab, Unfinished Walkout Basement

EPLANS.COM

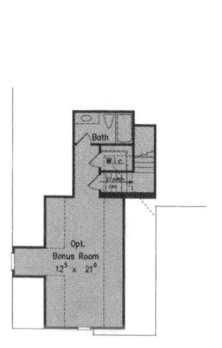

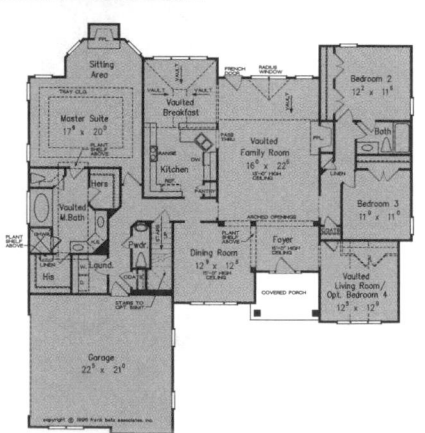

ORDER BLUEPRINTS ANYTIME AT EPLANS.COM OR 1-800-521-6797

HPK2100444

Style: French Country

Square Footage: 2,322

Bedrooms: 3

Bathrooms: 2 ½

Width: 62' - 0"

Depth: 61' - 0"

Foundation: Crawlspace, Slab, Unfinished Walkout Basement

EPLANS.COM

HPK2100445

Style: Tudor

Square Footage: 2,325

Bonus Space: 725 sq. ft.

Bedrooms: 3

Bathrooms: 2 ½

Width: 64' - 6"

Depth: 88' - 4"

Foundation: Crawlspace, Unfinished Walkout Basement

EPLANS.COM

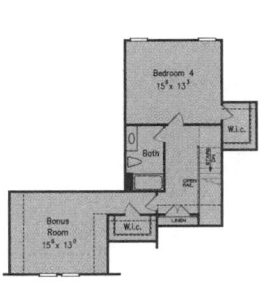

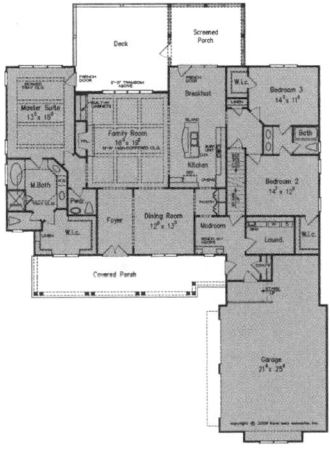

HPK2100446

Style: Country
Square Footage: 2,329
Bedrooms: 3
Bathrooms: 2 ½
Width: 72' - 0"
Depth: 73' - 10"
Foundation: Crawlspace

©The Sater Design Collection, Inc.

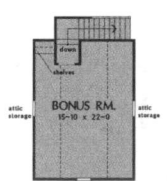

HPK2100447

Style: Craftsman
Square Footage: 2,353
Bonus Space: 353 sq. ft.
Bedrooms: 4
Bathrooms: 2
Width: 65' - 8"
Depth: 67' - 10"

ORDER BLUEPRINTS ANYTIME AT EPLANS.COM OR 1-800-521-6797

HPK2100448

Style: Mediterranean
Square Footage: 2,362
Bedrooms: 4
Bathrooms: 3
Width: 65' - 8"
Depth: 73' - 4"
Foundation: Slab

EPLANS.COM

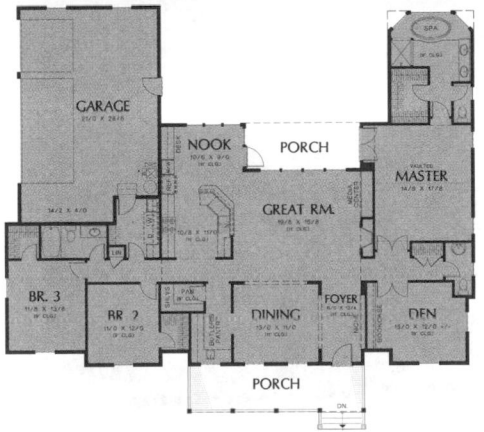

HPK2100449

Style: Country
Square Footage: 2,367
Bedrooms: 3
Bathrooms: 2 ½
Width: 72' - 0"
Depth: 62' - 0"
Foundation: Crawlspace

EPLANS.COM

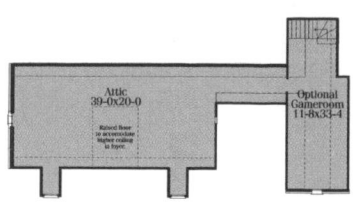

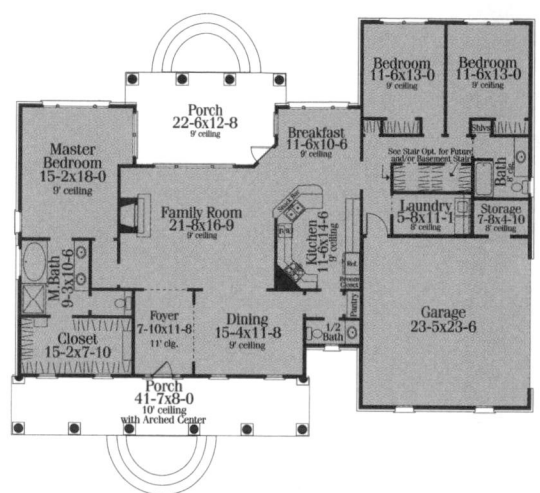

HPK2100450

Style: Country

Square Footage: 2,373

Bonus Space: 1,178 sq. ft.

Bedrooms: 3

Bathrooms: 2 ½

Width: 73' - 1"

Depth: 58' - 6"

Foundation: Crawlspace, Slab, Unfinished Basement

EPLANS.COM

HPK2100451

Style: Mediterranean

Square Footage: 2,376

Bedrooms: 4

Bathrooms: 3

Width: 59' - 6"

Depth: 72' - 0"

Foundation: Slab

EPLANS.COM

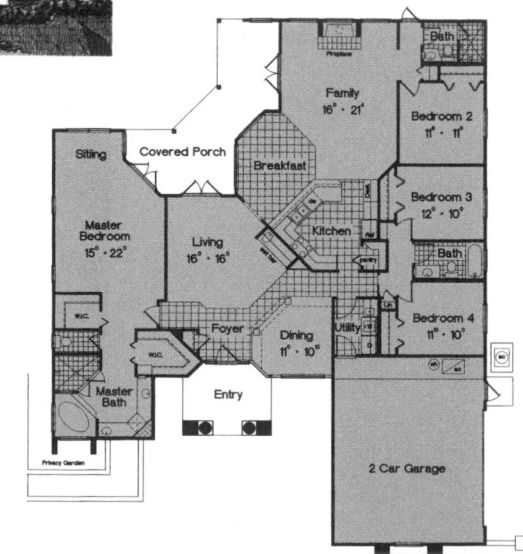

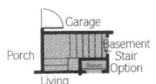

HPK2100452

Style: Greek Revival

Square Footage: 2,379

Bonus Space: 367 sq. ft.

Bedrooms: 3

Bathrooms: 2 ½

Width: 61' - 0"

Depth: 81' - 9"

Foundation: Crawlspace, Slab, Unfinished Basement

EPLANS.COM

©The Sater Design Collection, Inc.

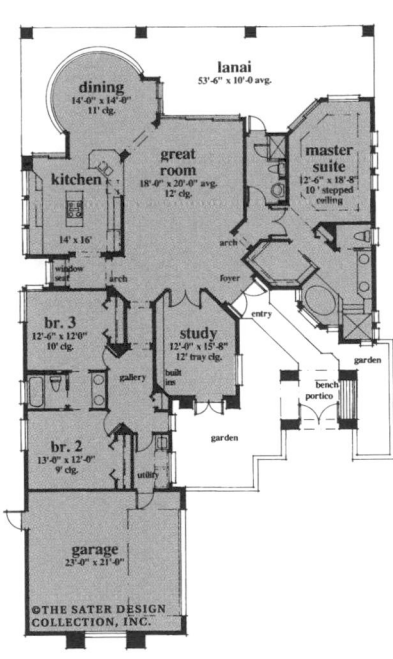

©THE SATER DESIGN COLLECTION, INC.

HPK2100453

Style: Mediterranean

Square Footage: 2,387

Bedrooms: 3

Bathrooms: 3

Width: 53' - 6"

Depth: 94' - 6"

Foundation: Slab

EPLANS.COM

2,000 TO 2,499 SQUARE FEET

HPK2100454

Style: Colonial Revival

Square Footage: 2,387

Bonus Space: 377 sq. ft.

Bedrooms: 3

Bathrooms: 2 ½

Width: 69' - 6"

Depth: 68' - 11"

Foundation: Crawlspace, Slab

EPLANS.COM

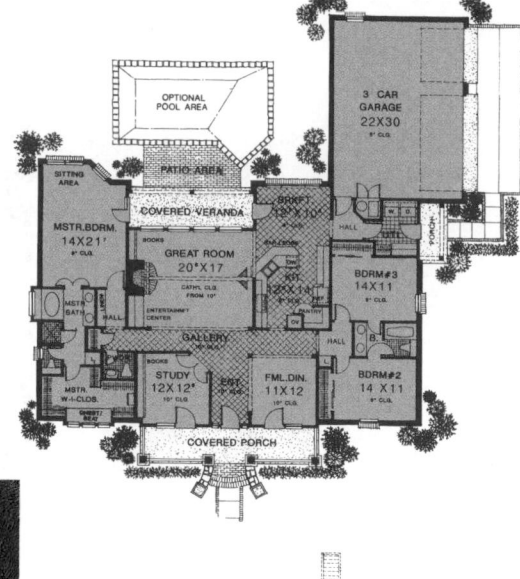

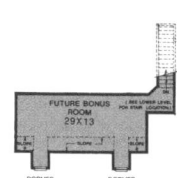

HPK2100455

Style: European

Square Footage: 2,388

Bedrooms: 3

Bathrooms: 2 ½

Width: 63' - 0"

Depth: 60' - 0"

Foundation: Crawlspace, Slab, Unfinished Walkout Basement

EPLANS.COM

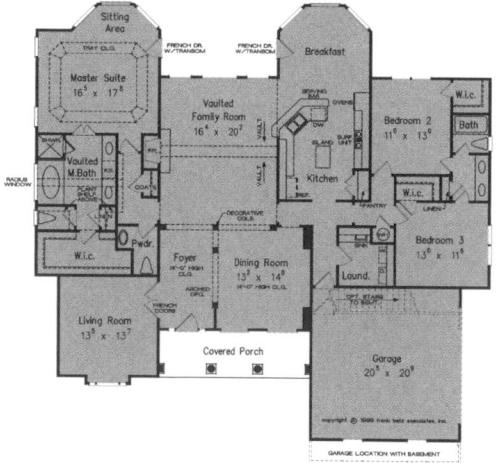

ORDER BLUEPRINTS ANYTIME AT EPLANS.COM OR 1-800-521-6797

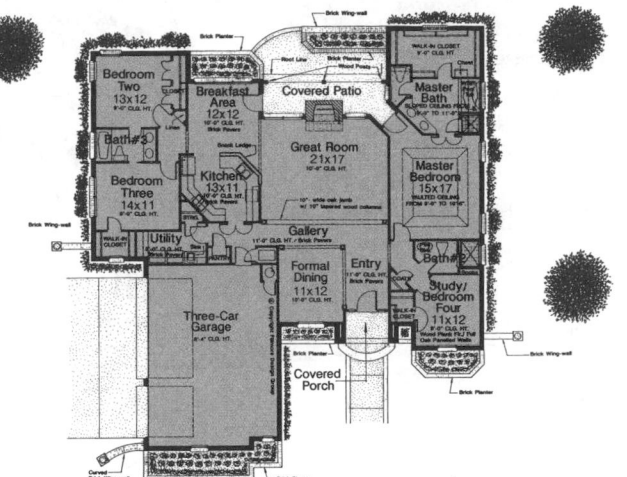

HPK2100456

Style: French Country

Square Footage: 2,391

Bedrooms: 4

Bathrooms: 3

Width: 64' - 0"

Depth: 68' - 5"

Foundation: Crawlspace, Slab

EPLANS.COM

HPK2100457

Style: Georgian

Square Footage: 2,394

Bedrooms: 3

Bathrooms: 3

Width: 82' - 6"

Depth: 52' - 8"

Foundation: Crawlspace

EPLANS.COM

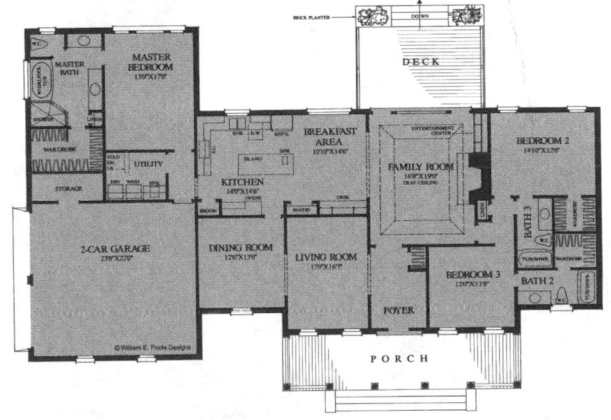

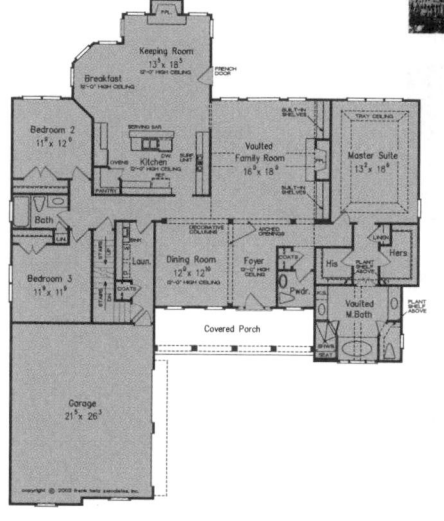

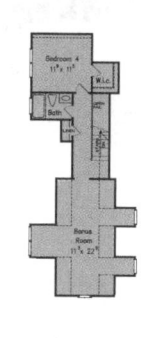

HPK2100458

Style: Country
Square Footage: 2,395
Bonus Space: 660 sq. ft.
Bedrooms: 3
Bathrooms: 2 ½
Width: 62' - 6"
Depth: 77' - 4"
Foundation: Crawlspace, Unfinished Walkout Basement

EPLANS.COM

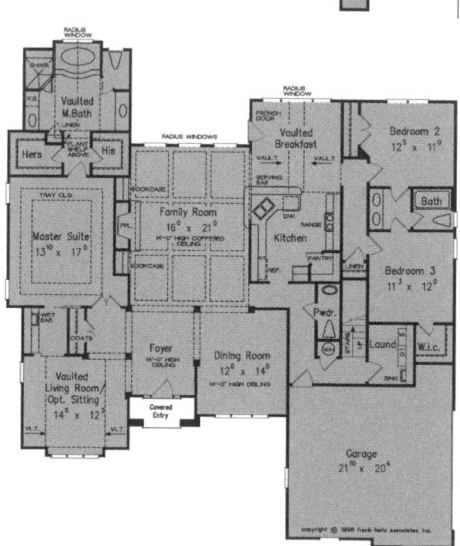

HPK2100459

Style: French Country
Square Footage: 2,403
Bonus Space: 285 sq. ft.
Bedrooms: 3
Bathrooms: 2 ½
Width: 60' - 0"
Depth: 67' - 0"
Foundation: Crawlspace, Slab, Unfinished Walkout Basement

EPLANS.COM

HPK2100460

Style: Mediterranean

Square Footage: 2,409

Bedrooms: 4

Bathrooms: 3

Width: 65' - 0"

Depth: 85' - 0"

Foundation: Slab

EPLANS.COM

This classic design is impressive at every turn. The entry is adorned with square and round columns and a keystone lintel above a transom and double doors. The tiled foyer faces the living room with its wall of glass. To the right is the dining room, featuring a clerestory window. The master wing enjoys a sitting area and a luxurious bath. Two family bedrooms share a full bath.

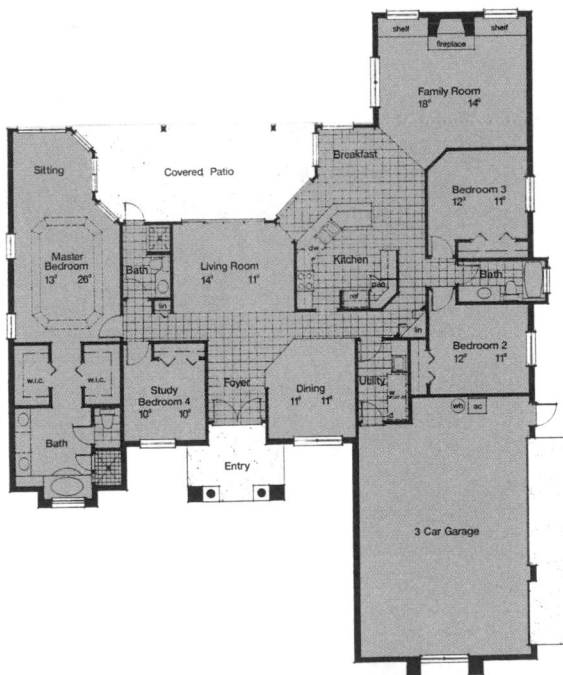

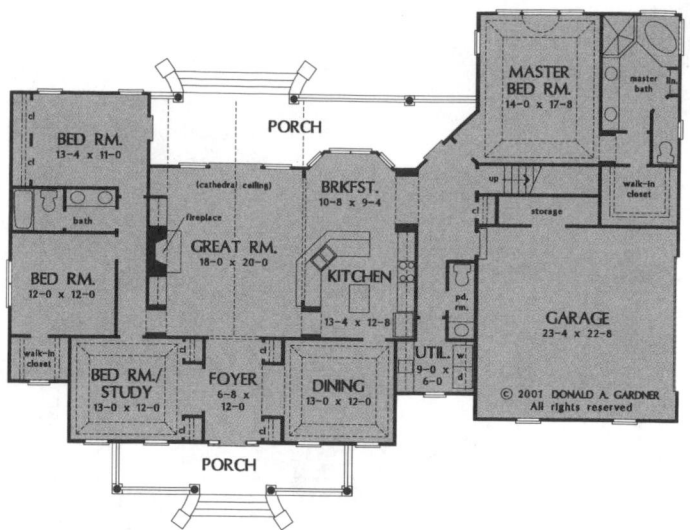

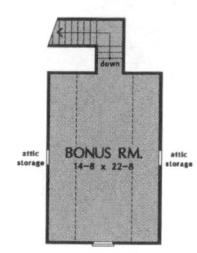

Dormers set above a charming porch and a beautiful entry door with arched transoms lend eye appeal to this wonderful four-bedroom design. The foyer leads to the dining room to the right and a bedroom or study to the left—both featuring exciting ceiling treatments. The hearth-warmed great room shares an open area with the island kitchen and bayed breakfast nook.

HPK2100461

Style: Country
Square Footage: 2,413
Bonus Space: 417 sq. ft.
Bedrooms: 4
Bathrooms: 2 ½
Width: 78' - 8"
Depth: 57' - 8"

EPLANS.COM

© 2001 Donald A. Gardner, Inc.

HPK2100462

Style: New American

Square Footage: 2,416

Bedrooms: 4

Bathrooms: 3

Width: 58' - 0"

Depth: 68' - 0"

Foundation: Crawlspace, Unfinished Walkout Basement

EPLANS.COM

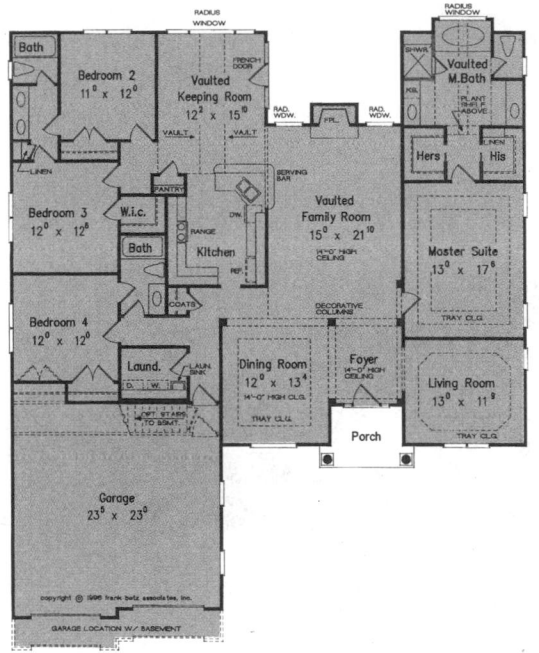

Arches and quoins lend a quaint appearance to this 21st-Century country home and harmonize with a thoroughly up-to-date interior. Decorative columns define formal rooms that feature soaring interior vistas of the vaulted family room with wide views of the outdoors through radius windows. The lavish master suite boasts two walk-in closets, a windowed whirlpool tub, and a knee-space vanity. Three family bedrooms share a full bath. A curved serving bar makes kitchen service to the keeping and family rooms simple.

2,000 TO 2,499 SQUARE FEET

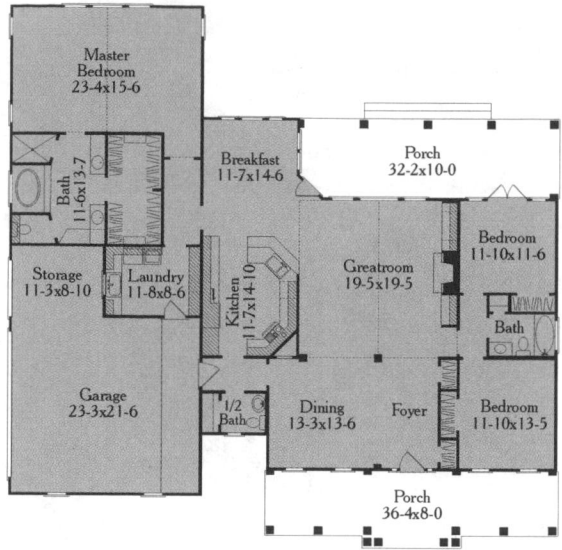

Columns on the front of this home mark it with grace and style and dress up its sunny stucco facade. The floor plan holds open living areas: a great room with a fireplace, a dining room, a U-shaped kitchen, and a breakfast room. Family bedrooms on the right side of the plan are separated by a full bath. The master suite is tucked away behind the garage and contains a huge walk-in closet and bath with a whirlpool tub.

HPK2100463

Style: Colonial Revival

Square Footage: 2,424

Bedrooms: 3

Bathrooms: 2 ½

Width: 68' - 2"

Depth: 67' - 6"

Foundation: Crawlspace, Slab, Unfinished Basement

EPLANS.COM

HPK2100464

Style: Country

Square Footage: 2,426

Bonus Space: 767 sq. ft.

Bedrooms: 4

Bathrooms: 2 ½

Width: 63' - 0"

Depth: 72' - 4"

Foundation: Crawlspace, Unfinished Walkout Basement

EPLANS.COM

The covered front porch adds an element of Greek Revival to this Southern Country home. The dining room is defined by archways that open to the foyer and vaulted family room, where a fireplace offers warmth and a window wall offers beautiful views. The master wing is impressive with a bayed sitting area with a private fireplace. Two family bedrooms on the opposite side of the home share a hall bath. The formal living room converts to a fourth bedroom, providing flexible space.

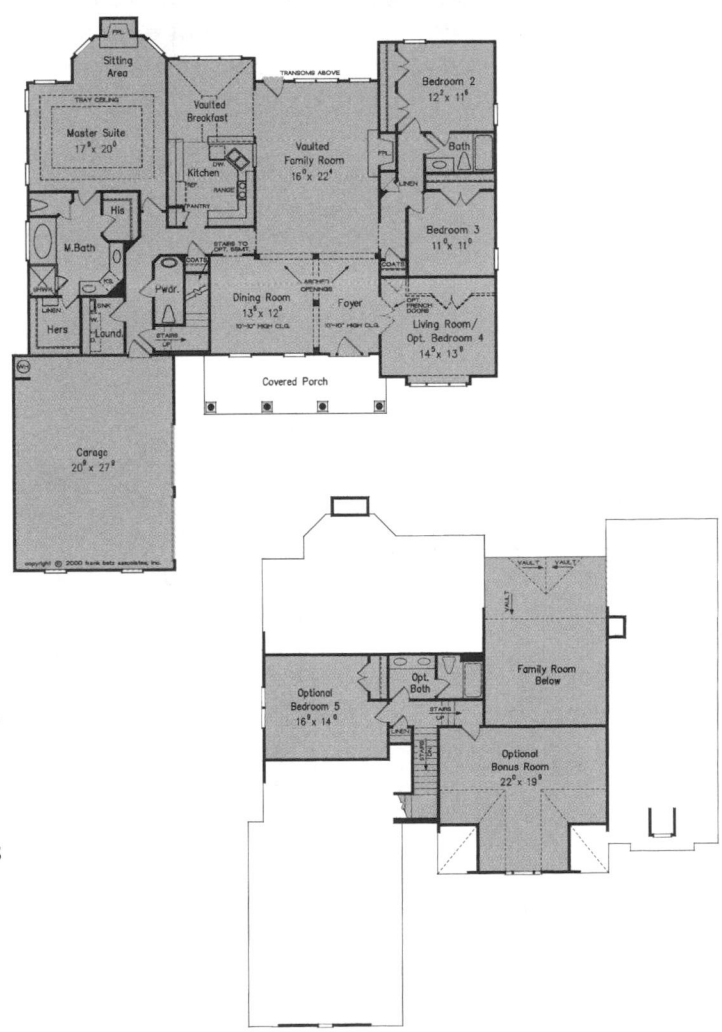

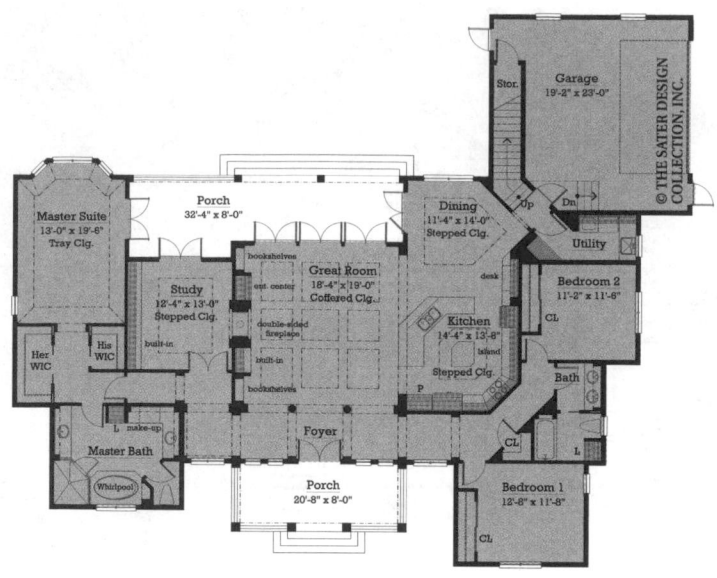

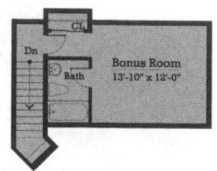

HPK2100465

Style: Colonial Revival
Square Footage: 2,454
Bonus Space: 256 sq. ft.
Bedrooms: 3
Bathrooms: 2
Width: 80' - 6"
Depth: 66' - 0"
Foundation: Crawlspace

EPLANS.COM

This traditional home offers a wide variety of modern amenities. The spacious foyer opens to the great room, which boasts built-in bookshelves, a wall of double doors to the rear porch, and a double-sided fireplace shared with the study. To the far left, the master suite is enhanced by a bay window, His and Hers walk-in closets, and a luxury whirlpool bath. The island cook-top kitchen serves the dining area with ease.

© The Sater Design Collection, Inc.

© The Sater Design Collection, Inc.

HPK2100466

Style: Country

Square Footage: 2,454

Bonus Space: 256 sq. ft.

Bedrooms: 3

Bathrooms: 2

Width: 80' - 6"

Depth: 66' - 6"

Foundation: Crawlspace

EPLANS.COM

A neat row of classic front-porch pillars opens this beautiful one-story plan. The bay window in the master suite offers a front-row seat to views. The pentagonal dining room is large enough for special occasions. A double-sided fireplace lights the great room and adjacent study. To the right of the entry is an angled hallway that leads to two bedrooms and a hall bath. A bonus room with a full bath sits above the double garage.

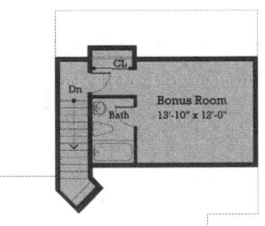

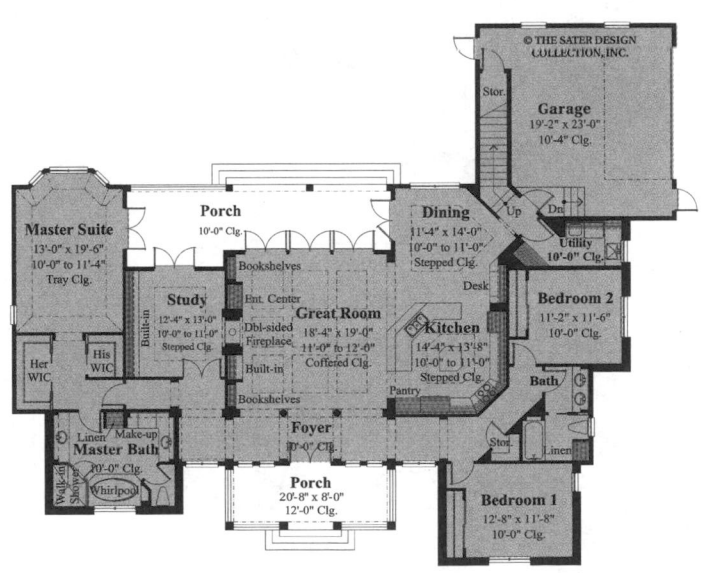

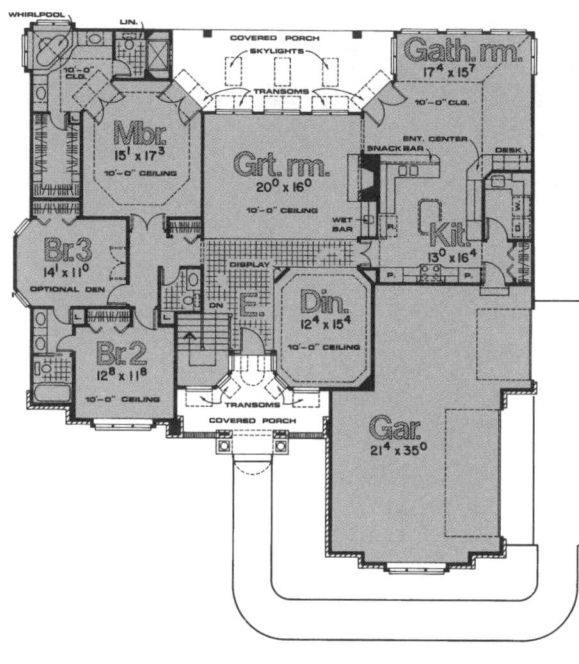

Gently tapered columns set off an elegant arched entry framed by multipane windows. Inside, an open great room features a wet bar, fireplace, tall transom windows, and access to a covered porch. The gourmet kitchen boasts a food-preparation island and a snack bar. Double doors open to the master suite, where French doors lead to a private bath with an angled whirlpool tub. One of two nearby family bedrooms could serve as a den, with optional French doors opening to a hall central to the sleeping wing.

HPK2100467

Style: New American
Square Footage: 2,456
Bedrooms: 3
Bathrooms: 2 ½
Width: 66' - 0"
Depth: 68' - 0"

EPLANS.COM

© 2001 Donald A. Gardner, Inc.

HPK2100468

Style: Colonial Revival
Square Footage: 2,461
Bonus Space: 397 sq. ft.
Bedrooms: 4
Bathrooms: 2
Width: 71' - 2"
Depth: 67' - 2"

Turret-style bay windows, an arched entryway, and an elegant balustrade add timeless appeal to a remarkable facade, yet this refined exterior encompasses a very practical layout. Separated from the kitchen by an angled island, the great room features built-in shelves on both sides of the fireplace as well as French doors leading to the rear porch with wet bar. Custom-style details include tray ceilings in the dining room and study/bedroom as well as columns found in the foyer and master bath.

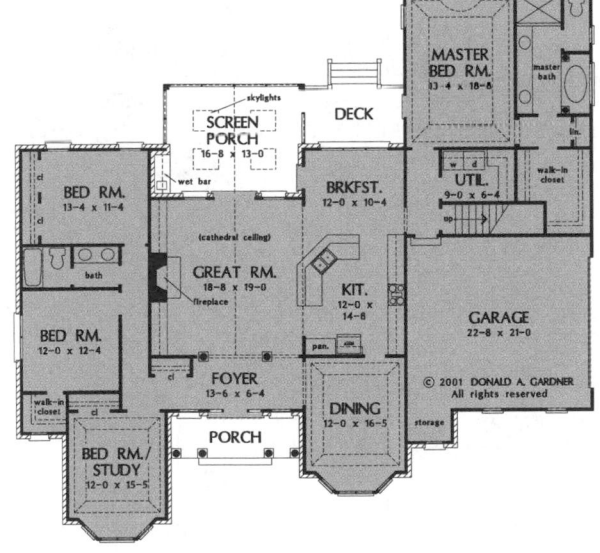

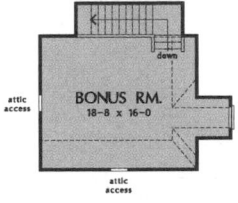

2,000 TO 2,499 SQUARE FEET

HPK2100469

Style: Colonial Revival

Square Footage: 2,465

Bedrooms: 4

Bathrooms: 2 ½

Width: 65' - 1"

Depth: 73' - 7"

Foundation: Crawlspace, Slab, Unfinished Basement

EPLANS.COM

This home boasts a well-laid-out design that promotes comfort and flow. The great room offers two sets of French doors to the rear porch, a fireplace, and a spacious layout that's perfect for entertaining. The open island kitchen shares an area with the breakfast room and connects to the dining room. The master suite delights in a room-sized sitting area, His and Hers walk-in closets and vanities, a compartmented toilet, and a separate tub and shower.

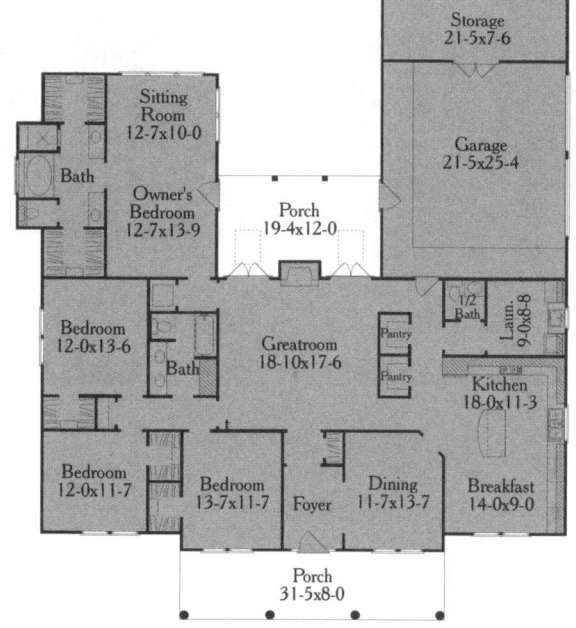

This lovely one-story home is spacious and efficient. An island kitchen is handy for extra space and opens to a breakfast nook, which accesses a rear porch. The master suite also privately accesses the porch and boasts a walk-in closet and a whirlpool tub.

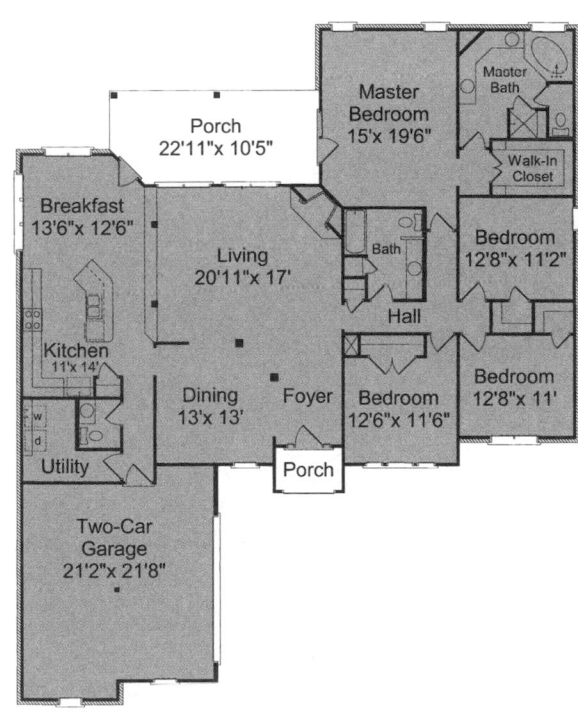

HPK2100470

EPLANS.COM

Style: New American

Square Footage: 2,471

Bedrooms: 4

Bathrooms: 2 ½

Width: 62' - 10"

Depth: 75' - 3"

Foundation: Slab

2,000 TO 2,499 SQUARE FEET

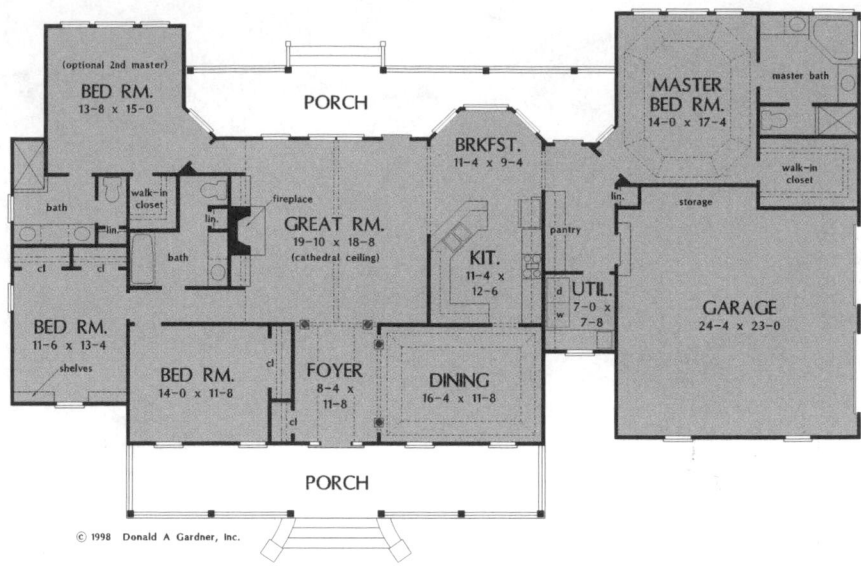

(optional 2nd master)

BED RM.
13-8 x 15-0

PORCH

MASTER
BED RM.
14-0 x 17-4

master bath

BRKFST.
11-4 x 9-4

walk-in
closet

bath

walk-in
closet

fireplace

lin.

GREAT RM.
19-10 x 18-8
(cathedral ceiling)

lin.

storage

bath

KIT.
11-4 x
12-6

pantry

BED RM.
11-6 x 13-4

shelves

UTIL.
7-0 x
7-8

GARAGE
24-4 x 23-0

cl

cl

BED RM.
14-0 x 11-8

cl

FOYER
8-4 x
11-8

DINING
16-4 x 11-8

cl

PORCH

© 1998   Donald A Gardner, Inc.

The central great room forms the heart of this country home. The warming fireplace, access to the rear porch, and a snack bar make it the perfect spot for comfortable living. The kitchen is flanked by the breakfast area and provides a large pantry. The master suite is located at the rear for seclusion. Three family bedrooms share a full hall bath on the left of the plan.

HPK2100471

Style: Farmhouse
Square Footage: 2,487
Bedrooms: 4
Bathrooms: 3
Width: 86' - 2"
Depth: 51' - 8"

EPLANS.COM

© 1998 Donald A. Gardner, Inc.

© The Sater Design Collection, Inc.

HPK2100472

Style: French Country

Square Footage: 2,487

Bedrooms: 3

Bathrooms: 2

Width: 70' - 0"

Depth: 72' - 0"

Foundation: Slab

EPLANS.COM

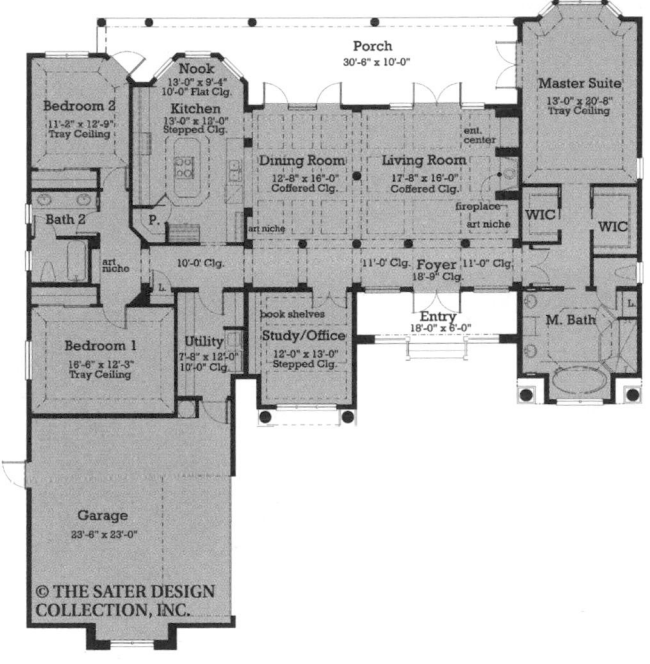

© THE SATER DESIGN COLLECTION, INC.

This petite cottage opens to a foyer facing a formal area made up of the combined living and dining rooms. The connecting island kitchen expands into a bayed nook. Just off the main living area is the study/office. Two family bedrooms share a hall bath. Double doors open into the master suite, which offers two walk-in closets and a private bath.

2,000 TO 2,499 SQUARE FEET

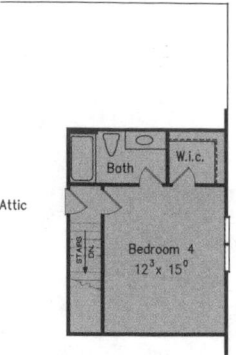

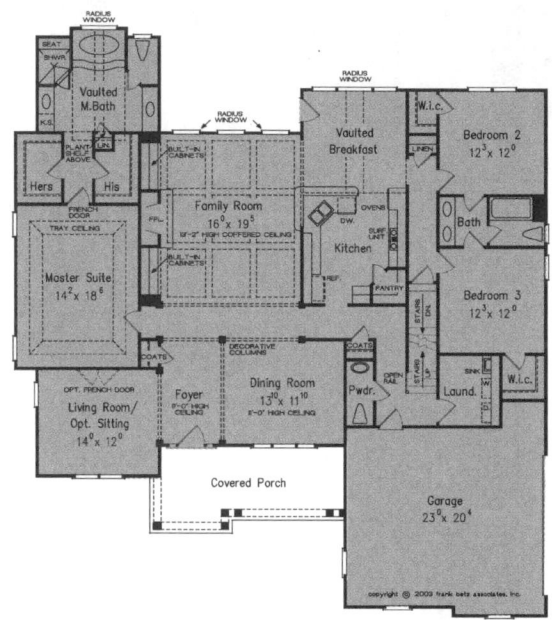

One story is all you need when the floor plan is as perfect as this one. Family and friends will feel right at home in the family room. The nearby kitchen connects to a convenient breakfast room. The master suite and bath are spectacular—feel free to turn the living room into a master sitting room for more space. Two more bedrooms are on the opposite side of the plan and share a full bath.

HPK2100473

Style: Bungalow
Square Footage: 2,487
Bonus Space: 306 sq. ft.
Bedrooms: 3
Bathrooms: 2 ½
Width: 61' - 6"
Depth: 67' - 6"
Foundation: Crawlspace, Slab, Unfinished Walkout Basement

EPLANS.COM

HPK2100474

Style: Bungalow

Square Footage: 2,487

Bonus Space: 306 sq. ft.

Bedrooms: 3

Bathrooms: 2 ½

Width: 61' - 6"

Depth: 67' - 6"

Foundation: Crawlspace, Slab, Unfinished Walkout Basement

EPLANS.COM

Experience the benefits of bunglaow living in this well-appointed single story home. Lofty ceilings with decorative touches add appeal throughout. The master suite indulges with a lavish bath equipped for two. Two secondary bedrooms share a Jack-and-Jill bath. The spacious deck accessed from the breakfast area encourages outdoor gatherings.

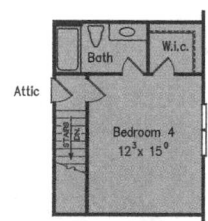

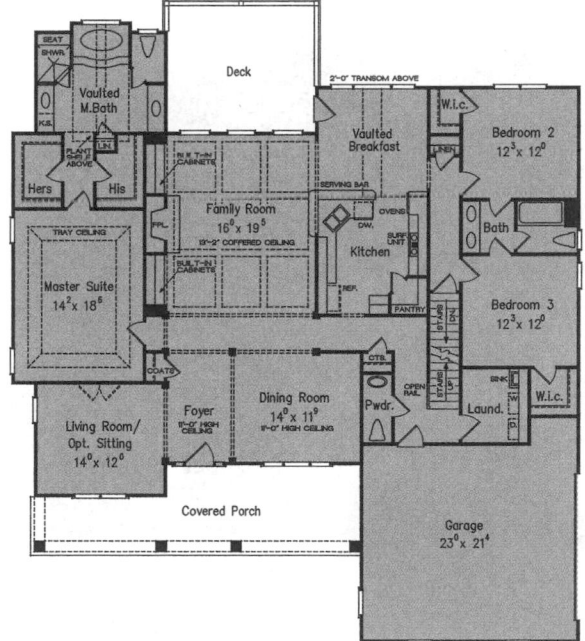

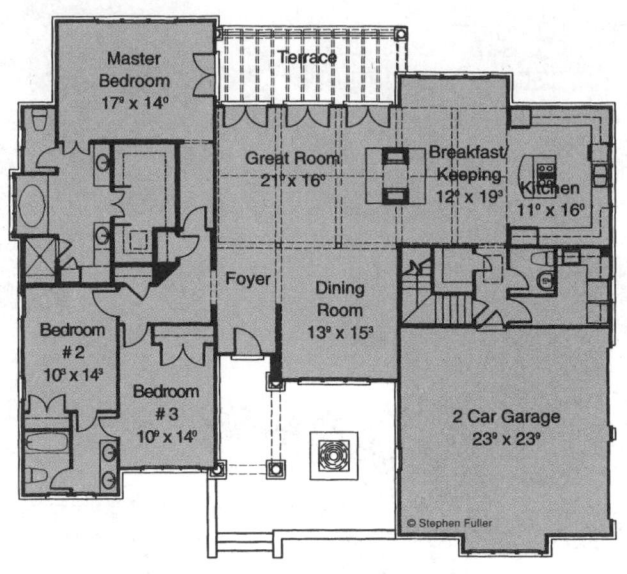

HPK2100475

Style: Bungalow
Square Footage: 2,489
Bedrooms: 3
Bathrooms: 2 ½
Width: 68' - 3"
Depth: 62' - 0"
Foundation: Finished Walkout Basement

EPLANS.COM

This fine bungalow will be the envy of any neighborhood. The great room is enhanced by a beam ceiling, a through-fireplace, and French doors to the rear terrace. The U-shaped kitchen features a cooktop island. The master suite features a walk-in closet, a separate shower, and access to the terrace. Two secondary bedrooms share a full bath.

HPK2100476

Style: French Country

Square Footage: 2,491

Bonus Space: 588 sq. ft.

Bedrooms: 3

Bathrooms: 2 ½

Width: 64' - 0"

Depth: 72' - 4"

Foundation: Crawlspace, Slab, Unfinished Walkout Basement

EPLANS.COM

European details bring charm and a bit of joie de vivre to this traditional home, and a thoughtful floor plan warms up to a variety of lifestyles. Comfortable living space includes a vaulted family room with a centered fireplace. A sizable gourmet kitchen offers a walk-in pantry and a center cooktop island counter. The master suite offers a tray ceiling and a private sitting room, bright with windows and a warming hearth.

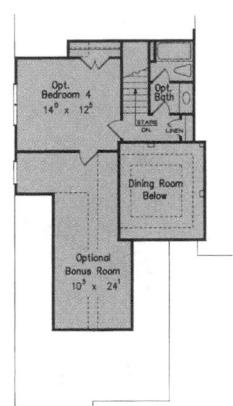

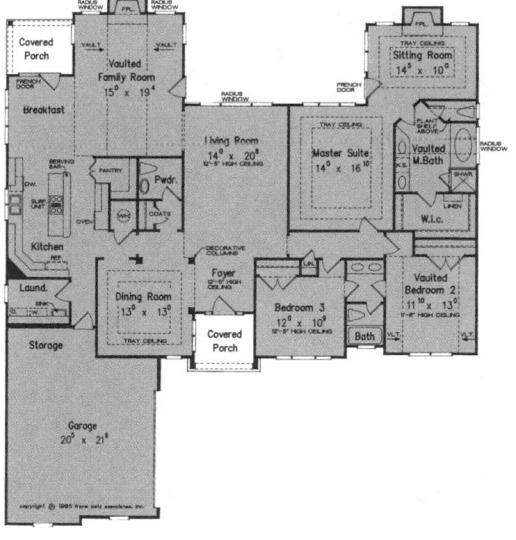

2,000 TO 2,499 SQUARE FEET

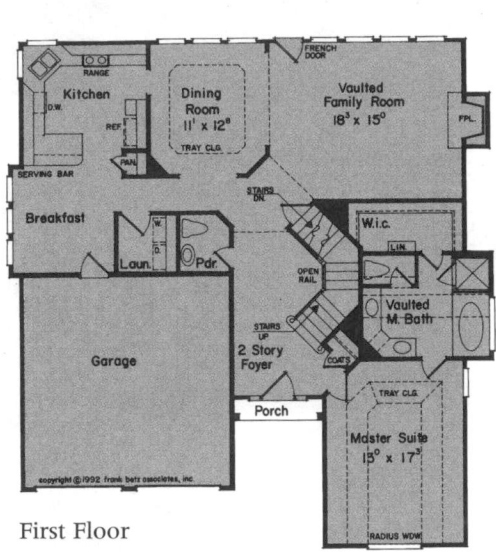

First Floor

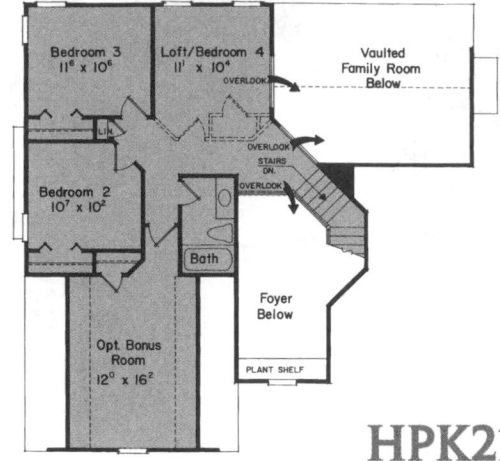

Second Floor

HPK2100477

Style: Colonial Revival

First Floor: 1,426 sq. ft.

Second Floor: 574 sq. ft.

Total: 2,000 sq. ft.

Bonus Space: 233 sq. ft.

Bedrooms: 4

Bathrooms: 2 ½

Width: 45' - 6"

Depth: 48' - 0"

Foundation: Crawlspace, Unfinished Walkout Basement

EPLANS.COM

This home—with a gabled roof, keystone lintels above arched windows, and stone accents—gives a warm and welcoming appeal. To the right is the luxurious master suite. The hall leads to the massive family room, which enjoys a fireplace and accesses the rear through French doors. The tray-ceilinged dining room gives access to the elaborate kitchen with a pantry, plenty of counter space, and a serving bar. The second floor is complete with three spacious family bedrooms that share a hall bath.

HPK2100478

Style: Craftsman
First Floor: 1,060 sq. ft.
Second Floor: 950 sq. ft.
Total: 2,010 sq. ft.
Bedrooms: 3
Bathrooms: 3
Width: 32' - 0"
Depth: 35' - 0"
Foundation: Crawlspace

EPLANS.COM

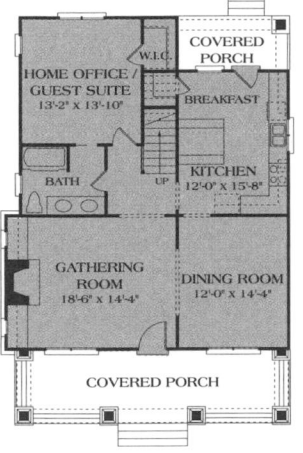

First Floor

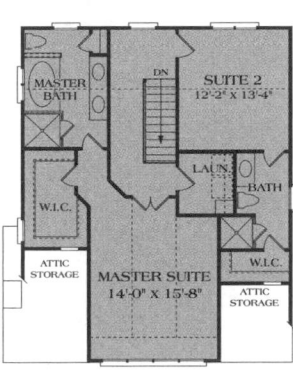

Second Floor

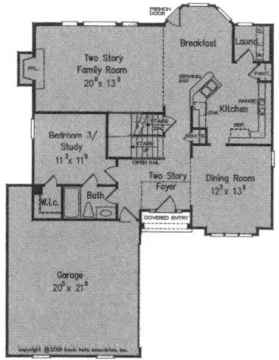

First Floor

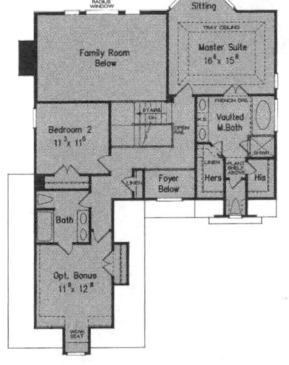

Second Floor

HPK2100479

Style: French Country
First Floor: 1,191 sq. ft.
Second Floor: 824 sq. ft.
Total: 2,015 sq. ft.
Bonus Space: 199 sq. ft.
Bedrooms: 3
Bathrooms: 3
Width: 41' - 6"
Depth: 55' - 0"
Foundation: Crawlspace, Unfinished Walkout Basement

EPLANS.COM

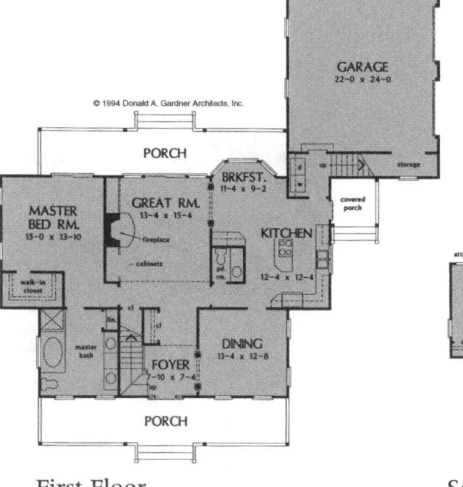

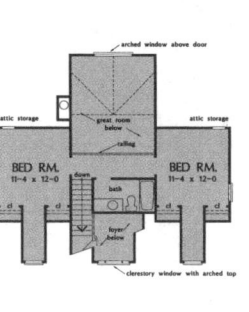

First Floor

Second Floor

HPK2100480

Style: Farmhouse

First Floor: 1,506 sq. ft.

Second Floor: 513 sq. ft.

Total: 2,019 sq. ft.

Bonus Space: 397 sq. ft.

Bedrooms: 3

Bathrooms: 2 ½

Width: 65' - 4"

Depth: 67' - 10"

EPLANS.COM

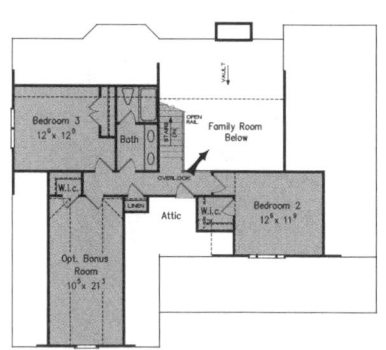

First Floor

Second Floor

HPK2100481

Style: Country

First Floor: 1,480 sq. ft.

Second Floor: 544 sq. ft.

Total: 2,024 sq. ft.

Bonus Space: 253 sq. ft.

Bedrooms: 3

Bathrooms: 2 ½

Width: 52' - 0"

Depth: 46' - 4"

Foundation: Crawlspace, Slab, Unfinished Walkout Basement

EPLANS.COM

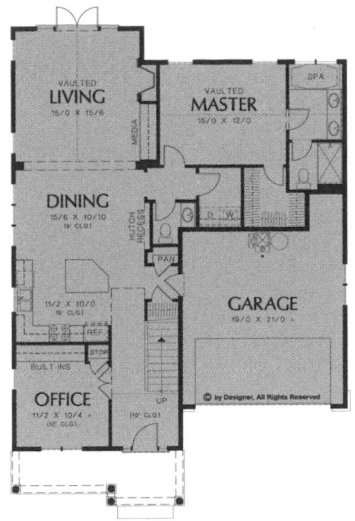

First Floor

Second Floor

HPK2100482

Style: Cottage

First Floor: 1,407 sq. ft.

Second Floor: 625 sq. ft.

Total: 2,032 sq. ft.

Bedrooms: 3

Bathrooms: 2 ½

Width: 40' - 0"

Depth: 56' - 0"

Foundation: Crawlspace

EPLANS.COM

HPK2100483

Style: Country

First Floor: 1,559 sq. ft.

Second Floor: 475 sq. ft.

Total: 2,034 sq. ft.

Bonus Space: 321 sq. ft.

Bedrooms: 4

Bathrooms: 3

Width: 50' - 0"

Depth: 56' - 4"

Foundation: Crawlspace, Slab, Unfinished Walkout Basement

EPLANS.COM

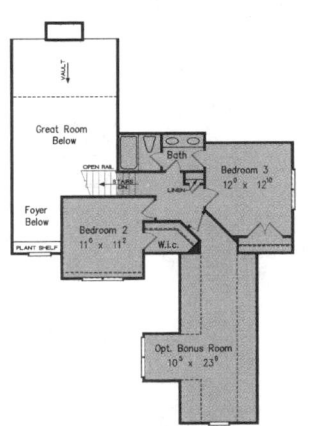

Second Floor

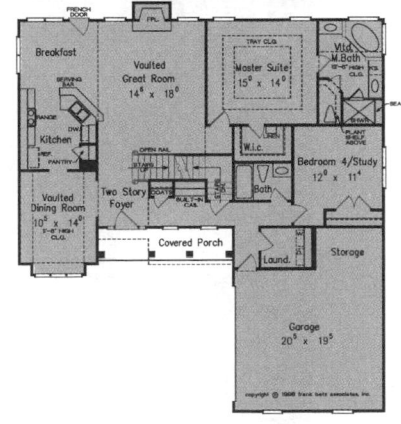

First Floor

2,000 TO 2,499 SQUARE FEET

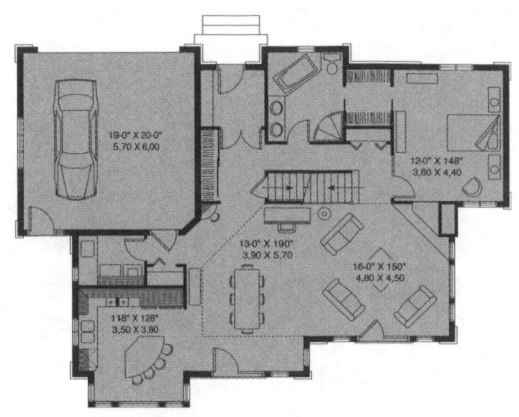

First Floor

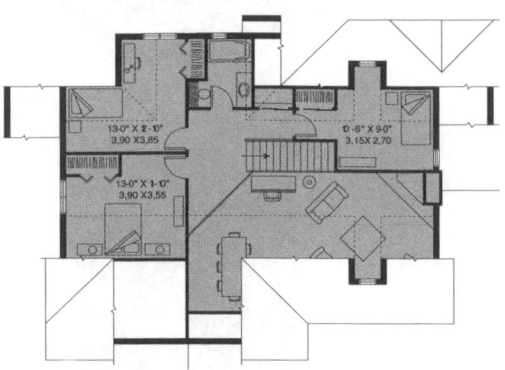

Second Floor

HPK2100484

Style: Cottage

First Floor: 1,347 sq. ft.

Second Floor: 690 sq. ft.

Total: 2,037 sq. ft.

Bedrooms: 4

Bathrooms: 2

Width: 55' - 0"

Depth: 41' - 0"

Foundation: Unfinished Basement

EPLANS.COM

First Floor

Second Floor

HPK2100485

Style: Greek Revival

First Floor: 1,370 sq. ft.

Second Floor: 668 sq. ft.

Total: 2,038 sq. ft.

Bonus Space: 421 sq. ft.

Bedrooms: 3

Bathrooms: 2 ½

Width: 71' - 8"

Depth: 49' - 4"

Foundation: Crawlspace

EPLANS.COM

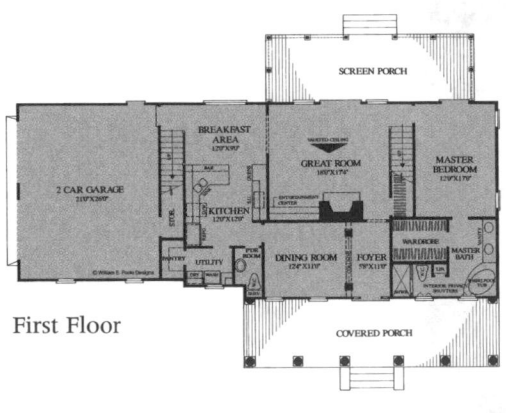

First Floor

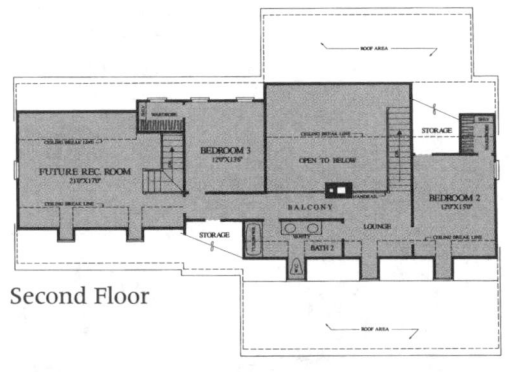

Second Floor

© William E. Poole Designs, Inc.

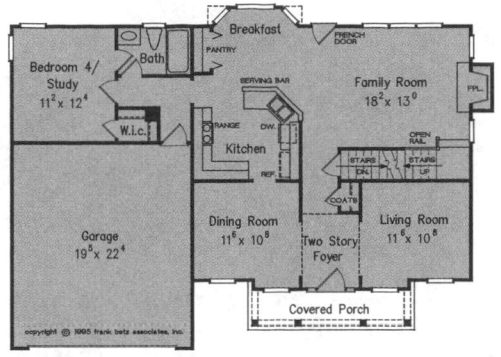

First Floor

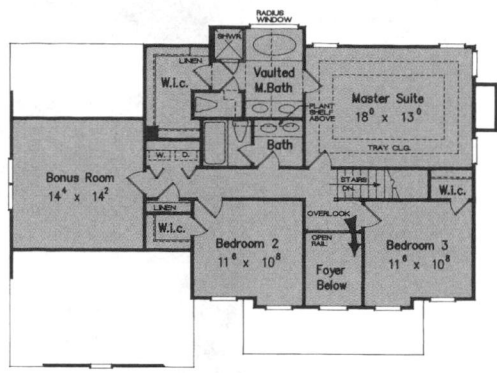

Second Floor

HPK2100486

Style: Colonial Revival

First Floor: 1,135 sq. ft.

Second Floor: 917 sq. ft.

Total: 2,052 sq. ft.

Bonus Space: 216 sq. ft.

Bedrooms: 4

Bathrooms: 3

Width: 52' - 4"

Depth: 37' - 6"

Foundation: Crawlspace, Slab, Unfinished Walkout Basement

EPLANS.COM

HPK2100487

Second Floor

Style: Country

First Floor: 1,562 sq. ft.

Second Floor: 502 sq. ft.

Total: 2,064 sq. ft.

Bonus Space: 416 sq. ft.

Bedrooms: 3

Bathrooms: 2 ½

Width: 54' - 0"

Depth: 55' - 10"

EPLANS.COM

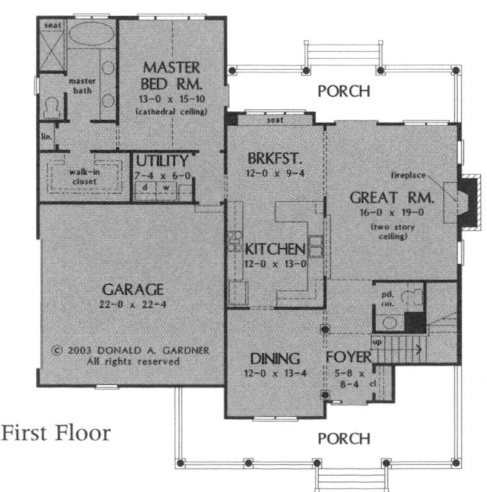

First Floor

HPK2100488

Style: New American
First Floor: 1,605 sq. ft.
Second Floor: 467 sq. ft.
Total: 2,072 sq. ft.
Bonus Space: 217 sq. ft.
Bedrooms: 4
Bathrooms: 3
Width: 52' - 0"
Depth: 46' - 6"
Foundation: Crawlspace, Unfinished Walkout Basement

EPLANS.COM

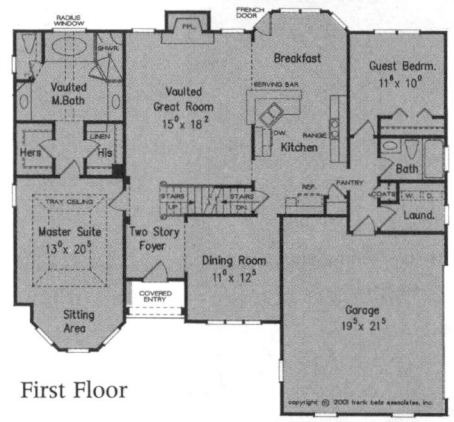

First Floor

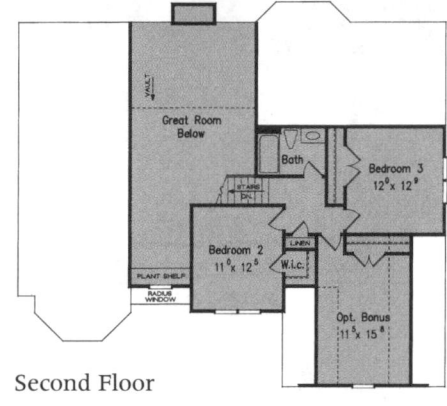

Second Floor

© 1999 Donald A. Gardner, Inc.

B. NATHAN

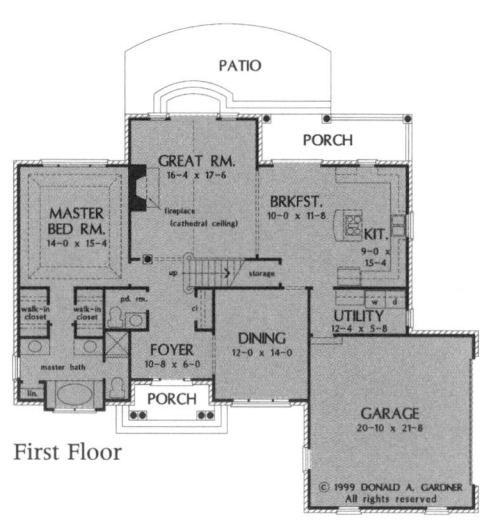

First Floor

© 1999 DONALD A. GARDNER
All rights reserved

HPK2100489

Style: New American
First Floor: 1,588 sq. ft.
Second Floor: 487 sq. ft.
Total: 2,075 sq. ft.
Bonus Space: 363 sq. ft.
Bedrooms: 3
Bathrooms: 2 ½
Width: 60' - 1"
Depth: 50' - 11"

EPLANS.COM

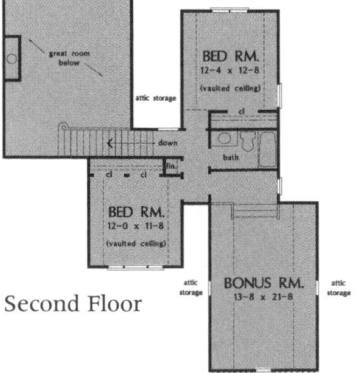

Second Floor

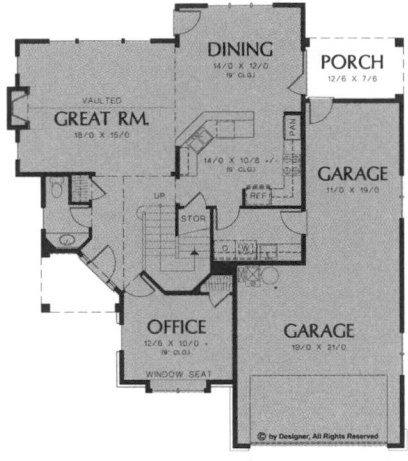

First Floor

Second Floor

HPK2100490

Style: Cottage

First Floor: 1,109 sq. ft.

Second Floor: 970 sq. ft.

Total: 2,079 sq. ft.

Bedrooms: 3

Bathrooms: 2 ½

Width: 45' - 0"

Depth: 52' - 0"

Foundation: Crawlspace

EPLANS.COM

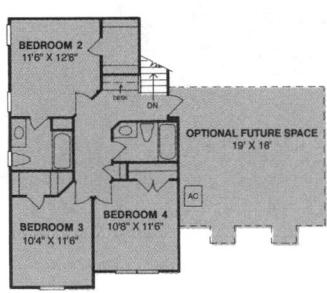

Second Floor

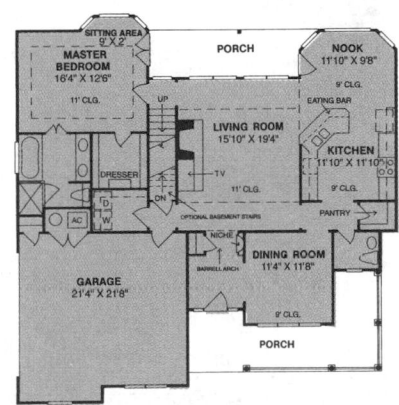

First Floor

HPK2100491

Style: Country

First Floor: 1,383 sq. ft.

Second Floor: 703 sq. ft.

Total: 2,086 sq. ft.

Bonus Space: 342 sq. ft.

Bedrooms: 4

Bathrooms: 3 ½

Width: 49' - 0"

Depth: 50' - 0"

EPLANS.COM

HPK2100492

Style: New American
First Floor: 1,139 sq. ft.
Second Floor: 948 sq. ft.
Total: 2,087 sq. ft.
Bedrooms: 3
Bathrooms: 2 ½
Width: 32' - 0"
Depth: 59' - 4"
Foundation: Unfinished Basement

EPLANS.COM

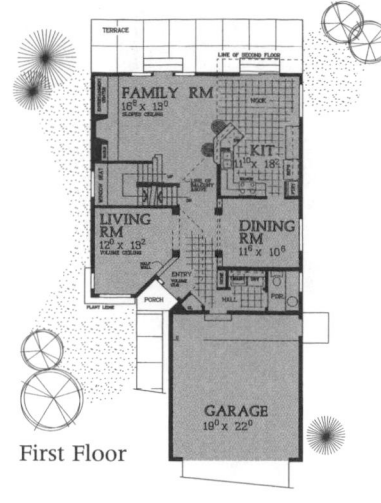

First Floor

Second Floor

HPK2100493

Style: Country
First Floor: 1,377 sq. ft.
Second Floor: 714 sq. ft.
Total: 2,091 sq. ft.
Bonus Space: 375 sq. ft.
Bedrooms: 4
Bathrooms: 2 ½
Width: 55' - 8"
Depth: 62' - 4"

EPLANS.COM

Second Floor

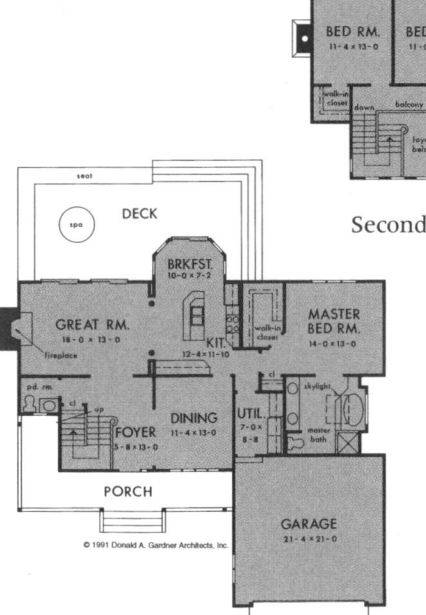

First Floor

© 1991 Donald A. Gardner Architects, Inc.

ORDER BLUEPRINTS ANYTIME AT EPLANS.COM OR 1-800-521-6797

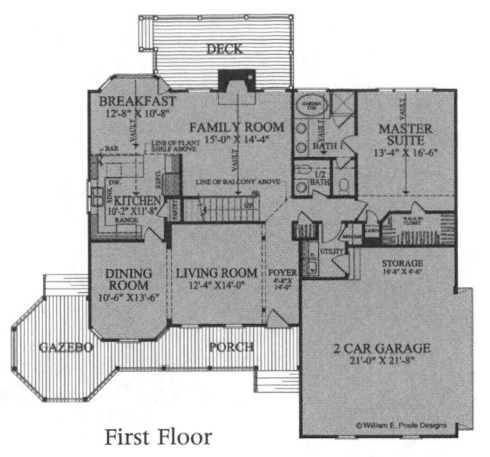

First Floor

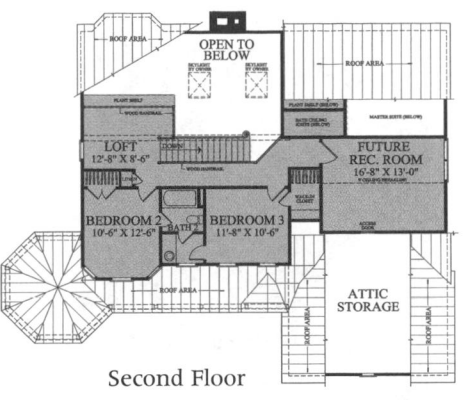

Second Floor

©2003 William E. Poole Designs, Inc.

HPK2100494

Style: Queen Anne
First Floor: 1,492 sq. ft.
Second Floor: 607 sq. ft.
Total: 2,099 sq. ft.
Bonus Space: 233 sq. ft.
Bedrooms: 3
Bathrooms: 2 ½
Width: 61' - 2"
Depth: 58' - 4"
Foundation: Crawlspace

EPLANS.COM

HPK2100495

Style: Craftsman
First Floor: 1,392 sq. ft.
Second Floor: 708 sq. ft.
Total: 2,100 sq. ft.
Bedrooms: 3
Bathrooms: 2 ½
Width: 32' - 0"
Depth: 55' - 0"
Foundation: Crawlspace

EPLANS.COM

First Floor   Second Floor

HPK2100496

Style: French Country

First Floor: 1,626 sq. ft.

Second Floor: 475 sq. ft.

Total: 2,101 sq. ft.

Bedrooms: 3

Bathrooms: 2 ½

Width: 59' - 0"

Depth: 60' - 8"

Foundation: Unfinished Basement

EPLANS.COM

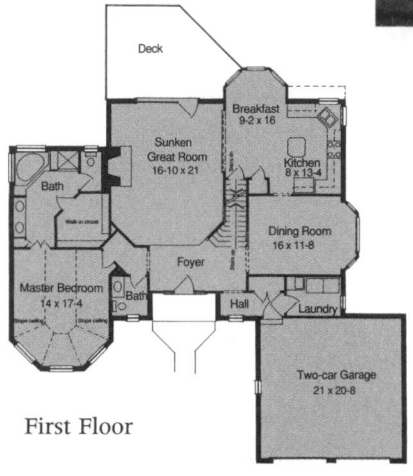

First Floor

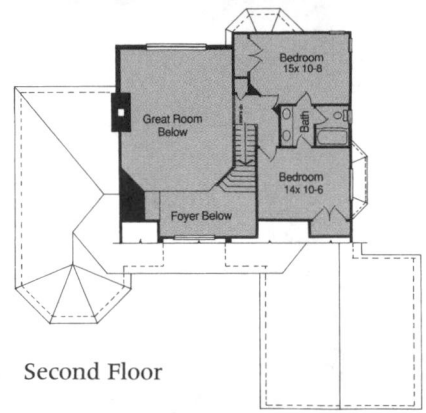

Second Floor

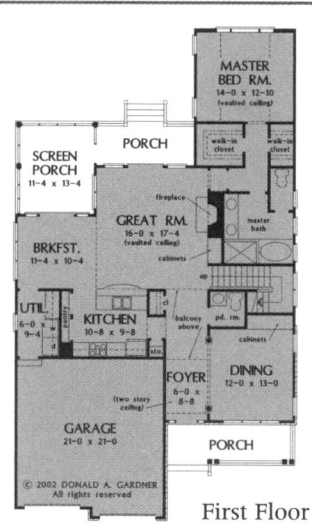

First Floor

HPK2100497

Style: Cottage

First Floor: 1,496 sq. ft.

Second Floor: 615 sq. ft.

Total: 2,111 sq. ft.

Bonus Space: 277 sq. ft.

Bedrooms: 3

Bathrooms: 2 ½

Width: 40' - 4"

Depth: 70' - 0"

EPLANS.COM

Second Floor

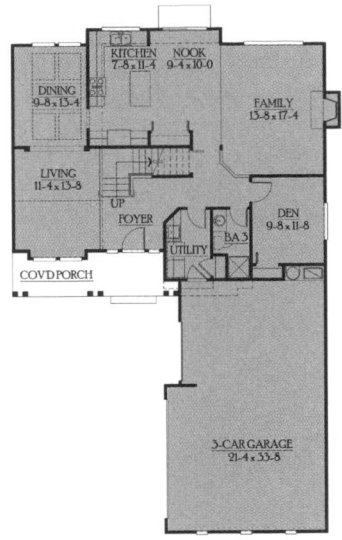

First Floor

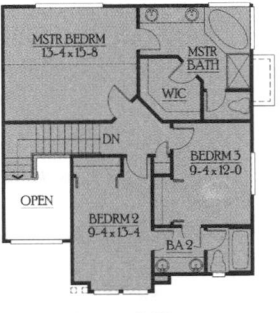

Second Floor

HPK2100498

Style: Craftsman

First Floor: 1,296 sq. ft.

Second Floor: 819 sq. ft.

Total: 2,115 sq. ft.

Bedrooms: 3

Bathrooms: 3

Width: 42' - 0"

Depth: 68' - 0"

Foundation: Crawlspace

EPLANS.COM

HPK2100499

Style: Cottage

First Floor: 878 sq. ft.

Second Floor: 1,245 sq. ft.

Total: 2,123 sq. ft.

Bedrooms: 3

Bathrooms: 2 ½

Width: 27' - 6"

Depth: 64' - 0"

Foundation: Crawlspace

EPLANS.COM

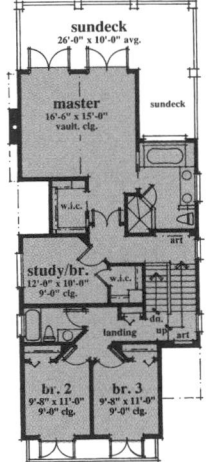

First Floor

Second Floor

2,000 TO 2,499 SQUARE FEET

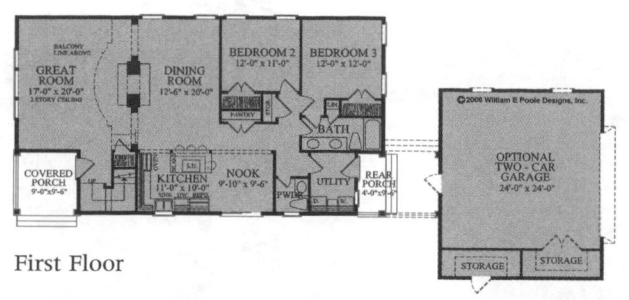

First Floor

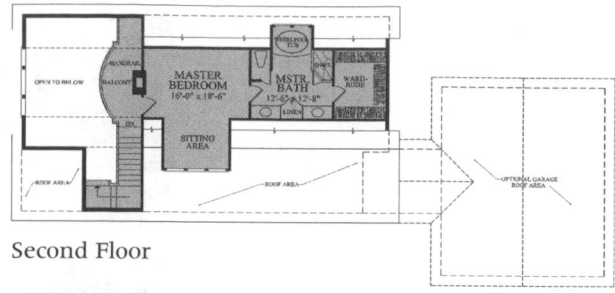

Second Floor

©2006 William E Poole Designs, Inc.

HPK2100500

Style: Cottage

First Floor: 1,588 sq. ft.

Second Floor: 537 sq. ft.

Total: 2,125 sq. ft.

Bedrooms: 3

Bathrooms: 2 ½

Width: 30' - 8"

Depth: 56' - 2"

Foundation: Crawlspace

EPLANS.COM

HPK2100501

Style: Craftsman

First Floor: 985 sq. ft.

Second Floor: 1,162 sq. ft.

Total: 2,147 sq. ft.

Bedrooms: 3

Bathrooms: 2 ½

Width: 30' - 0"

Depth: 56' - 0"

Foundation: Crawlspace

EPLANS.COM

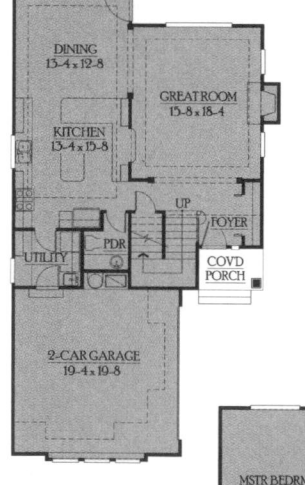

First Floor

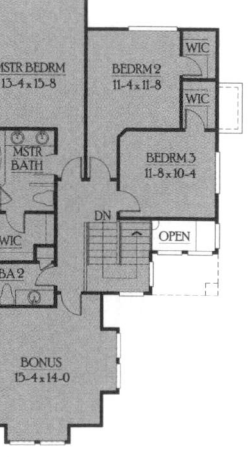

Second Floor

HPK2100502

Style: Colonial Revival

Square Footage: 2,127

Bedrooms: 3

Bathrooms: 2 ½

Width: 69' - 0"

Depth: 67' - 4"

Foundation: Crawlspace, Slab, Unfinished Basement

EPLANS.COM

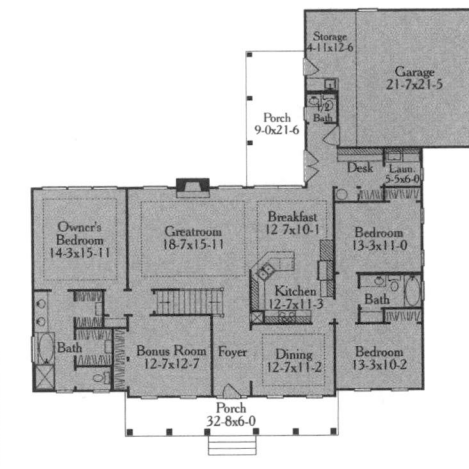

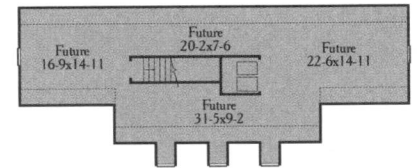

HPK2100503

Style: Craftsman

First Floor: 1,085 sq. ft.

Second Floor: 1,045 sq. ft.

Total: 2,130 sq. ft.

Bedrooms: 3

Bathrooms: 2 ½

Width: 48' - 0"

Depth: 38' - 0"

Foundation: Crawlspace

EPLANS.COM

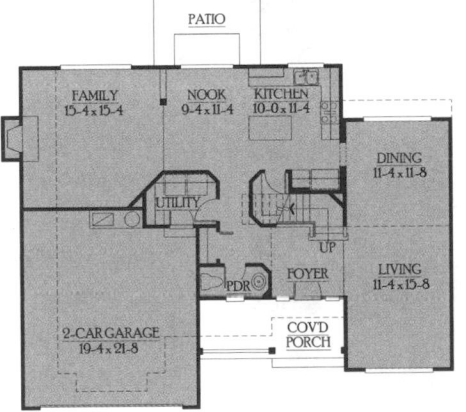

First Floor

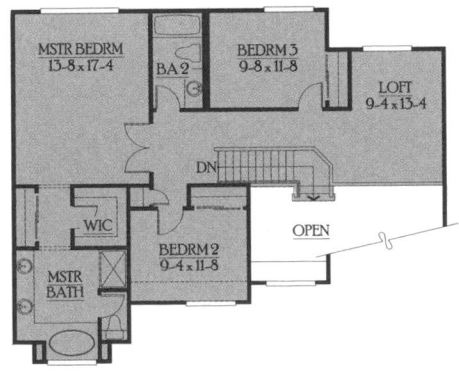

Second Floor

HPK2100504

Style: Farmhouse
First Floor: 1,501 sq. ft.
Second Floor: 631 sq. ft.
Total: 2,132 sq. ft.
Bedrooms: 3
Bathrooms: 2 ½
Width: 76' - 0"
Depth: 48' - 4"
Foundation: Crawlspace, Slab, Unfinished Basement

EPLANS.COM

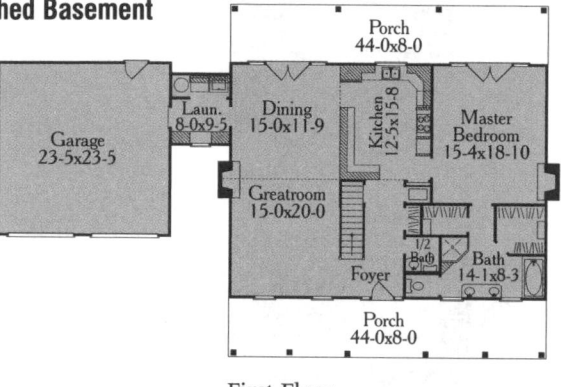

First Floor

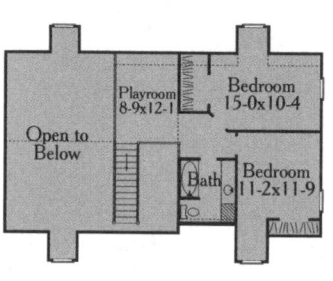

Second Floor

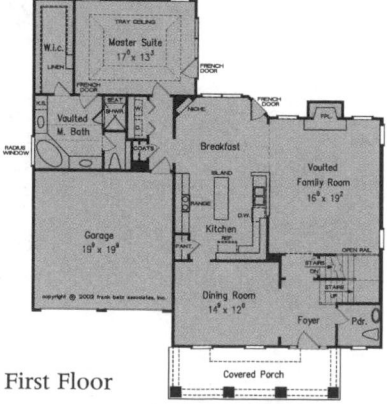

First Floor

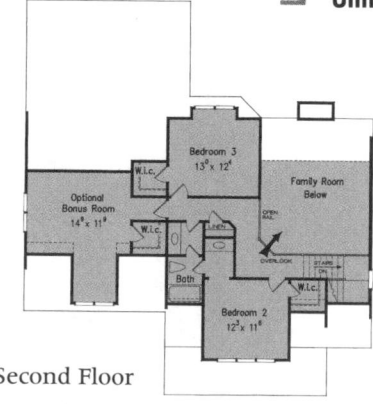

Second Floor

HPK2100505

Style: Craftsman
First Floor: 1,561 sq. ft.
Second Floor: 578 sq. ft.
Total: 2,139 sq. ft.
Bonus Space: 238 sq. ft.
Bedrooms: 3
Bathrooms: 2 ½
Width: 50' - 0"
Depth: 56' - 6"
Foundation: Crawlspace, Slab, Unfinished Walkout Basement

EPLANS.COM

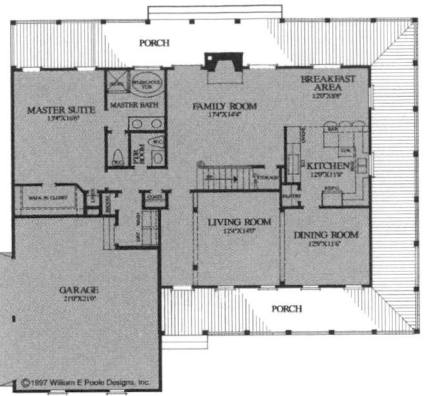

First Floor

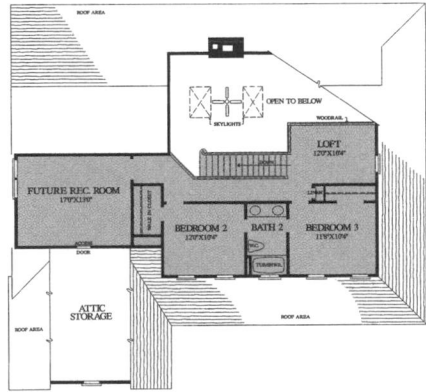

Second Floor

©1997 William E Poole Designs, Inc

HPK2100506

Style: Farmhouse

First Floor: 1,529 sq. ft.

Second Floor: 613 sq. ft.

Total: 2,142 sq. ft.

Bedrooms: 3

Bathrooms: 2 ½

Width: 59' - 8"

Depth: 55' - 4"

Foundation: Crawlspace

EPLANS.COM

HPK2100507

Style: Colonial Revival

First Floor: 1,142 sq. ft.

Second Floor: 1,004 sq. ft.

Total: 2,146 sq. ft.

Bonus Space: 156 sq. ft.

Bedrooms: 4

Bathrooms: 3

Width: 52' - 4"

Depth: 38' - 6"

Foundation: Crawlspace, Slab, Unfinished Walkout Basement

EPLANS.COM

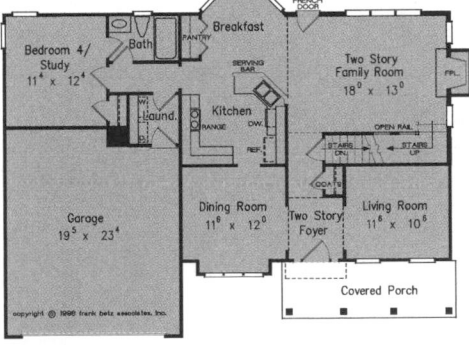

First Floor

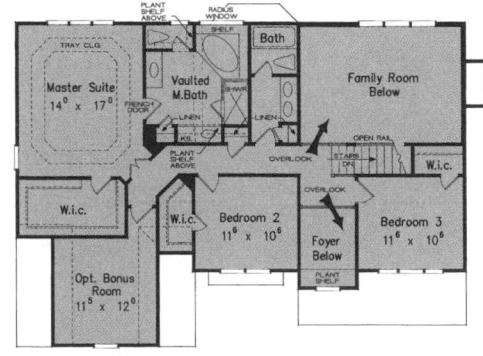

Second Floor

HPK2100508

Style: Colonial Revival
First Floor: 1,092 sq. ft.
Second Floor: 1,059 sq. ft.
Total: 2,151 sq. ft.
Bedrooms: 3
Bathrooms: 2 ½
Width: 48' - 0"
Depth: 38' - 4"
Foundation: Crawlspace, Unfinished Walkout Basement

EPLANS.COM

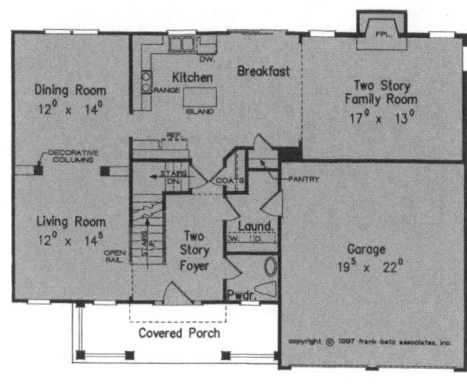

First Floor

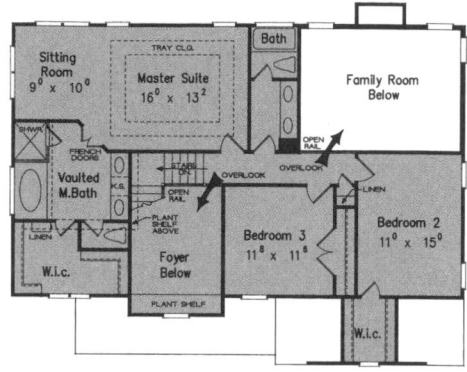

Second Floor

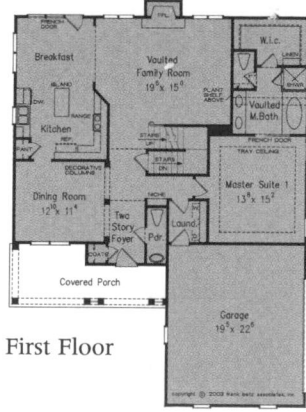

First Floor

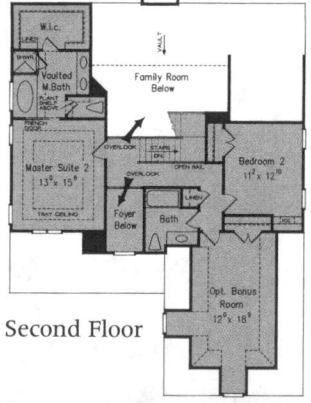

Second Floor

HPK2100509

Style: Country
First Floor: 1,390 sq. ft.
Second Floor: 764 sq. ft.
Total: 2,154 sq. ft.
Bonus Space: 282 sq. ft.
Bedrooms: 3
Bathrooms: 3 ½
Width: 42' - 0"
Depth: 57' - 4"
Foundation: Crawlspace, Unfinished Walkout Basement

EPLANS.COM

ORDER BLUEPRINTS ANYTIME AT EPLANS.COM OR 1-800-521-6797

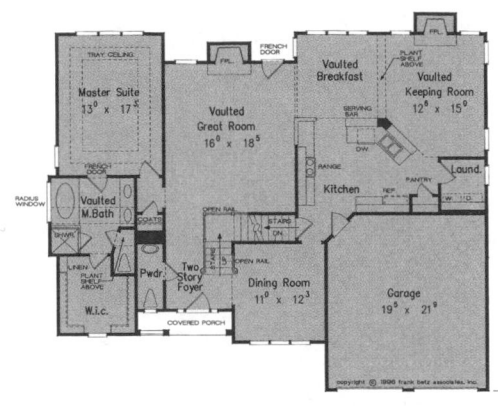

First Floor

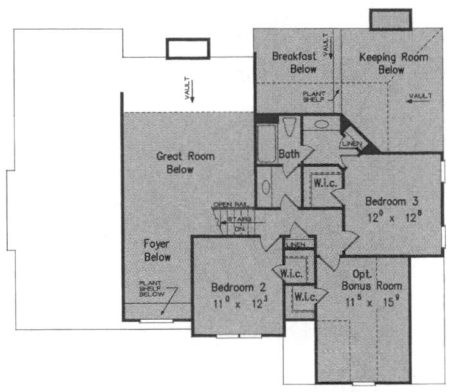

Second Floor

HPK2100510

Style: French Country

First Floor: 1,628 sq. ft.

Second Floor: 527 sq. ft.

Total: 2,155 sq. ft.

Bonus Space: 207 sq. ft.

Bedrooms: 3

Bathrooms: 2 ½

Width: 54' - 0"

Depth: 46' - 10"

Foundation: Crawlspace, Slab, Unfinished Walkout Basement

EPLANS.COM

HPK2100511

Style: Craftsman

First Floor: 1,100 sq. ft.

Second Floor: 1,054 sq. ft.

Total: 2,154 sq. ft.

Bedrooms: 3

Bathrooms: 2 ½

Width: 58' - 0"

Depth: 40' - 0"

Foundation: Crawlspace

EPLANS.COM

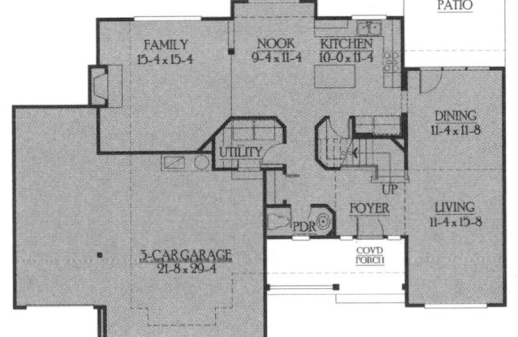

First Floor

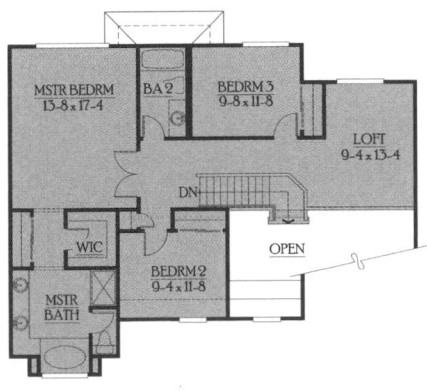

Second Floor

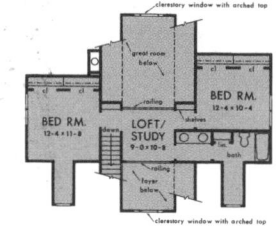

First Floor

Second Floor

BONUS RM.
27-0 x 12-0

HPK2100512

Style: Farmhouse
First Floor: 1,526 sq. ft.
Second Floor: 635 sq. ft.
Total: 2,161 sq. ft.
Bonus Space: 355 sq. ft.
Bedrooms: 3
Bathrooms: 2 ½
Width: 76' - 4"
Depth: 74' - 2"

EPLANS.COM

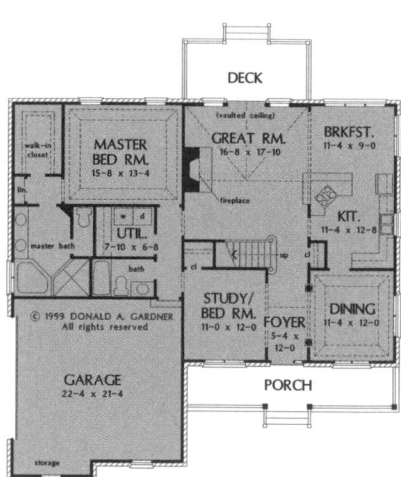

First Floor

HPK2100513

Style: Country
First Floor: 1,668 sq. ft.
Second Floor: 495 sq. ft.
Total: 2,163 sq. ft.
Bonus Space: 327 sq. ft.
Bedrooms: 4
Bathrooms: 3
Width: 52' - 7"
Depth: 50' - 11"

EPLANS.COM

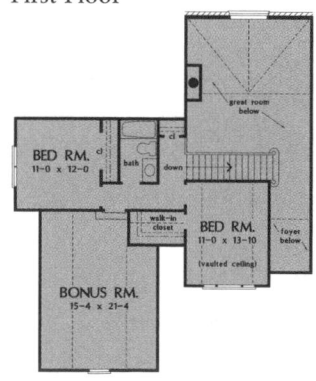

Second Floor

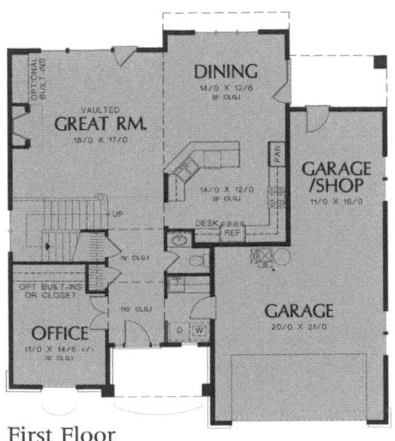

First Floor

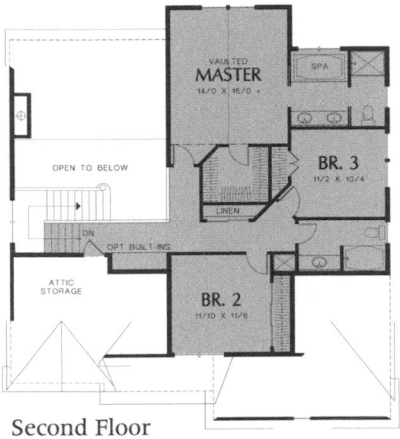

Second Floor

HPK2100514

Style: Cottage
First Floor: 1,171 sq. ft.
Second Floor: 993 sq. ft.
Total: 2,164 sq. ft.
Bedrooms: 3
Bathrooms: 2 ½
Width: 45' - 0"
Depth: 49' - 0"
Foundation: Crawlspace

EPLANS.COM

HPK2100515

Style: Prairie
First Floor: 1,538 sq. ft.
Second Floor: 628 sq. ft.
Total: 2,166 sq. ft.
Bedrooms: 3
Bathrooms: 2 ½
Width: 53' - 0"
Depth: 35' - 0"
Foundation: Crawlspace, Unfinished Basement

EPLANS.COM

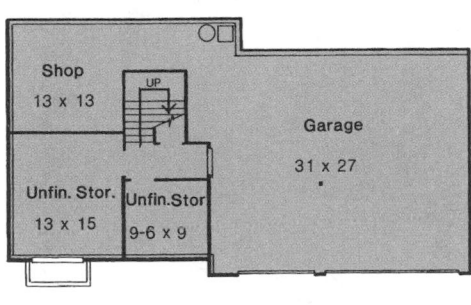

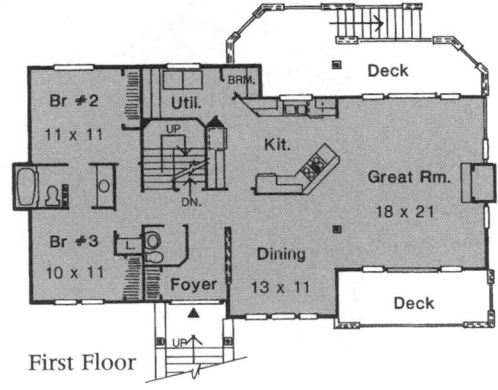

First Floor

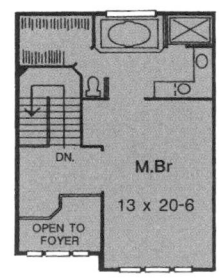

Second Floor

HPK2100516

Style: Neoclassical

First Floor: 1,176 sq. ft.

Second Floor: 993 sq. ft.

Total: 2,169 sq. ft.

Bonus Space: 322 sq. ft.

Bedrooms: 3

Bathrooms: 2 ½

Width: 56' - 7"

Depth: 32' - 0"

Foundation: Slab

EPLANS.COM

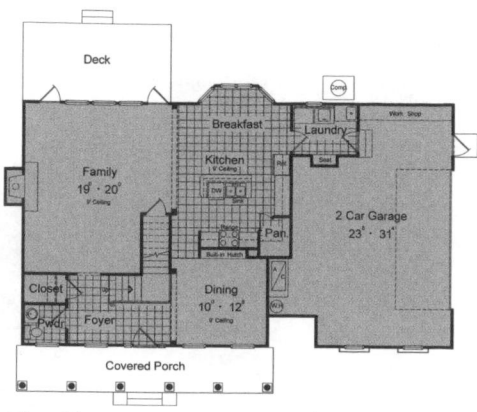

First Floor

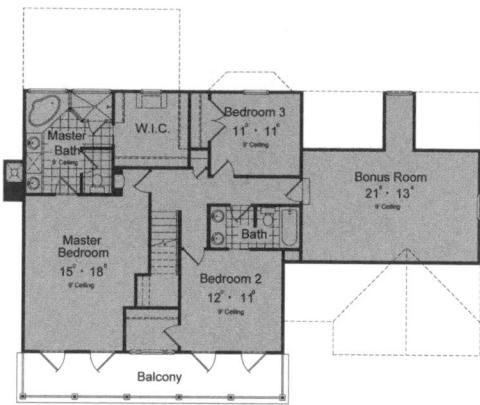

Second Floor

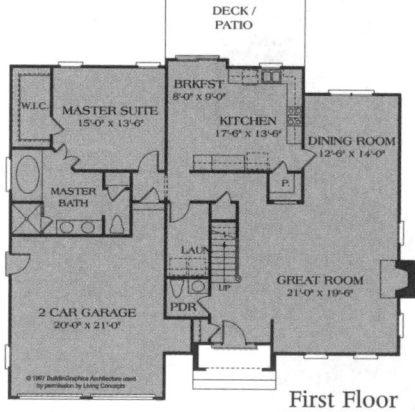

First Floor

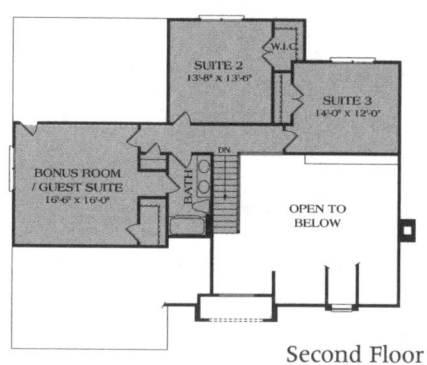

Second Floor

HPK2100517

Style: New American

First Floor: 1,577 sq. ft.

Second Floor: 593 sq. ft.

Total: 2,170 sq. ft.

Bonus Space: 320 sq. ft.

Bedrooms: 3

Bathrooms: 2 ½

Width: 52' - 10"

Depth: 45' - 10"

Foundation: Crawlspace

EPLANS.COM

HPK2100518

EPLANS.COM

Style: Cottage

First Floor: 1,580 sq. ft.

Second Floor: 595 sq. ft.

Total: 2,175 sq. ft.

Bedrooms: 3

Bathrooms: 2 ½

Width: 50' - 2"

Depth: 70' - 11"

Foundation: Finished Walkout Basement

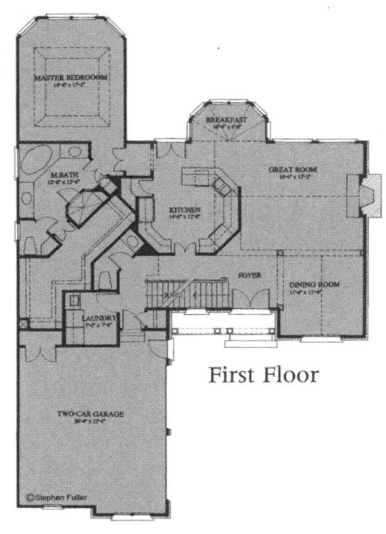

First Floor

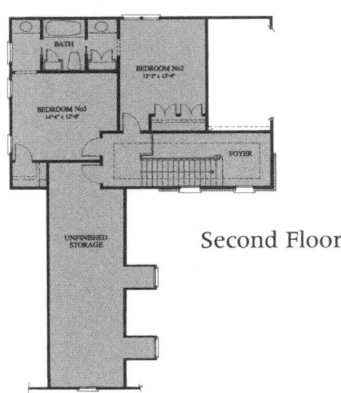

Second Floor

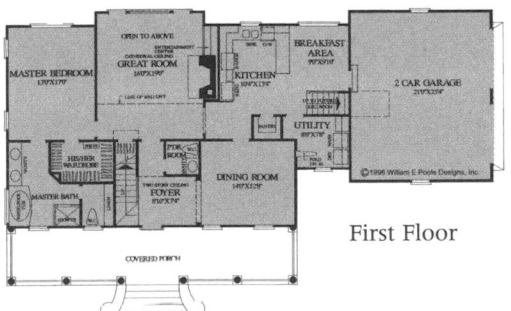

First Floor

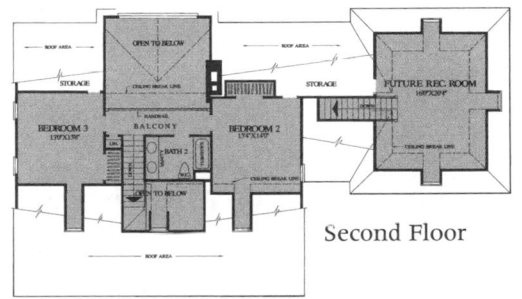

Second Floor

HPK2100519

EPLANS.COM

Style: Cottage

First Floor: 1,556 sq. ft.

Second Floor: 623 sq. ft.

Total: 2,179 sq. ft.

Bonus Space: 368 sq. ft.

Bedrooms: 3

Bathrooms: 2 ½

Width: 73' - 4"

Depth: 41' - 4"

Foundation: Crawlspace, Finished Basement

2,000 TO 2,499 SQUARE FEET

HPK2100520

Style: Country
First Floor: 1,232 sq. ft.
Second Floor: 951 sq. ft.
Total: 2,183 sq. ft.
Bonus Space: 365 sq. ft.
Bedrooms: 3
Bathrooms: 2 ½
Width: 56' - 0"
Depth: 38' - 0"
Foundation: Unfinished Basement

EPLANS.COM

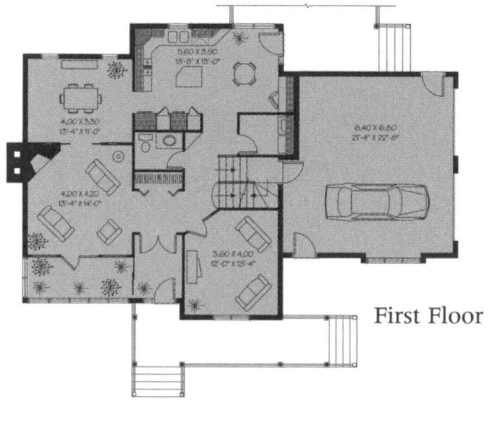

First Floor

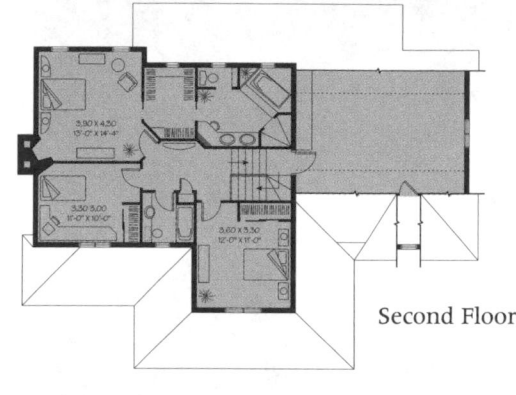

Second Floor

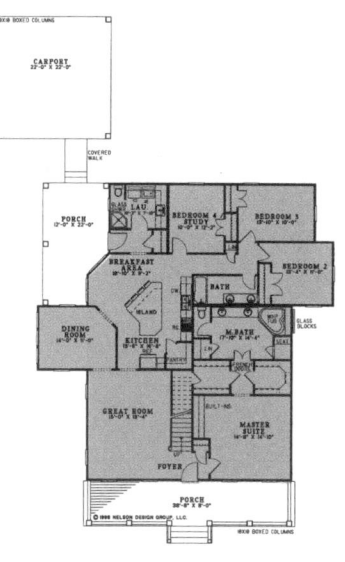

HPK2100521

Style: Farmhouse
Square Footage: 2,186
Bonus Space: 1,283 sq. ft.
Bedrooms: 4
Bathrooms: 3
Width: 62' - 10"
Depth: 91' - 4"
Foundation: Crawlspace, Slab, Unfinished Basement

EPLANS.COM

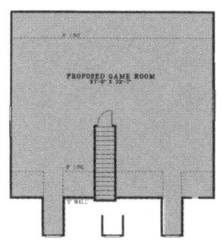

HPK2100522

Style: Farmhouse
First Floor: 1,618 sq. ft.
Second Floor: 570 sq. ft.
Total: 2,188 sq. ft.
Bonus Space: 495 sq. ft.
Bedrooms: 3
Bathrooms: 2 ½
Width: 87' - 0"
Depth: 57' - 0"

EPLANS.COM

© 1993 Donald A. Gardner Architects, Inc.

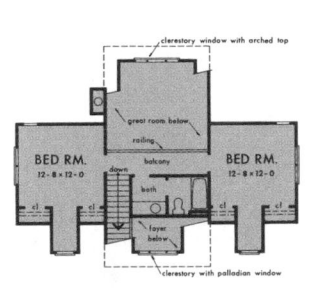

First Floor

Second Floor

©Stephen Fuller

HPK2100523

Style: Cottage
First Floor: 1,652 sq. ft.
Second Floor: 543 sq. ft.
Total: 2,195 sq. ft.
Bonus Space: 470 sq. ft.
Bedrooms: 4
Bathrooms: 3 ½
Width: 46' - 6"
Depth: 72' - 0"
Foundation: Unfinished Basement

EPLANS.COM

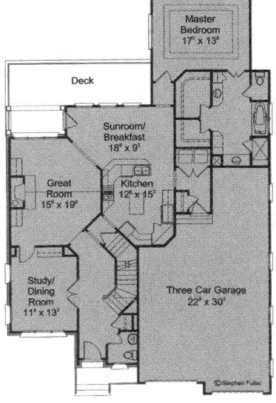

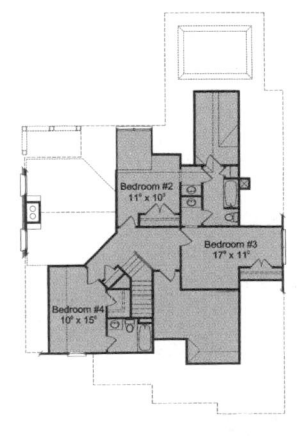

First Floor

Second Floor

2,000 TO 2,499 SQUARE FEET

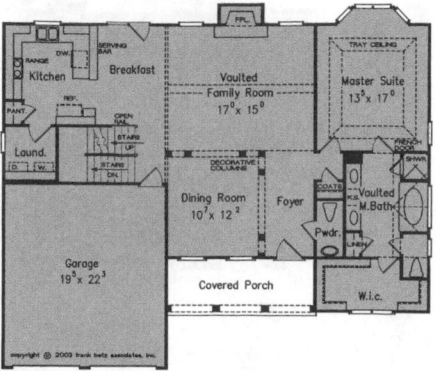

Lower Level

Main Level

HPK2100524

Style: Bungalow

Lower Level: 820 sq. ft.

Main Level: 1,381 sq. ft.

Total: 2,201 sq. ft.

Bonus Space: 331 sq. ft.

Bedrooms: 3

Bathrooms: 2 ½

Width: 51' - 0"

Depth: 44' - 0"

Foundation: Unfinished Walkout Basement

EPLANS.COM

First Floor

Second Floor

HPK2100525

Style: Craftsman

First Floor: 1,460 sq. ft.

Second Floor: 753 sq. ft.

Total: 2,213 sq. ft.

Bonus Space: 249 sq. ft.

Bedrooms: 3

Bathrooms: 2 ½

Width: 50' - 0"

Depth: 45' - 0"

Foundation: Crawlspace

EPLANS.COM

HPK2100526

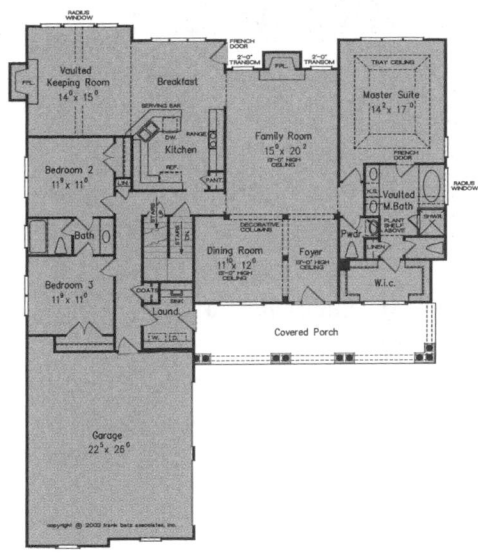

Style: Country

Square Footage: 2,214

Bonus Space: 377 sq. ft.

Bedrooms: 3

Bathrooms: 2 ½

Width: 59' - 4"

Depth: 73' - 0"

Foundation: Crawlspace, Unfinished Walkout Basement

EPLANS.COM

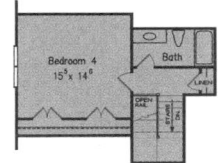

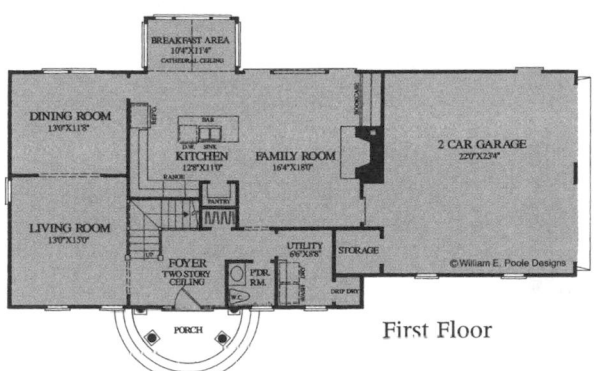

First Floor

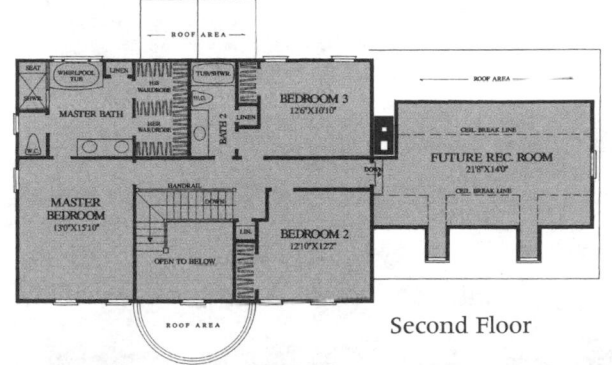

Second Floor

HPK2100527

EPLANS.COM

Style: Georgian

First Floor: 1,209 sq. ft.

Second Floor: 1,005 sq. ft.

Total: 2,214 sq. ft.

Bonus Space: 366 sq. ft.

Bedrooms: 3

Bathrooms: 2 ½

Width: 65' - 4"

Depth: 40' - 4"

Foundation: Crawlspace

HPK2100528

Style: French Country
First Floor: 1,293 sq. ft.
Second Floor: 922 sq. ft.
Total: 2,215 sq. ft.
Bonus Space: 235 sq. ft.
Bedrooms: 3
Bathrooms: 3
Width: 40' - 0"
Depth: 57' - 0"
Foundation: Crawlspace, Unfinished Walkout Basement

EPLANS.COM

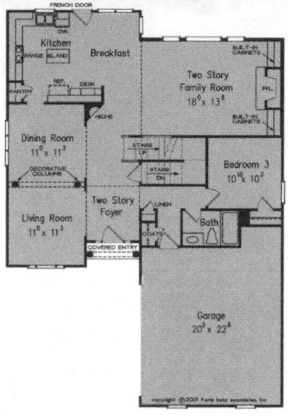

First Floor

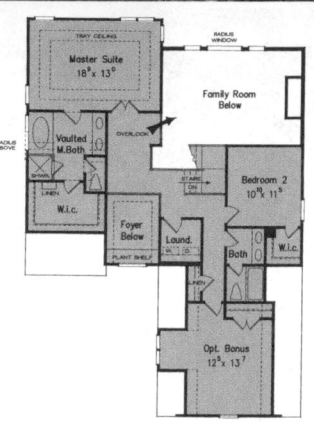

Second Floor

Find a matching garage on page 182.

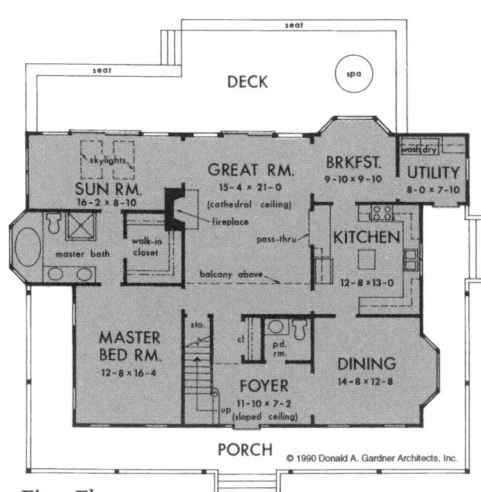

First Floor

HPK2100529

Style: Tidewater
First Floor: 1,651 sq. ft.
Second Floor: 567 sq. ft.
Total: 2,218 sq. ft.
Bedrooms: 3
Bathrooms: 2 ½
Width: 55' - 0"
Depth: 42' - 4"

EPLANS.COM

Second Floor

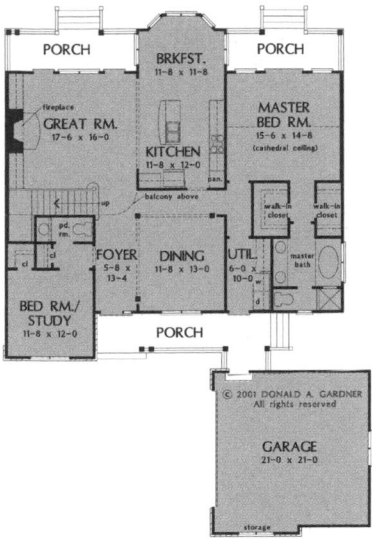

First Floor

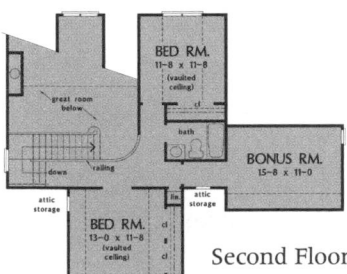

Second Floor

HPK2100530

Style: Cottage
First Floor: 1,707 sq. ft.
Second Floor: 514 sq. ft.
Total: 2,221 sq. ft.
Bonus Space: 211 sq. ft.
Bedrooms: 4
Bathrooms: 2 ½
Width: 50' - 0"
Depth: 71' - 8"

EPLANS.COM

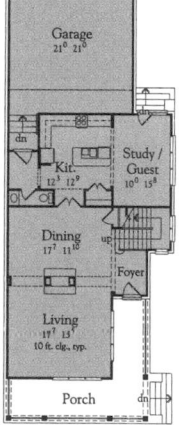

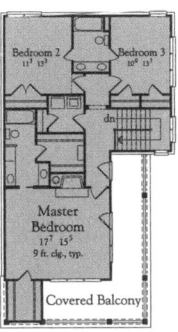

First Floor   Second Floor

HPK2100531

Style: Neoclassical
First Floor: 1,135 sq. ft.
Second Floor: 1,092 sq. ft.
Total: 2,227 sq. ft.
Bedrooms: 3
Bathrooms: 2 ½
Width: 28' - 8"
Depth: 74' - 2"
Foundation: Crawlspace

EPLANS.COM

2,000 TO 2,499 SQUARE FEET

First Floor

MASTER BED RM.
15-0 x 14-0
(vaulted ceiling)

master bath

walk-in closet

storage

UTILITY
7-8 x 6-0

w d

pd. rm.

KIT.
8-8 x 14-0

pantry

sto.

up

BRKFST.
10-0 x 10-8

PORCH

GREAT RM.
15-6 x 20-0
(cathedral ceiling)

fireplace

balcony above

FOYER
6-6 x 9-0

GARAGE
21-0 x 21-0

DINING
12-0 x 13-8

PORCH

storage

© 2001 Donald A. Gardner
All rights reserved

First Floor

Second Floor

attic storage

bath

lin

attic storage

down

sto.

attic stor.

BONUS RM.
13-0 x 21-0

BED RM.
12-10 x 14-0

cl

cl

down

LOFT
9-4 x 11-4

railing

cl

BED RM.
12-0 x 11-4

great room below

foyer below

Second Floor

HPK2100532

Style: French Country

First Floor: 1,547 sq. ft.

Second Floor: 684 sq. ft.

Total: 2,231 sq. ft.

Bonus Space: 300 sq. ft.

Bedrooms: 3

Bathrooms: 2 ½

Width: 59' - 2"

Depth: 44' - 4"

EPLANS.COM

HPK2100533

Style: French Country

First Floor: 1,701 sq. ft.

Second Floor: 534 sq. ft.

Total: 2,235 sq. ft.

Bonus Space: 274 sq. ft.

Bedrooms: 3

Bathrooms: 2 ½

Width: 65' - 11"

Depth: 43' - 5"

EPLANS.COM

First Floor

PATIO

MASTER BED RM.
13-4 x 16-8

(cathedral ceiling)

FAMILY RM.
18-0 x 16-6

fireplace

balcony above

BRKFST.
13-4 x 10-0

UTILITY
8-4 x 6-0

storage

walk-in closet

walk-in closet

pd. rm.

lin.

KIT.
11-4 x 12-0

cl

GARAGE
21-0 x 24-0

master bath

LIVING RM./ STUDY
12-0 x 12-0

DINING
11-4 x 13-0

FOYER
9-8 x 11-10

shelves

storage

PORCH

© 1998 Donald A Gardner, Inc.

First Floor

Second Floor

family room below

railing

LOFT
9-0 x 9-0

down

down

BED RM.
11-4 x 11-4

cl

attic storage

BONUS RM.
14-9 x 13-0

6-3 x 5-10

bath

lin

cl

attic storage

BED RM.
11-4 x 11-4

foyer below

Second Floor

HPK2100534

Style: Craftsman
First Floor: 1,252 sq. ft.
Second Floor: 985 sq. ft.
Total: 2,237 sq. ft.
Bonus Space: 183 sq. ft.
Bedrooms: 4
Bathrooms: 3
Width: 40' - 0"
Depth: 51' - 0"
Foundation: Crawlspace

EPLANS.COM

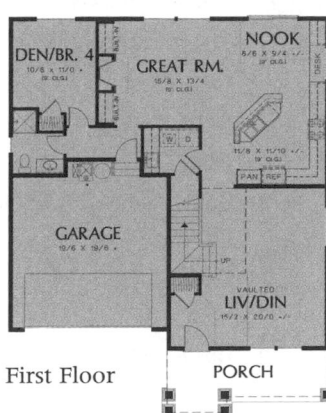

First Floor

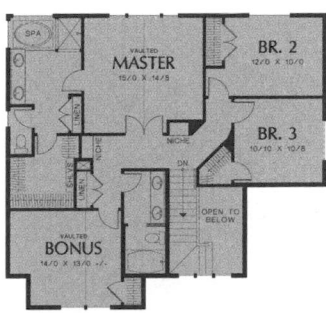

Second Floor

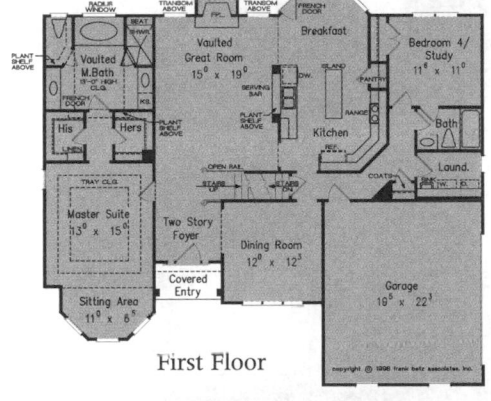

First Floor

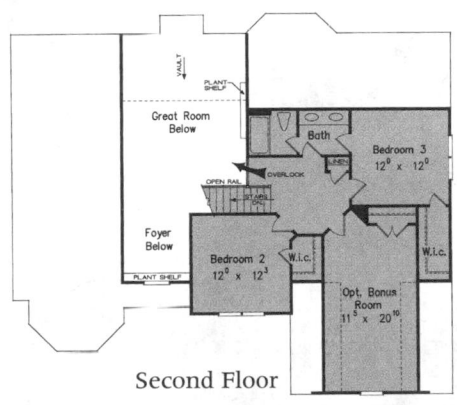

Second Floor

HPK2100535

EPLANS.COM

Style: New American
First Floor: 1,688 sq. ft.
Second Floor: 558 sq. ft.
Total: 2,246 sq. ft.
Bonus Space: 269 sq. ft.
Bedrooms: 4
Bathrooms: 3
Width: 54' - 0"
Depth: 48' - 0"
Foundation: Crawlspace, Slab, Unfinished Walkout Basement

HPK2100536

Style: Farmhouse
First Floor: 1,569 sq. ft.
Second Floor: 682 sq. ft.
Total: 2,251 sq. ft.
Bonus Space: 332 sq. ft.
Bedrooms: 3
Bathrooms: 2 ½
Width: 64' - 8"
Depth: 43' - 4"

EPLANS.COM

©1998 Donald A. Gardner, Inc.

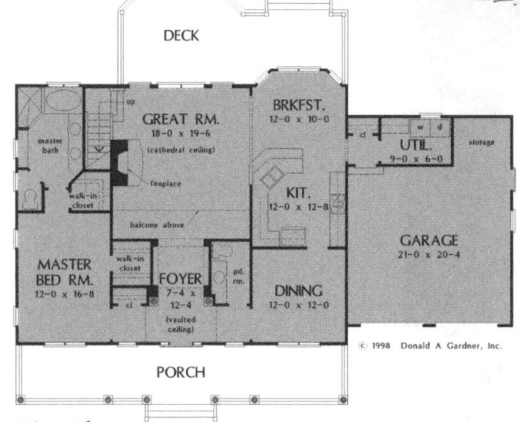

First Floor

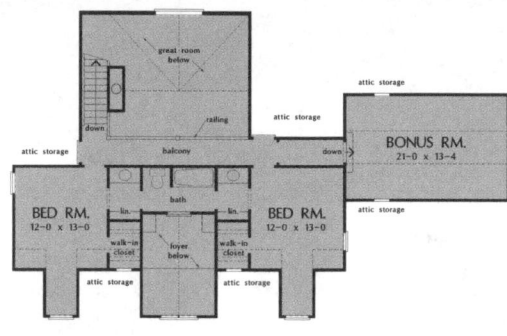

Second Floor

First Floor

HPK2100537

Style: Country
First Floor: 1,714 sq. ft.
Second Floor: 537 sq. ft.
Total: 2,251 sq. ft.
Bonus Space: 260 sq. ft.
Bedrooms: 4
Bathrooms: 3
Width: 60' - 0"
Depth: 42' - 10"
Foundation: Crawlspace, Unfinished Walkout Basement

EPLANS.COM

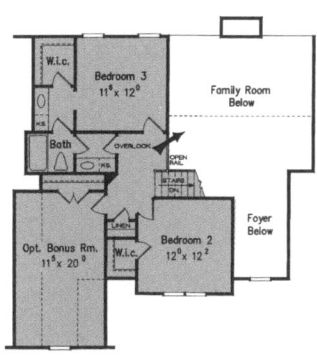

Second Floor

ORDER BLUEPRINTS ANYTIME AT EPLANS.COM OR 1-800-521-6797

HPK2100538

Style: Craftsman

First Floor: 1,302 sq. ft.

Second Floor: 960 sq. ft.

Total: 2,262 sq. ft.

Bedrooms: 3

Bathrooms: 2 ½

Width: 40' - 0"

Depth: 40' - 0"

Foundation: Slab

EPLANS.COM

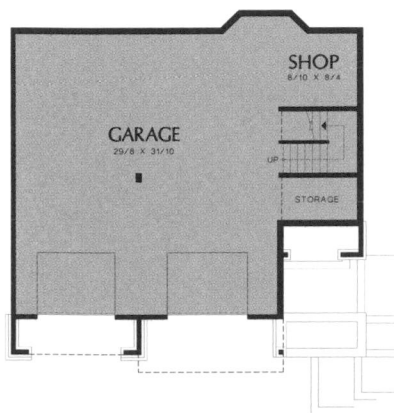

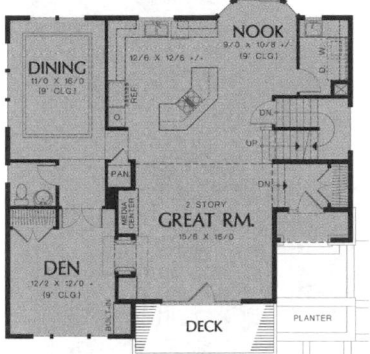

First Floor

Second Floor

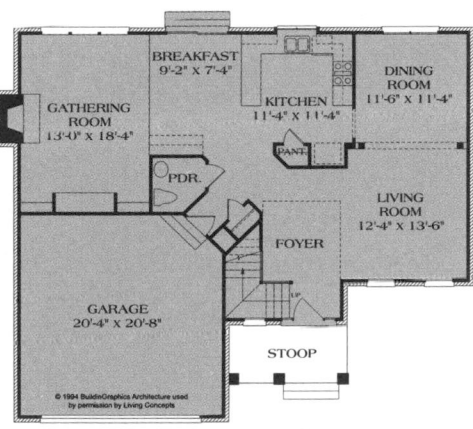

First Floor

HPK2100539

Style: Colonial Revival

First Floor: 1,118 sq. ft.

Second Floor: 1,144 sq. ft.

Total: 2,262 sq. ft.

Bedrooms: 4

Bathrooms: 2 ½

Width: 46' - 0"

Depth: 40' - 0"

Foundation: Crawlspace

EPLANS.COM

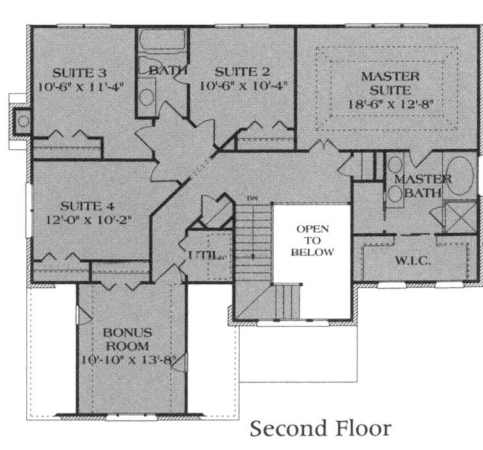

Second Floor

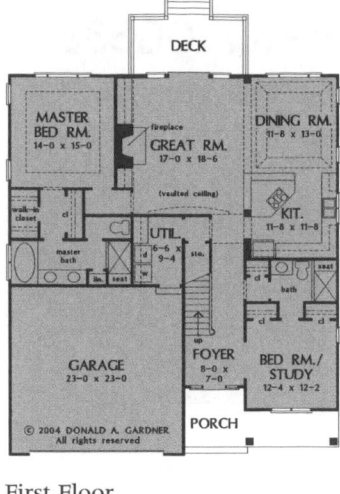

HPK2100540

Style: Country
First Floor: 1,635 sq. ft.
Second Floor: 629 sq. ft.
Total: 2,264 sq. ft.
Bonus Space: 351 sq. ft.
Bedrooms: 4
Bathrooms: 4
Width: 44' - 8"
Depth: 52' - 4"

EPLANS.COM

First Floor

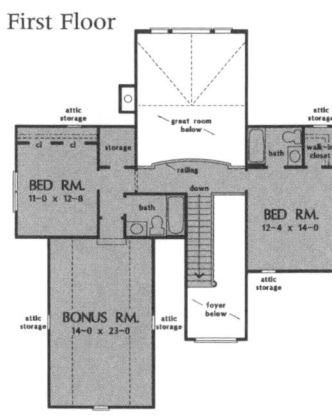

Second Floor

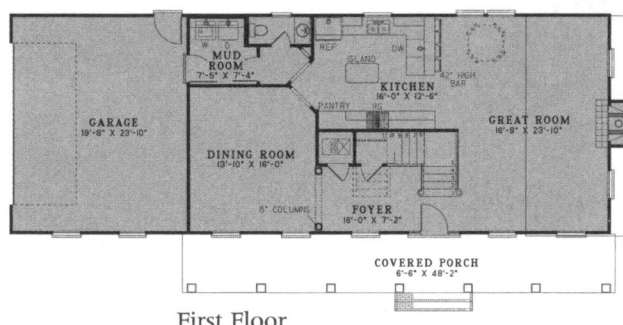

First Floor

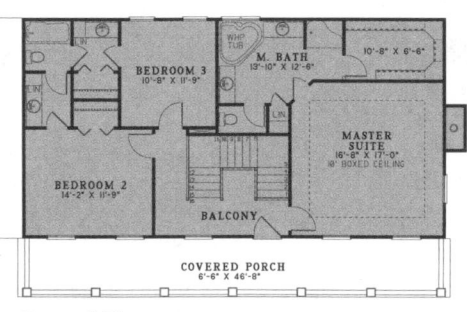

Second Floor

HPK2100541

Style: Neoclassical
First Floor: 1,168 sq. ft.
Second Floor: 1,100 sq. ft.
Total: 2,268 sq. ft.
Bedrooms: 3
Bathrooms: 2 ½
Width: 69' - 6"
Depth: 31' - 0"
Foundation: Crawlspace, Slab, Unfinished Basement, Block

EPLANS.COM

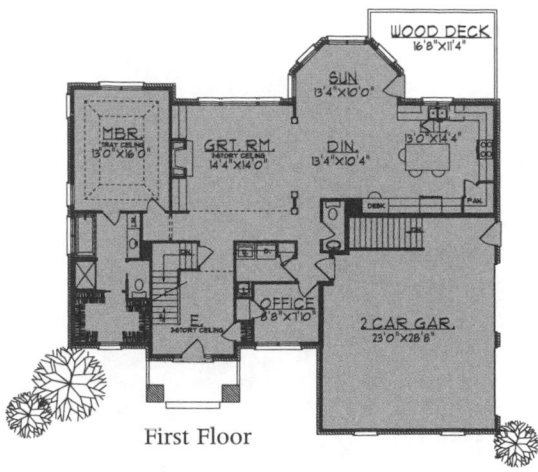

First Floor

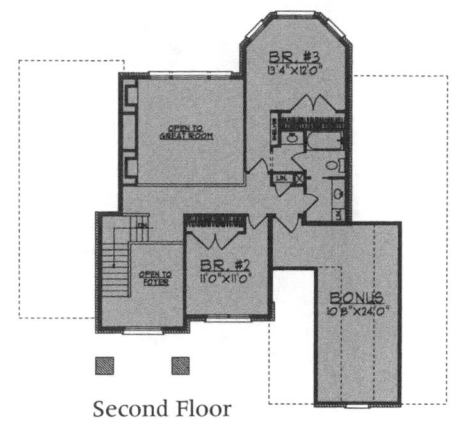

Second Floor

HPK2100542

Style: New American

First Floor: 1,649 sq. ft.

Second Floor: 622 sq. ft.

Total: 2,271 sq. ft.

Bonus Space: 250 sq. ft.

Bedrooms: 3

Bathrooms: 2 ½

Width: 57' - 4"

Depth: 52' - 4"

Foundation: Unfinished Walkout Basement

EPLANS.COM

HPK2100543

Style: Bungalow

First Floor: 1,587 sq. ft.

Second Floor: 685 sq. ft.

Total: 2,272 sq. ft.

Bedrooms: 3

Bathrooms: 2 ½

Width: 38' - 0"

Depth: 55' - 0"

Foundation: Slab

EPLANS.COM

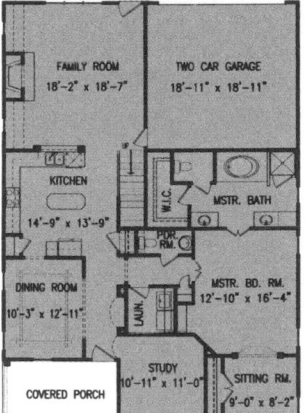

First Floor

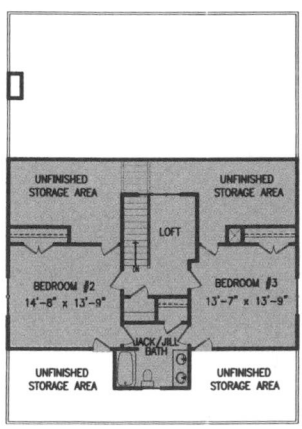

Second Floor

HPK2100544

Style: Federal - Adams

First Floor: 1,981 sq. ft.

Second Floor: 291 sq. ft.

Total: 2,272 sq. ft.

Bonus Space: 412 sq. ft.

Bedrooms: 4

Bathrooms: 3 ½

Width: 58' - 0"

Depth: 53' - 0"

Foundation: Crawlspace

© 1994 William E Poole Designs, Inc.

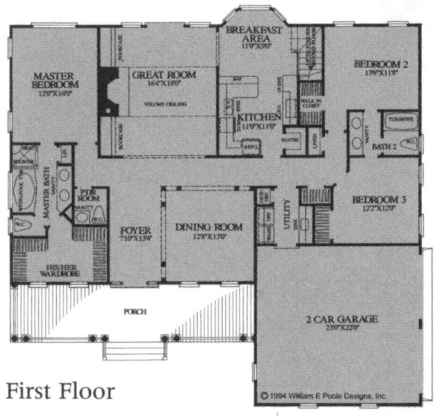

First Floor

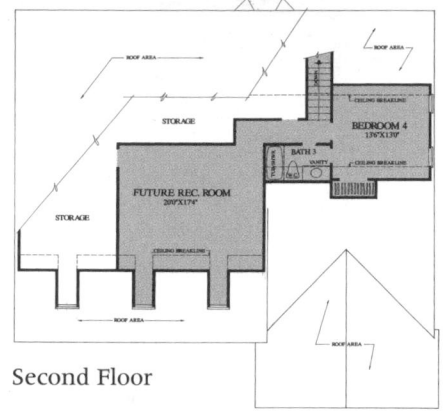

Second Floor

HPK2100545

Style: New American

First Floor: 1,290 sq. ft.

Second Floor: 985 sq. ft.

Total: 2,275 sq. ft.

Bonus Space: 186 sq. ft.

Bedrooms: 4

Bathrooms: 3

Width: 45' - 0"

Depth: 43' - 4"

Foundation: Crawlspace, Slab, Unfinished Walkout Basement

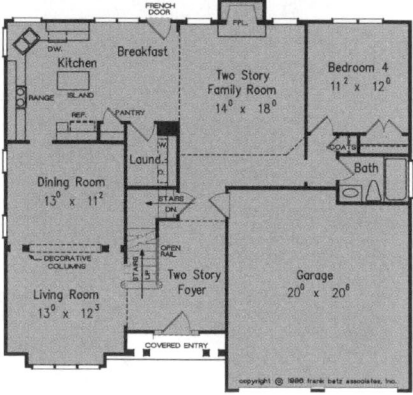

First Floor

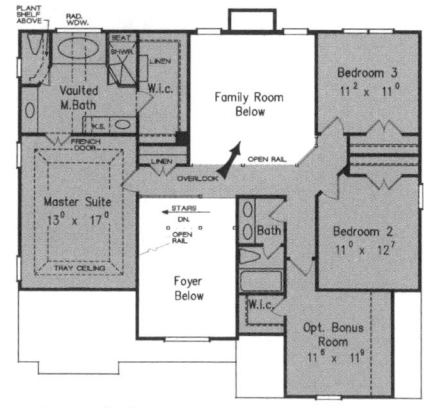

Second Floor

HPK2100546

Style: Mission
First Floor: 1,731 sq. ft.
Second Floor: 554 sq. ft.
Total: 2,285 sq. ft.
Bedrooms: 3
Bathrooms: 2 ½
Width: 90' - 2"
Depth: 69' - 10"
Foundation: Slab

EPLANS.COM

First Floor

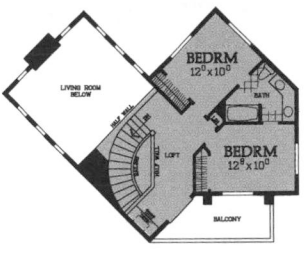

Second Floor

HPK2100547

Style: Farmhouse
First Floor: 1,371 sq. ft.
Second Floor: 916 sq. ft.
Total: 2,287 sq. ft.
Bedrooms: 3
Bathrooms: 2 ½
Width: 43' - 0"
Depth: 69' - 0"
Foundation: Crawlspace

EPLANS.COM

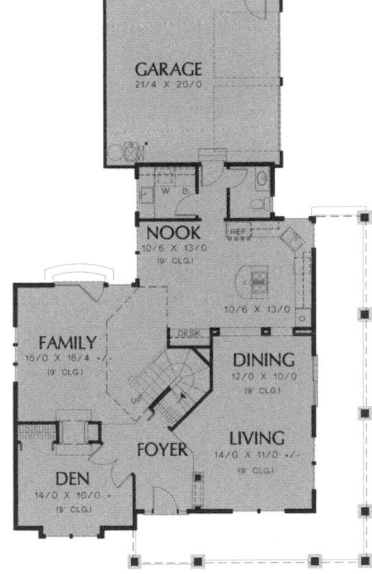

First Floor

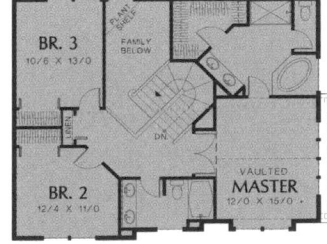

Second Floor

2,000 TO 2,499 SQUARE FEET

HPK2100548

Style: Greek Revival

First Floor: 1,344 sq. ft.

Second Floor: 947 sq. ft.

Total: 2,291 sq. ft.

Bedrooms: 3

Bathrooms: 2 ½

Width: 48' - 0"

Depth: 51' - 4"

Foundation: Unfinished Basement

EPLANS.COM

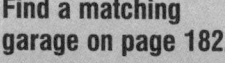

Find a matching garage on page 182.

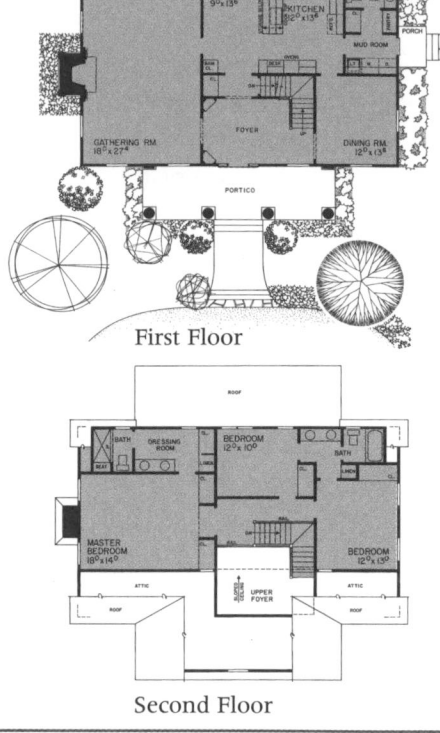

First Floor

Second Floor

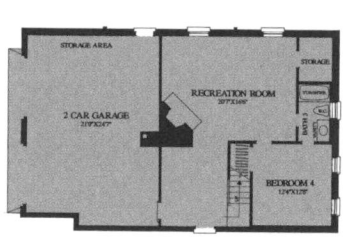

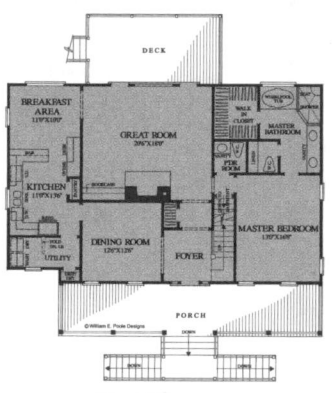

First Floor

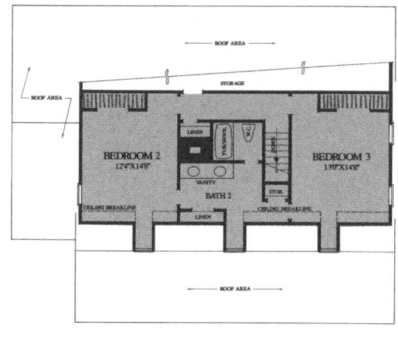

Second Floor

HPK2100549

Style: Farmhouse

First Floor: 1,542 sq. ft.

Second Floor: 755 sq. ft.

Total: 2,297 sq. ft.

Bedrooms: 3

Bathrooms: 2 ½

Width: 48' - 4"

Depth: 39' - 6"

Foundation: Unfinished Walkout Basement

EPLANS.COM

© William E. Poole Designs, Inc.

ORDER BLUEPRINTS ANYTIME AT EPLANS.COM OR 1-800-521-6797

HPK2100550

Style: Farmhouse
First Floor: 1,743 sq. ft.
Second Floor: 555 sq. ft.
Total: 2,298 sq. ft.
Bonus Space: 350 sq. ft.
Bedrooms: 4
Bathrooms: 3
Width: 77' - 11"
Depth: 53' - 2"

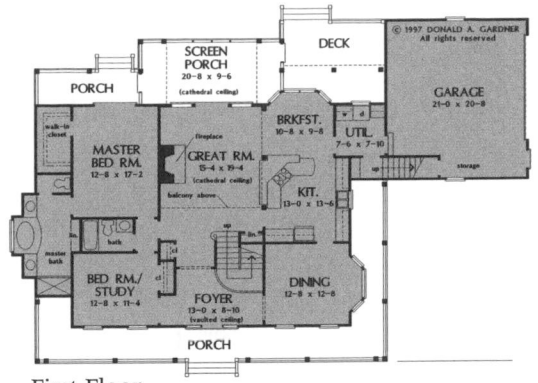

First Floor

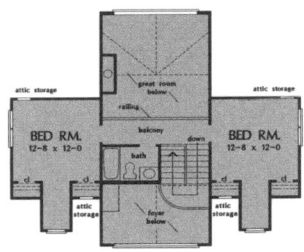

Second Floor

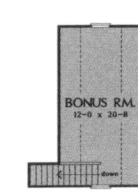

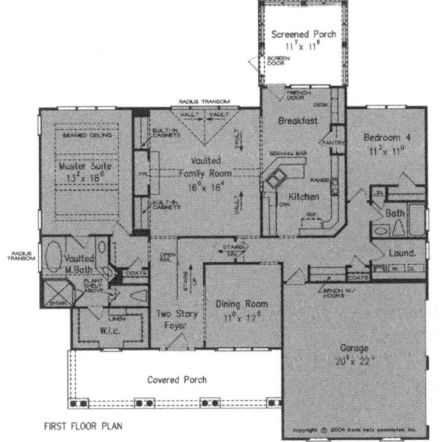

First Floor

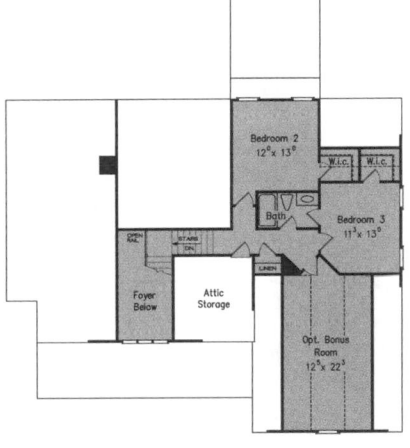

Second Floor

HPK2100551

Style: Craftsman
First Floor: 1,774 sq. ft.
Second Floor: 525 sq. ft.
Total: 2,299 sq. ft.
Bonus Space: 300 sq. ft.
Bedrooms: 4
Bathrooms: 3
Width: 56' - 0"
Depth: 63' - 4"
Foundation: Crawlspace, Slab, Unfinished Walkout Basement

HPK2100552

Style: Cottage
First Floor: 1,752 sq. ft.
Second Floor: 555 sq. ft.
Total: 2,307 sq. ft.
Bonus Space: 300 sq. ft.
Bedrooms: 3
Bathrooms: 2 ½
Width: 56' - 0"
Depth: 51' - 0"
Foundation: Crawlspace, Slab, Unfinished Walkout Basement

EPLANS.COM

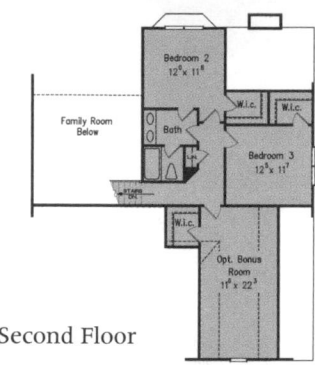

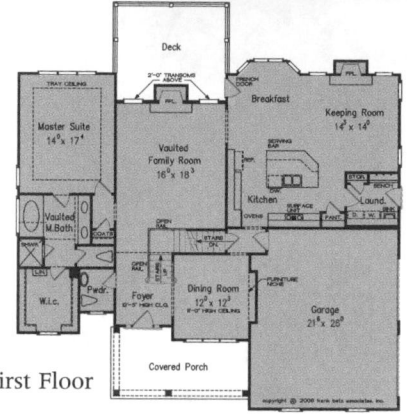

First Floor

Second Floor

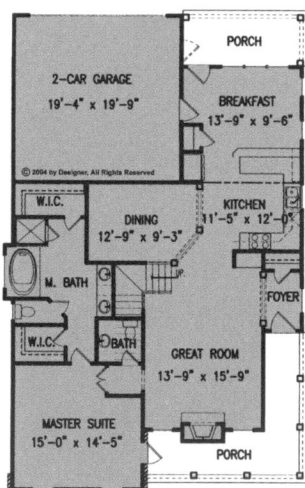

First Floor

HPK2100553

Style: Country
First Floor: 1,260 sq. ft.
Second Floor: 1,057 sq. ft.
Total: 2,317 sq. ft.
Bedrooms: 5
Bathrooms: 2 ½
Width: 35' - 0"
Depth: 56' - 0"
Foundation: Slab

EPLANS.COM

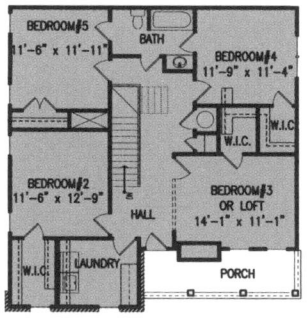

Second Floor

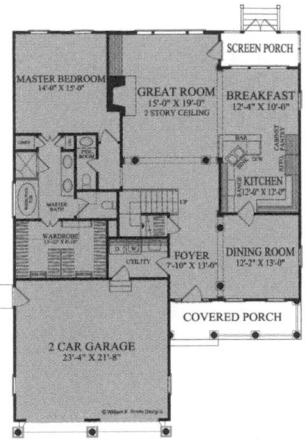

First Floor

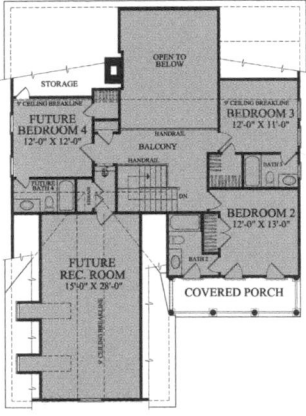

Second Floor

© William E. Poole Designs, Inc.

HPK2100554

Style: Federal - Adams

First Floor: 1,688 sq. ft.

Second Floor: 630 sq. ft.

Total: 2,318 sq. ft.

Bonus Space: 506 sq. ft.

Bedrooms: 3

Bathrooms: 3 ½

Width: 44' - 4"

Depth: 62' - 4"

Foundation: Crawlspace

EPLANS.COM

© 1991 Donald A. Gardner Architects, Inc.

Find a matching garage on page 182.

HPK2100555

Style: Tidewater

First Floor: 1,756 sq. ft.

Second Floor: 565 sq. ft.

Total: 2,321 sq. ft.

Bedrooms: 4

Bathrooms: 3

Width: 56' - 8"

Depth: 42' - 4"

EPLANS.COM

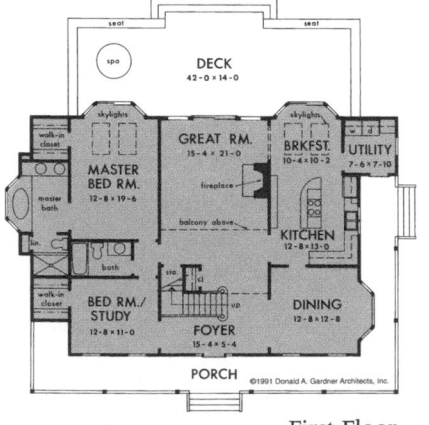

First Floor

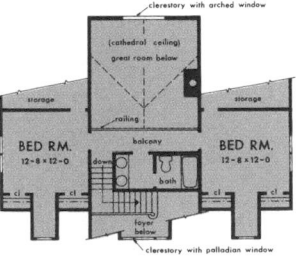

Second Floor

2,000 TO 2,499 SQUARE FEET

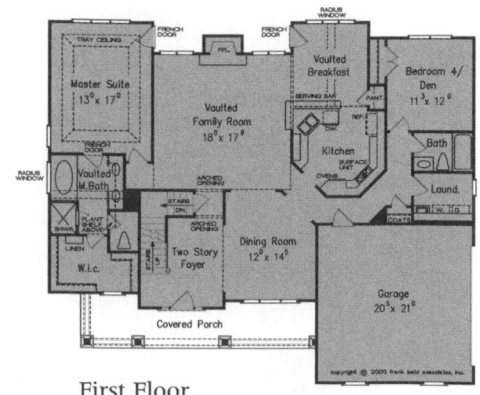

First Floor

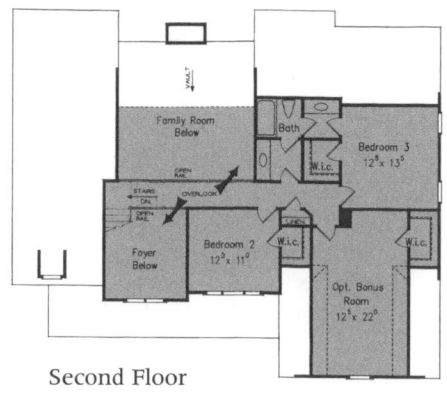

Second Floor

HPK2100556

Style: Craftsman

First Floor: 1,761 sq. ft.

Second Floor: 577 sq. ft.

Total: 2,338 sq. ft.

Bonus Space: 305 sq. ft.

Bedrooms: 4

Bathrooms: 3

Width: 56' - 0"

Depth: 48' - 0"

Foundation: Crawlspace, Unfinished Walkout Basement

EPLANS.COM

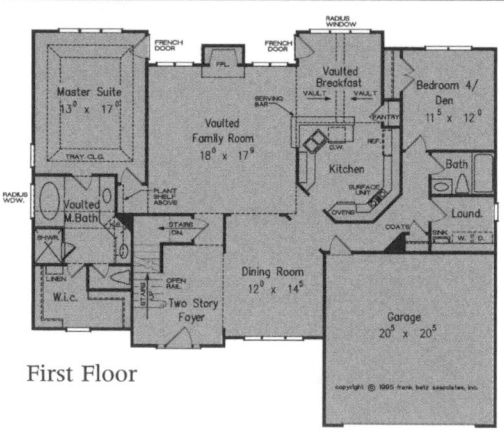

First Floor

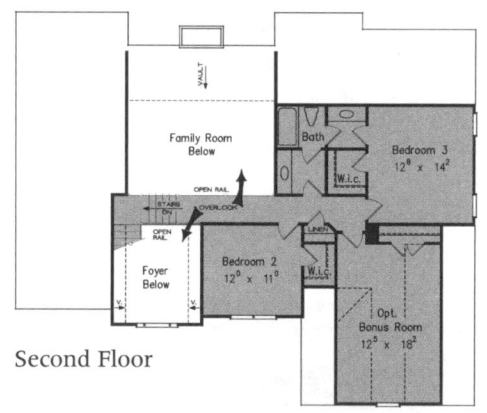

Second Floor

HPK2100557

Style: New American

First Floor: 1,761 sq. ft.

Second Floor: 580 sq. ft.

Total: 2,341 sq. ft.

Bonus Space: 276 sq. ft.

Bedrooms: 4

Bathrooms: 3

Width: 56' - 0"

Depth: 47' - 6"

Foundation: Crawlspace, Slab, Unfinished Walkout Basement

EPLANS.COM

ORDER BLUEPRINTS ANYTIME AT EPLANS.COM OR 1-800-521-6797

HPK2100558

Style: Victorian Eclectic

First Floor: 1,107 sq. ft.

Second Floor: 1,243 sq. ft.

Total: 2,350 sq. ft.

Bedrooms: 3

Bathrooms: 2 ½

Width: 58' - 0"

Depth: 33' - 0"

Foundation: Unfinished Basement

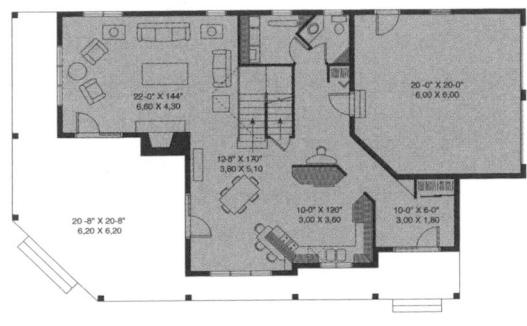

First Floor

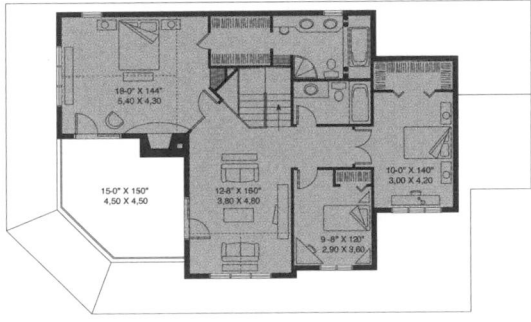

Second Floor

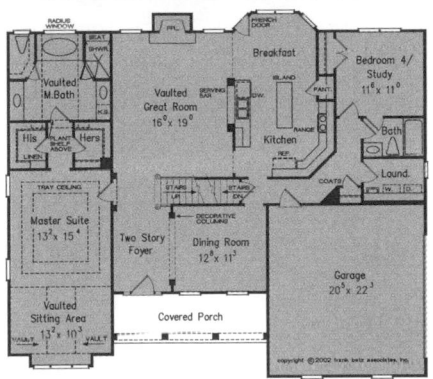

First Floor

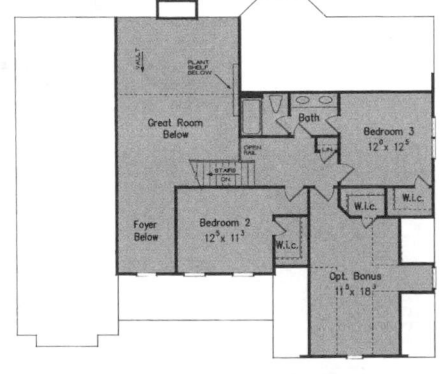

Second Floor

HPK2100559

Style: Country

First Floor: 1,803 sq. ft.

Second Floor: 548 sq. ft.

Total: 2,351 sq. ft.

Bonus Space: 277 sq. ft.

Bedrooms: 4

Bathrooms: 3

Width: 55' - 0"

Depth: 48' - 0"

Foundation: Crawlspace, Slab, Unfinished Walkout Basement

HPK2100560

Style: Farmhouse
First Floor: 1,718 sq. ft.
Second Floor: 638 sq. ft.
Total: 2,356 sq. ft.
Bonus Space: 348 sq. ft.
Bedrooms: 4
Bathrooms: 3
Width: 71' - 0"
Depth: 42' - 8"

EPLANS.COM

© 1999 Donald A. Gardner, Inc.

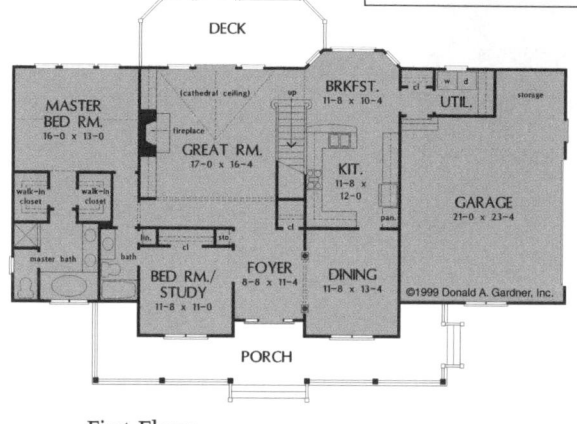

First Floor

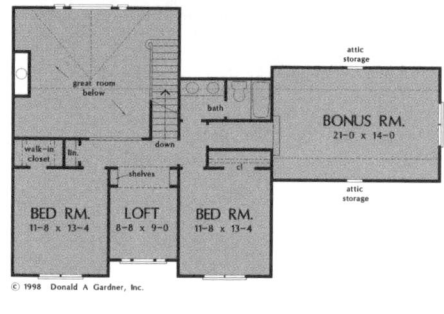

Second Floor

HPK2100561

Style: French Country
First Floor: 1,120 sq. ft.
Second Floor: 1,250 sq. ft.
Total: 2,370 sq. ft.
Bedrooms: 3
Bathrooms: 2 ½
Width: 41' - 4"
Depth: 51' - 0"
**Foundation: Crawlspace, Slab,
Unfinished Walkout Basement**

EPLANS.COM

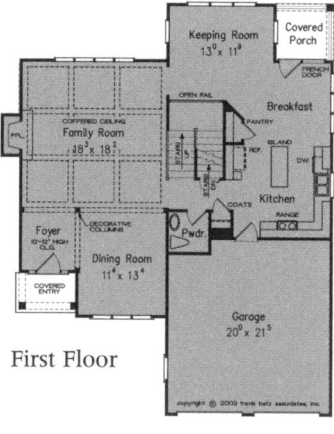

First Floor

Second Floor

HPK2100562

Style: New American

First Floor: 1,665 sq. ft.

Second Floor: 707 sq. ft.

Total: 2,372 sq. ft.

Bonus Space: 164 sq. ft.

Bedrooms: 4

Bathrooms: 2 ½

Width: 54' - 6"

Depth: 44' - 10"

Foundation: Crawlspace, Unfinished Walkout Basement

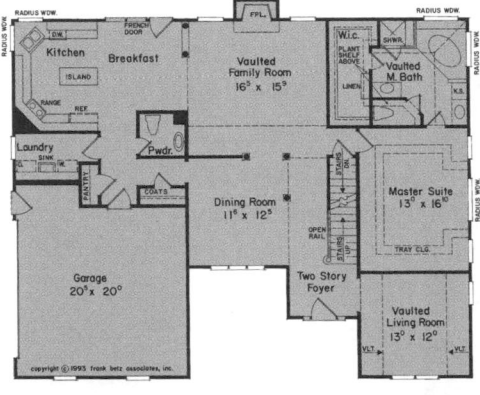

First Floor

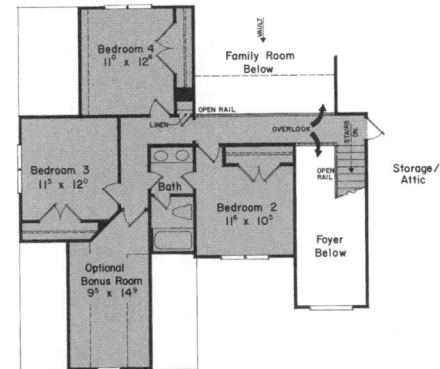

Second Floor

HPK2100563

Style: Country

First Floor: 1,656 sq. ft.

Second Floor: 717 sq. ft.

Total: 2,373 sq. ft.

Bonus Space: 717 sq. ft.

Bedrooms: 4

Bathrooms: 3

Width: 54' - 0"

Depth: 54' - 0"

Foundation: Crawlspace, Slab, Unfinished Walkout Basement

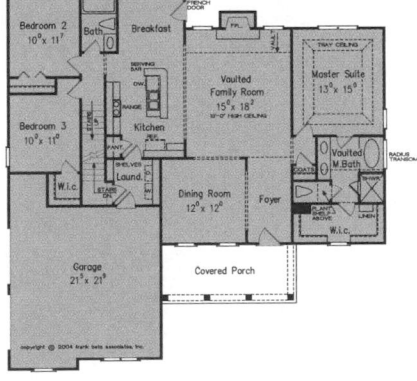

First Floor

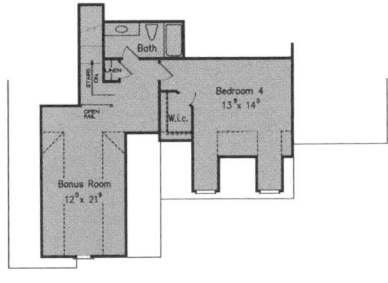

Second Floor

EPLANS.COM

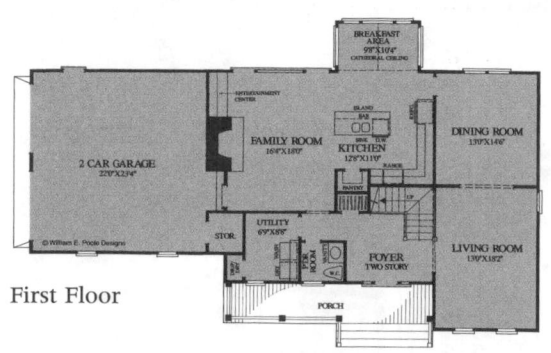

First Floor

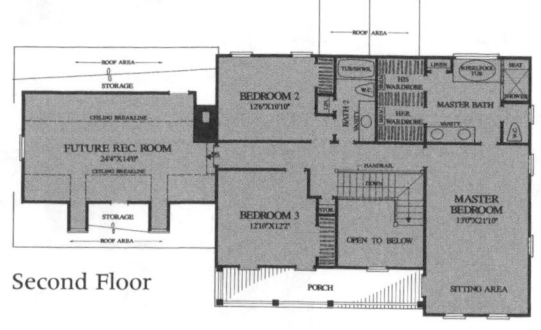

Second Floor

© William E. Poole Designs, Inc.

HPK2100564

EPLANS.COM

Style: Federal - Adams
First Floor: 1,291 sq. ft.
Second Floor: 1,087 sq. ft.
Total: 2,378 sq. ft.
Bonus Space: 366 sq. ft.
Bedrooms: 3
Bathrooms: 2 ½
Width: 65' - 4"
Depth: 40' - 0"
Foundation: Crawlspace

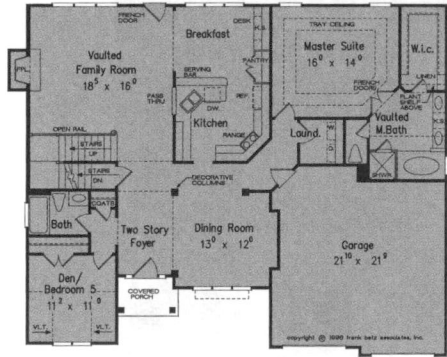

First Floor

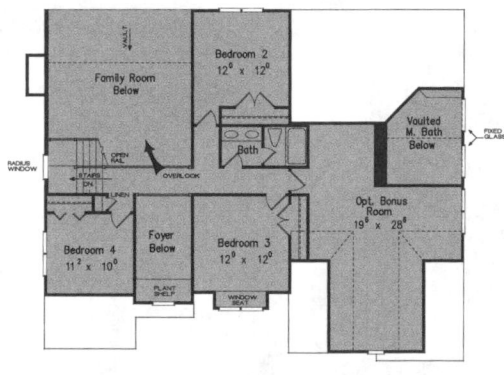

Second Floor

HPK2100565

EPLANS.COM

Style: New American
First Floor: 1,687 sq. ft.
Second Floor: 694 sq. ft.
Total: 2,381 sq. ft.
Bonus Space: 407 sq. ft.
Bedrooms: 5
Bathrooms: 3
Width: 55' - 10"
Depth: 44' - 6"
Foundation: Crawlspace,
Unfinished Walkout Basement

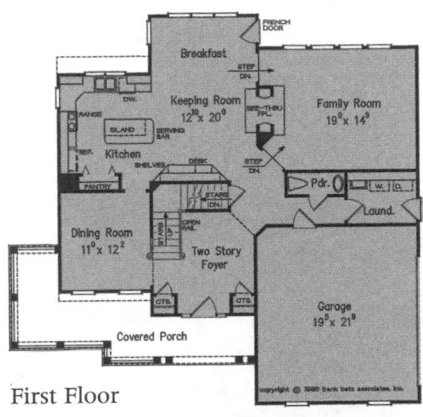

First Floor

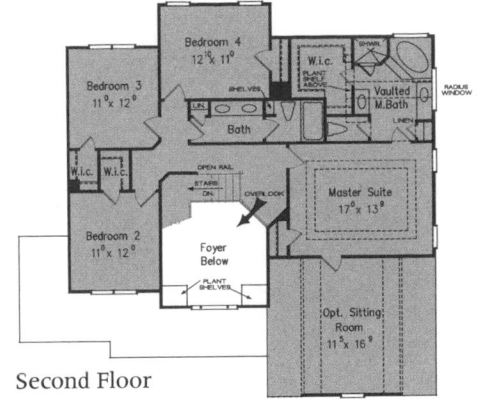

Second Floor

HPK2100566

Style: Country

First Floor: 1,223 sq. ft.

Second Floor: 1,163 sq. ft.

Total: 2,386 sq. ft.

Bonus Space: 204 sq. ft.

Bedrooms: 4

Bathrooms: 2 ½

Width: 50' - 0"

Depth: 48' - 0"

Foundation: Crawlspace, Unfinished Walkout Basement

EPLANS.COM

HPK2100567

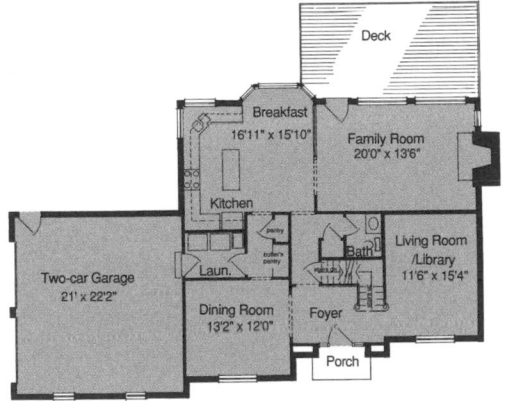

First Floor

Second Floor

Style: New American

First Floor: 1,207 sq. ft.

Second Floor: 1,181 sq. ft.

Total: 2,388 sq. ft.

Bedrooms: 4

Bathrooms: 2 ½

Width: 59' - 10"

Depth: 37' - 4"

Foundation: Unfinished Basement

EPLANS.COM

2,000 TO 2,499 SQUARE FEET

First Floor

DECK

PORCH

PORCH

GREAT RM.
21-0 x 16-0
(vaulted ceiling)
fireplace

© 2000 DAG
All rights reserved

DINING
12-0 x 14-0

shelves

MASTER
BED RM.
14-0 x 16-0

balcony above

KIT.
12-0 x 12-0

down up

FOYER
7-4 x 10-4

cl

walk-in closet

walk-in closet

d
w
UTILITY
12-0 x 6-0

pd. rm.

master bath

PORCH

Second Floor

PORCH

PORCH

BED RM.
12-0 x 14-0

great room below

BED RM.
14-0 x 14-0

railing

cl cl

down

foyer below

cl cl

bath

lin.

bath

© 2000 Donald A. Gardner, Inc.

HPK2100568

Style: Country
First Floor: 1,620 sq. ft.
Second Floor: 770 sq. ft.
Total: 2,390 sq. ft.
Bedrooms: 3
Bathrooms: 3 ½
Width: 49' - 0"
Depth: 58' - 8"

EPLANS.COM

HPK2100569

Style: Country
First Floor: 1,783 sq. ft.
Second Floor: 611 sq. ft.
Total: 2,394 sq. ft.
Bedrooms: 4
Bathrooms: 3
Width: 70' - 0"
Depth: 79' - 2"

EPLANS.COM

© 1993 DONALD A. GARDNER
All rights reserved

GARAGE
22-4 x 21-4

spa

DECK

covered breezeway

clerestory with arched window

GREAT RM.
19-8 x 19-2
(cathedral ceiling)
fireplace

walk-in closet

skylight

master bath

cabs

balcony above

wet bar

BRKFST.
9-6 x 10-6

UTIL
8-0 x 9-4

pantry

KITCHEN
13-0 x 16-4

MASTER
BED RM.
13-0 x 15-4

bath

up

BED RM./
STUDY
12-0 x 11-0

FOYER
5-0 x 13-6

DINING
12-0 x 13-2

PORCH
30-4 x 8-0

First Floor

great room below

railing

balcony

down

bath

BED RM.
12-8 x 14-10

cl

cl

BED RM.
12-0 x 12-6

Second Floor

HPK2100570

Style: New American

First Floor: 1,814 sq. ft.

Second Floor: 580 sq. ft.

Total: 2,394 sq. ft.

Bonus Space: 259 sq. ft.

Bedrooms: 4

Bathrooms: 3

Width: 55' - 4"

Depth: 52' - 0"

Foundation: Crawlspace, Slab, Unfinished Walkout Basement

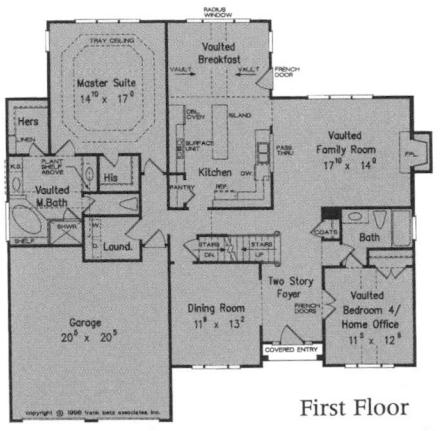

First Floor

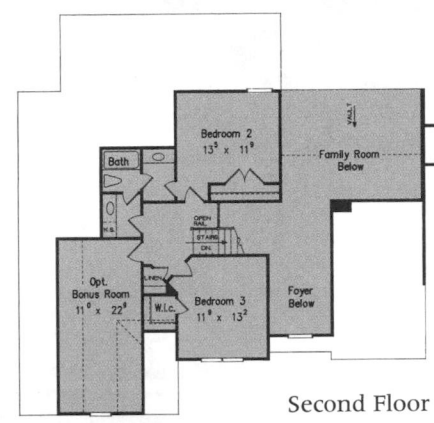

Second Floor

HPK2100571

Style: New American

First Floor: 1,847 sq. ft.

Second Floor: 548 sq. ft.

Total: 2,395 sq. ft.

Bonus Space: 395 sq. ft.

Bedrooms: 3

Bathrooms: 2 ½

Width: 60' - 0"

Depth: 66' - 4"

Foundation: Crawlspace, Unfinished Walkout Basement

First Floor

Second Floor

2,000 TO 2,499 SQUARE FEET

HPK2100572

Style: Greek Revival
First Floor: 1,714 sq. ft.
Second Floor: 683 sq. ft.
Total: 2,397 sq. ft.
Bonus Space: 287 sq. ft.
Bedrooms: 3
Bathrooms: 2 ½
Width: 53' - 8"
Depth: 56' - 8"
Foundation: Crawlspace

EPLANS.COM

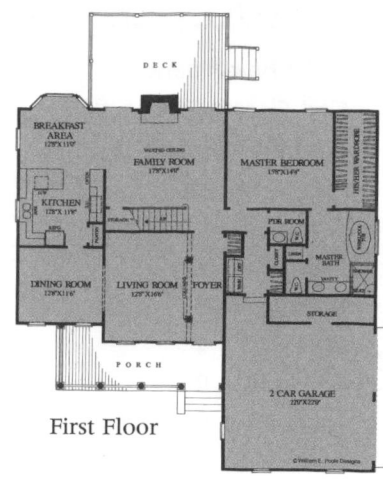

First Floor

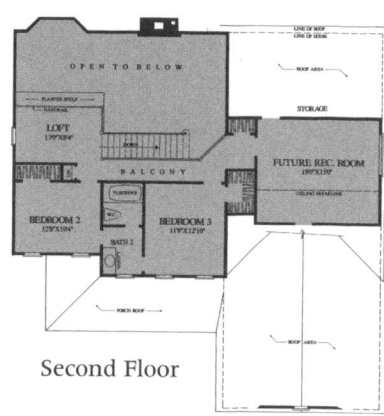

Second Floor

© William E. Poole Designs, Inc.

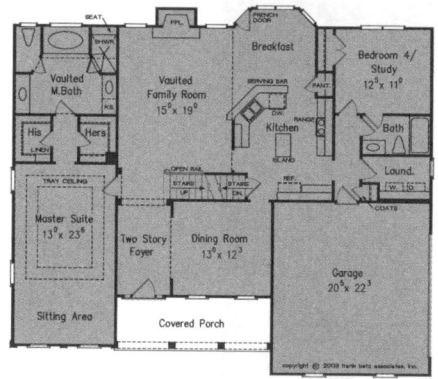

First Floor

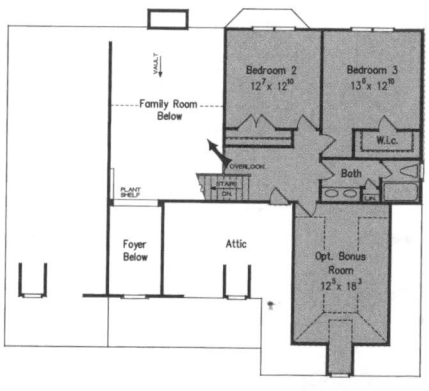

Second Floor

HPK2100573

Style: Greek Revival
First Floor: 1,805 sq. ft.
Second Floor: 593 sq. ft.
Total: 2,398 sq. ft.
Bonus Space: 255 sq. ft.
Bedrooms: 4
Bathrooms: 3
Width: 55' - 0"
Depth: 48' - 0"
Foundation: Crawlspace, Slab, Unfinished Walkout Basement

EPLANS.COM

ORDER BLUEPRINTS ANYTIME AT EPLANS.COM OR 1-800-521-6797

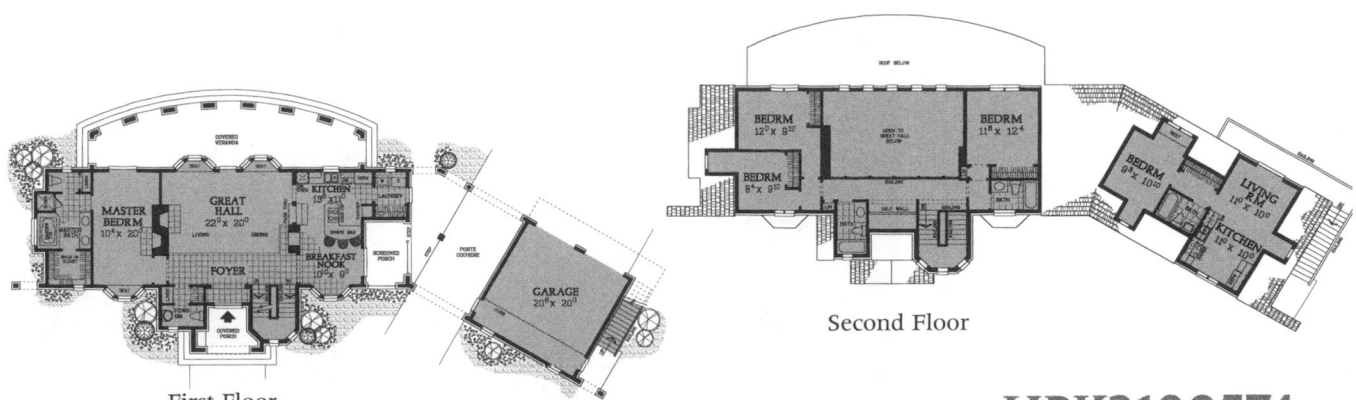

First Floor

Second Floor

HPK2100574

Style: French Country

First Floor: 1,566 sq. ft.

Second Floor: 837 sq. ft.

Total: 2,403 sq. ft.

Bedrooms: 5

Bathrooms: 4 ½

Width: 116' - 3"

Depth: 55' - 1"

Foundation: Unfinished Basement

EPLANS.COM

HPK2100575

Style: Farmhouse

First Floor: 1,832 sq. ft.

Second Floor: 574 sq. ft.

Total: 2,406 sq. ft.

Bonus Space: 410 sq. ft.

Bedrooms: 4

Bathrooms: 3

Width: 77' - 10"

Depth: 41' - 4"

Foundation: Crawlspace

EPLANS.COM

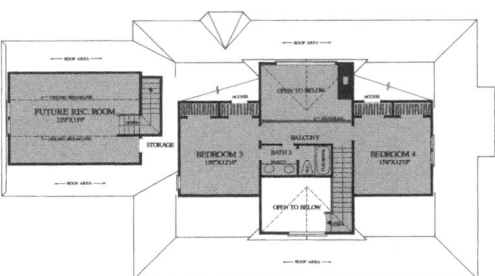

First Floor

Second Floor

© WILLIAM E POOLE DESIGNS, INC.

2,000 TO 2,499 SQUARE FEET

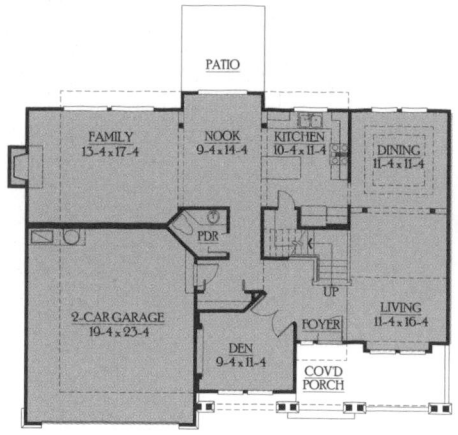

First Floor

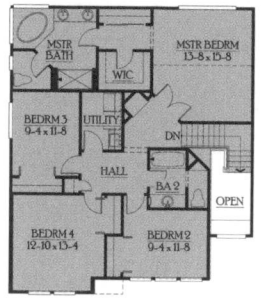

Second Floor

HPK2100576

Style: Craftsman
First Floor: 1,239 sq. ft.
Second Floor: 1,168 sq. ft.
Total: 2,407 sq. ft.
Bedrooms: 4
Bathrooms: 2 ½
Width: 50' - 0"
Depth: 40' - 0"
Foundation: Crawlspace

EPLANS.COM

©1994 William E Poole Designs, Inc.

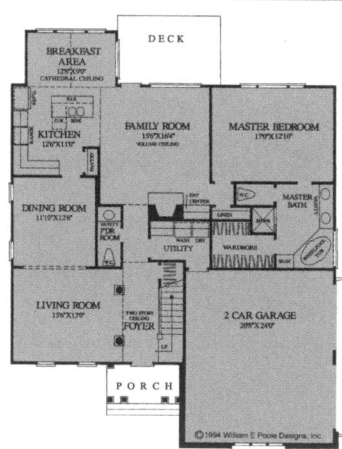

First Floor

HPK2100577

Style: French Country
First Floor: 1,627 sq. ft.
Second Floor: 783 sq. ft.
Total: 2,410 sq. ft.
Bonus Space: 418 sq. ft.
Bedrooms: 4
Bathrooms: 2 ½
Width: 46' - 0"
Depth: 58' - 6"
Foundation: Crawlspace

EPLANS.COM

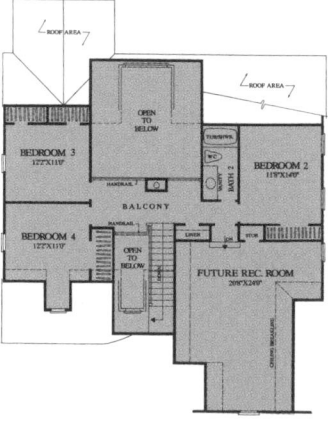

Second Floor

HPK2100578

Style: Cottage

First Floor: 1,627 sq. ft.

Second Floor: 783 sq. ft.

Total: 2,410 sq. ft.

Bonus Space: 418 sq. ft.

Bedrooms: 4

Bathrooms: 2 ½

Width: 46' - 0"

Depth: 58' - 0"

Foundation: Crawlspace

EPLANS.COM

© William E. Poole Designs, Inc.

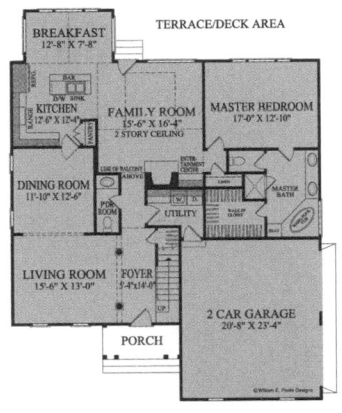

First Floor

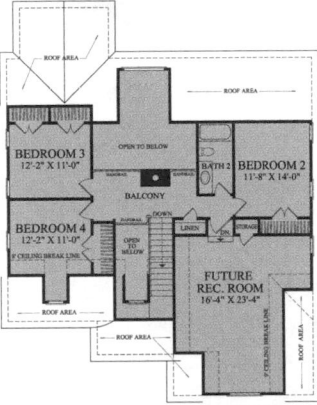

Second Floor

© 1997 William E. Poole Designs, Inc.

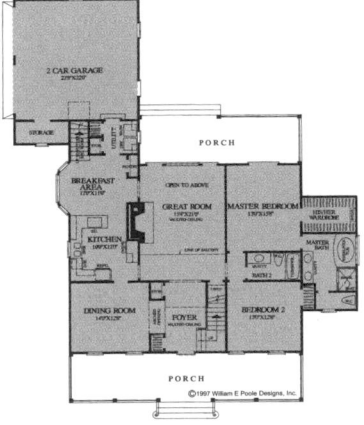

First Floor

HPK2100579

Style: Farmhouse

First Floor: 1,776 sq. ft.

Second Floor: 643 sq. ft.

Total: 2,419 sq. ft.

Bonus Space: 367 sq. ft.

Bedrooms: 4

Bathrooms: 3

Width: 61' - 8"

Depth: 74' - 4"

Foundation: Crawlspace, Unfinished Basement

EPLANS.COM

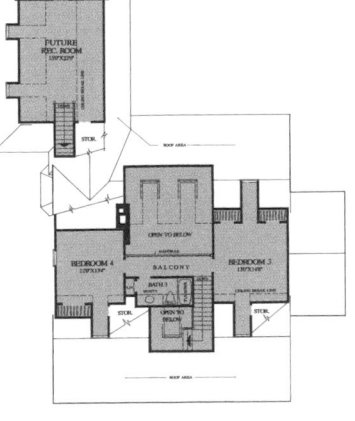

Second Floor

2,000 TO 2,499 SQUARE FEET

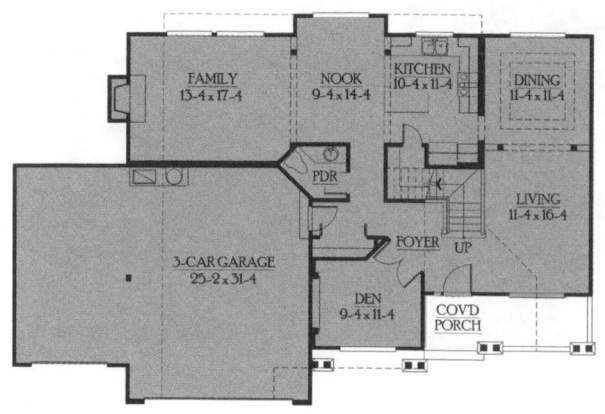

First Floor

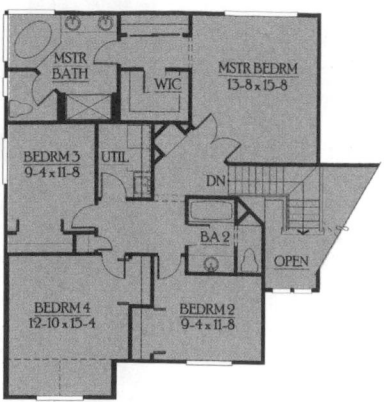

Second Floor

HPK2100580

Style: Craftsman
First Floor: 1,230 sq. ft.
Second Floor: 1,190 sq. ft.
Total: 2,420 sq. ft.
Bedrooms: 4
Bathrooms: 2 ½
Width: 62' - 0"
Depth: 42' - 0"
Foundation: Crawlspace

EPLANS.COM

HPK2100581

Style: French Country
First Floor: 1,724 sq. ft.
Second Floor: 700 sq. ft.
Total: 2,424 sq. ft.
Bedrooms: 3
Bathrooms: 2 ½
Width: 47' - 10"
Depth: 63' - 8"
Foundation: Finished Walkout Basement

EPLANS.COM

First Floor

Second Floor

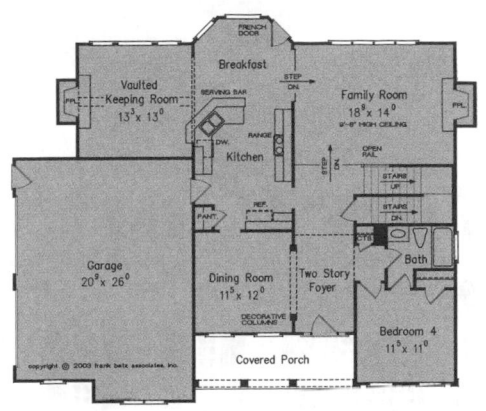

First Floor

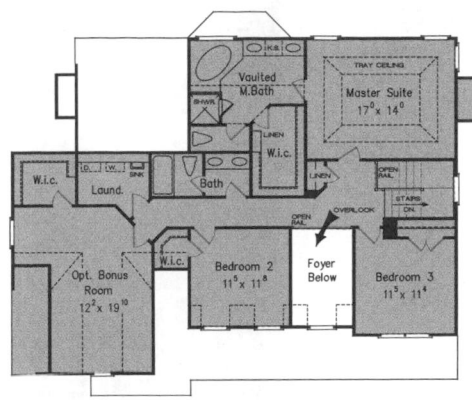

Second Floor

HPK2100582

Style: Country

First Floor: 1,353 sq. ft.

Second Floor: 1,072 sq. ft.

Total: 2,425 sq. ft.

Bonus Space: 322 sq. ft.

Bedrooms: 4

Bathrooms: 3

Width: 54' - 4"

Depth: 45' - 6"

Foundation: Crawlspace, Unfinished Walkout Basement

EPLANS.COM

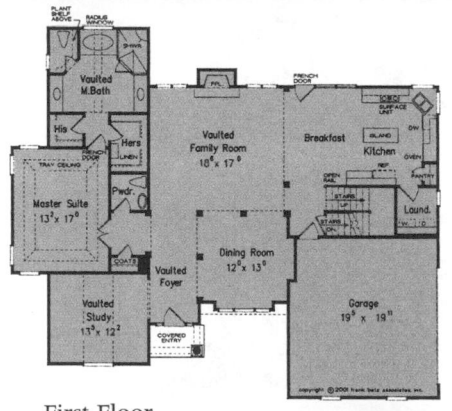

First Floor

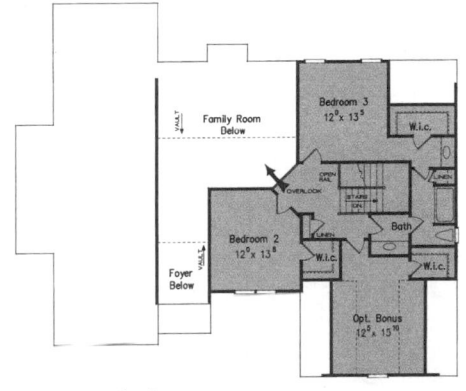

Second Floor

HPK2100583

Style: French Country

First Floor: 1,788 sq. ft.

Second Floor: 639 sq. ft.

Total: 2,427 sq. ft.

Bonus Space: 235 sq. ft.

Bedrooms: 3

Bathrooms: 2 ½

Width: 59' - 0"

Depth: 51' - 0"

Foundation: Crawlspace, Unfinished Walkout Basement

EPLANS.COM

2,000 TO 2,499 SQUARE FEET

HPK2100584

Style: Country
First Floor: 1,415 sq. ft.
Second Floor: 1,015 sq. ft.
Total: 2,430 sq. ft.
Bonus Space: 169 sq. ft.
Bedrooms: 4
Bathrooms: 3 ½
Width: 54' - 0"
Depth: 43' - 4"
Foundation: Crawlspace, Unfinished Walkout Basement

EPLANS.COM

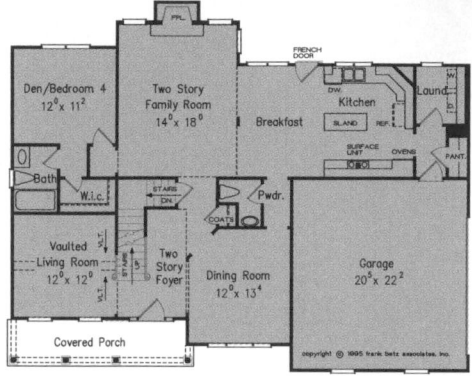

First Floor

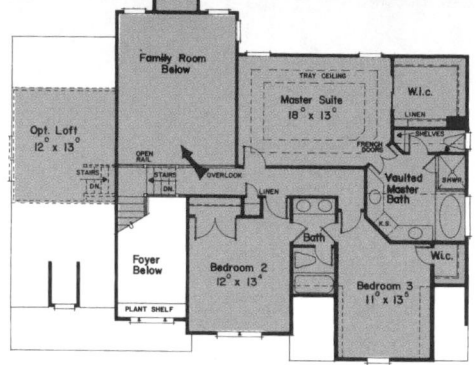

Second Floor

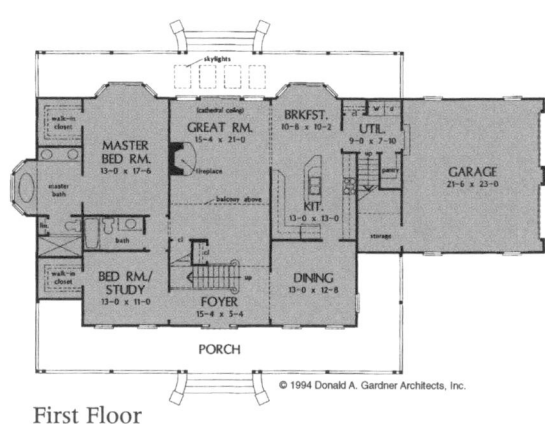

First Floor

HPK2100585

Style: Farmhouse
First Floor: 1,841 sq. ft.
Second Floor: 594 sq. ft.
Total: 2,435 sq. ft.
Bonus Space: 391 sq. ft.
Bedrooms: 4
Bathrooms: 3
Width: 82' - 2"
Depth: 48' - 10"

EPLANS.COM

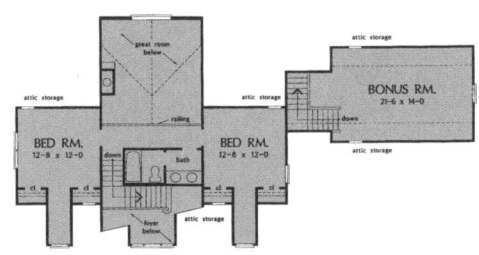

Second Floor

ORDER BLUEPRINTS ANYTIME AT EPLANS.COM OR 1-800-521-6797

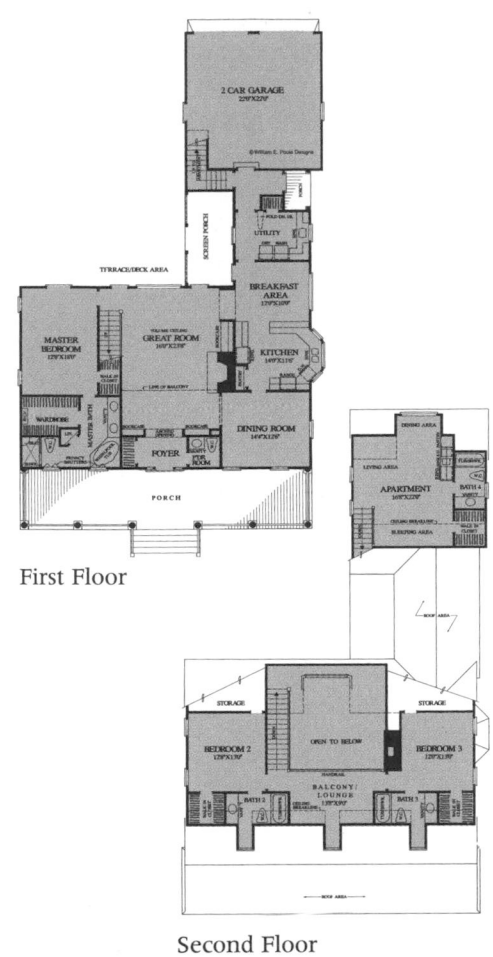

First Floor

Second Floor

HPK2100586

Style: Farmhouse

First Floor: 1,704 sq. ft.

Second Floor: 734 sq. ft.

Total: 2,438 sq. ft.

Bonus Space: 479 sq. ft.

Bedrooms: 3

Bathrooms: 3 ½

Width: 50' - 0"

Depth: 82' - 6"

Foundation: Crawlspace

EPLANS.COM

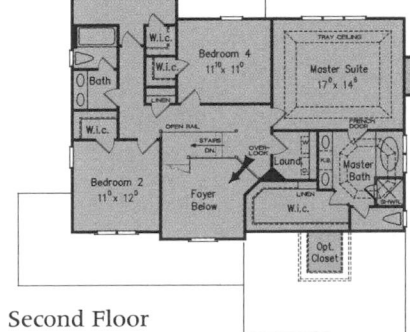

First Floor

Second Floor

HPK2100587

Style: Country

First Floor: 1,214 sq. ft.

Second Floor: 1,229 sq. ft.

Total: 2,443 sq. ft.

Bedrooms: 4

Bathrooms: 2 ½

Width: 52' - 4"

Depth: 55' - 10"

Foundation: Crawlspace, Unfinished Walkout Basement

EPLANS.COM

2,000 TO 2,499 SQUARE FEET

HPK2100588

Style: French Country

First Floor: 1,758 sq. ft.

Second Floor: 685 sq. ft.

Total: 2,443 sq. ft.

Bonus Space: 260 sq. ft.

Bedrooms: 3

Bathrooms: 3 ½

Width: 55' - 10"

Depth: 63' - 6"

Foundation: Crawlspace

EPLANS.COM

First Floor

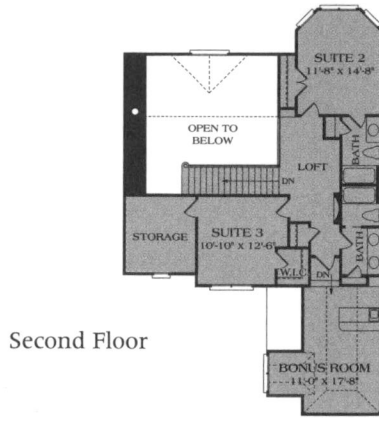

Second Floor

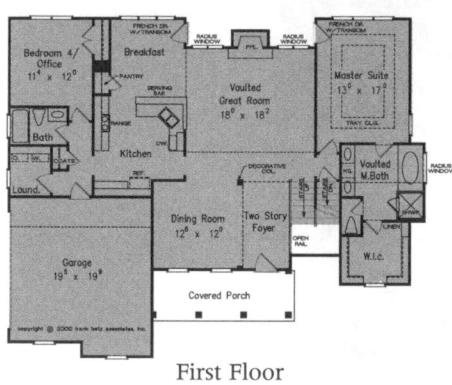

First Floor

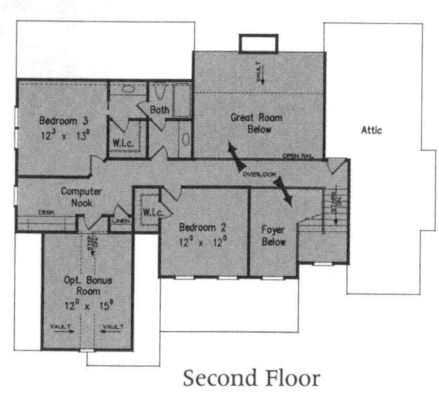

Second Floor

HPK2100589

Style: New American

First Floor: 1,720 sq. ft.

Second Floor: 724 sq. ft.

Total: 2,444 sq. ft.

Bonus Space: 212 sq. ft.

Bedrooms: 4

Bathrooms: 3

Width: 58' - 0"

Depth: 47' - 0"

Foundation: Crawlspace, Unfinished Walkout Basement

EPLANS.COM

HPK2100590

Style: Craftsman

First Floor: 1,118 sq. ft.

Second Floor: 1,335 sq. ft.

Total: 2,453 sq. ft.

Bedrooms: 4

Bathrooms: 2 ½

Width: 48' - 0"

Depth: 40' - 0"

Foundation: Crawlspace

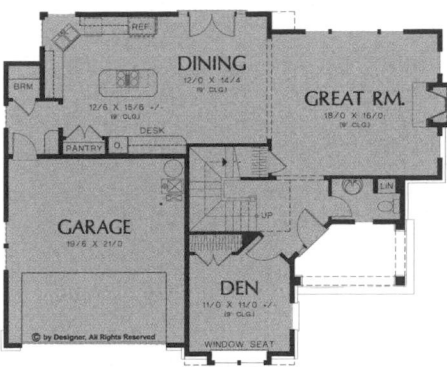

First Floor

Second Floor

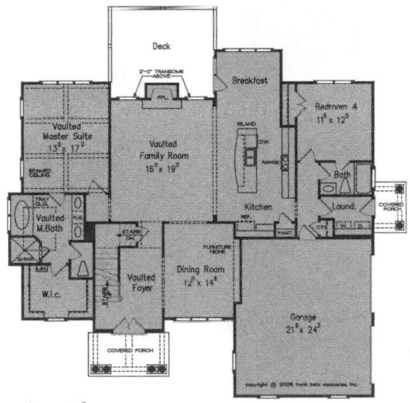

First Floor

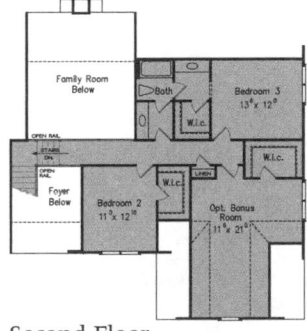

Second Floor

HPK2100591

Style: Cottage

First Floor: 1,831 sq. ft.

Second Floor: 628 sq. ft.

Total: 2,459 sq. ft.

Bonus Space: 360 sq. ft.

Bedrooms: 4

Bathrooms: 3 ½

Width: 62' - 0"

Depth: 54' - 0"

Foundation: Crawlspace, Unfinished Walkout Basement

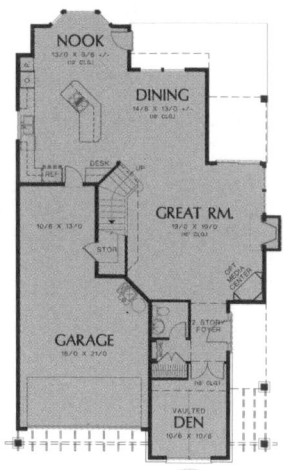

First Floor

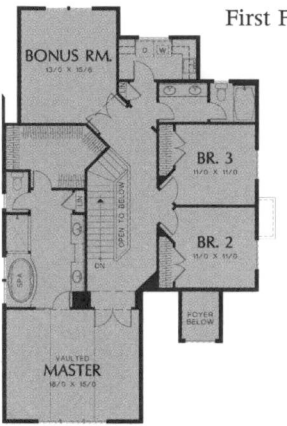

Second Floor

HPK2100592

Style: Cottage

First Floor: 1,204 sq. ft.

Second Floor: 1,264 sq. ft.

Total: 2,468 sq. ft.

Bonus Space: 213 sq. ft.

Bedrooms: 3

Bathrooms: 2 ½

Width: 35' - 0"

Depth: 63' - 0"

Foundation: Crawlspace

EPLANS.COM

© The Sater Design Collection, Inc.

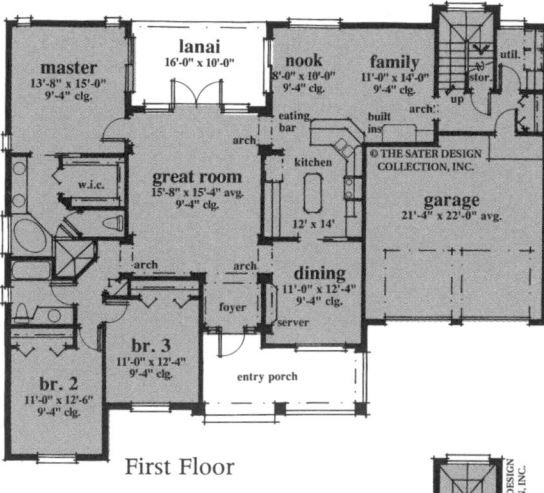

First Floor

Second Floor

HPK2100593

Style: New American

First Floor: 2,052 sq. ft.

Second Floor: 419 sq. ft.

Total: 2,471 sq. ft.

Bedrooms: 5

Bathrooms: 3

Width: 65' - 0"

Depth: 54' - 0"

Foundation: Slab

EPLANS.COM

HPK2100594

Style: Country

First Floor: 1,822 sq. ft.

Second Floor: 649 sq. ft.

Total: 2,471 sq. ft.

Bedrooms: 3

Bathrooms: 2 ½

Width: 64' - 9"

Depth: 52' - 7"

Foundation: Unfinished Walkout Basement

EPLANS.COM

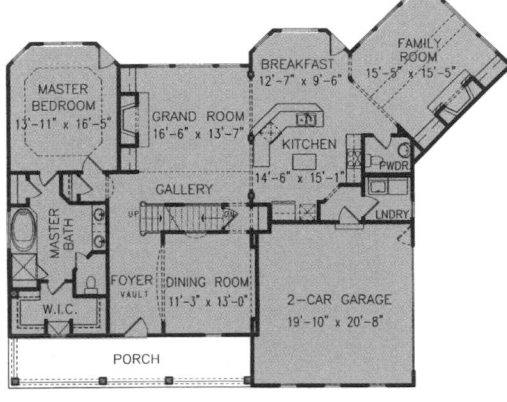

First Floor

Second Floor

HPK2100595

Style: Country

First Floor: 1,961 sq. ft.

Second Floor: 520 sq. ft.

Total: 2,481 sq. ft.

Bonus Space: 265 sq. ft.

Bedrooms: 4

Bathrooms: 3

Width: 60' - 0"

Depth: 53' - 0"

Foundation: Crawlspace, Unfinished Walkout Basement

EPLANS.COM

First Floor

Second Floor

HPK2100596

Style: Farmhouse
First Floor: 1,706 sq. ft.
Second Floor: 776 sq. ft.
Total: 2,482 sq. ft.
Bonus Space: 414 sq. ft.
Bedrooms: 4
Bathrooms: 2 ½
Width: 54' - 8"
Depth: 43' - 0"

EPLANS.COM

First Floor

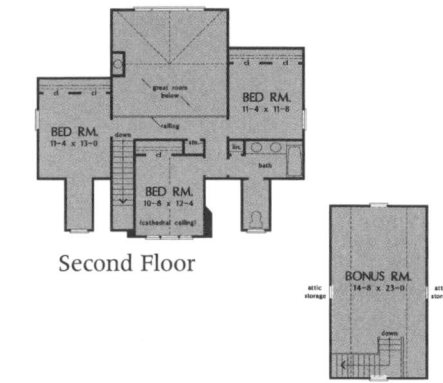

Second Floor

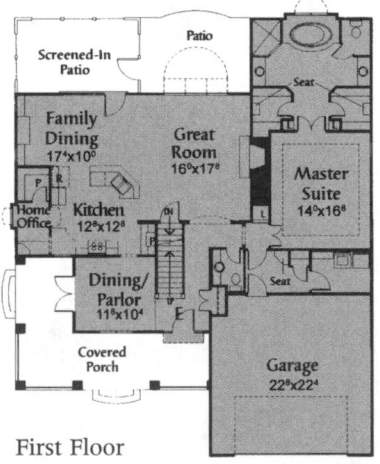

First Floor

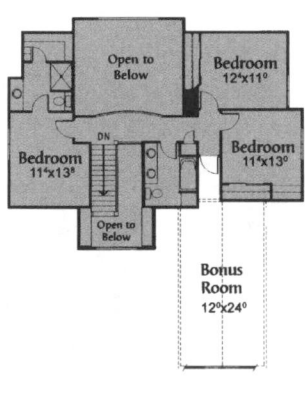

Second Floor

HPK2100597

Style: Craftsman
First Floor: 1,711 sq. ft.
Second Floor: 773 sq. ft.
Total: 2,484 sq. ft.
Bonus Space: 323 sq. ft.
Bedrooms: 4
Bathrooms: 3 ½
Width: 50' - 8"
Depth: 62' - 0"
Foundation: Unfinished Basement

EPLANS.COM

© 2002 Donald A. Gardner, Inc.

HPK2100598

Style: Farmhouse
First Floor: 1,420 sq. ft.
Second Floor: 1,065 sq. ft.
Total: 2,485 sq. ft.
Bonus Space: 411 sq. ft.
Bedrooms: 4
Bathrooms: 3
Width: 57' - 8"
Depth: 49' - 0"

EPLANS.COM

Looking every bit like the big country homes of yesteryear, this plan's traditional facade belies the up-to-date floor plan inside. The roomy island kitchen flows into a sunny breakfast room, which, in turn, accesses the hearth-warmed great room. The rear porch can be reached from the great room and the breakfast room. Upstairs, two family bedrooms share a hall bath, and the deluxe master suite boasts His and Hers amenities. There is bonus space to the right that can convert to a number of uses.

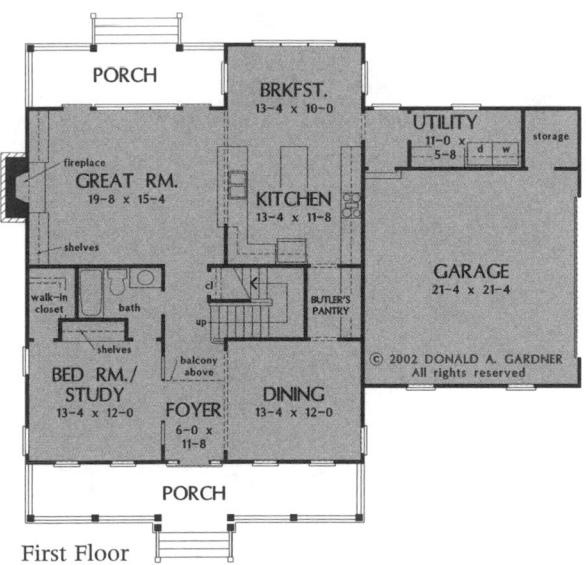

First Floor

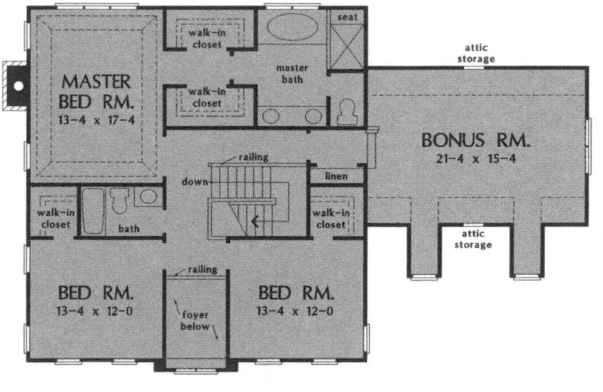

Second Floor

2,000 TO 2,499 SQUARE FEET

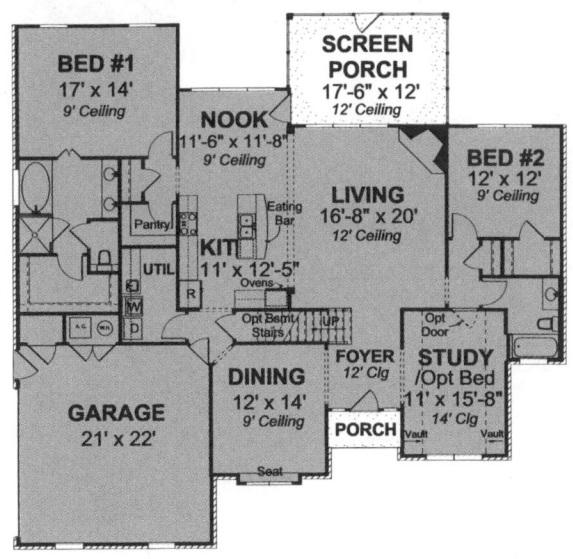

First Floor

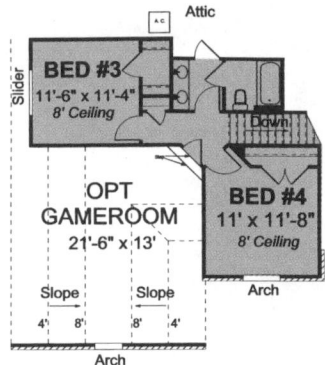

Second Floor

HPK2100599

This plan offers a well-designed, compact home ideal for a growing family with hopes of future expansion. Upstairs houses an optional game room, and a study on the first floor doubles as an optional bedroom. The open kitchen layout serves the adjoining breakfast nook, and an eating bar backs the living room. A rear screened porch makes outdoor dining a possibility. The spacious master suite sits on the first floor. A second first-floor bedroom equipped with a full bath could serve as a guest suite. Two additional family bedrooms sharing a full bath are on the second floor.

Style: New American
First Floor: 2,019 sq. ft.
Second Floor: 468 sq. ft.
Total: 2,487 sq. ft.
Bonus Space: 286 sq. ft.
Bedrooms: 4
Bathrooms: 3
Width: 59' - 0"
Depth: 58' - 0"

EPLANS.COM

HPK2100600

Style: New American
First Floor: 1,751 sq. ft.
Second Floor: 740 sq. ft.
Total: 2,491 sq. ft.
Bedrooms: 4
Bathrooms: 2 ½
Width: 54' - 0"
Depth: 49' - 0"
Foundation: Slab

EPLANS.COM

Large, multipaned windows grace the front of this exterior, promising light-filled interiors. The grand room and the breakfast area are two stories, creating a spacious and ethereal feel. The kitchen is sufficiently roomy to fashion all of your culinary needs, with a wraparound counter, corner pantry, and center work island. Access to the dining area from the kitchen is afforded through the keeping room and across the hall. The master suite boasts His and Hers walk-in closets in between the bedroom and bath.

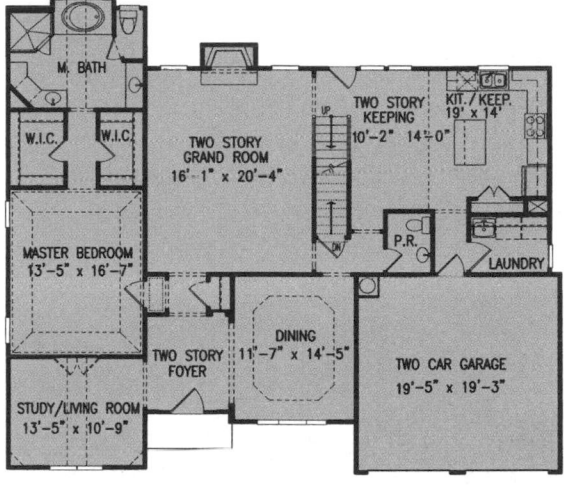

First Floor

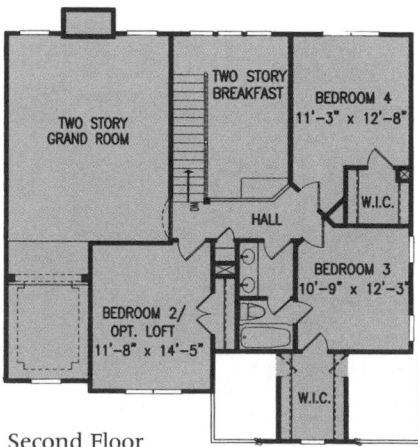

Second Floor

HPK2100601

Style: Craftsman

First Floor: 1,687 sq. ft.

Second Floor: 807 sq. ft.

Total: 2,494 sq. ft.

Bedrooms: 4

Bathrooms: 2 ½

Width: 52' - 8"

Depth: 67' - 0"

EPLANS.COM

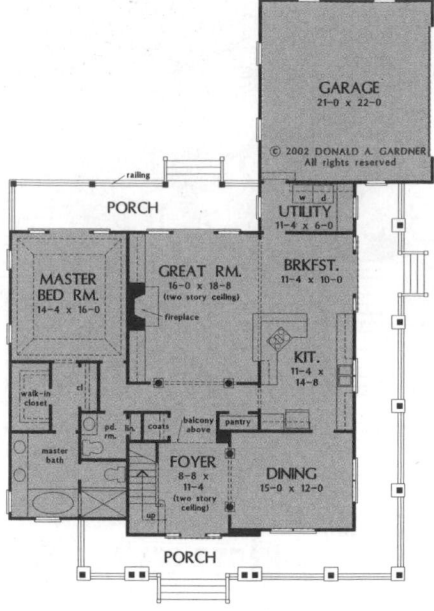

First Floor

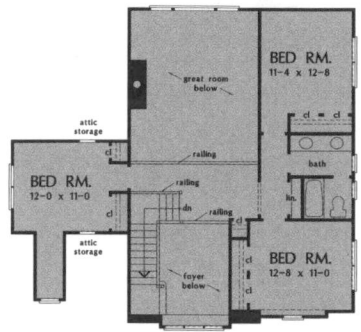

Second Floor

This glorious farmhouse was designed with the best of family living in mind. The beautiful wraparound porch is accented with stone and columns, and varying window detail. The swanky master suite takes up the entire left wing of the plan with its enormous private bath and double closets. To the right of the plan, the spacious kitchen is bookended by a formal dining room at the front and a cozy breakfast nook to the rear. A utility room opens to the garage. Upstairs, three bedrooms share a bath as well as attic storage.

HPK2101523

Style: New American
First Floor: 1,777 sq. ft.
Second Floor: 719 sq. ft.
Total: 2,496 sq. ft.
Bedrooms: 4
Bathrooms: 2 ½
Width: 58' - 0"
Depth: 59' - 4"

This charming 2,496-square-foot country cottage features spacious open rooms and an easy flow from the welcoming stone front porch to the breezy screened porch off the family room and master suite. Perfect for entertaining, the well-appointed kitchen serves a breakfast room as well as a spacious dining room. The family room features a cozy corner fireplace. Isolated from the secondary bedrooms, the master suite is an owner's retreat with a sitting area, large walk-in closet and private bath with separate tub and shower. The secondary bedrooms share a hall bath. A laundry room is conveniently located off the breakfast room. Garage access to a bonus room and handy workshop complete this delightful design.

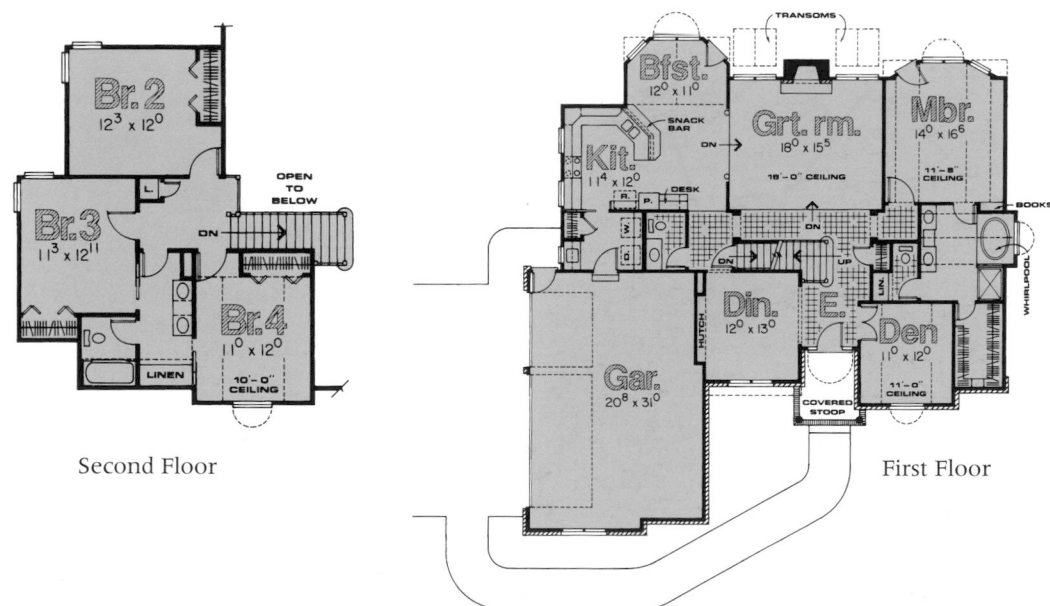

Second Floor

First Floor

HOW TO READ A
FLOOR PLAN

When you have 1,500 plans to choose from, it's easy to overlook the care and skill that goes into the creation of every home design. In fact, residential designers and architects typically spend many months—even years—drawing a home, seeing it built, then refining it before the design is released as a predrawn plan to the public. Every plan is the culmination of talent, professional know-how, hard work, and prevailing consumer trends. You owe it to yourself to read these plans carefully, and in this feature, we'll show you how.

PLOT PLAN

LEFT SIDE ELEVATION

FRONT ELEVATION

RIGHT SIDE ELEVATION

REAR ELEVATION

HOME PLANNERS, INC.

3343

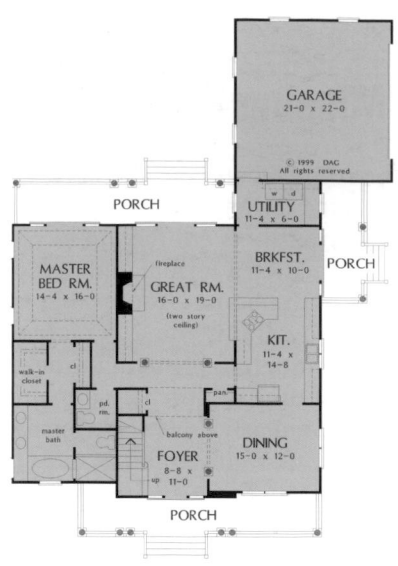

First Floor

Second Floor

A prominent center gable and an inviting front porch create excellent curb appeal for this two-story family home. An exciting balcony that overlooks the two-story foyer as well as the two-story great room provides an impressive welcome. Elegant columns mark entry to both the dining room and great room. The generously proportioned kitchen features a nearby pantry and is open to the breakfast room and great room for easy entertaining and family togetherness. Located on the first floor, the master bedroom enjoys a tray ceiling, back-porch access, a private bath, and ample closet space. Upstairs, three more bedrooms share a spacious bath.

HPK2101524

Style: Country
First Floor: 1,685 sq. ft.
Second Floor: 815 sq. ft.
Total: 2,500 sq. ft.
Bedrooms: 4
Bathrooms: 2 ½
Width: 52' - 8"
Depth: 72' - 4"

EPLANS.COM

HPK2100602

Style: Country
First Floor: 1,428 sq. ft.
Second Floor: 1,067 sq. ft.
Total: 2,495 sq. ft.
Bonus Space: 342 sq. ft.
Bedrooms: 3
Bathrooms: 2 ½
Width: 74' - 0"
Depth: 64' - 8"

EPLANS.COM

Eye-catching twin chimneys dominate the exterior of this grand design, but on closer approach you will delight in the covered porch with decorated pediment and the tall windows across the front of the house. A long hallway separates the family room, with fireplace, from the rest of the house. A large U-shaped kitchen features an island work center and direct access to the sunny breakfast room and the formal dining room. A study/living room (with optional second fireplace) completes the first floor. Upstairs, you'll find a well-appointed master suite, two family bedrooms, and a bonus room over the garage.

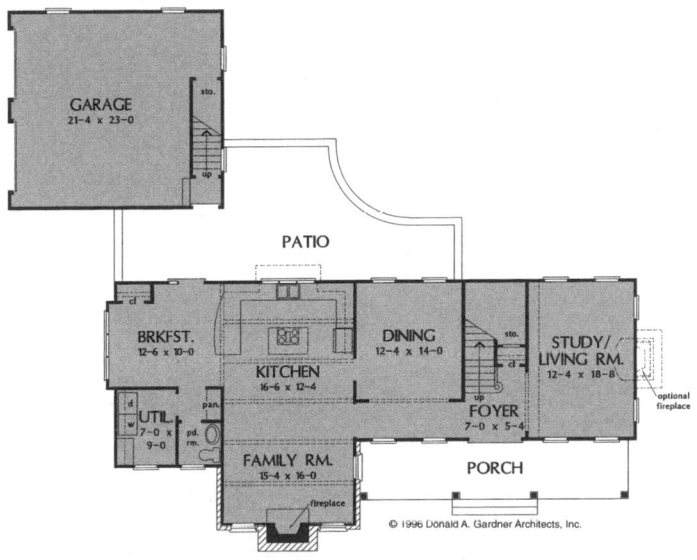

First Floor

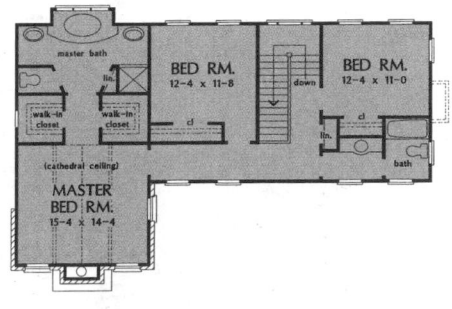

Second Floor

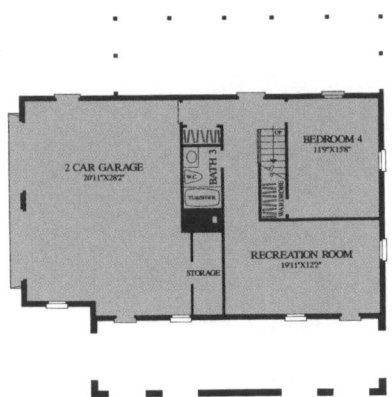

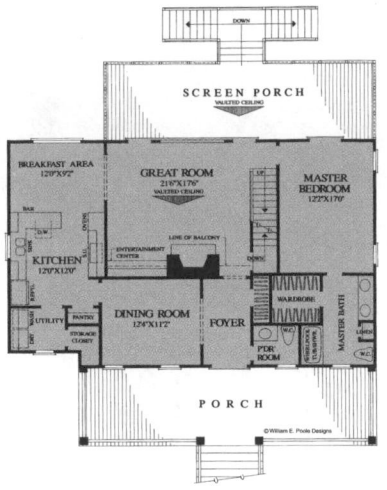

First Floor

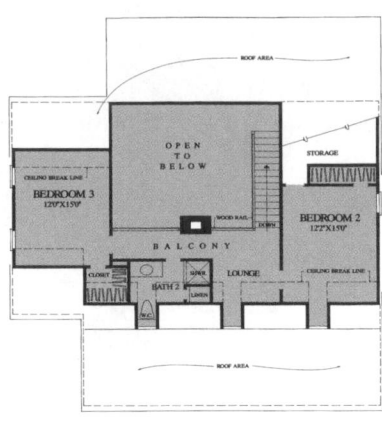

Second Floor

The unique charm of this farmhouse begins with a flight of steps and a welcoming, covered front porch. Just inside, the foyer leads to the formal dining room on the left—with easy access to the kitchen—and straight ahead to the great room. The first-floor master suite provides plenty of privacy; upstairs, two family bedrooms share a full bath. The lower level offers space for a fourth bedroom, a recreation room, and a garage.

HPK2100603

Style: Georgian

First Floor: 1,376 sq. ft.

Second Floor: 695 sq. ft.

Total: 2,071 sq. ft.

Bedrooms: 3

Bathrooms: 2 ½

Width: 47' - 0"

Depth: 49' - 8"

Foundation: Finished Walkout Basement

EPLANS.COM

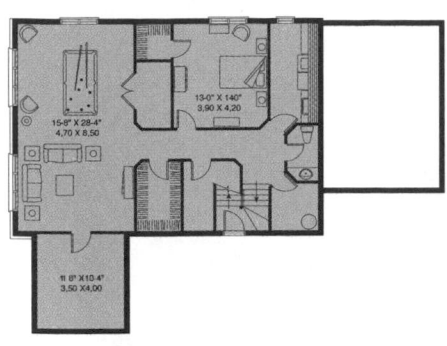

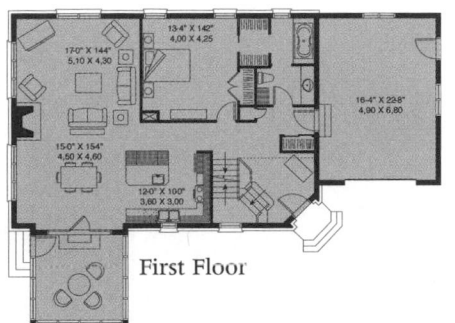

First Floor

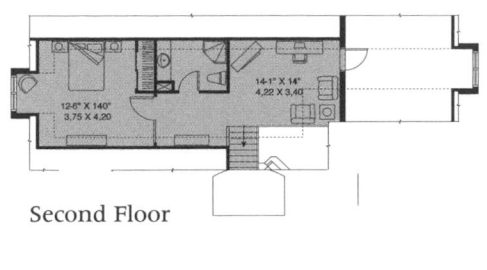

Second Floor

HPK2100604

Style: Cottage

First Floor: 1,488 sq. ft.

Second Floor: 602 sq. ft.

Total: 2,090 sq. ft.

Bonus Space: 1,321 sq. ft.

Bedrooms: 2

Bathrooms: 2

Width: 60' - 0"

Depth: 44' - 0"

Foundation: Finished Basement

EPLANS.COM

HPK2100605

Style: Country

Square Footage: 2,097

Bonus Space: 452 sq. ft.

Bedrooms: 3

Bathrooms: 3

Width: 70' - 2"

Depth: 59' - 0"

Foundation: Crawlspace, Slab

EPLANS.COM

2,000 TO 2,499 SQUARE FEET

HPK2100606

Style: New American

First Floor: 1,583 sq. ft.

Second Floor: 543 sq. ft.

Total: 2,126 sq. ft.

Bonus Space: 251 sq. ft.

Bedrooms: 4

Bathrooms: 3

Width: 53' - 0"

Depth: 47' - 0"

Foundation: Crawlspace, Slab, Unfinished Walkout Basement

EPLANS.COM

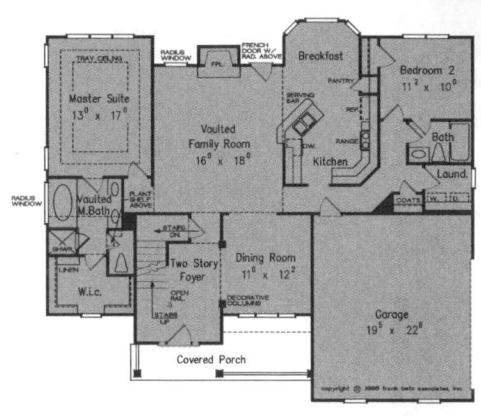

First Floor

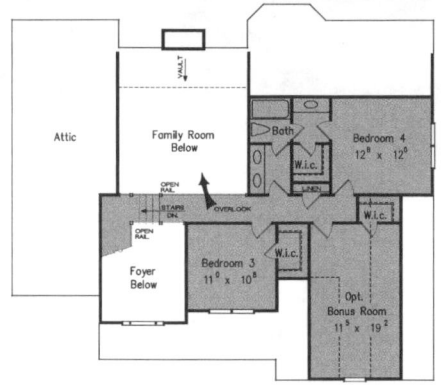

Second Floor

Find a matching garage on page 182.

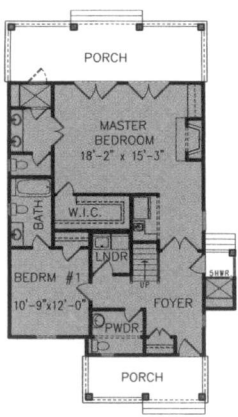

First Floor

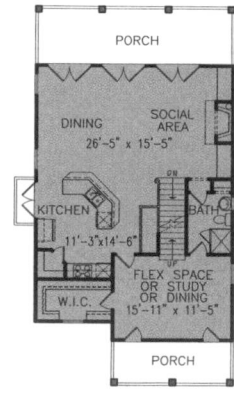

Second Floor

HPK2100607

Style: Tidewater

First Floor: 1,000 sq. ft.

Second Floor: 958 sq. ft.

Third Floor: 178 sq. ft.

Total: 2,136 sq. ft.

Bedrooms: 2

Bathrooms: 3 ½

Width: 31' - 4"

Depth: 52' - 0"

Foundation: Crawlspace

EPLANS.COM

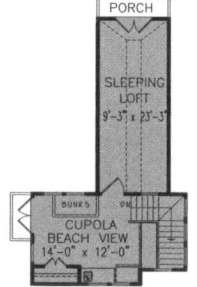

Third Floor

HPK2100608

Style: French Country

Square Footage: 2,170

Bedrooms: 4

Bathrooms: 3

Width: 62' - 0"

Depth: 61' - 6"

Foundation: Unfinished Walkout Basement

© Stephen Fuller, Inc.

©Stephen Fuller

Rear Exterior

HPK2100609

Style: Cottage

First Floor: 1,580 sq. ft.

Second Floor: 595 sq. ft.

Total: 2,175 sq. ft.

Bedrooms: 3

Bathrooms: 2 ½

Width: 50' - 0"

Depth: 69' - 9"

Foundation: Unfinished Walkout Basement

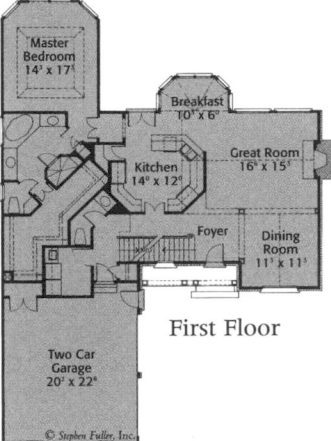

First Floor

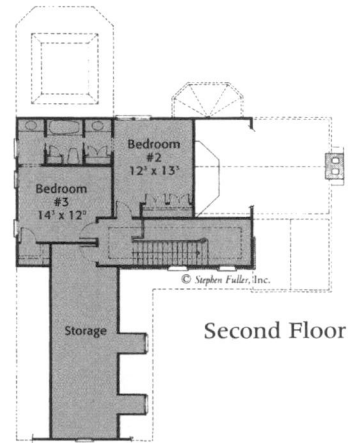

© Stephen Fuller, Inc.

Second Floor

2,000 TO 2,499 SQUARE FEET

HPK2100610

Style: Cottage

First Floor: 1,042 sq. ft.

Second Floor: 1,150 sq. ft.

Total: 2,192 sq. ft.

Bedrooms: 4

Bathrooms: 3

Width: 41' - 0"

Depth: 43' - 0"

Foundation: Crawlspace, Unfinished Walkout Basement

EPLANS.COM

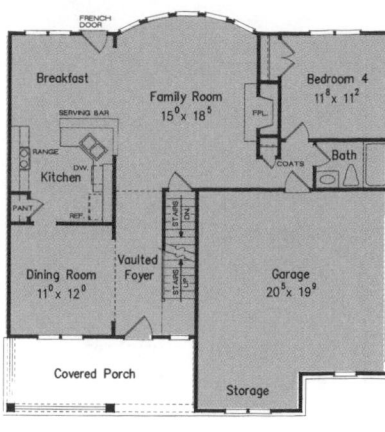

First Floor

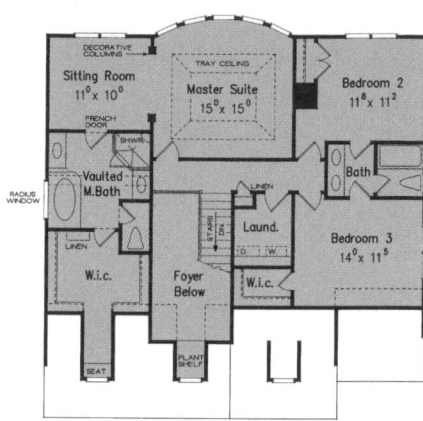

Second Floor

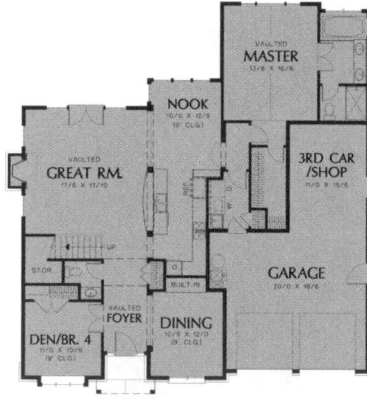

First Floor

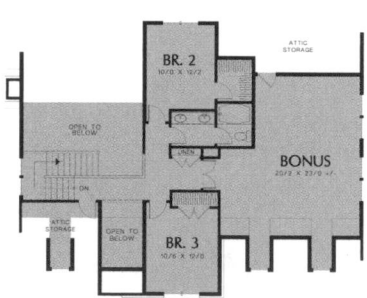

Second Floor

HPK2100611

Style: French Country

First Floor: 1,658 sq. ft.

Second Floor: 538 sq. ft.

Total: 2,196 sq. ft.

Bonus Space: 496 sq. ft.

Bedrooms: 4

Bathrooms: 2 ½

Width: 50' - 0"

Depth: 56' - 0"

Foundation: Crawlspace

EPLANS.COM

HPK2100612

Style: French Country

First Floor: 1,732 sq. ft.

Second Floor: 504 sq. ft.

Total: 2,236 sq. ft.

Bedrooms: 3

Bathrooms: 2 ½

Width: 47' - 3"

Depth: 63' - 6"

Foundation: Unfinished Walkout Basement

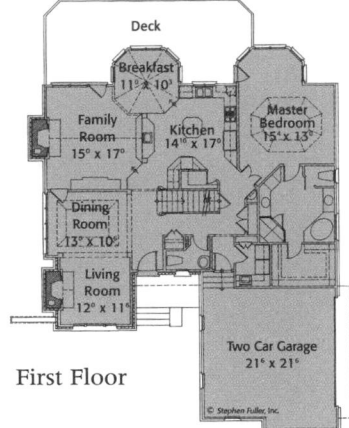

First Floor

© Stephen Fuller, Inc.

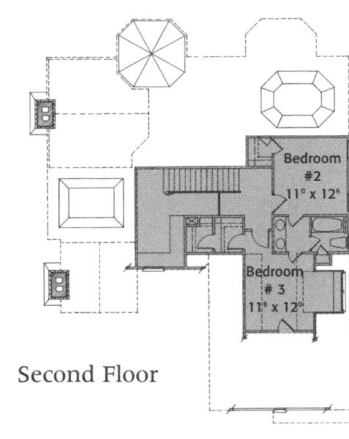

Second Floor

HPK2100613

Style: Craftsman

Square Footage: 2,326

Bonus Space: 358 sq. ft.

Bedrooms: 3

Bathrooms: 2 ½

Width: 64' - 0"

Depth: 72' - 4"

Foundation: Finished Walkout Basement

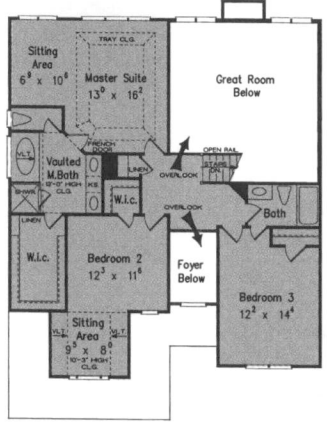

First Floor

Second Floor

HPK2100614

Style: New American
First Floor: 1,208 sq. ft.
Second Floor: 1,137 sq. ft.
Total: 2,345 sq. ft.
Bedrooms: 3
Bathrooms: 3
Width: 38' - 6"
Depth: 51' - 4"
Foundation: Crawlspace,
Unfinished Walkout Basement

EPLANS.COM

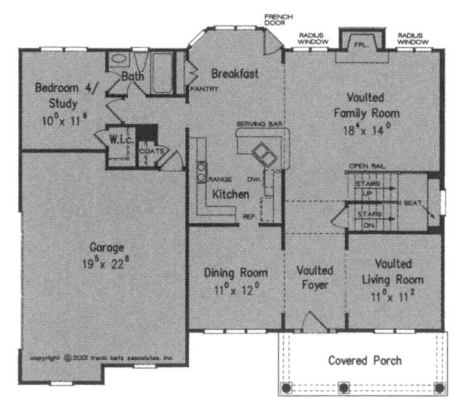

First Floor

HPK2100615

Style: Country
First Floor: 1,279 sq. ft.
Second Floor: 1,071 sq. ft.
Total: 2,350 sq. ft.
Bedrooms: 4
Bathrooms: 3
Width: 50' - 0"
Depth: 42' - 6"
Foundation: Crawlspace,
Unfinished Walkout Basement

EPLANS.COM

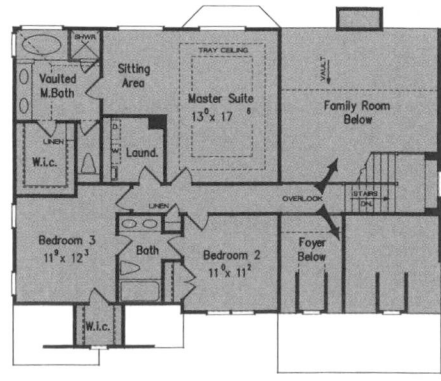

Second Floor

HPK2100616

Style: Colonial Revival
First Floor: 1,186 sq. ft.
Second Floor: 1,210 sq. ft.
Total: 2,396 sq. ft.
Bedrooms: 4
Bathrooms: 2 ½
Width: 50' - 0"
Depth: 47' - 6"
Foundation: Crawlspace, Unfinished Walkout Basement

EPLANS.COM

Brick and shake create a weathered look for this Colonial home, complemented by a pedimented entry; use recycled materials for a more vintage appeal. The serving-bar kitchen is conveniently central to the bayed breakfast nook and formal dining room. Upstairs, three family bedrooms—one lit by dormer windows—share a full bath. The master suite resides in luxury with a sumptuous private bath that includes a vaulted ceiling and a corner tub.

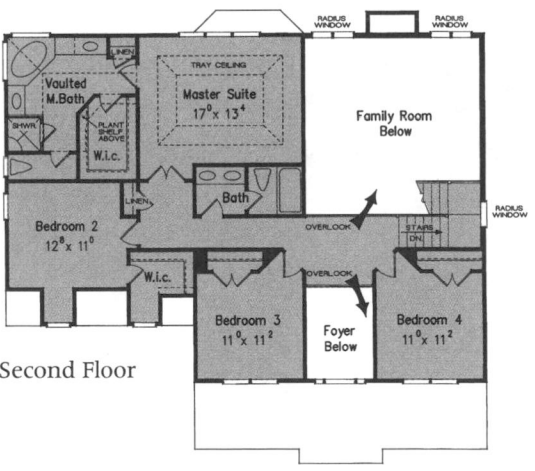

Second Floor

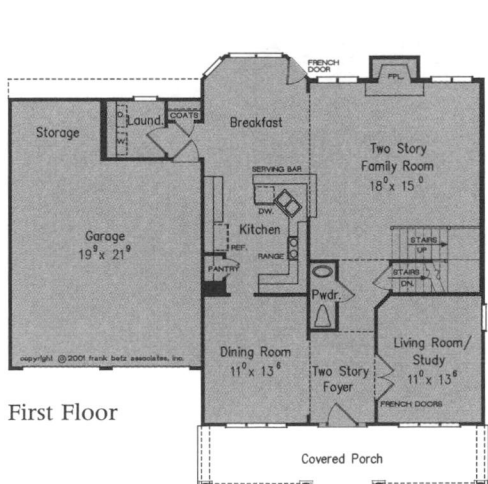

First Floor

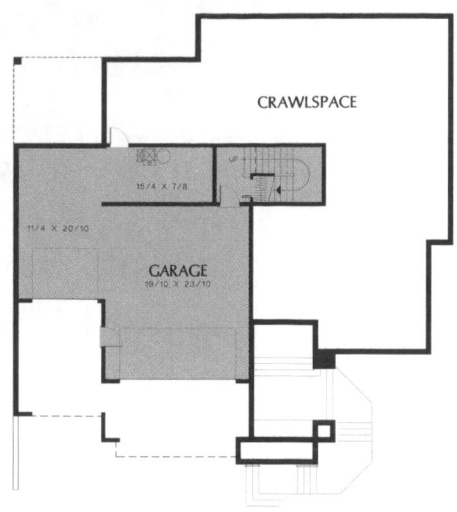

CRAWLSPACE

15/4 X 7/8

11/4 X 20/10

GARAGE
19/10 X 23/10

With windows and glass panels to take in the view, this design would make an exquisite seaside resort. A grand great room sets the tone inside, with an elegant tray ceiling and French doors to a private front balcony. Three steps up from the foyer, the sleeping level includes a spacious master suite with a sizable private bath. The two additional bedrooms access a shared bath with two vanities.

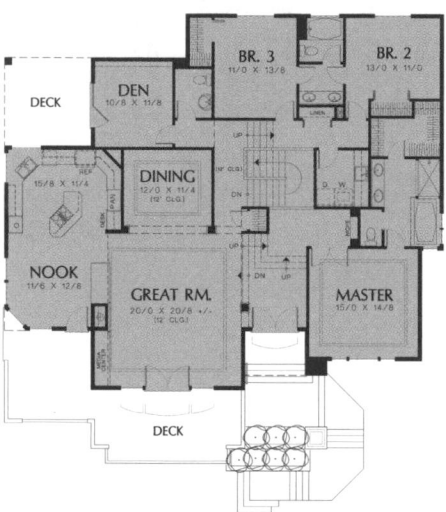

DECK

BR. 3
11/0 X 13/8

BR. 2
13/0 X 11/0

DEN
10/8 X 11/8

DINING
12/0 X 11/4
(12' CLG)

15/8 X 11/4

NOOK
11/6 X 12/8

GREAT RM.
20/0 X 20/8 +/-
(12' CLG)

MASTER
15/0 X 14/8

DECK

HPK2100617

Style: Mediterranean

Square Footage: 2,412

Bedrooms: 3

Bathrooms: 2 ½

Width: 60' - 0"

Depth: 59' - 0"

Foundation: Slab

EPLANS.COM

© Sater Design Collection, Inc.

HPK2100618

Style: Mediterranean
Main Level: 2,385 sq. ft.
Lower Level: 109 sq. ft.
Total: 2,494 sq. ft.
Bedrooms: 3
Bathrooms: 3
Width: 60' - 0"
Depth: 52' - 0"
Foundation: Slab

EPLANS.COM

This Mediterranean villa boasts Italian charm and a distinct coastal feel. Once inside, the foyer leads up to a study on the left and the vaulted great room and rear views straight ahead. The island kitchen is conveniently open to a breakfast nook. Guest quarters reside on the right side of the plan: one suite boasts a private bath and the other uses a full hall bath. The master suite is secluded and features two walk-in closets and a pampering master bath.

2,000 TO 2,499 SQUARE FEET

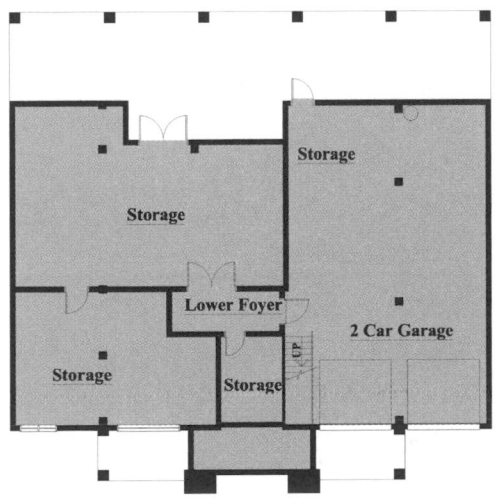

Lower Level

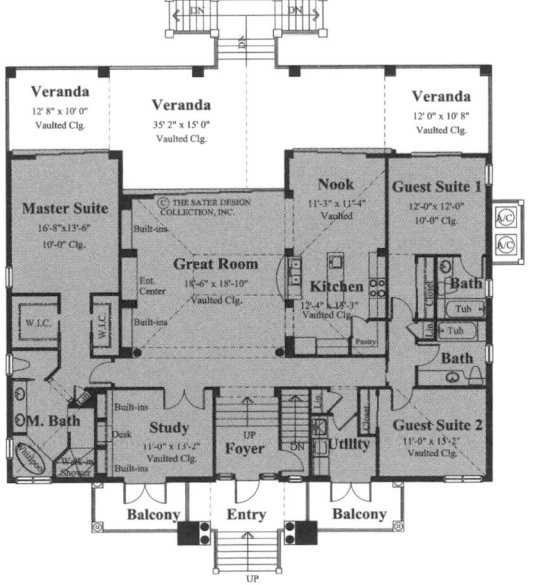

Main Level

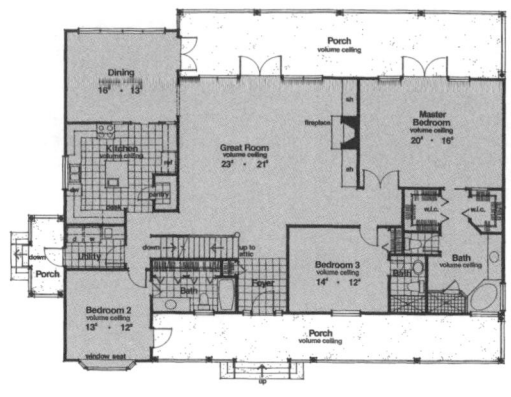

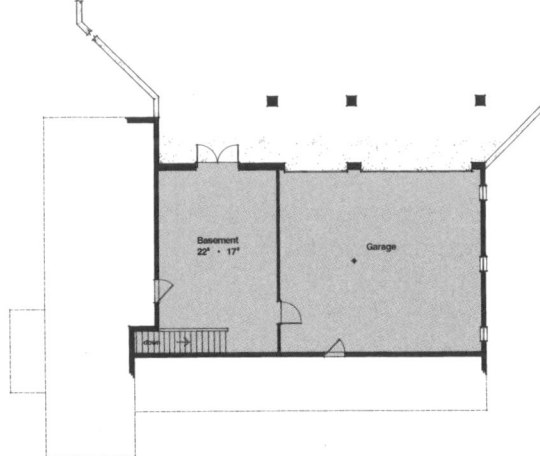

HPK2100619

Style: Farmhouse

Square Footage: 2,500

Bedrooms: 3

Bathrooms: 3

Width: 64' - 0"

Depth: 52' - 0"

Foundation: Unfinished Basement

EPLANS.COM

Unpretentious use of space is the hallmark of the Florida "Cracker"-style home. This design shows the style at its best. The huge great room, which sports a volume ceiling, opens to the expansive rear porch for extended entertaining. The master suite has a lavish bedchamber and a luxurious bath with His and Hers closets. Perfect for a sloping lot, this home can be expanded with a lower garage and bonus space in the basement.

ORDER BLUEPRINTS ANYTIME AT EPLANS.COM OR 1-800-521-6797

Rear Exterior

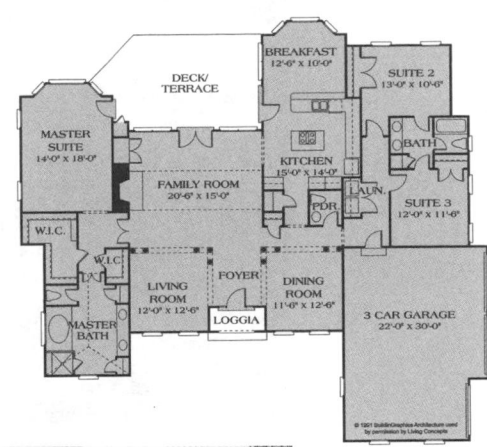

HPK2100620

Style: Norman
Square Footage: 2,500
Bedrooms: 3
Bathrooms: 2 ½
Width: 73' - 0"
Depth: 65' - 10"
Foundation: Crawlspace

EPLANS.COM

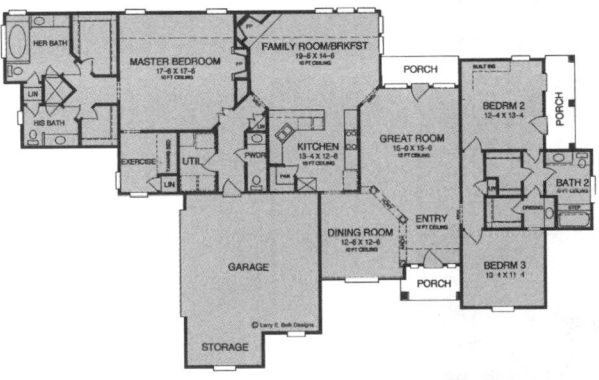

HPK2100621

Style: New American
Square Footage: 2,506
Bedrooms: 3
Bathrooms: 2 ½
Width: 89' - 6"
Depth: 54' - 2"
Foundation: Crawlspace, Slab

EPLANS.COM

HPK2100622

Style: Country

Square Footage: 2,506

Bedrooms: 4

Bathrooms: 2 ½

Width: 72' - 2"

Depth: 66' - 4"

Foundation: Crawlspace, Slab, Unfinished Basement

EPLANS.COM

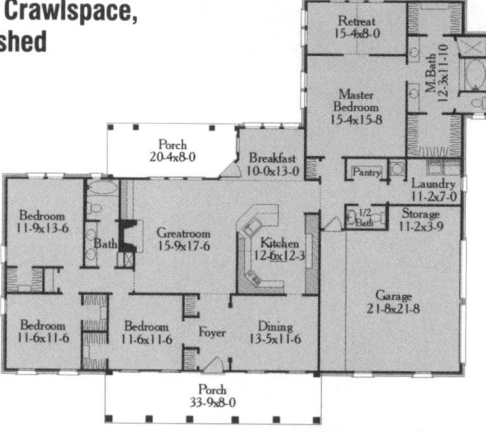

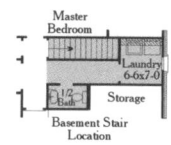

© The Sater Design Collection, Inc.

HPK2100623

Style: New American

Square Footage: 2,508

Bedrooms: 4

Bathrooms: 3

Width: 60' - 0"

Depth: 78' - 9"

Foundation: Slab

EPLANS.COM

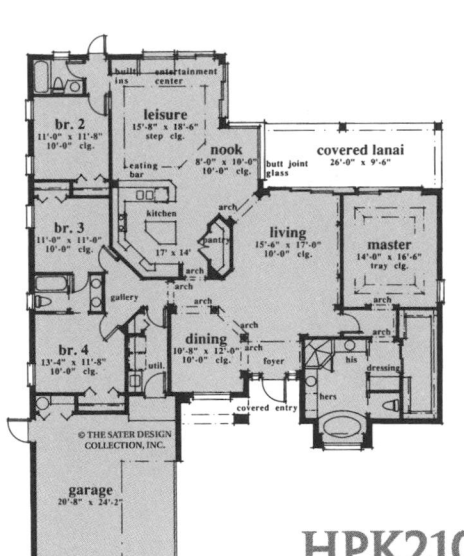

© THE SATER DESIGN COLLECTION, INC.

© The Sater Design Collection, Inc.

HPK2100624

Style: New American
Square Footage: 2,508
Bedrooms: 4
Bathrooms: 3
Width: 60' - 0"
Depth: 78' - 9"
Foundation: Slab

EPLANS.COM

HPK2100625

Style: New American
Square Footage: 2,517
Bedrooms: 3
Bathrooms: 2 ½
Width: 77' - 0"
Depth: 59' - 0"

EPLANS.COM

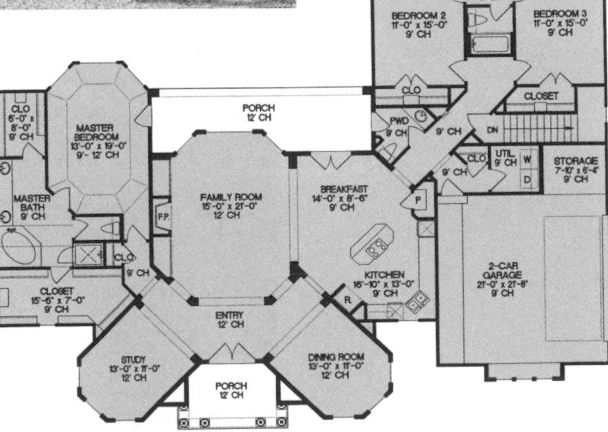

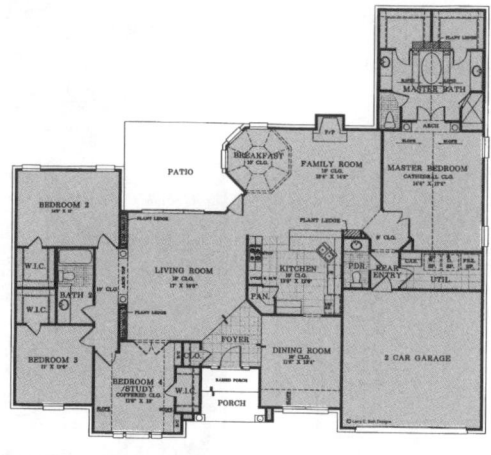

HPK2100626

Style: Cottage
Square Footage: 2,517
Bedrooms: 4
Bathrooms: 2 ½
Width: 69' - 0"
Depth: 63' - 6"
Foundation: Crawlspace, Slab

EPLANS.COM

HPK2100627

Style: Chateauesque
Square Footage: 2,526
Bedrooms: 4
Bathrooms: 3
Width: 64' - 0"
Depth: 81' - 7"
Foundation: Slab

EPLANS.COM

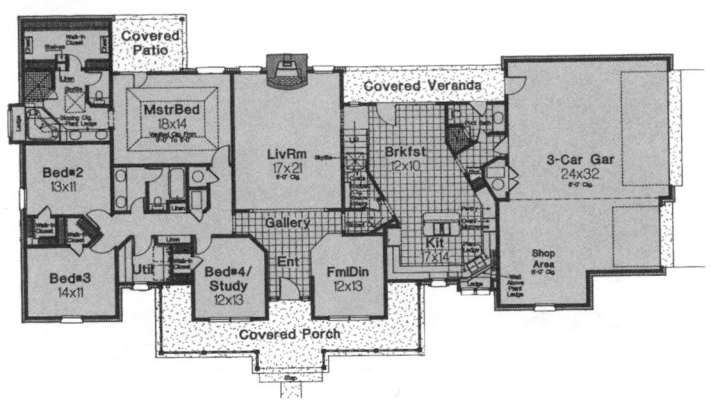

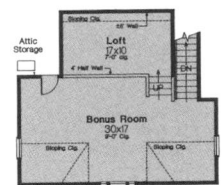

HPK2100628

Style: Gothic Revival

Square Footage: 2,539

Bonus Space: 636 sq. ft.

Bedrooms: 4

Bathrooms: 3

Width: 98' - 0"

Depth: 53' - 11"

Foundation: Crawlspace, Slab, Unfinished Basement

EPLANS.COM

HPK2100629

Style: New American

Square Footage: 2,540

Bedrooms: 4

Bathrooms: 2 ½

Width: 70' - 0"

Depth: 65' - 0"

Foundation: Crawlspace, Slab

EPLANS.COM

© Larry E. Belk Designs

2,500 TO 2,999 SQUARE FEET

HPK2100630

Style: Craftsman
Square Footage: 2,541
Bedrooms: 4
Bathrooms: 3
Width: 81' - 0"
Depth: 54' - 0"
Foundation: Crawlspace, Slab, Unfinished Basement

EPLANS.COM

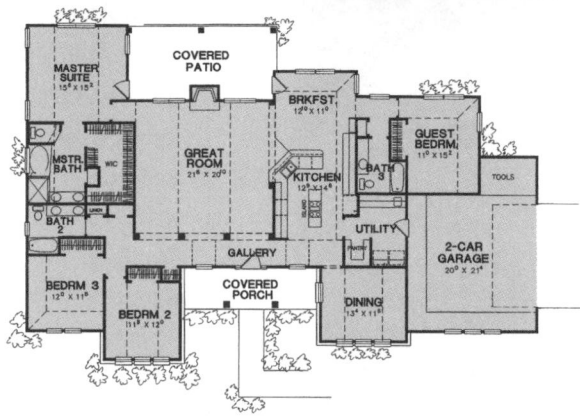

HPK2100631

Style: New American
Square Footage: 2,542
Bedrooms: 4
Bathrooms: 3 ½
Width: 80' - 0"
Depth: 64' - 0"
Foundation: Slab

EPLANS.COM

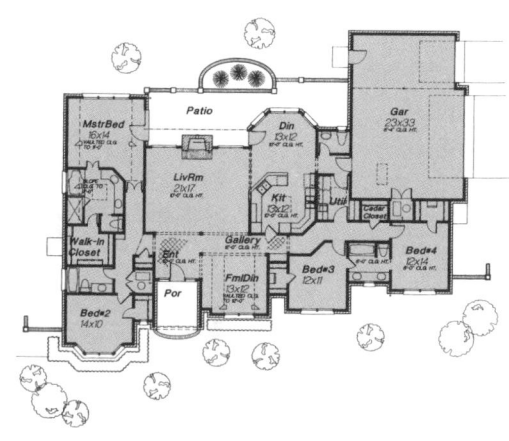

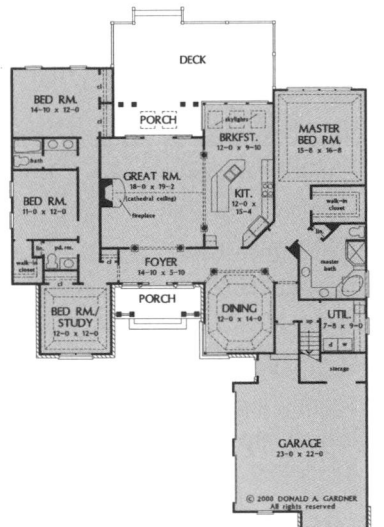

HPK2100632

Style: Cottage

Square Footage: 2,544

Bonus Space: 394 sq. ft.

Bedrooms: 4

Bathrooms: 2 ½

Width: 62' - 8"

Depth: 82' - 1"

EPLANS.COM

HPK2100633

Style: Craftsman

Square Footage: 2,545

Bedrooms: 2

Bathrooms: 2

Width: 80' - 0"

Depth: 65' - 0"

Foundation: Crawlspace

EPLANS.COM

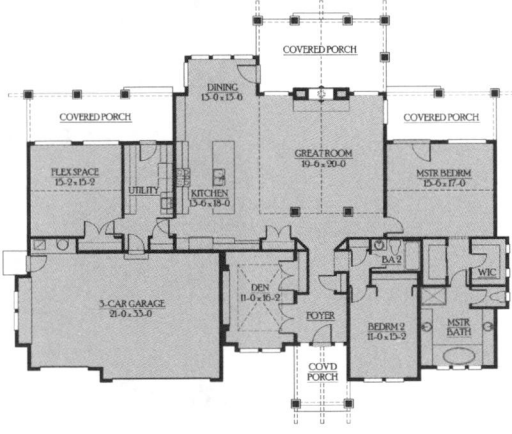

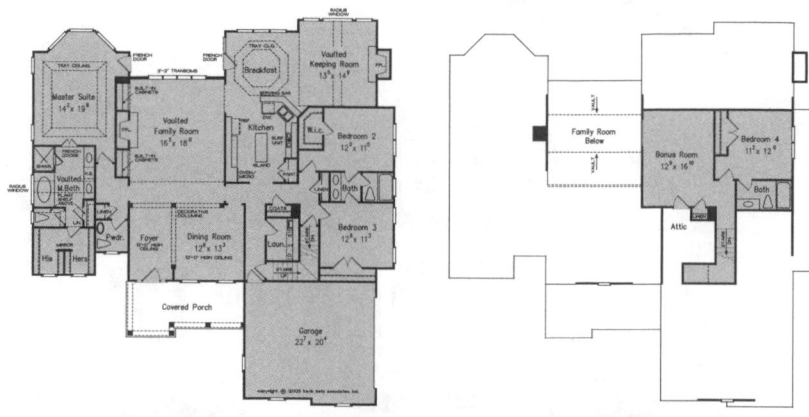

HPK2100634

Style: Country

Square Footage: 2,548

Bonus Space: 490 sq. ft.

Bedrooms: 3

Bathrooms: 2 ½

Width: 63' - 0"

Depth: 67' - 6"

Foundation: Crawlspace, Unfinished Walkout Basement

EPLANS.COM

HPK2100635

Style: Neoclassical

Square Footage: 2,551

Bonus Space: 287 sq. ft.

Bedrooms: 4

Bathrooms: 3

Width: 69' - 8"

Depth: 71' - 4"

Foundation: Slab

EPLANS.COM

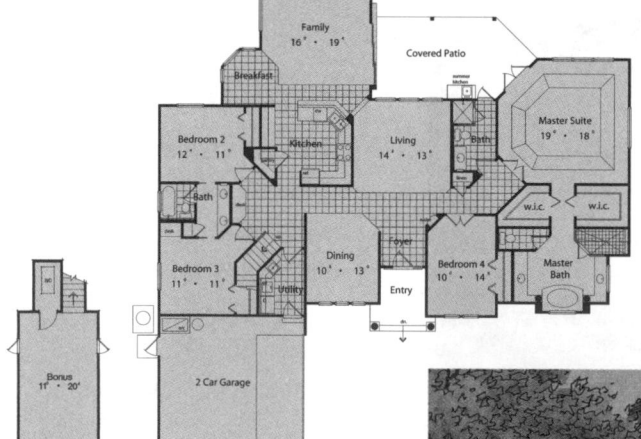

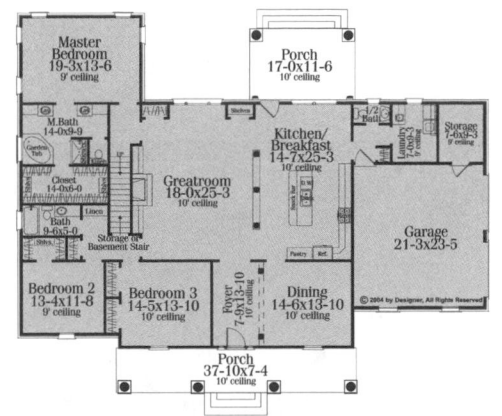

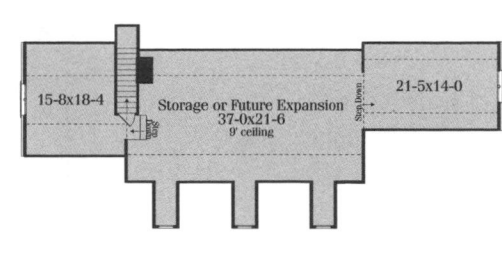

HPK2100636

Style: Greek Revival

Square Footage: 2,561

Bonus Space: 1,494 sq. ft.

Bedrooms: 3

Bathrooms: 2 ½

Width: 76' - 8"

Depth: 62' - 0"

Foundation: Crawlspace, Slab, Unfinished Basement

EPLANS.COM

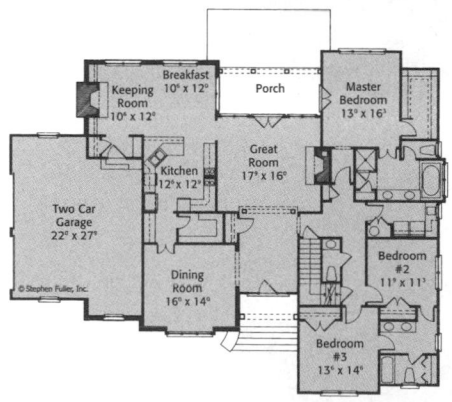

HPK2100637

Style: Country

Square Footage: 2,570

Bedrooms: 3

Bathrooms: 2 ½

Width: 73' - 9"

Depth: 58' - 6"

Foundation: Unfinished Walkout Basement

EPLANS.COM

2,500 TO 2,999 SQUARE FEET

HPK2100638

Style: New American
Square Footage: 2,585
Bonus Space: 519 sq. ft.
Bedrooms: 3
Bathrooms: 2 ½
Width: 62' - 6"
Depth: 83' - 10"
Foundation: Crawlspace

EPLANS.COM

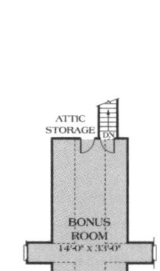

HPK2100639

Style: French Country
Square Footage: 2,590
Bedrooms: 4
Bathrooms: 3 ½
Width: 73' - 6"
Depth: 64' - 10"
Foundation: Slab

EPLANS.COM

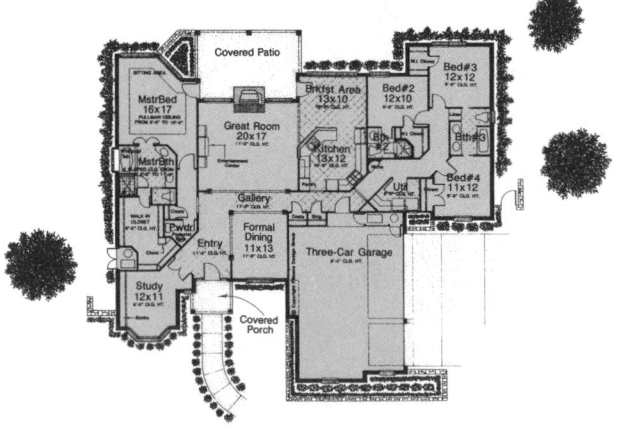

HPK2100640

Style: Mediterranean

Square Footage: 2,597

Bedrooms: 4

Bathrooms: 3

Width: 96' - 6"

Depth: 50' - 0"

Foundation: Slab

EPLANS.COM

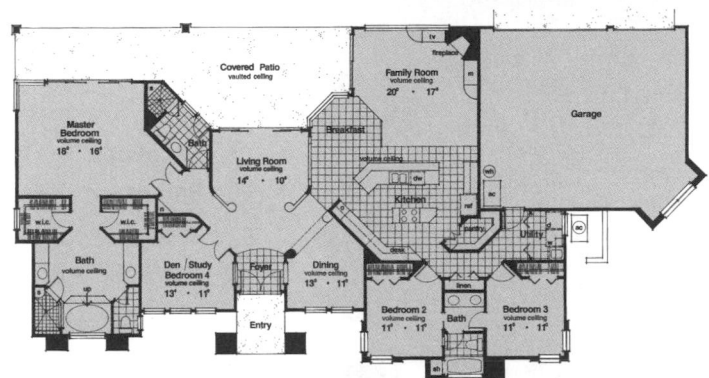

HPK2100641

Style: New American

Square Footage: 2,600

Bonus Space: 311 sq. ft.

Bedrooms: 3

Bathrooms: 2 ½

Width: 57' - 0"

Depth: 70' - 0"

Foundation: Crawlspace, Slab, Unfinished Walkout Basement

EPLANS.COM

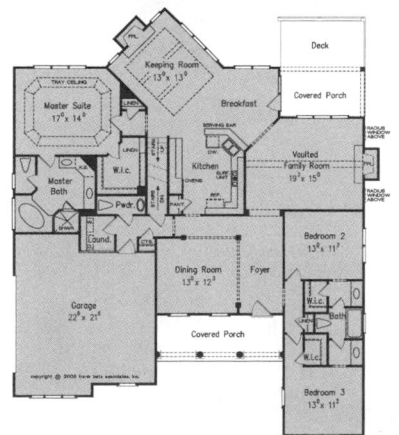

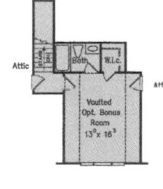

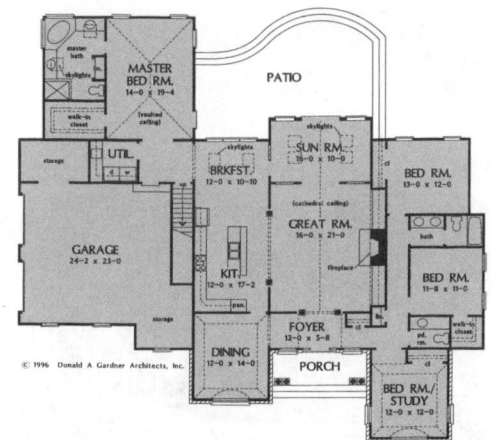

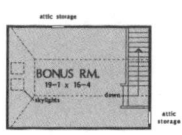

HPK2100642

Style: Cottage
Square Footage: 2,602
Bonus Space: 399 sq. ft.
Bedrooms: 4
Bathrooms: 2 ½
Width: 75' - 3"
Depth: 69' - 6"

EPLANS.COM

© 1996 Donald A. Gardner Architects, Inc.

HPK2100643

Style: New American
Square Footage: 2,622
Bonus Space: 478 sq. ft.
Bedrooms: 3
Bathrooms: 2 ½
Width: 69' - 0"
Depth: 71' - 4"
Foundation: Crawlspace,
Unfinished Walkout Basement

EPLANS.COM

HPK2100644

Style: Pueblo

Square Footage: 2,624

Bedrooms: 3

Bathrooms: 2 ½

Width: 88' - 8"

Depth: 69' - 0"

Foundation: Slab

EPLANS.COM

HPK2100645

Style: New American

Square Footage: 2,625

Bonus Space: 447 sq. ft.

Bedrooms: 4

Bathrooms: 2 ½

Width: 63' - 1"

Depth: 90' - 2"

EPLANS.COM

2,500 TO 2,999 SQUARE FEET

HPK2100646

Style: French Country
Square Footage: 2,630
Bonus Space: 627 sq. ft.
Bedrooms: 4
Bathrooms: 3 ½
Width: 73' - 6"
Depth: 67' - 7"
Foundation: Slab

EPLANS.COM

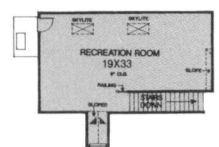

HPK2100647

Style: Cottage
Square Footage: 2,648
Bonus Space: 616 sq. ft.
Bedrooms: 3
Bathrooms: 2 ½
Width: 65' - 0"
Depth: 86' - 0"
Foundation: Crawlspace,
Unfinished Walkout Basement

EPLANS.COM

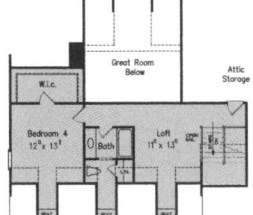

HPK2100648

Style: Country

Square Footage: 2,656

Bonus Space: 484 sq. ft.

Bedrooms: 3

Bathrooms: 2 ½

Width: 63' - 0"

Depth: 76' - 6"

Foundation: Crawlspace, Unfinished Walkout Basement

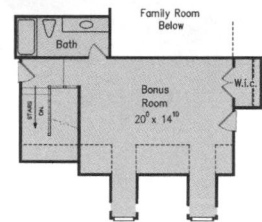

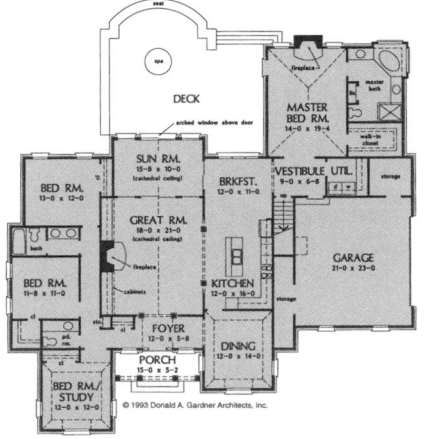

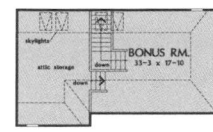

HPK2100649

Style: Country

Square Footage: 2,663

Bonus Space: 653 sq. ft.

Bedrooms: 4

Bathrooms: 2 ½

Width: 72' - 7"

Depth: 71' - 5"

2,500 TO 2,999 SQUARE FEET

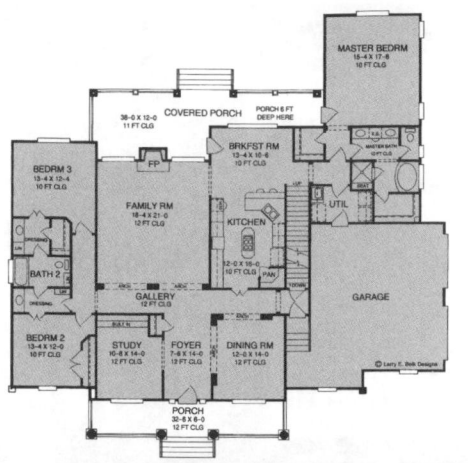
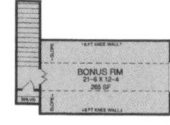

© Larry E. Belk Designs

HPK2100650

Style: Country
Square Footage: 2,684
Bonus Space: 265 sq. ft.
Bedrooms: 3
Bathrooms: 2
Width: 71' - 10"
Depth: 71' - 2"
Foundation: Crawlspace, Slab, Unfinished Basement

EPLANS.COM

HPK2100651

Style: New American
Square Footage: 2,696
Bedrooms: 4
Bathrooms: 3 ½
Width: 80' - 0"
Depth: 64' - 1"
Foundation: Slab

EPLANS.COM

HPK2100652

Style: Federal - Adams

Square Footage: 2,697

Bedrooms: 3

Bathrooms: 2 ½

Width: 65' - 3"

Depth: 67' - 3"

Foundation: Finished Walkout Basement

EPLANS.COM

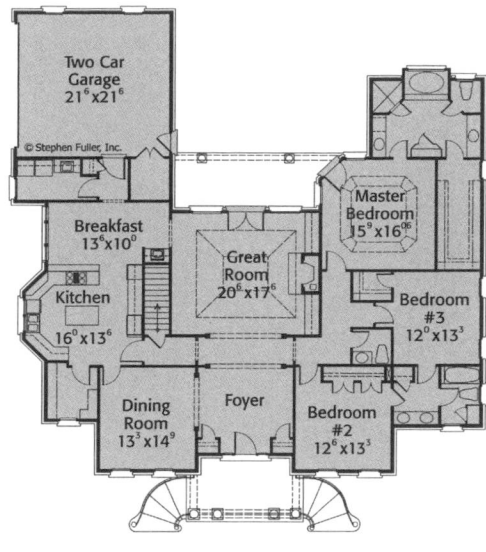

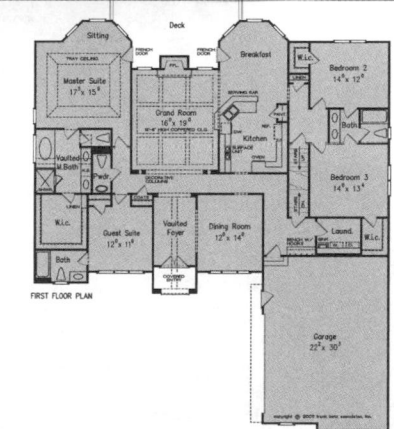

HPK2100653

Style: New American

Square Footage: 2,699

Bonus Space: 418 sq. ft.

Bedrooms: 4

Bathrooms: 3 ½

Width: 65' - 0"

Depth: 75' - 4"

Foundation: Crawlspace, Slab, Unfinished Walkout Basement

EPLANS.COM

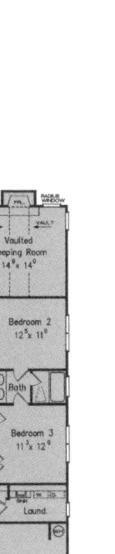

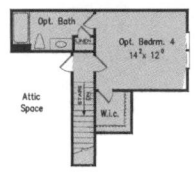

HPK2100654

Style: European
Square Footage: 2,713
Bonus Space: 324 sq. ft.
Bedrooms: 3
Bathrooms: 2 ½
Width: 60' - 0"
Depth: 79' - 4"
Foundation: Crawlspace, Unfinished Walkout Basement

HPK2100655

Style: New American
Square Footage: 2,713
Bonus Space: 440 sq. ft.
Bedrooms: 3
Bathrooms: 3
Width: 66' - 4"
Depth: 80' - 8"
Foundation: Slab

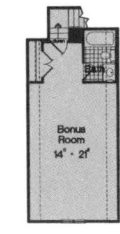

HPK2100656

Style: New American

Square Footage: 2,733

Bedrooms: 4

Bathrooms: 2 ½

Width: 88' - 0"

Depth: 54' - 2"

Foundation: Crawlspace, Slab

EPLANS.COM

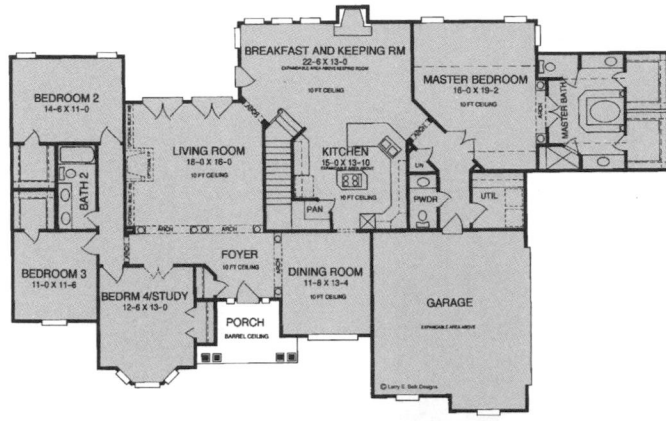

HPK2100657

Style: French Country

Square Footage: 2,745

Bedrooms: 4

Bathrooms: 2 ½

Width: 69' - 6"

Depth: 76' - 8"

Foundation: Crawlspace, Slab, Unfinished Basement

EPLANS.COM

2,500 TO 2,999 SQUARE FEET

HPK2100658

Style: New American
Square Footage: 2,755
Bonus Space: 440 sq. ft.
Bedrooms: 4
Bathrooms: 3
Width: 73' - 0"
Depth: 82' - 8"
Foundation: Slab

EPLANS.COM

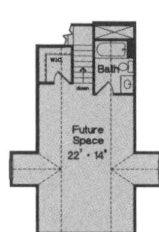

HPK2100659

Style: French Country
Square Footage: 2,757
Bedrooms: 4
Bathrooms: 2 ½
Width: 69' - 6"
Depth: 68' - 8"
Foundation: Crawlspace, Slab,
Unfinished Basement

EPLANS.COM

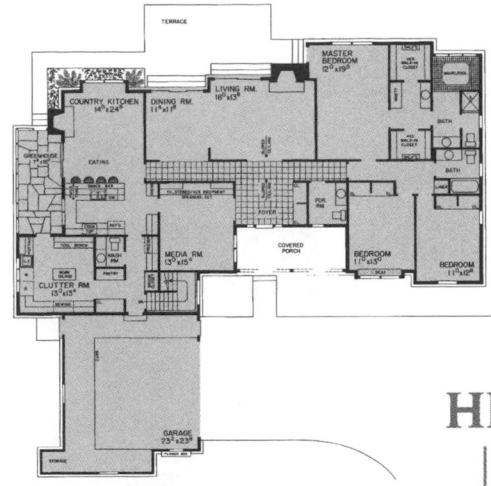

HPK2100660

Style: Ranch

Square Footage: 2,758

Bedrooms: 3

Bathrooms: 2 ½ + ½

Width: 81' - 4"

Depth: 76' - 0"

Foundation: Unfinished Basement

EPLANS.COM

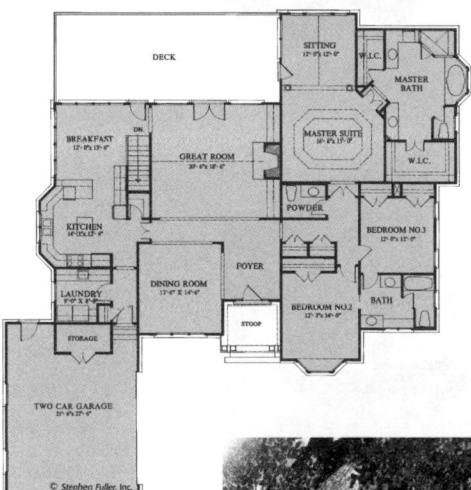

HPK2100661

EPLANS.COM

Style: French Country

Square Footage: 2,770

Bedrooms: 3

Bathrooms: 2 ½

Width: 73' - 6"

Depth: 78' - 0"

Foundation: Finished Walkout Basement

© 1995 William E Poole Designs,

HPK2100662

Style: Federal - Adams
Square Footage: 2,777
Bonus Space: 424 sq. ft.
Bedrooms: 3
Bathrooms: 2 ½
Width: 75' - 6"
Depth: 60' - 2"
Foundation: Crawlspace, Unfinished Basement

EPLANS.COM

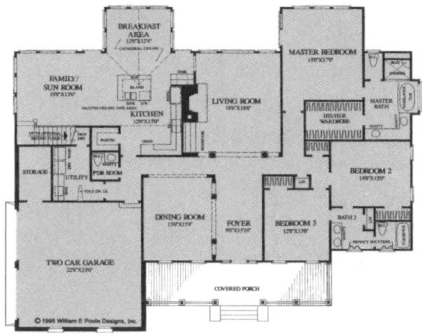

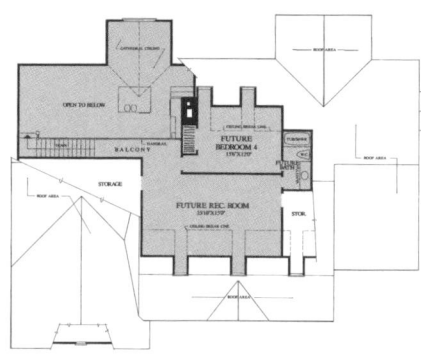

HPK2100663

Style: French Country
Square Footage: 2,778
Bedrooms: 4
Bathrooms: 3 ½
Width: 74' - 0"
Depth: 74' - 1"
Foundation: Slab

EPLANS.COM

HPK2100664

Style: Mediterranean

Square Footage: 2,791

Bedrooms: 3

Bathrooms: 2

Width: 84' - 0"

Depth: 54' - 0"

Foundation: Crawlspace, Slab

EPLANS.COM

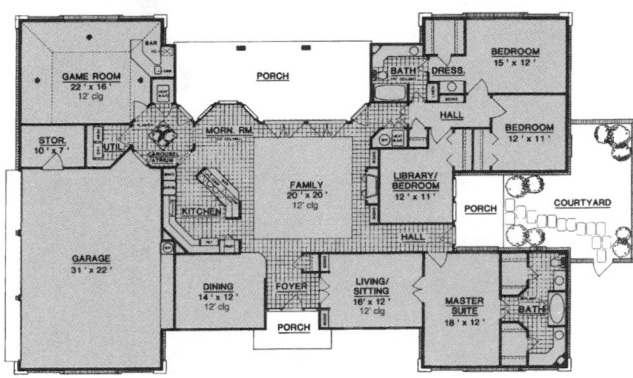

HPK2100665

Style: Ranch

Square Footage: 2,791

Bedrooms: 4

Bathrooms: 2 ½

Width: 84' - 0"

Depth: 54' - 0"

Foundation: Crawlspace, Slab

EPLANS.COM

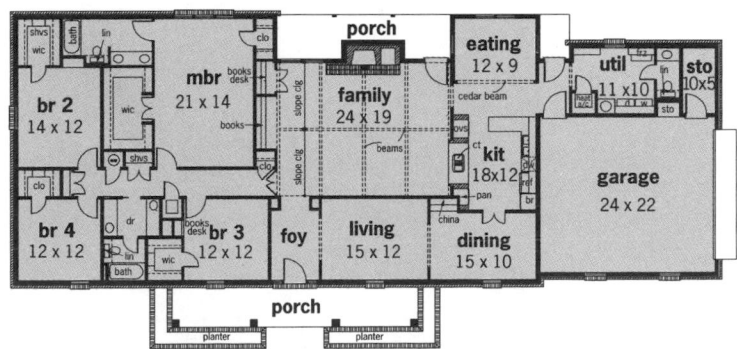

© 2002 Donald A. Gardner
All rights reserved.

HPK2100666

EPLANS.COM

Style: Pueblo

Square Footage: 2,792

Bedrooms: 3

Bathrooms: 2 ½

Width: 89' - 2"

Depth: 88' - 9"

© 2002 Donald A. Gardner, Inc.

© THE SATER DESIGN COLLECTION, INC.

HPK2100667

EPLANS.COM

Style: Mediterranean

Square Footage: 2,794

Bedrooms: 3

Bathrooms: 3

Width: 70' - 0"

Depth: 98' - 0"

Foundation: Slab

HPK2100668

Style: Cottage
Square Footage: 2,796
Bedrooms: 3
Bathrooms: 2 ½
Width: 70' - 9"
Depth: 66' - 6"
Foundation: Finished Walkout Basement

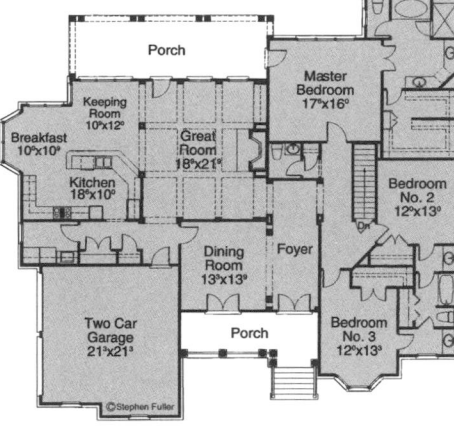

HPK2100669

Style: New American
Square Footage: 2,816
Bonus Space: 290 sq. ft.
Bedrooms: 4
Bathrooms: 3 ½ + ½
Width: 94' - 0"
Depth: 113' - 6"
Foundation: Slab

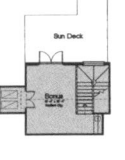

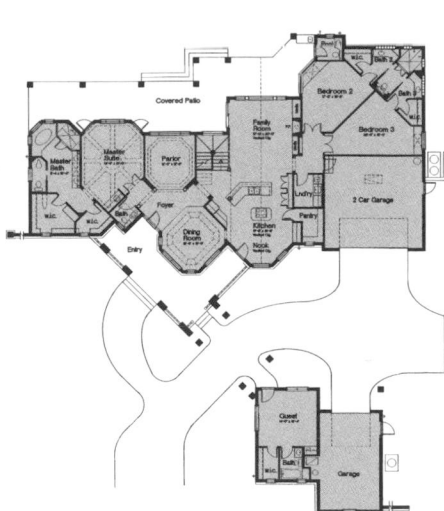

2,500 TO 2,999 SQUARE FEET

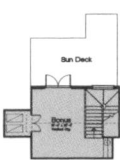

HPK2100670

Style: Craftsman

Square Footage: 2,816

Bonus Space: 290 sq. ft.

Bedrooms: 4

Bathrooms: 3 ½ + ½

Width: 94' - 0"

Depth: 113' - 6"

Foundation: Slab

EPLANS.COM

© 2003 Donald A. Gardner, Inc.

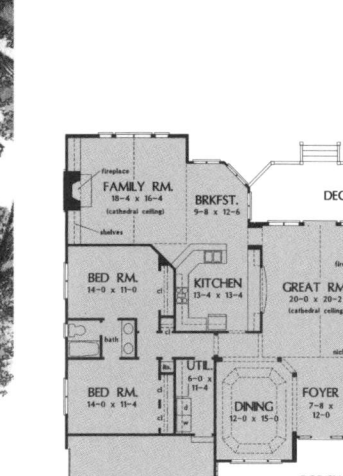

HPK2100671

Style: French Country

Square Footage: 2,818

Bedrooms: 4

Bathrooms: 3

Width: 70' - 0"

Depth: 69' - 10"

EPLANS.COM

©The Sater Design Collection, Inc.

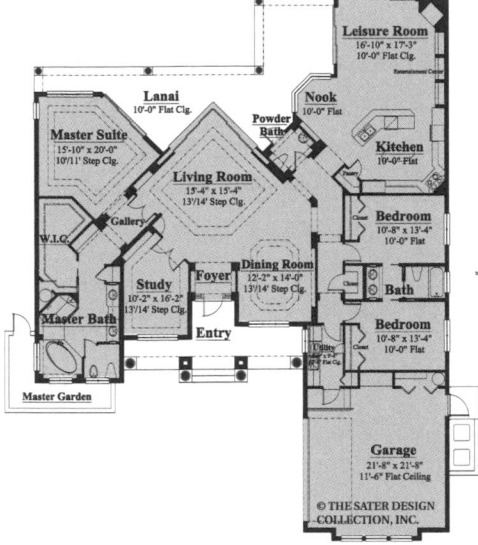

© THE SATER DESIGN COLLECTION, INC.

HPK2100672

Style: Mediterranean

Square Footage: 2,823

Bedrooms: 3

Bathrooms: 2 ½

Width: 65' - 0"

Depth: 85' - 4"

Foundation: Slab

EPLANS.COM

HPK2100673

Style: Mediterranean

Square Footage: 2,831

Bedrooms: 4

Bathrooms: 3

Width: 84' - 0"

Depth: 77' - 0"

Foundation: Slab

EPLANS.COM

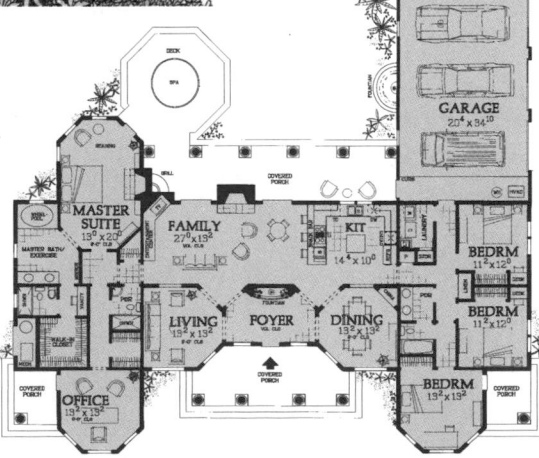

2,500 TO 2,999 SQUARE FEET

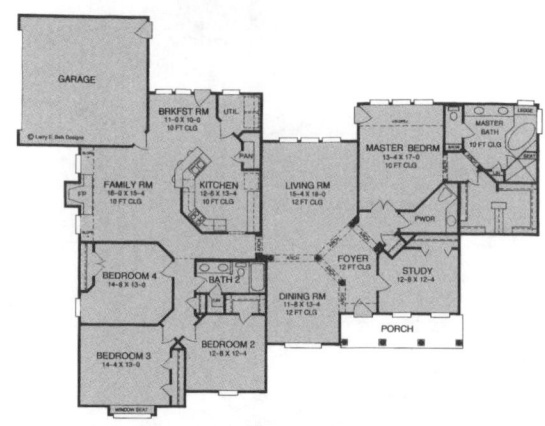

HPK2100674

Style: Colonial Revival

Square Footage: 2,846

Bedrooms: 4

Bathrooms: 2 ½

Width: 84' - 6"

Depth: 64' - 2"

Foundation: Crawlspace, Slab

EPLANS.COM

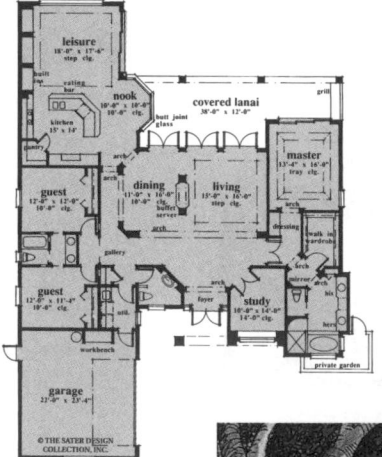

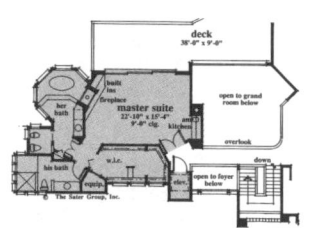

HPK2100675

Style: French Country

Square Footage: 2,856

Bedrooms: 3

Bathrooms: 2 ½

Width: 63' - 4"

Depth: 87' - 0"

Foundation: Slab

EPLANS.COM

HPK2100676

Style: Greek Revival

Square Footage: 2,863

Bedrooms: 4

Bathrooms: 3

Width: 73' - 8"

Depth: 97' - 9"

Foundation: Crawlspace, Slab, Unfinished Basement

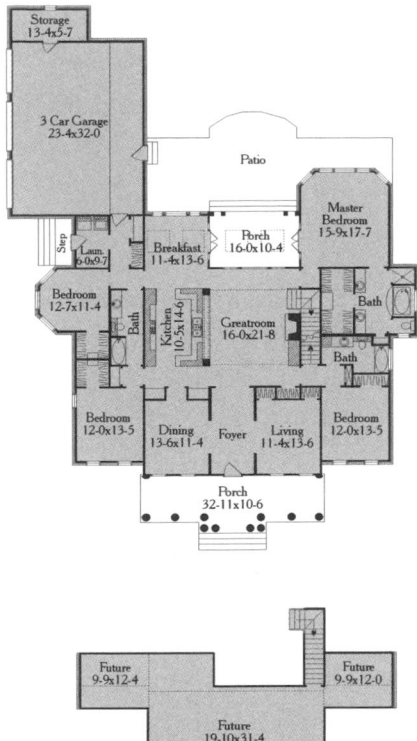

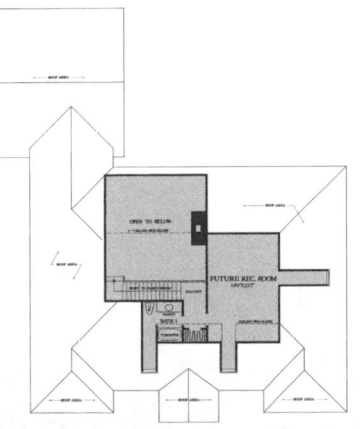

HPK2100677

Style: Federal - Adams

Square Footage: 2,869

Bedrooms: 3

Bathrooms: 3 ½

Width: 68' - 6"

Depth: 79' - 8"

Foundation: Crawlspace

2 William E. Poole Designs, Inc.

2,500 TO 2,999 SQUARE FEET

HPK2100678

Style: New American
Square Footage: 2,881
Bedrooms: 3
Bathrooms: 2 ½
Width: 77' - 11"
Depth: 73' - 11"
Foundation: Unfinished Basement

EPLANS.COM

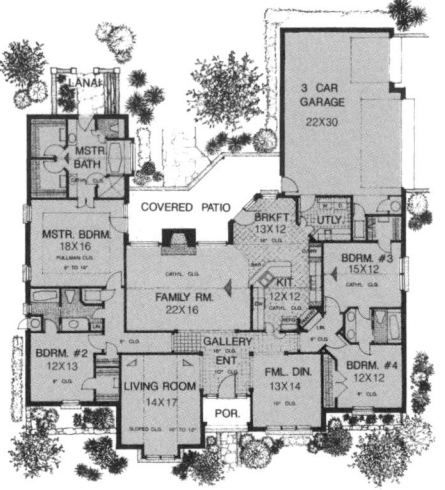

HPK2100679

Style: Norman
Square Footage: 2,888
Bedrooms: 4
Bathrooms: 3
Width: 68' - 6"
Depth: 78' - 1"
Foundation: Slab

EPLANS.COM

HPK2100680

Style: French Country

Square Footage: 2,902

Bedrooms: 3

Bathrooms: 2 ½

Width: 71' - 3"

Depth: 66' - 3"

Foundation: Finished Walkout Basement

EPLANS.COM

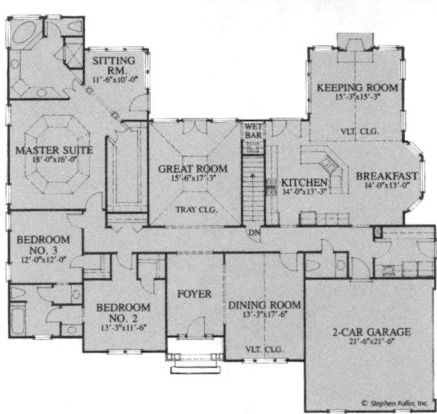

© The Sater Design Collection, Inc.

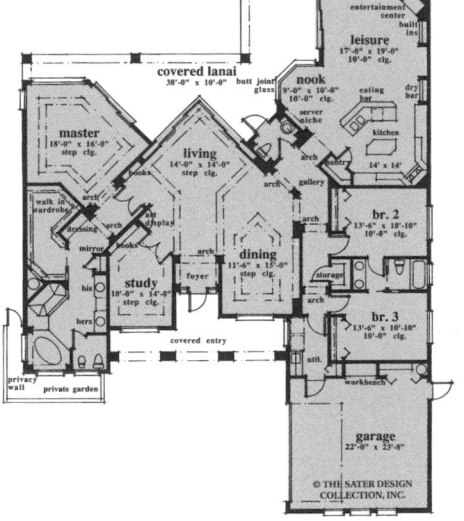

© THE SATER DESIGN COLLECTION, INC.

HPK2100681

EPLANS.COM

Style: Prairie

Square Footage: 2,907

Bedrooms: 3

Bathrooms: 2 ½

Width: 65' - 0"

Depth: 84' - 0"

Foundation: Slab

2,500 TO 2,999 SQUARE FEET

HPK2100682

Style: Mediterranean
Square Footage: 2,907
Bedrooms: 3
Bathrooms: 2 ½
Width: 65' - 0"
Depth: 84' - 0"
Foundation: Slab

EPLANS.COM

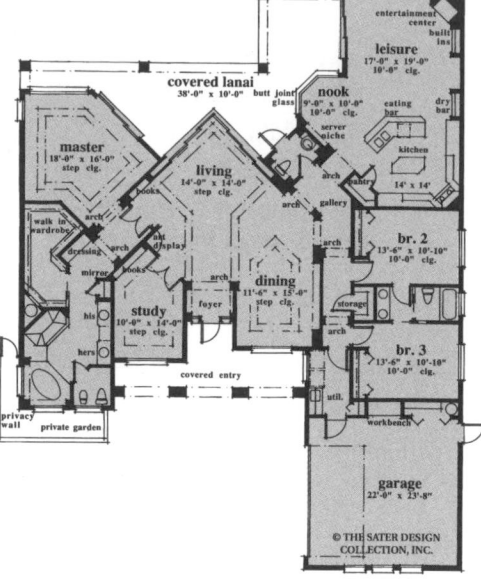

© The Sater Design Collection, Inc.

HPK2100683

Style: Chateauesque
Square Footage: 2,927
Bedrooms: 4
Bathrooms: 3 ½
Width: 80' - 0"
Depth: 73' - 10"
Foundation: Slab

EPLANS.COM

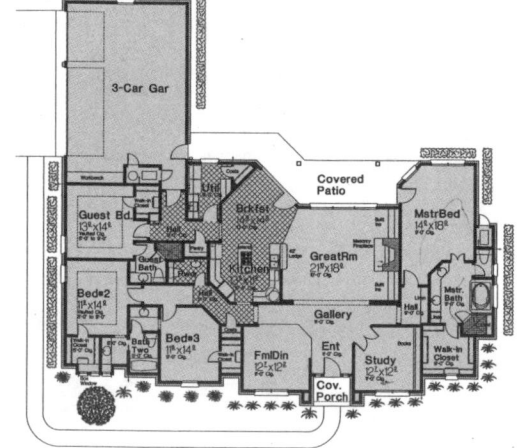

HPK2100684

Style: French Country

Square Footage: 2,935

Bedrooms: 3

Bathrooms: 2 ½

Width: 71' - 0"

Depth: 66' - 0"

Foundation: Finished Walkout Basement

EPLANS.COM

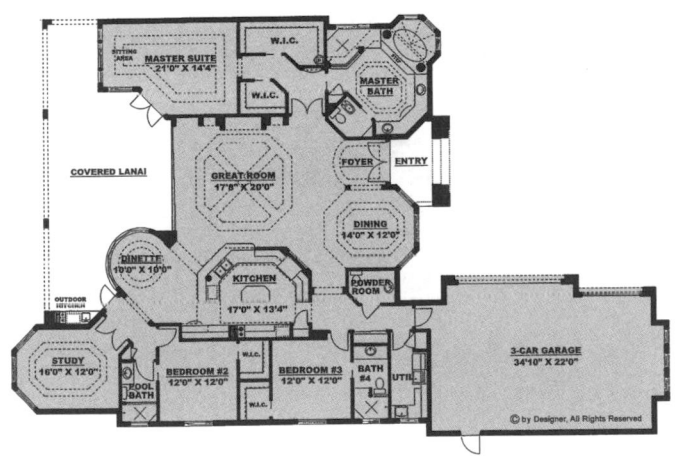

HPK2100685

Style: Italianate

Square Footage: 2,951

Bedrooms: 3

Bathrooms: 3 ½

Width: 64' - 0"

Depth: 102' - 2"

Foundation: Slab

EPLANS.COM

HPK2100686

Style: New American

Square Footage: 2,962

Bedrooms: 4

Bathrooms: 3

Width: 70' - 0"

Depth: 76' - 0"

Foundation: Slab

EPLANS.COM

©The Sater Design Collection, Inc.

HPK2100687

Style: Neoclassical

Square Footage: 2,974

Bedrooms: 4

Bathrooms: 3 ½

Width: 74' - 8"

Depth: 118' - 0"

Foundation: Slab

EPLANS.COM

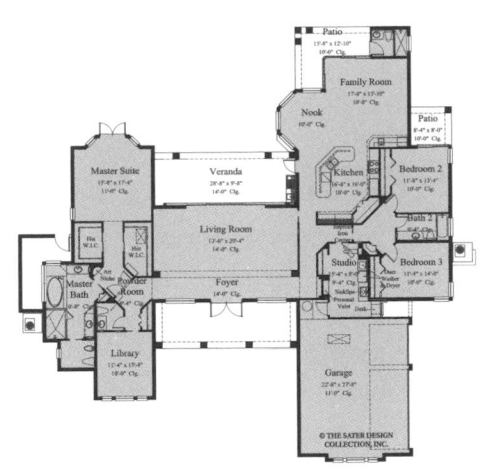

HPK2100688

Style: Neoclassical

Square Footage: 2,978

Bedrooms: 3

Bathrooms: 3 ½

Width: 84' - 0"

Depth: 90' - 0"

Foundation: Slab

EPLANS.COM

HPK2100689

Style: Greek Revival

Square Footage: 2,987

Bedrooms: 3

Bathrooms: 2 ½

Width: 74' - 0"

Depth: 62' - 0"

Foundation: Finished Walkout Basement

EPLANS.COM

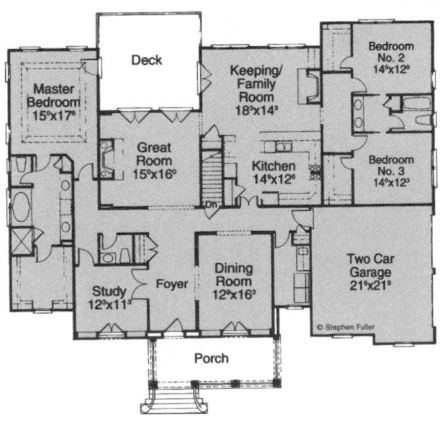

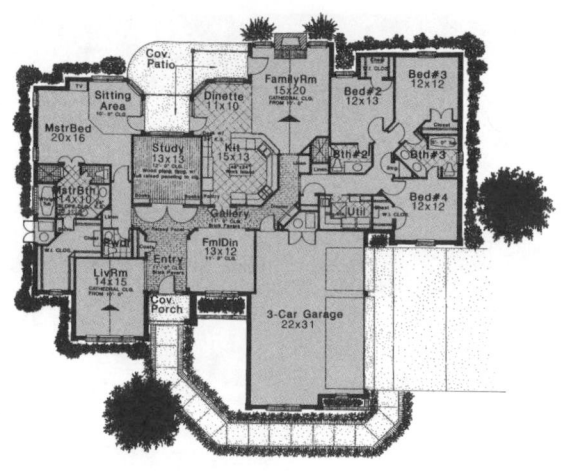

HPK2100690

Style: New American

Square Footage: 2,990

Bedrooms: 4

Bathrooms: 3 ½

Width: 80' - 0"

Depth: 68' - 0"

Foundation: Slab

EPLANS.COM

HPK2100691

Style: French Country

Square Footage: 2,998

Bonus Space: 345 sq. ft.

Bedrooms: 4

Bathrooms: 3 ½

Width: 69' - 7"

Depth: 81' - 6"

Foundation: Slab

EPLANS.COM

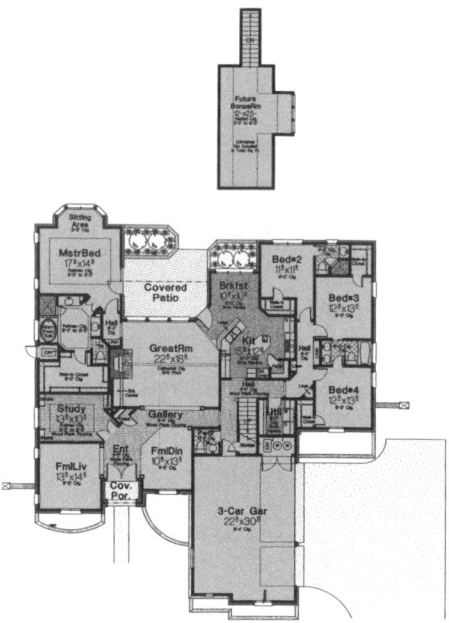

HPK2100692

Style: Farmhouse
First Floor: 1,319 sq. ft.
Second Floor: 1,181 sq. ft.
Total: 2,500 sq. ft.
Bonus Space: 371 sq. ft.
Bedrooms: 4
Bathrooms: 2 ½
Width: 60' - 0"
Depth: 42' - 0"
Foundation: Crawlspace

EPLANS.COM

A stunning shingle home with stone accents (including a stone fireplace!), this Cape Cod-style home will complement any neighborhood. Multi-pane windows light up the living room; an archway connects it to the family room. The island kitchen is designed with extra space, to accommodate two cooks. Upstairs, three bedrooms share a full bath and a bonus room. The master suite has a vaulted ceiling and a private bath with a spa tub.

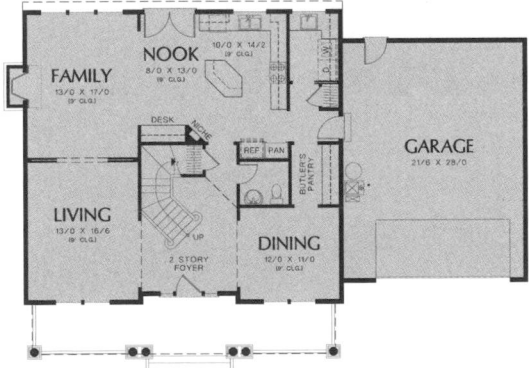

First Floor

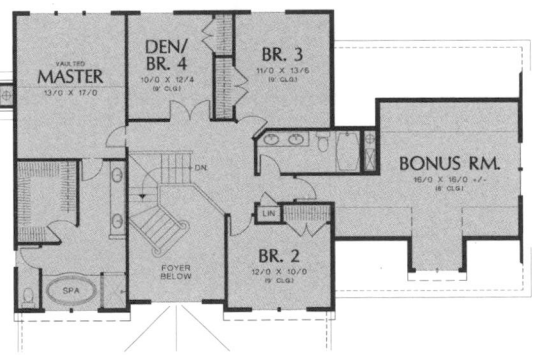

Second Floor

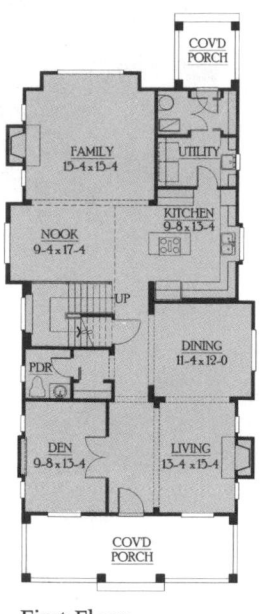

First Floor

Second Floor

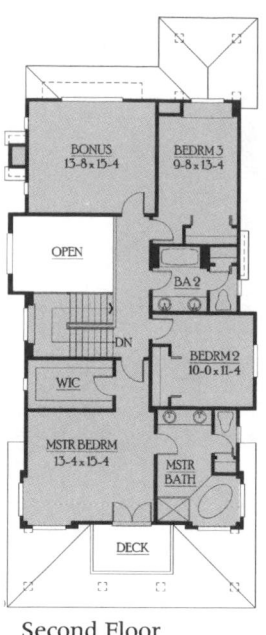

HPK2100693

Style: Craftsman
First Floor: 1,360 sq. ft.
Second Floor: 1,145 sq. ft.
Total: 2,505 sq. ft.
Bonus Space: 230 sq. ft.
Bedrooms: 3
Bathrooms: 2 ½
Width: 30' - 0"
Depth: 68' - 0"
Foundation: Crawlspace

EPLANS.COM

Find a matching garage on page 182.

© 1998 Donald A. Gardner Architects, Inc.

HPK2100694

Style: Farmhouse
First Floor: 1,614 sq. ft.
Second Floor: 892 sq. ft.
Total: 2,506 sq. ft.
Bonus Space: 341 sq. ft.
Bedrooms: 4
Bathrooms: 2 ½
Width: 71' - 10"
Depth: 50' - 0"

EPLANS.COM

First Floor

Second Floor

HPK2100695

Style: New American

First Floor: 1,946 sq. ft.

Second Floor: 562 sq. ft.

Total: 2,508 sq. ft.

Bonus Space: 366 sq. ft.

Bedrooms: 4

Bathrooms: 3 ½

Width: 54' - 0"

Depth: 63' - 4"

Foundation: Crawlspace, Unfinished Walkout Basement

EPLANS.COM

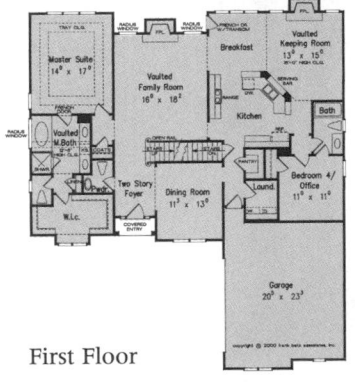

First Floor

Second Floor

HPK2100696

Style: Colonial Revival

First Floor: 1,788 sq. ft.

Second Floor: 720 sq. ft.

Total: 2,508 sq. ft.

Bonus Space: 384 sq. ft.

Bedrooms: 3

Bathrooms: 2 ½

Width: 78' - 8"

Depth: 77' - 10"

Foundation: Slab

EPLANS.COM

First Floor

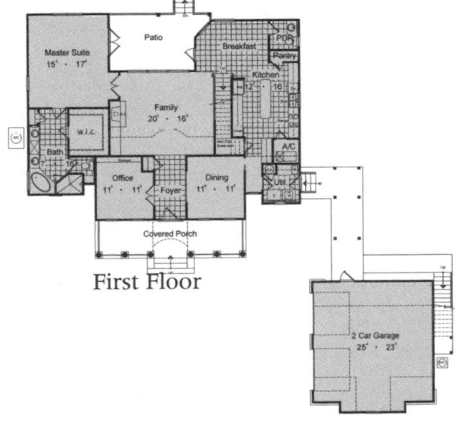

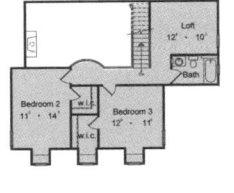

Second Floor

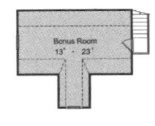

2,500 TO 2,999 SQUARE FEET

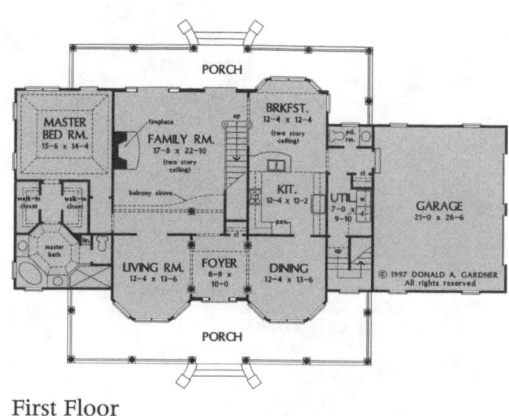

First Floor

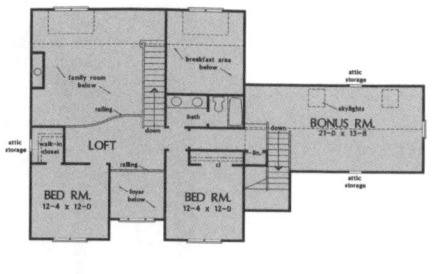

Second Floor

1997 Donald A. Gardner, Inc.

HPK2100697

Style: Farmhouse

First Floor: 1,914 sq. ft.

Second Floor: 597 sq. ft.

Total: 2,511 sq. ft.

Bonus Space: 487 sq. ft.

Bedrooms: 3

Bathrooms: 2 ½

Width: 79' - 2"

Depth: 51' - 6"

EPLANS.COM

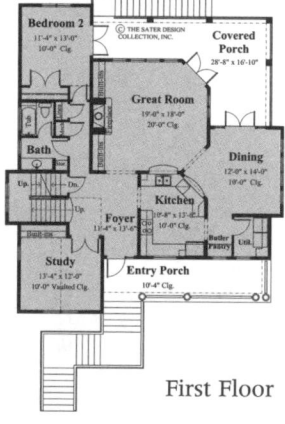

First Floor

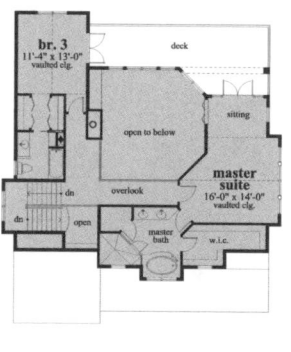

Second Floor

HPK2100698

Style: Cottage

First Floor: 1,542 sq. ft.

Second Floor: 971 sq. ft.

Total: 2,513 sq. ft.

Bedrooms: 3

Bathrooms: 3

Width: 46' - 0"

Depth: 51' - 0"

Foundation: Island Basement

EPLANS.COM

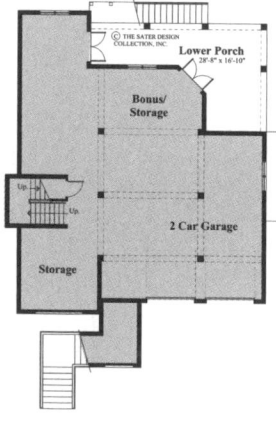

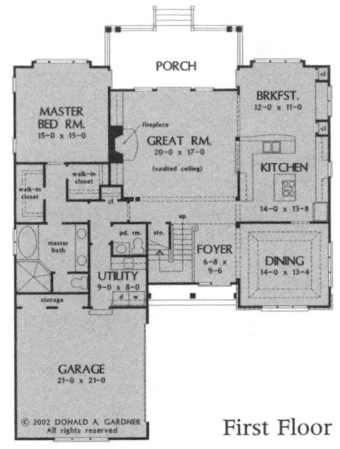

First Floor

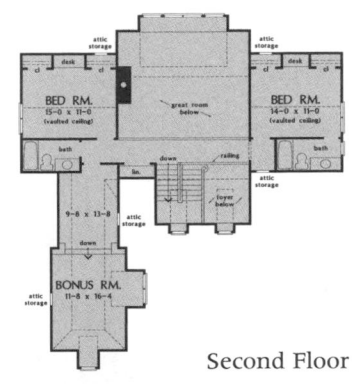

Second Floor

HPK2100699

Style: French Country
First Floor: 1,834 sq. ft.
Second Floor: 681 sq. ft.
Total: 2,515 sq. ft.
Bonus Space: 365 sq. ft.
Bedrooms: 3
Bathrooms: 3 ½
Width: 50' - 8"
Depth: 66' - 8"

First Floor

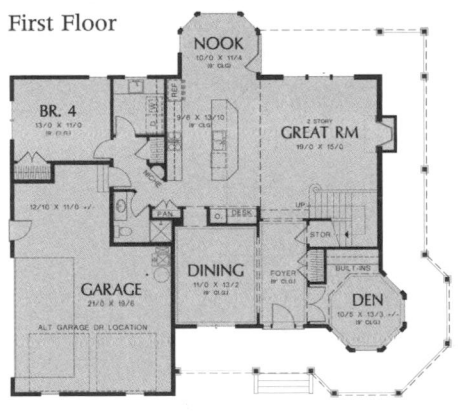

Second Floor

HPK2100700

Style: Victorian Eclectic
First Floor: 1,464 sq. ft.
Second Floor: 1,054 sq. ft.
Total: 2,518 sq. ft.
Bonus Space: 332 sq. ft.
Bedrooms: 4
Bathrooms: 3
Width: 59' - 0"
Depth: 51' - 6"
Foundation: Crawlspace

2,500 TO 2,999 SQUARE FEET

HPK2100701

Style: Craftsman
First Floor: 1,365 sq. ft.
Second Floor: 1,155 sq. ft.
Total: 2,520 sq. ft.
Bedrooms: 3
Bathrooms: 2 ½
Width: 40' - 0"
Depth: 52' - 0"
Foundation: Crawlspace

EPLANS.COM

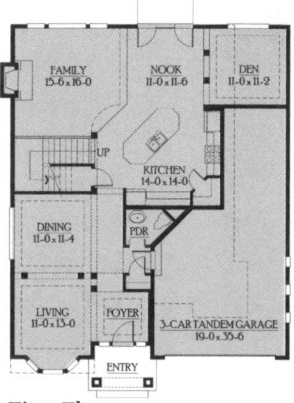

First Floor

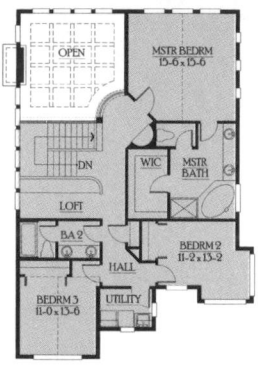

Second Floor

HPK2100702

Style: Cottage
First Floor: 1,305 sq. ft.
Second Floor: 1,215 sq. ft.
Total: 2,520 sq. ft.
Bonus Space: 935 sq. ft.
Bedrooms: 3
Bathrooms: 2 ½
Width: 30' - 6"
Depth: 72' - 2"
Foundation: Slab

EPLANS.COM

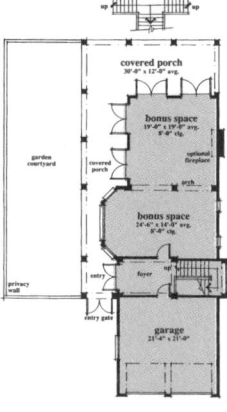

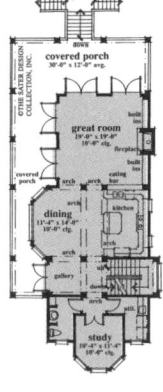

First Floor

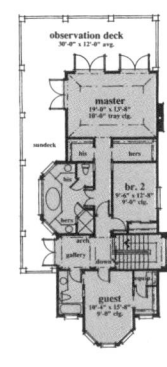

Second Floor

HPK2100703

Style: Farmhouse
First Floor: 1,798 sq. ft.
Second Floor: 723 sq. ft.
Total: 2,521 sq. ft.
Bonus Space: 349 sq. ft.
Bedrooms: 4
Bathrooms: 3 ½
Width: 66' - 8"
Depth: 49' - 8"

© 2002 Donald A. Gardner, Inc.

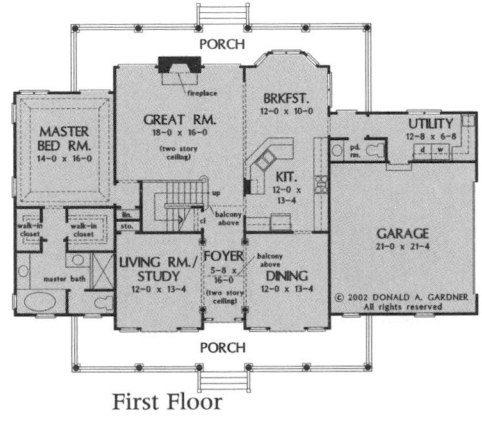

First Floor

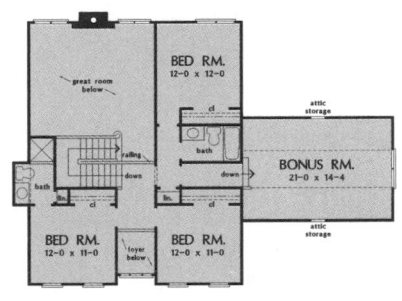

Second Floor

© The Sater Design Collection, Inc.

HPK2100704

Style: Country
First Floor: 1,676 sq. ft.
Second Floor: 851 sq. ft.
Total: 2,527 sq. ft.
Bedrooms: 5
Bathrooms: 2 ½
Width: 55' - 0"
Depth: 50' - 0"
Foundation: Slab

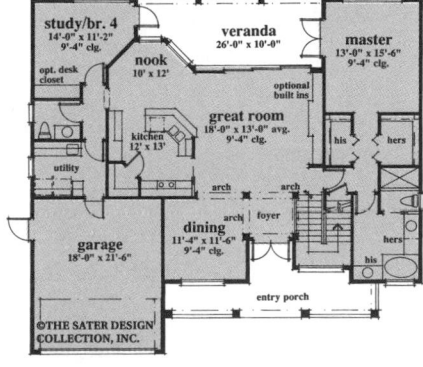

First Floor

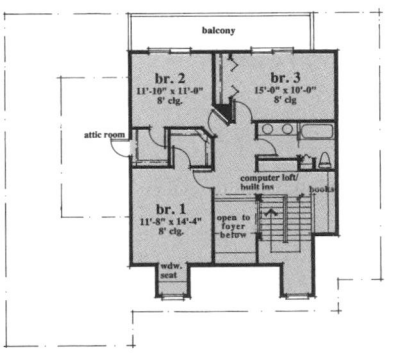

Second Floor

2,500 TO 2,999 SQUARE FEET

HPK2100705

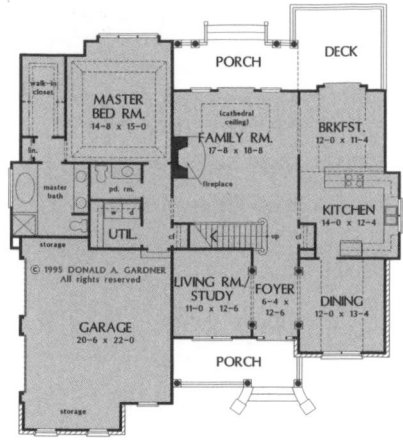

Style: New American
First Floor: 1,799 sq. ft.
Second Floor: 730 sq. ft.
Total: 2,529 sq. ft.
Bonus Space: 328 sq. ft.
Bedrooms: 4
Bathrooms: 2 ½
Width: 55' - 4"
Depth: 61' - 4"

EPLANS.COM

First Floor

Second Floor

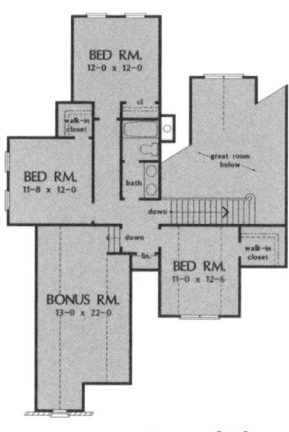

First Floor

Second Floor

HPK2100706

EPLANS.COM

Style: Country
First Floor: 1,598 sq. ft.
Second Floor: 932 sq. ft.
Total: 2,530 sq. ft.
Bonus Space: 415 sq. ft.
Bedrooms: 4
Bathrooms: 3 ½
Width: 55' - 8"
Depth: 61' - 0"
Foundation: Crawlspace,
Unfinished Basement

ORDER BLUEPRINTS ANYTIME AT EPLANS.COM OR 1-800-521-6797

First Floor

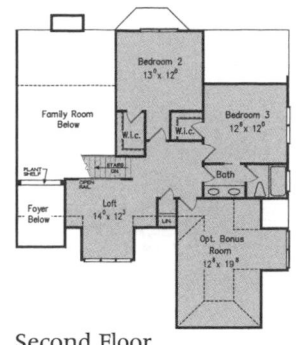

Second Floor

HPK2100707

Style: European

First Floor: 1,811 sq. ft.

Second Floor: 721 sq. ft.

Total: 2,532 sq. ft.

Bonus Space: 286 sq. ft.

Bedrooms: 4

Bathrooms: 3

Width: 58' - 0"

Depth: 55' - 0"

Foundation: Crawlspace, Unfinished Walkout Basement

EPLANS.COM

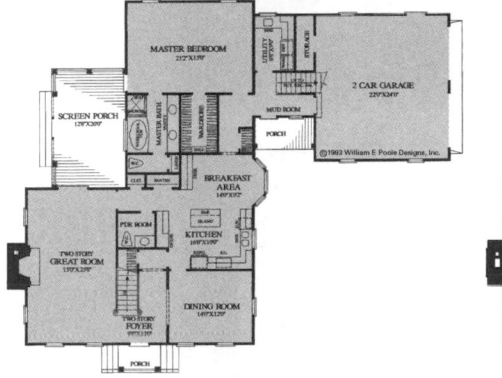

First Floor

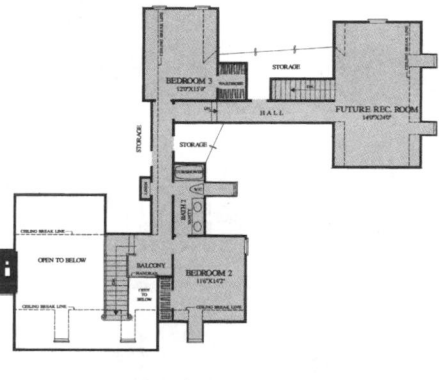

Second Floor

HPK2100708

EPLANS.COM

Style: Cape Cod

First Floor: 1,884 sq. ft.

Second Floor: 661 sq. ft.

Total: 2,545 sq. ft.

Bonus Space: 489 sq. ft.

Bedrooms: 3

Bathrooms: 2 ½

Width: 71' - 4"

Depth: 62' - 2"

Foundation: Crawlspace

©1993 William E Poole Designs, Inc.

2,500 TO 2,999 SQUARE FEET

HPK2100709

Style: New American
First Floor: 1,904 sq. ft.
Second Floor: 645 sq. ft.
Total: 2,549 sq. ft.
Bonus Space: 434 sq. ft.
Bedrooms: 3
Bathrooms: 2 ½
Width: 71' - 2"
Depth: 45' - 8"

EPLANS.COM

First Floor

Second Floor

HPK2100710

Style: New American
First Floor: 1,972 sq. ft.
Second Floor: 579 sq. ft.
Total: 2,551 sq. ft.
Bonus Space: 256 sq. ft.
Bedrooms: 3
Bathrooms: 2 ½
Width: 57' - 4"
Depth: 51' - 2"
Foundation: Crawlspace, Slab, Unfinished Walkout Basement

EPLANS.COM

First Floor

Second Floor

HPK2100711

Style: Mediterranean
First Floor: 1,490 sq. ft.
Second Floor: 1,061 sq. ft.
Total: 2,551 sq. ft.
Bedrooms: 2
Bathrooms: 2 ½
Width: 44' - 8"
Depth: 51' - 0"
Foundation: Slab

EPLANS.COM

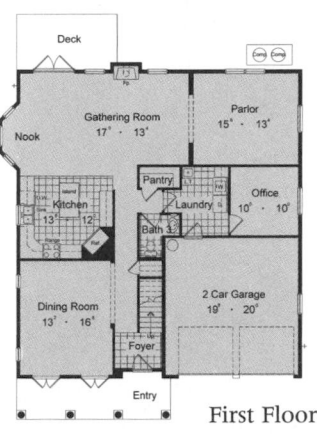

First Floor

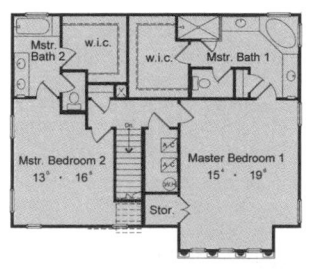

Second Floor

HPK2100712

Style: Craftsman
First Floor: 1,235 sq. ft.
Second Floor: 1,325 sq. ft.
Total: 2,560 sq. ft.
Bedrooms: 3
Bathrooms: 2 ½
Width: 62' - 0"
Depth: 41' - 0"
Foundation: Crawlspace

EPLANS.COM

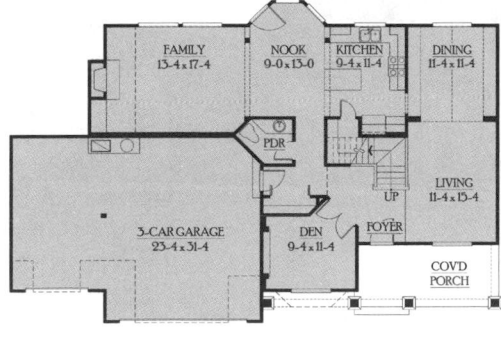

First Floor

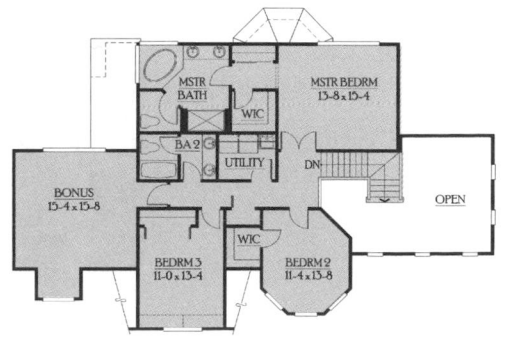

Second Floor

HPK2100713

Style: Farmhouse

First Floor: 1,357 sq. ft.

Second Floor: 1,204 sq. ft.

Total: 2,561 sq. ft.

Bedrooms: 4

Bathrooms: 2 ½

Width: 80' - 0"

Depth: 57' - 0"

EPLANS.COM

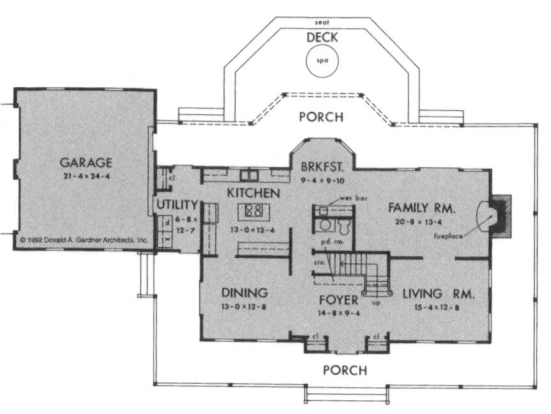

First Floor

Second Floor

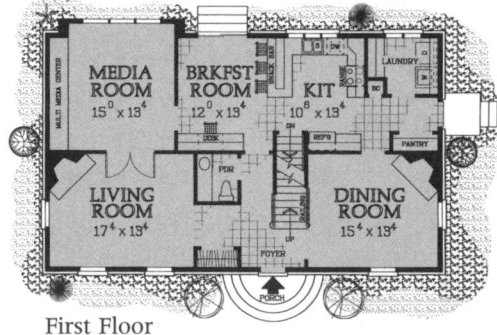

First Floor

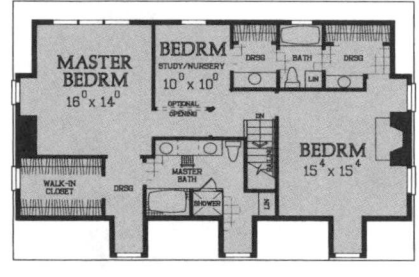

Second Floor

Find a matching garage on page 182.

HPK2100714

Style: Cape Cod

First Floor: 1,396 sq. ft.

Second Floor: 1,169 sq. ft.

Total: 2,565 sq. ft.

Bedrooms: 3

Bathrooms: 2 ½

Width: 48' - 0"

Depth: 28' - 8"

Foundation: Unfinished Basement

EPLANS.COM

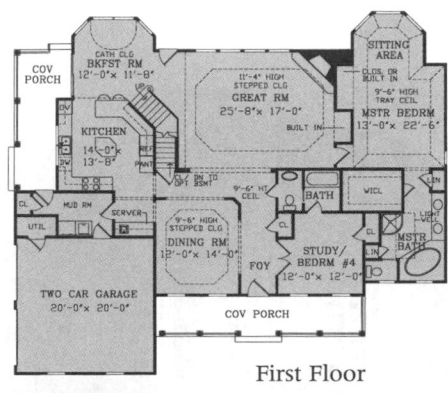

First Floor

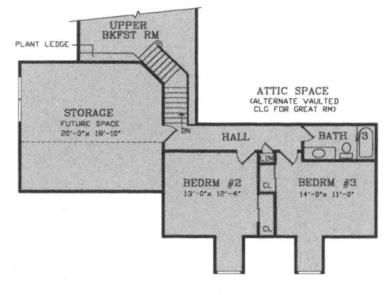

Second Floor

HPK2100715

Style: Country
First Floor: 2,017 sq. ft.
Second Floor: 550 sq. ft.
Total: 2,567 sq. ft.
Bedrooms: 4
Bathrooms: 3
Width: 62' - 4"
Depth: 52' - 6"
Foundation: Crawlspace, Slab, Unfinished Basement

EPLANS.COM

HPK2100716

Style: Craftsman
First Floor: 1,780 sq. ft.
Second Floor: 790 sq. ft.
Total: 2,570 sq. ft.
Bedrooms: 5
Bathrooms: 3
Width: 40' - 0"
Depth: 83' - 0"
Foundation: Crawlspace

EPLANS.COM

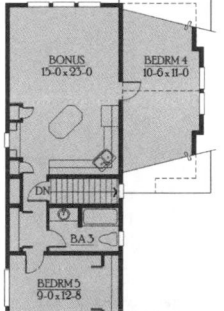

Second Floor

First Floor

2,500 TO 2,999 SQUARE FEET

HPK2100717

Style: New American
First Floor: 1,668 sq. ft.
Second Floor: 905 sq. ft.
Total: 2,573 sq. ft.
Bedrooms: 3
Bathrooms: 2 ½
Width: 83' - 8"
Depth: 59' - 8"
Foundation: Unfinished Basement

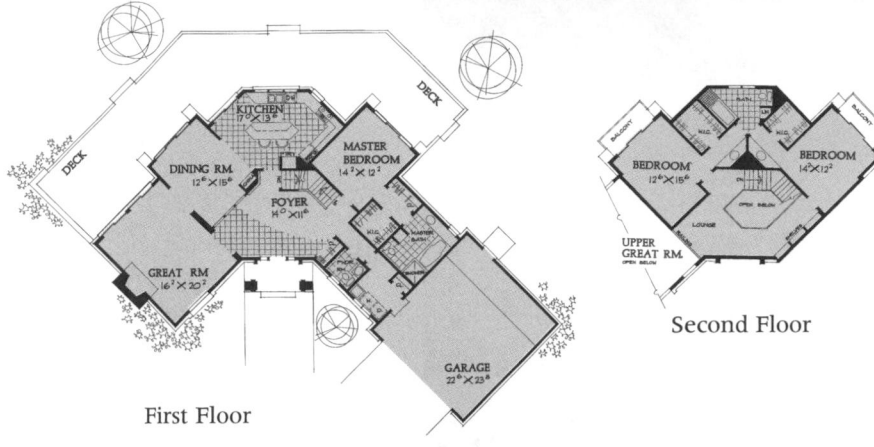

First Floor

Second Floor

First Floor

HPK2100718

Style: Queen Anne
First Floor: 1,790 sq. ft.
Second Floor: 792 sq. ft.
Total: 2,582 sq. ft.
Bedrooms: 4
Bathrooms: 3 ½
Width: 63' - 0"
Depth: 80' - 4"

Second Floor

HPK2100719

Style: New American

First Floor: 2,003 sq. ft.

Second Floor: 579 sq. ft.

Total: 2,582 sq. ft.

Bonus Space: 262 sq. ft.

Bedrooms: 4

Bathrooms: 3

Width: 54' - 0"

Depth: 60' - 0"

Foundation: Crawlspace, Slab, Unfinished Walkout Basement

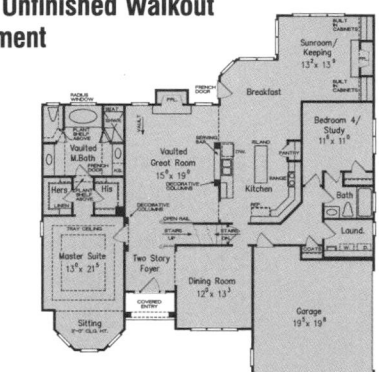

First Floor

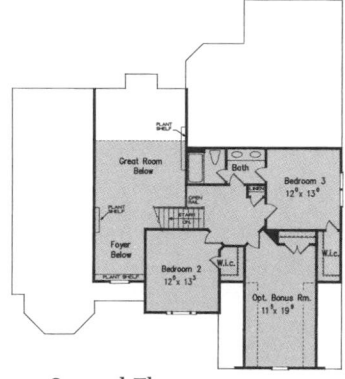

Second Floor

HPK2100720

Style: Craftsman

First Floor: 1,322 sq. ft.

Second Floor: 1,262 sq. ft.

Total: 2,584 sq. ft.

Bedrooms: 4

Bathrooms: 3

Width: 48' - 0"

Depth: 50' - 0"

Foundation: Crawlspace, Slab, Unfinished Walkout Basement

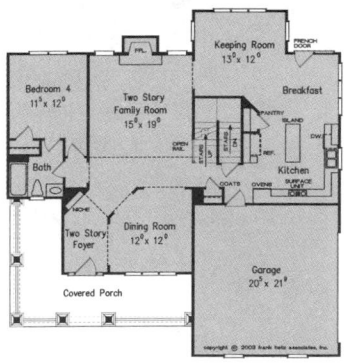

First Floor

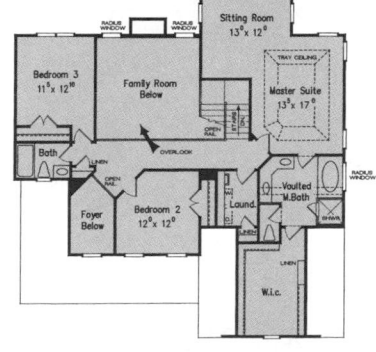

Second Floor

2,500 TO 2,999 SQUARE FEET

EPLANS.COM

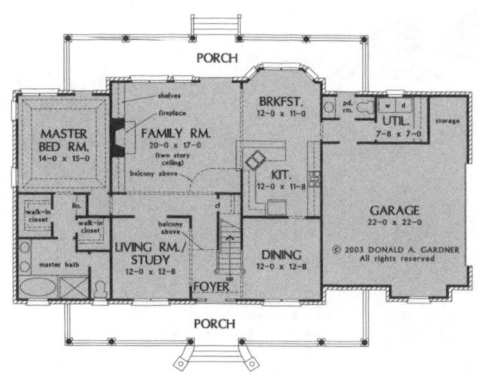

First Floor

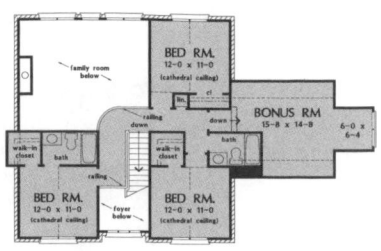

Second Floor

HPK2100721

Style: Farmhouse
First Floor: 1,809 sq. ft.
Second Floor: 777 sq. ft.
Total: 2,586 sq. ft.
Bonus Space: 264 sq. ft.
Bedrooms: 4
Bathrooms: 3 ½
Width: 70' - 7"
Depth: 48' - 4"

EPLANS.COM

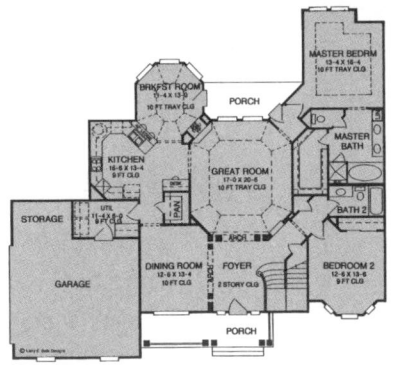

First Floor

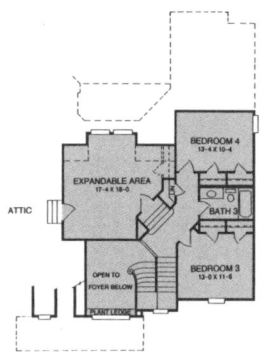

Second Floor

HPK2100722

Style: Country
First Floor: 2,028 sq. ft.
Second Floor: 558 sq. ft.
Total: 2,586 sq. ft.
Bonus Space: 272 sq. ft.
Bedrooms: 4
Bathrooms: 3
Width: 64' - 10"
Depth: 61' - 0"
Foundation: Crawlspace, Slab, Unfinished Basement

EPLANS.COM

First Floor

Second Floor

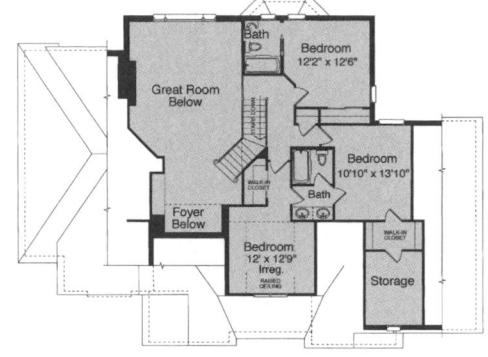

HPK2100723

Style: French Country
First Floor: 1,790 sq. ft.
Second Floor: 797 sq. ft.
Total: 2,587 sq. ft.
Bedrooms: 4
Bathrooms: 3 ½
Width: 64' - 4"
Depth: 50' - 0"
Foundation: Unfinished Basement

EPLANS.COM

First Floor

Second Floor

HPK2100724

Style: Country
First Floor: 1,896 sq. ft.
Second Floor: 692 sq. ft.
Total: 2,588 sq. ft.
Bedrooms: 3
Bathrooms: 2 ½
Width: 60' - 0"
Depth: 84' - 10"

EPLANS.COM

2,500 TO 2,999 SQUARE FEET

HPK2100725

Style: Italianate

First Floor: 1,266 sq. ft.

Second Floor: 1,324 sq. ft.

Total: 2,590 sq. ft.

Bedrooms: 3

Bathrooms: 2 ½

Width: 34' - 0"

Depth: 63' - 2"

Foundation: Slab

EPLANS.COM

© The Sater Design Collection, Inc.

Find a matching garage on page 203.

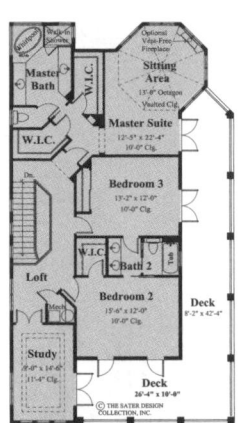

First Floor

Second Floor

© THE SATER DESIGN COLLECTION, INC.

HPK2100726

Style: Colonial Revival

First Floor: 1,809 sq. ft.

Second Floor: 785 sq. ft.

Total: 2,594 sq. ft.

Bonus Space: 353 sq. ft.

Bedrooms: 5

Bathrooms: 4

Width: 72' - 7"

Depth: 51' - 5"

Foundation: Crawlspace, Slab, Unfinished Walkout Basement

EPLANS.COM

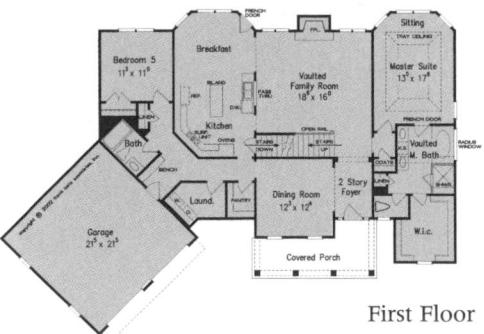

First Floor

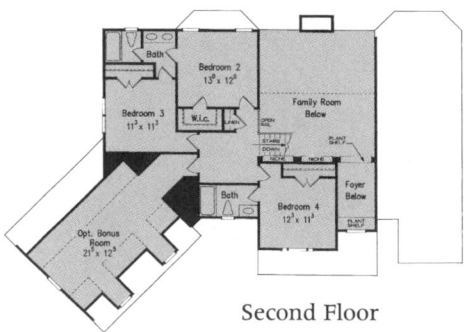

Second Floor

HPK2100727

Style: New American

First Floor: 2,003 sq. ft.

Second Floor: 598 sq. ft.

Total: 2,601 sq. ft.

Bonus Space: 321 sq. ft.

Bedrooms: 4

Bathrooms: 3

Width: 60' - 0"

Depth: 61' - 0"

Foundation: Crawlspace, Slab, Unfinished Walkout Basement

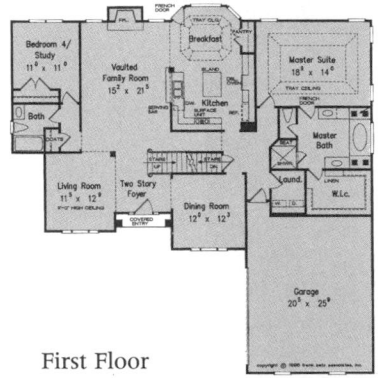

First Floor

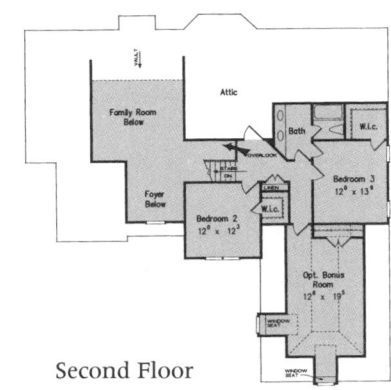

Second Floor

© 1993 Donald A. Gardner Architects, Inc.

HPK2100728

Style: Farmhouse

First Floor: 1,871 sq. ft.

Second Floor: 731 sq. ft.

Total: 2,602 sq. ft.

Bonus Space: 402 sq. ft.

Bedrooms: 4

Bathrooms: 3

Width: 77' - 6"

Depth: 70' - 0"

First Floor

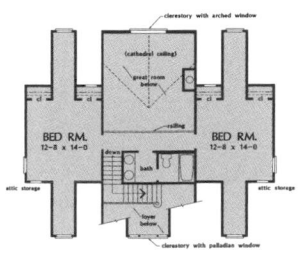

Second Floor

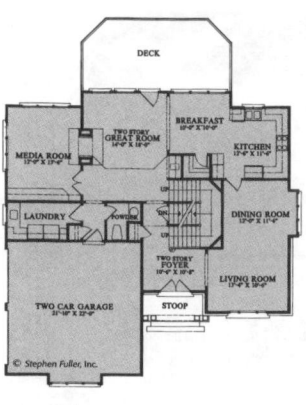

First Floor

Second Floor

HPK2100729

Style: French Country

First Floor: 1,395 sq. ft.

Second Floor: 1,210 sq. ft.

Total: 2,605 sq. ft.

Bonus Space: 225 sq. ft.

Bedrooms: 3

Bathrooms: 2 ½

Width: 47' - 0"

Depth: 49' - 6"

Foundation: Unfinished Basement

EPLANS.COM

© Stephen Fuller, Inc.

HPK2100730

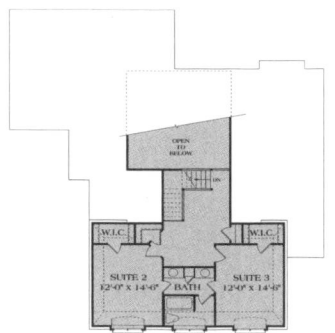

First Floor

Style: Norman

First Floor: 1,836 sq. ft.

Second Floor: 775 sq. ft.

Total: 2,611 sq. ft.

Bedrooms: 3

Bathrooms: 2 ½

Width: 54' - 10"

Depth: 56' - 7"

Foundation: Crawlspace

EPLANS.COM

Second Floor

First Floor

Second Floor

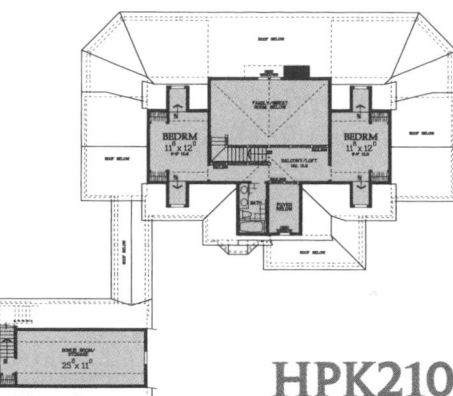

HPK2100731

Style: Farmhouse
First Floor: 1,969 sq. ft.
Second Floor: 660 sq. ft.
Total: 2,629 sq. ft.
Bonus Space: 360 sq. ft.
Bedrooms: 4
Bathrooms: 3
Width: 90' - 8"
Depth: 80' - 4"
Foundation: Unfinished Basement

EPLANS.COM

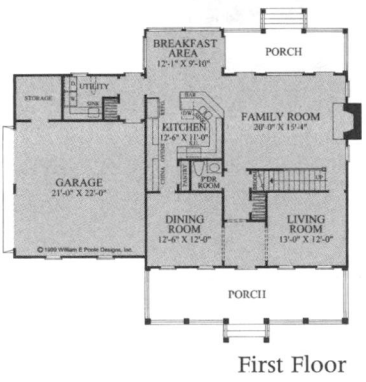

First Floor

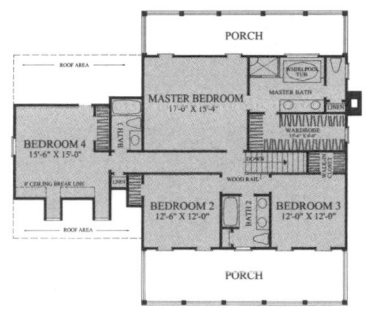

Second Floor

HPK2100732

Style: Neoclassical
First Floor: 1,273 sq. ft.
Second Floor: 1,358 sq. ft.
Total: 2,631 sq. ft.
Bedrooms: 4
Bathrooms: 3 ½
Width: 54' - 10"
Depth: 48' - 6"
Foundation: Crawlspace

EPLANS.COM

2,500 TO 2,999 SQUARE FEET

HPK2100733

Style: Queen Anne

First Floor: 1,362 sq. ft.

Second Floor: 1,270 sq. ft.

Total: 2,632 sq. ft.

Bedrooms: 4

Bathrooms: 2 ½

Width: 79' - 0"

Depth: 44' - 0"

Foundation: Crawlspace, Unfinished Basement

EPLANS.COM

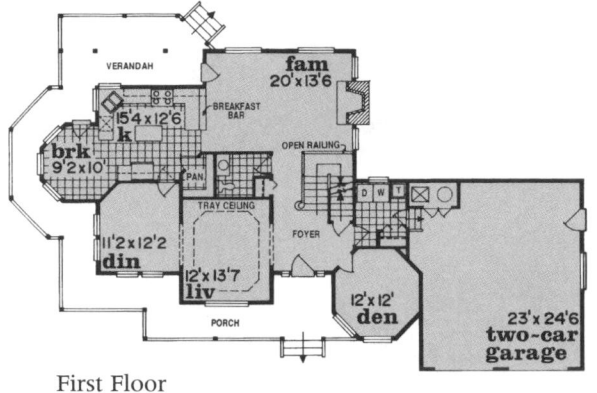

First Floor

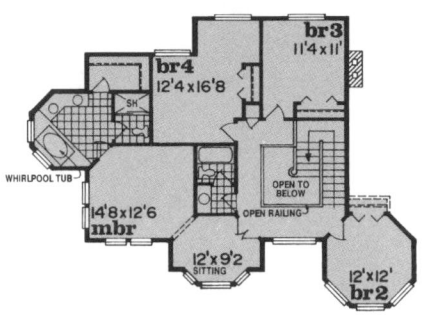

Second Floor

HPK2100734

Style: French Country

First Floor: 1,844 sq. ft.

Second Floor: 794 sq. ft.

Total: 2,638 sq. ft.

Bedrooms: 4

Bathrooms: 3 ½

Width: 65' - 6"

Depth: 56' - 10"

EPLANS.COM

First Floor

Second Floor

HPK2100735

Style: New American

First Floor: 2,015 sq. ft.

Second Floor: 628 sq. ft.

Total: 2,643 sq. ft.

Bonus Space: 315 sq. ft.

Bedrooms: 4

Bathrooms: 3

Width: 56' - 0"

Depth: 52' - 6"

Foundation: Crawlspace, Slab, Unfinished Walkout Basement

EPLANS.COM

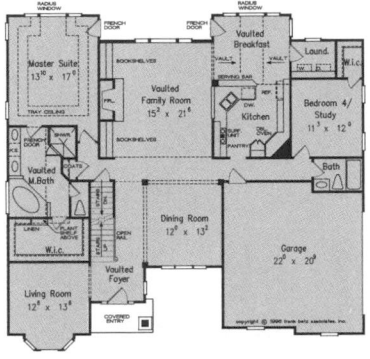

First Floor

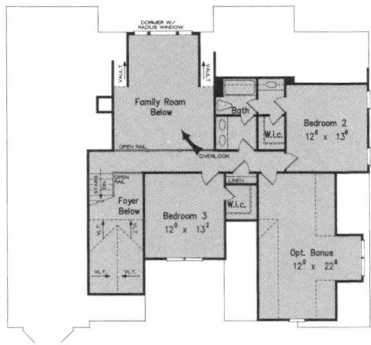

Second Floor

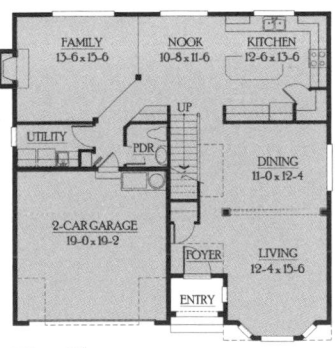

First Floor

HPK2100736

Style: Craftsman

First Floor: 1,190 sq. ft.

Second Floor: 1,461 sq. ft.

Total: 2,651 sq. ft.

Bedrooms: 4

Bathrooms: 2 ½

Width: 40' - 0"

Depth: 42' - 0"

Foundation: Crawlspace

EPLANS.COM

Second Floor

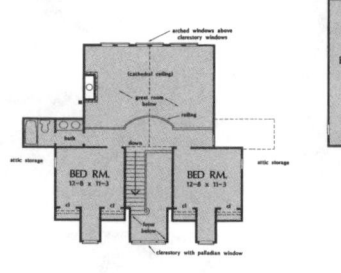

First Floor

Second Floor

HPK2100737

Style: Farmhouse

First Floor: 2,064 sq. ft.

Second Floor: 594 sq. ft.

Total: 2,658 sq. ft.

Bonus Space: 483 sq. ft.

Bedrooms: 4

Bathrooms: 3 ½

Width: 92' - 0"

Depth: 57' - 8"

EPLANS.COM

© 1993 Donald A. Gardner Architects, Inc.

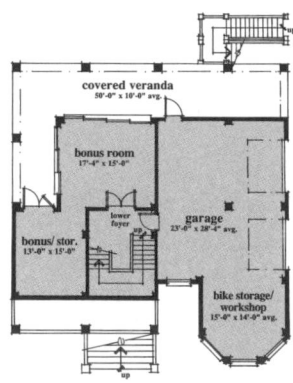

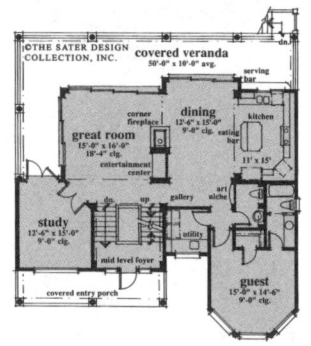

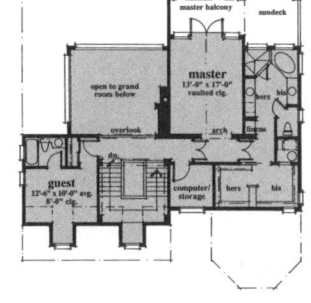

First Floor

Second Floor

HPK2100738

Style: Victorian Eclectic

First Floor: 1,637 sq. ft.

Second Floor: 1,022 sq. ft.

Total: 2,659 sq. ft.

Bonus Space: 532 sq. ft.

Bedrooms: 3

Bathrooms: 3 ½

Width: 50' - 0"

Depth: 53' - 0"

Foundation: Pier (same as Piling)

EPLANS.COM

HPK2100739

Style: Farmhouse
First Floor: 1,907 sq. ft.
Second Floor: 758 sq. ft.
Total: 2,665 sq. ft.
Bedrooms: 3
Bathrooms: 2 ½
Width: 50' - 0"
Depth: 86' - 0"
Foundation: Slab

EPLANS.COM

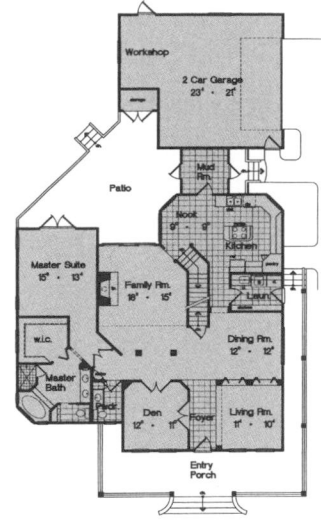

First Floor

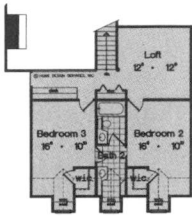

Second Floor

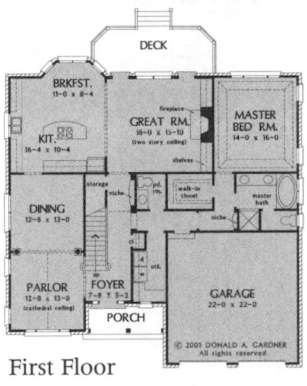

First Floor

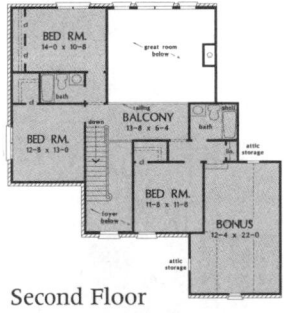

Second Floor

HPK2100740

Style: New American
First Floor: 1,809 sq. ft.
Second Floor: 869 sq. ft.
Total: 2,678 sq. ft.
Bonus Space: 320 sq. ft.
Bedrooms: 4
Bathrooms: 3 ½
Width: 50' - 7"
Depth: 52' - 7"

EPLANS.COM

2,500 TO 2,999 SQUARE FEET

HPK2100741

Style: French Country
First Floor: 1,840 sq. ft.
Second Floor: 840 sq. ft.
Total: 2,680 sq. ft.
Bonus Space: 295 sq. ft.
Bedrooms: 3
Bathrooms: 2 ½
Width: 66' - 0"
Depth: 65' - 10"
Foundation: Crawlspace

EPLANS.COM

First Floor

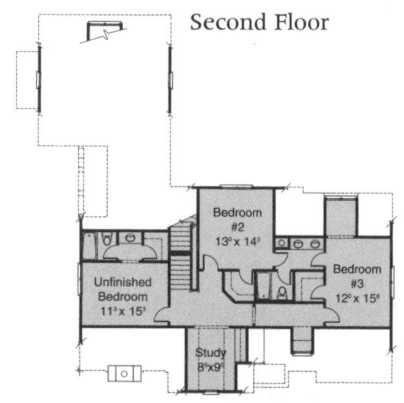

Second Floor

HPK2100742

Style: New American
First Floor: 1,424 sq. ft.
Second Floor: 1,256 sq. ft.
Total: 2,680 sq. ft.
Bedrooms: 5
Bathrooms: 3
Width: 57' - 0"
Depth: 41' - 0"
Foundation: Crawlspace, Slab, Unfinished Walkout Basement

EPLANS.COM

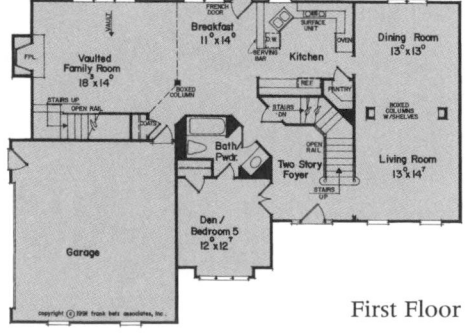

First Floor

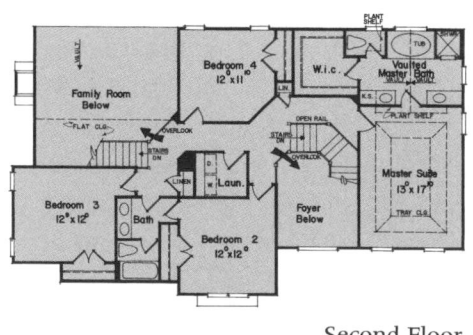

Second Floor

ORDER BLUEPRINTS ANYTIME AT EPLANS.COM OR 1-800-521-6797

HPK2100743

Style: New American
First Floor: 1,374 sq. ft.
Second Floor: 1,311 sq. ft.
Total: 2,685 sq. ft.
Bedrooms: 4
Bathrooms: 2 ½
Width: 57' - 4"
Depth: 42' - 0"
Foundation: Crawlspace, Slab, Unfinished Walkout Basement

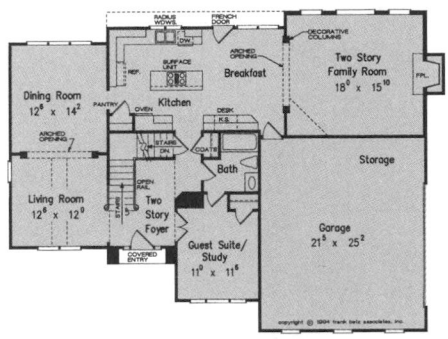

First Floor

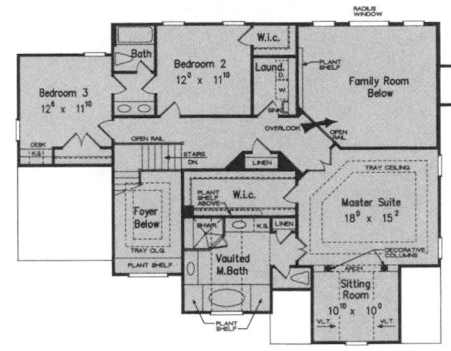

Second Floor

HPK2100744

Style: New American
First Floor: 1,883 sq. ft.
Second Floor: 803 sq. ft.
Total: 2,686 sq. ft.
Bedrooms: 4
Bathrooms: 3 ½
Width: 58' - 6"
Depth: 59' - 4"
Foundation: Crawlspace, Unfinished Walkout Basement

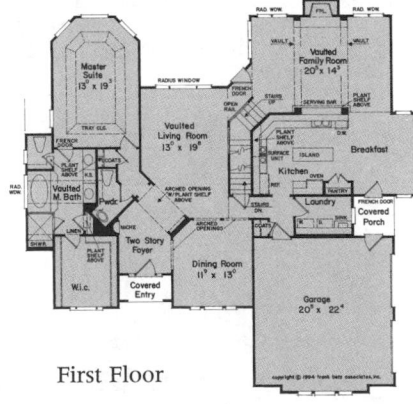

First Floor

Second Floor

2,500 TO 2,999 SQUARE FEET

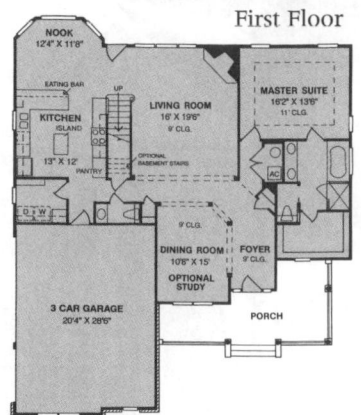

First Floor

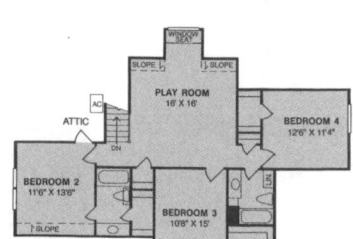

Second Floor

HPK2100745

Style: Country

First Floor: 1,650 sq. ft.

Second Floor: 1,038 sq. ft.

Total: 2,688 sq. ft.

Bedrooms: 4

Bathrooms: 3 ½

Width: 50' - 0"

Depth: 60' - 0"

EPLANS.COM

HPK2100746

Style: Craftsman

First Floor: 2,042 sq. ft.

Second Floor: 647 sq. ft.

Total: 2,689 sq. ft.

Bonus Space: 243 sq. ft.

Bedrooms: 4

Bathrooms: 4

Width: 60' - 0"

Depth: 56' - 0"

Foundation: Crawlspace, Slab, Unfinished Walkout Basement

EPLANS.COM

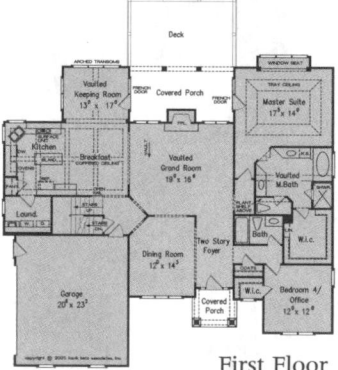

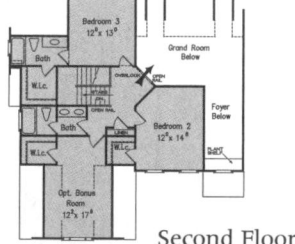

First Floor

Second Floor

ORDER BLUEPRINTS ANYTIME AT EPLANS.COM OR 1-800-521-6797

HPK2100747

Style: Neoclassical
First Floor: 1,792 sq. ft.
Second Floor: 899 sq. ft.
Total: 2,691 sq. ft.
Bedrooms: 4
Bathrooms: 2 ½
Width: 32' - 9"
Depth: 99' - 5"
Foundation: Slab

EPLANS.COM

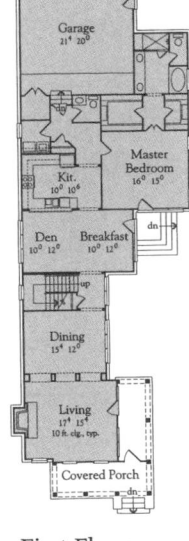

First Floor

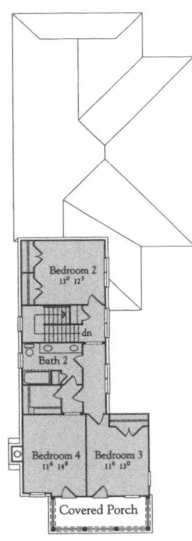

Second Floor

HPK2100748

Style: Farmhouse
First Floor: 1,734 sq. ft.
Second Floor: 958 sq. ft.
Total: 2,692 sq. ft.
Bedrooms: 4
Bathrooms: 3 ½
Width: 55' - 0"
Depth: 59' - 10"

EPLANS.COM

First Floor

Second Floor

Find a matching garage on page 182.

© 1990 Donald A. Gardner Architects, Inc.

2,500 TO 2,999 SQUARE FEET

HPK2100749

Style: Farmhouse

First Floor: 1,798 sq. ft.

Second Floor: 900 sq. ft.

Total: 2,698 sq. ft.

Bedrooms: 3

Bathrooms: 3 ½

Width: 54' - 0"

Depth: 57' - 0"

Foundation: Crawlspace

EPLANS.COM

Find a matching garage on page 182.

First Floor

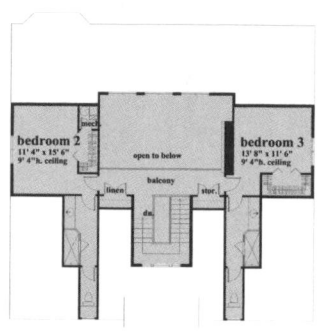

Second Floor

HPK2100750

Style: French Country

First Floor: 1,355 sq. ft.

Second Floor: 1,347 sq. ft.

Total: 2,702 sq. ft.

Bonus Space: 285 sq. ft.

Bedrooms: 4

Bathrooms: 4

Width: 41' - 0"

Depth: 66' - 0"

Foundation: Crawlspace, Unfinished Walkout Basement

EPLANS.COM

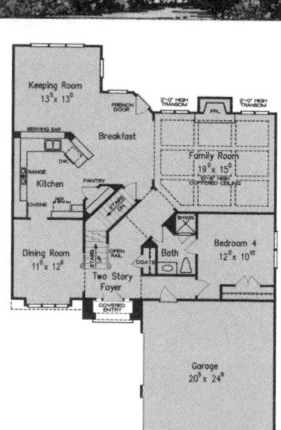

First Floor

Second Floor

HPK2100751

Style: Cottage

First Floor: 1,650 sq. ft.

Second Floor: 1,060 sq. ft.

Total: 2,710 sq. ft.

Bedrooms: 4

Bathrooms: 3 ½

Width: 53' - 0"

Depth: 68' - 2"

Foundation: Finished Walkout Basement

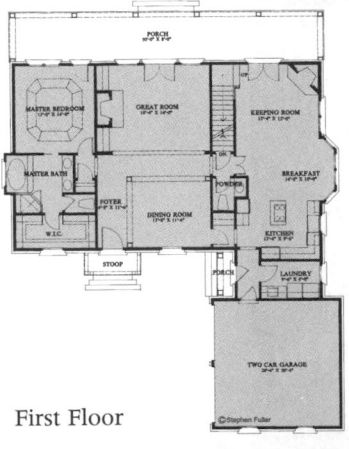

First Floor

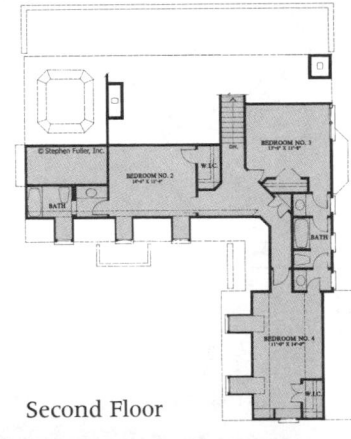

Second Floor

HPK2100752

Style: French Country

First Floor: 1,763 sq. ft.

Second Floor: 947 sq. ft.

Total: 2,710 sq. ft.

Bedrooms: 3

Bathrooms: 2 ½

Width: 50' - 0"

Depth: 75' - 4"

Foundation: Unfinished Walkout Basement

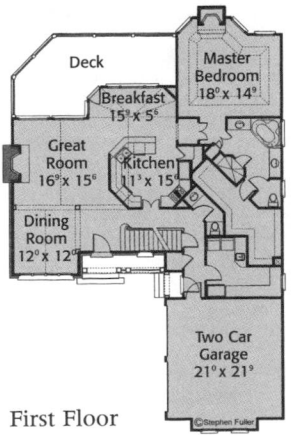

First Floor

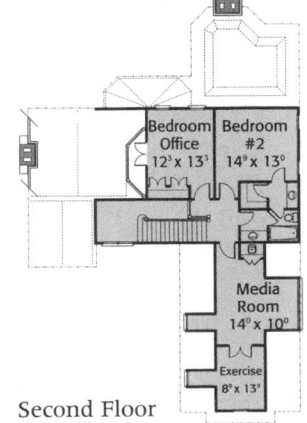

Second Floor

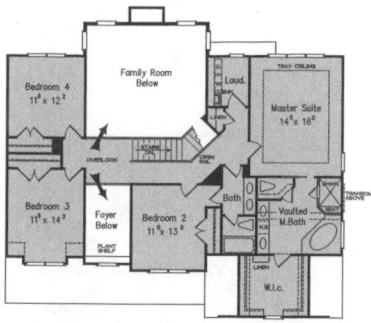

First Floor

Second Floor

HPK2100753

Style: New American

First Floor: 1,349 sq. ft.

Second Floor: 1,368 sq. ft.

Total: 2,717 sq. ft.

Bedrooms: 5

Bathrooms: 3

Width: 51' - 0"

Depth: 45' - 0"

Foundation: Crawlspace, Slab, Unfinished Walkout Basement

EPLANS.COM

First Floor

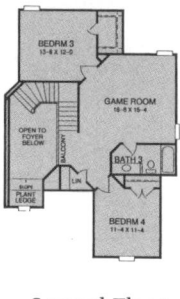

Second Floor

HPK2100754

Style: New American

First Floor: 1,930 sq. ft.

Second Floor: 791 sq. ft.

Total: 2,721 sq. ft.

Bedrooms: 4

Bathrooms: 3

Width: 64' - 4"

Depth: 62' - 0"

Foundation: Crawlspace, Slab, Unfinished Basement

EPLANS.COM

© Larry E. Belk Designs

HPK2100755

Style: Cottage

First Floor: 1,904 sq. ft.

Second Floor: 819 sq. ft.

Total: 2,723 sq. ft.

Bedrooms: 4

Bathrooms: 4

Width: 39' - 8"

Depth: 78' - 8"

Foundation: Crawlspace

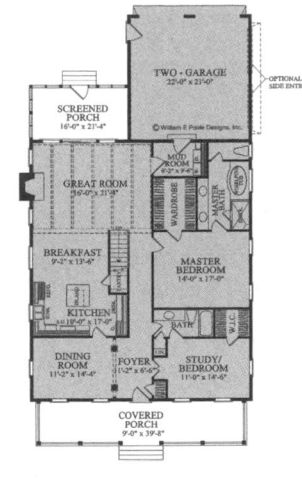

First Floor

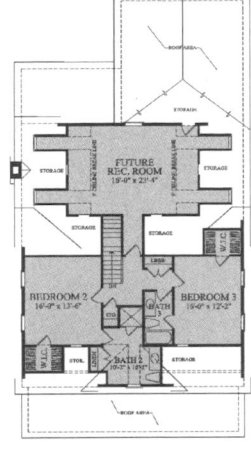

Second Floor

©2005 William E Poole Designs, Inc.

First Floor

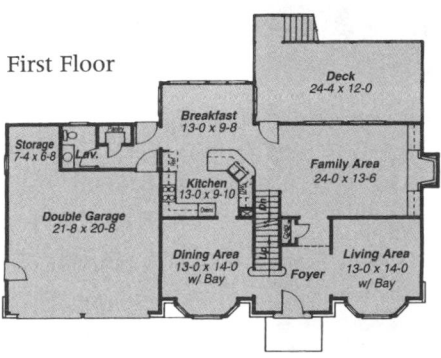

Second Floor

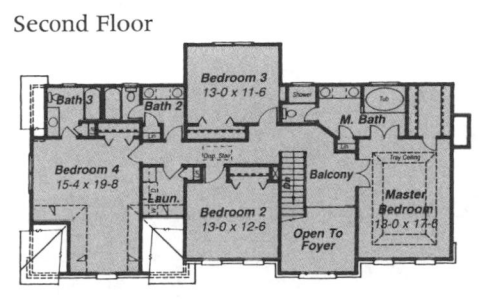

HPK2100756

Style: Colonial Revival

First Floor: 1,230 sq. ft.

Second Floor: 1,496 sq. ft.

Total: 2,726 sq. ft.

Bedrooms: 4

Bathrooms: 3 ½

Width: 60' - 0"

Depth: 34' - 6"

Foundation: Crawlspace, Slab, Unfinished Basement

2,500 TO 2,999 SQUARE FEET

EPLANS.COM

HPK2100757

Style: Mediterranean

First Floor: 2,365 sq. ft.

Second Floor: 364 sq. ft.

Total: 2,729 sq. ft.

Bedrooms: 3

Bathrooms: 3

Width: 69' - 0"

Depth: 70' - 0"

Foundation: Slab

EPLANS.COM

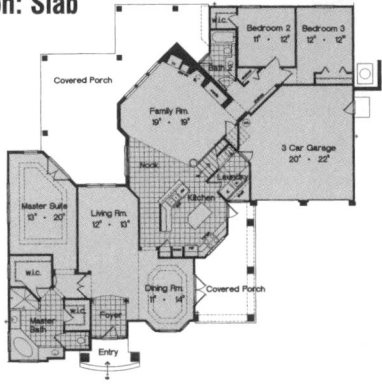

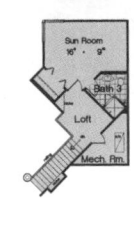

HPK2100758

Style: Bungalow

First Floor: 2,270 sq. ft.

Second Floor: 461 sq. ft.

Total: 2,731 sq. ft.

Bedrooms: 3

Bathrooms: 3

Width: 70' - 0"

Depth: 73' - 8"

Foundation: Slab

EPLANS.COM

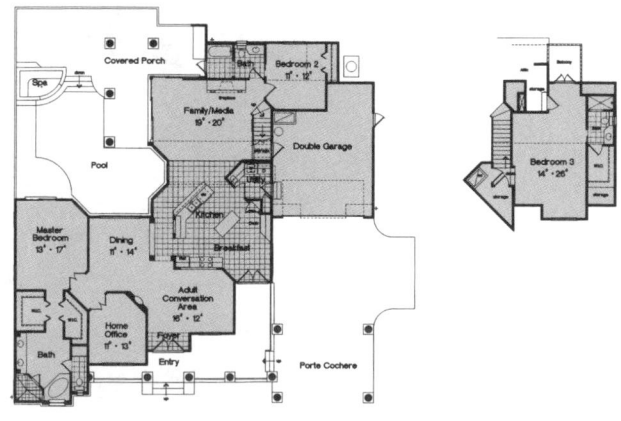

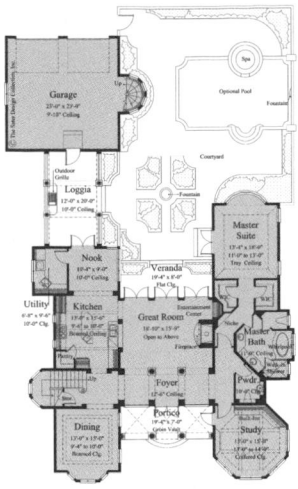

First Floor

© The Sater Design Collection, Inc.

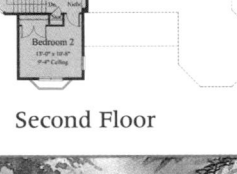

Second Floor

HPK2100759

Style: Italianate

First Floor: 2,084 sq. ft.

Second Floor: 652 sq. ft.

Total: 2,736 sq. ft.

Bonus Space: 375 sq. ft.

Bedrooms: 3

Bathrooms: 2 ½

Width: 60' - 6"

Depth: 94' - 0"

Foundation: Slab

EPLANS.COM

First Floor

HPK2100760

Style: Bungalow

First Floor: 1,814 sq. ft.

Second Floor: 923 sq. ft.

Total: 2,737 sq. ft.

Bedrooms: 4

Bathrooms: 2 ½

Width: 50' - 0"

Depth: 54' - 0"

Foundation: Crawlspace

EPLANS.COM

Second Floor

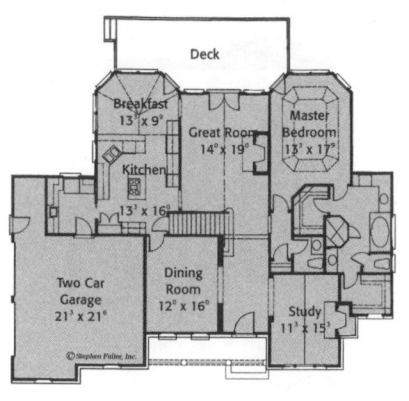

First Floor

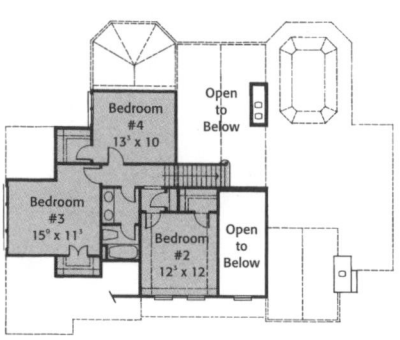

Second Floor

HPK2100761

Style: Colonial Revival

First Floor: 1,932 sq. ft.

Second Floor: 807 sq. ft.

Total: 2,739 sq. ft.

Bedrooms: 4

Bathrooms: 2 ½

Width: 63' - 0"

Depth: 51' - 6"

Foundation: Finished Walkout Basement

EPLANS.COM

First Floor

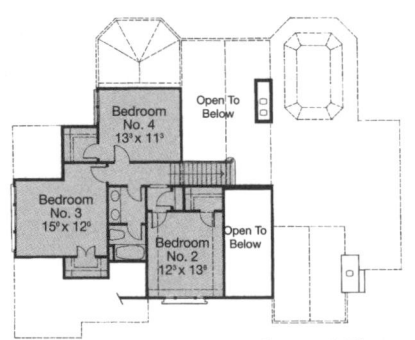

Second Floor

HPK2100762

Style: French Country

First Floor: 1,932 sq. ft.

Second Floor: 807 sq. ft.

Total: 2,739 sq. ft.

Bedrooms: 4

Bathrooms: 2 ½

Width: 63' - 0"

Depth: 51' - 6"

Foundation: Finished Walkout Basement

EPLANS.COM

2,500 TO 2,999 SQUARE FEET

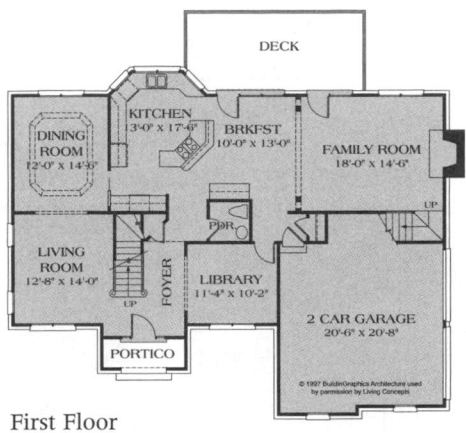

First Floor

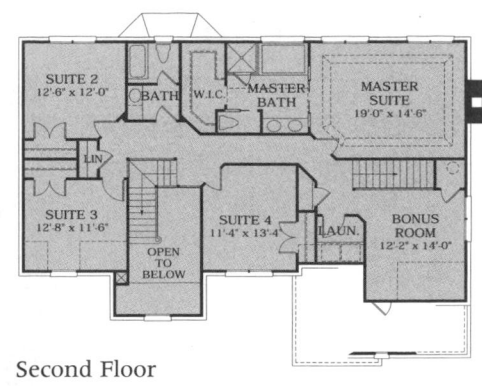

Second Floor

HPK2100763

Style: New American
First Floor: 1,426 sq. ft.
Second Floor: 1,315 sq. ft.
Total: 2,741 sq. ft.
Bonus Space: 200 sq. ft.
Bedrooms: 4
Bathrooms: 2 ½
Width: 57' - 7"
Depth: 44' - 10"
Foundation: Crawlspace

EPLANS.COM

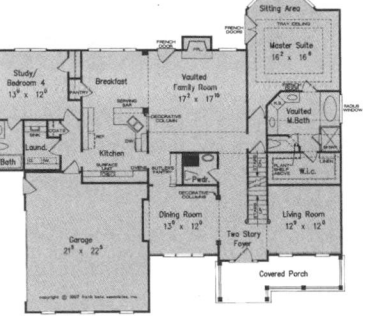

First Floor

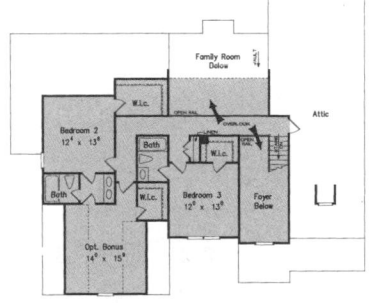

Second Floor

HPK2100764

Style: New American
First Floor: 2,026 sq. ft.
Second Floor: 726 sq. ft.
Total: 2,752 sq. ft.
Bonus Space: 277 sq. ft.
Bedrooms: 4
Bathrooms: 4 ½
Width: 61' - 6"
Depth: 56' - 0"
**Foundation: Crawlspace,
Slab, Unfinished Walkout
Basement**

EPLANS.COM

2,500 TO 2,999 SQUARE FEET

HPK2100765

Style: French Country

First Floor: 2,084 sq. ft.

Second Floor: 671 sq. ft.

Total: 2,755 sq. ft.

Bedrooms: 4

Bathrooms: 3

Width: 57' - 4"

Depth: 55' - 10"

Foundation: Crawlspace, Slab

EPLANS.COM

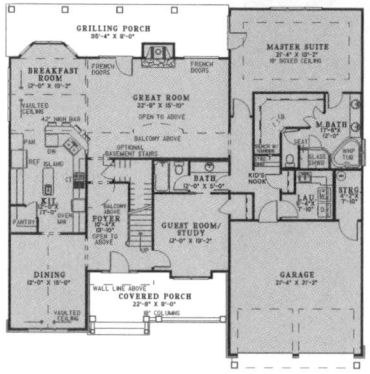

First Floor

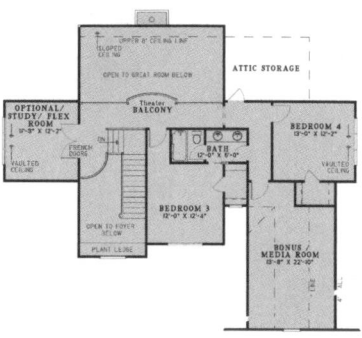

Second Floor

HPK2100766

Style: Plantation

First Floor: 1,855 sq. ft.

Second Floor: 901 sq. ft.

Total: 2,756 sq. ft.

Bedrooms: 3

Bathrooms: 3 ½

Width: 66' - 0"

Depth: 50' - 0"

Foundation: Island Basement

EPLANS.COM

First Floor

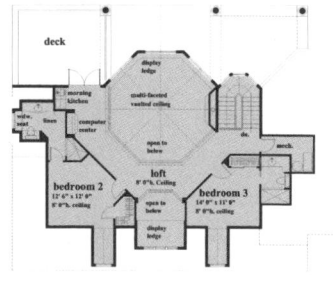

Second Floor

HPK2100767

Style: French Country
First Floor: 1,805 sq. ft.
Second Floor: 952 sq. ft.
Total: 2,757 sq. ft.
Bonus Space: 475 sq. ft.
Bedrooms: 4
Bathrooms: 3 ½
Width: 48' - 10"
Depth: 64' - 10"
Foundation: Crawlspace, Unfinished Basement

EPLANS.COM

© 1997 William E Poole Designs, Inc.

First Floor

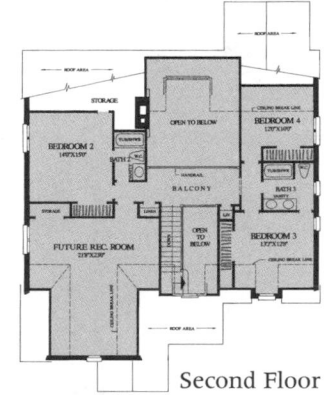

Second Floor

HPK2100768

Style: French Country
First Floor: 1,889 sq. ft.
Second Floor: 869 sq. ft.
Total: 2,758 sq. ft.
Bedrooms: 4
Bathrooms: 3 ½
Width: 66' - 4"
Depth: 57' - 8"
Foundation: Unfinished Basement

EPLANS.COM

First Floor

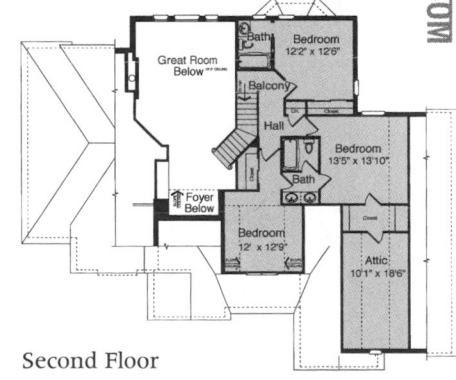

Second Floor

2,500 TO 2,999 SQUARE FEET

HPK2100769

First Floor

Second Floor

Style: Norman
First Floor: 1,360 sq. ft.
Second Floor: 1,400 sq. ft.
Total: 2,760 sq. ft.
Bedrooms: 4
Bathrooms: 3 ½
Width: 52' - 0"
Depth: 49' - 0"
Foundation: Finished Walkout Basement

EPLANS.COM

First Floor

Second Floor

HPK2100770

Style: Colonial Revival
First Floor: 1,364 sq. ft.
Second Floor: 1,398 sq. ft.
Total: 2,762 sq. ft.
Bedrooms: 5
Bathrooms: 4
Width: 51' - 0"
Depth: 45' - 4"
Foundation: Crawlspace, Unfinished Walkout Basement

EPLANS.COM

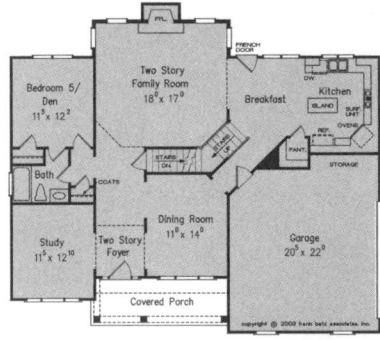

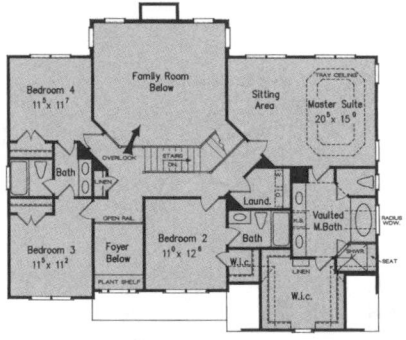

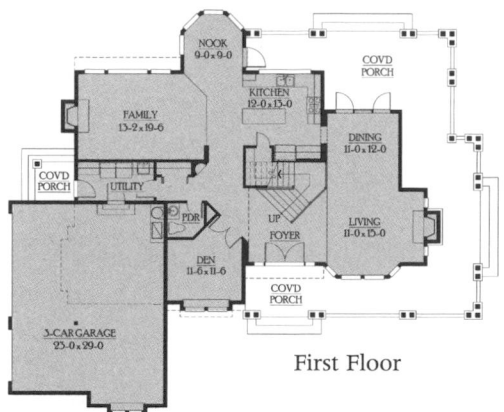

First Floor

Second Floor

HPK2100771

Style: Craftsman
First Floor: 1,510 sq. ft.
Second Floor: 1,260 sq. ft.
Total: 2,770 sq. ft.
Bedrooms: 4
Bathrooms: 2 ½
Width: 72' - 0"
Depth: 61' - 0"
Foundation: Crawlspace

EPLANS.COM

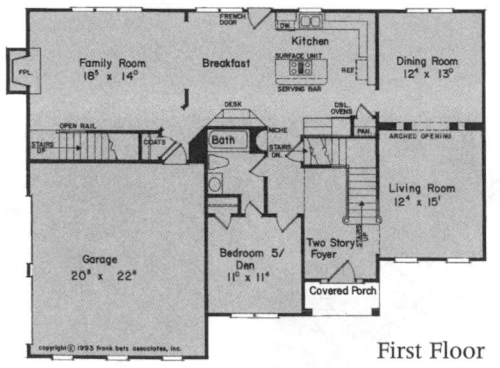

First Floor

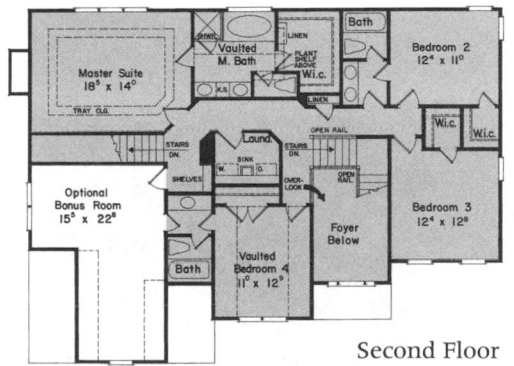

Second Floor

HPK2100772

Style: New American
First Floor: 1,447 sq. ft.
Second Floor: 1,325 sq. ft.
Total: 2,772 sq. ft.
Bonus Space: 301 sq. ft.
Bedrooms: 5
Bathrooms: 4
Width: 56' - 4"
Depth: 41' - 0"
Foundation: Crawlspace, Unfinished Walkout Basement

EPLANS.COM

First Floor

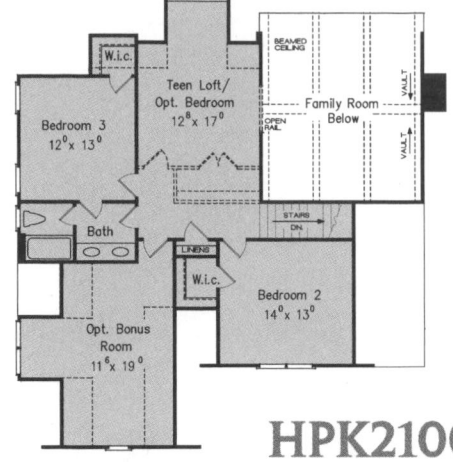

Second Floor

HPK2100773

Stone embellishments distinguish this French Country home. Inside, upgraded amenities set it apart. The vaulted master suite occupies the right wing and comfortably pampers both homeowners. The tray ceiling in the master bath is an elegant touch. Bedroom 4 is positioned perfectly for a guest or in-law. Upstairs, flex space is useful as additional sleeping quarters or recreation space.

Style: Cottage
First Floor: 1,959 sq. ft.
Second Floor: 817 sq. ft.
Total: 2,776 sq. ft.
Bonus Space: 271 sq. ft.
Bedrooms: 5
Bathrooms: 3
Width: 59' - 0"
Depth: 52' - 0"
Foundation: Crawlspace, Unfinished Walkout Basement

EPLANS.COM

© 1994 Donald A. Gardner Architects, Inc.

With its long wraparound porches and expansive informal living spaces stretching across the back, this farmhouse projects a graceful, relaxed attitude. Nine-foot ceilings on the first level with a vaulted ceiling in the great room, ventilating skylights in the sunroom, a two-level foyer, and bay windows combine to make this home feel much larger than 2,777 square feet. The first-level bedroom can double as a study, while the master bedroom upstairs features double vanities and a large walk-in closet.

HPK2100774

Style: Farmhouse

First Floor: 1,821 sq. ft.

Second Floor: 956 sq. ft.

Total: 2,777 sq. ft.

Bedrooms: 4

Bathrooms: 3

Width: 77' - 0"

Depth: 58' - 8"

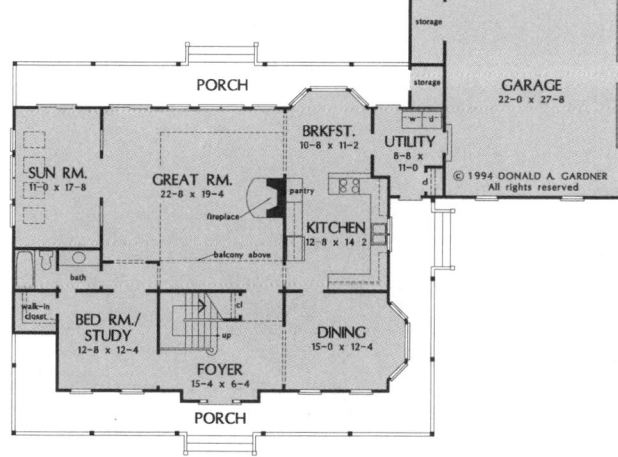

First Floor

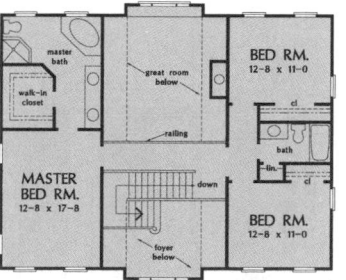

Second Floor

2,500 TO 2,999 SQUARE FEET

HPK2100775

Style: Greek Revival
First Floor: 1,279 sq. ft.
Second Floor: 1,499 sq. ft.
Total: 2,778 sq. ft.
Bonus Space: 240 sq. ft.
Bedrooms: 4
Bathrooms: 2 ½
Width: 53' - 0"
Depth: 46' - 6"
Foundation: Crawlspace, Unfinished Walkout Basement

EPLANS.COM

A variety of materials abounds on the facade of this classic Colonial design: brick, siding, and mouldings. The pedimented entry gives way to the two-story foyer that opens to the living room, dining room, and the engaging two-story family room. The second floor holds the master suite along with three bedrooms and a shared full bath.

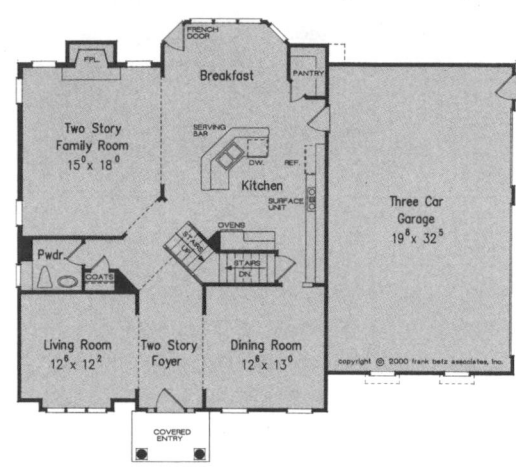

Optional Layout

First Floor

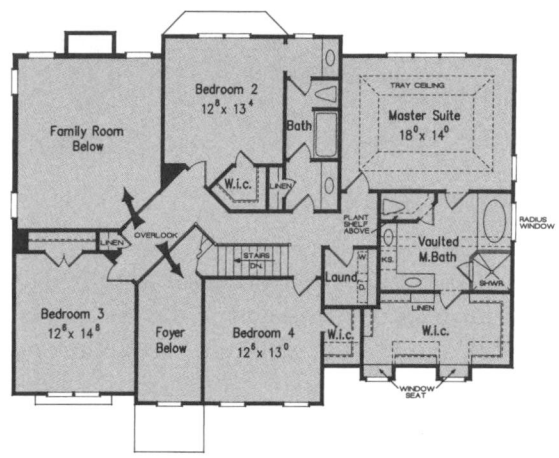

Second Floor

ORDER BLUEPRINTS ANYTIME AT EPLANS.COM OR 1-800-521-6797

HPK2100776

Style: Mediterranean

Square Footage: 2,781

Bedrooms: 4

Bathrooms: 3

Width: 64' - 10"

Depth: 76' - 9"

Foundation: Crawlspace, Slab

EPLANS.COM

A multi-faceted facade and classic arches blend with a hipped roof design to dress this home with a sheer sense of elegance. The dining and living rooms meld with the breakfast nook, creating an expansive common area that spills out onto the rear covered porch. The four bedrooms are split with two on each side of the plan; the master suite on the left boasts a lavish master bath and twin walk-in closets.

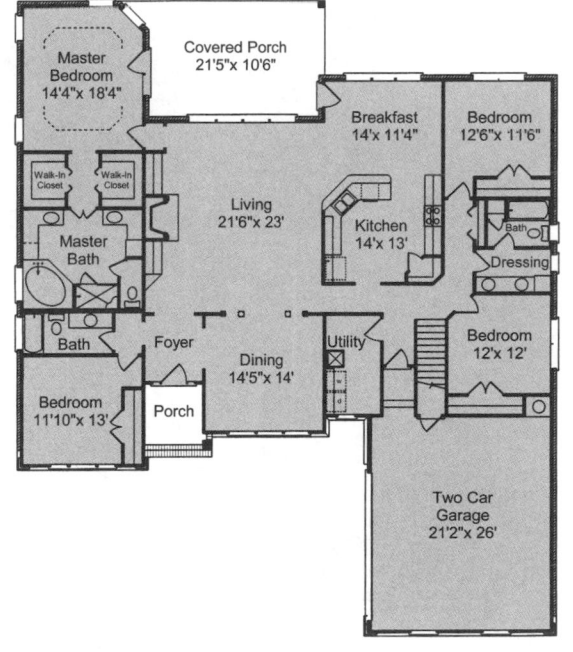

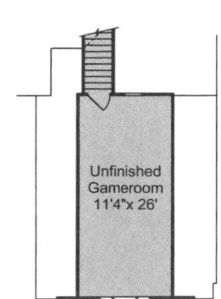

2,500 TO 2,999 SQUARE FEET

First Floor

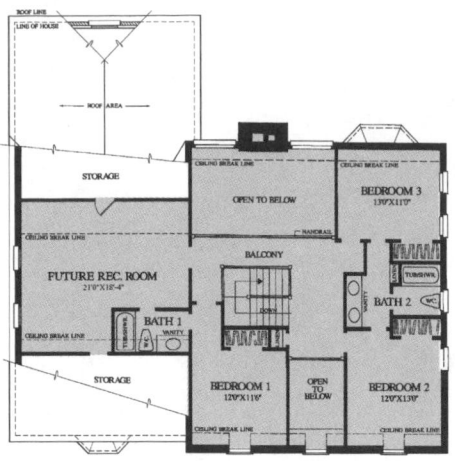

Second Floor

Pediments and lintels adorn the front of this brick Colonial home guided by Federal-style symmetry. Inset dormers decorate the roofline while increasing floor space in two of the three upstairs bedrooms. A traditional layout separates the front rooms with partial walls and columns, while contemporary design keeps the kitchen and breakfast area open to the two-story family room. The master bedroom awaits homeowners with a bay window, amenity-filled bath, and long walk-in closet. The two-bay garage can be customized to suit your lot.

HPK2100777

Style: Georgian
First Floor: 1,816 sq. ft.
Second Floor: 968 sq. ft.
Total: 2,784 sq. ft.
Bedrooms: 4
Bathrooms: 3 ½
Width: 54' - 6"
Depth: 52' - 5"
Foundation: Crawlspace

EPLANS.COM

©2005 William E Poole Designs, Inc.

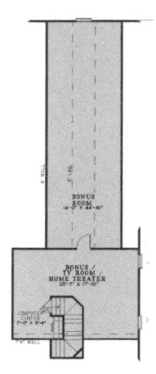

HPK2100778

Style: French Country

Square Footage: 2,788

Bedrooms: 4

Bathrooms: 3 ½

Width: 73' - 2"

Depth: 91' - 6"

Foundation: Crawlspace, Slab

EPLANS.COM

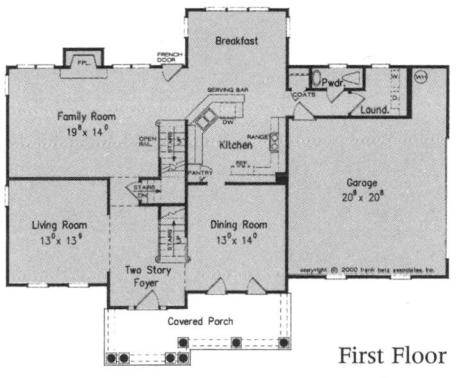

First Floor

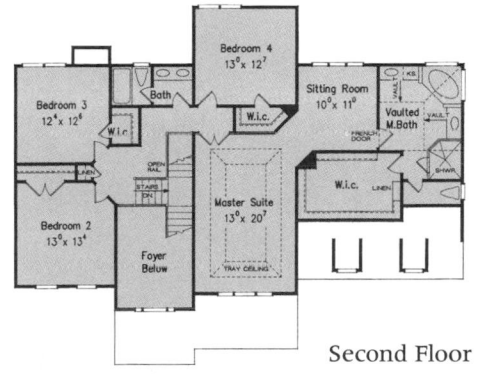

Second Floor

HPK2100779

EPLANS.COM

Style: Greek Revival

First Floor: 1,332 sq. ft.

Second Floor: 1,457 sq. ft.

Total: 2,789 sq. ft.

Bedrooms: 4

Bathrooms: 2 ½

Width: 58' - 0"

Depth: 46' - 6"

Foundation: Crawlspace, Unfinished Walkout Basement

2,500 TO 2,999 SQUARE FEET

HPK2100780

Style: French Country

First Floor: 1,900 sq. ft.

Second Floor: 890 sq. ft.

Total: 2,790 sq. ft.

Bedrooms: 4

Bathrooms: 2 ½

Width: 63' - 0"

Depth: 51' - 0"

Foundation: Finished Walkout Basement

EPLANS.COM

First Floor   Second Floor

HPK2100781

Style: Country

First Floor: 1,840 sq. ft.

Second Floor: 950 sq. ft.

Total: 2,790 sq. ft.

Bedrooms: 4

Bathrooms: 3 ½

Width: 58' - 6"

Depth: 62' - 0"

Foundation: Finished Walkout Basement

EPLANS.COM

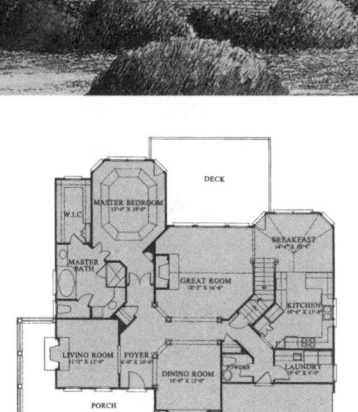

First Floor   Second Floor

HPK2100782

Style: Craftsman

First Floor: 1,919 sq. ft.

Second Floor: 876 sq. ft.

Total: 2,795 sq. ft.

Bonus Space: 167 sq. ft.

Bedrooms: 4

Bathrooms: 3 ½

Width: 56' - 0"

Depth: 53' - 4"

Foundation: Crawlspace, Slab, Unfinished Walkout Basement

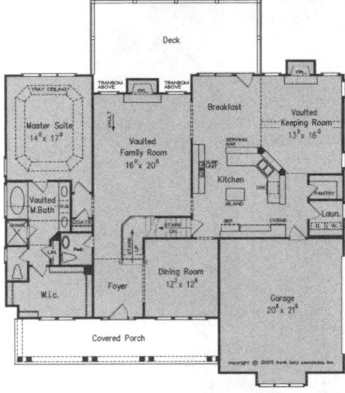

First Floor

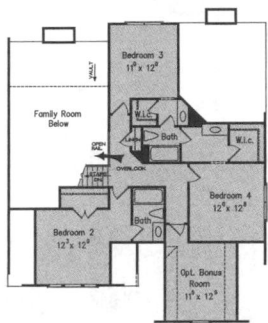

Second Floor

© The Sater Design Collection, Inc.

First Floor

HPK2100783

Style: Mediterranean

First Floor: 2,368 sq. ft.

Second Floor: 428 sq. ft.

Total: 2,796 sq. ft.

Bedrooms: 3

Bathrooms: 3

Width: 72' - 8"

Depth: 72' - 0"

Foundation: Slab

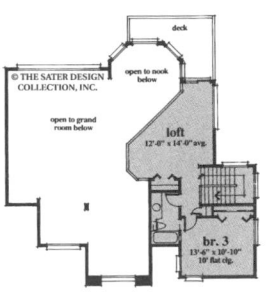

Second Floor

2,500 TO 2,999 SQUARE FEET

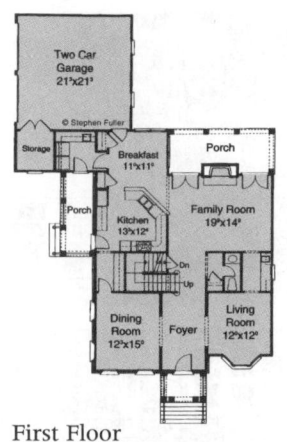

First Floor

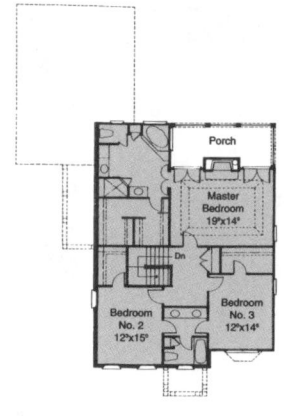

Second Floor

HPK2100784

Style: Federal - Adams
First Floor: 1,465 sq. ft.
Second Floor: 1,332 sq. ft.
Total: 2,797 sq. ft.
Bedrooms: 3
Bathrooms: 2 ½
Width: 49' - 0"
Depth: 75' - 0"
Foundation: Finished Walkout Basement

EPLANS.COM

First Floor

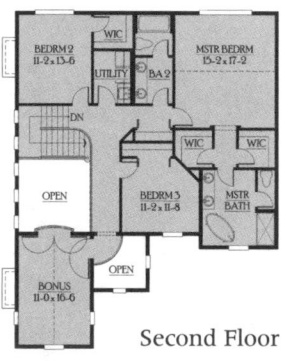

Second Floor

HPK2100785

Style: Craftsman
First Floor: 1,425 sq. ft.
Second Floor: 1,380 sq. ft.
Total: 2,805 sq. ft.
Bedrooms: 3
Bathrooms: 2 ½
Width: 48' - 0"
Depth: 60' - 0"
Foundation: Crawlspace

EPLANS.COM

First Floor

Second Floor

HPK2100786

Style: Craftsman
First Floor: 1,330 sq. ft.
Second Floor: 1,475 sq. ft.
Total: 2,805 sq. ft.
Bonus Space: 272 sq. ft.
Bedrooms: 4
Bathrooms: 2 ½
Width: 40' - 0"
Depth: 60' - 0"
Foundation: Crawlspace

EPLANS.COM

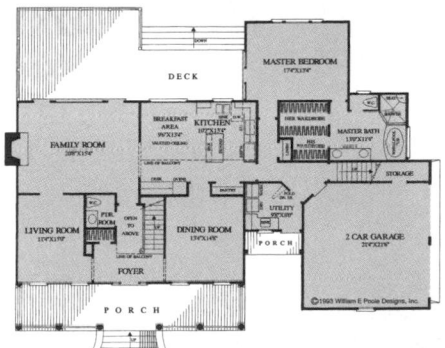

First Floor

Second Floor

HPK2100787

Style: Federal - Adams
First Floor: 1,927 sq. ft.
Second Floor: 879 sq. ft.
Total: 2,806 sq. ft.
Bonus Space: 459 sq. ft.
Bedrooms: 4
Bathrooms: 3 ½
Width: 71' - 0"
Depth: 53' - 0"
Foundation: Crawlspace

EPLANS.COM

2,500 TO 2,999 SQUARE FEET

HPK2100788

Style: Queen Anne

First Floor: 1,632 sq. ft.

Second Floor: 1,188 sq. ft.

Total: 2,820 sq. ft.

Bedrooms: 3

Bathrooms: 2 ½

Width: 61' - 3"

Depth: 68' - 6"

Foundation: Slab

EPLANS.COM

First Floor

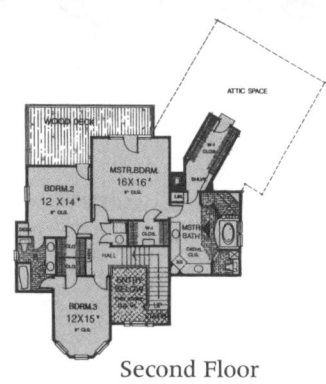

Second Floor

© William E. Poole Designs, Inc.

HPK2100789

Style: Farmhouse

First Floor: 1,734 sq. ft.

Second Floor: 1,091 sq. ft.

Total: 2,825 sq. ft.

Bonus Space: 488 sq. ft.

Bedrooms: 4

Bathrooms: 3 ½

Width: 57' - 6"

Depth: 80' - 11"

Foundation: Crawlspace, Unfinished Basement

EPLANS.COM

First Floor

Second Floor

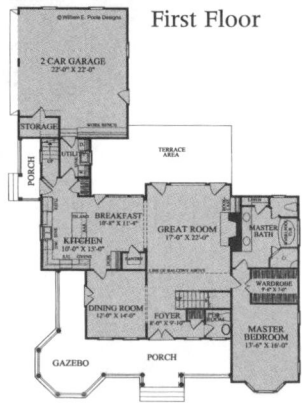

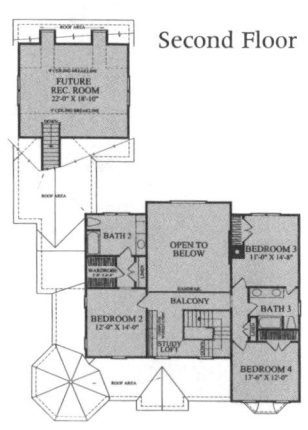

HPK2100790

Style: Country
First Floor: 1,426 sq. ft.
Second Floor: 1,408 sq. ft.
Total: 2,834 sq. ft.
Bedrooms: 5
Bathrooms: 4
Width: 60' - 0"
Depth: 41' - 4"
Foundation: Crawlspace, Slab, Unfinished Walkout Basement

EPLANS.COM

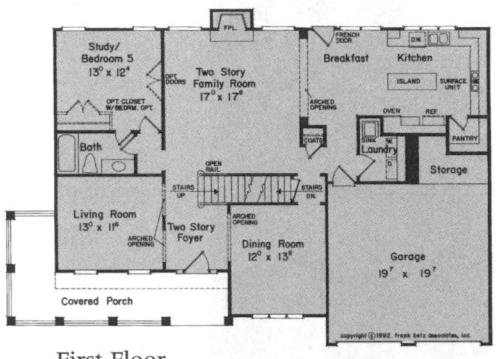

First Floor

Second Floor

HPK2100791

Style: New American
First Floor: 1,466 sq. ft.
Second Floor: 1,369 sq. ft.
Total: 2,835 sq. ft.
Bedrooms: 4
Bathrooms: 2 ½
Width: 50' - 0"
Depth: 60' - 6"
Foundation: Crawlspace

EPLANS.COM

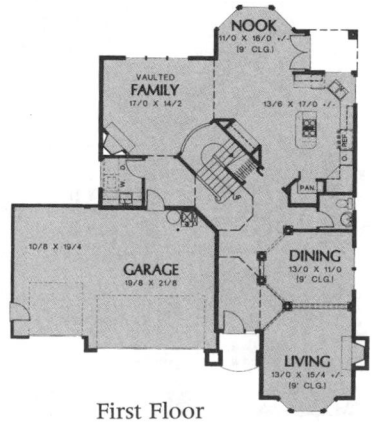

First Floor

Second Floor

2,500 TO 2,999 SQUARE FEET

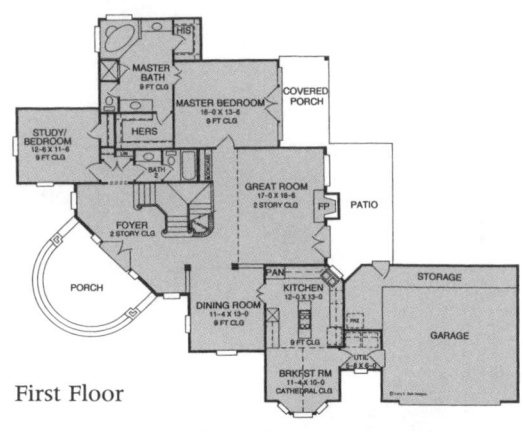

First Floor

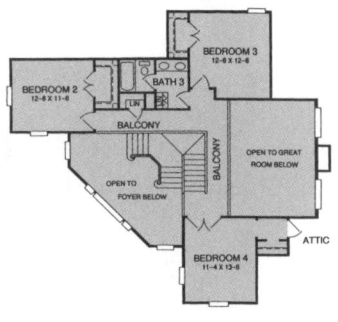

Second Floor

HPK2100792

Style: New American

First Floor: 1,966 sq. ft.

Second Floor: 872 sq. ft.

Total: 2,838 sq. ft.

Bedrooms: 5

Bathrooms: 3

Width: 79' - 10"

Depth: 63' - 10"

Foundation: Crawlspace, Slab, Unfinished Basement

EPLANS.COM

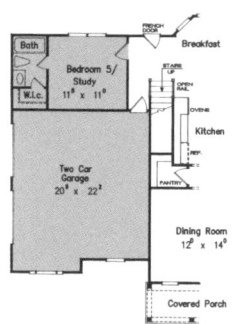

Optional Layout

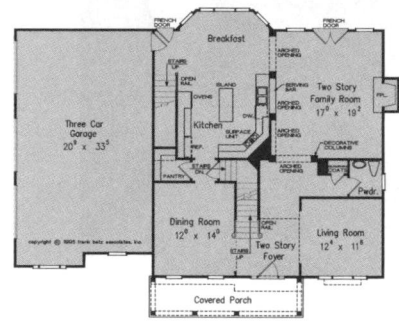

First Floor

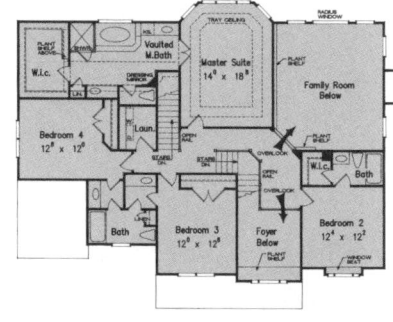

Second Floor

HPK2100793

Style: Country

First Floor: 1,347 sq. ft.

Second Floor: 1,493 sq. ft.

Total: 2,840 sq. ft.

Bonus Space: 243 sq. ft.

Bedrooms: 4

Bathrooms: 3 ½

Width: 58' - 4"

Depth: 46' - 6"

Foundation: Crawlspace, Slab, Unfinished Walkout Basement

EPLANS.COM

First Floor

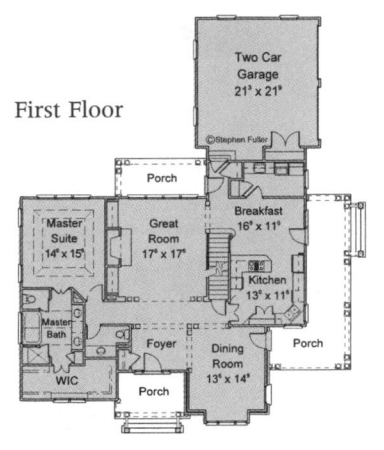

Second Floor

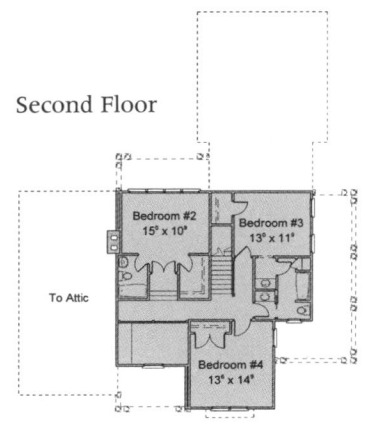

HPK2100794

Style: Country
First Floor: 1,804 sq. ft.
Second Floor: 1,041 sq. ft.
Total: 2,845 sq. ft.
Bedrooms: 4
Bathrooms: 3 ½
Width: 57' - 3"
Depth: 71' - 0"
Foundation: Finished Walkout Basement

EPLANS.COM

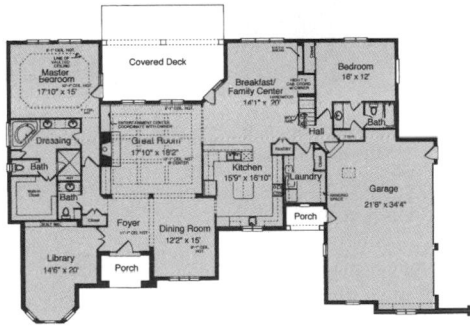

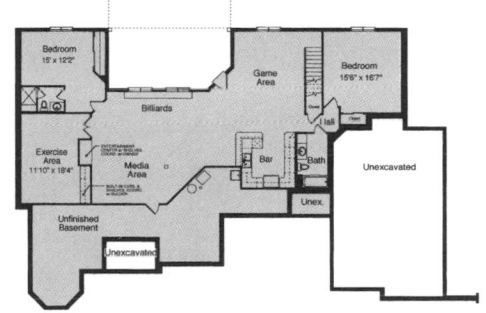

HPK2100795

Style: French Country
Square Footage: 2,850
Bedrooms: 2
Bathrooms: 2 ½
Width: 86' - 2"
Depth: 57' - 5"
Foundation: Finished Walkout Basement

EPLANS.COM

2,500 TO 2,999 SQUARE FEET

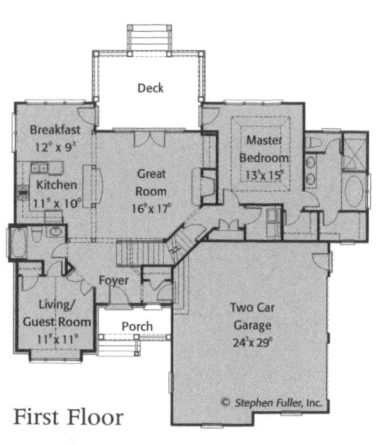

First Floor

© Stephen Fuller, Inc.

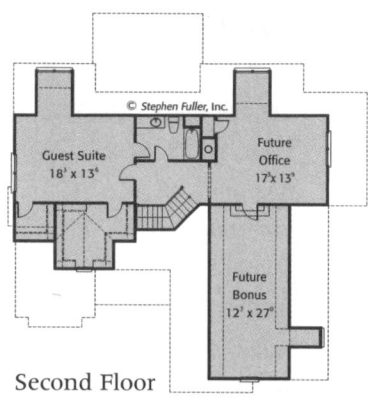

Second Floor

HPK2100796

Style: Cottage

First Floor: 1,498 sq. ft.

Second Floor: 1,353 sq. ft.

Total: 2,851 sq. ft.

Bedrooms: 3

Bathrooms: 3

Width: 55' - 9"

Depth: 51' - 9"

Foundation: Crawlspace

EPLANS.COM

HPK2100797

Style: Colonial Revival

First Floor: 1,482 sq. ft.

Second Floor: 1,373 sq. ft.

Total: 2,855 sq. ft.

Bonus Space: 537 sq. ft.

Bedrooms: 4

Bathrooms: 4

Width: 66' - 7"

Depth: 41' - 6"

Foundation: Unfinished Basement

EPLANS.COM

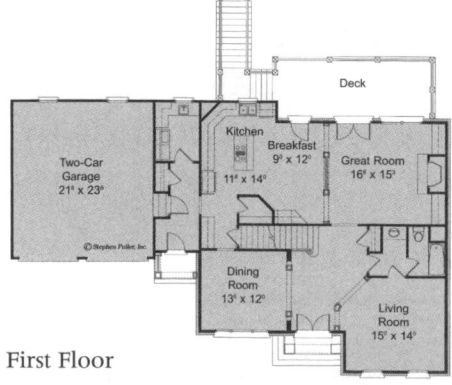

First Floor

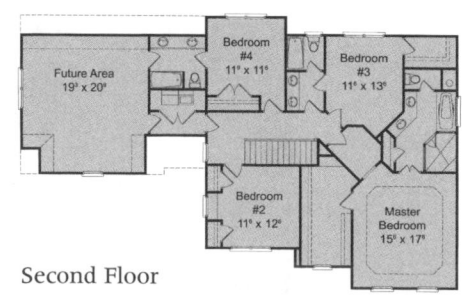

Second Floor

ORDER BLUEPRINTS ANYTIME AT EPLANS.COM OR 1-800-521-6797

HPK2100798

Style: New American

First Floor: 1,895 sq. ft.

Second Floor: 963 sq. ft.

Total: 2,858 sq. ft.

Bonus Space: 352 sq. ft.

Bedrooms: 5

Bathrooms: 4

Width: 54' - 0"

Depth: 70' - 4"

Foundation: Crawlspace, Unfinished Walkout Basement

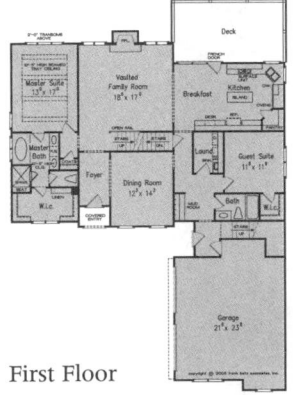

First Floor

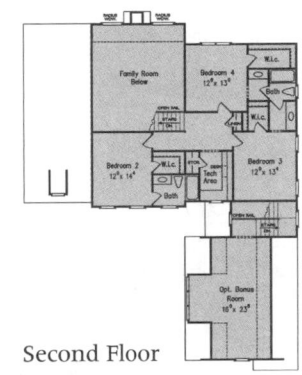

Second Floor

HPK2100799

Style: French Country

First Floor: 2,070 sq. ft.

Second Floor: 790 sq. ft.

Total: 2,860 sq. ft.

Bedrooms: 4

Bathrooms: 3 ½

Width: 57' - 6"

Depth: 54' - 0"

Foundation: Finished Walkout Basement

First Floor

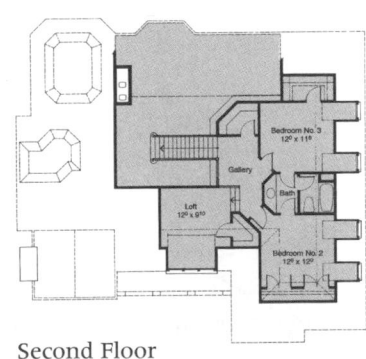

Second Floor

First Floor

Second Floor

HPK2100800

© Stephen Fuller, Inc.

Style: Georgian

First Floor: 1,960 sq. ft.

Second Floor: 905 sq. ft.

Total: 2,865 sq. ft.

Bonus Space: 297 sq. ft.

Bedrooms: 4

Bathrooms: 3 ½

Width: 61' - 0"

Depth: 70' - 6"

Foundation: Finished Walkout Basement

EPLANS.COM

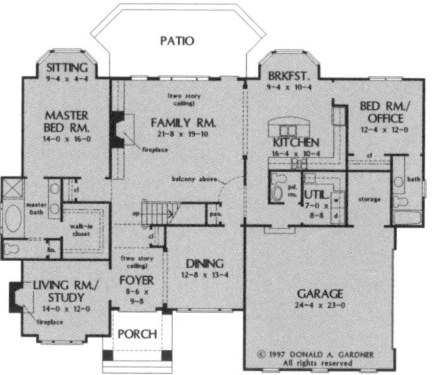

First Floor

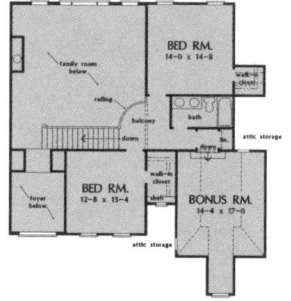

Second Floor

HPK2100801

Style: New American

First Floor: 2,249 sq. ft.

Second Floor: 620 sq. ft.

Total: 2,869 sq. ft.

Bonus Space: 308 sq. ft.

Bedrooms: 4

Bathrooms: 3 ½

Width: 69' - 6"

Depth: 52' - 0"

EPLANS.COM

HPK2100802

Style: Italianate

First Floor: 1,293 sq. ft.

Second Floor: 1,580 sq. ft.

Total: 2,873 sq. ft.

Bedrooms: 3

Bathrooms: 2 ½

Width: 50' - 0"

Depth: 90' - 0"

Foundation: Slab

EPLANS.COM

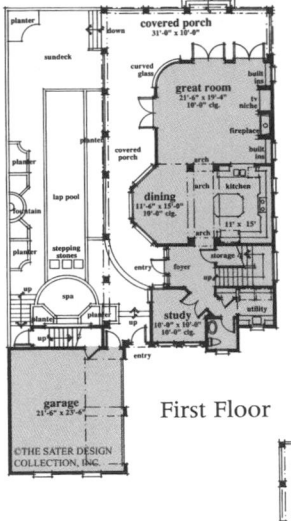

First Floor

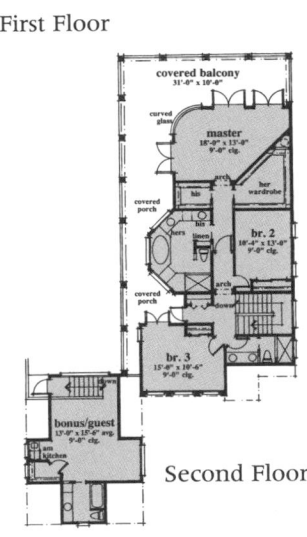

Second Floor

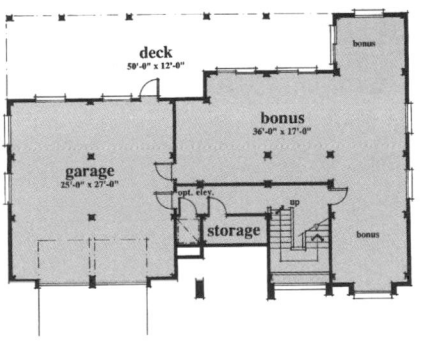

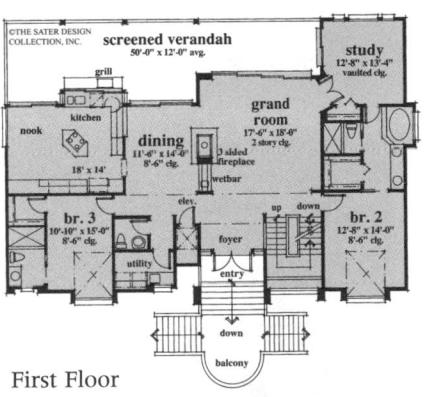

First Floor

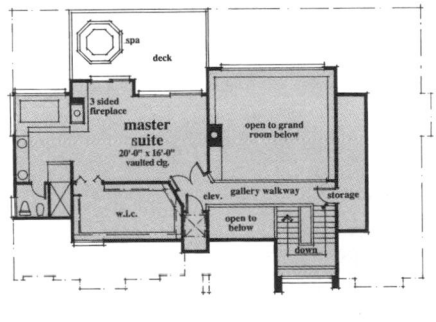

Second Floor

HPK2100803

Style: Cottage

First Floor: 2,066 sq. ft.

Second Floor: 809 sq. ft.

Total: 2,875 sq. ft.

Bonus Space: 1,260 sq. ft.

Bedrooms: 3

Bathrooms: 3 ½

Width: 64' - 0"

Depth: 45' - 0"

Foundation: Pier (same as Piling)

EPLANS.COM

2,500 TO 2,999 SQUARE FEET

HPK2100804

Style: Cottage

First Floor: 1,877 sq. ft.

Second Floor: 998 sq. ft.

Total: 2,875 sq. ft.

Bonus Space: 518 sq. ft.

Bedrooms: 4

Bathrooms: 3 ½

Width: 49' - 0"

Depth: 66' - 4"

Foundation: Crawlspace

EPLANS.COM

©2005 William E Poole Designs, Inc.

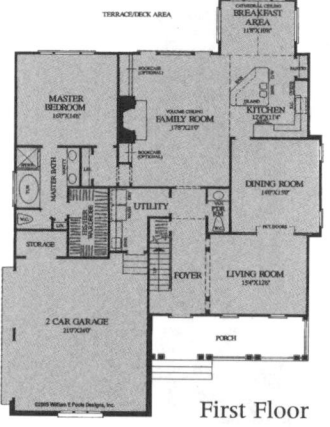

First Floor

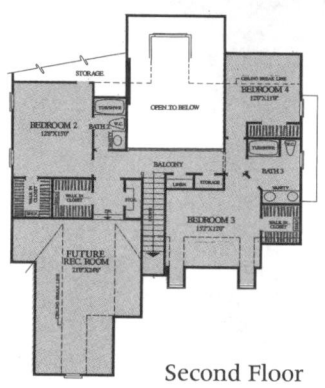

Second Floor

HPK2100805

Style: Cottage

First Floor: 1,684 sq. ft.

Second Floor: 1,195 sq. ft.

Total: 2,879 sq. ft.

Bonus Space: 674 sq. ft.

Bedrooms: 3

Bathrooms: 3

Width: 45' - 0"

Depth: 52' - 0"

Foundation: Pier (same as Piling)

EPLANS.COM

©The Sater Design Collection, Inc.

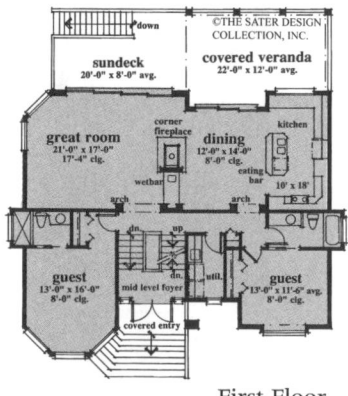

First Floor

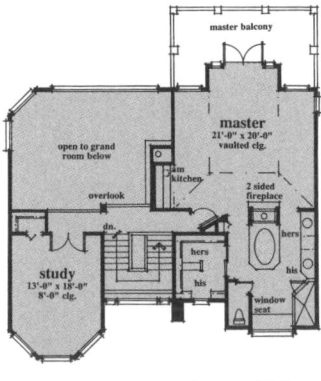

Second Floor

ORDER BLUEPRINTS ANYTIME AT EPLANS.COM OR 1-800-521-6797

HPK2100806

Style: Craftsman
First Floor: 1,400 sq. ft.
Second Floor: 1,482 sq. ft.
Total: 2,882 sq. ft.
Bedrooms: 3
Bathrooms: 2 ½
Width: 40' - 0"
Depth: 61' - 6"
Foundation: Crawlspace

EPLANS.COM

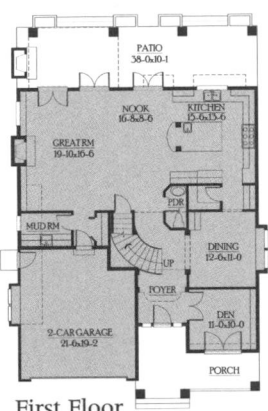

First Floor

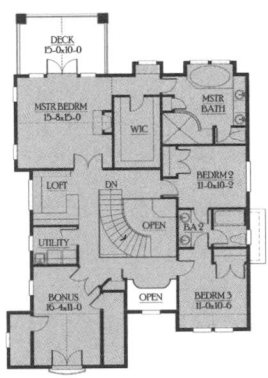

Second Floor

HPK2100807

Style: New American
First Floor: 2,247 sq. ft.
Second Floor: 637 sq. ft.
Total: 2,884 sq. ft.
Bonus Space: 235 sq. ft.
Bedrooms: 4
Bathrooms: 4
Width: 64' - 0"
Depth: 55' - 2"
Foundation: Crawlspace, Unfinished Walkout Basement

EPLANS.COM

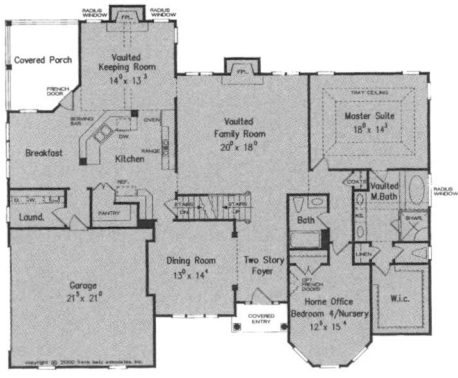

First Floor

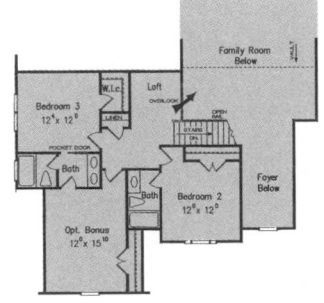

Second Floor

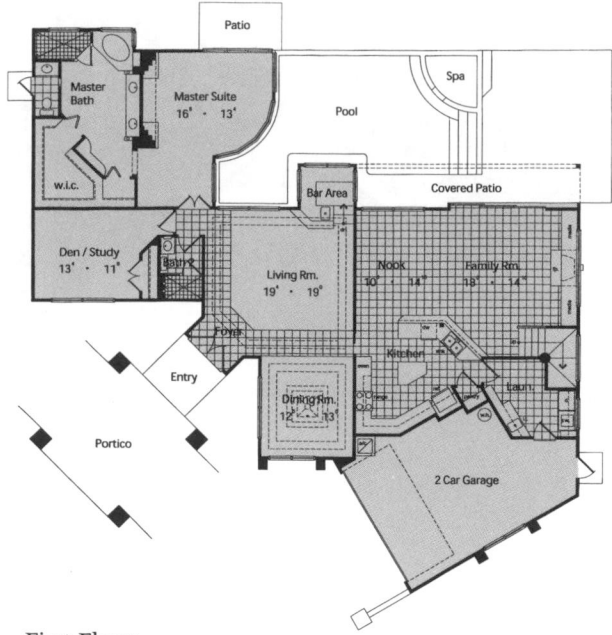

First Floor

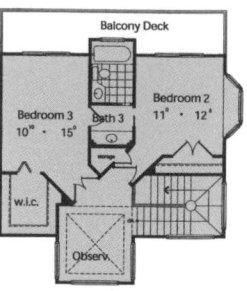

Second Floor

HPK2100808

EPLANS.COM

Style: Italianate
First Floor: 2,212 sq. ft.
Second Floor: 675 sq. ft.
Total: 2,887 sq. ft.
Bedrooms: 3
Bathrooms: 3
Width: 70' - 8"
Depth: 74' - 10"
Foundation: Slab

As you drive up to the porte-cochere entry of this home, the visual movement of the elevation is breathtaking. The foyer leads into the wide glass-walled living room. To the right, the formal dining room features a tiered pedestal ceiling. To the left is the master suite wing of the home. The master bath comes complete with a columned vanity area, a soaking tub, and a shower. Two large bedrooms on the second floor share a sundeck.

HPK2100809

Style: Farmhouse
First Floor: 2,151 sq. ft.
Second Floor: 738 sq. ft.
Total: 2,889 sq. ft.
Bonus Space: 534 sq. ft.
Bedrooms: 3
Bathrooms: 2 ½
Width: 99' - 0"
Depth: 56' - 0"
Foundation: Crawlspace

EPLANS.COM

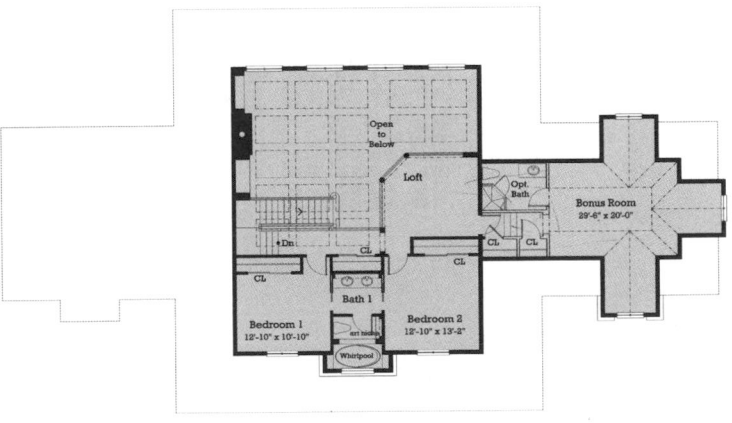

First Floor

Second Floor

A wide, welcoming porch and plenty of stone accents highlight the facade of this charming symmetrical design. From the great room, four sets of French doors open to a wraparound rear porch with a grilling area. The master bedroom, also with porch access, includes built-in shelves, a walk-in closet with a window seat, and a luxurious bath with a whirlpool tub. On the second floor, two family bedrooms share a full bath with a whirlpool tub.

2,500 TO 2,999 SQUARE FEET

HPK2100810

Style: Chateauesque

First Floor: 2,181 sq. ft.

Second Floor: 710 sq. ft.

Total: 2,891 sq. ft.

Bedrooms: 3

Bathrooms: 3

Width: 65' - 0"

Depth: 79' - 0"

Foundation: Slab

EPLANS.COM

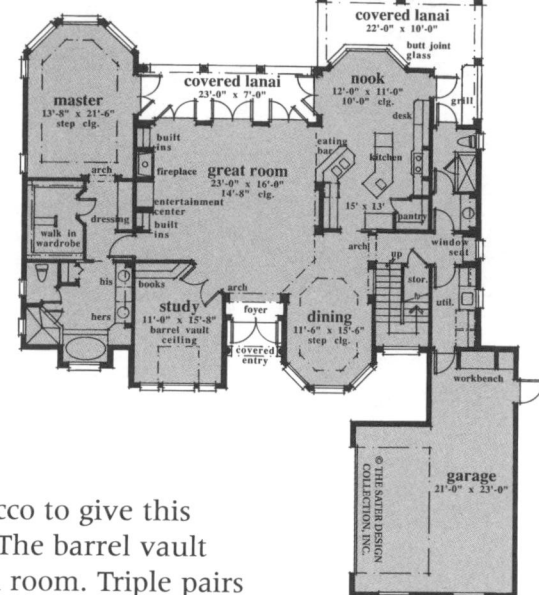

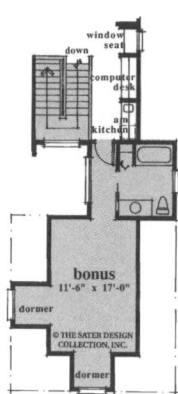

First Floor

Second Floor

A traditional exterior blends brick and stucco to give this two-story home a wonderful appearance. The barrel vault entryway opens up the home to the grand room. Triple pairs of French doors lead to the covered lanai and rear yard. A warming fireplace and built-in entertainment center will make any social or family gathering a joyous occasion.

© The Sater Design Collection, Inc.

HPK2100811

Style: New American
First Floor: 1,751 sq. ft.
Second Floor: 1,143 sq. ft.
Total: 2,894 sq. ft.
Bonus Space: 206 sq. ft.
Bedrooms: 4
Bathrooms: 3 ½
Width: 45' - 0"
Depth: 72' - 6"
Foundation: Crawlspace

Stately pilasters and a decorative balcony at a second-level window adorn this ornate four-bedroom design. Inside the recessed entryway, columns define the formal dining room. Ahead is a great room with a fireplace, built-in bookshelves, and access to the rear deck. A breakfast nook nestles in a bay window and joins an island kitchen. The master suite with a tray ceiling features a walk-in closet and a pampering garden tub. A versatile loft and three additional bedrooms are found upstairs.

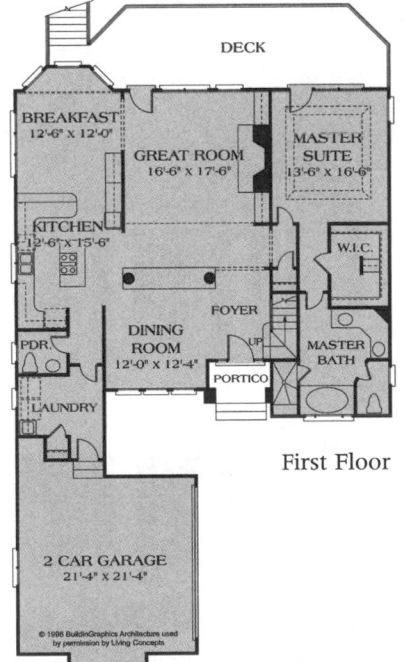

First Floor

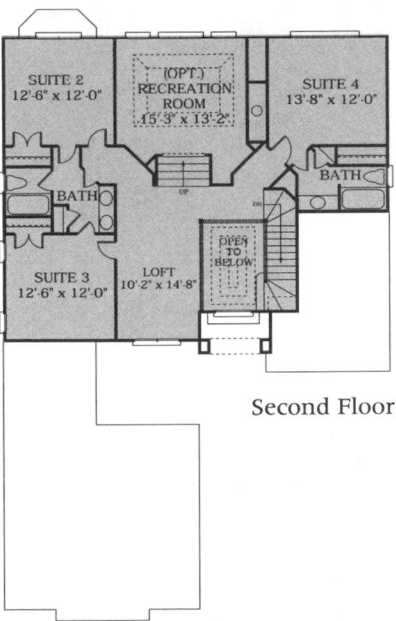

Second Floor

2,500 TO 2,999 SQUARE FEET

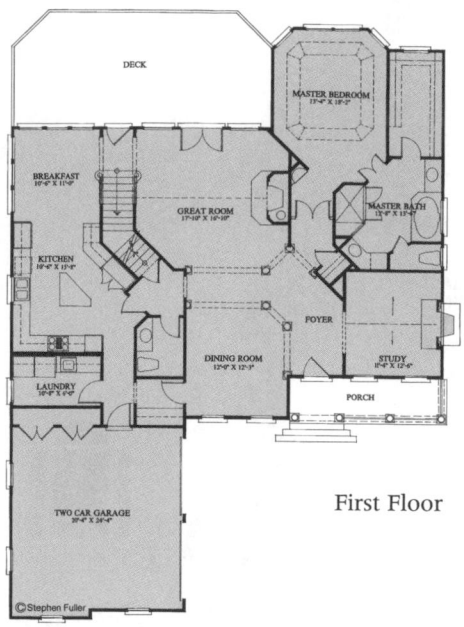

First Floor

Second Floor

HPK2100812

Style: Colonial Revival
First Floor: 1,944 sq. ft.
Second Floor: 954 sq. ft.
Total: 2,898 sq. ft.
Bedrooms: 4
Bathrooms: 3 ½
Width: 51' - 6"
Depth: 73' - 0"
Foundation: Unfinished Walkout Basement

EPLANS.COM

This gracious home combines warm informal materials with a modern livable floor plan to create a true southern classic. The dining room, study, and great room work together to create one large, exciting space. Plenty of counter space and storage make the kitchen user friendly. The master suite is a welcome retreat. Upstairs, two additional bedrooms each have their own vanities within a shared bath; the third bedroom includes its own bath.

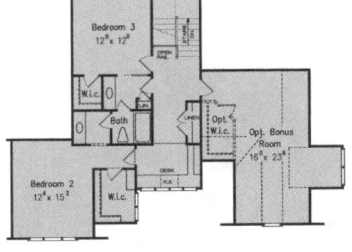

First Floor   Second Floor

HPK2100813

Style: Cottage

First Floor: 2,145 sq. ft.

Second Floor: 754 sq. ft.

Total: 2,899 sq. ft.

Bonus Space: 385 sq. ft.

Bedrooms: 4

Bathrooms: 3

Width: 62' - 4"

Depth: 64' - 0"

Foundation: Crawlspace, Slab, Unfinished Walkout Basement

EPLANS.COM

First Floor

Second Floor

HPK2100814

Style: New American

First Floor: 1,870 sq. ft.

Second Floor: 1,030 sq. ft.

Total: 2,900 sq. ft.

Bonus Space: 294 sq. ft.

Bedrooms: 4

Bathrooms: 3 ½

Width: 50' - 9"

Depth: 66' - 0"

Foundation: Finished Walkout Basement

EPLANS.COM

2,500 TO 2,999 SQUARE FEET

HPK2100815

Style: Farmhouse
First Floor: 1,913 sq. ft.
Second Floor: 997 sq. ft.
Total: 2,910 sq. ft.
Bonus Space: 377 sq. ft.
Bedrooms: 4
Bathrooms: 3 ½
Width: 63' - 0"
Depth: 59' - 4"
Foundation: Crawlspace,
Unfinished Basement

EPLANS.COM

First Floor

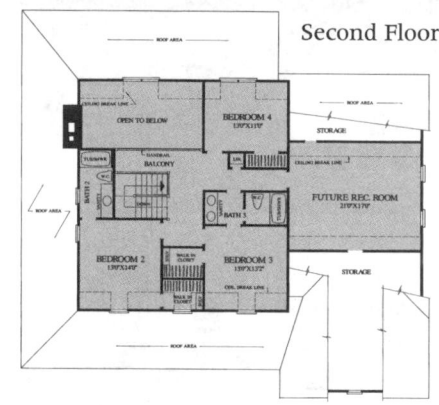

Second Floor

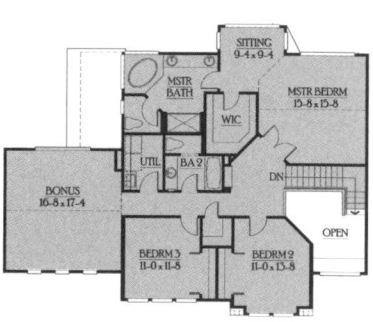

Second Floor

HPK2100816

Style: Craftsman
First Floor: 1,450 sq. ft.
Second Floor: 1,470 sq. ft.
Total: 2,920 sq. ft.
Bedrooms: 3
Bathrooms: 2 ½
Width: 65' - 0"
Depth: 54' - 0"
Foundation: Crawlspace

EPLANS.COM

First Floor

HPK2100817

Plan: HPK2100817

Style: French Country

First Floor: 2,142 sq. ft.

Second Floor: 779 sq. ft.

Total: 2,921 sq. ft.

Bonus Space: 393 sq. ft.

Bedrooms: 3

Bathrooms: 3 ½

Width: 57' - 0"

Depth: 81' - 0"

Foundation: Crawlspace

EPLANS.COM

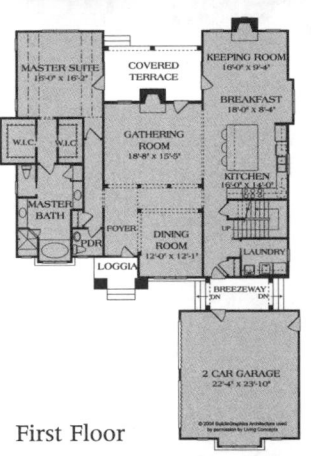

First Floor

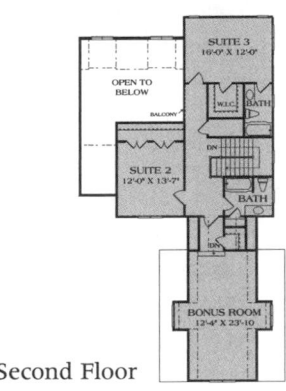

Second Floor

HPK2100818

Style: French Country

First Floor: 2,215 sq. ft.

Second Floor: 708 sq. ft.

Total: 2,923 sq. ft.

Bonus Space: 420 sq. ft.

Bedrooms: 3

Bathrooms: 3

Width: 76' - 4"

Depth: 69' - 10"

Foundation: Crawlspace

EPLANS.COM

First Floor

Second Floor

2,500 TO 2,999 SQUARE FEET

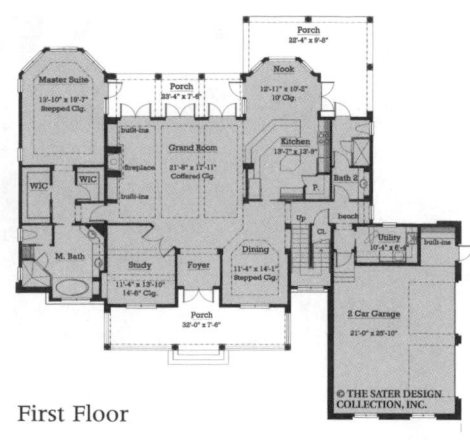

First Floor

Second Floor

©The Sater Design Collection, Inc.

HPK2100819

Style: Country

First Floor: 2,215 sq. ft.

Second Floor: 708 sq. ft.

Total: 2,923 sq. ft.

Bonus Space: 420 sq. ft.

Bedrooms: 3

Bathrooms: 3

Width: 76' - 4"

Depth: 69' - 10"

Foundation: Crawlspace

EPLANS.COM

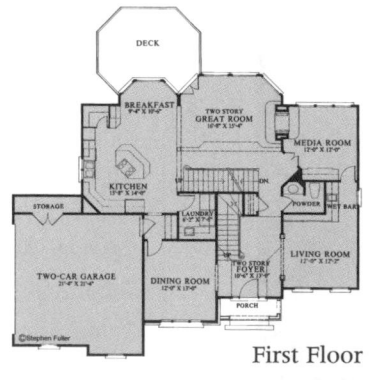

First Floor

Second Floor

HPK2100820

Style: French Country

First Floor: 1,475 sq. ft.

Second Floor: 1,460 sq. ft.

Total: 2,935 sq. ft.

Bedrooms: 4

Bathrooms: 3 ½

Width: 57' - 6"

Depth: 46' - 6"

Foundation: Unfinished Walkout Basement

EPLANS.COM

©Stephen Fuller, Inc.

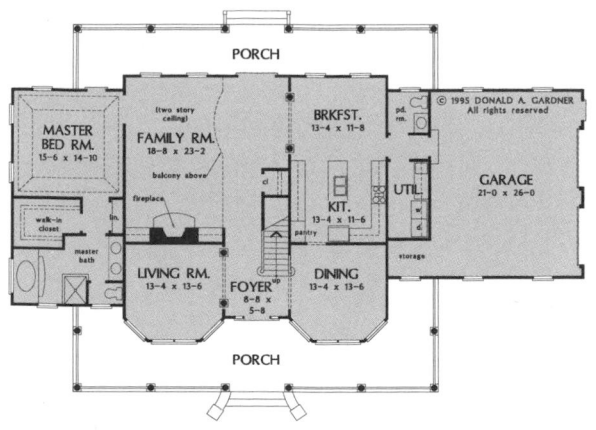

First Floor

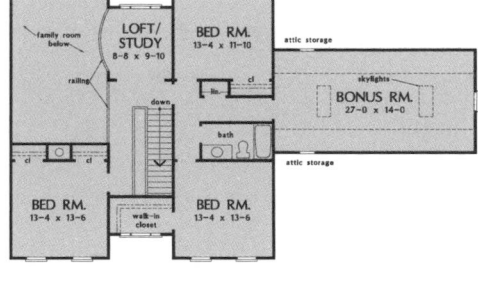

Second Floor

HPK2100821

Style: Farmhouse
First Floor: 1,943 sq. ft.
Second Floor: 1,000 sq. ft.
Total: 2,943 sq. ft.
Bonus Space: 403 sq. ft.
Bedrooms: 4
Bathrooms: 2 ½
Width: 79' - 10"
Depth: 51' - 8"

EPLANS.COM

HPK2100822

Style: Farmhouse
First Floor: 1,976 sq. ft.
Second Floor: 970 sq. ft.
Total: 2,946 sq. ft.
Bedrooms: 4
Bathrooms: 3 ½
Width: 58' - 8"
Depth: 66' - 4"

EPLANS.COM

First Floor

Find a matching garage on page 182.

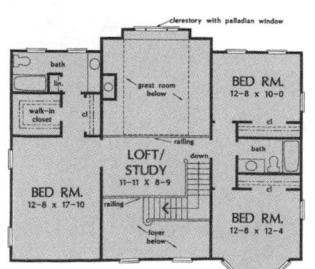

Second Floor

2,500 TO 2,999 SQUARE FEET

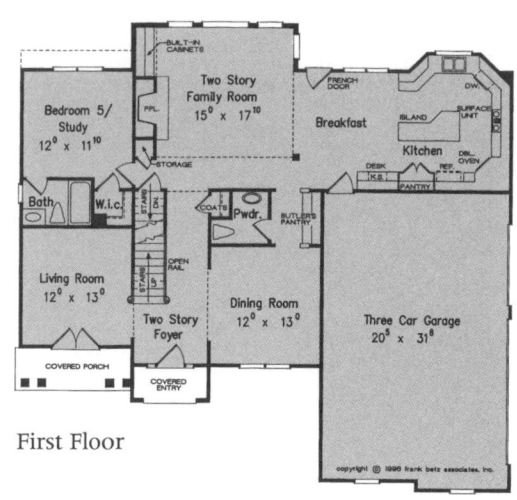

First Floor

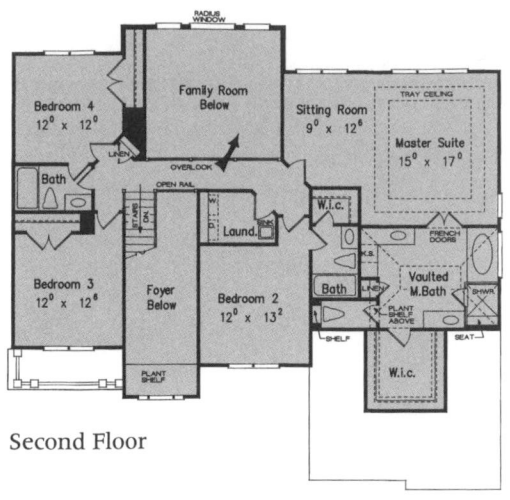

Second Floor

The nearly octagonal shape of the kitchen, with its long work island, will please the family's gourmet cook in this traditional design. The breakfast room opens to the back through a French door and flows into the two-story family room. A bedroom with a private bath and walk-in closet could be an in-law suite. The other four bedrooms are upstairs. The master suite includes a sitting room and luxurious bath.

HPK2100823

Style: New American

First Floor: 1,463 sq. ft.

Second Floor: 1,490 sq. ft.

Total: 2,953 sq. ft.

Bedrooms: 5

Bathrooms: 4 ½

Width: 54' - 0"

Depth: 51' - 6"

Foundation: Crawlspace, Slab, Unfinished Walkout Basement

EPLANS.COM

HPK2100824

Style: New American
First Floor: 2,270 sq. ft.
Second Floor: 685 sq. ft.
Total: 2,955 sq. ft.
Bonus Space: 563 sq. ft.
Bedrooms: 3
Bathrooms: 2 ½
Width: 75' - 1"
Depth: 53' - 6"

Hipped rooflines, sunburst windows, and French-style shutters are the defining elements of this home's exterior. The lavish great room is complete with a fireplace, built-in shelves, a vaulted ceiling, and views to the rear patio. The island kitchen easily accesses a pantry and a desk and flows into the bayed breakfast area. The first-floor master bedroom boasts a fireplace and an amenity-filled private bath. Two additional bedrooms reside upstairs, along with a sizable bonus room.

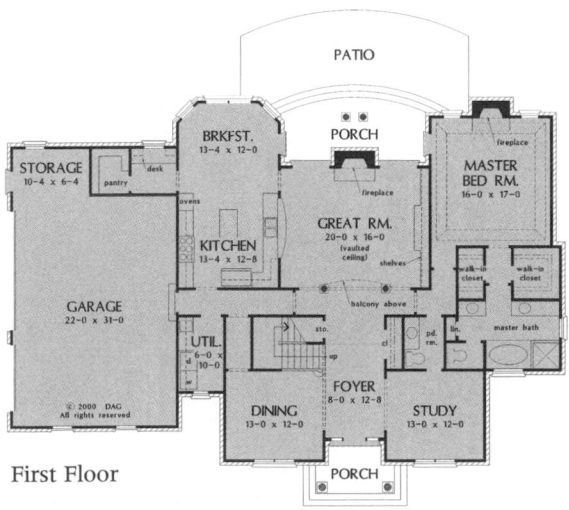

First Floor

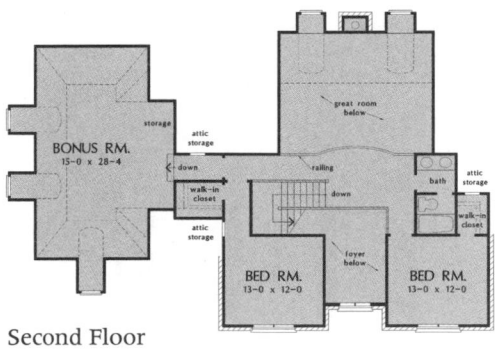

Second Floor

2,500 TO 2,999 SQUARE FEET

First Floor

Second Floor

HPK2100825

Style: Shingle
First Floor: 1,866 sq. ft.
Second Floor: 1,090 sq. ft.
Total: 2,956 sq. ft.
Bonus Space: 424 sq. ft.
Bedrooms: 4
Bathrooms: 3 ½
Width: 51' - 4"
Depth: 68' - 4"
Foundation: Crawlspace

EPLANS.COM

Muntin windows, keystone lintels, and steeply pitched rooflines mark this home's exterior with grace and style. A dining room situated to the right of the foyer is linked to the kitchen through a convenient door. The gathering room is enhanced with a fireplace and French doors to the backyard. The master suite, located on the first floor for privacy, includes amenities that homeowners love. Three suites reside upstairs, as do two full baths, an unfinished recreation room, and a balcony that looks to the foyer below.

HPK2100826

Style: Colonial Revival
First Floor: 1,940 sq. ft.
Second Floor: 1,025 sq. ft.
Total: 2,965 sq. ft.
Bedrooms: 4
Bathrooms: 3 ½
Width: 60' - 0"
Depth: 48' - 0"
Foundation: Finished Walkout Basement

EPLANS.COM

Wood siding, shutters, flower boxes, and an arched entrance give this home immediate appeal. Inside, the kitchen features an octagonal countertop and is open to a spacious breakfast area and a vaulted great room, both with access to the deck. The master suite boasts a bay window overlooking the backyard, a door to the deck, and a private bath with a garden tub. The second floor offers two bedrooms that share a full bath and another bedroom with a walk-in closet and a private bath.

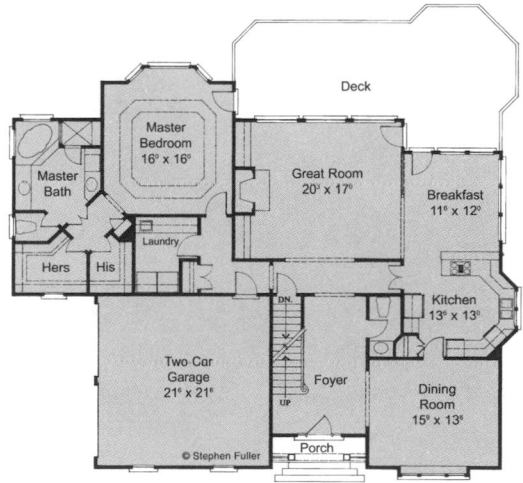

First Floor

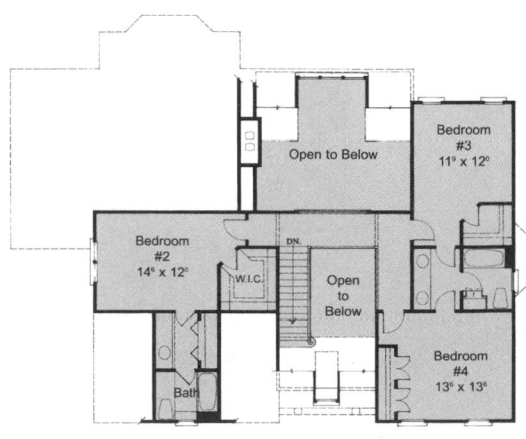

Second Floor

2,500 TO 2,999 SQUARE FEET

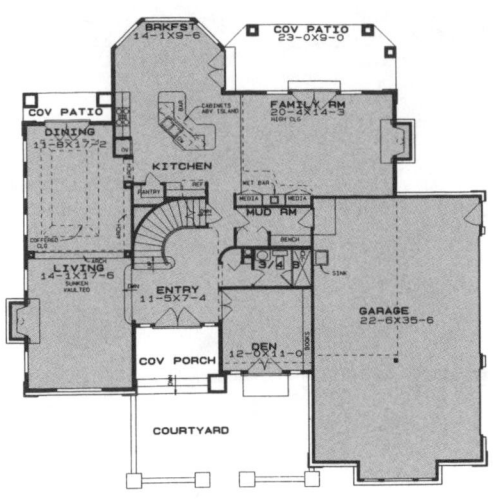

First Floor

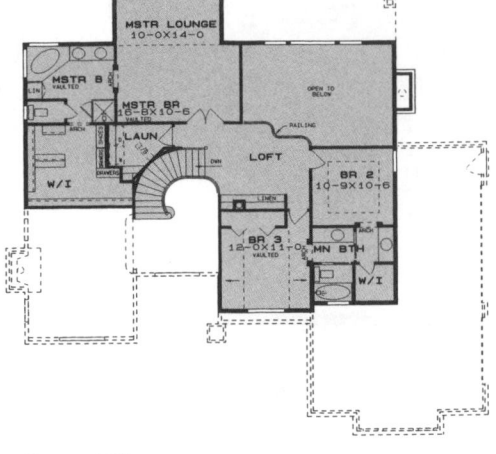

Second Floor

This home makes a strong statement of elegance and history. Federal and Colonial elements combine to create a timeless look. The dining room is oversized to accommodate large gatherings. Convert the den to a guest room or fourth bedroom as needed. The kitchen features a unique angular island bar and a large pantry. Expansive windows open the home to the covered rear patio and yard. The master suite is separated from the secondary bedrooms by a loft. The second-floor laundry can be moved to the main-floor mudroom if desired.

HPK2100827

Style: New American
First Floor: 1,715 sq. ft.
Second Floor: 1,257 sq. ft.
Total: 2,972 sq. ft.
Bedrooms: 3
Bathrooms: 3
Width: 62' - 0"
Depth: 63' - 6"
Foundation: Unfinished Basement

EPLANS.COM

©The Sater Design Collection, Inc.

HPK2100828

Style: New American
First Floor: 2,096 sq. ft.
Second Floor: 892 sq. ft.
Total: 2,988 sq. ft.
Bedrooms: 3
Bathrooms: 3 ½
Width: 56' - 0"
Depth: 54' - 0"
Foundation: Unfinished Walkout Basement

EPLANS.COM

Siding and shingles give this home a Craftsman look while columns and gables suggest a more traditional style. The foyer opens to a short flight of stairs that leads to the great room. To the left, the open island kitchen has a pass-through to the great room and easy service to the dining bay. The secluded master suite features two walk-in closets, a luxurious bath, and veranda access. Upstairs, two family bedrooms have their own full baths and share a loft area.

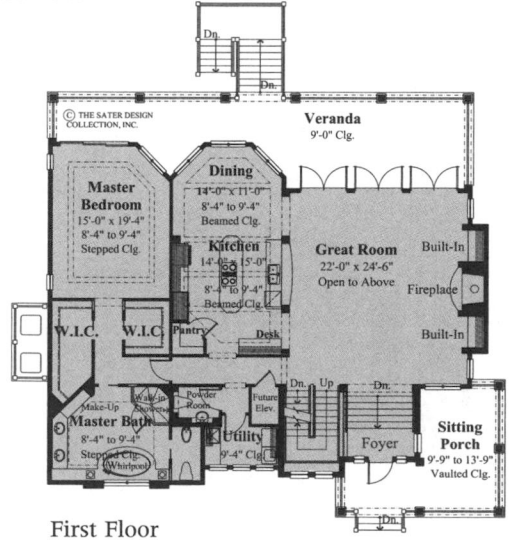

First Floor

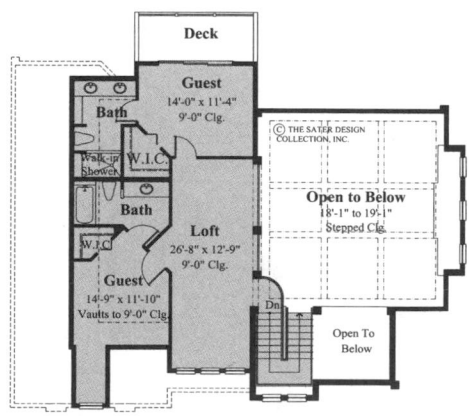

Second Floor

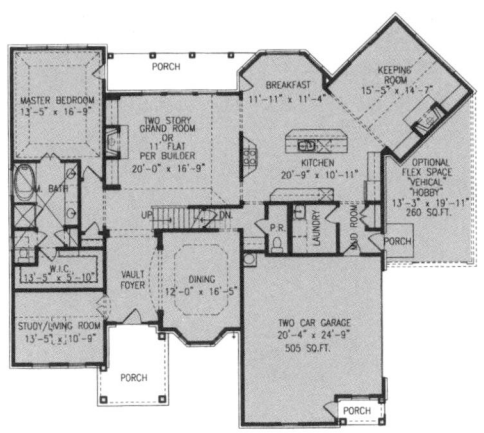

First Floor

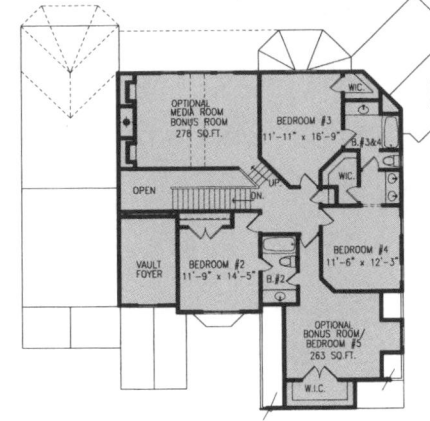

Second Floor

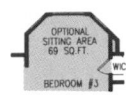

Optional Layout

HPK2100829

Style: New American

First Floor: 2,160 sq. ft.

Second Floor: 828 sq. ft.

Total: 2,988 sq. ft.

Bonus Space: 541 sq. ft.

Bedrooms: 4

Bathrooms: 3 ½

Width: 68' - 3"

Depth: 60' - 11"

Foundation: Unfinished Walkout Basement

EPLANS.COM

This delightful vacation home, designed for relaxation, will fit as well on a lakefront as in the mountains. Rear and front covered porches help to extend the living space outdoors. Three upstairs bedrooms, with an option for a fourth, offer plenty of room to put up family members and guests. A possible media room or office on the same level allows space to get some work done at home. The hub of family activity will be the area that includes the keeping room with a cozy fireplace.

©1997 William E Poole Designs, Inc.

HPK2100830

Style: Country
First Floor: 2,014 sq. ft.
Second Floor: 976 sq. ft.
Total: 2,990 sq. ft.
Bonus Space: 390 sq. ft.
Bedrooms: 4
Bathrooms: 3 ½
Width: 73' - 9"
Depth: 55' - 5"
**Foundation: Crawlspace,
Unfinished Basement**

EPLANS.COM

Wide steps lead up to a covered front porch, inviting one to step inside and appreciate the welcome expressed by this fine four-bedroom home. A pocket door leads from the living room into the spacious family room, where a fireplace waits to warm cool fall evenings. The L-shaped island kitchen offers an adjacent breakfast area, as well as a pantry and built-in desk. The first-floor master suite is designed to pamper with private outdoor access. Upstairs, three family bedrooms, two full baths, and a large future recreation room complete the plan.

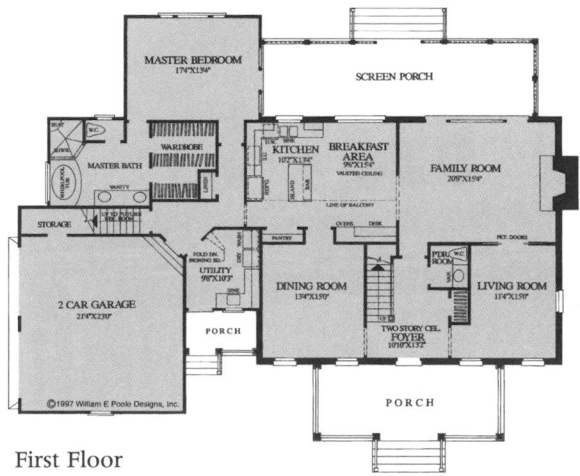

First Floor

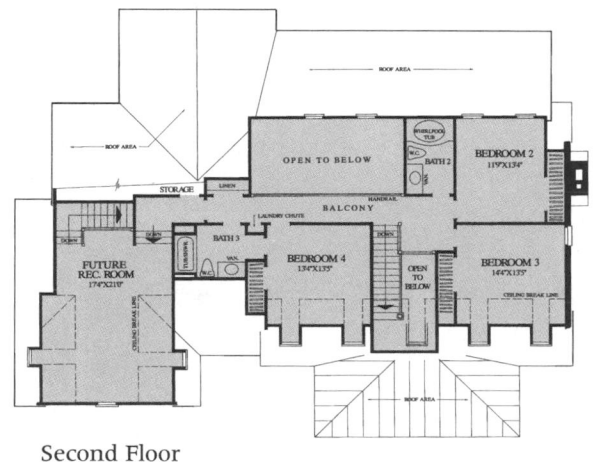

Second Floor

2,500 TO 2,999 SQUARE FEET

First Floor

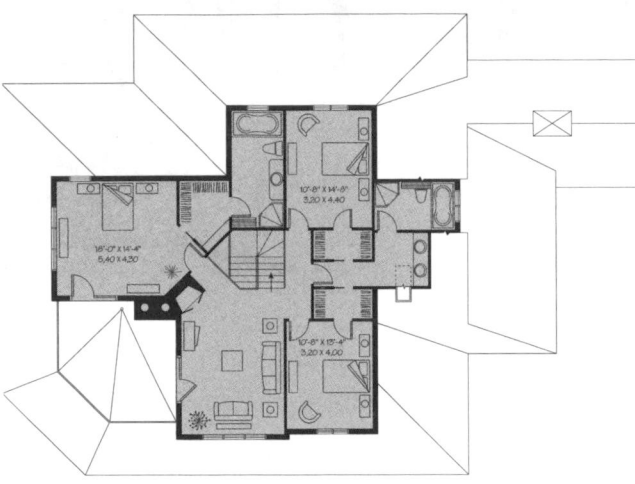

Second Floor

HPK2100831

Plan: HPK2100831

Style: Farmhouse

First Floor: 1,654 sq. ft.

Second Floor: 1,338 sq. ft.

Total: 2,992 sq. ft.

Bedrooms: 4

Bathrooms: 3 ½

Width: 72' - 0"

Depth: 52' - 0"

Foundation: Unfinished Basement

EPLANS.COM

You'll never find a more inviting home than this! Three French-door entrances open to a great layout; from the formal foyer, a showcase kitchen is on the left, joined by an airy dining room. Continue to the family room, warmed by a hearth. The master suite is located on this level, adorned with porch access. Rounding out the first floor is a three-car garage with plenty of storage space. Upstairs, three bedrooms, one of which could be a secondary master suite, share a loft sitting area with a fireplace and access to the upper-level porch.

HPK2100832

Style: Colonial Revival

First Floor: 1,581 sq. ft.

Second Floor: 1,415 sq. ft.

Total: 2,996 sq. ft.

Bedrooms: 4

Bathrooms: 3

Width: 55' - 0"

Depth: 52' - 0"

Foundation: Finished Walkout Basement

Classical details and a stately brick exterior accentuate the grace and timeless elegance of this home. The two-story great room awaits, featuring a wet bar and warming fireplace. To the left is the sunlit breakfast room and efficient kitchen. Upstairs, the master suite features a sun deck, while two large family bedrooms offer separate vanities and share a bath. This home is designed with a walkout basement foundation.

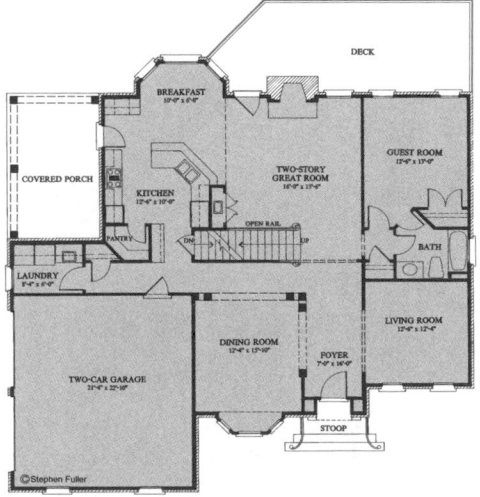

First Floor

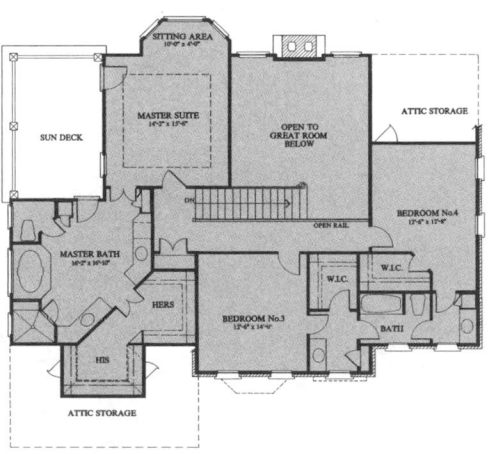

Second Floor

2,500 TO 2,999 SQUARE FEET

Deck

Master
Bedroom
13³ x 18³

Breakfast
10⁶ x 11⁰

Great
Room
17⁹ x 16⁹

Kitchen

10⁶ x 15⁹

Dining
Room
12⁰ x 12³

Study
11³ x 12⁶

Porch

© Stephen Fuller, Inc.

Two Car
Garage
20³ x 24³

©Stephen Fuller

First Floor

Bedroom
2
10⁶ x 14⁰

Bedroom
3
12⁰ x 12⁶

© Stephen Fuller, Inc.

Bedroom
4
11⁰ x 22⁰

Second Floor

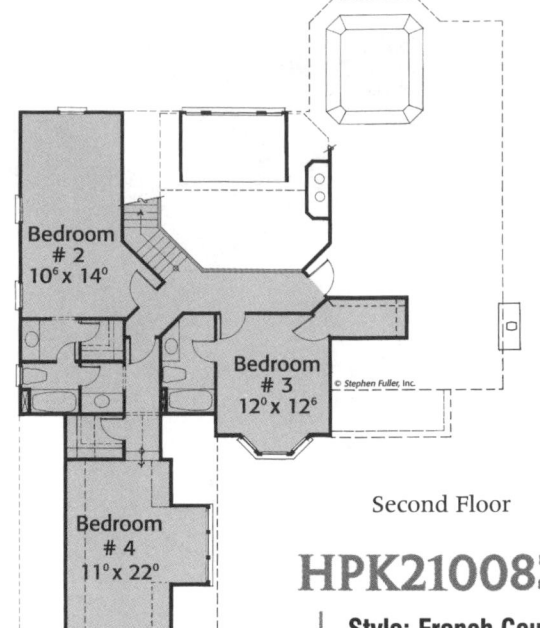

HPK2100833

Style: French Country

First Floor: 1,944 sq. ft.

Second Floor: 1,055 sq. ft.

Total: 2,999 sq. ft.

Bedrooms: 4

Bathrooms: 3 ½

Width: 51' - 6"

Depth: 72' - 0"

**Foundation: Finished
Walkout Basement**

EPLANS.COM

Interesting rooflines and a two-story bay window create a unique cottage farmhouse appearance. The foyer leads to the dining room and great room, both graced with columns. The great room features a fireplace and opens to the deck. The right wing is devoted to an amenity-filled master suite with convenient access to the study. The second floor contains three bedrooms and two baths.

HPK2100834

Style: Cottage
Main Level: 1,544 sq. ft.
Lower Level: 1,018 sq. ft.
Total: 2,562 sq. ft.
Bedrooms: 4
Bathrooms: 3
Width: 40' - 0"
Depth: 60' - 0"
Foundation: Finished Walkout Basement

EPLANS.COM

This Cape Cod design is enhanced with shingles, stone detailing, and muntin windows. The entry is flanked on the left by a bedroom/den, perfect for overnight guests or a cozy place to relax. The master bedroom features a private bath. Two family bedrooms and a spacious game room complete the lower level.

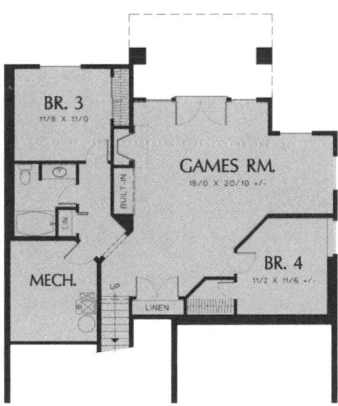

Lower Level

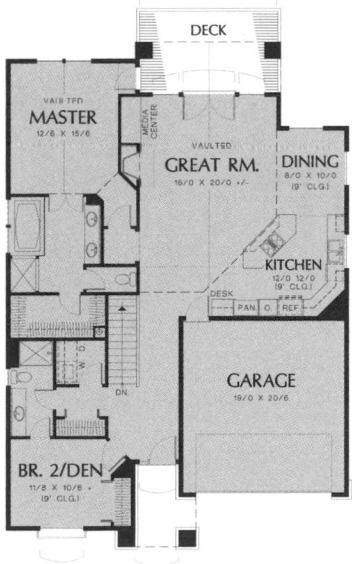

Main Level

HPK2100835

Style: Federal - Adams

First Floor: 1,694 sq. ft.

Second Floor: 874 sq. ft.

Total: 2,568 sq. ft.

Bonus Space: 440 sq. ft.

Bedrooms: 3

Bathrooms: 3 ½

Width: 74' - 2"

Depth: 46' - 8"

Foundation: Crawlspace, Unfinished Basement

EPLANS.COM

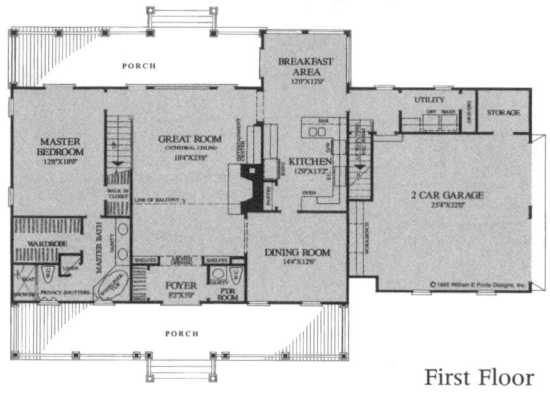

First Floor

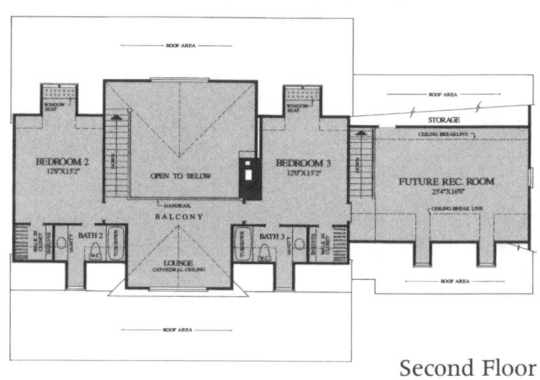

Second Floor

HPK2100836

Style: New American

First Floor: 1,642 sq. ft.

Second Floor: 927 sq. ft.

Total: 2,569 sq. ft.

Bedrooms: 3

Bathrooms: 2 ½

Width: 60' - 0"

Depth: 44' - 6"

Foundation: Slab

EPLANS.COM

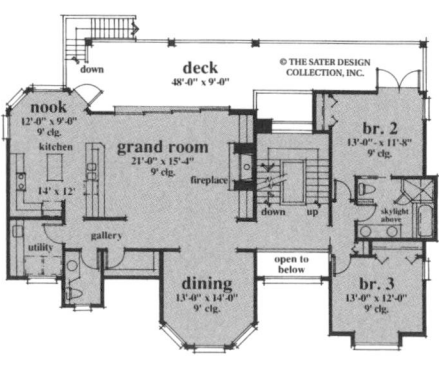

First Floor

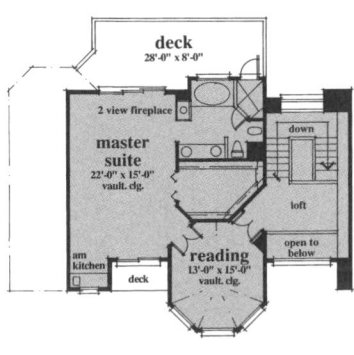

Second Floor

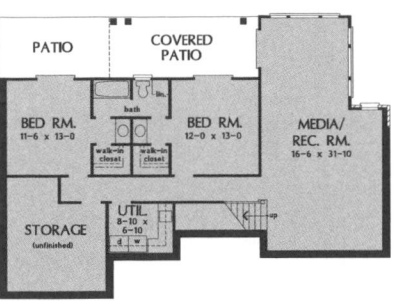

Lower Level

Main Level

HPK2100837

Style: French Country

Main Level: 1,472 sq. ft.

Lower Level: 1,211 sq. ft.

Total: 2,683 sq. ft.

Bedrooms: 3

Bathrooms: 2 ½

Width: 54' - 0"

Depth: 40' - 8"

EPLANS.COM

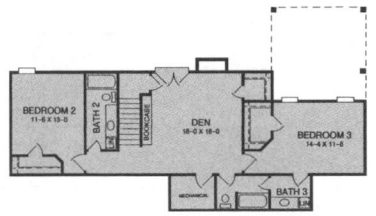

Lower Level

Main Level

HPK2100838

Style: Country

Main Level: 1,709 sq. ft.

Lower Level: 1,051 sq. ft.

Total: 2,760 sq. ft.

Bedrooms: 3

Bathrooms: 3 ½

Width: 60' - 10"

Depth: 69' - 3"

Foundation: Slab, Unfinished Basement

EPLANS.COM

2,500 TO 2,999 SQUARE FEET

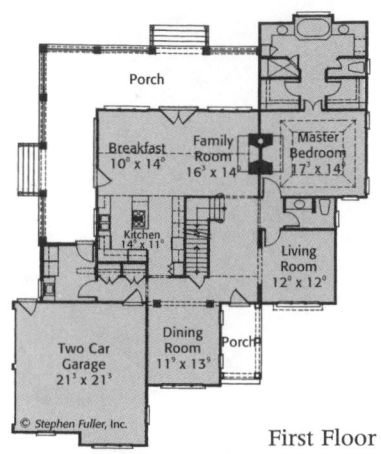

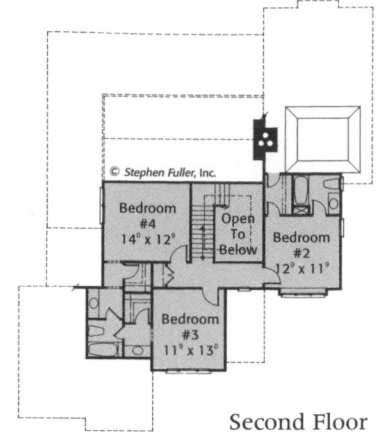

First Floor

Second Floor

© Stephen Fuller, Inc.

HPK2100839

Style: Cottage
First Floor: 1,870 sq. ft.
Second Floor: 910 sq. ft.
Total: 2,780 sq. ft.
Bedrooms: 4
Bathrooms: 3 ½
Width: 58' - 0"
Depth: 71' - 0"
Foundation: Unfinished Walkout Basement

EPLANS.COM

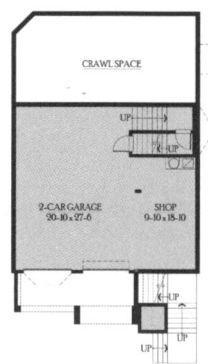

Lower Level

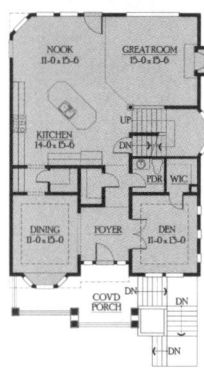

Main Level

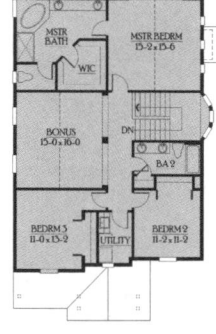

Upper Level

HPK2100840

Style: Craftsman
Main Level: 1,405 sq. ft.
Upper Level: 1,348 sq. ft.
Lower Level: 42 sq. ft.
Total: 2,795 sq. ft.
Bedrooms: 3
Bathrooms: 2 ½
Width: 32' - 0"
Depth: 52' - 6"
Foundation: Crawlspace

EPLANS.COM

ORDER BLUEPRINTS ANYTIME AT EPLANS.COM OR 1-800-521-6797

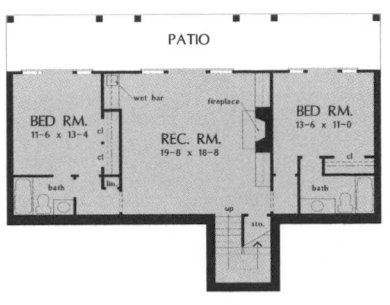

Lower Level

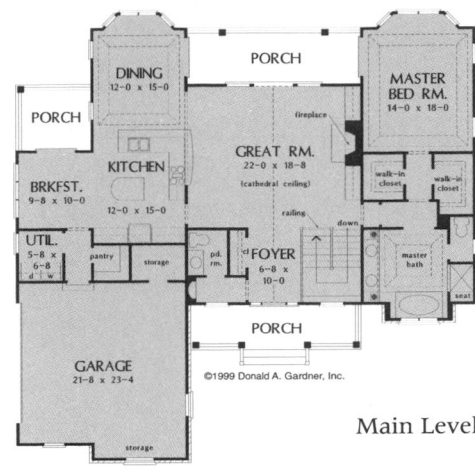

Main Level

© 1999 Donald A. Gardner, Inc.

HPK2100841

Style: French Country
Main Level: 1,725 sq. ft.
Lower Level: 1,090 sq. ft.
Total: 2,815 sq. ft.
Bedrooms: 3
Bathrooms: 3 ½
Width: 59' - 0"
Depth: 59' - 4"

EPLANS.COM

HPK2100842

Style: New American
First Floor: 2,044 sq. ft.
Second Floor: 896 sq. ft.
Total: 2,940 sq. ft.
Bonus Space: 197 sq. ft.
Bedrooms: 4
Bathrooms: 3 ½
Width: 63' - 0"
Depth: 54' - 0"
Foundation: Crawlspace, Slab, Unfinished Walkout Basement

EPLANS.COM

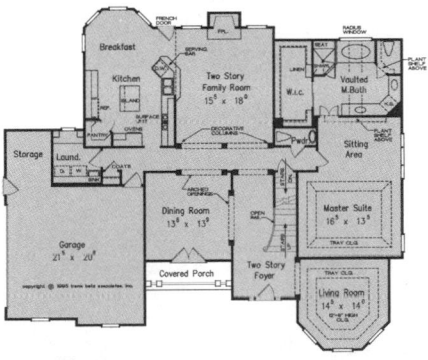

First Floor

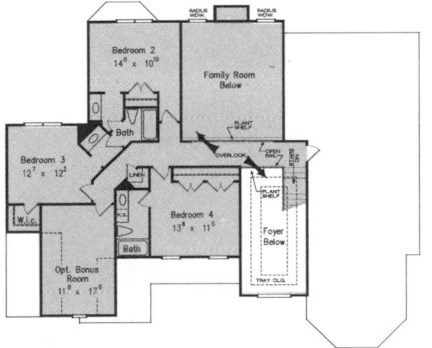

Second Floor

2,500 TO 2,999 SQUARE FEET

HPK2100843

Style: French Country
Main Level: 1,682 sq. ft.
Upper Level: 577 sq. ft.
Lower Level: 690 sq. ft.
Total: 2,949 sq. ft.
Bonus Space: 459 sq. ft.
Bedrooms: 4
Bathrooms: 3 ½
Width: 79' - 0"
Depth: 68' - 2"

EPLANS.COM

© 2000 Donald A. Gardner, Inc.

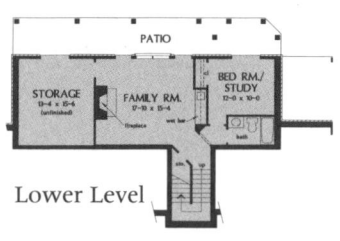

Lower Level

Main Level

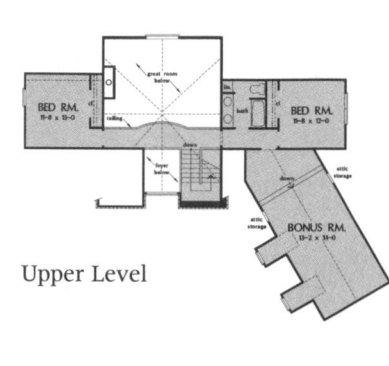

Upper Level

HPK2100844

Style: Country
Main Level: 1,662 sq. ft.
Upper Level: 585 sq. ft.
Lower Level: 706 sq. ft.
Total: 2,953 sq. ft.
Bonus Space: 575 sq. ft.
Bedrooms: 4
Bathrooms: 3 ½
Width: 81' - 4"
Depth: 68' - 8"

EPLANS.COM

© 1999 Donald A. Gardner, Inc.

Lower Level

Main Level

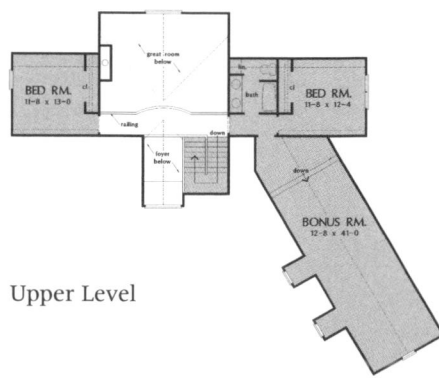

Upper Level

HPK2100845

© 1998 Donald A. Gardner, Inc.

Style: Craftsman
Main Level: 1,810 sq. ft.
Lower Level: 1,146 sq. ft.
Total: 2,956 sq. ft.
Bedrooms: 4
Bathrooms: 3
Width: 68' - 4"
Depth: 60' - 10"

EPLANS.COM

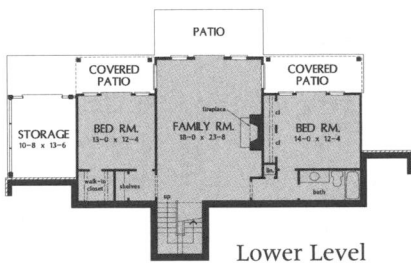

Lower Level

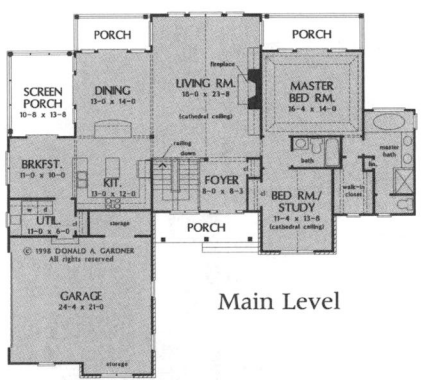

Main Level

HPK2100846

Style: New American
First Floor: 2,222 sq. ft.
Second Floor: 751 sq. ft.
Total: 2,973 sq. ft.
Bonus Space: 384 sq. ft.
Bedrooms: 3
Bathrooms: 3 ½
Width: 67' - 4"
Depth: 55' - 0"
Foundation: Unfinished Walkout Basement

EPLANS.COM

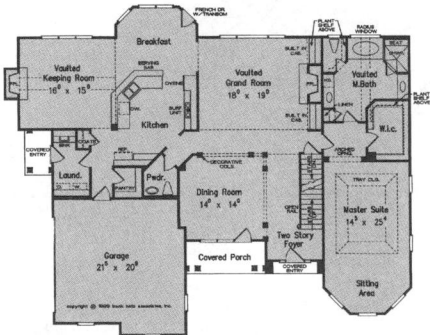

First Floor

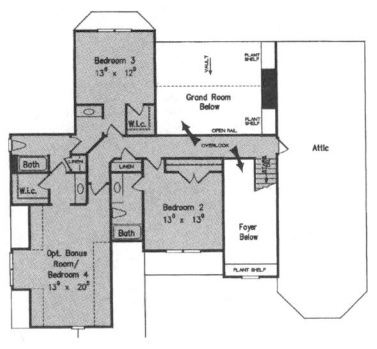

Second Floor

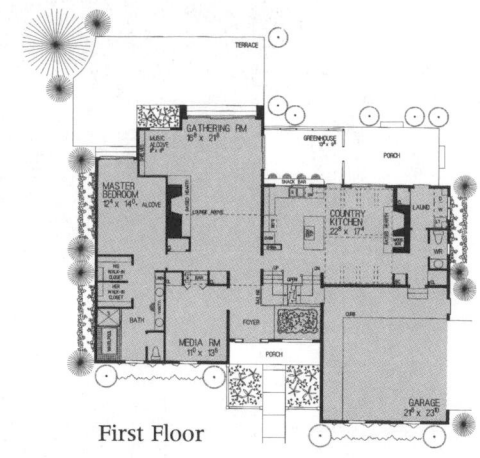

First Floor

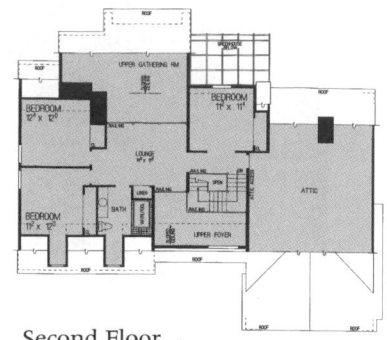

Second Floor

HPK2101525

Style: Cottage
First Floor: 1,953 sq. ft.
Second Floor: 895 sq. ft.
Total: 2,848 sq. ft.
Bedrooms: 4
Bathrooms: 2 1/2
Width: 63' - 0"
Depth: 56' - 8"
Foundation: Unfinished Basement

EPLANS.COM

HPK2100847

Style: French Country
Main Level: 1,901 sq. ft.
Lower Level: 1,075 sq. ft.
Total: 2,976 sq. ft.
Bedrooms: 4
Bathrooms: 3
Width: 64' - 0"
Depth: 62' - 4"

EPLANS.COM

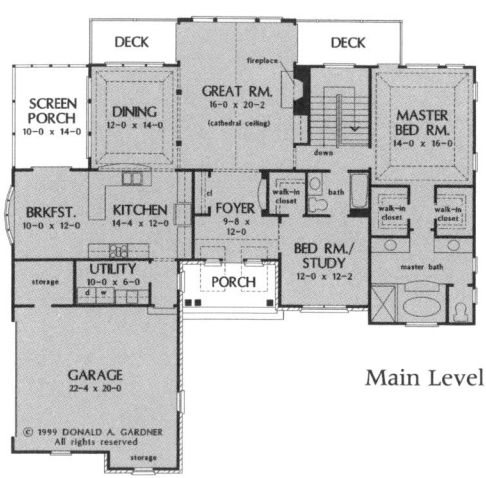

Lower Level

Main Level

© 1999 Donald A. Gardner, Inc.

© Stephen Fuller, Inc.

HPK2100848

Style: Tudor
First Floor: 1,983 sq. ft.
Second Floor: 1,006 sq. ft.
Total: 2,989 sq. ft.
Bedrooms: 4
Bathrooms: 3 ½
Width: 50' - 9"
Depth: 62' - 3"
Foundation: Unfinished Walkout Basement

EPLANS.COM

A sweeping storybook roofline and lovely cross-gabling lets this design take charge of corner lots and full-figured landscapes. Tudor details, including a charming off-center entry, beckon visitors inside, where a small foyer introduces the two-story family room and nook. A first-floor master suite resides at the corner of the plan, where it finds privacy and generous rearward views. Three more bedrooms, upstairs, share two baths. The integrated garage preserves period appearance of the exterior.

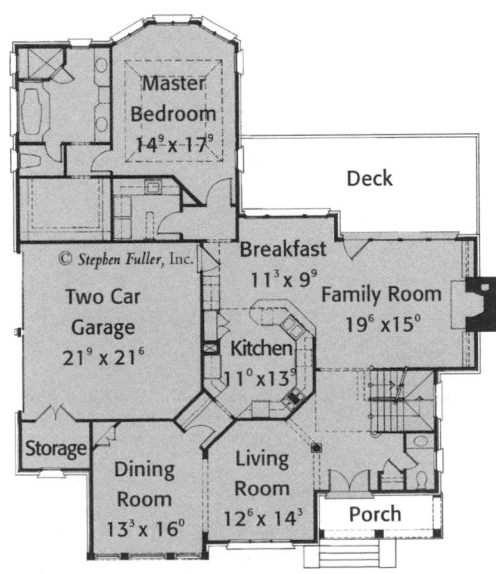

First Floor

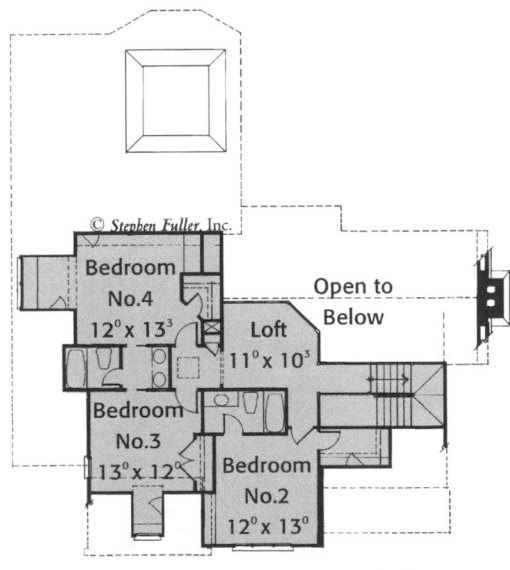

Second Floor

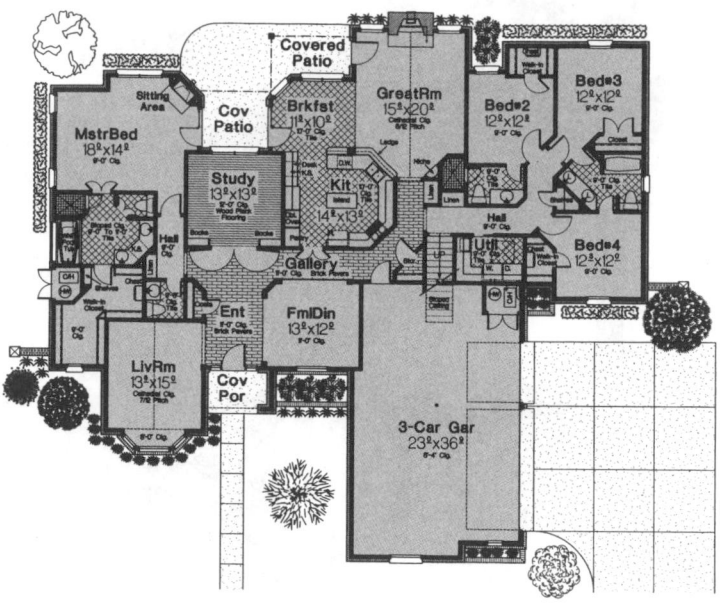

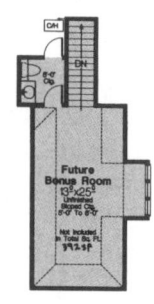

The European appeal of this spacious cottage plan features graceful elegance on the exterior, with abundant amenities found inside. The foyer is flanked by formal living and dining rooms. Straight ahead, double doors open into a study. The master suite features a sitting area with a fireplace and a private bath that extends into an enormous walk-in closet. The island kitchen is central and connects to the breakfast room, which is open to the great room at the rear of the plan. Three family bedrooms are located to the right of the plan. A future bonus room is available for additional expansion.

HPK2100849

EPLANS.COM

Style: French Country
Square Footage: 3,012
Bonus Space: 392 sq. ft.
Bedrooms: 4
Bathrooms: 3 ½
Width: 80' - 0"
Depth: 72' - 0"
Foundation: Crawlspace, Slab

HPK2100850

Style: Norman
Square Footage: 3,032
Bedrooms: 3
Bathrooms: 3
Width: 73' - 0"
Depth: 87' - 8"
Foundation: Slab

EPLANS.COM

HPK2100851

Style: Italianate
Square Footage: 3,034
Bedrooms: 3
Bathrooms: 3
Width: 112' - 0"
Depth: 74' - 6"
Foundation: Slab

EPLANS.COM

HPK2100852

Style: French Country

Square Footage: 3,049

Bonus Space: 868 sq. ft.

Bedrooms: 3

Bathrooms: 2 ½

Width: 72' - 6"

Depth: 78' - 10"

Foundation: Crawlspace, Unfinished Basement

EPLANS.COM

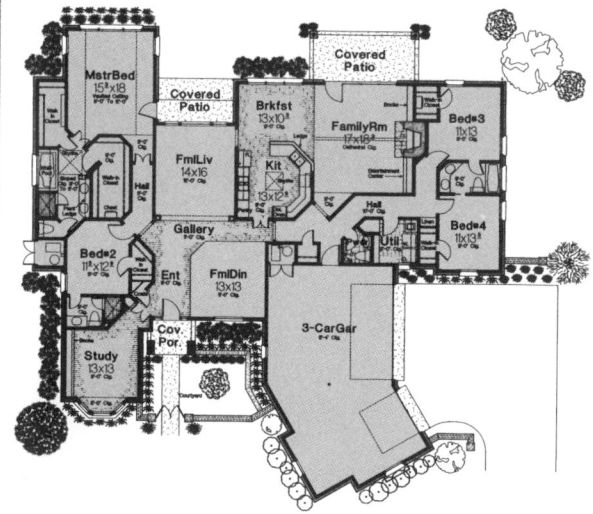

HPK2100853

Style: French Country

Square Footage: 3,056

Bedrooms: 4

Bathrooms: 3 ½

Width: 80' - 0"

Depth: 79' - 9"

Foundation: Slab, Unfinished Basement

EPLANS.COM

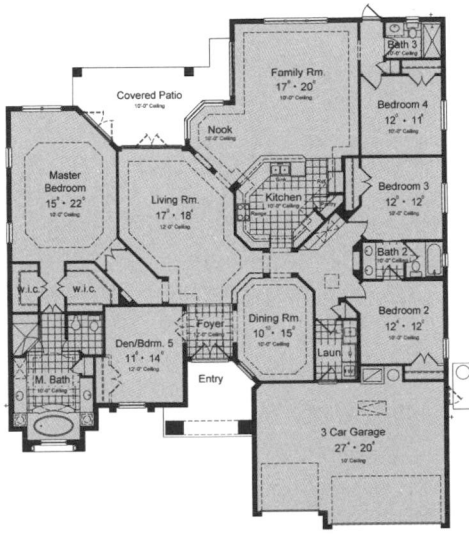

HPK2100854

Style: Mediterranean

Square Footage: 3,060

Bedrooms: 4

Bathrooms: 3

Width: 64' - 8"

Depth: 74' - 8"

Foundation: Slab

EPLANS.COM

© 2002 Donald A. Gardner, Inc.

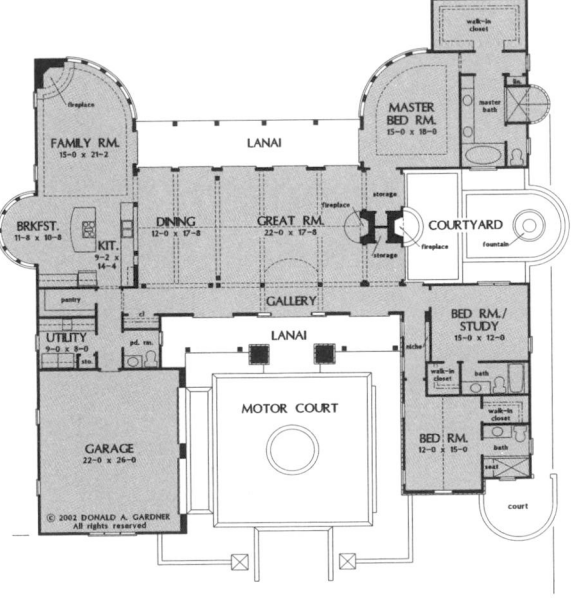

© 2002 DONALD A. GARDNER
All rights reserved

HPK2100855

Style: Southwest

Square Footage: 3,061

Bedrooms: 3

Bathrooms: 3 ½

Width: 86' - 1"

Depth: 84' - 8"

EPLANS.COM

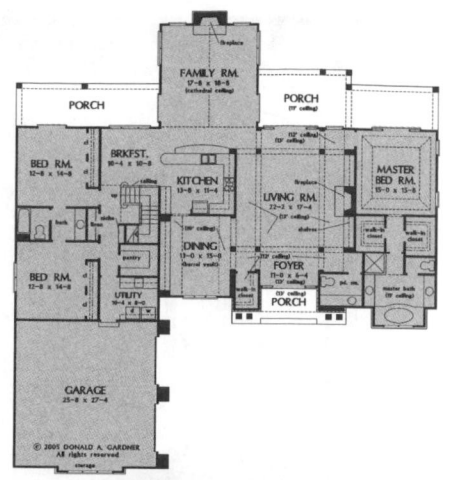

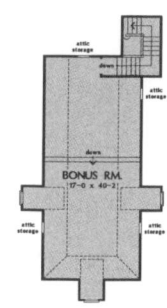

HPK2100856

Style: French Country

Square Footage: 3,068

Bonus Space: 746 sq. ft.

Bedrooms: 3

Bathrooms: 2 ½

Width: 78' - 4"

Depth: 86' - 3"

EPLANS.COM

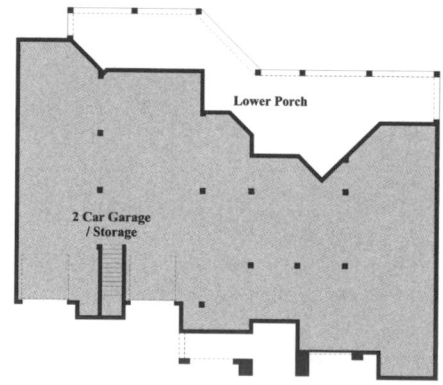

HPK2100857

Style: Cottage

Square Footage: 3,074

Bedrooms: 3

Bathrooms: 3 ½

Width: 77' - 0"

Depth: 66' - 8"

Foundation: Island Basement

EPLANS.COM

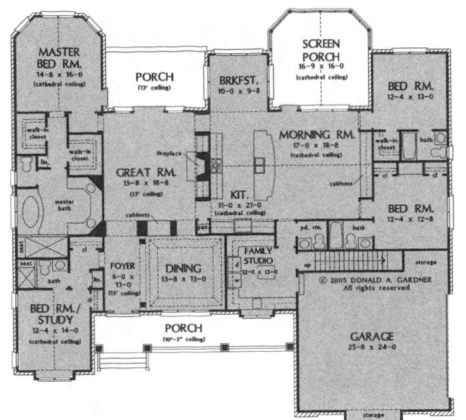

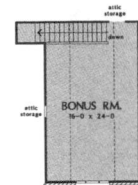

HPK2100858

Style: New American
Square Footage: 3,080
Bonus Space: 498 sq. ft.
Bedrooms: 4
Bathrooms: 4 ½
Width: 75' - 7"
Depth: 72' - 3"

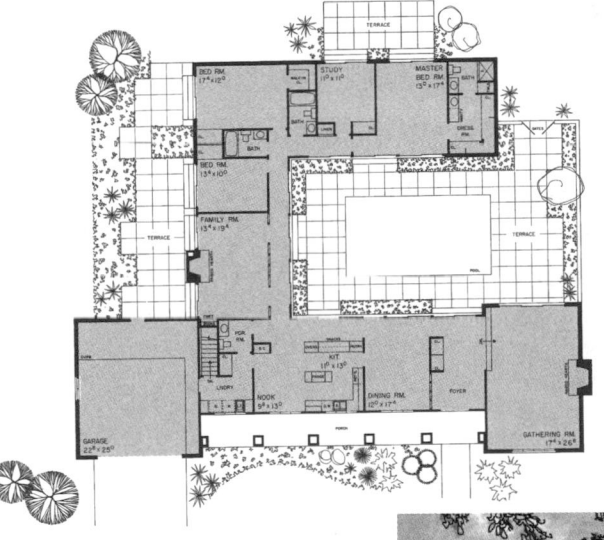

HPK2100859

Style: Ranch
Square Footage: 3,110
Bedrooms: 3
Bathrooms: 3 ½
Width: 95' - 8"
Depth: 74' - 4"
Foundation: Unfinished Basement

3,000 TO 3,499 SQUARE FEET

HPK2100860

Style: Country

Square Footage: 3,168

Bonus Space: 360 sq. ft.

Bedrooms: 3

Bathrooms: 2 ½

Width: 89' - 3"

Depth: 74' - 3"

Foundation: Crawlspace, Unfinished Walkout Basement

EPLANS.COM

© The Sater Design Collection, Inc.

HPK2100861

Style: New American

Square Footage: 3,185

Bedrooms: 3

Bathrooms: 3 ½

Width: 65' - 0"

Depth: 90' - 0"

Foundation: Slab

EPLANS.COM

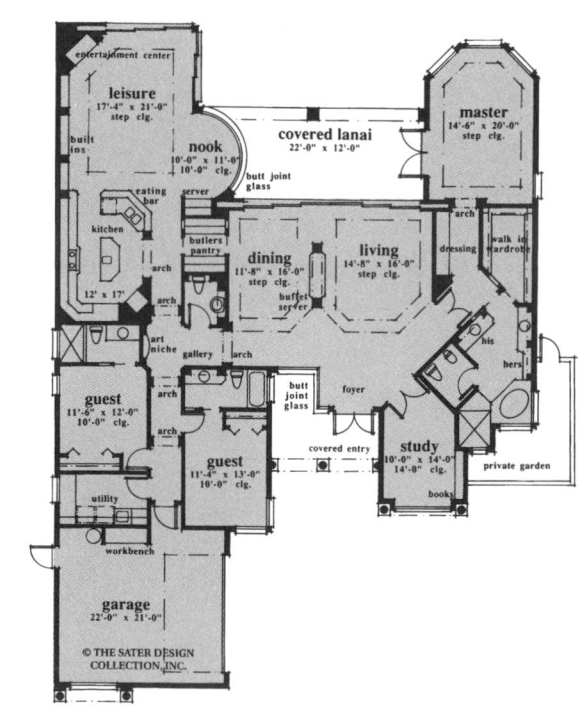

© THE SATER DESIGN COLLECTION, INC.

ORDER BLUEPRINTS ANYTIME AT EPLANS.COM OR 1-800-521-6797

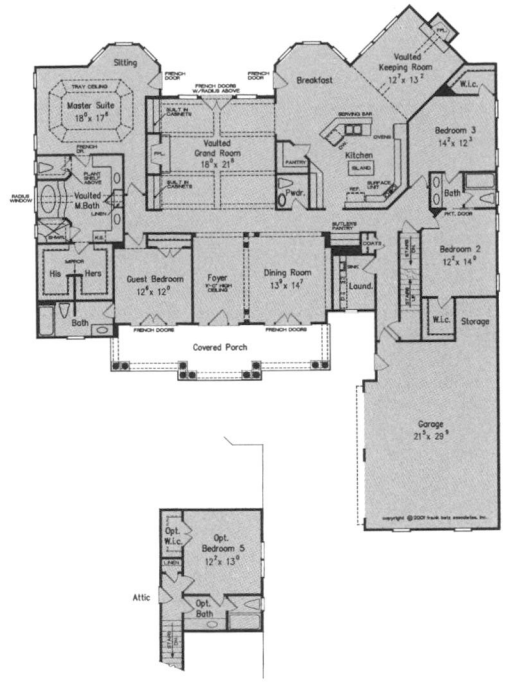

HPK2100862

Style: Federal - Adams

Square Footage: 3,190

Bonus Space: 305 sq. ft.

Bedrooms: 4

Bathrooms: 3 ½

Width: 74' - 0"

Depth: 84' - 6"

Foundation: Crawlspace, Unfinished Walkout Basement

EPLANS.COM

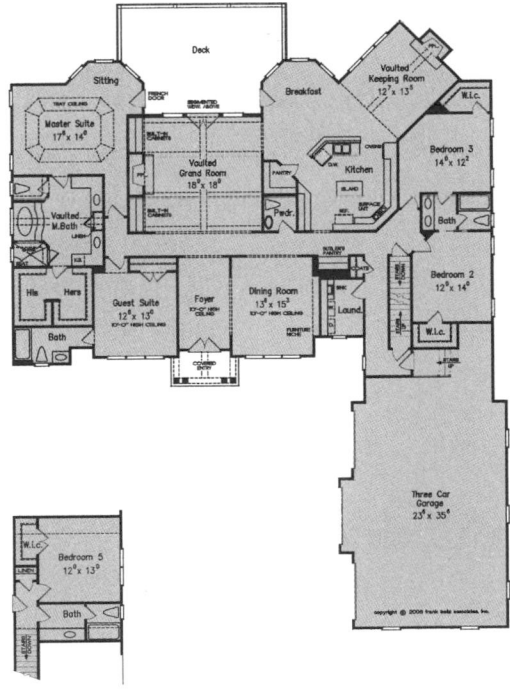

HPK2100863

Style: Cottage

Square Footage: 3,206

Bonus Space: 309 sq. ft.

Bedrooms: 4

Bathrooms: 3 ½

Width: 76' - 0"

Depth: 95' - 6"

Foundation: Crawlspace, Unfinished Walkout Basement

EPLANS.COM

HPK2100864

Style: Mediterranean

Square Footage: 3,231

Bedrooms: 4

Bathrooms: 3 ½

Width: 67' - 0"

Depth: 91' - 8"

Foundation: Slab

EPLANS.COM

©The Sater Design Collection, Inc

HPK2100865

Style: Mediterranean

Square Footage: 3,246

Bedrooms: 4

Bathrooms: 3 ½

Width: 67' - 0"

Depth: 90' - 8"

Foundation: Slab

EPLANS.COM

©The Sater Design Collection, Inc.

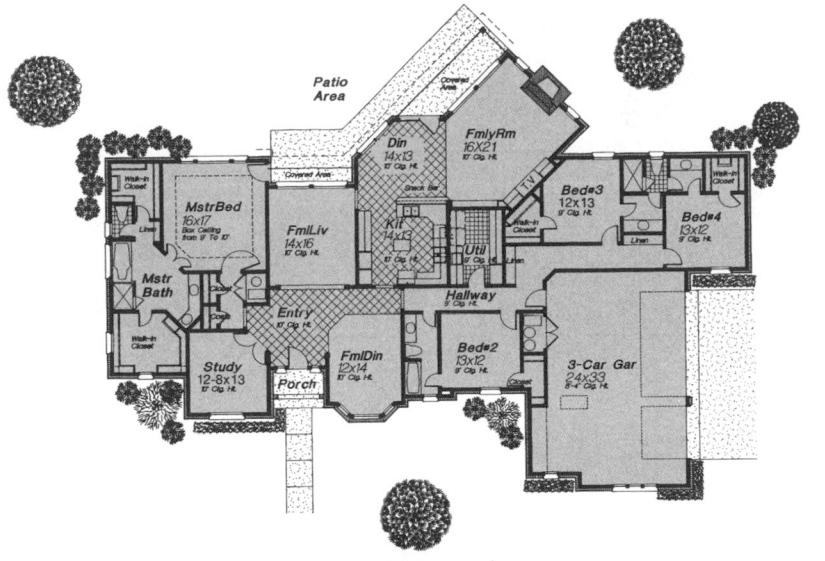

HPK2100866

EPLANS.COM

Style: French Country
Square Footage: 3,268
Bedrooms: 4
Bathrooms: 3
Width: 98' - 0"
Depth: 67' - 3"
Foundation: Slab

HPK2100867

EPLANS.COM

Style: Colonial
Square Footage: 3,270
Bedrooms: 4
Bathrooms: 3 ½
Width: 101' - 0"
Depth: 48' - 1"
Foundation: Crawlspace, Slab

3,000 TO 3,499 SQUARE FEET

HPK2100868

Style: Prairie

Square Footage: 3,278

Bedrooms: 4

Bathrooms: 3 ½

Width: 75' - 10"

Depth: 69' - 4"

Foundation: Crawlspace

EPLANS.COM

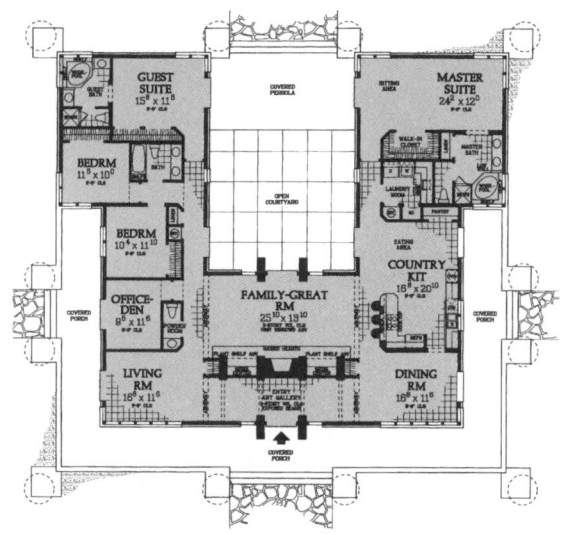

HPK2100869

Style: French Country

Square Footage: 3,281

Bedrooms: 3

Bathrooms: 2 ½

Width: 79' - 0"

Depth: 71' - 6"

Foundation: Crawlspace, Slab, Unfinished Basement

EPLANS.COM

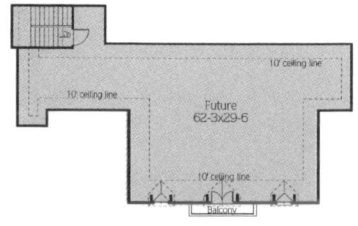

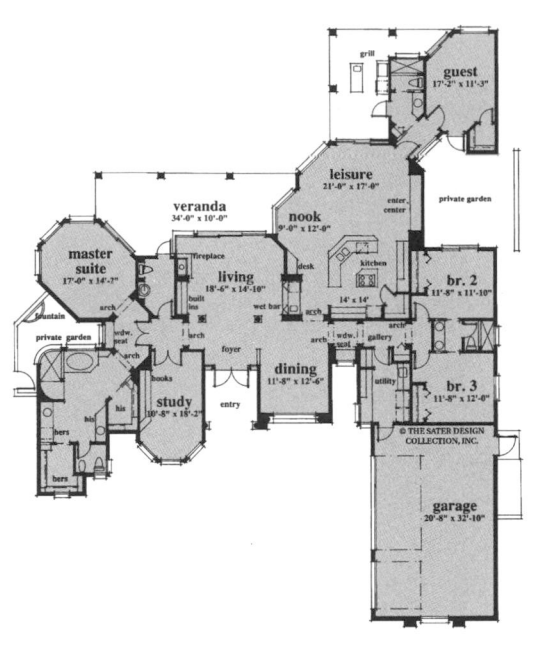

© The Sater Design Collection, Inc.

HPK2100870

Style: Mediterranean

Square Footage: 3,301

Bedrooms: 4

Bathrooms: 3 ½

Width: 80' - 0"

Depth: 103' - 8"

Foundation: Slab

EPLANS.COM

HPK2100871

Style: Ranch

Square Footage: 3,312

Bedrooms: 3

Bathrooms: 3 ½

Width: 90' - 11"

Depth: 81' - 3"

EPLANS.COM

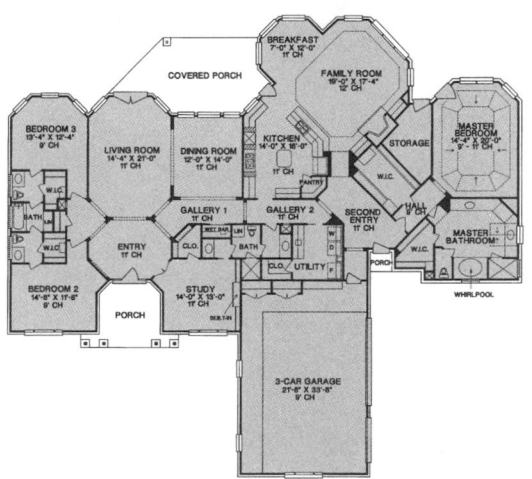

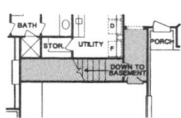

Optional Layout

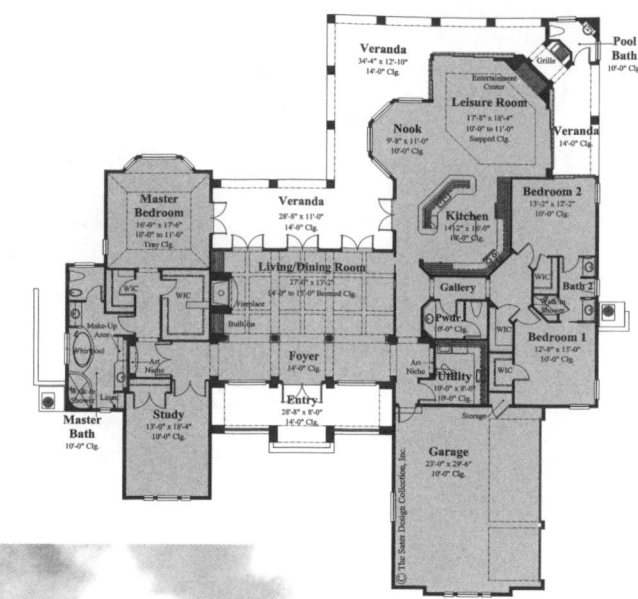

HPK2100872

Style: **Pueblo**

Square Footage: **3,343**

Bedrooms: **3**

Bathrooms: **2 ½ + ½**

Width: **84' - 0"**

Depth: **92' - 0"**

Foundation: **Slab**

EPLANS.COM

© The Sater Design Collection, Inc.

HPK2100873

Style: **Italianate**

Square Footage: **3,351**

Bedrooms: **3**

Bathrooms: **2 ½ + ½**

Width: **84' - 0"**

Depth: **92' - 2"**

Foundation: **Slab**

EPLANS.COM

© The Sater Design Collection, Inc.

ORDER BLUEPRINTS ANYTIME AT EPLANS.COM OR 1-800-521-6797

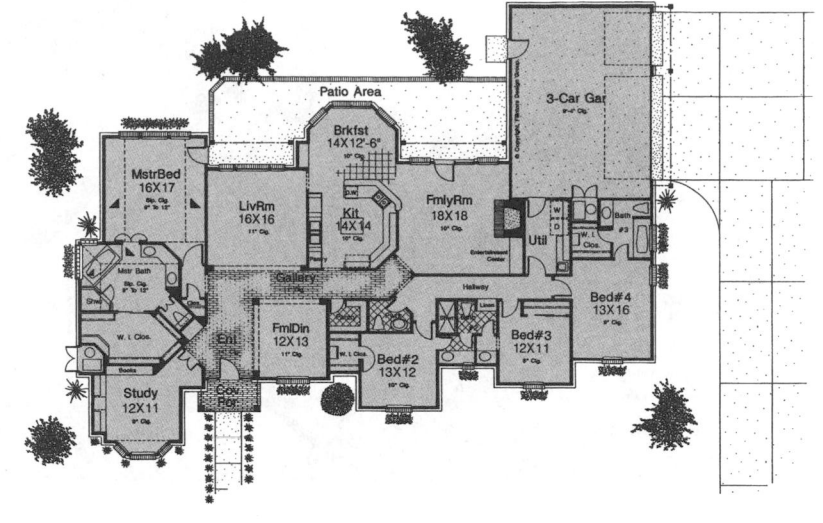

HPK2100874

Style: French Country
Square Footage: 3,352
Bedrooms: 4
Bathrooms: 3 ½
Width: 91' - 0"
Depth: 71' - 9"
Foundation: Crawlspace, Slab

EPLANS.COM

HPK2100875

Style: French Country
Square Footage: 3,359
Bonus Space: 459 sq. ft.
Bedrooms: 4
Bathrooms: 3 ½
Width: 73' - 4"
Depth: 89' - 4"
Foundation: Slab

EPLANS.COM

3,000 TO 3,499 SQUARE FEET

HPK2100876

Style: French Country

Square Footage: 3,394

Bonus Space: 816 sq. ft.

Bedrooms: 4

Bathrooms: 3 ½

Width: 83' - 0"

Depth: 77' - 0"

Foundation: Crawlspace, Unfinished Walkout Basement

EPLANS.COM

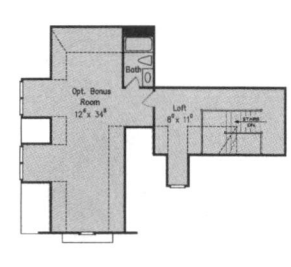

HPK2100877

Style: Mediterranean

Square Footage: 3,398

Bedrooms: 3

Bathrooms: 3 ½

Width: 121' - 5"

Depth: 96' - 2"

Foundation: Slab

EPLANS.COM

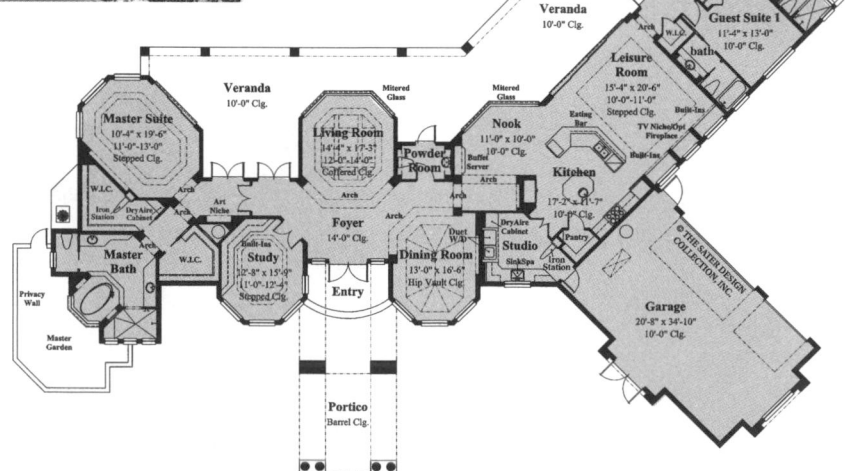

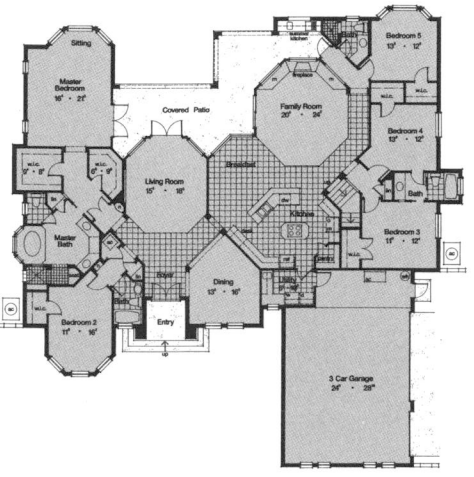

HPK2100878

Style: Italianate

Square Footage: 3,424

Bonus Space: 507 sq. ft.

Bedrooms: 5

Bathrooms: 4

Width: 82' - 4"

Depth: 83' - 8"

Foundation: Slab

EPLANS.COM

HPK2100879

Style: Mediterranean

Square Footage: 3,445

Bedrooms: 4

Bathrooms: 4

Width: 80' - 4"

Depth: 84' - 0"

Foundation: Slab

EPLANS.COM

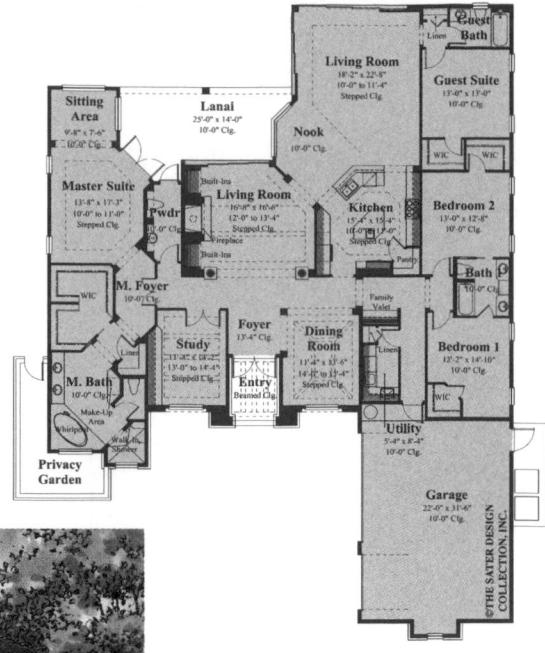

HPK2100880

Style: Italianate

Square Footage: 3,497

Bedrooms: 4

Bathrooms: 3 ½

Width: 68' - 8"

Depth: 91' - 8"

Foundation: Slab

EPLANS.COM

© The Sater Design Collection, Inc.

HPK2100881

Style: French Country

Square Footage: 3,497

Bedrooms: 4

Bathrooms: 3 ½

Width: 66' - 8"

Depth: 91' - 8"

Foundation: Slab

EPLANS.COM

© The Sater Design Collection, Inc.

ORDER BLUEPRINTS ANYTIME AT EPLANS.COM OR 1-800-521-6797

© 1993 Donald A. Gardner Architects, Inc.

HPK2100882

Style: Farmhouse

First Floor: 2,238 sq. ft.

Second Floor: 768 sq. ft.

Total: 3,006 sq. ft.

Bedrooms: 4

Bathrooms: 3 ½

Width: 94' - 1"

Depth: 59' - 10"

EPLANS.COM

This grand country farmhouse with a wraparound porch offers comfortable living at its finest. The open floor plan is accented by the great room's cathedral ceiling and the entrance foyer with clerestory windows. The large kitchen has lots of counter space, a sunny breakfast nook, and a cooktop island with a bumped-out snack bar. The master suite has beautiful bay windows, a well-designed private bath, and a spacious walk-in closet. The second level has two large bedrooms, a full bath, and plenty of attic storage.

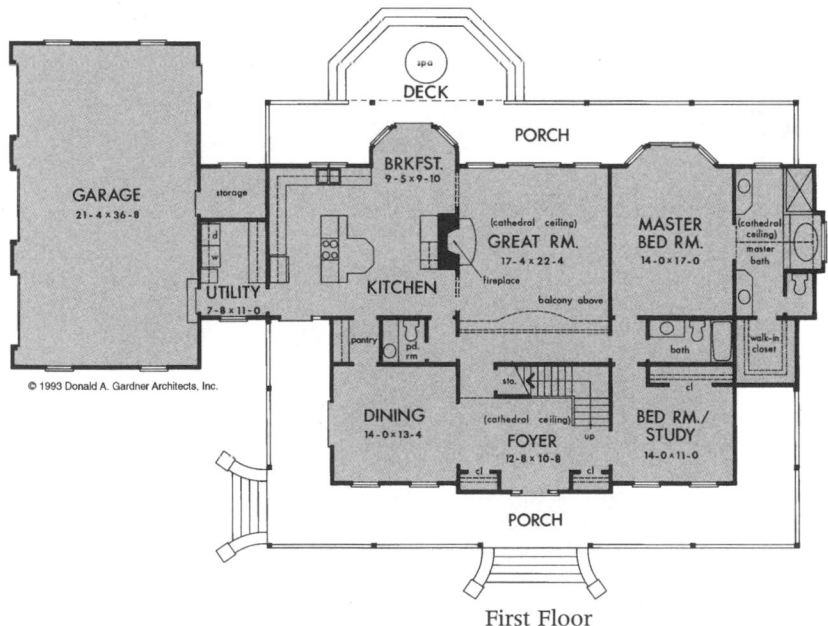

© 1993 Donald A. Gardner Architects, Inc.

First Floor

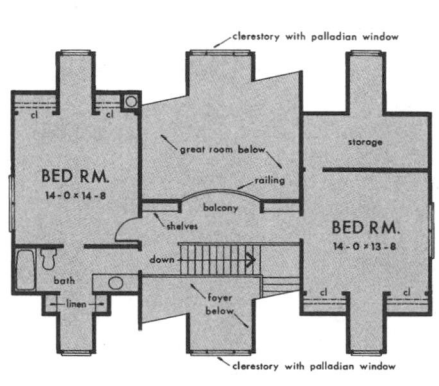

Second Floor

3,000 TO 3,499 SQUARE FEET

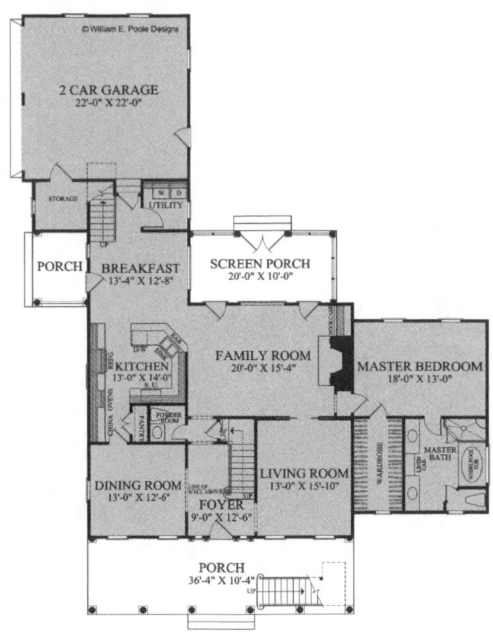

First Floor

Second Floor

HPK2100883

This beautiful Southern Colonial home will dazzle with a double-decker porch and generous family space. The family room features built-in bookshelves, a fireplace and screened-porch access. The dining room, kitchen, and breakfast nook flow effortlessly; porch access from the breakfast nook invites outdoor dining. In the master bedroom, an elongated walk-in closet and sumptuous bath with a whirlpool tub will soothe and refresh. Three upper-level bedrooms feature private baths and walk-in closets. Don't miss the future space above the garage.

Style: Neoclassical
First Floor: 1,887 sq. ft.
Second Floor: 1,133 sq. ft.
Total: 3,020 sq. ft.
Bonus Space: 444 sq. ft.
Bedrooms: 4
Bathrooms: 4 ½
Width: 63' - 4"
Depth: 82' - 2"
Foundation: Crawlspace, Unfinished Basement

EPLANS.COM

© William E. Poole Designs, Inc.

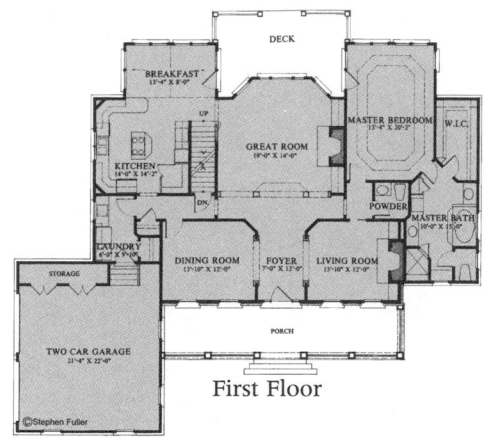

DECK

BREAKFAST
13'-4" x 8'-0"

UP

MASTER BEDROOM
15'-4" x 20'-2"

W.I.C.

KITCHEN
14'-0" x 14'-2"

GREAT ROOM
19'-0" x 14'-0"

DN.

POWDER

MASTER BATH
10'-0" x 15'-0"

LAUNDRY
6'-0" x 9'-10"

STORAGE

TWO CAR GARAGE
21'-4" x 22'-0"

DINING ROOM
13'-10" x 13'-0"

FOYER
7'-0" x 9'-0"

LIVING ROOM
13'-10" x 12'-0"

PORCH

©Stephen Fuller

First Floor

BEDROOM NO.2
14'-0" x 11'-0"

OPEN TO BELOW

UNFINISHED STORAGE
7'-10" x 12'-2"

DN.

BATH

BEDROOM NO.3
13'-10" x 12'-0"

BATH

BEDROOM NO.4
12'-4" x 12'-0"

Second Floor

HPK2100884

Style: Colonial Revival

First Floor: 2,081 sq. ft.

Second Floor: 940 sq. ft.

Total: 3,021 sq. ft.

Bedrooms: 4

Bathrooms: 3 ½

Width: 69' - 9"

Depth: 65' - 0"

Foundation: Walkout Basement

EPLANS.COM

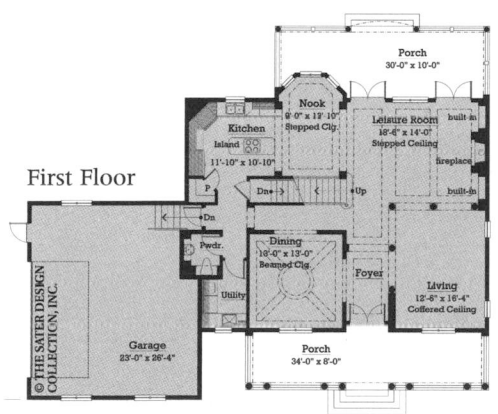

First Floor

Porch
30'-0" x 10'-0"

Nook
9'-0" x 13'-10"
Stepped Clg.

Kitchen
Island

Leisure Room
18'-4" x 14'-0"
Stepped Ceiling

built-in

fireplace

built-in

Dn

Up

Dining
18'-0" x 13'-0"
Beamed Clg.

Foyer

Living
12'-6" x 16'-4"
Coffered Ceiling

Pwdr.

Dn

Utility

Garage
23'-0" x 26'-4"

Porch
34'-0" x 8'-0"

© THE SATER DESIGN COLLECTION, INC.

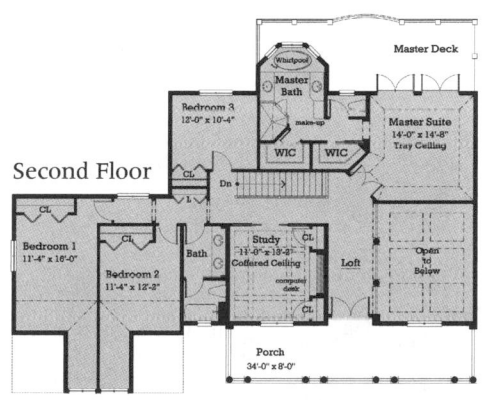

Second Floor

Master Deck

Whirlpool

Master Bath

Bedroom 3
13'-0" x 10'-4"

make-up

WIC

WIC

Master Suite
14'-0" x 14'-8"
Tray Ceiling

Bedroom 1
11'-4" x 16'-0"

CL

Bedroom 2
11'-4" x 12'-2"

Bath

Study
11'-0" x 13'-2"
Coffered Ceiling

CL

coffered decks

Loft

Open to Below

Porch
34'-0" x 8'-0"

HPK2100885

Style: Neoclassical

First Floor: 1,373 sq. ft.

Second Floor: 1,652 sq. ft.

Total: 3,025 sq. ft.

Bedrooms: 4

Bathrooms: 2 ½

Width: 64' - 0"

Depth: 51' - 8"

Foundation: Crawlspace

EPLANS.COM

©Sater Design Collection, Inc

3,000 TO 3,499 SQUARE FEET

© Sater Design Collection, Inc.

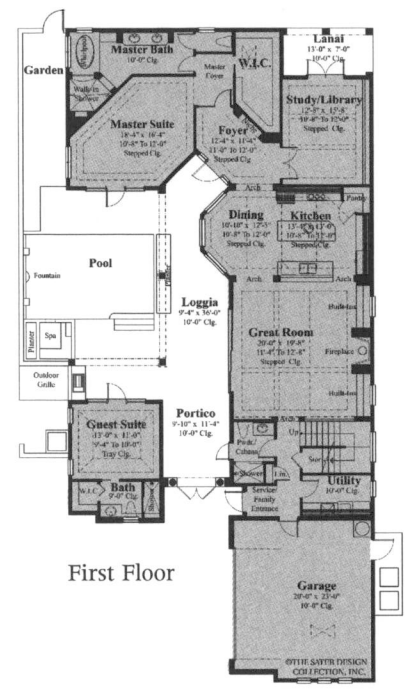

First Floor

Second Floor

HPK2100886

Style: Mediterranean
First Floor: 2,254 sq. ft.
Second Floor: 777 sq. ft.
Total: 3,031 sq. ft.
Bedrooms: 4
Bathrooms: 5
Width: 52' - 0"
Depth: 95' - 8"
Foundation: Slab

EPLANS.COM

© Stephen Fuller, Inc.

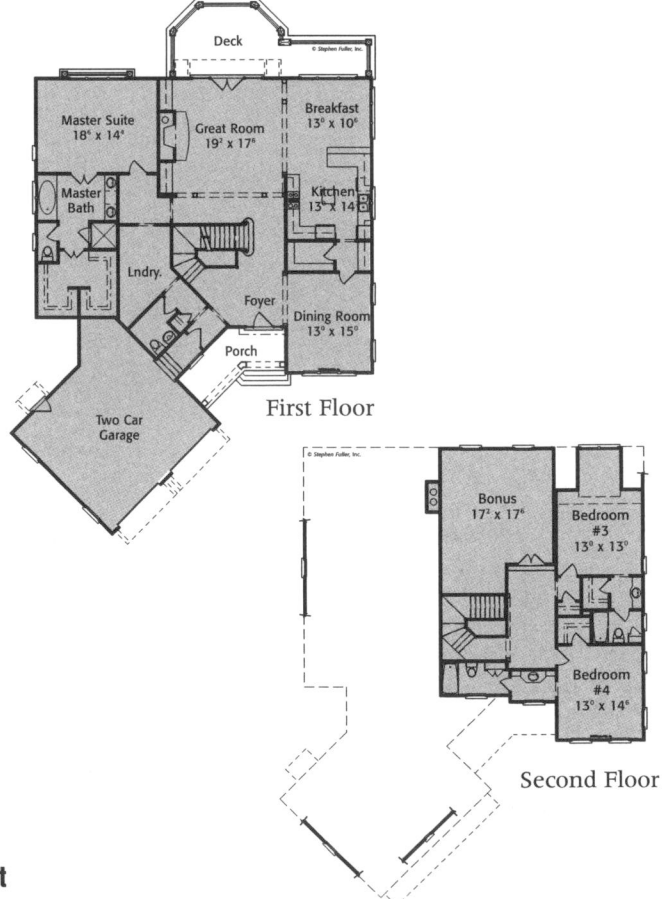

First Floor

Second Floor

HPK2100887

Style: Cape Cod
First Floor: 2,205 sq. ft.
Second Floor: 827 sq. ft.
Total: 3,032 sq. ft.
Bonus Space: 369 sq. ft.
Bedrooms: 3
Bathrooms: 3 ½
Width: 56' - 8"
Depth: 72' - 6"
Foundation: Walkout Basement

EPLANS.COM

HPK2100888

Style: Country
First Floor: 2,135 sq. ft.
Second Floor: 901 sq. ft.
Total: 3,036 sq. ft.
Bonus Space: 355 sq. ft.
Bedrooms: 3
Bathrooms: 3 ½
Width: 82' - 3"
Depth: 49' - 0"
Foundation: Crawlspace

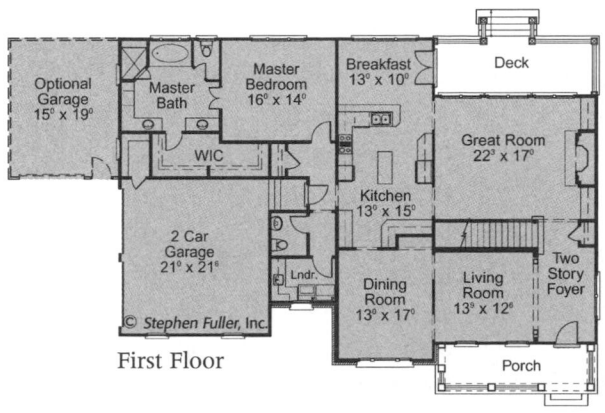

First Floor

Second Floor

HPK2100889

Style: Farmhouse
First Floor: 2,316 sq. ft.
Second Floor: 721 sq. ft.
Total: 3,037 sq. ft.
Bonus Space: 545 sq. ft.
Bedrooms: 4
Bathrooms: 3 ½
Width: 95' - 4"
Depth: 54' - 10"

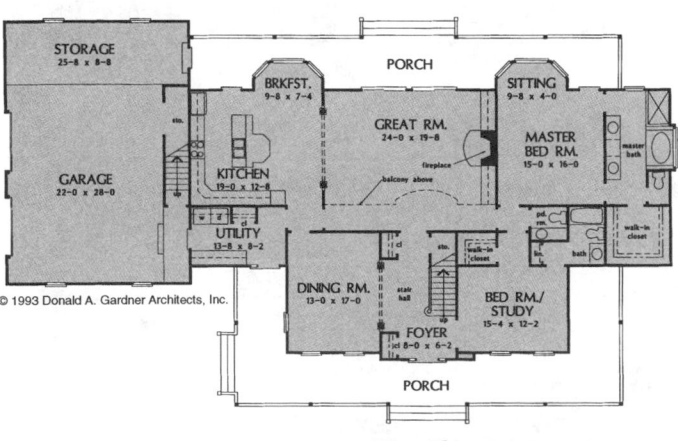

First Floor

Second Floor

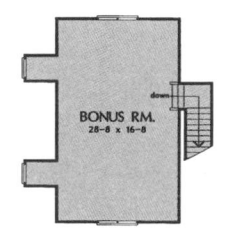

EPLANS.COM

3,000 TO 3,499 SQUARE FEET

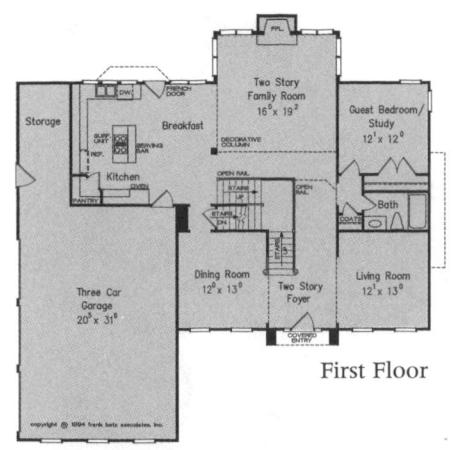

First Floor

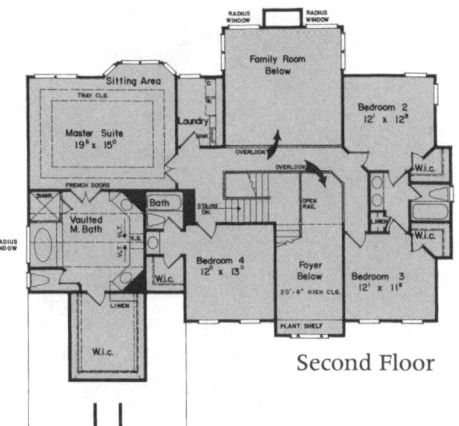

Second Floor

HPK2100890

Style: Colonial Revival

First Floor: 1,488 sq. ft.

Second Floor: 1,551 sq. ft.

Total: 3,039 sq. ft.

Bedrooms: 5

Bathrooms: 4

Width: 55' - 0"

Depth: 57' - 4"

Foundation: Crawlspace, Slab, Unfinished Walkout Basement

EPLANS.COM

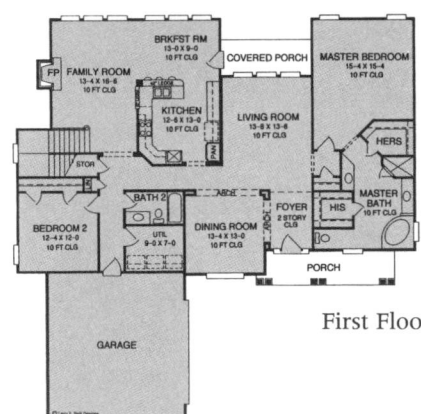

First Floor

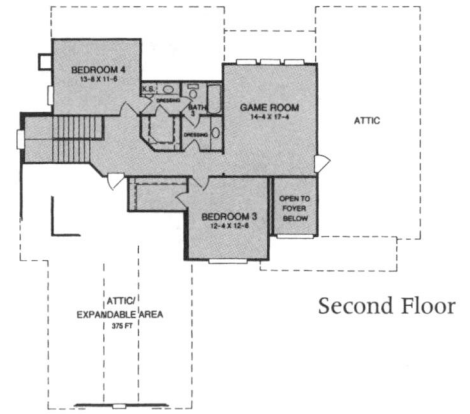

Second Floor

HPK2100891

Style: Colonial Revival

First Floor: 2,121 sq. ft.

Second Floor: 920 sq. ft.

Total: 3,041 sq. ft.

Bedrooms: 4

Bathrooms: 3

Width: 63' - 0"

Depth: 63' - 0"

Foundation: Crawlspace, Slab

EPLANS.COM

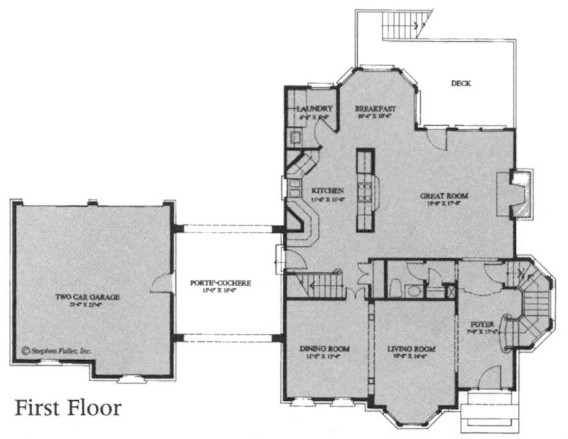

First Floor

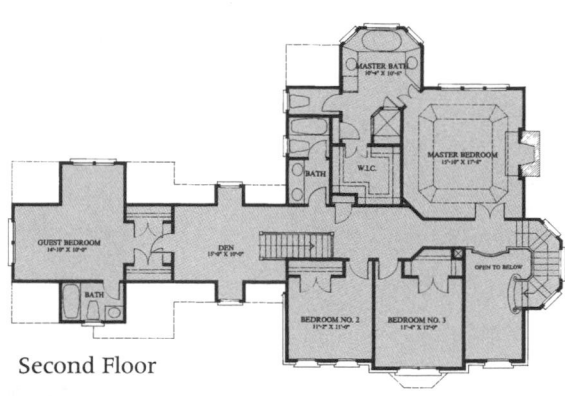

Second Floor

HPK2100892

Style: Colonial Revival

First Floor: 1,370 sq. ft.

Second Floor: 1,673 sq. ft.

Total: 3,043 sq. ft.

Bedrooms: 4

Bathrooms: 3 ½

Width: 73' - 6"

Depth: 49' - 0"

Foundation: Walkout Basement

EPLANS.COM

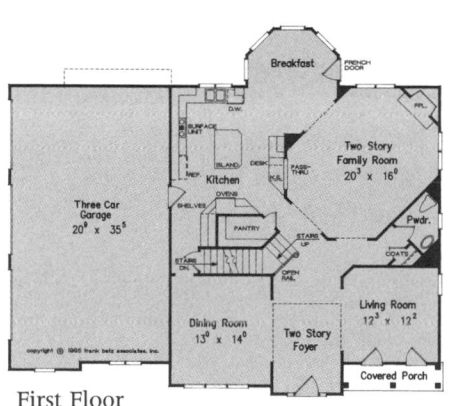

First Floor

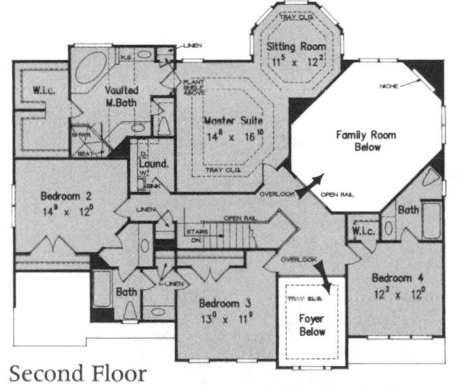

Second Floor

HPK2100893

Style: New American

First Floor: 1,415 sq. ft.

Second Floor: 1,632 sq. ft.

Total: 3,047 sq. ft.

Bedrooms: 4

Bathrooms: 3 ½

Width: 56' - 0"

Depth: 47' - 6"

Foundation: Crawlspace, Unfinished Walkout Basement

EPLANS.COM

3,000 TO 3,499 SQUARE FEET

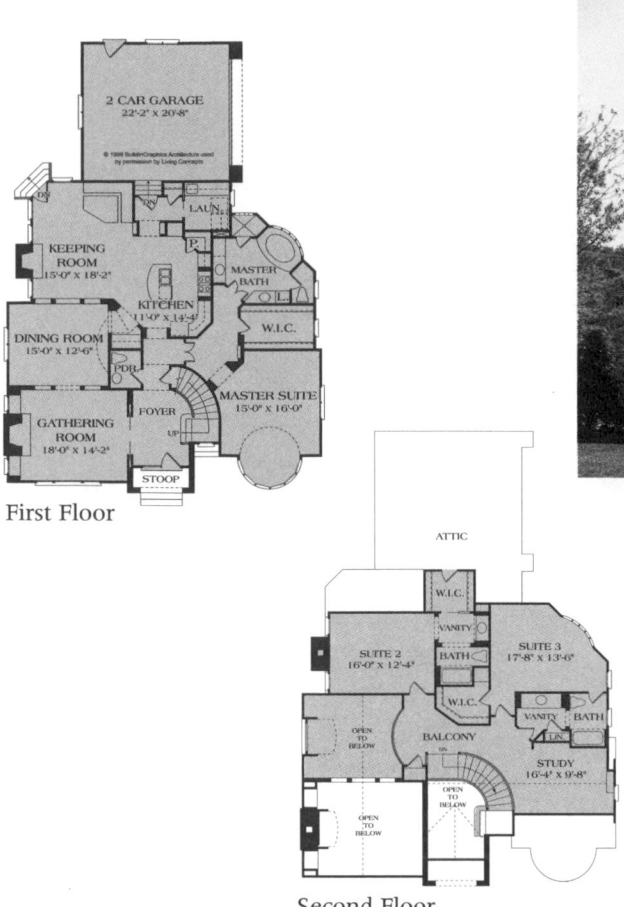

First Floor

Second Floor

HPK2100894

Style: French Country
First Floor: 1,982 sq. ft.
Second Floor: 1,071 sq. ft.
Total: 3,053 sq. ft.
Bedrooms: 3
Bathrooms: 3 ½
Width: 48' - 4"
Depth: 69' - 6"
Foundation: Crawlspace

EPLANS.COM

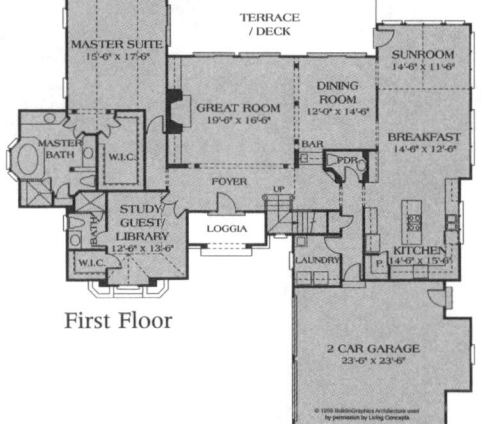

First Floor

Second Floor

HPK2100895

Style: French Country
First Floor: 2,398 sq. ft.
Second Floor: 657 sq. ft.
Total: 3,055 sq. ft.
Bonus Space: 374 sq. ft.
Bedrooms: 4
Bathrooms: 3 ½
Width: 72' - 8"
Depth: 69' - 1"
Foundation: Crawlspace, Unfinished Basement

EPLANS.COM

HPK2100896

Style: Country
First Floor: 2,047 sq. ft.
Second Floor: 1,014 sq. ft.
Total: 3,061 sq. ft.
Bonus Space: 393 sq. ft.
Bedrooms: 4
Bathrooms: 4 ½
Width: 81' - 0"
Depth: 45' - 0"
Foundation: Crawlspace

EPLANS.COM

© Stephen Fuller, Inc.

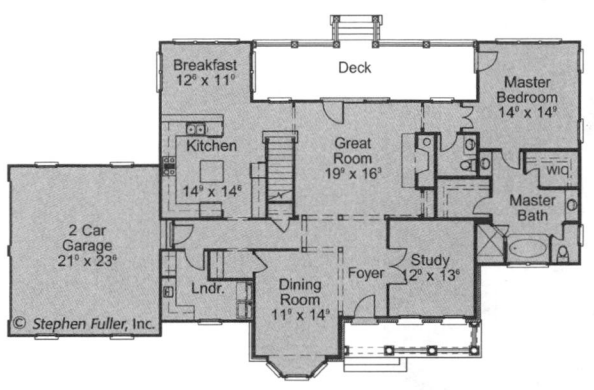

First Floor

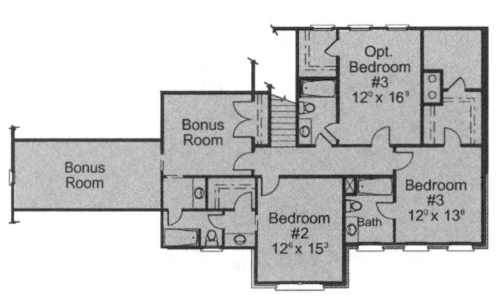

Second Floor

HPK2100897

Style: New American
First Floor: 2,115 sq. ft.
Second Floor: 947 sq. ft.
Total: 3,062 sq. ft.
Bonus Space: 216 sq. ft.
Bedrooms: 4
Bathrooms: 3 ½
Width: 68' - 10"
Depth: 58' - 1"
Foundation: Crawlspace, Slab, Unfinished Basement

EPLANS.COM

First Floor

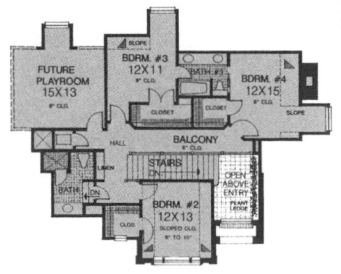

Second Floor

3,000 TO 3,499 SQUARE FEET

First Floor

Second Floor

HPK2100898

Style: French Country
First Floor: 2,440 sq. ft.
Second Floor: 626 sq. ft.
Total: 3,066 sq. ft.
Bonus Space: 302 sq. ft.
Bedrooms: 3
Bathrooms: 2 ½
Width: 83' - 0"
Depth: 77' - 0"
Foundation: Crawlspace

EPLANS.COM

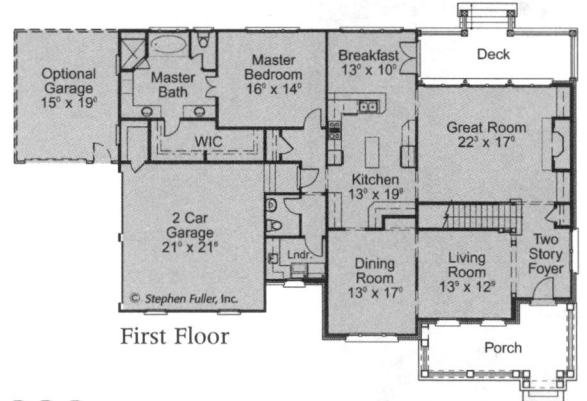

First Floor

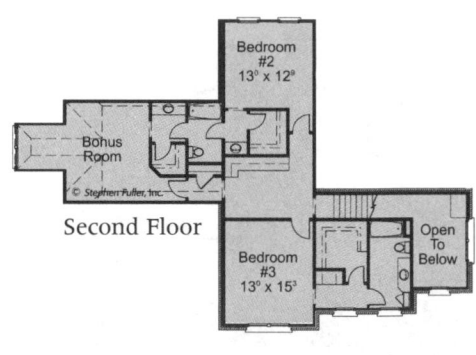

Second Floor

HPK2100899

Style: Colonial
First Floor: 2,150 sq. ft.
Second Floor: 931 sq. ft.
Total: 3,081 sq. ft.
Bedrooms: 3
Bathrooms: 3 ½
Width: 82' - 3"
Depth: 43' - 9"
Foundation: Crawlspace

EPLANS.COM

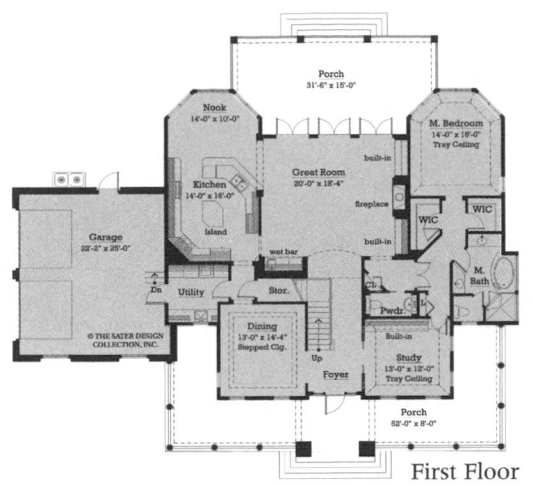

First Floor

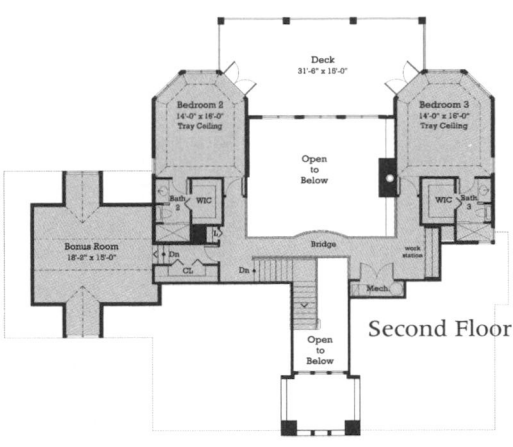

Second Floor

HPK2100900

Style: Country
First Floor: 2,138 sq. ft.
Second Floor: 944 sq. ft.
Total: 3,082 sq. ft.
Bonus Space: 427 sq. ft.
Bedrooms: 3
Bathrooms: 3 ½
Width: 77' - 2"
Depth: 64' - 0"
Foundation: Crawlspace

EPLANS.COM

©The Sater Design Collection, Inc.

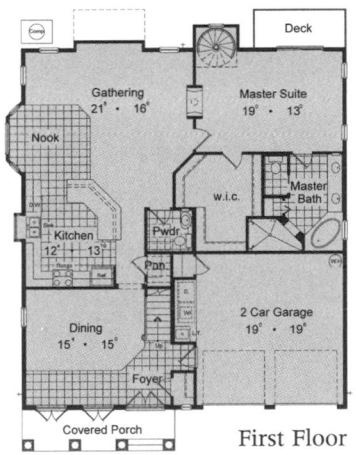

First Floor

Second Floor

HPK2100901

Style: Mediterranean
First Floor: 1,596 sq. ft.
Second Floor: 1,491 sq. ft.
Total: 3,087 sq. ft.
Bedrooms: 4
Bathrooms: 3 ½
Width: 42' - 0"
Depth: 52' - 0"
Foundation: Slab

EPLANS.COM

3,000 TO 3,499 SQUARE FEET

HPK2100902

Style: Country
First Floor: 1,866 sq. ft.
Second Floor: 1,222 sq. ft.
Total: 3,088 sq. ft.
Bedrooms: 4
Bathrooms: 3 ½
Width: 62' - 4"
Depth: 51' - 6"
Foundation: Crawlspace, Slab, Unfinished Walkout Basement

EPLANS.COM

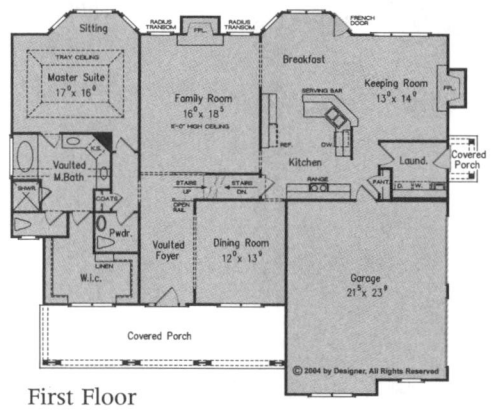

First Floor

Second Floor

HPK2100903

Style: New American
First Floor: 1,571 sq. ft.
Second Floor: 1,518 sq. ft.
Total: 3,089 sq. ft.
Bedrooms: 4
Bathrooms: 4
Width: 55' - 6"
Depth: 48' - 4"
Foundation: Crawlspace, Unfinished Walkout Basement

EPLANS.COM

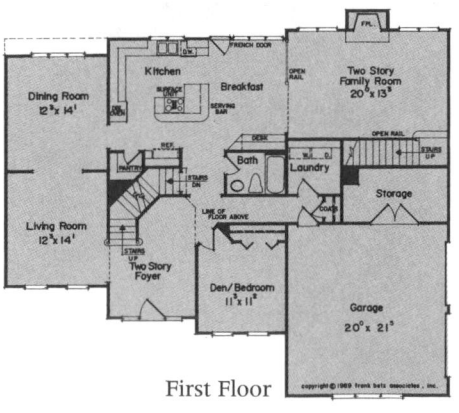

First Floor

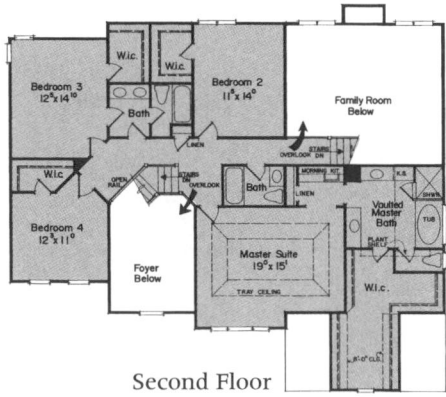

Second Floor

HPK2100904

Style: French Country

First Floor: 2,059 sq. ft.

Second Floor: 1,033 sq. ft.

Total: 3,092 sq. ft.

Bedrooms: 5

Bathrooms: 4

Width: 57' - 0"

Depth: 58' - 6"

Foundation: Crawlspace, Unfinished Walkout Basement

EPLANS.COM

First Floor

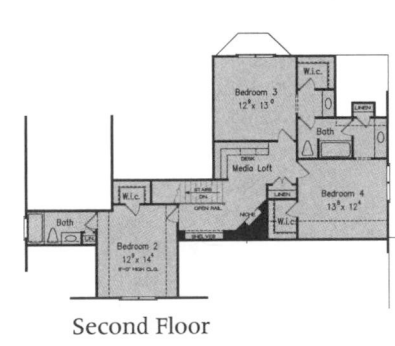

Second Floor

HPK2100905

Style: New American

First Floor: 1,846 sq. ft.

Second Floor: 1,249 sq. ft.

Total: 3,095 sq. ft.

Bonus Space: 394 sq. ft.

Bedrooms: 4

Bathrooms: 3 ½

Width: 52' - 2"

Depth: 66' - 2"

Foundation: Crawlspace

EPLANS.COM

First Floor

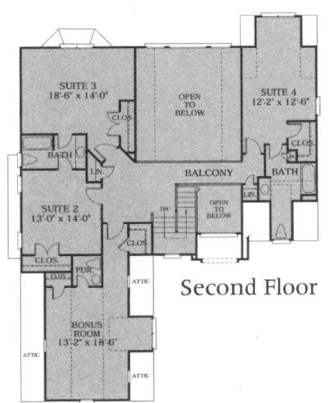

Second Floor

3,000 TO 3,499 SQUARE FEET

HPK2100906

Style: Queen Anne

First Floor: 2,083 sq. ft.

Second Floor: 1,013 sq. ft.

Total: 3,096 sq. ft.

Bedrooms: 4

Bathrooms: 3 ½

Width: 74' - 0"

Depth: 88' - 0"

Foundation: Crawlspace

EPLANS.COM

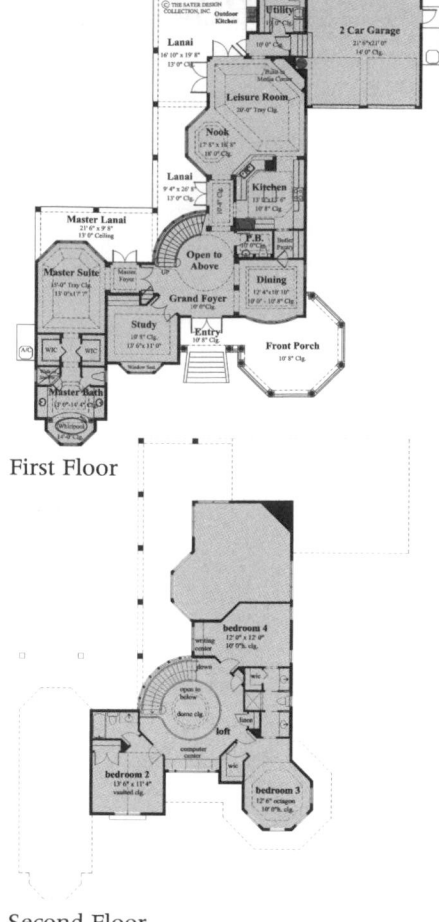

First Floor

Second Floor

©The Sater Design Collection, Inc.

First Floor

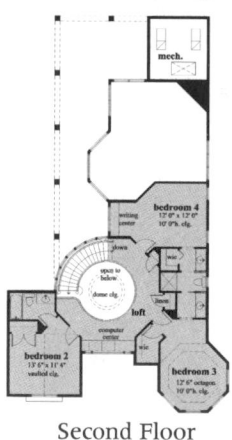

Second Floor

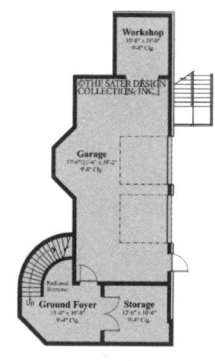

HPK2100907

Style: Victorian Eclectic

First Floor: 2,083 sq. ft.

Second Floor: 1,013 sq. ft.

Total: 3,096 sq. ft.

Bedrooms: 4

Bathrooms: 3 ½

Width: 59' - 6"

Depth: 88' - 0"

Foundation: Slab

EPLANS.COM

©The Sater Design Collection, Inc.

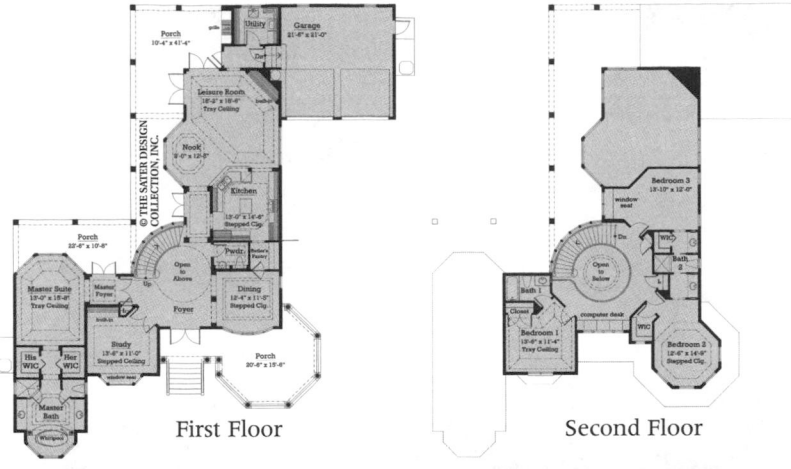

First Floor

Second Floor

HPK2100908

Style: Victorian Eclectic
First Floor: 2,083 sq. ft.
Second Floor: 1,013 sq. ft.
Total: 3,096 sq. ft.
Bedrooms: 4
Bathrooms: 3 ½
Width: 74' - 0"
Depth: 88' - 0"
Foundation: Crawlspace

©The Sater Design Collection, Inc.

First Floor

Second Floor

HPK2100909

Style: Country
First Floor: 2,083 sq. ft.
Second Floor: 1,013 sq. ft.
Total: 3,096 sq. ft.
Bedrooms: 4
Bathrooms: 3 ½
Width: 74' - 0"
Depth: 88' - 0"
Foundation: Crawlspace

©The Sater Design Collection, Inc.

HPK2100910

Style: Farmhouse
First Floor: 2,142 sq. ft.
Second Floor: 960 sq. ft.
Total: 3,102 sq. ft.
Bonus Space: 327 sq. ft.
Bedrooms: 4
Bathrooms: 3 ½
Width: 75' - 8"
Depth: 53' - 0"
Foundation: Crawlspace

EPLANS.COM

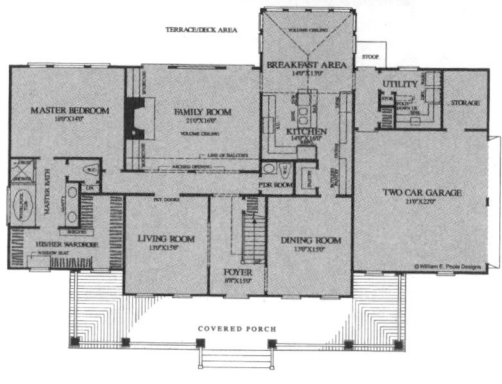

First Floor

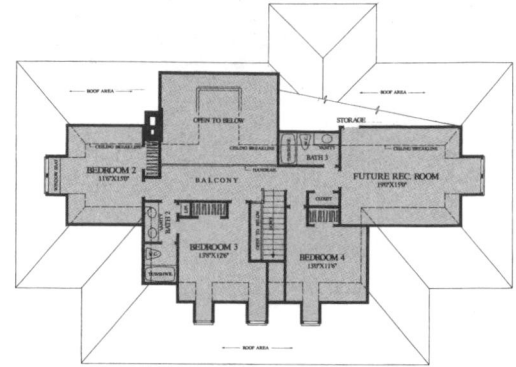

Second Floor

© Stephen Fuller, Inc.

HPK2100911

Style: Neoclassical
First Floor: 1,455 sq. ft.
Second Floor: 1,649 sq. ft.
Total: 3,104 sq. ft.
Bedrooms: 4
Bathrooms: 3 ½
Width: 54' - 4"
Depth: 46' - 0"
Foundation: Walkout Basement

EPLANS.COM

First Floor

Second Floor

HPK2100912

Style: Country

First Floor: 2,140 sq. ft.

Second Floor: 964 sq. ft.

Total: 3,104 sq. ft.

Bedrooms: 5

Bathrooms: 4

Width: 65' - 4"

Depth: 52' - 0"

Foundation: Crawlspace, Unfinished Walkout Basement

EPLANS.COM

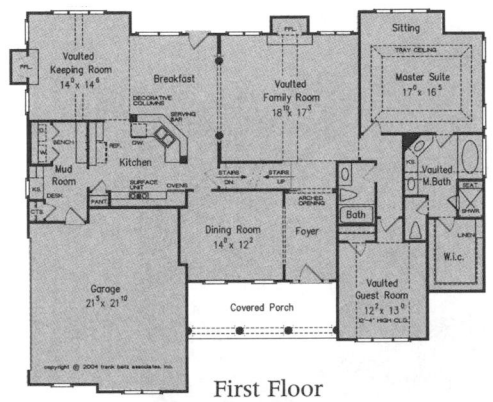

First Floor

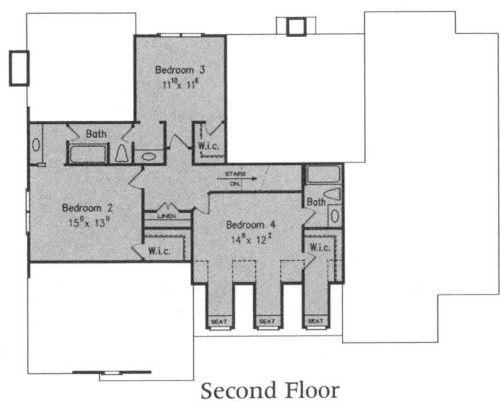

Second Floor

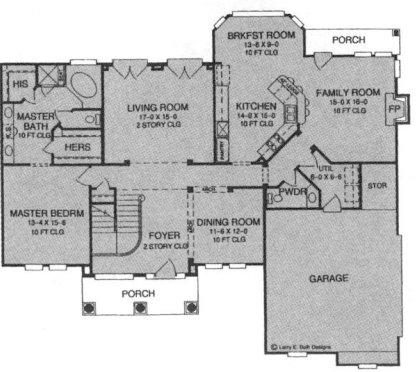

First Floor

Second Floor

HPK2100913

Style: New American

First Floor: 1,919 sq. ft.

Second Floor: 1,190 sq. ft.

Total: 3,109 sq. ft.

Bonus Space: 286 sq. ft.

Bedrooms: 4

Bathrooms: 3 ½

Width: 64' - 6"

Depth: 55' - 10"

Foundation: Crawlspace, Slab, Unfinished Basement

EPLANS.COM

3,000 TO 3,499 SQUARE FEET

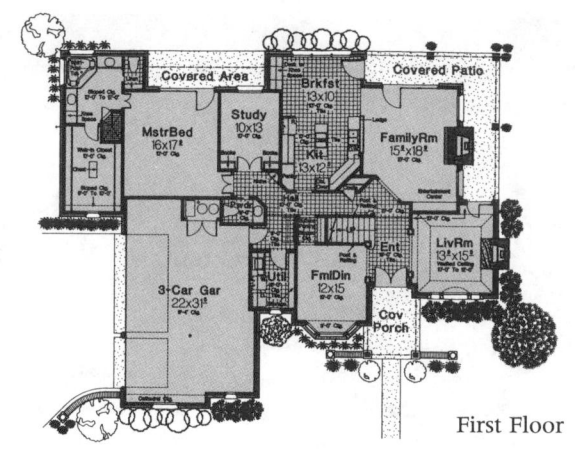

First Floor

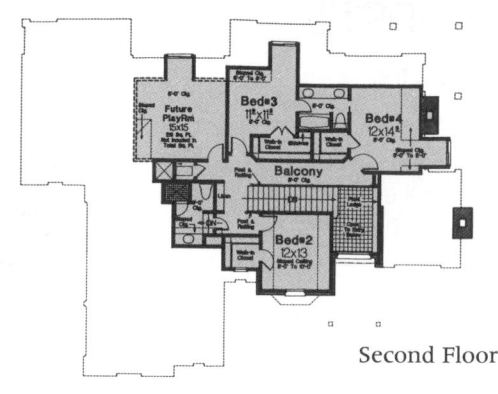

Second Floor

HPK2100914

Style: Chateauesque

First Floor: 2,162 sq. ft.

Second Floor: 947 sq. ft.

Total: 3,109 sq. ft.

Bonus Space: 225 sq. ft.

Bedrooms: 4

Bathrooms: 3 ½

Width: 71' - 10"

Depth: 58' - 1"

Foundation: Slab

EPLANS.COM

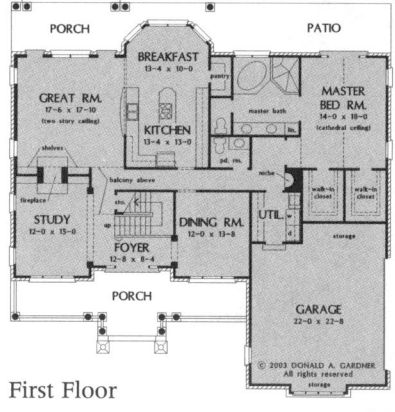

First Floor

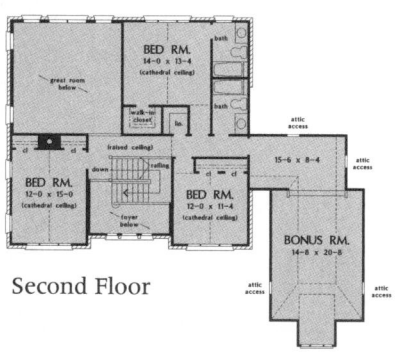

Second Floor

HPK2100915

Style: Country

First Floor: 2,160 sq. ft.

Second Floor: 951 sq. ft.

Total: 3,111 sq. ft.

Bonus Space: 491 sq. ft.

Bedrooms: 4

Bathrooms: 3 ½

Width: 61' - 11"

Depth: 63' - 11"

EPLANS.COM

First Floor

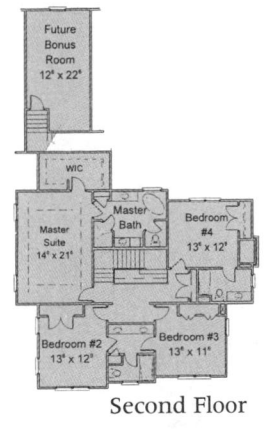

Second Floor

HPK2100916

Style: Colonial Revival

First Floor: 1,652 sq. ft.

Second Floor: 1,460 sq. ft.

Total: 3,112 sq. ft.

Bonus Space: 256 sq. ft.

Bedrooms: 4

Bathrooms: 3 ½

Width: 48' - 0"

Depth: 78' - 4"

Foundation: Walkout Basement

EPLANS.COM

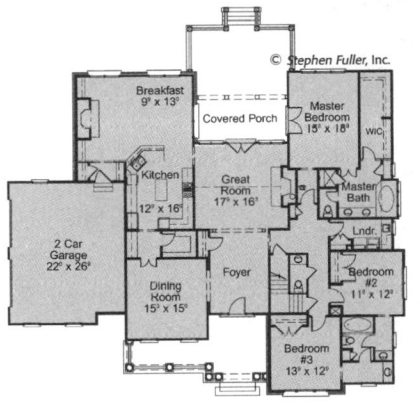

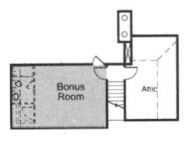

HPK2100917

Style: Colonial

First Floor: 2,807 sq. ft.

Second Floor: 310 sq. ft.

Total: 3,117 sq. ft.

Bedrooms: 3

Bathrooms: 2 ½

Width: 75' - 9"

Depth: 61' - 3"

Foundation: Crawlspace

EPLANS.COM

3,000 TO 3,499 SQUARE FEET

HPK2100918

Style: New American

First Floor: 2,188 sq. ft.

Second Floor: 932 sq. ft.

Total: 3,120 sq. ft.

Bonus Space: 488 sq. ft.

Bedrooms: 4

Bathrooms: 2 ½

Width: 60' - 8"

Depth: 66' - 4"

EPLANS.COM

© 2000 Donald A. Gardner, Inc.

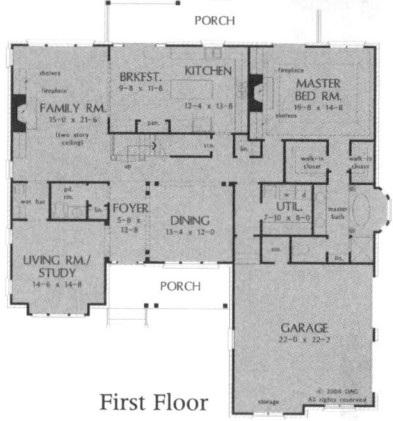

First Floor

Second Floor

First Floor

HPK2100919

Style: Cottage

First Floor: 2,399 sq. ft.

Second Floor: 726 sq. ft.

Total: 3,125 sq. ft.

Bonus Space: 425 sq. ft.

Bedrooms: 4

Bathrooms: 4

Width: 58' - 4"

Depth: 72' - 0"

Foundation: Crawlspace, Unfinished Walkout Basement

EPLANS.COM

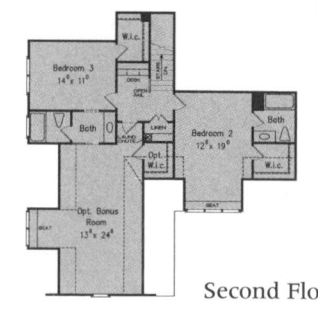

Second Floor

HPK2100920

Style: Country
First Floor: 1,526 sq. ft.
Second Floor: 1,600 sq. ft.
Total: 3,126 sq. ft.
Bedrooms: 4
Bathrooms: 2 ½
Width: 46' - 0"
Depth: 50' - 0"
Foundation: Unfinished Basement

EPLANS.COM

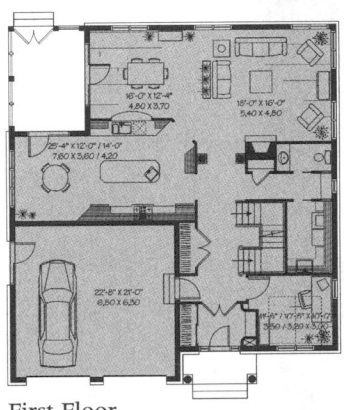

First Floor

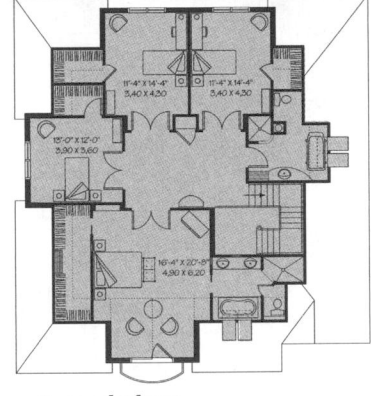

Second Floor

HPK2100921

Style: Craftsman
First Floor: 1,630 sq. ft.
Second Floor: 1,260 sq. ft.
Total: 2,890 sq. ft.
Bonus Space: 240 sq. ft.
Bedrooms: 3
Bathrooms: 2 ½
Width: 59' - 0"
Depth: 50' - 0"
Foundation: Crawlspace

EPLANS.COM

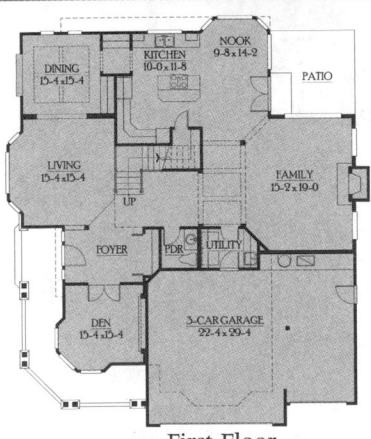

First Floor

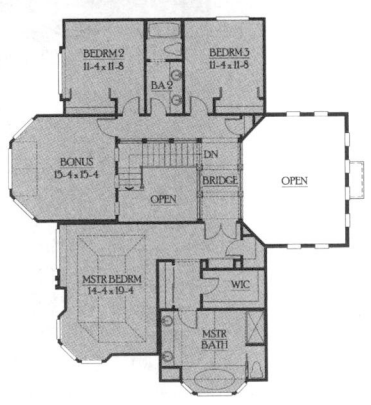

Second Floor

3,000 TO 3,499 SQUARE FEET

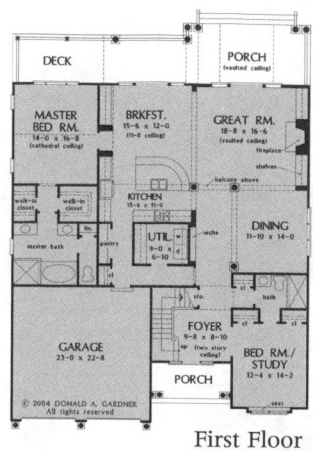

First Floor

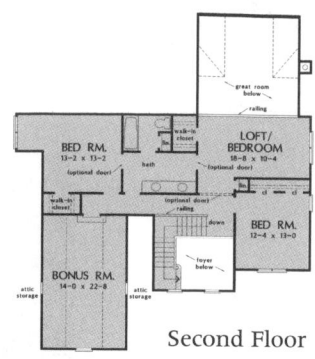

Second Floor

© 2004 Donald A. Gardner, Inc.

HPK2100922

Style: New American
First Floor: 2,172 sq. ft.
Second Floor: 962 sq. ft.
Total: 3,134 sq. ft.
Bedrooms: 4
Bathrooms: 3
Width: 50' - 0"
Depth: 67' - 6"

EPLANS.COM

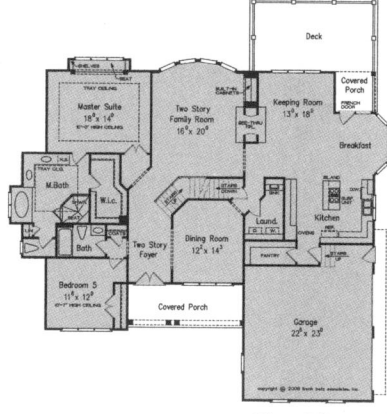

First Floor

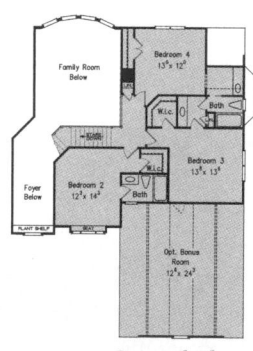

Second Floor

HPK2100923

Style: Country
First Floor: 2,233 sq. ft.
Second Floor: 902 sq. ft.
Total: 3,135 sq. ft.
Bonus Space: 319 sq. ft.
Bedrooms: 5
Bathrooms: 4
Width: 66' - 0"
Depth: 59' - 0"
Foundation: Crawlspace,
Unfinished Walkout Basement

EPLANS.COM

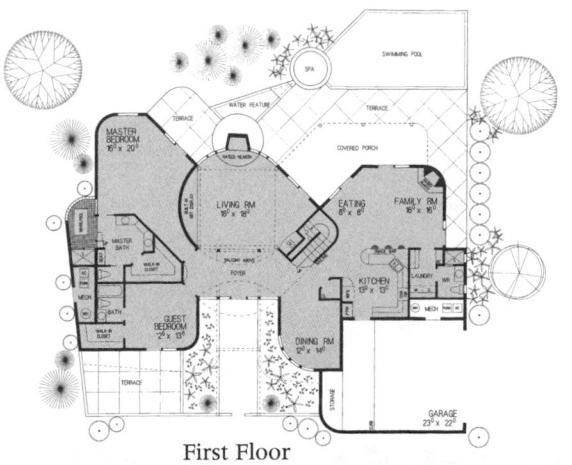

First Floor

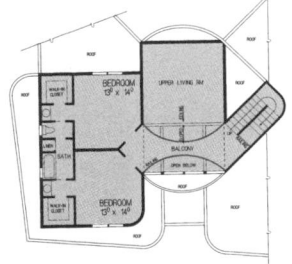

Second Floor

HPK2100924

Style: Pueblo
First Floor: 2,422 sq. ft.
Second Floor: 714 sq. ft.
Total: 3,136 sq. ft.
Bedrooms: 4
Bathrooms: 4
Width: 77' - 6"
Depth: 62' - 0"
Foundation: Slab

EPLANS.COM

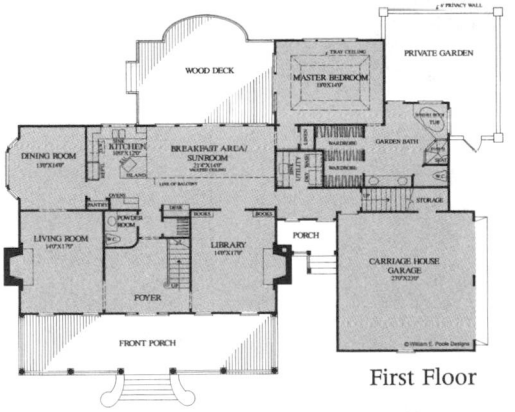

First Floor

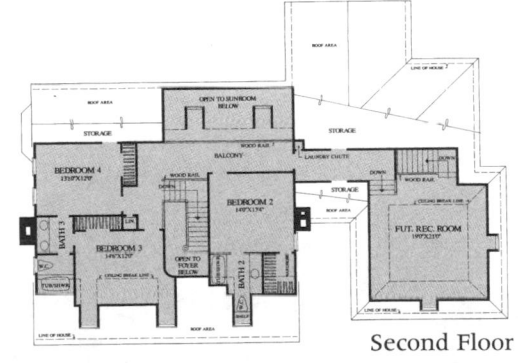

Second Floor

HPK2100925

Style: Federal - Adams
First Floor: 2,092 sq. ft.
Second Floor: 1,045 sq. ft.
Total: 3,137 sq. ft.
Bonus Space: 546 sq. ft.
Bedrooms: 4
Bathrooms: 3 ½
Width: 77' - 0"
Depth: 56' - 4"
Foundation: Crawlspace

EPLANS.COM

3,000 TO 3,499 SQUARE FEET

HPK2100926

Style: Cottage
First Floor: 2,285 sq. ft.
Second Floor: 854 sq. ft.
Total: 3,139 sq. ft.
Bonus Space: 327 sq. ft.
Bedrooms: 4
Bathrooms: 4
Width: 64' - 0"
Depth: 58' - 4"
Foundation: Crawlspace, Unfinished Walkout Basement

EPLANS.COM

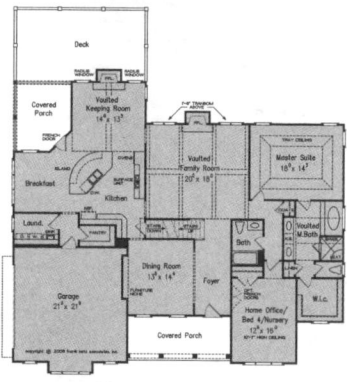

First Floor

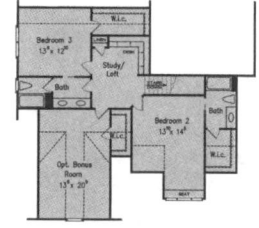

Second Floor

First Floor

HPK2100927

Style: Queen Anne
First Floor: 2,041 sq. ft.
Second Floor: 1,098 sq. ft.
Total: 3,139 sq. ft.
Bonus Space: 385 sq. ft.
Bedrooms: 4
Bathrooms: 3 ½
Width: 76' - 6"
Depth: 62' - 2"
Foundation: Slab

EPLANS.COM

Second Floor

ORDER BLUEPRINTS ANYTIME AT EPLANS.COM OR 1-800-521-6797

HPK2100928

Style: New American

First Floor: 2,302 sq. ft.

Second Floor: 845 sq. ft.

Total: 3,147 sq. ft.

Bonus Space: 247 sq. ft.

Bedrooms: 4

Bathrooms: 3 ½

Width: 64' - 0"

Depth: 59' - 4"

Foundation: Crawlspace, Slab, Unfinished Walkout Basement

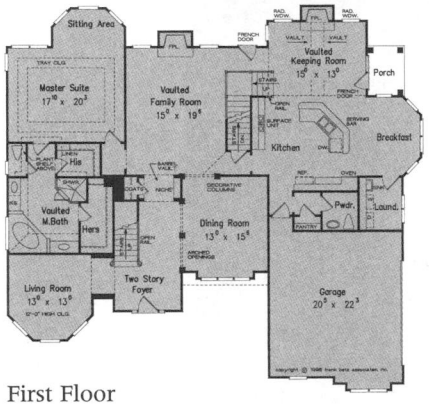

First Floor

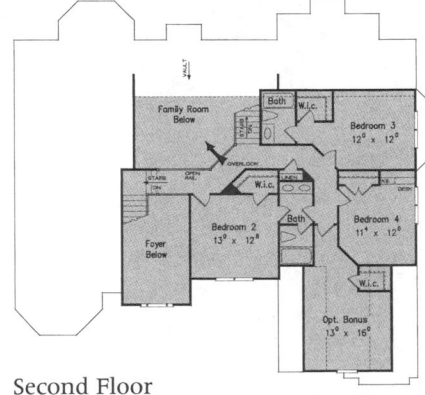

Second Floor

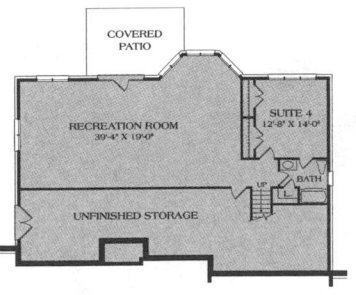

Lower Level

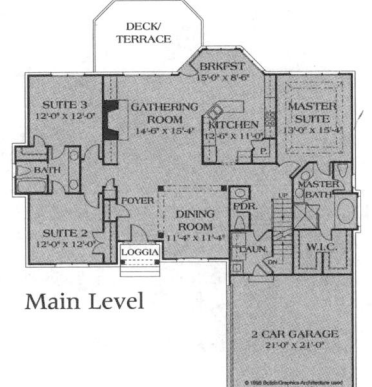

Main Level

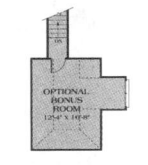

HPK2100929

Style: Cottage

Main Level: 1,947 sq. ft.

Lower Level: 1,200 sq. ft.

Total: 3,147 sq. ft.

Bonus Space: 255 sq. ft.

Bedrooms: 4

Bathrooms: 3 ½

Width: 59' - 4"

Depth: 62' - 2"

Foundation: Finished Basement

EPLANS.COM

3,000 TO 3,499 SQUARE FEET

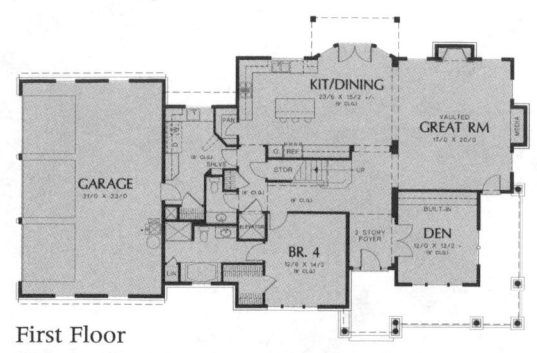

First Floor

Second Floor

HPK2100930

Style: Craftsman
First Floor: 1,846 sq. ft.
Second Floor: 1,309 sq. ft.
Total: 3,155 sq. ft.
Bonus Space: 563 sq. ft.
Bedrooms: 4
Bathrooms: 3 ½
Width: 77' - 6"
Depth: 48' - 8"
Foundation: Crawlspace

EPLANS.COM

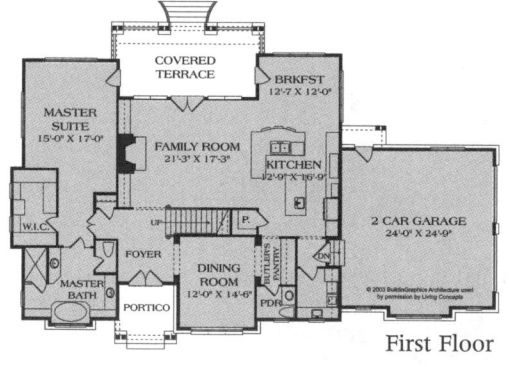

First Floor

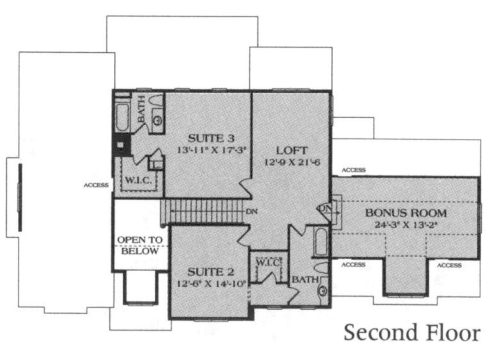

Second Floor

HPK2100931

Style: Craftsman
First Floor: 2,012 sq. ft.
Second Floor: 1,149 sq. ft.
Total: 3,161 sq. ft.
Bonus Space: 379 sq. ft.
Bedrooms: 3
Bathrooms: 3 ½
Width: 53' - 4"
Depth: 51' - 4"
Foundation: Crawlspace

EPLANS.COM

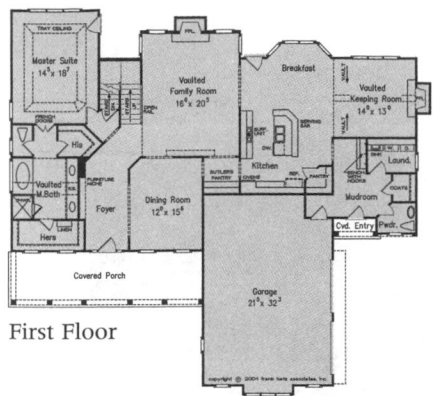

First Floor

Second Floor

HPK2100932

Style: Country

First Floor: 2,182 sq. ft.

Second Floor: 980 sq. ft.

Total: 3,162 sq. ft.

Bedrooms: 4

Bathrooms: 3 ½

Width: 70' - 4"

Depth: 65' - 0"

Foundation: Crawlspace, Slab, Unfinished Walkout Basement

EPLANS.COM

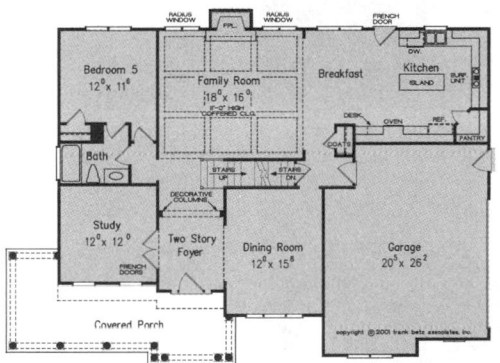

First Floor

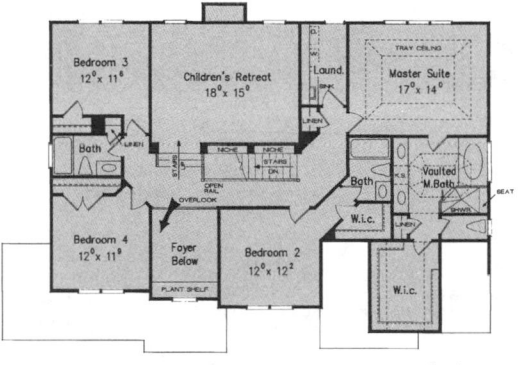

Second Floor

HPK2100933

Style: French Country

First Floor: 1,448 sq. ft.

Second Floor: 1,714 sq. ft.

Total: 3,162 sq. ft.

Bedrooms: 5

Bathrooms: 4

Width: 60' - 0"

Depth: 43' - 10"

Foundation: Crawlspace, Slab, Unfinished Walkout Basement

EPLANS.COM

3,000 TO 3,499 SQUARE FEET

HPK2100934

Style: Farmhouse
First Floor: 2,086 sq. ft.
Second Floor: 1,077 sq. ft.
Total: 3,163 sq. ft.
Bonus Space: 403 sq. ft.
Bedrooms: 4
Bathrooms: 3 ½
Width: 81' - 10"
Depth: 51' - 8"

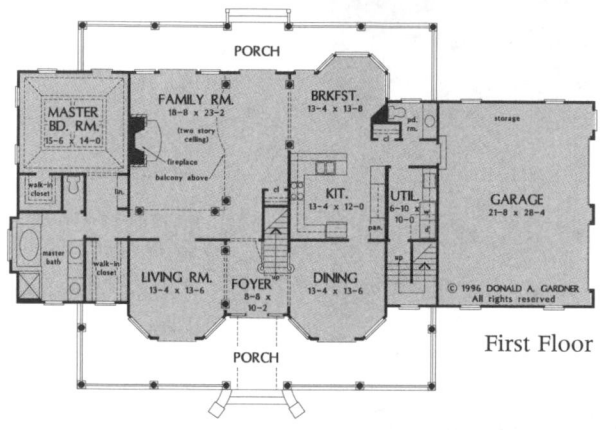

First Floor

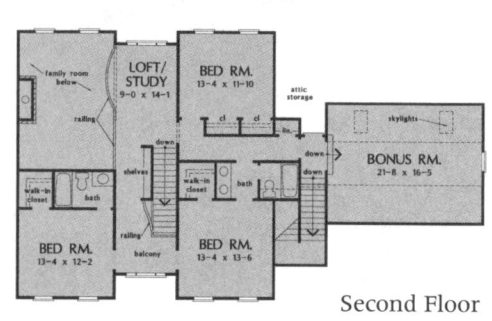

Second Floor

First Floor

HPK2100935

Style: New American
First Floor: 2,294 sq. ft.
Second Floor: 869 sq. ft.
Total: 3,163 sq. ft.
Bonus Space: 309 sq. ft.
Bedrooms: 4
Bathrooms: 3 ½
Width: 63' - 6"
Depth: 63' - 0"
Foundation: Crawlspace, Unfinished Walkout Basement

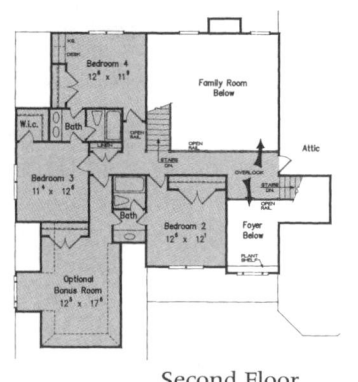

Second Floor

HPK2100936

Style: Farmhouse
First Floor: 2,194 sq. ft.
Second Floor: 973 sq. ft.
Total: 3,167 sq. ft.
Bonus Space: 281 sq. ft.
Bedrooms: 4
Bathrooms: 3 ½
Width: 71' - 11"
Depth: 54' - 4"

EPLANS.COM

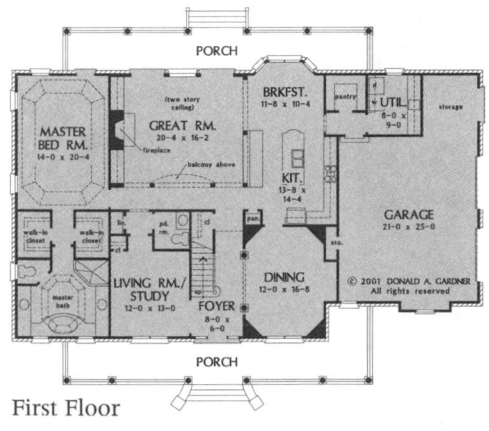

First Floor

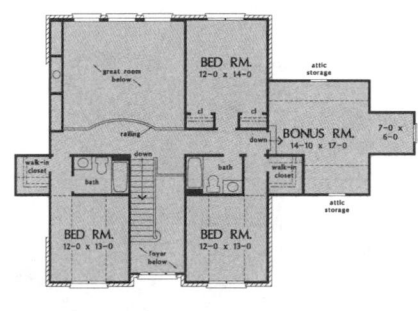

Second Floor

HPK2100937

Style: Chateauesque
First Floor: 2,056 sq. ft.
Second Floor: 1,111 sq. ft.
Total: 3,167 sq. ft.
Bedrooms: 4
Bathrooms: 3 ½
Width: 69' - 8"
Depth: 51' - 6"
Foundation: Crawlspace

EPLANS.COM

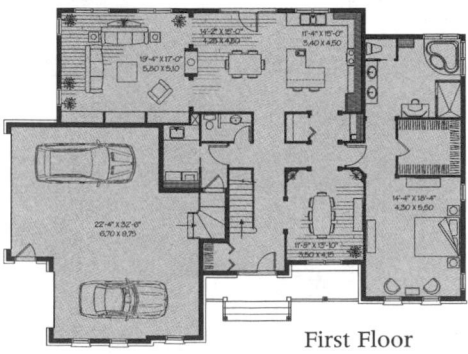

First Floor

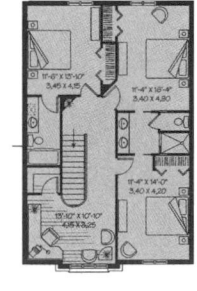

Second Floor

3,000 TO 3,499 SQUARE FEET

First Floor

Second Floor

HPK2100938

Style: New American
First Floor: 2,452 sq. ft.
Second Floor: 715 sq. ft.
Total: 3,167 sq. ft.
Bonus Space: 379 sq. ft.
Bedrooms: 4
Bathrooms: 3 ½
Width: 73' - 6"
Depth: 69' - 11"
Foundation: Crawlspace

EPLANS.COM

First Floor

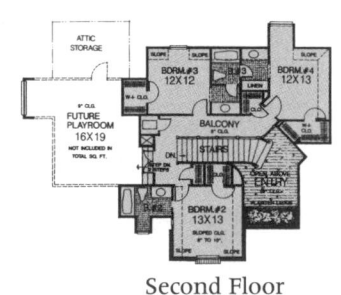

Second Floor

HPK2100939

Style: Chateauesque
First Floor: 2,237 sq. ft.
Second Floor: 931 sq. ft.
Total: 3,168 sq. ft.
Bonus Space: 304 sq. ft.
Bedrooms: 4
Bathrooms: 3 ½
Width: 68' - 0"
Depth: 55' - 6"
Foundation: Slab

EPLANS.COM

HPK2100940

Style: Georgian
First Floor: 2,183 sq. ft.
Second Floor: 993 sq. ft.
Total: 3,176 sq. ft.
Bedrooms: 4
Bathrooms: 3 ½
Width: 66' - 0"
Depth: 84' - 0"
Foundation: Slab

EPLANS.COM

First Floor

Second Floor

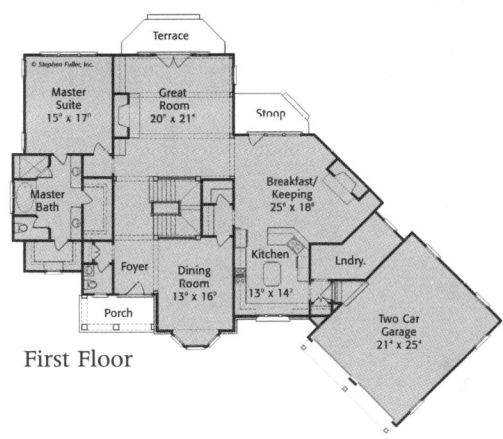

First Floor

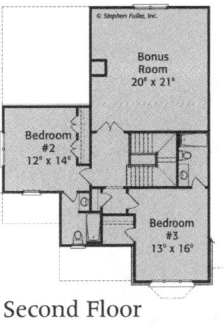

Second Floor

HPK2100941

EPLANS.COM

Style: Country
First Floor: 2,456 sq. ft.
Second Floor: 725 sq. ft.
Total: 3,181 sq. ft.
Bedrooms: 3
Bathrooms: 3 ½
Width: 85' - 6"
Depth: 60' - 0"
Foundation: Walkout Basement

© Stephen Fuller, Inc.

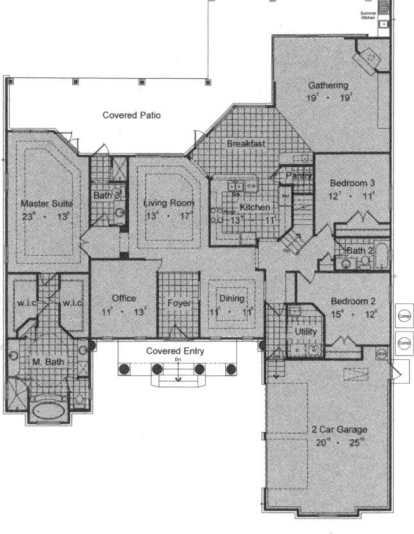

HPK2100942

Style: Georgian
First Floor: 2,782 sq. ft.
Second Floor: 401 sq. ft.
Total: 3,183 sq. ft.
Bedrooms: 3
Bathrooms: 4
Width: 65' - 0"
Depth: 88' - 3"
Foundation: Slab

EPLANS.COM

© Sater Design Collection, Inc.

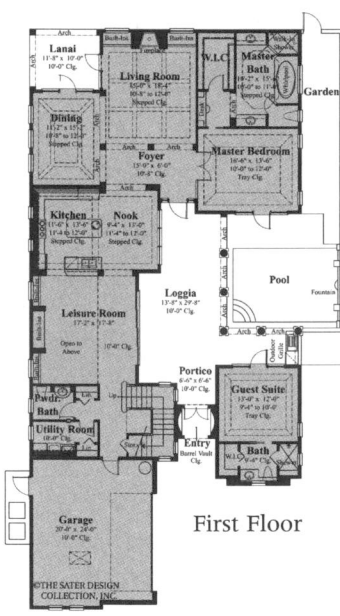

First Floor

HPK2100943

Style: Mediterranean
First Floor: 2,087 sq. ft.
Second Floor: 1,099 sq. ft.
Total: 3,186 sq. ft.
Bedrooms: 4
Bathrooms: 4 ½
Width: 52' - 2"
Depth: 94' - 0"
Foundation: Slab

EPLANS.COM

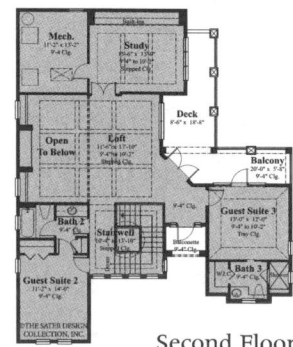

Second Floor

ORDER BLUEPRINTS ANYTIME AT EPLANS.COM OR 1-800-521-6797

HPK2100944

Style: Cottage
First Floor: 2,167 sq. ft.
Second Floor: 1,027 sq. ft.
Total: 3,194 sq. ft.
Bonus Space: 394 sq. ft.
Bedrooms: 4
Bathrooms: 3 ½
Width: 65' - 0"
Depth: 68' - 4"
Foundation: Crawlspace, Unfinished Walkout Basement

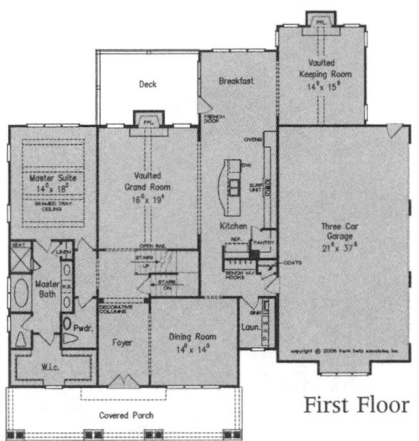

First Floor

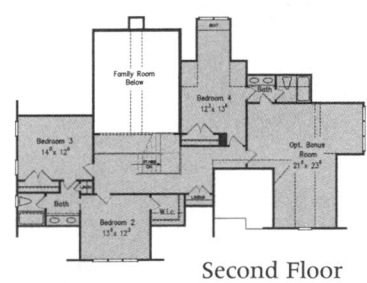

Second Floor

HPK2100945

Style: Shingle
First Floor: 1,595 sq. ft.
Second Floor: 1,600 sq. ft.
Total: 3,195 sq. ft.
Bedrooms: 5
Bathrooms: 4
Width: 54' - 0"
Depth: 43' - 0"
Foundation: Slab, Unfinished Walkout Basement

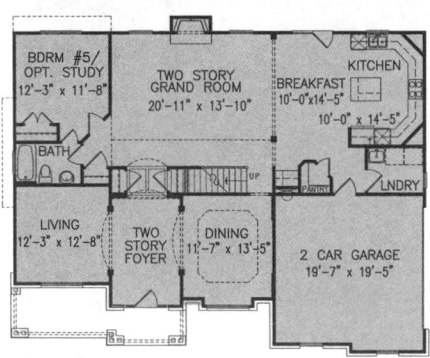

First Floor

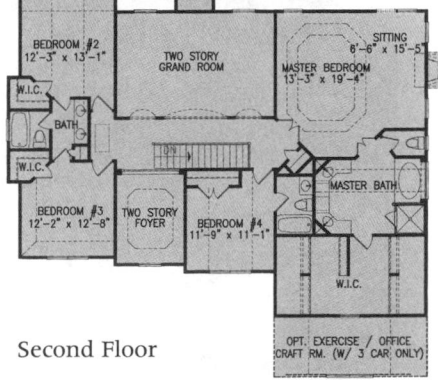

Second Floor

3,000 TO 3,499 SQUARE FEET

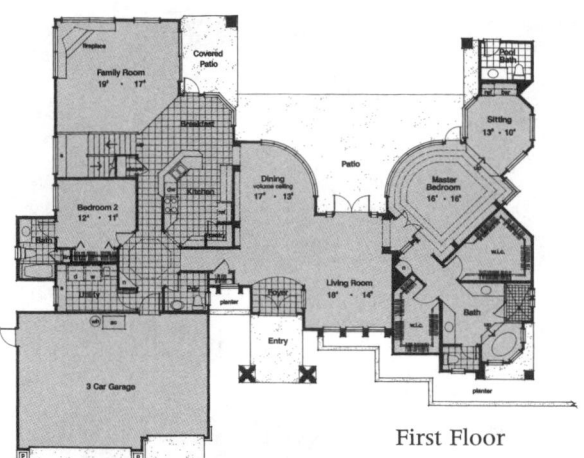

First Floor

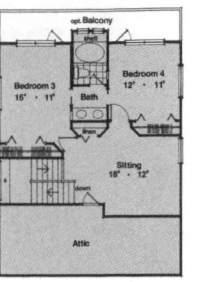

Second Floor

HPK2100946

Style: Prairie

First Floor: 2,531 sq. ft.

Second Floor: 669 sq. ft.

Total: 3,200 sq. ft.

Bedrooms: 4

Bathrooms: 3 ½ + ½

Width: 82' - 4"

Depth: 72' - 0"

Foundation: Slab

EPLANS.COM

First Floor

Second Floor

HPK2100947

Style: Federal - Adams

First Floor: 2,200 sq. ft.

Second Floor: 1,001 sq. ft.

Total: 3,201 sq. ft.

Bonus Space: 674 sq. ft.

Bedrooms: 4

Bathrooms: 3 ½

Width: 70' - 4"

Depth: 74' - 4"

Foundation: Crawlspace

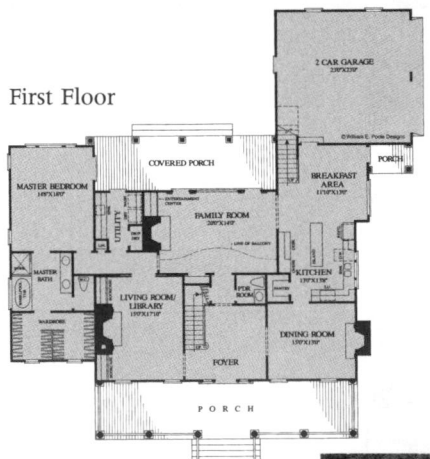

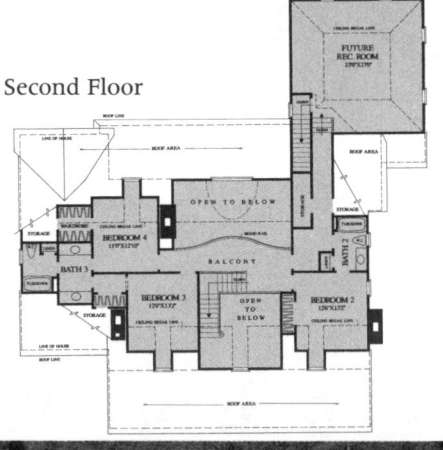

EPLANS.COM

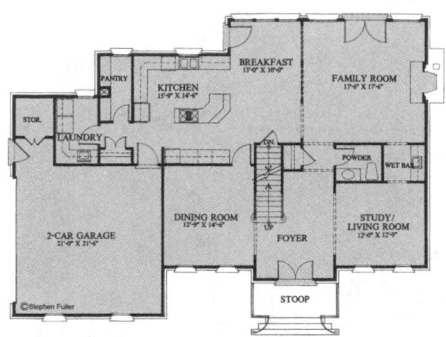

First Floor

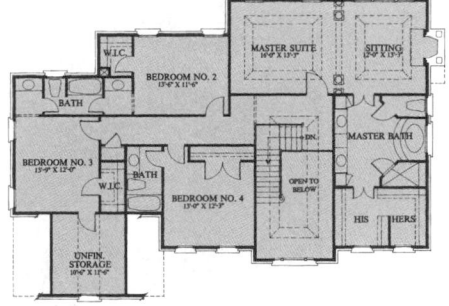

Second Floor

HPK2100948

Style: Federal - Adams

First Floor: 1,554 sq. ft.

Second Floor: 1,648 sq. ft.

Total: 3,202 sq. ft.

Bedrooms: 4

Bathrooms: 3 ½

Width: 60' - 0"

Depth: 43' - 0"

Foundation: Walkout Basement

EPLANS.COM

HPK2100949

First Floor

Style: New American

First Floor: 2,107 sq. ft.

Second Floor: 1,099 sq. ft.

Total: 3,206 sq. ft.

Bonus Space: 298 sq. ft.

Bedrooms: 4

Bathrooms: 3

Width: 61' - 0"

Depth: 66' - 4"

Foundation: Crawlspace, Slab

EPLANS.COM

Second Floor

3,000 TO 3,499 SQUARE FEET

HPK2100950

Style: French Country

First Floor: 1,746 sq. ft.

Second Floor: 1,464 sq. ft.

Total: 3,210 sq. ft.

Bedrooms: 5

Bathrooms: 4

Width: 61' - 4"

Depth: 51' - 0"

Foundation: Crawlspace, Slab, Unfinished Walkout Basement

EPLANS.COM

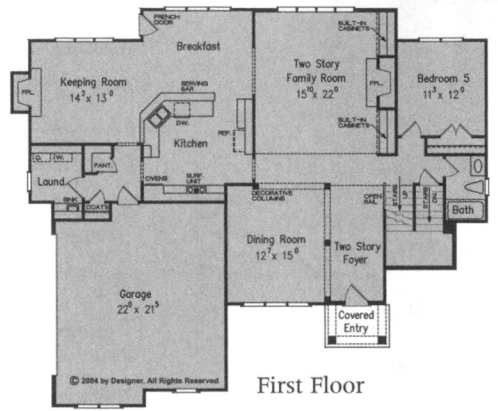

First Floor

Second Floor

HPK2100951

Style: Colonial Revival

First Floor: 1,548 sq. ft.

Second Floor: 1,666 sq. ft.

Total: 3,214 sq. ft.

Bedrooms: 5

Bathrooms: 4

Width: 55' - 4"

Depth: 54' - 0"

Foundation: Crawlspace, Unfinished Walkout Basement

EPLANS.COM

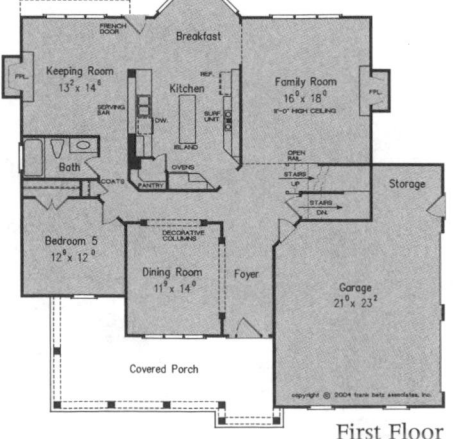

First Floor

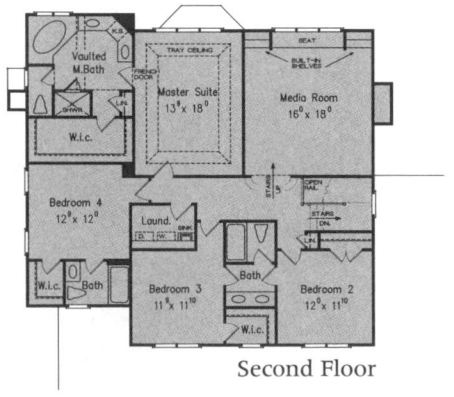

Second Floor

HPK2100952

Style: New American

First Floor: 1,583 sq. ft.

Second Floor: 1,632 sq. ft.

Total: 3,215 sq. ft.

Bedrooms: 5

Bathrooms: 4 ½

Width: 58' - 4"

Depth: 50' - 0"

Foundation: Crawlspace, Slab, Unfinished Walkout Basement

EPLANS.COM

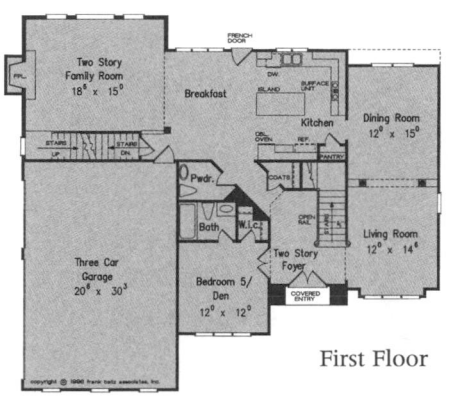

First Floor

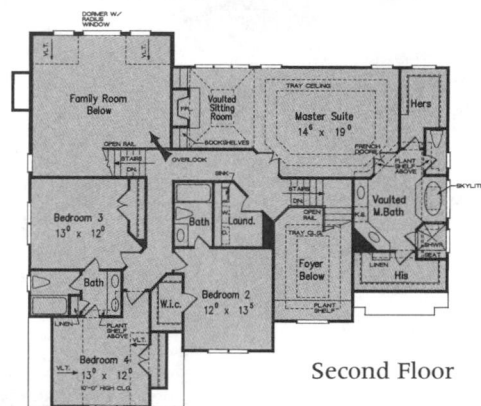

Second Floor

HPK2100953

Style: Craftsman

First Floor: 2,477 sq. ft.

Second Floor: 742 sq. ft.

Total: 3,219 sq. ft.

Bonus Space: 419 sq. ft.

Bedrooms: 4

Bathrooms: 4

Width: 100' - 0"

Depth: 66' - 2"

EPLANS.COM

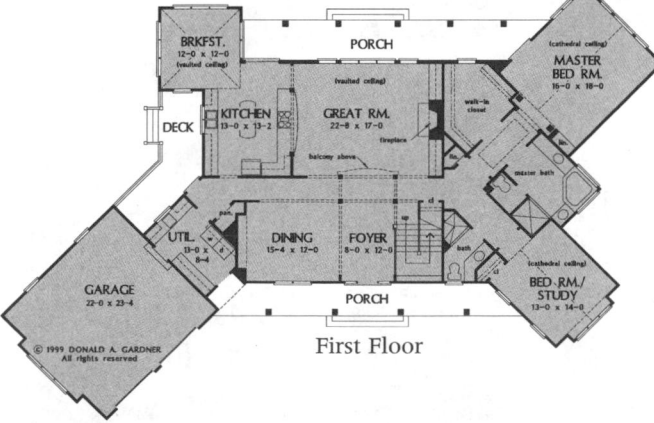

© 1999 Donald A. Gardner, Inc.

First Floor

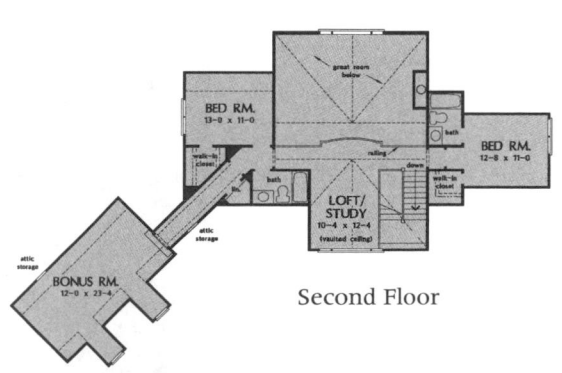

Second Floor

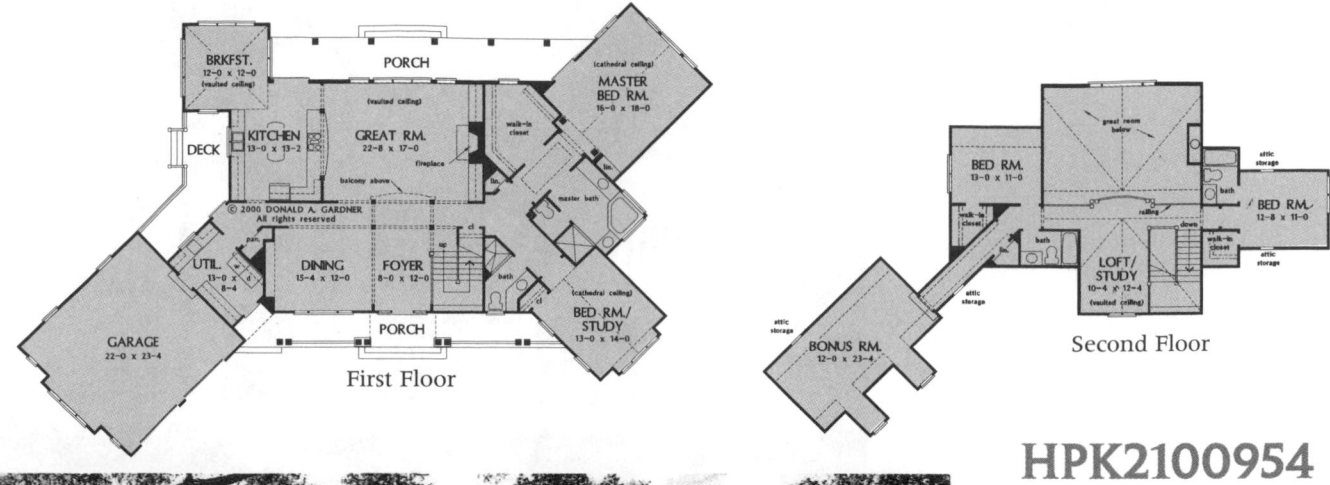

First Floor

Second Floor

HPK2100954

Style: Craftsman

First Floor: 2,477 sq. ft.

Second Floor: 742 sq. ft.

Total: 3,219 sq. ft.

Bonus Space: 419 sq. ft.

Bedrooms: 4

Bathrooms: 4

Width: 99' - 10"

Depth: 66' - 2"

EPLANS.COM

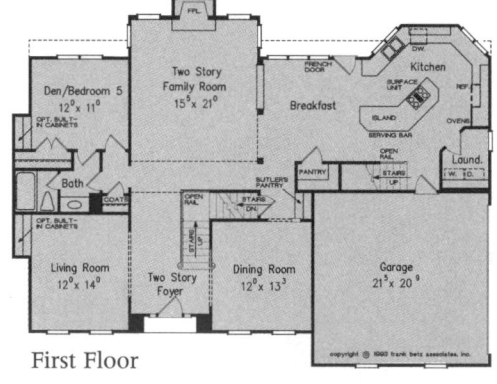

First Floor

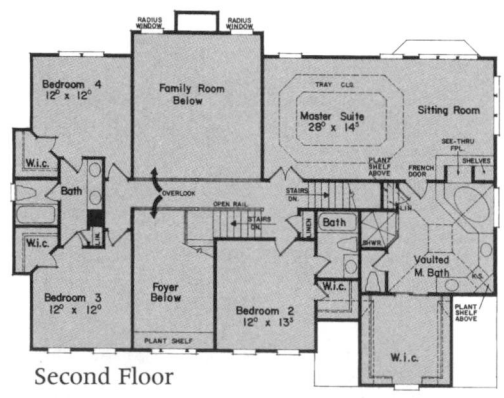

Second Floor

HPK2100955

Style: Georgian

First Floor: 1,665 sq. ft.

Second Floor: 1,554 sq. ft.

Total: 3,219 sq. ft.

Bedrooms: 5

Bathrooms: 4

Width: 58' - 6"

Depth: 44' - 10"

Foundation: Crawlspace, Unfinished Walkout Basement

EPLANS.COM

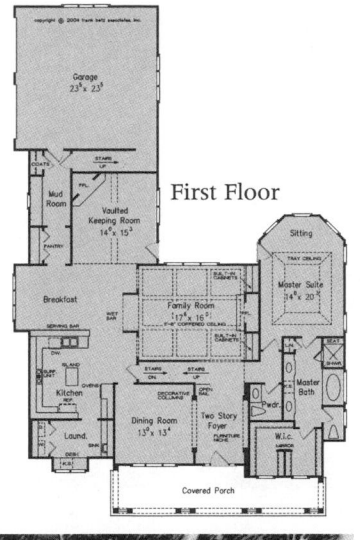

First Floor

HPK2100956

Style: Country

First Floor: 2,284 sq. ft.

Second Floor: 940 sq. ft.

Total: 3,224 sq. ft.

Bonus Space: 545 sq. ft.

Bedrooms: 4

Bathrooms: 3 ½

Width: 55' - 0"

Depth: 85' - 0"

Foundation: Crawlspace, Unfinished Walkout Basement

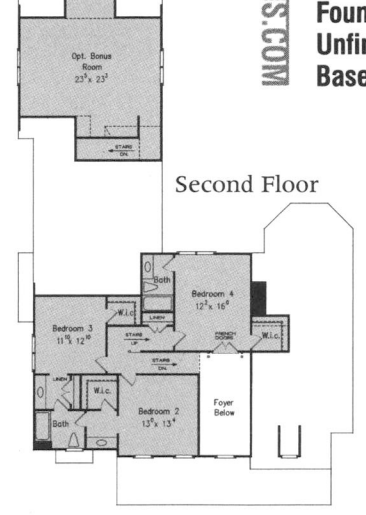

Second Floor

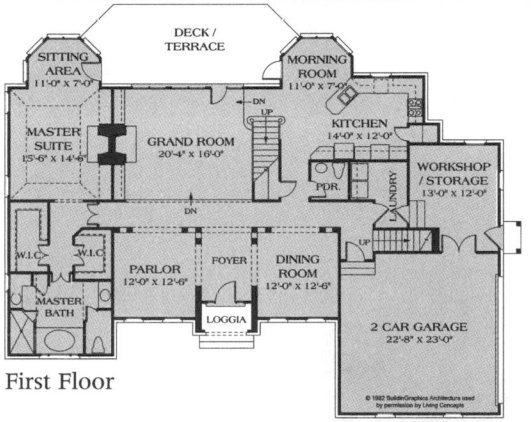

First Floor

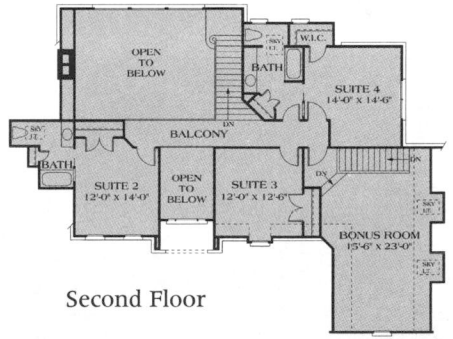

Second Floor

HPK2100957

Style: New American

First Floor: 2,198 sq. ft.

Second Floor: 1,028 sq. ft.

Total: 3,226 sq. ft.

Bonus Space: 466 sq. ft.

Bedrooms: 4

Bathrooms: 3 ½

Width: 72' - 8"

Depth: 56' - 6"

Foundation: Crawlspace

EPLANS.COM

3,000 TO 3,499 SQUARE FEET

HPK2100958

Style: Craftsman

First Floor: 2,063 sq. ft.

Second Floor: 1,170 sq. ft.

Total: 3,233 sq. ft.

Bonus Space: 370 sq. ft.

Bedrooms: 3

Bathrooms: 3 ½

Width: 40' - 0"

Depth: 63' - 0"

Foundation: Walkout Basement

EPLANS.COM

© Stephen Fuller, Inc.

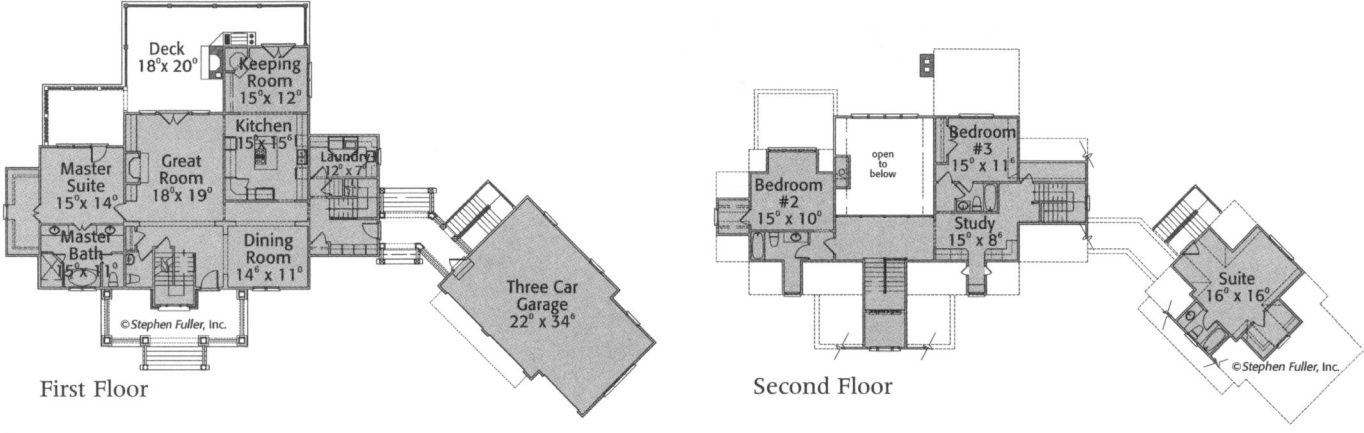

First Floor

Second Floor

HPK2100959

Style: New American

First Floor: 2,450 sq. ft.

Second Floor: 787 sq. ft.

Total: 3,237 sq. ft.

Bedrooms: 4

Bathrooms: 3 ½

Width: 68' - 11"

Depth: 65' - 7"

Foundation: Crawlspace, Unfinished Basement

EPLANS.COM

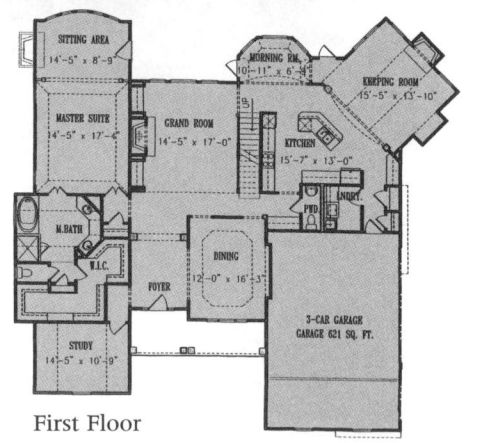

First Floor

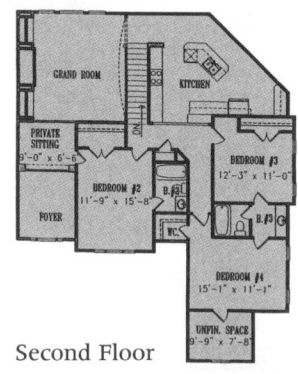

Second Floor

ORDER BLUEPRINTS ANYTIME AT EPLANS.COM OR 1-800-521-6797

HPK2100960

Style: Farmhouse
First Floor: 2,260 sq. ft.
Second Floor: 986 sq. ft.
Total: 3,246 sq. ft.
Bedrooms: 4
Bathrooms: 3 ½
Width: 64' - 4"
Depth: 61' - 0"
Foundation: Crawlspace, Unfinished Walkout Basement

EPLANS.COM

First Floor

Second Floor

HPK2100961

Style: French Country
First Floor: 1,586 sq. ft.
Second Floor: 1,664 sq. ft.
Total: 3,250 sq. ft.
Bedrooms: 4
Bathrooms: 3
Width: 44' - 4"
Depth: 65' - 4"
Foundation: Crawlspace, Slab, Unfinished Walkout Basement

EPLANS.COM

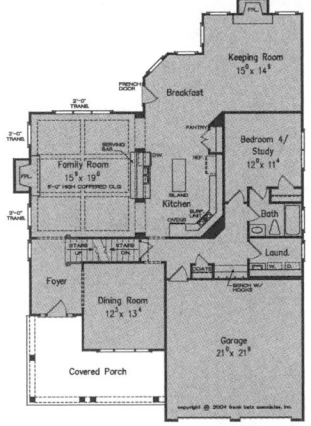

First Floor

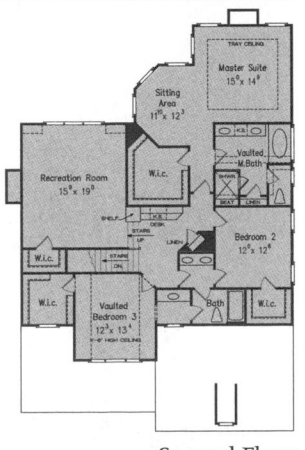

Second Floor

3,000 TO 3,499 SQUARE FEET

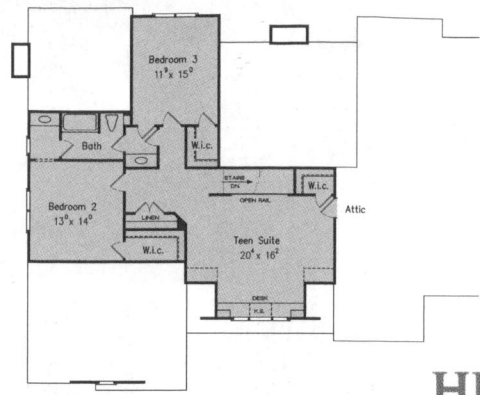

First Floor

Second Floor

HPK2100962

Style: French Country
First Floor: 2,224 sq. ft.
Second Floor: 1,030 sq. ft.
Total: 3,254 sq. ft.
Bedrooms: 4
Bathrooms: 3
Width: 65' - 4"
Depth: 53' - 8"
Foundation: Crawlspace, Unfinished Walkout Basement

EPLANS.COM

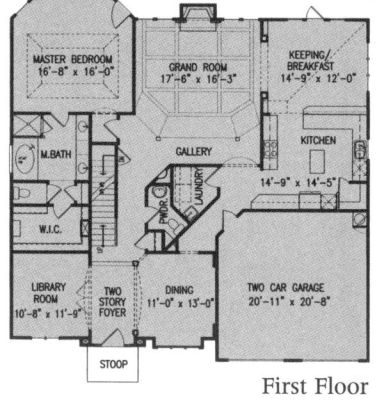

First Floor

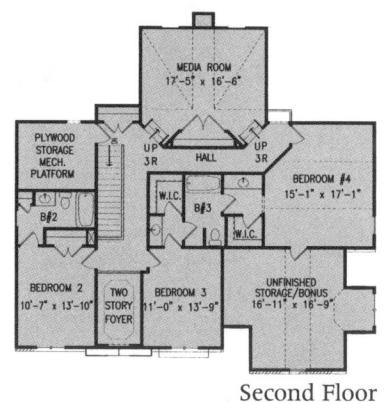

Second Floor

HPK2100963

Style: French Country
First Floor: 1,932 sq. ft.
Second Floor: 1,327 sq. ft.
Total: 3,259 sq. ft.
Bedrooms: 4
Bathrooms: 3 ½
Width: 50' - 0"
Depth: 51' - 0"
Foundation: Slab, Finished Walkout Basement

EPLANS.COM

HPK2100964

Style: Georgian

First Floor: 1,591 sq. ft.

Second Floor: 1,669 sq. ft.

Total: 3,260 sq. ft.

Bedrooms: 5

Bathrooms: 4 ½

Width: 58' - 4"

Depth: 58' - 6"

Foundation: Crawlspace, Unfinished Walkout Basement

EPLANS.COM

The classic red brick facade evokes a timeless quality from this traditional home. The minimal use of walls lends a roomy feel and encourages gatherings. French doors access the screened porch where year-round outdoor dining is an option. Four of the five bedrooms reside on the second floor, but the lone first-floor suite is ideal for guests or in-laws. The master suite is unmatched, with a private sitting area adorned with a personal fireplace. The second-floor laundry room is a thoughtful touch.

3,000 TO 3,499 SQUARE FEET

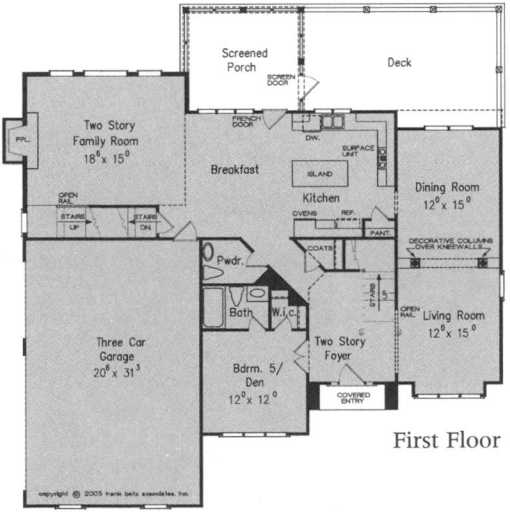

First Floor

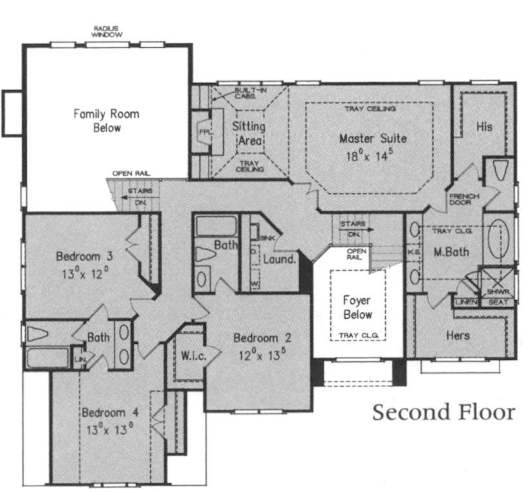

Second Floor

First Floor

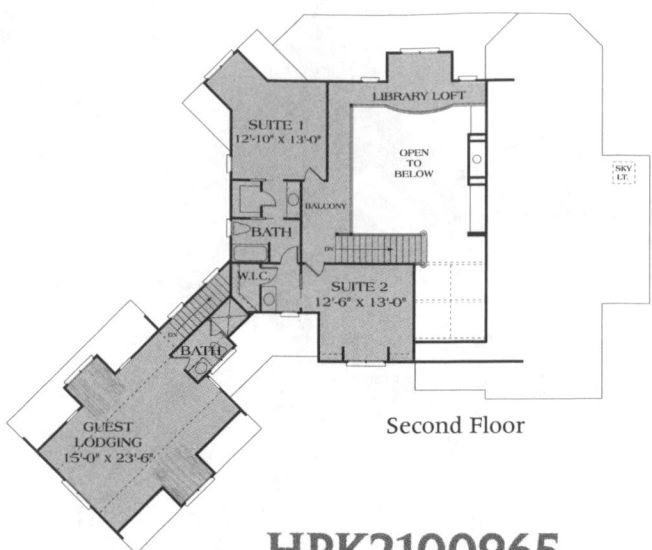

Second Floor

HPK2100965

Style: French Country
First Floor: 2,394 sq. ft.
Second Floor: 867 sq. ft.
Total: 3,261 sq. ft.
Bonus Space: 524 sq. ft.
Bedrooms: 3
Bathrooms: 2 ½
Width: 87' - 11"
Depth: 75' - 2"
Foundation: Crawlspace

EPLANS.COM

Columns flank the entrance to this attractive home. Inside, the study and the gathering room both feature fireplaces. The kitchen has a large work island and extended counter space, and serves the morning and gathering rooms. The master suite is truly luxurious, with a walk-in closet, lavish bath, and access to the rear veranda. Upstairs, two suites share a full bath and access to a loft overlooking the gathering room.

HPK2100966

Style: New American
First Floor: 1,418 sq. ft.
Second Floor: 1,844 sq. ft.
Total: 3,262 sq. ft.
Bedrooms: 4
Bathrooms: 3 ½
Width: 63' - 0"
Depth: 41' - 0"
Foundation: Crawlspace, Slab, Unfinished Walkout Basement

EPLANS.COM

Hipped rooflines, lintels, and French-style shutters give this home a taste of Europe. The two-story foyer is flanked by the formal living and dining rooms, and the living room opens through French doors to a private covered porch. A spacious, sunken family room features a warming fireplace framed by windows. The second floor overlooks the breakfast area and foyer. The lavish master bedroom provides a tray ceiling, a sitting room, a through-fireplace, and a sumptuous bath. Three family bedrooms and two full baths complete this level.

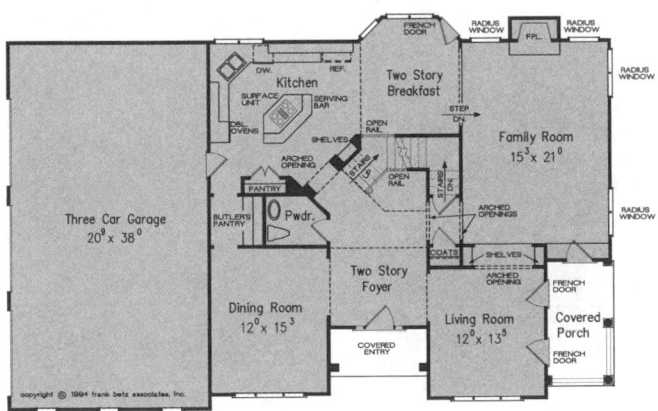

First Floor

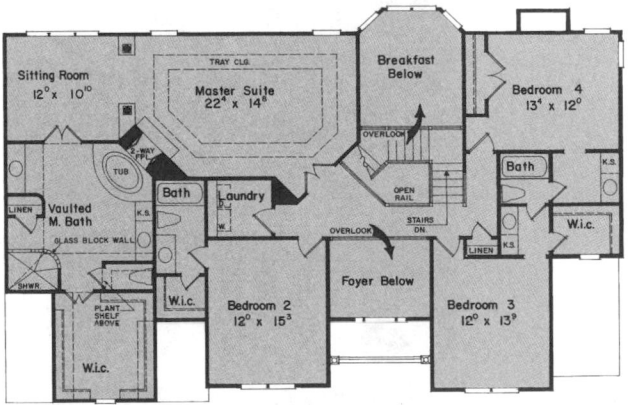

Second Floor

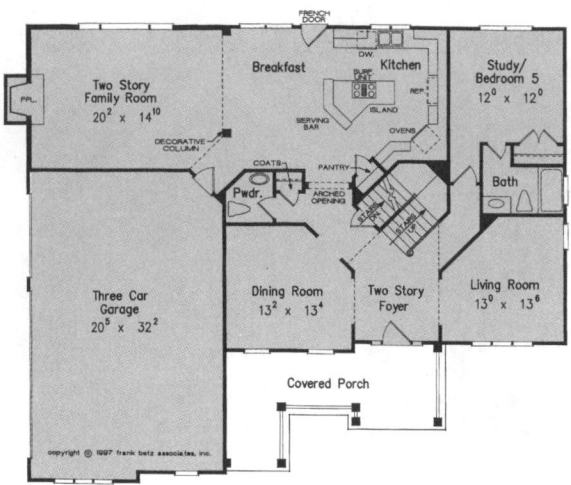

First Floor

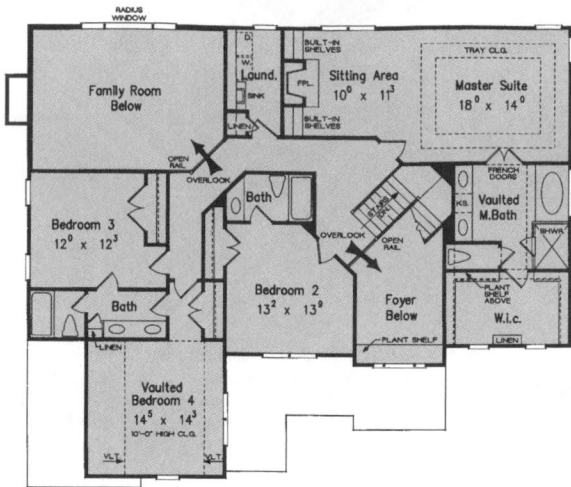

Second Floor

HPK2100967

Style: New American

First Floor: 1,577 sq. ft.

Second Floor: 1,689 sq. ft.

Total: 3,266 sq. ft.

Bedrooms: 5

Bathrooms: 4 ½

Width: 59' - 4"

Depth: 49' - 0"

Foundation: Crawlspace, Unfinished Walkout Basement

A variety of textures add interest and curb appeal to this two-story home. Past the U-shaped staircase, the spacious kitchen provides a pantry, cooktop island with a serving bar, and plenty of counter and cabinet space. A study/bedroom completes this floor. Upstairs, Bedrooms 3 and 4 share a full bath, while Bedroom 2 offers privacy with its own bath. The master suite is complete with a sitting area, fireplace, built-ins, and a lavish bath.

EPLANS.COM

© Stephen Fuller, Inc.

HPK2100968

Style: Farmhouse

First Floor: 2,210 sq. ft.

Second Floor: 1,070 sq. ft.

Total: 3,280 sq. ft.

Bedrooms: 4

Bathrooms: 3 ½

Width: 60' - 6"

Depth: 58' - 6"

Foundation: Walkout Basement

EPLANS.COM

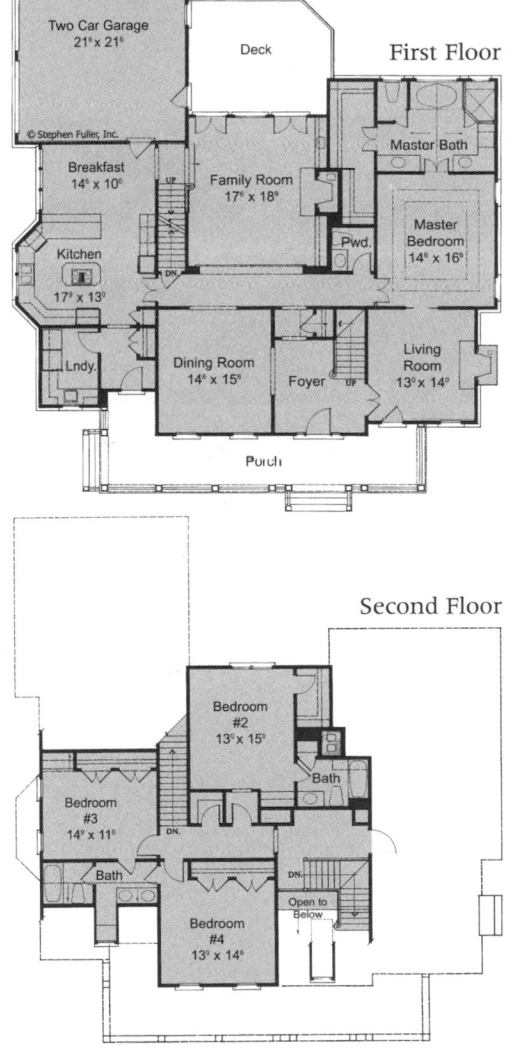

First Floor

Two Car Garage
21⁶ x 21⁶

Deck

© Stephen Fuller, Inc.

Breakfast
14⁶ x 10⁰

Family Room
17⁶ x 18⁹

Master Bath

Master
Bedroom
14⁶ x 16⁹

Kitchen
17⁹ x 13⁰

UP

DN

Pwd.

Lndy.

Dining Room
14⁶ x 15⁰

Foyer

Living
Room
13⁰ x 14⁰

Porch

Second Floor

Bedroom
#2
13⁶ x 15⁰

Bath

Bedroom
#3
14⁹ x 11⁰

DN.

Bath

Bedroom
#4
13⁹ x 14⁰

Open to
Below

DN.

A generous front porch enhances the living area of this home with a sheltering welcome. Double doors open into the study with an exposed-beam ceiling and fireplace. Left of the foyer lies the dining room, drenched in natural sunlight. The master suite features a complete master bath with separate shower and a large walk-in closet. The second floor contains three bedrooms and two baths.

3,000 TO 3,499 SQUARE FEET

HPK2100969

Style: French Country

First Floor: 1,685 sq. ft.

Second Floor: 1,596 sq. ft.

Total: 3,281 sq. ft.

Bedrooms: 5

Bathrooms: 4 ½

Width: 51' - 0"

Depth: 66' - 10"

Foundation: Crawlspace, Unfinished Walkout Basement

EPLANS.COM

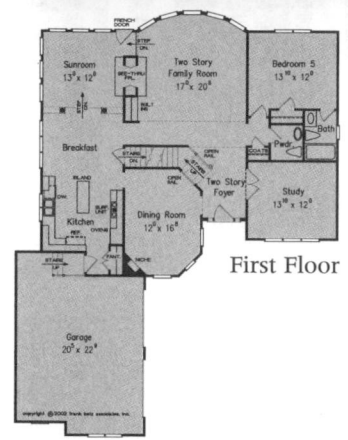

First Floor

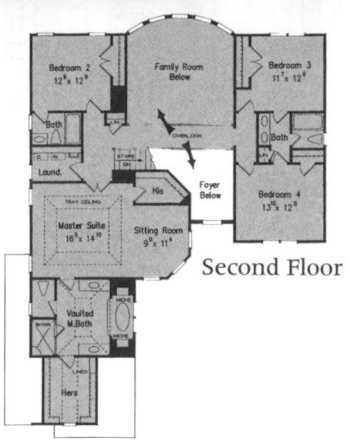

Second Floor

HPK2100970

Style: French Country

First Floor: 2,293 sq. ft.

Second Floor: 992 sq. ft.

Total: 3,285 sq. ft.

Bonus Space: 131 sq. ft.

Bedrooms: 4

Bathrooms: 3 ½

Width: 71' - 0"

Depth: 62' - 0"

Foundation: Crawlspace, Slab, Unfinished Walkout Basement

EPLANS.COM

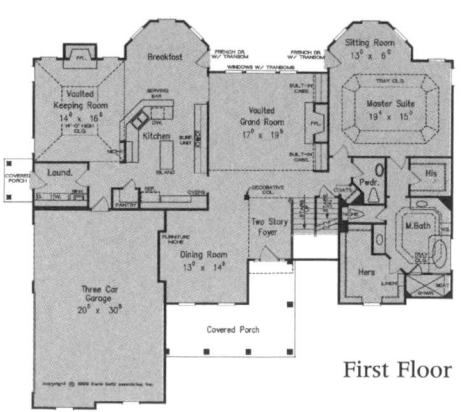

First Floor

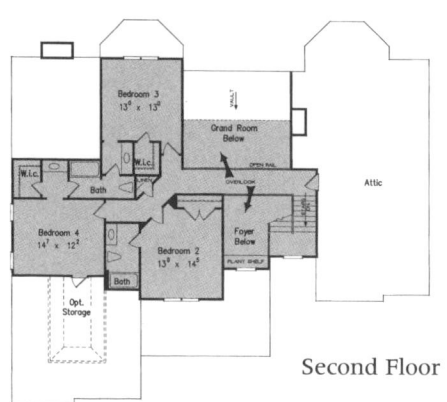

Second Floor

HPK2100971

Style: Cottage
First Floor: 2,492 sq. ft.
Second Floor: 798 sq. ft.
Total: 3,290 sq. ft.
Bedrooms: 3
Bathrooms: 3
Width: 59' - 9"
Depth: 76' - 9"
Foundation: Walkout Basement

EPLANS.COM

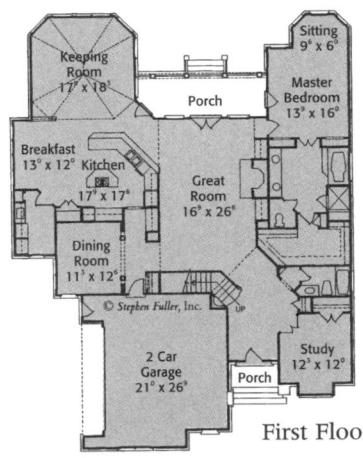

First Floor

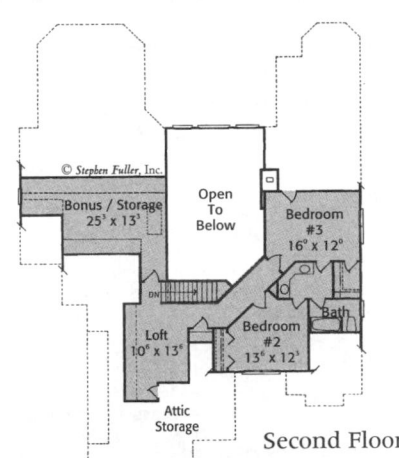

Second Floor

© 2004 Donald A. Gardner, Inc.

HPK2100972

Style: Country
First Floor: 2,314 sq. ft.
Second Floor: 978 sq. ft.
Total: 3,292 sq. ft.
Bonus Space: 358 sq. ft.
Bedrooms: 4
Bathrooms: 4
Width: 60' - 3"
Depth: 61' - 11"

EPLANS.COM

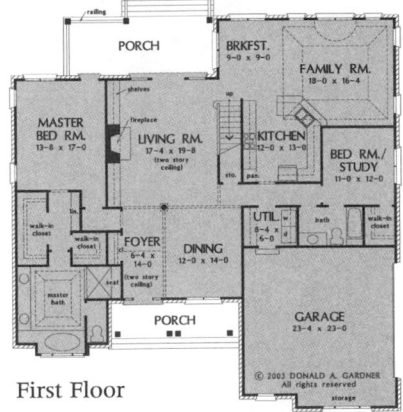

First Floor

Second Floor

3,000 TO 3,499 SQUARE FEET

HPK2100973

Style: Cottage
First Floor: 1,744 sq. ft.
Second Floor: 1,551 sq. ft.
Total: 3,295 sq. ft.
Bonus Space: 443 sq. ft.
Bedrooms: 4
Bathrooms: 3
Width: 47' - 4"
Depth: 79' - 4"
Foundation: Crawlspace, Unfinished Walkout Basement

EPLANS.COM

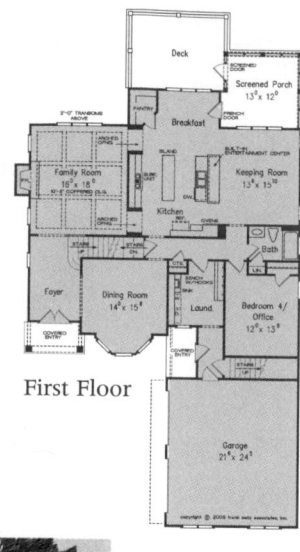

First Floor

Second Floor

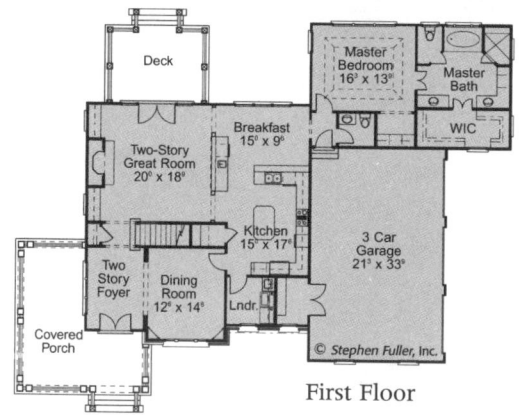

First Floor

Second Floor

HPK2100974

Style: Colonial
First Floor: 1,986 sq. ft.
Second Floor: 1,312 sq. ft.
Total: 3,298 sq. ft.
Bedrooms: 4
Bathrooms: 3 ½
Width: 79' - 0"
Depth: 59' - 4"
Foundation: Crawlspace

EPLANS.COM

© Stephen-Fuller, Inc.

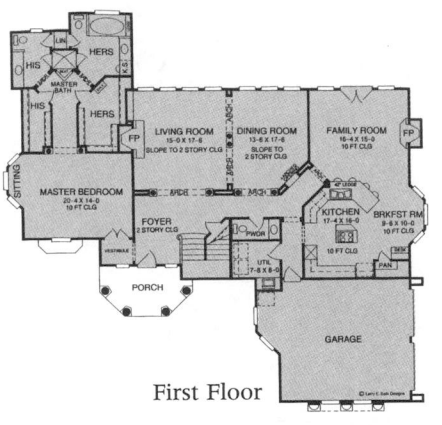

First Floor

Second Floor

HPK2100975

Style: Norman
First Floor: 2,188 sq. ft.
Second Floor: 1,110 sq. ft.
Total: 3,298 sq. ft.
Bedrooms: 4
Bathrooms: 3 ½
Width: 69' - 0"
Depth: 64' - 8"
Foundation: Slab

EPLANS.COM

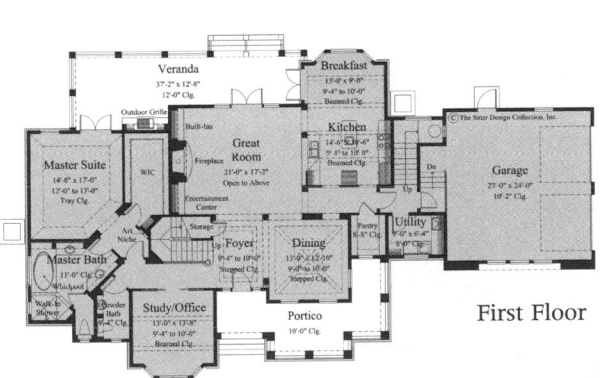

First Floor

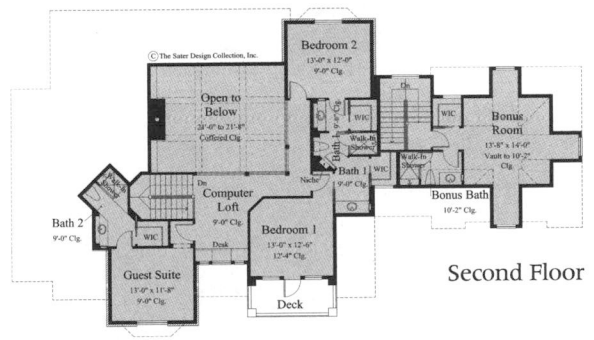

Second Floor

HPK2100976

Style: Italianate
First Floor: 2,219 sq. ft.
Second Floor: 1,085 sq. ft.
Total: 3,304 sq. ft.
Bonus Space: 404 sq. ft.
Bedrooms: 4
Bathrooms: 3 ½
Width: 91' - 0"
Depth: 52' - 8"
Foundation: Slab

EPLANS.COM

© The Sater Design Collection, Inc.

3,000 TO 3,499 SQUARE FEET

HPK2100977

Style: French Country
First Floor: 2,278 sq. ft.
Second Floor: 1,028 sq. ft.
Total: 3,306 sq. ft.
Bedrooms: 4
Bathrooms: 3 ½
Width: 62' - 0"
Depth: 66' - 0"
Foundation: Crawlspace, Unfinished Walkout Basement

EPLANS.COM

First Floor

Second Floor

HPK2100978

Style: Craftsman
First Floor: 1,719 sq. ft.
Second Floor: 1,589 sq. ft.
Total: 3,308 sq. ft.
Bonus Space: 515 sq. ft.
Bedrooms: 4
Bathrooms: 4
Width: 65' - 0"
Depth: 52' - 0"
Foundation: Crawlspace

EPLANS.COM

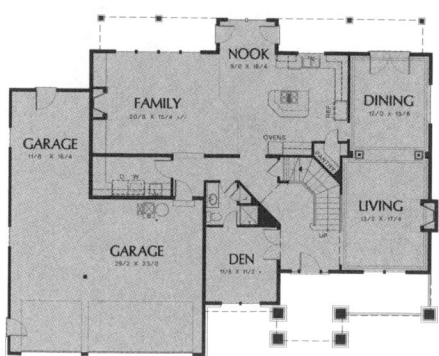

First Floor

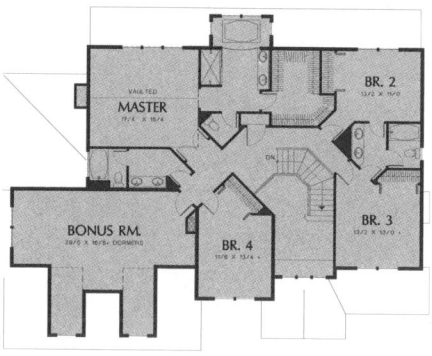

Second Floor

HPK2100979

Style: Craftsman
First Floor: 1,788 sq. ft.
Second Floor: 1,527 sq. ft.
Total: 3,315 sq. ft.
Bedrooms: 3
Bathrooms: 2 ½
Width: 64' - 0"
Depth: 54' - 0"
Foundation: Crawlspace

EPLANS.COM

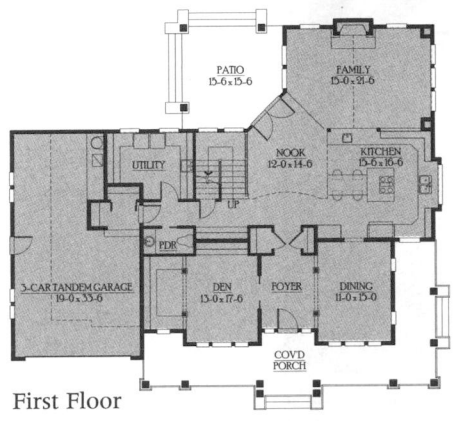

First Floor

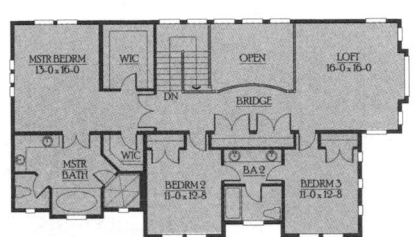

Second Floor

© The Sater Design Collection, Inc.

HPK2100980

Style: Cottage
First Floor: 2,159 sq. ft.
Second Floor: 1,160 sq. ft.
Total: 3,319 sq. ft.
Bonus Space: 317 sq. ft.
Bedrooms: 4
Bathrooms: 5
Width: 63' - 0"
Depth: 114' - 10"
Foundation: Pier (same as Piling)

EPLANS.COM

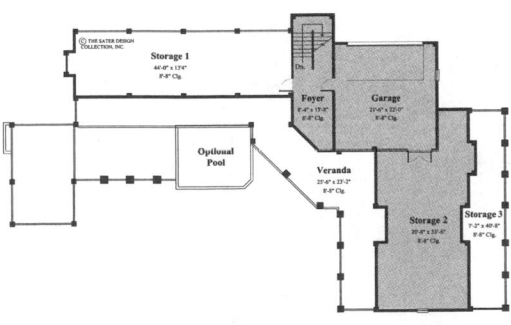

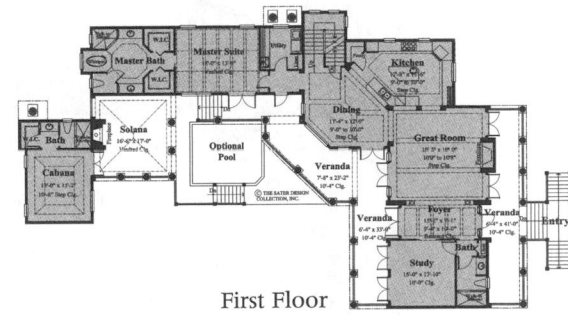

First Floor

Second Floor

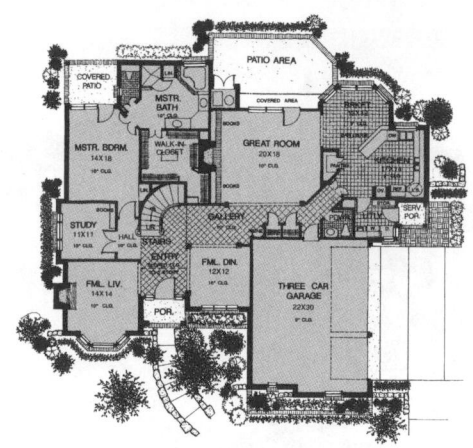

First Floor

Second Floor

HPK2100981

Style: French Country
First Floor: 2,438 sq. ft.
Second Floor: 882 sq. ft.
Total: 3,320 sq. ft.
Bonus Space: 230 sq. ft.
Bedrooms: 4
Bathrooms: 4 ½
Width: 70' - 0"
Depth: 63' - 2"
Foundation: Slab, Unfinished Basement

EPLANS.COM

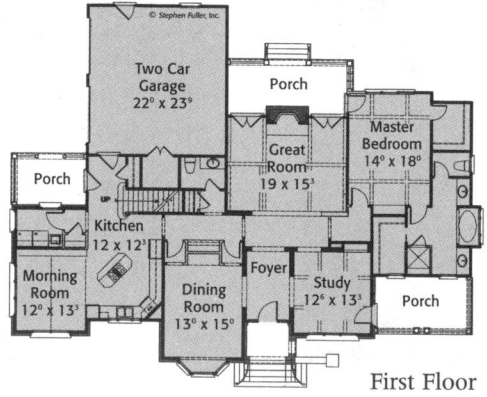

First Floor

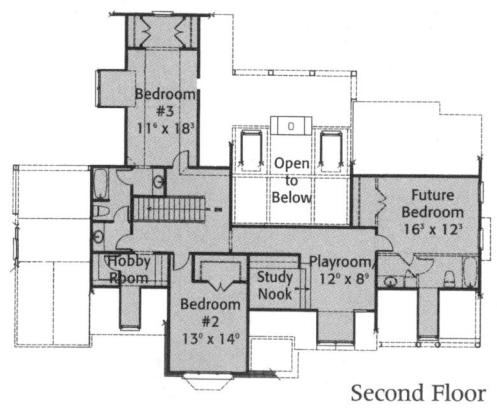

Second Floor

HPK2100982

Style: French Country
First Floor: 2,175 sq. ft.
Second Floor: 1,150 sq. ft.
Total: 3,325 sq. ft.
Bedrooms: 3
Bathrooms: 2 ½
Width: 73' - 9"
Depth: 56' - 6"
Foundation: Crawlspace

EPLANS.COM

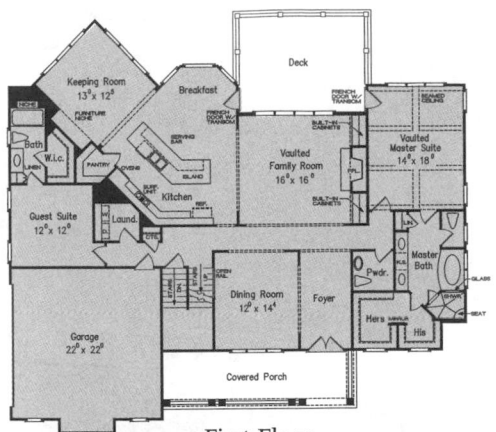

First Floor

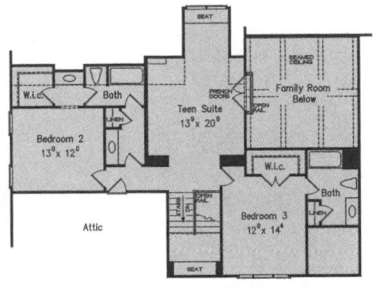

Second Floor

HPK2100983

Style: Craftsman
First Floor: 2,348 sq. ft.
Second Floor: 977 sq. ft.
Total: 3,325 sq. ft.
Bedrooms: 4
Bathrooms: 4 ½
Width: 66' - 6"
Depth: 61' - 0"
Foundation: Crawlspace, Unfinished Walkout Basement

First Floor

Second Floor

HPK2100984

Style: Cottage
First Floor: 2,372 sq. ft.
Second Floor: 955 sq. ft.
Total: 3,327 sq. ft.
Bonus Space: 325 sq. ft.
Bedrooms: 4
Bathrooms: 3 ½
Width: 61' - 0"
Depth: 66' - 4"
Foundation: Crawlspace, Unfinished Walkout Basement

EPLANS.COM

3,000 TO 3,499 SQUARE FEET

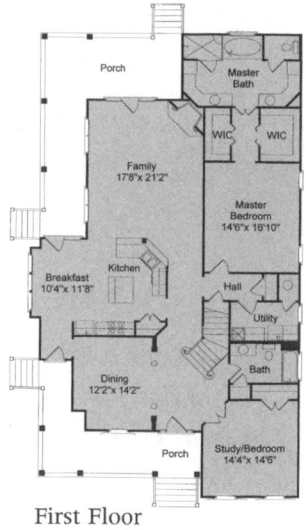

Porch

Master Bath

WIC | WIC

Family
17'8"x 21'2"

Master
Bedroom
14'6"x 16'10"

Breakfast
10'4"x 11'8"

Kitchen

Hall

Utility

Dining
12'2"x 14'2"

Bath

Porch

Study/Bedroom
14'4"x 14'6"

First Floor

Future Gameroom
19'4"x 14'8"

Bedroom
13'x 14'6"

Bedroom
11'4"x 13'10"

Computer/Library
17'8"x 8'10"

Bath

Bedroom
14'8"x 13'4"

Second Floor

HPK2100985

Style: Country

First Floor: 2,193 sq. ft.

Second Floor: 1,136 sq. ft.

Total: 3,329 sq. ft.

Bedrooms: 4

Bathrooms: 4

Width: 41' - 6"

Depth: 71' - 4"

Foundation: Pier (same as Piling)

EPLANS.COM

HPK2100986

Style: Federal - Adams

First Floor: 2,432 sq. ft.

Second Floor: 903 sq. ft.

Total: 3,335 sq. ft.

Bedrooms: 4

Bathrooms: 3 ½

Width: 90' - 0"

Depth: 53' - 10"

Foundation: Crawlspace, Slab, Unfinished Basement

EPLANS.COM

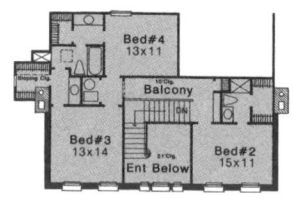

Pool

Gar
22x23

Covered Patio

Covered Patio

FamilyRm
18x22

Kit
15x15

Brkfst
10x15

MstrBed
15x21

Pwdr

GolfCart
Stor.
15x20

Bar

Util

LivRm/
Parlor
15x17

WorkShop

FmlDin
13x15

Ent

Covered
Por

First Floor

Bed#4
13x11

Balcony

Bed#3
13x14

Bed#2
15x11

Ent Below

Second Floor

HPK2100987

Style: Country
First Floor: 2,298 sq. ft.
Second Floor: 1,039 sq. ft.
Total: 3,337 sq. ft.
Bedrooms: 4
Bathrooms: 3 ½
Width: 65' - 0"
Depth: 56' - 10"
Foundation: Crawlspace

EPLANS.COM

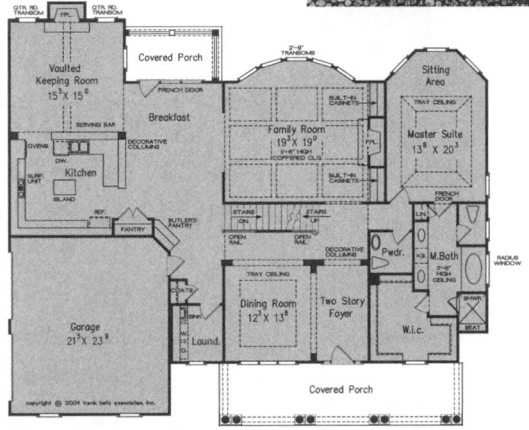

First Floor

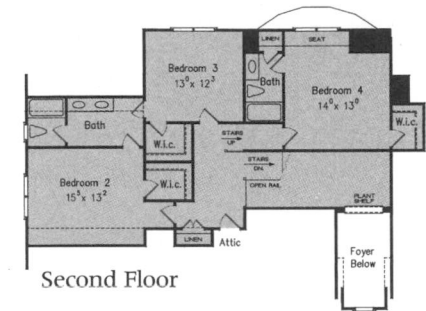

Second Floor

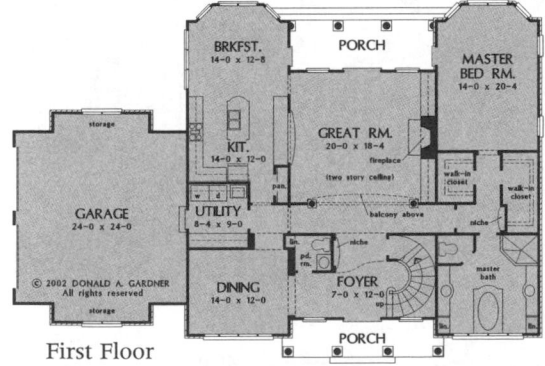

First Floor

HPK2100988

Style: Norman
First Floor: 2,062 sq. ft.
Second Floor: 1,279 sq. ft.
Total: 3,341 sq. ft.
Bonus Space: 386 sq. ft.
Bedrooms: 5
Bathrooms: 4 ½
Width: 73' - 8"
Depth: 50' - 0"

EPLANS.COM

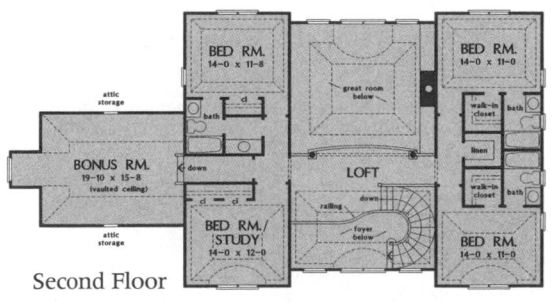

Second Floor

3,000 TO 3,499 SQUARE FEET

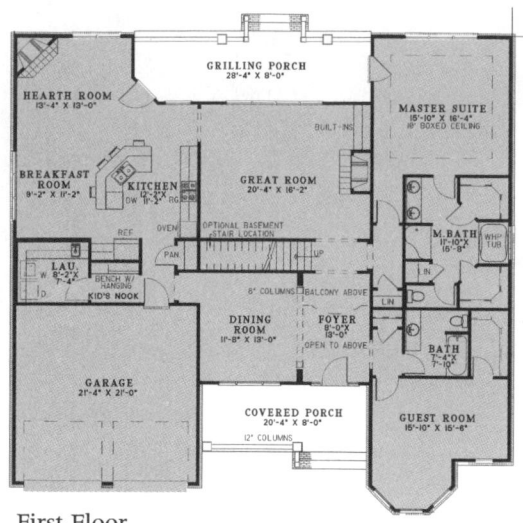

First Floor

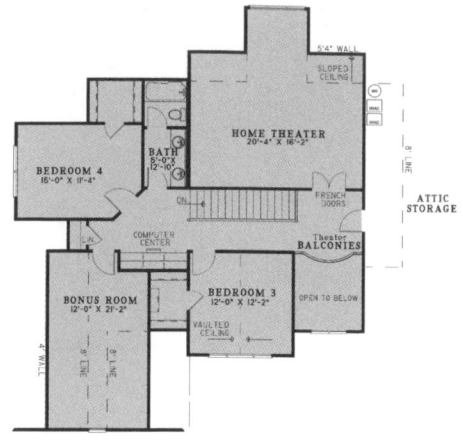

Second Floor

HPK2100989

Style: New American
First Floor: 2,245 sq. ft.
Second Floor: 1,098 sq. ft.
Total: 3,343 sq. ft.
Bonus Space: 261 sq. ft.
Bedrooms: 4
Bathrooms: 3
Width: 58' - 10"
Depth: 57' - 0"
Foundation: Crawlspace, Slab

EPLANS.COM

This home is a welcome addition to any neighborhood. The exterior appeal is punctuated by a generous front porch. Inside, sizable rooms and unexpected amenities will delight. The master suite is highlighted by a private entrance to the rear porch. The nearby guest suite is well-appointed. Upstairs, an immense home theater is a compelling feature. Two additional family bedrooms share a full bath.

HPK2100990

Style: Farmhouse
First Floor: 2,357 sq. ft.
Second Floor: 995 sq. ft.
Total: 3,352 sq. ft.
Bonus Space: 545 sq. ft.
Bedrooms: 4
Bathrooms: 3 ½
Width: 95' - 4"
Depth: 54' - 10"

EPLANS.COM

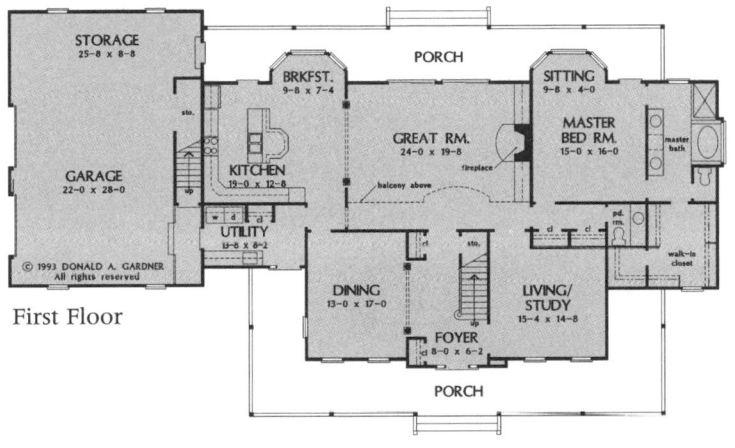

First Floor

From the two-story foyer with a Palladian clerestory window and graceful stairway to the large great room with a cathedral ceiling and curved balcony, impressive spaces prevail in this open plan. The master suite is situated privately on the first floor. Three bedrooms and two full baths make up the second floor, perfect for friends and family. A bonus room and attic storage offer expansion opportunities for the future.

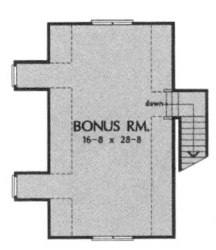

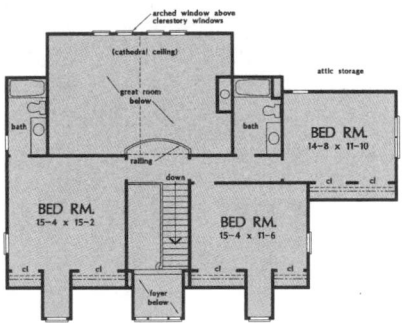

Second Floor

3,000 TO 3,499 SQUARE FEET

First Floor

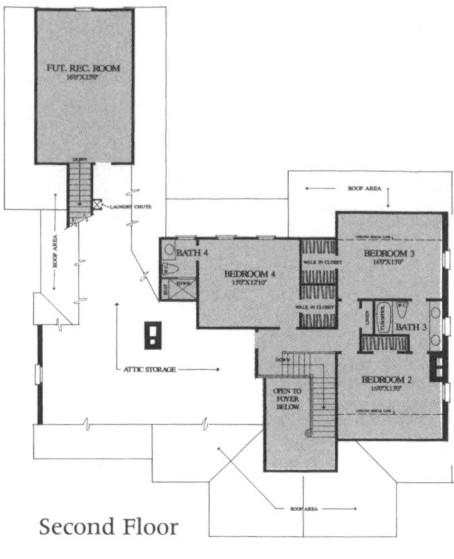

Second Floor

HPK2100991

EPLANS.COM

Style: Greek Revival
First Floor: 2,337 sq. ft.
Second Floor: 1,016 sq. ft.
Total: 3,353 sq. ft.
Bonus Space: 394 sq. ft.
Bedrooms: 4
Bathrooms: 3 ½
Width: 66' - 2"
Depth: 71' - 2"
Foundation: Crawlspace

With an abundance of natural light and amenities, this home is sure to please. The sunporch doubles as a delightful area to enjoy meals with a view. A mudroom off the utility room accesses a side porch and serves as a place to hang coats or shed dirty shoes before entering the kitchen or family room. The master bedroom, family room, and living room/library each boast a private fireplace. Upstairs houses three additional bedrooms, two sharing a full bath and one with an attached full bath.

© William E. Poole Designs, Inc.

© 2004 Donald A. Gardner, Inc.

HPK2100992

Style: Country

First Floor: 2,113 sq. ft.

Second Floor: 1,243 sq. ft.

Total: 3,356 sq. ft.

Bedrooms: 4

Bathrooms: 4

Width: 68' - 8"

Depth: 51' - 4"

EPLANS.COM

Using columns, dormers, and a prominent gable, the front elevation showcases architectural interest for striking curb appeal. A sweeping staircase makes a stunning focal point upon entering the foyer. With distinct room definition, the kitchen, breakfast nook, and great room remain open to each other. The first floor features 10-foot ceilings, with special treatment given to the great room and master suite. Upstairs there is a rec room with a cathedral ceiling and columns. Two secondary bedrooms access the upper porch through French doors.

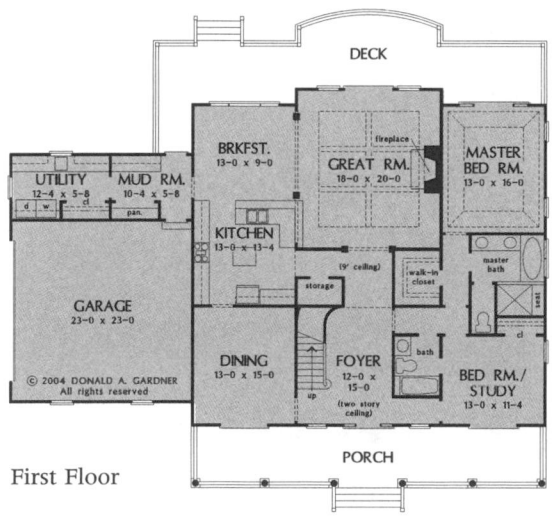

First Floor

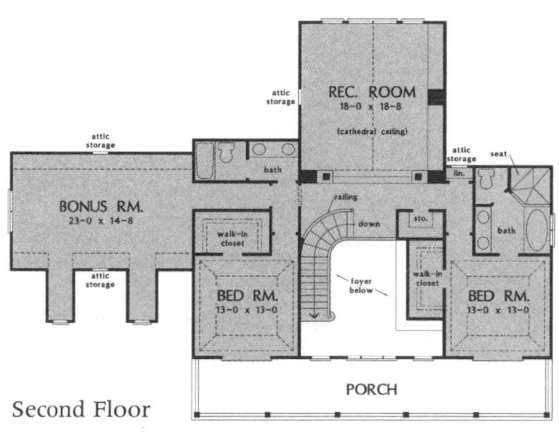

Second Floor

3,000 TO 3,499 SQUARE FEET

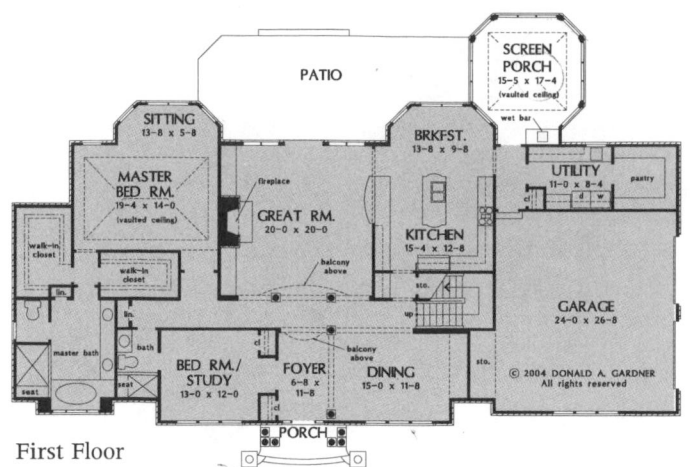

First Floor

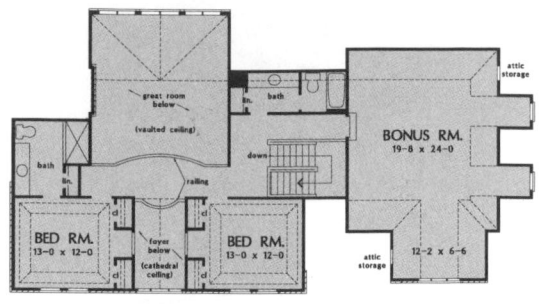

Second Floor

Evoking stately manors of the past, this traditional plan would be at home in any neighborhood. Inside, the design balances formal and informal spaces. Decorative windows usher in natural light, while columns and built-in cabinetry enhance elegance. The master bedroom is not to be missed, with a sitting nook, two walk-in closets, and a lavish bath. Two bedrooms upstairs—each with two wall closets, one with an attached bath—accommodate additional family members. The first-floor study easily converts to a guest room.

HPK2100993

Style: Federal - Adams
First Floor: 2,562 sq. ft.
Second Floor: 805 sq. ft.
Total: 3,367 sq. ft.
Bonus Space: 622 sq. ft.
Bedrooms: 4
Bathrooms: 4
Width: 87' - 7"
Depth: 59' - 6"

EPLANS.COM

First Floor

Second Floor

© William E. Poole Designs, Inc.

HPK2100994

Style: Georgian
First Floor: 2,168 sq. ft.
Second Floor: 1,203 sq. ft.
Total: 3,371 sq. ft.
Bonus Space: 452 sq. ft.
Bedrooms: 4
Bathrooms: 4 ½
Width: 71' - 2"
Depth: 63' - 4"
Foundation: Crawlspace, Unfinished Basement

EPLANS.COM

First Floor

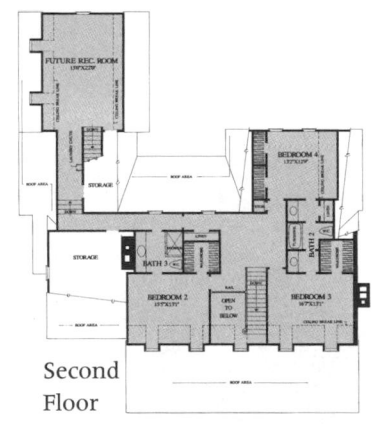

Second Floor

HPK2100995

EPLANS.COM

Style: Federal - Adams
First Floor: 2,193 sq. ft.
Second Floor: 1,179 sq. ft.
Total: 3,372 sq. ft.
Bonus Space: 558 sq. ft.
Bedrooms: 4
Bathrooms: 3 ½ + ½
Width: 66' - 5"
Depth: 75' - 5"
Foundation: Crawlspace

© William E. Poole Designs, Inc.

3,000 TO 3,499 SQUARE FEET

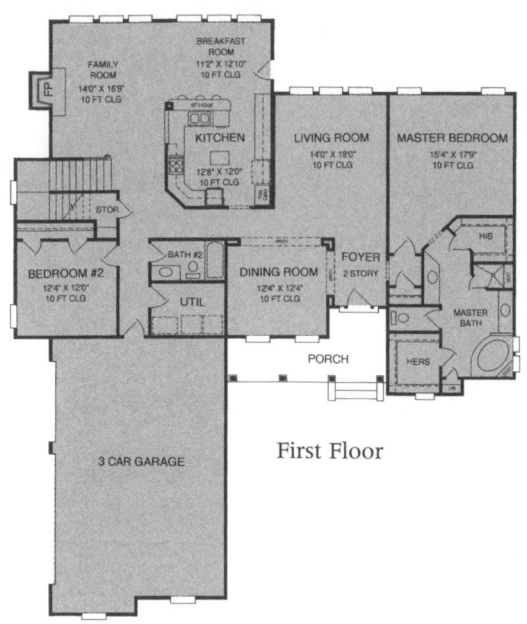

First Floor

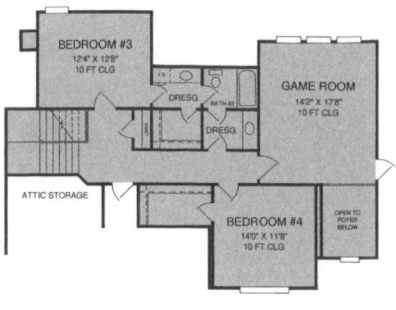

Second Floor

HPK2100996

Efficient to build, this charming country cottage orients all major living areas with wide open views to the rear. The kitchen features an eating bar and is open to the breakfast room and adjoining family room. The master bedroom is downstairs, along with a private second bedroom and bath. Two additional bedrooms and a game room are located upstairs. A large expandable area is available over the three car garage.

Style: Cottage
First Floor: 2,360 sq. ft.
Second Floor: 1,024 sq. ft.
Total: 3,384 sq. ft.
Bedrooms: 4
Bathrooms: 3
Width: 63' - 0"
Depth: 75' - 0"
Foundation: Slab

EPLANS.COM

HPK2100997

Style: Mediterranean
First Floor: 2,335 sq. ft.
Second Floor: 1,059 sq. ft.
Total: 3,394 sq. ft.
Bedrooms: 4
Bathrooms: 3 ½
Width: 67' - 1"
Depth: 65' - 10"

EPLANS.COM

First Floor

Second Floor

HPK2100998

Style: Mediterranean
First Floor: 2,144 sq. ft.
Second Floor: 1,253 sq. ft.
Total: 3,397 sq. ft.
Bedrooms: 3
Bathrooms: 3 ½
Width: 64' - 11"
Depth: 76' - 7"

EPLANS.COM

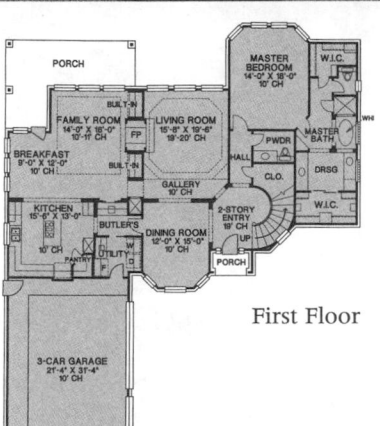

First Floor

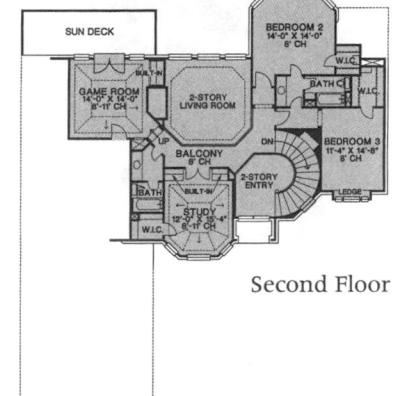

Second Floor

3,000 TO 3,499 SQUARE FEET

First Floor

Second Floor

HPK2100999

Style: French Country
First Floor: 1,821 sq. ft.
Second Floor: 1,577 sq. ft.
Total: 3,398 sq. ft.
Bedrooms: 4
Bathrooms: 2 ½
Width: 60' - 0"
Depth: 50' - 0"
Foundation: Crawlspace

EPLANS.COM

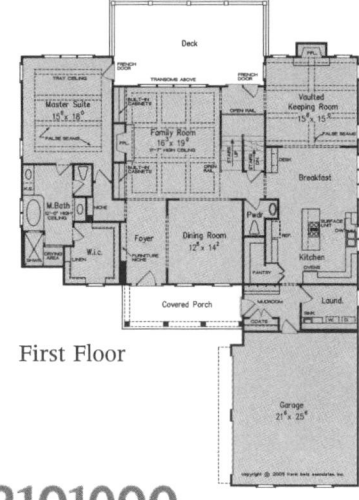

First Floor

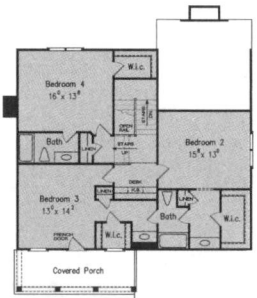

Second Floor

HPK2101000

Style: Farmhouse
First Floor: 2,272 sq. ft.
Second Floor: 1,127 sq. ft.
Total: 3,399 sq. ft.
Bedrooms: 4
Bathrooms: 3 ½
Width: 58' - 0"
Depth: 75' - 4"
Foundation: Crawlspace,
Unfinished Walkout Basement

EPLANS.COM

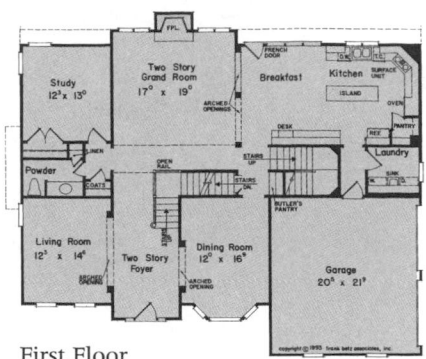

First Floor

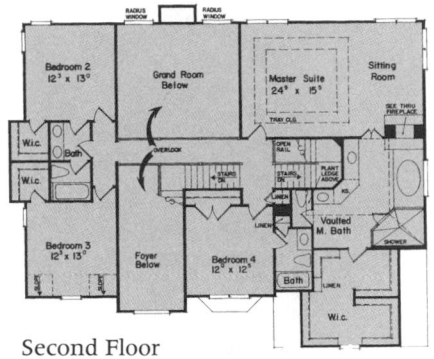

Second Floor

HPK2101001

Style: New American
First Floor: 1,738 sq. ft.
Second Floor: 1,665 sq. ft.
Total: 3,403 sq. ft.
Bedrooms: 4
Bathrooms: 3 ½
Width: 55' - 0"
Depth: 47' - 4"
Foundation: Crawlspace, Unfinished Walkout Basement

EPLANS.COM

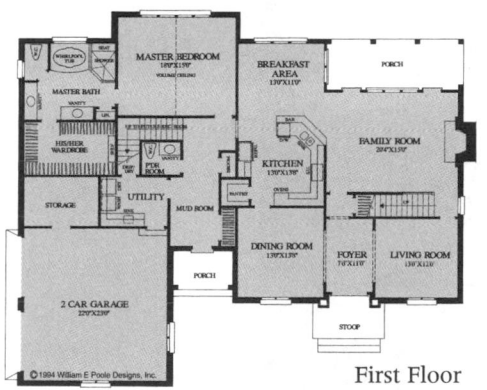

First Floor

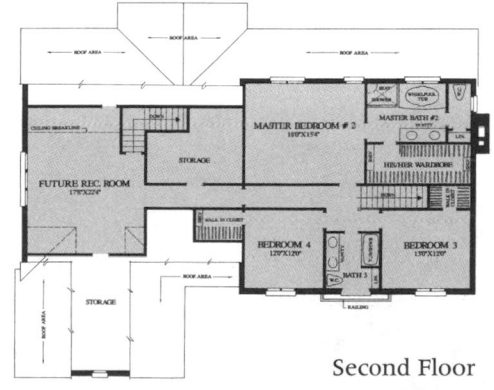

Second Floor

HPK2101002

EPLANS.COM

Style: Norman
First Floor: 2,216 sq. ft.
Second Floor: 1,192 sq. ft.
Total: 3,408 sq. ft.
Bonus Space: 458 sq. ft.
Bedrooms: 4
Bathrooms: 3 ½
Width: 67' - 10"
Depth: 56' - 10"
Foundation: Crawlspace

©1994 William E Poole Designs, Inc.

3,000 TO 3,499 SQUARE FEET

HPK2101003

Style: Farmhouse
First Floor: 2,237 sq. ft.
Second Floor: 1,182 sq. ft.
Total: 3,419 sq. ft.
Bonus Space: 475 sq. ft.
Bedrooms: 4
Bathrooms: 3 ½
Width: 85' - 4"
Depth: 56' - 4"

EPLANS.COM

© 2002 Donald A. Gardner, Inc.

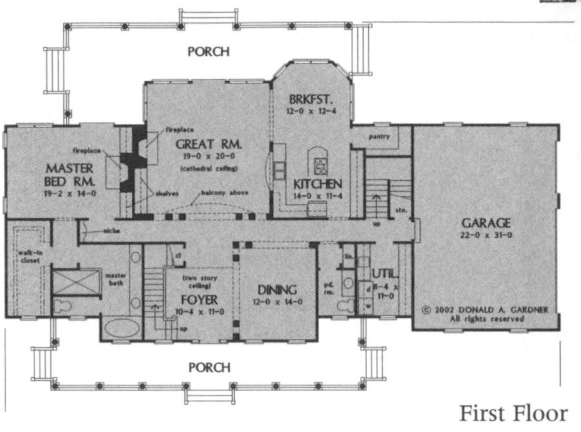

First Floor

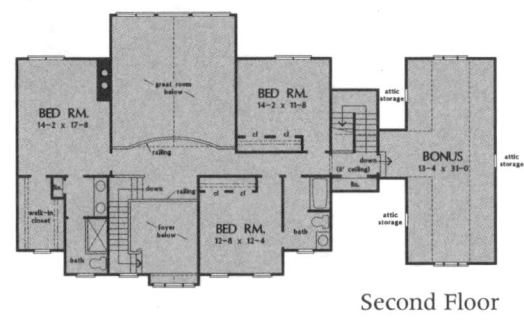

Second Floor

© William E. Poole Designs, Inc.

HPK2101004

Style: Chateauesque
First Floor: 2,272 sq. ft.
Second Floor: 1,154 sq. ft.
Total: 3,426 sq. ft.
Bonus Space: 513 sq. ft.
Bedrooms: 4
Bathrooms: 3 ½
Width: 102' - 8"
Depth: 49' - 6"
**Foundation: Crawlspace,
Unfinished Basement**

EPLANS.COM

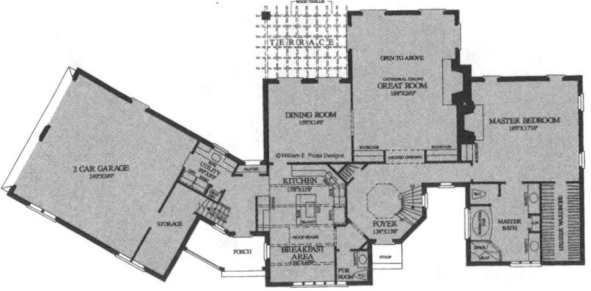

First Floor

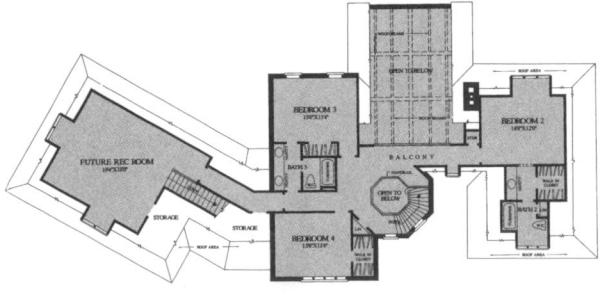

Second Floor

HPK2101005

Style: New American

First Floor: 2,108 sq. ft.

Second Floor: 1,319 sq. ft.

Total: 3,427 sq. ft.

Bonus Space: 340 sq. ft.

Bedrooms: 4

Bathrooms: 3 ½

Width: 55' - 0"

Depth: 78' - 0"

Foundation: Crawlspace, Slab, Unfinished Walkout Basement

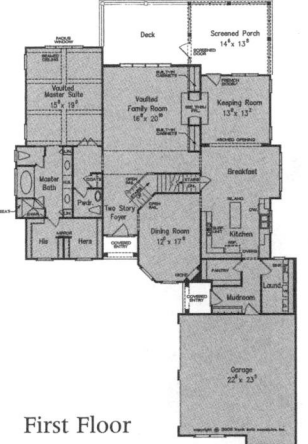

First Floor

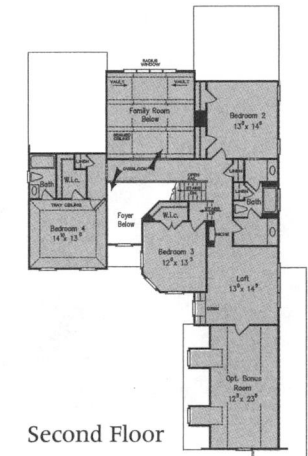

Second Floor

First Floor

Second Floor

HPK2101006

Style: New American

First Floor: 2,384 sq. ft.

Second Floor: 1,050 sq. ft.

Total: 3,434 sq. ft.

Bonus Space: 228 sq. ft.

Bedrooms: 4

Bathrooms: 3 ½

Width: 65' - 8"

Depth: 57' - 0"

Foundation: Crawlspace, Unfinished Walkout Basement

3,000 TO 3,499 SQUARE FEET

First Floor

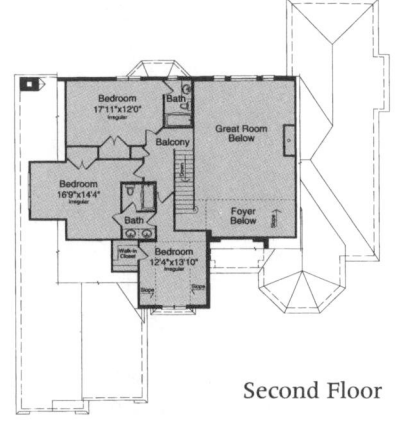

Second Floor

HPK2101007

Style: French Country

First Floor: 2,479 sq. ft.

Second Floor: 956 sq. ft.

Total: 3,435 sq. ft.

Bedrooms: 4

Bathrooms: 3 ½

Width: 67' - 6"

Depth: 75' - 6"

Foundation: Unfinished Walkout Basement

EPLANS.COM

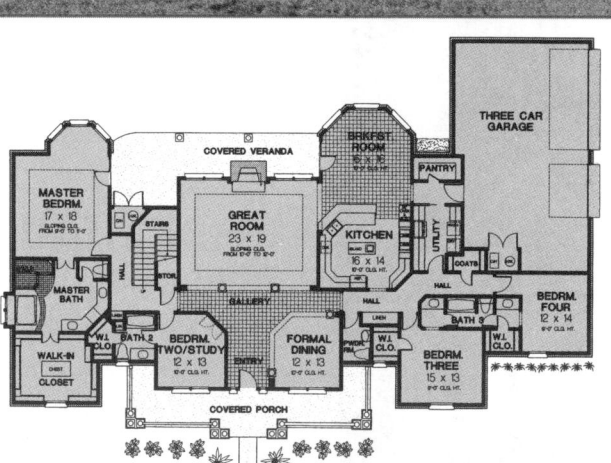

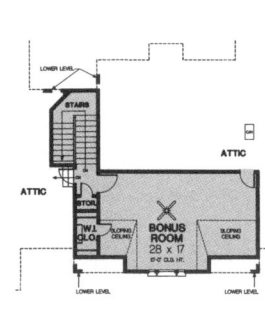

HPK2101008

Style: Gothic Revival

Square Footage: 3,439

Bonus Space: 514 sq. ft.

Bedrooms: 4

Bathrooms: 3 ½

Width: 100' - 0"

Depth: 67' - 11"

Foundation: Crawlspace, Slab, Unfinished Basement

EPLANS.COM

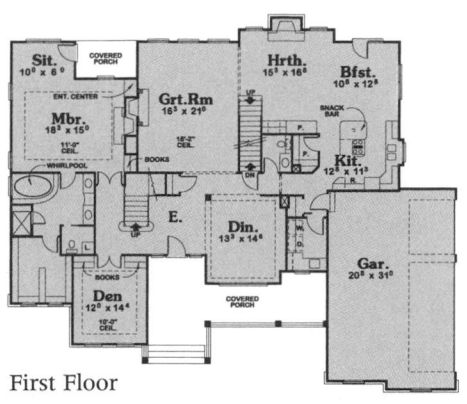

First Floor

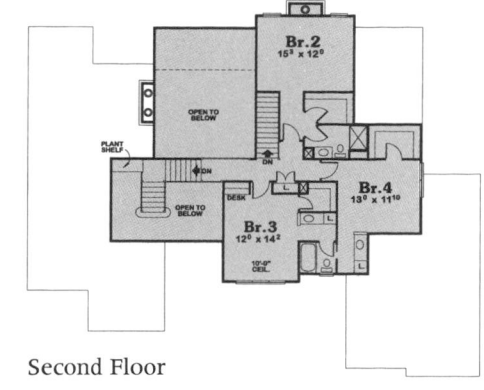

Second Floor

HPK2101009

Style: Country
First Floor: 2,454 sq. ft.
Second Floor: 986 sq. ft.
Total: 3,440 sq. ft.
Bedrooms: 4
Bathrooms: 3 ½
Width: 73' - 4"
Depth: 59' - 4"

EPLANS.COM

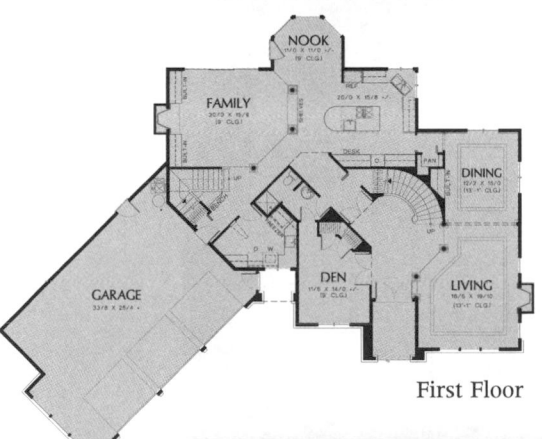

First Floor

Second Floor

HPK2101010

Style: New American
First Floor: 2,148 sq. ft.
Second Floor: 1,300 sq. ft.
Total: 3,448 sq. ft.
Bonus Space: 444 sq. ft.
Bedrooms: 4
Bathrooms: 4
Width: 85' - 5"
Depth: 73' - 0"
Foundation: Crawlspace

EPLANS.COM

3,000 TO 3,499 SQUARE FEET

HPK2101011

Style: New American
First Floor: 2,468 sq. ft.
Second Floor: 981 sq. ft.
Total: 3,449 sq. ft.
Bedrooms: 4
Bathrooms: 4
Width: 58' - 7"
Depth: 79' - 6"

EPLANS.COM

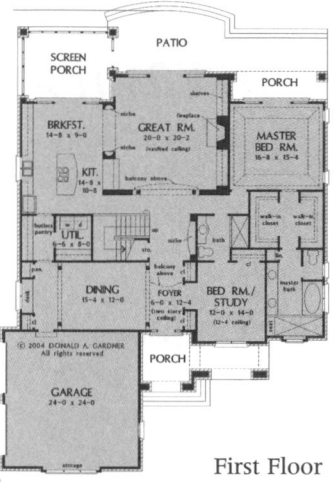

First Floor

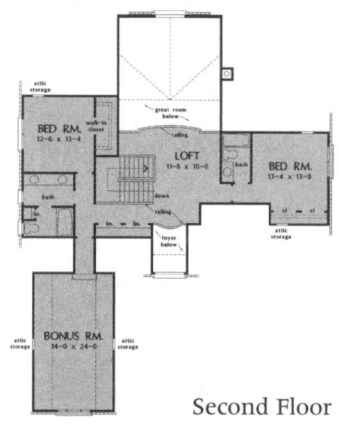

Second Floor

HPK2101012

Style: Greek Revival
First Floor: 1,773 sq. ft.
Second Floor: 1,676 sq. ft.
Total: 3,449 sq. ft.
Bedrooms: 5
Bathrooms: 4
Width: 68' - 7"
Depth: 62' - 8"
Foundation: Crawlspace, Unfinished Walkout Basement

EPLANS.COM

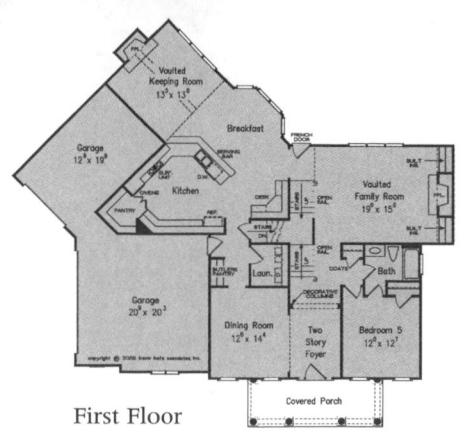

First Floor

Second Floor

HPK2101013

Style: French Country
First Floor: 2,304 sq. ft.
Second Floor: 1,147 sq. ft.
Total: 3,451 sq. ft.
Bedrooms: 4
Bathrooms: 3 ½
Width: 64' - 0"
Depth: 55' - 0"

EPLANS.COM

The decorative juliet balcony beckons while hinting at the adornments that await inside. Vaulted ceilings are peppered throughout. Square columns announce entryways lending an elegant feel. The first-floor master suite is positioned for privacy. Three additional bedrooms reside on the second floor and share two full baths.

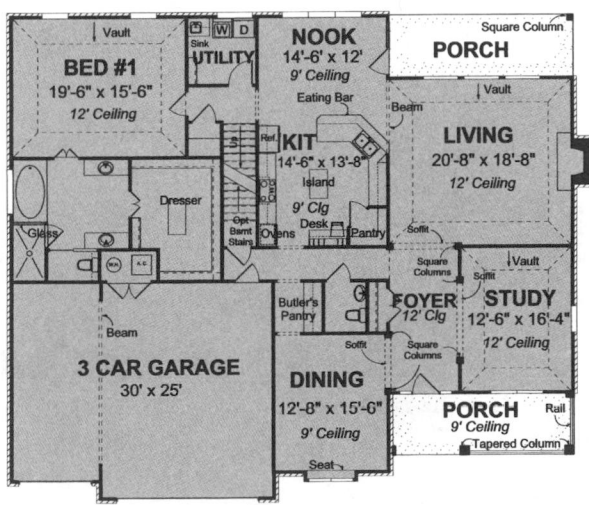

First Floor

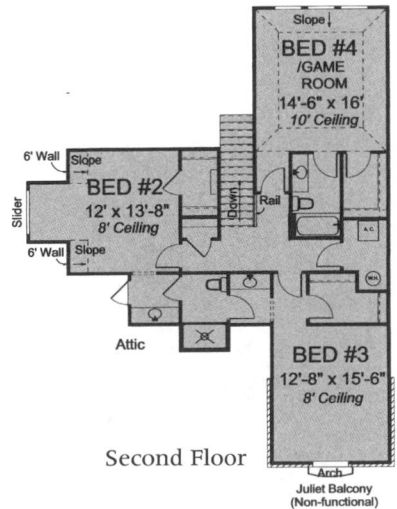

Second Floor

3,000 TO 3,499 SQUARE FEET

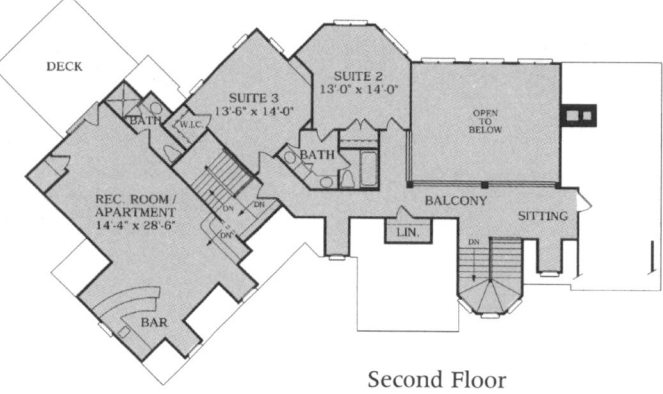

First Floor

Second Floor

HPK2101014

Style: French Country
First Floor: 2,391 sq. ft.
Second Floor: 1,071 sq. ft.
Total: 3,462 sq. ft.
Bonus Space: 609 sq. ft.
Bedrooms: 3
Bathrooms: 3 ½
Width: 113' - 7"
Depth: 57' - 5"
Foundation: Crawlspace

EPLANS.COM

If you've ever dreamed of living in a castle, this could be the home for you. The interior is fit for royalty, from the formal dining room and the multipurpose grand room to the comfortable sitting area off the kitchen. The master suite has its own fireplace and luxurious bath. One of two staircases, housed in the turret, leads to a sitting area and a balcony overlooking the grand room.

HPK2101015

Style: New American
First Floor: 2,550 sq. ft.
Second Floor: 917 sq. ft.
Total: 3,467 sq. ft.
Bonus Space: 736 sq. ft.
Bedrooms: 4
Bathrooms: 4
Width: 61' - 6"
Depth: 85' - 0"
Foundation: Crawlspace, Slab, Unfinished Walkout Basement

EPLANS.COM

Fanciful touches, like a swooping roofline and overflowing window boxes, lend fairy-tale charm to this country-style home, while a courtyard entry and a thoughtful floorplan make it practical as well. The fantasy continues inside as luxurious features turn up around every corner. The vaulted family room boasts a warming hearth flanked by built-ins. The master suite consumes the right wing of the plan with a tray ceiling, lavish bath, and His and Hers walk-in closet.

First Floor

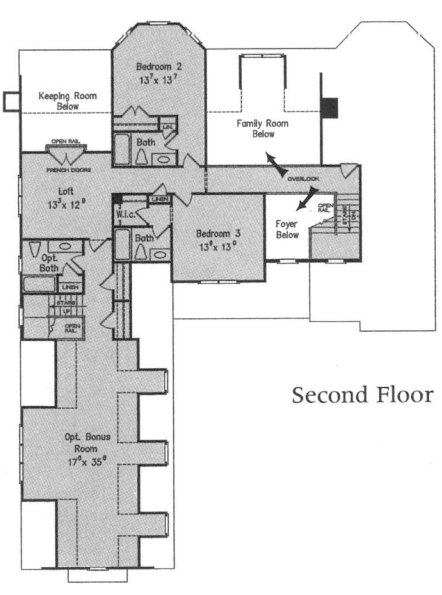

Second Floor

3,000 TO 3,499 SQUARE FEET

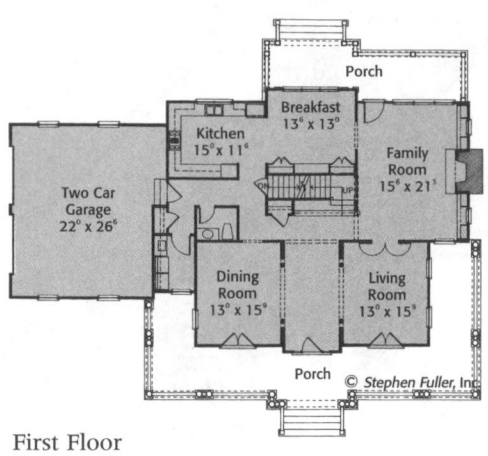

First Floor

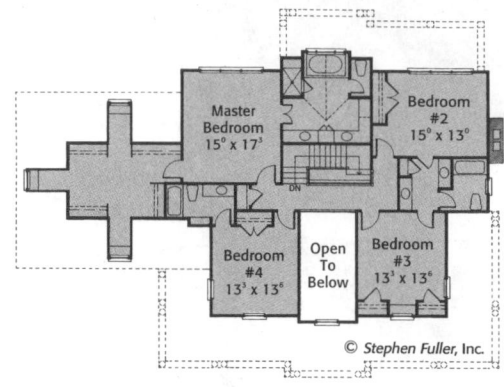

Second Floor

HPK2101016

This may be the perfect traditional country plan. From the foyer, a formal living room is on the right and a dining room is on the left. Each has access to the wrapping front porch. Straight ahead, stairs lead to the second floor, where every bedroom directly accesses a full bath. The master suite's walk-in closet lies above the garage. Beyond the staircase, a U-shaped kitchen serves a nook, and a pass-through connects to the family room. The back porch extends living space outdoors.

EPLANS.COM

Style: Country
First Floor: 1,748 sq. ft.
Second Floor: 1,720 sq. ft.
Total: 3,468 sq. ft.
Bedrooms: 4
Bathrooms: 3 ½
Width: 73' - 3"
Depth: 55' - 6"
Foundation: Walkout Basement

© Stephen Fuller, Inc.

HPK2101017

Style: Plantation

First Floor: 2,033 sq. ft.

Second Floor: 1,447 sq. ft.

Total: 3,480 sq. ft.

Bonus Space: 411 sq. ft.

Bedrooms: 3

Bathrooms: 3 ½

Width: 67' - 10"

Depth: 64' - 4"

Foundation: Crawlspace, Unfinished Basement

EPLANS.COM

Southern grandeur is evident in this wonderful two-story design with a magnificent second-floor balcony. The family room resides in the rear and opens to the terrace. The sunny breakfast bay adjoins the island kitchen for efficient planning. The right wing holds the two-car garage, utility room, a secondary staircase, and a study that can easily be converted to a guest suite with a private bath. The master suite and Bedrooms 2 and 3 are on the second floor.

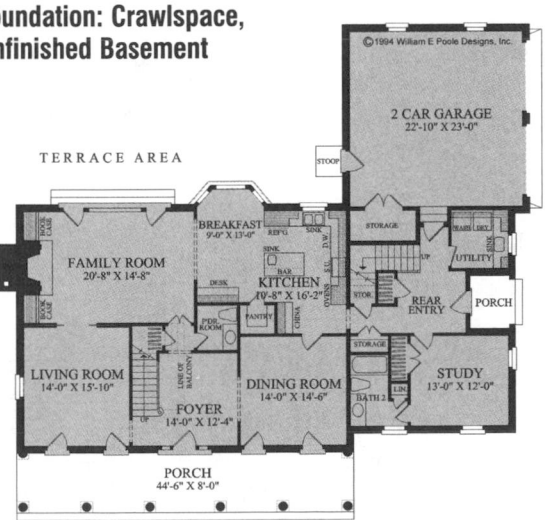

First Floor

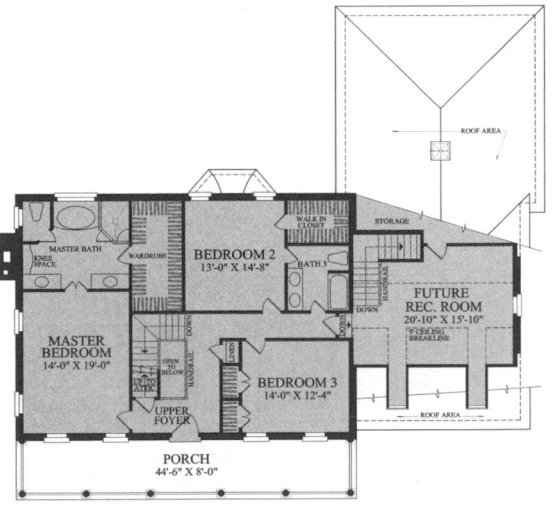

Second Floor

3,000 TO 3,499 SQUARE FEET

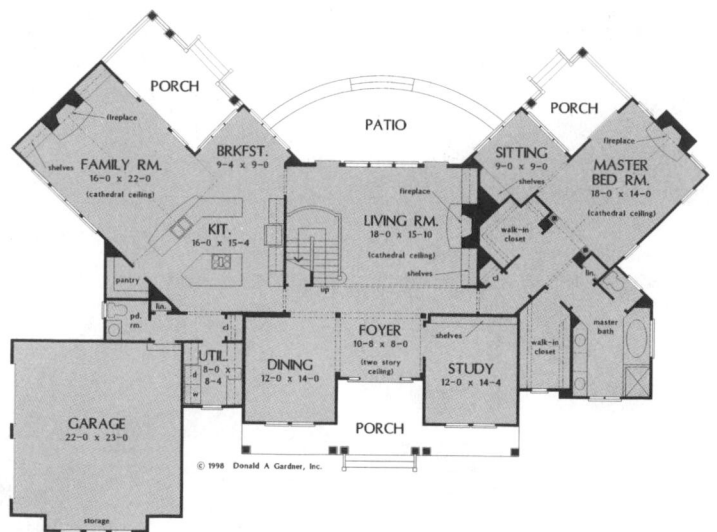

First Floor

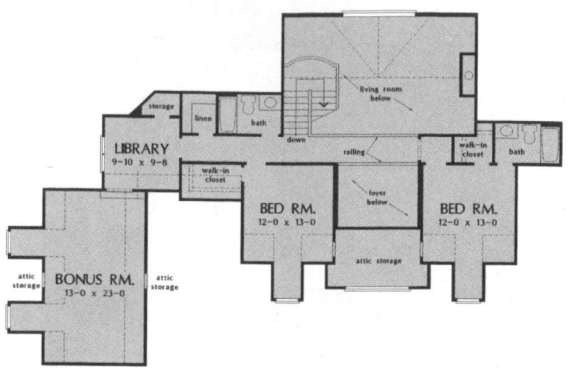

Second Floor

HPK2101018

Style: Craftsman
First Floor: 2,755 sq. ft.
Second Floor: 735 sq. ft.
Total: 3,490 sq. ft.
Bonus Space: 481 sq. ft.
Bedrooms: 3
Bathrooms: 3 ½
Width: 92' - 6"
Depth: 69' - 10"

EPLANS.COM

One can always count on a covered porch and charming dormers to bring curb appeal, but the interior amenities of this house make it a home. The open foyer is flanked by the study and formal dining room, and the family-oriented living room separates the master bedroom, with its porch access and cozy sitting room, from the open kitchen, breakfast nook, and family room. A library, two bedrooms, a bonus room, and two full bathrooms make up the second floor.

© 1998 Donald A. Gardner, Inc.

© Larry E. Belk Designs

HPK2101019

Style: New American

First Floor: 2,469 sq. ft.

Second Floor: 1,025 sq. ft.

Total: 3,494 sq. ft.

Bonus Space: 320 sq. ft.

Bedrooms: 4

Bathrooms: 3 ½

Width: 67' - 8"

Depth: 74' - 2"

Foundation: Crawlspace, Slab, Unfinished Basement

EPLANS.COM

A lovely double arch gives this European-style home a commanding presence. Once inside, a two-story foyer provides an open view directly through the formal living room to the rear grounds beyond. The private master suite features dual sinks, twin walk-in closets, a corner garden tub, and a separate shower. A second bedroom and a full bath are located nearby.

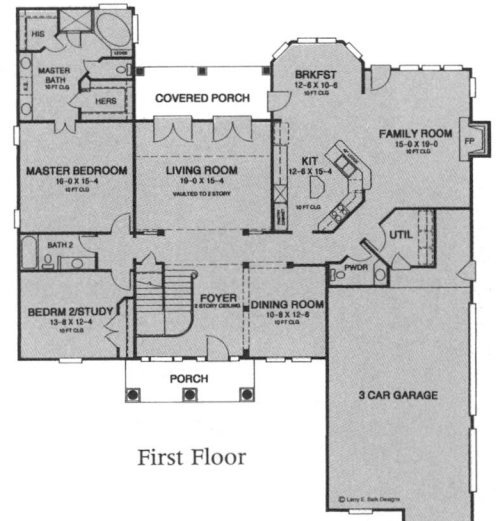

First Floor

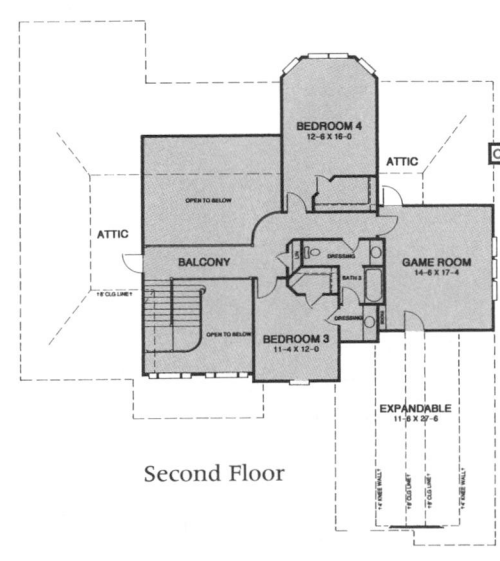

Second Floor

First Floor

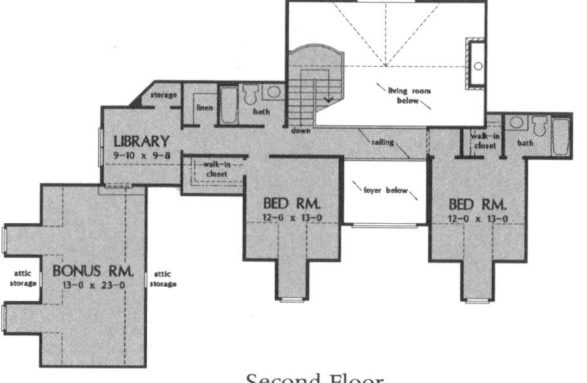

Second Floor

HPK2101020

Style: Country

First Floor: 2,755 sq. ft.

Second Floor: 744 sq. ft.

Total: 3,499 sq. ft.

Bonus Space: 481 sq. ft.

Bedrooms: 3

Bathrooms: 3 ½

Width: 92' - 6"

Depth: 69' - 10"

EPLANS.COM

Small- and medium-sized families will find comfortably spaced private areas and generous amounts of family rooms. At the left of the plan, a brief foyer sets off the master suite, which includes a fireplace, separate sitting area, and two walk-in closets. At the other end of the home, the large island kitchen works well with the breakfast nook and family room to provide the home's casual gathering space.

ORDER BLUEPRINTS ANYTIME AT EPLANS.COM OR 1-800-521-6797

HPK2101021

Style: Italianate

First Floor: 2,114 sq. ft.

Second Floor: 924 sq. ft.

Total: 3,038 sq. ft.

Bedrooms: 3

Bathrooms: 4

Width: 60' - 0"

Depth: 62' - 8"

Foundation: Slab

EPLANS.COM

A Mediterranean dream—amenities abound throughout this three-bedroom home. With large rooms and spacious outdoor living areas, this home is great for entertaining. A summer kitchen on the covered lanai and a full pool bath invite the possibility of warm weather fun. The lavish master suite sits to the right of the first floor, equipped with a sitting area. Upstairs houses two additional family bedrooms—both with full baths—a loft area, and a large study.

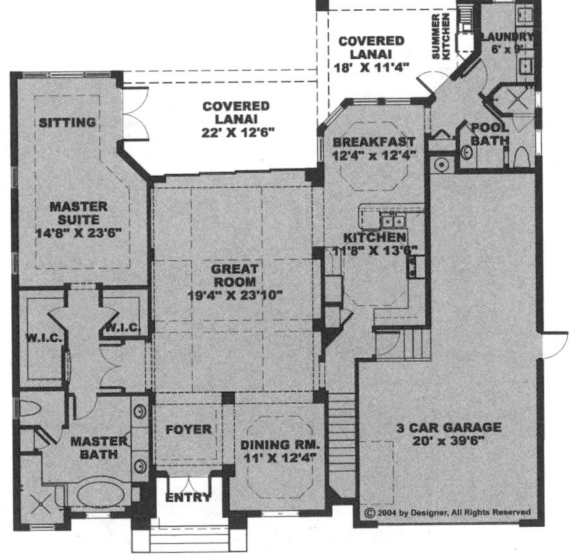

First Floor

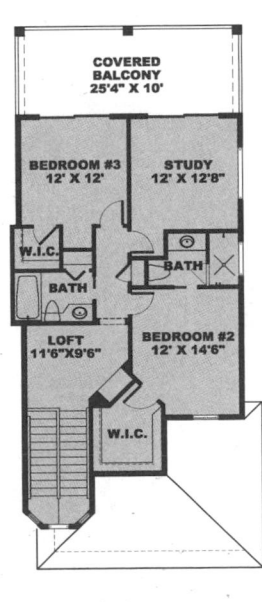

Second Floor

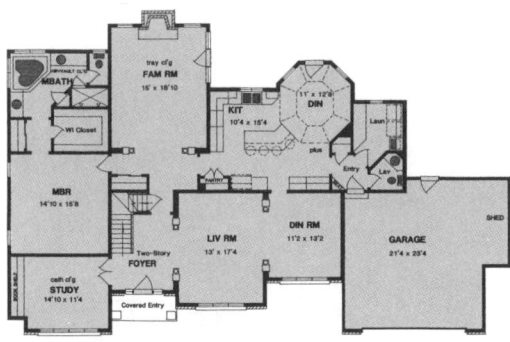

First Floor

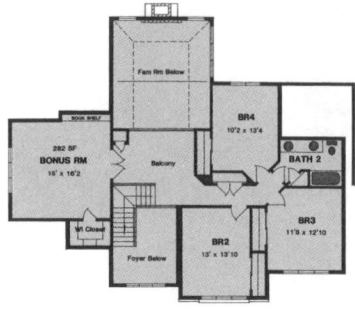

Second Floor

This brick- and clapboard-sided transitional front elevation is signatured by its repeating elliptical transom glass. The adjoining living and dining rooms with pillared entries provide a luxurious formal area off the front foyer. The first-floor master suite features a walk-through dressing area with generous closets opening to a luxurious master bath with His and Hers vanities, a corner tub with windows, a compartmented water closet and a large shower. The spacious kitchen opens to an octagon-shaped dinette and tray ceiling. The second floor features a large balcony/loft with three spacious bedrooms and a bonus room.

HPK2101022

Style: French Country
First Floor: 2,190 sq. ft.
Second Floor: 854 sq. ft.
Total: 3,044 sq. ft.
Bonus Space: 282 sq. ft.
Bedrooms: 4
Bathrooms: 2 ½
Width: 77' - 8"
Depth: 48' - 0"
Foundation: Unfinished Basement

EPLANS.COM

ORDER BLUEPRINTS ANYTIME AT EPLANS.COM OR 1-800-521-6797

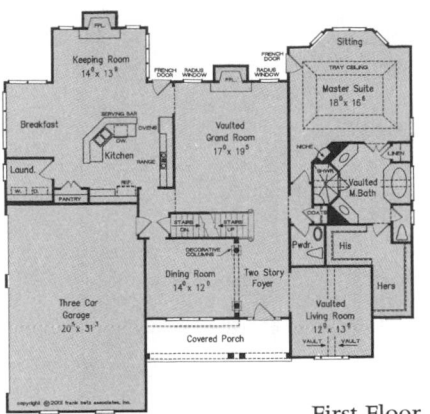

First Floor

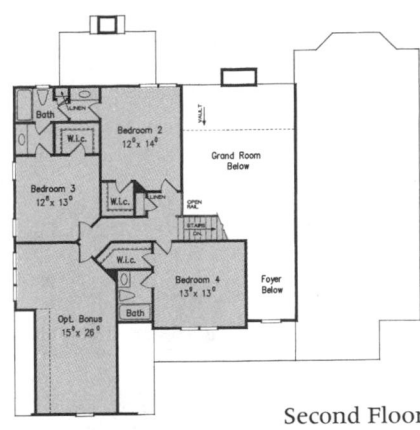

Second Floor

HPK2101023

Style: Colonial Revival

First Floor: 2,146 sq. ft.

Second Floor: 878 sq. ft.

Total: 3,024 sq. ft.

Bonus Space: 341 sq. ft.

Bedrooms: 4

Bathrooms: 3 ½

Width: 61' - 0"

Depth: 60' - 4"

Foundation: Crawlspace, Unfinished Walkout Basement

EPLANS.COM

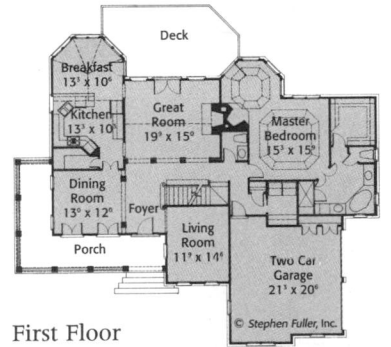

First Floor

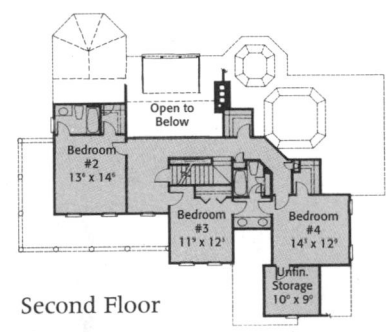

Second Floor

HPK2101024

Style: Cottage

First Floor: 1,935 sq. ft.

Second Floor: 1,115 sq. ft.

Total: 3,050 sq. ft.

Bedrooms: 4

Bathrooms: 3 ½

Width: 69' - 9"

Depth: 60' - 0"

Foundation: Walkout Basement

EPLANS.COM

3,000 TO 3,499 SQUARE FEET

HPK2101025

Style: Neoclassical
First Floor: 1,995 sq. ft.
Second Floor: 1,062 sq. ft.
Total: 3,057 sq. ft.
Bonus Space: 459 sq. ft.
Bedrooms: 4
Bathrooms: 3 ½
Width: 71' - 0"
Depth: 57' - 4"
Foundation: Unfinished Basement

EPLANS.COM

©1995 William E Poole Designs, Inc.

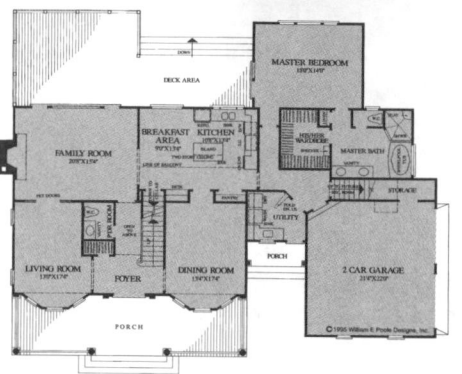

First Floor

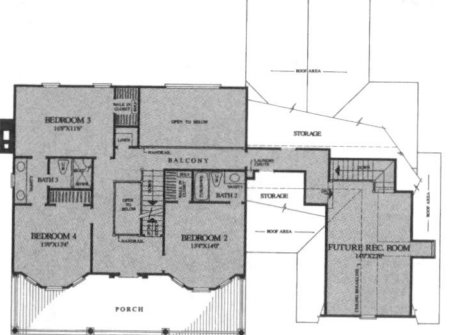

Second Floor

© Stephen Fuller, Inc.

HPK2101026

Style: Cottage
First Floor: 2,710 sq. ft.
Second Floor: 389 sq. ft.
Total: 3,099 sq. ft.
Bedrooms: 4
Bathrooms: 3 ½
Width: 58' - 3"
Depth: 66' - 3"
Foundation: Walkout Basement

EPLANS.COM

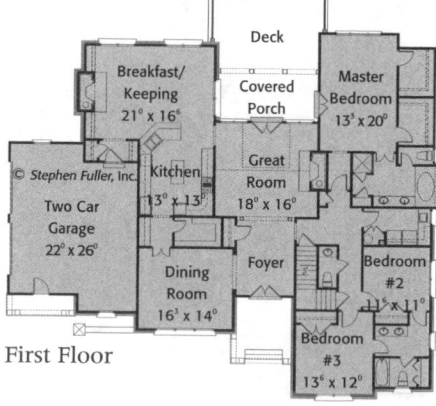

First Floor

Second Floor

ORDER BLUEPRINTS ANYTIME AT EPLANS.COM OR 1-800-521-6797

HPK2101027

© Stephen Fuller, Inc.

Style: Country

Square Footage: 3,110

Bedrooms: 4

Bathrooms: 3 ½

Width: 73' - 9"

Depth: 80' - 9"

Foundation: Walkout Basement

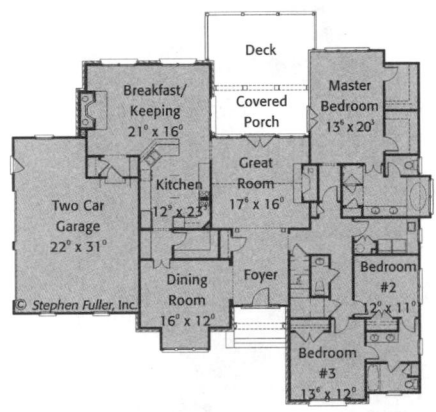

© Stephen Fuller, Inc.

HPK2101028

Style: Craftsman

Main Level: 1,268 sq. ft.

Upper Level: 931 sq. ft.

Lower Level: 949 sq. ft.

Total: 3,148 sq. ft.

Bedrooms: 4

Bathrooms: 3 ½

Width: 53' - 6"

Depth: 73' - 0"

Foundation: Finished Walkout Basement

Lower Level   Main Level   Upper Level

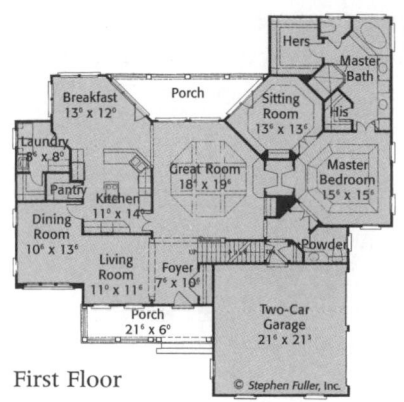

First Floor

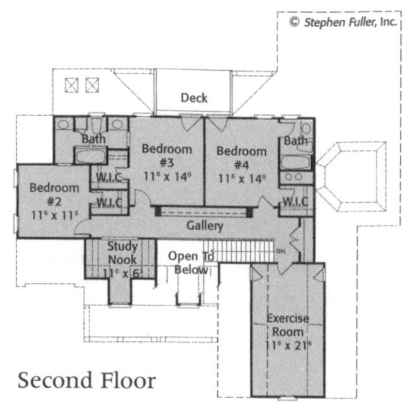

Second Floor

© Stephen Fuller, Inc.

HPK2101029

Style: Farmhouse
First Floor: 2,155 sq. ft.
Second Floor: 1,020 sq. ft.
Total: 3,175 sq. ft.
Bedrooms: 4
Bathrooms: 3 ½
Width: 62' - 3"
Depth: 63' - 3"
Foundation: Walkout Basement

EPLANS.COM

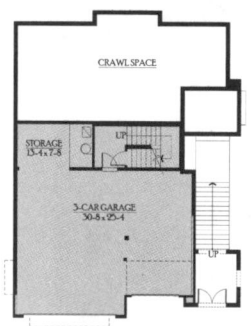

Lower Level

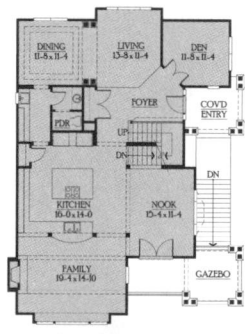

Main Level

Upper Level

HPK2101030

Style: Craftsman
Main Level: 1,630 sq. ft.
Upper Level: 1,460 sq. ft.
Lower Level: 130 sq. ft.
Total: 3,220 sq. ft.
Bedrooms: 3
Bathrooms: 2 ½
Width: 40' - 0"
Depth: 55' - 6"
Foundation: Crawlspace

EPLANS.COM

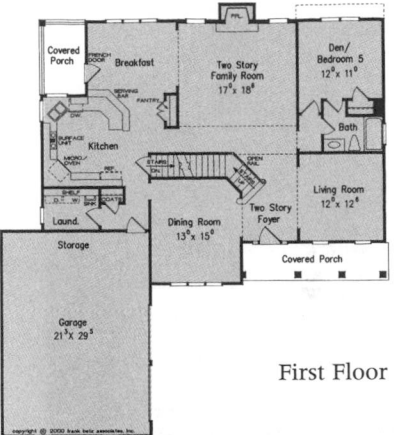

First Floor

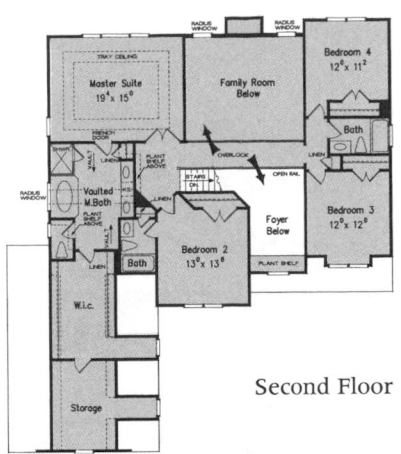

Second Floor

HPK2101031

Style: Colonial Revival
First Floor: 1,570 sq. ft.
Second Floor: 1,650 sq. ft.
Total: 3,220 sq. ft.
Bedrooms: 5
Bathrooms: 4
Width: 55' - 6"
Depth: 60' - 0"
Foundation: Crawlspace, Unfinished Walkout Basement

EPLANS.COM

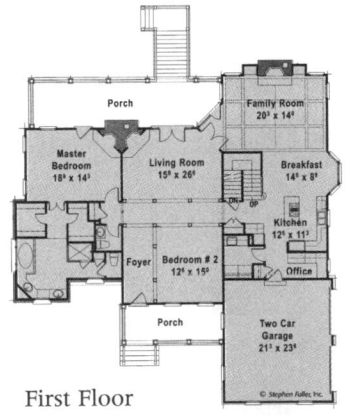

First Floor

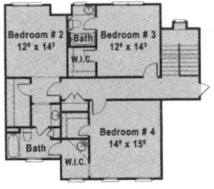

Second Floor

HPK2101032

Style: Country
First Floor: 2,205 sq. ft.
Second Floor: 1,035 sq. ft.
Total: 3,240 sq. ft.
Bedrooms: 4
Bathrooms: 3 ½
Width: 63' - 3"
Depth: 64' - 0"
Foundation: Walkout Basement

EPLANS.COM

3,000 TO 3,499 SQUARE FEET

HPK2101033

Style: Craftsman
Main Level: 1,993 sq. ft.
Lower Level: 1,251 sq. ft.
Total: 3,244 sq. ft.
Bedrooms: 3
Bathrooms: 3 ½
Width: 66' - 0"
Depth: 57' - 6"
Foundation: Finished Walkout Basement

EPLANS.COM

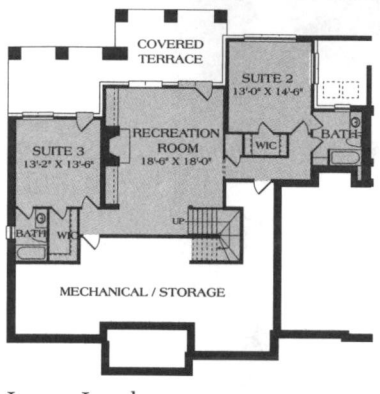

Lower Level

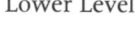

Main Level

HPK2101034

Style: Bungalow
Main Level: 2,170 sq. ft.
Lower Level: 1,076 sq. ft.
Total: 3,246 sq. ft.
Bedrooms: 3
Bathrooms: 2 ½
Width: 74' - 0"
Depth: 54' - 0"
Foundation: Slab, Finished Walkout Basement

EPLANS.COM

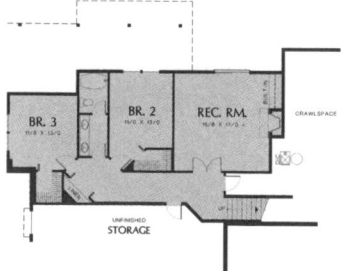

Lower Level

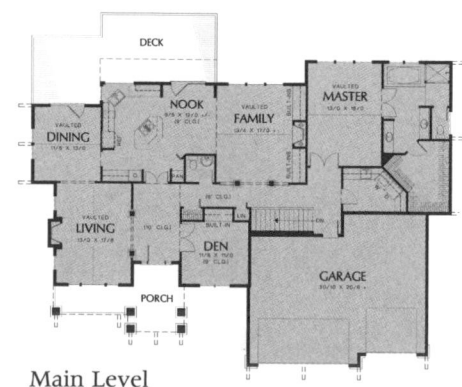

Main Level

HPK2101035

Style: Federal - Adams
First Floor: 2,335 sq. ft.
Second Floor: 936 sq. ft.
Total: 3,271 sq. ft.
Bonus Space: 958 sq. ft.
Bedrooms: 3
Bathrooms: 3 ½
Width: 91' - 4"
Depth: 54' - 6"
Foundation: Unfinished Walkout Basement

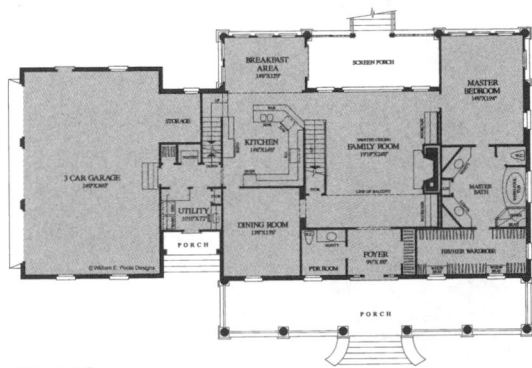

First Floor

Second Floor

© 1999 Donald A. Gardner, Inc.

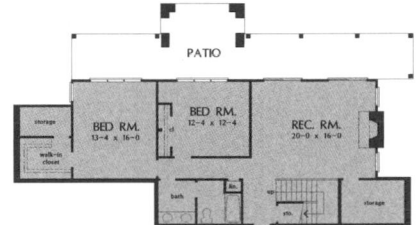

Lower Level

HPK2101036

Style: Craftsman
Main Level: 2,122 sq. ft.
Lower Level: 1,150 sq. ft.
Total: 3,272 sq. ft.
Bedrooms: 4
Bathrooms: 3
Width: 83' - 0"
Depth: 74' - 4"

Main Level

3,000 TO 3,499 SQUARE FEET

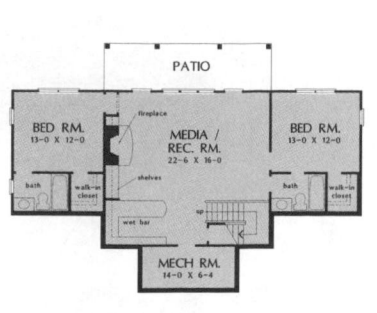

Lower Level

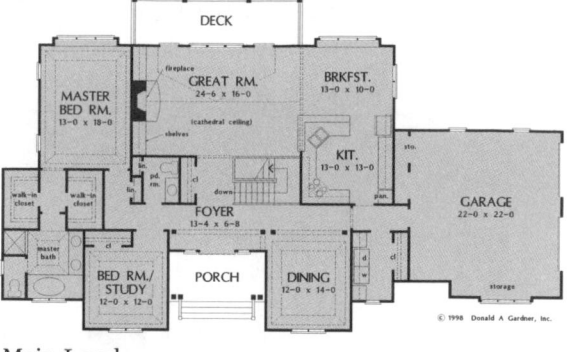

Main Level

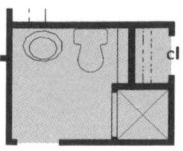

(optional bath)

©1998 Donald A. Gardner, Inc.

HPK2101037

Style: French Country
Main Level: 2,065 sq. ft.
Lower Level: 1,216 sq. ft.
Total: 3,281 sq. ft.
Bedrooms: 4
Bathrooms: 3 ½
Width: 82' - 2"
Depth: 43' - 6"

EPLANS.COM

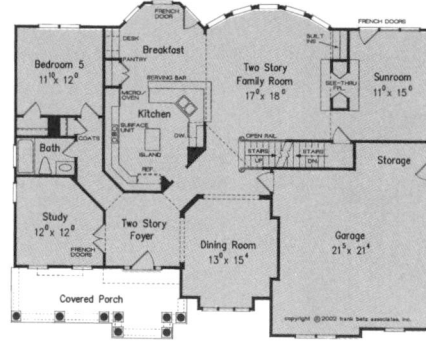

First Floor

Second Floor

HPK2101038

Style: New American
First Floor: 1,679 sq. ft.
Second Floor: 1,605 sq. ft.
Total: 3,284 sq. ft.
Bedrooms: 5
Bathrooms: 4
Width: 57' - 0"
Depth: 45' - 4"
Foundation: Crawlspace, Unfinished Walkout Basement

EPLANS.COM

HPK2101039

Style: Plantation
Main Level: 2,146 sq. ft.
Upper Level: 952 sq. ft.
Lower Level: 187 sq. ft.
Total: 3,285 sq. ft.
Bedrooms: 3
Bathrooms: 3 ½
Width: 52' - 0"
Depth: 65' - 4"
Foundation: Island Basement

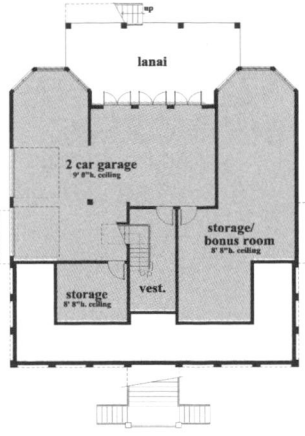

Lower Level

© The Sater Design Collection, Inc.

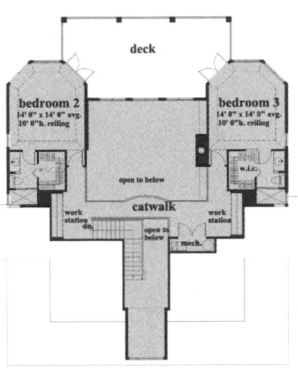

Upper Level

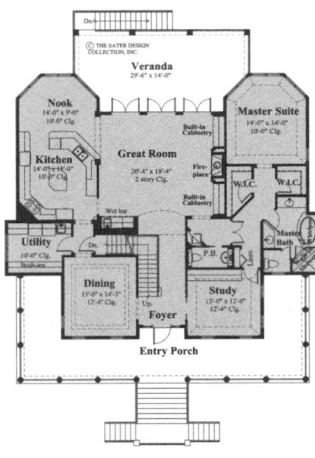

Main Level

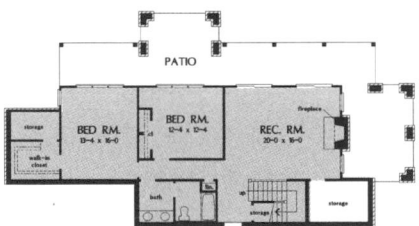
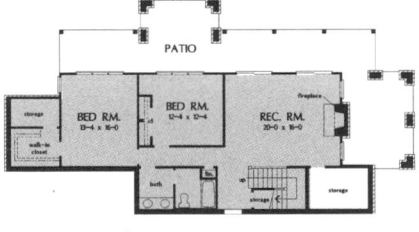

Lower Level

Main Level

© 1999 DONALD A. GARDNER
All rights reserved

HPK2101040

Style: Craftsman
Main Level: 2,151 sq. ft.
Lower Level: 1,150 sq. ft.
Total: 3,301 sq. ft.
Bedrooms: 4
Bathrooms: 3
Width: 83' - 0"
Depth: 74' - 4"

3,000 TO 3,499 SQUARE FEET

HPK2101041

Style: French Country

Main Level: 1,720 sq. ft.

Lower Level: 1,600 sq. ft.

Total: 3,320 sq. ft.

Bedrooms: 4

Bathrooms: 3 ½

Width: 59' - 0"

Depth: 59' - 4"

EPLANS.COM

© 2002 Donald A. Gardner, Inc.

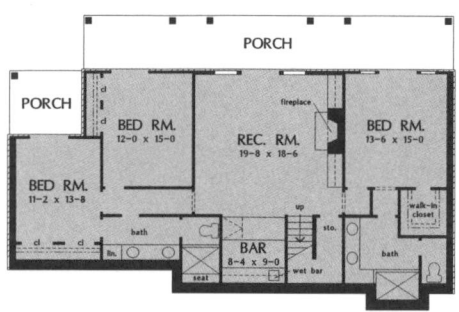

Lower Level

Main Level

© 2002 DONALD A. GARDNER
All rights reserved

© Stephen Fuller, Inc.

HPK2101042

Style: Cottage

First Floor: 1,846 sq. ft.

Second Floor: 1,476 sq. ft.

Total: 3,322 sq. ft.

Bedrooms: 3

Bathrooms: 3

Width: 70' - 3"

Depth: 54' - 0"

Foundation: Walkout Basement

EPLANS.COM

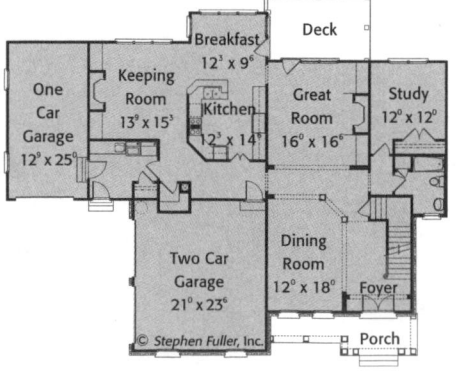

First Floor

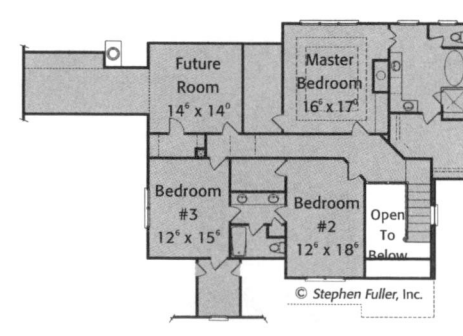

Second Floor

©1998 Donald A. Gardner, Inc.

HPK2101043

Style: Country
First Floor: 2,623 sq. ft.
Second Floor: 748 sq. ft.
Total: 3,371 sq. ft.
Bonus Space: 738 sq. ft.
Bedrooms: 4
Bathrooms: 4 ½
Width: 85' - 8"
Depth: 51' - 4"

EPLANS.COM

This charming country estate is a welcome retreat with plenty of room for everyone. Marked by columns, the formal living and dining rooms are positioned up front, and the family gathering areas are at the back. The first-floor master suite features an elegant tray ceiling, and a bayed sitting area offers a private spot for relaxation. Upstairs, two bedrooms, both with cathedral ceilings, two full baths, and an enormous bonus room provide plenty of room for the family.

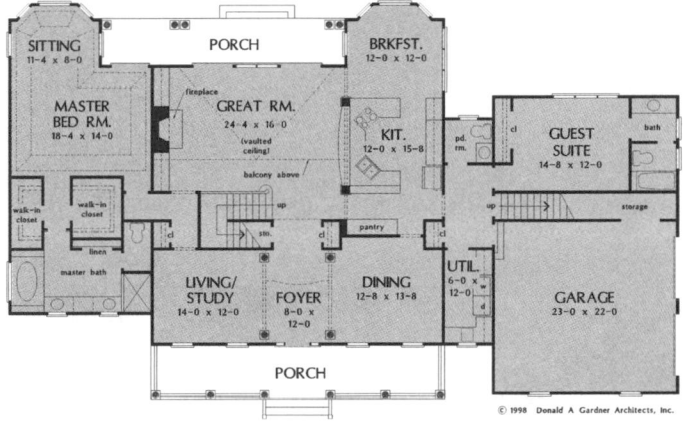

First Floor

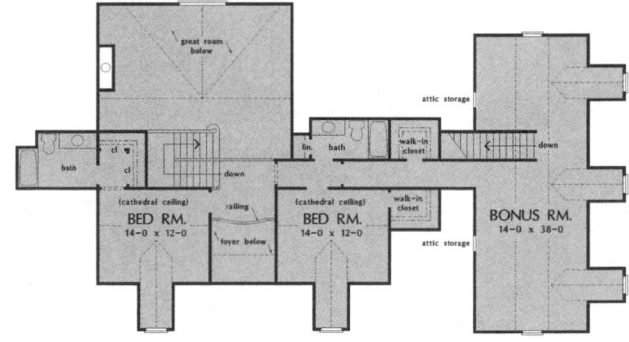

Second Floor

3,000 TO 3,499 SQUARE FEET

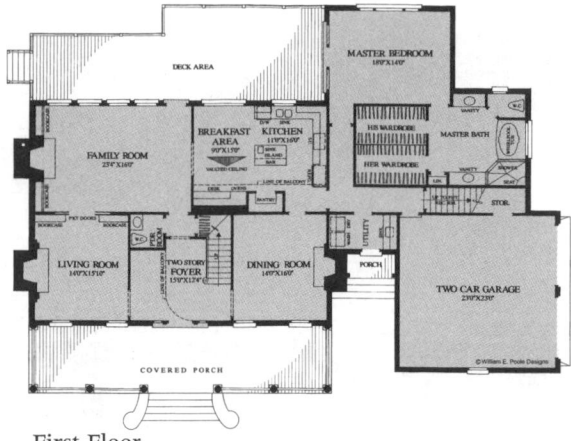

First Floor

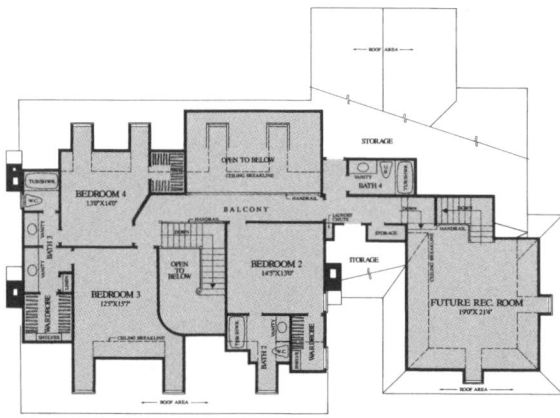

Second Floor

This unique design uses a wall of windows at the rear of the home to showcase the deck area and attempt to expand the living space to the outdoors. Built-in bookcases in the family and living rooms are an added bonus. Three fireplaces on the first floor make a grand impression and provide extra warmth. The lavish master suite boasts large, side-by-side His and Hers wardrobes. Upstairs, Bedrooms 3 and 4 share a full-bath with a dual-sink vanity. A third family bedroom—a possible guest suite—has a private, full bath. A laundry chute is conveniently located on this level.

HPK2101044

Style: Federal - Adams
First Floor: 2,320 sq. ft.
Second Floor: 1,057 sq. ft.
Total: 3,377 sq. ft.
Bonus Space: 608 sq. ft.
Bedrooms: 4
Bathrooms: 4 ½
Width: 81' - 4"
Depth: 58' - 2"
Foundation: Crawlspace

EPLANS.COM

© William E. Poole Designs, Inc.

HPK2101045

Style: Craftsman
Main Level: 1,685 sq. ft.
Upper Level: 1,490 sq. ft.
Lower Level: 200 sq. ft.
Total: 3,375 sq. ft.
Bedrooms: 3
Bathrooms: 2 ½
Width: 37' - 0"
Depth: 58' - 0"
Foundation: Crawlspace

EPLANS.COM

A side entry makes this home perfect for a corner lot; or, take advantage of the interesting Craftsman architecture that makes the garage side of the home stand out. The family room is the focus of the design, with a wide picture window overlooking the side deck. Double doors from the deck to the den and the nook on either side of the family room invite lots of indoor/outdoor activities. For quiet seclusion, retreat to the second-floor master suite. Two additional bedrooms, a full bath, and a bonus room are also on this level.

3,000 TO 3,499 SQUARE FEET

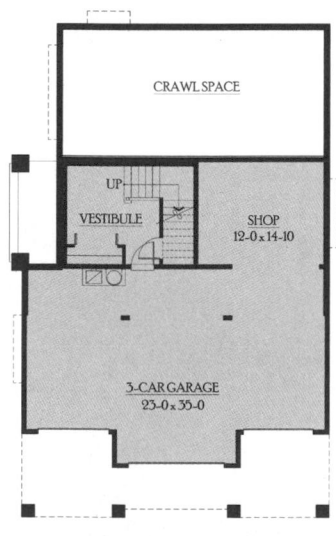

Lower Level

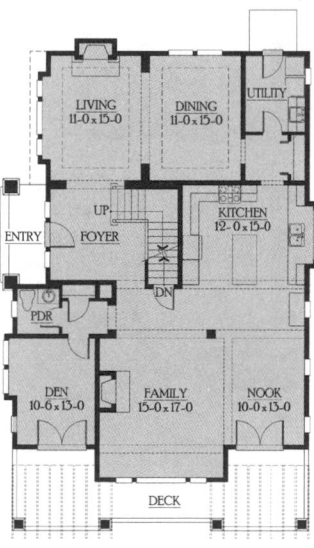

Main Level

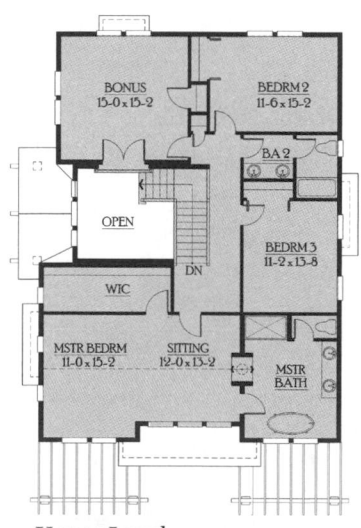

Upper Level

First Floor

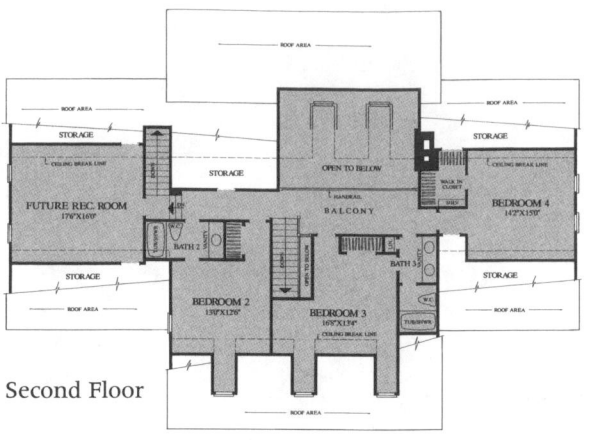

Second Floor

This Colonial farmhouse will be the showpiece of your neighborhood. Come in from the wide front porch through French doors topped by a sunburst window. Continue past the formal dining and living rooms to a columned gallery and a large family room with a focal fireplace. The kitchen astounds with a unique layout, an island, and abundant counter and cabinet space. The master bath balances luxury with efficiency. Three upstairs bedrooms enjoy amenities such as dormer windows or walk-in closets. Bonus space is ready for expansion as your needs change.

HPK2101046

Style: Federal - Adams
First Floor: 2,191 sq. ft.
Second Floor: 1,220 sq. ft.
Total: 3,411 sq. ft.
Bonus Space: 280 sq. ft.
Bedrooms: 4
Bathrooms: 3 ½
Width: 75' - 8"
Depth: 54' - 4"
Foundation: Crawlspace, Unfinished Basement

EPLANS.COM

© 1995 William E Poole Designs, Inc.

HPK2101047

Style: New American

Main Level: 2,300 sq. ft.

Lower Level: 1,114 sq. ft.

Total: 3,414 sq. ft.

Bedrooms: 5

Bathrooms: 3

Width: 56' - 0"

Depth: 61' - 6"

Foundation: Finished Walkout Basement

EPLANS.COM

Looking for all the world like a one-story plan, this elegant hillside design has a surprise on the lower level. The formal dining room is on the right, next to a cozy den or Bedroom 3. The breakfast nook and kitchen are just steps away. Lower-level space includes another great room and two family bedrooms sharing a full bath.

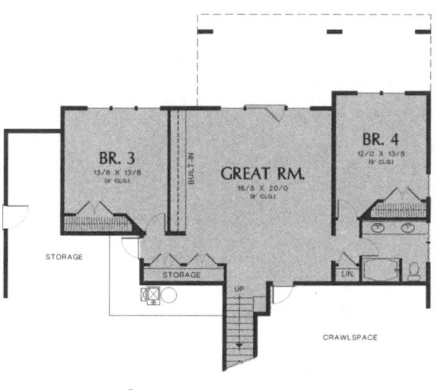

Lower Level

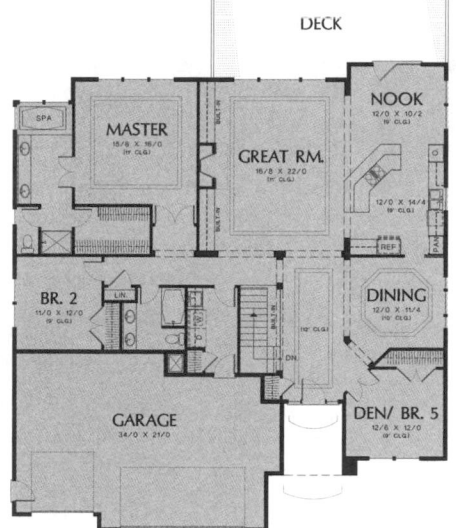

Main Level

3,000 TO 3,499 SQUARE FEET

HPK2101048

Style: Queen Anne
First Floor: 1,329 sq. ft.
Second Floor: 1,917 sq. ft.
Third Floor: 189 sq. ft.
Total: 3,435 sq. ft.
Bedrooms: 3
Bathrooms: 2 ½
Width: 40' - 4"
Depth: 62' - 0"
Foundation: Crawlspace

EPLANS.COM

While speaking clearly of the past, the inside of this Victorian home coincides with the open, flowing interiors of today. Have meals in the elegant dining room with its tray ceiling, or move through the double French doors between the formal living room and informal family room to sense the comfort of this charming home. The kitchen boasts a large pantry and a corner sink with a window. The lovely master suite resides upstairs. The raised sitting area off the master bedroom provides the owner with a mini retreat for reading and relaxing. The second floor also includes two large bedrooms and a library/music room.

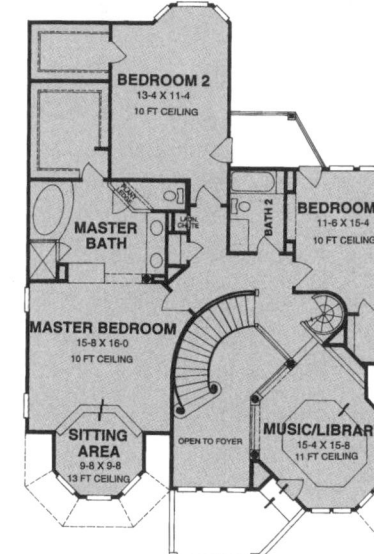

First Floor

Second Floor

Third Floor

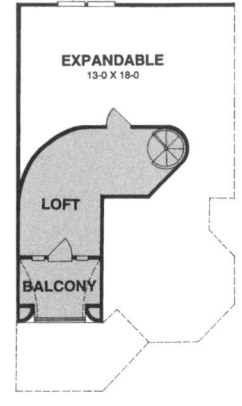

© Larry E. Belk Designs

HPK2101049

Style: Country
First Floor: 2,420 sq. ft.
Second Floor: 1,020 sq. ft.
Total: 3,440 sq. ft.
Bedrooms: 4
Bathrooms: 3 ½
Width: 80' - 0"
Depth: 63' - 3"
Foundation: Walkout Basement

Reminiscent of decades ago, simplicity and symmetry combine to give this home a timeless appearance. The half round window and fanlight window above the front door are common features of the Early Classical Revival style. The study and adjoining computer nook can be converted to a guest bedroom and full bath, if desired. Upstairs houses three bedrooms and two baths.

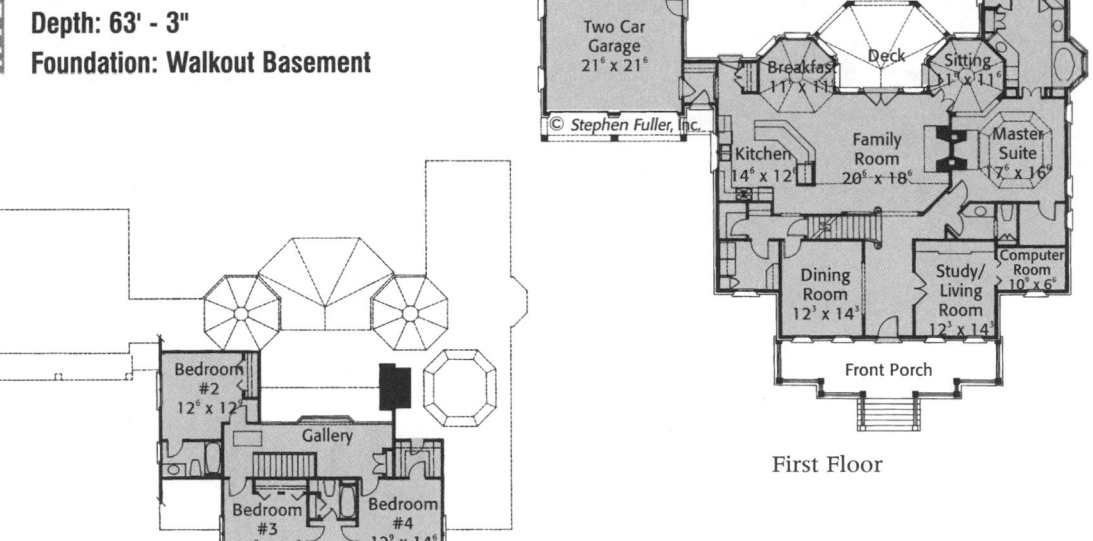

Second Floor

First Floor

3,000 TO 3,499 SQUARE FEET

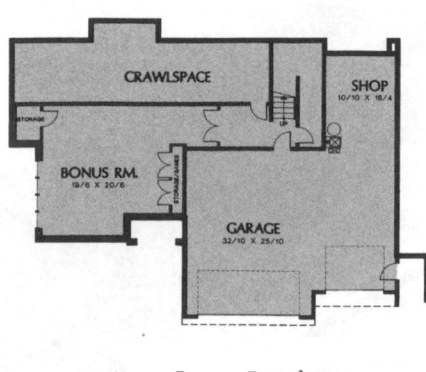

Lower Level

Main Level

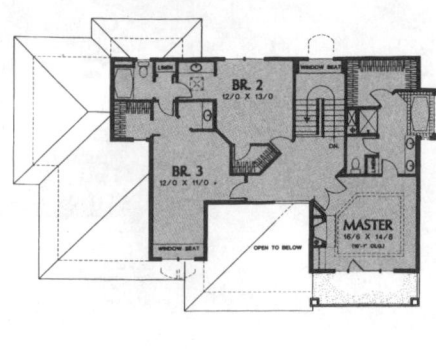

Upper Level

HPK2101050

Style: Mediterranean
Main Level: 1,989 sq. ft.
Upper Level: 1,349 sq. ft.
Lower Level: 105 sq. ft.
Total: 3,443 sq. ft.
Bonus Space: 487 sq. ft.
Bedrooms: 3
Bathrooms: 2 ½
Width: 63' - 0"
Depth: 48' - 0"
Foundation: Finished Walkout Basement

EPLANS.COM

Dramatic balconies and spectacular window treatments enhance this stunning luxury home. Inside, a through-fireplace warms the formal living room and a restful den. Both living spaces open to a balcony that invites quiet reflection on starry nights. The banquet-sized dining room is easily served from the adjacent kitchen. Here, space is shared with an eating nook that provides access to the rear grounds and a family room with a corner fireplace—for casual gatherings. The upper level contains two family bedrooms and a luxurious master suite that enjoys its own private balcony. The lower level accommodates a shop and a bonus room for future development.

The spacious grand room of this home is open to the foyer and the pentagonal dining room, which is defined by decorative columns. An angled gathering room offers a fireplace and wide views of the rear of the home. The master suite boasts two walk-in closets, a bath with a garden tub, and access to the covered lanai.

HPK2101051

Style: New American
Main Level: 2,585 sq. ft.
Lower Level: 874 sq. ft.
Total: 3,459 sq. ft.
Bonus Space: 519 sq. ft.
Bedrooms: 6
Bathrooms: 4 ½
Width: 61' - 0"
Depth: 80' - 0"
Foundation: Finished Walkout Basement

EPLANS.COM

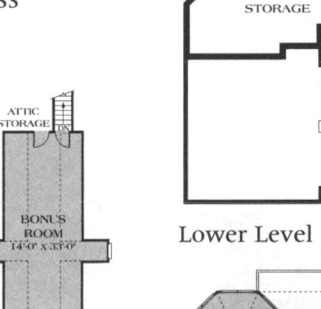

Lower Level

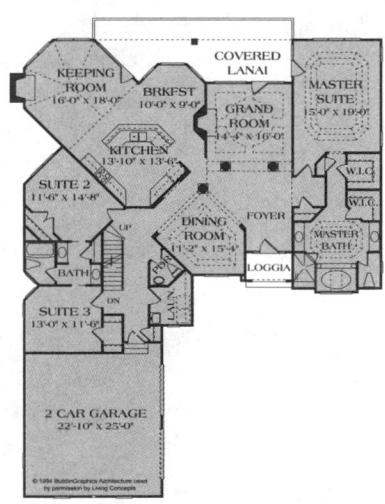

Main Level

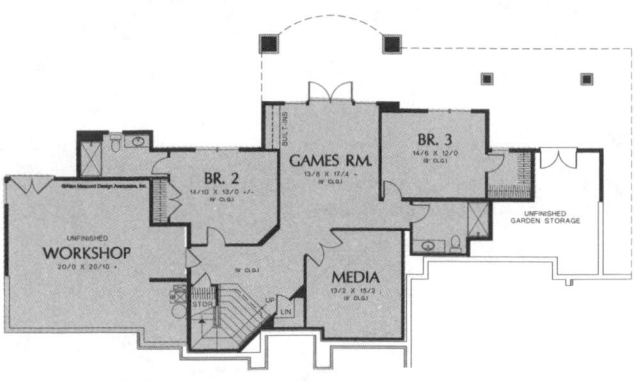

Lower Level

HPK2101052

Style: French Country
Main Level: 2,095 sq. ft.
Lower Level: 1,373 sq. ft.
Total: 3,468 sq. ft.
Bedrooms: 3
Bathrooms: 3 ½
Width: 83' - 6"
Depth: 62' - 0"
Foundation: Slab, Finished Walkout Basement

EPLANS.COM

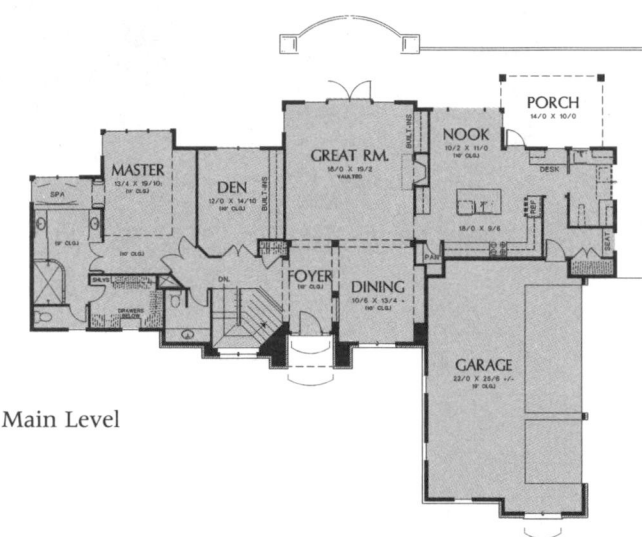

Main Level

Stone touches accent the exterior of this multilevel home. Inside, the sprawling design highlights an expansive great room and gourmet kitchen. The main level master suite is a pampering retreat. On the lower level, entertainment options abound with a games room and media room. Two additional family bedrooms access full, private baths.

© Stephen Fuller, Inc.

HPK2101053

Style: Cottage
First Floor: 2,360 sq. ft.
Second Floor: 1,133 sq. ft.
Total: 3,493 sq. ft.
Bedrooms: 4
Bathrooms: 3 ½
Width: 68' - 0"
Depth: 62' - 5"
Foundation: Walkout Basement

EPLANS.COM

Farmhouse life has never been as good as it is in this two-story classic. The foyer opens to a fanned staircase, but all of the common rooms are on the first floor. The kitchen's peninsula snack bar separates it from the nook and faces the nearby family room. A second set of stairs leads down to an unfinished walk-out basement or up to the second floor, where there are three bedrooms and two baths. The master suite remains quiet and secluded on the first floor.

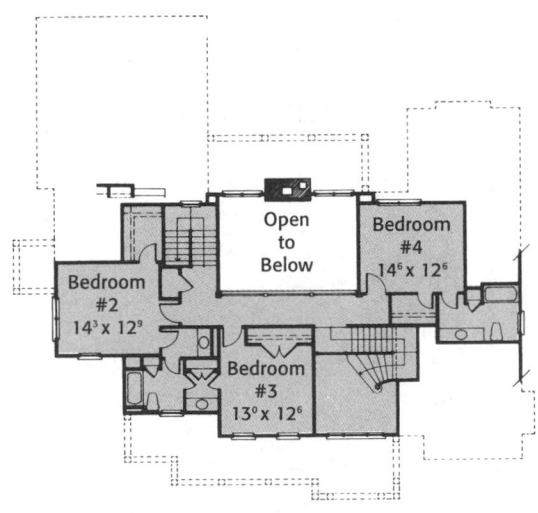

Second Floor

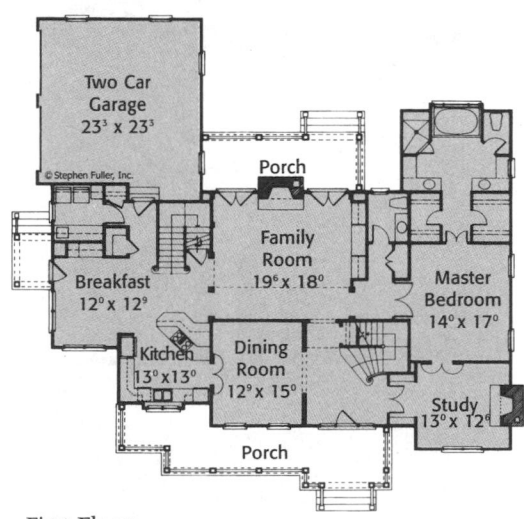

First Floor

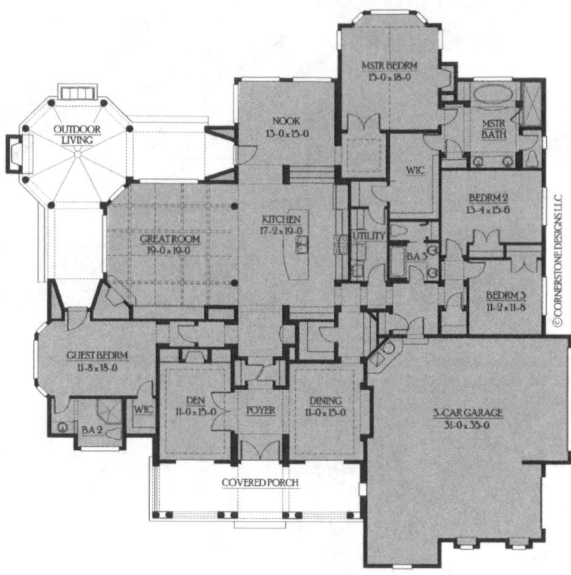

Stunning exterior architecture complements the dramatic interiors of this elegant beauty. The gracious columned front porch leads to a carefully crafted floor plan with warm living spaces and spacious covered porches highlighted by columns and ceiling details. Intimate private suites are full of luxurious features and ample storage. Laundry access from the large master walk-in closet is a special convenience. The grand kitchen and adjacent great room make a bold statement upon entry. A fireplace in the outdoor living area is an added bonus.

HPK2101054

Style: Craftsman
Square Footage: 3,500
Bedrooms: 4
Bathrooms: 3
Width: 87' - 0"
Depth: 86' - 6"
Foundation: Crawlspace

EPLANS.COM

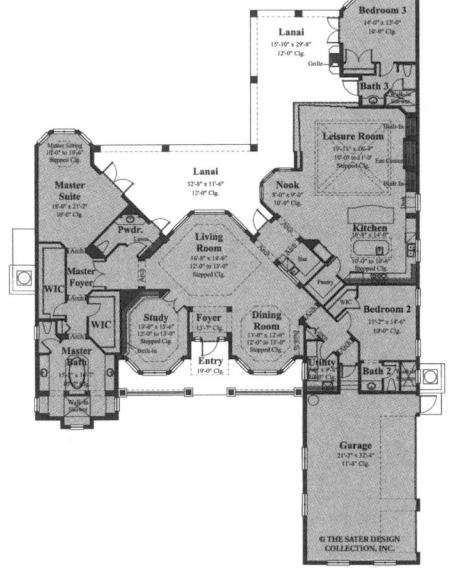

HPK2101055

Style: Farmhouse

Square Footage: 3,553

Bedrooms: 3

Bathrooms: 3 ½

Width: 75' - 0"

Depth: 111' - 4"

Foundation: Slab

EPLANS.COM

HPK2101056

Plan: HPK2101056

Style: Mediterranean

Square Footage: 3,556

Bedrooms: 4

Bathrooms: 3 ½

Width: 85' - 0"

Depth: 85' - 0"

Foundation: Slab

EPLANS.COM

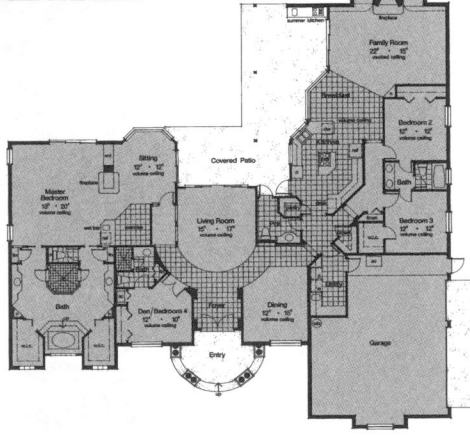

3,500 TO 3,999 SQUARE FEET

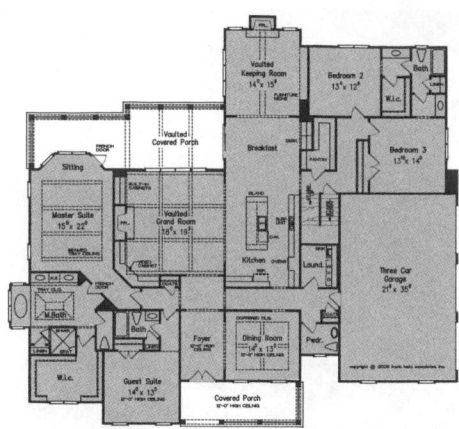
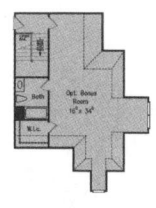

HPK2101057

Style: French Country
Square Footage: 3,590
Bonus Space: 718 sq. ft.
Bedrooms: 4
Bathrooms: 3 ½
Width: 83' - 0"
Depth: 76' - 4"
Foundation: Crawlspace, Unfinished Basement

EPLANS.COM

HPK2101058

Style: Neoclassical
Square Footage: 3,600
Bedrooms: 4
Bathrooms: 3 ½
Width: 76' - 2"
Depth: 100' - 10"
Foundation: Crawlspace, Unfinished Basement

EPLANS.COM

ORDER BLUEPRINTS ANYTIME AT EPLANS.COM OR 1-800-521-6797

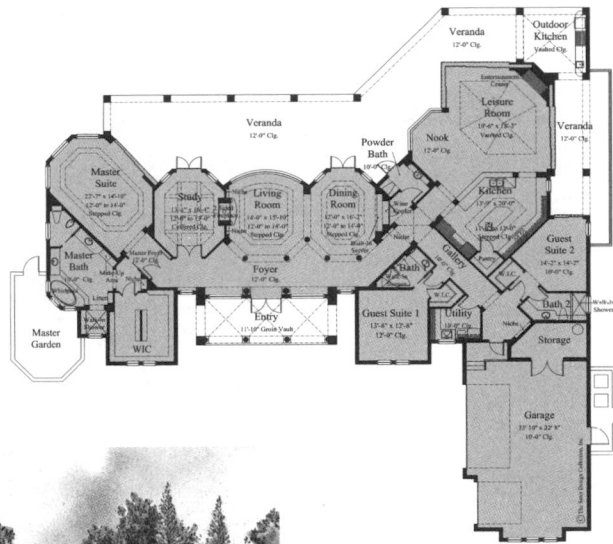

HPK2101059

© The Sater Design Collection, Inc.

Style: Italianate
Square Footage: 3,640
Bedrooms: 3
Bathrooms: 3 ½
Width: 106' - 4"
Depth: 102' - 4"
Foundation: Slab

EPLANS.COM

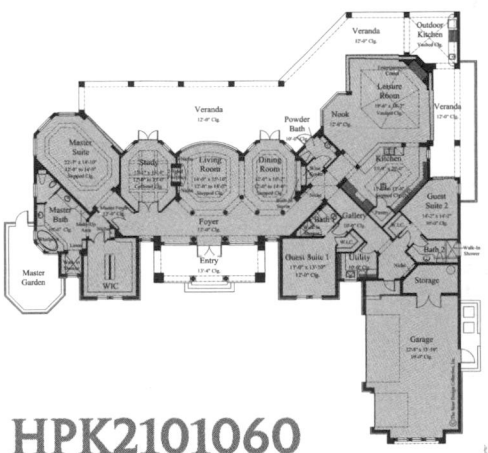

HPK2101060

EPLANS.COM

Style: Beaux Arts
Square Footage: 3,640
Bedrooms: 3
Bathrooms: 3 ½
Width: 106' - 4"
Depth: 102' - 4"
Foundation: Slab

© The Sater Design Collection, Inc.

3,500 TO 3,999 SQUARE FEET

HPK2101061

Style: Mediterranean

Square Footage: 3,640

Bedrooms: 3

Bathrooms: 3 ½

Width: 106' - 4"

Depth: 102' - 4"

Foundation: Slab

EPLANS.COM

© The Sater Design Collection, Inc.

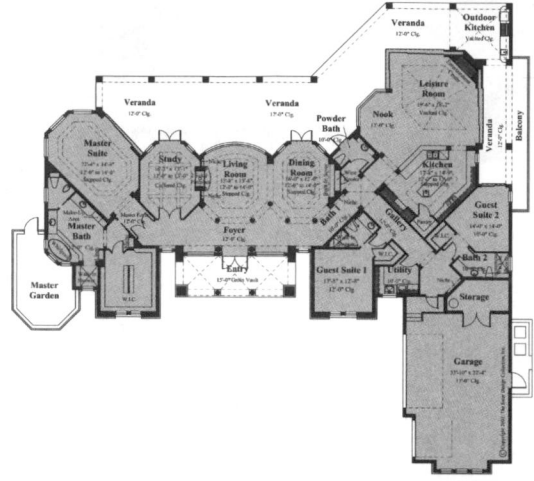

HPK2101062

Style: Mediterranean

Square Footage: 3,688

Bedrooms: 3

Bathrooms: 3 ½

Width: 129' - 0"

Depth: 102' - 0"

Foundation: Slab

EPLANS.COM

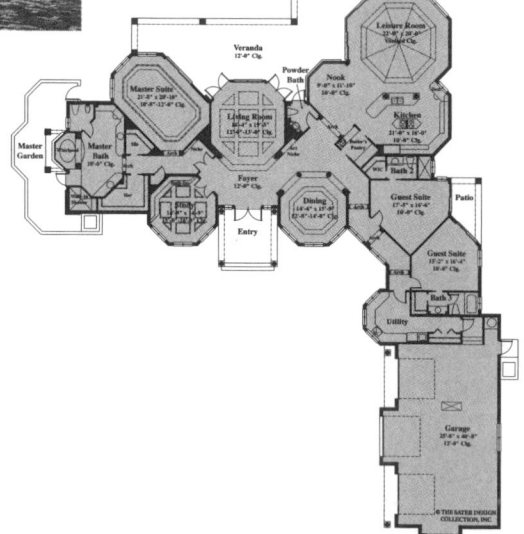

The Sater Design Collection, Inc. This home, as shown in photographs, may differ from the actual blueprints. For more detailed information, please check the floor plans carefully.

ORDER BLUEPRINTS ANYTIME AT EPLANS.COM OR 1-800-521-6797

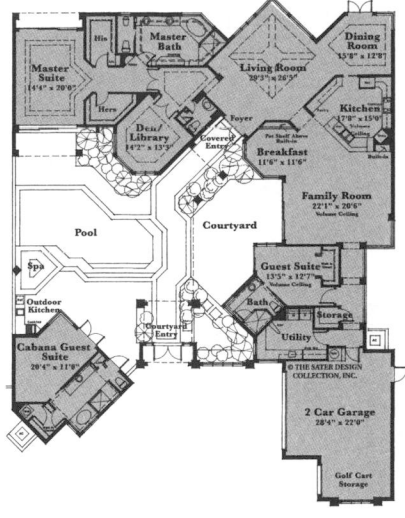

© The Sater Design Collection, Inc.

HPK2101063

Style: Mediterranean

Square Footage: 3,696

Bedrooms: 3

Bathrooms: 3 ½

Width: 80' - 0"

Depth: 107' - 3"

Foundation: Slab

EPLANS.COM

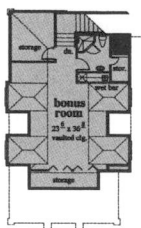

HPK2101064

Style: Mediterranean

Square Footage: 3,725

Bonus Space: 595 sq. ft.

Bedrooms: 3

Bathrooms: 3 ½

Width: 84' - 3"

Depth: 115' - 2"

Foundation: Slab

EPLANS.COM

3,500 TO 3,999 SQUARE FEET

HPK2101065

Style: Italianate
Square Footage: 3,743
Bedrooms: 4
Bathrooms: 3 ½
Width: 80' - 0"
Depth: 103' - 8"
Foundation: Slab

The Sater Design Collection, Inc.

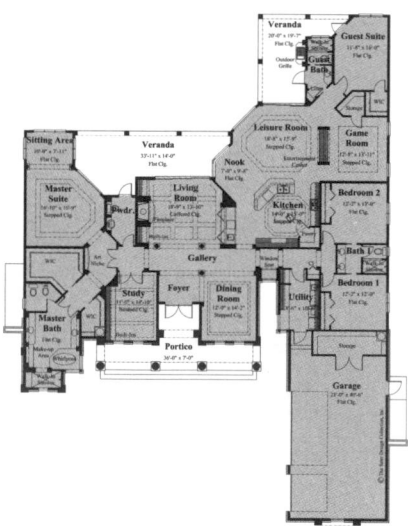

Optional Layout

HPK2101066

Style: Greek Revival
Square Footage: 3,764
Bedrooms: 4
Bathrooms: 3 ½
Width: 80' - 6"
Depth: 111' - 0"
Foundation: Slab

© The Sater Design Collection, Inc.

HPK2101067

Style: Beaux Arts
Square Footage: 3,790
Bedrooms: 4
Bathrooms: 3 ½
Width: 80' - 8"
Depth: 107' - 8"
Foundation: Slab

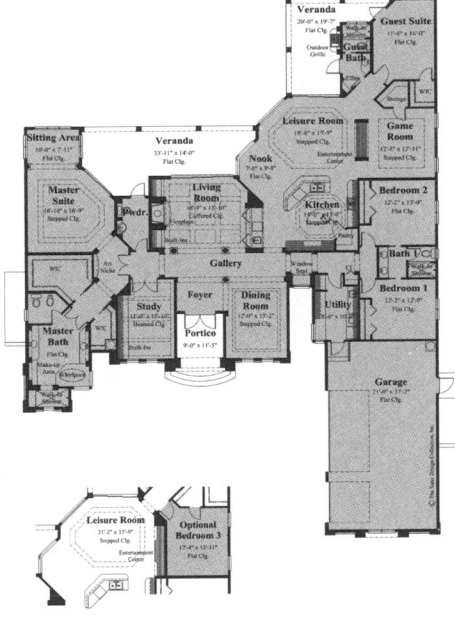

© The Sater Design Collection, Inc.

Optional Layout

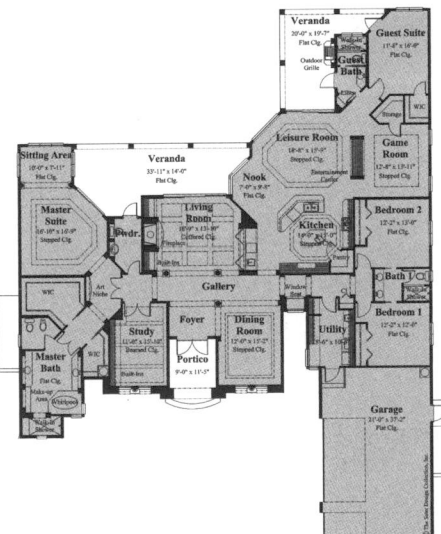

Optional Layout

HPK2101068

Style: Mediterranean
Square Footage: 3,790
Bedrooms: 4
Bathrooms: 3 ½
Width: 80' - 0"
Depth: 107' - 8"
Foundation: Slab

© Sater Design Collection, Inc.

HPK2101069

Style: Mediterranean

Square Footage: 3,817

Bedrooms: 4

Bathrooms: 3 ½

Width: 102' - 4"

Depth: 102' - 4"

Foundation: Slab

EPLANS.COM

Photo By: CJ Walker. This home, as shown in photographs, may differ from the actual blueprints. For more detailed information, please check the floor plans carefully.

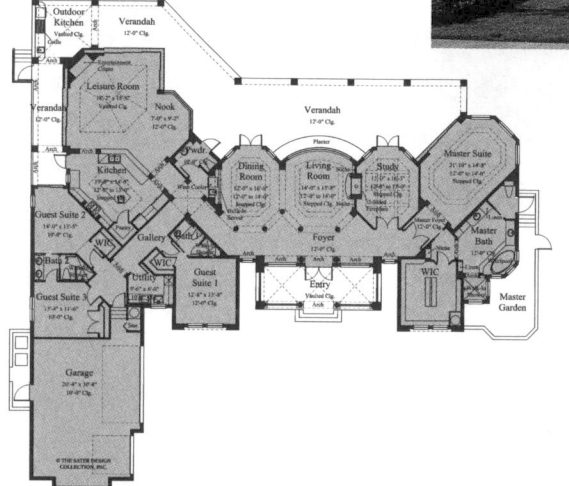

©The Sater Design Collection, Inc.

HPK2101070

Style: Mediterranean

Square Footage: 3,825

Bedrooms: 3

Bathrooms: 3

Width: 89' - 9"

Depth: 104' - 0"

Foundation: Slab

EPLANS.COM

Photo by: Laurence Taylor. This home, as shown in photographs, may differ from the actual blueprints. For more detailed information, please check the floor plans carefully.

HPK2101071

Style: Pueblo

Square Footage: 3,838

Bedrooms: 4

Bathrooms: 3 ½

Width: 127' - 6"

Depth: 60' - 10"

Foundation: Slab

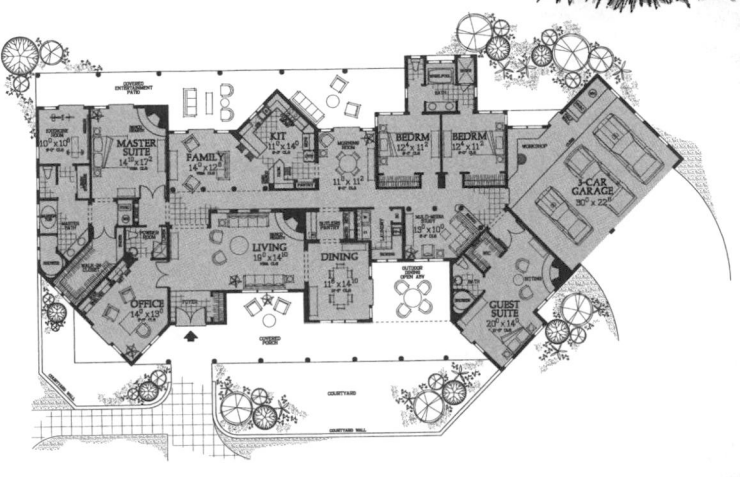

HPK2101072

Style: Mediterranean

Square Footage: 3,866

Bedrooms: 3

Bathrooms: 3 ½

Width: 120' - 0"

Depth: 89' - 0"

Foundation: Slab

© The Sater Design Collection, Inc.

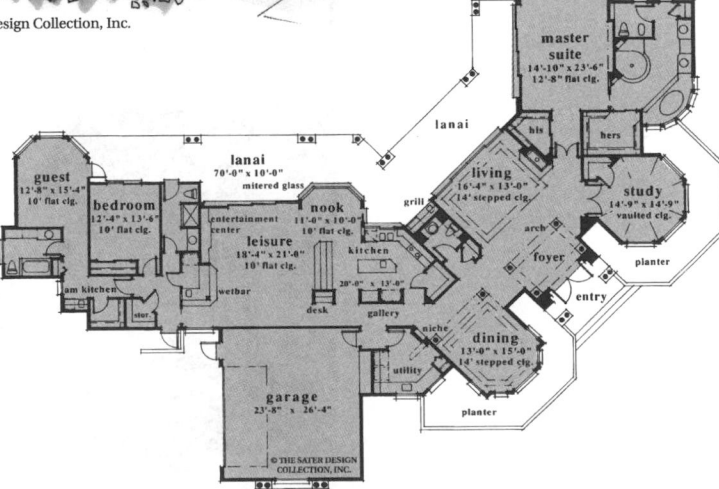

HPK2101073

Style: Italianate

Square Footage: 3,877

Bedrooms: 3

Bathrooms: 3 ½

Width: 102' - 4"

Depth: 98' - 10"

Foundation: Slab

EPLANS.COM

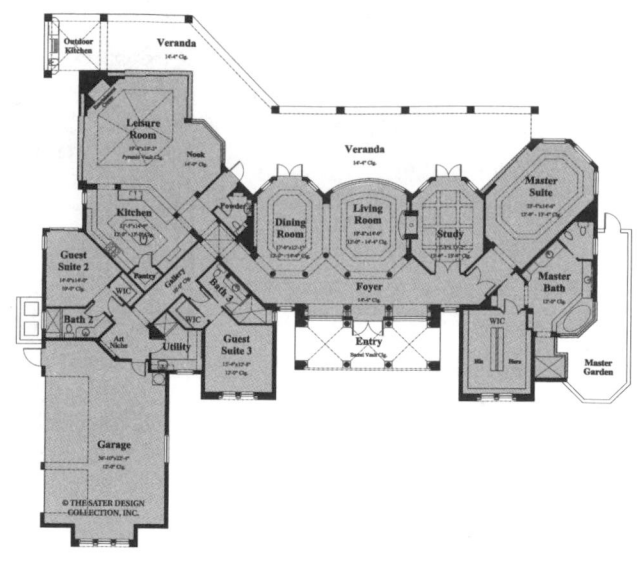

© Laurence Taylor Photography. This home, as shown in photographs, may differ from the actual blueprints. For more detailed information, please check the floor plans carefully.

HPK2101074

Style: Mediterranean

Square Footage: 3,883

Bedrooms: 3

Bathrooms: 3 ½

Width: 101' - 4"

Depth: 106' - 0"

Foundation: Slab

EPLANS.COM

Oscar Thompson; Courtesy of The Sater Design Collection, Inc. This home, as shown in photographs, may differ from the actual blueprints. For more detailed information, please check the floor plans carefully.

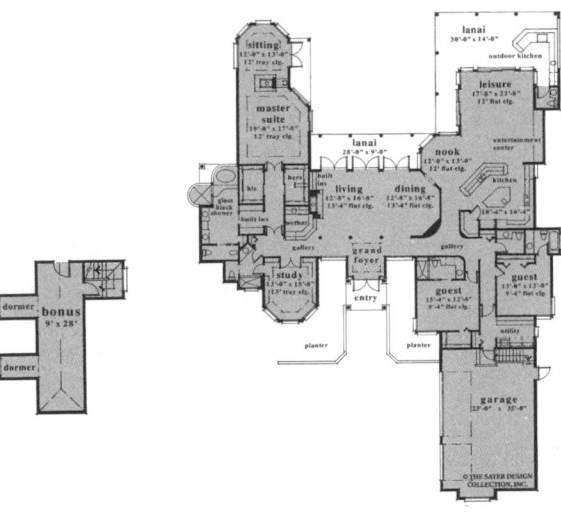

© The Sater Design Collection, Inc.

HPK2101075

Style: Mediterranean

Square Footage: 3,896

Bonus Space: 356 sq. ft.

Bedrooms: 3

Bathrooms: 4 ½

Width: 90' - 0"

Depth: 120' - 8"

Foundation: Slab

EPLANS.COM

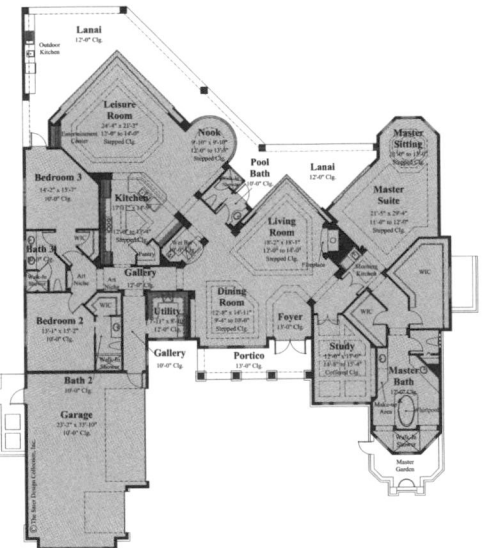

HPK2101076

Style: Italianate

Square Footage: 3,942

Bedrooms: 3

Bathrooms: 4

Width: 83' - 10"

Depth: 106' - 0"

Foundation: Slab

EPLANS.COM

© The Sater Design Collection, Inc.

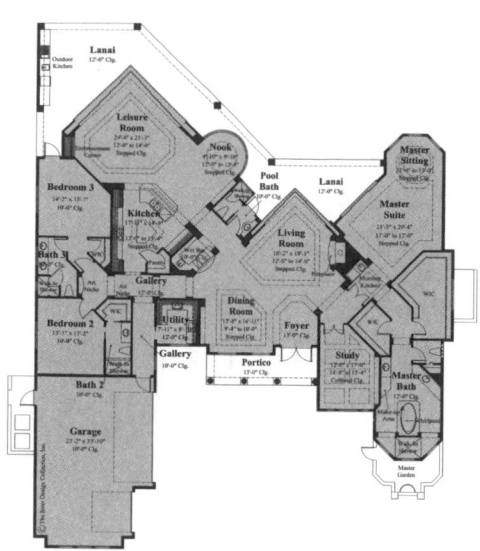

© The Sater Design Collection, Inc.

HPK2101077

Style: Italianate

Square Footage: 3,942

Bedrooms: 3

Bathrooms: 4

Width: 83' - 10"

Depth: 106' - 0"

Foundation: Slab

EPLANS.COM

© The Sater Design Collection, Inc.

HPK2101078

Style: Gothic Revival

Square Footage: 3,942

Bedrooms: 3

Bathrooms: 4

Width: 83' - 10"

Depth: 106' - 0"

Foundation: Slab

EPLANS.COM

© The Sater Design Collection, Inc.

HPK2101079

EPLANS.COM

Style: Italianate

Square Footage: 3,993

Bedrooms: 5

Bathrooms: 3 ½

Width: 80' - 0"

Depth: 104' - 0"

Foundation: Slab

The Teodora redefines the interplay between indoor and outdoor spaces, creating a wonderfully livable Italianate home with elegant touches at every turn. Doors open to two verandas, and windows bring light into the home from a variety of locations. In every room, the relationship to the outdoors takes center stage, whether through French doors, as in the bedroom, or the sliding glass door in the guest room. Special touches on the verandas, like the fireplace outside the master suite or the grill outside the leisure room, create destinations outdoors, as well.

3,500 TO 3,999 SQUARE FEET

First Floor

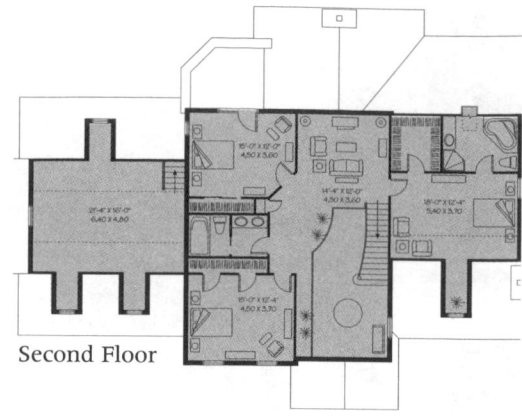

Second Floor

Step into this country home through an arched entrance and handsome columns, and immediately be dazzled by the comfort and efficiency of the layout. Two fireplaces—one in the living room, the other in the den—will strike your eye. A large, lavishly furnished guest suite on the first floor invites visitors. A country-style kitchen can easily serve meals in both the sunny family nook and the formal dining room. Upstairs, two bedrooms share a bath, and the master suite comes with a deluxe bath and a walk-in closet. A sitting room is accessible to all the upstairs sleeping quarters.

HPK2101080

Style: Colonial Revival

First Floor: 2,182 sq. ft.

Second Floor: 1,318 sq. ft.

Total: 3,500 sq. ft.

Bonus Space: 442 sq. ft.

Bedrooms: 4

Bathrooms: 3 ½

Width: 70' - 0"

Depth: 50' - 0"

Foundation: Unfinished Basement

EPLANS.COM

ORDER BLUEPRINTS ANYTIME AT EPLANS.COM OR 1-800-521-6797

HPK2101081

Style: Italianate

First Floor: 2,232 sq. ft.

Second Floor: 1,269 sq. ft.

Total: 3,501 sq. ft.

Bedrooms: 4

Bathrooms: 4 ½

Width: 63' - 9"

Depth: 80' - 0"

Foundation: Slab

EPLANS.COM

© The Sater Design Collection, Inc.

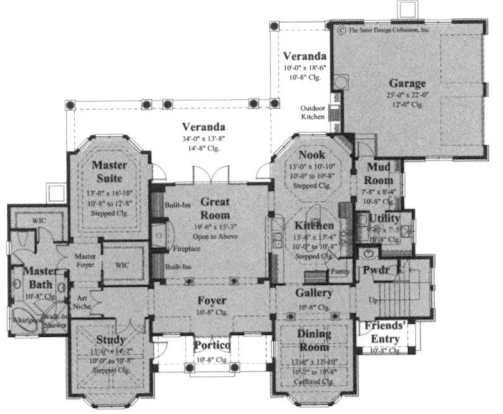

First Floor

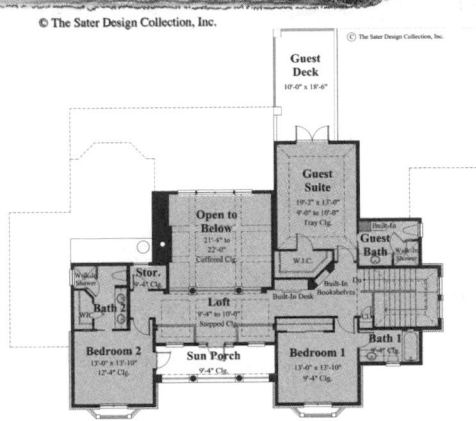

Second Floor

HPK2101082

Style: Neoclassical

First Floor: 2,232 sq. ft.

Second Floor: 1,269 sq. ft.

Total: 3,501 sq. ft.

Bedrooms: 4

Bathrooms: 4 ½

Width: 80' - 0"

Depth: 63' - 9"

Foundation: Slab

EPLANS.COM

© The Sater Design Collection, Inc.

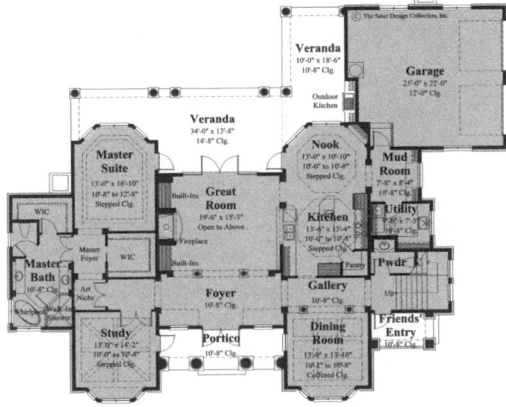

First Floor

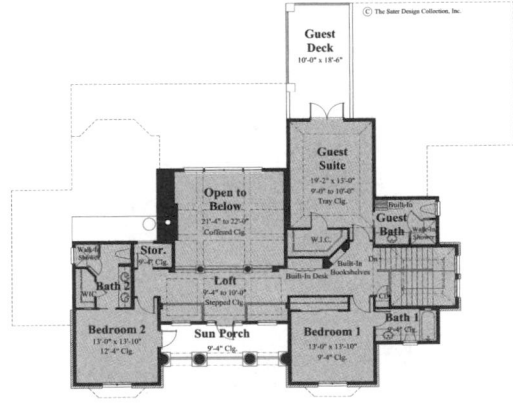

Second Floor

HPK2101083

Style: Mediterranean

First Floor: 2,227 sq. ft.

Second Floor: 1,278 sq. ft.

Total: 3,505 sq. ft.

Bedrooms: 4

Bathrooms: 4 ½

Width: 80' - 0"

Depth: 63' - 0"

Foundation: Slab

EPLANS.COM

© The Sater Design Collection, Inc.

First Floor

Second Floor

HPK2101084

Style: French Country

First Floor: 2,658 sq. ft.

Second Floor: 854 sq. ft.

Total: 3,512 sq. ft.

Bonus Space: 150 sq. ft.

Bedrooms: 4

Bathrooms: 3 ½

Width: 86' - 0"

Depth: 58' - 1"

Foundation: Crawlspace, Slab, Unfinished Basement

EPLANS.COM

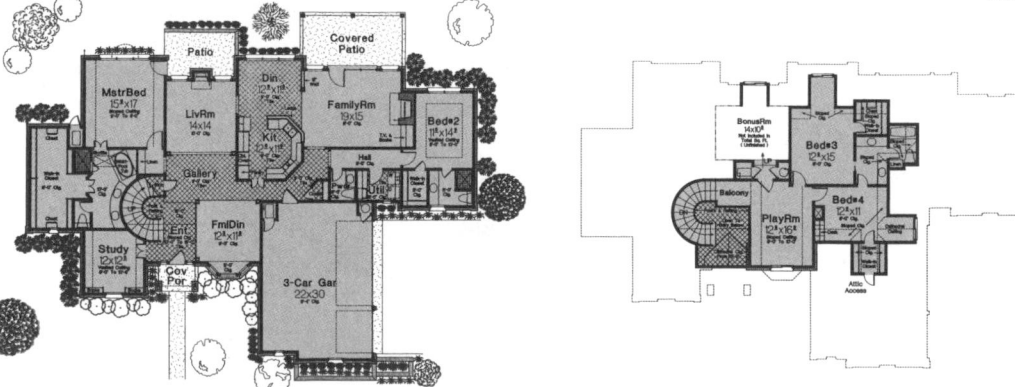

First Floor

Second Floor

HPK2101085

Style: French Country
First Floor: 2,698 sq. ft.
Second Floor: 819 sq. ft.
Total: 3,517 sq. ft.
Bonus Space: 370 sq. ft.
Bedrooms: 3
Bathrooms: 3 ½
Width: 90' - 6"
Depth: 84' - 0"
Foundation: Crawlspace

EPLANS.COM

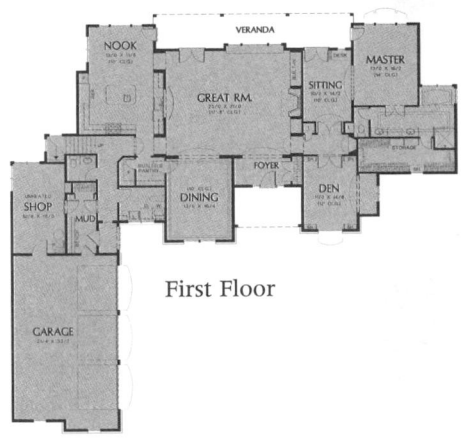

First Floor

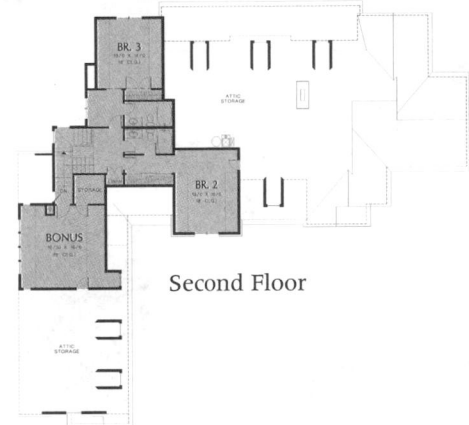

Second Floor

HPK2101086

Style: Craftsman
First Floor: 2,049 sq. ft.
Second Floor: 1,468 sq. ft.
Total: 3,517 sq. ft.
Bedrooms: 4
Bathrooms: 4 ½
Width: 57' - 0"
Depth: 44' - 0"
Foundation: Crawlspace

EPLANS.COM

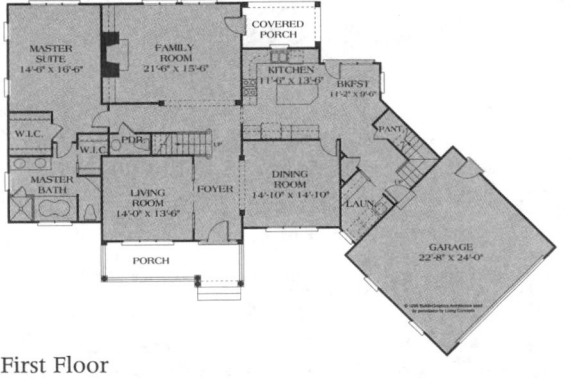

First Floor

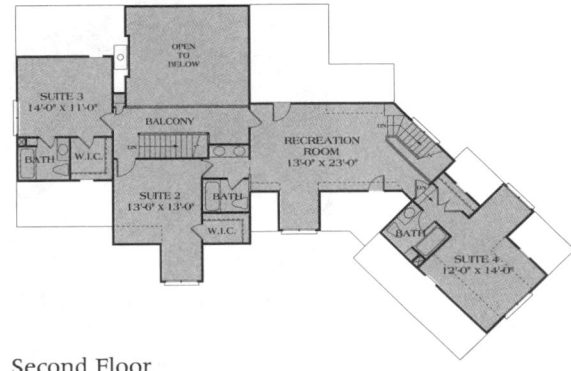

Second Floor

3,500 TO 3,999 SQUARE FEET

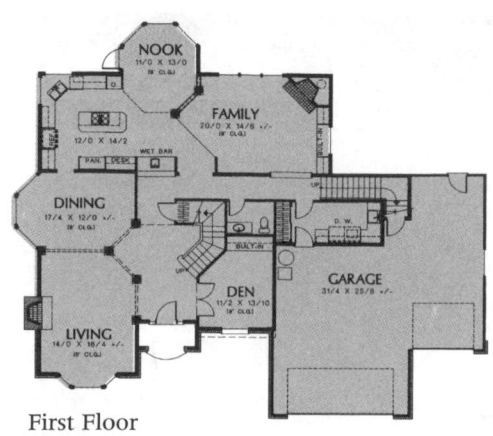

First Floor

Second Floor

HPK2101087

Style: **New American**

First Floor: **1,940 sq. ft.**

Second Floor: **1,578 sq. ft.**

Total: **3,518 sq. ft.**

Bonus Space: **292 sq. ft.**

Bedrooms: **4**

Bathrooms: **3 ½**

Width: **70' - 6"**

Depth: **59' - 6"**

Foundation: **Crawlspace**

EPLANS.COM

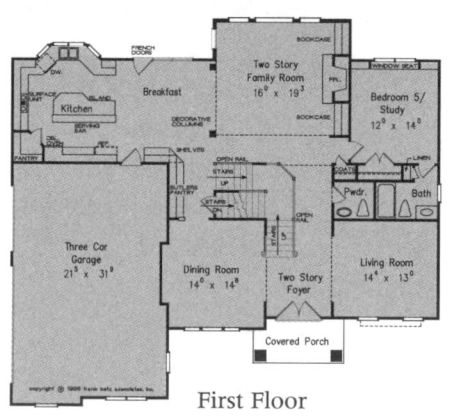

First Floor

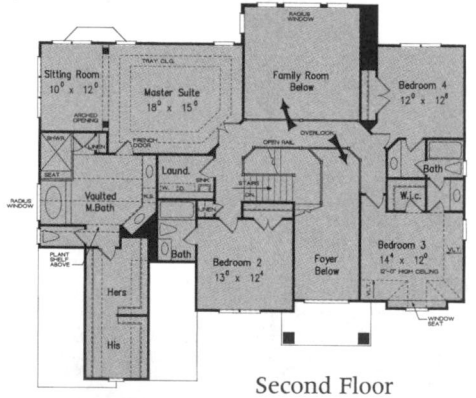

Second Floor

HPK2101088

Style: **New American**

First Floor: **1,786 sq. ft.**

Second Floor: **1,739 sq. ft.**

Total: **3,525 sq. ft.**

Bedrooms: **5**

Bathrooms: **4 ½**

Width: **59' - 0"**

Depth: **53' - 0"**

Foundation: **Crawlspace, Slab, Unfinished Walkout Basement**

EPLANS.COM

ORDER BLUEPRINTS ANYTIME AT EPLANS.COM OR 1-800-521-6797

First Floor

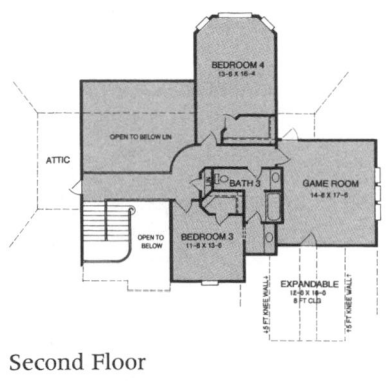

Second Floor

COPYRIGHT LARRY E. BELK

HPK2101089

Style: French Country
First Floor: 2,518 sq. ft.
Second Floor: 1,013 sq. ft.
Total: 3,531 sq. ft.
Bonus Space: 192 sq. ft.
Bedrooms: 4
Bathrooms: 3 ½
Width: 67' - 8"
Depth: 74' - 2"
Foundation: Crawlspace, Slab, Unfinished Basement

EPLANS.COM

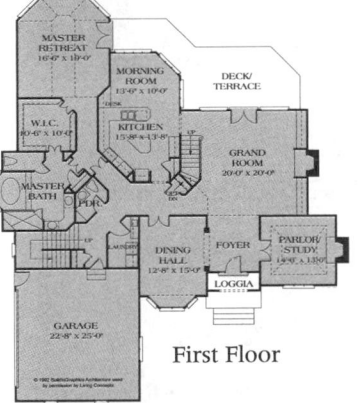

First Floor

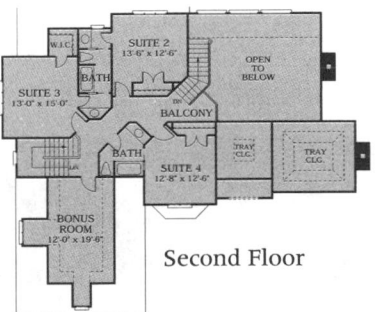

Second Floor

HPK2101090

Style: French Country
First Floor: 2,452 sq. ft.
Second Floor: 1,079 sq. ft.
Total: 3,531 sq. ft.
Bonus Space: 273 sq. ft.
Bedrooms: 4
Bathrooms: 3 ½
Width: 68' - 0"
Depth: 77' - 8"
Foundation: Crawlspace, Unfinished Basement

EPLANS.COM

3,500 TO 3,999 SQUARE FEET

HPK2101091

Style: New American
First Floor: 2,200 sq. ft.
Second Floor: 1,338 sq. ft.
Total: 3,538 sq. ft.
Bedrooms: 4
Bathrooms: 3 ½
Width: 83' - 5"
Depth: 68' - 11"

eplans.com

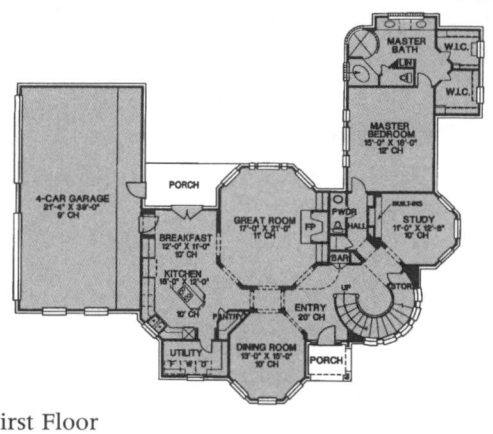

First Floor

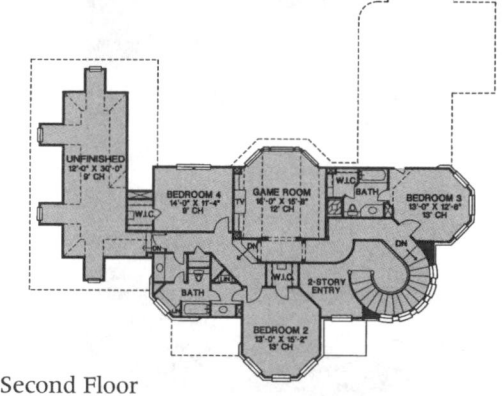

Second Floor

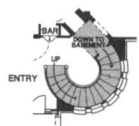

Optional Layout

HPK2101092

Style: Tudor
First Floor: 2,361 sq. ft.
Second Floor: 1,177 sq. ft.
Total: 3,538 sq. ft.
Bonus Space: 465 sq. ft.
Bedrooms: 4
Bathrooms: 4 ½
Width: 62' - 4"
Depth: 99' - 9"
Foundation: Crawlspace

EPLANS.COM

First Floor

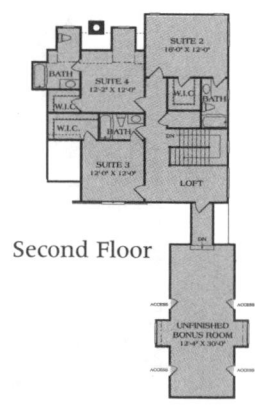

Second Floor

HPK2101093

Style: Greek Revival
First Floor: 2,449 sq. ft.
Second Floor: 1,094 sq. ft.
Total: 3,543 sq. ft.
Bonus Space: 409 sq. ft.
Bedrooms: 4
Bathrooms: 3 ½
Width: 89' - 0"
Depth: 53' - 10"
Foundation: Crawlspace

© William E. Poole Designs, Inc.

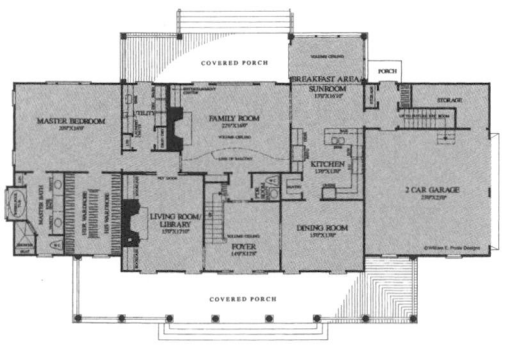

First Floor

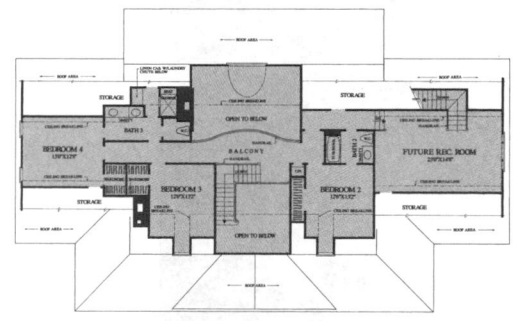

Second Floor

©1995 William E Poole Designs, Inc.

HPK2101094

Style: French Country
First Floor: 2,568 sq. ft.
Second Floor: 981 sq. ft.
Total: 3,549 sq. ft.
Bedrooms: 4
Bathrooms: 4 ½
Width: 66' - 8"
Depth: 71' - 0"
Foundation: Unfinished Basement

First Floor

Second Floor

eplans.com

3,500 TO 3,999 SQUARE FEET

HPK2101095

Style: Craftsman

First Floor: 1,602 sq. ft.

Second Floor: 1,948 sq. ft.

Total: 3,550 sq. ft.

Bedrooms: 4

Bathrooms: 3 ½

Width: 40' - 0"

Depth: 60' - 0"

Foundation: Crawlspace

EPLANS.COM

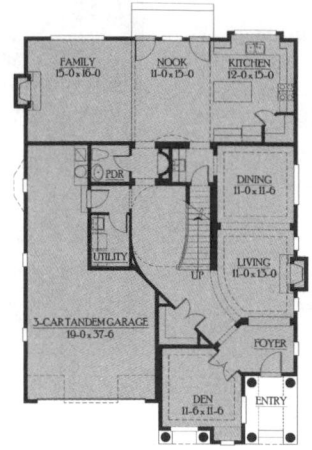

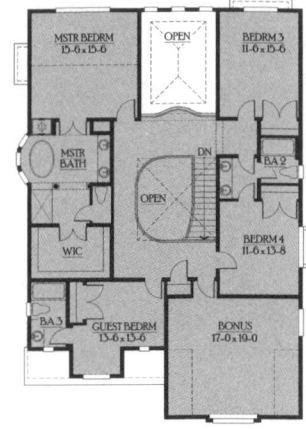

First Floor   Second Floor

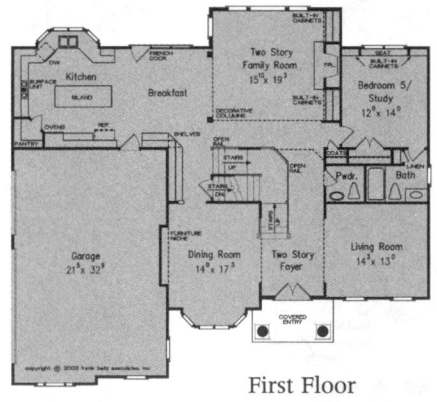

First Floor

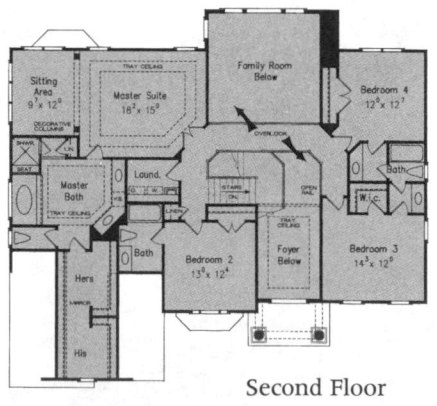

Second Floor

HPK2101096

Style: Neoclassical

First Floor: 1,810 sq. ft.

Second Floor: 1,740 sq. ft.

Total: 3,550 sq. ft.

Bedrooms: 5

Bathrooms: 4 ½

Width: 59' - 0"

Depth: 53' - 0"

Foundation: Crawlspace, Unfinished Walkout Basement

EPLANS.COM

HPK2101097

Style: Mediterranean

First Floor: 2,761 sq. ft.

Second Floor: 796 sq. ft.

Total: 3,557 sq. ft.

Bonus Space: 284 sq. ft.

Bedrooms: 4

Bathrooms: 4 ½

Width: 85' - 0"

Depth: 72' - 0"

Foundation: Slab

EPLANS.COM

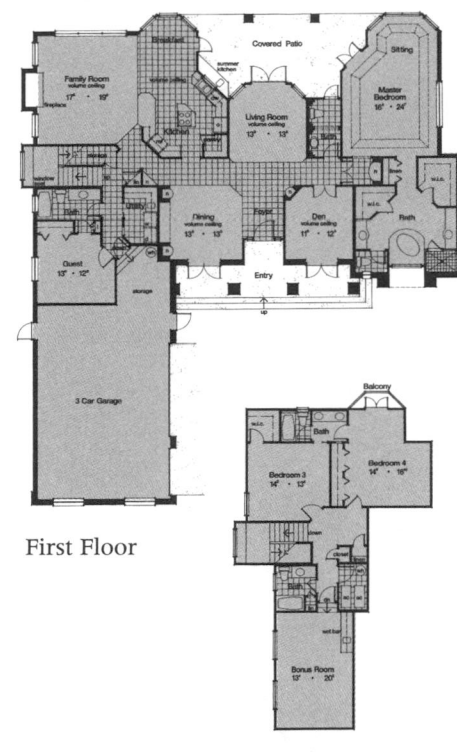

First Floor

Second Floor

First Floor

Second Floor

HPK2101098

Style: Cottage

First Floor: 2,202 sq. ft.

Second Floor: 1,355 sq. ft.

Total: 3,557 sq. ft.

Bonus Space: 523 sq. ft.

Bedrooms: 4

Bathrooms: 3 ½

Width: 66' - 0"

Depth: 65' - 10"

Foundation: Crawlspace

EPLANS.COM

3,500 TO 3,999 SQUARE FEET

HPK2101099

Style: Cottage
First Floor: 2,493 sq. ft.
Second Floor: 1,065 sq. ft.
Total: 3,558 sq. ft.
Bonus Space: 277 sq. ft.
Bedrooms: 4
Bathrooms: 3 ½
Width: 76' - 0"
Depth: 68' - 0"
Foundation: Crawlspace, Slab

EPLANS.COM

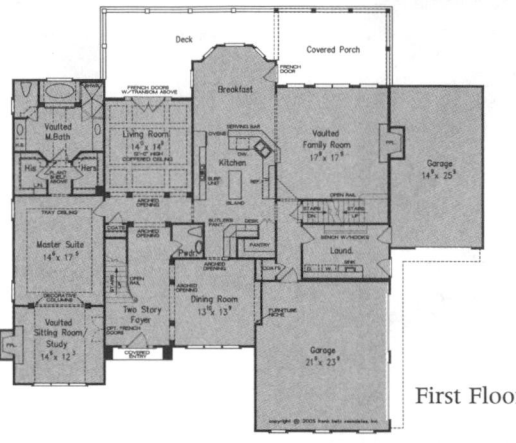

First Floor

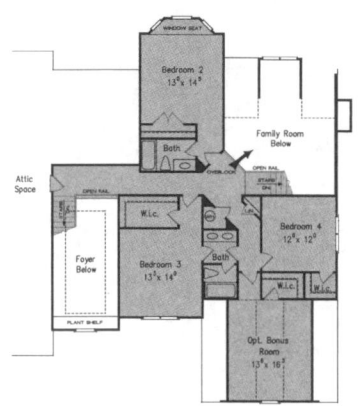

Second Floor

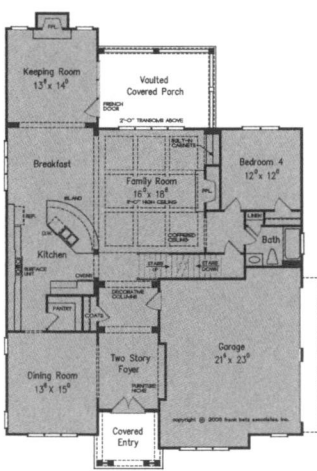

First Floor

HPK2101100

Style: Tudor
First Floor: 1,737 sq. ft.
Second Floor: 1,821 sq. ft.
Total: 3,558 sq. ft.
Bedrooms: 4
Bathrooms: 4
Width: 45' - 0"
Depth: 67' - 10"
Foundation: Crawlspace

EPLANS.COM

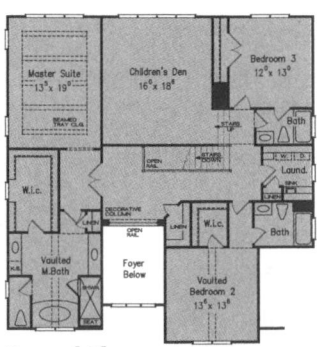

Second Floor

HPK2101101

Style: Federal - Adams
First Floor: 2,093 sq. ft.
Second Floor: 1,469 sq. ft.
Total: 3,562 sq. ft.
Bonus Space: 589 sq. ft.
Bedrooms: 4
Bathrooms: 3 ½
Width: 69' - 0"
Depth: 74' - 2"
Foundation: Crawlspace

EPLANS.COM

First Floor

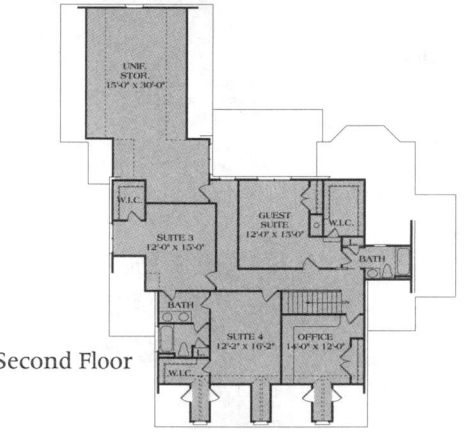

Second Floor

HPK2101102

Style: French Country
First Floor: 2,630 sq. ft.
Second Floor: 935 sq. ft.
Total: 3,565 sq. ft.
Bedrooms: 4
Bathrooms: 3 ½
Width: 78' - 5"
Depth: 65' - 2"
Foundation: Unfinished Basement

EPLANS.COM

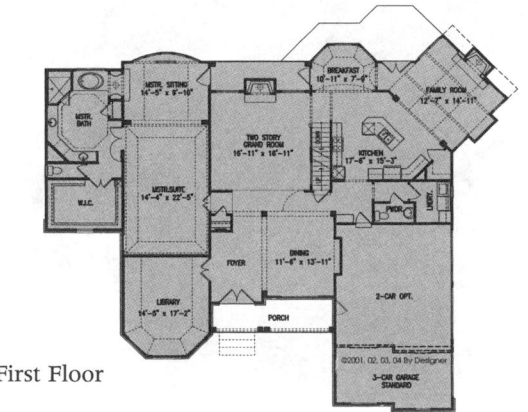

First Floor

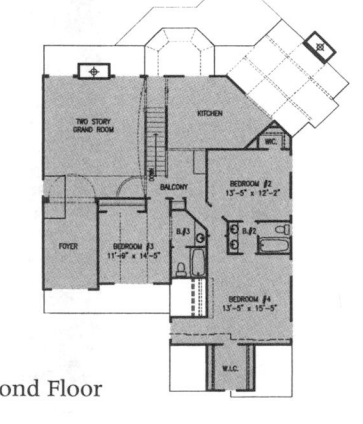

Second Floor

3,500 TO 3,999 SQUARE FEET

HPK2101103

Style: Craftsman
First Floor: 1,815 sq. ft.
Second Floor: 1,755 sq. ft.
Total: 3,570 sq. ft.
Bedrooms: 4
Bathrooms: 2 ½
Width: 56' - 0"
Depth: 54' - 0"
Foundation: Crawlspace

EPLANS.COM

First Floor

Second Floor

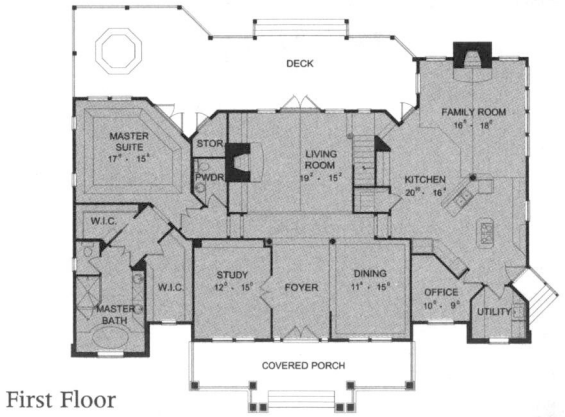

First Floor

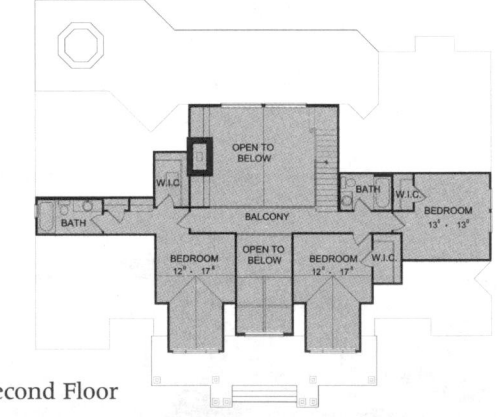

Second Floor

HPK2101104

Style: Log House
First Floor: 2,589 sq. ft.
Second Floor: 981 sq. ft.
Total: 3,570 sq. ft.
Bedrooms: 4
Bathrooms: 3 ½
Width: 70' - 8"
Depth: 61' - 10"
Foundation: Crawlspace

EPLANS.COM

HPK2101105

Style: New American
First Floor: 2,216 sq. ft.
Second Floor: 1,356 sq. ft.
Total: 3,572 sq. ft.
Bonus Space: 409 sq. ft.
Bedrooms: 4
Bathrooms: 3 ½
Width: 49' - 0"
Depth: 89' - 4"
Foundation: Crawlspace

First Floor

Second Floor

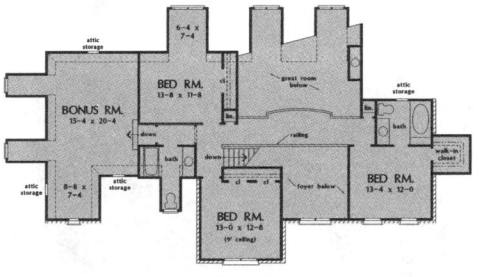

First Floor

Second Floor

HPK2101106

Style: New American
First Floor: 2,511 sq. ft.
Second Floor: 1,062 sq. ft.
Total: 3,573 sq. ft.
Bonus Space: 465 sq. ft.
Bedrooms: 4
Bathrooms: 3 ½
Width: 84' - 11"
Depth: 55' - 11"

EPLANS.COM

HPK2101107

Style: Farmhouse
First Floor: 1,737 sq. ft.
Second Floor: 1,837 sq. ft.
Total: 3,574 sq. ft.
Bedrooms: 5
Bathrooms: 4
Width: 55' - 0"
Depth: 50' - 6"
Foundation: Crawlspace, Unfinished Walkout Basement

EPLANS.COM

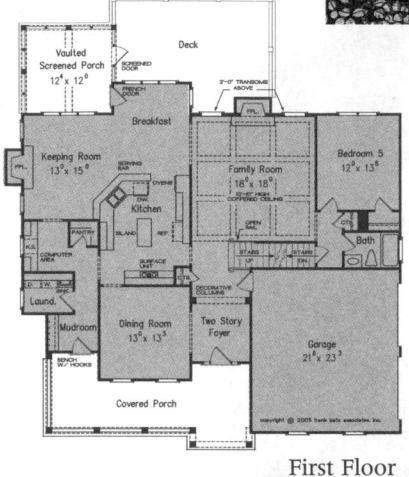

First Floor

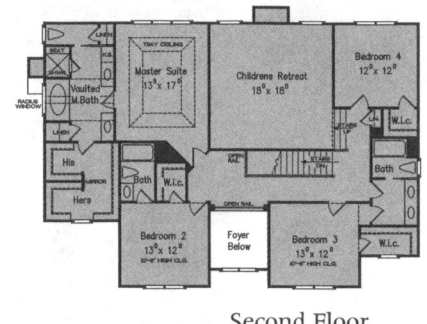

Second Floor

HPK2101108

Style: Mediterranean
First Floor: 2,688 sq. ft.
Second Floor: 887 sq. ft.
Total: 3,575 sq. ft.
Bedrooms: 4
Bathrooms: 3 ½
Width: 107' - 10"
Depth: 84' - 2"
Foundation: Slab

EPLANS.COM

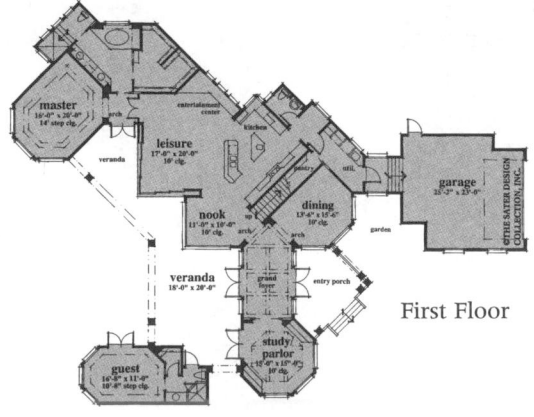

First Floor

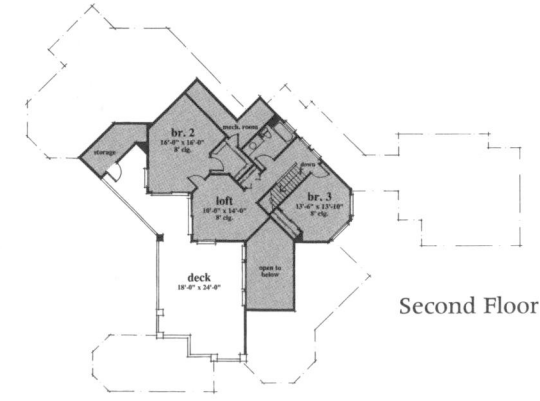

Second Floor

© The Sater Design Collection, Inc.

HPK2101109

Style: Italianate
First Floor: 2,163 sq. ft.
Second Floor: 1,415 sq. ft.
Total: 3,578 sq. ft.
Bedrooms: 5
Bathrooms: 3 ½
Width: 71' - 0"
Depth: 72' - 0"
Foundation: Slab

EPLANS.COM

The arched portico, balcony, and low-pitched roof combine to form a pleasingly Italianate facade in this European design. Matching arches top front-facing windows. In the interior, the foyer opens into the great room, featuring a fireplace, built-in entertainment center, and access to the rear terrace. The left wing of the plan comprises the large island kitchen, dining room with beamed ceiling, and an airy breakfast nook. The right wing is reserved for the study, master suite, and master bath. Upstairs, four bedrooms share two full baths and access to the balcony. Art niches adorn the walls throughout the house.

First Floor

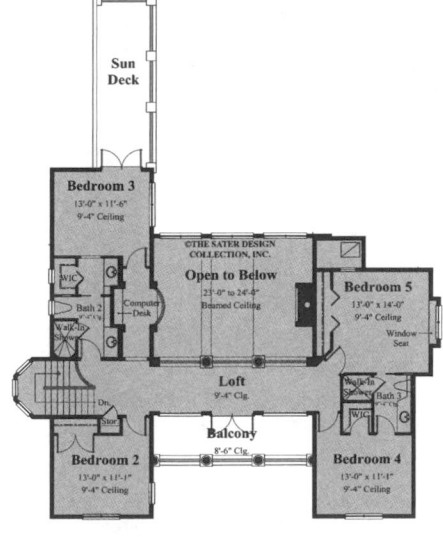

Second Floor

3,500 TO 3,999 SQUARE FEET

First Floor

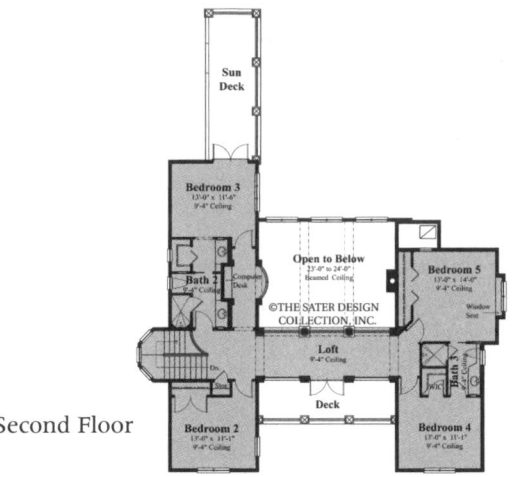

Second Floor

The portico yields to an open foyer that is defined by tapered columns and graceful arches. Well-defined formal rooms flank the gallery that leads to the great room. Three sets of French doors invite a sense of nature within, and link the space to an outdoor room: a patio terrace. Nearby, a splendid loggia boasts an outdoor grill and a link to the morning nook and kitchen. The right wing of the home is dedicated to the owners' retreat. On the upper level, a gallery loft permits views of the great room below, and links four secondary bedrooms—one with private access to a sun deck.

HPK2101110

Style: French Country
First Floor: 2,163 sq. ft.
Second Floor: 1,415 sq. ft.
Total: 3,578 sq. ft.
Bedrooms: 5
Bathrooms: 3 ½
Width: 71' - 0"
Depth: 72' - 0"
Foundation: Slab

EPLANS.COM

©The Sater Design Collection, Inc.

HPK2101111

Style: Neoclassical
First Floor: 2,240 sq. ft.
Second Floor: 1,220 sq. ft.
Total: 3,460 sq. ft.
Bedrooms: 5
Bathrooms: 4
Width: 64' - 0"
Depth: 68' - 6"
Foundation: Crawlspace

EPLANS.COM

A double-height, arched portico and careful fenestration provide for maximum penetration of daylight to this plan's interior. Inside holds ample opportunity for indulgence in the form of carefully and attractively designed rooms. A main hallway on the first floor connects either wing. Open spaces create an expansive feel throughout. The master suite features an exquisite tray ceiling, private outdoor access, and the biggest walk-in closet you've ever seen!

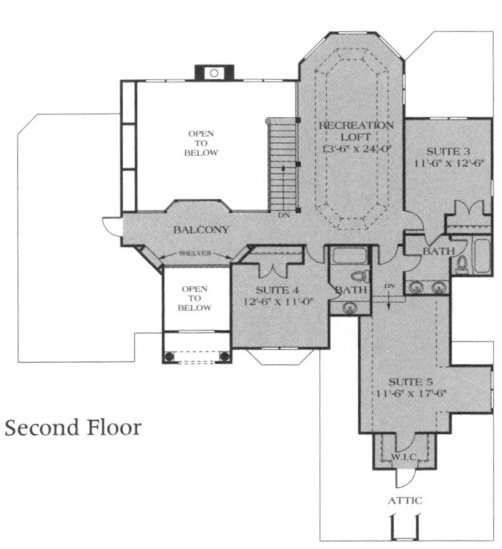

Second Floor

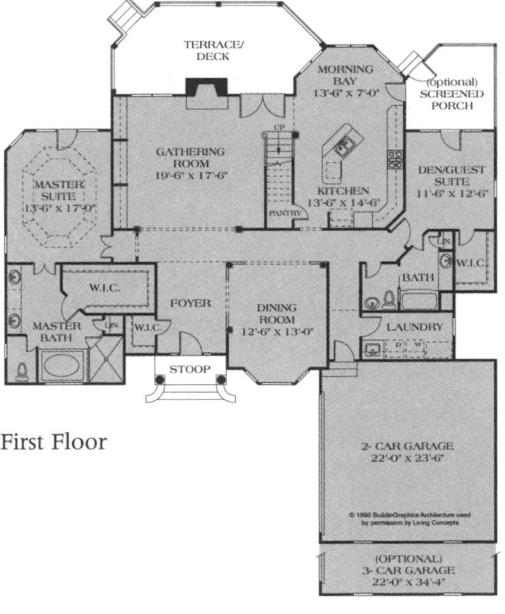

First Floor

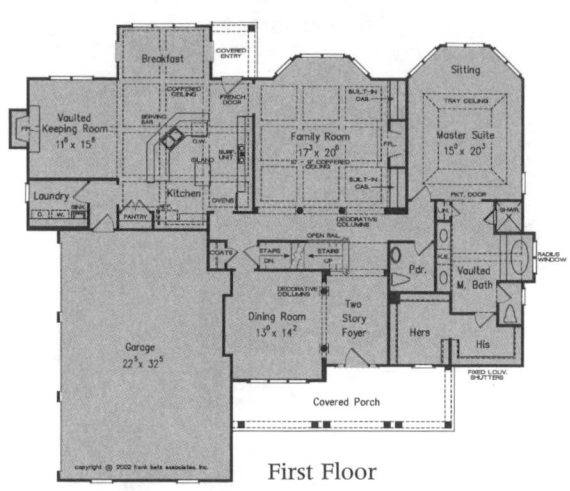

First Floor

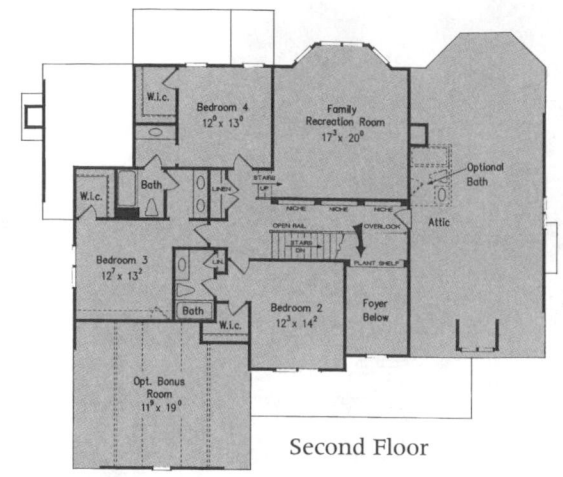

Second Floor

HPK2101112

This breathtaking stone-and-shingle European cottage will turn the home of your dreams into a reality. The fireplace gives a definite focus; tall windows bring in floods of natural light. An expansive kitchen makes it easy for multiple cooks to share space. A vaulted keeping room at the rear is a cozy hideaway. The master suite shines with a bayed sitting area and majestic vaulted bath with a garden tub.

Style: Country
First Floor: 2,225 sq. ft.
Second Floor: 1,360 sq. ft.
Total: 3,585 sq. ft.
Bonus Space: 277 sq. ft.
Bedrooms: 4
Bathrooms: 3 ½
Width: 68' - 10"
Depth: 60' - 0"
Foundation: Crawlspace, Unfinished Walkout Basement

EPLANS.COM

HPK2101113

Style: Federal - Adams
First Floor: 2,064 sq. ft.
Second Floor: 1,521 sq. ft.
Total: 3,585 sq. ft.
Bonus Space: 427 sq. ft.
Bedrooms: 4
Bathrooms: 3
Width: 84' - 8"
Depth: 65' - 0"
Foundation: Crawlspace

The best of southern tradition combines with an easygoing floor plan to make this home a sure neighborhood favorite. The elegant portico at the front is a unique touch. In the very back, the kitchen is amplified by a gorgeous vaulted sunroom featuring two walls of windows to let in light. The second floor is home to a deluxe master suite as well as two family bedrooms that share a bath. A utility room is conveniently located upstairs as well. Future space is available for expansion over the garage.

3,500 TO 3,999 SQUARE FEET

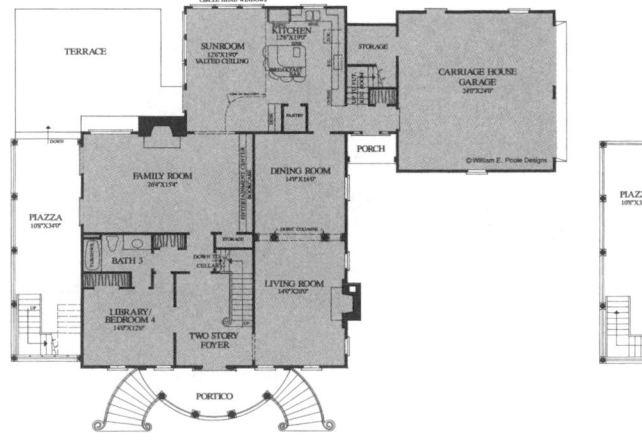

First Floor

Second Floor

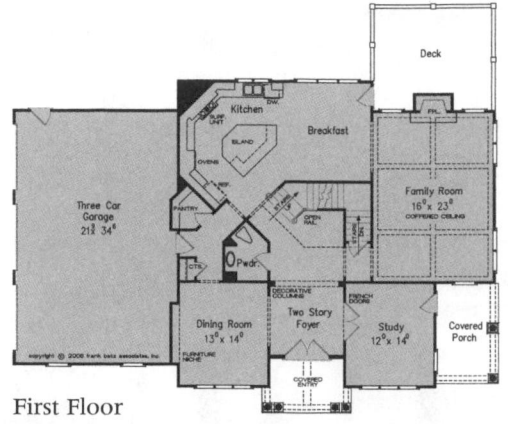

First Floor

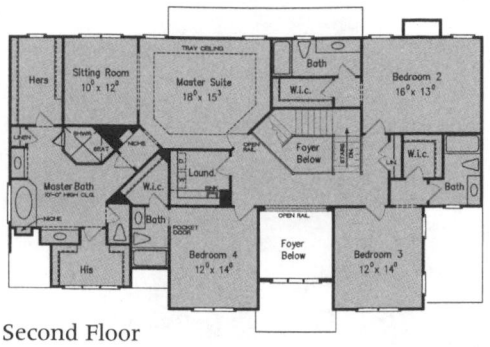

Second Floor

HPK2101114

Style: Cottage

First Floor: 1,599 sq. ft.

Second Floor: 1,987 sq. ft.

Total: 3,586 sq. ft.

Bedrooms: 4

Bathrooms: 4 ½

Width: 65' - 0"

Depth: 45' - 0"

Foundation: Crawlspace, Unfinished Walkout Basement

EPLANS.COM

HPK2101115

Style: New American

First Floor: 2,551 sq. ft.

Second Floor: 1,037 sq. ft.

Total: 3,588 sq. ft.

Bedrooms: 3

Bathrooms: 3 ½

Width: 76' - 0"

Depth: 90' - 0"

Foundation: Slab

EPLANS.COM

First Floor

Second Floor

© The Sater Design Collection, Inc.

HPK2101116

Style: Tidewater

First Floor: 2,390 sq. ft.

Second Floor: 1,200 sq. ft.

Total: 3,590 sq. ft.

Bedrooms: 4

Bathrooms: 3

Width: 61' - 0"

Depth: 64' - 4"

Foundation: Pier (same as Piling)

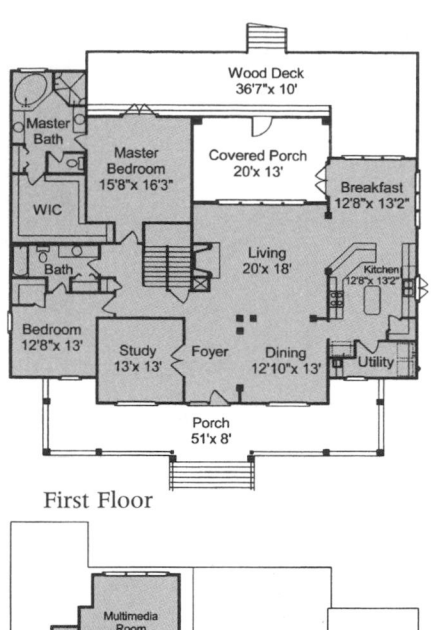

First Floor

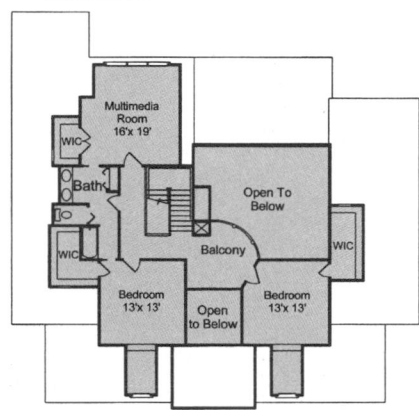

Second Floor

First Floor

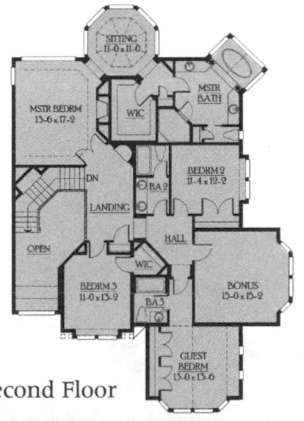

Second Floor

HPK2101117

Style: Craftsman

First Floor: 1,735 sq. ft.

Second Floor: 1,855 sq. ft.

Total: 3,590 sq. ft.

Bedrooms: 4

Bathrooms: 3 ½

Width: 74' - 0"

Depth: 72' - 0"

Foundation: Crawlspace

HPK2101118

Style: Cottage
First Floor: 2,436 sq. ft.
Second Floor: 1,155 sq. ft.
Total: 3,591 sq. ft.
Bedrooms: 4
Bathrooms: 4 ½
Width: 80' - 0"
Depth: 65' - 3"
Foundation: Crawlspace, Unfinished Walkout Basement

EPLANS.COM

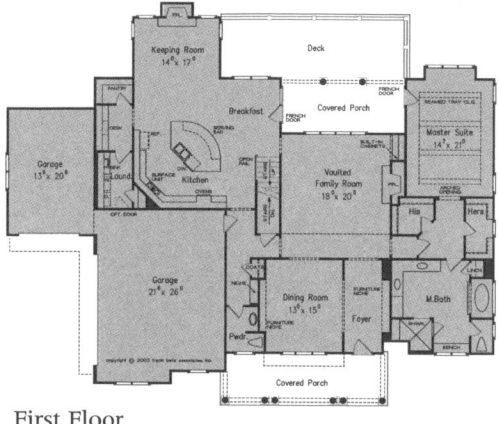

First Floor

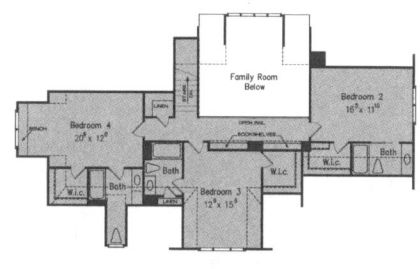

Second Floor

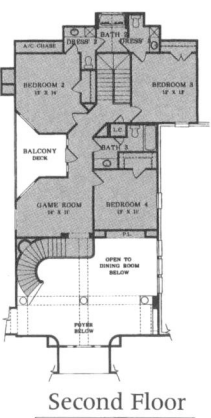

Second Floor

HPK2101119

Style: New American
First Floor: 2,528 sq. ft.
Second Floor: 1,067 sq. ft.
Total: 3,595 sq. ft.
Bedrooms: 4
Bathrooms: 3 ½ + ½
Width: 69' - 2"
Depth: 73' - 10"
Foundation: Slab

EPLANS.COM

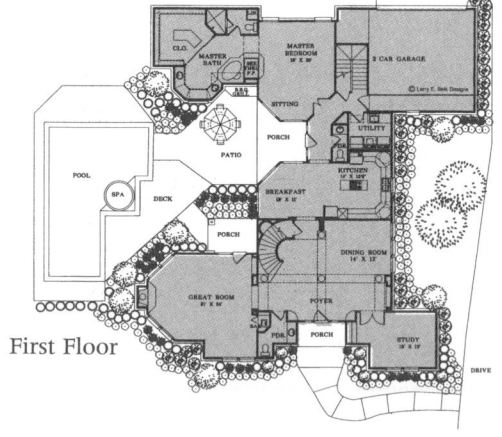

First Floor

ORDER BLUEPRINTS ANYTIME AT EPLANS.COM OR 1-800-521-6797

HPK2101120

Style: New American
First Floor: 2,369 sq. ft.
Second Floor: 1,230 sq. ft.
Total: 3,599 sq. ft.
Bedrooms: 3
Bathrooms: 3
Width: 89' - 8"
Depth: 53' - 9"
Foundation: Slab

EPLANS.COM

© The Sater Design Collection, Inc.

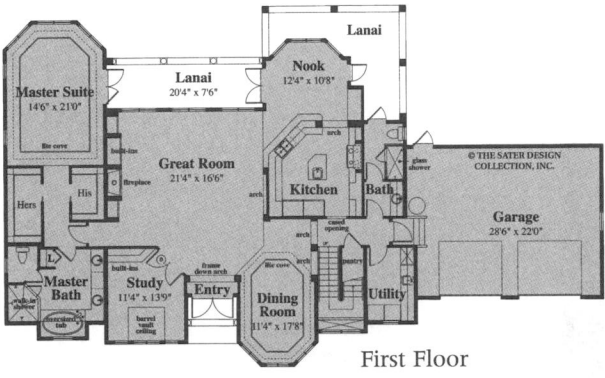

First Floor

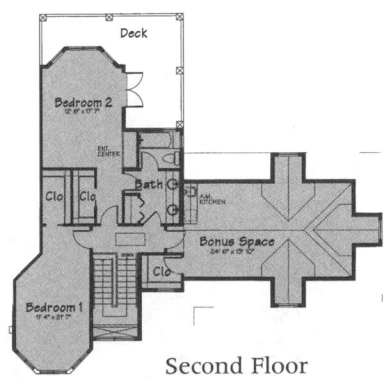

Second Floor

HPK2101121

Style: Cottage
First Floor: 2,334 sq. ft.
Second Floor: 1,265 sq. ft.
Total: 3,599 sq. ft.
Bedrooms: 4
Bathrooms: 3 ½
Width: 74' - 8"
Depth: 58' - 9"
Foundation: Crawlspace, Unfinished Walkout Basement

EPLANS.COM

First Floor

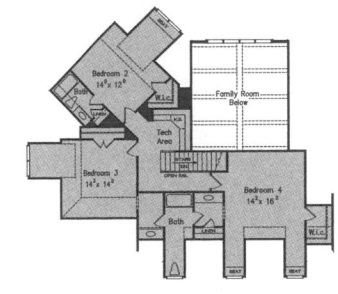

Second Floor

First Floor

Second Floor

© Stephen Fuller, Inc.

HPK2101122

Style: French Country

First Floor: 2,346 sq. ft.

Second Floor: 1,260 sq. ft.

Total: 3,606 sq. ft.

Bedrooms: 4

Bathrooms: 3 ½

Width: 68' - 11"

Depth: 58' - 9"

Foundation: Walkout Basement

EPLANS.COM

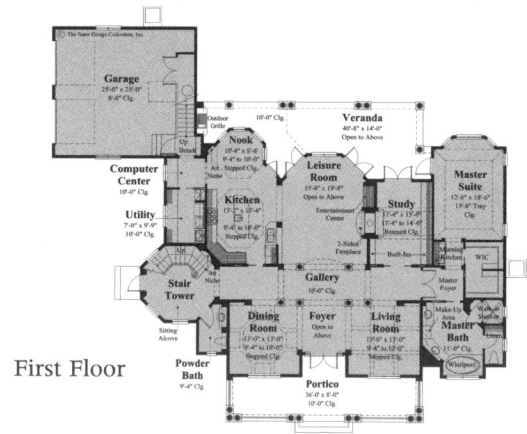

First Floor

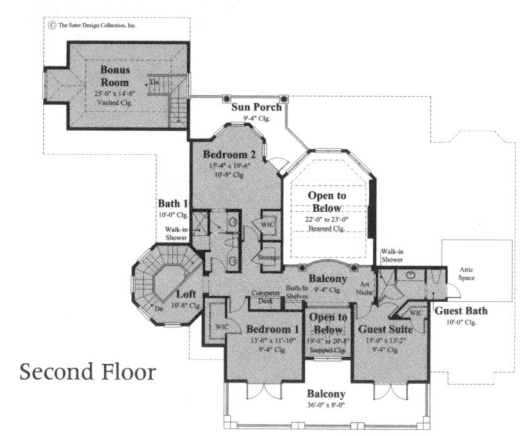

Second Floor

HPK2101123

Style: Beaux Arts

First Floor: 2,483 sq. ft.

Second Floor: 1,127 sq. ft.

Total: 3,610 sq. ft.

Bonus Space: 332 sq. ft.

Bedrooms: 4

Bathrooms: 3 ½

Width: 83' - 0"

Depth: 71' - 8"

Foundation: Slab

EPLANS.COM

© The Sater Design Collection, Inc.

HPK2101124

Style: Neoclassical
First Floor: 2,484 sq. ft.
Second Floor: 1,127 sq. ft.
Total: 3,611 sq. ft.
Bonus Space: 332 sq. ft.
Bedrooms: 4
Bathrooms: 3 ½
Width: 83' - 0"
Depth: 71' - 8"
Foundation: Slab

EPLANS.COM

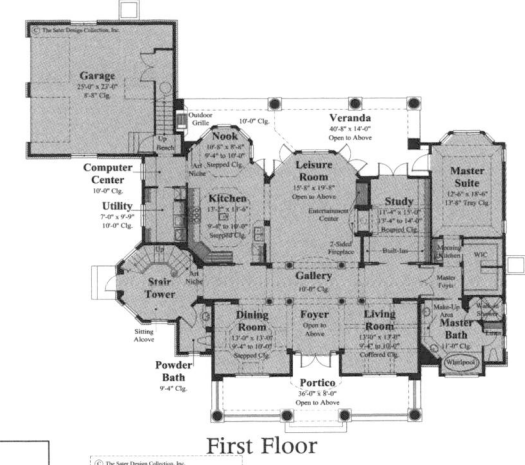

First Floor

© The Sater Design Collection, Inc.

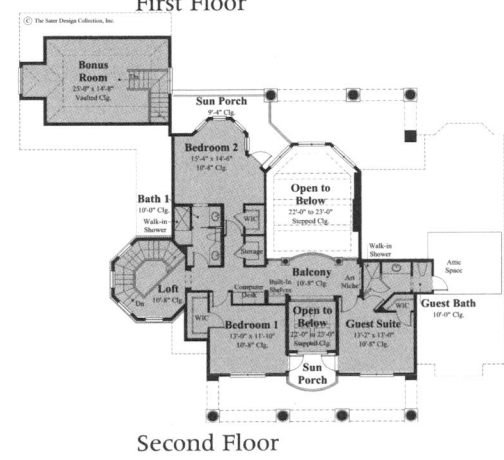

Second Floor

First Floor

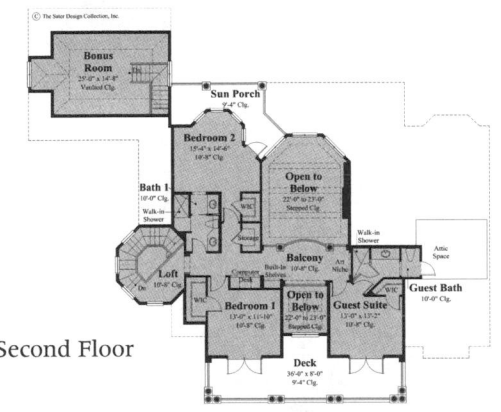

Second Floor

HPK2101125

Style: Plantation
First Floor: 2,481 sq. ft.
Second Floor: 1,132 sq. ft.
Total: 3,613 sq. ft.
Bonus Space: 332 sq. ft.
Bedrooms: 4
Bathrooms: 3 ½
Width: 83' - 0"
Depth: 71' - 8"
Foundation: Slab

EPLANS.COM

© The Sater Design Collection, Inc.

3,500 TO 3,999 SQUARE FEET

HPK2101126

Style: French Country

First Floor: 2,248 sq. ft.

Second Floor: 1,367 sq. ft.

Total: 3,615 sq. ft.

Bonus Space: 160 sq. ft.

Bedrooms: 4

Bathrooms: 3 ½

Width: 67' - 4"

Depth: 62' - 0"

Foundation: Crawlspace, Unfinished Walkout Basement

EPLANS.COM

First Floor

Second Floor

HPK2101127

Style: French Country

First Floor: 2,384 sq. ft.

Second Floor: 1,234 sq. ft.

Total: 3,618 sq. ft.

Bonus Space: 344 sq. ft.

Bedrooms: 5

Bathrooms: 4 ½

Width: 64' - 6"

Depth: 57' - 10"

Foundation: Crawlspace, Slab, Unfinished Walkout Basement

EPLANS.COM

First Floor

Second Floor

HPK2101128

Style: Neoclassical
First Floor: 2,411 sq. ft.
Second Floor: 1,207 sq. ft.
Total: 3,618 sq. ft.
Bonus Space: 691 sq. ft.
Bedrooms: 4
Bathrooms: 4 ½ + ½
Width: 84' - 2"
Depth: 93' - 4"
Foundation: Crawlspace

EPLANS.COM

©2006 William E Poole Designs, Inc

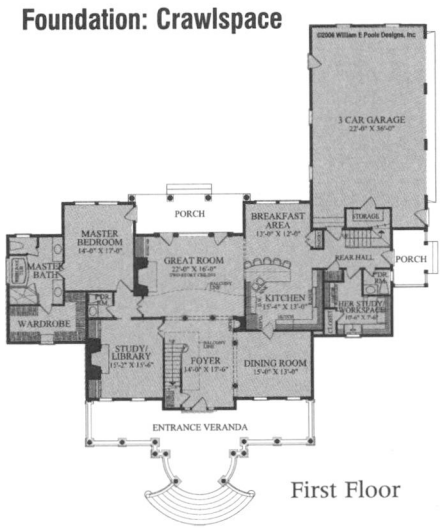

First Floor

Second Floor

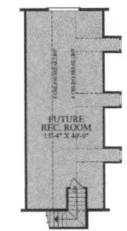

HPK2101129

Style: New American
First Floor: 2,778 sq. ft.
Second Floor: 841 sq. ft.
Total: 3,619 sq. ft.
Bedrooms: 4
Bathrooms: 3 ½ + ½
Width: 100' - 9"
Depth: 67' - 5"
Foundation: Unfinished Basement

EPLANS.COM

First Floor

Second Floor

3,500 TO 3,999 SQUARE FEET

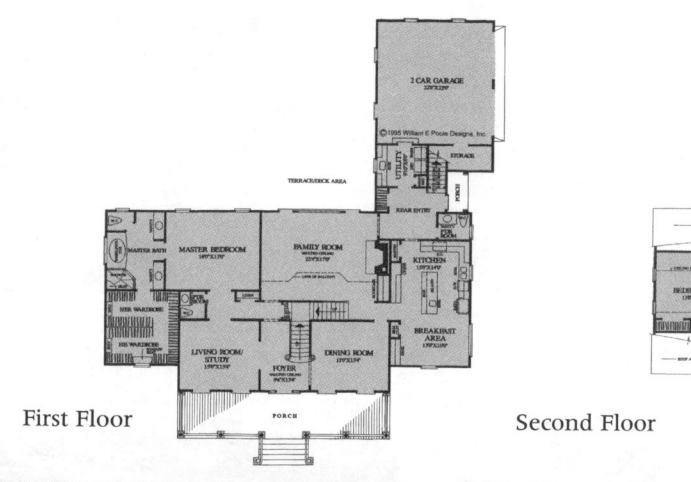

First Floor

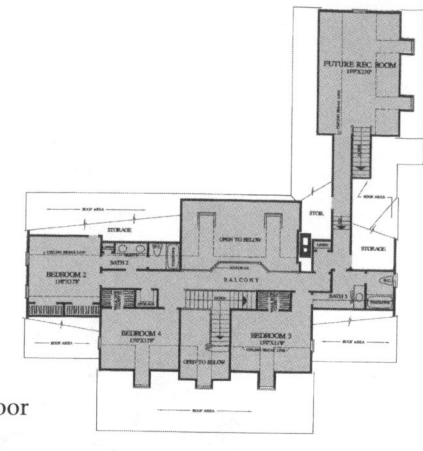

Second Floor

HPK2101130

Style: Federal - Adams
First Floor: 2,467 sq. ft.
Second Floor: 1,152 sq. ft.
Total: 3,619 sq. ft.
Bonus Space: 510 sq. ft.
Bedrooms: 4
Bathrooms: 3 ½ + ½
Width: 74' - 0"
Depth: 80' - 4"
Foundation: Crawlspace, Unfinished Basement

EPLANS.COM

© 1995 William E Poole Designs, Inc.

HPK2101131

Style: Chateauesque
First Floor: 2,423 sq. ft.
Second Floor: 1,197 sq. ft.
Total: 3,620 sq. ft.
Bonus Space: 551 sq. ft.
Bedrooms: 4
Bathrooms: 3 ½
Width: 56' - 6"
Depth: 97' - 3"
Foundation: Crawlspace

EPLANS.COM

First Floor

Second Floor

HPK2101132

Style: New American
First Floor: 2,603 sq. ft.
Second Floor: 1,020 sq. ft.
Total: 3,623 sq. ft.
Bedrooms: 4
Bathrooms: 4 ½
Width: 76' - 8"
Depth: 68' - 0"

EPLANS.COM

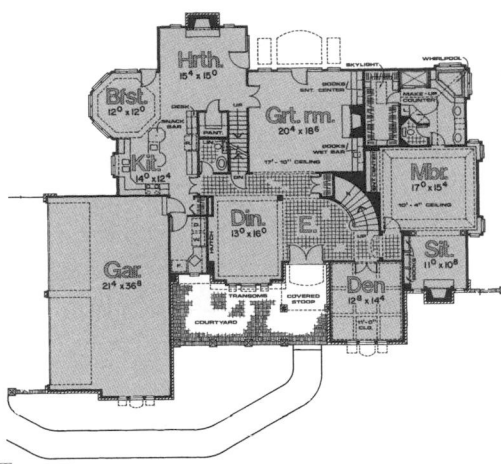

First Floor

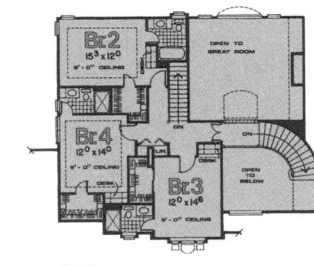

Second Floor

First Floor

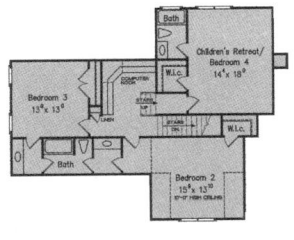

Second Floor

HPK2101133

Style: French Country
First Floor: 2,499 sq. ft.
Second Floor: 1,130 sq. ft.
Total: 3,629 sq. ft.
Bedrooms: 5
Bathrooms: 4
Width: 67' - 6"
Depth: 69' - 10"
Foundation: Crawlspace, Slab, Unfinished Walkout Basement

EPLANS.COM

3,500 TO 3,999 SQUARE FEET

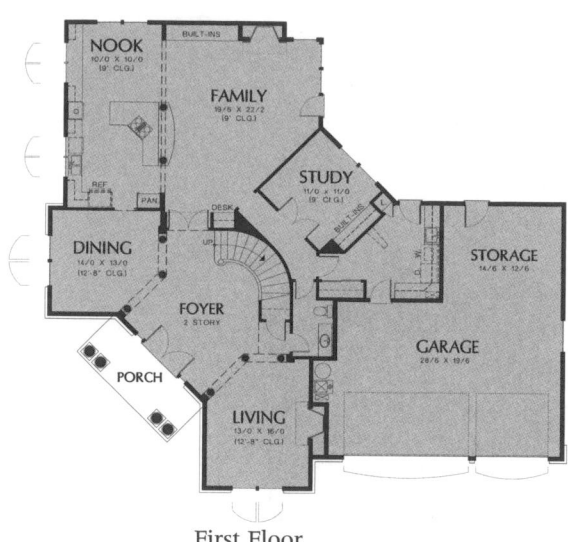

First Floor

Second Floor

HPK2101134

Style: New American
First Floor: 1,923 sq. ft.
Second Floor: 1,710 sq. ft.
Total: 3,633 sq. ft.
Bedrooms: 4
Bathrooms: 2 ½
Width: 66' - 0"
Depth: 60' - 0"
Foundation: Crawlspace

EPLANS.COM

This uniquely designed home is dazzled in Mediterranean influences and eye-catching luxury. A grand arching entrance welcomes you inside to a spacious foyer. Casual areas of the home are clustered to the rear left of the plan. The professional study is a quiet retreat. Upstairs, the master bedroom enjoys a private bath and roomy walk-in closet. Three additional bedrooms share a hall bath and open playroom.

HPK2101135

Style: European

First Floor: 2,648 sq. ft.

Second Floor: 987 sq. ft.

Total: 3,635 sq. ft.

Bonus Space: 338 sq. ft.

Bedrooms: 4

Bathrooms: 4

Width: 82' - 0"

Depth: 69' - 4"

Foundation: Crawlspace, Unfinished Walkout Basement

EPLANS.COM

First Floor

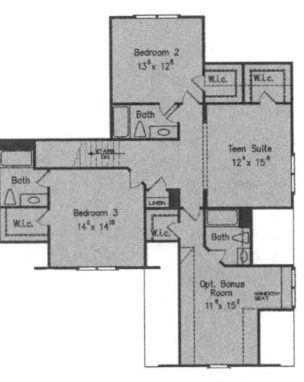

Second Floor

Much larger than it appears curbside, this multilevel home can easily accomodate a family of five. Upgraded ceiling treatments are featured throughout. The well-equipped kitchen is a chef's dream. Two fireplaces warm the first floor. Rear covered porches make outdoor dining an option. The second floor houses three additional family bedrooms, two full baths, and the option to expand.

3,500 TO 3,999 SQUARE FEET

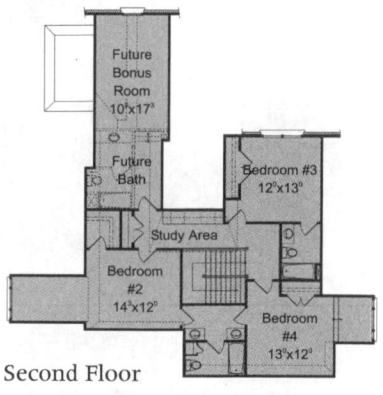

Second Floor

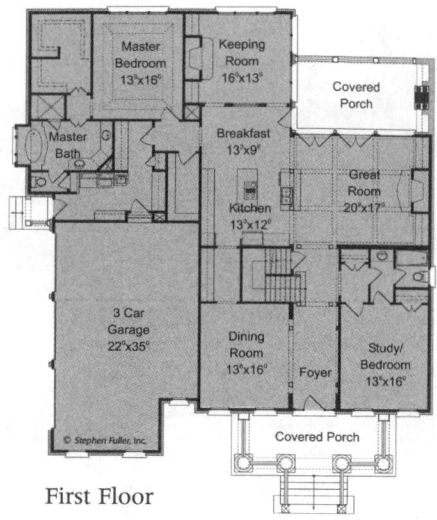

First Floor

HPK2101136

This Greek Revival home displays a stately manner appreciated by all. The four bold columns offer a gracious entrance. The floor plan is both functional and spacious. Open to the great room, the kitchen and keeping room provide a place for casual entertaining. Special features in the kitchen include a walk-in storage pantry and a butler's pantry off the dining room. The mudroom acts as an extension of the laundry room and includes a variety of storage options. The master suite provides the ultimate in convenience and privacy. The second floor has three bedrooms with an optional bonus room.

Style: Greek Revival
First Floor: 2,569 sq. ft.
Second Floor: 1,068 sq. ft.
Total: 3,637 sq. ft.
Bonus Space: 339 sq. ft.
Bedrooms: 5
Bathrooms: 4
Width: 63' - 0"
Depth: 69' - 9"
Foundation: Unfinished Walkout Basement

EPLANS.COM

HPK2101137

Style: Country

First Floor: 2,521 sq. ft.

Second Floor: 1,116 sq. ft.

Total: 3,637 sq. ft.

Bonus Space: 650 sq. ft.

Bedrooms: 4

Bathrooms: 4 ½

Width: 70' - 0"

Depth: 82' - 0"

Foundation: Crawlspace, Unfinished Walkout Basement

EPLANS.COM

The exterior appeal of this Country Cottage is just the beginning. The foyer connects with the coffered-ceiling family room adding warmth to the space with a fireplace. The master suite, enhanced by a tray ceiling, boasts a private sitting room, His and Hers closets, a roomy bath with dual-sink vanities, a separate shower and tub, and a private toilet. Upstairs houses three additional bedrooms, each with a full bath, and a large bonus space.

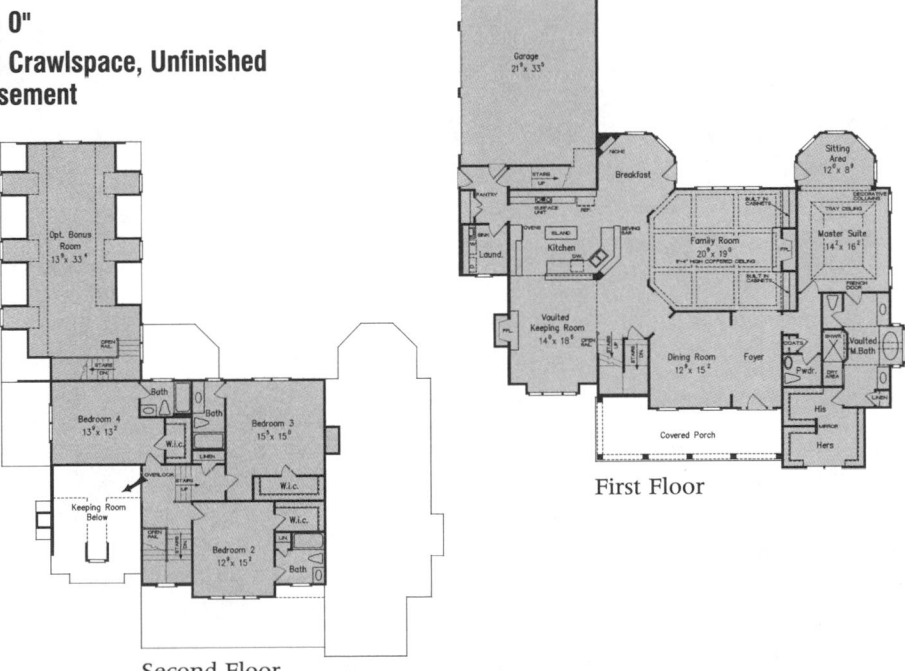

First Floor

Second Floor

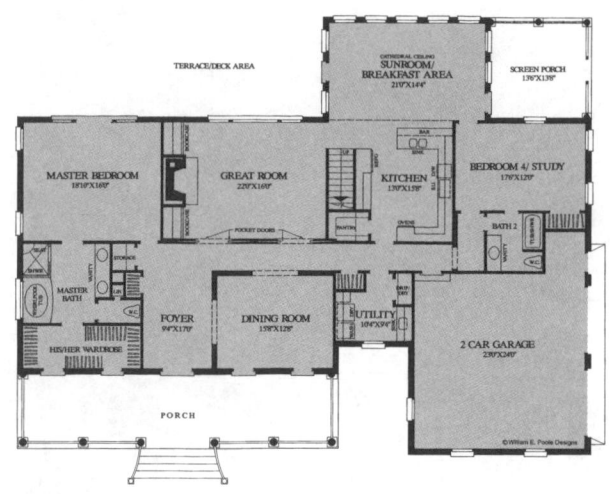

First Floor

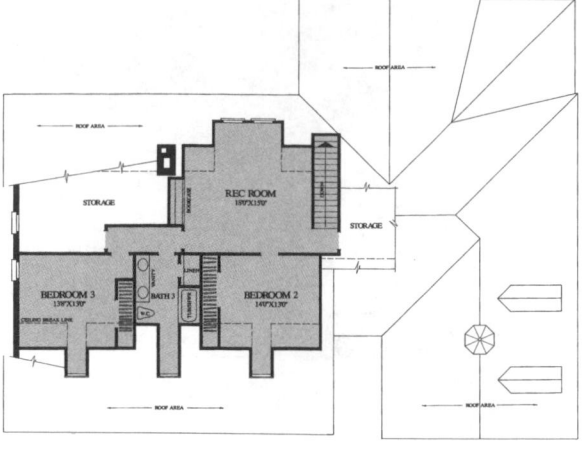

Second Floor

A country cottage with curb appeal, this design will surely please. The master suite, nestled in the far left corner of the first floor, is a quiet retreat for the homeowners. The great room is centrally located with a fireplace on the left wall and built-in bookcases. The U-shaped kitchen features a corner snack bar that serves the adjoining sunroom/breakfast area. A rear screen porch is accessed from here. A first-floor bedroom with full bath could serve as a guest suite or study. Upstairs houses two additional family bedrooms sharing a full bath, two storage areas, and a rec room.

HPK2101138

Style: Farmhouse
First Floor: 2,620 sq. ft.
Second Floor: 1,019 sq. ft.
Total: 3,639 sq. ft.
Bedrooms: 4
Bathrooms: 3
Width: 77' - 6"
Depth: 59' - 10"
Foundation: Crawlspace

EPLANS.COM

© William E. Poole Designs, Inc.

HPK2101139

Style: European
First Floor: 2,673 sq. ft.
Second Floor: 968 sq. ft.
Total: 3,641 sq. ft.
Bonus Space: 787 sq. ft.
Bedrooms: 4
Bathrooms: 4
Width: 64' - 4"
Depth: 87' - 0"
Foundation: Crawlspace, Unfinished Walkout Basement

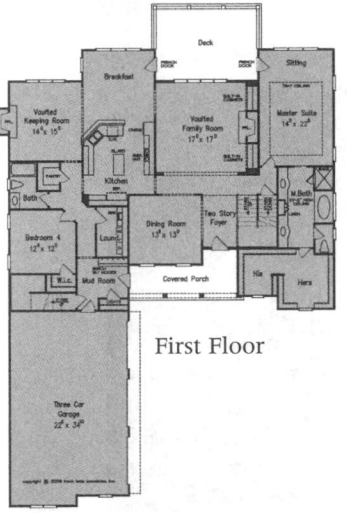

First Floor

Second Floor

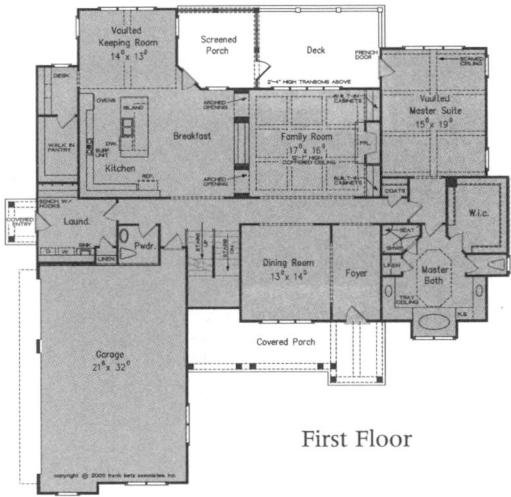

First Floor

HPK2101140

Style: Cottage
First Floor: 2,458 sq. ft.
Second Floor: 1,186 sq. ft.
Total: 3,644 sq. ft.
Bedrooms: 4
Bathrooms: 3 ½
Width: 73' - 0"
Depth: 72' - 6"
Foundation: Crawlspace, Unfinished Walkout Basement

Second Floor

3,500 TO 3,999 SQUARE FEET

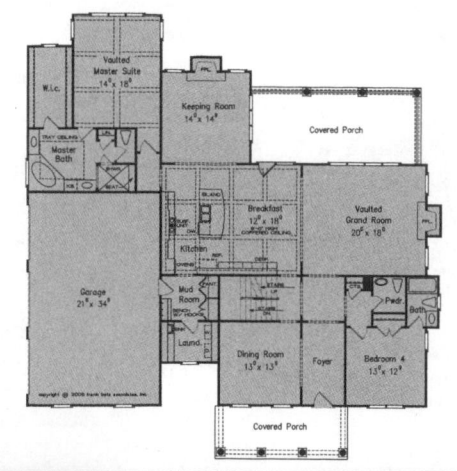

First Floor

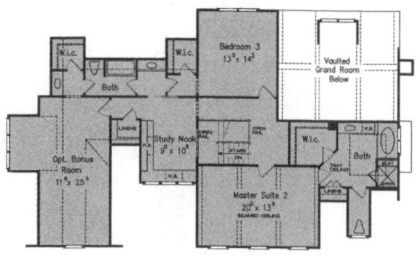

Second Floor

HPK2101141

Style: Cottage
First Floor: 2,498 sq. ft.
Second Floor: 1,146 sq. ft.
Total: 3,644 sq. ft.
Bonus Space: 405 sq. ft.
Bedrooms: 4
Bathrooms: 4 ½
Width: 67' - 4"
Depth: 72' - 0"
Foundation: Crawlspace,
Unfinished Walkout Basement

EPLANS.COM

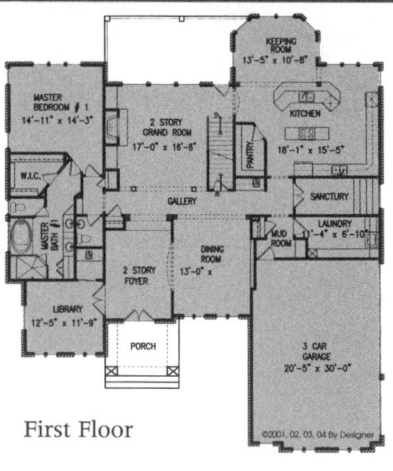

First Floor

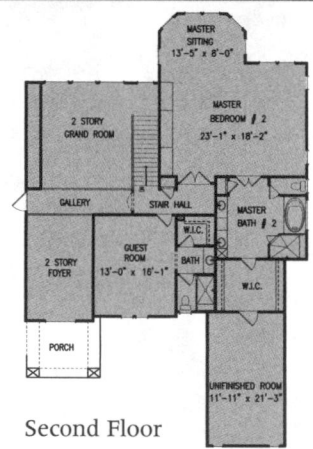

Second Floor

HPK2101142

Style: New American
First Floor: 2,412 sq. ft.
Second Floor: 1,232 sq. ft.
Total: 3,644 sq. ft.
Bedrooms: 3
Bathrooms: 3 ½
Width: 59' - 11"
Depth: 70' - 5"
Foundation: Unfinished Walkout
Basement

EPLANS.COM

HPK2101143

Style: French Country
First Floor: 2,766 sq. ft.
Second Floor: 881 sq. ft.
Total: 3,647 sq. ft.
Bonus Space: 407 sq. ft.
Bedrooms: 3
Bathrooms: 3 ½
Width: 92' - 5"
Depth: 71' - 10"

First Floor

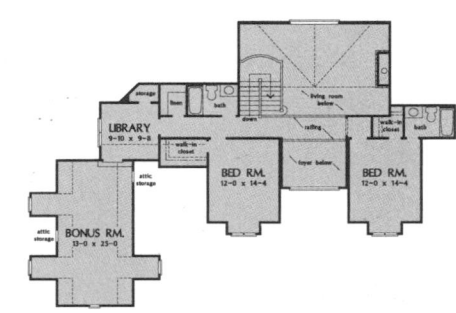

Second Floor

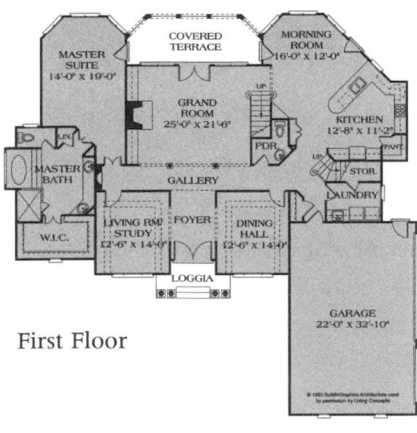

First Floor

Second Floor

HPK2101144

Style: Mediterranean
First Floor: 2,417 sq. ft.
Second Floor: 1,238 sq. ft.
Total: 3,655 sq. ft.
Bonus Space: 413 sq. ft.
Bedrooms: 4
Bathrooms: 3 ½
Width: 71' - 8"
Depth: 69' - 8"
Foundation: Crawlspace

HPK2101145

Style: French Country
First Floor: 2,660 sq. ft.
Second Floor: 1,000 sq. ft.
Total: 3,660 sq. ft.
Bonus Space: 856 sq. ft.
Bedrooms: 3
Bathrooms: 3 ½
Width: 114' - 8"
Depth: 75' - 10"
Foundation: Crawlspace

EPLANS.COM

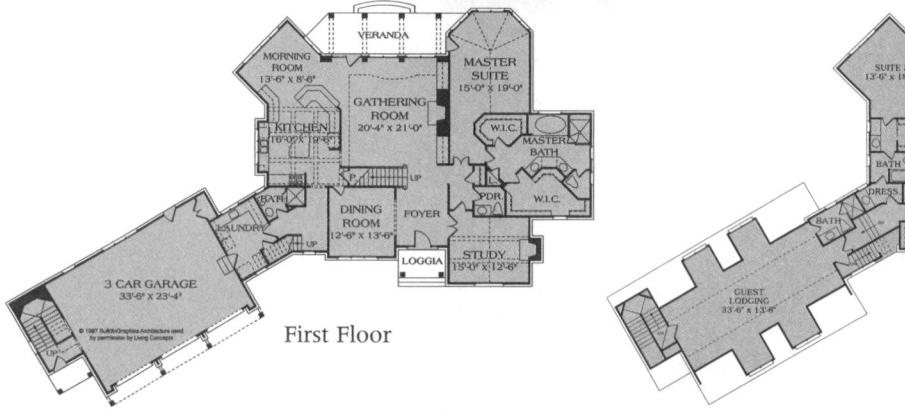

First Floor

Second Floor

HPK2101146

Style: Georgian
First Floor: 2,273 sq. ft.
Second Floor: 1,391 sq. ft.
Total: 3,664 sq. ft.
Bonus Space: 547 sq. ft.
Bedrooms: 4
Bathrooms: 4 ½
Width: 77' - 2"
Depth: 48' - 0"
Foundation: Crawlspace

EPLANS.COM

First Floor

Second Floor

HPK2101147

Style: French Country

First Floor: 2,654 sq. ft.

Second Floor: 1,013 sq. ft.

Total: 3,667 sq. ft.

Bedrooms: 4

Bathrooms: 3 ½

Width: 75' - 4"

Depth: 74' - 2"

Foundation: Crawlspace, Slab, Unfinished Basement

EPLANS.COM

© Larry E. Belk Designs

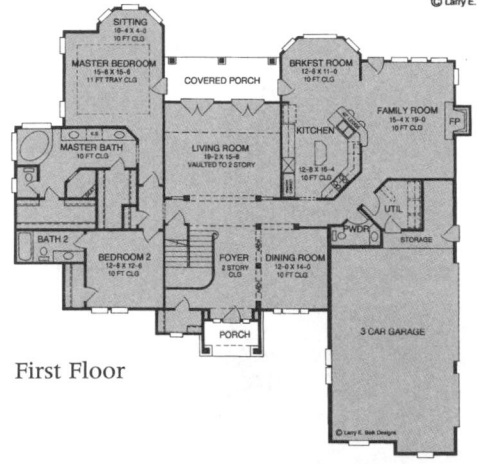

First Floor

© Larry E. Belk Designs

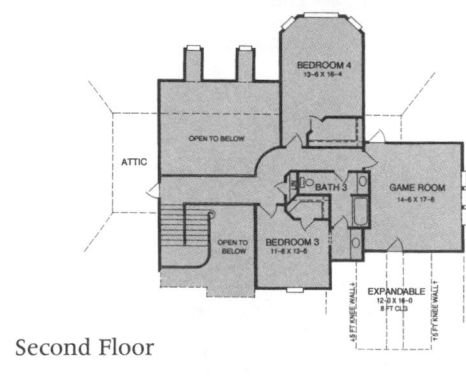

Second Floor

HPK2101148

Style: New American

First Floor: 2,638 sq. ft.

Second Floor: 1,032 sq. ft.

Total: 3,670 sq. ft.

Bedrooms: 4

Bathrooms: 3 ½

Width: 80' - 4"

Depth: 65' - 4"

Foundation: Slab

EPLANS.COM

© The Sater Design Collection, Inc.

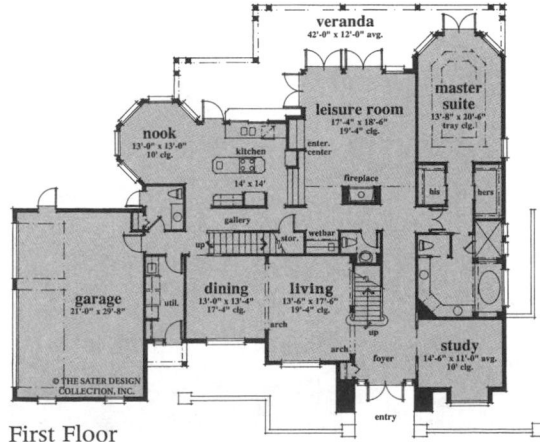

First Floor

Second Floor

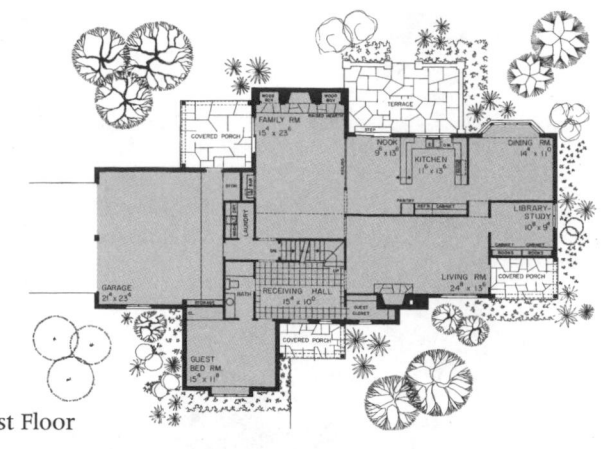

First Floor

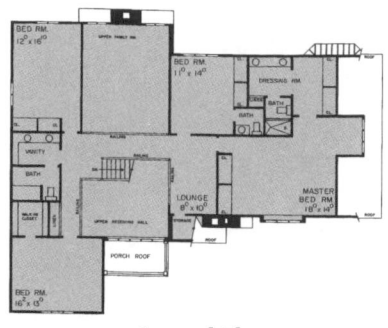

Second Floor

HPK2101149

Style: Tudor
First Floor: 1,969 sq. ft.
Second Floor: 1,702 sq. ft.
Total: 3,671 sq. ft.
Bedrooms: 5
Bathrooms: 3 ½
Width: 79' - 10"
Depth: 53' - 6"
Foundation: Crawlspace

EPLANS.COM

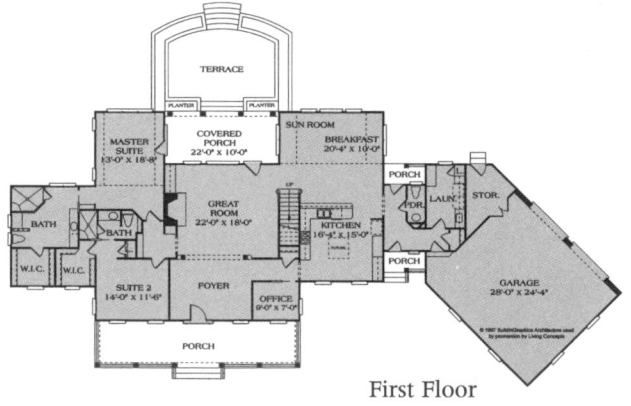

First Floor

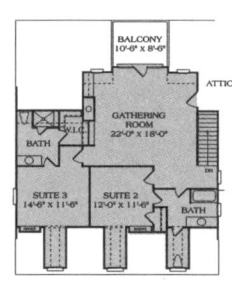

Second Floor

HPK2101150

Style: Farmhouse
First Floor: 2,507 sq. ft.
Second Floor: 1,165 sq. ft.
Total: 3,672 sq. ft.
Bedrooms: 4
Bathrooms: 4 ½
Width: 119' - 0"
Depth: 52' - 10"
Foundation: Crawlspace

EPLANS.COM

HPK2101151

Style: Neoclassical
First Floor: 2,380 sq. ft.
Second Floor: 1,295 sq. ft.
Total: 3,675 sq. ft.
Bedrooms: 4
Bathrooms: 3 ½
Width: 77' - 4"
Depth: 58' - 4"
Foundation: Walkout Basement

EPLANS.COM

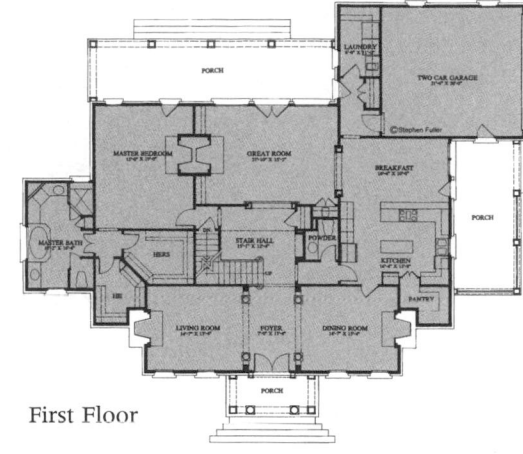

First Floor

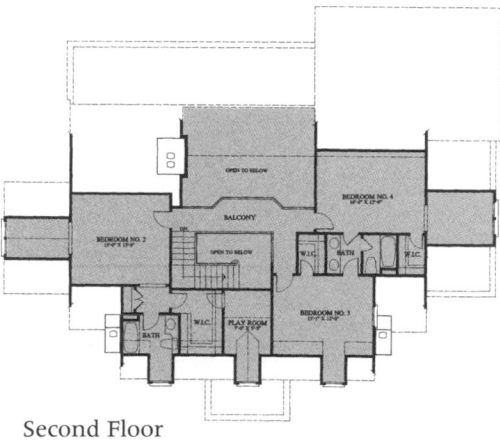

Second Floor

© Stephen Fuller, Inc.

First Floor

Second Floor

HPK2101152

Style: New American
First Floor: 2,657 sq. ft.
Second Floor: 1,026 sq. ft.
Total: 3,683 sq. ft.
Bonus Space: 308 sq. ft.
Bedrooms: 4
Bathrooms: 3 ½
Width: 75' - 8"
Depth: 74' - 2"
Foundation: Crawlspace, Slab, Unfinished Basement

EPLANS.COM

3,500 TO 3,999 SQUARE FEET

HPK2101153

Style: New American
First Floor: 1,935 sq. ft.
Second Floor: 1,753 sq. ft.
Total: 3,688 sq. ft.
Bedrooms: 5
Bathrooms: 4 ½
Width: 65' - 6"
Depth: 59' - 0"
Foundation: Crawlspace, Unfinished Walkout Basement

EPLANS.COM

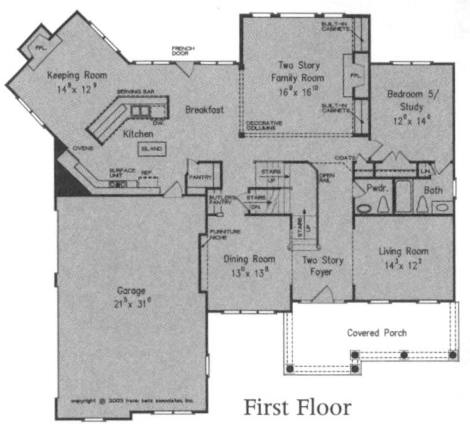

First Floor

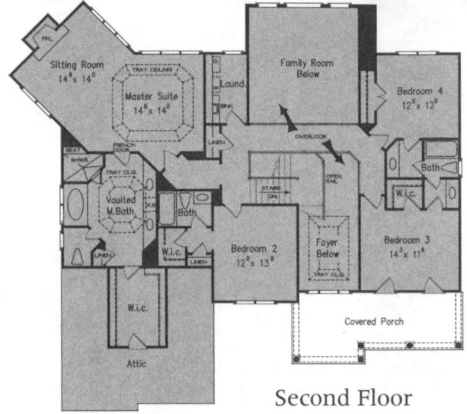

Second Floor

First Floor

HPK2101154

Style: French Country
First Floor: 2,700 sq. ft.
Second Floor: 990 sq. ft.
Total: 3,690 sq. ft.
Bonus Space: 365 sq. ft.
Bedrooms: 4
Bathrooms: 3 ½
Width: 76' - 0"
Depth: 74' - 1"
Foundation: Crawlspace, Slab, Unfinished Basement

EPLANS.COM

Second Floor

ORDER BLUEPRINTS ANYTIME AT EPLANS.COM OR 1-800-521-6797

HPK2101155

Style: New American
First Floor: 2,908 sq. ft.
Second Floor: 790 sq. ft.
Total: 3,698 sq. ft.
Bonus Space: 521 sq. ft.
Bedrooms: 4
Bathrooms: 4 ½
Width: 86' - 11"
Depth: 59' - 5"

EPLANS.COM

© 2000 Donald A. Gardner, Inc.

First Floor

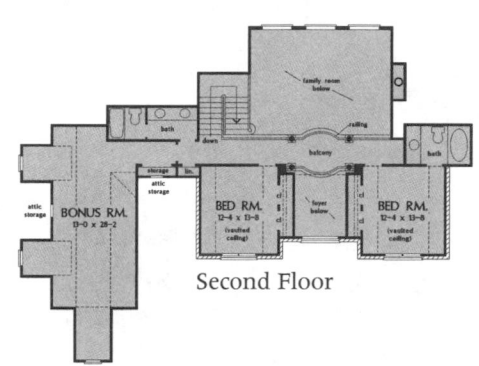

Second Floor

HPK2101156

Style: Italianate
First Floor: 2,699 sq. ft.
Second Floor: 1,006 sq. ft.
Total: 3,705 sq. ft.
Bedrooms: 4
Bathrooms: 5
Width: 65' - 0"
Depth: 95' - 0"
Foundation: Slab

EPLANS.COM

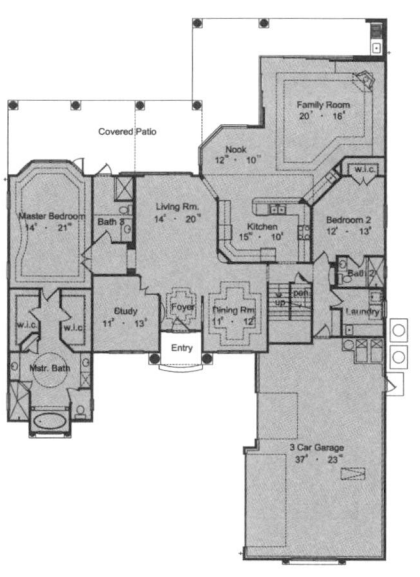

First Floor

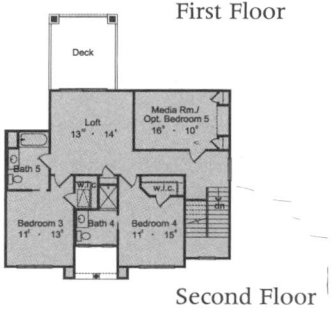

Second Floor

3,500 TO 3,999 SQUARE FEET

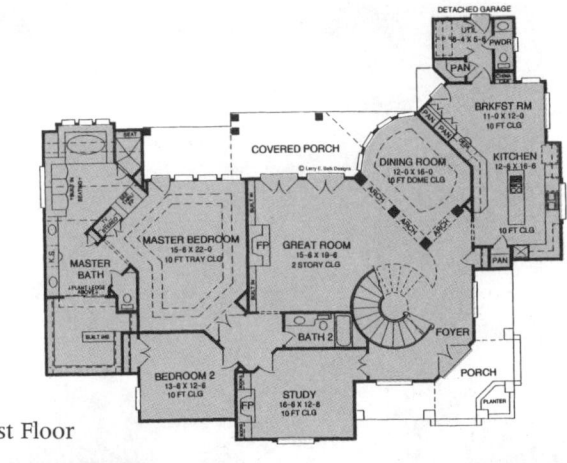

First Floor

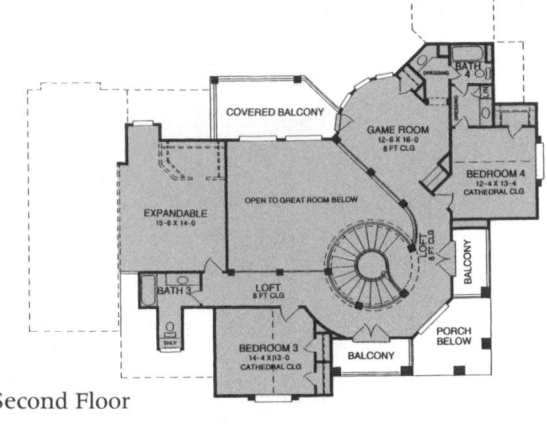

Second Floor

HPK2101157

Style: Neoclassical
First Floor: 2,772 sq. ft.
Second Floor: 933 sq. ft.
Total: 3,705 sq. ft.
Bedrooms: 4
Bathrooms: 4 ½
Width: 74' - 8"
Depth: 61' - 10"
Foundation: Crawlspace, Slab

EPLANS.COM

First Floor

Second Floor

HPK2101158

Style: French Country
First Floor: 2,727 sq. ft.
Second Floor: 981 sq. ft.
Total: 3,708 sq. ft.
Bedrooms: 5
Bathrooms: 4 ½
Width: 69' - 0"
Depth: 79' - 0"
Foundation: Crawlspace, Unfinished Walkout Basement

EPLANS.COM

ORDER BLUEPRINTS ANYTIME AT EPLANS.COM OR 1-800-521-6797

HPK2101159

Style: French Country
First Floor: 2,778 sq. ft.
Second Floor: 931 sq. ft.
Total: 3,709 sq. ft.
Bonus Space: 140 sq. ft.
Bedrooms: 4
Bathrooms: 3 ½
Width: 86' - 0"
Depth: 60' - 1"
Foundation: Slab

EPLANS.COM

This brick-and-stone combination features a country-fresh look with a contemporary interior floor plan. Step into the gallery, and directly to your left is the sweeping staircase; to the right, you will find a large kitchen and breakfast area. The family room is enhanced with an entertainment center, fireplace, and access to the rear patio. The first-floor master suite boasts a sumptuous bath. Along with two bedrooms, the second floor holds a playroom and a bonus room.

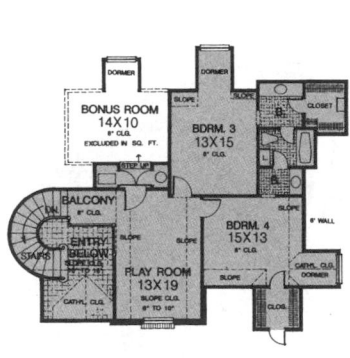

Second Floor

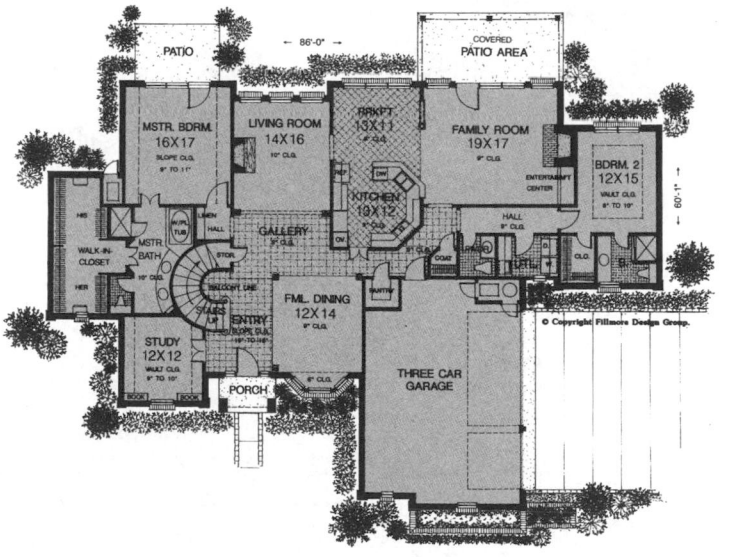

First Floor

3,500 TO 3,999 SQUARE FEET

HPK2101160

Style: New American

First Floor: 2,495 sq. ft.

Second Floor: 1,233 sq. ft.

Total: 3,728 sq. ft.

Bonus Space: 351 sq. ft.

Bedrooms: 4

Bathrooms: 3 ½

Width: 66' - 10"

Depth: 57' - 6"

Foundation: Crawlspace, Slab, Unfinished Walkout Basement

EPLANS.COM

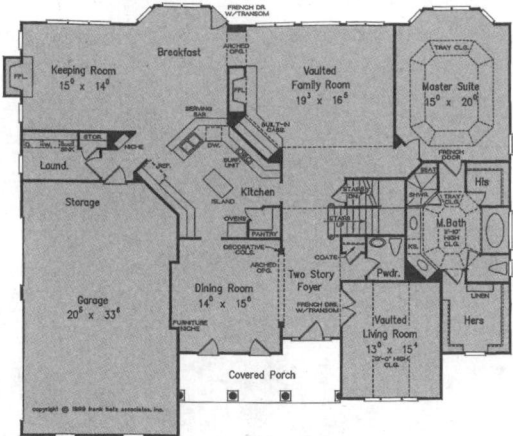

First Floor

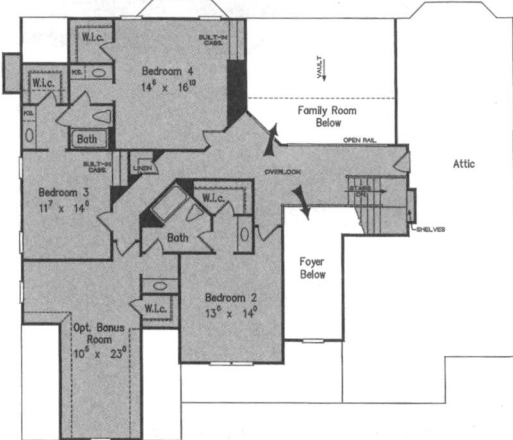

Second Floor

The brick-and-siding exterior and hipped roof lend a country aura to this home. Amenities abound inside, including a walk-in pantry in the island kitchen and fireplaces in the family and keeping rooms. Vaulted ceilings enhance the family and living rooms, and the keeping room features a lovely bay window. Note the elegant master suite on the first floor and three family bedrooms on the second. An optional bonus room offers plenty of space for future expansion.

HPK2101526

Style: Tudor
First Floor: 1,920 sq. ft.
Second Floor: 1,801 sq. ft.
Total: 3,721 sq. ft.
Bedrooms: 4
Bathrooms: 3 ½
Width: 60' - 9"
Depth: 61' - 8"
Foundation: Crawlspace

EPLANS.COM

The sloping roof line lends an aristocratic feel to this Tudor home. Stone accents enhance the appeal. The first floor houses spacious, common areas including hearth-warmed keeping and family rooms. Abundant outdoor living spaces encourage alfresco dining. Decorative columns and arches add a graceful touch. The sleeping quarters reside on the second floor, including the well-appointed master suite. Three secondary bedrooms share two full baths.

3,500 TO 3,999 SQUARE FEET

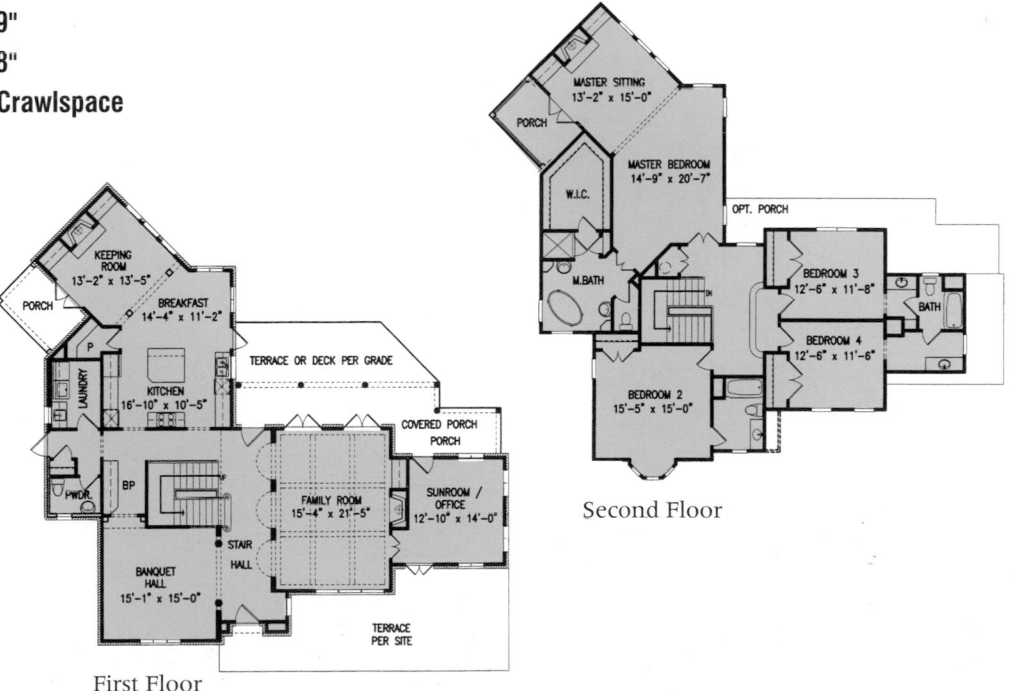

First Floor

Second Floor

Traditional and Colonial details beautify the front of this deceptively larger home. For dimensions and ordering information on this home, please turn to page 781.

LARGER HOMES
DONE RIGHT

Besides square footage, what really distinguishes a larger home from a smaller one is the presence of dedicated specialized spaces. There is less demand on rooms to function in hybrid roles or need for subtlety in transition between areas. Instead, designers must take up the challenge of bringing a sense of intimacy to larger spaces. A two-story great room with a roaring fireplace is a great waste of space if it feels cavernous and cold. Such a room communicates absence and uncomfortable silence, instead of warmth and welcome. Likewise, a larger home must provide adequate privacy to its owners—assumed to be a larger family. Indeed, zoning for privacy can be more difficult in a larger home than a smaller one because there are more family members to please.

Decorative columns and mouldings help define the one-story height in the two-story great room.

HPK2101527

Style: French Country

First Floor: 2,702 sq. ft.

Second Floor: 986 sq. ft.

Total: 3,688 sq. ft.

Bedrooms: 4

Bathrooms: 3 ½

Width: 75' - 0"

Depth: 64' - 11"

Foundation: Unfinished Basement

First Floor

This traditional design is accented in Craftsman architecture and features two lavish levels of livability for the whole family. Inside, a formal dining room and library flank the foyer. The two-story great room is warmed by an enormous fireplace flanked by built-ins. Casual areas of the home include the island kitchen, breakfast nook, and bay-windowed hearth room. The first-floor master suite offers two walk-in closets and a lavish private bath enjoying a whirlpool tub. A three-car garage and laundry room complete the first floor. Three additional bedrooms and two baths are located upstairs.

Second Floor

© 1997 William E Poole Designs, Inc.

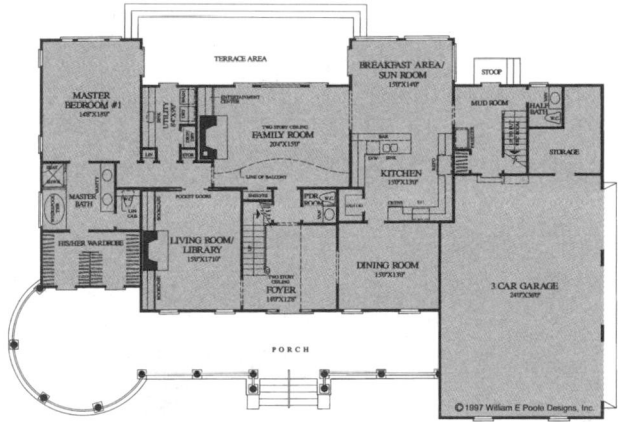

First Floor

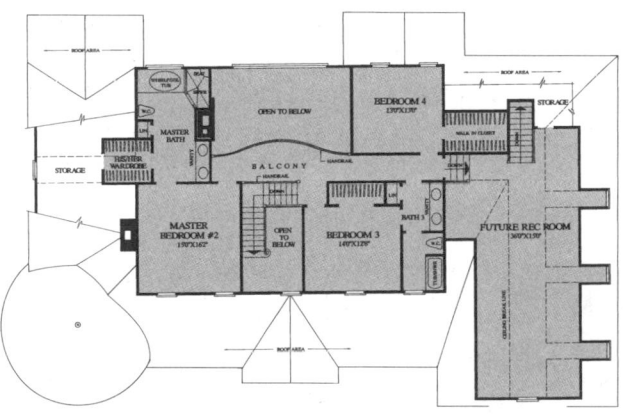

Second Floor

With a gazebo-style corner and careful exterior details, you can't help but imagine tea parties, porch swings, and lazy summer evenings spent on this covered porch. Inside, a living room/library will comfort with its fireplace and built-ins. The family room is graced with a fireplace and a curved, two-story ceiling with an overlook above. The master bedroom is a private retreat with a lovely bath, twin walk-in closets, and rear-porch access. Upstairs, three bedrooms with sizable closets share access to expandable space.

EPLANS.COM

HPK2101161

Style: Farmhouse
First Floor: 2,442 sq. ft.
Second Floor: 1,286 sq. ft.
Total: 3,728 sq. ft.
Bonus Space: 681 sq. ft.
Bedrooms: 4
Bathrooms: 3 ½ + ½
Width: 84' - 8"
Depth: 60' - 0"
Foundation: Crawlspace

3,500 TO 3,999 SQUARE FEET

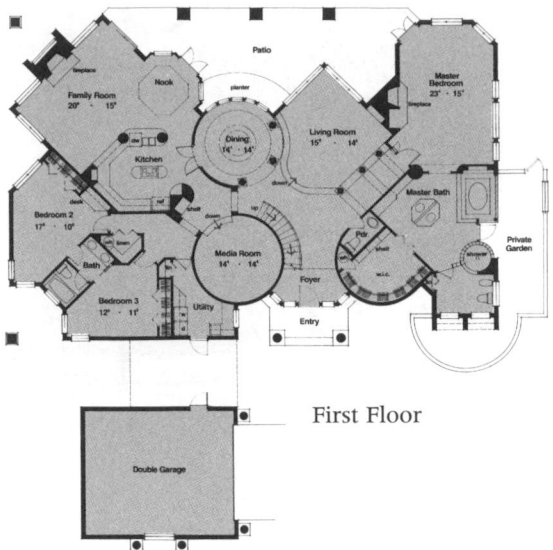

First Floor

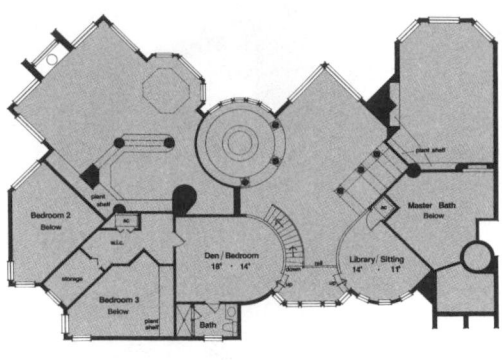

Second Floor

If you want to build a home light years ahead of most other designs, nontraditional, yet addresses every need for your family, this showcase home is for you. From the moment you walk into it you are confronted with wonderful interior architecture that reflects modern, yet refined taste. The exterior says contemporary; the interior creates special excitement. Note the special rounded corners found throughout the home and the many amenities. The master suite is especially appealing with fireplace and grand bath. Upstairs are a library/sitting room and a very private den or guest bedroom.

HPK2101162

Style: Mediterranean
First Floor: 3,236 sq. ft.
Second Floor: 494 sq. ft.
Total: 3,730 sq. ft.
Bedrooms: 4
Bathrooms: 3 ½
Width: 80' - 0"
Depth: 89' - 10"
Foundation: Slab

EPLANS.COM

© Larry E. Belk Designs

Formal and informal needs are met in this attractive four-bedroom home. For fine dinner parties, the formal dining room flows into the formal living room. A warming fireplace in the spacious family room will add just the right glow to festivities. The nearby kitchen will make serving a breeze. For more intimate meetings, the study is available. Located on the main floor for privacy, the master bedroom suite is designed to pamper. Upstairs, three secondary bedrooms share two full baths, a walk-in linen closet, and access to a large game room.

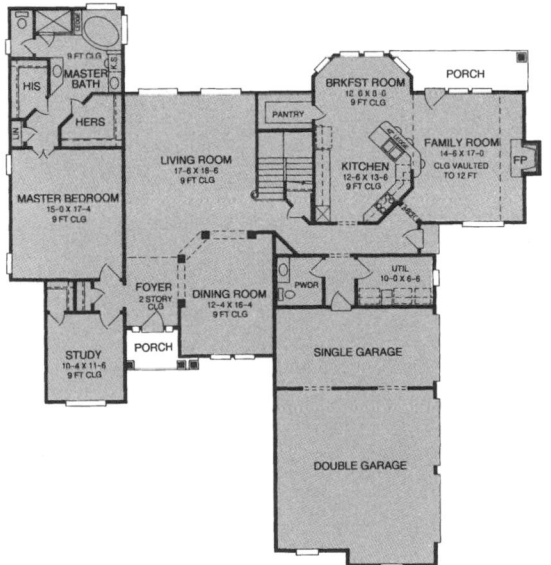

First Floor

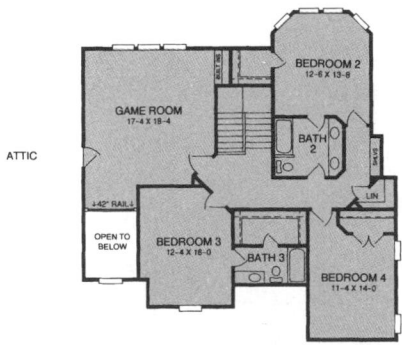

Second Floor

HPK2101163

Style: New American
First Floor: 2,369 sq. ft.
Second Floor: 1,363 sq. ft.
Total: 3,732 sq. ft.
Bedrooms: 4
Bathrooms: 3 ½
Width: 71' - 10"
Depth: 75' - 6"
Foundation: Crawlspace, Slab

EPLANS.COM

First Floor

Second Floor

An eye-catching roofline and a gently arched entry draw attention to this home's exterior; the interior contains a wide variety of amenity-packed rooms. On the first floor, the central grand room overlooks both the rear screened porch and a side deck; a wet bar sits just outside the nearby dining room. The gourmet kitchen offers a walk-in pantry and adjoins a cozy "good morning" room, suitable for quiet family meals and open to a small dining deck. A library and gathering room round out the first-floor living space, and a luxurious master suite with a private lounge comprises the sleeping space. Three more family bedrooms—one with a private bath and deck—are found upstairs.

HPK2101164

Style: French Country
First Floor: 2,345 sq. ft.
Second Floor: 1,336 sq. ft.
Total: 3,681 sq. ft.
Bedrooms: 4
Bathrooms: 3 ½
Width: 65' - 0"
Depth: 66' - 0"
Foundation: Crawlspace

EPLANS.COM

HPK2101165

Style: Colonial Revival
First Floor: 1,930 sq. ft.
Second Floor: 1,807 sq. ft.
Total: 3,737 sq. ft.
Bonus Space: 372 sq. ft.
Bedrooms: 4
Bathrooms: 4
Width: 55' - 2"
Depth: 60' - 2"
Foundation: Crawlspace

EPLANS.COM

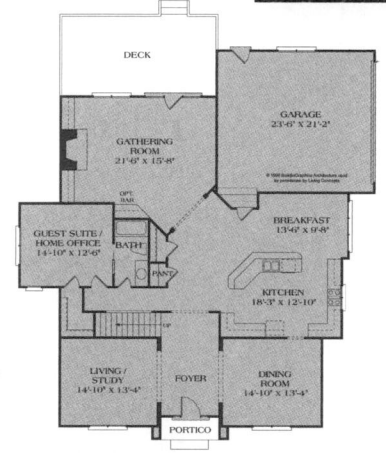

First Floor

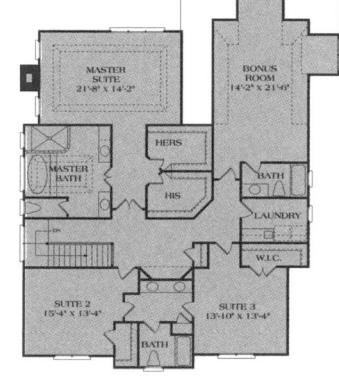

Second Floor

HPK2101166

Style: Federal - Adams
First Floor: 2,746 sq. ft.
Second Floor: 992 sq. ft.
Total: 3,738 sq. ft.
Bonus Space: 453 sq. ft.
Bedrooms: 4
Bathrooms: 3 ½
Width: 80' - 0"
Depth: 58' - 6"
Foundation: Crawlspace

EPLANS.COM

© William E. Poole Designs, Inc.

First Floor

Second Floor

3,500 TO 3,999 SQUARE FEET

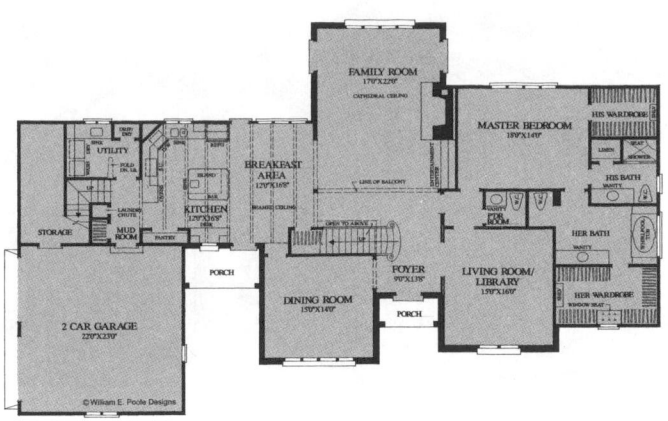

First Floor

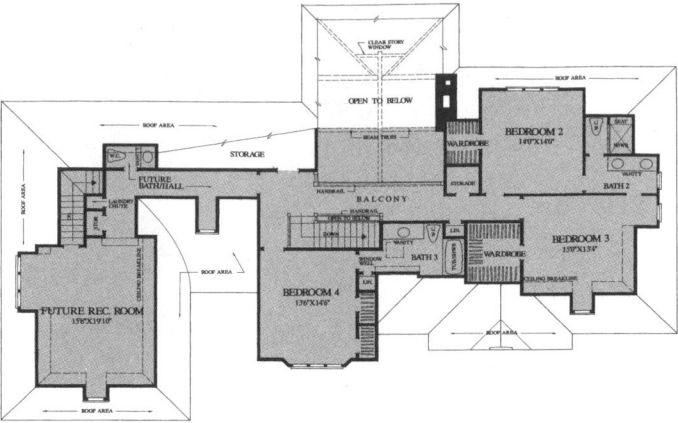

Second Floor

HPK2101167

Style: Tudor
First Floor: 2,526 sq. ft.
Second Floor: 1,215 sq. ft.
Total: 3,741 sq. ft.
Bonus Space: 547 sq. ft.
Bedrooms: 4
Bathrooms: 4 ½
Width: 88' - 6"
Depth: 53' - 6"
Foundation: Crawlspace

EPLANS.COM

A farmhouse with a French flourish, this plan is comfortable and distinctive in the Provencial style. The foyer, opening through a charming round-arch doorway, opens to a dining room on the left, and a formal living room/library on the right. A large family room serves as the perfect gathering place in this home. Find plenty of space and a large island in the kitchen, with a convenient private entry.

© William E. Poole Designs, Inc.

HPK2101168

Style: Mediterranean

First Floor: 3,134 sq. ft.

Second Floor: 610 sq. ft.

Total: 3,744 sq. ft.

Bedrooms: 4

Bathrooms: 3 ½

Width: 80' - 0"

Depth: 96' - 0"

Foundation: Slab

EPLANS.COM

A unique courtyard provides a happy medium for indoor/outdoor living in this design. Inside, a grand salon provides unobstructed views of the backyard. Informal areas include a leisure room with an entertainment center and access to a covered poolside lanai. The master suite boasts a bayed sitting area, His and Hers closets, and access to the rear lanai. Upstairs, two family bedrooms—both with private decks—share a full bath. A detached guest house has a cabana bath and an outdoor grill area.

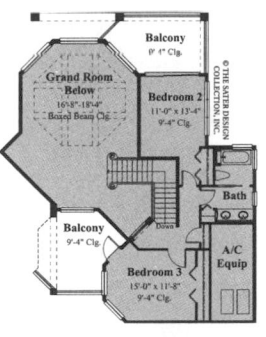

Second Floor

First Floor

3,500 TO 3,999 SQUARE FEET

HPK2101169

Style: New American
First Floor: 1,870 sq. ft.
Second Floor: 1,881 sq. ft.
Total: 3,751 sq. ft.
Bedrooms: 5
Bathrooms: 4 ½
Width: 60' - 0"
Depth: 55' - 0"
Foundation: Crawlspace, Unfinished Walkout Basement

EPLANS.COM

First Floor

A grand entrance is just one of the highlights of this fine brick home. Inside, the two-story foyer leads through French doors to a quiet study—or make it a private guest suite. The spacious kitchen provides a large island with a serving bar as well as an adjacent breakfast area. Upstairs, Bedrooms 2 and 3 share a full bath, while Bedroom 4 offers a private bath and a large walk-in closet. The master suite is sure to please with its pampering bath and tray ceiling treatment.

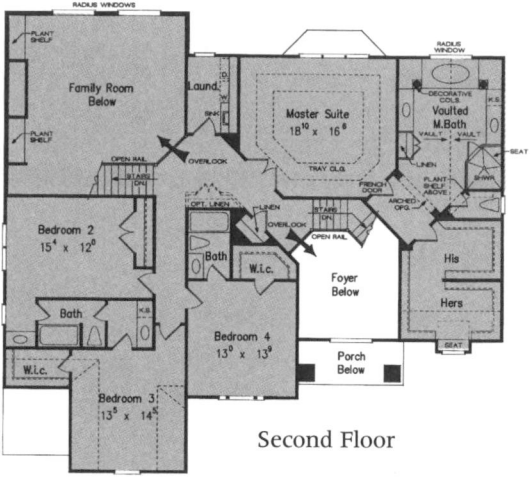

Second Floor

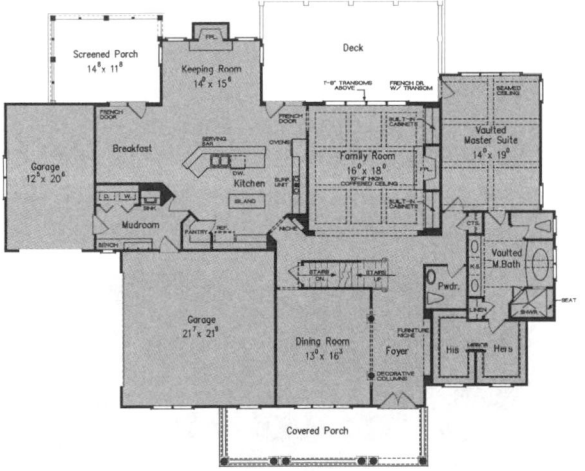

First Floor

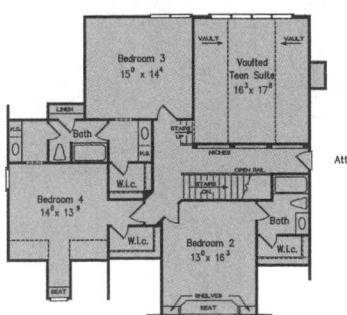

Second Floor

Craftsman charm is reflected in the exterior architectural elements, adding curb appeal. The interior relies on a well-crafted design that centers around the impressive kitchen space. The vaulted master suite occupies the right wing. On the second floor, three bedrooms share two full baths and a spacious teen suite/recreation room is housed a short stairwell above it all.

HPK2101170

EPLANS.COM

Style: Country
First Floor: 2,308 sq. ft.
Second Floor: 1,445 sq. ft.
Total: 3,753 sq. ft.
Bedrooms: 4
Bathrooms: 3 ½
Width: 78' - 0"
Depth: 52' - 0"
Foundation: Crawlspace, Slab, Unfinished Walkout Basement

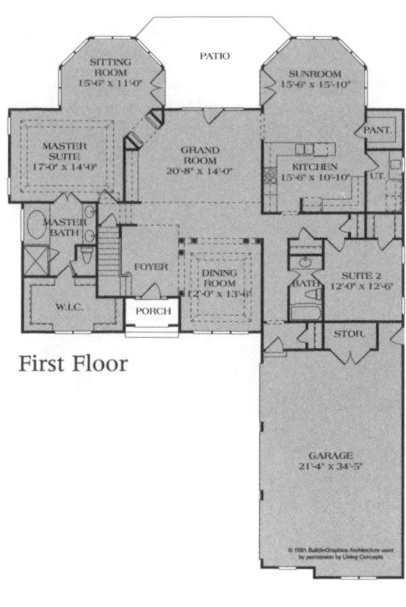

First Floor

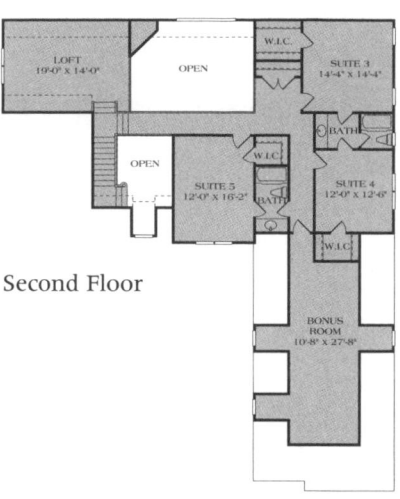

Second Floor

HPK2101171

Style: New American
First Floor: 2,330 sq. ft.
Second Floor: 1,426 sq. ft.
Total: 3,756 sq. ft.
Bonus Space: 405 sq. ft.
Bedrooms: 5
Bathrooms: 4
Width: 60' - 4"
Depth: 83' - 4"
Foundation: Crawlspace

EPLANS.COM

Tasteful stucco surrounds arches and quoins on the exterior, while an abundance of comfortable, contemporary living is ensconced inside. The master suite has a separate sitting room surrounded with windows, which also opens to the patio. The foyer and dining room, with tray ceiling, share a large, open area. The kitchen has an attached sunroom, which can be used as an airy breakfast nook.

HPK2101172

Style: New American
First Floor: 2,292 sq. ft.
Second Floor: 1,465 sq. ft.
Total: 3,757 sq. ft.
Bedrooms: 4
Bathrooms: 3 ½
Width: 67' - 6"
Depth: 78' - 0"
Foundation: Crawlspace

EPLANS.COM

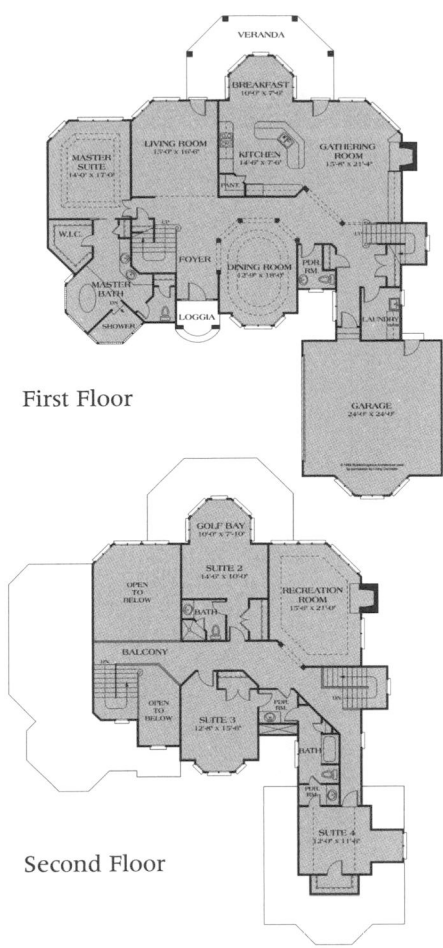

First Floor

Second Floor

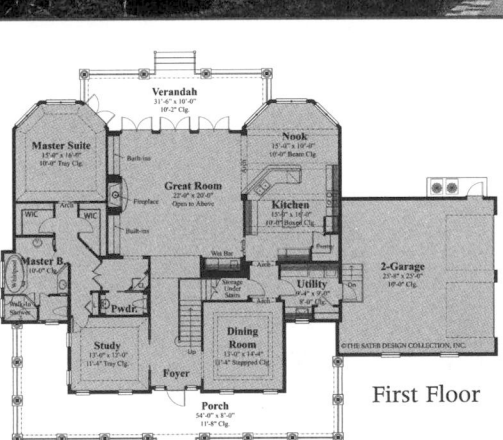

First Floor

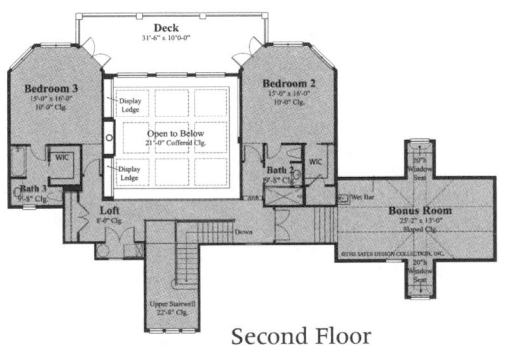

Second Floor

HPK2101173

Style: Country
First Floor: 2,253 sq. ft.
Second Floor: 1,510 sq. ft.
Total: 3,763 sq. ft.
Bedrooms: 3
Bathrooms: 3 ½
Width: 77' - 2"
Depth: 64' - 0"
Foundation: Crawlspace

EPLANS.COM

3,500 TO 3,999 SQUARE FEET

HPK2101174

Style: New American
First Floor: 2,534 sq. ft.
Second Floor: 1,230 sq. ft.
Total: 3,764 sq. ft.
Bonus Space: 454 sq. ft.
Bedrooms: 3
Bathrooms: 3 ½
Width: 67' - 8"
Depth: 77' - 4"
Foundation: Crawlspace

EPLANS.COM

First Floor

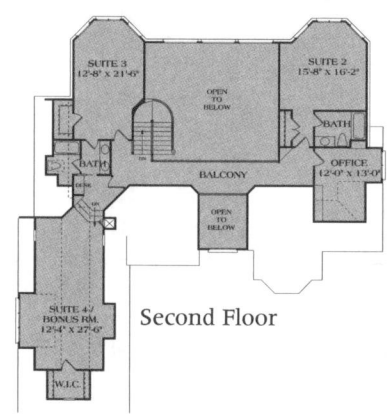

Second Floor

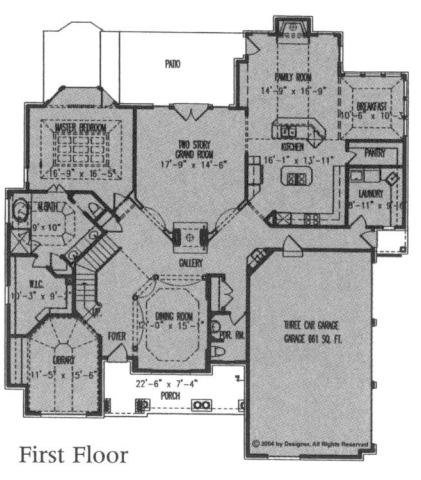

First Floor

HPK2101175

Style: French Country
First Floor: 2,522 sq. ft.
Second Floor: 1,244 sq. ft.
Total: 3,766 sq. ft.
Bedrooms: 4
Bathrooms: 3 ½
Width: 63' - 10"
Depth: 70' - 6"
Foundation: Slab, Unfinished Walkout Basement

EPLANS.COM

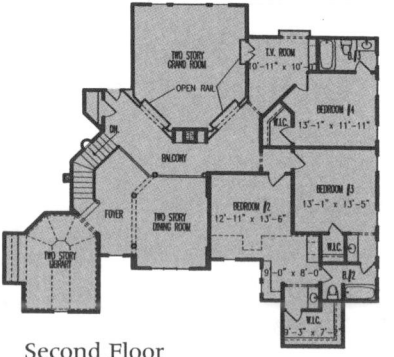

Second Floor

First Floor

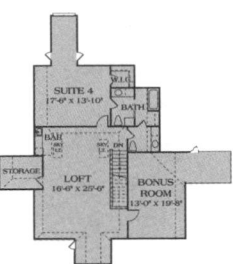

Second Floor

HPK2101176

Style: Cottage

First Floor: 2,600 sq. ft.

Second Floor: 1,174 sq. ft.

Total: 3,774 sq. ft.

Bonus Space: 340 sq. ft.

Bedrooms: 4

Bathrooms: 4

Width: 58' - 1"

Depth: 125' - 4"

Foundation: Crawlspace

EPLANS.COM

HPK2101177

Style: Plantation

First Floor: 1,901 sq. ft.

Second Floor: 1,874 sq. ft.

Total: 3,775 sq. ft.

Bedrooms: 4

Bathrooms: 3 ½

Width: 50' - 0"

Depth: 70' - 0"

Foundation: Pier (same as Piling)

EPLANS.COM

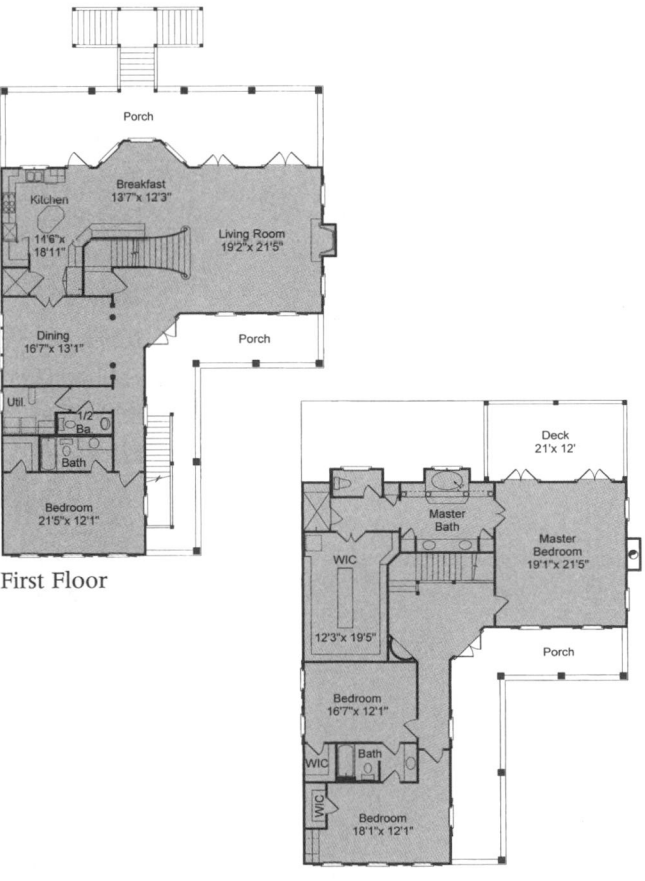

First Floor

Second Floor

First Floor

Second Floor

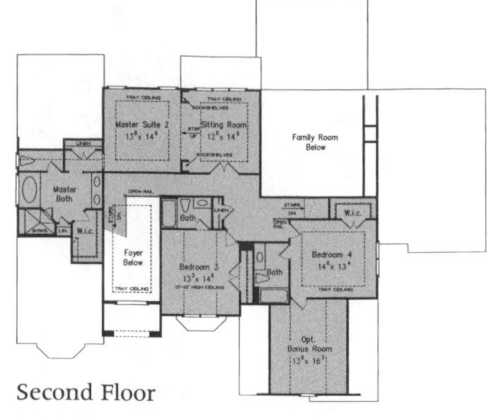

HPK2101178

Style: French Country
First Floor: 2,350 sq. ft.
Second Floor: 1,425 sq. ft.
Total: 3,775 sq. ft.
Bonus Space: 219 sq. ft.
Bedrooms: 4
Bathrooms: 4 ½
Width: 79' - 0"
Depth: 69' - 6"
Foundation: Crawlspace, Unfinished Walkout Basement

EPLANS.COM

HPK2101179

First Floor

Style: Beaux Arts
First Floor: 1,807 sq. ft.
Second Floor: 1,970 sq. ft.
Total: 3,777 sq. ft.
Bedrooms: 4
Bathrooms: 3 ½
Width: 57' - 4"
Depth: 53' - 6"
Foundation: Unfinished Walkout Basement

EPLANS.COM

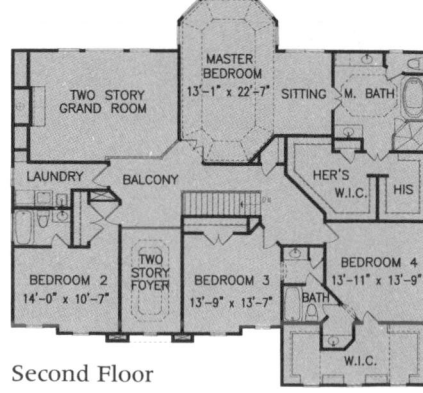

Second Floor

ORDER BLUEPRINTS ANYTIME AT EPLANS.COM OR 1-800-521-6797

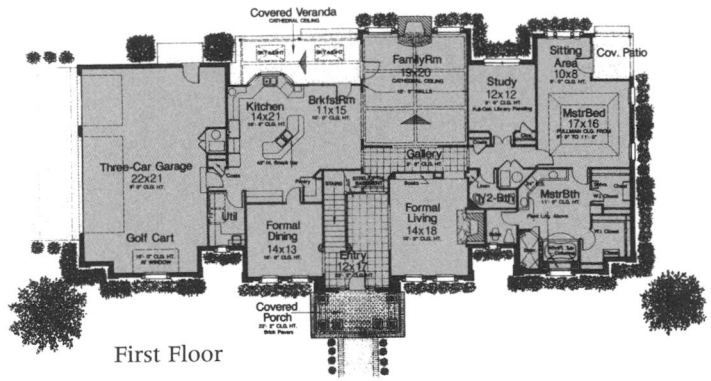

First Floor

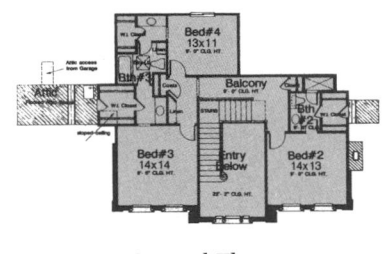

Second Floor

HPK2101180

Style: Federal - Adams
First Floor: 2,814 sq. ft.
Second Floor: 979 sq. ft.
Total: 3,793 sq. ft.
Bedrooms: 4
Bathrooms: 3 ½
Width: 98' - 0"
Depth: 45' - 10"
Foundation: Slab, Unfinished Basement

First Floor

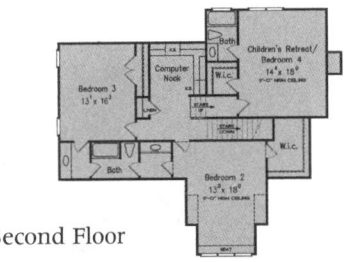

Second Floor

HPK2101181

Style: Cottage
First Floor: 2,537 sq. ft.
Second Floor: 1,258 sq. ft.
Total: 3,795 sq. ft.
Bedrooms: 5
Bathrooms: 4
Width: 67' - 0"
Depth: 69' - 10"
Foundation: Crawlspace, Slab, Unfinished Walkout Basement

3,500 TO 3,999 SQUARE FEET

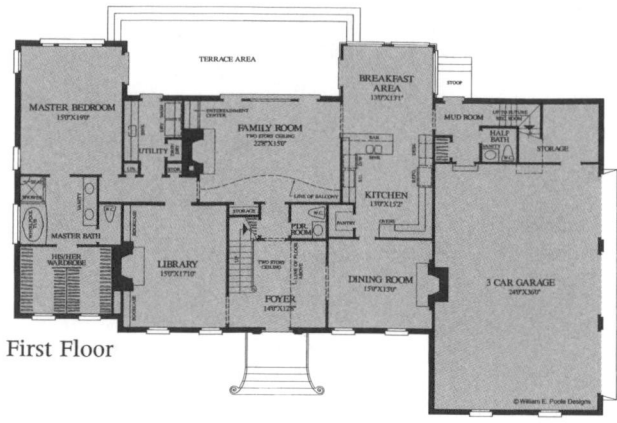

First Floor

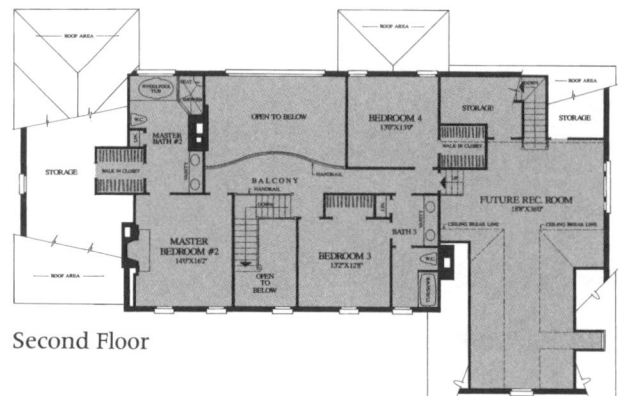

Second Floor

HPK2101182

Style: Georgian

First Floor: 2,492 sq. ft.

Second Floor: 1,313 sq. ft.

Total: 3,805 sq. ft.

Bonus Space: 687 sq. ft.

Bedrooms: 4

Bathrooms: 3 ½ + ½

Width: 85' - 10"

Depth: 54' - 6"

Foundation: Crawlspace, Unfinished Basement

EPLANS.COM

Although the exterior of this Georgian home is entirely classical, the interior boasts an up-to-date floor plan that's a perfect fit for today's lifestyles. The large central family room includes a fireplace and access to the rear terrace. The master suite, also with terrace access, features a spacious walk-in closet and a bath with a whirlpool tub. Upstairs, a second master suite—great for guests—joins two family bedrooms. Nearby, a large open area can serve as a recreation room.

© William E. Poole Designs, Inc.

ORDER BLUEPRINTS ANYTIME AT EPLANS.COM OR 1-800-521-6797

HPK2101183

Style: New American
First Floor: 1,858 sq. ft.
Second Floor: 1,952 sq. ft.
Total: 3,810 sq. ft.
Bedrooms: 5
Bathrooms: 4
Width: 59' - 0"
Depth: 56' - 0"
Foundation: Crawlspace,
Unfinished Walkout Basement

EPLANS.COM

Formal elegance is highlighted by stucco detailing and graceful window treatments on this fine two-story home. The two-story family room features a fireplace, built-in bookshelves, and a wall of windows. The U-shaped kitchen provides a cooktop island and plenty of cabinet and counter space. A den—or make it a guest bedroom—has a built-in bookshelf. Upstairs, Bedrooms 3 and 4 each have walk-in closets and share a bath, while Bedroom 2 provides a private bath and another walk-in closet. The master suite is filled with amenities, including a bayed sitting area and a fireplace.

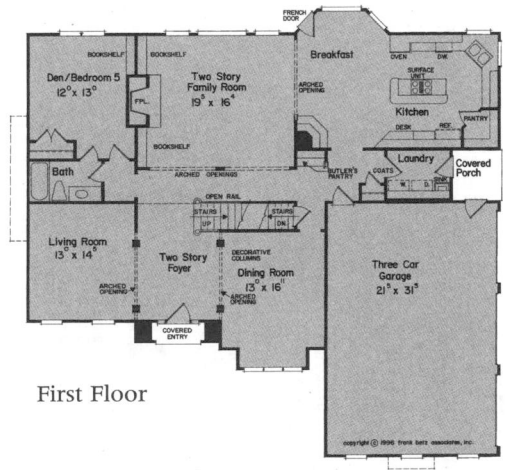

First Floor

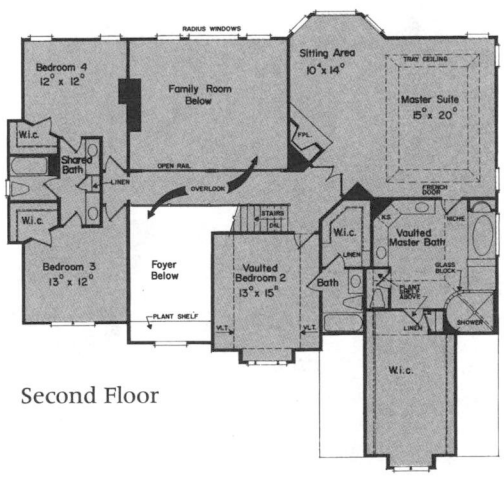

Second Floor

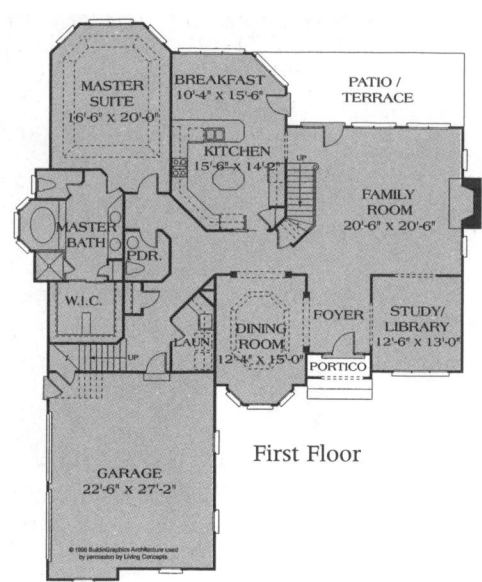

MASTER SUITE 16'-6" X 20'-0"

BREAKFAST 10'-4" X 15'-6"

PATIO / TERRACE

KITCHEN 15'-6" X 14'-2"

FAMILY ROOM 20'-6" X 20'-6"

MASTER BATH

PDR.

W.I.C.

DINING ROOM 12'-4" X 15'-0"

FOYER

STUDY/ LIBRARY 12'-6" X 13'-0"

LAUN.

PORTICO

GARAGE 22'-6" X 27'-2"

First Floor

SUITE 3 15'-4" X 14'-6"

SUITE 4 12'-6" X 15'-8"

BATH

ROOM 20'-5" X 20'-6"

STOR.

W.I.C.

BATH

SUITE 2 12'-4" X 15'-0"

BONUS ROOM 19'-0" X 22'-10"

Second Floor

HPK2101184

Style: New American
First Floor: 2,302 sq. ft.
Second Floor: 1,517 sq. ft.
Total: 3,819 sq. ft.
Bonus Space: 482 sq. ft.
Bedrooms: 4
Bathrooms: 3 ½
Width: 60' - 3"
Depth: 75' - 6"
Foundation: Crawlspace

EPLANS.COM

Decorative, round windows enhance the exterior of this compact three-bedroom Southern contemporary with covered porch framed by ornate columns. The foyer opens into a large living area. A short hall leads past the angled kitchen to the gathering room with fireplace. The morning room is fully framed with windows and opens onto the covered veranda. Upstairs, a fine master retreat includes a fireplace, a garden tub, a large walk-in closet, and private access to the second-level covered veranda.

ORDER BLUEPRINTS ANYTIME AT EPLANS.COM OR 1-800-521-6797

First Floor

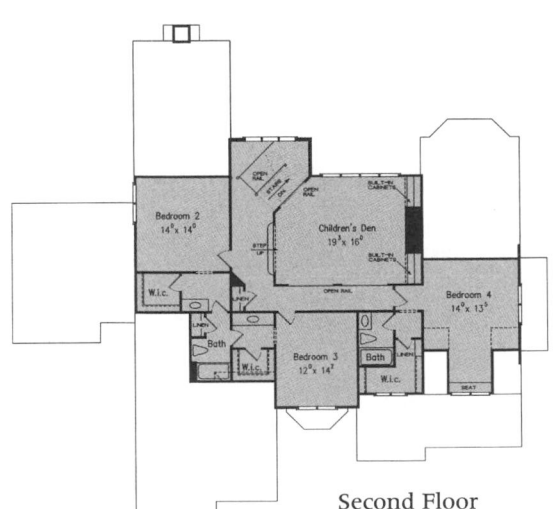

Second Floor

Multiple gables with trusses and a brick exterior evidence European cottage influences in the design. The layout is thoroughly modern and American: family room with coffered ceiling, flow-through kitchen and nook, vaulted keeping room with fireplace, and a luxurious master suite. Upstairs, three more bedrooms share two baths, surrounding a common area to be used as a den, media room, or recreation room.

HPK2101185

Style: French Country
First Floor: 2,269 sq. ft.
Second Floor: 1,551 sq. ft.
Total: 3,820 sq. ft.
Bedrooms: 4
Bathrooms: 3 ½
Width: 79' - 0"
Depth: 73' - 4"
Foundation: Crawlspace, Unfinished Walkout Basement

EPLANS.COM

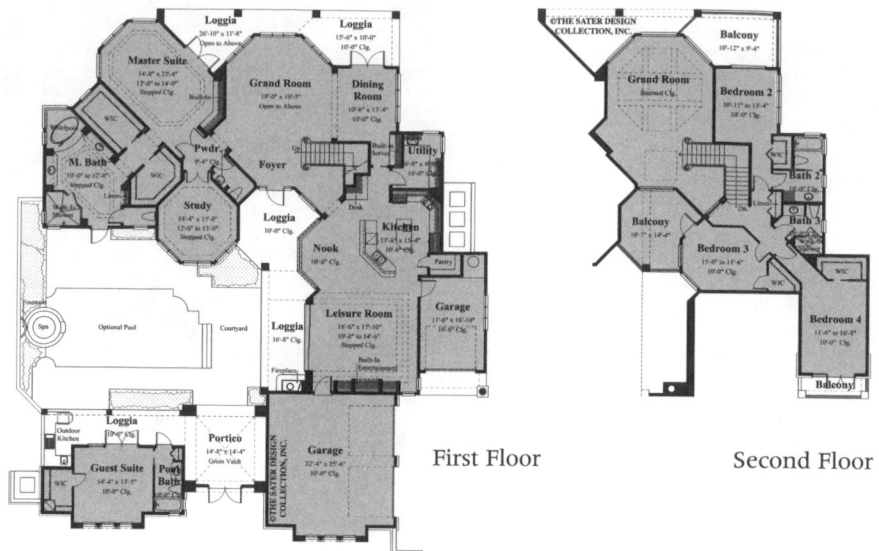

First Floor

Second Floor

HPK2101186

Earth-hued stone turrets pronounce elements of timeless architecture. Powerful forms address the streetscape with this English Country home. A recessed entry opens to an unexpected outdoor space that proceeds through a magnificent courtyard to the formal entry. Near the outer portal, a guest house offers a cabana-style bath and opens to an eating area of the courtyard, complete with a grille and food-prep area. Near the front door, a separate sitting area designed for conversation provides a fireplace. A pocket door protects guests from kitchen noises from the formal dining room which, in a stroke of genius, opens to a private loggia.

Style: Chateauesque
First Floor: 2,852 sq. ft.
Second Floor: 969 sq. ft.
Total: 3,821 sq. ft.
Bonus Space: 337 sq. ft.
Bedrooms: 4
Bathrooms: 4 ½
Width: 80' - 0"
Depth: 96' - 0"
Foundation: Slab

EPLANS.COM

©The Sater Design Collection, Inc.

First Floor

Second Floor

HPK2101187

Style: Mediterranean
First Floor: 2,852 sq. ft.
Second Floor: 969 sq. ft.
Total: 3,821 sq. ft.
Bedrooms: 5
Bathrooms: 4 ½
Width: 80' - 0"
Depth: 96' - 6"
Foundation: Slab

EPLANS.COM

©The Sater Design Collection, Inc.

HPK2101188

Style: Mediterranean
First Floor: 2,107 sq. ft.
Second Floor: 1,717 sq. ft.
Total: 3,824 sq. ft.
Bonus Space: 310 sq. ft.
Bedrooms: 4
Bathrooms: 4
Width: 69' - 0"
Depth: 68' - 0"
Foundation: Crawlspace

EPLANS.COM

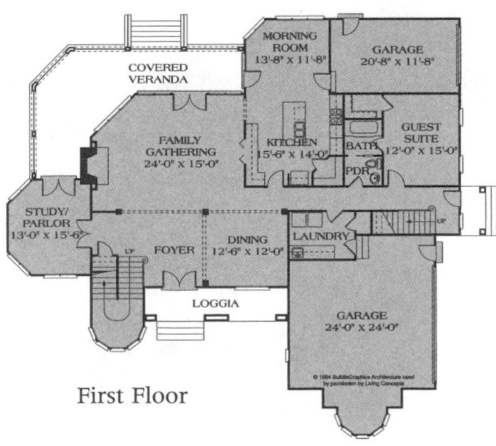

First Floor

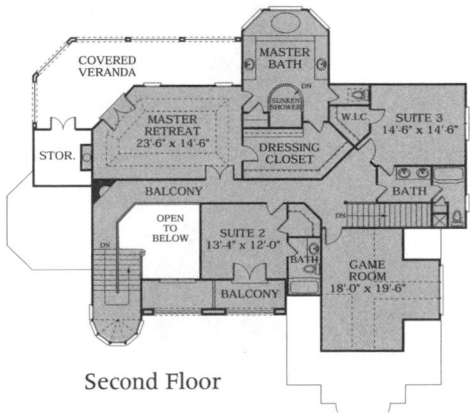

Second Floor

3,500 TO 3,999 SQUARE FEET

First Floor

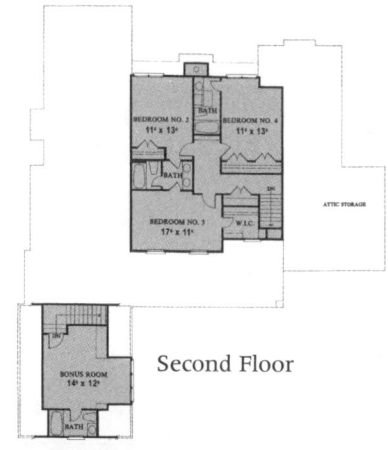

Second Floor

HPK2101189

Style: Country

First Floor: 2,895 sq. ft.

Second Floor: 945 sq. ft.

Total: 3,840 sq. ft.

Bonus Space: 305 sq. ft.

Bedrooms: 4

Bathrooms: 3 ½

Width: 70' - 8"

Depth: 85' - 2"

Foundation: Walkout Basement

EPLANS.COM

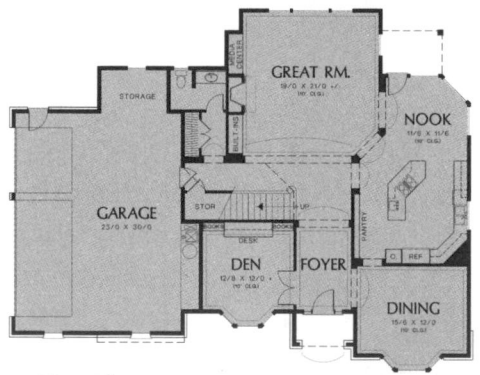

First Floor

Second Floor

HPK2101190

Style: French Country

First Floor: 1,634 sq. ft.

Second Floor: 2,207 sq. ft.

Total: 3,841 sq. ft.

Bedrooms: 4

Bathrooms: 3 ½

Width: 64' - 0"

Depth: 50' - 0"

Foundation: Crawlspace

EPLANS.COM

HPK2101191

Style: Greek Revival
First Floor: 1,992 sq. ft.
Second Floor: 1,851 sq. ft.
Total: 3,843 sq. ft.
Bedrooms: 5
Bathrooms: 4 ½
Width: 66' - 4"
Depth: 53' - 0"
Foundation: Crawlspace, Unfinished Walkout Basement

EPLANS.COM

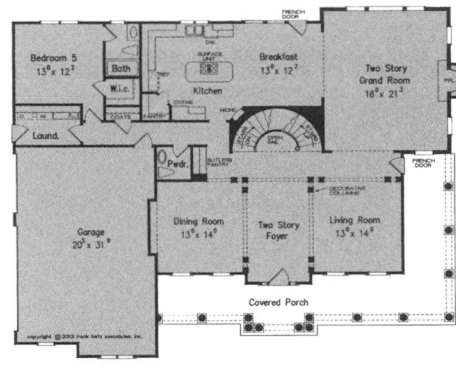

First Floor

Second Floor

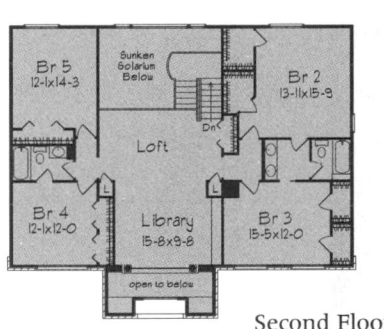

Second Floor

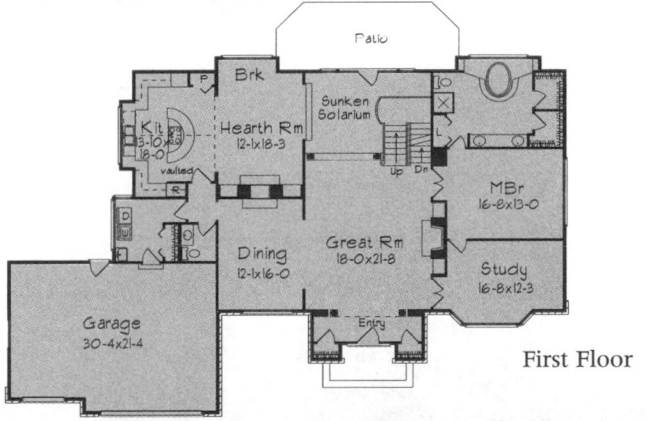

First Floor

HPK2101192

Style: New American
First Floor: 2,306 sq. ft.
Second Floor: 1,544 sq. ft.
Total: 3,850 sq. ft.
Bedrooms: 5
Bathrooms: 3 ½
Width: 80' - 8"
Depth: 51' - 8"
Foundation: Unfinished Basement

EPLANS.COM

3,500 TO 3,999 SQUARE FEET

HPK2101193

Style: Beaux Arts

First Floor: 1,948 sq. ft.

Second Floor: 1,903 sq. ft.

Total: 3,851 sq. ft.

Bedrooms: 5

Bathrooms: 4 ½

Width: 61' - 0"

Depth: 56' - 0"

Foundation: Crawlspace, Unfinished Walkout Basement

EPLANS.COM

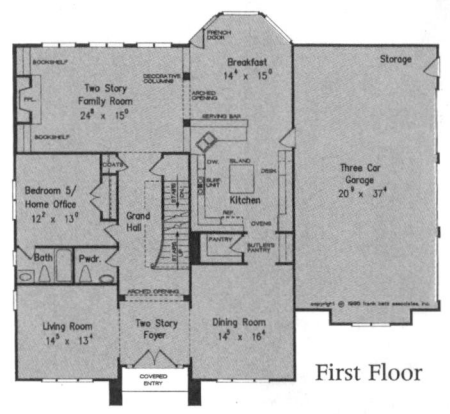

First Floor

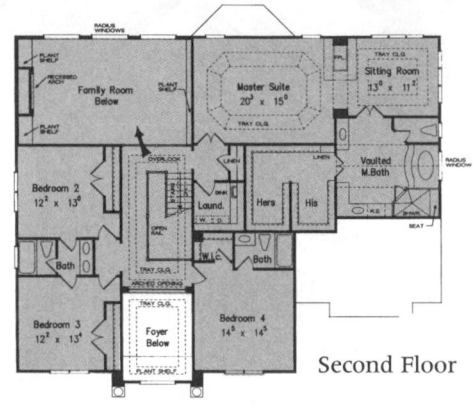

Second Floor

HPK2101194

Style: French Country

First Floor: 2,598 sq. ft.

Second Floor: 1,255 sq. ft.

Total: 3,853 sq. ft.

Bonus Space: 401 sq. ft.

Bedrooms: 5

Bathrooms: 4 ½

Width: 71' - 6"

Depth: 61' - 0"

Foundation: Crawlspace, Slab, Unfinished Walkout Basement

EPLANS.COM

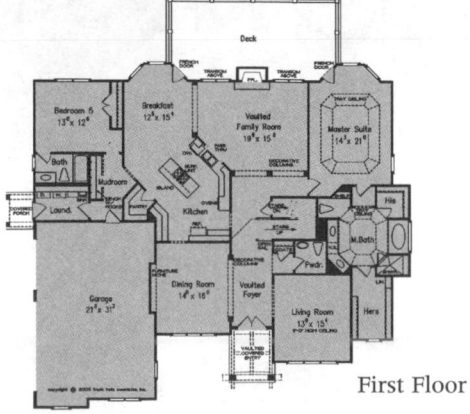

First Floor

Second Floor

ORDER BLUEPRINTS ANYTIME AT EPLANS.COM OR 1-800-521-6797

HPK2101195

Style: Plantation

First Floor: 2,578 sq. ft.

Second Floor: 1,277 sq. ft.

Total: 3,855 sq. ft.

Bedrooms: 4

Bathrooms: 3 ½

Width: 53' - 6"

Depth: 97' - 0"

Foundation: Pier
(same as Piling)

eplans.com

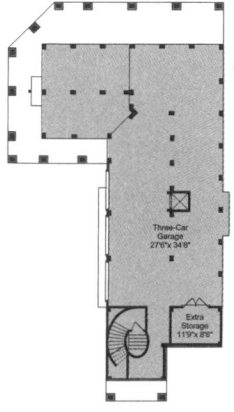

First Floor

Second Floor

HPK2101196

eplans.com

Style: Mediterranean

Square Footage: 3,437

Bedrooms: 3

Bathrooms: 3

Width: 86' - 4"

Depth: 60' - 0"

Foundation: Slab

3,500 TO 3,999 SQUARE FEET

3,500 TO 3,999 SQUARE FEET

HPK2101197

Style: New American
First Floor: 2,523 sq. ft.
Second Floor: 1,337 sq. ft.
Total: 3,860 sq. ft.
Bonus Space: 517 sq. ft.
Bedrooms: 4
Bathrooms: 3 ½
Width: 83' - 0"
Depth: 79' - 3"
Foundation: Crawlspace

EPLANS.COM

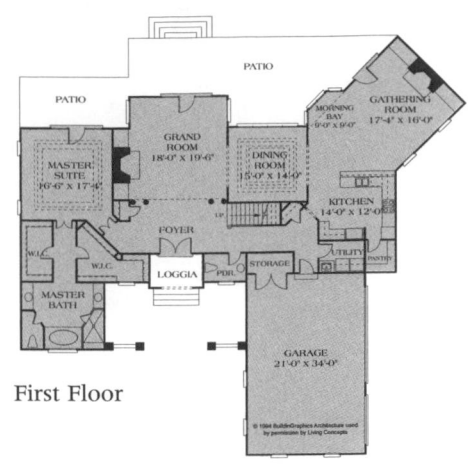

First Floor

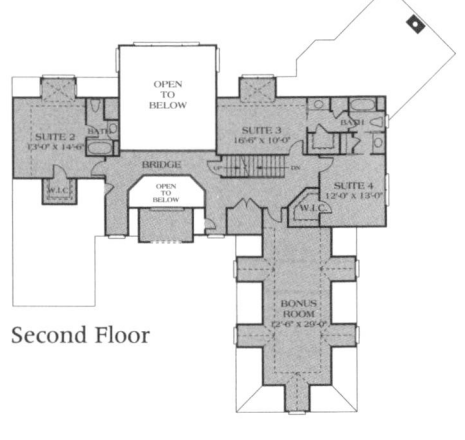

Second Floor

First Floor

Second Floor

HPK2101198

Style: Tudor
First Floor: 2,190 sq. ft.
Second Floor: 1,680 sq. ft.
Total: 3,870 sq. ft.
Bonus Space: 697 sq. ft.
Bedrooms: 4
Bathrooms: 4
Width: 70' - 0"
Depth: 76' - 8"
Foundation: Crawlspace

EPLANS.COM

Dave Rowland. This home, as shown in photographs, may differ from the actual blueprints. For more detailed information, please check the floor plans carefully.

HPK2101199

Style: Country
First Floor: 2,924 sq. ft.
Second Floor: 948 sq. ft.
Total: 3,872 sq. ft.
Bedrooms: 4
Bathrooms: 3 ½
Width: 65' - 0"
Depth: 91' - 0"
Foundation: Slab

First Floor

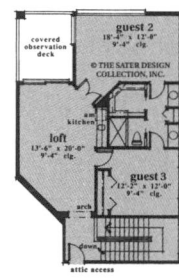

Second Floor

© The Sater Design Collection, Inc.

HPK2101200

Style: New American
First Floor: 2,060 sq. ft.
Second Floor: 1,817 sq. ft.
Total: 3,877 sq. ft.
Bedrooms: 5
Bathrooms: 4 ½
Width: 54' - 0"
Depth: 78' - 4"
Foundation: Crawlspace, Slab, Unfinished Walkout Basement

First Floor

Second Floor

HPK2101201

Style: Craftsman

First Floor: 2,745 sq. ft.

Second Floor: 1,133 sq. ft.

Total: 3,878 sq. ft.

Bonus Space: 649 sq. ft.

Bedrooms: 4

Bathrooms: 4 ½

Width: 69' - 0"

Depth: 85' - 6"

Foundation: Crawlspace, Unfinished Walkout Basement

EPLANS.COM

First Floor

Second Floor

Second Floor

HPK2101202

Style: Chateauesque

First Floor: 3,030 sq. ft.

Second Floor: 848 sq. ft.

Total: 3,878 sq. ft.

Bonus Space: 320 sq. ft.

Bedrooms: 4

Bathrooms: 4 ½

Width: 88' - 0"

Depth: 72' - 1"

Foundation: Slab

EPLANS.COM

First Floor

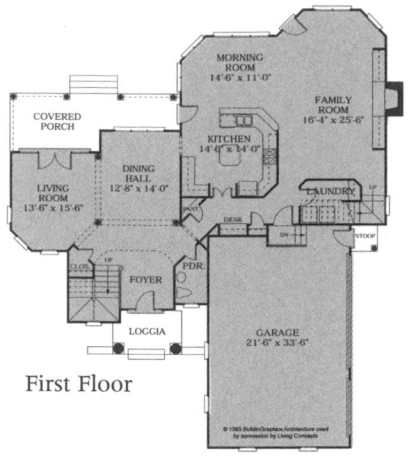

First Floor

Second Floor

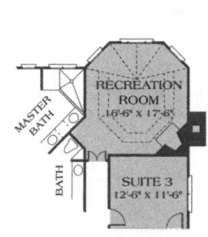

Optional Layout

HPK2101203

Style: New American

First Floor: 1,741 sq. ft.

Second Floor: 2,141 sq. ft.

Total: 3,882 sq. ft.

Bedrooms: 4

Bathrooms: 3 ½

Width: 61' - 8"

Depth: 69' - 6"

Foundation: Crawlspace

EPLANS.COM

HPK2101204

Style: French Country

First Floor: 2,729 sq. ft.

Second Floor: 1,157 sq. ft.

Total: 3,886 sq. ft.

Bedrooms: 4

Bathrooms: 3 ½

Width: 64' - 6"

Depth: 70' - 11"

Foundation: Unfinished Walkout Basement

EPLANS.COM

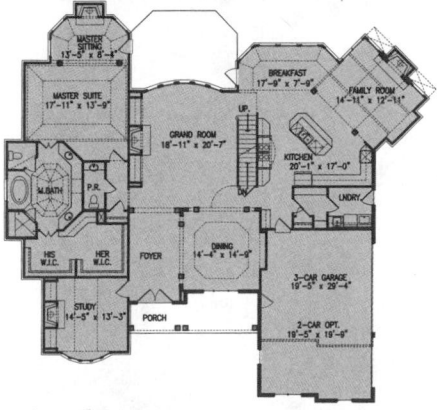

First Floor

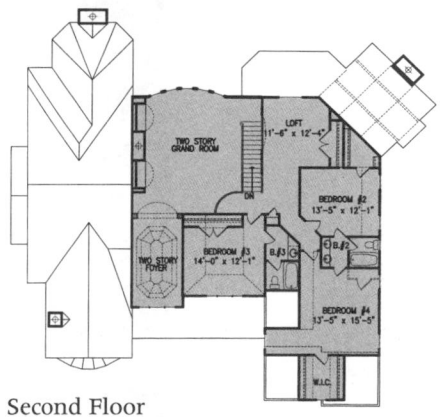

Second Floor

3,500 TO 3,999 SQUARE FEET

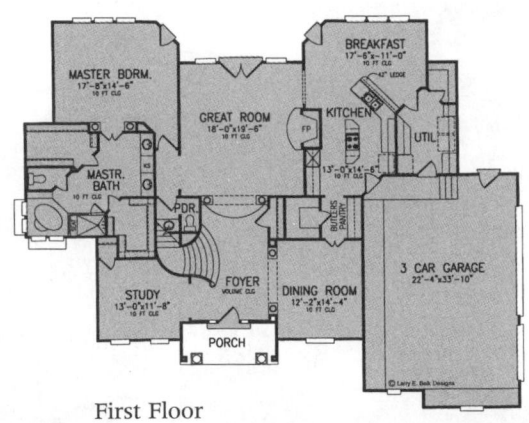

First Floor

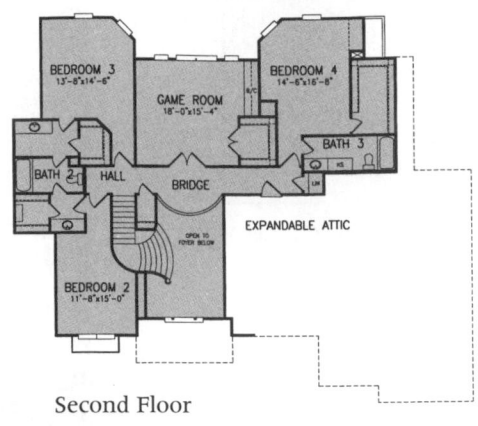

Second Floor

HPK2101205

Style: New American
First Floor: 2,319 sq. ft.
Second Floor: 1,570 sq. ft.
Total: 3,889 sq. ft.
Bedrooms: 4
Bathrooms: 3 ½
Width: 72' - 0"
Depth: 58' - 0"
Foundation: Crawlspace

EPLANS.COM

HPK2101206

Style: Craftsman
First Floor: 2,950 sq. ft.
Second Floor: 943 sq. ft.
Total: 3,893 sq. ft.
Bedrooms: 4
Bathrooms: 3 ½
Width: 75' - 0"
Depth: 83' - 0"
Foundation: Crawlspace

EPLANS.COM

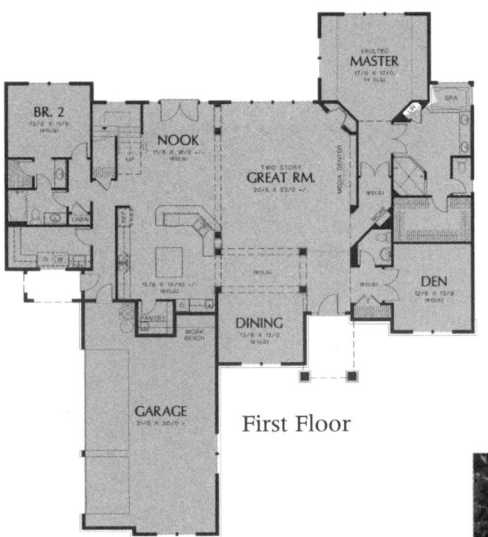

First Floor

Second Floor

© The Sater Design Collection, Inc.

HPK2101207

Style: Italianate

First Floor: 2,841 sq. ft.

Second Floor: 1,052 sq. ft.

Total: 3,893 sq. ft.

Bedrooms: 4

Bathrooms: 3 ½

Width: 85' - 0"

Depth: 76' - 8"

Foundation: Slab

EPLANS.COM

A turret, two-story bay windows, and plenty of arched glass impart a graceful style to the exterior and rich amenities inside furnish contentment. A grand foyer decked with columns introduces the living room with a curve of glass windows viewing the rear gardens. The master suite fills the entire right section of the design and enjoys a tray ceiling, two walk-in closets, a separate shower, and a garden tub set in a bay window.

3,500 TO 3,999 SQUARE FEET

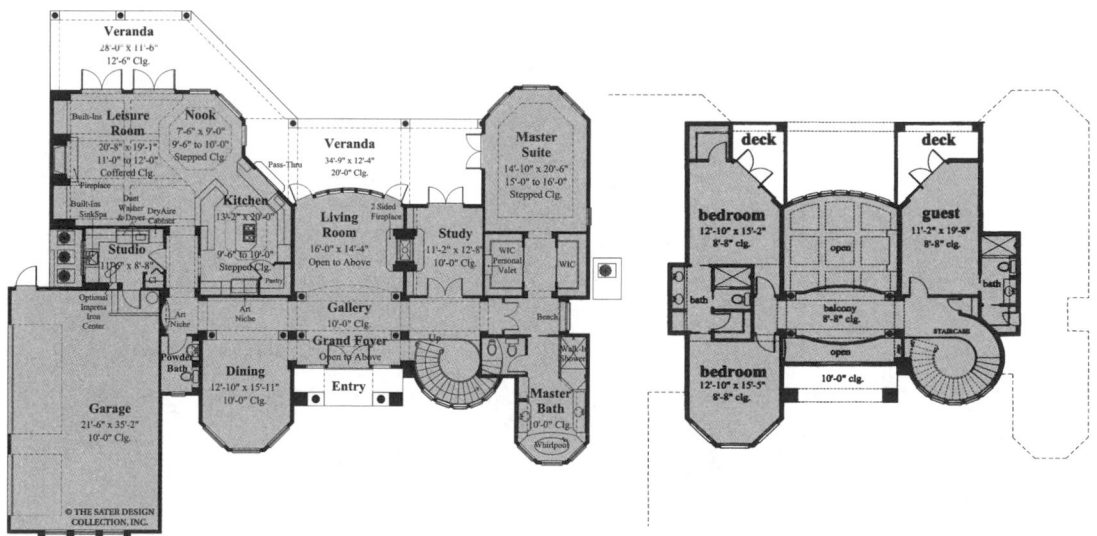

First Floor

Second Floor

HPK2101208

Style: New American

First Floor: 2,772 sq. ft.

Second Floor: 1,127 sq. ft.

Total: 3,899 sq. ft.

Bonus Space: 374 sq. ft.

Bedrooms: 4

Bathrooms: 4 ½

Width: 75' - 0"

Depth: 68' - 0"

Foundation: Crawlspace, Slab, Unfinished Walkout Basement

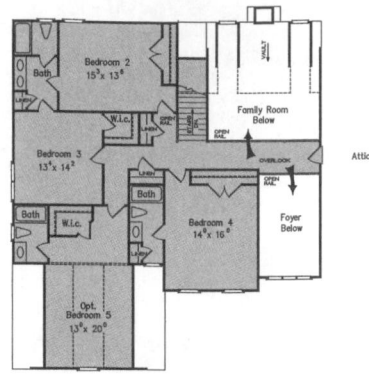

Second Floor

A blend of styles culminated in this handsome design. The equally impressive interior offers spacious room dimensions, upgraded amenities, and decorative flourishes throughout. The master suite is a haven of indulgence, complete with a personal fireplace nestled in the vaulted sitting room. The second floor houses three well-appointed secondary bedrooms, plus the option for a fourth on this level.

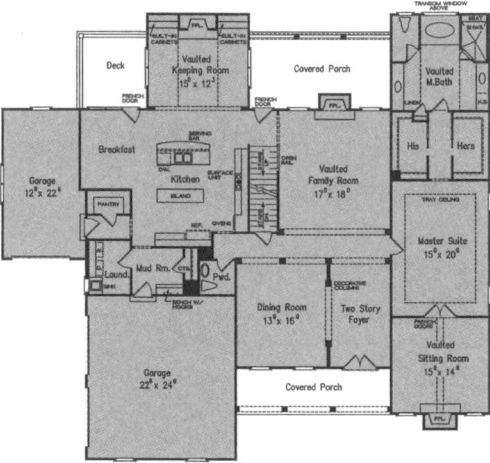

First Floor

This plan is definitely the house of sun. A complex roofline astrides a brick facade, with bay and dormer windows dappling this sweeping exterior. Inside, you'll be in awe of the corner master suite on the main level, which provides plenty of views through the windows, and private outdoor access, not to mention its own spectacular bath. The great room has more of those views in store, plus a pair of stunning French doors.

HPK2101209

Style: New American

First Floor: 2,346 sq. ft.

Second Floor: 1,554 sq. ft.

Total: 3,900 sq. ft.

Bonus Space: 455 sq. ft.

Bedrooms: 3

Bathrooms: 2 ½

Width: 97' - 4"

Depth: 58' - 6"

Foundation: Crawlspace

EPLANS.COM

First Floor

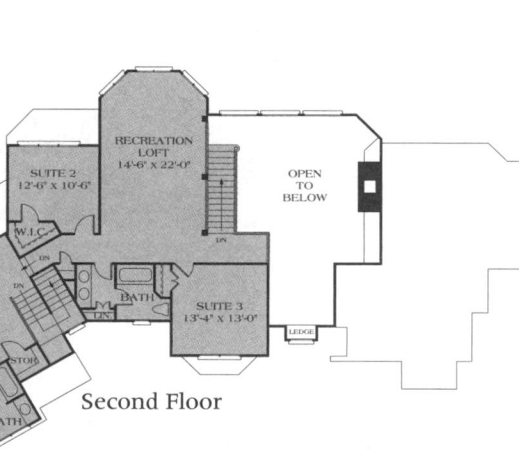

Second Floor

3,500 TO 3,999 SQUARE FEET

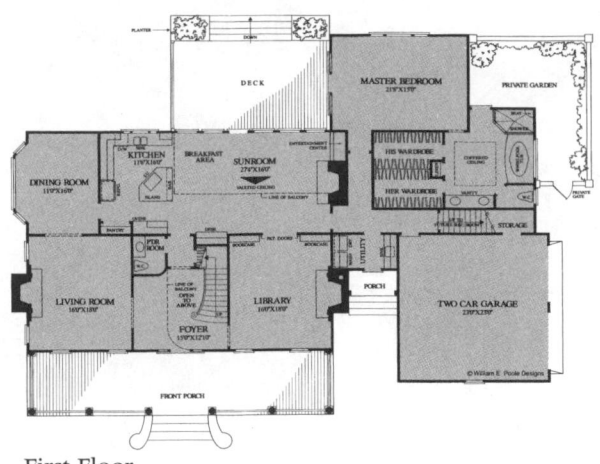

First Floor

Second Floor

HPK2101210

Style: Federal - Adams
First Floor: 2,648 sq. ft.
Second Floor: 1,253 sq. ft.
Total: 3,901 sq. ft.
Bonus Space: 540 sq. ft.
Bedrooms: 4
Bathrooms: 3 ½
Width: 82' - 0"
Depth: 60' - 4"
Foundation: Crawlspace

EPLANS.COM

This delightful home packs quite a punch. The grand staircase in the elegant foyer makes a dazzling first impression. The library opens to the sunroom, which overlooks the deck. The master suite finds privacy on the far right. Three additional bedrooms are found on the second floor, along with two full baths. Future space provides an additional bedroom, bath, and rec room.

© William E. Poole Designs, Inc.

Keystone lintels, an arched transom over the entry, and sidelights spell classic design for this four-bedroom home. The tiled foyer offers entry to any room you choose, whether it be the secluded den with its built-in bookshelves, the formal dining room, the formal living room with its fireplace, wet bar, and wall of windows, or the spacious rear family and kitchen area with its sunny breakfast nook. The master suite offers privacy on the first floor and features a sitting room with bookshelves, two walk-in closets, and a private bath with a corner whirlpool tub. Upstairs, two family bedrooms share a bath and enjoy separate vanities.

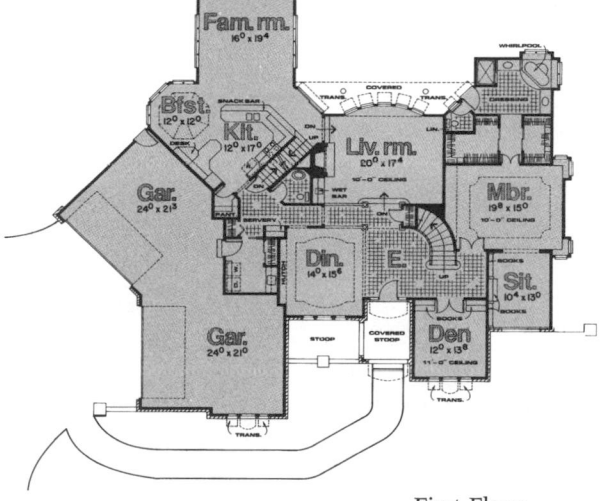

First Floor

HPK2101211

Style: French Country

First Floor: 2,813 sq. ft.

Second Floor: 1,091 sq. ft.

Total: 3,904 sq. ft.

Bedrooms: 4

Bathrooms: 3 ½

Width: 85' - 5"

Depth: 74' - 8"

EPLANS.COM

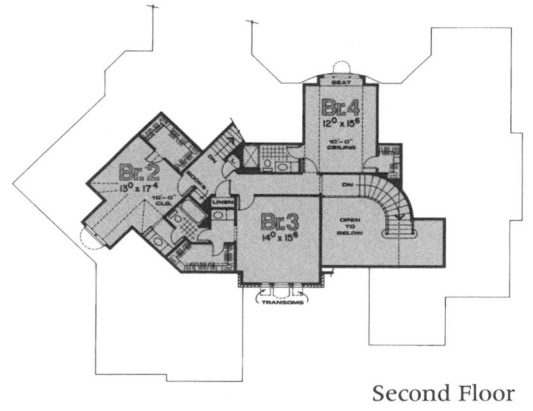

Second Floor

HPK2101212

Style: New American

First Floor: 3,613 sq. ft.

Second Floor: 297 sq. ft.

Total: 3,910 sq. ft.

Bedrooms: 4

Bathrooms: 3 ½ + ½

Width: 87' - 0"

Depth: 64' - 2"

Foundation: Crawlspace, Slab, Unfinished Basement

EPLANS.COM

First Floor

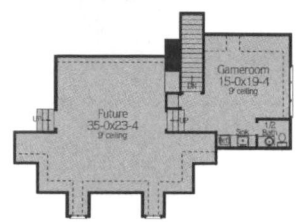

Second Floor

HPK2101213

Style: Country

First Floor: 2,554 sq. ft.

Second Floor: 1,361 sq. ft.

Total: 3,915 sq. ft.

Bedrooms: 4

Bathrooms: 3 ½

Width: 79' - 0"

Depth: 64' - 4"

Foundation: Crawlspace, Unfinished Walkout Basement

EPLANS.COM

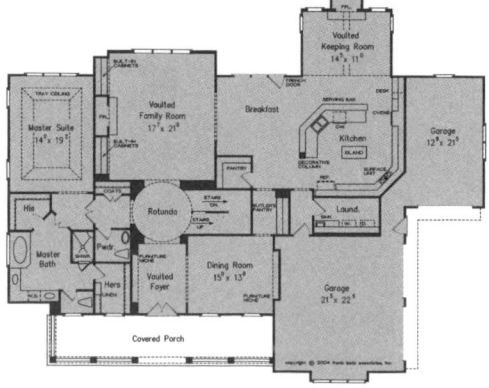

First Floor

Second Floor

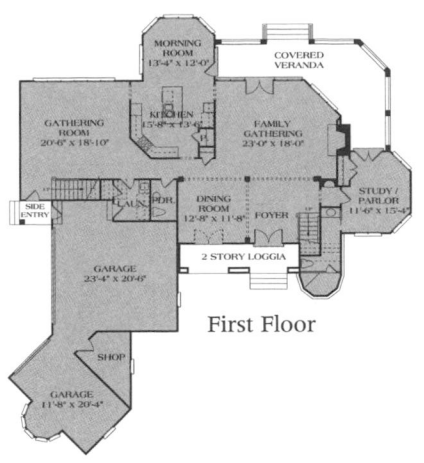

First Floor

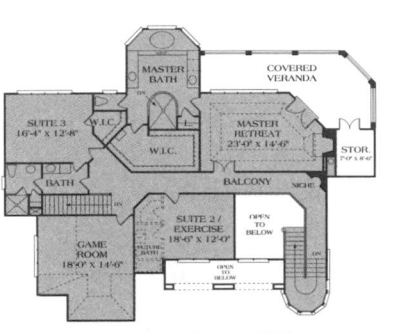

Second Floor

HPK2101214

Style: New American

First Floor: 2,154 sq. ft.

Second Floor: 1,764 sq. ft.

Total: 3,918 sq. ft.

Bonus Space: 339 sq. ft.

Bedrooms: 3

Bathrooms: 2 ½

Width: 77' - 2"

Depth: 83' - 8"

Foundation: Crawlspace

EPLANS.COM

HPK2101215

Style: Greek Revival

First Floor: 2,473 sq. ft.

Second Floor: 1,447 sq. ft.

Total: 3,920 sq. ft.

Bonus Space: 428 sq. ft.

Bedrooms: 4

Bathrooms: 3 ½

Width: 68' - 8"

Depth: 80' - 0"

Foundation: Crawlspace, Unfinished Walkout Basement

EPLANS.COM

© William E. Poole Designs, Inc.

First Floor

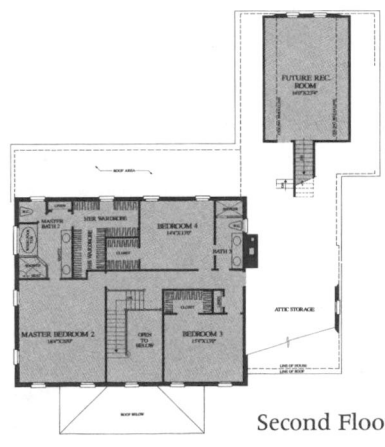

Second Floor

3,500 TO 3,999 SQUARE FEET

First Floor

Second Floor

© The Sater Design Collection, Inc.

HPK2101216

Style: New American
First Floor: 2,794 sq. ft.
Second Floor: 1,127 sq. ft.
Total: 3,921 sq. ft.
Bedrooms: 4
Bathrooms: 3 ½
Width: 85' - 0"
Depth: 76' - 8"
Foundation: Slab

EPLANS.COM

HPK2101217

Style: French Country
First Floor: 2,985 sq. ft.
Second Floor: 938 sq. ft.
Total: 3,923 sq. ft.
Bedrooms: 4
Bathrooms: 3 ½
Width: 86' - 0"
Depth: 68' - 6"
Foundation: Slab, Unfinished Basement

EPLANS.COM

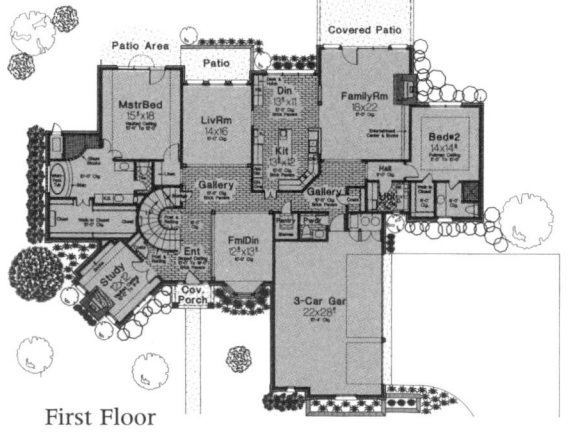

First Floor

Second Floor

First Floor

Second Floor

HPK2101218

Style: French Country
First Floor: 2,641 sq. ft.
Second Floor: 1,290 sq. ft.
Total: 3,931 sq. ft.
Bonus Space: 399 sq. ft.
Bedrooms: 4
Bathrooms: 3 ½
Width: 71' - 0"
Depth: 72' - 4"
Foundation: Crawlspace, Unfinished Walkout Basement

EPLANS.COM

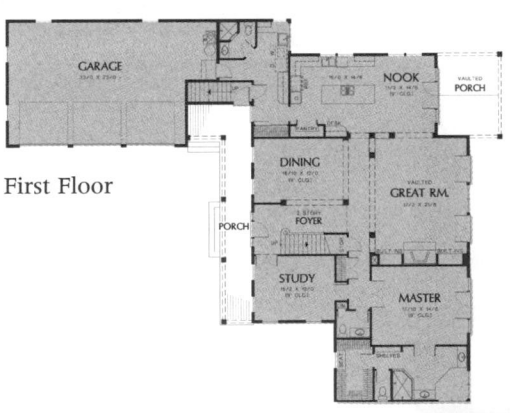

First Floor

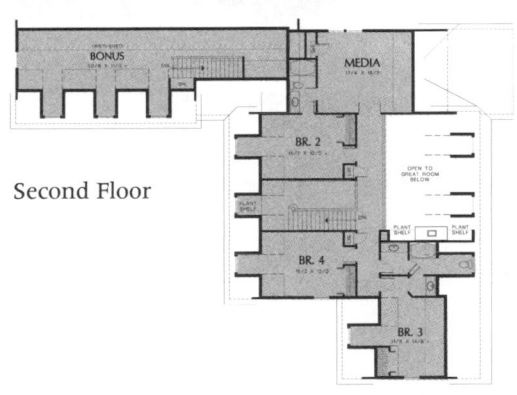

Second Floor

HPK2101219

Style: Farmhouse
First Floor: 2,513 sq. ft.
Second Floor: 1,421 sq. ft.
Total: 3,934 sq. ft.
Bonus Space: 596 sq. ft.
Bedrooms: 4
Bathrooms: 4 ½
Width: 72' - 0"
Depth: 93' - 0"
Foundation: Crawlspace

EPLANS.COM

3,500 TO 3,999 SQUARE FEET

HPK2101220

Style: New American
First Floor: 2,751 sq. ft.
Second Floor: 1,185 sq. ft.
Total: 3,936 sq. ft.
Bedrooms: 4
Bathrooms: 3 ½
Width: 79' - 0"
Depth: 66' - 4"
Foundation: Slab, Unfinished Basement

EPLANS.COM

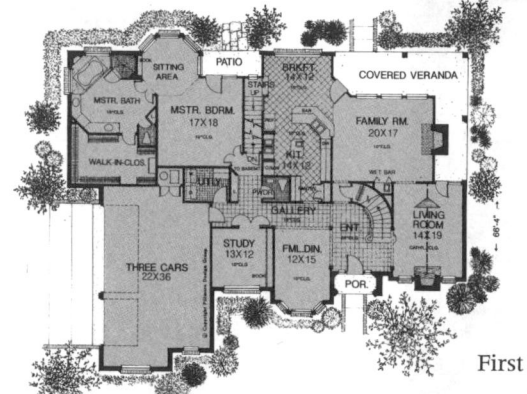

First Floor

Second Floor

© William E. Poole Designs, Inc.

HPK2101221

Style: Farmhouse
First Floor: 2,653 sq. ft.
Second Floor: 1,286 sq. ft.
Total: 3,939 sq. ft.
Bonus Space: 583 sq. ft.
Bedrooms: 4
Bathrooms: 3 ½
Width: 77' - 8"
Depth: 81' - 6"
Foundation: Crawlspace

EPLANS.COM

First Floor

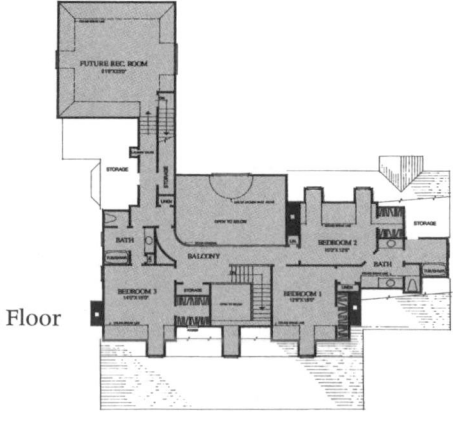

Second Floor

HPK2101222

Style: Federal - Adams
First Floor: 2,565 sq. ft.
Second Floor: 1,375 sq. ft.
Total: 3,940 sq. ft.
Bedrooms: 4
Bathrooms: 3 ½
Width: 88' - 6"
Depth: 58' - 6"
Foundation: Walkout Basement

© Stephen Fuller, Inc.

EPLANS.COM

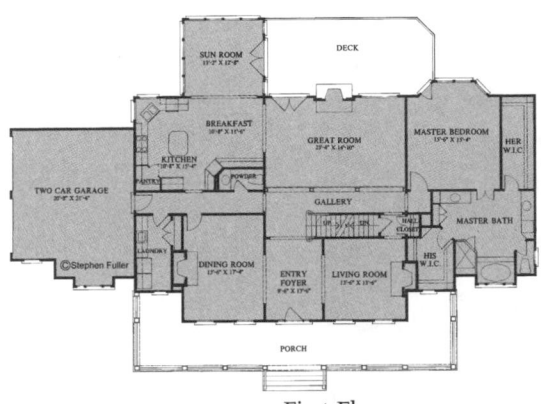

First Floor

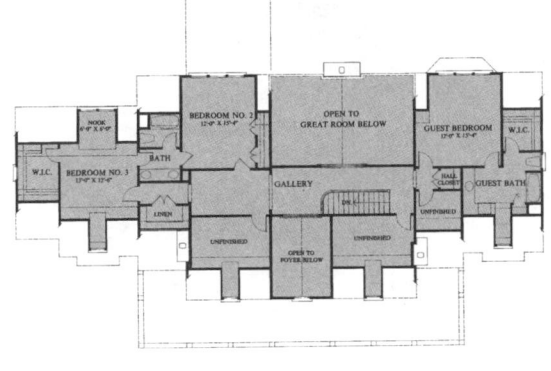

Second Floor

© The Sater Design Collection, Inc.

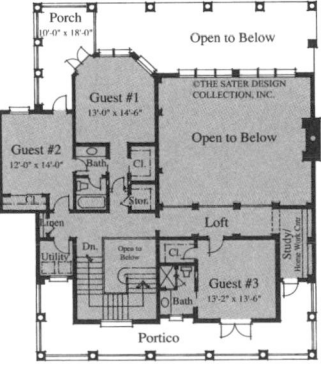

Second Floor

HPK2101223

Style: Neoclassical
First Floor: 2,705 sq. ft.
Second Floor: 1,241 sq. ft.
Total: 3,946 sq. ft.
Bedrooms: 4
Bathrooms: 4
Width: 98' - 0"
Depth: 60' - 0"
Foundation: Crawlspace, Slab

EPLANS.COM

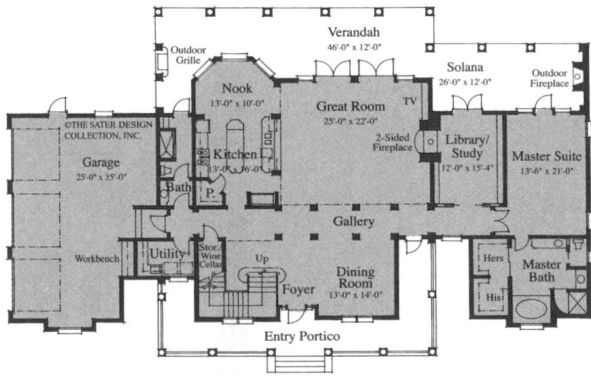

First Floor

3,500 TO 3,999 SQUARE FEET

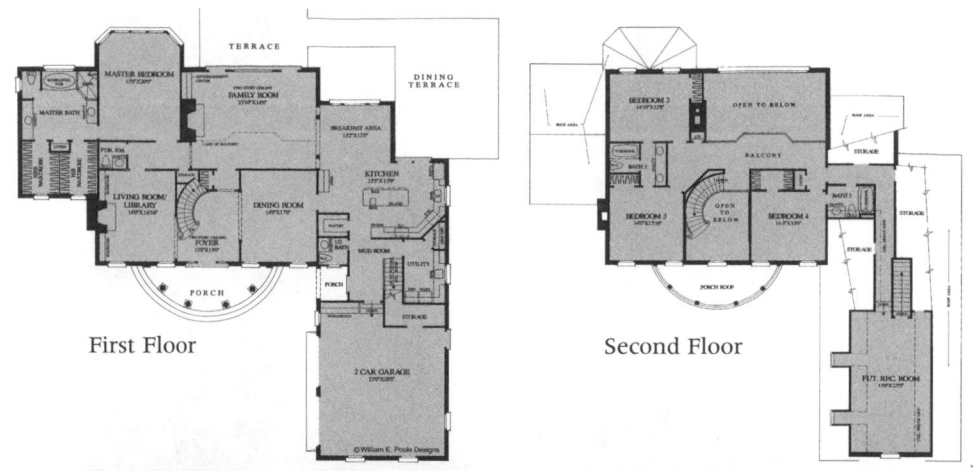

First Floor

Second Floor

HPK2101224

Style: Federal - Adams
First Floor: 2,767 sq. ft.
Second Floor: 1,179 sq. ft.
Total: 3,946 sq. ft.
Bonus Space: 591 sq. ft.
Bedrooms: 4
Bathrooms: 3 ½ + ½
Width: 79' - 11"
Depth: 80' - 6"
Foundation: Crawlspace

EPLANS.COM

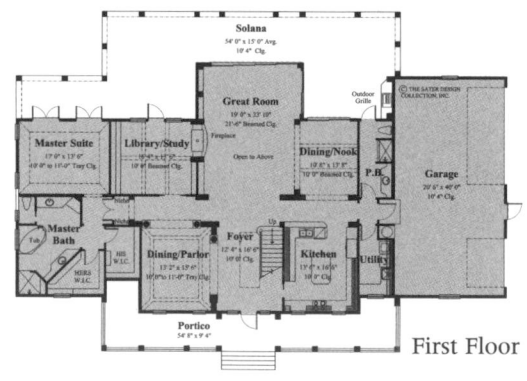

First Floor

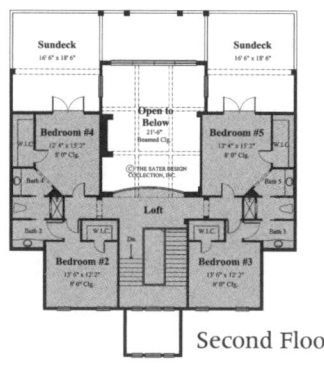

Second Floor

HPK2101225

Style: Farmhouse
First Floor: 2,628 sq. ft.
Second Floor: 1,320 sq. ft.
Total: 3,948 sq. ft.
Bedrooms: 5
Bathrooms: 4
Width: 92' - 0"
Depth: 63' - 0"
Foundation: Slab

EPLANS.COM

ORDER BLUEPRINTS ANYTIME AT EPLANS.COM OR 1-800-521-6797

HPK2101226

Style: Cottage

First Floor: 2,576 sq. ft.

Second Floor: 1,374 sq. ft.

Total: 3,950 sq. ft.

Bedrooms: 4

Bathrooms: 2 ½

Width: 46' - 4"

Depth: 57' - 4"

Foundation: Crawlspace, Unfinished Walkout Basement

EPLANS.COM

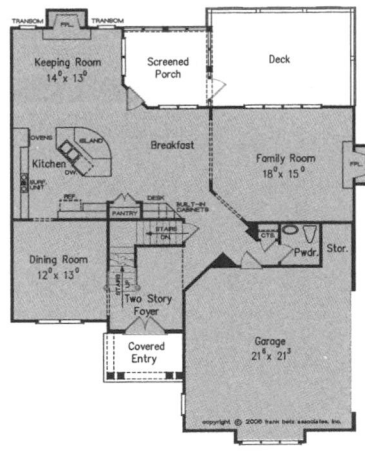

First Floor

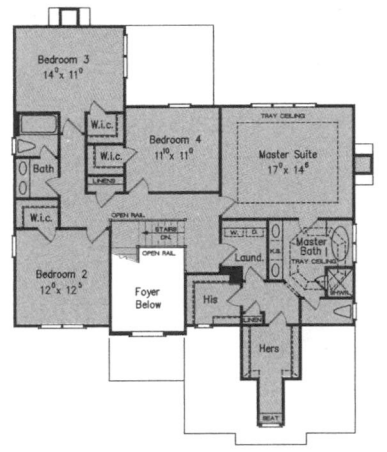

Second Floor

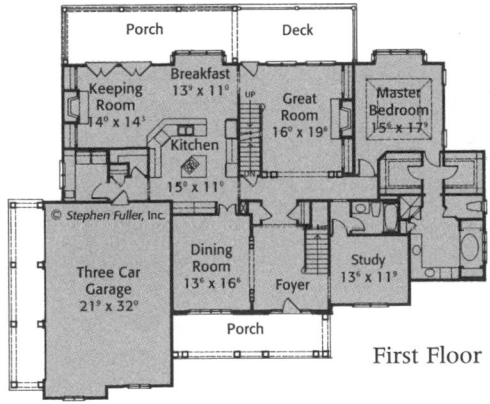

First Floor

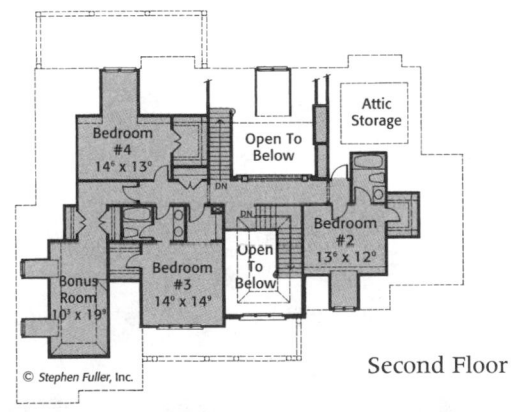

Second Floor

HPK2101227

Style: French Country

First Floor: 2,727 sq. ft.

Second Floor: 1,224 sq. ft.

Total: 3,951 sq. ft.

Bedrooms: 4

Bathrooms: 4

Width: 83' - 3"

Depth: 69' - 3"

Foundation: Walkout Basement

EPLANS.COM

3,500 TO 3,999 SQUARE FEET

HPK2101228

Style: Italianate

First Floor: 2,829 sq. ft.

Second Floor: 1,127 sq. ft.

Total: 3,956 sq. ft.

Bedrooms: 4

Bathrooms: 3 ½

Width: 85' - 0"

Depth: 76' - 8"

Foundation: Slab

EPLANS.COM

© The Sater Design Collection, Inc.

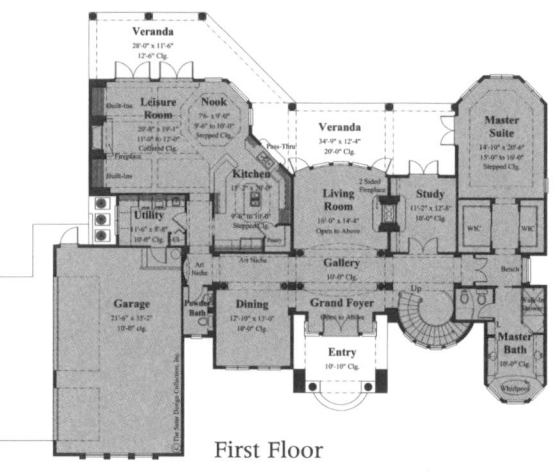

First Floor

Second Floor

© The Sater Design Collection, Inc.

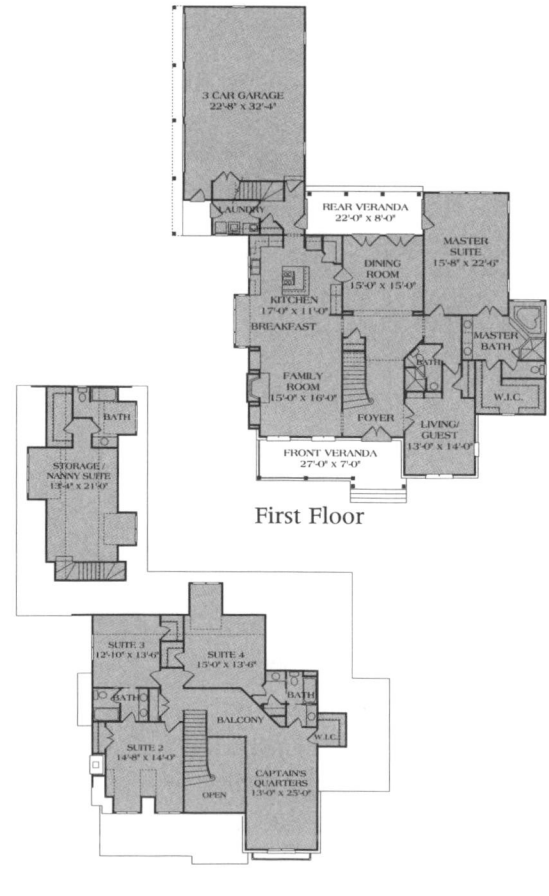

First Floor

HPK2101229

Style: French Country

First Floor: 2,414 sq. ft.

Second Floor: 1,543 sq. ft.

Total: 3,957 sq. ft.

Bonus Space: 544 sq. ft.

Bedrooms: 5

Bathrooms: 5

Width: 70' - 4"

Depth: 88' - 6"

Foundation: Crawlspace

EPLANS.COM

Second Floor

First Floor

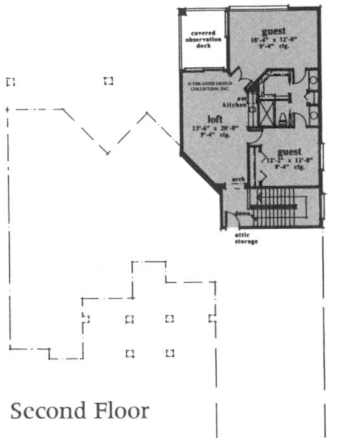

Second Floor

HPK2101230

Style: New American
First Floor: 3,010 sq. ft.
Second Floor: 948 sq. ft.
Total: 3,958 sq. ft.
Bedrooms: 4
Bathrooms: 3 ½
Width: 65' - 0"
Depth: 91' - 0"
Foundation: Slab

EPLANS.COM

HPK2101231

Style: French Country
First Floor: 2,588 sq. ft.
Second Floor: 1,375 sq. ft.
Total: 3,963 sq. ft.
Bonus Space: 460 sq. ft.
Bedrooms: 4
Bathrooms: 3 ½
Width: 91' - 4"
Depth: 51' - 10"
Foundation: Crawlspace

EPLANS.COM

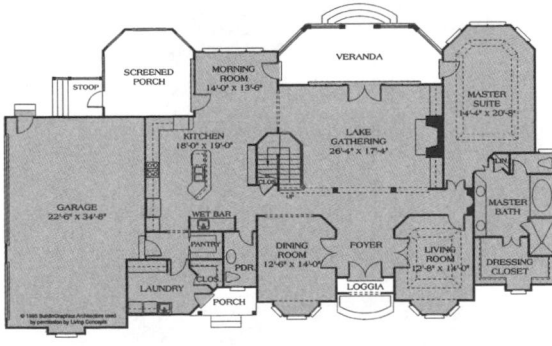

First Floor

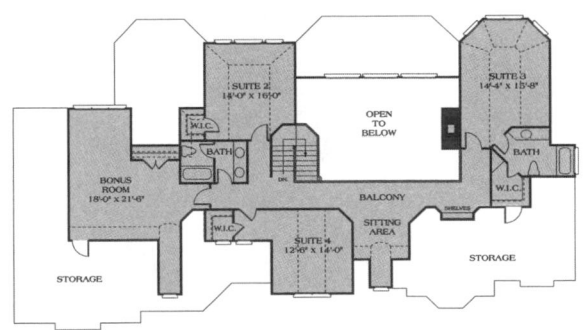

Second Floor

3,500 TO 3,999 SQUARE FEET

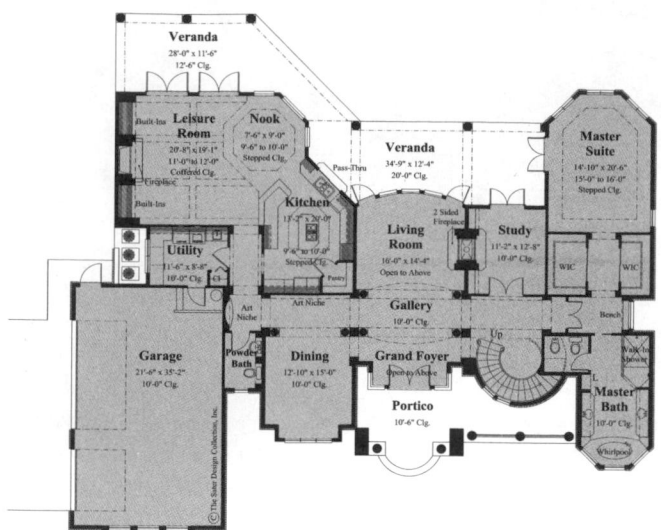

First Floor

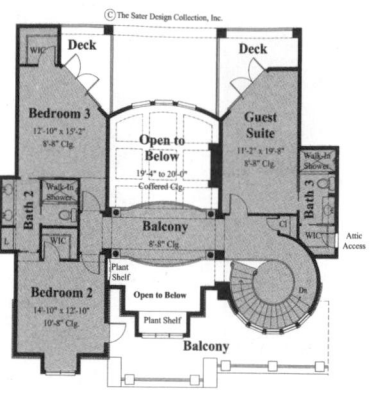

Second Floor

Mediterranean accents enhance the facade of this contemporary estate home. Two fanciful turret bays add a sense of grandeur to the exterior. Double doors open inside to a grand two-story foyer. A two-sided fireplace warms the study and living room, which has a two-story coffered ceiling. To the right, the master suite includes a private bath, two walk-in closets, and double-door access to the sweeping rear veranda.

HPK2101232

Style: Italianate
First Floor: 2,834 sq. ft.
Second Floor: 1,143 sq. ft.
Total: 3,977 sq. ft.
Bedrooms: 4
Bathrooms: 3 ½
Width: 85' - 0"
Depth: 76' - 8"
Foundation: Slab

EPLANS.COM

ORDER BLUEPRINTS ANYTIME AT EPLANS.COM OR 1-800-521-6797

French and Tudor design elements delight the exterior with intriguing rooflines, surface materials, and window placement. The entry portico sits next to a stunning spiral-staircase tower and well-appointed, private study. Built-ins line the walls of the library/dining space, which is efficiently served by the Butler's pantry. The glorious counter, cabinet, and pantry space offered by the kitchen is further extended to a planning office. A first-floor master suite features a bumped-out alcove, full baths, and twin walk-in closets. Two family bedroom suites share a library with built-ins, a loft area, and a large bonus room with a balcony and wet bar.

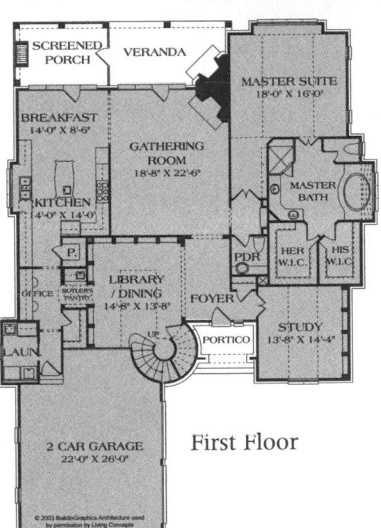

First Floor

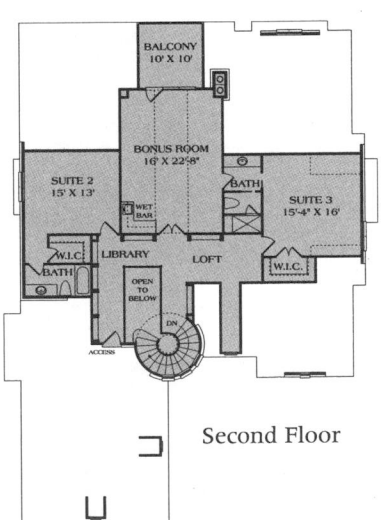

Second Floor

HPK2101233

Style: Chateauesque
First Floor: 2,507 sq. ft.
Second Floor: 1,472 sq. ft.
Total: 3,979 sq. ft.
Bedrooms: 3
Bathrooms: 3 ½
Width: 59' - 6"
Depth: 82' - 8"
Foundation: Crawlspace

EPLANS.COM

HPK2101234

Style: Federal - Adams
First Floor: 2,436 sq. ft.
Second Floor: 1,548 sq. ft.
Total: 3,984 sq. ft.
Bonus Space: 330 sq. ft.
Bedrooms: 3
Bathrooms: 3 ½
Width: 107' - 0"
Depth: 60' - 0"
Foundation: Crawlspace

EPLANS.COM

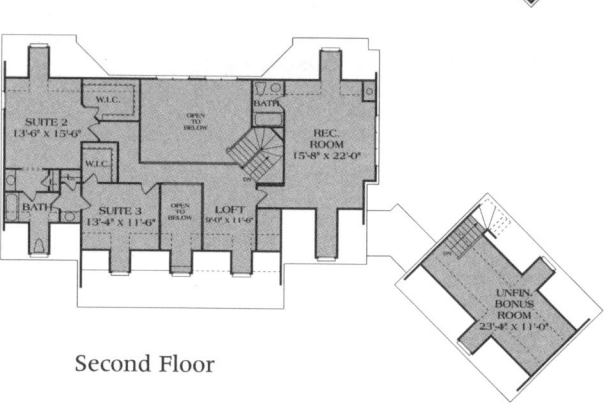

First Floor

Second Floor

A beautiful arched entry begins the country charm of this plantation cottage. The grand room is aptly named and serves as a comfortable receiving area. At the rear, the gathering room is a casual place to relax in front of a warming fire. Situated for privacy, the master suite excels with a unique room shape, patio access, and a soothing bath designed for two. Upstairs, dormer windows light every room, including the bonus space over the garage.

ORDER BLUEPRINTS ANYTIME AT EPLANS.COM OR 1-800-521-6797

HPK2101235

Style: Mediterranean
First Floor: 3,008 sq. ft.
Second Floor: 983 sq. ft.
Total: 3,991 sq. ft.
Bedrooms: 4
Bathrooms: 3 ½
Width: 65' - 0"
Depth: 115' - 0"
Foundation: Slab

EPLANS.COM

Stone balustrades create an entryway patio, making this home ultra-impressive. The interior impresses too, with zero-corner pocket doors in the living room, a private master suite with a privacy garden, and a fabulous Solana with an outdoor grill and fireplace. The second floor offers two guest rooms with a shared bath, a bonus room with its own lanai and deck, and even a wet bar complete with popcorn maker.

First Floor

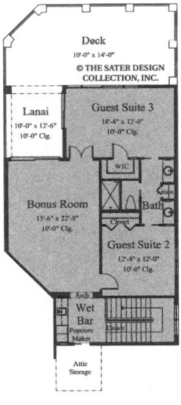

Second Floor

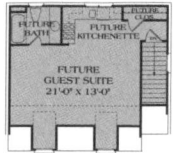

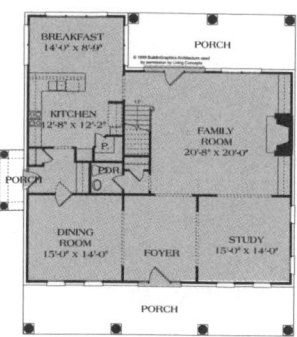

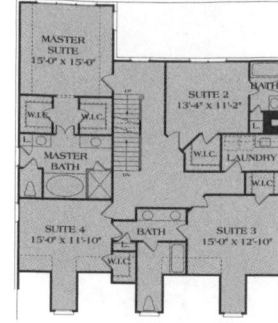

First Floor

Second Floor

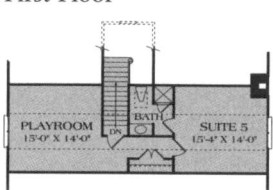

HPK2101236

Style: Federal - Adams
First Floor: 1,630 sq. ft.
Second Floor: 1,763 sq. ft.
Total: 3,393 sq. ft.
Bonus Space: 539 sq. ft.
Bedrooms: 4
Bathrooms: 3 ½
Width: 47' - 10"
Depth: 52' - 10"
Foundation: Crawlspace

EPLANS.COM

This Southern-raised country cottage offers style, comfort, and a floor plan that is ready to meet your needs. The side-lit foyer opens on the right to a study, or make it a formal living room. The dining room is to the left with a unique butler's pantry that leads to a well-planned kitchen. In the family room, a fireplace framed by built-ins and rear-porch access make it a favorite gathering spot. Bedrooms are located upstairs, including three generously appointed secondary suites and a lavish master suite. The two-car garage provides extra storage and a future guest suite above.

ORDER BLUEPRINTS ANYTIME AT EPLANS.COM OR 1-800-521-6797

HPK2101237

Style: Contemporary
Main Level: 1,604 sq. ft.
Upper Level: 655 sq. ft.
Lower Level: 1,247 sq. ft.
Total: 3,506 sq. ft.
Bonus Space: 307 sq. ft.
Bedrooms: 5
Bathrooms: 3 ½
Width: 59' - 0"
Depth: 59' - 8"
Foundation: Finished Basement

EPLANS.COM

Expansive rear views invite the scenic imagery of the outdoors. French doors flank the fireplace on the second-floor deck, providing access to the great room and kitchen. A covered sunroom off the kitchen makes alfresco meals an option, despite the weather. The master suite, nestled in the corner, is cozy and private. The first floor houses two family bedrooms, a large full bath, a rec room, and the laundry room. On the upper level, two additional bedrooms and a full bath are ideal for guests.

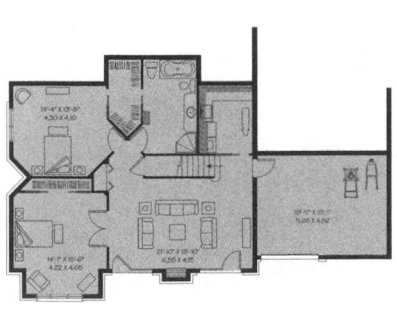

Lower Level

Main Level

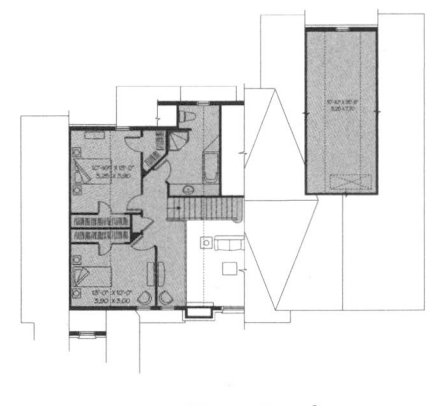

Upper Level

HPK2101238

Style: Country
Main Level: 2,297 sq. ft.
Lower Level: 1,212 sq. ft.
Total: 3,509 sq. ft.
Bedrooms: 5
Bathrooms: 5 ½
Width: 70' - 10"
Depth: 69' - 0"

EPLANS.COM

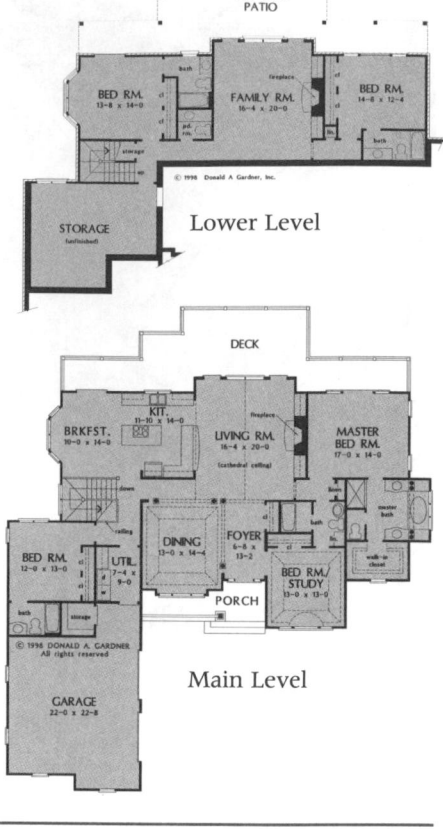

Lower Level

Main Level

©1998 Donald A. Gardner, Inc.

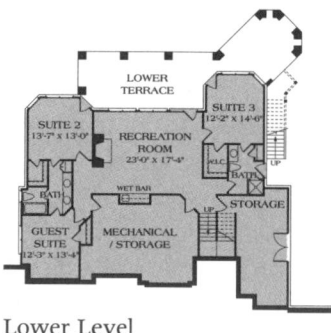

Lower Level

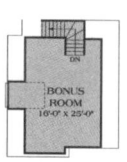

Main Level

HPK2101239

Style: Craftsman
Main Level: 2,213 sq. ft.
Lower Level: 1,333 sq. ft.
Total: 3,546 sq. ft.
Bonus Space: 430 sq. ft.
Bedrooms: 4
Bathrooms: 3 ½
Width: 67' - 2"
Depth: 93' - 1"
Foundation: Finished Walkout Basement

EPLANS.COM

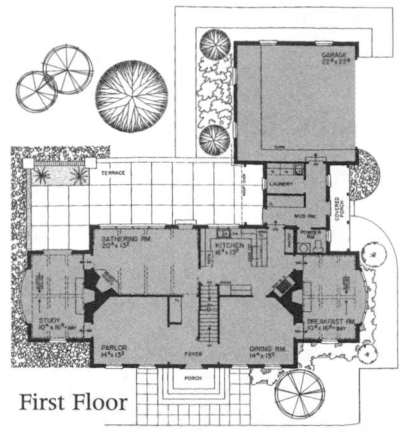

First Floor

Second Floor

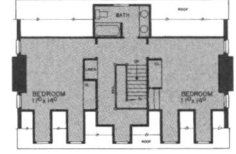

Third Floor

HPK2101240

Style: Georgian
First Floor: 1,735 sq. ft.
Second Floor: 1,075 sq. ft.
Third Floor: 746 sq. ft.
Total: 3,556 sq. ft.
Bedrooms: 5
Bathrooms: 3 ½
Width: 64' - 0"
Depth: 64' - 0"
Foundation: Unfinished Basement

EPLANS.COM

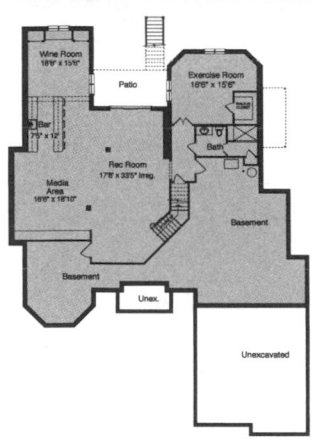

First Floor

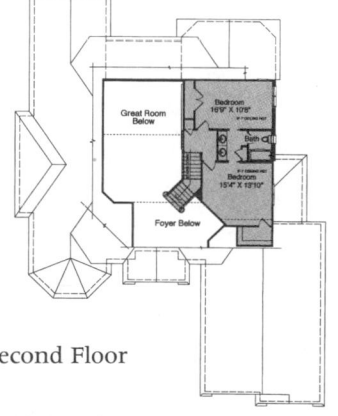

Second Floor

HPK2101241

Style: French Country
First Floor: 3,014 sq. ft.
Second Floor: 621 sq. ft.
Total: 3,635 sq. ft.
Bedrooms: 3
Bathrooms: 2 ½ + ½
Width: 65' - 0"
Depth: 88' - 11"
Foundation: Unfinished Walkout Basement

EPLANS.COM

3,500 TO 3,999 SQUARE FEET

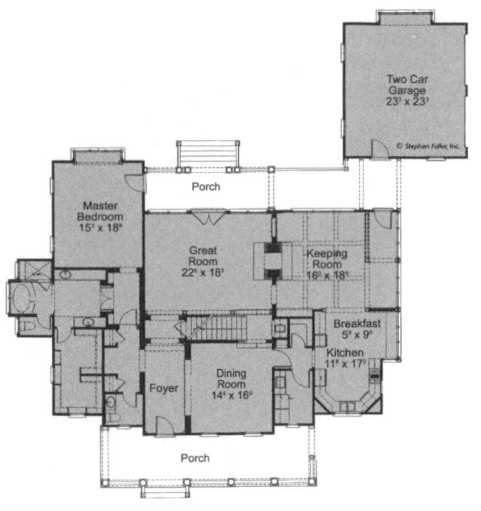

First Floor

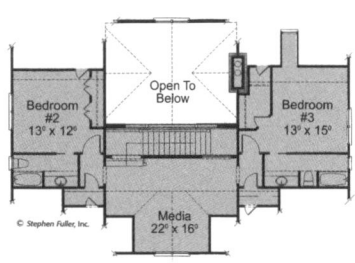

Second Floor

HPK2101242

Style: Cottage
First Floor: 2,565 sq. ft.
Second Floor: 1,075 sq. ft.
Total: 3,640 sq. ft.
Bedrooms: 3
Bathrooms: 3 ½
Width: 68' - 3"
Depth: 31' - 3"
Foundation: Walkout Basement

HPK2101243

Style: Craftsman
Main Level: 1,977 sq. ft.
Lower Level: 1,668 sq. ft.
Total: 3,645 sq. ft.
Bedrooms: 3
Bathrooms: 4
Width: 108' - 6"
Depth: 56' - 0"
Foundation: Finished Basement

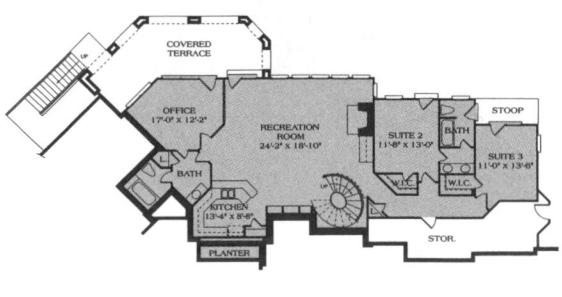

Lower Level

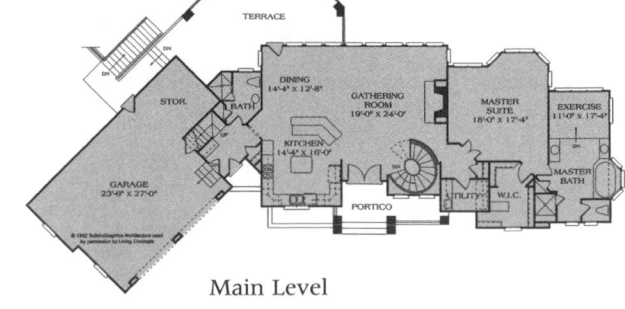

Main Level

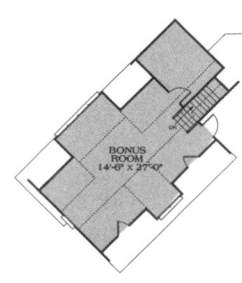

3,500 TO 3,999 SQUARE FEET

HPK2101244

Style: New American
Main Level: 1,458 sq. ft.
Upper Level: 1,513 sq. ft.
Lower Level: 707 sq. ft.
Total: 3,678 sq. ft.
Bedrooms: 4
Bathrooms: 3 ½
Width: 55' - 8"
Depth: 44' - 10"
Foundation: Unfinished Basement

EPLANS.COM

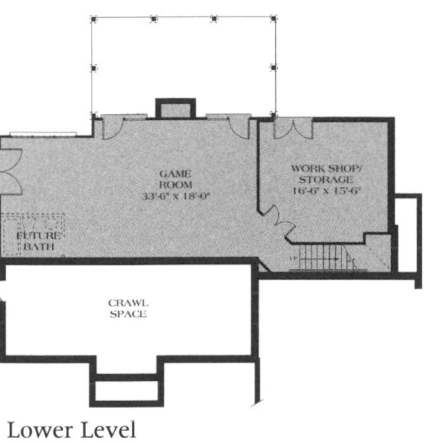

Lower Level

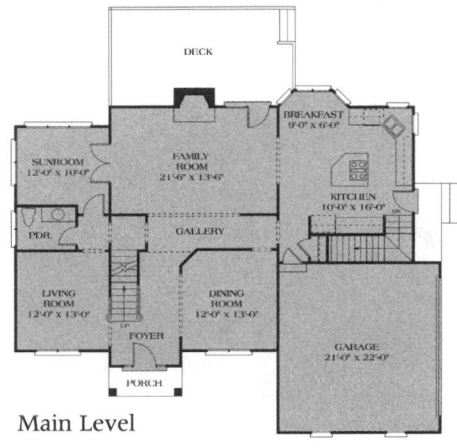

Main Level

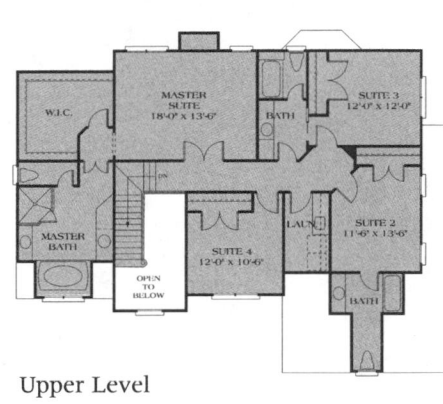

Upper Level

HPK2101245

EPLANS.COM

Style: Queen Anne
First Floor: 1,538 sq. ft.
Second Floor: 1,526 sq. ft.
Third Floor: 658 sq. ft.
Total: 3,722 sq. ft.
Bedrooms: 5
Bathrooms: 3 ½
Width: 67' - 0"
Depth: 66' - 0"
Foundation: Unfinished Basement

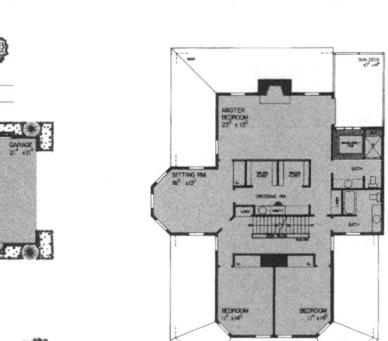

First Floor

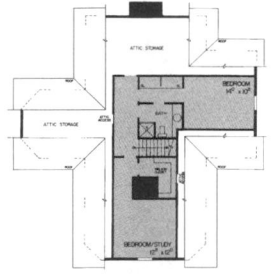

Second Floor

Third Floor

3,500 TO 3,999 SQUARE FEET

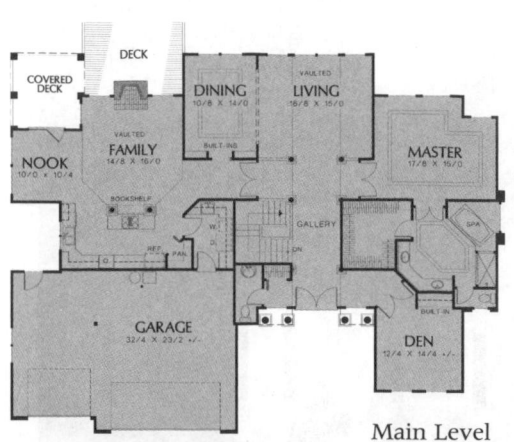

Main Level

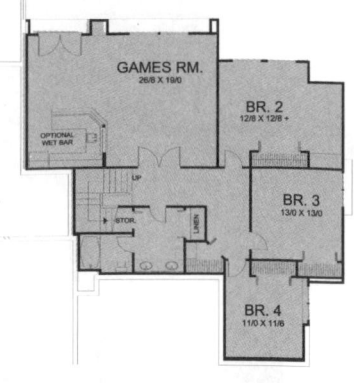

Lower Level

HPK2101246

Style: Mediterranean

Main Level: 2,196 sq. ft.

Lower Level: 1,542 sq. ft.

Total: 3,738 sq. ft.

Bedrooms: 4

Bathrooms: 2 ½

Width: 72' - 0"

Depth: 56' - 0"

Foundation: Crawlspace, Finished Walkout Basement

EPLANS.COM

Bob Greenspan. This home, as shown in photographs, may differ from the actual blueprints. For more detailed information, please check the floor plans carefully.

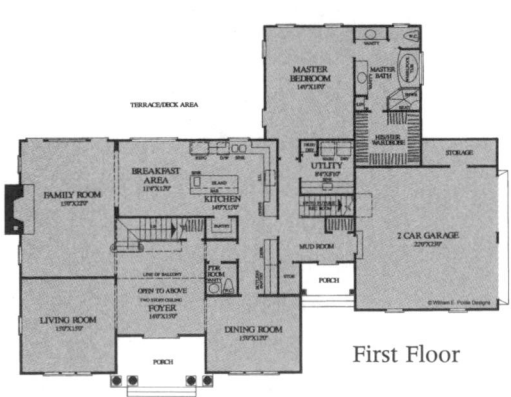

First Floor

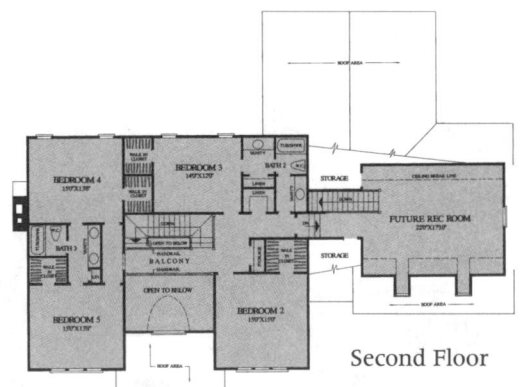

Second Floor

HPK2101247

Style: Colonial Revival

First Floor: 2,327 sq. ft.

Second Floor: 1,431 sq. ft.

Total: 3,758 sq. ft.

Bonus Space: 473 sq. ft.

Bedrooms: 5

Bathrooms: 3 ½

Width: 78' - 10"

Depth: 58' - 2"

Foundation: Crawlspace, Unfinished Basement

EPLANS.COM

© William E. Poole Designs, Inc.

Lower Level

Main Level

Upper Level

HPK2101248

Style: New American

Main Level: 1,878 sq. ft.

Upper Level: 886 sq. ft.

Lower Level: 1,042 sq. ft.

Total: 3,806 sq. ft.

Bedrooms: 5

Bathrooms: 4 ½

Width: 67' - 10"

Depth: 56' - 4"

Foundation: Finished Walkout Basement

EPLANS.COM

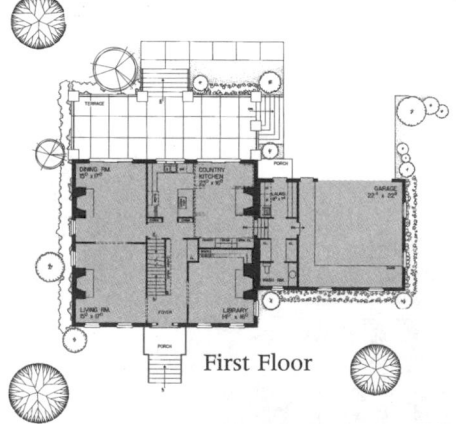

First Floor

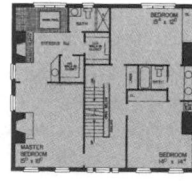

Second Floor

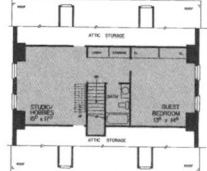

Third Floor

HPK2101249

Style: Federal - Adams

First Floor: 1,656 sq. ft.

Second Floor: 1,440 sq. ft.

Third Floor: 715 sq. ft.

Total: 3,811 sq. ft.

Bedrooms: 4

Bathrooms: 3 ½

Width: 72' - 0"

Depth: 36' - 0"

Foundation: Unfinished Basement

EPLANS.COM

3,500 TO 3,999 SQUARE FEET

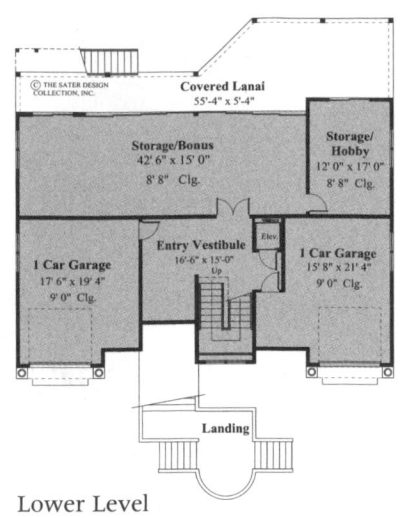

Lower Level

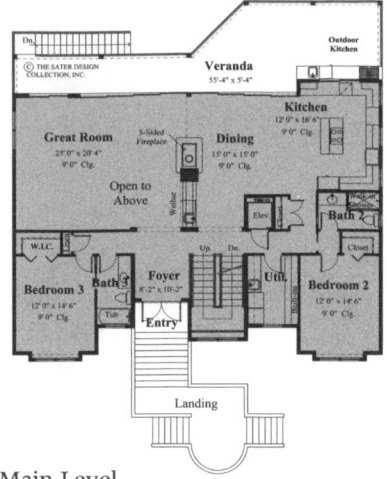

Main Level

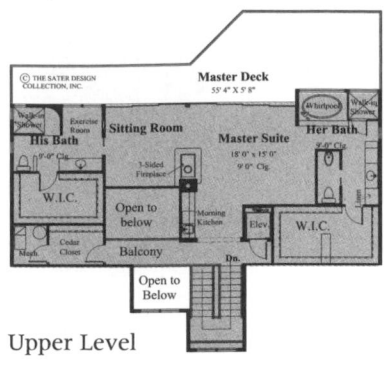

Upper Level

A transom creates a picture-perfect entry and complements the arch-top windows of this exquisite villa. The foyer opens to a central gallery with extensive views through the interior. The great room creates an environment for grand entertaining or cozy gatherings; a wet bar and three-sided fireplace help define the space. The upper floor is dedicated to a rambling master suite, which provides a sitting area, three-sided fireplace, and separate baths and wardrobes. An elevator connects three levels.

HPK2101250

Style: Italianate
Main Level: 2,039 sq. ft.
Upper Level: 1,426 sq. ft.
Lower Level: 374 sq. ft.
Total: 3,839 sq. ft.
Bedrooms: 3
Bathrooms: 4
Width: 56' - 0"
Depth: 54' - 0"
Foundation: Island Basement

EPLANS.COM

HPK2101251

Style: French Country
Main Level: 1,742 sq. ft.
Upper Level: 777 sq. ft.
Lower Level: 1,386 sq. ft.
Total: 3,905 sq. ft.
Bonus Space: 644 sq. ft.
Bedrooms: 3
Bathrooms: 2 ½
Width: 53' - 4"
Depth: 63' - 4"
Foundation: Finished Basement

Extremely cost-effective to build, this house makes great use of interior space. The foyer opens to a two-story grand room, which features a fireplace and an elegant Palladian window. A full kitchen connects the dining room and brightly lit morning room. The master suite overlooks the backyard through a bay window. An expansive walk-in closet and garden tub grace the master bath. A U-shaped staircase leads up to a loft and two additional suites that share a bath. The bonus room provides space for a home office or playroom.

3,500 TO 3,999 SQUARE FEET

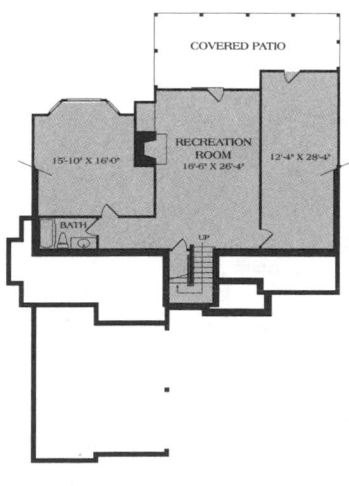

Lower Level

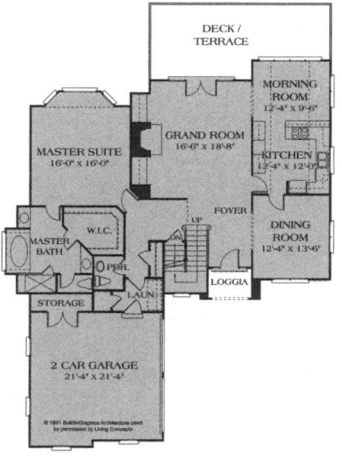

Main Level

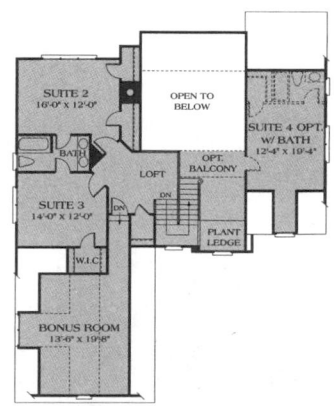

Upper Level

HPK2101252

Style: French Country
Main Level: 2,075 sq. ft.
Upper Level: 859 sq. ft.
Lower Level: 987 sq. ft.
Total: 3,921 sq. ft.
Bonus Space: 262 sq. ft.
Bedrooms: 4
Bathrooms: 4 ½
Width: 70' - 4"
Depth: 67' - 4"
Foundation: Finished Walkout Basement

EPLANS.COM

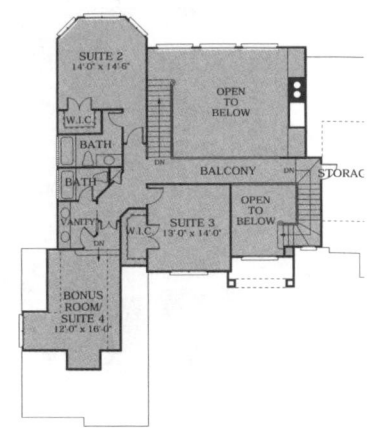

Upper Level

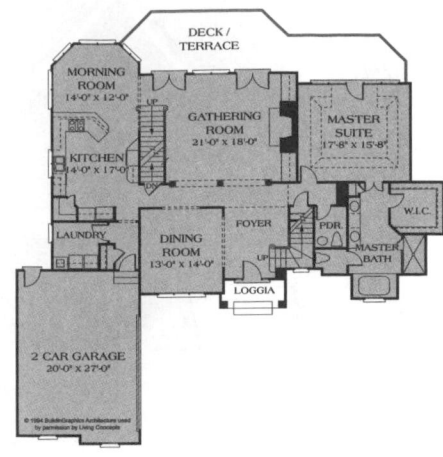

Main Level

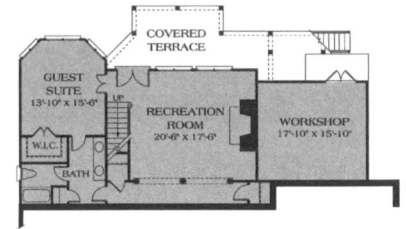

Lower Level

A European-influenced stone entrance graces the exterior of this magnificent house. Inside, a columned entry ushers guests into a two-story gathering room that includes a pair of spectacular arched windows and a fireplace. The dining room is just a step away from the generous kitchen, which opens into a bay-windowed morning room. An immense master suite features a tray ceiling, walk-in closet, and dual vanities in the relaxing bath. A second-floor balcony overlooking the gathering room and foyer leads to two additional suites and a bonus room.

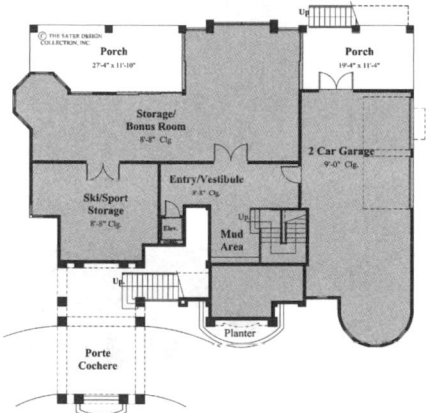

First Floor

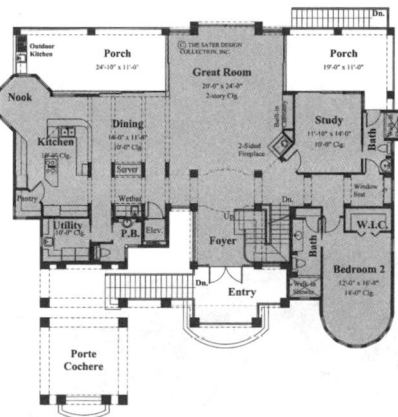

First Floor

Second Floor

HPK2101253

Style: Craftsman

First Floor: 2,391 sq. ft.

Second Floor: 1,539 sq. ft.

Total: 3,930 sq. ft.

Bedrooms: 3

Bathrooms: 4 ½

Width: 71' - 0"

Depth: 69' - 0"

Foundation: Island Basement

Climate is a key component of any mountain retreat, and outdoor living is an integral part of its design. This superior cabin features open and covered porches. A mix of matchstick details and rugged stone sets off this lodge-house facade, concealing a well-defined interior. Windows line the breakfast bay and brighten the kitchen, which features a center cooktop island. A door leads out to a covered porch with a summer kitchen. The upper level features a secluded master suite with a spacious bath. A two-sided fireplace extends warmth to the whirlpool spa-style tub.

EPLANS.COM

3,500 TO 3,999 SQUARE FEET

HPK2101254

Style: Georgian

First Floor: 2,416 sq. ft.

Second Floor: 1,535 sq. ft.

Total: 3,951 sq. ft.

Bonus Space: 552 sq. ft.

Bedrooms: 5

Bathrooms: 3 ½

Width: 79' - 2"

Depth: 63' - 6"

Foundation: Crawlspace, Unfinished Basement

EPLANS.COM

A curved front porch, graceful symmetry in the details, and the sturdiness of brick all combine to enhance this beautiful two-story home. The L-shaped kitchen provides a walk-in pantry, an island with a sink, a butler's pantry, and an adjacent breakfast area. Perfect for casual gatherings, the family room features a fireplace and backyard access. Located on the first floor for privacy, the master suite offers a large walk-in closet and a lavish bath. Upstairs, four bedrooms—each with a walk-in closet—share two full baths and access to the future recreation room over the garage.

First Floor

Second Floor

© William E. Poole Designs, Inc.

HPK2101255

Style: Federal - Adams
First Floor: 1,541 sq. ft.
Second Floor: 1,408 sq. ft.
Third Floor: 1,016 sq. ft.
Total: 3,965 sq. ft.
Bedrooms: 4
Bathrooms: 3 ½
Width: 44' - 0"
Depth: 43' - 0"
Foundation: Unfinished Basement

EPLANS.COM

This Federal-style home is beautiful in its simplicity. The interior is a traditional center-hall layout, with formal rooms toward the front and more relaxed spaces in the back. A U-shaped kitchen is ideally positioned for serving the dining room, and also the nearby circular breakfast room. Three fireplaces warm the rooms on the first floor, while a fourth hearth warms the master bedroom upstairs. The two remaining bedrooms upstairs share a full hall bath. There is an additional guest suite on the third floor, complete with its own bath and walk-in closet, as well as a spacious studio.

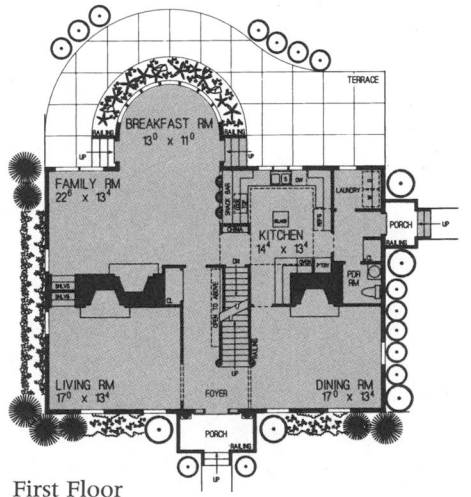

First Floor

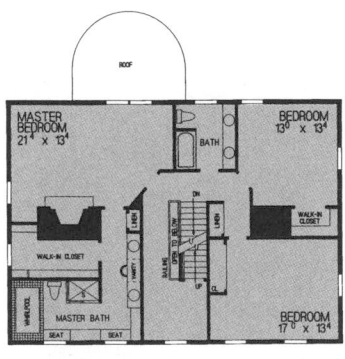

Second Floor

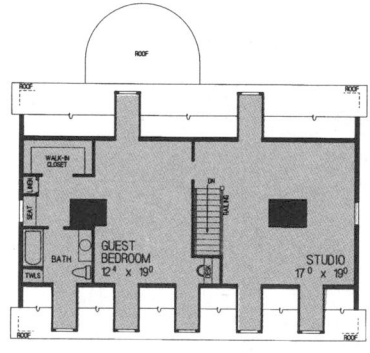

Third Floor

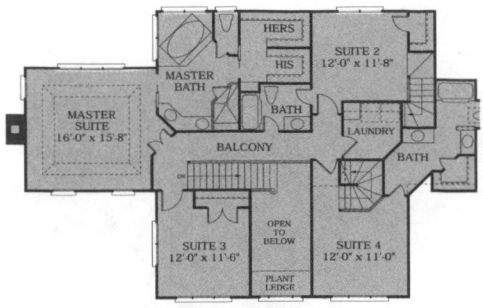

Upper Level

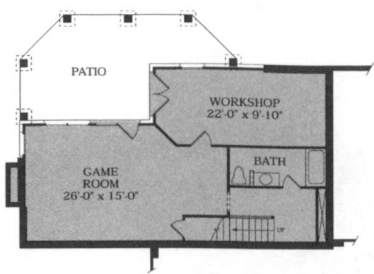

Lower Level

Main Level

HPK2101256

Style: Colonial Revival
Main Level: 1,318 sq. ft.
Upper Level: 1,575 sq. ft.
Lower Level: 824 sq. ft.
Total: 3,969 sq. ft.
Bedrooms: 4
Bathrooms: 3 ½
Width: 67' - 8"
Depth: 45' - 6"
Foundation: Finished Walkout Basement

EPLANS.COM

A handsome brick facade and elegant window treatments introduce this lavish Colonial estate. In the family room, a cozy fireplace and deck access are sure to make this room a favorite. The gourmet kitchen will delight with a cooktop island. The upper-level master suite is romantic with a tray ceiling and a lush bath with a unique garden tub. Three family suites share two full baths. An optional loft and the finished basement allow room to grow.

HPK2101257

Style: French Country

Main Level: 2,172 sq. ft.

Lower Level: 1,813 sq. ft.

Total: 3,985 sq. ft.

Bedrooms: 4

Bathrooms: 3 ½

Width: 75' - 0"

Depth: 49' - 0"

Foundation: Finished Walkout Basement

EPLANS.COM

With the Craftsman stylings of a mountain lodge, this rustic four-bedroom home is full of surprises. The foyer opens to the right to the great room, warmed by a stone hearth. A corner media center is convenient for entertaining. The dining room, with a furniture alcove, opens to the side terrace, inviting meals alfresco. The master suite is expansive, with French doors, a private bath, and spa tub. On the lower level, two bedrooms share a bath; a third enjoys a private suite. The games room includes a fireplace, media center, wet bar, and wine cellar.

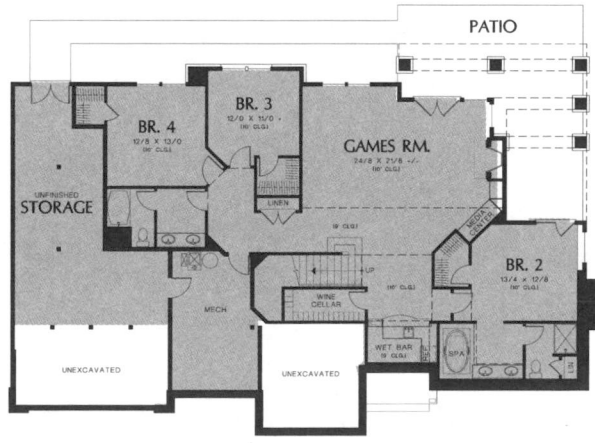

Lower Level

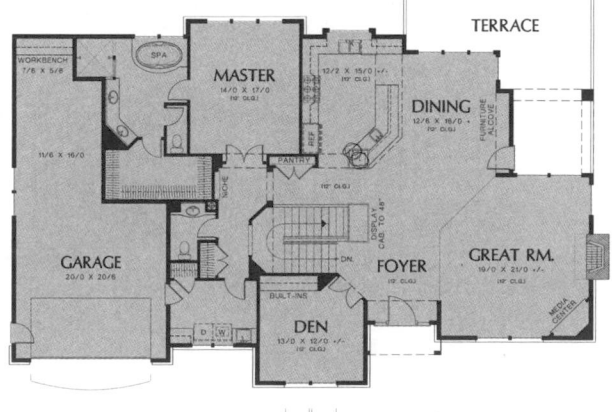

Main Level

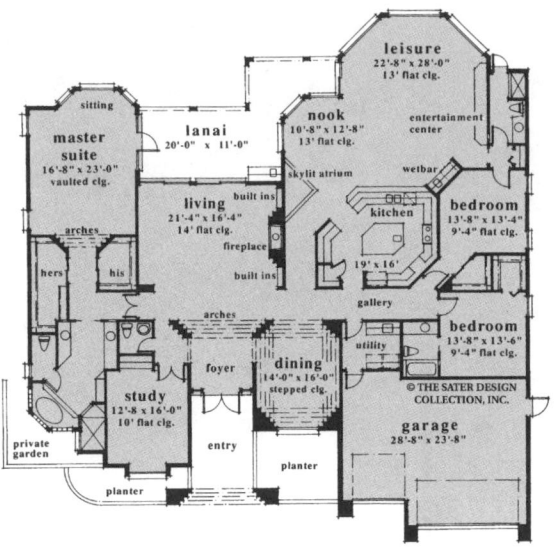

sitting

master suite
16'-8" x 23'-0"
vaulted clg.

lanai
20'-0" x 11'-0"

nook
10'-8" x 12'-8"
13' flat clg.

leisure
22'-8" x 28'-0"
13' flat clg.

entertainment center

arches

hers   his

living
21'-4" x 16'-4"
14' flat clg.

fireplace

built ins

built ins

skylit atrium

kitchen

wetbar

bedroom
13'-8" x 13'-4"
9'-4" flat clg.

19' x 16'

gallery

arches

foyer

dining
14'-0" x 16'-0"
stepped clg.

utility

bedroom
13'-8" x 13'-6"
9'-4" flat clg.

© THE SATER DESIGN COLLECTION, INC.

study
12'-8" x 16'-0"
10' flat clg.

private garden

entry

planter

planter

garage
28'-8" x 23'-8"

planter

HPK2101258

Style: Mediterranean

Square Footage: 4,028

Bedrooms: 3

Bathrooms: 3 ½

Width: 80' - 0"

Depth: 82' - 8"

Foundation: Slab

EPLANS.COM

An interesting roofline adds charm to this home; custom details make it luxurious. The foyer and dining room feature stepped arches and ceiling treatments. The gallery leads past the indoor planter to the large kitchen, nook, and leisure room. A built-in entertainment center and wet bar are nice touches. The secondary bedrooms are full guest suites in their own right, but do not overshadow the master bedroom with bayed sitting area and marvelous bath. A three-car garage connects to the main house via a utility room.

© The Sater Design Collection, Inc.

HPK2101259

Style: Mediterranean

Square Footage: 4,222

Bonus Space: 590 sq. ft.

Bedrooms: 4

Bathrooms: 5

Width: 83' - 10"

Depth: 112' - 0"

Foundation: Slab

EPLANS.COM

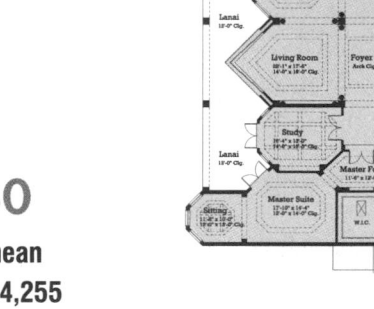

HPK2101260

Style: Mediterranean

Square Footage: 4,255

Bedrooms: 3

Bathrooms: 3 ½

Width: 91' - 6"

Depth: 116' - 11"

Foundation: Slab

EPLANS.COM

4,000 SQUARE FEET AND OVER

HPK2101261

Style: Italianate
Square Footage: 4,282
Bedrooms: 3
Bathrooms: 4
Width: 88' - 0"
Depth: 133' - 0"
Foundation: Slab

EPLANS.COM

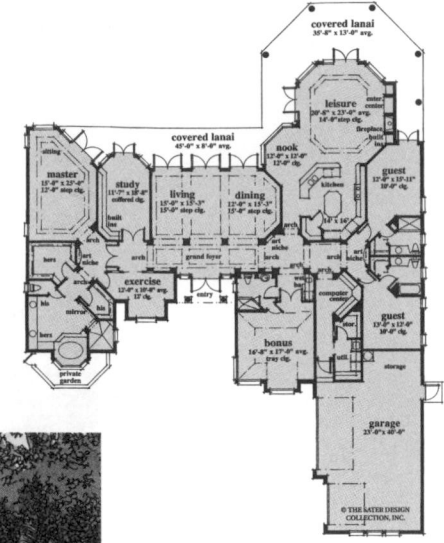

HPK2101262

Style: Colonial
Square Footage: 4,302
Bedrooms: 3
Bathrooms: 3 ½
Width: 104' - 0"
Depth: 111' - 0"
Foundation: Slab

EPLANS.COM

Rear Exterior

ORDER BLUEPRINTS ANYTIME AT EPLANS.COM OR 1-800-521-6797

Photo by: Tom Harper. This home, as shown in photographs, may differ from the actual blueprints. For more detailed information, please check the floor plans carefully.

HPK2101263

Style: New American

Square Footage: 4,523

Bedrooms: 4

Bathrooms: 4 ½

Width: 114' - 4"

Depth: 82' - 3"

EPLANS.COM

Rear Exterior

Rear Exterior

HPK2101264

Style: Italianate

Square Footage: 4,534

Bedrooms: 3

Bathrooms: 4 ½

Width: 87' - 2"

Depth: 127' - 11"

Foundation: Slab

EPLANS.COM

4,000 SQUARE FEET AND OVER

HPK2101265

Style: Italianate
Square Footage: 4,534
Bedrooms: 3
Bathrooms: 4 ½
Width: 98' - 5"
Depth: 126' - 11"
Foundation: Slab

EPLANS.COM

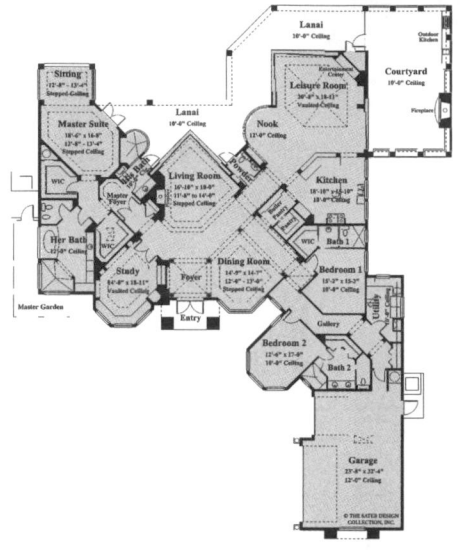

Rear Exterior

HPK2101266

Style: Mission
Square Footage: 4,565
Bedrooms: 3
Bathrooms: 3 ½
Width: 88' - 0"
Depth: 95' - 0"
Foundation: Slab

EPLANS.COM

Rear Exterior

ORDER BLUEPRINTS ANYTIME AT EPLANS.COM OR 1-800-521-6797

HPK2101267

Style: French Country

Square Footage: 4,615

Bedrooms: 4

Bathrooms: 4 ½

Width: 109' - 10"

Depth: 89' - 4"

Foundation: Slab

EPLANS.COM

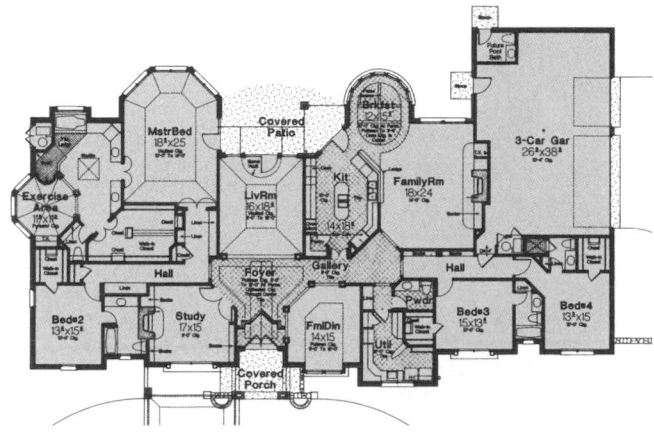

HPK2101268

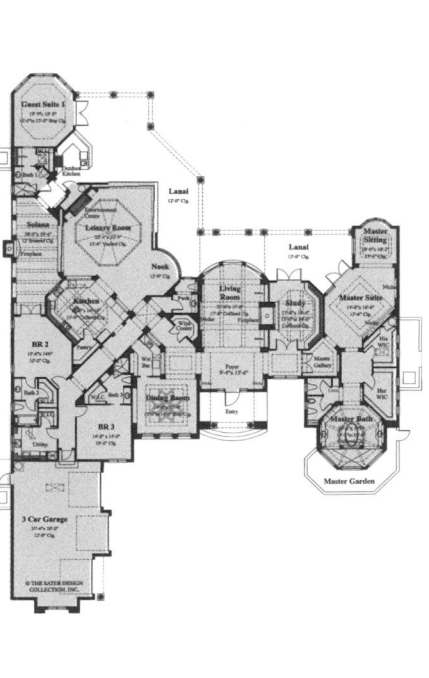

EPLANS.COM

Style: Mediterranean

Square Footage: 5,109

Bedrooms: 4

Bathrooms: 4 ½

Width: 100' - 0"

Depth: 138' - 10"

Foundation: Slab

4,000 SQUARE FEET AND OVER

HPK2101269

Style: Italianate

Square Footage: 5,169

Bonus Space: 565 sq. ft.

Bedrooms: 3

Bathrooms: 4 ½

Width: 98' - 5"

Depth: 126' - 11"

Foundation: Slab

EPLANS.COM

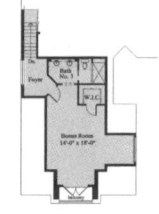

HPK2101270

Style: Mediterranean

Square Footage: 5,199

Bonus Space: 554 sq. ft.

Bedrooms: 3

Bathrooms: 4 ½

Width: 99' - 9"

Depth: 127' - 3"

Foundation: Slab

EPLANS.COM

ORDER BLUEPRINTS ANYTIME AT EPLANS.COM OR 1-800-521-6797

HPK2101271

Style: Prairie

Square Footage: 5,628

Bedrooms: 5

Bathrooms: 5 ½

Width: 165' - 0"

Depth: 115' - 8"

Foundation: Slab

A unique X-shaped floor plan manages to accommodate over 5,000 square feet of living space and amenities on one level. Raised and recessed planters greet visitors at the entryway and along the exterior, and a raised planter subtly yet elegantly separates the great room from the foyer.

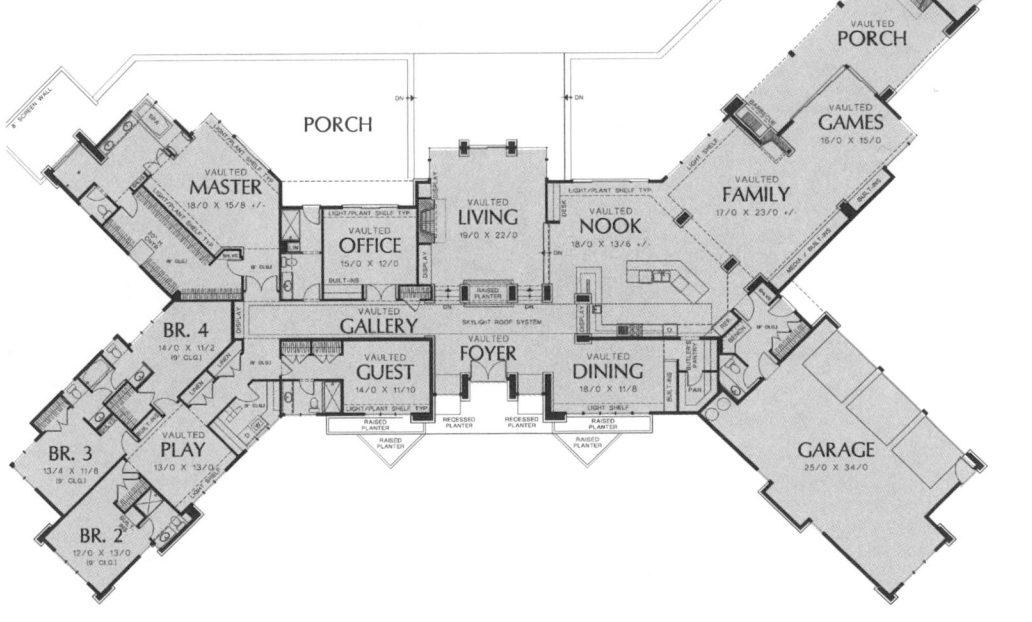

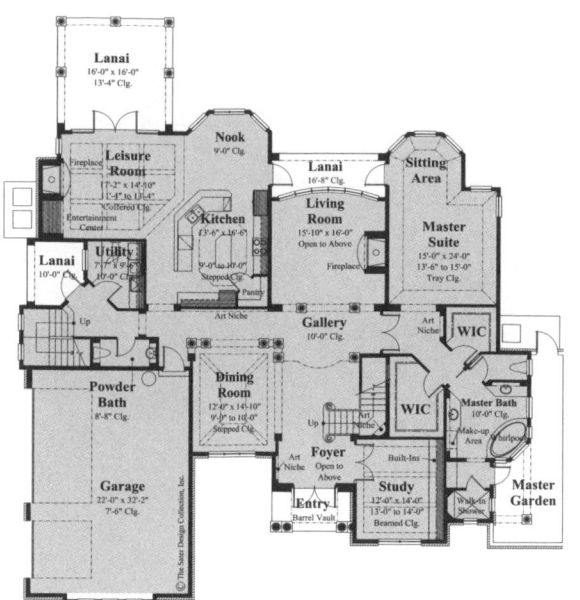

First Floor

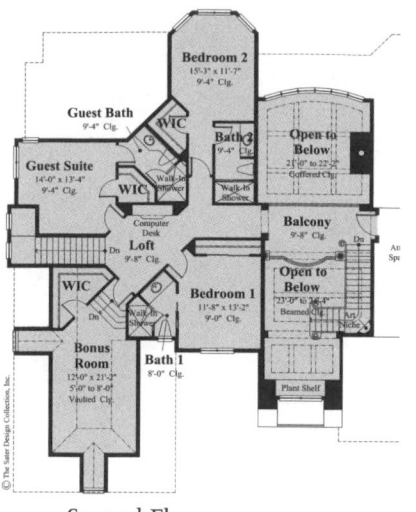

Second Floor

HPK2101272

Style: Italianate

First Floor: 2,850 sq. ft.

Second Floor: 1,155 sq. ft.

Total: 4,005 sq. ft.

Bonus Space: 371 sq. ft.

Bedrooms: 4

Bathrooms: 4 ½

Width: 71' - 6"

Depth: 83' - 0"

Foundation: Slab

EPLANS.COM

Stone, stucco, and soaring rooflines combine to give this elegant Mediterranean design a stunning exterior. The interior is packed with luxurious amenities, from the wall of glass in the living room to the whirlpool tub in the master bath. A dining room and study serve as formal areas, while a leisure room with a fireplace offers a relaxing retreat. The first-floor master suite boasts a private bayed sitting area. Upstairs, all three bedrooms include private baths; Bedroom 2 and the guest suite also provide walk-in closets.

© The Sater Design Collection, Inc.

© The Sater Design Collection, Inc.

First Floor

Second Floor

HPK2101273

Style: New American

First Floor: 2,850 sq. ft.

Second Floor: 1,155 sq. ft.

Total: 4,005 sq. ft.

Bonus Space: 371 sq. ft.

Bedrooms: 4

Bathrooms: 4 ½

Width: 71' - 6"

Depth: 83' - 0"

Foundation: Slab

EPLANS.COM

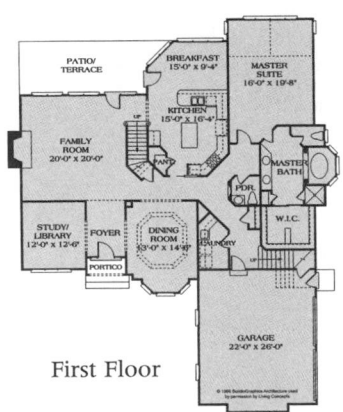

First Floor

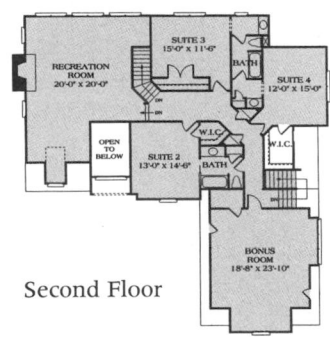

Second Floor

HPK2101274

Style: New American

First Floor: 2,340 sq. ft.

Second Floor: 1,666 sq. ft.

Total: 4,006 sq. ft.

Bonus Space: 570 sq. ft.

Bedrooms: 4

Bathrooms: 3 ½

Width: 62' - 8"

Depth: 75' - 6"

Foundation: Crawlspace

EPLANS.COM

4,000 SQUARE FEET AND OVER

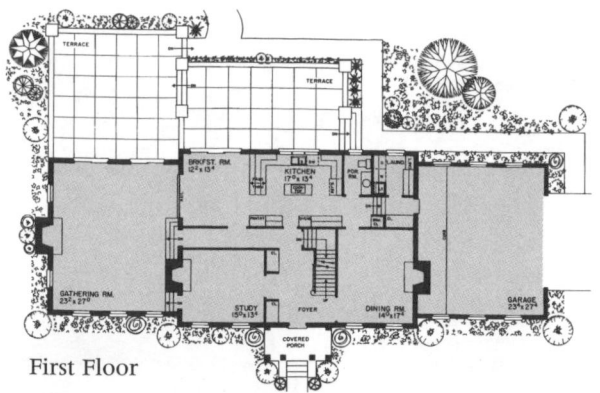

First Floor

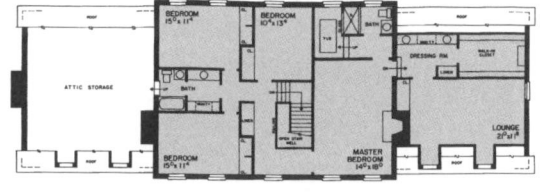

Second Floor

HPK2101275

Style: Georgian
First Floor: 2,126 sq. ft.
Second Floor: 1,882 sq. ft.
Total: 4,008 sq. ft.
Bedrooms: 4
Bathrooms: 2 ½
Width: 92' - 0"
Depth: 64' - 4"
Foundation: Unfinished Basement

EPLANS.COM

HPK2101276

Style: New American
First Floor: 2,867 sq. ft.
Second Floor: 1,155 sq. ft.
Total: 4,022 sq. ft.
Bonus Space: 371 sq. ft.
Bedrooms: 4
Bathrooms: 4 ½
Width: 71' - 6"
Depth: 82' - 2"
Foundation: Slab

EPLANS.COM

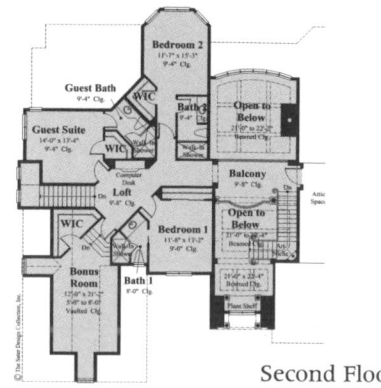

First Floor

Second Floor

© The Sater Design Collection, Inc.

ORDER BLUEPRINTS ANYTIME AT EPLANS.COM OR 1-800-521-6797

First Floor

Second Floor

HPK2101277

Style: New American

First Floor: 2,430 sq. ft.

Second Floor: 1,594 sq. ft.

Total: 4,024 sq. ft.

Bonus Space: 405 sq. ft.

Bedrooms: 4

Bathrooms: 4 ½

Width: 81' - 0"

Depth: 77' - 0"

Foundation: Crawlspace, Unfinished Walkout Basement

EPLANS.COM

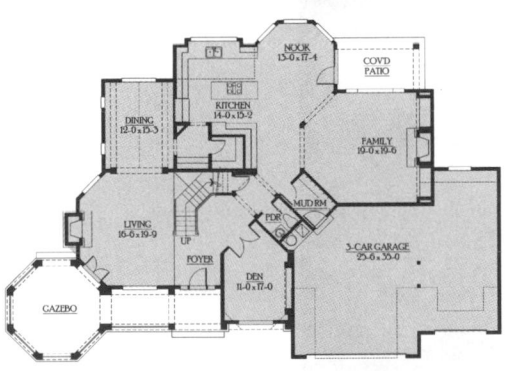

First Floor

Second Floor

HPK2101278

EPLANS.COM

Style: Craftsman

First Floor: 2,010 sq. ft.

Second Floor: 2,020 sq. ft.

Total: 4,030 sq. ft.

Bedrooms: 4

Bathrooms: 3 ½

Width: 85' - 0"

Depth: 58' - 0"

Foundation: Crawlspace

4,000 SQUARE FEET AND OVER

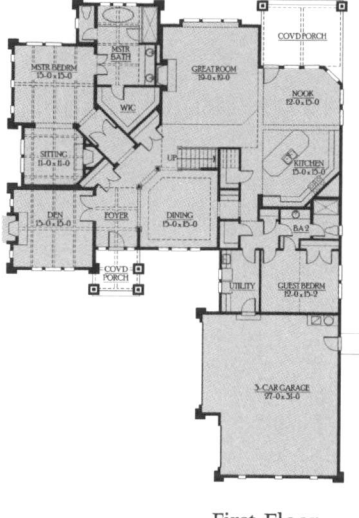

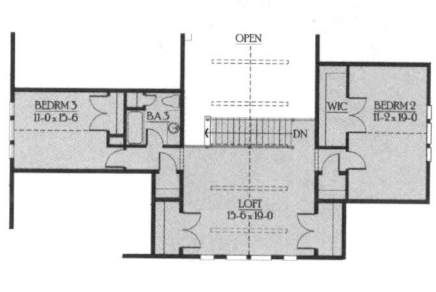

First Floor   Second Floor

HPK2101279

Style: Craftsman

First Floor: 3,005 sq. ft.

Second Floor: 1,030 sq. ft.

Total: 4,035 sq. ft.

Bedrooms: 4

Bathrooms: 3

Width: 66' - 9"

Depth: 93' - 6"

Foundation: Crawlspace

EPLANS.COM

HPK2101280

Style: Beaux Arts

First Floor: 2,608 sq. ft.

Second Floor: 1,432 sq. ft.

Total: 4,040 sq. ft.

Bedrooms: 4

Bathrooms: 3 ½

Width: 89' - 10"

Depth: 63' - 8"

Foundation: Crawlspace, Slab

EPLANS.COM

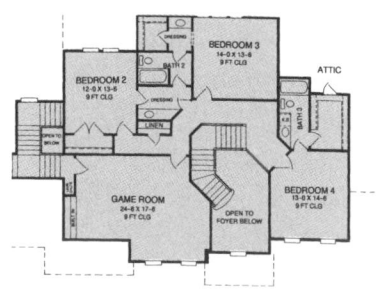

First Floor   Second Floor

HPK2101281

Style: Country
First Floor: 1,999 sq. ft.
Second Floor: 2,046 sq. ft.
Total: 4,045 sq. ft.
Bedrooms: 5
Bathrooms: 4 ½
Width: 66' - 4"
Depth: 64' - 0"
Foundation: Crawlspace, Unfinished Walkout Basement

EPLANS.COM

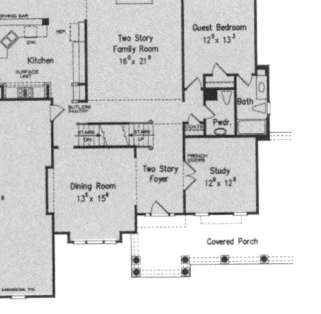

First Floor

Second Floor

HPK2101282

Style: Federal - Adams
First Floor: 2,814 sq. ft.
Second Floor: 1,231 sq. ft.
Total: 4,045 sq. ft.
Bedrooms: 5
Bathrooms: 3 ½
Width: 98' - 0"
Depth: 45' - 10"
Foundation: Slab, Unfinished Basement

EPLANS.COM

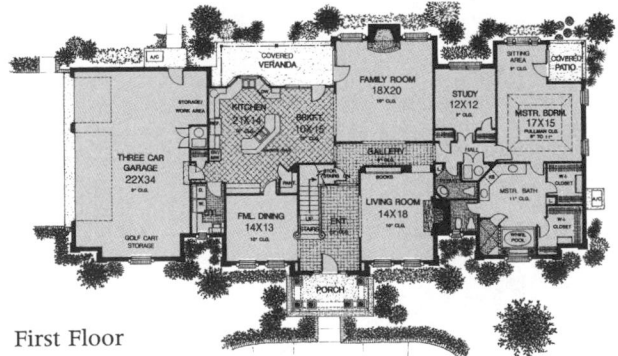

First Floor

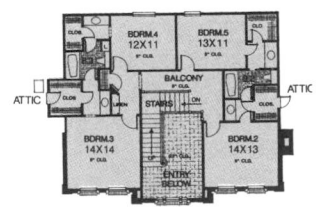

Second Floor

First Floor

Second Floor

HPK2101283

Style: New American

First Floor: 2,095 sq. ft.

Second Floor: 1,954 sq. ft.

Total: 4,049 sq. ft.

Bedrooms: 5

Bathrooms: 4 ½

Width: 56' - 0"

Depth: 63' - 0"

Foundation: Crawlspace, Unfinished Walkout Basement

EPLANS.COM

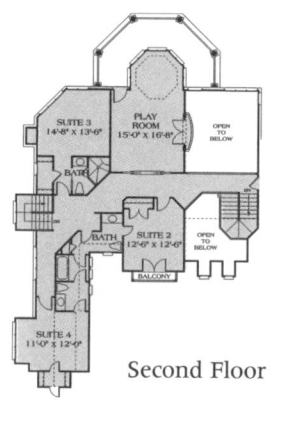

First Floor

Second Floor

HPK2101284

Style: Craftsman

First Floor: 2,430 sq. ft.

Second Floor: 1,624 sq. ft.

Total: 4,054 sq. ft.

Bedrooms: 4

Bathrooms: 3 ½ + ½

Width: 70' - 4"

Depth: 95' - 9"

Foundation: Crawlspace

EPLANS.COM

Rear Exterior

ORDER BLUEPRINTS ANYTIME AT EPLANS.COM OR 1-800-521-6797

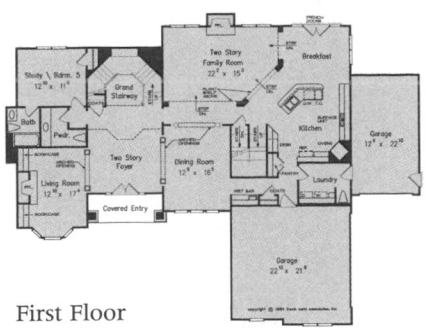

First Floor

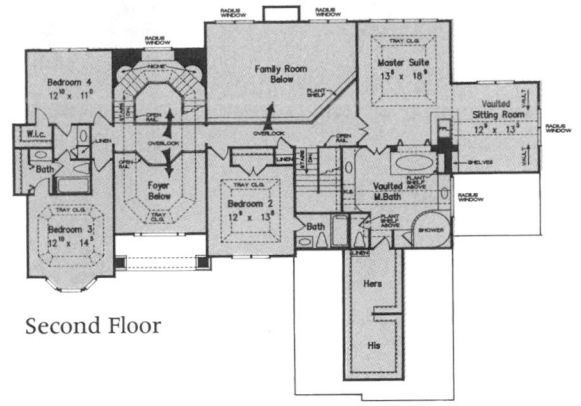

Second Floor

HPK2101285

Style: New American

First Floor: 2,190 sq. ft.

Second Floor: 1,865 sq. ft.

Total: 4,055 sq. ft.

Bedrooms: 5

Bathrooms: 4 ½ + ½

Width: 79' - 0"

Depth: 60' - 4"

Foundation: Slab, Unfinished Walkout Basement

EPLANS.COM

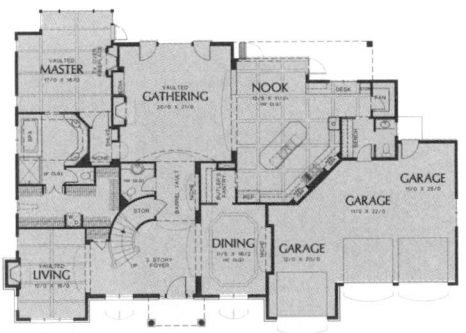

First Floor

Second Floor

HPK2101286

Style: European

First Floor: 2,672 sq. ft.

Second Floor: 1,392 sq. ft.

Total: 4,064 sq. ft.

Bedrooms: 4

Bathrooms: 3 ½ + ½

Width: 80' - 0"

Depth: 57' - 0"

Foundation: Crawlspace

EPLANS.COM

4,000 SQUARE FEET AND OVER

HPK2101287

Style: Colonial Revival

First Floor: 1,773 sq. ft.

Second Floor: 2,293 sq. ft.

Total: 4,066 sq. ft.

Bedrooms: 5

Bathrooms: 4 ½

Width: 69' - 0"

Depth: 54' - 4"

Foundation: Crawlspace, Unfinished Walkout Basement

EPLANS.COM

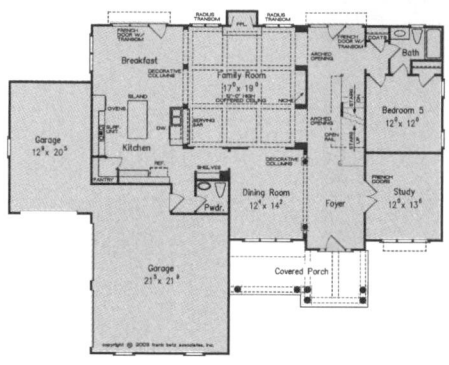

First Floor

Second Floor

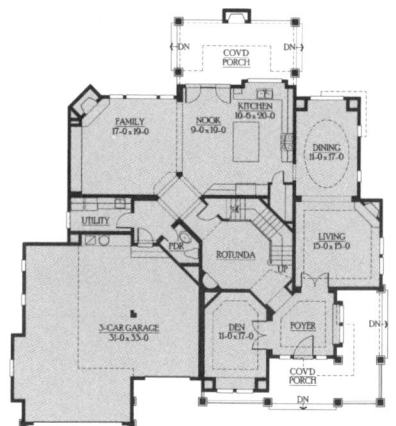

First Floor

HPK2101288

Style: Craftsman

First Floor: 2,000 sq. ft.

Second Floor: 2,084 sq. ft.

Total: 4,084 sq. ft.

Bedrooms: 4

Bathrooms: 3 ½

Width: 66' - 6"

Depth: 74' - 0"

Foundation: Crawlspace

EPLANS.COM

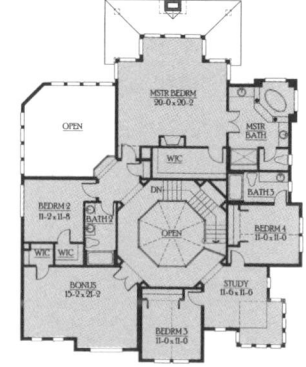

Second Floor

HPK2101289

Style: French Country
First Floor: 2,995 sq. ft.
Second Floor: 1,102 sq. ft.
Total: 4,097 sq. ft.
Bedrooms: 4
Bathrooms: 3 ½
Width: 120' - 6"
Depth: 58' - 8"
Foundation: Slab

EPLANS.COM

First Floor

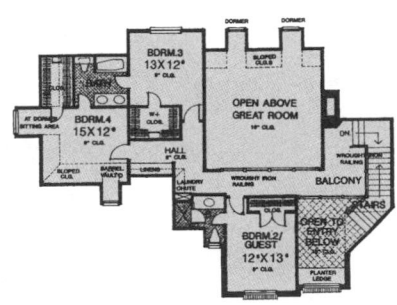

Second Floor

HPK2101290

Style: French Country
First Floor: 2,484 sq. ft.
Second Floor: 1,615 sq. ft.
Total: 4,099 sq. ft.
Bonus Space: 572 sq. ft.
Bedrooms: 4
Bathrooms: 4 ½
Width: 71' - 8"
Depth: 74' - 3"
Foundation: Crawlspace

EPLANS.COM

First Floor

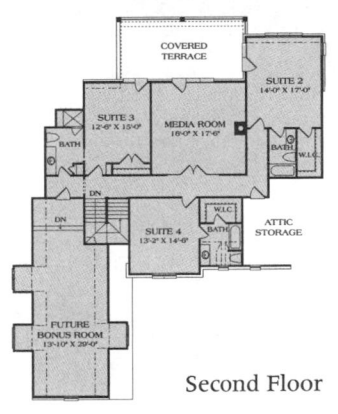

Second Floor

4,000 SQUARE FEET AND OVER

First Floor

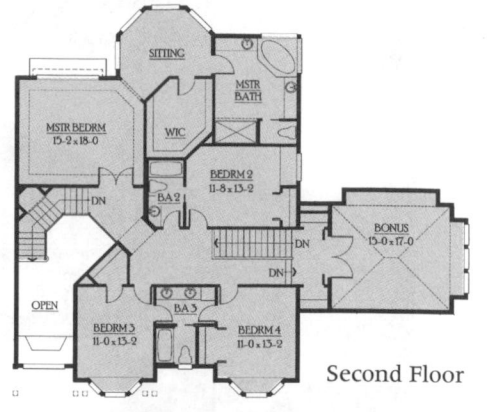

Second Floor

HPK2101291

Style: Craftsman

First Floor: 2,010 sq. ft.

Second Floor: 2,090 sq. ft.

Total: 4,100 sq. ft.

Bedrooms: 4

Bathrooms: 3 ½

Width: 90' - 0"

Depth: 66' - 6"

Foundation: Crawlspace

EPLANS.COM

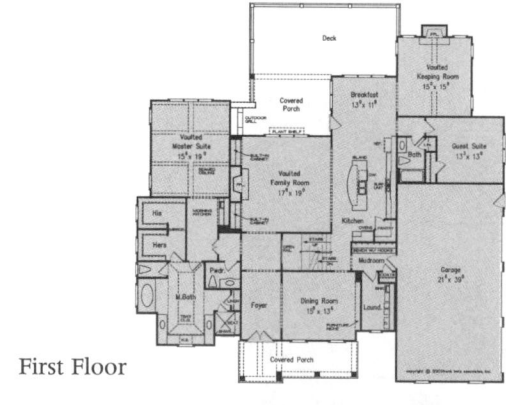

First Floor

Second Floor

HPK2101292

Style: Cottage

First Floor: 2,896 sq. ft.

Second Floor: 1,211 sq. ft.

Total: 4,107 sq. ft.

Bonus Space: 227 sq. ft.

Bedrooms: 5

Bathrooms: 4 ½

Width: 74' - 0"

Depth: 71' - 4"

Foundation: Crawlspace, Unfinished Walkout Basement

EPLANS.COM

ORDER BLUEPRINTS ANYTIME AT EPLANS.COM OR 1-800-521-6797

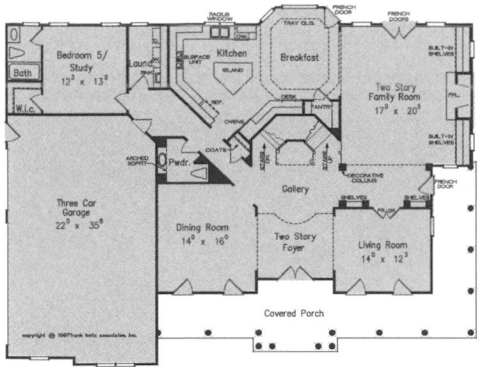

First Floor

Second Floor

HPK2101293

Style: Farmhouse

First Floor: 2,037 sq. ft.

Second Floor: 2,098 sq. ft.

Total: 4,135 sq. ft.

Bedrooms: 5

Bathrooms: 4 ½

Width: 68' - 6"

Depth: 53' - 0"

Foundation: Crawlspace, Slab, Unfinished Walkout Basement

EPLANS.COM

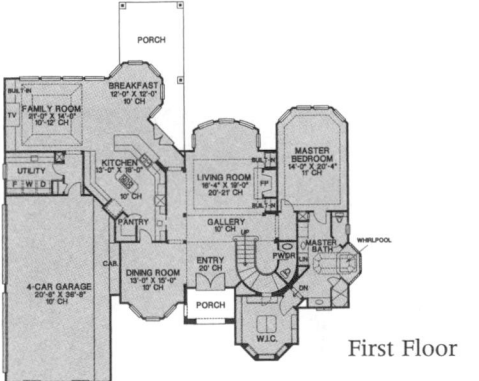

First Floor

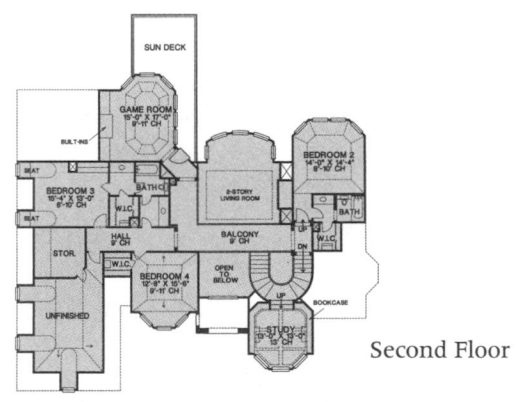

Second Floor

HPK2101294

Style: Mediterranean

First Floor: 2,489 sq. ft.

Second Floor: 1,650 sq. ft.

Total: 4,139 sq. ft.

Bonus Space: 366 sq. ft.

Bedrooms: 4

Bathrooms: 3 ½

Width: 72' - 8"

Depth: 77' - 0"

EPLANS.COM

4,000 SQUARE FEET AND OVER

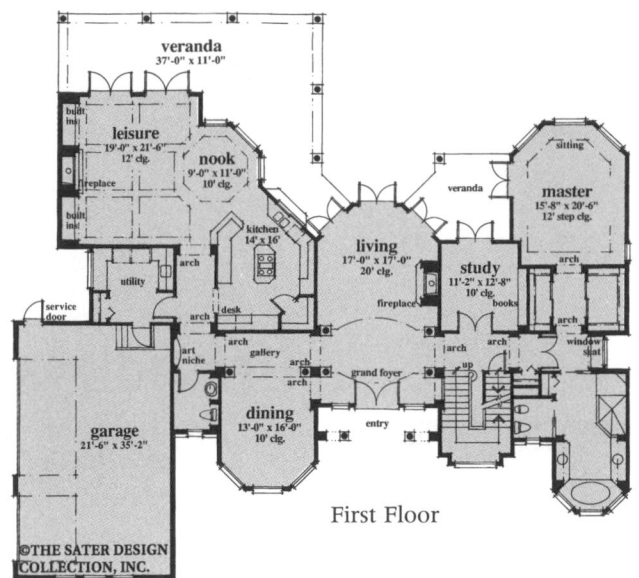

First Floor

©THE SATER DESIGN COLLECTION, INC.

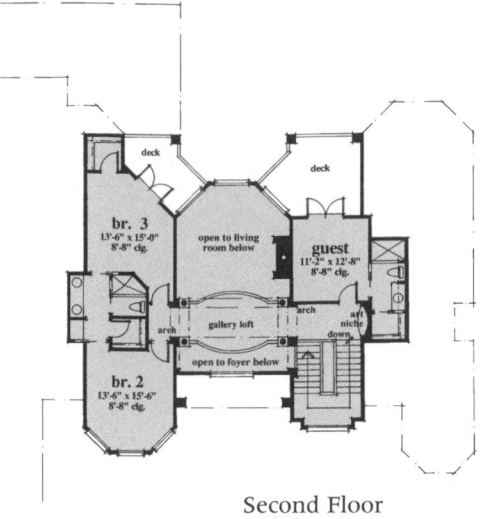

Second Floor

HPK2101295

Style: New American
First Floor: 3,053 sq. ft.
Second Floor: 1,087 sq. ft.
Total: 4,140 sq. ft.
Bedrooms: 4
Bathrooms: 3 ½
Width: 87' - 4"
Depth: 80' - 4"
Foundation: Unfinished Basement

EPLANS.COM

The inside of this design is just as majestic as the outside. The grand foyer opens to a two-story living room with a fireplace and magnificent views. Dining in the bayed formal dining room will be a memorable experience. The master wing includes a separate study and an elegant private bath. The second level features a guest suite with its own bath and deck, two family bedrooms (Bedroom 3 also has its own deck), and a gallery loft with views to the living room below.

© The Sater Design Collection, Inc.

© The Sater Design Collection, Inc.

HPK2101296

Style: New American
First Floor: 2,725 sq. ft.
Second Floor: 1,418 sq. ft.
Total: 4,143 sq. ft.
Bedrooms: 4
Bathrooms: 5 ½
Width: 61' - 4"
Depth: 62' - 0"
Foundation: Pier (same as Piling)

EPLANS.COM

Florida living takes off in this design. A grand room gains attention as an entertaining area. Here, a see-through fireplace divides the room from the dining room. A full bath connects the study to the front right bedroom. Another bedroom sits on the opposite side of the house with its own bath. The kitchen features a large work island and a connecting breakfast nook. Upstairs, the master bedroom suite contains His and Hers baths, a see-through fireplace, and access to the upper deck.

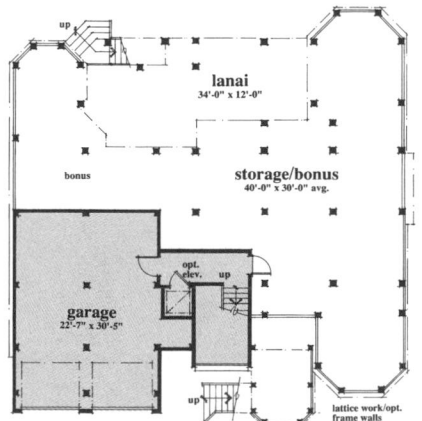

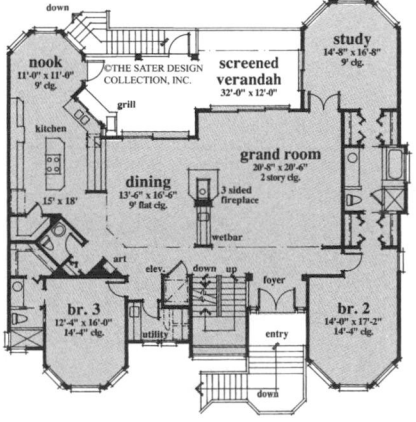

First Floor

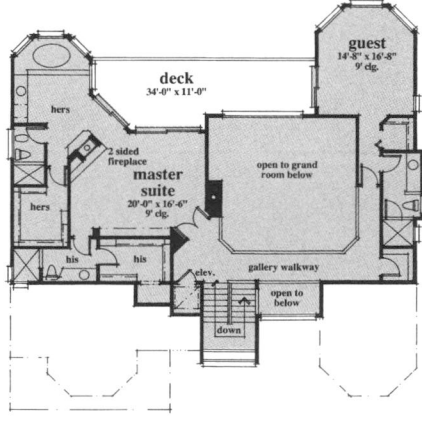

Second Floor

First Floor

Second Floor

HPK2101297

Style: New American
First Floor: 2,502 sq. ft.
Second Floor: 1,645 sq. ft.
Total: 4,147 sq. ft.
Bedrooms: 5
Bathrooms: 3 ½
Width: 95' - 0"
Depth: 51' - 0"
Foundation: Unfinished Basement

EPLANS.COM

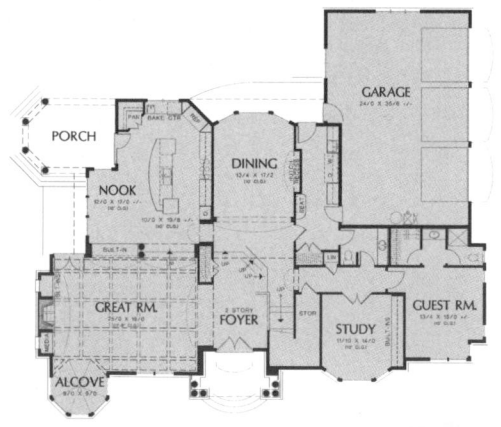

First Floor

Second Floor

HPK2101298

Style: Shingle
First Floor: 2,572 sq. ft.
Second Floor: 1,578 sq. ft.
Total: 4,150 sq. ft.
Bonus Space: 315 sq. ft.
Bedrooms: 4
Bathrooms: 4 ½
Width: 78' - 2"
Depth: 68' - 0"
Foundation: Crawlspace

EPLANS.COM

First Floor

Second Floor

HPK2101299

Style: Italianate

First Floor: 2,852 sq. ft.

Second Floor: 969 sq. ft.

Total: 4,151 sq. ft.

Bonus Space: 330 sq. ft.

Bedrooms: 5

Bathrooms: 4 ½

Width: 80' - 0"

Depth: 96' - 0"

Foundation: Slab

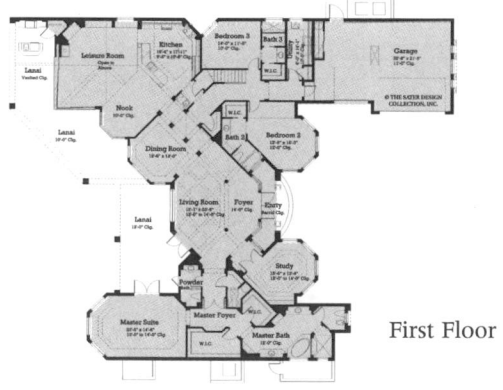

First Floor

Second Floor

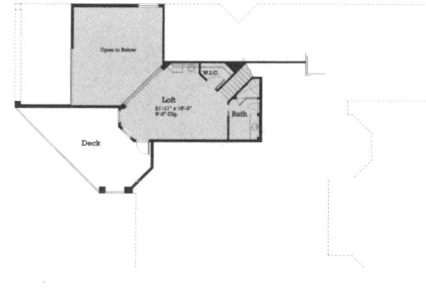

HPK2101300

Style: Mediterranean

First Floor: 3,734 sq. ft.

Second Floor: 418 sq. ft.

Total: 4,152 sq. ft.

Bedrooms: 3

Bathrooms: 4 ½

Width: 82' - 0"

Depth: 107' - 8"

Foundation: Slab

4,000 SQUARE FEET AND OVER

First Floor

Second Floor

HPK2101301

Style: Country
First Floor: 1,839 sq. ft.
Second Floor: 2,320 sq. ft.
Total: 4,159 sq. ft.
Bedrooms: 5
Bathrooms: 3 ½
Width: 61' - 6"
Depth: 61' - 0"
Foundation: Crawlspace, Unfinished Walkout Basement

EPLANS.COM

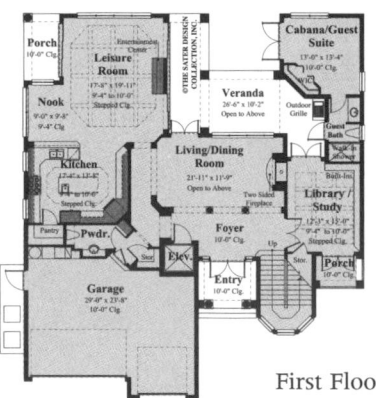

First Floor

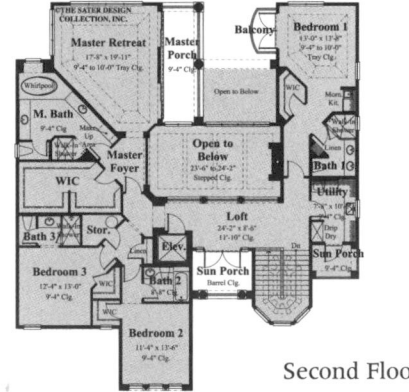

Second Floor

HPK2101302

Style: Italianate
First Floor: 1,995 sq. ft.
Second Floor: 2,165 sq. ft.
Total: 4,160 sq. ft.
Bedrooms: 5
Bathrooms: 5 ½
Width: 58' - 0"
Depth: 65' - 0"
Foundation: Slab

EPLANS.COM

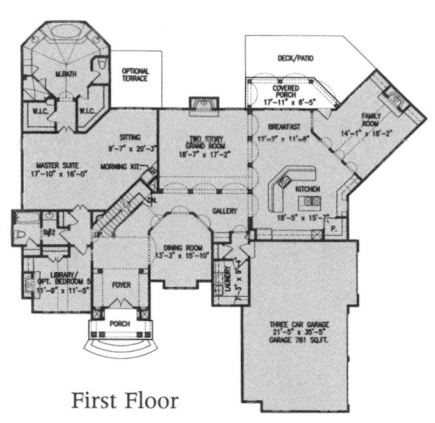

First Floor

Second Floor

HPK2101303

Style: New American

First Floor: 3,011 sq. ft.

Second Floor: 1,151 sq. ft.

Total: 4,162 sq. ft.

Bonus Space: 378 sq. ft.

Bedrooms: 4

Bathrooms: 5

Width: 85' - 2"

Depth: 81' - 4"

Foundation: Unfinished Basement

EPLANS.COM

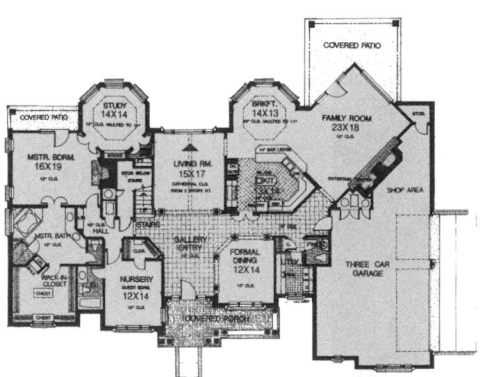

First Floor

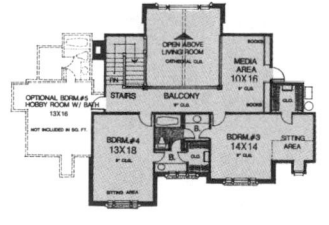

Second Floor

HPK2101304

Style: New American

First Floor: 3,168 sq. ft.

Second Floor: 998 sq. ft.

Total: 4,166 sq. ft.

Bonus Space: 210 sq. ft.

Bedrooms: 4

Bathrooms: 3 ½

Width: 90' - 0"

Depth: 63' - 5"

Foundation: Crawlspace, Slab, Unfinished Basement

EPLANS.COM

4,000 SQUARE FEET AND OVER

HPK2101305

Style: New American

First Floor: 2,547 sq. ft.

Second Floor: 1,637 sq. ft.

Total: 4,184 sq. ft.

Bonus Space: 802 sq. ft.

Bedrooms: 4

Bathrooms: 3 ½

Width: 74' - 0"

Depth: 95' - 6"

Foundation: Crawlspace

EPLANS.COM

First Floor

Second Floor

HPK2101306

Style: Neoclassical

First Floor: 3,129 sq. ft.

Second Floor: 1,058 sq. ft.

Total: 4,187 sq. ft.

Bonus Space: 551 sq. ft.

Bedrooms: 4

Bathrooms: 4 ½

Width: 68' - 0"

Depth: 117' - 10"

Foundation: Slab

EPLANS.COM

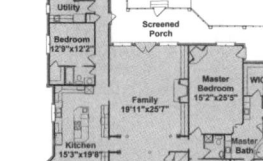

First Floor

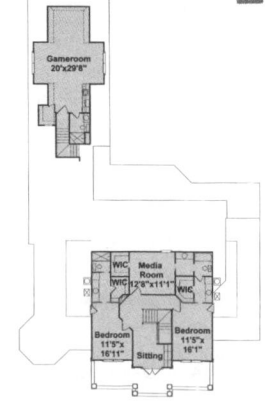

Second Floor

HPK2101307

Style: Craftsman
First Floor: 2,979 sq. ft.
Second Floor: 1,209 sq. ft.
Total: 4,188 sq. ft.
Bedrooms: 3
Bathrooms: 3 ½
Width: 101' - 8"
Depth: 78' - 5"
Foundation: Crawlspace

EPLANS.COM

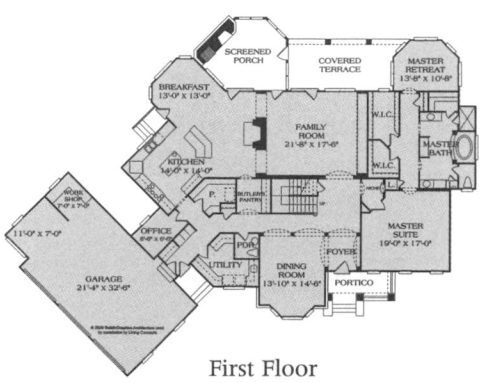

First Floor

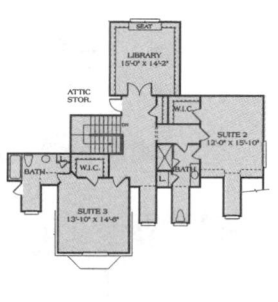

Second Floor

Rear Exterior

HPK2101308

Style: Colonial Revival
First Floor: 2,761 sq. ft.
Second Floor: 1,444 sq. ft.
Total: 4,205 sq. ft.
Bedrooms: 4
Bathrooms: 4 ½
Width: 82' - 0"
Depth: 59' - 0"
Foundation: Crawlspace, Unfinished Walkout Basement

EPLANS.COM

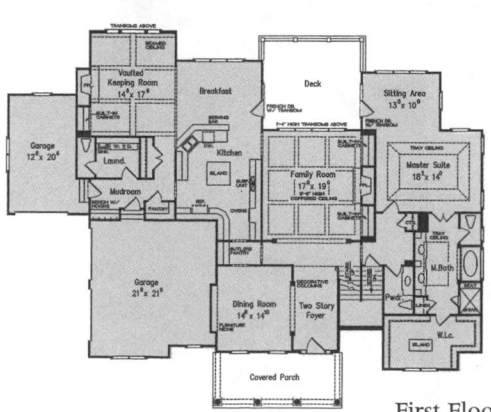

First Floor

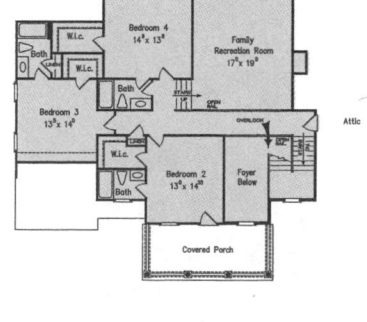

Second Floor

4,000 SQUARE FEET AND OVER

First Floor

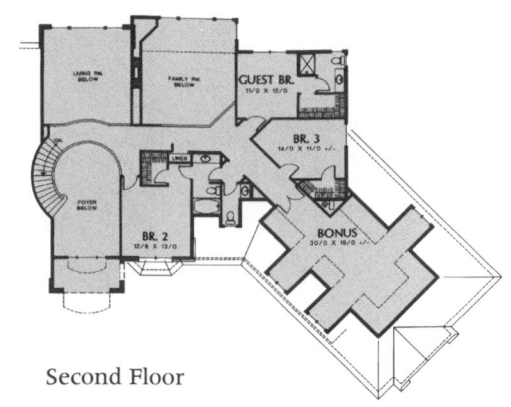

Second Floor

HPK2101309

Style: New American

First Floor: 3,098 sq. ft.

Second Floor: 1,113 sq. ft.

Total: 4,211 sq. ft.

Bonus Space: 567 sq. ft.

Bedrooms: 4

Bathrooms: 3 ½

Width: 112' - 0"

Depth: 69' - 9"

Foundation: Crawlspace

EPLANS.COM

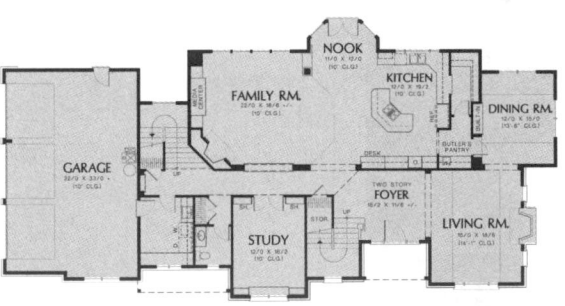

First Floor

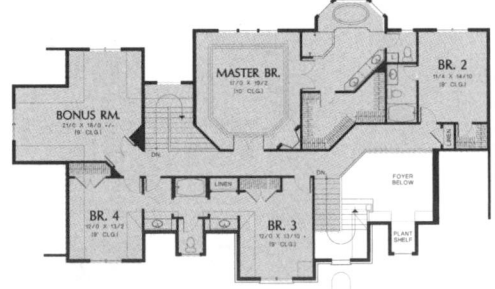

Second Floor

HPK2101310

Style: French Country

First Floor: 2,451 sq. ft.

Second Floor: 1,762 sq. ft.

Total: 4,213 sq. ft.

Bonus Space: 353 sq. ft.

Bedrooms: 4

Bathrooms: 3 ½

Width: 92' - 6"

Depth: 46' - 0"

Foundation: Crawlspace

EPLANS.COM

First Floor

Second Floor

HPK2101311

Style: Neoclassical
First Floor: 2,696 sq. ft.
Second Floor: 1,518 sq. ft.
Total: 4,214 sq. ft.
Bonus Space: 360 sq. ft.
Bedrooms: 4
Bathrooms: 4 ½ + ½
Width: 72' - 6"
Depth: 97' - 10"
Foundation: Crawlspace

EPLANS.COM

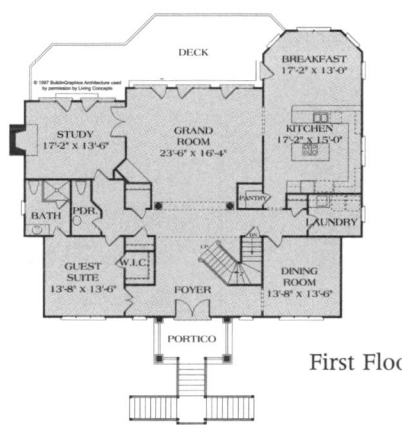

First Floor

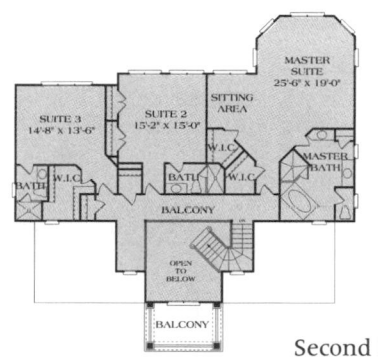

Second Floor

HPK2101312

Style: Mediterranean
First Floor: 2,297 sq. ft.
Second Floor: 1,929 sq. ft.
Total: 4,226 sq. ft.
Bedrooms: 4
Bathrooms: 4 ½
Width: 59' - 2"
Depth: 49' - 4"
Foundation: Unfinished Basement

EPLANS.COM

4,000 SQUARE FEET AND OVER

HPK2101313

Style: Tidewater

First Floor: 2,891 sq. ft.

Second Floor: 1,336 sq. ft.

Total: 4,227 sq. ft.

Bonus Space: 380 sq. ft.

Bedrooms: 4

Bathrooms: 3 ½ + ½

Width: 90' - 8"

Depth: 56' - 4"

Foundation: Crawlspace, Unfinished Basement

EPLANS.COM

First Floor

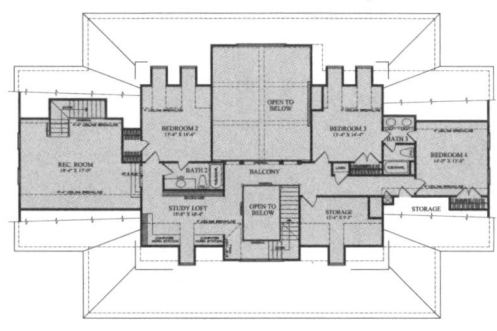

Second Floor

HPK2101314

Style: French Country

First Floor: 2,950 sq. ft.

Second Floor: 1,278 sq. ft.

Total: 4,228 sq. ft.

Bedrooms: 4

Bathrooms: 4 ½

Width: 91' - 8"

Depth: 71' - 10"

Foundation: Crawlspace, Slab, Unfinished Basement

EPLANS.COM

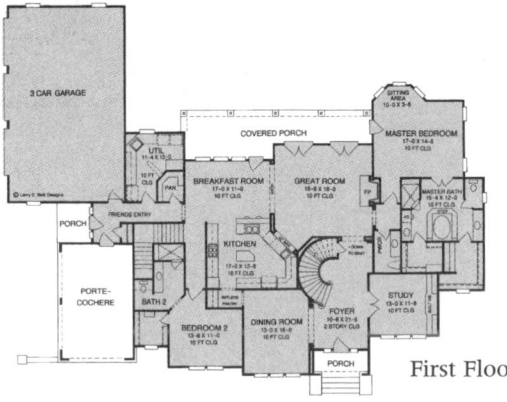

First Floor

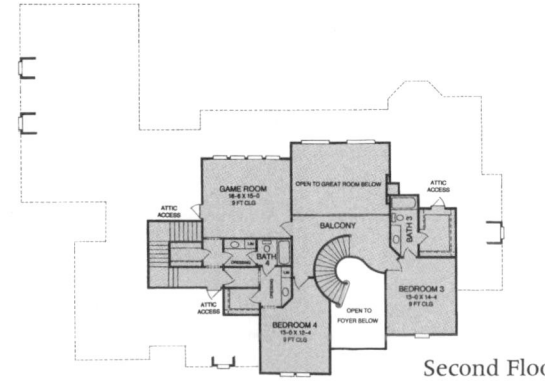

Second Floor

HPK2101315

Style: French Country
First Floor: 2,672 sq. ft.
Second Floor: 1,586 sq. ft.
Total: 4,258 sq. ft.
Bonus Space: 650 sq. ft.
Bedrooms: 5
Bathrooms: 4 ½ + 2 half baths
Width: 89' - 6"
Depth: 63' - 0"
Foundation: Crawlspace, Unfinished Basement

First Floor

Second Floor

HPK2101316

Style: Federal - Adams
First Floor: 2,603 sq. ft.
Second Floor: 1,660 sq. ft.
Total: 4,263 sq. ft.
Bonus Space: 669 sq. ft.
Bedrooms: 4
Bathrooms: 4 ½ + 2 half baths
Width: 98' - 0"
Depth: 56' - 8"
Foundation: Unfinished Basement

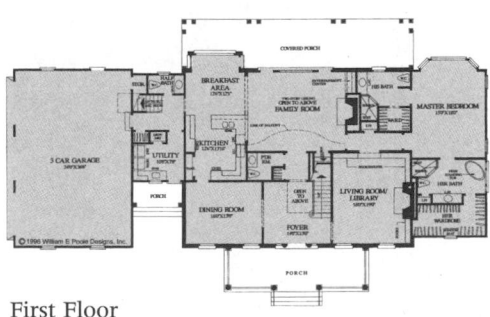

First Floor

Second Floor

EPLANS.COM

4,000 SQUARE FEET AND OVER

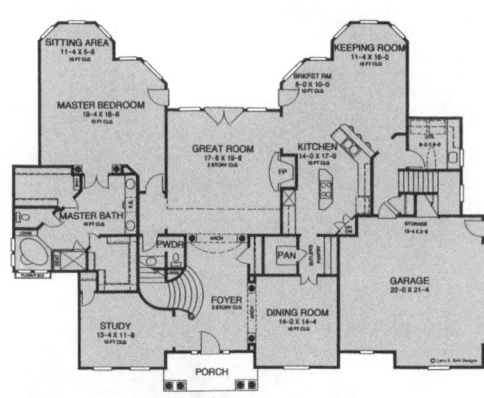

First Floor

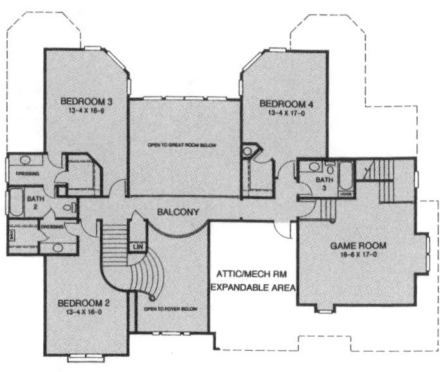

Second Floor

HPK2101317

Style: New American

First Floor: 2,639 sq. ft.

Second Floor: 1,625 sq. ft.

Total: 4,264 sq. ft.

Bedrooms: 4

Bathrooms: 3 ½

Width: 73' - 8"

Depth: 58' - 6"

Foundation: Crawlspace, Slab, Unfinished Basement

EPLANS.COM

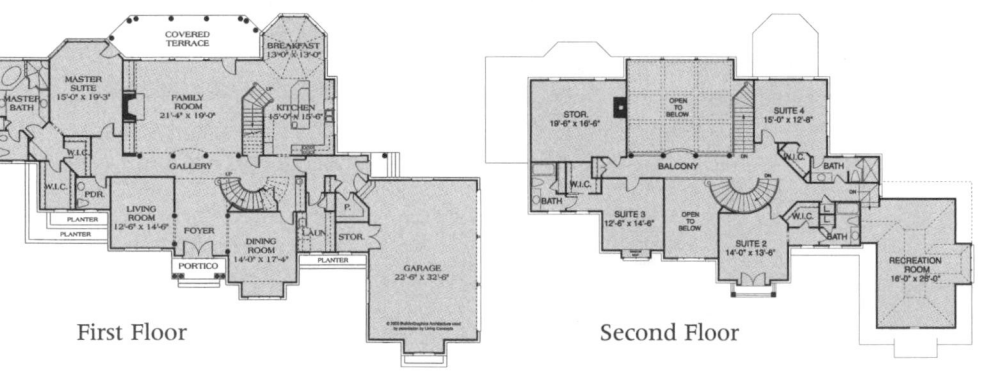

First Floor

Second Floor

Rear Exterior

HPK2101318

Style: Italianate

First Floor: 2,887 sq. ft.

Second Floor: 1,387 sq. ft.

Total: 4,274 sq. ft.

Bonus Space: 517 sq. ft.

Bedrooms: 4

Bathrooms: 4 ½

Width: 102' - 2"

Depth: 73' - 5"

Foundation: Crawlspace

EPLANS.COM

First Floor

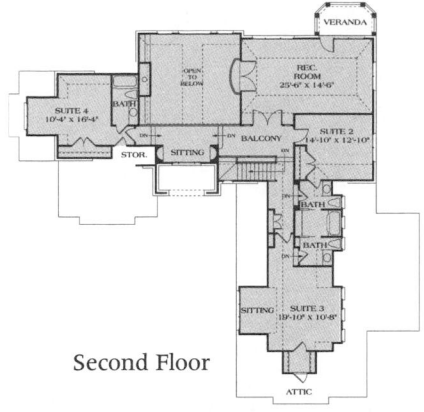

Second Floor

HPK2101319

Style: New American
First Floor: 2,577 sq. ft.
Second Floor: 1,703 sq. ft.
Total: 4,280 sq. ft.
Bedrooms: 4
Bathrooms: 3 ½
Width: 80' - 4"
Depth: 85' - 11"
Foundation: Crawlspace

EPLANS.COM

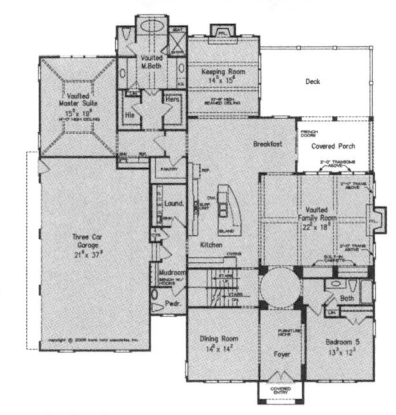

First Floor

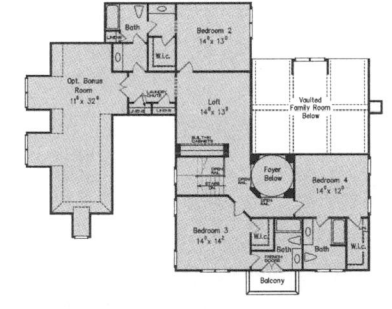

Second Floor

HPK2101320

Style: European
First Floor: 2,896 sq. ft.
Second Floor: 1,388 sq. ft.
Total: 4,284 sq. ft.
Bonus Space: 498 sq. ft.
Bedrooms: 5
Bathrooms: 5 ½
Width: 68' - 4"
Depth: 76' - 0"
Foundation: Crawlspace, Unfinished Walkout Basement

EPLANS.COM

4,000 SQUARE FEET AND OVER

HPK2101321

Style: Neoclassical
First Floor: 2,913 sq. ft.
Second Floor: 1,380 sq. ft.
Total: 4,293 sq. ft.
Bonus Space: 905 sq. ft.
Bedrooms: 4
Bathrooms: 4 ½
Width: 88' - 4"
Depth: 100' - 8"
Foundation: Crawlspace

EPLANS.COM

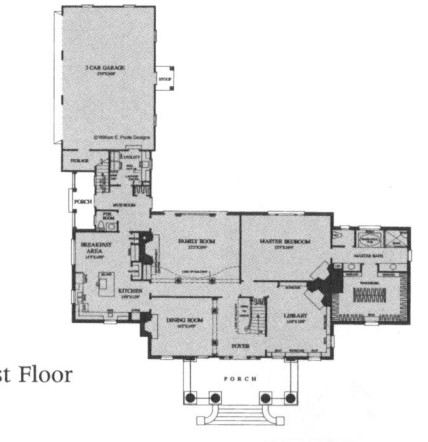

First Floor

Second Floor

HPK2101322

Style: Georgian
First Floor: 2,798 sq. ft.
Second Floor: 1,496 sq. ft.
Total: 4,294 sq. ft.
Bonus Space: 515 sq. ft.
Bedrooms: 4
Bathrooms: 3 ½
Width: 91' - 10"
Depth: 57' - 2"
Foundation: Crawlspace,
Unfinished Basement

EPLANS.COM

First Floor

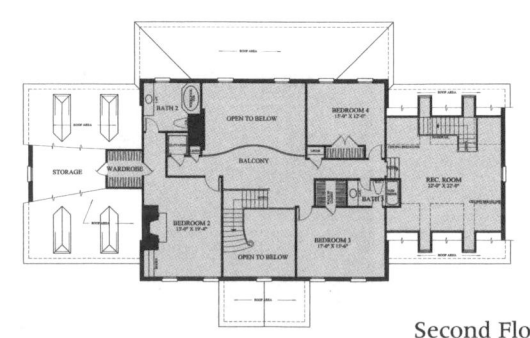

Second Floor

HPK2101323

Style: Plantation
First Floor: 2,945 sq. ft.
Second Floor: 1,353 sq. ft.
Total: 4,298 sq. ft.
Bedrooms: 4
Bathrooms: 4 ½
Width: 61' - 4"
Depth: 72' - 2"
Foundation: Finished Walkout Basement

© William E. Poole Designs, Inc.

First Floor

Second Floor

HPK2101324

Style: Dutch
First Floor: 3,016 sq. ft.
Second Floor: 1,283 sq. ft.
Total: 4,299 sq. ft.
Bonus Space: 757 sq. ft.
Bedrooms: 4
Bathrooms: 4 ½ + ½
Width: 105' - 0"
Depth: 69' - 0"
Foundation: Crawlspace

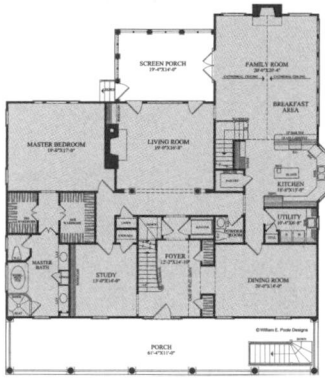

First Floor

Second Floor

4,000 SQUARE FEET AND OVER

First Floor

Second Floor

HPK2101325

Style: Craftsman
First Floor: 2,360 sq. ft.
Second Floor: 1,940 sq. ft.
Total: 4,300 sq. ft.
Bedrooms: 4
Bathrooms: 3 ½
Width: 105' - 4"
Depth: 53' - 0"
Foundation: Crawlspace

EPLANS.COM

An abundance of windows provides a wealth of natural light and exceptional views throughout this luxurious Craftsman home. The open floor plan adds spaciousness and invites the possibility for entertaining. A guest suite accesses a full, private bath ideal for an elderly visitor. Upstairs, the master suite enjoys a private deck that overlooks the backyard. A bridge separates the master suite from the remaining bedrooms creating a private retreat. The large playroom is great for kids and adults alike.

First Floor

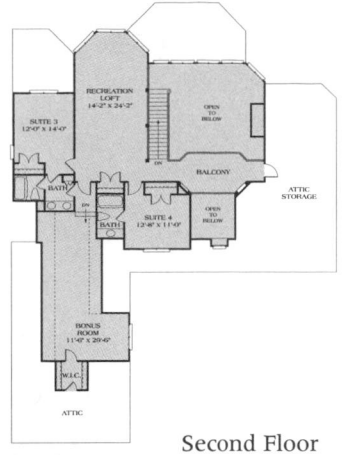

Second Floor

HPK2101326

Style: New American

First Floor: 2,591 sq. ft.

Second Floor: 1,715 sq. ft.

Total: 4,306 sq. ft.

Bedrooms: 4

Bathrooms: 4

Width: 64' - 10"

Depth: 90' - 4"

Foundation: Crawlspace

EPLANS.COM

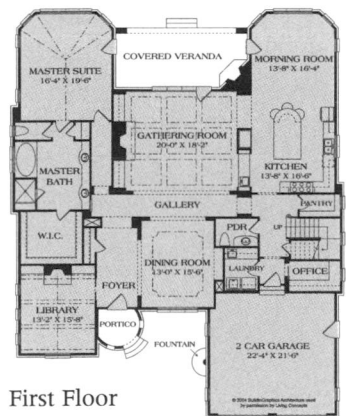

First Floor

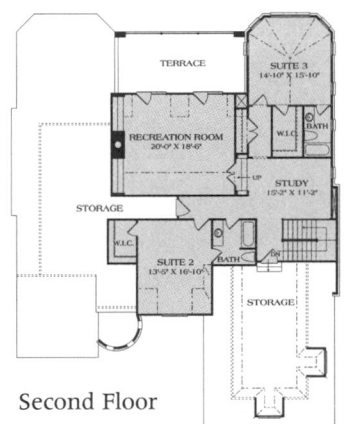

Second Floor

Rear Exterior

HPK2101327

Style: French Country

First Floor: 2,763 sq. ft.

Second Floor: 1,543 sq. ft.

Total: 4,306 sq. ft.

Bedrooms: 3

Bathrooms: 3 ½

Width: 59' - 10"

Depth: 73' - 2"

Foundation: Crawlspace

EPLANS.COM

4,000 SQUARE FEET AND OVER

HPK2101328

Style: Neoclassical
First Floor: 2,635 sq. ft.
Second Floor: 1,682 sq. ft.
Total: 4,317 sq. ft.
Bedrooms: 4
Bathrooms: 4 ½
Width: 79' - 0"
Depth: 74' - 5"
Foundation: Crawlspace, Unfinished Walkout Basement

EPLANS.COM

First Floor

Second Floor

HPK2101329

Style: French Country
Main Level: 2,582 sq. ft.
Lower Level: 1,746 sq. ft.
Total: 4,328 sq. ft.
Bedrooms: 3
Bathrooms: 3 ½
Width: 70' - 8"
Depth: 64' - 0"
Foundation: Finished Basement

EPLANS.COM

Main Level

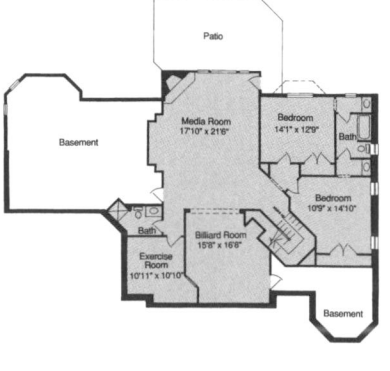

Lower Level

HPK2101330

Style: French Country

First Floor: 3,185 sq. ft.

Second Floor: 1,168 sq. ft.

Total: 4,353 sq. ft.

Bonus Space: 315 sq. ft.

Bedrooms: 4

Bathrooms: 4 ½

Width: 78' - 5"

Depth: 84' - 6"

Foundation: Unfinished Basement

EPLANS.COM

First Floor   Second Floor

HPK2101331

Style: Mediterranean

Main Level: 2,391 sq. ft.

Upper Level: 1,539 sq. ft.

Lower Level: 429 sq. ft.

Total: 4,359 sq. ft.

Bedrooms: 3

Bathrooms: 4 ½

Width: 71' - 0"

Depth: 69' - 0"

Foundation: Island Basement

EPLANS.COM

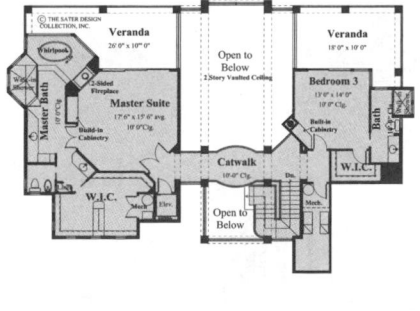

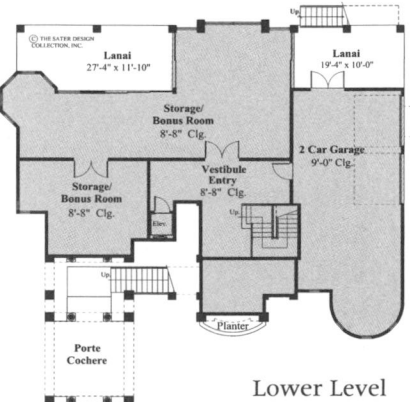

Main Level   Upper Level   Lower Level

4,000 SQUARE FEET AND OVER

First Floor

Second Floor

HPK2101332

Style: Neoclassical
First Floor: 2,764 sq. ft.
Second Floor: 1,598 sq. ft.
Total: 4,362 sq. ft.
Bedrooms: 4
Bathrooms: 3 ½
Width: 74' - 6"
Depth: 65' - 10"
Foundation: Crawlspace, Unfinished Walkout Basement

Photo by: Happy Terrebone. This home, as shown in photographs, may differ from the actual blueprints. For more detailed information, please check the floor plans carefully.

EPLANS.COM

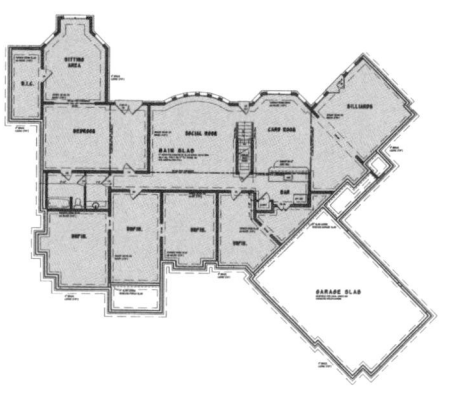

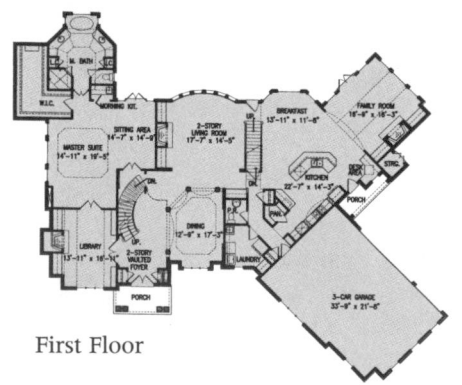

First Floor

Second Floor

Photographs: Jim Sink - Artech, Builder: Spectum Homes, Inc., Design by Garrell Associates, Inc.; Interiors: Susan Stone Interiors. This home, as shown in photographs, may differ from the actual blueprints. For more detailed information, please check the floor plans carefully.

HPK2101333

Style: French Country
First Floor: 3,056 sq. ft.
Second Floor: 1,307 sq. ft.
Total: 4,363 sq. ft.
Bonus Space: 692 sq. ft.
Bedrooms: 4
Bathrooms: 4 ½
Width: 94' - 4"
Depth: 79' - 2"
Foundation: Crawlspace, Unfinished Basement

EPLANS.COM

ORDER BLUEPRINTS ANYTIME AT EPLANS.COM OR 1-800-521-6797

First Floor

Second Floor

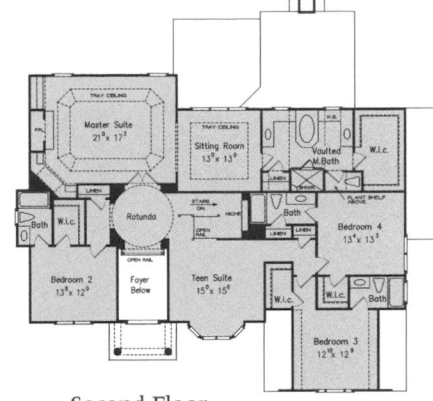

HPK2101334

Style: New American
First Floor: 2,173 sq. ft.
Second Floor: 2,202 sq. ft.
Total: 4,375 sq. ft.
Bedrooms: 5
Bathrooms: 5 ½
Width: 74' - 6"
Depth: 63' - 4"
Foundation: Crawlspace, Unfinished Walkout Basement

EPLANS.COM

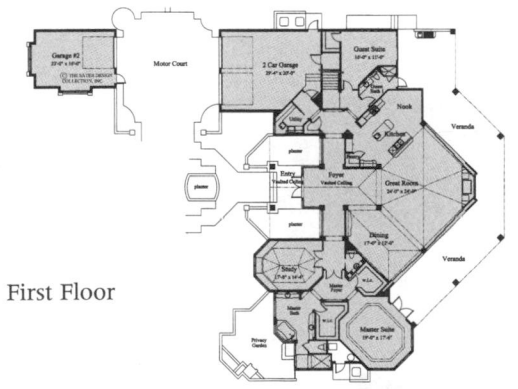

First Floor

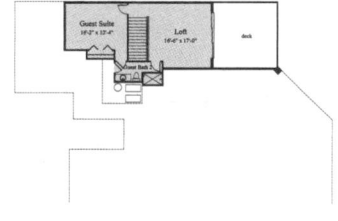

Second Floor

HPK2101335

Style: Contemporary
First Floor: 3,741 sq. ft.
Second Floor: 657 sq. ft.
Total: 4,398 sq. ft.
Bedrooms: 3
Bathrooms: 3 ½
Width: 139' - 11"
Depth: 99' - 10"
Foundation: Slab

EPLANS.COM

4,000 SQUARE FEET AND OVER

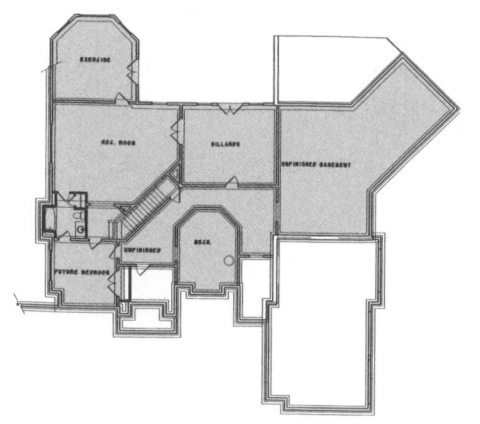

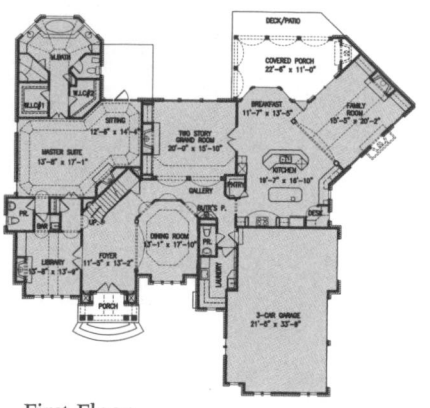

First Floor

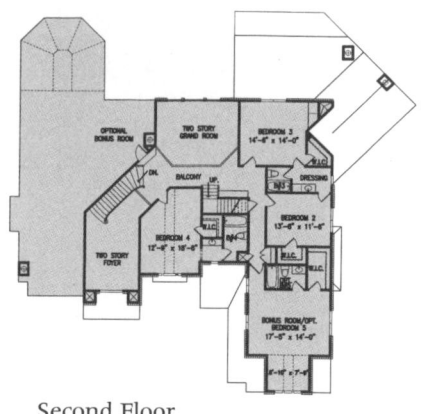

Second Floor

A brick/stone facade creates the solid exterior of this French Country design. Inside, a library in the front is warmed by a fireplace, but the heart of the house is found in a large, open great room with a second fireplace. The spacious gourmet kitchen enjoys warmth from the grand room to the left and a third fireplace in the adjoining family room on the right. Access to a rear covered porch and deck/patio can be gained from the family room. There are three bedrooms upstairs and a bonus room/optional fifth bedroom.

HPK2101336

Style: French Country
First Floor: 3,121 sq. ft.
Second Floor: 1,278 sq. ft.
Total: 4,399 sq. ft.
Bedrooms: 4
Bathrooms: 3 ½ + ½
Width: 86' - 7"
Depth: 81' - 4"
Foundation: Unfinished Walkout Basement

EPLANS.COM

HPK2101528

Style: Colonial Revival

First Floor: 2,628 sq. ft.

Second Floor: 1,775 sq. ft.

Total: 4,403 sq. ft.

Bedrooms: 5

Bathrooms: 3 ½

Width: 79' - 6"

Depth: 65' - 1"

Foundation: Unfinished Walkout Basement

EPLANS.COM

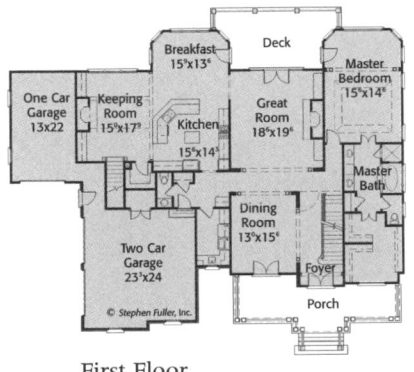

First Floor

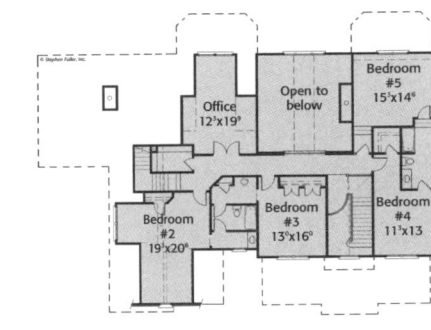

Second Floor

HPK2101337

EPLANS.COM

Style: Italianate

First Floor: 3,633 sq. ft.

Second Floor: 695 sq. ft.

Total: 4,328 sq. ft.

Bedrooms: 5

Bathrooms: 5 ½

Width: 115' - 7"

Depth: 109' - 8"

Foundation: Slab

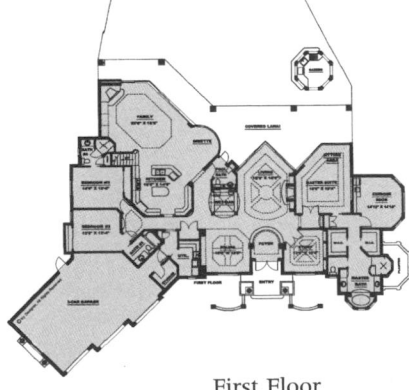

First Floor

Second Floor

4,000 SQUARE FEET AND OVER

HPK2101338

Style: Colonial Revival

First Floor: 2,768 sq. ft.

Second Floor: 1,662 sq. ft.

Total: 4,430 sq. ft.

Bedrooms: 4

Bathrooms: 3 ½

Width: 75' - 6"

Depth: 96' - 6"

Foundation: Crawlspace

EPLANS.COM

First Floor

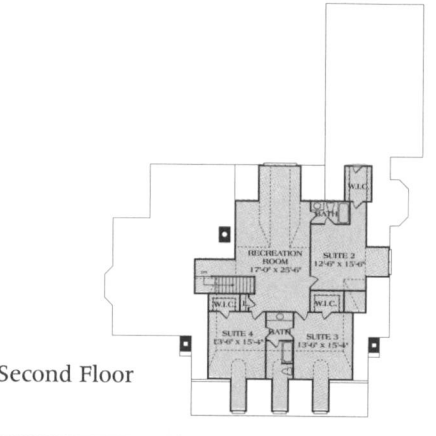

Second Floor

HPK2101339

Style: Norman

First Floor: 2,446 sq. ft.

Second Floor: 1,988 sq. ft.

Total: 4,434 sq. ft.

Bonus Space: 651 sq. ft.

Bedrooms: 5

Bathrooms: 4 ½

Width: 61' - 2"

Depth: 78' - 10"

Foundation: Crawlspace

EPLANS.COM

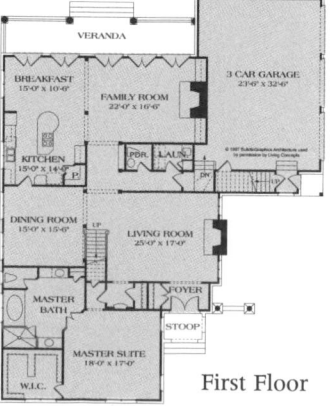

First Floor

Second Floor

HPK2101340

Style: Federal - Adams
First Floor: 2,993 sq. ft.
Second Floor: 1,452 sq. ft.
Total: 4,445 sq. ft.
Bonus Space: 611 sq. ft.
Bedrooms: 4
Bathrooms: 5
Width: 113' - 0"
Depth: 65' - 4"
Foundation: Crawlspace

EPLANS.COM

© William E. Poole Designs, Inc.

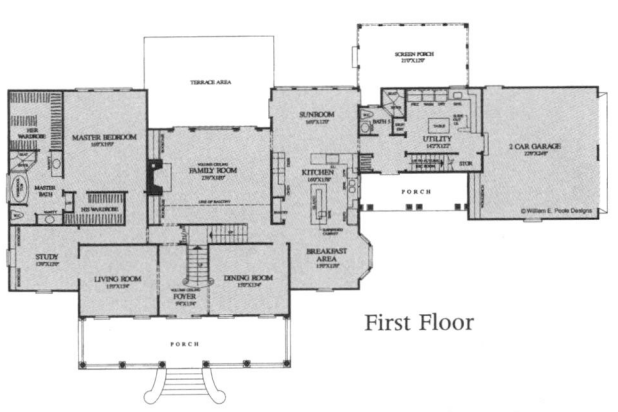

First Floor

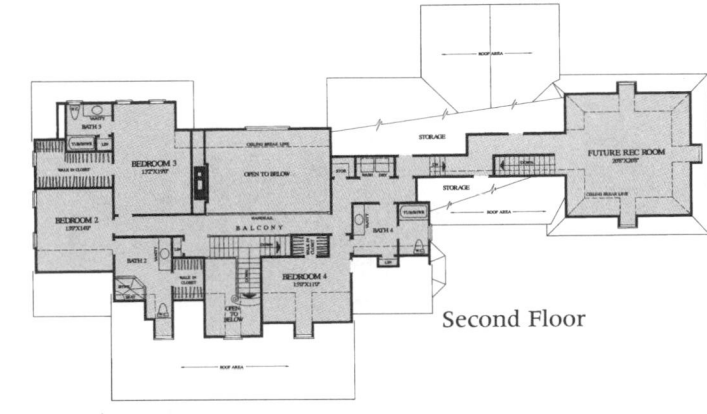

Second Floor

HPK2101341

Style: Craftsman
First Floor: 2,119 sq. ft.
Second Floor: 2,331 sq. ft.
Total: 4,450 sq. ft.
Bedrooms: 4
Bathrooms: 3
Width: 59' - 0"
Depth: 85' - 0"
Foundation: Crawlspace

EPLANS.COM

First Floor

Second Floor

4,000 SQUARE FEET AND OVER

Main Level

Lower Level

HPK2101342

Style: Mediterranean

Main Level: 2,195 sq. ft.

Lower Level: 2,262 sq. ft.

Total: 4,457 sq. ft.

Bedrooms: 4

Bathrooms: 3 ½

Width: 76' - 0"

Depth: 59' - 4"

Foundation: Finished Basement

EPLANS.COM

First Floor

Second Floor

HPK2101343

Style: New American

First Floor: 3,218 sq. ft.

Second Floor: 1,240 sq. ft.

Total: 4,458 sq. ft.

Bonus Space: 656 sq. ft.

Bedrooms: 4

Bathrooms: 3 ½

Width: 76' - 0"

Depth: 73' - 10"

Foundation: Crawlspace, Unfinished Walkout Basement

EPLANS.COM

ORDER BLUEPRINTS ANYTIME AT EPLANS.COM OR 1-800-521-6797

First Floor

Second Floor

HPK2101344

Style: Italianate

First Floor: 2,569 sq. ft.

Second Floor: 1,890 sq. ft.

Total: 4,459 sq. ft.

Bedrooms: 4

Bathrooms: 3 ½

Width: 69' - 1"

Depth: 85' - 1"

Foundation: Crawlspace

EPLANS.COM

Rear Exterior

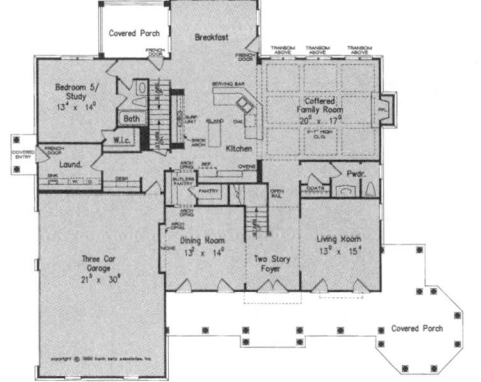

First Floor

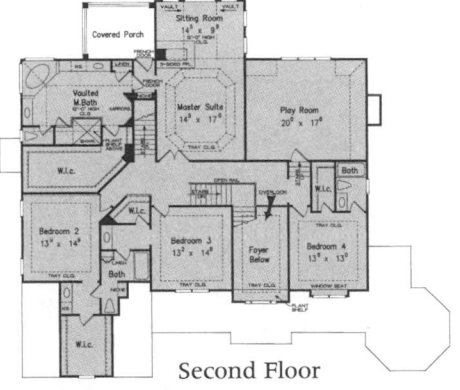

Second Floor

HPK2101345

Style: Farmhouse

First Floor: 2,092 sq. ft.

Second Floor: 2,372 sq. ft.

Total: 4,464 sq. ft.

Bedrooms: 5

Bathrooms: 4 ½

Width: 75' - 5"

Depth: 64' - 0"

Foundation: Crawlspace, Unfinished Walkout Basement

EPLANS.COM

4,000 SQUARE FEET AND OVER

HPK2101346

Style: Italianate

First Floor: 2,163 sq. ft.

Second Floor: 2,302 sq. ft.

Total: 4,465 sq. ft.

Bedrooms: 5

Bathrooms: 5 ½

Width: 58' - 0"

Depth: 65' - 0"

Foundation: Slab

EPLANS.COM

© The Sater Design Collection, Inc.

First Floor

Second Floor

© William E. Poole Designs, Inc.

HPK2101347

Style: Neoclassical

First Floor: 2,670 sq. ft.

Second Floor: 1,795 sq. ft.

Total: 4,465 sq. ft.

Bonus Space: 744 sq. ft.

Bedrooms: 5

Bathrooms: 4 ½ + ½

Width: 74' - 8"

Depth: 93' - 10"

Foundation: Crawlspace, Unfinished Basement

EPLANS.COM

First Floor

Second Floor

HPK2101348

Style: French Country

First Floor: 2,267 sq. ft.

Second Floor: 2,209 sq. ft.

Total: 4,476 sq. ft.

Bedrooms: 4

Bathrooms: 3 ½

Width: 67' - 2"

Depth: 64' - 10"

Foundation: Crawlspace

EPLANS.COM

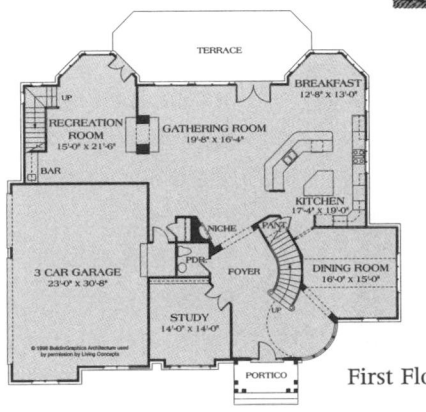

First Floor

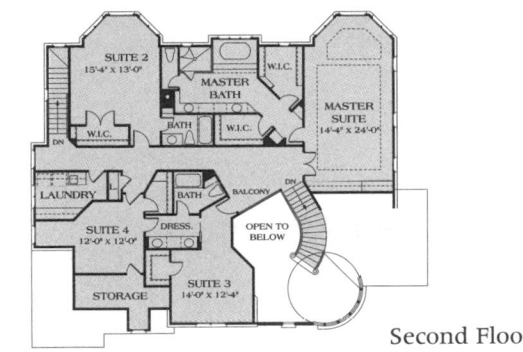

Second Floor

First Floor

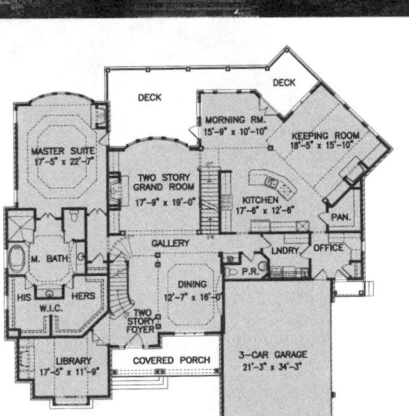

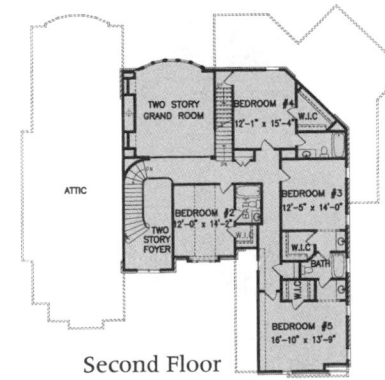

Second Floor

HPK2101349

Style: French Country

First Floor: 3,072 sq. ft.

Second Floor: 1,406 sq. ft.

Total: 4,478 sq. ft.

Bedrooms: 5

Bathrooms: 4 ½

Width: 75' - 5"

Depth: 73' - 11"

Foundation: Unfinished Basement

EPLANS.COM

Photo courtesy of Garrell Associates Inc. This home, as shown in photographs, may differ from the actual blueprints. For more detailed information, please check the floor plans carefully.

4,000 SQUARE FEET AND OVER

First Floor

Second Floor

HPK2101350

Style: Federal - Adams
First Floor: 2,968 sq. ft.
Second Floor: 1,521 sq. ft.
Total: 4,489 sq. ft.
Bonus Space: 522 sq. ft.
Bedrooms: 4
Bathrooms: 4 ½ + ½
Width: 82' - 6"
Depth: 81' - 8"
Foundation: Crawlspace

EPLANS.COM

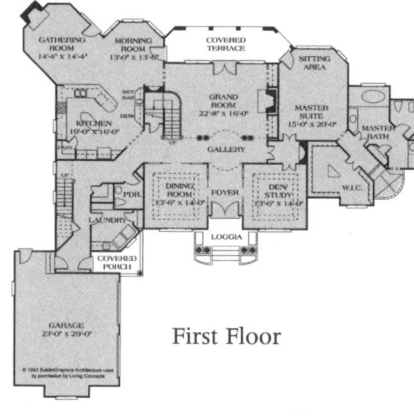

First Floor

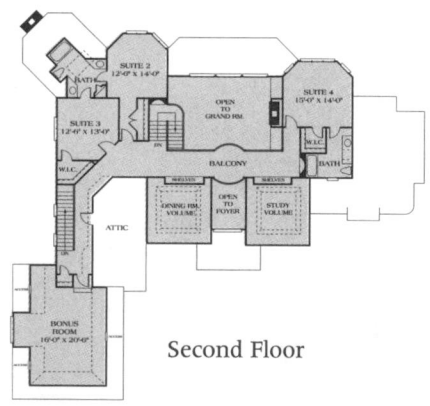

Second Floor

HPK2101351

Style: New American
First Floor: 3,143 sq. ft.
Second Floor: 1,348 sq. ft.
Total: 4,491 sq. ft.
Bonus Space: 368 sq. ft.
Bedrooms: 4
Bathrooms: 3 ½
Width: 89' - 4"
Depth: 85' - 9"
Foundation: Crawlspace

EPLANS.COM

First Floor

Second Floor

HPK2101352

Style: Italianate

First Floor: 3,947 sq. ft.

Second Floor: 545 sq. ft.

Total: 4,492 sq. ft.

Bedrooms: 4

Bathrooms: 4 ½

Width: 105' - 9"

Depth: 100' - 9"

Foundation: Slab

EPLANS.COM

HPK2101353

Style: Italianate

First Floor: 3,947 sq. ft.

Second Floor: 545 sq. ft.

Total: 4,492 sq. ft.

Bedrooms: 4

Bathrooms: 4 ½

Width: 105' - 9"

Depth: 100' - 9"

Foundation: Slab

EPLANS.COM

First Floor

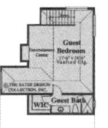

Second Floor

4,000 SQUARE FEET AND OVER

HPK2101354

Style: Italianate
First Floor: 3,745 sq. ft.
Second Floor: 747 sq. ft.
Total: 4,492 sq. ft.
Bedrooms: 4
Bathrooms: 4 ½
Width: 94' - 10"
Depth: 103' - 5"
Foundation: Slab

EPLANS.COM

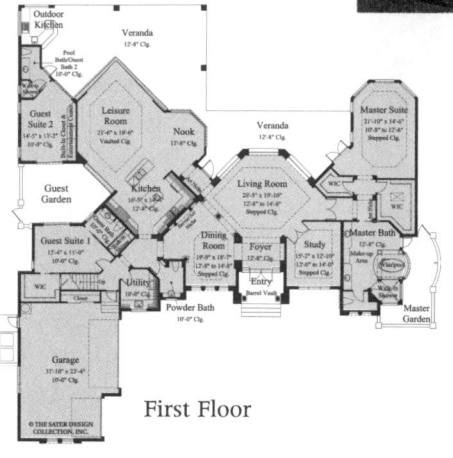

First Floor

Second Floor

HPK2101355

Style: New American
First Floor: 3,348 sq. ft.
Second Floor: 1,154 sq. ft.
Total: 4,502 sq. ft.
Bedrooms: 4
Bathrooms: 4 ½
Width: 91' - 3"
Depth: 94' - 6"
Foundation: Unfinished Basement

EPLANS.COM

First Floor

Second Floor

First Floor

Second Floor

Rear Exterior

HPK2101356

Style: Mediterranean

First Floor: 3,633 sq. ft.

Second Floor: 895 sq. ft.

Total: 4,528 sq. ft.

Bedrooms: 4

Bathrooms: 4 ½

Width: 91' - 6"

Depth: 122' - 4"

Foundation: Slab

EPLANS.COM

HPK2101357

Style: Federal - Adams

First Floor: 3,027 sq. ft.

Second Floor: 1,509 sq. ft.

Total: 4,536 sq. ft.

Bedrooms: 5

Bathrooms: 4 ½

Width: 85' - 0"

Depth: 82' - 6"

Foundation: Crawlspace, Unfinished Basement

EPLANS.COM

First Floor

Second Floor

4,000 SQUARE FEET AND OVER

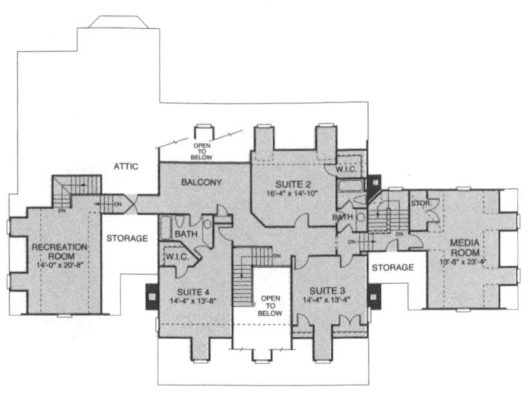

First Floor

Second Floor

HPK2101358

Style: Federal - Adams
First Floor: 2,722 sq. ft.
Second Floor: 1,991 sq. ft.
Total: 4,713 sq. ft.
Bonus Space: 364 sq. ft.
Bedrooms: 4
Bathrooms: 3 ½
Width: 99' - 8"
Depth: 71' - 8"
Foundation: Crawlspace

EPLANS.COM

Photo Courtesy of Living Concepts. This home, as shown in photographs, may differ from the actual blueprints. For more detailed information, please check the floor plans carefully.

First Floor

Second Floor

HPK2101359

Style: Federal - Adams
First Floor: 2,998 sq. ft.
Second Floor: 1,556 sq. ft.
Total: 4,554 sq. ft.
Bonus Space: 741 sq. ft.
Bedrooms: 4
Bathrooms: 4 ½
Width: 75' - 6"
Depth: 91' - 2"
Foundation: Crawlspace

EPLANS.COM

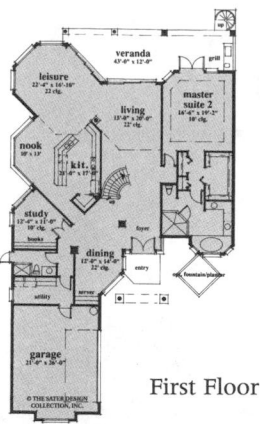

First Floor

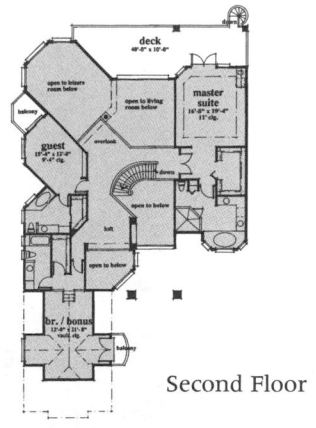

Second Floor

© The Sater Design Collection, Inc.

HPK2101360

Style: Mediterranean

First Floor: 2,618 sq. ft.

Second Floor: 1,945 sq. ft.

Total: 4,563 sq. ft.

Bedrooms: 4

Bathrooms: 5

Width: 54' - 8"

Depth: 97' - 4"

Foundation: Slab

EPLANS.COM

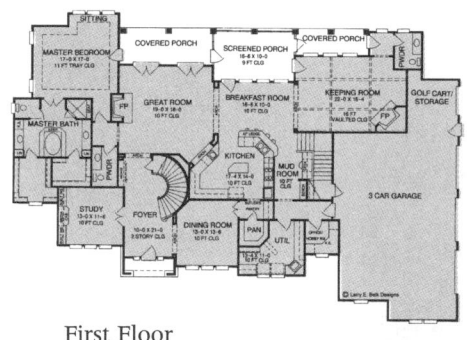

First Floor

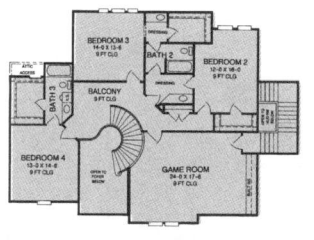

Second Floor

HPK2101361

Style: French Country

First Floor: 3,033 sq. ft.

Second Floor: 1,545 sq. ft.

Total: 4,578 sq. ft.

Bedrooms: 4

Bathrooms: 3 ½ + ½

Width: 91' - 6"

Depth: 63' - 8"

Foundation: Crawlspace, Slab, Unfinished Basement

EPLANS.COM

© Larry E. Belk Designs

4,000 SQUARE FEET AND OVER

HPK2101362

Style: Georgian
First Floor: 3,327 sq. ft.
Second Floor: 1,260 sq. ft.
Total: 4,587 sq. ft.
Bedrooms: 4
Bathrooms: 3 ½
Width: 75' - 4"
Depth: 73' - 6"
Foundation: Finished Walkout Basement

EPLANS.COM

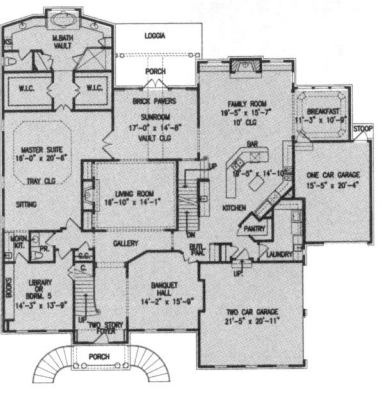

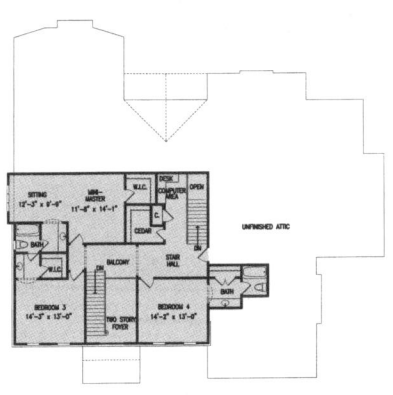

First Floor   Second Floor

© Peter Fownes, Backlight Photography. This home, as shown in photographs, may differ from the actual blueprints. For more detailed information, please check the floor plans carefully.

HPK2101363

Plan: HPK2101363
Style: Chateauesque
First Floor: 2,453 sq. ft.
Second Floor: 2,138 sq. ft.
Total: 4,591 sq. ft.
Bedrooms: 5
Bathrooms: 4
Width: 80' - 0"
Depth: 67' - 0"
Foundation: Unfinished Basement

EPLANS.COM

Photo courtesy of David Marck Loftus, Archival Designs, Inc. This home, as shown in photographs, may differ from the actual blueprints. For more detailed information, please check the floor plans carefully.

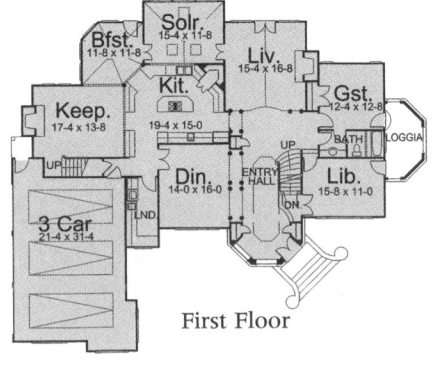

First Floor

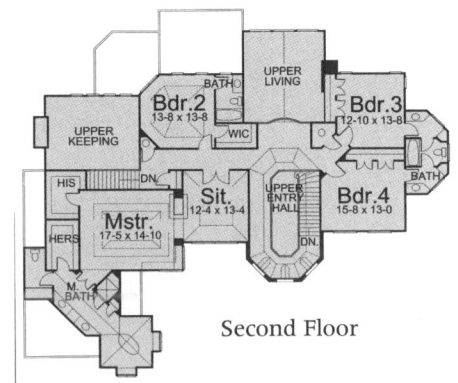

Second Floor

HPK2101364

Style: Chateauesque

First Floor: 3,337 sq. ft.

Second Floor: 1,292 sq. ft.

Total: 4,629 sq. ft.

Bedrooms: 4

Bathrooms: 4 ½

Width: 84' - 10"

Depth: 102' - 3"

EPLANS.COM

Dreaming of a home with estate-like elegance and cottage allure? Explore this flexible small-scale chateau. Allow your guests the delight of wandering through the garden courtyard, just off the dining room, before dinner. Retire to the handsome den, with soaring 14-foot ceilings, for a nightcap and conversation. Prepare holiday pastries in the chef's kitchen with friends to keep you company in the comfortable breakfast room. Feel closer without sacrificing space in the open family room fully outfitted with built-ins and a stunning extended-hearth fireplace.

First Floor

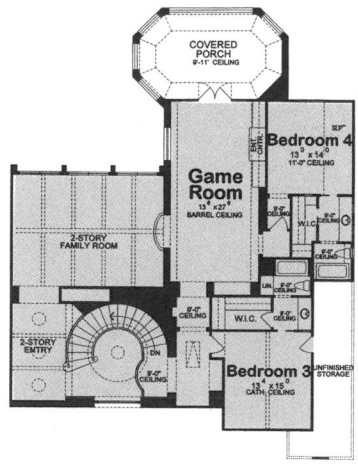

Second Floor

4,000 SQUARE FEET AND OVER

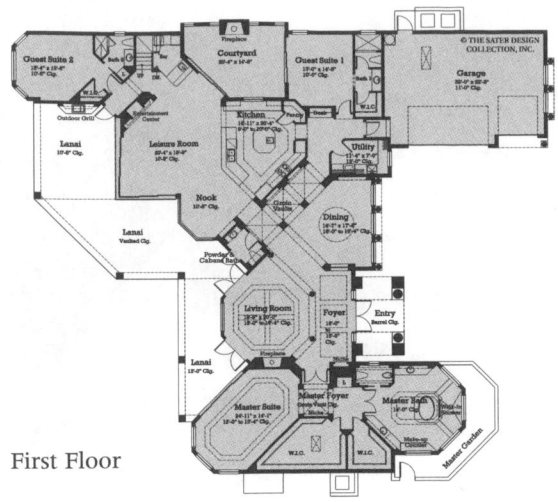

First Floor

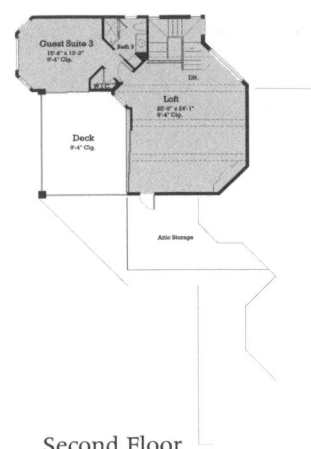

Second Floor

HPK2101365

Style: Italianate
First Floor: 3,933 sq. ft.
Second Floor: 719 sq. ft.
Total: 4,652 sq. ft.
Bedrooms: 4
Bathrooms: 4 ½
Width: 91' - 4"
Depth: 109' - 0"
Foundation: Slab

EPLANS.COM

Beautiful and spacious, the artful disposition of this luxurious villa owns a distinctly Mediterranean flavor. The octagonal living room provides a fireplace and opens through two sets of doors to the rear lanai. The master wing is a sumptuous retreat with double doors that open from a private vaulted foyer. One of the spacious guest suites can easily convert to personal quarters for a live-in relative. An upper-level loft leads to a third guest suite.

© Sater Design Collection, Inc.

HPK2101366

Style: French Country
First Floor: 3,018 sq. ft.
Second Floor: 1,646 sq. ft.
Total: 4,664 sq. ft.
Bonus Space: 294 sq. ft.
Bedrooms: 4
Bathrooms: 4 ½
Width: 70' - 0"
Depth: 100' - 0"
Foundation: Slab

EPLANS.COM

European accents and intriguing details make this stone-and-stucco home a unique addition to any neighborhood. From the foyer, the dining room is defined by columns. The two-story great room is graced with a bowed window wall for excellent views and a two-sided fireplace, shared with the study. The hexagonal kitchen includes a wet bar and overlooks the bayed breakfast nook and family-friendly leisure room. The master suite is designed to pamper highlighted by a private garden. Upstairs, two bedrooms and a guest suite all enjoy private baths and walk-in closets.

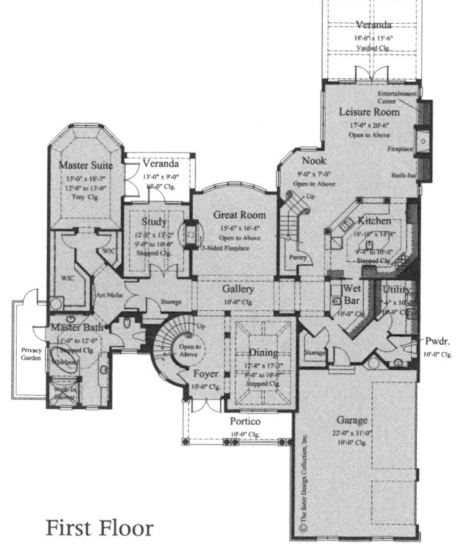

First Floor

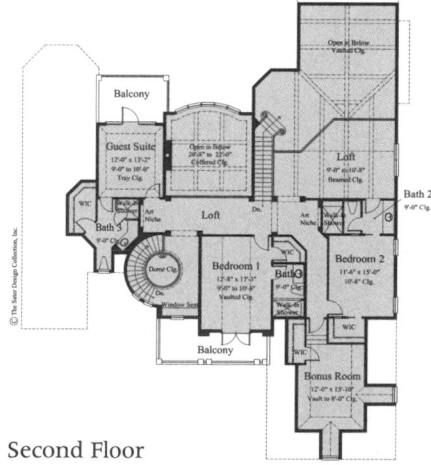

Second Floor

Optional Layout

HPK2101367

Style: French Country
First Floor: 3,248 sq. ft.
Second Floor: 1,426 sq. ft.
Total: 4,674 sq. ft.
Bedrooms: 5
Bathrooms: 5 ½ + ½
Width: 99' - 10"
Depth: 74' - 10"
Foundation: Slab, Unfinished Basement

EPLANS.COM

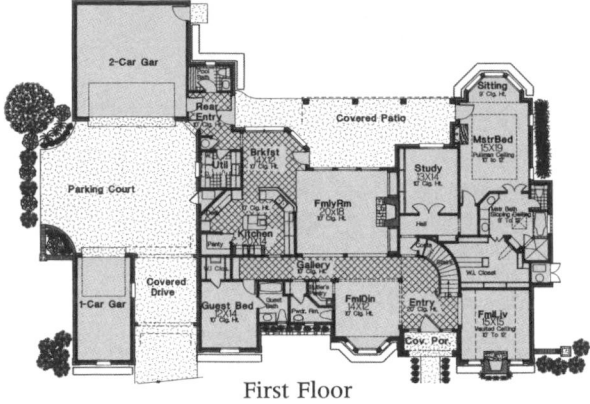
First Floor

Second Floor

HPK2101368

Style: Mediterranean
First Floor: 3,103 sq. ft.
Second Floor: 1,616 sq. ft.
Total: 4,719 sq. ft.
Bedrooms: 4
Bathrooms: 3 ½ + ½
Width: 86' - 9"
Depth: 84' - 6"

EPLANS.COM

First Floor

Second Floor

HPK2101369

Style: New American
First Floor: 3,297 sq. ft.
Second Floor: 1,453 sq. ft.
Total: 4,750 sq. ft.
Bedrooms: 5
Bathrooms: 4 ½
Width: 80' - 10"
Depth: 85' - 6"
Foundation: Slab

EPLANS.COM

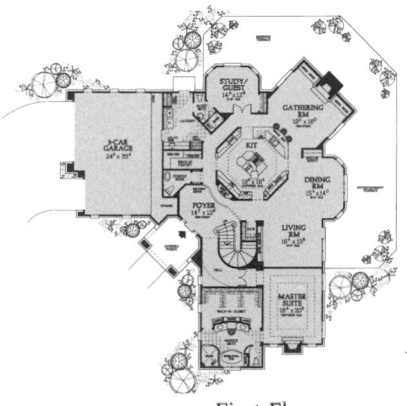

First Floor

Second Floor

© The Sater Design Collection, Inc.

HPK2101370

Style: Italianate
First Floor: 3,546 sq. ft.
Second Floor: 1,213 sq. ft.
Total: 4,759 sq. ft.
Bedrooms: 4
Bathrooms: 3 ½
Width: 96' - 0"
Depth: 83' - 0"
Foundation: Unfinished Basement

EPLANS.COM

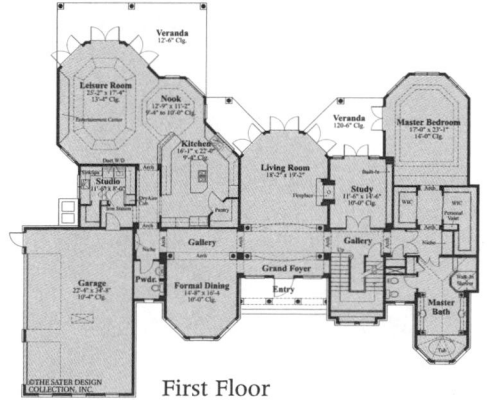

First Floor

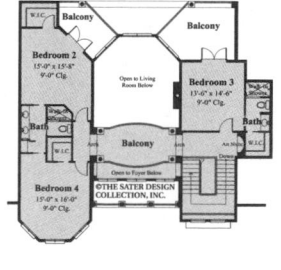

Second Floor

4,000 SQUARE FEET AND OVER

First Floor

Second Floor

HPK2101371

Style: Craftsman
First Floor: 2,597 sq. ft.
Second Floor: 2,171 sq. ft.
Total: 4,768 sq. ft.
Bedrooms: 4
Bathrooms: 4 ½
Width: 76' - 6"
Depth: 68' - 6"
Foundation: Crawlspace

EPLANS.COM

This splendid Craftsman home will look good in any neighborhood. Inside, the foyer offers a beautiful wooden bench to the right, flanked by built-in curio cabinets. On the left, double French doors lead to a cozy study. The large L-shaped kitchen includes a work island/snack bar, plenty of storage, and an adjacent sunny nook. The two-story great room offers a massive stone fireplace and a two-story wall of windows. Upstairs, two family bedrooms share a full bath, and the guest suite features its own bath. The lavish master bedroom suite pampers the homeowner with a fireplace and a private deck.

HPK2101372

Style: Shingle
First Floor: 3,800 sq. ft.
Second Floor: 990 sq. ft.
Total: 4,790 sq. ft.
Bedrooms: 4
Bathrooms: 5 ½
Width: 116' - 0"
Depth: 88' - 0"
Foundation: Crawlspace

Entertaining is easy in this spacious home with an expansive U-shaped interior. To the right of the foyer is a formal dining room with a built-in hutch. A butler's pantry leads to the island kitchen. In the opposite wing lies a guest room, pool bath, and master suite with His and Hers amenities. Joining the home's two wings is the great room. Here, a built-in media center and access to the bar and the veranda make it an excellent room for entertaining. Upstairs, two private bedroom suites flank a flexible media/playroom area.

First Floor

Second Floor

4,000 SQUARE FEET AND OVER

First Floor

Second Floor

HPK2101373

Style: Neoclassical

First Floor: 3,064 sq. ft.

Second Floor: 1,726 sq. ft.

Total: 4,790 sq. ft.

Bonus Space: 793 sq. ft.

Bedrooms: 4

Bathrooms: 4 ½ + ½

Width: 94' - 2"

Depth: 92' - 2"

Foundation: Crawlspace

EPLANS.COM

First Floor

Second Floor

HPK2101374

Style: Italianate

First Floor: 2,856 sq. ft.

Second Floor: 2,662 sq. ft.

Total: 5,518 sq. ft.

Bedrooms: 4

Bathrooms: 4 ½

Width: 115' - 4"

Depth: 53' - 4"

Foundation: Slab

EPLANS.COM

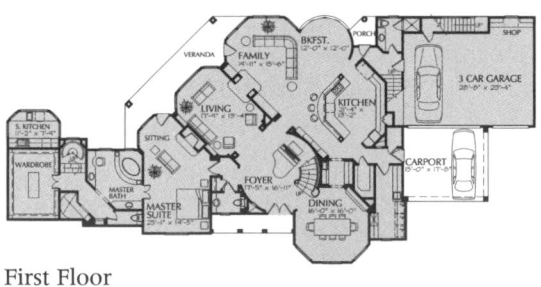

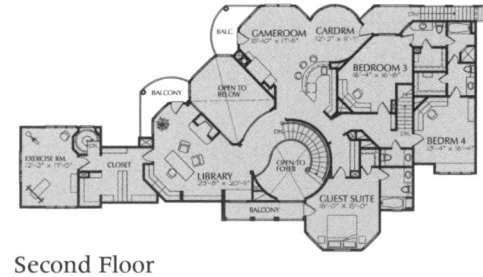

Design by: Jack Preston Wood: Design, Inc., Photographs by Tanya Scherbin. This home, as shown in photographs, may differ from the actual blueprints. For more detailed information, please check the floor plans carefully.

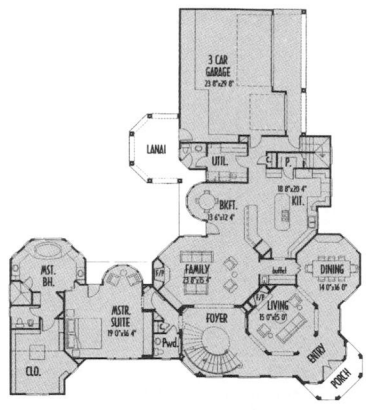

First Floor

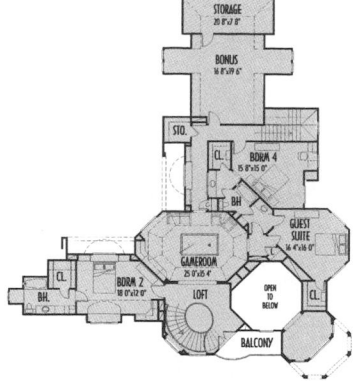

Second Floor

HPK2101375

Style: Neoclassical
First Floor: 2,744 sq. ft.
Second Floor: 1,727 sq. ft.
Total: 4,471 sq. ft.
Bonus Space: 572 sq. ft.
Bedrooms: 4
Bathrooms: 3 ½ + ½
Width: 78' - 4"
Depth: 88' - 4"
Foundation: Slab

EPLANS.COM

First Floor

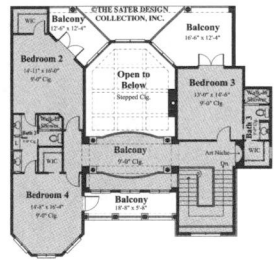

Second Floor

HPK2101376

Style: Italianate
First Floor: 3,556 sq. ft.
Second Floor: 1,308 sq. ft.
Total: 4,864 sq. ft.
Bedrooms: 4
Bathrooms: 3 ½
Width: 95' - 0"
Depth: 84' - 8"
Foundation: Slab

EPLANS.COM

© The Sater Design Collection, Inc.

4,000 SQUARE FEET AND OVER

HPK2101377

Style: Cottage

First Floor: 3,269 sq. ft.

Second Floor: 1,612 sq. ft.

Total: 4,881 sq. ft.

Bonus Space: 739 sq. ft.

Bedrooms: 4

Bathrooms: 4 ½ + ½

Width: 96' - 3"

Depth: 73' - 8"

Foundation: Crawlspace

EPLANS.COM

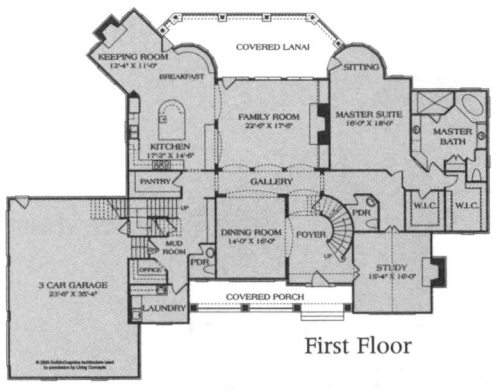

First Floor

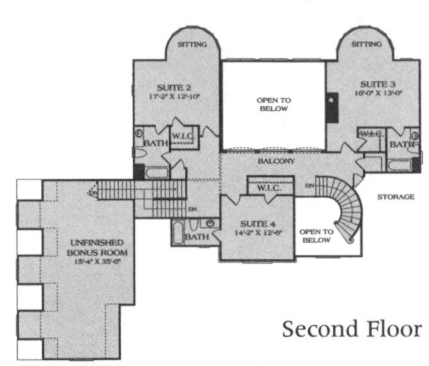

Second Floor

HPK2101378

Style: New American

First Floor: 2,733 sq. ft.

Second Floor: 2,206 sq. ft.

Total: 4,939 sq. ft.

Bonus Space: 350 sq. ft.

Bedrooms: 4

Bathrooms: 4 ½ + ½

Width: 93' - 7"

Depth: 78' - 8"

Foundation: Crawlspace

EPLANS.COM

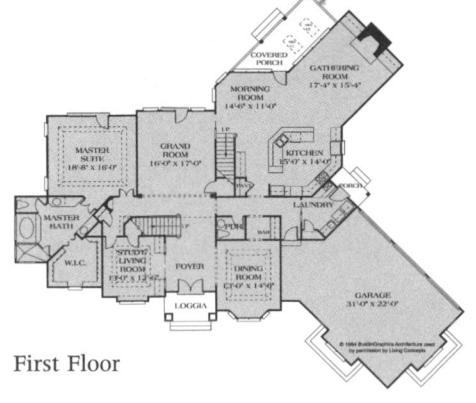

First Floor

Second Floor

HPK2101379

Style: Neoclassical
First Floor: 3,129 sq. ft.
Second Floor: 1,812 sq. ft.
Total: 4,941 sq. ft.
Bedrooms: 4
Bathrooms: 4 ½
Width: 85' - 0"
Depth: 61' - 6"
Foundation: Crawlspace

EPLANS.COM

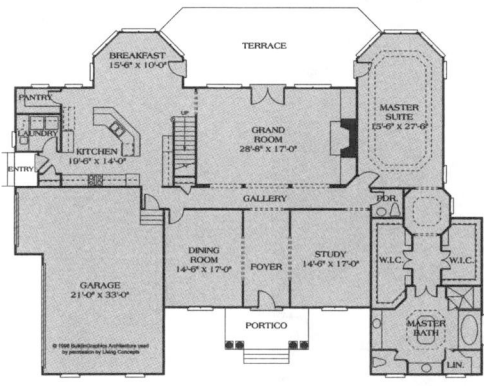

First Floor

Second Floor

First Floor

Second Floor

HPK2101380

Style: Neoclassical
First Floor: 3,635 sq. ft.
Second Floor: 1,357 sq. ft.
Total: 4,992 sq. ft.
Bonus Space: 759 sq. ft.
Bedrooms: 4
Bathrooms: 4 ½ + ½
Width: 121' - 6"
Depth: 60' - 4"
Foundation: Crawlspace, Unfinished Basement

EPLANS.COM

4,000 SQUARE FEET AND OVER

HPK2101381

Style: Italianate
First Floor: 4,137 sq. ft.
Second Floor: 876 sq. ft.
Total: 5,013 sq. ft.
Bedrooms: 4
Bathrooms: 5
Width: 81' - 10"
Depth: 113' - 0"
Foundation: Slab

EPLANS.COM

First Floor

Second Floor

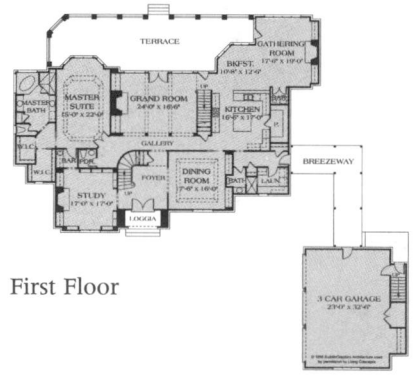

First Floor

Second Floor

HPK2101382

Style: French Country
First Floor: 3,347 sq. ft.
Second Floor: 1,696 sq. ft.
Total: 5,043 sq. ft.
Bedrooms: 5
Bathrooms: 6 ½
Width: 120' - 0"
Depth: 99' - 11"
Foundation: Crawlspace

EPLANS.COM

First Floor

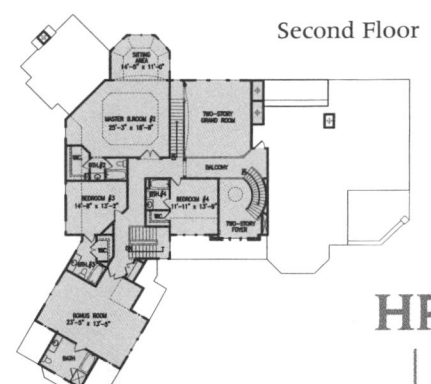
Second Floor

HPK2101383

Style: French Country

First Floor: 3,538 sq. ft.

Second Floor: 1,540 sq. ft.

Total: 5,078 sq. ft.

Bonus Space: 524 sq. ft.

Bedrooms: 4

Bathrooms: 4 ½

Width: 96' - 2"

Depth: 96' - 8"

Foundation: Crawlspace, Unfinished Basement

EPLANS.COM

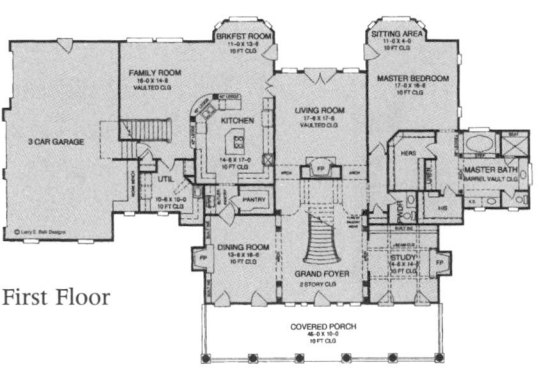
First Floor

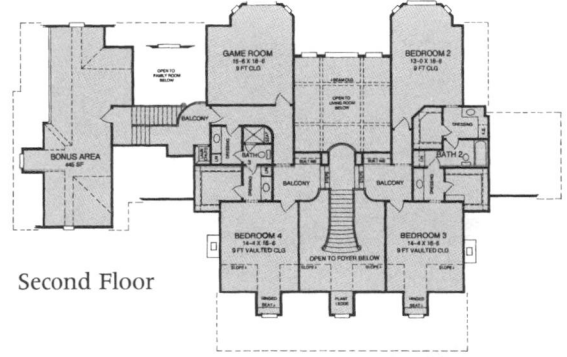
Second Floor

HPK2101384

Style: Federal - Adams

First Floor: 3,170 sq. ft.

Second Floor: 1,914 sq. ft.

Total: 5,084 sq. ft.

Bonus Space: 445 sq. ft.

Bedrooms: 4

Bathrooms: 3 ½

Width: 100' - 10"

Depth: 65' - 5"

Foundation: Crawlspace

EPLANS.COM

© Larry E. Belk Designs

4,000 SQUARE FEET AND OVER

HPK2101385

Style: Beaux Arts
First Floor: 3,703 sq. ft.
Second Floor: 1,427 sq. ft.
Total: 5,130 sq. ft.
Bonus Space: 1,399 sq. ft.
Bedrooms: 4
Bathrooms: 3 ½ + ½
Width: 125' - 2"
Depth: 58' - 10"
Foundation: Finished Walkout Basement

EPLANS.COM

Photographs Courtesy of Stephen Fuller, Inc. This home, as shown in photographs, may differ from the actual blueprints. For more detailed information, please check the floor plans carefully.

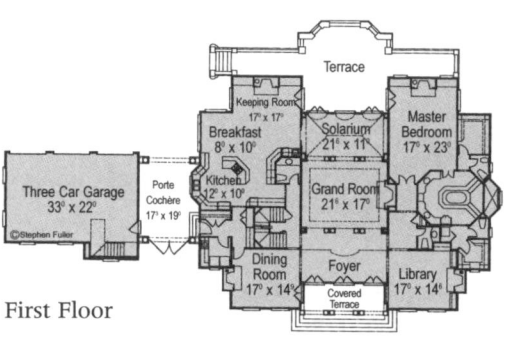

First Floor

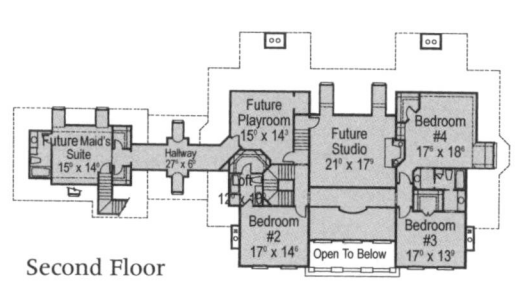

Second Floor

HPK2101386

Style: Chateauesque
First Floor: 3,058 sq. ft.
Second Floor: 2,076 sq. ft.
Total: 5,134 sq. ft.
Bedrooms: 4
Bathrooms: 4 ½
Width: 79' - 6"
Depth: 73' - 10"
Foundation: Crawlspace, Slab, Unfinished Basement

EPLANS.COM

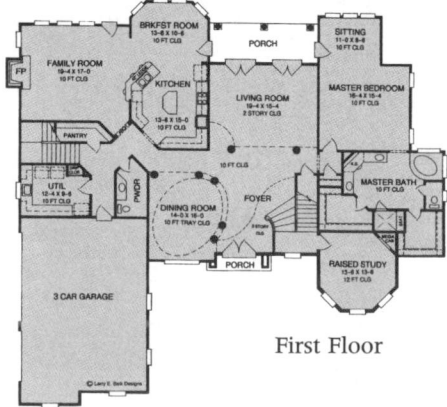

First Floor

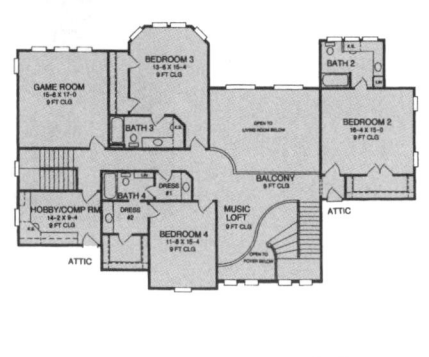

Second Floor

HPK2101387

Style: Chateauesque

First Floor: 3,520 sq. ft.

Second Floor: 1,638 sq. ft.

Total: 5,158 sq. ft.

Bonus Space: 411 sq. ft.

Bedrooms: 5

Bathrooms: 4 ½

Width: 96' - 6"

Depth: 58' - 8"

EPLANS.COM

First Floor

Second Floor

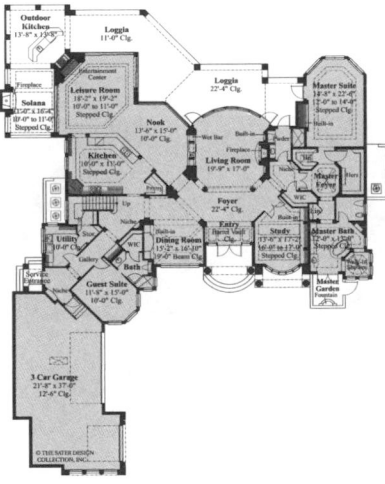

First Floor

HPK2101388

Style: Mediterranean

First Floor: 3,873 sq. ft.

Second Floor: 1,289 sq. ft.

Total: 5,162 sq. ft.

Bedrooms: 4

Bathrooms: 5

Width: 98' - 0"

Depth: 119' - 9"

Foundation: Slab

EPLANS.COM

Second Floor

4,000 SQUARE FEET AND OVER

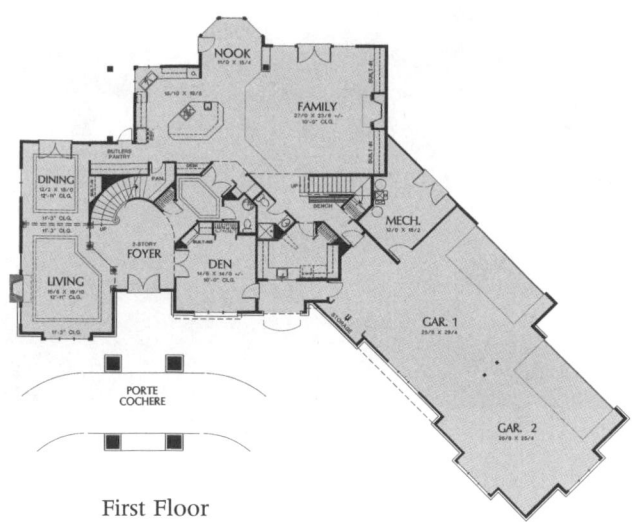

First Floor

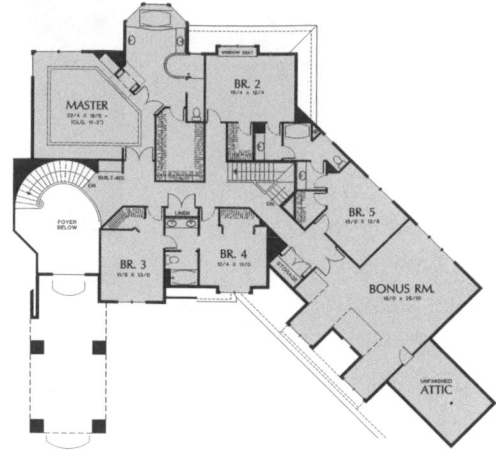

Second Floor

HPK2101389

Style: Craftsman
First Floor: 2,790 sq. ft.
Second Floor: 2,382 sq. ft.
Total: 5,172 sq. ft.
Bonus Space: 599 sq. ft.
Bedrooms: 5
Bathrooms: 4 ½
Width: 111' - 10"
Depth: 92' - 8"
Foundation: Crawlspace

EPLANS.COM

Rustic stone accents on the exterior of this home balance the grandeur found inside. A magnificent stairway spirals up through the foyer. A convenient butler's pantry leads to the spacious island kitchen, where yards of counter space and cabinetry will delight. French doors in the family room allow the company to spill out onto the grass. A back stair leads to the second floor, which includes a spacious bonus room. Four family bedrooms are paired around two compartmented baths, and the master suite features a plush spa-like getaway.

ORDER BLUEPRINTS ANYTIME AT EPLANS.COM OR 1-800-521-6797

HPK2101390

Style: Victorian Eclectic
First Floor: 3,030 sq. ft.
Second Floor: 2,150 sq. ft.
Total: 5,180 sq. ft.
Bedrooms: 6
Bathrooms: 5
Width: 117' - 6"
Depth: 63' - 6"
Foundation: Crawlspace

EPLANS.COM

Farmhouse style brings to this home a delightful appeal. The main floor holds great livability with a great room, a club room, a formal dining room, and a tucked-away office. The second floor holds the master suite and three family bedrooms. The master bedroom has a private deck. An apartment over the three-car garage offers living/dining space, a kitchen, and two bedrooms.

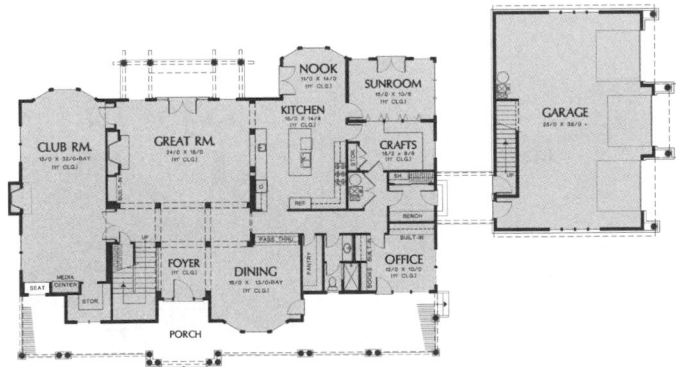

First Floor

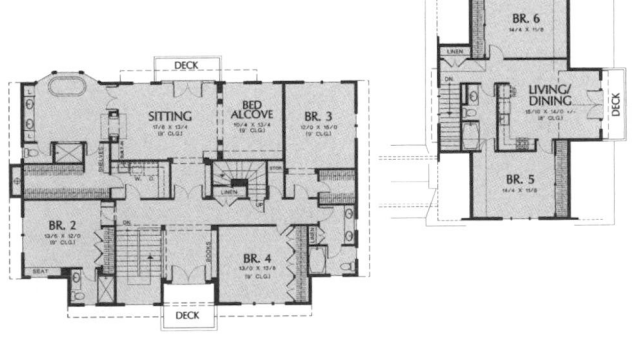

Second Floor

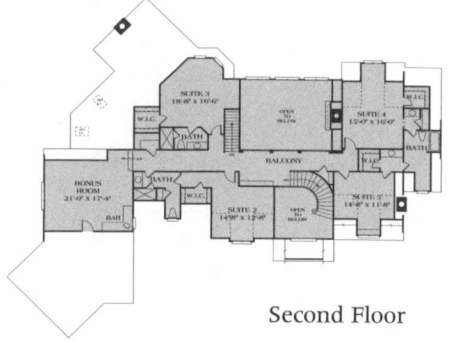

First Floor

Second Floor

HPK2101391

Style: Chateauesque
First Floor: 3,387 sq. ft.
Second Floor: 1,799 sq. ft.
Total: 5,186 sq. ft.
Bonus Space: 379 sq. ft.
Bedrooms: 5
Bathrooms: 4 ½ + ½
Width: 110' - 10"
Depth: 84' - 6"
Foundation: Crawlspace

EPLANS.COM

HPK2101392

Style: French Country
First Floor: 3,310 sq. ft.
Second Floor: 1,881 sq. ft.
Total: 5,191 sq. ft.
Bonus Space: 929 sq. ft.
Bedrooms: 5
Bathrooms: 4 ½ + ½
Width: 111' - 6"
Depth: 71' - 0"
Foundation: Crawlspace

EPLANS.COM

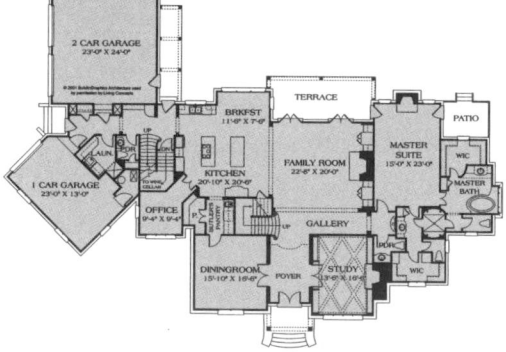

First Floor

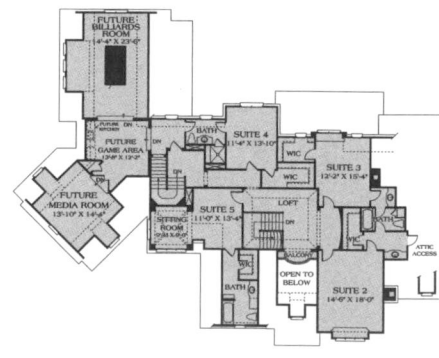

Second Floor

Rear Exterior

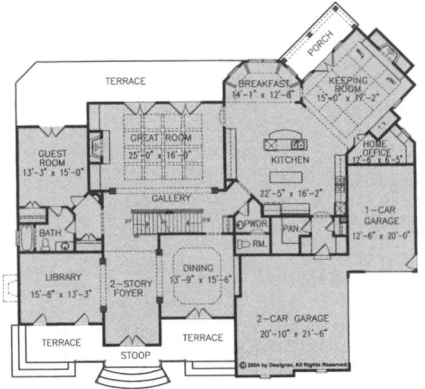

First Floor

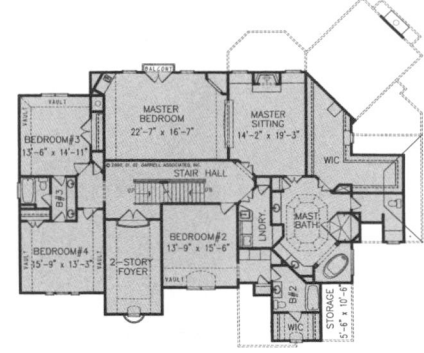

Second Floor

HPK2101393

Style: Chateauesque

First Floor: 2,702 sq. ft.

Second Floor: 2,494 sq. ft.

Total: 5,196 sq. ft.

Bedrooms: 5

Bathrooms: 4 ½

Width: 74' - 10"

Depth: 65' - 9"

Foundation: Unfinished Walkout Basement

EPLANS.COM

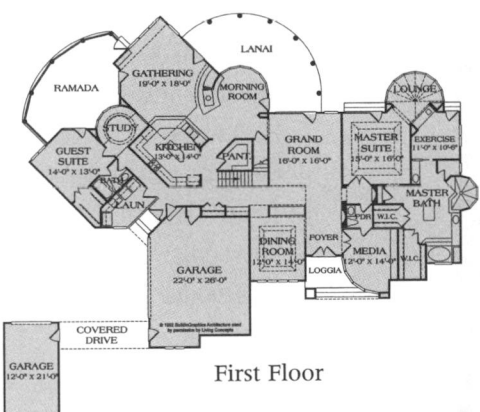

First Floor

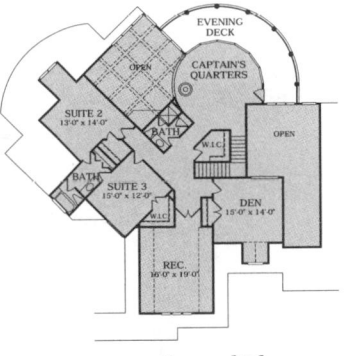

Second Floor

HPK2101394

Style: New American

First Floor: 3,322 sq. ft.

Second Floor: 1,897 sq. ft.

Total: 5,219 sq. ft.

Bedrooms: 4

Bathrooms: 4 ½

Width: 106' - 6"

Depth: 89' - 10"

Foundation: Crawlspace

EPLANS.COM

HPK2101395

Style: New American
First Floor: 3,599 sq. ft.
Second Floor: 1,621 sq. ft.
Total: 5,220 sq. ft.
Bonus Space: 537 sq. ft.
Bedrooms: 4
Bathrooms: 5 ½
Width: 108' - 10"
Depth: 53' - 10"
Foundation: Slab, Unfinished Basement

EPLANS.COM

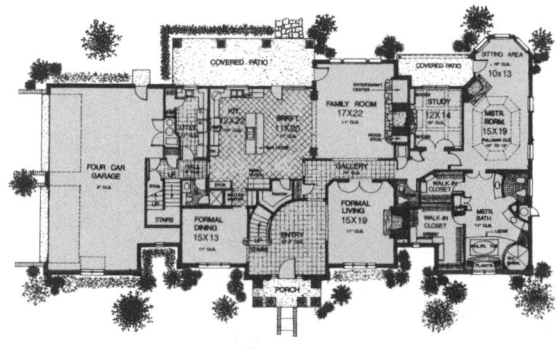

First Floor

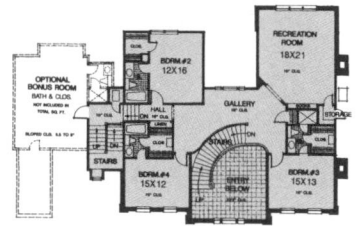

Second Floor

HPK2101396

Style: Chateauesque
First Floor: 3,568 sq. ft.
Second Floor: 1,667 sq. ft.
Total: 5,235 sq. ft.
Bedrooms: 4
Bathrooms: 3 ½
Width: 86' - 8"
Depth: 79' - 0"
Foundation: Finished Walkout Basement

EPLANS.COM

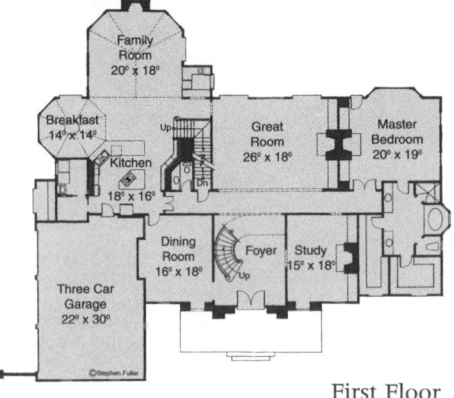

First Floor

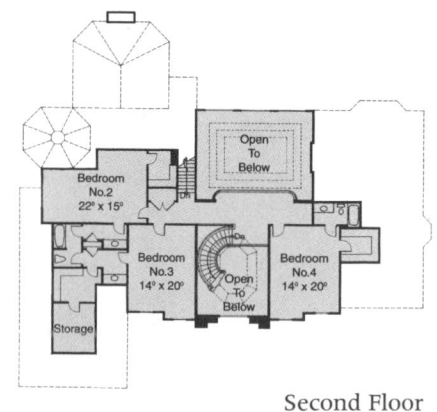

Second Floor

Photography by: Dave Dawson. This home, as shown in photographs, may differ from the actual blueprints. For more detailed information, please check the floor plans carefully.

HPK2101397

Style: Craftsman
First Floor: 2,750 sq. ft.
Second Floor: 2,500 sq. ft.
Total: 5,250 sq. ft.
Bedrooms: 5
Bathrooms: 4 ½
Width: 98' - 0"
Depth: 74' - 0"
Foundation: Crawlspace

EPLANS.COM

First Floor

Second Floor

HPK2101398

Style: Victorian Eclectic
First Floor: 2,375 sq. ft.
Second Floor: 2,875 sq. ft.
Total: 5,250 sq. ft.
Bedrooms: 4
Bathrooms: 4 ½
Width: 71' - 0"
Depth: 91' - 6"
Foundation: Crawlspace

EPLANS.COM

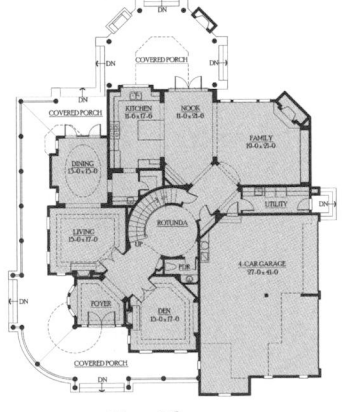

First Floor

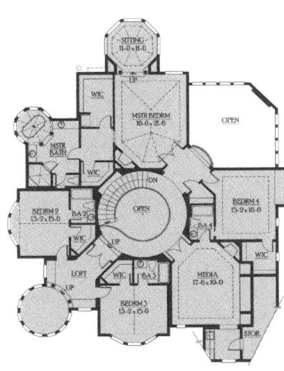

Second Floor

4,000 SQUARE FEET AND OVER

First Floor

Second Floor

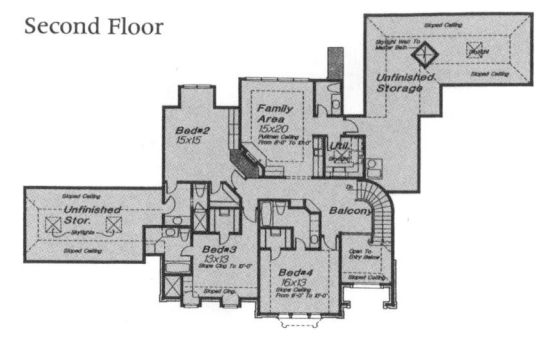

HPK2101399

Style: New American
First Floor: 3,594 sq. ft.
Second Floor: 1,656 sq. ft.
Total: 5,250 sq. ft.
Bedrooms: 4
Bathrooms: 4 ½ + ½
Width: 112' - 4"
Depth: 72' - 10"
Foundation: Crawlspace, Slab, Unfinished Basement

EPLANS.COM

First Floor

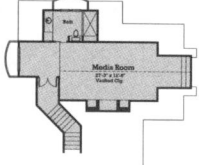

Second Floor

HPK2101400

Style: Mediterranean
First Floor: 4,784 sq. ft.
Second Floor: 481 sq. ft.
Total: 5,265 sq. ft.
Bedrooms: 4
Bathrooms: 6 ½
Width: 106' - 6"
Depth: 106' - 0"
Foundation: Slab

EPLANS.COM

First Floor

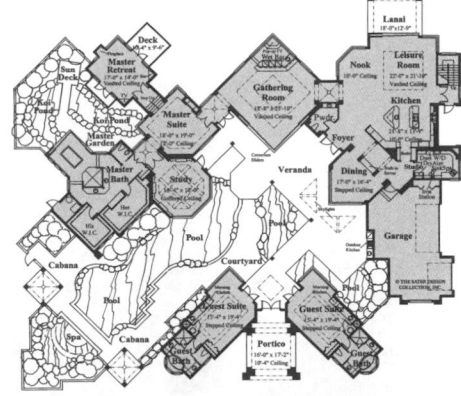

Second Floor

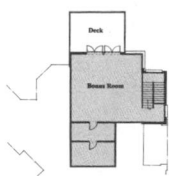

HPK2101401

Style: Mediterranean

First Floor: 5,887 sq. ft.

Second Floor: 570 sq. ft.

Total: 6,457 sq. ft.

Bedrooms: 3

Bathrooms: 3 ½

Width: 137' - 4"

Depth: 103' - 0"

Foundation: Slab

EPLANS.COM

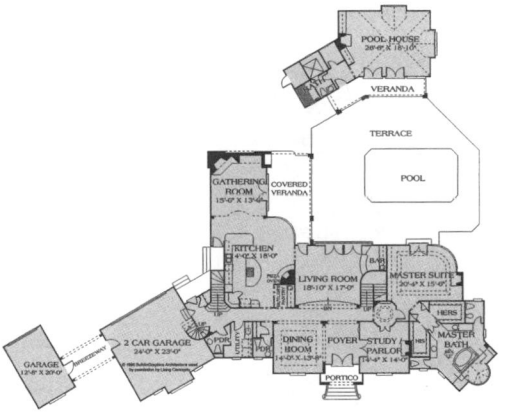

First Floor

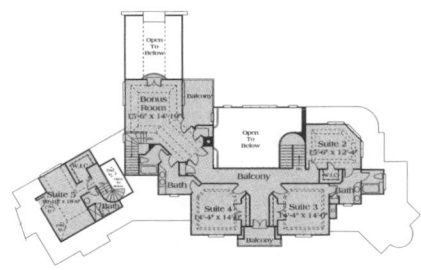

Second Floor

HPK2101402

Style: Mediterranean

First Floor: 3,307 sq. ft.

Second Floor: 2,015 sq. ft.

Total: 5,322 sq. ft.

Bonus Space: 373 sq. ft.

Bedrooms: 5

Bathrooms: 5 ½ + ½

Width: 143' - 3"

Depth: 71' - 2"

Foundation: Crawlspace

EPLANS.COM

4,000 SQUARE FEET AND OVER

First Floor

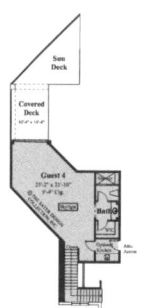

Second Floor

HPK2101403

Style: Mediterranean

First Floor: 4,716 sq. ft.

Second Floor: 619 sq. ft.

Total: 5,335 sq. ft.

Bedrooms: 4

Bathrooms: 5 ½

Width: 95' - 0"

Depth: 134' - 6"

Foundation: Slab

EPLANS.COM

HPK2101404

Style: French Country

First Floor: 3,560 sq. ft.

Second Floor: 1,783 sq. ft.

Total: 5,343 sq. ft.

Bedrooms: 4

Bathrooms: 3 ½

Width: 121' - 2"

Depth: 104' - 4"

Foundation: Crawlspace

EPLANS.COM

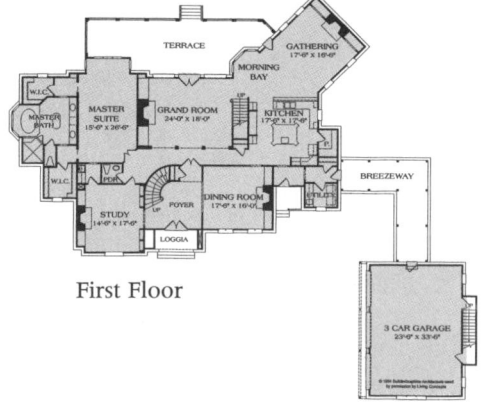

First Floor

Second Floor

HPK2101405

Style: Neoclassical

First Floor: 3,749 sq. ft.

Second Floor: 1,631 sq. ft.

Total: 5,380 sq. ft.

Bonus Space: 1,171 sq. ft.

Bedrooms: 4

Bathrooms: 4 ½ + ½

Width: 92' - 4"

Depth: 112' - 0"

Foundation: Crawlspace, Unfinished Basement

EPLANS.COM

First Floor

Second Floor

HPK2101406

©1999 William E Poole Designs, Inc.

Style: Federal - Adams

First Floor: 3,463 sq. ft.

Second Floor: 1,924 sq. ft.

Total: 5,387 sq. ft.

Bedrooms: 4

Bathrooms: 5 ½

Width: 88' - 6"

Depth: 98' - 0"

Foundation: Crawlspace, Basement

EPLANS.COM

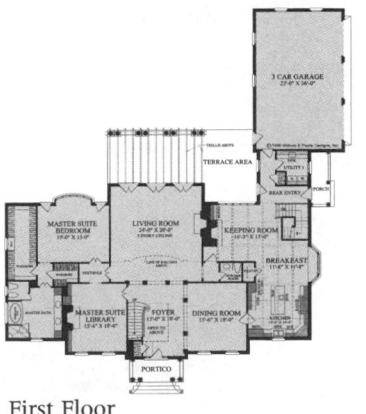

First Floor

Second Floor

4,000 SQUARE FEET AND OVER

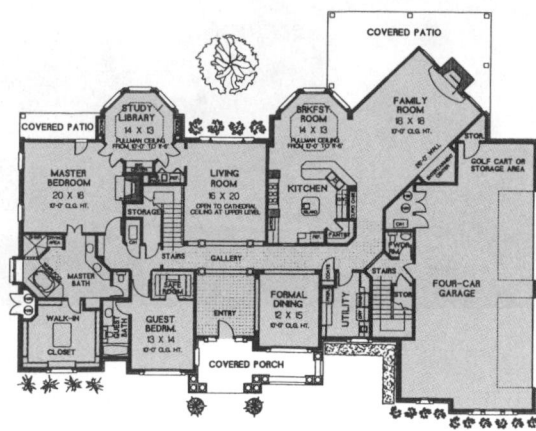

First Floor

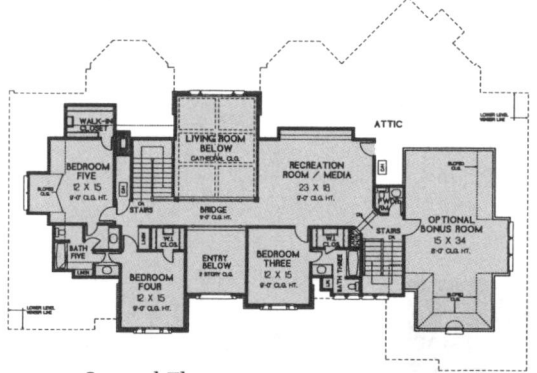

Second Floor

HPK2101407

Style: New American

First Floor: 3,745 sq. ft.

Second Floor: 1,643 sq. ft.

Total: 5,388 sq. ft.

Bonus Space: 510 sq. ft.

Bedrooms: 5

Bathrooms: 4 ½ + ½

Width: 100' - 0"

Depth: 70' - 1"

Foundation: Crawlspace, Slab, Unfinished Basement

EPLANS.COM

Steep rooflines and plenty of windows create a sophisticated aura around this home. An angled family room featuring a fireplace is great for rest and relaxation. A ribbon of windows in the living room makes for an open feel. The master bedroom offers a bath with dual vanities and a spacious walk-in closet. Three family bedrooms are located on the upper level with a recreation/media room and an optional bonus room.

HPK2101408

Style: Mediterranean
First Floor: 4,138 sq. ft.
Second Floor: 1,269 sq. ft.
Total: 5,407 sq. ft.
Bedrooms: 3
Bathrooms: 3 ½ + ½
Width: 90' - 0"
Depth: 85' - 0"
Foundation: Slab

EPLANS.COM

Most of the living in this grand home takes place on the first floor. An open arrangement of the living and dining rooms allows interior vistas to extend from the entry to the rear veranda. A gourmet kitchen with wrapping counters and a food-preparation island links the formal and casual dining spaces. The master suite features a private study, a marvelous bath, and a bedroom with a step ceiling. Two guest suites are perfect for family and friends. The leisure room features corner sliding glass doors and a wet bar.

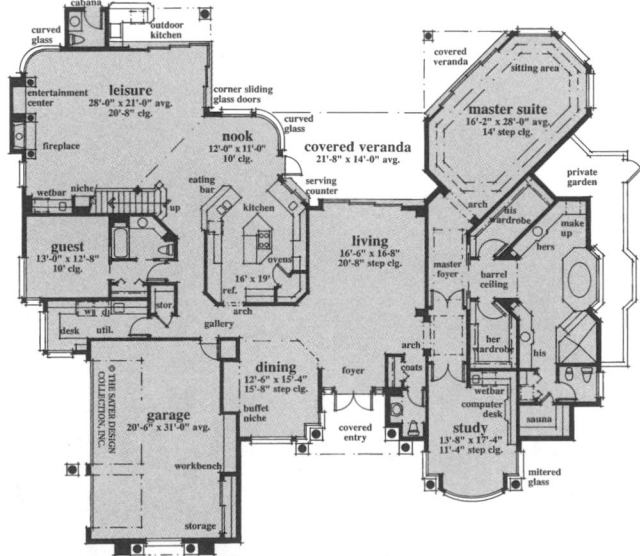

First Floor

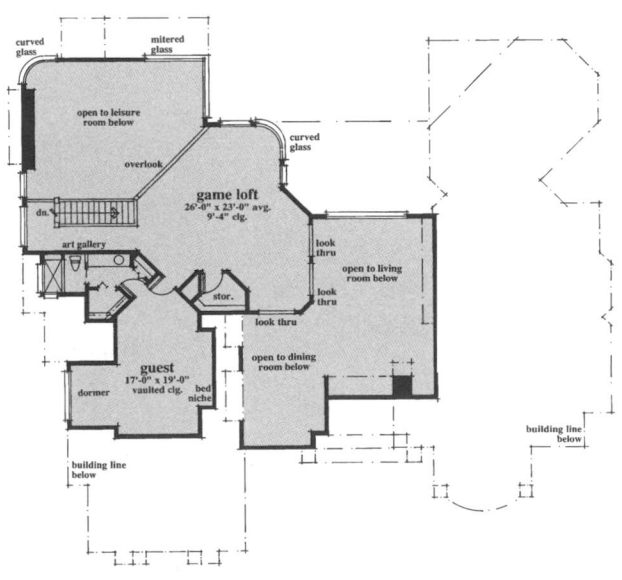

Second Floor

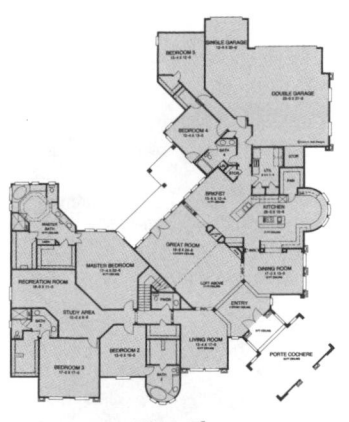
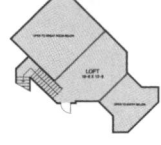

First Floor

Second Floor

HPK2101409

Style: Mediterranean
First Floor: 5,183 sq. ft.
Second Floor: 238 sq. ft.
Total: 5,421 sq. ft.
Bedrooms: 5
Bathrooms: 4 ½
Width: 93' - 5"
Depth: 113' - 0"
Foundation: Slab

EPLANS.COM

© Larry E. Belk Designs

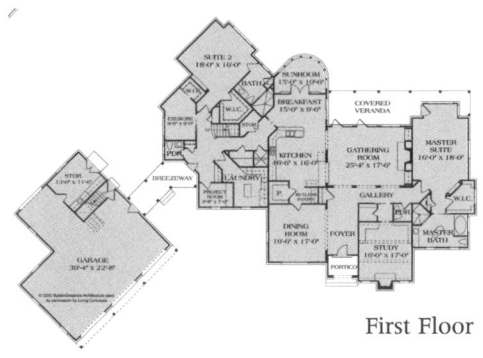

First Floor

Second Floor

HPK2101410

Style: French Country
First Floor: 4,218 sq. ft.
Second Floor: 1,208 sq. ft.
Total: 5,426 sq. ft.
Bedrooms: 5
Bathrooms: 5 ½ + ½
Width: 138' - 0"
Depth: 98' - 6"
Foundation: Crawlspace

EPLANS.COM

First Floor

Second Floor

HPK2101411

Style: Georgian
First Floor: 3,487 sq. ft.
Second Floor: 1,945 sq. ft.
Total: 5,432 sq. ft.
Bedrooms: 5
Bathrooms: 5 ½
Width: 82' - 4"
Depth: 105' - 10"
Foundation: Crawlspace

EPLANS.COM

First Floor

Second Floor

HPK2101412

Style: French Country
First Floor: 3,559 sq. ft.
Second Floor: 1,888 sq. ft.
Total: 5,447 sq. ft.
Bedrooms: 5
Bathrooms: 5 ½
Width: 106' - 6"
Depth: 89' - 5"
Foundation: Unfinished Walkout Basement

EPLANS.COM

4,000 SQUARE FEET AND OVER

HPK2101413

Style: French Country
First Floor: 3,229 sq. ft.
Second Floor: 2,219 sq. ft.
Total: 5,448 sq. ft.
Bonus Space: 603 sq. ft.
Bedrooms: 5
Bathrooms: 5 ½ + ½
Width: 72' - 11"
Depth: 99' - 6"
Foundation: Crawlspace

EPLANS.COM

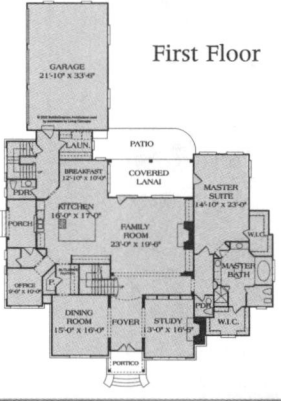

First Floor

Second Floor

First Floor

HPK2101414

Style: Mediterranean
First Floor: 4,470 sq. ft.
Second Floor: 680 sq. ft.
Total: 5,150 sq. ft.
Bonus Space: 314 sq. ft.
Bedrooms: 4
Bathrooms: 5 ½
Width: 102' - 0"
Depth: 131' - 0"
Foundation: Slab

EPLANS.COM

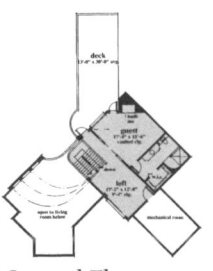

Second Floor

HPK2101415

Style: Farmhouse

First Floor: 2,732 sq. ft.

Second Floor: 2,734 sq. ft.

Total: 5,466 sq. ft.

Bedrooms: 5

Bathrooms: 5 ½ + ½

Width: 85' - 0"

Depth: 85' - 6"

Foundation: Crawlspace, Slab, Unfinished Walkout Basement

A wraparound covered porch adds plenty of outdoor space to this already impressive home. Built-in cabinets flank the fireplace in the grand room; a fireplace also warms the hearthroom. The gourmet kitchen includes an island counter, large walk-in pantry, and serving bar. A secluded home office, with a separate entrance nearby, provides a quiet work place. A front parlor provides even more room for entertaining or relaxing. The second floor is home to the spacious master suite, an enormous exercise room, and three additional bedrooms.

First Floor

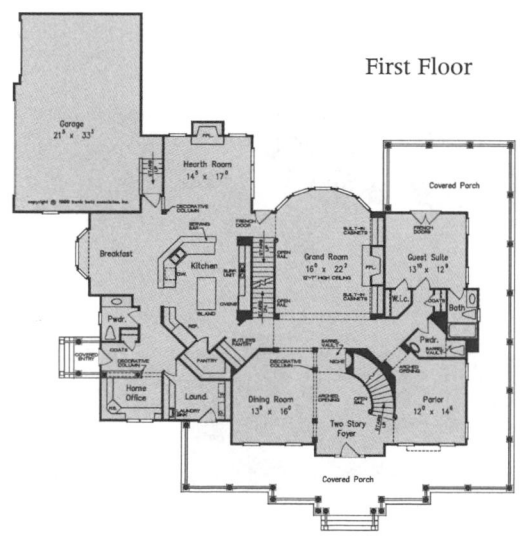

Second Floor

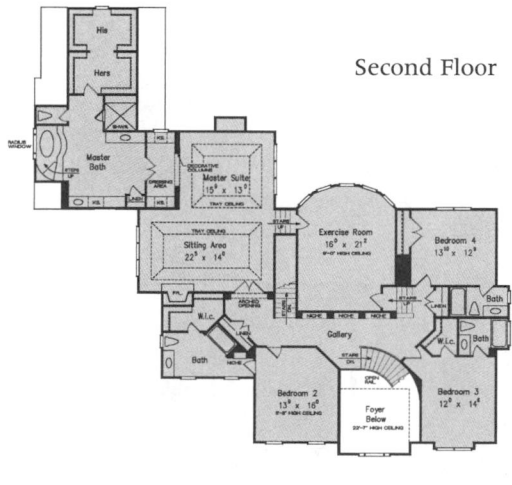

4,000 SQUARE FEET AND OVER

First Floor

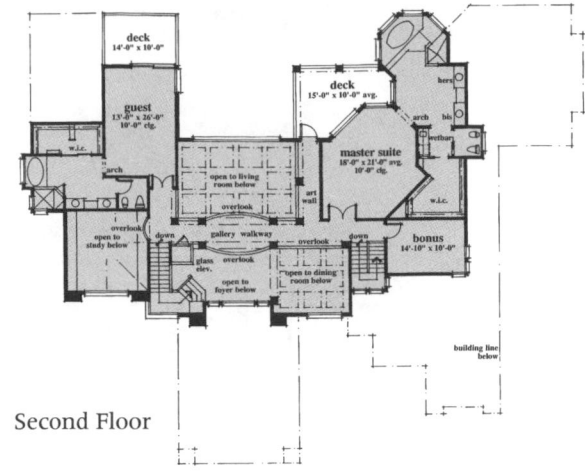

Second Floor

HPK2101416

Sweeping heights lend a grand stroke to many of the rooms in this estate: the study, the grand foyer, the dining room, and the living room. The living and dining room ceilings are also coffered. Upstairs, the master suite enjoys a full list of appointments, including an exercise (or bonus) room, a tub tower with vaulted cove-lit ceiling, and a private deck. Also on this floor is a guest bedroom with an observation deck (or make this a spectacular study to complement the master suite). Other special details: a pass-through outdoor bar, an outdoor kitchen, a workshop area, two verandas, and a glass elevator.

Style: Mediterranean
First Floor: 3,667 sq. ft.
Second Floor: 1,862 sq. ft.
Total: 5,529 sq. ft.
Bonus Space: 140 sq. ft.
Bedrooms: 4
Bathrooms: 5 ½
Width: 102' - 0"
Depth: 87' - 0"
Foundation: Slab

EPLANS.COM

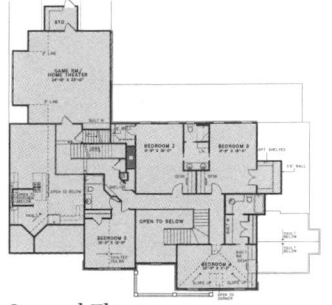

First Floor   Second Floor

HPK2101417

Style: New American

First Floor: 3,276 sq. ft.

Second Floor: 2,272 sq. ft.

Total: 5,548 sq. ft.

Bedrooms: 5

Bathrooms: 4 ½

Width: 81' - 6"

Depth: 93' - 2"

Foundation: Crawlspace, Slab, Unfinished Basement

EPLANS.COM

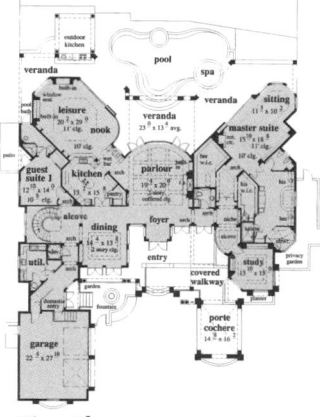

First Floor

Second Floor

HPK2101418

Style: Mediterranean

First Floor: 4,351 sq. ft.

Second Floor: 1,200 sq. ft.

Total: 5,551 sq. ft.

Bedrooms: 4

Bathrooms: 5 ½

Width: 90' - 1"

Depth: 114' - 3"

Foundation: Slab

EPLANS.COM

4,000 SQUARE FEET AND OVER

HPK2101419

Style: French Country
First Floor: 3,289 sq. ft.
Second Floor: 2,266 sq. ft.
Total: 5,555 sq. ft.
Bedrooms: 5
Bathrooms: 5 ½ + ½
Width: 96' - 4"
Depth: 69' - 0"
Foundation: Crawlspace

EPLANS.COM

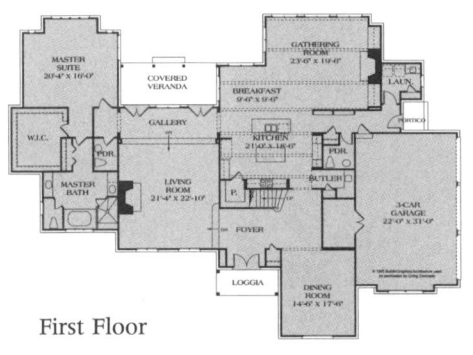

First Floor

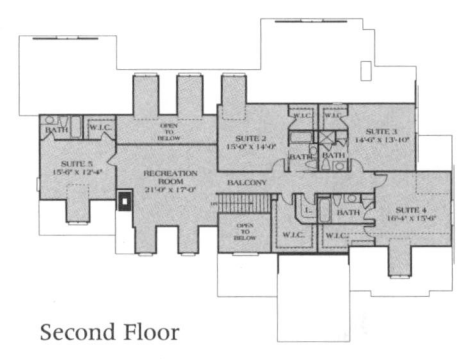

Second Floor

HPK2101420

Style: Mediterranean
First Floor: 4,208 sq. ft.
Second Floor: 1,352 sq. ft.
Total: 5,560 sq. ft.
Bedrooms: 4
Bathrooms: 4 ½ + ½
Width: 94' - 0"
Depth: 68' - 0"
Foundation: Crawlspace, Slab

EPLANS.COM

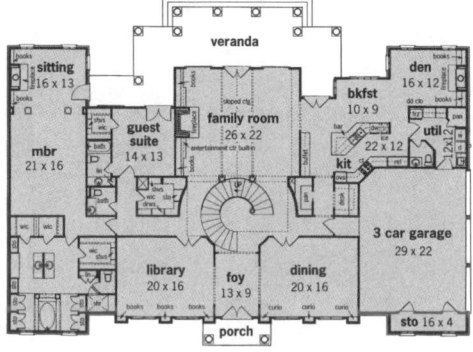

First Floor

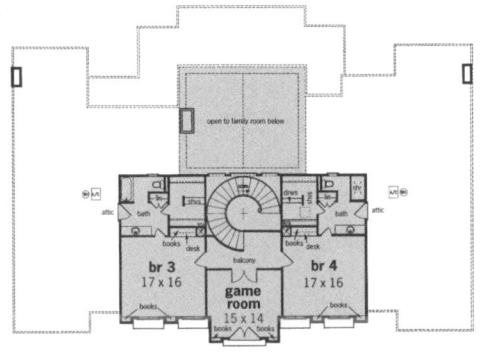

Second Floor

HPK2101421

Style: Mediterranean
First Floor: 4,186 sq. ft.
Second Floor: 1,378 sq. ft.
Total: 5,564 sq. ft.
Bedrooms: 5
Bathrooms: 6
Width: 96' - 0"
Depth: 111' - 0"
Foundation: Slab

EPLANS.COM

First Floor

Second Floor

Rear Exterior

HPK2101422

Style: Neoclassical
First Floor: 3,545 sq. ft.
Second Floor: 2,019 sq. ft.
Total: 5,564 sq. ft.
Bonus Space: 928 sq. ft.
Bedrooms: 4
Bathrooms: 4 ½ + ½
Width: 124' - 4"
Depth: 79' - 3"
Foundation: Crawlspace, Unfinished Basement

EPLANS.COM

© WILLIAM E POOLE DESIGNS, INC.

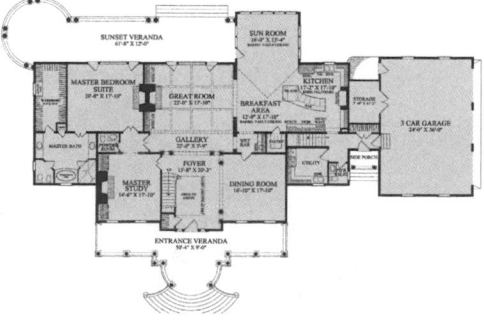

First Floor

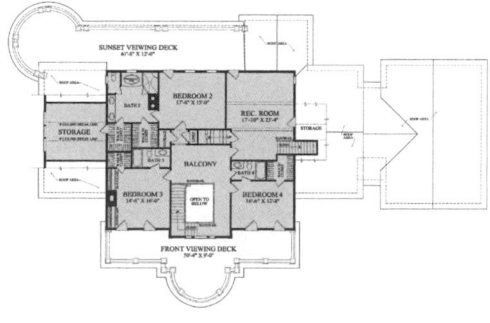

Second Floor

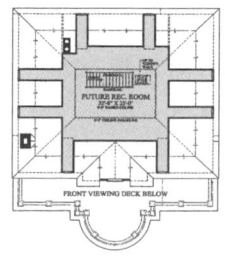

4,000 SQUARE FEET AND OVER

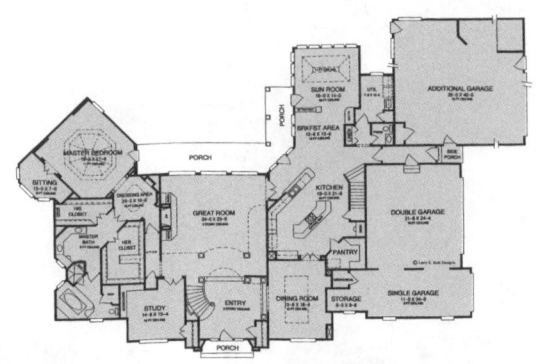

First Floor

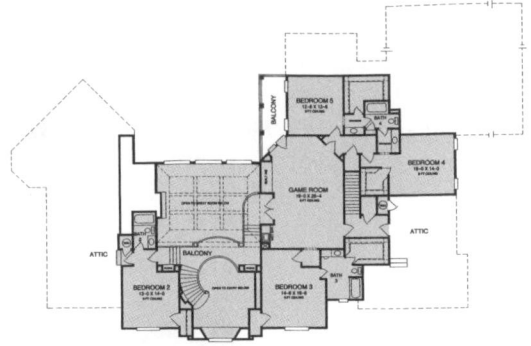

Second Floor

HPK2101423

Style: Colonial Revival

First Floor: 3,722 sq. ft.

Second Floor: 1,859 sq. ft.

Total: 5,581 sq. ft.

Bedrooms: 5

Bathrooms: 4 ½

Width: 127' - 10"

Depth: 83' - 9"

Foundation: Slab

EPLANS.COM

© Larry E. Belk Designs

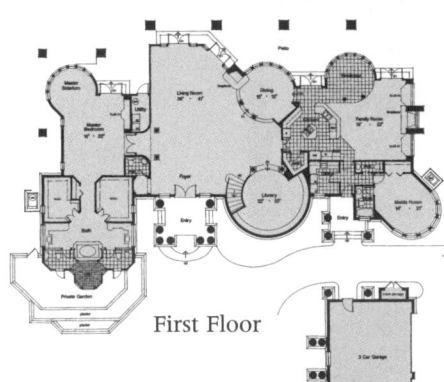

First Floor

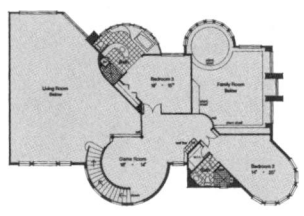

Second Floor

HPK2101424

Style: Mediterranean

First Floor: 4,284 sq. ft.

Second Floor: 1,319 sq. ft.

Total: 5,603 sq. ft.

Bedrooms: 4

Bathrooms: 4 ½ + ½

Width: 109' - 4"

Depth: 73' - 2"

Foundation: Slab

EPLANS.COM

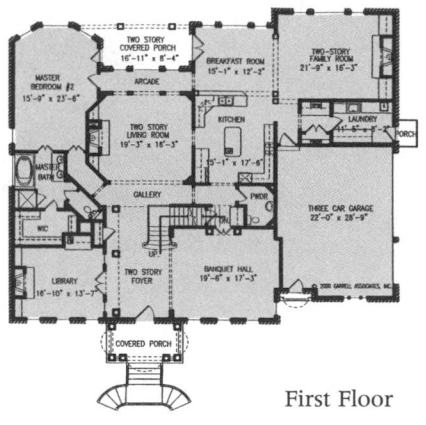

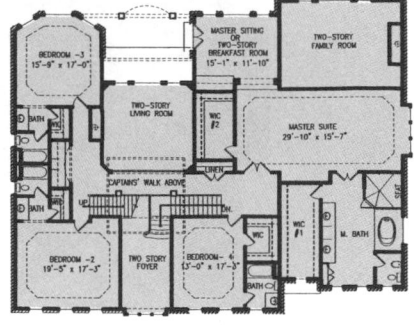

First Floor

Second Floor

HPK2101425

Style: Italianate

First Floor: 3,156 sq. ft.

Second Floor: 2,557 sq. ft.

Total: 5,713 sq. ft.

Bedrooms: 5

Bathrooms: 5 ½

Width: 71' - 0"

Depth: 58' - 8"

Foundation: Unfinished Basement

EPLANS.COM

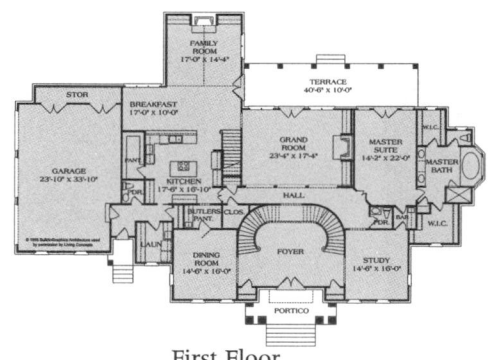

First Floor

Second Floor

HPK2101426

Style: Neoclassical

First Floor: 3,669 sq. ft.

Second Floor: 2,048 sq. ft.

Total: 5,717 sq. ft.

Bonus Space: 375 sq. ft.

Bedrooms: 5

Bathrooms: 4 ½ + ½

Width: 108' - 10"

Depth: 72' - 0"

Foundation: Crawlspace

EPLANS.COM

HPK2101427

Style: Georgian
First Floor: 3,712 sq. ft.
Second Floor: 2,083 sq. ft.
Total: 5,795 sq. ft.
Bonus Space: 409 sq. ft.
Bedrooms: 5
Bathrooms: 5 ½ + 2 Half Baths
Width: 107' - 8"
Depth: 46' - 6"
Foundation: Crawlspace

EPLANS.COM

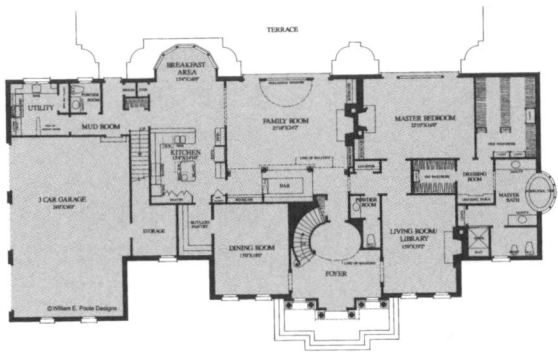

First Floor

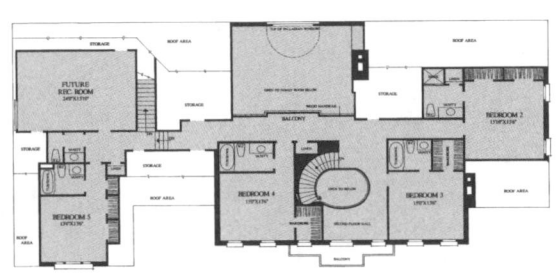

Second Floor

HPK2101428

Style: Mediterranean
First Floor: 5,307 sq. ft.
Second Floor: 497 sq. ft.
Total: 5,804 sq. ft.
Bedrooms: 4
Bathrooms: 4 ½
Width: 132' - 8"
Depth: 117' - 3"
Foundation: Slab

EPLANS.COM

Rear Exterior

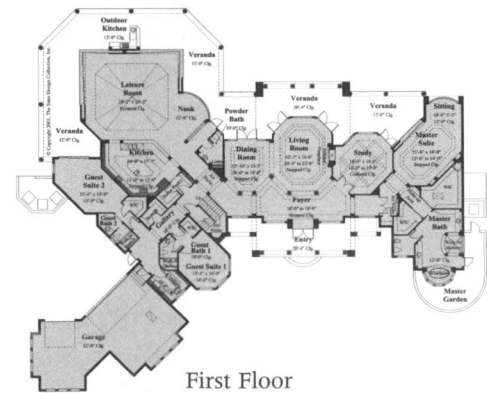

First Floor

Second Floor

HPK2101429

Style: Mediterranean

First Floor: 4,385 sq. ft.

Second Floor: 1,431 sq. ft.

Total: 5,816 sq. ft.

Bedrooms: 5

Bathrooms: 6

Width: 88' - 0"

Depth: 110' - 1"

Foundation: Slab

EPLANS.COM

Grand arches lend Mediterranean flavor to this contemporary estate. An open interior of decorative columns and stone arches defines the formal living and dining rooms. Leisure space invites relaxation in front of a built-in entertainment center, while the outdoor kitchen encourages dining alfresco. A master suite stretches across the left wing, which includes a quiet study. Among the four additional bedroom suites, one boasts a morning kitchen and two have access to a private deck or veranda.

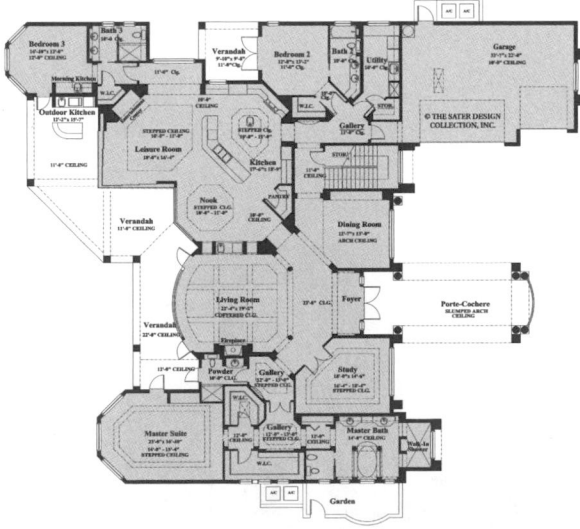

First Floor

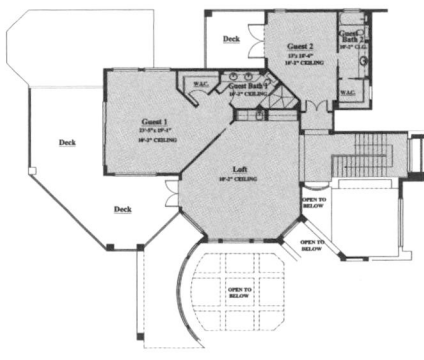

Second Floor

4,000 SQUARE FEET AND OVER

First Floor

Second Floor

HPK2101430

Style: New American
First Floor: 4,205 sq. ft.
Second Floor: 1,618 sq. ft.
Total: 5,823 sq. ft.
Bonus Space: 504 sq. ft.
Bedrooms: 4
Bathrooms: 5 ½
Width: 104' - 0"
Depth: 97' - 0"
Foundation: Crawlspace

EPLANS.COM

First Floor

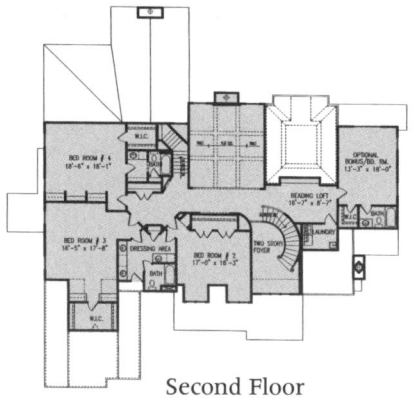

Second Floor

HPK2101431

Style: French Country
First Floor: 3,607 sq. ft.
Second Floor: 2,238 sq. ft.
Total: 5,845 sq. ft.
Bonus Space: 329 sq. ft.
Bedrooms: 4
Bathrooms: 3 ½ + ½
Width: 83' - 6"
Depth: 88' - 4"
Foundation: Unfinished Basement

EPLANS.COM

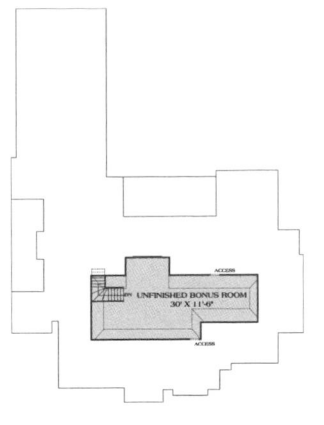

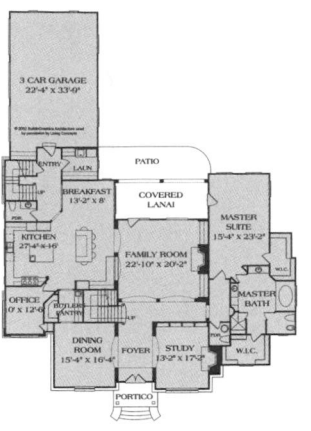

First Floor

Second Floor

HPK2101432

Style: Chateauesque
First Floor: 3,352 sq. ft.
Second Floor: 2,520 sq. ft.
Total: 5,872 sq. ft.
Bonus Space: 592 sq. ft.
Bedrooms: 5
Bathrooms: 5 ½ + ½
Width: 72' - 10"
Depth: 99' - 6"
Foundation: Crawlspace

EPLANS.COM

HPK2101433

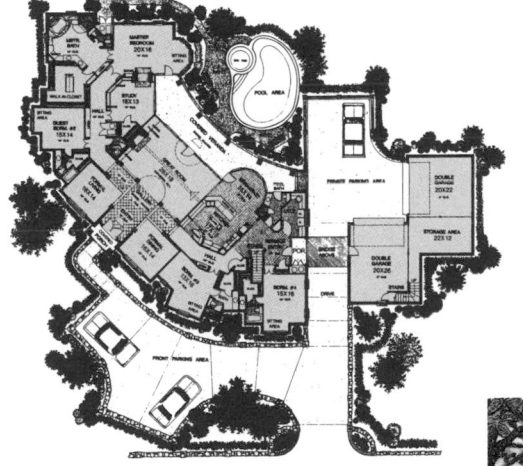

First Floor

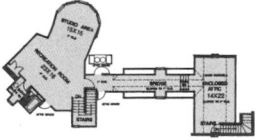

Second Floor

EPLANS.COM

Style: Chateauesque
First Floor: 5,152 sq. ft.
Second Floor: 726 sq. ft.
Total: 5,878 sq. ft.
Bedrooms: 4
Bathrooms: 5 ½
Width: 146' - 7"
Depth: 106' - 7"
Foundation: Slab

4,000 SQUARE FEET AND OVER

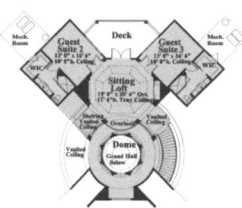

First Floor

Second Floor

HPK2101434

Style: Italianate

First Floor: 4,715 sq. ft.

Second Floor: 1,209 sq. ft.

Total: 5,924 sq. ft.

Bedrooms: 3

Bathrooms: 3 ½

Width: 117' - 2"

Depth: 131' - 7"

Foundation: Slab

EPLANS.COM

HPK2101435

Style: Chateauesque

First Floor: 3,736 sq. ft.

Second Floor: 2,264 sq. ft.

Total: 6,000 sq. ft.

Bedrooms: 5

Bathrooms: 5 ½ + ½

Width: 133' - 4"

Depth: 65' - 5"

Foundation: Slab

EPLANS.COM

First Floor

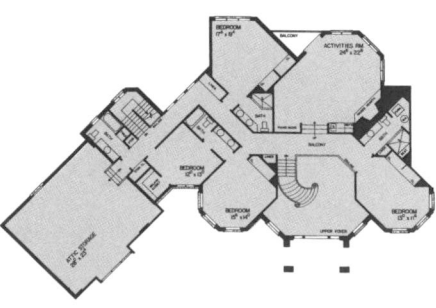

Second Floor

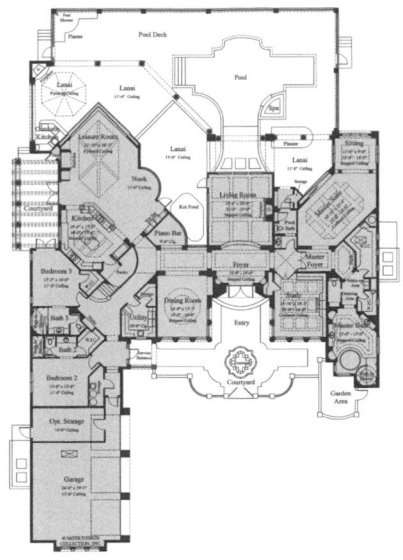

First Floor

Second Floor

HPK2101436

Style: Italianate
First Floor: 5,265 sq. ft.
Second Floor: 746 sq. ft.
Total: 6,011 sq. ft.
Bedrooms: 4
Bathrooms: 4 ½
Width: 100' - 0"
Depth: 140' - 0"
Foundation: Slab

EPLANS.COM

HPK2101437

Style: New American
First Floor: 3,620 sq. ft.
Second Floor: 2,440 sq. ft.
Total: 6,060 sq. ft.
Bedrooms: 4
Bathrooms: 3 ½ + ½
Width: 139' - 6"
Depth: 91' - 1"
Foundation: Crawlspace

EPLANS.COM

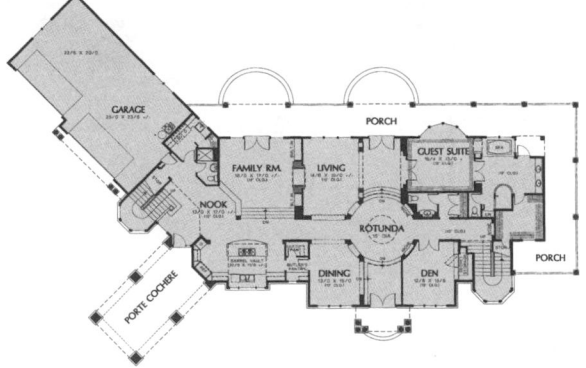

First Floor

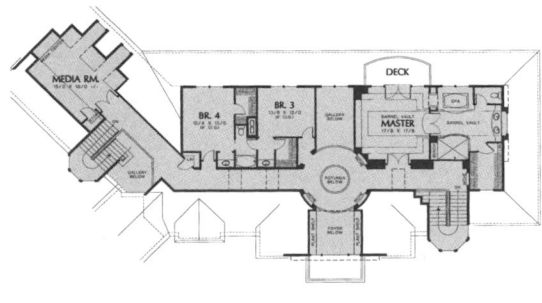

Second Floor

4,000 SQUARE FEET AND OVER

HPK2101438

Style: Italianate
First Floor: 4,742 sq. ft.
Second Floor: 1,531 sq. ft.
Total: 6,273 sq. ft.
Bedrooms: 4
Bathrooms: 4 ½ + ½
Width: 96' - 0"
Depth: 134' - 8"
Foundation: Slab

EPLANS.COM

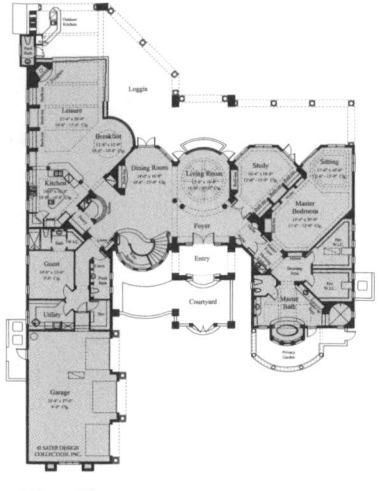

First Floor

Second Floor

HPK2101439

Style: Mediterranean
First Floor: 4,760 sq. ft.
Second Floor: 1,552 sq. ft.
Total: 6,312 sq. ft.
Bedrooms: 5
Bathrooms: 6 ½
Width: 98' - 0"
Depth: 103' - 8"
Foundation: Slab

EPLANS.COM

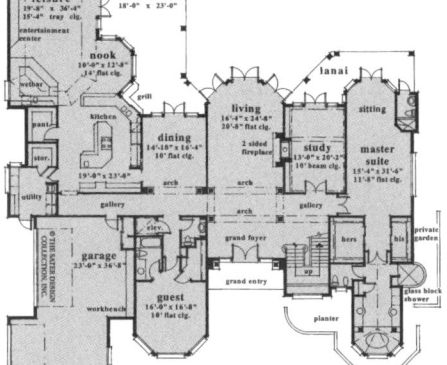

First Floor

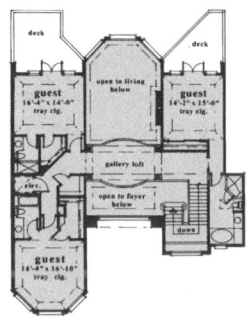

Second Floor

© The Sater Design Collection, Inc.

Photo By: Laurence Taylor. This home, as shown in photographs, may differ from the actual blueprints. For more detailed information, please check the floor plans carefully.

Rear Exterior

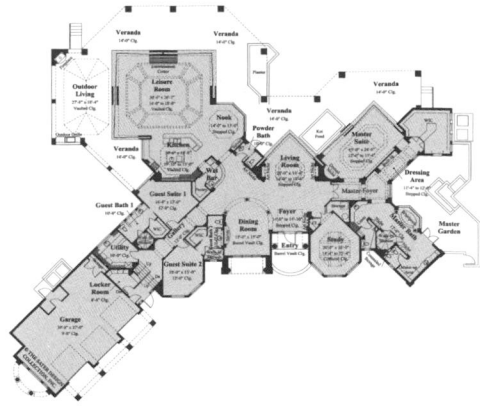

First Floor

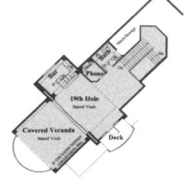

Second Floor

HPK2101440

Style: Mediterranean
First Floor: 5,696 sq. ft.
Second Floor: 644 sq. ft.
Total: 6,340 sq. ft.
Bedrooms: 3
Bathrooms: 4 ½
Width: 146' - 0"
Depth: 132' - 5"
Foundation: Slab

EPLANS.COM

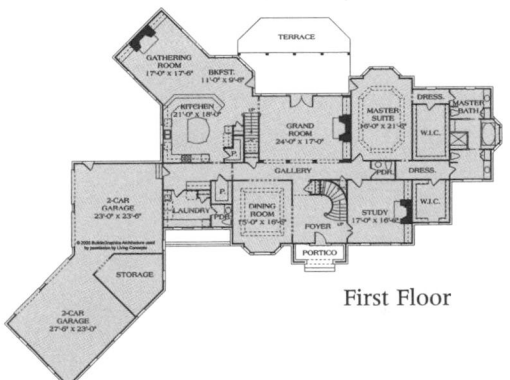

First Floor

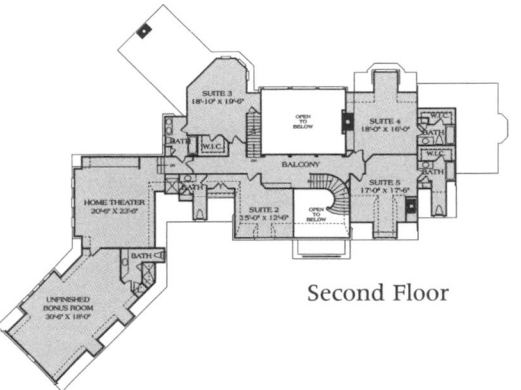

Second Floor

HPK2101441

EPLANS.COM

Style: Craftsman
First Floor: 3,767 sq. ft.
Second Floor: 2,665 sq. ft.
Total: 6,432 sq. ft.
Bonus Space: 780 sq. ft.
Bedrooms: 5
Bathrooms: 6 ½ + ½
Width: 133' - 10"
Depth: 102' - 8"
Foundation: Crawlspace

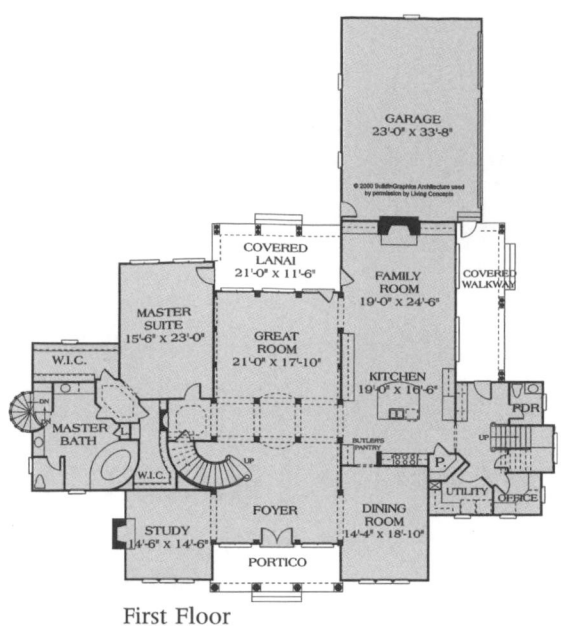

First Floor

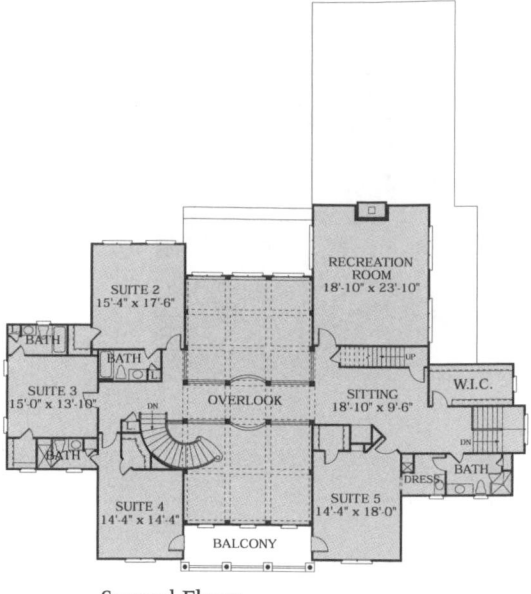

Second Floor

HPK2101442

Stunning Mediterranean style gives this home a sense of palatial elegance. Arches frame the portico, which leads inside to an impressive two-story foyer. The first-floor master suite enjoys a deluxe whirlpool bath and two walk-in closets. The island kitchen opens to the casual family room, warmed by a second fireplace. Four additional suites reside upstairs for other family members. A romantic overlook views the great room and foyer. A sitting room is placed just outside of the second-floor recreation room.

Style: Italianate
First Floor: 3,592 sq. ft.
Second Floor: 2,861 sq. ft.
Total: 6,453 sq. ft.
Bedrooms: 5
Bathrooms: 5 ½
Width: 96' - 5"
Depth: 91' - 6"
Foundation: Crawlspace

EPLANS.COM

ORDER BLUEPRINTS ANYTIME AT EPLANS.COM OR 1-800-521-6797

HPK2101443

Style: Chateauesque

First Floor: 3,874 sq. ft.

Second Floor: 2,588 sq. ft.

Total: 6,462 sq. ft.

Bedrooms: 4

Bathrooms: 5 ½ + ½

Width: 146' - 8"

Depth: 84' - 4"

Foundation: Slab

An oversized front entry beckons your attention to the wonderful amenities inside this home: a raised marble vestibule with a circular stair, a formal library and dining hall with views to the veranda and pool beyond, and a family gathering hall open to the kitchen and connected to the outdoor grill. The master suite is embellished with a nature garden and a fireplace. The second floor offers a media presentation room and a game room. Each of the family bedrooms features a private bath.

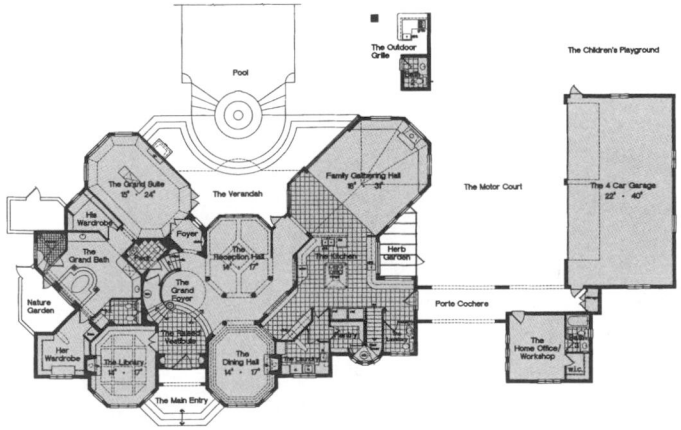

First Floor

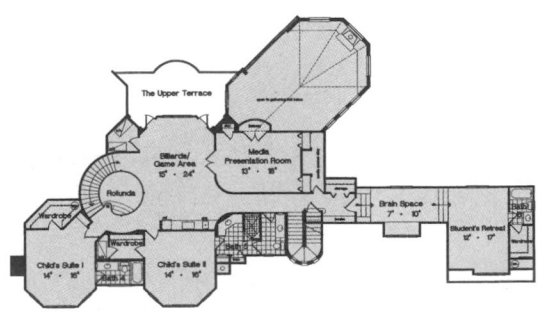

Second Floor

The facade is a mix of California Mission style and Italianate with stone siding, thoroughly modern interior is nearly mansion-sized and designed for luxury living. Choose formal or casual dining spaces—they flank the island kitchen, which also boasts a pizza oven and walk-in pantry. A butler's pantry and a wet bar add convenience to entertaining. Enjoy the outdoor spaces with three trellised porches at the rear of the plan. A three-car garage accesses the main part of the house via a handy mudroom.

HPK2101444

Style: Mission
First Floor: 4,747 sq. ft.
Second Floor: 1,737 sq. ft.
Total: 6,484 sq. ft.
Bedrooms: 5
Bathrooms: 4 ½ + ½
Width: 161' - 10"
Depth: 64' - 6"
Foundation: Crawlspace

EPLANS.COM

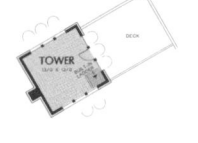

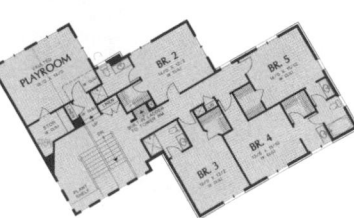

Second Floor

First Floor

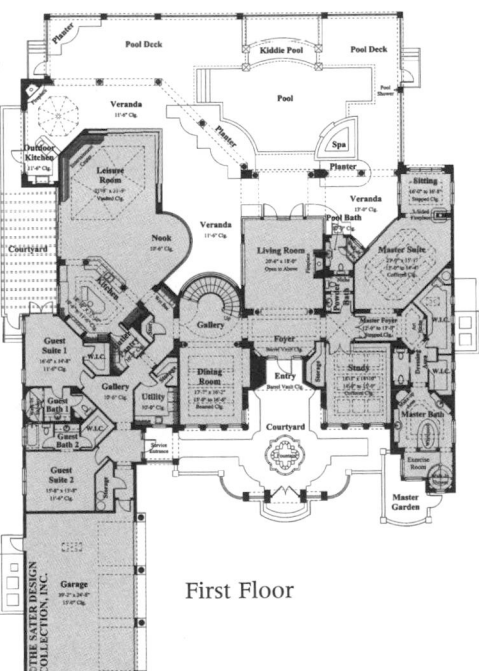

First Floor

A characteristic feature in Mediterranean villas, the courtyard entry creates a personal introduction into the home. The Mediterranean undertones in this courtyard, however, are anything but common, with a formal medallion-shaped fountain and lush landscaping. An elegant circular staircase curves leisurely upward from the first floor gallery to an impressive conclusion—a spacious game room with wet bar and a guest suite with private balcony.

Rear Exterior

HPK2101445

Style: Mediterranean

First Floor: 5,391 sq. ft.

Second Floor: 1,133 sq. ft.

Total: 6,524 sq. ft.

Bedrooms: 4

Bathrooms: 5 ½

Width: 104' - 0"

Depth: 140' - 0"

Foundation: Slab

EPLANS.COM

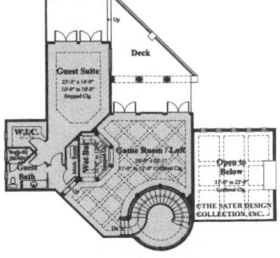

Second Floor

First Floor

Second Floor

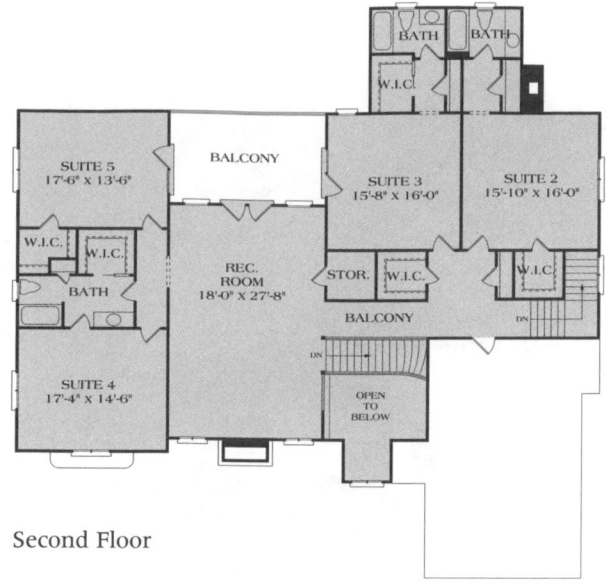

HPK2101446

Style: French Country
First Floor: 3,276 sq. ft.
Second Floor: 3,260 sq. ft.
Total: 6,536 sq. ft.
Bedrooms: 5
Bathrooms: 4 ½
Width: 68' - 8"
Depth: 68' - 6"
Foundation: Crawlspace

EPLANS.COM

A charming set of features—slate stone fireplace, arched dormer, and hipped roof—adorns the exterior of this five-bedroom home. A dramatic foyer introduces a sunken living room with a warming fireplace to the left. The roomy kitchen features abundant counter space. The luxurious master suite occupies its own wing on the left side of the plan. Four bedroom suites—all with walk-in closets—nestle on the second floor alongside a roomy recreation room and three full baths.

ORDER BLUEPRINTS ANYTIME AT EPLANS.COM OR 1-800-521-6797

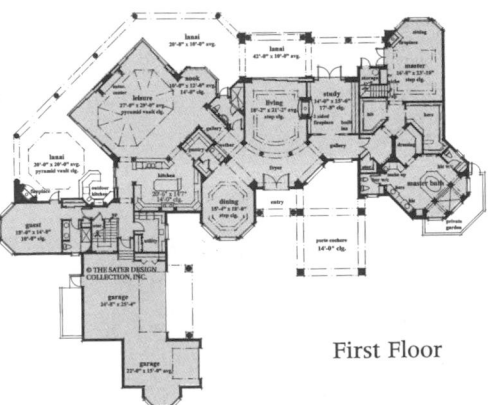

First Floor

Barrel dormers and cupola add architectural interest to this home, which offers Southern contemporary inspirations through the use of columns, arches, stone ornamentation and a porte-cochere. The living room's two-sided fireplace is shared by the adjoining study, and sliding glass doors pocket into the wall, opening up the room to a generously sized covered lanai. The lanai embraces the rear of the home, wrapping around to the leisure room, where zero-corner sliding glass doors open up two corners-an effect that pushes the room outside.

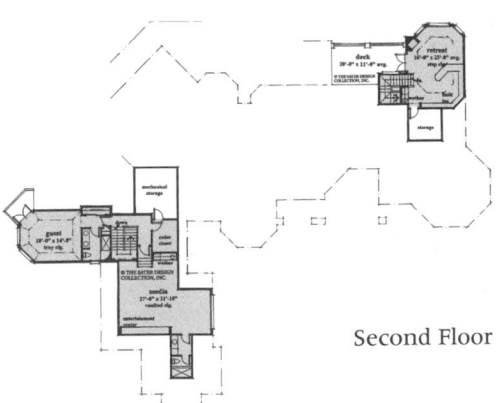

Second Floor

Rear Exterior

HPK2101447

Style: Mediterranean

First Floor: 5,170 sq. ft.

Second Floor: 1,600 sq. ft.

Total: 6,770 sq. ft.

Bedrooms: 3

Bathrooms: 4

Width: 140' - 7"

Depth: 118' - 3"

Foundation: Slab

EPLANS.COM

4,000 SQUARE FEET AND OVER

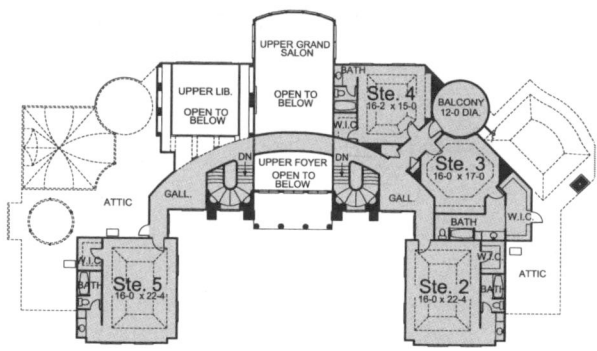

First Floor

Second Floor

HPK2101448

Style: Neoclassical
First Floor: 4,463 sq. ft.
Second Floor: 2,507 sq. ft.
Total: 6,970 sq. ft.
Bedrooms: 5
Bathrooms: 5 ½
Width: 131' - 0"
Depth: 73' - 0"
Foundation: Unfinished Basement

EPLANS.COM

Soaring ceiling heights allow full walls of glass for gorgeous views within this estate home. More intimate in ambience, the keeping room and attached morning room are designed for casual gatherings. The kitchen features a curved work counter, a walk-in pantry, and a built-in desk. Sharing a through-fireplace with the grand salon, the formal library is tucked away beyond gathering spaces. Sitting-room space complements the master suite. Twin staircases lead to four staterooms upstairs—each has a private bath.

HPK2101449

Style: Mediterranean
First Floor: 6,134 sq. ft.
Second Floor: 1,075 sq. ft.
Total: 7,209 sq. ft.
Bedrooms: 4
Bathrooms: 4 ½
Width: 142' - 7"
Depth: 118' - 0"
Foundation: Slab

EPLANS.COM

The steeple-style front entrance brings focus to the center of the design, while the plan dictates long reaches of stucco to the left and far right. From the moment of entry, eyes immediately capture the backyard view through the great room and gravitate to the winding staircase to the second level. The master suite is to the left, where it encapsulates an entire wing with a uniquely shaped bedroom and turreted master bath. The right wing of the plan houses the design's common areas, plus a second bedroom suite and a fully-equipped guest suite.

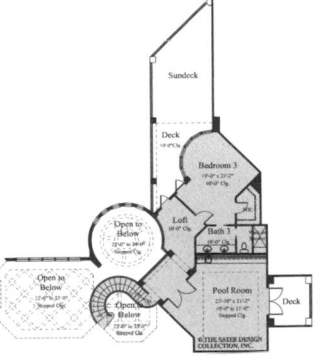

Second Floor

Rear Exterior

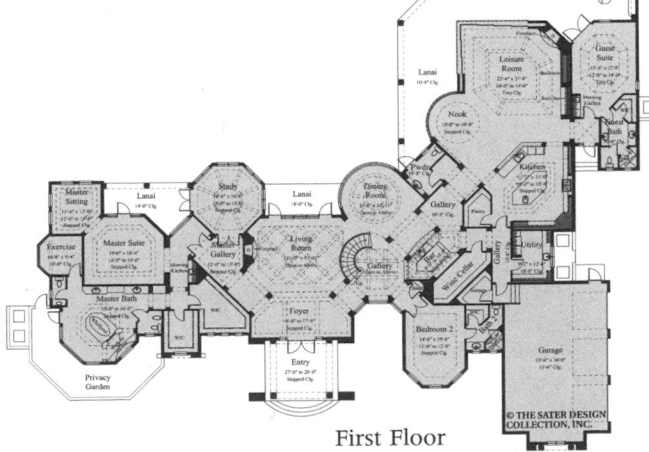

First Floor

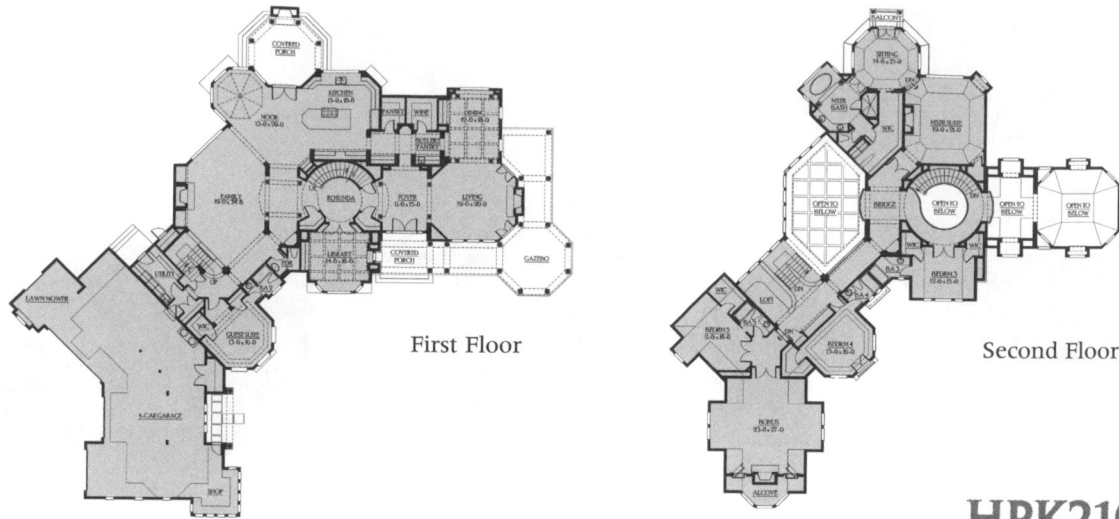

First Floor

Second Floor

HPK2101450

A shingle-style mansion on a grand scale, this American classic displays charm on the outside and luxury within. Its sweeping elevations are highlighted by sculptural columned porches, gazebos, bays, turrets, and dormers. Carefully designed alignments and interior volumes create dramatic spatial sequences, the impact of which are not diminished by their practicality. Packed with elegant detail and thoughtful features, this design is a perfect place to escape from the routine of everyday life.

Style: Craftsman
First Floor: 3,970 sq. ft.
Second Floor: 3,430 sq. ft.
Total: 7,400 sq. ft.
Bedrooms: 5
Bathrooms: 5 ½
Width: 136' - 2"
Depth: 125' - 6"
Foundation: Crawlspace

EPLANS.COM

ORDER BLUEPRINTS ANYTIME AT EPLANS.COM OR 1-800-521-6797

HPK2101451

Style: Chateauesque
First Floor: 4,613 sq. ft.
Second Floor: 3,446 sq. ft.
Total: 8,059 sq. ft.
Bonus Space: 583 sq. ft.
Bedrooms: 5
Bathrooms: 6 ½
Width: 138' - 8"
Depth: 99' - 3"
Foundation: Unfinished Basement

EPLANS.COM

Looking like a French Provencal castle, this estate recalls the grandeur of an era of grace and charm. Nothing is left to chance in the elegant floor plan. A spectacular entry reveals double-curved staircases with a columned gallery beyond. The great room is sunken a few steps and has a warming hearth and connecting lounge. Boasting a quaint sunroom, the master suite shares the left wing of the home with an office or library. Upstairs are four sizable bedrooms, each with its own bath and balcony access.

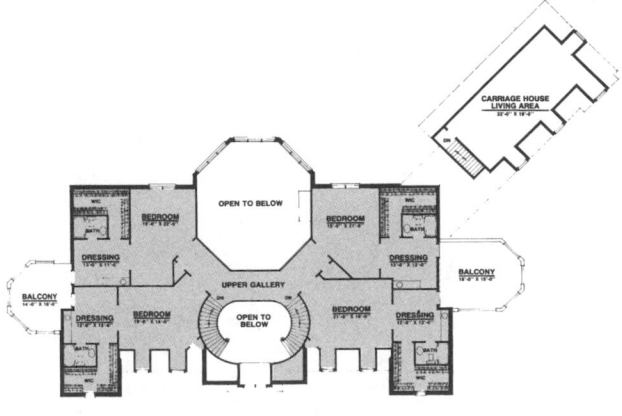

First Floor   Second Floor

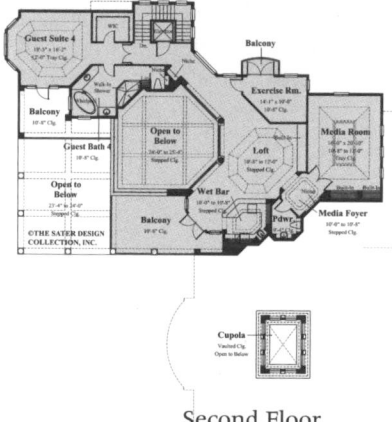

First Floor

Second Floor

HPK2101452

Style: Mediterranean
First Floor: 6,122 sq. ft.
Second Floor: 1,966 sq. ft.
Total: 8,088 sq. ft.
Bedrooms: 5
Bathrooms: 5 ½ + ½
Width: 118' - 0"
Depth: 147' - 10"
Foundation: Slab

EPLANS.COM

Rear Exterior

True to its Spanish Revival heritage—low-pitched hipped roofs, an elaborate carved entry, red barrel tile, and a stately cupola— this spectacular estate home is an 8,000-square-foot work of art. This award-winning design garners instant recognition. No detail is overlooked, embellishment is the norm. Awe-inspiring highlights include an exercise room with private balcony, a massive media room, an outdoor kitchen, two wet bars, and ample space for entertaining.

HPK2101453

Style: French Country

First Floor: 3,501 sq. ft.

Second Floor: 2,582 sq. ft.

Total: 8,733 sq. ft.

Bedrooms: 6

Bathrooms: 5 ½ + ½

Width: 89' - 8"

Depth: 116' - 7"

Foundation: Unfinished Basement

The portico of this stunning European-style cottage offers a touch of whimsy to a stately facade. Inside, the foyer opens to a formal dining room and a quiet study. The grand room boasts a fireplace and leads outdoors to a covered lanai. The gourmet kitchen overlooks a spacious gathering room and shares the warmth of its fireplace. Upstairs, four additional suites share a balcony hall. A recreation room leads to an upper hall and Suite 6.

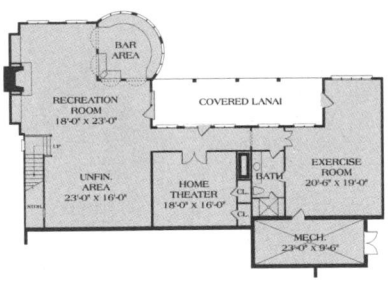

First Floor

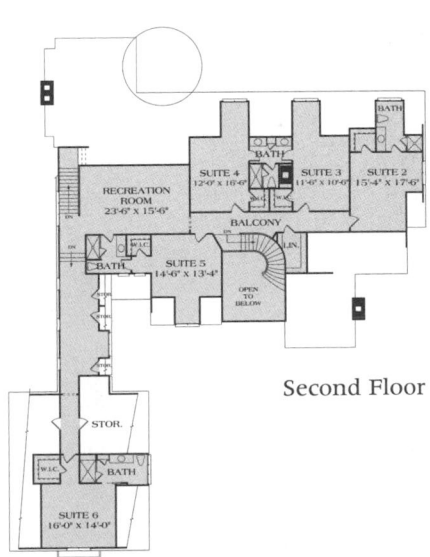

Second Floor

First Floor

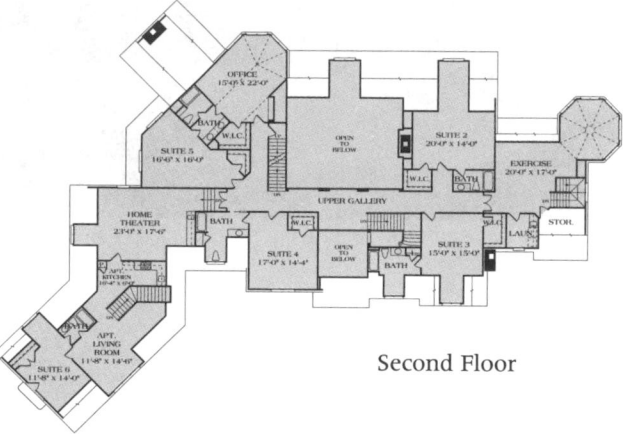

Second Floor

HPK2101454

Style: French Country
First Floor: 5,200 sq. ft.
Second Floor: 4,177 sq. ft.
Total: 9,377 sq. ft.
Bedrooms: 6
Bathrooms: 7 ½
Width: 155' - 9"
Depth: 107' - 11"
Foundation: Crawlspace

EPLANS.COM

The details of this stone manor are exquisite! The foyer opens through arches to the formal dining room and the grand room, with fireplace, built-ins, and French doors to the lanai. The informal zone includes an island kitchen, breakfast nook, and family room with fireplace and screened porch. The master suite is loaded with extras, including a stairway to the upper-level exercise room. The second floor also offers a theater, office, four bedroom suites, and maid's apartment. Note four staircases and a laundry room on each level.

HPK2101455

Style: New American
Main Level: 1,894 sq. ft.
Upper Level: 1,031 sq. ft.
Lower Level: 1,084 sq. ft.
Total: 4,009 sq. ft.
Bedrooms: 4
Bathrooms: 2 ½
Width: 63' - 4"
Depth: 70' - 8"
Foundation: Unfinished Basement

eplans.com

A recessed entryway and decorative planter introduce this interesting four-bedroom plan. Open to the second floor, the great room features a fireplace with built-in bookshelves. The master bedroom suite has a high sloping ceiling with private bath and generous walk-in closet. Stairs from the foyer lead to three additional bedrooms with shared bath and dressing area arranged along a balcony open to the great room below.

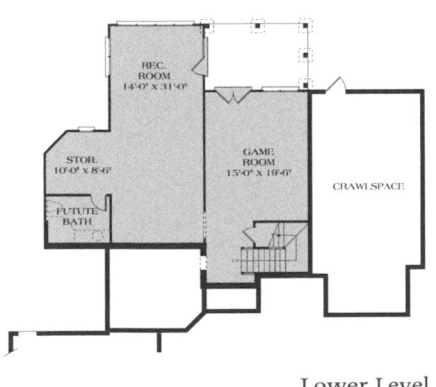

Lower Level

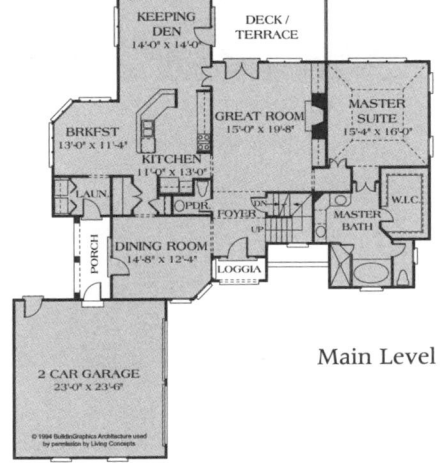

Main Level

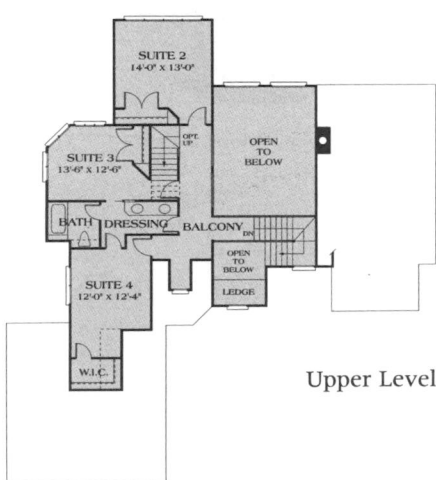

Upper Level

HPK2101456

Style: New American
Main Level: 1,404 sq. ft.
Upper Level: 1,613 sq. ft.
Lower Level: 1,073 sq. ft.
Total: 4,090 sq. ft.
Bedrooms: 4
Bathrooms: 3 ½
Width: 55' - 6"
Depth: 46' - 10"
Foundation: Unfinished Basement

EPLANS.COM

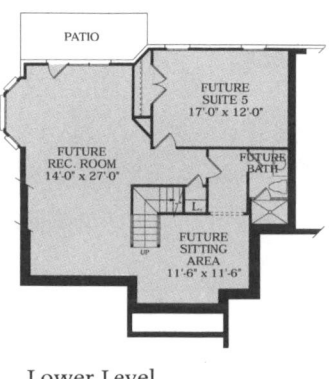

Lower Level

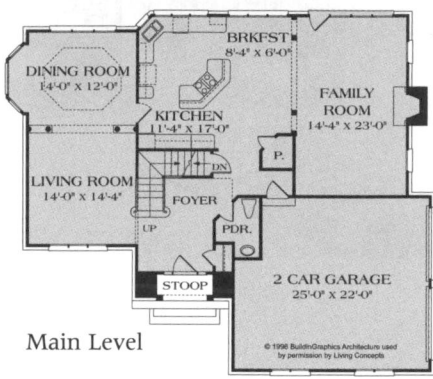

Main Level

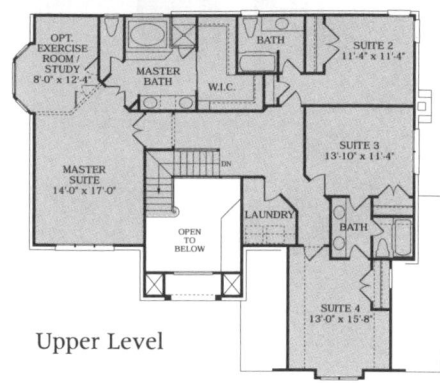

Upper Level

HPK2101457

Style: French Country
Main Level: 1,793 sq. ft.
Upper Level: 1,115 sq. ft.
Lower Level: 1,223 sq. ft.
Total: 4,131 sq. ft.
Bedrooms: 5
Bathrooms: 5 ½
Width: 103' - 8"
Depth: 57' - 6"
Foundation: Unfinished Basement

EPLANS.COM

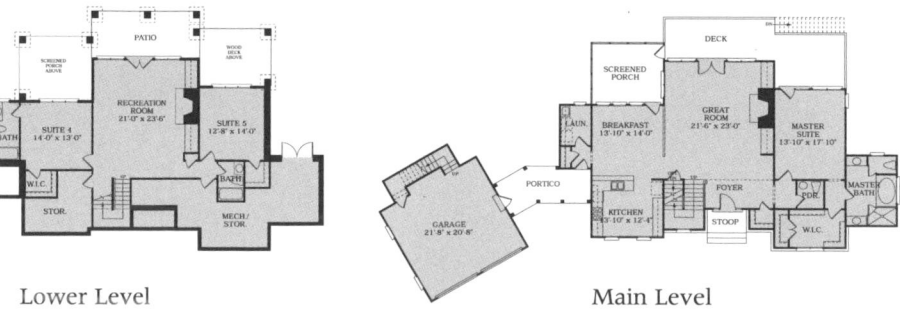

Lower Level

Main Level

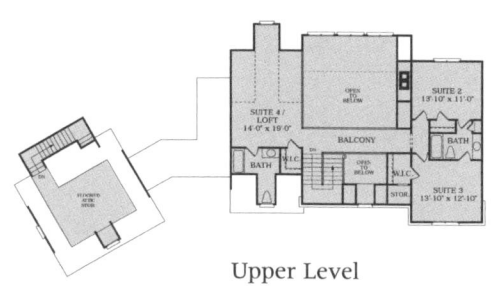

Upper Level

ORDER BLUEPRINTS ANYTIME AT EPLANS.COM OR 1-800-521-6797

HPK2101458

Style: Farmhouse

First Floor: 2,073 sq. ft.

Second Floor: 2,079 sq. ft.

Total: 4,152 sq. ft.

Bedrooms: 5

Bathrooms: 4 ½

Width: 72' - 3"

Depth: 78' - 6"

Foundation: Crawlspace, Unfinished Walkout Basement

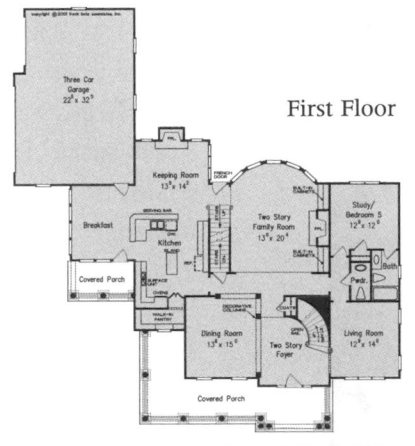

First Floor

Second Floor

HPK2101459

Style: New American

First Floor: 2,207 sq. ft.

Second Floor: 1,993 sq. ft.

Total: 4,200 sq. ft.

Bedrooms: 4

Bathrooms: 3 ½

Width: 74' - 6"

Depth: 46' - 0"

Foundation: Unfinished Basement

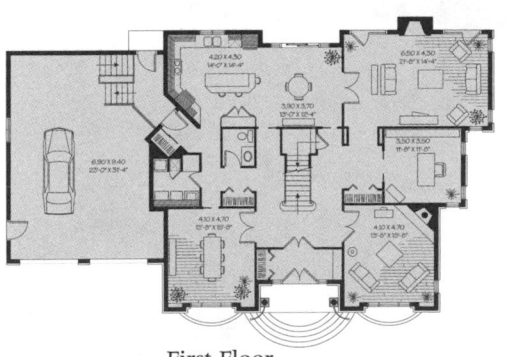

First Floor

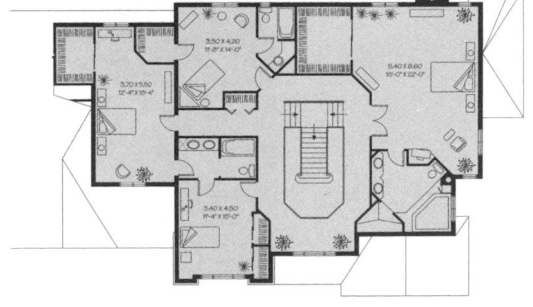

Second Floor

First Floor

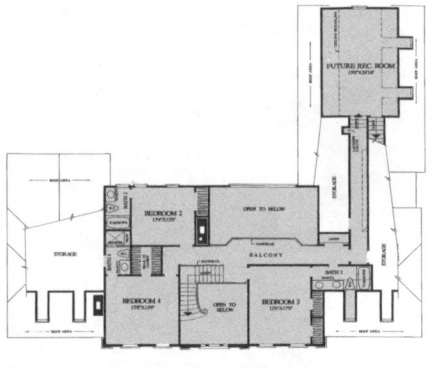

Second Floor

HPK2101460

Style: Georgian

First Floor: 2,988 sq. ft.

Second Floor: 1,216 sq. ft.

Total: 4,204 sq. ft.

Bonus Space: 485 sq. ft.

Bedrooms: 4

Bathrooms: 4 ½ + ½

Width: 83' - 0"

Depth: 70' - 4"

Foundation: Crawlspace, Unfinished Basement

EPLANS.COM

First Floor

Second Floor

HPK2101461

Style: Country

First Floor: 2,928 sq. ft.

Second Floor: 1,296 sq. ft.

Total: 4,224 sq. ft.

Bedrooms: 4

Bathrooms: 3 ½

Width: 67' - 0"

Depth: 70' - 10"

Foundation: Crawlspace, Unfinished Walkout Basement

EPLANS.COM

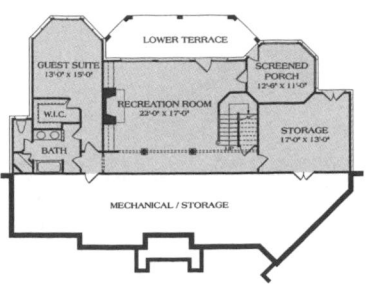

Lower Level

Main Level

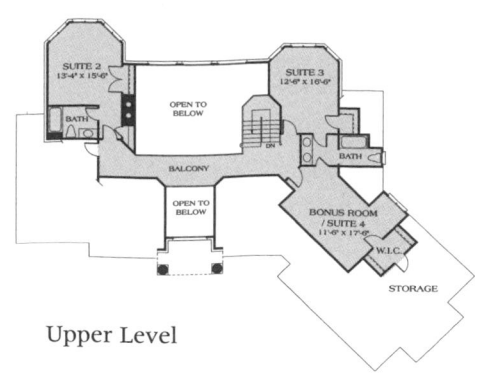

Upper Level

HPK2101462

Style: Neoclassical

Main Level: 2,293 sq. ft.

Upper Level: 949 sq. ft.

Lower Level: 1,088 sq. ft.

Total: 4,330 sq. ft.

Bonus Space: 373 sq. ft.

Bedrooms: 4

Bathrooms: 4 ½

Width: 82' - 6"

Depth: 67' - 2"

Foundation: Finished Walkout Basement

EPLANS.COM

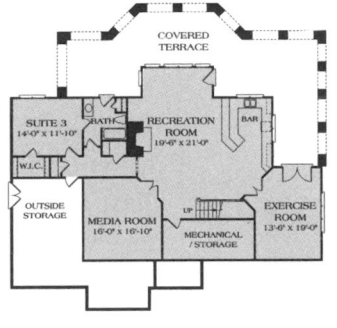

Lower Level

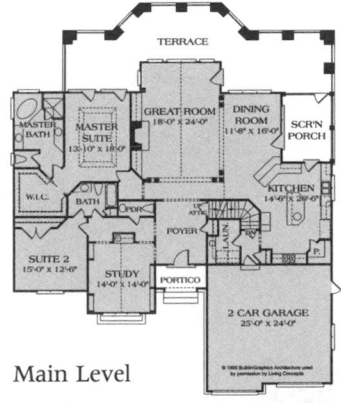

Main Level

HPK2101463

Style: French Country

Main Level: 2,546 sq. ft.

Lower Level: 1,814 sq. ft.

Total: 4,360 sq. ft.

Bedrooms: 3

Bathrooms: 3 ½

Width: 66' - 4"

Depth: 80' - 8"

Foundation: Finished Basement

EPLANS.COM

HPK2101464

Style: Craftsman
Main Level: 2,285 sq. ft.
Upper Level: 1,726 sq. ft.
Lower Level: 368 sq. ft.
Total: 4,379 sq. ft.
Bedrooms: 4
Bathrooms: 2 ½
Width: 59' - 0"
Depth: 58' - 6"
Foundation: Crawlspace

EPLANS.COM

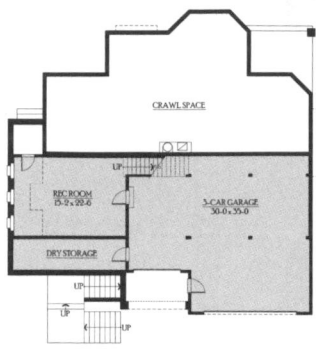

Lower Level

Main Level

Upper Level

HPK2101465

Style: New American
Main Level: 2,022 sq. ft.
Upper Level: 1,556 sq. ft.
Lower Level: 836 sq. ft.
Total: 4,414 sq. ft.
Bonus Space: 273 sq. ft.
Bedrooms: 5
Bathrooms: 4 ½
Width: 62' - 2"
Depth: 54' - 10"
Foundation: Unfinished Basement

EPLANS.COM

Lower Level

Main Level

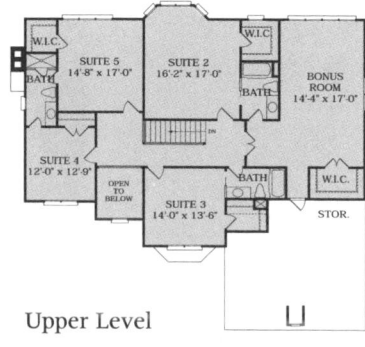

Upper Level

HPK2101466

Style: Craftsman
Main Level: 2,932 sq. ft.
Lower Level: 1,556 sq. ft.
Total: 4,488 sq. ft.
Bedrooms: 3
Bathrooms: 3 ½ + ½
Width: 114' - 0"
Depth: 82' - 11"
Foundation: Finished Walkout Basement

EPLANS.COM

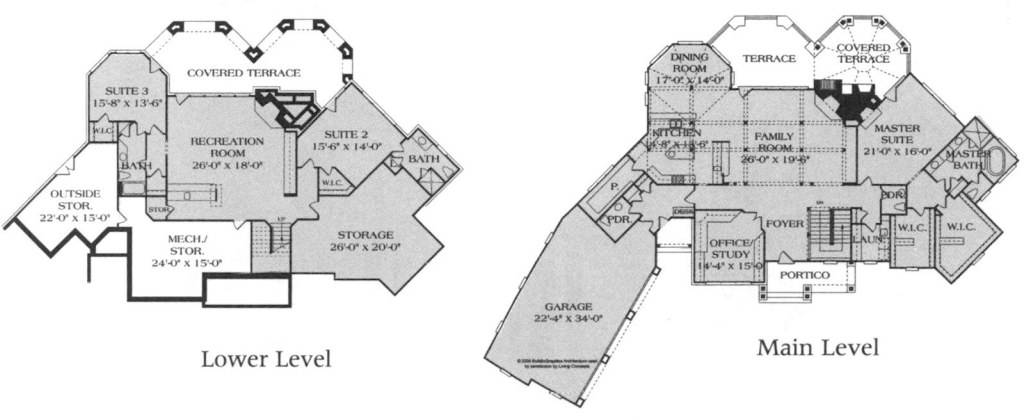

Lower Level

Main Level

HPK2101467

Style: French Country
Main Level: 2,562 sq. ft.
Lower Level: 1,955 sq. ft.
Total: 4,517 sq. ft.
Bedrooms: 3
Bathrooms: 2 ½ + ½
Width: 75' - 8"
Depth: 70' - 6"
Foundation: Finished Walkout Basement

EPLANS.COM

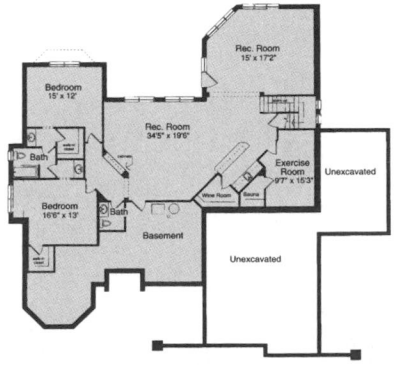

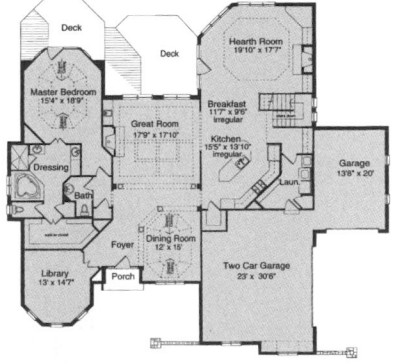

Lower Level

Main Level

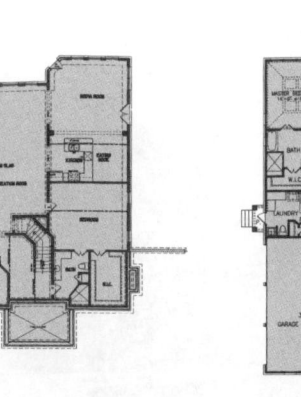

First Floor

Second Floor

HPK2101468

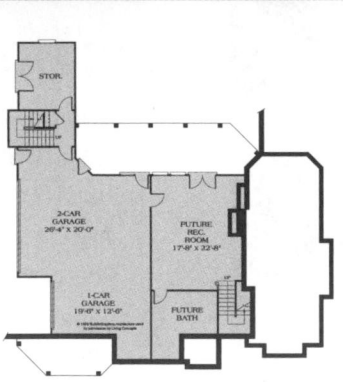

Style: Colonial Revival

First Floor: 3,364 sq. ft.

Second Floor: 1,160 sq. ft.

Total: 4,524 sq. ft.

Bedrooms: 4

Bathrooms: 4 ½ + ½

Width: 69' - 0"

Depth: 75' - 0"

Foundation: Basement

Lower Level

Main Level

Upper Level

HPK2101469

Style: New American

Main Level: 2,425 sq. ft.

Upper Level: 1,398 sq. ft.

Lower Level: 705 sq. ft.

Total: 4,528 sq. ft.

Bonus Space: 176 sq. ft.

Bedrooms: 4

Bathrooms: 3 ½

Width: 64' - 10"

Depth: 66' - 4"

Foundation: Finished Basement

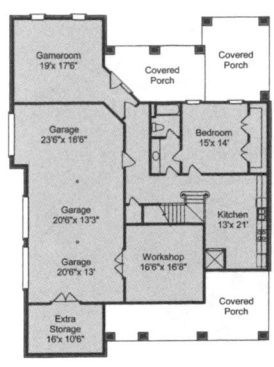

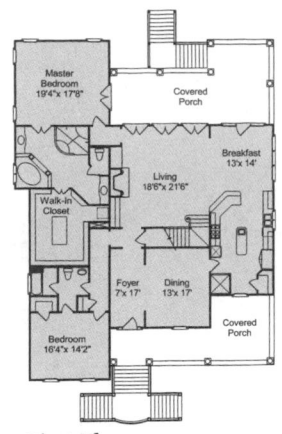

First Floor

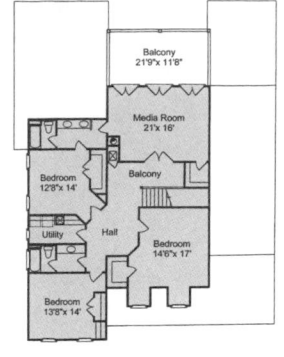

Second Floor

HPK2101470

Style: Plantation
First Floor: 2,782 sq. ft.
Second Floor: 1,767 sq. ft.
Total: 4,549 sq. ft.
Bedrooms: 5
Bathrooms: 4
Width: 55' - 0"
Depth: 73' - 0"
Foundation: Slab

EPLANS.COM

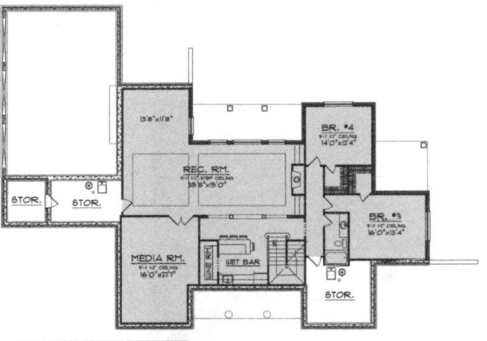

Lower Level

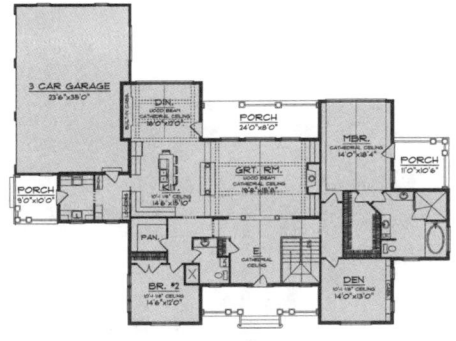

Main Level

HPK2101471

Style: Ranch
Main Level: 2,551 sq. ft.
Lower Level: 2,028 sq. ft.
Total: 4,579 sq. ft.
Bedrooms: 4
Bathrooms: 3
Width: 89' - 4"
Depth: 67' - 0"
Foundation: Finished Basement

EPLANS.COM

4,000 SQUARE FEET AND OVER

HPK2101472

Style: Contemporary

Main Level: 2,624 sq. ft.

Lower Level: 1,976 sq. ft.

Total: 4,600 sq. ft.

Bedrooms: 4

Bathrooms: 3 ½

Width: 76' - 6"

Depth: 65' - 0"

Foundation: Finished Walkout Basement

EPLANS.COM

Photo by Alan Mascord. This home, as shown in photographs, may differ from the actual blueprints. For more detailed information, please check the floor plans carefully.

Lower Level

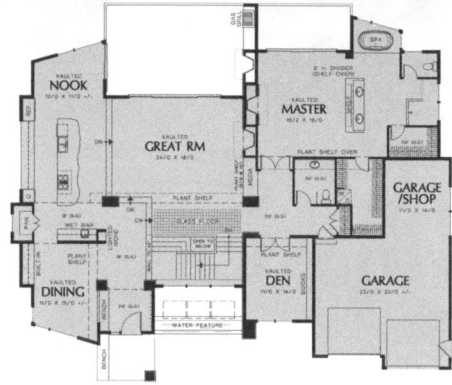

Main Level

HPK2101473

Style: New American

Main Level: 2,394 sq. ft.

Upper Level: 792 sq. ft.

Lower Level: 1,486 sq. ft.

Total: 4,672 sq. ft.

Bonus Space: 450 sq. ft.

Bedrooms: 4

Bathrooms: 4 ½

Width: 67' - 0"

Depth: 93' - 2"

Foundation: Finished Walkout Basement

EPLANS.COM

Photo Courtesy of: Living Concepts. This home, as shown in photographs, may differ from the actual blueprints. For more detailed information, please check the floor plans carefully.

Lower Level

Main Level

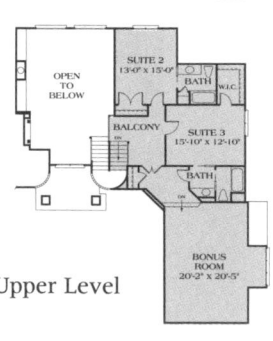

Upper Level

HPK2101474

Style: Shingle
First Floor: 2,030 sq. ft.
Second Floor: 1,967 sq. ft.
Third Floor: 688 sq. ft.
Total: 4,685 sq. ft.
Bedrooms: 5
Bathrooms: 6
Width: 80' - 8"
Depth: 111' - 8"
Foundation: Crawlspace

EPLANS.COM

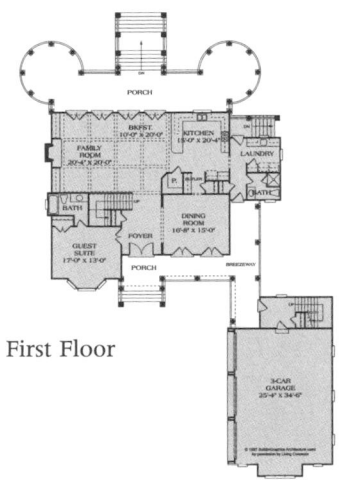

First Floor

Second Floor

Third Floor

HPK2101475

Style: Chateauesque
Main Level: 2,138 sq. ft.
Upper Level: 1,252 sq. ft.
Lower Level: 1,332 sq. ft.
Total: 4,722 sq. ft.
Bedrooms: 5
Bathrooms: 4 ½
Width: 72' - 10"
Depth: 49' - 1"
Foundation: Finished Basement

EPLANS.COM

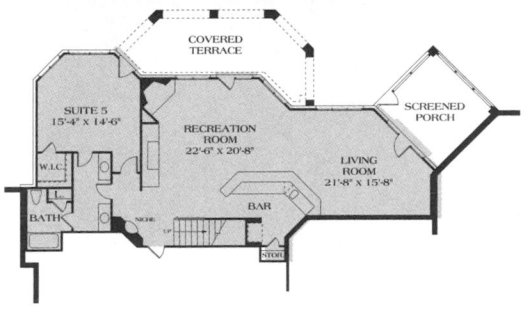

Lower Level

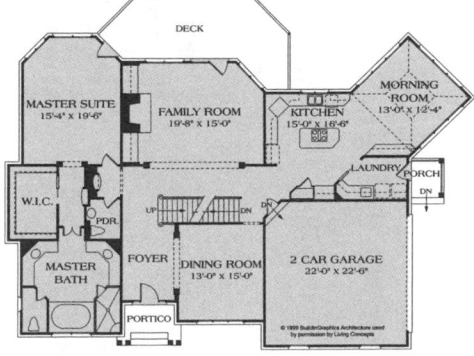

Main Level

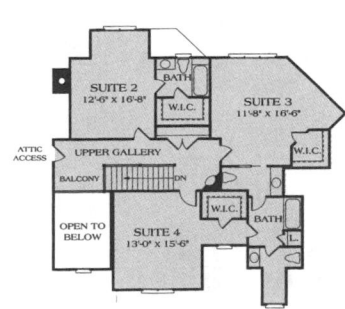

Upper Level

4,000 SQUARE FEET AND OVER

Lower Level

Main Level

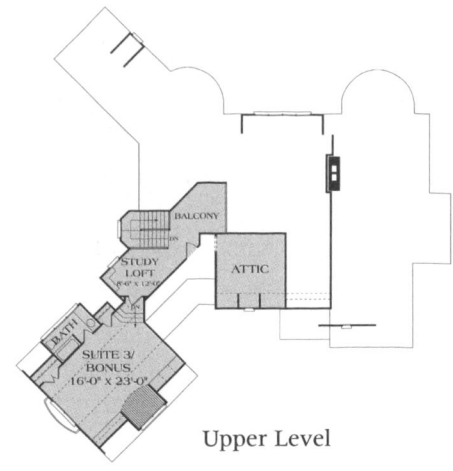

Upper Level

HPK2101476

Style: French Country

Main Level: 2,563 sq. ft.

Upper Level: 298 sq. ft.

Lower Level: 1,870 sq. ft.

Total: 4,731 sq. ft.

Bonus Space: 532 sq. ft.

Bedrooms: 3

Bathrooms: 3 ½

Width: 84' - 2"

Depth: 89' - 3"

Foundation: Finished Walkout Basement

EPLANS.COM

Varying rooflines and arched windows complement the brick and stone of a French Country facade. Inside, a generous gathering room has a fireplace and the island kitchen accesses a screened porch. The master bedroom is to the right, complete with a walk-in closet, separate tub and shower, dual vanities, and a sitting area that leads to the veranda. Downstairs, two bedrooms each have a full bath and doors to a veranda. A wet bar and wine cellar make the space perfect for entertaining. The top level harbors a bonus room, full bath, and study loft.

HPK2101477

Style: Craftsman
Main Level: 3,040 sq. ft.
Lower Level: 1,736 sq. ft.
Total: 4,776 sq. ft.
Bedrooms: 5
Bathrooms: 4 ½ + ½
Width: 106' - 5"
Depth: 104' - 2"

EPLANS.COM

This rustic-style home is sure to be the envy of your neighborhood. Entering through the elegant front door, find an open staircase to the right and a spacious great room directly ahead. A lavish hearth-warmed master suite features a private porch, large walk-in closet, and sumptuous bedroom area. The gourmet kitchen adjoins a sunny dining room that offers access to a screened porch.

4,000 SQUARE FEET AND OVER

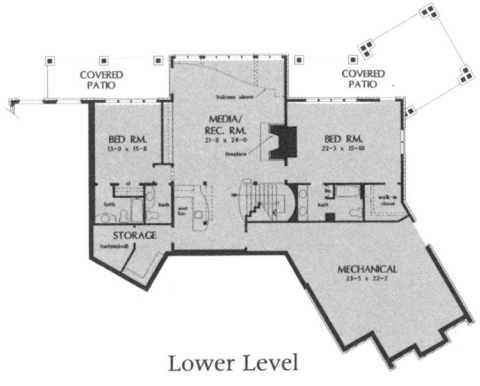

Lower Level

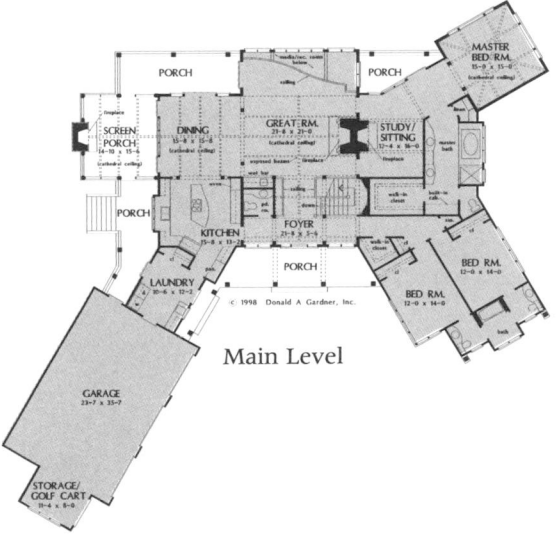

Main Level

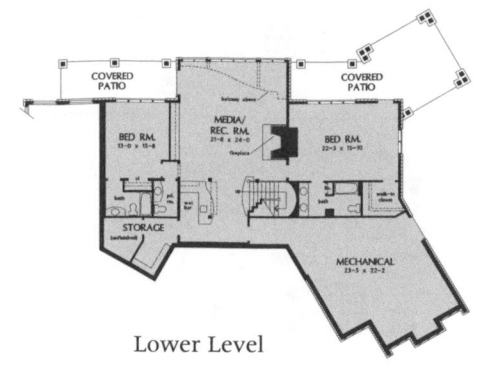

Lower Level

Main Level

HPK2101478

Style: Country
Main Level: 3,040 sq. ft.
Lower Level: 1,736 sq. ft.
Total: 4,776 sq. ft.
Bedrooms: 5
Bathrooms: 4 ½ + ½
Width: 106' - 1"
Depth: 104' - 2"

EPLANS.COM

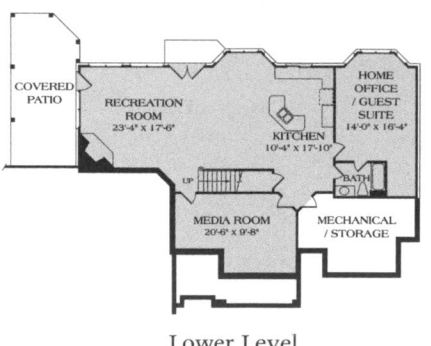

Lower Level

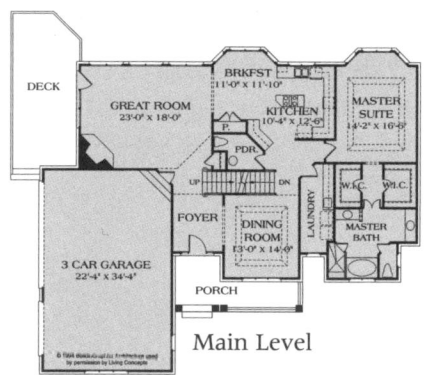

Main Level

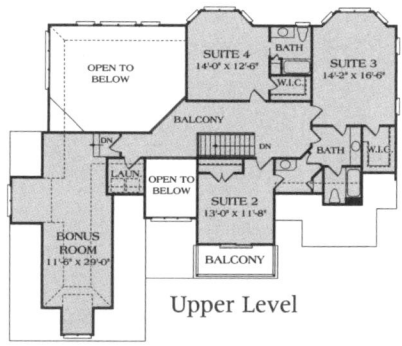

Upper Level

HPK2101479

Style: Craftsman
Main Level: 1,890 sq. ft.
Upper Level: 1,286 sq. ft.
Lower Level: 1,615 sq. ft.
Total: 4,791 sq. ft.
Bonus Space: 431 sq. ft.
Bedrooms: 5
Bathrooms: 4 ½
Width: 67' - 0"
Depth: 56' - 8"
Foundation: Finished Basement

EPLANS.COM

Lower Level

Main Level

HPK2101480

Style: French Country

Main Level: 2,792 sq. ft.

Lower Level: 2,016 sq. ft.

Total: 4,808 sq. ft.

Bedrooms: 4

Bathrooms: 4 ½

Width: 81' - 0"

Depth: 66' - 0"

Foundation: Finished Walkout Basement

EPLANS.COM

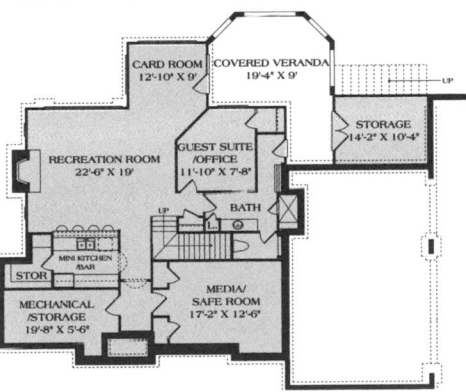

Lower Level

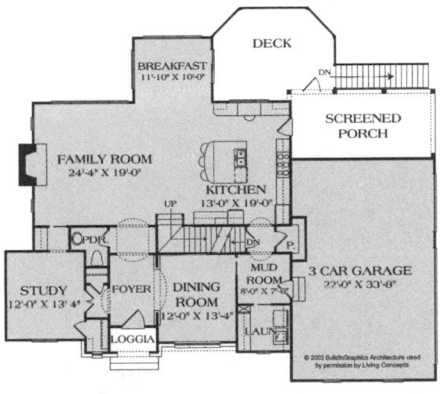

Main Level

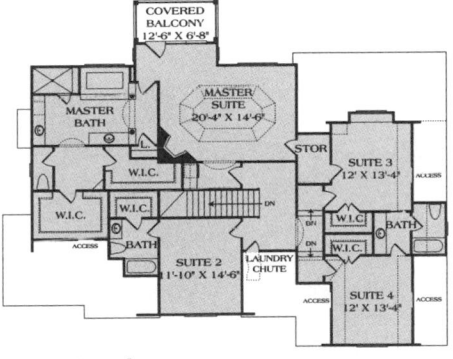

Upper Level

HPK2101481

Style: French Country

Main Level: 1,703 sq. ft.

Upper Level: 1,930 sq. ft.

Lower Level: 1,233 sq. ft.

Total: 4,866 sq. ft.

Bedrooms: 4

Bathrooms: 4 ½

Width: 67' - 0"

Depth: 58' - 0"

Foundation: Finished Walkout Basement

EPLANS.COM

HPK2101482

Style: French Country
Main Level: 2,911 sq. ft.
Upper Level: 1,345 sq. ft.
Lower Level: 857 sq. ft.
Total: 5,113 sq. ft.
Bonus Space: 721 sq. ft.
Bedrooms: 2
Bathrooms: 2 ½
Width: 107' - 1"
Depth: 67' - 7"
Foundation: Finished Basement

EPLANS.COM

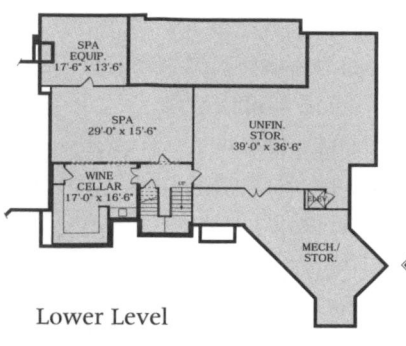

Lower Level

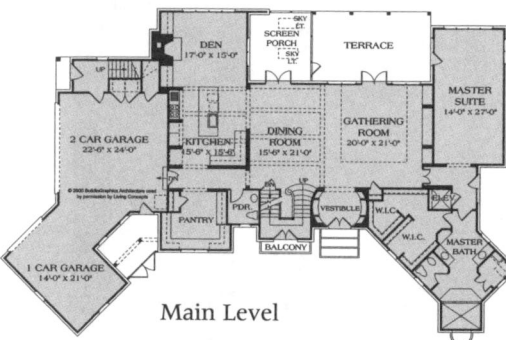

Main Level

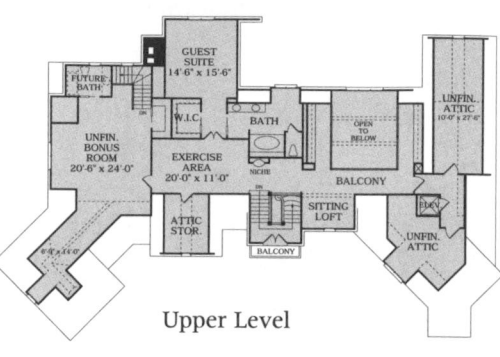

Upper Level

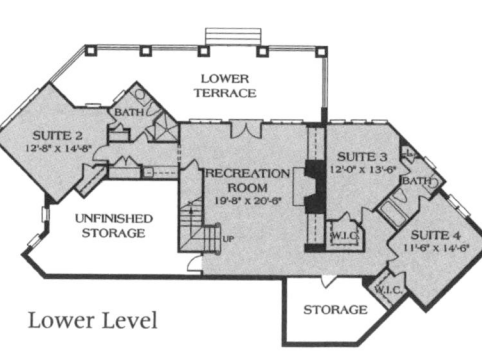

Lower Level

HPK2101483

Style: French Country
Main Level: 3,054 sq. ft.
Lower Level: 2,092 sq. ft.
Total: 5,146 sq. ft.
Bedrooms: 5
Bathrooms: 4 ½
Width: 115' - 8"
Depth: 83' - 0"
Foundation: Finished Walkout Basement

EPLANS.COM

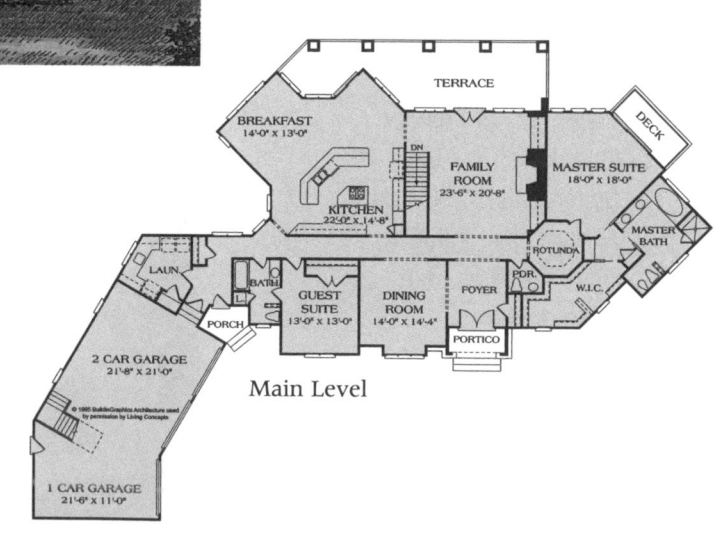

Main Level

ORDER BLUEPRINTS ANYTIME AT EPLANS.COM OR 1-800-521-6797

HPK2101484

Style: Mediterranean

Main Level: 2,391 sq. ft.

Upper Level: 922 sq. ft.

Lower Level: 1,964 sq. ft.

Total: 5,277 sq. ft.

Bonus Space: 400 sq. ft.

Bedrooms: 4

Bathrooms: 4 ½

Width: 63' - 10"

Depth: 85' - 6"

Foundation: Finished Walkout Basement

EPLANS.COM

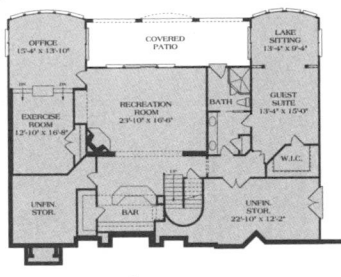

Lower Level

Main Level

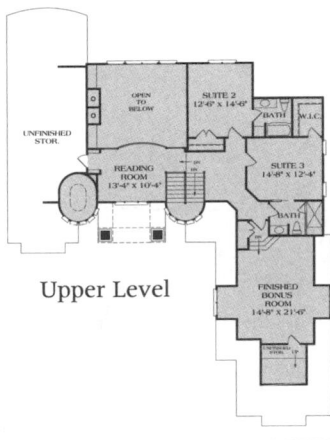

Upper Level

HPK2101485

EPLANS.COM

Style: French Country

Main Level: 1,805 sq. ft.

Upper Level: 2,098 sq. ft.

Lower Level: 1,393 sq. ft.

Total: 5,296 sq. ft.

Bedrooms: 5

Bathrooms: 4 ½

Width: 62' - 2"

Depth: 54' - 0"

Foundation: Finished Walkout Basement

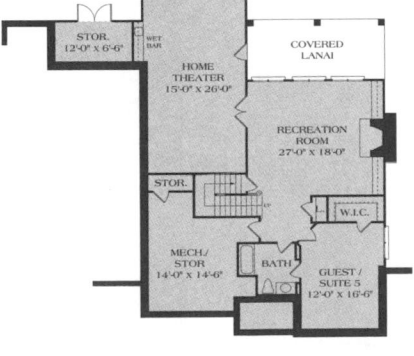

Lower Level

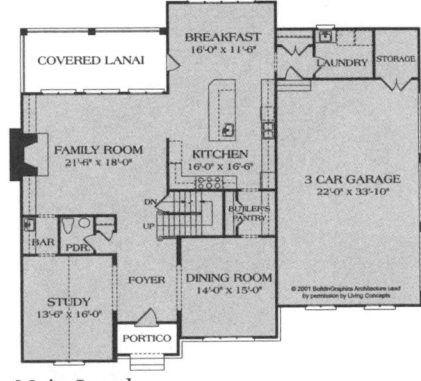

Main Level

Upper Level

4,000 SQUARE FEET AND OVER

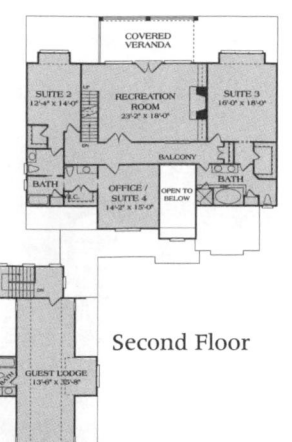

First Floor

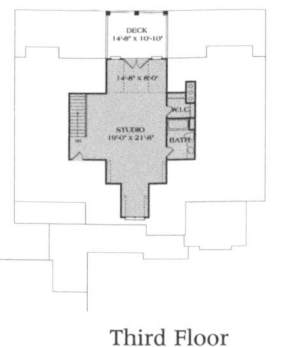

Second Floor

Third Floor

HPK2101486

Style: Craftsman

First Floor: 2,620 sq. ft.

Second Floor: 2,001 sq. ft.

Third Floor: 684 sq. ft.

Total: 5,305 sq. ft.

Bedrooms: 4

Bathrooms: 5 ½ + ½

Width: 67' - 0"

Depth: 103' - 8"

Foundation: Crawlspace

EPLANS.COM

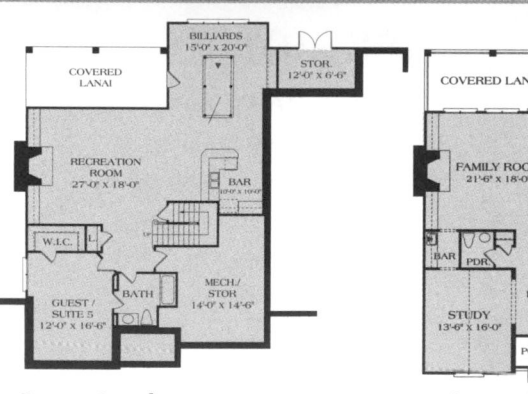

Lower Level

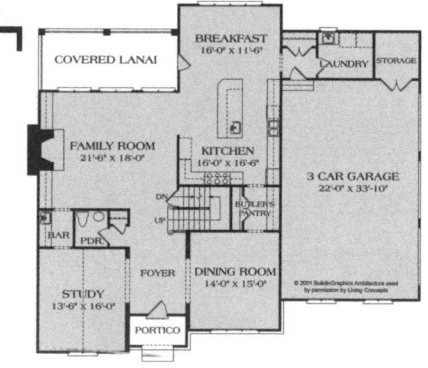

Main Level

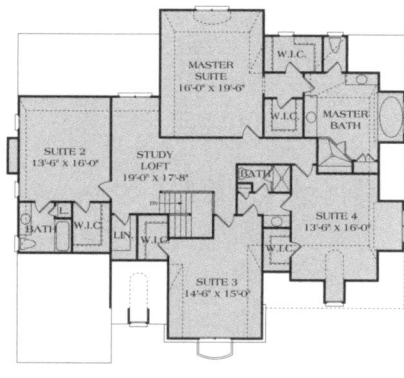

Upper Level

HPK2101487

Style: French Country

Main Level: 1,805 sq. ft.

Upper Level: 2,096 sq. ft.

Lower Level: 1,414 sq. ft.

Total: 5,315 sq. ft.

Bedrooms: 5

Bathrooms: 4 ½

Width: 62' - 2"

Depth: 54' - 0"

Foundation: Finished Walkout Basement

EPLANS.COM

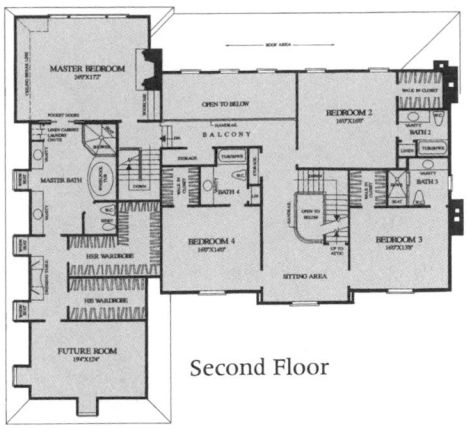

First Floor

Second Floor

HPK2101488

Style: Beaux Arts

First Floor: 2,870 sq. ft.

Second Floor: 2,502 sq. ft.

Total: 5,372 sq. ft.

Bedrooms: 5

Bathrooms: 5 ½

Width: 72' - 0"

Depth: 66' - 6"

Foundation: Crawlspace, Unfinished Basement

EPLANS.COM

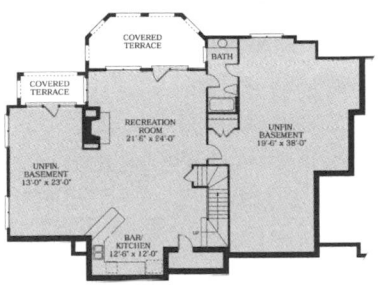

Lower Level

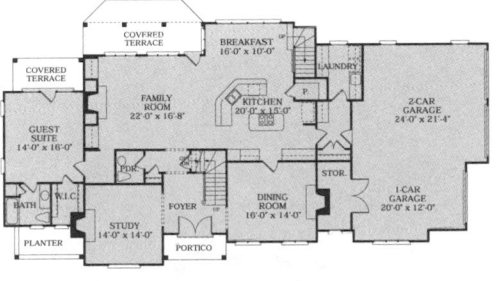

Main Level

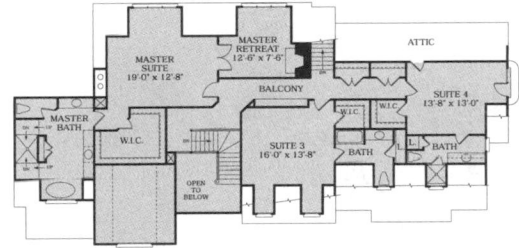

Upper Level

HPK2101489

Style: French Country

Main Level: 2,124 sq. ft.

Upper Level: 1,962 sq. ft.

Lower Level: 1,295 sq. ft.

Total: 5,381 sq. ft.

Bedrooms: 4

Bathrooms: 4 ½

Width: 88' - 0"

Depth: 48' - 0"

Foundation: Unfinished Basement

EPLANS.COM

4,000 SQUARE FEET AND OVER

HPK2101490

Style: Craftsman
Main Level: 3,793 sq. ft.
Lower Level: 1,588 sq. ft.
Total: 5,381 sq. ft.
Bedrooms: 4
Bathrooms: 3 ½
Width: 99' - 8"
Depth: 68' - 8"
Foundation: Finished Walkout Basement

EPLANS.COM

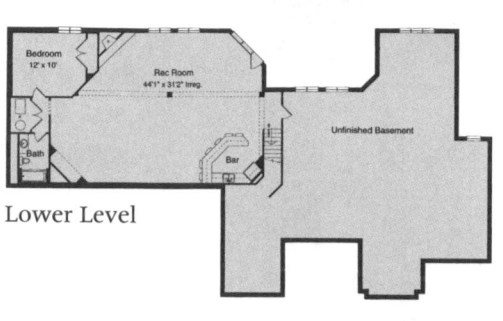

Lower Level

Main Level

HPK2101491

Style: French Country
Main Level: 1,924 sq. ft.
Upper Level: 1,774 sq. ft.
Lower Level: 1,098 sq. ft.
Total: 4,796 sq. ft.
Bedrooms: 5
Bathrooms: 4 ½ + ½
Width: 99' - 2"
Depth: 64' - 4"
Foundation: Finished Walkout Basement

EPLANS.COM

Lower Level

Main Level

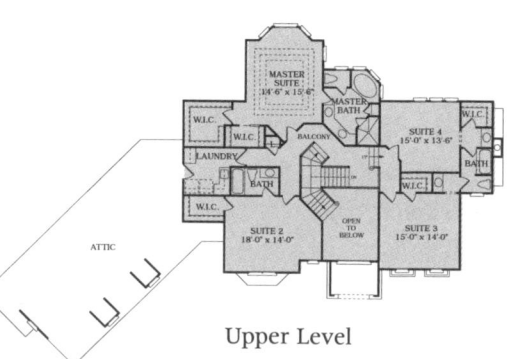

Upper Level

ORDER BLUEPRINTS ANYTIME AT EPLANS.COM OR 1-800-521-6797

HPK2101492

Style: Chateauesque
Main Level: 2,981 sq. ft.
Upper Level: 1,017 sq. ft.
Lower Level: 1,471 sq. ft.
Total: 5,469 sq. ft.
Bedrooms: 4
Bathrooms: 4 ½ + ½
Width: 79' - 4"
Depth: 91' - 0"
Foundation: Finished Walkout Basement

EPLANS.COM

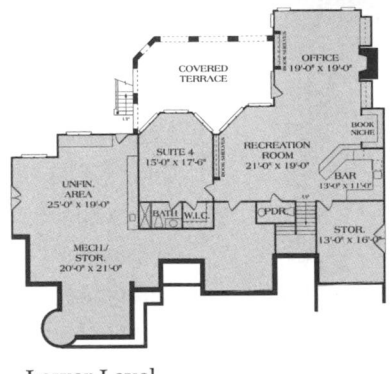

Lower Level

Main Level

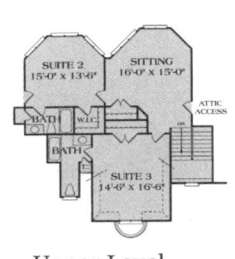

Upper Level

HPK2101493

Style: Federal - Adams
Main Level: 2,137 sq. ft.
Upper Level: 1,901 sq. ft.
Lower Level: 1,528 sq. ft.
Total: 5,566 sq. ft.
Bedrooms: 3
Bathrooms: 3 ½
Width: 79' - 4"
Depth: 83' - 3"
Foundation: Unfinished Basement

EPLANS.COM

Lower Level

Main Level

Upper Level

Lower Level

Main Level

Upper Level

HPK2101494

Style: French Country

Main Level: 2,689 sq. ft.

Upper Level: 1,180 sq. ft.

Lower Level: 1,734 sq. ft.

Total: 5,603 sq. ft.

Bonus Space: 723 sq. ft.

Bedrooms: 4

Bathrooms: 5

Width: 126' - 7"

Depth: 86' - 0"

Foundation: Finished Basement

EPLANS.COM

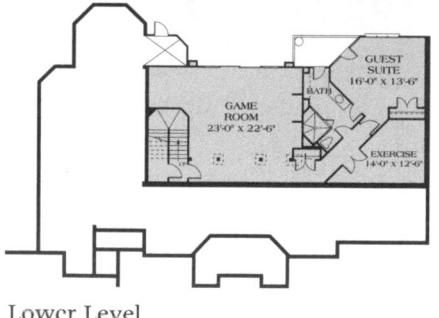

Lower Level

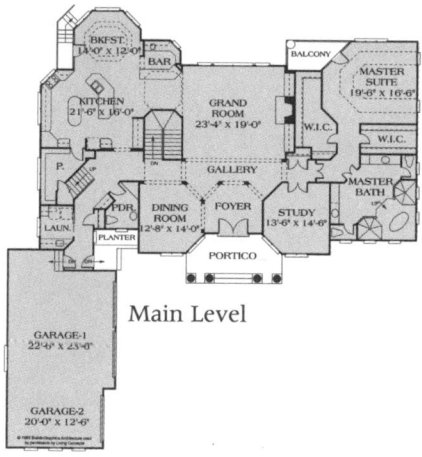

Main Level

Upper Level

HPK2101495

Style: Mediterranean

Main Level: 3,187 sq. ft.

Upper Level: 1,000 sq. ft.

Lower Level: 1,500 sq. ft.

Total: 5,687 sq. ft.

Bedrooms: 4

Bathrooms: 4 ½

Width: 85' - 4"

Depth: 90' - 10"

Foundation: Finished Walkout Basement

EPLANS.COM

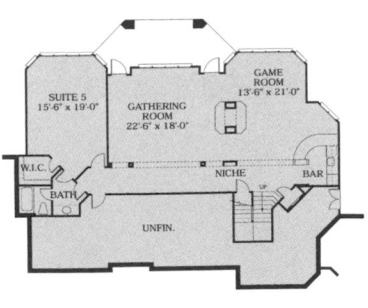

Lower Level

Main Level

Upper Level

HPK2101496

Style: Prairie
Main Level: 2,450 sq. ft.
Upper Level: 1,674 sq. ft.
Lower Level: 1,568 sq. ft.
Total: 5,692 sq. ft.
Bedrooms: 5
Bathrooms: 4 ½
Width: 65' - 10"
Depth: 85' - 2"
Foundation: Finished Basement

EPLANS.COM

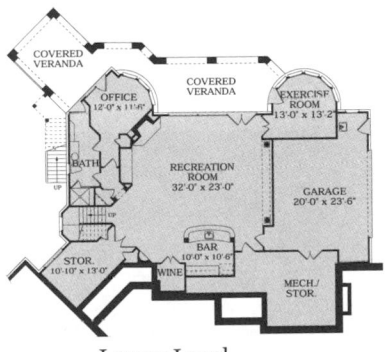

Lower Level

Main Level

Upper Level

HPK2101497

Style: French Country
Main Level: 2,734 sq. ft.
Upper Level: 1,258 sq. ft.
Lower Level: 1,839 sq. ft.
Total: 5,831 sq. ft.
Bonus Space: 529 sq. ft.
Bedrooms: 3
Bathrooms: 4 ½
Width: 88' - 0"
Depth: 92' - 8"
Foundation: Finished Walkout Basement

EPLANS.COM

4,000 SQUARE FEET AND OVER

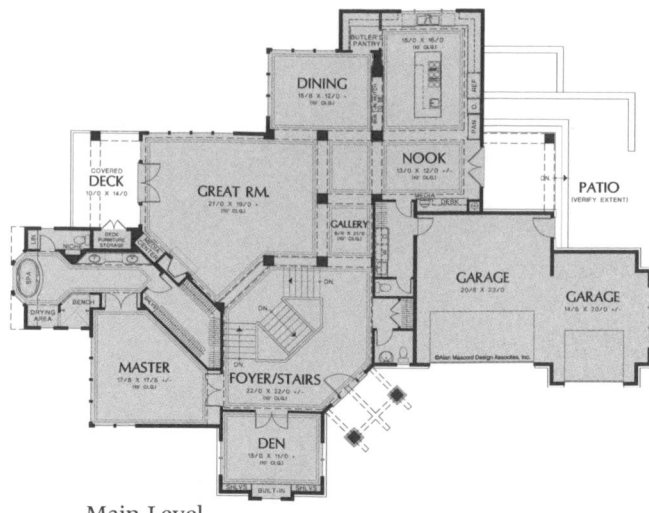

Lower Level

Main Level

Although the exterior of this home appears rustic, the interior is nothing but lavish. The great room has a warming fireplace and built-in media center. Covered-deck access is perfect year-round, with built-in deck furniture storage. The kitchen is marvelous, with a six-burner cooktop island and a butler's pantry. The inspiring master suite relishes a luxurious spa bath and tons of natural light. Downstairs, a games room, wine cellar, and theater are special touches. Two generous bedrooms share a full bath and a computer center to the right; to the left, a fourth bedroom has its own private spa bath.

HPK2101498

Style: Craftsman
Main Level: 2,922 sq. ft.
Lower Level: 3,027 sq. ft.
Total: 5,949 sq. ft.
Bedrooms: 4
Bathrooms: 4 ½+ ½
Width: 98' - 0"
Depth: 76' - 0"
Foundation: Finished Walkout Basement

EPLANS.COM

ORDER BLUEPRINTS ANYTIME AT EPLANS.COM OR 1-800-521-6797

HPK2101499

Style: French Country
Main Level: 2,534 sq. ft.
Upper Level: 1,578 sq. ft.
Lower Level: 1,857 sq. ft.
Total: 5,969 sq. ft.
Bonus Space: 685 sq. ft.
Bedrooms: 6
Bathrooms: 4 ½ + 2 Half Baths
Width: 126' - 4"
Depth: 74' - 5"
Foundation: Finished Basement

EPLANS.COM

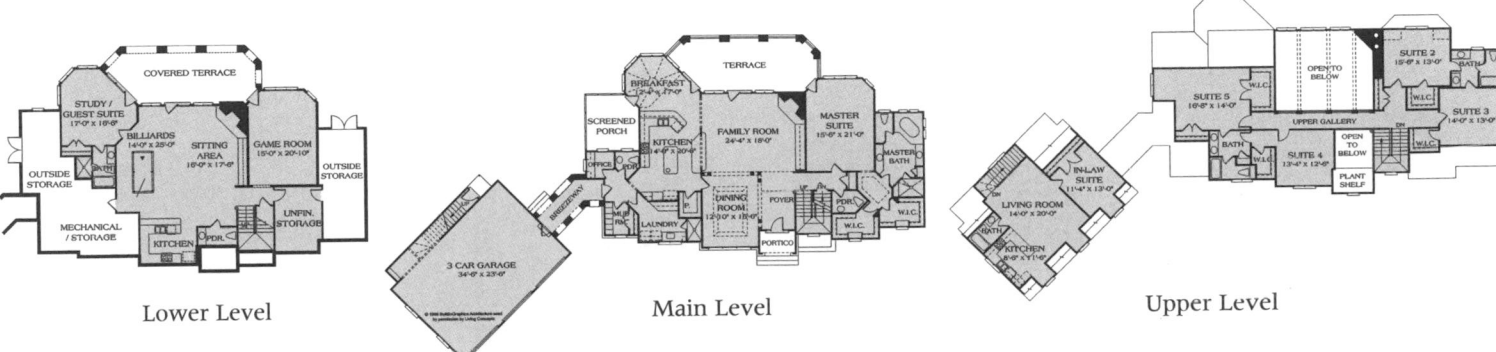

Lower Level

Main Level

Upper Level

HPK2101500

Style: Chateauesque
Main Level: 3,566 sq. ft.
Upper Level: 864 sq. ft.
Lower Level: 1,619 sq. ft.
Total: 6,049 sq. ft.
Bedrooms: 4
Bathrooms: 4 ½
Width: 127' - 9"
Depth: 75' - 8"
Foundation: Finished Basement

EPLANS.COM

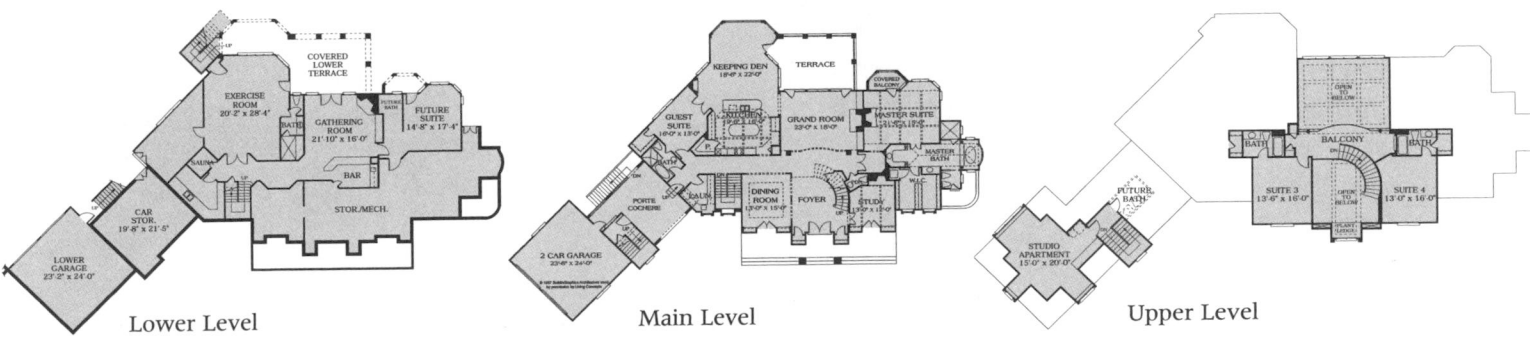

Lower Level

Main Level

Upper Level

4,000 SQUARE FEET AND OVER

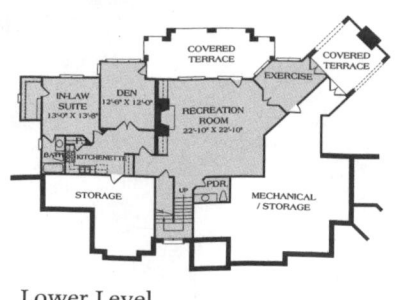

Lower Level

Main Level

Upper Level

HPK2101501

Style: French Country

Main Level: 3,177 sq. ft.

Upper Level: 1,390 sq. ft.

Lower Level: 1,565 sq. ft.

Total: 6,132 sq. ft.

Bedrooms: 5

Bathrooms: 4 ½

Width: 120' - 11"

Depth: 85' - 4"

Foundation: Finished Basement

EPLANS.COM

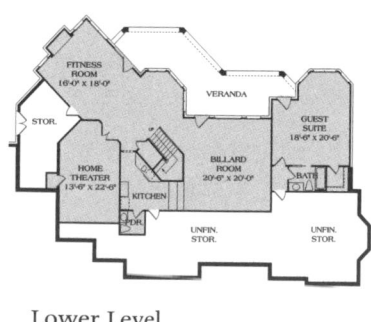

Lower Level

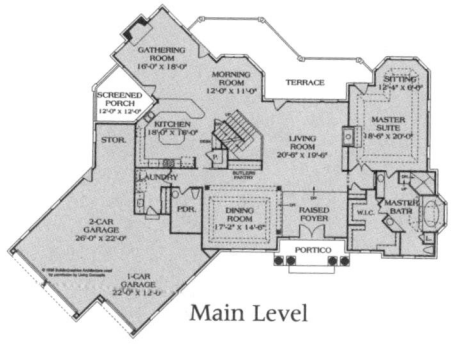

Main Level

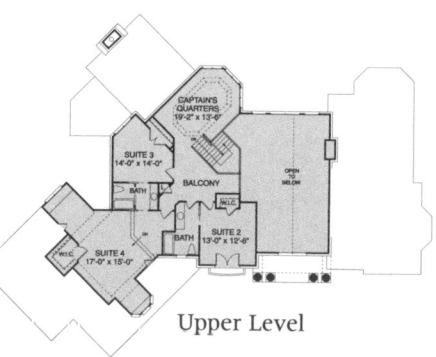

Upper Level

HPK2101502

Style: Mediterranean

Main Level: 2,943 sq. ft.

Upper Level: 1,510 sq. ft.

Lower Level: 2,010 sq. ft.

Total: 6,463 sq. ft.

Bedrooms: 5

Bathrooms: 4 ½ + ½

Width: 104' - 2"

Depth: 78' - 1"

Foundation: Finished Basement

EPLANS.COM

HPK2101503

Style: French Country
Main Level: 3,040 sq. ft.
Upper Level: 1,899 sq. ft.
Lower Level: 1,526 sq. ft.
Total: 6,465 sq. ft.
Bonus Space: 542 sq. ft.
Bedrooms: 5
Bathrooms: 5 ½ + 2 Half Baths
Width: 102' - 0"
Depth: 89' - 1"
Foundation: Finished Walkout Basement

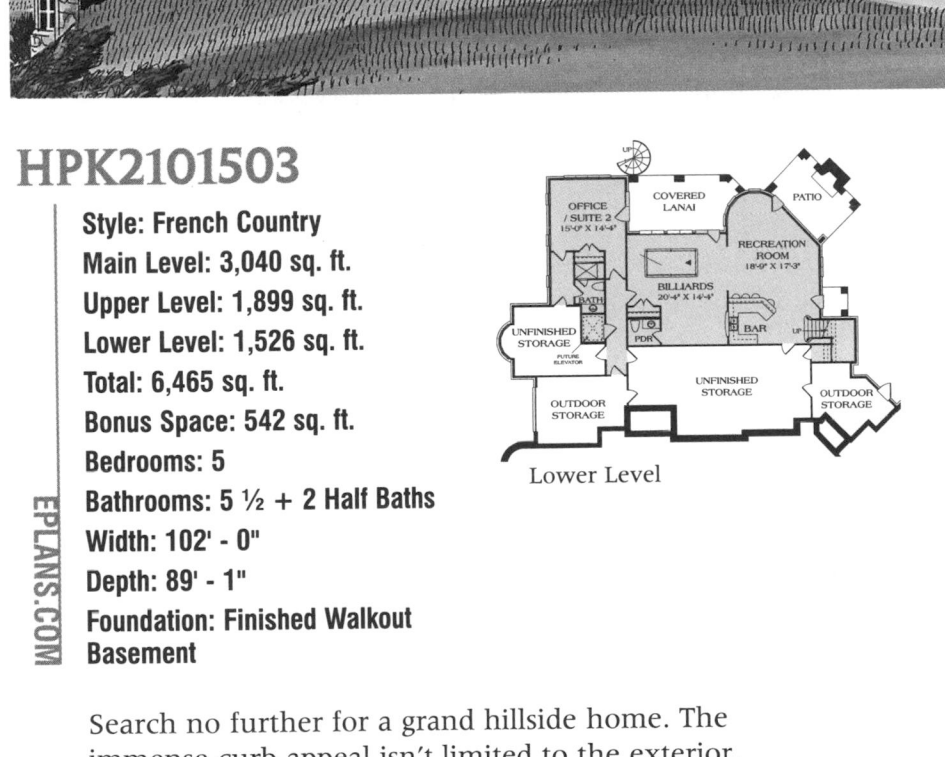

Lower Level

Main Level

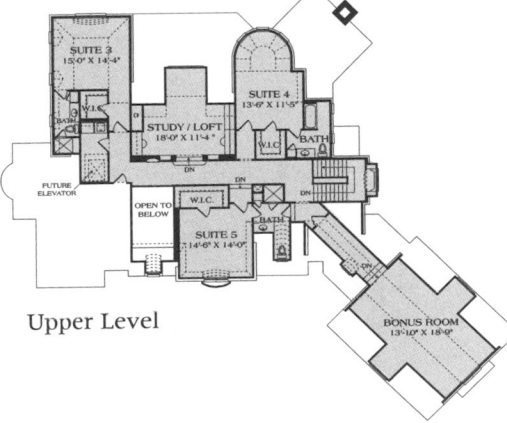

Upper Level

Search no further for a grand hillside home. The immense curb appeal isn't limited to the exterior. Inside, the lower level houses entertainment options and extra storage. A fireplace on the patio is sure to please. On the main level, the kitchen is a chef's dream with abundant space and two islands, one a workspace with a sink, the other a snack bar for informal meals. Three secondary bedrooms reside on the upper level, each with a full bath. Don't miss the optional elevator, an added convenience

4,000 SQUARE FEET AND OVER

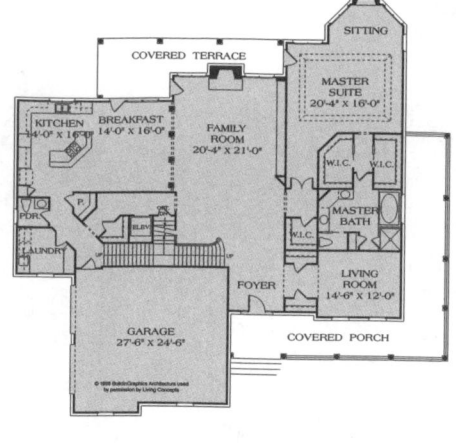

Lower Level

Main Level

Upper Level

HPK2101504

A wraparound covered porch offers shelter from the elements and introduces the two-story foyer of this attractive home. Inside, a large family room beckons with a cozy fireplace. A secluded first-floor master suite includes a luxurious bedroom with an attractive tray ceiling, a bay sitting area, and a fireplace. A second and equally luxurious master suite is located on the upper level. A vaulted ceiling in the master bedroom's sitting area is a special feature here. Three additional bedroom suites complete this floor.

Style: Farmhouse
Main Level: 2,799 sq. ft.
Upper Level: 2,336 sq. ft.
Lower Level: 1,334 sq. ft.
Total: 6,469 sq. ft.
Bonus Space: 464 sq. ft.
Bedrooms: 6
Bathrooms: 4 ½ + ½
Width: 78' - 10"
Depth: 79' - 0"
Foundation: Finished Walkout Basement

EPLANS.COM

Delight in all that this lavish Craftsman home has to offer. The attractive wraparound porch adds instant curb appeal to the front and side of the home. A generous rear deck highlights the back of the home. Entertainment possibilities are endless. A fireplace in the library proffers a cozy sanctuary to read or work at home. On the second floor, the master suite enjoys a private deck. Unique room shapes add space and interest to the remaining family bedrooms. Each accesses a private, full bath. The third floor houses an office or additional storage space.

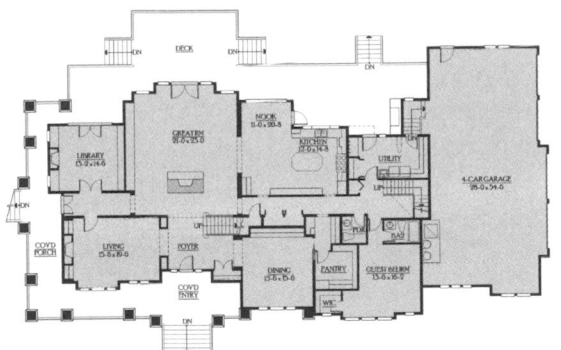

First Floor

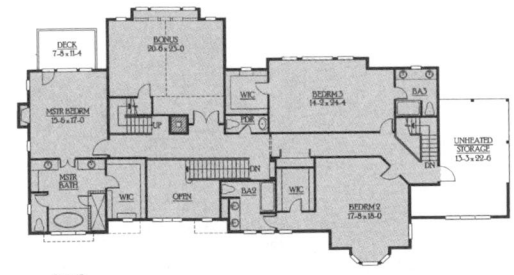

Second Floor

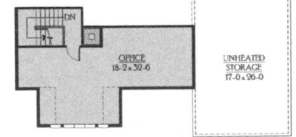

Third Floor

HPK2101505

Style: Craftsman
First Floor: 3,413 sq. ft.
Second Floor: 2,675 sq. ft.
Third Floor: 494 sq. ft.
Total: 6,582 sq. ft.
Bonus Space: 843 sq. ft.
Bedrooms: 4
Bathrooms: 4 ½
Width: 118' - 0"
Depth: 61' - 6"
Foundation: Crawlspace

EPLANS.COM

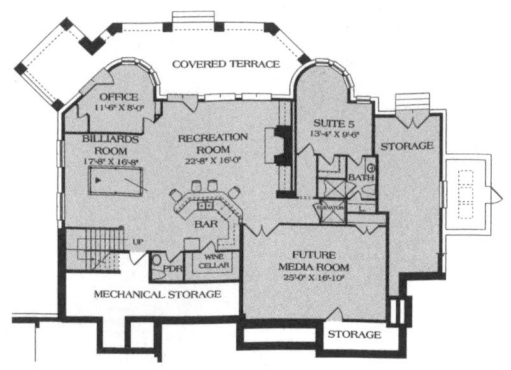

Lower Level

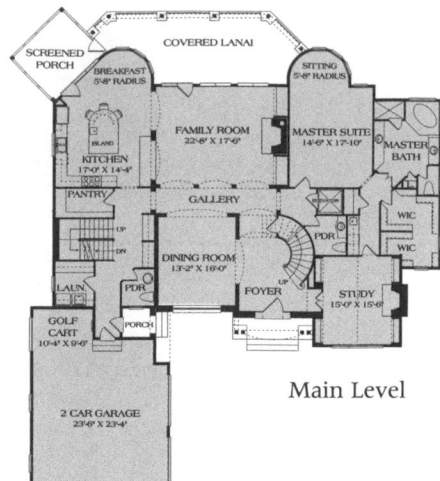

Main Level

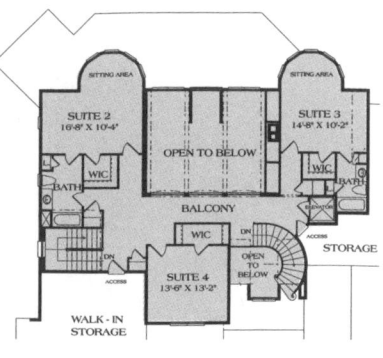

Upper Level

HPK2101506

Style: Cottage

Main Level: 2,962 sq. ft.

Upper Level: 1,522 sq. ft.

Lower Level: 2,105 sq. ft.

Total: 6,589 sq. ft.

Bedrooms: 5

Bathrooms: 4 ½ + 2 Half Baths

Width: 76' - 3"

Depth: 88' - 1"

Foundation: Finished Walkout Basement

A deceptively modest exterior reveals an extravagant hillside home of over 6,500 square feet. The basement level entices with a recreation room, an impressive wet bar, a billiards area, and space for a future media room. A fireplace here ensures year-round comfort. On the main level, access to the study from the master suite is an added bonus. The covered lanai and screened porch invite the possibility of outdoor gatherings or meals. On the upper level, three additional secondary bedrooms share two full baths. An elevator conveniently services all three levels.

This three-level Norman design flows with the tradition of European luxury. A stately portico welcomes guests inside. The two-story family room is warmed by a fireplace flanked by built-ins. The informal areas of the home include the island kitchen and the casual dining and gathering rooms. The first-floor master suite features private veranda access. Three additional bedrooms, two baths, and a recreation room with a balcony reside upstairs. The lower level includes a guest suite, a bath, and a wet bar with a wine cellar, ideal for the lower recreation and game rooms.

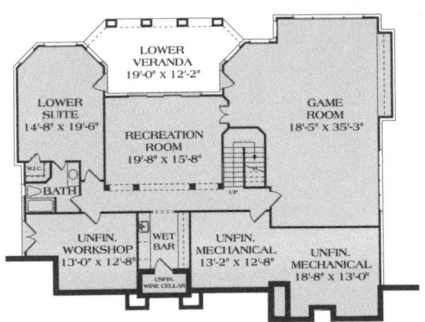

Lower Level

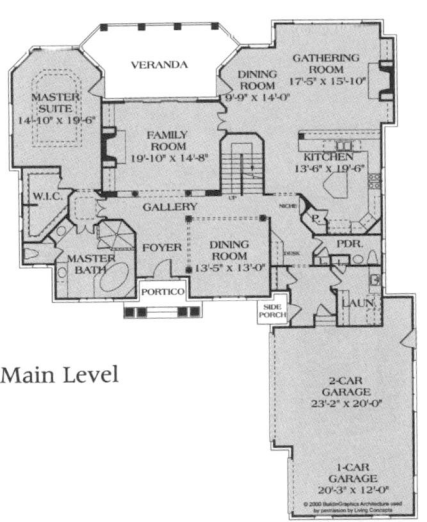

Main Level

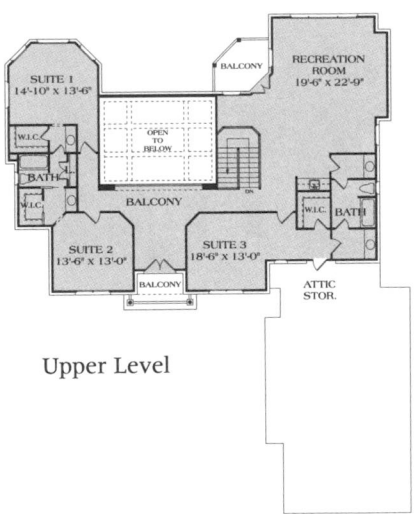

Upper Level

HPK2101507

Style: Norman
Main Level: 2,663 sq. ft.
Upper Level: 2,083 sq. ft.
Lower Level: 1,949 sq. ft.
Total: 6,695 sq. ft.
Bedrooms: 5
Bathrooms: 4 ½
Width: 69' - 1"
Depth: 85' - 1"
Foundation: Finished Walkout Basement

EPLANS.COM

4,000 SQUARE FEET AND OVER

HPK2101508

Style: Chateauesque
Main Level: 3,388 sq. ft.
Upper Level: 2,302 sq. ft.
Lower Level: 1,130 sq. ft.
Total: 6,820 sq. ft.
Bedrooms: 5
Bathrooms: 4 ½ + ½
Width: 117' - 1"
Depth: 90' - 11"
Foundation: Finished Basement

EPLANS.COM

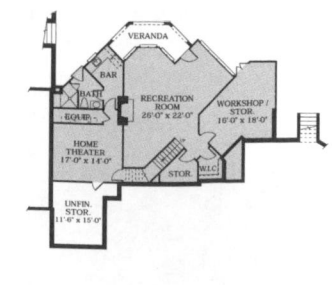

Lower Level

Main Level

This expansive mansion provides something for everyone in the family. The vivacious members will appreciate the large gathering room, formal dining room, and music room, while the resident chef enjoys the gourmet kitchen. The opposite corner of the main level holds a spectacular master suite, highlighted by a central soaking tub and huge Mediterranean shower. The lower level features space for entertaining, including a wet bar and a home theater room. There is also a workshop with direct access to the backyard. Verandas on every level will appeal to the outdoors-lovers.

Upper Level

HPK2101509

Style: Mediterranean

First Floor: 2,347 sq. ft.

Second Floor: 1,800 sq. ft.

Third Floor: 1,688 sq. ft.

Total: 7,017 sq. ft.

Bedrooms: 4

Bathrooms: 5 ½

Width: 75' - 5"

Depth: 76' - 4"

Foundation: Finished Walkout Basement

EPLANS.COM

A level for everyone! On the first floor, there's a study with a full bath, a formal dining room, a grand room with a fireplace, and a fabulous kitchen with an adjacent morning room. The second floor contains three suites—each with a walk-in closet—two full baths, a loft, and a reading nook. A lavish master suite on the third floor is full of amenities, including His and Hers walk-in closets, a huge private bath, and a balcony. In the basement, casual entertaining takes off with a large gathering room, a home theater, and a spacious game room.

4,000 SQUARE FEET AND OVER

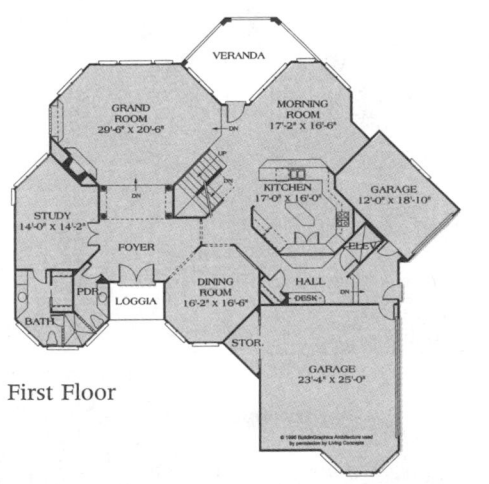

First Floor

Second Floor

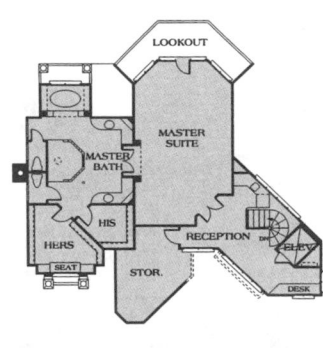

Third Floor

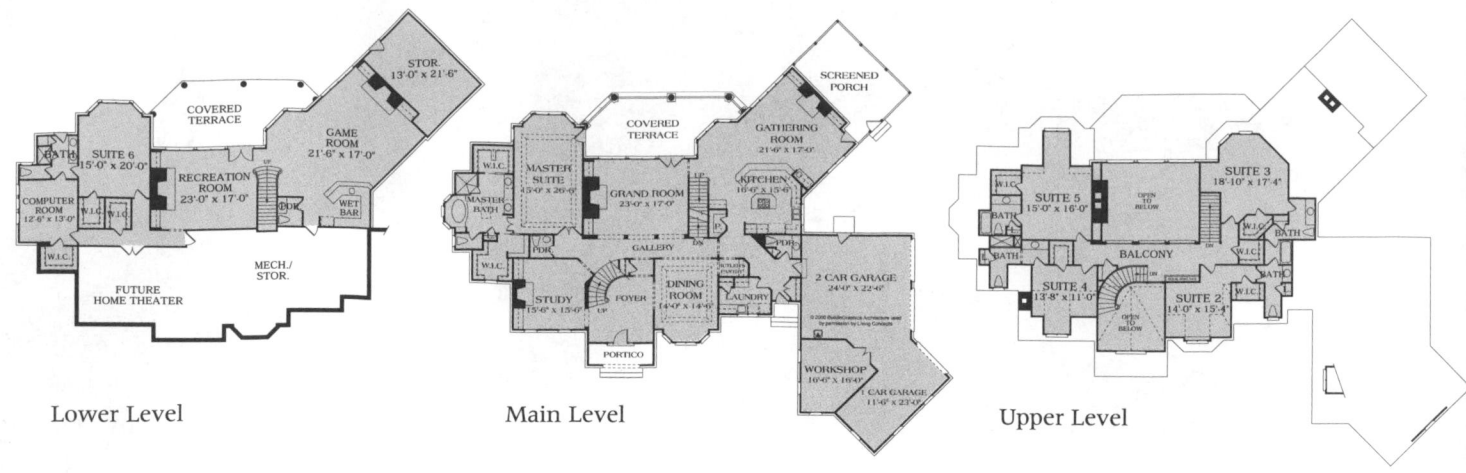

Lower Level

Main Level

Upper Level

Three levels of luxury highlight the livability of this French Country manor. To the left, the study features a fireplace with flanking built-ins. The grand room presents a massive hearth and accesses the rear terrace. The gathering room and nook are also warmed by a fireplace and access a rear screened porch. The first-floor master suite offers privacy. Upstairs, four additional family bedrooms reside on this level. The basement level is reserved for pure entertainment and includes a recreation room, game room complete with a wet bar, a sitting room, future home theater, guest suite, and computer room.

HPK2101510

Style: French Country
Main Level: 3,309 sq. ft.
Upper Level: 1,694 sq. ft.
Lower Level: 2,235 sq. ft.
Total: 7,238 sq. ft.
Bedrooms: 6
Bathrooms: 5 ½ + 2 Half Baths
Width: 112' - 9"
Depth: 97' - 0"
Foundation: Finished Walkout Basement

EPLANS.COM

ORDER BLUEPRINTS ANYTIME AT EPLANS.COM OR 1-800-521-6797

HPK2101511

Style: Italianate

Main Level: 3,850 sq. ft.

Upper Level: 1,783 sq. ft.

Lower Level: 1,785 sq. ft.

Total: 7,418 sq. ft.

Bedrooms: 4

Bathrooms: 3 ½ + ½

Width: 89' - 10"

Depth: 89' - 4"

Foundation: Finished Walkout Basement

The center of this imposing home is the striking great room, which truly lives up to its name. At one end a huge extended hearth fireplace offers many cozy evenings. French doors open to the rear deck. From the great room, ascend a magnificent stairway to the upper level where three bedrooms, two baths, and inside and outside balconies can be found. On the main floor, the kitchen, set up for multiple cooks to work comfortably, adjoins a large breakfast alcove, which opens to a rear patio.

4,000 SQUARE FEET AND OVER

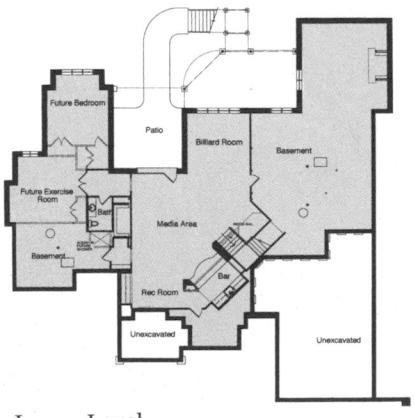

Lower Level

Main Level

Upper Level

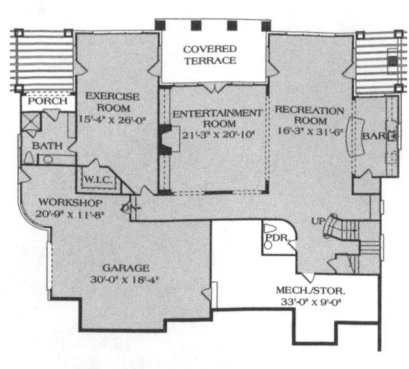

Lower Level

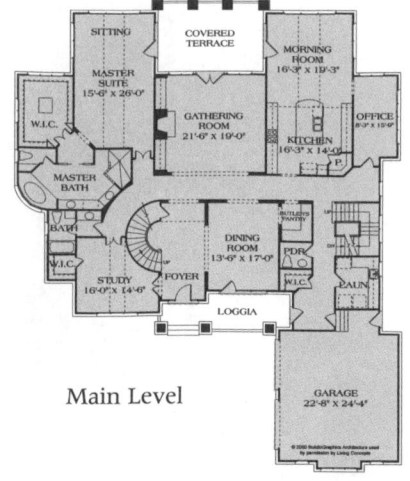

Main Level

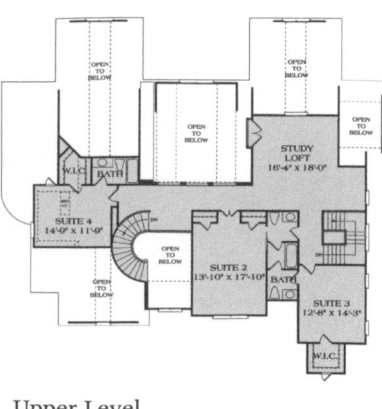

Upper Level

Exquisite Craftsman character is the hallmark of this incredible design. A front loggia welcomes you inside. The gathering room is warmed by a fireplace flanked by built-ins. The master suite is enhanced with a spacious sitting area. The gourmet kitchen extends into a morning nook that accesses the rear covered terrace. Three additional suites are located upstairs, along with a spacious study loft. Don't miss the impressive basement level, with a recreation room served by a bar, an entertainment room with a fireplace, an exercise room, and a handy workshop area.

HPK2101513

Style: Craftsman
Main Level: 3,562 sq. ft.
Upper Level: 1,594 sq. ft.
Lower Level: 2,346 sq. ft.
Total: 7,502 sq. ft.
Bedrooms: 4
Bathrooms: 4 ½
Width: 74' - 6"
Depth: 92' - 0"
Foundation: Finished Walkout Basement

EPLANS.COM

HPK2101515

EPLANS.COM

Style: New American

Main Level: 2,893 sq. ft.

Upper Level: 2,865 sq. ft.

Lower Level: 1,747 sq. ft.

Total: 7,505 sq. ft.

Bedrooms: 5

Bathrooms: 5 ½

Width: 74' - 2"

Depth: 86' - 11"

Foundation: Finished Basement

Stucco detailing, varied window treatments, and elegant design give this home plenty of curb appeal. Lavish with its luxuries inside as well as out, this plan is designed to please. A bayed study opens off the foyer and offers the warmth of a fireplace. The formal dining room is defined from the spacious gathering room by graceful columns. The master suite is designed to pamper. With elegant angles, the efficient kitchen works well with the bayed breakfast area. Three suites-each with a private bath-reside on the second floor. A huge home office completes this level.

4,000 SQUARE FEET AND OVER

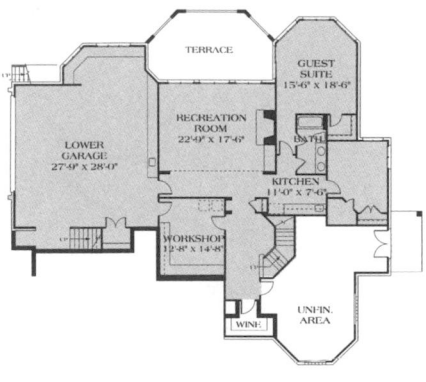

Lower Level

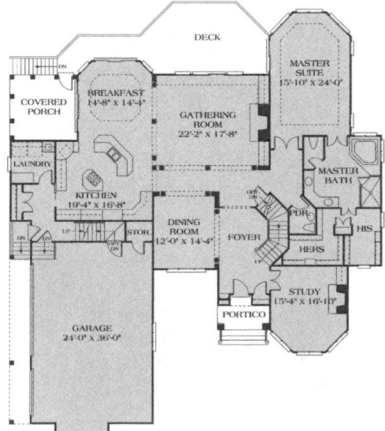

Main Level

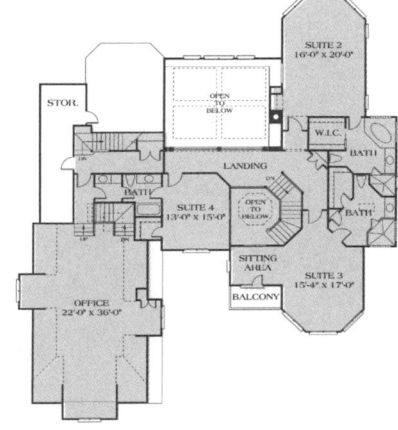

Upper Level

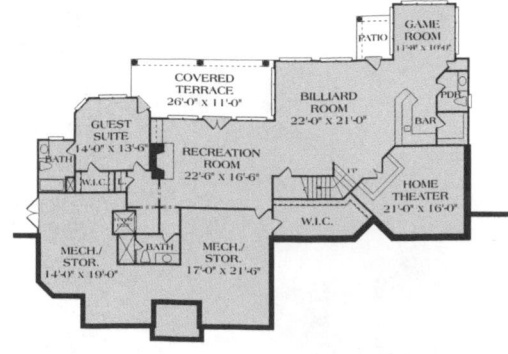

Lower Level

HPK2101512

Style: Mediterranean
Main Level: 3,060 sq. ft.
Upper Level: 2,530 sq. ft.
Lower Level: 2,232 sq. ft.
Total: 7,822 sq. ft.
Bedrooms: 6
Bathrooms: 7 ½ + ½
Width: 81' - 4"
Depth: 80' - 2"
Foundation: Finished Walkout Basement

EPLANS.COM

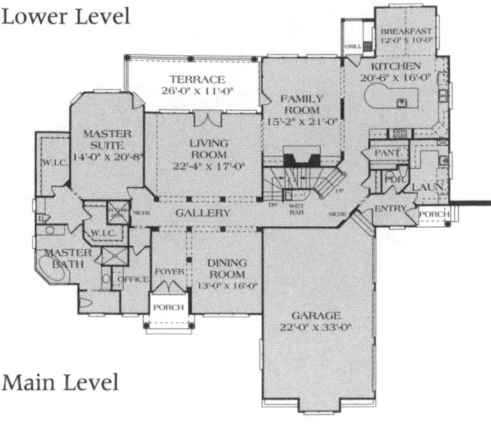

Main Level

A distinctively Mediterranean feel is found in this plan. A fully-appointed basement provides three floors of living. A main floor gallery connects the master suite, foyer, dining and living rooms, and kitchen. The upper floor contains an attic, library, sitting room, and a nanny suite, along with three bedrooms with private baths and walk-in closets.

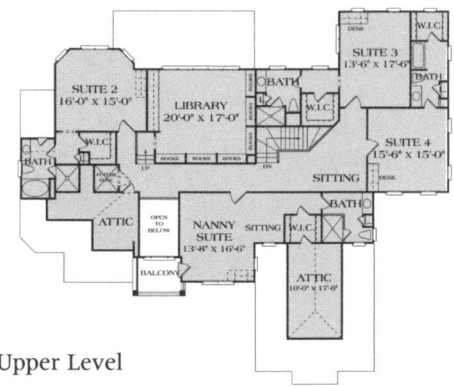

Upper Level

HPK2101514

Style: Mediterranean

First Floor: 2,971 sq. ft.

Second Floor: 2,199 sq. ft.

Third Floor: 1,040 sq. ft.

Basement 1,707 sq. ft.

Total: 7,917 sq. ft.

Bedrooms: 5

Bathrooms: 5 ½

Width: 84' - 4"

Depth: 64' - 11"

Foundation: Unfinished Basement

EPLANS.COM

From the gathering room to the master suite on the third floor, this plan provides a comfortable home, office, showplace, private retreat, and entertainment center. The first floor includes living areas, a guest suite, a music room, and an office. Three bedroom suites and a reception room are on the second floor. An elevator to the right of the front entrance carries you between the four floors.

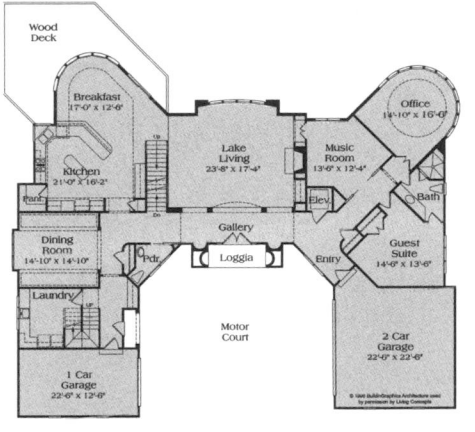

First Floor

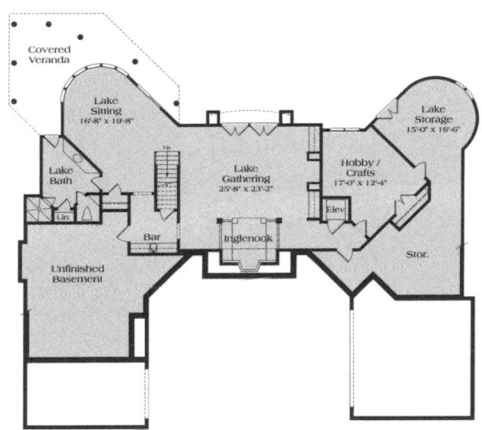

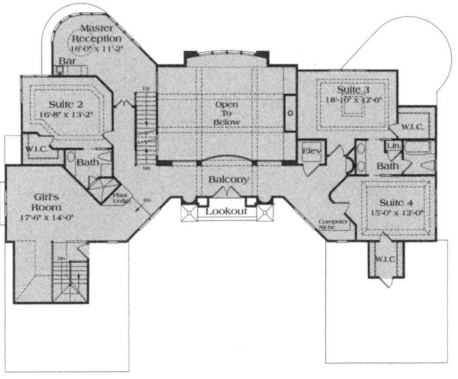

Second Floor

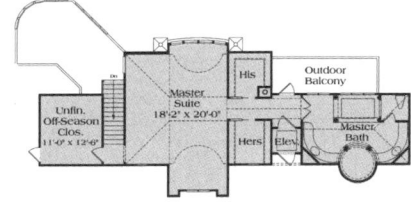

Third Floor

4,000 SQUARE FEET AND OVER

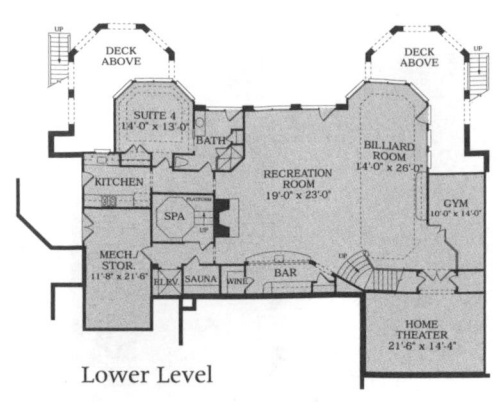

Lower Level

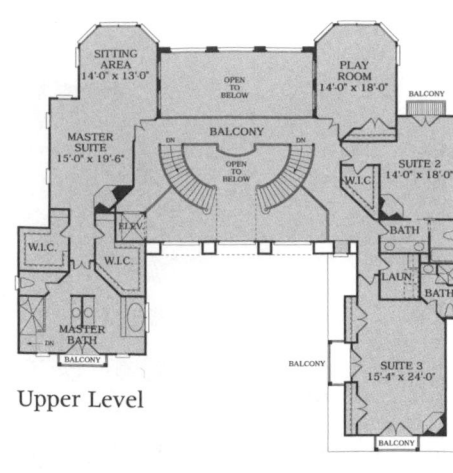

Main Level

Upper Level

HPK2101516

Style: Italianate

Main Level: 2,710 sq. ft.

Upper Level: 2,784 sq. ft.

Lower Level: 2,574 sq. ft.

Total: 8,068 sq. ft.

Bedrooms: 4

Bathrooms: 5 ½

Width: 79' - 4"

Depth: 76' - 8"

Foundation: Finished Walkout Basement

EPLANS.COM

This Mediterranean estate features palatial elegance with all the comfortable amenities of the modern world. The second floor offers a plush master suite. Two additional suites and a playroom also reside here. The basement level is an impressive entertainment center that provides a recreation room served by a wet bar, a billiard room, home theater, gym, indoor spa, sauna, guest suite, second kitchen, and a mechanical/storage room. An elevator provides easy access to all levels.

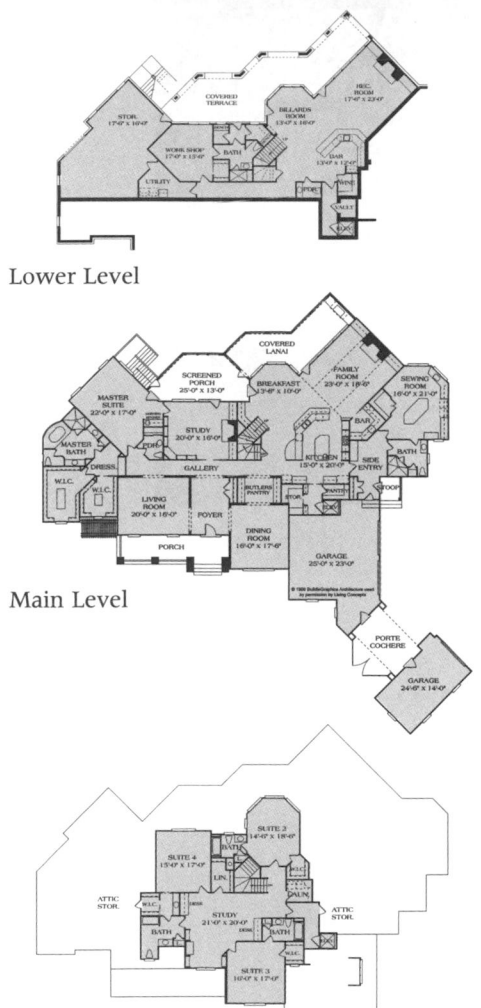

Lower Level

Main Level

Upper Level

Shingles and stone add charismatic splendor to this magnificent Early American-style home. A gallery hall leads to the hearth-warmed study or to the main living areas, including a kitchen, a breakfast nook, a comfortable family room, and a quiet sewing room. The master suite is on this level, secluded for privacy with an indulgent spa bath and two room-sized walk-in closets. Upstairs, three bedroom suites enjoy private baths and share a central study loft. The lower level can be finished to hold an extensive recreation room with a billiards bay and a wet bar.

HPK2101517

Style: Shingle
Main Level: 4,593 sq. ft.
Upper Level: 1,855 sq. ft.
Lower Level: 1,725 sq. ft.
Total: 8,173 sq. ft.
Bedrooms: 4
Bathrooms: 5 ½ + 2 Half Baths
Width: 113' - 10"
Depth: 93' - 7"
Foundation: Unfinished Basement

EPLANS.COM

4,000 SQUARE FEET AND OVER

Dreaming is free.
And now, so are shipping & handling.

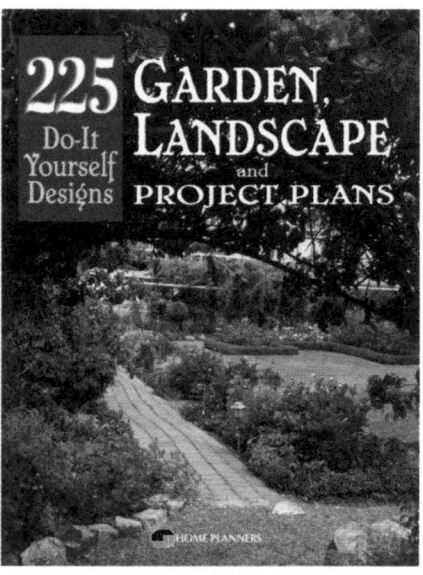

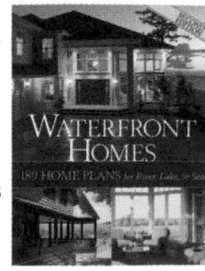

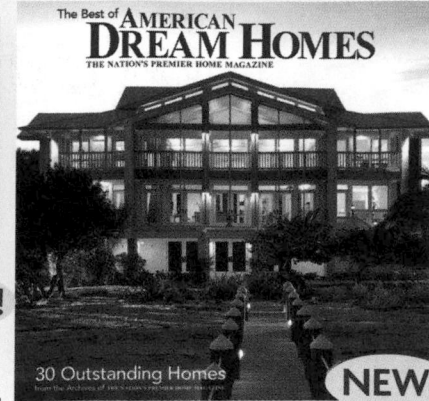

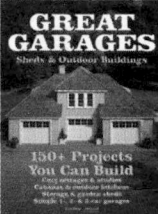
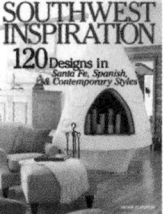

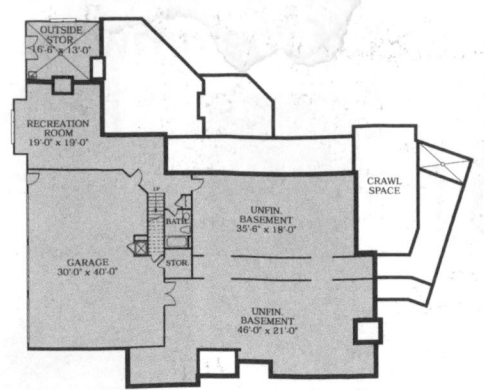

Lower Level

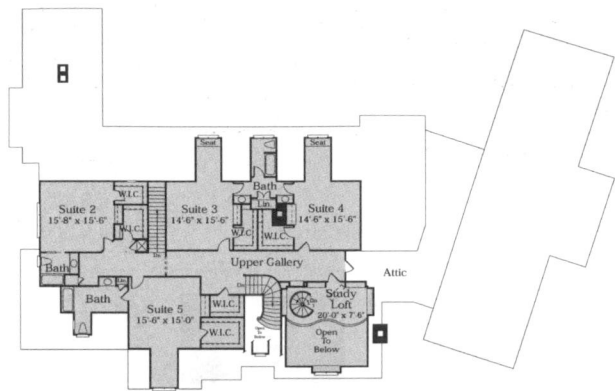

Main Level

HPK2101518

Style: Chateauesque

Main Level: 4,002 sq. ft.

Upper Level: 2,338 sq. ft.

Lower Level: 3,271 sq. ft.

Total: 9,611 sq. ft.

Bedrooms: 5

Bathrooms: 5 ½ + ½

Width: 133' - 4"

Depth: 84' - 0

Foundation: Finished Basement

Upper Level

Stone and shutters on the outside are a prelude to the attractiveness of the interior. Flanking the foyer is the two-story study—complete with a fireplace and spiral staircase to the study loft. The grand room is aptly named, with a second fireplace and direct access to the rear covered terrace. A third fireplace is shared with the family room and a covered porch. A lavish master suite is designed to pamper with direct access to the indoor pool! Upstairs, four suites—each with a walk-in closet—share three bathrooms and access to the study loft.

HPK2101529

Style: New American

Main Level: 4,232 sq. ft.

Upper Level: 1,841 sq. ft.

Lower Level: 3,962 sq. ft.

Total: 10,035 sq. ft.

Bedrooms: 4

Bathrooms: 5 ½ + ½

Width: 108' - 4"

Depth: 82' - 4"

Foundation: Finished Walkout Basement

EPLANS.COM

Main Level

Upper Level

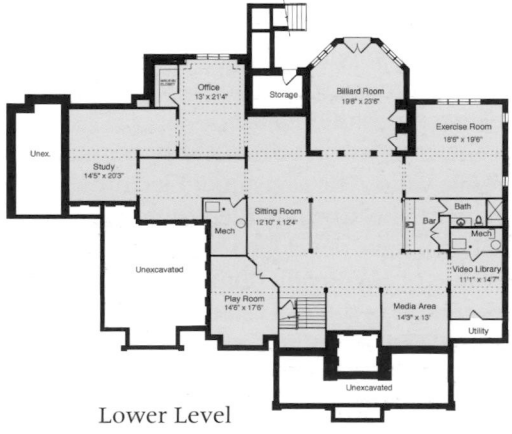

Lower Level

A spectacular brick exterior with limestone trim, decorative carvings, and various window styles creates an elegant European manor. A gas fireplace decorates the great room, while a wood-burning fireplace warms the hearth room. The master bedroom offers a quiet retreat for the homeowner, with a stepped ceiling and luxurious bath. The gourmet kitchen with island and walk-in pantry easily serves the breakfast and dining rooms. A wood-burning fireplace is the highlight of the covered porch, with access from the breakfast room, great room, and master suite. Split stairs lead to a second floor where three bedrooms, each with a walk-in closet and private bath, access a raised computer room. Let the good times roll in the lower level; there's a room for every activity.

4,000 SQUARE FEET AND OVER

IT'S ALL IN THE DETAILS.

Our strict standards ensure that all blueprint packages contain detailed, high-quality working drawings designed to show exactly how the house is to be built. You can expect to find the following standard elements in most sets of plans:

< Front Perspective

This sheet depicts a fully landscaped architectural rendering of the home as it would appear when complete…a great tool for discussions with the builder.

Foundation and Basement Plans >

This sheet contains the foundation layout including concrete walls, footings, pads, posts, beams, bearing walls, and foundation sizes, configuration, reinforcing details and notes. The first-floor framing details may be included in this plan if your home includes a basement or crawlspace; otherwise, details and specifications for a monolithic slab are provided.

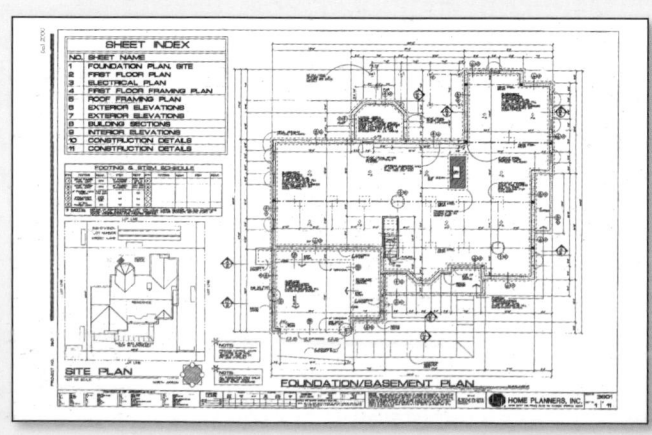

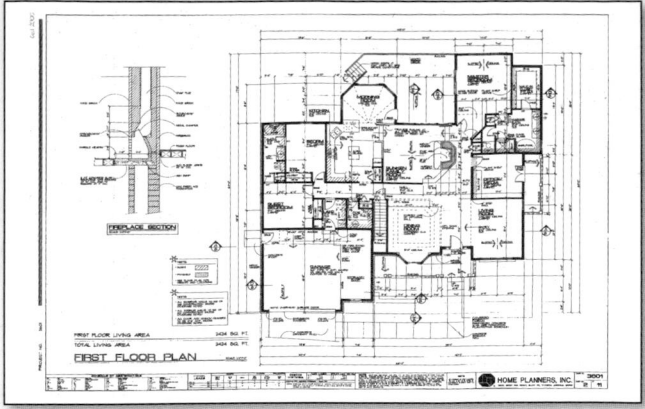

∧ Detailed Floor Plans

These plans show the layout of each floor of the house. Rooms and interior spaces are dimensioned; stairways, doors, and windows located; and keys are given for cross-section details provided elsewhere in the plans. They may also contain floor and roof framing information, including beam locations and joist/rafter sizes, directions, and span.

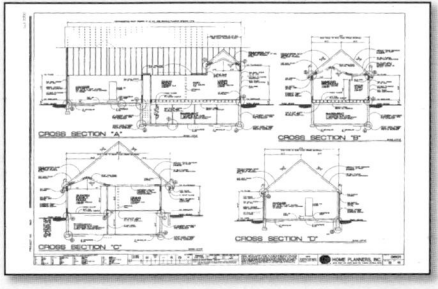

∧ House Details and Cross-Sections

These views show sections or cutaways through the house highlighting the foundation, interior and exterior walls assemblies, floors, stairways, insulation levels, and roof details. Additional cross-sections or details may be included to explain important changes in floor, ceiling, or roof heights.

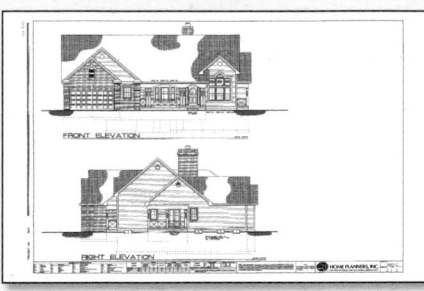

∧ Exterior Elevations

These drawings show the front, rear, and side views of the house, roof slope, pitch and overhang dimensions, cladding information with particular attention to cornice detail, brick and stone accents, or other exterior finish details that make a home unique.

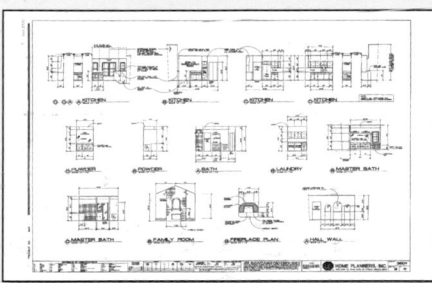

∧ Kitchen and Bath Elevations

These elevations, when included in the working drawings, show the arrangement and size of each fixture in the room, including cabinets. They provide the basic information needed to create customized layouts with a cabinet manufacturer.

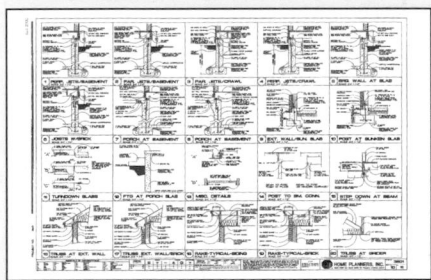

∧ Plan Details

Most plan sets include basic detail sheets that show typical wall sections, foundation, and other construction details. Some designs also offer customization options, such as interior trim and fireplace details.

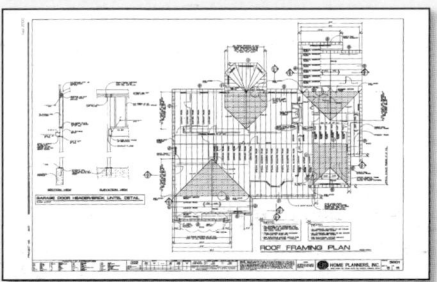

∧ Roof and Floor Framing Plans

These sheets, when included separately in the working drawings, include floor joist, ceiling joist, rafter and roof joist size, spacing, direction, span, and specifications. Beam and window headers, along with necessary details for framing connections, stairways, skylights, or dormers are also detailed. This information, when not isolated on a separate sheet, may be included on the detailed floor plans.

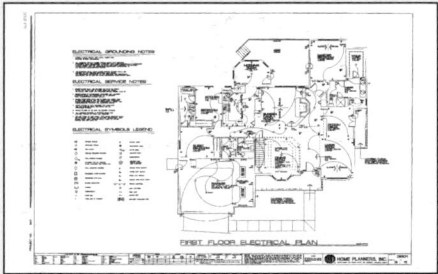

∧ Schematic Electrical Layout

Available with most plans, this layout suggests the location for wall plugs, fixtures, and switches, and may be shown on the detailed floor plans or on a separate diagram.

BLUEPRINT PRICE SCHEDULE

PRICE TIERS	1-SET STUDY PACKAGE	5-SET BUILDING PACKAGE	8-SET BUILDING PACKAGE	1-SET REPRODUCIBLE*	I-SET CAD*
A1	$470	$520	$575	$700	$1,055
A2	$510	$565	$620	$765	$1,230
A3	$575	$630	$690	$870	$1,400
A4	$620	$685	$750	$935	$1,570
C1	$665	$740	$810	$1,000	$1,735
C2	$715	$795	$855	$1,065	$1,815
C3	$785	$845	$910	$1,145	$1,915
C4	$840	$915	$970	$1,225	$2,085
L1	$930	$1,030	$1,115	$1,390	$2,500
L2	$1,010	$1,105	$1,195	$1,515	$2,575
L3	$1,115	$1,220	$1,325	$1,665	$2,835
L4	$1,230	$1,350	$1,440	$1,850	$3,140
SQ1				$0.40/SQ. FT.	$0.68/SQ. FT.
SQ3				$0.55/SQ. FT.	$0.94/SQ. FT.
SQ5				$0.80/SQ. FT	$1.36/SQ. FT.
SQ7				$1.00/SQ. FT.	$1.70/SQ. FT.
SQ9				$1.25/SQ. FT.	$2.13/SQ. FT.
SQ11				$1.50/SQ. FT.	$2.55/SQ. FT.

PRICES SUBJECT TO CHANGE   * REQUIRES AN E-MAIL ADDRESS OR FAX NUMBER

PLAN #	PRICE TIER	PAGE	MATERIALS LIST	DECK	DECK PRICE	LANDSCAPE	LANDSCAPE PRICE	REGIONS
HPK2100001	A1	8	Y					
HPK2100003	A1	9	Y					
HPK2100002	A1	9	Y					
HPK2100004	A2	10						
HPK2100005	A2	10	Y					
HPK2100006	A3	11	Y	ODA014	D1	OLA003	P3	
HPK2100007	A2	11						
HPK2100009	A2	12	Y					
HPK2100008	SQ3	12						
HPK2100010	A3	13	Y			OLA091	P3	
HPK2100011	A2	13						
HPK2100013	A4	14						
HPK2100012	A2	14						
HPK2100015	A2	15	Y					
HPK2100014	A1	15						
HPK2100016	A2	16						
HPK2100017	A2	16	Y					
HPK2100019	A2	17						
HPK2100018	A2	17						
HPK2100020	A3	18						
HPK2100021	A3	18	Y					
HPK2100023	A2	19	Y					
HPK2100022	A3	19	Y					
HPK2100024	A2	20	Y					
HPK2100025	A2	20	Y					
HPK2100027	A1	21						
HPK2100026	A2	21	Y					
HPK2100028	A3	22	Y					
HPK2100029	A2	22						
HPK2100030	A2	23	Y					
HPK2100031	A2	23						
HPK2100032	A3	24	Y					
HPK2100033	SQ3	24	Y					
HPK2100035	A3	25	Y					
HPK2100034	A2	25	Y					
HPK2100036	A2	26						
HPK2100037	A3	26	Y					
HPK2100039	A3	27						
HPK2100038	A2	27	Y					
HPK2100040	A2	28						
HPK2100041	SQ3	28						
HPK2100043	A2	29						
HPK2100042	A2	29	Y					
HPK2100044	A3	30	Y					
HPK2100045	A2	30	Y					

PLAN #	PRICE TIER	PAGE	MATERIALS LIST	DECK	DECK PRICE	LANDSCAPE	LANDSCAPE PRICE	REGIONS
HPK2100046	A4	31	Y					
HPK2100047	A2	31						
HPK2100048	A2	32						
HPK2100049	A2	32	Y					
HPK2100050	A3	33						
HPK2100051	A2	33						
HPK2100052	A3	34	Y					
HPK2100053	A2	34	Y					
HPK2100054	A3	35	Y					
HPK2100055	A3	35	Y					
HPK2100057	A2	36	Y					
HPK2100056	A3	36	Y			OLA001	P3	
HPK2100058	A2	37	Y					
HPK2100059	A2	37						
HPK2100060	A3	38	Y					
HPK2100061	A4	38						
HPK2100063	A4	39						
HPK2100062	A2	39						
HPK2100065	A4	40						
HPK2100064	A2	40						
HPK2100067	A4	41	Y					
HPK2100066	A4	41						
HPK2100068	A2	42	Y					
HPK2100069	A3	42						
HPK2100071	A2	43						
HPK2100070	A3	43						
HPK2100072	A3	44	Y					
HPK2100073	A3	44	Y					
HPK2100075	A3	45	Y					
HPK2100074	A1	45						
HPK2100076	A3	46	Y					
HPK2100077	A4	46						
HPK2100079	A3	47						
HPK2100078	A3	47						
HPK2100081	A2	48	Y					
HPK2100080	A2	48	Y					
HPK2100082	SQ3	49						
HPK2100083	A3	50	Y					
HPK2100084	A4	51						
HPK2100085	A4	52						
HPK2100086	A2	53	Y					
HPK2100087	A3	54						
HPK2100088	A3	55	Y					
HPK2100089	A3	56	Y					
HPK2100090	A3	57						
HPK2100091	A3	58	Y					
HPK2100092	A3	59	Y					
HPK2100093	A3	60	Y					
HPK2100094	C2	61						
HPK2100095	SQ3	62	Y			OLA012	P3	
HPK2100096	A3	63	Y					
HPK2100097	A3	64	Y					
HPK2101520	A2	64						
HPK2101521	A2	64						
HPK2101522	A3	64						
HPK2100098	A3	65	Y					
HPK2100099	A2	66						
HPK2100100	A2	67						
HPK2100101	A2	67						
HPK2100102	C3	68						
HPK2100103	A2	68						
HPK2100105	A2	69	Y					
HPK2100104	A4	69	Y					
HPK2100106	A2	70						
HPK2100107	A2	70						
HPK2100108	SQ3	71						
HPK2100109	A2	71	Y					
HPK2100110	A4	72						
HPK2100111	A1	73						
HPK2100112	A3	74						
HPK2100113	A2	75	Y					
HPK2100114	A2	76	Y					
HPK2100115	SQ3	77						
HPK2100116	A2	78						
HPK2100117	A2	79	Y					
HPK2100118	A1	80						
HPK2100119	A3	81						
HPK2100120	A3	82	Y					
HPK2100121	A3	83						

PLAN #	PRICE TIER	PAGE	MATERIALS LIST	DECK	DECK PRICE	LANDSCAPE	LANDSCAPE PRICE	REGIONS
HPK2100123	A3	84						
HPK2100122	A2	84						
HPK2100124	A2	85						
HPK2100125	A4	85						
HPK2100127	A2	86						
HPK2100126	A2	86						
HPK2100128	A3	87						
HPK2100129	A4	88						
HPK2100130	A3	89						
HPK2100131	A4	90						
HPK2100132	A4	91						
HPK2100133	A3	91	Y					
HPK2100134	A4	92	Y					
HPK2100135	SQ3	92						
HPK2100137	A4	93	Y					
HPK2100136	A4	93	Y					
HPK2100139	A4	94	Y					
HPK2100138	A4	94	Y					
HPK2100140	A3	95						
HPK2100141	A3	95						
HPK2100143	A3	96	Y					
HPK2100142	A4	96	Y					
HPK2100145	A4	97						
HPK2100144	SQ3	97						
HPK2100146	A4	98	Y					
HPK2100147	A3	98	Y					
HPK2100149	A3	99	Y					
HPK2100148	C2	99						
HPK2100150	A3	100	Y					
HPK2100151	A4	100	Y					
HPK2100153	A4	101	Y					
HPK2100152	A4	101						
HPK2100154	A4	102	Y					
HPK2100155	SQ3	102						
HPK2100156	SQ3	103						
HPK2100157	A4	103	Y					
HPK2100159	A3	104	Y					
HPK2100158	A4	104	Y					
HPK2100160	A3	105						
HPK2100161	A3	105						
HPK2100162	A4	106	Y					
HPK2100163	A4	106	Y					
HPK2100164	SQ3	107						
HPK2100165	A4	107						
HPK2100167	A4	108	Y					
HPK2100166	A3	108	Y					
HPK2100168	A3	109						
HPK2100169	A4	109	Y					
HPK2100171	A4	110	Y					
HPK2100170	A3	110	Y					
HPK2100173	A4	111	Y					
HPK2100172	A3	111	Y					
HPK2100174	A3	112	Y					
HPK2100175	A3	112	Y					
HPK2100176	A4	113	Y					
HPK2100177	A3	113	Y					
HPK2100178	A3	114						
HPK2100179	A3	114	Y					
HPK2100180	A3	115						
HPK2100181	A4	115						
HPK2100182	A4	116						
HPK2100183	A4	116	Y					
HPK2100185	A3	117	Y					
HPK2100184	A3	117	Y					
HPK2100187	C3	118	Y					
HPK2100186	A3	118	Y					
HPK2100188	A4	119	Y					
HPK2100189	A3	119				OLA004	P3	
HPK2100190	SQ3	120						
HPK2100191	A4	120						
HPK2100192	A4	121						
HPK2100193	SQ3	121						
HPK2100195	A3	122						
HPK2100194	A4	122	Y					
HPK2100196	A4	123						
HPK2100197	A3	123	Y					
HPK2100198	A4	124	Y					
HPK2100199	A3	124	Y					

PLAN #	PRICE TIER	PAGE	MATERIALS LIST	DECK	DECK PRICE	LANDSCAPE	LANDSCAPE PRICE	REGIONS
HPK2100200	A3	125						
HPK2100201	A4	125						
HPK2100203	A4	126	Y					
HPK2100202	A3	126						
HPK2100204	A4	127	Y					
HPK2100205	C3	127						
HPK2100206	A4	128	Y					
HPK2100207	SQ3	128						
HPK2100209	A4	129	Y					
HPK2100208	SQ3	129						
HPK2100211	A4	130	Y					
HPK2100210	A4	130	Y	ODA013	D1	OLA001	P3	
HPK2100212	A4	131						
HPK2100213	A3	131						
HPK2100214	A4	132	Y					
HPK2100215	SQ3	132						
HPK2100217	A4	133	Y					
HPK2100216	A3	133	Y					
HPK2100219	A4	134	Y					
HPK2100218	A3	134	Y					
HPK2100220	A4	135						
HPK2100221	A3	135	Y					
HPK2100222	A4	136	Y					
HPK2100223	A4	136	Y					
HPK2100224	A4	137	Y					
HPK2100225	A4	137						
HPK2100227	C1	138						
HPK2100226	C1	138	Y					
HPK2100228	A4	139	Y					
HPK2100229	A4	139	Y					
HPK2100231	A4	140	Y					
HPK2100230	C2	140						
HPK2100232	A3	141						
HPK2100233	SQ3	142						
HPK2100234	A4	143						
HPK2100235	A4	144	Y					
HPK2100236	A4	145	Y			OLA088	P4	
HPK2100237	C1	146						
HPK2100238	C1	147						
HPK2100239	C1	148						
HPK2100240	A4	149	Y					
HPK2100241	A4	150	Y					
HPK2100242	A4	151	Y					
HPK2100243	A3	152						
HPK2100244	A4	153	Y					
HPK2100245	A3	154						
HPK2100246	A4	155	Y					
HPK2100247	A4	156	Y					
HPK2100248	C1	157						
HPK2100249	A4	158	Y					
HPK2100250	SQ3	159						
HPK2100251	A3	160	Y					
HPK2100252	A4	161	Y					
HPK2100253	A4	162						
HPK2100254	A2	163	Y					
HPK2100255	A3	163						
HPK2100257	A4	164	Y					
HPK2100256	A4	164						
HPK2100259	A3	165	Y					
HPK2100258	C2	165						
HPK2100261	C3	166						
HPK2100260	A3	166						
HPK2100262	A4	167	Y					
HPK2100263	C1	167	Y					
HPK2100265	A3	168	Y					
HPK2100264	A3	168						
HPK2100267	A3	169						
HPK2100266	SQ3	169						
HPK2100268	A4	170	Y					
HPK2100269	C2	170						
HPK2100270	A4	171	Y					
HPK2100271	A4	171	Y	ODA012	D2	OLA083	P3	
HPK2100272	A3	172						
HPK2100273	A4	172	Y	ODA011	D1	OLA024	P4	
HPK2100274	A3	173	Y					
HPK2100275	A4	173						
HPK2100276	A4	174	Y					
HPK2100277	A4	174	Y					

PLAN #	PRICE TIER	PAGE	MATERIALS LIST	DECK	DECK PRICE	LANDSCAPE	LANDSCAPE PRICE	REGIONS
HPK2100278	A4	175	Y	ODA012	D2	OLA083	P3	
HPK2100279	A3	175	Y			OLA001	P3	
HPK2100280	A4	176	Y					
HPK2100281	A4	176						
HPK2100283	A3	177	Y					
HPK2100282	A3	177						
HPK2100285	A3	178	Y					
HPK2100284	A4	178	Y					
HPK2100286	C1	179						
HPK2100287	A3	180						
HPK2100288	C3	181						
HPK2100342	P5	182	Y					
HPK2100336	P4	182	Y					
HPK2100341	P5	182	Y					
HPK2100338	P5	182	Y					
HPK2100343	P5	182						
HPK2100344	P6	182	Y					
HPK2100339	P5	182	Y					
HPK2100340	P5	182	Y					
HPK2100337	P4	182	Y					
HPK2100290	P4	183	Y					
HPK2100292	P4	183	Y					
HPK2100297	P4	183	Y					
HPK2100293	P4	183	Y					
HPK2100295	P5	183	Y					
HPK2100291	P4	183	Y					
HPK2100294	P5	183	Y					
HPK2100296	P4	183	Y					
HPK2100298	P6	183	Y					
HPK2100300	A4	184	Y					
HPK2100299	A4	184	Y					
HPK2100302	A3	185	Y					
HPK2100301	C1	185						
HPK2100303	A4	186	Y					
HPK2100304	A3	186	Y			OLA004	P3	
HPK2100306	A4	187						
HPK2100305	A4	187	Y					
HPK2100307	SQ3	188	Y					
HPK2100308	SQ3	188	Y					
HPK2100310	A4	189	Y					
HPK2100309	SQ3	189	Y					
HPK2100312	A4	190						
HPK2100311	A4	190	Y					
HPK2100313	A3	191						
HPK2100314	A3	191	Y					
HPK2100316	C1	192						
HPK2100315	C2	192						
HPK2100317	A4	193						
HPK2100318	A3	193	Y					
HPK2100320	A4	194	Y					
HPK2100319	A4	194	Y					
HPK2100322	A4	195	Y					
HPK2100321	A4	195						
HPK2100323	A4	196	Y					
HPK2100324	A3	196	Y					
HPK2100325	A3	197	Y					
HPK2100326	C2	197						
HPK2100328	C1	198						
HPK2100327	A4	198	Y					
HPK2100329	SQ3	199						
HPK2100330	A3	199	Y	ODA015	D1	OLA003	P3	
HPK2100331	A4	200	Y					
HPK2100332	C1	200						
HPK2100334	C1	201	Y					
HPK2100333	C3	201						
HPK2100335	A3	202						
HPK2100289	A4	203						
HPK2100346	A4	204						
HPK2100345	A3	204	Y					
HPK2100348	A3	205	Y					
HPK2100347	A3	205	Y					
HPK2100349	C1	206	Y					
HPK2100350	A4	207	Y					
HPK2100351	A4	208	Y	ODA011	D1	OLA083	P3	
HPK2100352	C1	209						
HPK2100353	SQ3	210	Y					
HPK2100354	SQ3	211	Y					
HPK2100355	SQ3	212	Y					
HPK2100356	A4	213						
HPK2100357	A4	214	Y					
HPK2100358	A3	215						
HPK2100359	A4	216						
HPK2100360	A4	217	Y	ODA014	D1	OLA021	P3	
HPK2100361	A3	218	Y					
HPK2100362	C1	219	Y			OLA017	P3	
HPK2100363	A3	220						
HPK2100364	A3	221						
HPK2100365	A4	221						
HPK2100367	A3	222						
HPK2100366	C3	222	Y					
HPK2100368	SQ3	223						
HPK2100369	C1	223						
HPK2100370	SQ3	224	Y					
HPK2100371	A3	224	Y					
HPK2100373	A4	225						
HPK2100372	A4	225						
HPK2100375	C3	226						
HPK2100374	SQ3	226						
HPK2100376	C1	227						
HPK2100377	A3	228	Y					
HPK2100378	A3	229	Y					
HPK2100379	A4	230	Y					
HPK2100380	C1	231	Y					
HPK2100381	A4	231	Y					
HPK2100382	C1	232	Y					
HPK2100383	C4	232						
HPK2100385	C1	233	Y					
HPK2100384	C1	233	Y					
HPK2100386	C1	234	Y					
HPK2100387	A4	234	Y					
HPK2100389	C1	235	Y					
HPK2100388	A4	235						
HPK2100390	A4	236	Y					
HPK2100391	C1	236	Y					
HPK2100392	A4	237						
HPK2100393	C1	237	Y	ODA006	D1	OLA021	P3	
HPK2100394	C1	238	Y					
HPK2100395	SQ3	238						
HPK2100396	C1	239						
HPK2100397	C1	239	Y	ODA012	D2	OLA010	P3	
HPK2100399	C1	240	Y					
HPK2100398	C2	240						
HPK2100400	C1	241	Y					
HPK2100401	C4	241	Y					
HPK2100403	C1	242	Y					
HPK2100402	A4	242	Y					
HPK2100405	C1	243	Y					
HPK2100404	A4	243	Y					
HPK2100406	C4	244	Y					
HPK2100407	C2	244	Y					
HPK2100408	C1	245						
HPK2100409	C3	245						
HPK2100410	A4	246						
HPK2100411	A4	246						
HPK2100412	C1	247	Y					
HPK2100413	SQ3	247	Y					
HPK2100414	SQ3	248	Y					
HPK2100415	SQ3	248						
HPK2100416	C1	249	Y					
HPK2100417	C1	249						
HPK2100418	C1	250	Y					
HPK2100419	A4	250	Y					
HPK2100420	C1	251	Y					
HPK2100421	C1	251	Y					
HPK2100422	C2	252	Y					
HPK2100423	A4	252						
HPK2100425	C1	253						
HPK2100424	C1	253	Y					
HPK2100427	C1	254	Y					
HPK2100426	C3	254						
HPK2100428	C1	255	Y					
HPK2100429	C2	255						
HPK2100431	C1	256	Y					
HPK2100430	A4	256						
HPK2100433	C1	257	Y					
HPK2100432	C2	257						

PLAN #	PRICE TIER	PAGE	MATERIALS LIST	DECK	DECK PRICE	LANDSCAPE	LANDSCAPE PRICE	REGIONS
HPK2100434	C1	258	Y					
HPK2100435	C3	258						
HPK2100437	C3	259						
HPK2100436	A4	259	Y					
HPK2100439	C1	260	Y					
HPK2100438	A4	260	Y					
HPK2100441	C3	261	Y					
HPK2100440	C4	261	Y					
HPK2100443	C3	262						
HPK2100442	C1	262	Y					
HPK2100444	C3	263						
HPK2100445	C3	263						
HPK2100447	C1	264	Y					
HPK2100446	SQ3	264	Y					
HPK2100449	A4	265	Y					
HPK2100448	A4	265	Y					
HPK2100451	A4	266						
HPK2100450	A4	266	Y					
HPK2100453	SQ3	267						
HPK2100452	A4	267						
HPK2100455	C3	268						
HPK2100454	A4	268	Y					
HPK2100457	C2	269						
HPK2100456	C1	269						
HPK2100459	C3	270						
HPK2100458	C3	270						
HPK2100460	A4	271						
HPK2100461	C1	272	Y					
HPK2100462	C1	273						
HPK2100463	SQ1	274	Y					
HPK2100464	C1	275						
HPK2100465	SQ3	276						
HPK2100466	SQ3	277	Y					
HPK2100467	C1	278	Y					
HPK2100468	C1	279	Y					
HPK2100469	SQ1	280	Y					
HPK2100470	A4	281						
HPK2100471	C1	282	Y					
HPK2100472	SQ3	283	Y					
HPK2100473	C1	284						
HPK2100474	C3	285						
HPK2100475	C4	286						
HPK2100476	C3	287						
HPK2100477	A4	288						
HPK2100479	A4	289						
HPK2100478	C1	289						
HPK2100480	C1	290	Y					
HPK2100481	C1	290						
HPK2100483	C1	291						
HPK2100482	A4	291	Y					
HPK2100484	A4	292	Y					
HPK2100485	C2	292						
HPK2100487	C1	293	Y					
HPK2100486	C1	293						
HPK2100489	C1	294	Y					
HPK2100488	A4	294						
HPK2100491	C2	295	Y					
HPK2100490	A4	295	Y					
HPK2100492	A4	296	Y	ODA006	D1	OLA001	P3	
HPK2100493	C1	296	Y					
HPK2100495	C1	297						
HPK2100494	C2	297						
HPK2100497	C1	298	Y					
HPK2100496	A4	298	Y					
HPK2100499	SQ3	299	Y					
HPK2100498	C1	299						
HPK2100501	C1	300						
HPK2100500	C2	300						
HPK2100502	A4	301	Y					
HPK2100503	C1	301						
HPK2100505	C3	302						
HPK2100504	A4	302	Y					
HPK2100506	C2	303						
HPK2100507	C1	303						
HPK2100508	C1	304						
HPK2100509	C1	304						
HPK2100511	C1	305						
HPK2100510	C4	305						

PLAN #	PRICE TIER	PAGE	MATERIALS LIST	DECK	DECK PRICE	LANDSCAPE	LANDSCAPE PRICE	REGIONS
HPK2100513	C1	306	Y					
HPK2100512	C1	306	Y					
HPK2100515	A4	307						
HPK2100514	A4	307						
HPK2100516	A4	308						
HPK2100517	C1	308						
HPK2100518	C4	309	Y					
HPK2100519	C2	309						
HPK2100520	C2	310	Y					
HPK2100521	A4	310	Y					
HPK2100522	C1	311	Y					
HPK2100523	C4	311						
HPK2100525	C1	312						
HPK2100524	C1	312						
HPK2100527	C2	313						
HPK2100526	C1	313						
HPK2100529	C1	314	Y					
HPK2100528	C1	314						
HPK2100530	C1	315	Y					
HPK2100531	C2	315						
HPK2100533	C1	316	Y					
HPK2100532	C1	316	Y					
HPK2100535	C4	317						
HPK2100534	A4	317	Y					
HPK2100536	C1	318	Y					
HPK2100537	C1	318						
HPK2100539	C1	319						
HPK2100538	A4	319	Y					
HPK2100540	C1	320	Y					
HPK2100541	A4	320	Y					
HPK2100542	C1	321						
HPK2100543	SQ3	321						
HPK2100545	C1	322						
HPK2100544	C2	322						
HPK2100546	A4	323	Y					
HPK2100547	A4	323	Y					
HPK2100549	C2	324						
HPK2100548	A4	324	Y					
HPK2100551	C1	325						
HPK2100550	C1	325	Y					
HPK2100552	C4	326						
HPK2100553	SQ3	326						
HPK2100555	C1	327	Y					
HPK2100554	C2	327						
HPK2100557	C3	328						
HPK2100556	C1	328						
HPK2100559	C3	329						
HPK2100558	C2	329	Y					
HPK2100560	C1	330	Y					
HPK2100561	C1	330						
HPK2100562	C1	331						
HPK2100563	A4	331						
HPK2100565	C1	332						
HPK2100564	C2	332						
HPK2100566	C3	333						
HPK2100567	A4	333						
HPK2100568	C1	334	Y					
HPK2100569	C1	334	Y					
HPK2100571	C1	335						
HPK2100570	C1	335						
HPK2100573	C3	336						
HPK2100572	C2	336						
HPK2100575	C2	337						
HPK2100574	C1	337	Y			OLA025	P3	
HPK2100577	C2	338	Y					
HPK2100576	C1	338						
HPK2100578	C2	339						
HPK2100579	C1	339	Y					
HPK2100581	C4	340	Y					
HPK2100580	C1	340						
HPK2100582	C1	341						
HPK2100583	C1	341						
HPK2100585	C1	342	Y					
HPK2100584	C1	342						
HPK2100586	C1	343	Y					
HPK2100587	C3	343						
HPK2100589	C3	344						
HPK2100588	C1	344	Y					

PLAN #	PRICE TIER	PAGE	MATERIALS LIST	DECK	DECK PRICE	LANDSCAPE	LANDSCAPE PRICE	REGIONS
HPK2100590	A4	345	Y					
HPK2100591	C3	345						
HPK2100592	A4	346						
HPK2100593	SQ3	346						
HPK2100594	SQ3	347						
HPK2100595	C1	347						
HPK2100596	C1	348	Y					
HPK2100597	C3	348						
HPK2100598	C1	349	Y					
HPK2100599	A4	350						
HPK2100600	SQ3	351						
HPK2100601	C1	352	Y					
HPK2101523	C1	352	Y					
HPK2101524	C2	352	Y					
HPK2100602	C1	353	Y					
HPK2100603	C2	354	Y					
HPK2100604	C2	355	Y					
HPK2100605	A4	355	Y					
HPK2100607	SQ3	356						
HPK2100606	C3	356						
HPK2100608	C4	357	Y					
HPK2100609	A4	357						
HPK2100610	C1	358						
HPK2100611	A4	358	Y					
HPK2100612	C4	359						
HPK2100613	C1	359						
HPK2100615	C1	360						
HPK2100614	C1	360						
HPK2100616	C1	361						
HPK2100617	C1	362	Y					
HPK2100618	SQ3	363						
HPK2100619	C2	364						
HPK2100620	C2	365	Y					
HPK2100621	C1	365				OLA012	P3	
HPK2100622	C2	366	Y					
HPK2100623	SQ3	366						
HPK2100625	SQ1	367	Y					
HPK2100624	SQ3	367						
HPK2100627	C2	368	Y					
HPK2100626	C1	368				OLA004	P3	
HPK2100628	C3	369	Y					
HPK2100629	C1	369				OLA008	P4	
HPK2100630	C1	370						
HPK2100631	C2	370						
HPK2100632	C2	371	Y					
HPK2100633	C2	371						
HPK2100635	C2	372	Y					
HPK2100634	C3	372						
HPK2100637	C4	373						
HPK2100636	C1	373						
HPK2100638	C2	374	Y					
HPK2100639	C2	374	Y					
HPK2100640	C2	375						
HPK2100641	C3	375						
HPK2100642	C2	376	Y					
HPK2100643	C1	376						
HPK2100644	C1	377	Y			OLA033	P3	
HPK2100645	C2	377	Y					
HPK2100647	C3	378						
HPK2100646	C1	378	Y					
HPK2100649	C2	379	Y					
HPK2100648	C1	379						
HPK2100651	C2	380	Y					
HPK2100650	C1	380						
HPK2100652	C4	381	Y					
HPK2100653	C3	381						
HPK2100654	C4	382						
HPK2100655	C2	382						
HPK2100657	C2	383						
HPK2100656	C1	383				OLA005	P3	
HPK2100658	C1	384	Y					
HPK2100659	C1	384	Y					
HPK2100661	C4	385						
HPK2100660	C2	385	Y	ODA015	D1	OLA013	P4	
HPK2100662	C2	386	Y					
HPK2100663	C1	386						
HPK2100664	C1	387	Y					
HPK2100665	C1	387	Y					
HPK2100666	C2	388	Y					
HPK2100667	SQ3	388	Y			OLA004	P3	
HPK2100669	SQ1	389	Y					
HPK2100668	C4	389						
HPK2100671	C2	390	Y					
HPK2100670	C3	390						
HPK2100672	SQ3	391						
HPK2100673	C2	391	Y			OLA015	P4	
HPK2100674	C1	392	Y			OLA010	P3	
HPK2100675	SQ3	392						
HPK2100677	C4	393						
HPK2100676	SQ1	393	Y					
HPK2100679	C2	394						
HPK2100678	C1	394	Y	ODA011	D1	OLA018	P3	
HPK2100681	SQ3	395						
HPK2100680	C4	395	Y					
HPK2100682	SQ3	396						
HPK2100683	C3	396						
HPK2100684	C4	397						
HPK2100685	L1	397						
HPK2100686	C1	398	Y					
HPK2100687	SQ3	398						
HPK2100688	SQ3	399	Y					
HPK2100689	C4	399						
HPK2100690	C2	400	Y					
HPK2100691	C3	400	Y					
HPK2100692	A4	401	Y					
HPK2100694	C2	402	Y					
HPK2100693	C2	402						
HPK2100695	C1	403						
HPK2100696	C1	403						
HPK2100697	C2	404	Y					
HPK2100698	SQ3	404	Y					
HPK2100700	C1	405	Y					
HPK2100699	C2	405	Y					
HPK2100702	SQ3	406	Y					
HPK2100701	C2	406						
HPK2100703	C2	407	Y					
HPK2100704	SQ3	407						
HPK2100705	C2	408	Y					
HPK2100706	C2	408						
HPK2100708	C3	409						
HPK2100707	C4	409						
HPK2100710	C3	410						
HPK2100709	C2	410	Y					
HPK2100712	C2	411						
HPK2100711	C1	411						
HPK2100713	C2	412	Y					
HPK2100714	C3	412	Y			OLA083	P3	
HPK2100716	C2	413						
HPK2100715	C2	413	Y					
HPK2100718	C2	414	Y					
HPK2100717	C1	414	Y	ODA012	D2	OLA028	P4	
HPK2100720	C3	415						
HPK2100719	C3	415						
HPK2100721	C2	416	Y					
HPK2100722	C3	416	Y					
HPK2100724	C2	417	Y					
HPK2100723	C1	417	Y					
HPK2100725	SQ3	418	Y					
HPK2100726	C1	418						
HPK2100728	C2	419	Y					
HPK2100727	C1	419						
HPK2100730	C2	420						
HPK2100729	C4	420	Y					
HPK2100732	C2	421	Y					
HPK2100731	C2	421	Y	ODA011	D1	OLA025	P3	
HPK2100734	C2	422	Y					
HPK2100733	C1	422	Y					
HPK2100735	C3	423						
HPK2100736	C2	423						
HPK2100737	C2	424	Y					
HPK2100738	SQ3	424	Y					
HPK2100740	C2	425	Y					
HPK2100739	C1	425						
HPK2100742	C1	426						
HPK2100741	C4	426						
HPK2100744	C1	427						

PLAN #	PRICE TIER	PAGE	MATERIALS LIST	DECK	DECK PRICE	LANDSCAPE	LANDSCAPE PRICE	REGIONS
HPK2100743	C1	427						
HPK2100746	C4	428						
HPK2100745	C3	428	Y					
HPK2100748	C2	429	Y					
HPK2100747	C2	429						
HPK2100749	SQ3	430						
HPK2100750	C4	430						
HPK2100752	C4	431						
HPK2100751	C4	431						
HPK2100754	C1	432	Y			OLA014	P4	
HPK2100753	C4	432						
HPK2100755	C2	433						
HPK2100756	C1	433						
HPK2100757	C1	434						
HPK2100758	C2	434	Y					
HPK2100760	C1	435						
HPK2100759	SQ3	435	Y					
HPK2100761	C4	436						
HPK2100762	C4	436						
HPK2100764	C3	437						
HPK2100763	C2	437	Y					
HPK2100766	SQ3	438	Y					
HPK2100765	C1	438	Y					
HPK2100767	C2	439						
HPK2100768	C1	439	Y					
HPK2100770	C4	440						
HPK2100769	C4	440						
HPK2100772	C3	441						
HPK2100771	C2	441						
HPK2100773	C3	442						
HPK2100774	C2	443	Y					
HPK2100775	C3	444						
HPK2100776	C1	445						
HPK2100777	C2	446						
HPK2100779	C3	447						
HPK2100778	C1	447						
HPK2100780	C4	448	Y					
HPK2100781	C4	448						
HPK2100783	SQ3	449	Y			OLA008	P4	
HPK2100782	C4	449						
HPK2100784	C4	450						
HPK2100785	C2	450						
HPK2100787	C2	451	Y					
HPK2100786	C2	451						
HPK2100788	C1	452						
HPK2100789	C2	452	Y					
HPK2100791	C1	453	Y					
HPK2100790	C3	453						
HPK2100793	C4	454						
HPK2100792	C1	454	Y					
HPK2100794	C4	455						
HPK2100795	C3	455	Y					
HPK2100797	C4	456						
HPK2100796	C1	456						
HPK2100799	C4	457						
HPK2100798	C3	457						
HPK2100801	C2	458	Y					
HPK2100800	C4	458	Y					
HPK2100803	SQ3	459	Y			OLA004	P3	
HPK2100802	SQ3	459	Y					
HPK2100804	C3	460						
HPK2100805	SQ3	460	Y					
HPK2100807	C4	461						
HPK2100806	C2	461						
HPK2100808	C1	462	Y					
HPK2100809	SQ3	463	Y					
HPK2100810	SQ3	464						
HPK2100811	C2	465	Y					
HPK2100812	C4	466	Y					
HPK2100814	C4	467						
HPK2100813	C4	467						
HPK2100815	C2	468	Y					
HPK2100816	C2	468						
HPK2100817	C2	469						
HPK2100818	SQ3	469						
HPK2100819	SQ3	470	Y					
HPK2100820	C4	470	Y					
HPK2100822	C2	471	Y					
HPK2100821	C2	471	Y					
HPK2100823	C3	472						
HPK2100824	C2	473	Y					
HPK2100825	C2	474						
HPK2100826	C4	475						
HPK2100827	C4	476						
HPK2100828	SQ3	477						
HPK2100829	SQ3	478						
HPK2100830	C2	479						
HPK2100831	C2	480	Y					
HPK2100832	C4	481						
HPK2100833	C4	482						
HPK2100834	C1	483	Y					
HPK2100835	C2	484	Y					
HPK2100836	SQ3	484	Y			OLA024	P4	
HPK2100837	C2	485	Y					
HPK2100838	C1	485						
HPK2100840	C2	486						
HPK2100839	C1	486						
HPK2100841	C2	487	Y					
HPK2100842	C4	487						
HPK2100844	C2	488	Y					
HPK2100843	C2	488	Y					
HPK2100845	C2	489	Y					
HPK2100846	C3	489						
HPK2100847	C2	490	Y					
HPK2101525	C3	490	Y			OLA003	P3	
HPK2100848	C1	491						
HPK2100849	C2	492	Y					
HPK2100850	C3	493						
HPK2100851	C3	493	Y			OLA010	P3	
HPK2100852	C4	494	Y					
HPK2100853	SQ1	494						
HPK2100855	C3	495	Y					
HPK2100854	C2	495						
HPK2100857	SQ3	496						
HPK2100856	C3	496	Y					
HPK2100859	C2	497	Y					
HPK2100858	C3	497	Y					
HPK2100861	SQ3	498						
HPK2100860	SQ3	498						
HPK2100863	C4	499						
HPK2100862	C1	499						
HPK2100865	SQ3	500						
HPK2100864	SQ3	500						
HPK2100867	C3	501	Y					
HPK2100866	C3	501						
HPK2100868	C3	502	Y			OLA036	P4	
HPK2100869	C2	502	Y					
HPK2100871	SQ3	503	Y					
HPK2100870	SQ3	503	Y					
HPK2100872	SQ3	504	Y					
HPK2100873	SQ3	504	Y					
HPK2100874	C3	505	Y					
HPK2100875	C3	505						
HPK2100877	SQ3	506	Y					
HPK2100876	C4	506						
HPK2100879	C2	507						
HPK2100878	SQ1	507	Y					
HPK2100881	SQ3	508						
HPK2100880	SQ3	508						
HPK2100882	C3	509	Y					
HPK2100883	C4	510						
HPK2100884	C4	511						
HPK2100885	SQ3	511						
HPK2100886	SQ3	512						
HPK2100887	C4	512						
HPK2100889	C3	513	Y					
HPK2100888	C2	513						
HPK2100890	C4	514						
HPK2100891	C2	514						
HPK2100892	C4	515	Y					
HPK2100893	C3	515						
HPK2100894	C3	516						
HPK2100895	C3	516	Y					
HPK2100896	C2	517						
HPK2100897	C2	517						
HPK2100899	C2	518						

PLAN #	PRICE TIER	PAGE	MATERIALS LIST	DECK	DECK PRICE	LANDSCAPE	LANDSCAPE PRICE	REGIONS
HPK2100898	C2	518						
HPK2100901	C2	519						
HPK2100900	SQ3	519						
HPK2100903	C3	520						
HPK2100902	C3	520						
HPK2100905	C3	521	Y					
HPK2100904	C4	521						
HPK2100906	SQ3	522						
HPK2100907	SQ3	522						
HPK2100908	SQ3	523						
HPK2100909	SQ3	523						
HPK2100911	C4	524	Y					
HPK2100910	C4	524	Y					
HPK2100913	C4	525	Y					
HPK2100912	C3	525						
HPK2100914	C2	526						
HPK2100915	C3	526	Y					
HPK2100916	C4	527						
HPK2100917	C2	527						
HPK2100919	C4	528						
HPK2100918	C3	528	Y					
HPK2100921	C2	529						
HPK2100920	C4	529	Y					
HPK2100922	C3	530	Y					
HPK2100923	C4	530						
HPK2100924	C3	531	Y			OLA038	P3	
HPK2100925	C4	531						
HPK2100926	C4	532						
HPK2100927	SQ1	532	Y					
HPK2100928	C4	533						
HPK2100929	C3	533	Y					
HPK2100931	C3	534						
HPK2100930	C2	534	Y					
HPK2100933	C3	535						
HPK2100932	C3	535						
HPK2100934	C3	536	Y					
HPK2100935	C3	536						
HPK2100936	C3	537	Y					
HPK2100937	C4	537	Y					
HPK2100938	C3	538						
HPK2100939	C2	538	Y					
HPK2100941	C4	539						
HPK2100940	SQ1	539						
HPK2100943	SQ3	540						
HPK2100942	C2	540						
HPK2100944	C4	541						
HPK2100945	SQ3	541						
HPK2100946	C3	542	Y					
HPK2100947	C4	542	Y					
HPK2100948	C4	543	Y					
HPK2100949	C2	543	Y					
HPK2100951	C3	544						
HPK2100950	C3	544						
HPK2100953	C3	545	Y					
HPK2100952	C4	545						
HPK2100954	C3	546	Y					
HPK2100955	C3	546						
HPK2100957	C3	547	Y					
HPK2100956	C3	547						
HPK2100958	C4	548						
HPK2100959	SQ3	548	Y					
HPK2100960	C4	549						
HPK2100961	C3	549						
HPK2100962	C4	550						
HPK2100963	SQ3	550						
HPK2100964	C4	551						
HPK2100965	C3	552	Y					
HPK2100966	C4	553						
HPK2100967	C3	554						
HPK2100968	C4	555						
HPK2100970	C4	556						
HPK2100969	C4	556						
HPK2100972	C3	557	Y					
HPK2100971	C4	557						
HPK2100974	C2	558						
HPK2100973	C4	558						
HPK2100976	SQ3	559						
HPK2100975	C2	559	Y			OLA008	P4	

PLAN #	PRICE TIER	PAGE	MATERIALS LIST	DECK	DECK PRICE	LANDSCAPE	LANDSCAPE PRICE	REGIONS
HPK2100977	C4	560						
HPK2100978	C2	560	Y					
HPK2100980	SQ3	561						
HPK2100979	C2	561						
HPK2100982	C4	562						
HPK2100981	C3	562	Y					
HPK2100983	C4	563						
HPK2100984	C4	563						
HPK2100985	SQ5	564						
HPK2100986	C3	564						
HPK2100988	C3	565	Y					
HPK2100987	C4	565						
HPK2100989	C2	566	Y					
HPK2100990	C3	567	Y					
HPK2100991	C4	568						
HPK2100992	C3	569	Y					
HPK2100993	C3	570	Y					
HPK2100995	C4	571						
HPK2100994	C4	571						
HPK2100996	C2	572						
HPK2100998	C2	573						
HPK2100997	SQ1	573	Y					
HPK2101000	C4	574						
HPK2100999	C2	574	Y					
HPK2101002	C4	575	Y					
HPK2101001	A4	575						
HPK2101004	C4	576						
HPK2101003	C3	576	Y					
HPK2101006	C4	577						
HPK2101005	C4	577	Y					
HPK2101007	SQ1	578						
HPK2101008	C3	578	Y					
HPK2101009	C4	579	Y					
HPK2101010	C3	579						
HPK2101012	C4	580						
HPK2101011	C3	580	Y					
HPK2101013	C2	581	Y					
HPK2101014	C3	582	Y					
HPK2101015	C4	583						
HPK2101016	C4	584						
HPK2101017	C4	585						
HPK2101018	C3	586	Y					
HPK2101019	L1	587	Y			OLA008	P4	
HPK2101020	C3	588	Y					
HPK2101021	C4	589						
HPK2101022	C2	590						
HPK2101023	C4	591						
HPK2101024	C4	591						
HPK2101025	C4	592	Y					
HPK2101026	C2	592						
HPK2101028	C2	593	Y					
HPK2101027	C2	593						
HPK2101030	C2	594						
HPK2101029	C2	594						
HPK2101031	C3	595						
HPK2101032	C2	595						
HPK2101034	C2	596	Y					
HPK2101033	C3	596						
HPK2101036	C3	597	Y					
HPK2101035	C4	597						
HPK2101038	C3	598						
HPK2101037	C3	598	Y					
HPK2101039	SQ3	599	Y					
HPK2101040	C2	599	Y					
HPK2101042	C2	600						
HPK2101041	C3	600	Y					
HPK2101043	C3	601	Y					
HPK2101530	C4	602						
HPK2101045	C2	603						
HPK2101046	C4	604	Y					
HPK2101047	C2	605	Y					
HPK2101048	L1	606	Y			OLA010	P3	
HPK2101049	C2	607						
HPK2101050	SQ1	608	Y					
HPK2101051	C3	609	Y					
HPK2101052	C2	610	Y					
HPK2101053	C4	611						
HPK2101054	C3	612						

PLAN #	PRICE TIER	PAGE	MATERIALS LIST	DECK	DECK PRICE	LANDSCAPE	LANDSCAPE PRICE	REGIONS
HPK2101056	SQ1	613	Y					
HPK2101055	SQ3	613						
HPK2101058	C4	614						
HPK2101057	C4	614						
HPK2101059	SQ3	615						
HPK2101060	SQ3	615						
HPK2101062	SQ3	616						
HPK2101061	SQ3	616						
HPK2101064	SQ1	617						
HPK2101063	SQ3	617						
HPK2101065	SQ3	618	Y					
HPK2101066	SQ5	618	Y					
HPK2101067	SQ5	619	Y					
HPK2101068	SQ5	619						
HPK2101069	SQ5	620						
HPK2101070	SQ5	620						
HPK2101071	SQ1	621	Y					
HPK2101072	SQ5	621	Y	ODA011	D1	OLA012	P3	
HPK2101074	SQ5	622						
HPK2101073	SQ5	622	Y					
HPK2101075	SQ5	623	Y			OLA017	P3	
HPK2101076	SQ5	623	Y					
HPK2101078	SQ5	624						
HPK2101077	SQ5	624	Y					
HPK2101079	SQ5	625						
HPK2101080	C3	626	Y					
HPK2101081	SQ3	627	Y					
HPK2101082	SQ3	627	Y					
HPK2101083	SQ3	628						
HPK2101084	C4	628						
HPK2101086	C4	629						
HPK2101085	SQ1	629	Y					
HPK2101088	C4	630						
HPK2101087	C3	630	Y			OLA001	P3	
HPK2101089	L1	631						
HPK2101090	C4	631						
HPK2101091	C3	632						
HPK2101092	C4	632						
HPK2101094	C4	633						
HPK2101093	C4	633						
HPK2101095	C3	634						
HPK2101096	C4	634						
HPK2101097	C3	635						
HPK2101098	C4	635						
HPK2101099	C4	636						
HPK2101100	C4	636						
HPK2101102	SQ3	637						
HPK2101101	C4	637						
HPK2101103	C3	638						
HPK2101104	C3	638						
HPK2101106	C4	639	Y					
HPK2101105	C4	639						
HPK2101108	SQ3	640						
HPK2101107	C4	640						
HPK2101109	SQ3	641	Y					
HPK2101110	SQ3	642						
HPK2101111	C4	643						
HPK2101112	C4	644						
HPK2101113	C4	645						
HPK2101115	SQ3	646				OLA008	P4	
HPK2101114	C4	646						
HPK2101116	SQ5	647						
HPK2101117	C3	647						
HPK2101118	C4	648						
HPK2101119	L1	648				OLA017	P3	
HPK2101120	SQ3	649						
HPK2101121	C4	649						
HPK2101123	SQ3	650						
HPK2101122	C4	650						
HPK2101124	SQ3	651						
HPK2101125	SQ3	651	Y					
HPK2101127	C4	652						
HPK2101126	L1	652						
HPK2101129	L1	653	Y	ODA011	D1	OLA028	P4	
HPK2101128	L4	653						
HPK2101131	C4	654						
HPK2101130	C4	654						
HPK2101132	SQ1	655	Y					
HPK2101133	C4	655						
HPK2101134	C3	656						
HPK2101135	C4	657						
HPK2101136	C4	658						
HPK2101137	C4	659						
HPK2101138	C4	660						
HPK2101139	C4	661						
HPK2101140	C4	661						
HPK2101141	C4	662						
HPK2101142	SQ3	662						
HPK2101144	C4	663						
HPK2101143	C4	663	Y					
HPK2101145	C4	664	Y					
HPK2101146	C4	664	Y					
HPK2101147	L2	665	Y					
HPK2101148	SQ3	665						
HPK2101149	C3	666	Y	ODA020	D2	OLA020	P4	
HPK2101150	C4	666						
HPK2101151	C4	667	Y					
HPK2101152	C3	667						
HPK2101154	SQ1	668						
HPK2101153	C4	668						
HPK2101155	C4	669	Y					
HPK2101156	C3	669						
HPK2101157	L1	670						
HPK2101158	C4	670						
HPK2101159	C3	671						
HPK2101160	C4	672						
HPK2101526	SQ3	672						
HPK2101527	SQ1	672	Y					
HPK2101161	C4	673	Y					
HPK2101162	SQ1	674						
HPK2101163	C3	675						
HPK2101164	C4	676						
HPK2101165	C4	677						
HPK2101166	C4	677						
HPK2101167	C4	678						
HPK2101168	SQ3	679	Y			OLA008	P4	
HPK2101169	C4	680						
HPK2101170	C4	681	Y					
HPK2101171	C4	682						
HPK2101173	SQ5	683						
HPK2101172	C4	683						
HPK2101175	SQ3	684						
HPK2101174	C4	684						
HPK2101177	SQ5	685						
HPK2101176	C4	685						
HPK2101178	C4	686						
HPK2101179	SQ3	686						
HPK2101180	SQ1	687	Y					
HPK2101181	L1	687						
HPK2101182	C4	688						
HPK2101183	C4	689						
HPK2101184	C4	690						
HPK2101185	C4	691						
HPK2101186	SQ5	692						
HPK2101188	C4	693	Y					
HPK2101187	SQ5	693						
HPK2101190	C3	694	Y					
HPK2101189	C3	694						
HPK2101191	C4	695						
HPK2101192	C3	695	Y					
HPK2101193	A4	696						
HPK2101194	C4	696						
HPK2101195	SQ5	697						
HPK2101196	SQ3	697						
HPK2101197	C4	698						
HPK2101198	C3	698	Y					
HPK2101200	L1	699						
HPK2101199	SQ5	699						
HPK2101202	SQ1	700	Y					
HPK2101201	L1	700						
HPK2101204	SQ3	701						
HPK2101203	C4	701						
HPK2101206	C3	702						
HPK2101205	L2	702	Y					
HPK2101207	SQ5	703	Y					
HPK2101208	L1	704						

PLAN #	PRICE TIER	PAGE	MATERIALS LIST	DECK	DECK PRICE	LANDSCAPE	LANDSCAPE PRICE	REGIONS
HPK2101209	C4	705						
HPK2101210	C4	706						
HPK2101211	SQ1	707	Y					
HPK2101212	C3	708	Y					
HPK2101213	C4	708						
HPK2101214	C4	709						
HPK2101215	C4	709						
HPK2101216	SQ5	710						
HPK2101217	C3	710						
HPK2101219	C3	711	Y					
HPK2101218	L1	711						
HPK2101220	SQ1	712						
HPK2101221	C4	712						
HPK2101222	C4	713	Y					
HPK2101223	SQ5	713						
HPK2101224	C4	714						
HPK2101225	SQ5	714						
HPK2101227	C4	715						
HPK2101226	C4	715						
HPK2101228	SQ5	716	Y					
HPK2101229	C4	716						
HPK2101231	C4	717						
HPK2101230	SQ5	717						
HPK2101232	SQ5	718	Y					
HPK2101233	C4	719						
HPK2101234	C4	720						
HPK2101235	SQ5	721						
HPK2101236	C4	722						
HPK2101237	L1	723	Y					
HPK2101238	C4	724	Y					
HPK2101239	C4	724	Y					
HPK2101240	C3	725	Y			OLA017	P3	
HPK2101241	C3	725						
HPK2101242	C3	726						
HPK2101243	C4	726						
HPK2101245	C3	727	Y			OLA024	P4	
HPK2101244	C4	727						
HPK2101247	C4	728						
HPK2101246	C3	728	Y			OLA001	P3	
HPK2101249	C3	729	Y					
HPK2101248	C4	729	Y					
HPK2101250	SQ5	730	Y					
HPK2101251	C4	731	Y					
HPK2101252	C4	732	Y					
HPK2101253	SQ5	733						
HPK2101254	C4	734						
HPK2101255	L2	735	Y	ODA004	D1	OLA004	P3	
HPK2101256	C4	736						
HPK2101257	SQ1	737	Y					
HPK2101258	SQ5	738	Y			OLA004	P3	
HPK2101260	SQ5	739						
HPK2101259	SQ1	739	Y					
HPK2101261	SQ5	740						
HPK2101262	SQ5	740	Y					
HPK2101263	L2	741	Y					
HPK2101264	SQ5	741	Y					
HPK2101265	SQ5	742						
HPK2101266	SQ5	742	Y			OLA008	P4	
HPK2101267	L1	743	Y					
HPK2101268	SQ7	743						
HPK2101269	SQ7	744						
HPK2101270	SQ7	744						
HPK2101271	SQ1	745	Y					
HPK2101272	SQ5	746	Y					
HPK2101273	SQ5	747						
HPK2101274	L1	747						
HPK2101276	SQ5	748						
HPK2101275	L1	748	Y	ODA002	D1	OLA015	P4	
HPK2101278	L1	749						
HPK2101277	L1	749						
HPK2101280	L2	750	Y					
HPK2101279	L1	750						
HPK2101281	L1	751						
HPK2101282	SQ1	751						
HPK2101283	L1	752						
HPK2101284	L1	752						
HPK2101285	L1	753						
HPK2101286	C4	753						
HPK2101287	L1	754						
HPK2101288	L1	754						
HPK2101289	SQ1	755						
HPK2101290	L1	755						
HPK2101291	L1	756						
HPK2101292	L1	756						
HPK2101294	C4	757						
HPK2101293	L1	757						
HPK2101295	SQ5	758	Y					
HPK2101296	SQ5	759	Y			OLA024	P4	
HPK2101298	SQ1	760	Y					
HPK2101297	C4	760	Y					
HPK2101299	SQ5	761	Y					
HPK2101300	SQ5	761	Y					
HPK2101302	SQ5	762	Y					
HPK2101301	C2	762						
HPK2101304	C4	763	Y					
HPK2101303	SQ3	763						
HPK2101305	L1	764	Y					
HPK2101306	SQ1	764						
HPK2101308	L1	765						
HPK2101307	L1	765						
HPK2101309	SQ1	766	Y					
HPK2101310	SQ1	766	Y					
HPK2101312	L1	767						
HPK2101311	L1	767						
HPK2101314	L2	768						
HPK2101313	L1	768	Y					
HPK2101316	L1	769						
HPK2101315	L1	769						
HPK2101317	L2	770	Y			OLA008	P4	
HPK2101318	L1	770						
HPK2101320	L1	771						
HPK2101319	L1	771						
HPK2101321	L1	772						
HPK2101322	L1	772						
HPK2101324	L1	773						
HPK2101323	C2	773						
HPK2101325	L1	774						
HPK2101326	L1	775						
HPK2101327	L1	775						
HPK2101329	C4	776	Y					
HPK2101328	L1	776						
HPK2101330	SQ3	777						
HPK2101331	SQ5	777	Y					
HPK2101333	SQ3	778	Y					
HPK2101332	L1	778						
HPK2101335	SQ5	779						
HPK2101334	L1	779						
HPK2101336	SQ3	780						
HPK2101337	SQ1	781						
HPK2101528	L1	781						
HPK2101339	L1	782						
HPK2101338	L1	782						
HPK2101341	L1	783						
HPK2101340	L1	783						
HPK2101342	C4	784						
HPK2101343	L1	784						
HPK2101345	L1	785						
HPK2101344	L1	785						
HPK2101346	SQ5	786						
HPK2101347	L1	786						
HPK2101348	L1	787						
HPK2101349	SQ3	787	Y					
HPK2101350	L1	788						
HPK2101351	L1	788						
HPK2101352	SQ5	789						
HPK2101353	SQ5	789						
HPK2101355	SQ3	790						
HPK2101354	SQ5	790	Y					
HPK2101356	SQ5	791						
HPK2101357	C4	791						
HPK2101359	L1	792						
HPK2101358	L2	792						
HPK2101361	L2	793	Y					
HPK2101360	SQ5	793				OLA009	P4	
HPK2101363	L2	794						
HPK2101362	SQ3	794						

PLAN #	PRICE TIER	PAGE	MATERIALS LIST	DECK	DECK PRICE	LANDSCAPE	LANDSCAPE PRICE	REGIONS
HPK2101364	C4	795						
HPK2101365	SQ5	796	Y					
HPK2101366	SQ5	797	Y					
HPK2101368	C4	798						
HPK2101367	SQ1	798	Y					
HPK2101369	L1	799	Y					
HPK2101370	SQ7	799	Y					
HPK2101371	C4	800	Y					
HPK2101372	SQ1	801	Y					
HPK2101374	SQ1	802						
HPK2101373	L1	802						
HPK2101375	SQ1	803						
HPK2101376	SQ7	803	Y					
HPK2101378	L2	804						
HPK2101377	L2	804						
HPK2101379	L2	805						
HPK2101380	SQ1	805	Y					
HPK2101381	SQ7	806	Y					
HPK2101382	L3	806						
HPK2101384	L3	807	Y					
HPK2101383	SQ3	807						
HPK2101385	L2	808	Y					
HPK2101386	L3	808	Y					
HPK2101387	L3	809	Y					
HPK2101388	SQ7	809						
HPK2101389	L1	810	Y					
HPK2101390	L1	811	Y					
HPK2101391	L3	812	Y					
HPK2101392	L3	812						
HPK2101394	L3	813	Y					
HPK2101393	SQ3	813	Y					
HPK2101396	L2	814						
HPK2101395	SQ1	814	Y					
HPK2101397	L3	815						
HPK2101398	L3	815						
HPK2101399	L2	816						
HPK2101400	SQ7	816						
HPK2101402	L3	817	Y					
HPK2101401	SQ7	817	Y					
HPK2101403	SQ7	818						
HPK2101404	L3	818	Y					
HPK2101406	SQ1	819						
HPK2101405	L3	819						
HPK2101407	SQ1	820						
HPK2101408	SQ7	821	Y					
HPK2101409	L3	822	Y					
HPK2101410	L3	822						
HPK2101411	L3	823						
HPK2101412	SQ3	823						
HPK2101414	SQ7	824						
HPK2101413	L3	824						
HPK2101415	L1	825						
HPK2101416	SQ7	826						
HPK2101418	SQ1	827						
HPK2101417	L1	827	Y					
HPK2101420	SQ3	828	Y					
HPK2101419	L3	828						
HPK2101421	SQ7	829						
HPK2101422	L4	829						
HPK2101424	SQ1	830						
HPK2101423	SQ1	830	Y			OLA017	P3	
HPK2101426	L3	831						
HPK2101425	SQ3	831						
HPK2101428	SQ7	832						
HPK2101427	SQ1	832						
HPK2101429	SQ7	833	Y					
HPK2101430	SQ1	834	Y					
HPK2101431	SQ3	834						
HPK2101433	SQ1	835	Y					
HPK2101432	L3	835						
HPK2101435	SQ1	836	Y			OLA028	P4	
HPK2101434	SQ7	836						
HPK2101437	SQ1	837	Y					
HPK2101436	SQ7	837						
HPK2101439	SQ7	838	Y			OLA008	P4	
HPK2101438	SQ7	838	Y					
HPK2101440	SQ7	839						
HPK2101441	L4	839						

PLAN #	PRICE TIER	PAGE	MATERIALS LIST	DECK	DECK PRICE	LANDSCAPE	LANDSCAPE PRICE	REGIONS
HPK2101442	L4	840						
HPK2101443	SQ1	841	Y					
HPK2101444	SQ1	842	Y					
HPK2101445	SQ7	843						
HPK2101446	L4	844						
HPK2101447	SQ9	845						
HPK2101448	SQ1	846						
HPK2101449	SQ9	847						
HPK2101450	L4	848						
HPK2101451	L4	849						
HPK2101452	SQ9	850						
HPK2101453	L4	851						
HPK2101454	L4	852						
HPK2101455	L1	853						
HPK2101456	L1	854						
HPK2101457	L1	854						
HPK2101459	C4	855	Y					
HPK2101458	L1	855						
HPK2101461	L1	856						
HPK2101460	L1	856						
HPK2101462	L1	857	Y					
HPK2101463	L1	857						
HPK2101465	L1	858						
HPK2101464	L1	858						
HPK2101466	L1	859						
HPK2101467	C4	859	Y					
HPK2101468	SQ3	860						
HPK2101469	L2	860						
HPK2101471	C4	861						
HPK2101470	SQ3	861						
HPK2101472	SQ1	862						
HPK2101473	L2	862						
HPK2101474	L2	863	Y					
HPK2101475	L2	863						
HPK2101476	L2	864						
HPK2101477	L2	865	Y					
HPK2101478	L2	866	Y					
HPK2101479	L2	866						
HPK2101480	SQ1	867	Y					
HPK2101481	L2	867						
HPK2101482	L3	868						
HPK2101483	L3	868						
HPK2101485	L3	869						
HPK2101484	L3	869	Y					
HPK2101486	L3	870						
HPK2101487	L3	870						
HPK2101489	L3	871						
HPK2101488	SQ1	871						
HPK2101490	C4	872	Y					
HPK2101491	L3	872						
HPK2101492	L3	873						
HPK2101493	L3	873						
HPK2101495	L3	874						
HPK2101494	L3	874						
HPK2101497	L3	875	Y					
HPK2101496	L3	875						
HPK2101498	SQ1	876	Y					
HPK2101500	L4	877						
HPK2101499	L3	877	Y					
HPK2101501	L4	878						
HPK2101502	L4	878						
HPK2101503	L4	879						
HPK2101504	L4	880						
HPK2101505	L4	881						
HPK2101506	L4	882						
HPK2101507	L4	883						
HPK2101508	L4	884						
HPK2101509	L4	885	Y					
HPK2101510	L4	886						
HPK2101511	SQ1	887						
HPK2101513	L4	888						
HPK2101515	L4	889						
HPK2101512	L4	890						
HPK2101514	L4	891						
HPK2101516	L4	892						
HPK2101517	L4	893						
HPK2101518	L4	896						
HPK2101529	L4	896						

STYLE INDEX

BEAUX ARTS	PLAN #	PRICE TIER	PAGE	SQUARE FEET
HPK2101123	SQ3	650	3610	
HPK2101060	SQ3	615	3640	
HPK2101179	SQ3	686	3777	
HPK2101067	SQ5	619	3790	
HPK2101193	A4	696	3851	
HPK2101280	L2	750	4040	
HPK2101385	L2	808	5130	
HPK2101488	SQ1	871	5372	
BUNGALOW				
HPK2100003	A1	9	984	
HPK2100004	A2	10	996	
HPK2100030	A2	23	1275	
HPK2100070	A3	43	1407	
HPK2100109	A2	71	1430	
HPK2100089	A3	56	1473	
HPK2100097	A3	64	1488	
HPK2100133	A3	91	1509	
HPK2100261	C3	166	1606	
HPK2100265	A3	168	1637	
HPK2100185	A3	117	1728	
HPK2100195	A3	122	1771	
HPK2100202	A3	126	1797	
HPK2100216	A3	133	1850	
HPK2100314	A3	191	1866	
HPK2100324	A3	196	1904	
HPK2100335	A3	202	1941	
HPK2100383	C4	232	2019	
HPK2100412	C1	247	2184	
HPK2100524	C1	312	2201	
HPK2100543	SQ3	321	2272	
HPK2100473	C1	284	2487	
HPK2100475	C4	286	2489	
HPK2100758	C2	434	2731	
HPK2100760	C1	435	2737	
HPK2101034	C2	596	3246	
CAPE COD				
HPK2100330	A3	199	1933	
HPK2100714	C3	412	2565	
HPK2100887	C4	512	3032	
CHATEAUESQUE				
HPK2100627	C2	368	2526	
HPK2100810	SQ3	464	2891	
HPK2100683	C3	396	2927	
HPK2100914	C2	526	3109	
HPK2100937	C4	537	3167	
HPK2100939	C2	538	3168	
HPK2101004	C4	576	3426	
HPK2101131	C4	654	3620	
HPK2101202	SQ1	700	3878	
HPK2101233	C4	719	3979	
HPK2101363	L2	794	4591	
HPK2101364	C4	795	4629	
HPK2101475	L2	863	4722	
HPK2101386	L3	808	5134	
HPK2101387	L3	809	5158	
HPK2101391	L3	812	5186	
HPK2101393	SQ3	813	5196	
HPK2101396	L2	814	5235	
HPK2101492	L3	873	5469	
HPK2101432	L3	835	5872	
HPK2101433	SQ1	835	5878	
HPK2101435	SQ1	836	6000	
HPK2101500	L4	877	6049	
HPK2101443	SQ1	841	6462	
HPK2101508	L4	884	6820	
HPK2101451	L4	849	8059	
HPK2101518	L4	896	9611	
COLONIAL REVIVAL				
HPK2100123	A3	84	1295	
HPK2100106	A2	70	1367	
HPK2100111	A1	73	1452	

PLAN #	PRICE TIER	PAGE	SQUARE FEET
HPK2100363	A3	220	1516
HPK2100256	A4	164	1550
HPK2100166	A3	108	1670
HPK2100272	A3	172	1671
HPK2100275	A4	173	1675
HPK2100174	A3	112	1688
HPK2100175	A3	112	1689
HPK2100186	A3	118	1730
HPK2100214	A4	132	1836
HPK2100306	A4	187	1850
HPK2100329	SQ3	199	1930
HPK2100252	A4	161	1997
HPK2100477	A4	288	2000
HPK2100486	C1	293	2052
HPK2100502	A4	301	2127
HPK2100507	C1	303	2146
HPK2100508	C1	304	2151
HPK2100516	A4	308	2169
HPK2100415	SQ3	248	2191
HPK2100539	C1	319	2262
HPK2100454	A4	268	2387
HPK2100616	C1	361	2396
HPK2100463	SQ1	274	2424
HPK2100465	SQ3	276	2454
HPK2100468	C1	279	2461
HPK2100469	SQ1	280	2465
HPK2100696	C1	403	2508
HPK2100726	C1	418	2594
HPK2100756	C1	433	2726
HPK2100761	C4	436	2739
HPK2100770	C4	440	2762
HPK2100674	C1	392	2846
HPK2100797	C4	456	2855
HPK2100812	C4	466	2898
HPK2100826	C4	475	2965
HPK2100832	C4	481	2996
HPK2100884	C4	511	3021
HPK2101023	C4	591	3024
HPK2100890	C4	514	3039
HPK2100891	C2	514	3041
HPK2100892	C4	515	3043
HPK2100916	C4	527	3112
HPK2100951	C3	544	3214
HPK2101031	C3	595	3220
HPK2101080	C3	626	3500
HPK2101165	C4	677	3737
HPK2101247	C4	728	3758
HPK2101256	C4	736	3969
HPK2101287	L1	754	4066
HPK2101308	L1	765	4205
HPK2101324	L1	773	4299
HPK2101528	L1	781	4403
HPK2101338	L1	782	4430
HPK2101468	SQ3	860	4524
HPK2101423	SQ1	830	5581
COTTAGE			
HPK2100001	A1	8	840
HPK2100002	A1	9	972
HPK2100007	A2	11	1085
HPK2100099	A2	66	1098
HPK2100011	A2	13	1124
HPK2100012	A2	14	1149
HPK2100013	A4	14	1151
HPK2100014	A1	15	1166
HPK2100015	A2	15	1195
HPK2100016	A2	16	1202
HPK2100017	A2	16	1208
HPK2100018	A2	17	1209
HPK2100019	A2	17	1218
HPK2100020	A3	18	1232
HPK2100023	A2	19	1248
HPK2100026	A2	21	1256
HPK2100028	A3	22	1264
HPK2100031	A2	23	1281
HPK2100103	A2	68	1288

PLAN #	PRICE TIER	PAGE	SQUARE FEET
HPK2100038	A2	27	1315
HPK2100039	A3	27	1317
HPK2100040	A2	28	1324
HPK2100041	SQ3	28	1328
HPK2100042	A2	29	1333
HPK2100043	A2	29	1342
HPK2100047	A2	31	1360
HPK2100051	A2	33	1374
HPK2100052	A3	34	1377
HPK2100054	A3	35	1380
HPK2100055	A3	35	1386
HPK2100056	A3	36	1389
HPK2100057	A2	36	1392
HPK2100058	A2	37	1392
HPK2100059	A2	37	1393
HPK2100063	A4	39	1402
HPK2100064	A2	40	1402
HPK2100065	A4	40	1402
HPK2100066	A4	41	1402
HPK2100069	A3	42	1405
HPK2100073	A3	44	1425
HPK2100074	A1	45	1425
HPK2100078	A3	47	1432
HPK2100128	A3	87	1441
HPK2100080	A2	48	1442
HPK2100110	A4	72	1445
HPK2100083	A3	50	1457
HPK2100084	A4	51	1458
HPK2100085	A4	52	1458
HPK2100112	A3	74	1462
HPK2100113	A2	75	1464
HPK2100129	A4	88	1467
HPK2100088	A3	55	1472
HPK2100090	A3	57	1477
HPK2100092	A3	59	1481
HPK2100130	A3	89	1482
HPK2100093	A3	60	1486
HPK2100096	A3	63	1488
HPK2100118	A1	80	1491
HPK2100120	A3	82	1492
HPK2101521	A2	64	1496
HPK2100254	A2	163	1500
HPK2100132	A4	91	1506
HPK2100143	A3	96	1580
HPK2100145	A4	97	1583
HPK2100258	C2	165	1583
HPK2100146	A4	98	1593
HPK2100153	A4	101	1608
HPK2100154	A4	102	1610
HPK2100365	A4	221	1634
HPK2100264	A3	168	1635
HPK2100165	A4	107	1664
HPK2100177	A3	113	1702
HPK2100279	A3	175	1707
HPK2100280	A4	176	1715
HPK2100181	A4	115	1725
HPK2100187	C3	118	1733
HPK2100284	A4	178	1756
HPK2100286	C1	179	1762
HPK2100192	A4	121	1768
HPK2100213	A3	131	1834
HPK2100307	SQ3	188	1853
HPK2100315	C2	192	1866
HPK2100320	A4	194	1884
HPK2100374	SQ3	226	1886
HPK2100228	A4	139	1892
HPK2100326	C2	197	1909
HPK2100332	C1	200	1936
HPK2100334	C1	201	1940
HPK2100241	A4	150	1955
HPK2100244	A4	153	1966
HPK2100352	C1	209	1975
HPK2100355	SQ3	212	1978
HPK2100356	A4	213	1985
HPK2100378	A3	229	1999

ORDER BLUEPRINTS ANYTIME AT EPLANS.COM OR 1-800-521-6797

PLAN #	PRICE TIER	PAGE	SQUARE FEET
HPK2100379	A4	230	2001
HPK2100382	C1	232	2017
HPK2100482	A4	291	2032
HPK2100484	A4	292	2037
HPK2100490	A4	295	2079
HPK2100395	SQ3	238	2086
HPK2100604	C2	355	2090
HPK2100399	C1	240	2097
HPK2100497	C1	298	2111
HPK2100499	SQ3	299	2123
HPK2100500	C2	300	2125
HPK2100407	C2	244	2151
HPK2100514	A4	307	2164
HPK2100518	C4	309	2175
HPK2100609	A4	357	2175
HPK2100519	C2	309	2179
HPK2100413	SQ3	247	2190
HPK2100610	C1	358	2192
HPK2100523	C4	311	2195
HPK2100422	C2	252	2215
HPK2100530	C1	315	2221
HPK2100428	C1	255	2252
HPK2100429	C2	255	2253
HPK2100431	C1	256	2259
HPK2100552	C4	326	2307
HPK2100578	C2	339	2410
HPK2100591	C3	345	2459
HPK2100592	A4	346	2468
HPK2100698	SQ3	404	2513
HPK2100626	C1	368	2517
HPK2100702	SQ3	406	2520
HPK2100632	C2	371	2544
HPK2100834	C1	483	2562
HPK2100642	C2	376	2602
HPK2100647	C3	378	2648
HPK2100751	C4	431	2710
HPK2100755	C2	433	2723
HPK2100773	C3	442	2776
HPK2100839	C1	486	2780
HPK2100668	C4	389	2796
HPK2101525	C3	490	2848
HPK2100796	C1	456	2851
HPK2100803	SQ3	459	2875
HPK2100804	C3	460	2875
HPK2100805	SQ3	460	2879
HPK2100813	C4	467	2899
HPK2101024	C4	591	3050
HPK2100857	SQ3	496	3074
HPK2101026	C2	592	3099
HPK2100919	C4	528	3125
HPK2100926	C4	532	3139
HPK2100929	C3	533	3147
HPK2100944	C4	541	3194
HPK2100863	C4	499	3206
HPK2100971	C4	557	3290
HPK2100973	C4	558	3295
HPK2101042	C2	600	3322
HPK2100984	C4	563	3327
HPK2100996	C2	572	3384
HPK2101053	C4	611	3493
HPK2101098	C4	635	3557
HPK2101099	C4	636	3558
HPK2101114	C4	646	3586
HPK2101118	C4	648	3591
HPK2101121	C4	649	3599
HPK2101242	C3	726	3640
HPK2101140	C4	661	3644
HPK2101141	C4	662	3644
HPK2100980	SQ3	561	3655
HPK2101176	C4	685	3774
HPK2101181	L1	687	3795
HPK2101226	C4	715	3950
HPK2101292	L1	756	4107
HPK2101377	L2	804	4881
HPK2101506	L4	882	6589

PLAN #	PRICE TIER	PAGE	SQUARE FEET
COUNTRY			
HPK2100006	A3	11	1080
HPK2100122	A2	84	1080
HPK2100008	SQ3	12	1093
HPK2100010	A3	13	1118
HPK2100100	A2	67	1170
HPK2100021	A3	18	1246
HPK2100022	A3	19	1246
HPK2100025	A2	20	1252
HPK2100032	A3	24	1287
HPK2100104	A4	69	1297
HPK2100037	A3	26	1310
HPK2100105	A3	69	1338
HPK2100044	A3	30	1346
HPK2100126	A2	86	1371
HPK2100050	A3	33	1373
HPK2100060	A3	38	1399
HPK2100067	A4	41	1404
HPK2100072	A3	44	1417
HPK2100075	A3	45	1426
HPK2100076	A3	46	1428
HPK2100079	A3	47	1439
HPK2100081	A2	48	1442
HPK2100091	A3	58	1480
HPK2100115	SQ3	77	1487
HPK2100117	A2	79	1488
HPK2100119	A3	81	1491
HPK2100121	A3	83	1497
HPK2100098	A3	65	1498
HPK2100255	A3	163	1505
HPK2100134	A4	92	1517
HPK2100136	A4	93	1540
HPK2100257	A4	164	1558
HPK2100138	A4	94	1559
HPK2100139	A4	94	1561
HPK2100260	A3	166	1597
HPK2100151	A4	100	1601
HPK2100152	A4	101	1604
HPK2100157	A4	103	1628
HPK2100158	A4	104	1632
HPK2100159	A4	104	1643
HPK2100160	A3	105	1644
HPK2100162	A4	106	1652
HPK2100163	A4	106	1655
HPK2100164	SQ3	107	1656
HPK2100270	A4	171	1669
HPK2100167	A4	108	1671
HPK2100168	A3	109	1671
HPK2100169	A4	109	1674
HPK2100171	A4	110	1680
HPK2100172	A3	111	1680
HPK2100276	A4	174	1684
HPK2100173	A4	111	1685
HPK2100277	A4	174	1689
HPK2100176	A4	113	1700
HPK2100281	A4	176	1719
HPK2100179	A3	114	1721
HPK2100183	A4	116	1727
HPK2100188	A4	119	1737
HPK2100283	A3	177	1737
HPK2100191	A4	120	1749
HPK2100193	SQ3	121	1768
HPK2100194	A4	122	1770
HPK2100197	A3	123	1787
HPK2100198	A4	124	1787
HPK2100200	A3	125	1792
HPK2100203	A4	126	1807
HPK2100301	C1	185	1811
HPK2100207	SQ3	128	1821
HPK2100208	SQ3	129	1822
HPK2100303	A4	186	1823
HPK2100209	A4	129	1827
HPK2100210	A4	130	1830
HPK2100211	A4	130	1832
HPK2100305	A4	187	1846

PLAN #	PRICE TIER	PAGE	SQUARE FEET
HPK2100217	A4	133	1850
HPK2100310	A4	189	1859
HPK2100312	A4	190	1862
HPK2100219	A4	134	1864
HPK2100222	A4	136	1879
HPK2100318	A3	193	1879
HPK2100223	A4	136	1882
HPK2100322	A4	195	1891
HPK2100327	A4	198	1918
HPK2100328	C1	198	1928
HPK2100234	A4	143	1932
HPK2100375	C3	226	1932
HPK2100331	A4	200	1936
HPK2100236	A4	145	1937
HPK2100346	A4	204	1948
HPK2100240	A4	149	1954
HPK2100247	A4	156	1972
HPK2100248	C1	157	1973
HPK2100250	SQ3	159	1985
HPK2100358	A3	215	1993
HPK2100359	A4	216	1995
HPK2100361	A3	218	1998
HPK2100380	C1	231	2006
HPK2100384	C1	233	2024
HPK2100481	C1	290	2024
HPK2100483	C1	291	2034
HPK2100385	C1	233	2037
HPK2100386	C1	234	2038
HPK2100388	A4	235	2050
HPK2100389	C1	235	2057
HPK2100487	C1	293	2064
HPK2100393	C1	237	2076
HPK2100394	C1	238	2078
HPK2100491	C2	295	2086
HPK2100493	C1	296	2091
HPK2100605	A4	355	2097
HPK2100405	C1	243	2136
HPK2100509	C1	304	2154
HPK2100513	C1	306	2163
HPK2100409	C3	245	2170
HPK2100410	A4	246	2172
HPK2100520	C2	310	2183
HPK2100416	C1	249	2192
HPK2100420	C1	251	2207
HPK2100421	C1	251	2207
HPK2100526	C1	313	2214
HPK2100537	C1	318	2251
HPK2100433	C1	257	2262
HPK2100540	C1	320	2264
HPK2100434	C1	258	2273
HPK2100439	C1	260	2290
HPK2100442	C1	262	2304
HPK2100553	SQ3	326	2317
HPK2100446	SQ3	264	2329
HPK2100615	C1	360	2350
HPK2100559	C3	329	2351
HPK2100449	A4	265	2367
HPK2100450	A4	266	2373
HPK2100563	A4	331	2373
HPK2100566	C3	333	2386
HPK2100568	C1	334	2390
HPK2100569	C1	334	2394
HPK2100458	C3	270	2395
HPK2100461	C1	272	2413
HPK2100582	C1	341	2425
HPK2100464	C1	275	2426
HPK2100584	C1	342	2430
HPK2100587	C3	343	2443
HPK2100466	SQ3	277	2454
HPK2100594	SQ3	347	2471
HPK2100595	C1	347	2481
HPK2100602	C1	353	2495
HPK2101524	C2	352	2500
HPK2100622	C2	366	2506
HPK2100704	SQ3	407	2527

PLAN #	PRICE TIER	PAGE	SQUARE FEET
HPK2100706	C2	408	2530
HPK2100634	C3	372	2548
HPK2100715	C2	413	2567
HPK2100637	C4	373	2570
HPK2100722	C3	416	2586
HPK2100724	C2	417	2588
HPK2100648	C1	379	2656
HPK2100649	C2	379	2663
HPK2100650	C1	380	2684
HPK2100745	C3	428	2688
HPK2100838	C1	485	2760
HPK2100781	C4	448	2790
HPK2100790	C3	453	2834
HPK2100793	C4	454	2840
HPK2100794	C4	455	2845
HPK2100819	SQ3	470	2923
HPK2100844	C2	488	2953
HPK2100830	C2	479	2990
HPK2100888	C2	513	3036
HPK2100896	C2	517	3061
HPK2100900	SQ3	519	3082
HPK2100902	C3	520	3088
HPK2100909	SQ3	523	3096
HPK2100912	C3	525	3104
HPK2101027	C2	593	3110
HPK2100915	C3	526	3111
HPK2100920	C4	529	3126
HPK2100923	C4	530	3135
HPK2100932	C3	535	3162
HPK2100941	C4	539	3181
HPK2100956	C3	547	3224
HPK2101032	C2	595	3240
HPK2100972	C3	557	3292
HPK2100985	SQ5	564	3329
HPK2100987	C4	565	3337
HPK2100992	C3	569	3356
HPK2101043	C3	601	3371
HPK2101009	C4	579	3440
HPK2101049	C2	607	3440
HPK2101016	C4	584	3468
HPK2101020	C3	588	3499
HPK2101238	C4	724	3509
HPK2101112	C4	644	3585
HPK2101137	C4	659	3637
HPK2101170	C4	681	3753
HPK2101173	SQ5	683	3763
HPK2101189	C3	694	3840
HPK2101199	SQ5	699	3872
HPK2101213	C4	708	3915
HPK2101281	L1	751	4045
HPK2101301	C2	762	4159
HPK2101461	L1	856	4224
HPK2101478	L2	866	4776
CRACKER			
HPK2100048	A2	32	1363
HPK2100082	SQ3	49	1456
CRAFTSMAN			
HPK2100102	C3	68	1226
HPK2100125	A4	85	1320
HPK2100114	A2	76	1466
HPK2100116	A2	78	1488
HPK2100137	A4	93	1544
HPK2100263	C1	167	1625
HPK2100180	A3	115	1724
HPK2100182	A4	116	1725
HPK2100206	A4	128	1821
HPK2100333	C3	201	1939
HPK2100345	A3	204	1946
HPK2100347	A3	205	1953
HPK2100348	A3	205	1958
HPK2100253	A4	162	1962
HPK2100246	A4	155	1971
HPK2100377	A3	228	1978
HPK2100478	C1	289	2010
HPK2100495	C1	297	2100

PLAN #	PRICE TIER	PAGE	SQUARE FEET
HPK2100498	C1	299	2115
HPK2100503	C1	301	2130
HPK2100505	C3	302	2139
HPK2100501	C1	300	2147
HPK2100511	C1	305	2154
HPK2100525	C1	312	2213
HPK2100534	A4	317	2237
HPK2100538	A4	319	2262
HPK2100551	C1	325	2299
HPK2100613	C1	359	2326
HPK2100556	C1	328	2338
HPK2100447	C1	264	2353
HPK2100576	C1	338	2407
HPK2100580	C1	340	2420
HPK2100590	A4	345	2453
HPK2100597	C3	348	2484
HPK2100474	C3	285	2487
HPK2100601	C1	352	2494
HPK2100693	C2	402	2505
HPK2100701	C2	406	2520
HPK2100630	C1	370	2541
HPK2100633	C2	371	2545
HPK2100712	C2	411	2560
HPK2100716	C2	413	2570
HPK2100720	C3	415	2584
HPK2100736	C2	423	2651
HPK2100746	C4	428	2689
HPK2100771	C2	441	2770
HPK2100782	C4	449	2795
HPK2100840	C2	486	2795
HPK2100785	C2	450	2805
HPK2100786	C2	451	2805
HPK2100806	C2	461	2882
HPK2100921	C2	529	2890
HPK2100816	C2	468	2920
HPK2100845	C2	489	2956
HPK2100860	SQ3	498	3126
HPK2100670	C3	390	3146
HPK2101028	C2	593	3148
HPK2100930	C2	534	3155
HPK2100931	C3	534	3161
HPK2100953	C3	545	3219
HPK2100954	C3	546	3219
HPK2101030	C2	594	3220
HPK2100958	C4	548	3233
HPK2101033	C3	596	3244
HPK2101036	C3	597	3272
HPK2101040	C2	599	3301
HPK2100978	C2	560	3308
HPK2100979	C2	561	3315
HPK2100983	C4	563	3325
HPK2101045	C2	603	3375
HPK2101018	C3	586	3490
HPK2101054	C3	612	3500
HPK2101086	C4	629	3517
HPK2101239	C4	724	3546
HPK2101095	C3	634	3550
HPK2101103	C3	638	3570
HPK2101117	C3	647	3590
HPK2101243	C4	726	3645
HPK2101201	L1	700	3878
HPK2101206	C3	702	3893
HPK2101253	SQ5	733	3930
HPK2101278	L1	749	4030
HPK2101279	L1	750	4035
HPK2101284	L1	752	4054
HPK2101288	L1	754	4084
HPK2101291	L1	756	4100
HPK2101307	L1	765	4188
HPK2101325	L1	774	4300
HPK2101464	L1	858	4379
HPK2101341	L1	783	4450
HPK2101466	L1	859	4488
HPK2101371	C4	800	4768
HPK2101477	L2	865	4776

PLAN #	PRICE TIER	PAGE	SQUARE FEET
HPK2101479	L2	866	4791
HPK2101389	L1	810	5172
HPK2101397	L3	815	5250
HPK2101486	L3	870	5305
HPK2101490	C4	872	5381
HPK2101498	SQ1	876	5949
HPK2101441	L4	839	6432
HPK2101505	L4	881	6582
HPK2101450	L4	848	7400
HPK2101513	L4	888	7502
FARMHOUSE			
HPK2100127	A2	86	1398
HPK2100107	A2	70	1399
HPK2100150	A3	100	1600
HPK2100156	SQ3	103	1616
HPK2100268	A4	170	1663
HPK2100273	A4	172	1673
HPK2100274	A3	173	1673
HPK2100278	A4	175	1696
HPK2100299	A4	184	1792
HPK2100201	A4	125	1794
HPK2100204	A4	127	1815
HPK2100370	SQ3	224	1822
HPK2100319	A4	194	1883
HPK2100237	C1	146	1942
HPK2100350	A4	207	1968
HPK2100351	A4	208	1974
HPK2100357	A4	214	1991
HPK2100480	C1	290	2019
HPK2100397	C1	239	2090
HPK2100398	C2	240	2096
HPK2100504	A4	302	2132
HPK2100506	C2	303	2142
HPK2100512	C1	306	2161
HPK2100521	A4	310	2186
HPK2100522	C1	311	2188
HPK2100418	C1	250	2195
HPK2100536	C1	318	2251
HPK2100547	A4	323	2287
HPK2100549	C2	324	2297
HPK2100550	C1	325	2298
HPK2100560	C1	330	2356
HPK2100575	C2	337	2406
HPK2100579	C2	339	2419
HPK2100585	C1	342	2435
HPK2100586	C2	343	2438
HPK2100596	C1	348	2482
HPK2100598	C1	349	2485
HPK2100471	C1	282	2487
HPK2100619	C2	364	2500
HPK2100692	A4	401	2500
HPK2100694	C2	402	2506
HPK2100697	C2	404	2511
HPK2100703	C2	407	2521
HPK2100713	C2	412	2561
HPK2100721	C2	416	2586
HPK2100728	C2	419	2602
HPK2100731	C2	421	2629
HPK2100737	C2	424	2658
HPK2100739	C1	425	2665
HPK2100748	C2	429	2692
HPK2100749	SQ3	430	2698
HPK2100774	C2	443	2777
HPK2100789	C2	452	2825
HPK2100809	SQ3	463	2889
HPK2100815	C2	468	2910
HPK2100821	C2	471	2943
HPK2100822	C2	471	2946
HPK2100831	C2	480	2992
HPK2100882	C3	509	3006
HPK2100889	C3	513	3037
HPK2100910	C4	524	3102
HPK2100934	C3	536	3163
HPK2100936	C3	537	3167
HPK2101029	C2	594	3175

ORDER BLUEPRINTS ANYTIME AT EPLANS.COM OR 1-800-521-6797

PLAN #	PRICE TIER	PAGE	SQUARE FEET
HPK2100960	C4	549	3246
HPK2100968	C4	555	3280
HPK2100990	C3	567	3352
HPK2101000	C4	574	3399
HPK2101003	C3	576	3419
HPK2101055	SQ3	613	3553
HPK2101107	C4	640	3574
HPK2101138	C4	660	3639
HPK2101150	C4	666	3672
HPK2101161	C4	673	3728
HPK2101219	C3	711	3934
HPK2101221	C4	712	3939
HPK2101225	SQ5	714	3948
HPK2101293	L1	757	4135
HPK2101458	L1	855	4152
HPK2101345	L1	785	4464
HPK2101415	L1	825	5466
HPK2101504	L4	880	6469
FEDERAL - ADAMS			
HPK2100316	C1	192	1871
HPK2100387	A4	234	2046
HPK2100544	C2	322	2272
HPK2100554	C2	327	2318
HPK2100564	C2	332	2378
HPK2100835	C2	484	2568
HPK2100652	C4	381	2697
HPK2100662	C2	386	2777
HPK2100777	C2	446	2784
HPK2100784	C4	450	2797
HPK2100787	C2	451	2806
HPK2100677	C4	393	2869
HPK2100925	C4	531	3137
HPK2100862	C1	499	3190
HPK2100947	C4	542	3201
HPK2100948	C4	543	3202
HPK2101035	C4	597	3271
HPK2100986	C3	564	3335
HPK2100993	C3	570	3367
HPK2100995	C4	571	3372
HPK2101530	C4	602	3377
HPK2101046	C4	604	3411
HPK2101101	C4	637	3562
HPK2101113	C4	645	3585
HPK2101130	C4	654	3619
HPK2101166	C4	677	3738
HPK2101180	SQ1	687	3793
HPK2101249	C3	729	3811
HPK2101210	C4	706	3901
HPK2101222	C4	713	3940
HPK2101224	C4	714	3946
HPK2101255	L2	735	3965
HPK2101234	C4	720	3984
HPK2101236	C4	722	3993
HPK2101282	SQ1	751	4045
HPK2101316	L1	769	4263
HPK2101340	L1	783	4445
HPK2101350	L1	788	4489
HPK2101357	C4	791	4536
HPK2101359	L1	792	4554
HPK2101358	L2	792	4713
HPK2101384	L3	807	5084
HPK2101406	SQ1	819	5387
HPK2101493	L3	873	5566
FRENCH COUNTRY			
HPK2100053	A2	34	1379
HPK2100061	A4	38	1400
HPK2100071	A2	43	1416
HPK2100077	A4	46	1429
HPK2100135	SQ3	92	1526
HPK2100147	A3	98	1593
HPK2100155	SQ3	102	1616
HPK2100269	C2	170	1666
HPK2100184	A3	117	1728
HPK2100285	A3	178	1760
HPK2100287	A3	180	1764
HPK2100300	A4	184	1797
HPK2100215	SQ3	132	1848
HPK2100220	A3	135	1869
HPK2100373	A4	225	1879
HPK2100231	A4	140	1904
HPK2100245	A3	154	1966
HPK2100479	A4	289	2015
HPK2100390	A4	236	2061
HPK2100391	C1	236	2065
HPK2100496	A4	298	2101
HPK2100406	C4	244	2150
HPK2100510	C4	305	2155
HPK2100608	C4	357	2170
HPK2100611	A4	358	2196
HPK2100419	A4	250	2199
HPK2100528	C1	314	2215
HPK2100532	C1	316	2231
HPK2100533	C1	316	2235
HPK2100612	C4	359	2236
HPK2100427	C1	254	2250
HPK2100435	C3	258	2275
HPK2100437	C3	259	2282
HPK2100438	A4	260	2282
HPK2100444	C3	263	2322
HPK2100561	C1	330	2370
HPK2100456	C1	269	2391
HPK2100459	C3	270	2403
HPK2100574	C1	337	2403
HPK2100577	C2	338	2410
HPK2100581	C4	340	2424
HPK2100583	C1	341	2427
HPK2100588	C1	344	2443
HPK2100472	SQ3	283	2487
HPK2100476	C3	287	2491
HPK2100699	C2	405	2515
HPK2100723	C1	417	2587
HPK2100639	C2	374	2590
HPK2100729	C4	420	2605
HPK2100646	C1	378	2630
HPK2100734	C2	422	2638
HPK2100741	C4	426	2680
HPK2100837	C2	485	2683
HPK2100750	C4	430	2702
HPK2100752	C4	431	2710
HPK2100762	C4	436	2739
HPK2100657	C2	383	2745
HPK2100765	C1	438	2755
HPK2100659	C1	384	2757
HPK2100767	C2	439	2757
HPK2100661	C4	385	2770
HPK2100663	C1	386	2778
HPK2100780	C4	448	2790
HPK2100841	C2	487	2815
HPK2100671	C2	390	2818
HPK2100795	C4	455	2850
HPK2100675	SQ3	392	2856
HPK2100799	C4	457	2860
HPK2100680	C4	395	2902
HPK2100817	C1	231	2921
HPK2100818	SQ3	469	2923
HPK2100684	C4	397	2935
HPK2100820	C4	470	2935
HPK2100843	C2	488	2949
HPK2100847	C2	490	2976
FRENCH COUNTRY			
HPK2100691	C3	400	2998
HPK2100833	C4	482	2999
HPK2100849	C2	492	3012
HPK2101022	C2	590	3044
HPK2100852	C4	494	3049
HPK2100894	C3	516	3053
HPK2100895	C3	516	3055
HPK2100853	SQ1	494	3056
HPK2100898	C2	518	3066
HPK2100856	C3	496	3068
HPK2100904	C4	521	3092
HPK2100933	C3	535	3162
HPK2100950	C3	544	3210
HPK2100961	C3	549	3250
HPK2100962	C4	550	3254
HPK2100963	SQ3	550	3259
HPK2100965	C3	552	3261
HPK2100866	C3	501	3268
HPK2100869	C2	502	3281
HPK2100969	C4	556	3281
HPK2101037	C3	598	3281
HPK2100970	C4	556	3285
HPK2100977	C4	560	3306
HPK2100981	C3	562	3320
HPK2101041	C3	600	3320
HPK2100982	C4	562	3325
HPK2100874	C3	505	3352
HPK2100875	C3	505	3359
HPK2100876	C4	506	3394
HPK2100999	C2	574	3398
HPK2101007	SQ1	578	3435
HPK2101013	C2	581	3451
HPK2101014	C3	582	3462
HPK2101052	C2	610	3468
HPK2100881	SQ3	508	3497
HPK2101084	C4	628	3512
HPK2101085	SQ1	629	3517
HPK2101089	L1	631	3531
HPK2101090	C4	631	3531
HPK2101094	C4	633	3549
HPK2101102	SQ3	637	3565
HPK2101110	SQ3	642	3578
HPK2101057	C4	614	3590
HPK2101122	C4	650	3606
HPK2101126	L1	652	3615
HPK2101127	C4	652	3618
HPK2101133	C4	655	3629
HPK2101241	C3	725	3635
HPK2101143	C4	663	3647
HPK2101145	C4	664	3660
HPK2101147	L2	665	3667
HPK2101527	SQ1	672	3688
HPK2101154	SQ1	668	3690
HPK2101158	C4	670	3708
HPK2101159	C3	671	3709
HPK2101164	C4	676	3736
HPK2101175	SQ3	684	3766
HPK2101178	C4	686	3775
HPK2101185	C4	691	3820
HPK2101190	C3	694	3841
HPK2101194	C4	696	3853
HPK2101204	SQ3	701	3886
HPK2101211	SQ1	707	3904
HPK2101251	C4	731	3905
HPK2101252	C4	732	3921
HPK2101217	C3	710	3923
HPK2101218	L1	711	3931
HPK2101227	C4	715	3951
HPK2101229	C4	716	3957
HPK2101231	C4	717	3963
HPK2101257	SQ1	737	3985
HPK2101289	SQ1	755	4097
HPK2101290	L1	755	4099
HPK2101457	L1	854	4131
HPK2101310	SQ1	766	4213
HPK2101314	L2	768	4228
HPK2101315	L1	769	4258
HPK2101327	L1	775	4306
HPK2101329	C4	776	4328
HPK2101330	SQ3	777	4353
HPK2101463	L1	857	4360
HPK2101333	SQ3	778	4363
HPK2101336	SQ3	780	4399
HPK2101348	L1	787	4476
HPK2101349	SQ3	787	4478
HPK2101467	C4	859	4517

PLAN #	PRICE TIER	PAGE	SQUARE FEET
HPK2101361	L2	793	4578
HPK2101267	L1	743	4615
HPK2101366	SQ5	797	4664
HPK2101367	SQ1	798	4674
HPK2101476	L2	864	4731
HPK2101491	L3	872	4796
HPK2101480	SQ1	867	4808
HPK2101481	L2	867	4866
HPK2101382	L3	806	5043
HPK2101383	SQ3	807	5078
HPK2101482	L3	868	5113
HPK2101483	L3	868	5146
HPK2101392	L3	812	5191
HPK2101485	L3	869	5296
HPK2101487	L3	870	5315
HPK2101404	L3	818	5343
HPK2101489	L3	871	5381
HPK2101410	L3	822	5426
HPK2101412	SQ3	823	5447
HPK2101413	L3	824	5448
HPK2101419	L3	828	5555
HPK2101494	L3	874	5603
HPK2101497	L3	875	5831
HPK2101431	SQ3	834	5845
HPK2101499	L3	877	5969
HPK2101501	L4	878	6132
HPK2101503	L4	879	6465
HPK2101446	L4	844	6536
HPK2101510	L4	886	7238
HPK2101453	L4	851	8733
HPK2101454	L4	852	9377

GARAGE

PLAN #	PRICE TIER	PAGE	SQUARE FEET
HPK2100290	P4	183	336
HPK2100291	P4	183	336
HPK2100292	P4	183	384
HPK2100293	P4	183	576
HPK2100295	P5	183	656
HPK2100296	P4	183	662
HPK2100297	P4	183	704
HPK2100298	P6	183	713
HPK2100336	P4	182	741
HPK2100337	P4	182	840
HPK2100338	P5	182	910
HPK2100339	P5	182	980
HPK2100340	P5	182	998
HPK2100341	P5	182	1031
HPK2100342	P5	182	1050
HPK2100343	P5	182	1071
HPK2100344	P6	182	1080

GEORGIAN

PLAN #	PRICE TIER	PAGE	SQUARE FEET
HPK2100603	C2	354	2071
HPK2100527	C2	313	2214
HPK2100457	C2	269	2394
HPK2100800	C4	458	2865
HPK2100940	SQ1	539	3176
HPK2100942	C2	540	3183
HPK2100955	C3	546	3219
HPK2100964	C4	551	3260
HPK2100994	C4	571	3371
HPK2101240	C3	725	3556
HPK2101146	C4	664	3664
HPK2101182	C4	688	3805
HPK2101254	C4	734	3951
HPK2101275	L1	748	4008
HPK2101460	L1	856	4204
HPK2101322	L1	772	4294
HPK2101362	SQ3	794	4587
HPK2101411	L3	823	5432
HPK2101427	SQ1	832	5795

GOTHIC REVIVAL

PLAN #	PRICE TIER	PAGE	SQUARE FEET
HPK2100628	C3	369	2539
HPK2101008	C3	578	3439
HPK2101078	SQ5	624	3942

GREEK REVIVAL

PLAN #	PRICE TIER	PAGE	SQUARE FEET
HPK2100068	A2	42	1404
HPK2100288	C3	181	1770
HPK2100372	A4	225	1844
HPK2100317	A4	193	1877
HPK2100376	C1	227	1933
HPK2100242	A4	151	1955
HPK2100485	C2	292	2038
HPK2100392	A4	237	2072
HPK2100402	A4	242	2122
HPK2100548	A4	324	2291
HPK2100452	A4	267	2379
HPK2100572	C2	336	2397
HPK2100573	C3	336	2398
HPK2100636	C1	373	2561
HPK2100775	C3	444	2778
HPK2100779	C3	447	2789
HPK2100676	SQ1	393	2863
HPK2100689	C4	399	2987
HPK2100991	C4	568	3353
HPK2101012	C4	580	3449
HPK2101093	C4	633	3543
HPK2101136	C4	658	3637
HPK2101066	SQ5	618	3764
HPK2101191	C4	695	3843
HPK2101215	C4	709	3920

ITALIANATE

PLAN #	PRICE TIER	PAGE	SQUARE FEET
HPK2100108	SQ3	71	1416
HPK2100368	SQ3	223	1754
HPK2100432	C2	257	2259
HPK2100725	SQ3	418	2590
HPK2100759	SQ3	435	2736
HPK2100802	SQ3	459	2873
HPK2100808	C1	462	2887
HPK2100685	L1	397	2951
HPK2100851	C3	493	3034
HPK2101021	C4	589	3038
HPK2100976	SQ3	559	3304
HPK2100873	SQ3	504	3351
HPK2100878	SQ1	507	3424
HPK2100880	SQ3	508	3497
HPK2101081	SQ3	627	3501
HPK2101109	SQ3	641	3578
HPK2101059	SQ3	615	3640
HPK2101156	C3	669	3705
HPK2101065	SQ3	618	3743
HPK2101250	SQ5	730	3839
HPK2101073	SQ5	622	3877
HPK2101207	SQ5	703	3893
HPK2101076	SQ5	623	3942
HPK2101077	SQ5	624	3942
HPK2101228	SQ5	716	3956
HPK2101232	SQ5	718	3977
HPK2101079	SQ5	625	3993
HPK2101272	SQ5	746	4005
HPK2101299	SQ5	761	4151
HPK2101302	SQ5	762	4160
HPK2101318	L1	770	4274
HPK2101261	SQ5	740	4282
HPK2101337	SQ1	781	4403
HPK2101344	L1	785	4459
HPK2101346	SQ5	786	4465
HPK2101352	SQ5	789	4492
HPK2101353	SQ5	789	4492
HPK2101354	SQ5	790	4492
HPK2101264	SQ5	741	4534
HPK2101365	SQ5	796	4652
HPK2101370	SQ7	799	4759
HPK2101376	SQ7	803	4864
HPK2101381	SQ7	806	5013
HPK2101269	SQ7	744	5169
HPK2101374	SQ1	802	5518
HPK2101425	SQ3	831	5713
HPK2101434	SQ7	836	5924

PLAN #	PRICE TIER	PAGE	SQUARE FEET
HPK2101436	SQ7	837	6011
HPK2101438	SQ7	838	6273
HPK2101442	L4	840	6453
HPK2101511	SQ1	887	7418
HPK2101516	L4	892	8068

MEDITERRANEAN

PLAN #	PRICE TIER	PAGE	SQUARE FEET
HPK2100095	SQ3	62	1487
HPK2100353	SQ3	210	1978
HPK2100396	C1	239	2089
HPK2100411	A4	246	2173
HPK2100414	SQ3	248	2191
HPK2100423	A4	252	2227
HPK2100430	A4	256	2258
HPK2100448	A4	265	2362
HPK2100451	A4	266	2376
HPK2100453	SQ3	267	2387
HPK2100460	A4	271	2409
HPK2100617	C1	362	2412
HPK2100618	SQ3	363	2494
HPK2100711	C1	411	2551
HPK2100640	C2	375	2597
HPK2100757	C1	434	2729
HPK2100776	C1	445	2781
HPK2100664	C1	387	2791
HPK2100667	SQ3	388	2794
HPK2100783	SQ3	449	2796
HPK2100672	SQ3	391	2823
HPK2100673	C2	391	2831
HPK2100886	SQ3	512	3031
HPK2100854	C2	495	3060
HPK2100901	C2	519	3087
HPK2100943	SQ3	540	3186
HPK2100864	SQ3	500	3231
HPK2100870	SQ3	503	3301
HPK2100997	SQ1	573	3394
HPK2100998	C2	573	3397
HPK2100877	SQ3	506	3398
HPK2101050	SQ1	608	3443
HPK2100879	C2	507	3445
HPK2101083	SQ3	628	3505
HPK2101056	SQ1	613	3556
HPK2101097	C3	635	3557
HPK2101108	SQ3	640	3575
HPK2101061	SQ3	616	3640
HPK2101144	C4	663	3655
HPK2101062	SQ3	616	3688
HPK2101063	SQ3	617	3696
HPK2101064	SQ1	617	3725
HPK2101162	SQ1	674	3730
HPK2101246	C3	728	3738
HPK2101168	SQ3	679	3744
HPK2101068	SQ5	619	3790
HPK2101069	SQ5	620	3817
HPK2101187	SQ5	693	3821
HPK2101188	C4	693	3824
HPK2101070	SQ5	620	3825
HPK2101196	SQ3	697	3857
HPK2101072	SQ5	621	3866
HPK2101074	SQ5	622	3883
HPK2101075	SQ5	623	3896
HPK2101235	SQ5	721	3991
HPK2101258	SQ5	738	4028
HPK2101294	C4	757	4139
HPK2101300	SQ5	761	4152
HPK2101259	SQ1	739	4222
HPK2101312	L1	767	4226
HPK2101260	SQ5	739	4255
HPK2101262	SQ5	740	4302
HPK2101331	SQ5	777	4359
HPK2101342	C4	784	4457
HPK2101356	SQ5	791	4528
HPK2101265	SQ5	742	4534
HPK2101360	SQ5	793	4563
HPK2101368	C4	798	4719
HPK2101268	SQ7	743	5109